CHAMBERS
An imprint of Larousse plc
7 Hopetoun Crescent, Edinburgh EH7 4AY

This edition first published by Chambers 1997
Previously published as *Chambers Compact Thesaurus* 199

ISBN 0-550-10586-7

D1328927

Typeset by Hewer Text Composition Services, Edinburgh
and Larousse plc, Edinburgh
Printed in Great Britain by Clays Ltd, St Ives plc

CHAMBERS

SUPER-MINI THESAURUS

Editor
Martin Manser

Assistant Editors
Rosalind Fergusson
Jenny Roberts
Gloria Wren

CHAMBERS

Introduction

A synonym is a word that means something similar to another word, and a thesaurus is a listing of such words. This thesaurus lists about 150,000 synonyms for common English words. *Chambers Super-Mini Thesaurus* is based on *Chambers Thesaurus*, which itself is drawn from the extensive *Chambers Dictionary* database.

This thesaurus has been compiled to help you find the most appropriate word for a particular occasion. You will be able to include a more exact term in an essay or a report, a livelier phrase in a speech or a simpler expression in a letter. We hope that not only will your skills in using English improve, but also that you will enjoy sampling more of the varied delights of the English language.

Suppose you want to find a synonym for the word *summarize*, either because you have used this word already, or because you want to vary the style of what you are writing or saying. If you look up the entry **summarize**, you will see a list of synonyms arranged according to shades of meaning, and in order from the most common to the least frequently used, or specialized, term: outline, précis, condense, abridge, abbreviate, shorten, sum up, encapsulate, review.

Many entries are divided into numbered sections, indicating that the word has several meanings. After each number comes either a key synonym in small capitals or an example to help you find precisely which meaning you want. For example:

arrest *v* **1** *arrest a criminal*: capture, catch, seize, nick (*infml*), run in, apprehend, detain. **2** STOP, stem, check, restrain, inhibit, halt, interrupt, stall, delay, slow, retard, block, obstruct, impede, hinder.

This means that for the sense shown by the example *arrest a criminal* the synonyms are capture, catch, seize, *etc*, and for the sense shown by the key synonym STOP, other possible synonyms are stress, check, restrain, *etc*.

Note that no one word can be used in the place of another word in every context. So if you are not sure of the meaning or use of one of the words included as a synonym, look up the word in a general dictionary such as *The Chambers Dictionary*.

At the end of many entries, antonyms – words that mean the opposite of another word – are shown after the symbol ≠ For example, at **boring**: interesting, exciting, stimulating, original.

Two hundred special entries are printed with a shaded background. These entries, *eg* at **animal**, **chemical elements**, **flower** and **sport**, are lists of related words which present examples of different flowers, sports, *etc*. A separate list of all these entries is given at the end of this introduction.

eg **sport**

> *Sports include*: badminton, fives, lacrosse, squash, table-tennis, ping-pong (*infml*), tennis; American football, baseball, basketball, billiards, boules, bowls, cricket, croquet, football, golf, handball, hockey, netball, pétanque, pitch and putt, polo, pool, putting, rounders, Rugby, snooker, soccer, tenpin bowling, volleyball;...

Abbreviations

adj	adjective		*prep*	preposition
adv	adverb		®	trademark
conj	conjunction		*sl*	slang
infml	informal		*US*	American English
interj	interjection		*v*	verb
fml	formal		≠	antonym(s)
n	noun			

Special entries

Lists of related words appear in the main text under the following entries:

accommodation
agriculture
aircraft
alphabets and
  writing systems
amphibian
anatomical terms
anchor
angel
animal
anniversary
arch
architecture and
  building
armed services
art
art and craft
artist
atom
ballet
biological terms
bird
boats and ships
bones
book
brain
bridge
building
bulb
butterfly
camera
canonical hours
car
castle

cat
cattle
celebration
cheese
chemical
  elements
chemistry
Chinese calendar
church
circle
class
clocks and
  watches
clothes
cloud
coat
collective nouns
collectors and
  enthusiasts
colour
communication
computing
cook
cosmetics
crime
crockery
currency
cutlery
cutter
dance
dinosaur
doctor
dog
drink

drug
ear
education
educational terms
engine
entertainer
entertainment
eye
fabric
family
farm
female
fencing
fish
flag
flower
food
footwear
fruit
fuel
fungus
furniture
game[1]
game[2]
gem
government
grass
hairstyle
hat
heart
heraldry
herbs and spices
house
insect

invertebrate
jewellery
Jewish calendar
karate
knot
language
languages
legal
literature
luggage
male
mammal
mania
marsupial
mathematical
  terms
meal
measurement
meat
medical terms
medicine
minerals
mollusc
monkey
mouth
mushrooms and
  toadstools
music
musical
  instruments
musical terms
musician
mythology
nobility

nut	politics	science	time
official	pottery	sexual	tool
paint	prosody	shape	tower
paper	punctuation	shop	travel
parliaments and	race	shrub	tree
political	rank[1]	singer	vegetable
assemblies	recording	smell	vehicle
party	region	soldier	vein
pasta	religion	song	vitamin
pastry	religious officer	sport	war
performance	reptile	star	weapon
philosophy	rhetoric	storm	weather
phobia	rock	story	wind
photography	rodent	study	wine
physics	room	sweets	wood
planet	ruler	symbol	writer
plant	sacred writing	taste	zodiac
plastic	sale	tax	
poem	say	theatrical	

Acknowledgements

The editor would like to thank Susan Rennie for her invaluable editorial advice and Peter Schwarz for his technical expertise in processing the text of this book.

A

abandon v **1** DESERT, leave, forsake, jilt, ditch (*sl*), leave in the lurch (*infml*), maroon, strand, leave behind, scrap. **2** *abandon ship*: vacate, evacuate, withdraw from, quit. **3** RENOUNCE, resign, give up, forgo, relinquish, surrender, yield, waive, drop.
F3 1 support, maintain, keep. **3** continue.

abandoned adj **1** DESERTED, unoccupied, derelict, neglected, forsaken, forlorn, desolate. **2** DISSOLUTE, wild, uninhibited, wanton, wicked.
F3 1 kept, occupied. **2** restrained.

abandonment n **1** DESERTION, leaving, forsaking, jilting, neglect, scrapping. **2** RENUNCIATION, resignation, giving up, relinquishment, surrender, sacrifice, waiver, dropping, discontinuation.

abashed adj **1** ASHAMED, shamefaced, embarrassed, mortified, humiliated, humbled. **2** CONFUSED, bewildered, nonplussed, confounded, perturbed, discomposed, disconcerted, taken aback, dumbfounded, floored (*infml*), dismayed.
F3 2 composed, at ease.

abate v **1** DECREASE, reduce, lessen, diminish, decline, sink, dwindle, taper off, fall off. **2** MODERATE, ease, relieve, alleviate, mitigate, remit, pacify, quell, subside, let up (*infml*), weaken, wane, slacken, slow, fade.
F3 1 increase. **2** strengthen.

abbey n monastery, priory, friary, seminary, convent, nunnery, cloister.

abbreviate v shorten, cut, trim, clip, truncate, curtail, abridge, summarize, précis, abstract, digest, condense, compress, reduce, lessen, shrink, contract.
F3 extend, lengthen, expand, amplify.

abbreviation n shortening, clipping, curtailment, abridgement, summarization, summary, synopsis, résumé, précis, abstract, digest, compression, reduction, contraction.
F3 extension, expansion, amplification.

abdicate v renounce, give up, relinquish, surrender, cede, yield, forgo, abandon, quit, vacate, retire, resign, step down (*infml*).

abdomen n belly, guts, stomach, tummy (*infml*), paunch, midriff.

abdominal adj ventral, intestinal, visceral, gastric.

abduct v carry off, run away with, run off with (*infml*), make off with, spirit away, seduce, kidnap, snatch, seize, appropriate.

aberration n deviation, straying, wandering, divergence, irregularity, nonconformity, anomaly, oddity, peculiarity, eccentricity, quirk, freak, lapse, defect.
F3 conformity.

abhor v hate, detest, loathe, abominate, shudder at, recoil from, shrink from, spurn, despise.
F3 love, adore.

abhorrence n hate, hatred, aversion, loathing, abomination, horror, repugnance, revulsion, disgust, distaste.
F3 love, adoration.

abhorrent adj detestable, loathsome, abominable, execrable, heinous, obnoxious, odious, hated, hateful, horrible, horrid, offensive,

repugnant, repellent, repulsive,
revolting, nauseating, disgusting,
distasteful.

⊟ delightful, attractive.

abide v 1 BEAR, stand, endure,
tolerate, put up with, stomach,
accept. 2 REMAIN, last, endure,
continue, persist.

abide by 1 *abide by the rules*: obey,
observe, follow, comply with, adhere
to, conform to, submit to, go along
with, agree to. 2 FULFIL, discharge,
carry out, stand by, hold to, keep to.

ability n 1 CAPABILITY, capacity,
faculty, facility, potentiality, power.
2 SKILL, dexterity, deftness,
adeptness, competence, proficiency,
qualification, aptitude, talent, gift,
endowment, knack, flair, touch,
expertise, know-how (*infml*), genius,
forte, strength.

⊟ 1 inability. 2 incompetence,
weakness.

abject adj 1 CONTEMPTIBLE,
worthless, low, mean, ignoble,
dishonourable, deplorable,
despicable, vile, sordid, debased,
degenerate, submissive, servile,
grovelling, slavish. 2 MISERABLE,
wretched, forlorn, hopeless, pitiable,
pathetic, outcast, degraded.

⊟ 1 proud, exalted.

ablaze adj 1 BLAZING, flaming,
burning, on fire, ignited, lighted,
alight, illuminated, luminous,
glowing, aglow, radiant, flashing,
gleaming, sparkling, brilliant.
2 IMPASSIONED, passionate, fervent,
ardent, fiery, enthusiastic, excited,
exhilarated, stimulated, aroused,
angry, furious, raging, incensed,
frenzied.

able adj capable, fit, fitted,
dexterous, adroit, deft, adept,
competent, proficient, qualified,
practised, experienced, skilled,
accomplished, clever, expert,
masterly, skilful, ingenious, talented,
gifted, strong, powerful, effective,

efficient, adequate.

⊟ unable, incapable, incompetent,
ineffective.

able-bodied adj fit, healthy, sound,
strong, robust, hardy, tough,
vigorous, powerful, hale, hearty,
lusty, sturdy, strapping, stout,
stalwart, staunch.

⊟ infirm, delicate.

abnormal adj odd, strange,
singular, peculiar, curious, queer,
weird, eccentric, paranormal,
unnatural, uncanny, extraordinary,
exceptional, unusual, uncommon,
unexpected, irregular, anomalous,
aberrant, erratic, wayward, deviant,
divergent, different.

⊟ normal, regular, typical.

abnormality n oddity, peculiarity,
singularity, eccentricity, strangeness,
bizarreness, unnaturalness,
unusualness, irregularity, exception,
anomaly, deformity, flaw,
aberration, deviation, divergence,
difference.

⊟ normality, regularity.

abolish v do away with, annul,
nullify, invalidate, quash, repeal,
rescind, revoke, cancel, obliterate,
blot out, suppress, destroy, eliminate,
eradicate, get rid of (*infml*), stamp
out, end, put an end to, terminate,
subvert, overthrow, overturn.

⊟ create, retain, authorize, continue.

abolition n annulment, nullification,
invalidation, quashing, repeal,
abrogation, cancellation,
obliteration, suppression,
eradication, extinction, end, ending,
termination, subversion, overturning,
dissolution.

⊟ creation, retention, continuance.

abominable adj loathsome,
detestable, hateful, horrid, horrible,
abhorrent, execrable, odious,
repugnant, repulsive, repellent,
disgusting, revolting, obnoxious,
nauseating, foul, vile, heinous,
atrocious, appalling, terrible,

reprehensible, contemptible, despicable, wretched.
🔄 delightful, pleasant, desirable.

abominate *v* hate, loathe, detest, abhor, execrate, despise, condemn.
🔄 love, adore.

abomination *n* hate, hatred, aversion, loathing, abhorrence, repugnance, revulsion, disgust, distaste, hostility, offence, outrage, disgrace, anathema, horror, evil, curse, plague, torment, bête noire.
🔄 adoration, delight.

abort *v* miscarry, terminate, end, stop, arrest, halt, check, frustrate, thwart, nullify, call off, fail.
🔄 continue.

abortion *n* miscarriage, termination, frustration, failure, misadventure.
🔄 continuation, success.

abortive *adj* failed, unsuccessful, fruitless, unproductive, barren, sterile, vain, idle, futile, useless, ineffective, unavailing.
🔄 successful, fruitful.

abound *v* be plentiful, proliferate, flourish, thrive, swell, increase, superabound, swarm, teem, run riot, overflow.

about *prep* **1** REGARDING, concerning, relating to, referring to, connected with, concerned with, as regards, with regard to, with respect to, with reference to. **2** CLOSE TO, near, nearby, beside, adjacent to. **3** ROUND, around, surrounding, encircling, encompassing, throughout, all over.
adv **1** *about twenty*: around, approximately, roughly, in the region of, more or less, almost, nearly, approaching, nearing. **2** *run about*: to and fro, here and there, from place to place.
about to on the point of, on the verge of, all but, ready to, intending to, preparing to.

above *prep* over, higher than, on top of, superior to, in excess of, exceeding, surpassing, beyond, before, prior to.
🔄 below, under.
adv overhead, aloft, on high, earlier.
🔄 below, underneath.
adj above-mentioned, above-stated, foregoing, preceding, previous, earlier, prior.

above-board *adj* honest, legitimate, straight, on the level, fair, fair and square, square, true, open, frank, candid, guileless, straightforward, forthright, truthful, veracious, trustworthy, honourable, reputable, upright.
🔄 dishonest, shady (*infml*), underhand.

abrasion *n* graze, scratch, scratching, scraping, scrape, scouring, grating, grinding, abrading, chafing, chafe, friction, rubbing, erosion, wearing away, wearing down.

abrasive *adj* scratching, scraping, grating, rough, harsh, chafing, frictional, galling, irritating, annoying, sharp, biting, caustic, hurtful, nasty, unpleasant.
🔄 smooth, pleasant.

abreast *adj* acquainted, informed, knowledgeable, in the picture, au courant, up to date, in touch, au fait, conversant, familiar.
🔄 unaware, out of touch.

abridge *v* shorten, cut (down), prune, curtail, abbreviate, contract, reduce, decrease, lessen, summarize, précis, abstract, digest, condense, compress, concentrate.
🔄 expand, amplify, pad out.

abridgement *n* **1** SHORTENING, cutting, reduction, decrease, diminishing, concentration, contraction, restriction, limitation. **2** SUMMARY, synopsis, résumé, outline, précis, abstract, digest, epitome.
🔄 **1** expansion, padding.

abroad *adv* **1** OVERSEAS, in foreign

parts, out of the country, far and
wide, widely, extensively. **2** AT
LARGE, around, about, circulating,
current.
🔁 at home.

abrupt *adj* **1** *abrupt departure*:
sudden, unexpected, unforeseen,
surprising, quick, rapid, swift, hasty,
hurried, precipitate. **2** SHEER,
precipitous, steep, sharp. **3**
BRUSQUE, curt, terse, short, brisk,
snappy, gruff, rude, uncivil, impolite,
blunt, direct.
🔁 **1** gradual, slow, leisurely.
3 expansive, ceremonious, polite.

abscond *v* run away, run off, make
off, decamp, flee, fly, escape, bolt,
quit, clear out (*infml*), disappear,
take French leave.

absence *n* **1** NON-ATTENDANCE,
non-appearance, truancy,
absenteeism, non-existence. **2** LACK,
need, want, deficiency, dearth,
scarcity, unavailability, default,
omission, vacancy.
🔁 **1** presence, attendance,
appearance. **2** existence.

absent *adj* **1** MISSING, not present,
away, out, unavailable, gone,
lacking, truant. **2** INATTENTIVE,
daydreaming, dreamy, faraway,
elsewhere, absent-minded, vacant,
vague, distracted, preoccupied,
unaware, oblivious, unheeding.
🔁 **1** present. **2** alert, aware.

absent-minded *adj* forgetful,
scatterbrained, absent, abstracted,
withdrawn, faraway, distracted,
preoccupied, absorbed, engrossed,
pensive, musing, dreaming, dreamy,
inattentive, unaware, oblivious,
unconscious, heedless, unheeding,
unthinking, impractical.
🔁 attentive, practical, matter-of-fact.

absolute *adj* **1** UTTER, total,
complete, entire, full, thorough,
exhaustive, supreme, consummate,
definitive, conclusive, final,
categorical, definite, unequivocal,

unquestionable, decided, decisive,
positive, sure, certain, genuine, pure,
perfect, sheer, unmixed, unqualified,
downright, out-and-out, outright.
2 OMNIPOTENT, totalitarian,
autocratic, tyrannical, despotic,
dictatorial, sovereign, unlimited,
unrestricted.

absolutely *adv* utterly, totally,
dead, completely, entirely, fully,
wholly, thoroughly, exhaustively,
perfectly, supremely,
unconditionally, conclusively, finally,
categorically, definitely, positively,
unequivocally, unambiguously,
unquestionably, decidedly, decisively,
surely, certainly, infallibly, genuinely,
truly, purely, exactly, precisely.

absorb *v* **1** TAKE IN, ingest, drink
in, imbibe, suck up, soak up,
consume, devour, engulf, digest,
assimilate, understand, receive, hold,
retain. **2** ENGROSS, involve,
fascinate, enthral, monopolize,
preoccupy, occupy, fill (up).
🔁 **1** exude.

absorbing *adj* interesting, amusing,
entertaining, diverting, engrossing,
preoccupying, intriguing, fascinating,
captivating, enthralling, spellbinding,
gripping, riveting, compulsive,
unputdownable (*infml*).
🔁 boring, off-putting.

abstain *v* refrain, decline, refuse,
reject, resist, forbear, shun, avoid,
keep from, stop, cease, desist, give
up, renounce, forgo, go without,
deny oneself.
🔁 indulge.

abstemious *adj* abstinent, self-
denying, self-disciplined, disciplined,
sober, temperate, moderate, sparing,
frugal, austere, ascetic, restrained.
🔁 intemperate, gluttonous, luxurious.

abstinence *n* abstaining,
abstention, abstemiousness, self-
denial, non-indulgence, avoidance,
forbearance, refraining, refusal,
restraint, self-restraint, self-control,

self-discipline, sobriety, teetotalism,
temperance, moderation, frugality,
asceticism.

☒ indulgence, self-indulgence.

abstract *adj* non-concrete,
conceptual, intellectual, hypothetical,
theoretical, unpractical, unrealistic,
general, generalized, indefinite,
metaphysical, philosophical,
academic, complex, abstruse, deep,
profound, subtle.

☒ concrete, real, actual.

n synopsis, outline, summary,
recapitulation, résumé, précis,
epitome, digest, abridgement,
compression.

v 1 SUMMARIZE, outline, précis,
digest, condense, compress, abridge,
abbreviate, shorten. 2 EXTRACT,
remove, withdraw, isolate, detach,
dissociate, separate.

☒ 1 expand. 2 insert.

abstraction *n* 1 IDEA, notion,
concept, thought, conception, theory,
hypothesis, theorem, formula,
generalization, generality.
2 INATTENTION, dream, dreaminess,
absent-mindedness, distraction,
pensiveness, preoccupation,
absorption. 3 EXTRACTION,
withdrawal, isolation, separation.

absurd *adj* ridiculous, ludicrous,
preposterous, fantastic, incongruous,
illogical, paradoxical, implausible,
untenable, unreasonable, irrational,
nonsensical, meaningless, senseless,
foolish, silly, stupid, idiotic, crazy,
daft (*infml*), farcical, comical, funny,
humorous, laughable, risible,
derisory.

☒ logical, rational, sensible.

abundant *adj* plentiful, in plenty,
full, filled, well-supplied, ample,
generous, bountiful, rich, copious,
profuse, lavish, exuberant, teeming,
overflowing.

☒ scarce, sparse.

abuse *v* 1 MISUSE, misapply,
exploit, take advantage of, oppress,

wrong, ill-treat, maltreat, hurt,
injure, molest, damage, spoil, harm.
2 INSULT, swear at, defame, libel,
slander, smear, disparage, malign,
revile, scold, upbraid.

☒ 1 cherish, care for. 2 compliment,
praise.

n 1 MISUSE, misapplication,
exploitation, imposition, oppression,
wrong, ill-treatment, maltreatment,
hurt, injury, molestation, damage,
spoiling, harm. 2 INSULTS, swearing,
cursing, offence, defamation, libel,
slander, disparagement, reproach,
scolding, upbraiding, tirade.

☒ 1 care, attention. 2 compliment,
praise.

abusive *adj* insulting, offensive,
rude, scathing, hurtful, injurious,
cruel, destructive, defamatory,
libellous, slanderous, derogatory,
disparaging, pejorative, vilifying,
maligning, reviling, censorious,
reproachful, scolding, upbraiding.

☒ complimentary, polite.

abyss *n* gulf, chasm, crevasse,
fissure, gorge, canyon, crater, pit,
depth, void.

academic *adj* 1 SCHOLARLY,
erudite, learned, well-read, studious,
bookish, scholastic, pedagogical,
educational, instructional, literary,
highbrow. 2 THEORETICAL,
hypothetical, conjectural,
speculative, notional, abstract,
impractical.

n professor, don, master, fellow,
lecturer, tutor, student, scholar, man
of letters, pedant.

accelerate *v* quicken, speed, speed
up, pick up speed, step up, expedite,
hurry, hasten, precipitate, stimulate,
facilitate, advance, further, promote,
forward.

☒ decelerate, slow down, delay.

accent *n* pronunciation,
enunciation, articulation, brogue,
twang (*infml*), tone, pitch,
intonation, inflection, accentuation,

stress, emphasis, intensity, force, cadence, rhythm, beat, pulse, pulsation.

accentuate v accent, stress, emphasize, underline, highlight, intensify, strengthen, deepen.
F3 play down, weaken.

accept v accept a gift: take, receive, obtain, acquire, gain, secure. **2** ACKNOWLEDGE, recognize, admit, allow, approve, agree to, consent to, take on, adopt. **3** TOLERATE, put up with, stand, bear, abide, face up to, yield to.
F3 1 refuse, turn down. **2** reject.

acceptable adj satisfactory, tolerable, moderate, passable, adequate, all right, OK (infml), so-so (infml), unexceptionable, admissible, suitable, conventional, correct, desirable, pleasant, gratifying, welcome.
F3 unacceptable, unsatisfactory, unwelcome.

acceptance n **1** TAKING, accepting, receipt, obtaining, getting, acquiring, gaining, securing.
2 ACKNOWLEDGEMENT, recognition, admission, concession, affirmation, concurrence, agreement, assent, consent, permission, ratification, approval, stamp of approval, OK (infml), adoption, undertaking, belief, credence.
F3 1 refusal. **2** rejection, dissent.

accepted adj authorized, approved, ratified, sanctioned, agreed, acknowledged, recognized, admitted, confirmed, acceptable, correct, conventional, unorthodox, traditional, customary, time-honoured, established, received, universal, regular, standard, normal, usual, common.
F3 unconventional, unorthodox, controversial.

access n admission, admittance, entry, entering, entrance, gateway, door, key, approach, passage, road,

path, course.
F3 exit, outlet.

accessible adj **1** REACHABLE, get-at-able (infml), attainable, achievable, possible, obtainable, available, on hand, ready, handy, convenient, near, nearby. **2** FRIENDLY, affable, approachable, sociable, informal.
F3 1 inaccessible, remote.
2 unapproachable.

accessory n **1** EXTRA, supplement, addition, appendage, attachment, extension, component, fitting, accompaniment, decoration, adornment, frill, trimming.
2 ACCOMPLICE, partner, associate, colleague, confederate, assistant, helper, help, aid.

accident n **1** CHANCE, hazard, fortuity, luck, fortune, fate, serendipity, contingency, fluke.
2 MISFORTUNE, mischance, misadventure, mishap, casualty, blow, calamity, disaster. **3** road accident: collision, crash, shunt (sl), prang (sl), pile-up.

accidental adj unintentional, unintended, inadvertent, unplanned, uncalculated, unexpected, unforeseen, unlooked-for, chance, fortuitous, flukey, uncertain, haphazard, random, casual, incidental.
F3 intentional, deliberate, calculated, premeditated.

acclaim v praise, commend, extol, exalt, honour, hail, salute, welcome, applaud, clap, cheer, celebrate.
n acclamation, praise, commendation, homage, tribute, eulogy, exaltation, honour, welcome, approbation, approval, applause, ovation, clapping, cheers, cheering, shouting, celebration.
F3 criticism, disapproval.

accommodate v **1** LODGE, board, put up, house, shelter. **2** OBLIGE, help, assist, aid, serve, provide, supply, comply, conform. **3** ADAPT, accustom, acclimatize, adjust, modify, fit, harmonize, reconcile, settle, compose.

accommodating *adj* obliging, indulgent, helpful, co-operative, willing, kind, considerate, unselfish, sympathetic, friendly, hospitable.
F3 disobliging, selfish.

accommodation

> *Types of accommodation include*: flat, apartment, bedsit, bedsitter, digs (*infml*), lodgings, hostel, halls of residence, rooms, residence, dwelling, shelter, pad (*infml*), squat (*infml*); bed and breakfast, board, guest house, hotel, youth hostel, villa, timeshare, motel, inn, pension, boarding-house; barracks, billet, married quarters. *see also* **house**; **room**.

accompany *v* **1** ESCORT, attend, convoy, chaperon, usher, conduct, follow. **2** COEXIST, coincide, belong to, go with, complement, supplement.

accomplice *n* assistant, helper, abettor, mate, henchman, conspirator, collaborator, ally, confederate, partner, associate, colleague, participator, accessory.

accomplish *v* achieve, attain, do, perform, carry out, execute, fulfil, discharge, finish, complete, conclude, consummate, realize, effect, bring about, engineer, produce, obtain.

accomplished *adj* skilled, professional, practised, proficient, gifted, talented, skilful, adroit, adept, expert, masterly, consummate, polished, cultivated.
F3 unskilled, inexpert, incapable.

accomplishment *n* **1** *the accomplishment of a task*: achievement, attainment, doing, performance, carrying out, execution, fulfilment, discharge, finishing, completion, conclusion,

consummation, perfection, realisation, fruition, production. **2** SKILL, art, aptitude, faculty, ability, capability, proficiency, gift, talent, forte. **3** EXPLOIT, feat, deed, stroke, triumph.

accord *v* **1** AGREE, concur, harmonize, match, conform, correspond, suit. **2** GIVE, tender, grant, allow, bestow, endow, confer.
F3 1 disagree. **2** deny.
n accordance, agreement, assent, unanimity, concert, unity, correspondence, conformity, harmony, sympathy.
F3 conflict, discord, disharmony.

according to in accordance with, in keeping with, obedient to, in conformity with, in line with, consistent with, commensurate with, in proportion to, in relation to, after, in the light of, in the manner of, after the manner of.

accordingly *adv* in accordance, in accord with, correspondingly, so, as a result, consequently, in consequence, therefore, thus, hence, appropriately, properly, suitably.

accost *v* approach, confront, buttonhole, waylay, stop, halt, detain, importune, solicit.

account *n* **1** *an account of what happened*: narrative, story, tale, chronicle, history, memoir, record, statement, report, communiqué, write-up, version, portrayal, sketch, description, presentation, explanation. **2** LEDGER, book, books, register, inventory, statement, invoice, bill, tab, charge, reckoning, computation, tally, score, balance.
account for explain, elucidate, illuminate, clear up, rationalize, justify, vindicate, answer for, put paid to, destroy, kill.

accountable *adj* answerable, responsible, liable, amenable, obliged, bound.

accumulate *v* gather, assemble,

collect, amass, aggregate, cumulate, accrue, grow, increase, multiply, build up, pile up, hoard, stockpile, stash (*infml*), store.
F3 disseminate.

accumulation *n* gathering, assembly, collection, growth, increase, build-up, conglomeration, mass, heap, pile, stack, stock, store, reserve, hoard, stockpile.

accuracy *n* correctness, precision, exactness, authenticity, truth, veracity, closeness, faithfulness, fidelity, carefulness.
F3 inaccuracy.

accurate *adj* correct, right, unerring, precise, exact, well-directed, spot-on (*infml*), faultless, perfect, word-perfect, sound, authentic, factual, nice, true, truthful, veracious, just, proper, close, faithful, well-judged, careful, rigorous, scrupulous, meticulous, strict, minute.
F3 inaccurate, wrong, imprecise, inexact.

accusation *n* charge, allegation, imputation, indictment, denunciation, impeachment, recrimination, complaint, incrimination.

accuse *v* charge, indict, impugn, denounce, arraign, impeach, cite, allege, attribute, impute, blame, censure, recriminate, incriminate, criminate, inform against.

accustomed *adj* used, in the habit of, given to, confirmed, seasoned, hardened, inured, disciplined, trained, adapted, acclimatized, acquainted, familiar, wonted, habitual, routine, regular, normal, usual, ordinary, everyday, conventional, customary, traditional, established, fixed, prevailing, general.
F3 unaccustomed, unusual.

ache *v* **1** HURT, be sore, pain, suffer, agonize, throb, pound, twinge, smart, sting. **2** YEARN, long, pine, hanker,

desire, crave, hunger, thirst, itch.
n **1** PAIN, hurt, soreness, suffering, anguish, agony, throb, throbbing, pounding, pang, twinge, smarting, stinging. **2** YEARNING, longing, craving, itch.

achieve *v* accomplish, attain, reach, get, obtain, acquire, procure, gain, earn, win, succeed, manage, do, perform, carry out, execute, fulfil, finish, complete, consummate, effect, bring about, realize, produce.
F3 miss, fail.

achievement *n* **1** *the achievement of our aims*: accomplishment, attainment, acquirement, performance, execution, fulfilment, completion, success, realization, fruition. **2** ACT, deed, exploit, feat, effort.

acid *adj* sour, bitter, tart, vinegary, sharp, pungent, acerbic, caustic, corrosive, stinging, biting, mordant, cutting, incisive, trenchant, harsh, hurtful.

acknowledge *v* **1** *acknowledge an error*: admit, confess, own up to, declare, recognize, accept, grant, allow, concede. **2** GREET, address, notice, recognize. **3** *acknowledge a letter*: answer, reply to, respond to, confirm.
F3 **1** deny. **2** ignore.

acknowledged *adj* recognized, accepted, approved, accredited, declared, professed, attested, avowed, confirmed.

acknowledgement *n* **1** ADMISSION, confession, declaration, profession, recognition, acceptance.
2 GREETING, salutation, notice, recognition. **3** ANSWER, reply, response, reaction, affirmation.
4 GRATITUDE, thanks, appreciation, tribute.

acquaint *v* accustom, familiarize, tell, notify, advise, inform, brief, enlighten, divulge, disclose, reveal, announce.

acquaintance *n* **1** AWARENESS, knowledge, understanding, experience, familiarity, intimacy, relationship, association, fellowship, companionship. **2** FRIEND, companion, colleague, associate, contact.

acquire *v* buy, purchase, procure, appropriate, obtain, get, cop (*sl*), receive, collect, pick up, gather, net, gain, secure, earn, win, achieve, attain, realize.
⊟ relinquish, forfeit.

acquisition *n* purchase, buy (*infml*), procurement, appropriation, gain, securing, achievement, attainment, accession, takeover, property, possession.

acquit *v* absolve, clear, reprieve, let off, exonerate, exculpate, excuse, vindicate, free, liberate, deliver, relieve, release, dismiss, discharge, settle, satisfy, repay.
⊟ convict.

acquittal *n* absolution, clearance, reprieve, exoneration, exculpation, excusing, vindication, freeing, liberation, deliverance, relief, release, dismissal, discharge.
⊟ conviction.

acrid *adj* pungent, sharp, stinging, acid, burning, caustic, acerbic, biting, cutting, incisive, trenchant, sarcastic, sardonic, bitter, acrimonious, virulent, harsh, vitriolic, nasty, malicious, venomous.

acrimonious *adj* bitter, biting, cutting, trenchant, sharp, virulent, severe, spiteful, censorious, abusive, ill-tempered.
⊟ peaceable, kindly.

acrimony *n* bitterness, rancour, resentment, ill-will, petulance, gall, ill temper, irascibility, trenchancy, sarcasm, astringency, acerbity, harshness, virulence.

act *n* **1** DEED, action, undertaking, enterprise, operation, manoeuvre, move, step, doing, execution,
accomplishment, achievement, exploit, feat, stroke. **2** *put on an act*: pretence, make-believe, sham, fake, feigning, dissimulation, affectation, show, front. **3** LAW, statute, ordinance, edict, decree, resolution, measure, bill. **4** TURN, item, routine, sketch, performance, gig (*sl*).
v **1** BEHAVE, conduct, exert, make, work, function, operate, do, execute, carry out. **2** PRETEND, feign, put on, assume, simulate, mimic, imitate, impersonate, portray, represent, mime, play, perform, enact.

act on 1 *act on orders*: carry out, fulfil, comply with, conform to, obey, follow, heed, take. **2** AFFECT, influence, alter, modify, change, transform.

acting *adj* temporary, provisional, interim, stopgap, supply, stand-by, substitute, reserve.
n theatre, stagecraft, artistry, performing, performance, play-acting, melodrama, dramatics, theatricals, portrayal, characterization, impersonation, imitating.

action *n* **1** ACT, move, deed, exploit, feat, accomplishment, achievement, performance, effort, endeavour, enterprise, undertaking, proceeding, process, activity, liveliness, spirit, energy, vigour, power, force, exercise, exertion, work, functioning, operation, mechanism, movement, motion. **2** *killed in action*: warfare, battle, conflict, combat, fight, fray, engagement, skirmish, clash. **3** LITIGATION, lawsuit, suit, case, prosecution.

activate *v* start, initiate, trigger, set off, fire, switch on, set in motion, mobilize, propel, move, stir, rouse, arouse, stimulate, motivate, prompt, animate, energize, impel, excite, galvanize.
⊟ deactivate, stop, arrest.

active *adj* **1** BUSY, occupied, on the go (*infml*), industrious, diligent,

hard-working, forceful, spirited, vital, forward, enterprising, enthusiastic, devoted, engaged, involved, committed, militant, activist. **2** AGILE, nimble, sprightly, light-footed, quick, alert, animated, lively, energetic, vigorous. **3** IN OPERATION, functioning, working, running.
F3 1 passive. **2** inert, dormant. **3** inactive.

activity n **1** LIVELINESS, life, activeness, action, motion, movement, commotion, bustle, hustle, industry, labour, exertion, exercise. **2** OCCUPATION, job, work, act, deed, project, scheme, task, venture, enterprise, endeavour, undertaking, pursuit, hobby, pastime, interest.

actor n actress, play-actor, comedian, tragedian, ham, player, performer, artist, impersonator, mime.

actual adj **1** REAL, existent, substantial, tangible, material, physical, concrete, positive, definite, absolute, certain, unquestionable, indisputable, confirmed, verified, factual, truthful, true, genuine, legitimate, bona fide, authentic, realistic. **2** CURRENT, present, present-day, prevailing, live, living.
F3 1 theoretical, apparent, imaginary.

actually adv in fact, as a matter of fact, as it happens, in truth, in reality, really, truly, indeed, absolutely.

acumen n astuteness, shrewdness, sharpness, keenness, quickness, penetration, insight, intuition, discrimination, discernment, judgement, perception, sense, wit, wisdom, intelligence, cleverness, ingenuity.

acute adj **1** SEVERE, intense, extreme, violent, dangerous, serious, grave, urgent, crucial, vital, decisive, sharp, cutting, poignant, distressing.

2 an acute mind: sharp, keen, incisive, penetrating, astute, shrewd, judicious, discerning, observant, perceptive.
F3 1 mild, slight.

adamant adj hard, resolute, determined, set, firm, insistent, rigid, stiff, inflexible, unbending, unrelenting, intransigent, unyielding, stubborn, uncompromising, tough, fixed, immovable, unshakable.
F3 hesitant, flexible, yielding.

adapt v alter, change, qualify, modify, adjust, convert, remodel, customize, fit, tailor, fashion, shape, harmonize, match, suit, conform, comply, prepare, familiarize, acclimatize.

adaptable adj alterable, changeable, variable, modifiable, adjustable, convertible, conformable, versatile, plastic, malleable, flexible, compliant, amenable, easy-going.
F3 inflexible, refractory.

adaptation n alteration, change, shift, transformation, modification, adjustment, accommodation, conversion, remodelling, reworking, reshaping, refitting, revision, variation, version.

add v append, annex, affix, attach, tack on, join, combine, supplement, augment.
F3 take away, remove.

add up 1 ADD, sum up, tot up, total, tally, count (up), reckon, compute. **2** AMOUNT, come to, constitute, include. **3** it doesn't add up: be consistent, hang together, fit, be plausible, be reasonable, make sense, mean, signify, indicate.
F3 1 subtract.

addict n **1** ENTHUSIAST, fan, buff (infml), fiend, freak, devotee, follower, adherent. **2** DRUG-ADDICT, user (infml), dope-fiend, junkie (infml), tripper (sl), mainliner (sl).

addicted adj dependent, hooked,

obsessed, absorbed, devoted, dedicated, fond, inclined, disposed, accustomed.

addiction *n* dependence, craving, habit, monkey (*sl*), obsession.

addition *n* **1** ADDING, annexation, accession, extension, enlargement, increasing, increase, gain.
2 ADJUNCT, supplement, additive, addendum, appendix, appendage, accessory, attachment, extra, increment. **3** SUMMING-UP, totting-up, totalling, counting, reckoning, inclusion.
Ξ 1 removal. **3** subtraction.

in addition additionally, too, also, as well, besides, moreover, further, furthermore, over and above.

additional *adj* added, extra, supplementary, spare, more, further, increased, other, new, fresh.

address *n* **1** RESIDENCE, dwelling, abode, house, home, lodging, direction, inscription, whereabouts, location, situation, place. **2** SPEECH, talk, lecture, sermon, discourse, dissertation.
v lecture, speak to, talk to, greet, salute, hail, invoke, accost, approach, buttonhole.

adept *adj* skilled, accomplished, expert, masterly, experienced, versed, practised, polished, proficient, able, adroit, deft, nimble.

adequate *adj* enough, sufficient, commensurate, requisite, suitable, fit, able, competent, capable, serviceable, acceptable, satisfactory, passable, tolerable, fair, respectable, presentable.
Ξ inadequate, insufficient.

adhere *v* **1** STICK, glue, paste, cement, fix, fasten, attach, join, link, combine, coalesce, cohere, hold, cling, cleave to. **2** *adhere to the agreement*: observe, follow, abide by, comply with, fulfil, obey, keep, heed, respect, stand by.

adherent *n* supporter, upholder,

advocate, partisan, follower, disciple, satellite, henchman, hanger-on, votary, devotee, admirer, fan, enthusiast, freak, nut.

adhesion *n* adherence, adhesiveness, bond, attachment, grip, cohesion.

adhesive *adj* sticky, tacky, self-adhesive, gummed, gummy, gluey, adherent, adhering, sticking, clinging, holding, attaching, cohesive.
n glue, gum, paste, cement.

adjacent *adj* adjoining, abutting, touching, contiguous, bordering, alongside, beside, juxtaposed, next-door, neighbouring, next, closest, nearest, close, near.
Ξ remote, distant.

adjoin *v* abut, touch, meet, border, verge, neighbour, interconnect, link, connect, join, combine, unite, couple, attach, annex, add.

adjourn *v* interrupt, suspend, discontinue, break off, delay, stay, defer, postpone, put off, recess, retire.
Ξ assemble, convene.

adjournment *n* interruption, suspension, discontinuation, break, pause, recess, delay, stay, deferment, deferral, postponement, putting off, dissolution.

adjudicate *v* judge, arbitrate, umpire, referee, settle, determine, decide, pronounce.

adjust *v* **1** MODIFY, change, adapt, alter, convert, dispose, shape, remodel, fit, accommodate, suit, measure, rectify, regulate, balance, temper, tune, fine-tune, fix, set, arrange, compose, settle, square.
2 ACCUSTOM, habituate, acclimatize, reconcile, harmonize, conform.
Ξ 1 disarrange, upset.

adjustment *n* **1** MODIFICATION, change, adaptation, alteration, conversion, remodelling, shaping, fitting, accommodation, rectification, regulation, tuning, fixing, setting, arranging, arrangement, ordering, settlement. **2** HABITUATION, orientation, acclimatization, naturalization, reconciliation, harmonization, conforming.

ad-lib *v* improvise, extemporize, make up, invent.

adj impromptu, improvised, extempore, extemporaneous, off-the-cuff, unprepared, unpremeditated, unrehearsed, spontaneous, made up. ☒ prepared.

adv impromptu, extempore, extemporaneously, off the cuff, off the top of one's head, spontaneously, impulsively.

administer *v* **1** *administer an organization*: govern, rule, lead, head, preside over, officiate, manage, run, organize, direct, conduct, control, regulate, superintend, supervise, oversee. **2** GIVE, provide, supply, distribute, dole out, dispense, measure out, mete out, execute, impose, apply.

administration *n* **1** ADMINISTERING, governing, ruling, leadership, management, execution, running, organization, direction, control, superintendence, supervision, overseeing. **2** GOVERNING BODY, regime, government, ministry, leadership, directorship, management, executive, term of office.

administrative *adj* governmental, legislative, authoritative, directorial, managerial, management, executive, organizational, regulatory, supervisory.

admirable *adj* praiseworthy, commendable, laudable, creditable, deserving, worthy, respected, fine, excellent, superior, wonderful, exquisite, choice, rare, valuable. ☒ contemptible, despicable, deplorable.

admiration *n* esteem, regard, respect, reverence, veneration,

worship, idolism, adoration, affection, approval, praise, appreciation, pleasure, delight, wonder, astonishment, amazement, surprise. ☒ contempt.

admire *v* esteem, respect, revere, venerate, worship, idolize, adore, approve, praise, laud, applaud, appreciate, value. ☒ despise, censure.

admirer *n* follower, disciple, adherent, supporter, fan, enthusiast, devotee, worshipper, idolizer, suitor, boyfriend, girlfriend, sweetheart, lover. ☒ critic, opponent.

admissible *adj* acceptable, tolerable, tolerated, passable, allowable, permissible, allowed, permitted, lawful, legitimate, justifiable. ☒ inadmissible, illegitimate.

admission *n* confession, granting, acknowledgement, recognition, acceptance, allowance, concession, affirmation, declaration, profession, disclosure, divulgence, revelation, exposé. ☒ denial.

admit *v* **1** CONFESS, own (up), grant, acknowledge, recognize, accept, allow, concede, agree, affirm, declare, profess, disclose, divulge, reveal. **2** LET IN, allow to enter, give access, accept, receive, take in, introduce, initiate. ☒ **1** deny. **2** shut out, exclude.

admittance *n* admitting, admission, letting in, access, entrance, entry, acceptance, reception, introduction, initiation. ☒ exclusion.

adolescence *n* teens, puberty, youth, minority, boyhood, girlhood, development, immaturity, youthfulness, boyishness, girlishness.

adolescent *adj* teenage, young, youthful, juvenile, puerile, boyish,

girlish, immature, growing, developing.

n teenager, youth, juvenile, minor.

adopt *v* take on, accept, assume, take up, appropriate, embrace, follow, choose, select, take in, foster, support, maintain, back, endorse, ratify, approve.

🔁 repudiate, disown.

adorable *adj* lovable, dear, darling, precious, appealing, sweet, winsome, charming, enchanting, captivating, winning, delightful, pleasing, attractive, fetching.

🔁 hateful, abominable.

adore *v* love, cherish, dote on, admire, esteem, honour, revere, venerate, worship, idolize, exalt, glorify.

🔁 hate, abhor.

adorn *v* decorate, deck, bedeck, ornament, crown, trim, garnish, gild, enhance, embellish, doll up, enrich, grace.

adult *adj* grown-up, of age, full-grown, fully grown, developed, mature, ripe, ripened.

🔁 immature.

adulterate *v* contaminate, pollute, taint, corrupt, defile, debase, dilute, water down, weaken, devalue, deteriorate.

🔁 purify.

advance *v* **1** PROCEED, go forward, move on, go ahead, progress, prosper, flourish, thrive, improve. **2** ACCELERATE, speed, hasten, send forward. **3** FURTHER, promote, upgrade, foster, support, assist, benefit, facilitate, increase, grow. **4** *advance an idea*: present, submit, suggest, allege, cite, bring forward, offer, provide, supply, furnish. **5** *advance a sum of money*: lend, loan, pay beforehand, pay, give.

🔁 **1** retreat. **3** retard. **3** impede.

n **1** PROGRESS, forward movement, onward movement, headway, step, advancement, furtherance,

breakthrough, development, growth, increase, improvement, amelioration. **2** DEPOSIT, down payment, prepayment, credit, loan.

🔁 **1** retreat, recession.

in advance beforehand, previously, early, earlier, sooner, ahead, in front, in the lead, in the forefront.

🔁 later, behind.

advanced *adj* leading, foremost, ahead, forward, precocious, progressive, forward-looking, avant-garde, ultra-modern, sophisticated, complex, higher.

🔁 backward, retarded, elementary.

advancement *n* furtherance, promotion, preferment, betterment, improvement, development, growth, rise, gain, advance, progress, headway.

🔁 demotion, retardation.

advantage *n* **1** ASSET, blessing, benefit, good, welfare, interest, service, help, aid, assistance, use, avail, convenience, usefulness, utility, profit, gain, start. **2** LEAD, edge, upper hand, superiority, precedence, pre-eminence, sway.

🔁 **1** disadvantage, drawback, hindrance.

advantageous *adj* beneficial, favourable, opportune, convenient, helpful, useful, worthwhile, valuable, profitable, gainful, remunerative, rewarding.

🔁 disadvantageous, adverse, damaging.

adventure *n* exploit, venture, undertaking, enterprise, risk, hazard, chance, speculation, experience, incident, occurrence.

adventurous *adj* daring, intrepid, bold, audacious, headstrong, impetuous, reckless, rash, risky, venturesome, enterprising.

🔁 cautious, chary, prudent.

adverse *adj* hostile, antagonistic, opposing, opposite, counter, contrary, conflicting, counter-

productive, negative,
disadvantageous, unfavourable,
inauspicious, unfortunate, unlucky,
inopportune, detrimental, harmful,
noxious, injurious, hurtful,
unfriendly, uncongenial.

E₃ advantageous, favourable.

adversity n misfortune, ill fortune,
bad luck, ill luck, reverse, hardship,
hard times, misery, wretchedness,
affliction, suffering, distress, sorrow,
woe, trouble, trial, tribulation,
calamity, disaster, catastrophe.

E₃ prosperity.

advertise v publicize, promote,
push, plug (infml), praise, hype (sl),
trumpet, blazon, herald, announce,
declare, proclaim, broadcast, publish,
display, make known, inform, notify.

advertisement n advert (infml), ad
(infml), commercial, publicity,
promotion, plug (infml), hype (sl),
display, blurb, announcement, notice,
poster, bill, placard, leaflet, handbill,
circular, handout, propaganda.

advice n **1** WARNING, caution, do's
and don'ts, injunction, instruction,
counsel, help, guidance, direction,
suggestion, recommendation,
opinion, view. **2** NOTIFICATION,
notice, memorandum,
communication, information,
intelligence.

advisable adj suggested,
recommended, sensible, wise,
prudent, judicious, sound, profitable,
beneficial, desirable, suitable,
appropriate, apt, fitting, fit, proper,
correct.

E₃ inadvisable, foolish.

advise v **1** COUNSEL, guide, warn,
forewarn, caution, instruct, teach,
tutor, suggest, recommend,
commend, urge. **2** NOTIFY, inform,
tell, acquaint, make known, report.

adviser n counsellor, consultant,
authority, guide, teacher, tutor,
instructor, coach, helper, aide, right-
hand man, mentor, confidant(e),

counsel, lawyer.

advocate v defend, champion,
campaign for, press for, argue for,
plead for, justify, urge, encourage,
advise, recommend, propose,
promote, endorse, support, uphold,
patronize, adopt, subscribe to,
favour, countenance.

E₃ impugn, disparage, deprecate.
n defender, supporter, upholder,
champion, campaigner, pleader,
vindicator, proponent, promoter,
speaker, spokesperson.

E₃ opponent, critic.

affable adj friendly, amiable,
approachable, open, expansive,
genial, good-humoured, good-
natured, mild, benevolent, kindly,
gracious, obliging, courteous,
amicable, congenial, cordial, warm,
sociable, pleasant, agreeable.

E₃ unfriendly, reserved, reticent, cool.

affair n **1** BUSINESS, transaction,
operation, proceeding, undertaking,
activity, project, responsibility,
interest, concern, matter, question,
issue, subject, topic, circumstance,
happening, occurrence, incident,
episode, event. **2** have an affair:
relationship, liaison, intrigue, love
affair, romance, amour.

affect v **1** CONCERN, regard,
involve, relate to, apply to, bear
upon, impinge upon, act on, change,
transform, alter, modify, influence,
sway, prevail over, attack, strike,
impress, interest, stir, move, touch,
upset, disturb, perturb, trouble,
overcome. **2** ADOPT, assume, put on,
feign, simulate, imitate, fake,
counterfeit, sham, pretend, profess,
aspire to.

affectation n airs, pretentiousness,
mannerism, pose, act, show,
appearance, façade, pretence, sham,
simulation, imitation, artificiality,
insincerity.

E₃ artlessness, ingenuousness.

affected adj assumed, put-on,

feigned, simulated, artificial, fake, counterfeit, sham, phoney (*infml*), contrived, studied, precious, mannered, pretentious, pompous, stiff, unnatural, insincere.
Ea genuine, natural.

affection *n* fondness, attachment, devotion, love, tenderness, care, warmth, feeling, kindness, friendliness, goodwill, favour, liking, partiality, inclination, penchant, passion, desire.
Ea dislike, antipathy.

affectionate *adj* fond, attached, devoted, doting, loving, tender, caring, warm, warm-hearted, kind, friendly, amiable, cordial.
Ea cold, undemonstrative.

affirm *v* confirm, corroborate, endorse, ratify, certify, witness, testify, swear, maintain, state, assert, declare, pronounce.
Ea refute, deny.

affirmative *adj* agreeing, concurring, approving, assenting, positive, confirming, corroborative, emphatic.
Ea negative, dissenting.

afflict *v* strike, visit, trouble, burden, oppress, distress, grieve, pain, hurt, wound, harm, try, harass, beset, plague, torment, torture.
Ea comfort, solace.

affliction *n* distress, grief, sorrow, misery, depression, suffering, pain, torment, disease, illness, sickness, plague, curse, cross, ordeal, trial, tribulation, trouble, hardship, adversity, misfortune, calamity, disaster.
Ea comfort, consolation, solace, blessing.

affluence *n* wealthiness, wealth, riches, fortune, substance, property, prosperity, opulence, abundance, profusion, plenty.
Ea poverty.

affluent *adj* wealthy, rich, moneyed, loaded (*sl*), flush (*infml*), well-off,

prosperous, well-to-do, opulent, comfortable.
Ea poor, impoverished.

afford *v* **1** HAVE ENOUGH FOR, spare, allow, manage, sustain, bear. **2** PROVIDE, supply, furnish, give, grant, offer, impart, produce, yield, generate.

affront *v* offend, insult, abuse, snub, slight, provoke, displease, irritate, annoy, anger, vex, incense, outrage.
Ea compliment, appease.
n offence, insult, slur, rudeness, discourtesy, disrespect, indignity, snub, slight, wrong, injury, abuse, provocation, vexation, outrage.
Ea compliment.

afraid *adj* frightened, scared, alarmed, terrified, fearful, timorous, daunted, intimidated, faint-hearted, cowardly, reluctant, apprehensive, anxious, nervous, timid, distrustful, suspicious.
Ea unafraid, brave, bold, confident.

after *prep* following, subsequent to, in consequence of, as a result of, behind, below.
Ea before.

again *adv* once more, once again, another time, over again, afresh, anew, encore.

against *prep* **1** *against the wall*: abutting, adjacent to, close up to, touching, in contact with, on. **2** OPPOSITE TO, facing, fronting, in the face of, confronting, opposing, versus, opposed to, in opposition to, hostile to, resisting, in defiance of, in contrast to.
Ea 2 for, pro.

age *n* **1** ERA, epoch, day, days, generation, date, time, period, duration, span, years, aeon. **2** OLD AGE, maturity, elderliness, seniority, dotage, senility, decline.
Ea 2 youth.
v grow old, mature, ripen, mellow, season, decline, deteriorate, degenerate.

agency *n* **1** *recruitment agency*: bureau, office, department, organization, business, work. **2** MEANS, medium, instrumentality, power, force, influence, effect, intervention, action, activity, operation, mechanism, workings.

agent *n* **1** SUBSTITUTE, deputy, delegate, envoy, emissary, representative, rep (*infml*), broker, middleman, go-between, intermediary, negotiator, mover, doer, performer, operator, operative, functionary, worker. **2** INSTRUMENT, vehicle, channel, means, agency, cause, force.

aggravate *v* **1** *aggravate a problem*: exacerbate, worsen, inflame, increase, intensify, heighten, magnify, exaggerate. **2** (*infml*) ANNOY, irritate, vex, irk, exasperate, incense, provoke, tease, pester, harass.
E3 **1** improve, alleviate. **2** appease, mollify.

aggregate *n* total, sum, amount, whole, totality, entirety, generality, combination, collection, accumulation.
adj cumulative, accumulated, collected, combined, united, added, total, complete, composite, mixed, collective.
E3 individual, particular.

aggression *n* **1** ANTAGONISM, provocation, offence, injury, attack, offensive, assault, onslaught, raid, incursion, invasion, intrusion. **2** AGGRESSIVENESS, militancy, belligerence, combativeness, hostility.
E3 **1** peace, resistance. **2** passivity, gentleness.

aggressive *adj* argumentative, quarrelsome, contentious, belligerent, hostile, offensive, provocative, intrusive, invasive, bold, assertive, pushy, go-ahead, forceful, vigorous, zealous, ruthless, destructive.
E3 peaceable, friendly, submissive,
timid.

aggrieved *adj* wronged, offended, hurt, injured, insulted, maltreated, ill-used, resentful, pained, distressed, saddened, unhappy, upset, annoyed.
E3 pleased.

aghast *adj* shocked, appalled, horrified, horror-struck, thunderstruck, stunned, stupefied, amazed, astonished, astounded, startled, confounded, dismayed.

agile *adj* active, lively, nimble, spry, sprightly, mobile, flexible, limber, lithe, fleet, quick, swift, brisk, prompt, sharp, acute, alert, quick-witted, clever, adroit, deft.
E3 clumsy, stiff.

agitate *v* **1** ROUSE, arouse, stir up, excite, stimulate, incite, inflame, ferment, work up, worry, trouble, upset, alarm, disturb, unsettle, disquiet, discompose, fluster, ruffle, flurry, unnerve, confuse, distract, disconcert. **2** SHAKE, rattle, rock, stir, beat, churn, toss, convulse.
E3 **1** calm, tranquillize.

agitator *n* troublemaker, rabble-rouser, revolutionary, stirrer (*sl*), inciter, instigator.

agony *n* anguish, torment, torture, pain, spasm, throes, suffering, affliction, tribulation, distress, woe, misery, wretchedness.

agree *v* **1** CONCUR, see eye to eye, get on, settle, accord, match, suit, fit, tally, correspond, conform. **2** CONSENT, allow, permit, assent, accede, grant, admit, concede, yield, comply.
E3 **1** disagree, differ, conflict. **2** refuse.

agreeable *adj* pleasant, congenial, likable, attractive, delightful, enjoyable, gratifying, satisfying, palatable, acceptable, proper, appropriate, suitable, fitting, in accord, consistent.
E3 disagreeable, nasty, distasteful.

agreement *n* **1** SETTLEMENT, compact, covenant, treaty, pact,

contract, deal, bargain, arrangement, understanding. **2** *be in agreement*: concurrence, accord, concord, unanimity, union, harmony, sympathy, affinity, compatibility, similarity, correspondence, consistency, conformity, compliance, adherence, acceptance.
⊟ 2 disagreement.

agricultural *adj* agronomic, agrarian, farming, farmed, cultivated, rural, pastoral, bucolic.

> *Types of agricultural implement and machinery include*: axe, chainsaw, clover broadcaster, fertilizer distributor, field sprinkler, fork, hayfork, pitchfork, hoe, potato planter, rake, hayrake, reaping hook, saw, scythe, shovel, sickle, spade, wheelbarrow, whetstone; all-terrain vehicle (ATV), baler, bale wrapper, cultivator, drill, corn drill, seed drill, fertilizer spreader, fork-lift truck, front end loader, harrow, combination seed-harrow, disc harrow, harvester, combine harvester, hedgecutter, irrigator, milking machine, mower, flail mower, muckspreader, potato planter, plough, reversible plough, wheel plough, power lift, rotary hoe, Rotovator®, scarifier, slurry tanker, sprayer, tedder, tractor, trailer.

agriculture *n* agronomics, farming, husbandry, cultivation, culture, tillage.

ahead *adv* forward, onward, leading, at the head, in front, in the lead, winning, at an advantage, advanced, superior, to the fore, in the forefront, in advance, before, earlier on.

aid *v* help, assist, succour, rally round, relieve, support, subsidize, sustain, second, serve, oblige, accommodate, favour, promote, boost, encourage, expedite, facilitate, ease.
⊟ hinder, impede, obstruct.
n help, assistance, prop, support, relief, benefit, subsidy, donation, contribution, funding, grant, sponsorship, patronage, favour, encouragement, service.
⊟ hindrance, impediment, obstruction.

ailing *adj* unwell, ill, sick, poorly, indisposed, out of sorts (*infml*), under the weather (*infml*), off-colour, suffering, languishing, sickly, diseased, invalid, infirm, unsound, frail, weak, feeble, failing.
⊟ healthy, thriving, flourishing.

ailment *n* illness, sickness, complaint, malady, disease, infection, disorder, affliction, infirmity, disability, weakness.

aim *v* **1** POINT, direct, take aim, level, train, sight, zero in on (*infml*), target. **2** *aim to achieve*: aspire, want, wish, seek, resolve, purpose, intend, propose, mean, plan, design, strive, try, attempt, endeavour.
n aspiration, ambition, hope, dream, desire, wish, plan, design, scheme, purpose, motive, end, intention, object, objective, target, mark, goal, direction, course.

aimless *adj* pointless, purposeless, unmotivated, irresolute, directionless, rambling, undirected, unguided, stray, chance, random, haphazard, erratic, unpredictable, wayward.
⊟ purposeful, positive, determined.

air *n* **1** ATMOSPHERE, oxygen, sky, heavens, breath, puff, waft, draught, breeze, wind, blast. **2** APPEARANCE, look, aspect, aura, bearing, demeanour, manner, character, effect, impression, feeling.
v **1** *air a room*: ventilate, aerate, freshen. **2** *air an opinion*: utter, voice, express, give vent to, make known, communicate, tell, declare, reveal, disclose, divulge, expose, make public, broadcast, publish, circulate,

aircraft 18

disseminate, exhibit, display, parade,
publicize.

aircraft

> *Types of aircraft include*: aeroplane,
> plane, jet, jumbo, Concorde, airbus,
> helicopter, monoplane, two-seater, air-
> ambulance, freighter, sea-plane, glider,
> hang-glider, microlight, hot-air
> balloon; fighter, spitfire, bomber, kite
> (*infml*), jump-jet, dive-bomber,
> chopper (*sl*), spy plane, delta-wing,
> swing-wing, troop-carrier, airship,
> turbojet, VTOL (vertical take-off and
> landing), warplane, zeppelin.

airless *adj* unventilated, stuffy,
musty, stale, suffocating, stifling,
sultry, muggy, close, heavy,
oppressive.
🔁 airy, fresh.

airy *adj* **1** ROOMY, spacious, open,
well-ventilated, draughty, breezy,
blowy, windy, gusty. **2** CHEERFUL,
happy, light-hearted, high-spirited,
lively, nonchalant, offhand.
🔁 **1** airless, stuffy, close, heavy,
oppressive.

aisle *n* gangway, corridor, passage,
passageway, alleyway, walkway,
path, lane.

alarm *v* frighten, scare, startle, put
the wind up (*infml*), terrify, panic,
unnerve, daunt, dismay, distress,
agitate.
🔁 reassure, calm, soothe.
n **1** FRIGHT, scare, fear, terror, panic,
horror, shock, consternation, dismay,
distress, anxiety, nervousness,
apprehension, trepidation, uneasiness.
2 DANGER SIGNAL, alert, warning,
distress signal, siren, bell, alarm-bell.
🔁 calmness, composure.

alarming *adj* frightening, scary,
startling, terrifying, unnerving,
daunting, ominous, threatening,
dismaying, disturbing, distressing,
shocking, dreadful.
🔁 reassuring.

alcohol *n* drink, booze (*sl*), liquor,
spirits, hard stuff (*sl*), intoxicant.

alcoholic *adj* intoxicating, brewed,
fermented, distilled, strong, hard.
n drunk, drunkard, inebriate, hard
drinker, dipsomaniac, wino (*sl*), alkie
(*sl*).

alcove *n* niche, nook, recess, bay,
corner, cubby-hole, compartment,
cubicle, booth, carrel.

alert *adj* attentive, wide-awake,
watchful, vigilant, on the lookout,
sharp-eyed, observant, perceptive,
sharp-witted, on the ball (*infml*),
active, lively, spirited, quick, brisk,
agile, nimble, ready, prepared,
careful, heedful, circumspect, wary.
🔁 slow, listless, unprepared.
v warn, forewarn, notify, inform, tip
off, signal, alarm.

alias *n* pseudonym, false name,
assumed name, nom de guerre, nom
de plume, pen name, stage name,
nickname, sobriquet.
prep also known as, also called,
otherwise, formerly.

alibi *n* defence, justification, story,
explanation, excuse, pretext, reason.

alien *adj* strange, unfamiliar,
outlandish, incongruous, foreign,
exotic, extraterrestrial, extraneous,
remote, estranged, separated,
opposed, contrary, conflicting,
antagonistic, incompatible.
🔁 akin.
n foreigner, immigrant, newcomer,
stranger, outsider.
🔁 native.

alight[1] *v* descend, get down,
dismount, get off, disembark, land,
touch down, come down, come to
rest, settle, light, perch.
🔁 ascend, board.

alight[2] *adj* lighted, lit, ignited, on
fire, burning, blazing, ablaze,
flaming, fiery, lit up, illuminated,
bright, radiant, shining, brilliant.
🔁 dark.

align *v* **1** STRAIGHTEN, range, line

up, make parallel, even (up), adjust, regulate, regularize, order, co-ordinate. **2** ALLY, side, sympathize, associate, affiliate, join, co-operate, agree.

alike *adj* similar, resembling, comparable, akin, analogous, corresponding, equivalent, equal, the same, identical, duplicate, parallel, even, uniform.
☒ dissimilar, unlike, different.
adv similarly, analogously, correspondingly, equally, in common.

alive *adj* **1** LIVING, having life, live, animate, breathing, existent, in existence, real. **2** LIVELY, animated, spirited, awake, alert, active, brisk, energetic, vigorous, zestful, vivacious, vibrant, vital.
☒ **1** dead, extinct. **2** lifeless, apathetic.

all *adj* **1** EACH, every, each and every, every single, every one of, the whole of, every bit of. **2** COMPLETE, entire, full, total, utter, outright, perfect, greatest.
☒ **1** no, none.
n everything, sum, total, aggregate, total amount, whole amount, whole, entirety, utmost, comprehensiveness, universality.
☒ nothing, none.
adv completely, entirely, wholly, fully, totally, utterly, altogether, wholesale.

all right *adj* **1** SATISFACTORY, passable, unobjectionable, acceptable, allowable, adequate, fair, average, OK (*infml*). **2** *are you all right?*: well, healthy, unhurt, uninjured, unharmed, unimpaired, whole, sound, safe, secure.
☒ **1** unacceptable, inadequate.
adv satisfactorily, well enough, passably, unobjectionably, acceptably, suitably, appropriately, adequately, reasonably, OK (*infml*).
☒ unsatisfactorily, unacceptably.

allay *v* alleviate, relieve, soothe, ease, smooth, calm, tranquillize, quiet, quell, pacify, mollify, soften,

blunt, lessen, reduce, diminish, check, moderate.
☒ exacerbate, intensify.

allegation *n* accusation, charge, claim, profession, assertion, affirmation, declaration, statement, testimony, plea.

allege *v* assert, affirm, declare, state, attest, maintain, insist, hold, contend, claim, profess, plead.

alleged *adj* supposed, reputed, putative, inferred, so-called, professed, declared, stated, claimed, described, designated, doubtful, dubious, suspect, suspicious.

allegiance *n* loyalty, fidelity, faithfulness, constancy, duty, obligation, obedience, devotion, support, adherence, friendship.
☒ disloyalty, enmity.

allergic *adj* sensitive, hypersensitive, susceptible, affected, incompatible, averse, disinclined, opposed, hostile, antagonistic.
☒ tolerant.

alleviate *v* relieve, soothe, ease, palliate, mitigate, soften, cushion, dull, deaden, allay, abate, lessen, reduce, diminish, check, moderate, temper, subdue.
☒ aggravate.

alliance *n* confederation, federation, association, affiliation, coalition, league, bloc, cartel, conglomerate, consortium, syndicate, guild, union, partnership, marriage, agreement, compact, bond, pact, treaty, combination, connection.
☒ separation, divorce, estrangement, enmity, hostility.

allocate *v* assign, designate, budget, allow, earmark, set aside, allot, apportion, share out, distribute, dispense, mete.

allocation *n* allotment, lot, apportionment, measure, share, portion, stint, ration, quota, budget, allowance, grant.

allot *v* divide, ration, apportion,

share out, distribute, dispense, mete, dole out, allocate, assign, designate, budget, allow, grant, earmark, set aside.

allotment n division, partition, allocation, apportionment, measure, percentage, lot, portion, share, stint, ration, quota, allowance, grant.

all-out adj complete, full, total, undivided, comprehensive, exhaustive, thorough, intensive, thoroughgoing, wholesale, vigorous, powerful, full-scale, no-holds-barred, maximum, utmost, unlimited, unrestrained, resolute, determined.
ᴈ perfunctory, half-hearted.

allow v **1** PERMIT, let, enable, authorize, sanction, approve, tolerate, put up with, endure, suffer. **2** ADMIT, confess, own, acknowledge, concede, grant. **3** *allow two hours for the journey*: allot, allocate, assign, apportion, afford, give, provide.
ᴈ **1** forbid, prevent. **2** deny.

allow for take into account, make provision for, make allowances for, provide for, foresee, plan for, arrange for, bear in mind, keep in mind, consider, include.
ᴈ discount.

allowance n **1** ALLOTMENT, lot, amount, allocation, portion, share, ration, quota. **2** REBATE, reduction, deduction, discount, concession, subsidy, weighting. **3** PAYMENT, remittance, pocket money, grant, maintenance, stipend, pension, annuity.

alloy n blend, compound, composite, amalgam, combination, mixture, fusion, coalescence.

allure v lure, entice, seduce, lead on, tempt, coax, cajole, persuade, win over, disarm, charm, enchant, attract, interest, fascinate, captivate, entrance, beguile.
ᴈ repel.
n lure, enticement, seduction,

temptation, appeal, attraction, magnetism, fascination, glamour, captivation, charm, enchantment.

allusion n mention, reference, citation, quotation, remark, observation, suggestion, hint, intimation, implication, insinuation.

ally n confederate, associate, leaguer, consort, partner, sidekick, colleague, co-worker, collaborator, helper, helpmate, accomplice, accessory, friend.
ᴈ antagonist, enemy.
v confederate, affiliate, league, associate, collaborate, join forces, band together, team up, fraternize, side, join, connect, link, marry, unite, unify, amalgamate, combine.
ᴈ estrange, separate.

almighty adj **1** OMNIPOTENT, all-powerful, supreme, absolute, great, invincible. **2** ENORMOUS, severe, intense, overwhelming, overpowering, terrible, awful, desperate.
ᴈ **1** impotent, weak.

almost adv nearly, well-nigh, practically, virtually, just about, as good as, all but, close to, not far from, approaching, nearing, not quite, about, approximately.

alone adj only, sole, single, unique, solitary, separate, detached, unconnected, isolated, apart, by oneself, by itself, on one's own, lonely, lonesome, deserted, abandoned, forsaken, forlorn, desolate, unaccompanied, unescorted, unattended, solo, single-handed, unaided, unassisted, mere.
ᴈ together, accompanied, escorted.

aloof adj distant, remote, offish, standoffish, haughty, supercilious, unapproachable, inaccessible, detached, forbidding, cool, chilly, cold, sympathetic, unresponsive, indifferent, uninterested, reserved, unforthcoming, unfriendly, unsociable, formal.

⊟ sociable, friendly, concerned.

aloud *adv* out loud, audibly, intelligibly, clearly, plainly, distinctly, loudly, resoundingly, sonorously, noisily, vociferously.

⊟ silently.

alphabets and writing systems

Alphabets and writing systems include: Byzantine, Chalcidian alphabet, cuneiform, Cyrillic, devanagari, estrangelo, finger-alphabet, futhark, Glagol, Glossic, Greek, Gurmukhi, hieroglyphs, hiragana, ideograph, initial teaching alphabet (i.t.a.), International Phonetic Alphabet (IPA), kana, kanji, katakana, Kufic, linear A, linear B, logograph, nagari, naskhi, ogam, pictograph, romaji, Roman, runic, syllabary.

also *adv* too, as well, and, plus, along with, including, as well as, additionally, in addition, besides, further, furthermore, moreover.

alter *v* change, vary, diversify, modify, qualify, shift, transpose, adjust, adapt, convert, turn, transmute, transform, reform, reshape, remodel, recast, revise, amend, emend.

⊟ fix.

alteration *n* change, variation, variance, difference, diversification, shift, transposition, modification, adjustment, adaptation, conversion, transformation, transfiguration, metamorphosis, reformation, reshaping, remodelling, revision, amendment.

⊟ fixity.

alternate *v* interchange, reciprocate, rotate, take turns, follow one another, replace each other, substitute, change, alter, vary, oscillate, fluctuate, intersperse.

adj alternating, every other, every second, interchanging, reciprocal, rotating, alternative.

alternative *n* option, choice, selection, preference, other, recourse, substitute, back-up.

adj substitute, second, another, other, different, unorthodox, unconventional, fringe, alternate.

altitude *n* height, elevation, loftiness, tallness, stature.

⊟ depth.

altogether *adv* totally, completely, entirely, wholly, fully, utterly, absolutely, quite, perfectly, thoroughly, in all, all told, in toto, all in all, as a whole, on the whole, generally, in general.

altruistic *adj* unselfish, self-sacrificing, disinterested, public-spirited, philanthropic, charitable, humanitarian, benevolent, generous, considerate, humane.

⊟ selfish.

always *adv* every time, consistently, invariably, without exception, unfailingly, regularly, repeatedly, continually, constantly, perpetually, unceasingly, eternally, endlessly, evermore, forever, ever.

⊟ never.

amalgamate *v* merge, blend, mingle, commingle, intermix, homogenize, incorporate, alloy, integrate, compound, fuse, coalesce, synthesize, combine, unite, unify, ally.

⊟ separate.

amateur *n* non-professional, layman, ham (*infml*), dilettante, dabbler, enthusiast, fancier, buff (*infml*).

⊟ professional.

adj non-professional, lay, unpaid, unqualified, untrained, amateurish, inexpert, unprofessional.

⊟ professional.

amaze *v* surprise, startle, astonish, astound, stun, stupefy, daze, stagger, floor (*infml*), dumbfound, flabbergast (*infml*), shock, dismay, disconcert, confound, bewilder.

amazement n surprise,
astonishment, shock, dismay,
confusion, perplexity, bewilderment,
admiration, wonderment, wonder,
marvel.

ambassador n emissary, envoy,
legate, diplomat, consul,
plenipotentiary, deputy,
representative, agent, minister,
apostle.

ambiguity n double meaning,
double entendre, equivocality,
equivocation, enigma, puzzle,
confusion, obscurity, unclearness,
vagueness, woolliness, dubiousness,
doubt, doubtfulness, uncertainty.
E3 clarity.

ambiguous adj double-meaning,
equivocal, multivocal, double-edged,
back-handed, cryptic, enigmatic,
puzzling, confusing, obscure, unclear,
vague, indefinite, woolly, confused,
dubious, doubtful, uncertain,
inconclusive, indeterminate.
E3 clear, definite.

ambition n **1** ASPIRATION, aim,
goal, target, objective, intent,
purpose, design, object, ideal, dream,
hope, wish, desire, yearning, longing,
hankering, craving, hunger. **2** *a
woman of ambition*: enterprise, drive,
push, thrust, striving, eagerness,
commitment, zeal.
E3 **2** apathy, diffidence.

ambitious adj **1** ASPIRING, hopeful,
desirous, intent, purposeful, pushy,
bold, assertive, go-ahead,
enterprising, driving, energetic,
enthusiastic, eager, keen, striving,
industrious, zealous. **2** FORMIDABLE,
hard, difficult, arduous, strenuous,
demanding, challenging, exacting,
impressive, grandiose, elaborate.
E3 **1** lazy, unassuming. **2** modest,
uninspiring.

ambivalent adj contradictory,
conflicting, clashing, warring,
opposed, inconsistent, mixed,

confused, fluctuating, vacillating,
wavering, hesitant, irresolute,
undecided, unresolved, unsettled,
uncertain, unsure, doubtful,
debatable, inconclusive.

amble v walk, saunter, toddle
(*infml*), stroll, promenade, wander,
drift, meander, ramble.
E3 stride, march.

ambush n waylaying, surprise
attack, trap, snare, cover, hiding-
place.
v lie in wait, waylay, surprise, trap,
ensnare.

amenable adj accommodating,
flexible, open, agreeable,
persuadable, compliant, tractable,
submissive, responsive, susceptible,
liable, responsible.
E3 intractable.

amend v revise, correct, rectify,
emend, fix, repair, mend, remedy,
redress, reform, change, alter, adjust,
modify, qualify, enhance, improve,
ameliorate, better.
E3 impair, worsen.

amendment n revision, correction,
corrigendum, rectification,
emendation, repair, remedy, reform,
change, alteration, adjustment,
modification, qualification,
clarification, addendum, addition,
adjunct, improvement.
E3 impairment, deterioration.

amends n atonement, expiation,
requital, satisfaction, recompense,
compensation, indemnification,
indemnity, reparation, redress,
restoration, restitution.

amiable adj affable, friendly,
approachable, genial, cheerful, good-
tempered, good-natured, kind,
obliging, charming, engaging, likable,
pleasant, agreeable, congenial,
companionable, sociable.
E3 unfriendly, curt, hostile.

amid prep amidst, midst, in the
midst of, in the thick of, among,
amongst, in the middle of,

surrounded by.

amnesty *n* pardon, forgiveness, absolution, mercy, lenience, indulgence, reprieve, remission, dispensation, immunity, oblivion.

among *prep* amongst, between, in the middle of, surrounded by, amid, amidst, midst, in the midst of, in the thick of, with, together with.

amount *n* quantity, number, sum, total, sum total, whole, entirety, aggregate, lot, quota, supply, volume, mass, bulk, measure, magnitude, extent, expanse.

 amount to add up to, total, aggregate, come to, make, equal, mean, be tantamount to, be equivalent to, approximate to, become, grow.

amphibian

> *Amphibians include*: frog, bullfrog, tree frog, toad, horned toad, midwife toad, natterjack, newt, eft, salamander, congo eel, axolotl.

ample *adj* large, big, extensive, expansive, broad, wide, full, voluminous, roomy, spacious, commodious, great, considerable, substantial, handsome, generous, bountiful, munificent, liberal, lavish, copious, abundant, plentiful, plenty, unrestricted, profuse, rich.
 Ↄ insufficient, inadequate, meagre.

amplify *v* enlarge, magnify, expand, dilate, fill out, bulk out, add to, supplement, augment, increase, extend, lengthen, widen, broaden, develop, elaborate, enhance, boost, intensify, strengthen, deepen, heighten, raise.
 Ↄ reduce, decrease, abridge.

amputate *v* cut off, remove, sever, dissever, separate, dock, lop, curtail, truncate.

amuse *v* entertain, divert, regale, make laugh, tickle (*infml*), crease (*infml*), slay (*infml*), cheer (up), gladden, enliven, please, charm,

delight, enthral, engross, absorb, interest, occupy, recreate, relax.
 Ↄ bore, displease.

amusement *n* entertainment, diversion, distraction, fun, enjoyment, pleasure, delight, merriment, mirth, hilarity, laughter, joke, prank, game, sport, recreation, hobby, pastime, interest.
 Ↄ boredom, monotony.

amusing *adj* funny, humorous, hilarious, comical, laughable, ludicrous, droll, witty, facetious, jocular, jolly, enjoyable, pleasant, charming, delightful, entertaining, interesting.
 Ↄ dull, boring.

anaemic *adj* bloodless, ashen, chalky, livid, pasty, pallid, sallow, whey-faced, pale, wan, colourless, insipid, weak, feeble, ineffectual, enervated, frail, infirm, sickly.
 Ↄ ruddy, sanguine, full-blooded.

anaesthetize *v* desensitize, numb, deaden, dull, drug, dope, stupefy.

analogy *n* comparison, simile, metaphor, likeness, resemblance, similarity, parallel, correspondence, equivalence, relation, correlation, agreement.

analyse *v* break down, separate, divide, take apart, dissect, anatomize, reduce, resolve, sift, investigate, study, examine, scrutinize, review, interpret, test, judge, evaluate, estimate, consider.

analysis *n* breakdown, separation, division, dissection, reduction, resolution, sifting, investigation, enquiry, study, examination, scrutiny, review, exposition, explication, explanation, interpretation, test, judgement, opinion, evaluation, estimation, reasoning.
 Ↄ synthesis.

analytic *adj* analytical, dissecting, detailed, in-depth, searching, critical, questioning, enquiring, inquisitive,

investigative, diagnostic, systematic,
methodical, logical, rational,
interpretative, explanatory,
expository, studious.

anarchic *adj* lawless, ungoverned,
anarchistic, libertarian, nihilist,
revolutionary, rebellious, mutinous,
riotous, chaotic, disordered,
confused, disorganized.
Ea submissive, orderly.

anarchist *n* revolutionary, rebel,
insurgent, libertarian, nihilist,
terrorist.

anarchy *n* lawlessness, unrule,
misrule, anarchism, revolution,
rebellion, insurrection, mutiny, riot,
pandemonium, chaos, disorder,
confusion.
Ea rule, control, order.

anathema *n* aversion, abhorrence,
abomination, object of loathing, bête
noire, bugbear, bane, curse,
proscription, taboo.

anatomical terms

Anatomical terms include: aural,
biceps, bone, cardiac, cartilage,
cerebral, dental, diaphragm, dorsal,
duodenal, elbow, epidermis, epiglottis,
Fallopian tubes, foreskin, funny bone,
gastric, genitalia, gingival, gristle,
groin, gullet, hamstring, helix,
hepatic, hock, intercostal, jugular,
lachrymal, ligament, lumbar,
mammary, membral, muscle, nasal,
neural, ocular, oesophagus, optical,
pectoral, pedal, pulmonary, renal,
spine, tendon, triceps, umbilicus,
uterus, uvula, voice-box, vulva,
windpipe, wisdom tooth, womb. *see
also* **bone**.

ancestor *n* forebear, forefather,
progenitor, predecessor, forerunner,
precursor, antecedent.
Ea descendant.

ancestral *adj* familial, parental,
genealogical, lineal, hereditary,
genetic.

ancestry *n* ancestors, forebears,
forefathers, progenitors, parentage,
family, lineage, line, descent, blood,
race, stock, roots, pedigree,
genealogy, extraction, derivation,
origin, heritage, heredity.

anchor *v* moor, berth, tie up, make
fast, fasten, attach, affix, fix.

Types of anchor include: car,
double fluked, grapnel, kedge, killick,
mushroom, navy, sea, stocked,
stockless, yachtsman.

ancient *adj* **1** OLD, aged, time-worn,
age-old, antique, antediluvian,
prehistoric, fossilized, primeval,
immemorial. **2** OLD-FASHIONED,
out-of-date, antiquated, archaic,
obsolete, bygone, early, original.
Ea **1** recent, contemporary. **2** modern,
up-to-date.

anecdote *n* story, tale, yarn, sketch,
reminiscence.

angel *n* **1** *angel of God*: archangel,
cherub, seraph, divine messenger,
principality. **2** DARLING, treasure,
saint, paragon, ideal.
Ea **1** devil, fiend.

The nine orders of angels are:
seraph, cherub, throne, domination,
dominion, virtue, power, principality,
archangel, angel.

angelic *adj* cherubic, seraphic,
celestial, heavenly, divine, holy,
pious, saintly, pure, innocent,
unworldly, virtuous, lovely,
beautiful, adorable.
Ea devilish, fiendish.

anger *n* annoyance, irritation,
antagonism, displeasure, irritability,
temper, pique, vexation, ire, rage,
fury, wrath, exasperation, outrage,
indignation, gall, bitterness, rancour,
resentment.
Ea forgiveness, forbearance.
v annoy, irritate, aggravate (*infml*)

wind up (*infml*), vex, irk, rile, miff (*infml*), needle, nettle, bother, ruffle, provoke, antagonize, offend, affront, gall, madden, enrage, incense, infuriate, exasperate, outrage.
E3 please, appease, calm.

angle *n* 1 CORNER, nook, bend, flexure, hook, crook, elbow, knee, crotch, edge, point. 2 ASPECT, outlook, facet, side, approach, direction, position, standpoint, viewpoint, point of view, slant, perspective.

angry *adj* annoyed, cross, irritated, aggravated (*infml*), displeased, uptight (*infml*), irate, mad (*infml*), enraged, incensed, infuriated, furious, raging, passionate, heated, hot, exasperated, outraged, indignant, bitter, resentful.
E3 content, happy, calm.

animal *n* creature, mammal, beast, brute, barbarian, savage, monster, cur, pig, swine.

> *Animals include*: cat, dog, hamster, gerbil, mouse, rat, rabbit, hare, fox, badger, beaver, mole, otter, weasel, ferret, ermine, mink, hedgehog, squirrel, horse, pig, cow, bull, goat, sheep; monkey, lemur, gibbon, ape, chimpanzee, orang-utan, baboon, gorilla; seal, sea lion, dolphin, walrus, whale; lion, tiger, cheetah, puma, panther, cougar, jaguar, ocelot, leopard; aardvark, armadillo, wolf, wolverine, hyena, mongoose, skunk, racoon, wombat, platypus, koala, polecat; deer, antelope, gazelle, eland, impala, reindeer, elk, caribou, moose; wallaby, kangaroo, bison, buffalo, gnu, camel, zebra, llama, panda, giant panda, grizzly bear, polar bear, giraffe, hippopotamus, rhinoceros, elephant. *see also* **amphibian**; **bird**; **cattle**; **dog**; **fish**; **insect**; **reptile**.

adj bestial, brutish, inhuman, savage, wild, instinctive, bodily, physical,

carnal, fleshly, sensual.

animate *adj* alive, living, live, breathing, conscious.
E3 inanimate.

animated *adj* lively, spirited, buoyant, vibrant, ebullient, vivacious, alive, vital, quick, brisk, vigorous, energetic, active, passionate, impassioned, vehement, ardent, fervent, glowing, radiant, excited, enthusiastic, eager.
E3 lethargic, sluggish, inert.

animosity *n* ill feeling, ill-will, acrimony, bitterness, rancour, resentment, spite, malice, malignity, malevolence, hate, hatred, loathing, antagonism, hostility, enmity, feud.
E3 goodwill.

annex *v* 1 ADD, append, affix, attach, fasten, adjoin, join, connect, unite, incorporate. 2 ACQUIRE, appropriate, seize, usurp, occupy, conquer, take over.

annexe *n* wing, extension, attachment, addition, supplement, expansion.

annihilate *v* eliminate, eradicate, obliterate, erase, wipe out, liquidate (*infml*), murder, assassinate, exterminate, extinguish, raze, destroy, abolish.

anniversary

> *Names of wedding anniversary include*: 1st cotton, 2nd paper, 3rd leather, 4th flowers/fruit, 5th wood, 6th iron/sugar, 7th copper/wool, 8th bronze/pottery, 9th pottery/willow, 10th tin, 11th steel, 12th silk/linen, 13th lace, 14th ivory, 15th crystal, 20th china, 25th silver, 30th pearl, 35th coral, 40th ruby, 45th sapphire, 50th gold, 55th emerald, 60th diamond, 70th platinum.

annotation *n* note, footnote, gloss, comment, commentary, exegesis, explanation, elucidation.

announce *v* declare, proclaim,

report, state, reveal, disclose, divulge, make known, notify, intimate, promulgate, propound, publish, broadcast, advertise, publicize, blazon.
🔁 suppress.

announcement n declaration, proclamation, report, statement, communiqué, dispatch, bulletin, notification, intimation, revelation, disclosure, divulgence, publication, broadcast, advertisement.

announcer n broadcaster, newscaster, newsreader, commentator, compère, master of ceremonies, MC, town crier, herald, messenger.

annoy v irritate, rile, aggravate (infml), displease, anger, vex, irk, madden, exasperate, tease, provoke, ruffle, trouble, disturb, bother, pester, plague, harass, molest.
🔁 please, gratify, comfort.

annoyance n **1** NUISANCE, pest, disturbance, bother, trouble, bore, bind (sl), pain (infml), headache (infml), tease, provocation. **2** express one's annoyance: irritation, aggravation (infml), displeasure, anger, vexation, exasperation, harassment.
🔁 **2** pleasure.

annoyed adj irritated, cross, displeased, angry, vexed, piqued, exasperated, provoked, harassed.
🔁 pleased.

annoying adj irritating, aggravating (infml), vexatious, irksome, troublesome, bothersome, tiresome, trying, maddening, exasperating, galling, offensive, teasing, provoking, harassing.
🔁 pleasing, welcome.

annul v nullify, invalidate, void, rescind, abrogate, suspend, cancel, abolish, quash, repeal, revoke, countermand, negate, retract, recall, reverse.
🔁 enact, restore.

anoint v **1** OIL, grease, lubricate, embrocate, rub, smear, daub.
2 BLESS, consecrate, sanctify, dedicate.

anomalous adj abnormal, atypical, exceptional, irregular, inconsistent, incongruous, deviant, freakish, eccentric, peculiar, odd, unusual, singular, rare.
🔁 normal, regular, ordinary.

anomaly n abnormality, exception, irregularity, inconsistency, incongruity, aberration, deviation, divergence, departure, freak, misfit, eccentricity, peculiarity, oddity, rarity.

anonymous adj unnamed, nameless, unsigned, unacknowledged, unspecified, unidentified, unknown, incognito, faceless, impersonal, nondescript, unexceptional.
🔁 named, signed, identifiable, distinctive.

answer n **1** REPLY, acknowledgement, response, reaction, rejoinder, retort, riposte, comeback, retaliation, rebuttal, vindication, defence, plea.
2 SOLUTION, explanation.
v **1** REPLY, acknowledge, respond, react, retort, retaliate, refute, solve.
2 answer one's needs: fulfil, fill, meet, satisfy, match up to, correspond, correlate, conform, agree, fit, suit, serve, pass.

answer back talk back, retort, riposte, retaliate, contradict, disagree, argue, dispute, rebut.

answerable adj liable, responsible, accountable, chargeable, blameworthy, to blame.

antagonism n hostility, opposition, rivalry, antipathy, ill feeling, ill-will, animosity, friction, discord, dissension, contention, conflict.
🔁 rapport, sympathy, agreement.

antagonist n opponent, adversary, enemy, foe, rival, competitor, contestant, contender.

⊟ ally, supporter.

antagonistic *adj* conflicting, opposed, adverse, at variance, incompatible, hostile, belligerent, contentious, unfriendly, ill-disposed, averse.

⊟ sympathetic, friendly.

antagonize *v* alienate, estrange, disaffect, repel, embitter, offend, insult, provoke, annoy, irritate, anger, incense.

⊟ disarm.

anthem *n* hymn, song, chorale, psalm, canticle, chant.

anthology *n* selection, collection, compilation, compendium, digest, treasury, miscellany.

anticipate *v* **1** FORESTALL, preempt, intercept, prevent, obviate, preclude. **2** EXPECT, foresee, predict, forecast, look for, await, look forward to, hope for, bank on, count upon.

anticlimax *n* bathos, comedown, let-down, disappointment, fiasco.

antics *n* foolery, tomfoolery, silliness, buffoonery, clowning, frolics, capers, skylarking, playfulness, mischief, tricks, monkey-tricks, pranks, stunts, doings.

antidote *n* remedy, cure, counter-agent, antitoxin, neutralizer, countermeasure, corrective.

antipathy *n* aversion, dislike, hate, hatred, loathing, abhorrence, distaste, disgust, repulsion, antagonism, animosity, ill-will, bad blood, enmity, hostility, opposition, incompatibility.

⊟ sympathy, affection, rapport.

antique *adj* antiquarian, ancient, old, veteran, vintage, quaint, antiquated, old-fashioned, outdated, archaic, obsolete.

n antiquity, relic, bygone, period piece, heirloom, curio, museum piece, curiosity, rarity.

antiquity *n* ancient times, time immemorial, distant past, olden days,

age, old age, oldness, agedness.

⊟ modernity, novelty.

antiseptic *adj* disinfectant, medicated, aseptic, germ-free, clean, pure, unpolluted, uncontaminated, sterile, sterilized, sanitized, sanitary, hygienic.

n disinfectant, germicide, bactericide, purifier, cleanser.

antisocial *adj* asocial, unacceptable, disruptive, disorderly, rebellious, belligerent, antagonistic, hostile, unfriendly, unsociable, uncommunicative, reserved, retiring, withdrawn, alienated, unapproachable.

⊟ sociable, gregarious.

anxiety *n* worry, concern, care, distress, nervousness, apprehension, dread, foreboding, misgiving, uneasiness, restlessness, fretfulness, impatience, suspense, tension, stress.

⊟ calm, composure, serenity.

anxious *adj* worried, concerned, nervous, apprehensive, afraid, fearful, uneasy, restless, fretful, impatient, in suspense, on tenterhooks, tense, taut, distressed, disturbed, troubled, tormented, tortured.

⊟ calm, composed.

apart *adv* **1** SEPARATELY, independently, individually, singly, alone, on one's own, by oneself, privately, aside, to one side, away, afar, distant, aloof, excluded, isolated, cut off, separated, divorced, separate, distinct. **2** *tear apart*: to pieces, to bits, into parts, in pieces, in bits, piecemeal.

⊟ 1 connected. **2** together.

apathetic *adj* uninterested, uninvolved, indifferent, cool, unemotional, emotionless, impassive, unmoved, unconcerned, cold, unfeeling, numb, unresponsive, passive, listless, unambitious.

⊟ enthusiastic, involved, concerned, feeling, responsive.

apathy n uninterestedness, indifference, coolness, impassivity, unconcern, coldness, insensibility, passivity, listlessness, lethargy, sluggishness, torpor, inertia.
🔁 enthusiasm, interest, concern.

ape v copy, imitate, echo, mirror, parrot, mimic, take off, caricature, parody, mock, counterfeit, affect.
n monkey, chimpanzee, gibbon, gorilla, baboon, orang-utan.

aplomb n composure, calmness, equanimity, poise, balance, coolness, confidence, assurance, self-assurance, audacity.
🔁 discomposure.

apocryphal adj unauthenticated, unverified, unsubstantiated, unsupported, questionable, spurious, equivocal, doubtful, dubious, fabricated, concocted, fictitious, imaginary, legendary, mythical.
🔁 authentic, true.

apologetic adj sorry, repentant, penitent, contrite, remorseful, conscience-stricken, regretful, rueful.
🔁 unrepentant, impenitent, defiant.

apology n acknowledgement, confession, excuse, explanation, justification, vindication, defence, plea.
🔁 defiance.

appal v horrify, shock, outrage, disgust, dismay, disconcert, daunt, intimidate, unnerve, alarm, scare, frighten, terrify.
🔁 reassure, encourage.

appalling adj horrifying, horrific, harrowing, shocking, outrageous, atrocious, disgusting, awful, dreadful, frightful, terrible, dire, grim, hideous, ghastly, horrible, horrid, loathsome, daunting, intimidating, unnerving, alarming, frightening, terrifying.
🔁 reassuring, encouraging.

apparatus n machine, appliance, gadget, device, contraption, equipment, gear, tackle, outfit, tools, implements, utensils, materials, machinery, system, mechanism, means.

apparent adj seeming, outward, visible, evident, noticeable, perceptible, plain, clear, distinct, marked, unmistakable, obvious, manifest, patent, open, declared.
🔁 hidden, obscure.

apparently adv seemingly, ostensibly, outwardly, superficially, plainly, clearly, obviously, manifestly, patently.

apparition n ghost, spectre, phantom, spirit, chimera, vision, manifestation, materialization, presence.

appeal n 1 REQUEST, application, petition, suit, solicitation, plea, entreaty, supplication, prayer, invocation. 2 ATTRACTION, allure, interest, fascination, enchantment, charm, attractiveness, winsomeness, beauty, charisma, magnetism.
v 1 appeal for help: ask, request, call, apply, address, petition, sue, solicit, plead, beg, beseech, implore, entreat, supplicate, pray, invoke, call upon.
2 ATTRACT, draw, allure, lure, tempt, entice, invite, interest, engage, fascinate, charm, please.

appear v 1 ARRIVE, enter, turn up, attend, materialize, develop, show (up), come into sight, come into view, loom, rise, surface, arise, occur, crop up, come to light, come out, emerge, issue, be published. 2 SEEM, look, turn out. 3 appear in a show: act, perform, play, take part.
🔁 1 disappear, vanish.

appearance n 1 APPEARING, arrival, advent, coming, rise, emergence, début, introduction.
2 LOOK, expression, face, aspect, air, bearing, demeanour, manner, looks, figure, form, semblance, show, front, guise, illusion, impression, image.
🔁 1 disappearance.

appendix n addition, appendage,

adjunct, addendum, supplement, epilogue, codicil, postscript, rider.

appetite n hunger, stomach, relish, zest, taste, propensity, inclination, liking, desire, longing, yearning, craving, eagerness, passion, zeal.
🔁 distaste.

appetizing adj mouthwatering, tempting, inviting, appealing, palatable, tasty, delicious, scrumptious (*infml*), succulent, piquant, savoury.
🔁 disgusting, distasteful.

applaud v clap, cheer, acclaim, compliment, congratulate, approve, commend, praise, laud, eulogize, extol.
🔁 criticize, censure.

applause n ovation, clapping, cheering, cheers, acclaim, acclamation, accolade, congratulation, approval, commendation, praise.
🔁 criticism, censure.

appliance n machine, device, contrivance, contraption, gadget, tool, implement, instrument, apparatus, mechanism.

applicable adj relevant, pertinent, apposite, apt, appropriate, fitting, suited, useful, suitable, fit, proper, valid, legitimate.
🔁 inapplicable, inappropriate.

applicant n candidate, interviewee, contestant, competitor, aspirant, suitor, petitioner, inquirer.

application n 1 REQUEST, appeal, petition, suit, claim, inquiry.
2 RELEVANCE, pertinence, function, purpose, use, value. 3 DILIGENCE, industry, assiduity, effort, commitment, dedication, perseverance, keenness, attentiveness.

apply v 1 REQUEST, ask for, requisition, put in for, appeal, petition, solicit, sue, claim, inquire.
2 *apply oneself to a task*: address, buckle down, settle down, commit, devote, dedicate, give, direct,

concentrate, study, persevere. 3 USE, exercise, utilize, employ, bring into play, engage, harness, ply, wield, administer, execute, implement, assign, direct, bring to bear, practise, resort to. 4 REFER, relate, be relevant, pertain, fit, suit. 5 *apply ointment*: put on, spread on, lay on, cover with, paint, anoint, smear, rub.

appoint v 1 NAME, nominate, elect, install, choose, select, engage, employ, take on, commission, delegate, assign, allot, designate, command, direct, charge, detail.
2 DECIDE, determine, arrange, settle, fix, set, establish, ordain, decree, destine.
🔁 1 reject, dismiss, discharge.

appointment n 1 ARRANGEMENT, engagement, date, meeting, rendezvous, interview, consultation.
2 JOB, position, situation, post, office, place. 3 NAMING, nomination, election, choosing, choice, selection, commissioning, delegation.

appraisal n valuation, rating, survey, inspection, review, examination, once-over (*infml*), evaluation, assessment, estimate, estimation, judgement, reckoning, opinion, appreciation.

appreciate v 1 ENJOY, relish, savour, prize, treasure, value, cherish, admire, respect, regard, esteem, like, welcome, take kindly to.
2 *appreciate in value*: grow, increase, rise, mount, inflate, gain, strengthen, improve, enhance. 3 UNDERSTAND, comprehend, perceive, realize, recognize, acknowledge, sympathize with, know.
🔁 1 despise. 2 depreciate. 3 overlook.

appreciation n 1 ENJOYMENT, relish, admiration, respect, regard, esteem, gratitude, gratefulness, thankfulness, indebtedness, obligation, liking, sensitivity, responsiveness, valuation, assessment, estimation, judgement.

2 GROWTH, increase, rise, inflation, gain, improvement, enhancement.
3 UNDERSTANDING, comprehension, perception, awareness, realization, recognition, acknowledgement, sympathy, knowledge.
⊟ 1 ingratitude. 2 depreciation.

appreciative *adj* **1** GRATEFUL, thankful, obliged, indebted, pleased.
2 ADMIRING, encouraging, enthusiastic, respectful, sensitive, responsive, perceptive, knowledgeable, conscious, mindful.
⊟ 1 ungrateful.

apprehension *n* dread, foreboding, misgiving, qualm, uneasiness, anxiety, worry, concern, disquiet, alarm, fear, doubt, suspicion, mistrust.

apprehensive *adj* nervous, anxious, worried, concerned, uneasy, doubtful, suspicious, mistrustful, distrustful, alarmed, afraid.
⊟ assured, confident.

apprentice *n* trainee, probationer, student, pupil, learner, novice, beginner, starter, recruit, newcomer.
⊟ expert.

approach *v* **1** ADVANCE, move towards, draw near, near, gain on, catch up, reach, meet. **2** APPLY TO, appeal to, sound out. **3** BEGIN, commence, set about, undertake, introduce, mention. **4** RESEMBLE, be like, compare with, approximate, come close.
n **1** *the approach of winter*: advance, coming, advent, arrival. **2** ACCESS, road, avenue, way, passage, entrance, doorway, threshold. **3** APPLICATION, appeal, overture, proposition, proposal. **4** ATTITUDE, manner, style, technique, procedure, method, means.

appropriate *adj* applicable, relevant, pertinent, to the point, well-chosen, apt, fitting, meet (*fml*), suitable, fit, befitting, becoming, proper, right, correct, spot-on (*infml*), well-timed, timely,

seasonable, opportune.
⊟ inappropriate, irrelevant, unsuitable.
v **1** SEIZE, take, expropriate, commandeer, requisition, confiscate, impound, assume, usurp. **2** STEAL, pocket, filch, pilfer, purloin, embezzle, misappropriate.

approval *n* **1** ADMIRATION, esteem, regard, respect, good opinion, liking, appreciation, approbation, favour, recommendation, praise, commendation, acclaim, acclamation, honour, applause.
2 AGREEMENT, concurrence, assent, consent, permission, leave, sanction, authorization, licence, mandate, go-ahead, green light (*infml*), blessing, OK (*infml*), certification, ratification, validation, confirmation, support.
⊟ 1 disapproval, condemnation.

approve *v* **1** ADMIRE, esteem, regard, like, appreciate, favour, recommend, praise, commend, acclaim, applaud. **2** *approve a proposal*: agree to, assent to, consent to, accede to, allow, permit, pass, sanction, authorize, mandate, bless, countenance, OK (*infml*), ratify, rubber-stamp (*infml*), validate, endorse, support, uphold, second, back, accept, adopt, confirm.
⊟ 1 disapprove, condemn.

approximate *adj* estimated, guessed, rough, inexact, loose, close, near, like, similar, relative.
⊟ exact.
v approach, border on, verge on, be tantamount to, resemble.

approximately *n* roughly, around, about, circa, more or less, loosely, approaching, close to, nearly, just about.

apt *adj* **1** RELEVANT, applicable, apposite, appropriate, fitting, suitable, fit, seemly, proper, correct, accurate, spot-on (*infml*), timely, seasonable. **2** CLEVER, gifted, talented, skilful, expert, intelligent,

quick, sharp. **3** LIABLE, prone,
given, disposed, likely, ready.
F3 1 inapt. **2** stupid.

aptitude *n* ability, capability,
capacity, faculty, gift, talent, flair,
facility, proficiency, cleverness,
intelligence, quickness, bent,
inclination, leaning, disposition,
tendency.
F3 inaptitude.

arbitrary *adj* **1** RANDOM, chance,
capricious, inconsistent,
discretionary, subjective, instinctive,
unreasoned, illogical, irrational,
unreasonable. **2** DESPOTIC,
tyrannical, dictatorial, autocratic,
absolute, imperious, magisterial,
domineering, overbearing, high-
handed, dogmatic.
F3 1 reasoned, rational, circumspect.

arbitrate *v* judge, adjudicate,
referee, umpire, mediate, settle,
decide, determine.

arbitration *n* judgement,
adjudication, intervention,
mediation, negotiation, settlement,
decision, determination.

arbitrator *n* judge, adjudicator,
arbiter, referee, umpire, moderator,
mediator, negotiator, intermediary,
go-between.

arch *n* archway, bridge, span, dome,
vault, concave, bend, curve,
curvature, bow, arc, semicircle.
v bend, curve, bow, arc, vault,
camber.

Types of arch include: basket
handle, convex, corbel, equilateral,
four-centre, Gothic, horseshoe, keel,
lancet, Norman, ogee, parabolic,
round, segmental, shouldered, skew,
stilted, tented, trefoil, Tudor.

archaic *adj* antiquated, old-
fashioned, outmoded, old hat (*infml*),
passé, outdated, out-of-date,
obsolete, old, ancient, antique,
quaint, primitive.

F3 modern, recent.

archetype *n* pattern, model,
standard, form, type, prototype,
original, precursor, classic,
paradigm, ideal.

architect *n* designer, planner, master
builder, prime mover, originator,
founder, instigator, creator, author,
inventor, engineer, maker,
constructor, shaper.

architecture and building

*Architectural and building terms
include*: alcove, annexe, architrave,
baluster, barge-board, baroque, bas
relief, capstone, casement window,
classical, coping stone, Corinthian,
corner-stone, cornice, coving, dado,
decorated, dogtooth, dome, Doric,
dormer, double-glazing, drawbridge,
dry-stone, duplex, Early English,
eaves, Edwardian, elevation,
Elizabethan, façade, fanlight, fascia,
festoon, fillet, finial, flamboyant,
Flemish bond, fletton, fluting, French
window, frieze, frontispiece, gable,
gargoyle, gatehouse, Georgian,
Gothic, groin, groundplan, half-
timbered, Ionic, jamb, lintel, mullion,
Norman, pagoda, pantile, parapet,
pinnacle, plinth, Queen-Anne, rafters,
Regency, reveal, ridge, rococo,
Romanesque, roof, rotunda,
roughcast, sacristy, scroll, soffit,
stucco, terrazzo, Tudor, Tuscan,
wainscot, weathering.

archives *n* records, annals,
chronicles, memorials, papers,
documents, deeds, ledgers, registers,
roll.

ardent *adj* fervent, fiery, warm,
passionate, impassioned, fierce,
vehement, intense, spirited,
enthusiastic, eager, keen, dedicated,
devoted, zealous.
F3 apathetic, unenthusiastic.

arduous *adj* hard, difficult, tough,
rigorous, severe, harsh, formidable,

strenuous, tiring, taxing, fatiguing, exhausting, backbreaking, punishing, gruelling, uphill, laborious, onerous. ✷ easy.

area n locality, neighbourhood, environment, environs, patch, terrain, district, region, zone, sector, department, province, domain, realm, territory, sphere, field, range, scope, compass, size, extent, expanse, width, breadth, stretch, tract, part, portion, section.

argue v **1** QUARREL, squabble, bicker, row, wrangle, haggle, remonstrate, join issue, fight, feud, fall out, disagree, dispute, question, debate, discuss. **2** REASON, assert, contend, hold, maintain, claim, plead, exhibit, display, show, manifest, demonstrate, indicate, denote, prove, evidence, suggest, imply.

argument n **1** QUARREL, squabble, row, wrangle, controversy, debate, discussion, dispute, disagreement, clash, conflict, fight, feud. **2** REASONING, reason, logic, assertion, contention, claim, demonstration, defence, case, synopsis, summary, theme.

argumentative adj quarrelsome, contentious, polemical, opinionated, belligerent, perverse, contrary. ✷ complaisant.

arid adj **1** arid landscape: dry, parched, waterless, desiccated, torrid, barren, infertile, unproductive, desert, waste. **2** DULL, uninteresting, boring, monotonous, tedious, dry, sterile, dreary, colourless, lifeless, spiritless, uninspired. ✷ **1** fertile. **2** lively.

arise v **1** ORIGINATE, begin, start, commence, derive, stem, spring, proceed, flow, emerge, issue, appear, come to light, crop up, occur, happen, result, ensue, follow. **2** RISE, get up, stand up, go up, ascend, climb, mount, lift, soar, tower.

aristocracy n upper class, gentry, nobility, peerage, ruling class, gentility, élite. ✷ common people.

aristocrat n noble, patrician, nobleman, noblewoman, peer, peeress, lord, lady. ✷ commoner.

aristocratic adj upper-class, highborn, well-born, noble, patrician, blue-blooded, titled, lordly, courtly, gentle, thoroughbred, élite. ✷ plebeian, vulgar.

arm¹ n limb, upper limb, appendage, bough, branch, projection, extension, offshoot, section, division, detachment, department.

arm² v provide, supply, furnish, issue, equip, rig, outfit, ammunition, prime, prepare, forearm, gird, steel, brace, reinforce, strengthen, fortify, protect.

armed services

Units in the armed services include: task-force, militia, garrison; *air force:* wing, squadron, flight; *army:* patrol, troop, corps, platoon, squad, battery, company, brigade, battalion, regiment; *marines:* Royal Marines, commandos; *navy:* fleet, flotilla, squadron, convoy. *see also* **rank**.

---

armoured adj armour-plated, steel-plated, iron-clad, reinforced, protected, bullet-proof, bomb-proof.

armoury n arsenal, ordnance depot, ammunition dump, magazine, depot, repository, stock, stockpile.

arms n **1** WEAPONS, weaponry, firearms, guns, artillery, instruments of war, armaments, ordnance, munitions, ammunition. **2** COAT-OF-ARMS, armorial bearings, insignia, heraldic device, escutcheon, shield, crest, heraldry, blazonry.

army n armed force, military, militia, land forces, soldiers, troops, legions, cohorts, multitude, throng, host, horde.

aroma n smell, odour, scent, perfume, fragrance, bouquet, savour.

aromatic adj perfumed, fragrant, sweet-smelling, balmy, redolent, savoury, spicy, pungent.

around prep **1** SURROUNDING, round, encircling, encompassing, enclosing, on all sides of, on every side of. **2** around a dozen: approximately, roughly, about, circa, more or less.

adv **1** EVERYWHERE, all over, in all directions, on all sides, about, here and there, to and fro. **2** CLOSE by, near, nearby, at hand.

arouse v rouse, startle, wake up, waken, awaken, instigate, summon up, call forth, spark, kindle, inflame, whet, sharpen, quicken, animate, excite, prompt, provoke, stimulate, galvanize, goad, spur, incite, agitate, stir up, whip up.

Fa calm, lull, quieten.

arrange v **1** ORDER, tidy, range, array, marshal, dispose, distribute, position, set out, lay out, align, group, class, classify, categorize, sort (out), sift, file, systematize, methodize, regulate, adjust. **2** ORGANIZE, co-ordinate, prepare, fix, plan, project, design, devise, contrive, determine, settle. **3** arrange music: adapt, set, score, orchestrate, instrument, harmonize.

Fa **1** untidy, disorganize, muddle.

arrangement n **1** ORDER, array, display, disposition, layout, line-up, grouping, classification, structure, system, method, set-up, organization, preparation, planning, plan, scheme, design, schedule. **2** AGREEMENT, settlement, contract, terms, compromise. **3** ADAPTATION, version, interpretation, setting, score, orchestration, instrumentation, harmonization.

array n ARRANGEMENT, display, show, exhibition, exposition,

assortment, collection, assemblage, muster, order, formation, line-up, parade.

v **1** ARRANGE, order, range, dispose, group, line up, align, draw up, marshal, assemble, muster, parade, display, show, exhibit. **2** CLOTHE, dress, robe, deck, adorn, decorate.

arrest v **1** arrest a criminal: capture, catch, seize, nick (infml), run in, apprehend, detain. **2** STOP, stem, check, restrain, inhibit, halt, interrupt, stall, delay, slow, retard, block, obstruct, impede, hinder.

arrival n appearance, entrance, advent, coming, approach, occurrence.

Fa departure.

arrive v reach, get to, appear, materialize, turn up, show up (infml), roll up (infml), enter, come, occur, happen.

Fa depart, leave.

arrogant adj haughty, supercilious, disdainful, scornful, contemptuous, superior, condescending, patronizing, high and mighty, lordly, overbearing, high-handed, imperious, self-important, presumptuous, assuming, insolent, proud, conceited, boastful.

Fa humble, unassuming, bashful.

art n **1** FINE ART, painting, sculpture, drawing, artwork, craft, artistry, draughtsmanship, craftsmanship. **2** SKILL, knack, technique, method, aptitude, facility, dexterity, finesse, ingenuity, mastery, expertise, profession, trade. **3** ARTFULNESS, cunning, craftiness, slyness, guile, deceit, trickery, astuteness, shrewdness.

Schools of art include: abstract, action painting, Aestheticism, Art Deco, Art Nouveau, Barbizon, Baroque, Bohemian, Byzantine, classical revival, classicism, Conceptual Art, Constructivism, Cubism, Dadaism, Etruscan art,

art and craft

Expressionism, Fauvism, Florentine, folk art, Futurism, Gothic, Hellenistic, Impressionism, junk art, Mannerism, medieval art, Minimal Art, Modernism, the Nabis, Naturalism, Neoclassicism, Neoexpressionism, Neoimpressionism, Neo-Plasticism, Op Art, plastic art, Pop Art, Postimpressionism, Post-Modernism, Purism, quattrocento, Realism, renaissance, Rococo, Romanesque, Romanticism, Suprematism, Surrealism, Symbolism, Venetian, Vorticism.

art and craft

Arts and crafts include: painting, oil painting, watercolour, fresco, portraiture; architecture, drawing, sketching, caricature, illustration; graphics, film, video; sculpture, modelling, woodcarving, woodcraft, marquetry, metalwork, enamelling, cloisonné, engraving, etching, pottery, ceramics, mosaic, jewellery, stained glass, photography, lithography, calligraphy, collage, origami, spinning, weaving, batik, silk-screen printing, needlework, tapestry, embroidery, patchwork, crochet, knitting.

artful *adj* cunning, crafty, sly, foxy, wily, tricky, scheming, designing, deceitful, devious, subtle, sharp, shrewd, smart, clever, masterly, ingenious, resourceful, skilful, dexterous.

🖝 artless, naïve, ingenuous.

article *n* **1** *article in a magazine*: feature, report, story, account, piece, review, commentary, composition, essay, paper. **2** ITEM, thing, object, commodity, unit, part, constituent, piece, portion, division.

articulate *adj* distinct, well-spoken, clear, lucid, intelligible, comprehensible, understandable, coherent, fluent, vocal, expressive, meaningful.

🖝 inarticulate, incoherent.

v say, utter, speak, talk, express, voice, vocalize, verbalize, state, pronounce, enunciate, breathe.

articulation *n* saying, utterance, speaking, talking, expression, voicing, vocalization, verbalization, pronunciation, enunciation, diction, delivery.

artificial *adj* false, fake, bogus, counterfeit, spurious, phoney (*infml*), pseudo, specious, sham, insincere, assumed, affected, mannered, forced, contrived, made-up, feigned, pretended, simulated, imitation, mock, synthetic, plastic, man-made, manufactured, non-natural, unnatural.

🖝 genuine, true, real, natural.

artisan *n* craftsman, craftswoman, artificer, journeyman, expert, skilled worker, mechanic, technician.

artist

Types of artist include: architect, graphic designer, designer, draughtsman, draughtswoman, illustrator, cartoonist, photographer, printer, engraver, goldsmith, silversmith, blacksmith, carpenter, potter, weaver, sculptor, painter; craftsman, craftswoman, master.

artiste *n* performer, entertainer, variety artist, vaudevillian, comic, comedian, comedienne, player, trouper, actor, actress.

artistic *adj* aesthetic, ornamental, decorative, beautiful, exquisite, elegant, stylish, graceful, harmonious, sensitive, tasteful, refined, cultured, cultivated, skilled, talented, creative, imaginative.

🖝 inelegant, tasteless.

artistry *n* craftsmanship, workmanship, skill, craft, talent, flair, brilliance, genius, finesse, style, mastery, expertise, proficiency, accomplishment, deftness, touch, sensitivity, creativity.

🔄 ineptitude.

as *conj, prep* **1** WHILE, when. **2** SUCH AS, for example, for instance, like, in the manner of. **3** BECAUSE, since, seeing that, considering that, inasmuch as, being.

as for with reference to, as regards, with regard to, on the subject of, in connection with, in relation to, with relation to, with respect to.

ascend *v* rise, take off, lift off, go up, move up, slope upwards, climb, scale, mount, tower, float up, fly up, soar.

🔄 descend, go down.

ascent *n* **1** ASCENDING, ascension, climb, climbing, scaling, escalation, rise, rising, mounting. **2** SLOPE, gradient, incline, ramp, hill, elevation.

🔄 **1** descent.

ascertain *v* find out, learn, discover, determine, fix, establish, settle, locate, detect, identify, verify, confirm, make certain.

ascribe *v* attribute, credit, accredit, put down, assign, impute, charge, chalk up to.

ashamed *adj* sorry, apologetic, remorseful, contrite, guilty, conscience-stricken, sheepish, embarrassed, blushing, red-faced, mortified, humiliated, abashed, humbled, crestfallen, distressed, discomposed, confused, reluctant, hesitant, shy, self-conscious, bashful, modest, prudish.

🔄 shameless, proud, defiant.

aside *adv* apart, on one side, in reserve, away, out of the way, separately, in isolation, alone, privately, secretly.

n digression, parenthesis, departure, soliloquy, stage whisper, whisper.

ask *v* **1** REQUEST, appeal, petition, sue, plead, beg, entreat, implore, clamour, beseech, pray, supplicate, crave, demand, order, bid, require, seek, solicit, invite, summon. **2** INQUIRE, query, question, interrogate, quiz, press.

asleep *adj* sleeping, napping, snoozing, fast asleep, sound asleep, dormant, resting, inactive, inert, unconscious, numb, dozing.

aspect *n* angle, direction, elevation, side, facet, feature, face, expression, countenance, appearance, look, air, manner, bearing, attitude, condition, situation, position, standpoint, point of view, view, outlook, prospect, scene.

aspiration *n* aim, intent, purpose, endeavour, object, objective, goal, ambition, hope, dream, ideal, wish, desire, yearning, longing, craving, hankering.

aspire *v* aim, intend, purpose, seek, pursue, hope, dream, wish, desire, yearn, long, crave, hanker.

aspiring *adj* would-be, aspirant, striving, endeavouring, ambitious, enterprising, keen, eager, hopeful, optimistic, wishful, longing.

assassin *n* murderer, killer, slayer, cut-throat, executioner, hatchet man (*infml*), gunman, hit-man (*sl*), liquidator (*infml*).

assassinate *v* murder, kill, slay, dispatch, hit (*sl*), eliminate (*infml*), liquidate (*infml*).

assault *n* **1** ATTACK, offensive, onslaught, blitz, strike, raid, invasion, incursion, storm, storming, charge. **2** *charged with assault*: battery, grievous bodily harm, GBH (*infml*), mugging (*sl*), rape, abuse. *v* attack, charge, invade, strike, hit, set upon, fall on, beat up (*infml*), mug (*sl*), rape, molest, abuse.

assemble *v* **1** GATHER, congregate, muster, rally, convene, meet, join up, flock, group, collect, accumulate, amass, bring together, round up, marshal, mobilize. **2** CONSTRUCT,

build, put together, piece together,
compose, make, fabricate,
manufacture.

F3 1 scatter, disperse. 2 dismantle.

assembly n 1 GATHERING, rally,
meeting, convention, conference,
convocation, congress, council,
group, body, company, congregation,
flock, crowd, multitude, throng,
collection, assemblage.
2 CONSTRUCTION, building,
fabrication, manufacture.

assert v affirm, attest, swear, testify
to, allege, claim, contend, maintain,
insist, stress, protest, defend,
vindicate, uphold, promote, declare,
profess, state, pronounce, lay down,
advance.

F3 deny, refute.

assertion n affirmation, attestation,
word, allegation, claim, contention,
insistence, vindication, declaration,
profession, statement,
pronouncement.

F3 denial.

assertive adj bold, confident, self-
assured, forward, pushy, insistent,
emphatic, forceful, firm, decided,
strong-willed, dogmatic, opinionated,
presumptuous, assuming,
overbearing, domineering,
aggressive.

F3 timid, diffident.

assess v gauge, estimate, evaluate,
appraise, review, judge, consider,
weigh, size up, compute, determine,
fix, value, rate, tax, levy, impose,
demand.

assessment n gauging, estimation,
estimate, evaluation, appraisal,
review, judgement, opinion,
consideration, calculation,
determination, valuation, rating,
taxation.

asset n strength, resource, virtue,
plus (infml), benefit, advantage,
blessing, boon, help, aid.

F3 liability.

assets n estate, property,

possessions, goods, holdings,
securities, money, wealth, capital,
funds, reserves, resources, means.

assign v 1 ALLOCATE, apportion,
grant, give, dispense, distribute, allot,
consign, delegate, name, nominate,
designate, appoint, choose, select,
determine, set, fix, specify, stipulate.
2 ATTRIBUTE, accredit, ascribe, put
down.

assignment n commission, errand,
task, project, job, position, post,
duty, responsibility, charge,
appointment, delegation,
designation, nomination, selection,
allocation, consignment, grant,
distribution.

assist v help, aid, abet, rally round,
co-operate, collaborate, back,
second, support, reinforce, sustain,
relieve, benefit, serve, enable,
facilitate, expedite, boost, further,
advance.

F3 hinder, thwart.

assistance n help, aid, succour, co-
operation, collaboration, backing,
support, reinforcement, relief,
benefit, service, boost, furtherance.

F3 hindrance, resistance.

assistant n helper, helpmate, aide,
right-hand man, auxiliary, ancillary,
subordinate, backer, second,
supporter, accomplice, accessory,
abettor, collaborator, colleague,
partner, ally, confederate, associate.

associate v 1 AFFILIATE,
confederate, ally, league, join,
amalgamate, combine, unite, link,
connect, correlate, relate, couple,
pair, yoke. 2 associate with bad
company: socialize, mingle, mix,
fraternize, consort, hang around
(infml).
n partner, ally, confederate, affiliate,
collaborator, co-worker, mate,
colleague, peer, compeer, fellow,
comrade, companion, friend, sidekick
(infml), assistant, follower.

association n 1 ORGANIZATION,

corporation, company, partnership, league, alliance, coalition, confederation, confederacy, federation, affiliation, consortium, cartel, syndicate, union, society, club, fraternity, fellowship, clique, group, band. **2** BOND, tie, connection, correlation, relation, relationship, involvement, intimacy, friendship, companionship, familiarity.

assorted *adj* miscellaneous, mixed, varied, different, differing, heterogeneous, diverse, sundry, various, several, manifold.

assortment *n* miscellany, medley, pot-pourri, jumble, mixture, variety, diversity, collection, selection, choice, arrangement, grouping.

assume *v* **1** PRESUME, surmise, accept, take for granted, expect, understand, deduce, infer, guess, postulate, suppose, think, believe, imagine, fancy. **2** AFFECT, take on, feign, counterfeit, simulate, put on, pretend. **3** *assume command*: undertake, adopt, embrace, seize, arrogate, commandeer, appropriate, usurp, take over.

assumed *adj* false, bogus, counterfeit, fake, phoney (*infml*), sham, affected, feigned, simulated, pretended, made-up, fictitious, hypothetical.
F3 true, real, actual.

assumption *n* presumption, surmise, inference, supposition, guess, conjecture, theory, hypothesis, premise, postulate, idea, notion, belief, fancy.

assurance *n* **1** ASSERTION, declaration, affirmation, guarantee, pledge, promise, vow, word, oath. **2** CONFIDENCE, self-confidence, aplomb, boldness, audacity, courage, nerve, conviction, sureness, certainty.
F3 **2** shyness, doubt, uncertainty.

assure *v* affirm, guarantee, warrant, pledge, promise, vow, swear, tell, convince, persuade, encourage,

hearten, reassure, soothe, comfort, boost, strengthen, secure, ensure, confirm.

assured *adj* **1** SURE, certain, indisputable, irrefutable, confirmed, positive, definite, settled, fixed, guaranteed, secure. **2** SELF-ASSURED, confident, self-confident, self-possessed, bold, audacious, assertive.
F3 **1** uncertain. **2** shy.

astonish *v* surprise, startle, amaze, astound, stun, stupefy, daze, stagger, floor (*infml*), dumbfound, flabbergast (*infml*), shock, confound, bewilder.

astonishment *n* surprise, amazement, shock, dismay, consternation, confusion, bewilderment, wonder.

astounding *adj* surprising, startling, amazing, astonishing, stunning, breathtaking, stupefying, overwhelming, staggering, shocking, bewildering.

astray *adv* adrift, off course, lost, amiss, wrong, off the rails (*infml*), awry, off the mark.

astute *adj* shrewd, prudent, sagacious, wise, canny, knowing, intelligent, sharp, penetrating, keen, perceptive, discerning, subtle, clever, crafty, cunning, sly, wily.
F3 stupid, slow.

asylum *n* haven, sanctuary, refuge, shelter, retreat, safety.

asymmetric *adj* unsymmetrical, unbalanced, uneven, crooked, awry, unequal, disproportionate, irregular.
F3 symmetrical.

atheism *n* unbelief, non-belief, disbelief, scepticism, irreligion, ungodliness, godlessness, impiety, infidelity, paganism, heathenism, free-thinking, rationalism.

atheist *n* unbeliever, non-believer, disbeliever, sceptic, infidel, pagan, heathen, free-thinker.

athlete *n* sportsman, sportswoman, runner, gymnast, competitor, contestant, contender.

athletic *adj* fit, energetic, vigorous, active, sporty, muscular, sinewy, brawny, strapping, robust, sturdy, strong, powerful, well-knit, well-proportioned, wiry.
F3 puny.

athletics *n* sports, games, races, track events, field events, exercises, gymnastics.

atmosphere *n* **1** AIR, sky, aerospace, heavens, ether.
2 AMBIENCE, environment, surroundings, aura, feel, feeling, mood, spirit, tone, tenor, character, quality, flavour.

atom *n* molecule, particle, bit, morsel, crumb, grain, spot, speck, mite, shred, scrap, hint, trace, scintilla, jot, iota, whit.

Subatomic particles include:
photon, electron, positron, neutrino,
anti-neutrino, muon, pion, kaon,
proton, anti-proton, neutron, anti-
neutron, lambda particle, sigma
particle, omega particle, psi particle.

atrocious *adj* shocking, appalling, abominable, dreadful, terrible, horrible, hideous, ghastly, heinous, grievous, savage, vicious, monstrous, fiendish, ruthless.
F3 admirable, fine.

atrocity *n* outrage, abomination, enormity, horror, monstrosity, savagery, barbarity, brutality, cruelty, viciousness, evil, villainy, wickedness, vileness, heinousness, hideousness, atrociousness.

attach *v* **1** *attach a label*: affix, stick, adhere, fasten, fix, secure, tie, bind, weld, join, unite, connect, link, couple, add, annex. **2** ASCRIBE, attribute, impute, assign, put, place, associate, relate to, belong.
F3 **1** detach, unfasten.

attachment *n* **1** ACCESSORY, fitting, fixture, extension, appendage, extra,

supplement, addition, adjunct, codicil. **2** FONDNESS, affection, tenderness, love, liking, partiality, loyalty, devotion, friendship, affinity, attraction, bond, tie, link.

attack *n* **1** OFFENSIVE, blitz, bombardment, invasion, incursion, foray, raid, strike, charge, rush, onslaught, assault, battery, aggression, criticism, censure, abuse. **2** SEIZURE, fit, convulsion, paroxysm, spasm, stroke.
v **1** invade, raid, strike, storm, charge, assail, assault, set about, set upon, fall on, lay into, do over (*sl*). **2** CRITICIZE, censure, blame, denounce, revile, malign, abuse.
F3 **1** defend, protect.

attacker *n* assailant, mugger (*sl*), aggressor, invader, raider, critic, detractor, reviler, abuser, persecutor.
F3 defender, supporter.

attain *v* accomplish, achieve, fulfil, complete, effect, realize, earn, reach, touch, arrive at, grasp, get, acquire, obtain, procure, secure, gain, win, net.

attainment *n* accomplishment, achievement, feat, fulfilment, completion, consummation, realization, success, ability, capability, competence, proficiency, skill, art, talent, gift, aptitude, facility, mastery.

attempt *n* try, endeavour, shot (*infml*), go (*infml*), stab (*infml*), bash (*infml*), push, effort, struggle, bid, undertaking, venture, trial, experiment.
v try, endeavour, have a go (*infml*), aspire, seek, strive, undertake, tackle, venture, experiment.

attend *v* **1** *attend a meeting*: be present, go to, frequent, visit. **2** ESCORT, chaperon, accompany, usher, follow, guard, look after, take care of, care for, nurse, tend, minister to, help, serve, wait on. **3** PAY ATTENTION, listen, hear, heed, mind, mark, note, notice, observe.

attend to deal with, see to, take care of, look after, manage, direct, control, oversee, supervise.

attendance n presence, appearance, turnout, audience, house, crowd, gate.

attendant n aide, helper, assistant, auxiliary, steward, waiter, servant, page, retainer, guide, marshal, usher, escort, companion, follower, guard, custodian.
adj accompanying, attached, associated, related, incidental, resultant, consequent, subsequent.

attention n alertness, vigilance, concentration, heed, notice, observation, regard, mindfulness, awareness, recognition, thought, contemplation, consideration, concern, care, treatment, service.
☒ inattention, disregard, carelessness.

attentive adj 1 ALERT, awake, vigilant, watchful, observant, concentrating, heedful, mindful, careful, conscientious.
2 CONSIDERATE, thoughtful, kind, obliging, accommodating, polite, courteous, devoted.
☒ 1 inattentive, heedless.
2 inconsiderate.

attitude n feeling, disposition, mood, aspect, manner, bearing, pose, posture, stance, position, point of view, opinion, view, outlook, perspective, approach.

attract v pull, draw, lure, allure, entice, seduce, tempt, invite, induce, incline, appeal to, interest, engage, fascinate, enchant, charm, bewitch, captivate, excite.
☒ repel, disgust.

attraction n pull, draw, magnetism, lure, allure, bait, enticement, inducement, seduction, temptation, invitation, appeal, interest, fascination, enchantment, charm, captivation.

☒ repulsion.

attractive adj pretty, fair, fetching, good-looking, handsome, beautiful, gorgeous, stunning, glamorous, lovely, pleasant, pleasing, agreeable, appealing, winsome, winning, enticing, seductive, tempting, inviting, interesting, engaging, fascinating, charming, captivating, magnetic.
☒ unattractive, repellent.

attribute v ascribe, accredit, credit, impute, assign, put down, blame, charge, refer, apply.
n property, quality, virtue, point, aspect, facet, feature, trait, characteristic, idiosyncrasy, peculiarity, quirk, note, mark, sign, symbol.

auburn adj red, chestnut, tawny, russet, copper, Titian.

audible adj clear, distinct, recognizable, perceptible, discernible, detectable, appreciable.
☒ inaudible, silent, unclear.

audience n spectators, onlookers, house, auditorium, listeners, viewers, crowd, turnout, gathering, assembly, congregation, fans, devotees, regulars, following, public.

audit n examination, inspection, check, verification, investigation, scrutiny, analysis, review, statement, balancing.

augur v bode, forebode, herald, presage, portend, prophesy, predict, promise, signify.

auspices n aegis, authority, patronage, sponsorship, backing, support, protection, charge, care, supervision, control, influence, guidance.

auspicious adj favourable, propitious, encouraging, cheerful, bright, rosy, promising, hopeful, optimistic, fortunate, lucky, opportune, happy, prosperous.
☒ inauspicious, ominous.

austere adj 1 STARK, bleak, plain,

austerity simple, unadorned, grim, forbidding.
2 SEVERE, stern, strict, cold, formal, rigid, rigorous, exacting, hard, harsh, spartan, grave, serious, solemn, sober, abstemious, self-denying, restrained, economical, frugal, ascetic, self-disciplined, puritanical, chaste.
1 ornate, elaborate. **2** genial.

austerity *n* plainness, simplicity, severity, coldness, formality, hardness, harshness, solemnity, abstemiousness, abstinence, economy, asceticism, puritanism.
elaborateness, materialism.

authentic *adj* genuine, true, real, actual, certain, bona fide, legitimate, honest, valid, original, pure, factual, accurate, true-to-life, faithful, reliable, trustworthy.
false, fake, counterfeit, spurious.

authenticate *v* guarantee, warrant, vouch for, attest, authorize, accredit, validate, certify, endorse, confirm, verify, corroborate.

authenticity *n* genuineness, certainty, authoritativeness, validity, truth, veracity, truthfulness, honesty, accuracy, correctness, faithfulness, fidelity, reliability, dependability, trustworthiness.
spuriousness, invalidity.

author *n* **1** WRITER, novelist, dramatist, playwright, composer, pen, penman, penwoman.
2 CREATOR, founder, originator, initiator, parent, prime mover, mover, inventor, designer, architect, planner, maker, producer.

authoritarian *adj* strict, disciplinarian, severe, harsh, rigid, inflexible, unyielding, dogmatic, doctrinaire, absolute, autocratic, dictatorial, despotic, tyrannical, oppressive, domineering, imperious.
liberal.

authoritative *adj* scholarly, learned, official, authorized, legitimate, valid, approved, sanctioned, accepted, definitive, decisive, authentic, factual, true, truthful, accurate, faithful, convincing, sound, reliable, dependable, trustworthy.
unofficial, unreliable.

authority *n* **1** SOVEREIGNTY, supremacy, rule, sway, control, dominion, influence, power, force, government, administration, officialdom. **2** AUTHORIZATION, permission, sanction, permit, warrant, licence, credentials, right, prerogative. **3** *an authority on antiques*: expert, pundit, connoisseur, specialist, professional, master, scholar.

authorize *v* legalize, validate, ratify, confirm, license, entitle, accredit, empower, enable, commission, warrant, permit, allow, consent to, sanction, approve, give the go-ahead.

autocracy *n* absolutism, totalitarianism, dictatorship, despotism, tyranny, authoritarianism, fascism.
democracy.

autocrat *n* absolutist, totalitarian, dictator, despot, tyrant, authoritarian, (little) Hitler (*infml*), fascist.

autocratic *adj* absolute, all-powerful, totalitarian, despotic, tyrannical, authoritarian, dictatorial, domineering, overbearing, imperious.
democratic, liberal.

automatic *adj* **1** AUTOMATED, self-activating, mechanical, mechanized, programmed, self-regulating, computerized, push-button, robotic, self-propelling, unmanned. **2** SPONTANEOUS, reflex, involuntary, unwilled, unconscious, unthinking, natural, instinctive, routine, necessary, certain, inevitable, unavoidable, inescapable.

autonomy *n* self-government, self-rule, home rule, sovereignty, independence, self-determination, freedom, free will.

& subjection, compulsion.

auxiliary *adj* ancillary, assistant, subsidiary, accessory, secondary, supporting, supportive, helping, assisting, aiding, extra, supplementary, spare, reserve, back-up, emergency, substitute.

available *adj* free, vacant, to hand, within reach, at hand, accessible, handy, convenient, on hand, ready, on tap, obtainable.

& unavailable.

avalanche *n* landslide, landslip, cascade, torrent, deluge, flood, inundation, barrage.

avant-garde *adj* innovative, innovatory, pioneering, experimental, unconventional, far-out (*sl*), way-out (*sl*), progressive, advanced, forward-looking, enterprising, inventive.

& conservative.

avarice *n* covetousness, rapacity, acquisitiveness, greed, greediness, meanness.

& generosity, liberality.

avaricious *adj* covetous, grasping, rapacious, acquisitive, greedy, mercenary, mean, miserly.

& generous.

avenge *v* take revenge for, take vengeance for, punish, requite, repay, retaliate.

average *n* mean, mid-point, norm, standard, rule, par, medium, run.

& extreme, exception.

adj mean, medial, median, middle, intermediate, medium, moderate, satisfactory, fair, mediocre, middling, indifferent, so-so (*infml*), passable, tolerable, undistinguished, run-of-the-mill, ordinary, everyday, common, usual, normal, regular, standard, typical, unexceptional.

& extreme, exceptional, remarkable.

averse *adj* reluctant, unwilling, loth, disinclined, ill-disposed, hostile, opposed, antagonistic, unfavourable.

& willing, keen, sympathetic.

aversion *n* dislike, hate, hatred, loathing, detestation, abhorrence, abomination, horror, phobia, reluctance, unwillingness, disinclination, distaste, disgust, revulsion, repugnance, repulsion, hostility, opposition, antagonism.

& liking, sympathy, desire.

avert *v* turn away, deflect, turn aside, parry, fend off, ward off, stave off, forestall, frustrate, prevent, obviate, avoid, evade.

aviation *n* aeronautics, flying, flight, aircraft industry.

avid *adj* eager, earnest, keen, enthusiastic, fanatical, devoted, dedicated, zealous, ardent, fervent, intense, passionate, insatiable, ravenous, hungry, thirsty, greedy, grasping, covetous.

& indifferent.

avoid *v* evade, elude, sidestep, dodge, shirk, duck (*infml*), escape, get out of, bypass, circumvent, balk, prevent, avert, shun, abstain from, refrain from, steer clear of.

avoidable *adj* escapable, preventable.

& inevitable.

avowed *adj* sworn, declared, professed, self-proclaimed, self-confessed, confessed, admitted, acknowledged, open, overt.

awake *v* awaken, waken, wake, wake up, rouse, arouse.

adj wakeful, wide-awake, aroused, alert, vigilant, watchful, observant, attentive, conscious, aware, sensitive, alive.

awakening *n* awaking, wakening, waking, rousing, arousal, stimulation, animating, enlivening, activation, revival, birth.

award *v* give, present, distribute, dispense, bestow, confer, accord, endow, gift, grant, allot, apportion, assign, allow, determine.

n prize, trophy, decoration, medal, presentation, dispensation, bestowal, conferral, endowment, gift, grant, allotment, allowance, adjudication, judgement, decision, order.

aware *adj* conscious, alive to, sensitive, appreciative, sentient, familiar, conversant, acquainted, informed, enlightened, au courant, knowing, knowledgeable, cognizant, mindful, heedful, attentive, observant, sharp, alert, on the ball (*infml*), shrewd, sensible.

⊟ unaware, oblivious, insensitive.

awe *n* wonder, veneration, reverence, respect, admiration, amazement, astonishment, fear, terror, dread, apprehension.

⊟ contempt.

awe-inspiring *adj* wonderful, sublime, magnificent, stupendous, overwhelming, breathtaking, stupefying, stunning, astonishing, amazing, impressive, imposing, majestic, solemn, moving, awesome, formidable, daunting, intimidating, fearsome.

⊟ contemptible, tame.

awful *adj* terrible, dreadful, fearful, frightful, ghastly, unpleasant, nasty, horrible, hideous, ugly, gruesome, dire, abysmal, atrocious, horrific, shocking, appalling, alarming, spine-chilling.

⊟ wonderful, excellent.

awkward *adj* **1** CLUMSY, gauche, inept, inexpert, unskilful, bungling, ham-fisted, unco-ordinated, ungainly, graceless, ungraceful, inelegant, cumbersome, unwieldy, inconvenient, difficult, fiddly, delicate, troublesome, perplexing. **2** *feeling awkward in their presence*: uncomfortable, ill at ease, embarrassed. **3** OBSTINATE, stubborn, unco-operative, irritable, touchy, prickly, rude, unpleasant.

⊟ **1** graceful, elegant, convenient, handy. **2** comfortable, relaxed. **3** amenable, pleasant.

axe *n* hatchet, chopper, cleaver, tomahawk, battle-axe.

v **1** CUT (DOWN), fell, hew, chop, cleave, split. **2** CANCEL, terminate, discontinue, remove, withdraw, eliminate, get rid of, throw out, dismiss, discharge, sack (*infml*), fire (*infml*).

axiom *n* principle, fundamental, truth, truism, precept, dictum, byword, maxim, adage, aphorism.

axis *n* centre-line, vertical, horizontal, pivot, hinge.

axle *n* shaft, spindle, rod, pin, pivot.

B

babble *v* **1** CHATTER, gabble, jabber, cackle, prate, mutter, mumble, murmur. **2** *the stream babbled*: burble, gurgle.

n chatter, gabble, clamour, hubbub, gibberish, burble, murmur.

baby *n* babe, infant, suckling, child, tiny, toddler.

adj miniature, small-scale, mini (*infml*), midget, small, little, tiny, minute, diminutive.

babyish *adj* childish, juvenile,

puerile, infantile, silly, foolish, soft (*infml*), sissy (*infml*), baby, young, immature, naïve.

⊟ mature, precocious.

back *n* rear, stern, end, tail, tail end, hind part, hindquarters, posterior, backside, reverse.

⊟ front, face.

v **1** GO BACKWARDS, reverse, recede, regress, backtrack, retreat, retire, withdraw, back away, recoil. **2** SUPPORT, sustain, assist, side with, champion, advocate, encourage, promote, boost, favour, sanction, countenance, endorse, second, countersign, sponsor, finance, subsidize, underwrite.

F₃ 1 advance, approach. 2 discourage, weaken.

adj rear, end, tail, posterior, hind, hindmost, reverse.

F₃ 1 front.

back down concede, yield, give in, surrender, submit, retreat, withdraw, back-pedal.

back out abandon, give up, chicken out (*infml*), withdraw, pull out (*infml*), resign, recant, go back on, cancel.

back up confirm, corroborate, substantiate, endorse, second, champion, support, reinforce, bolster, assist, aid.

F₃ let down.

backbone *n* 1 SPINE, spinal column, vertebrae, vertebral column, mainstay, support, core, foundation, basis, character. 2 COURAGE, mettle, pluck, nerve, grit, determination, resolve, tenacity, steadfastness, toughness, stamina, strength, power.

F₃ 2 spinelessness, weakness.

backfire *v* recoil, rebound, ricochet, boomerang, miscarry, fail, flop.

background *n* 1 SETTING, surroundings, environment, context, circumstances. 2 HISTORY, record, credentials, experience, grounding, preparation, education, upbringing, breeding, culture, tradition.

backing *n* support, accompaniment, aid, assistance, helpers, championing, advocacy, encouragement, moral support, favour, sanction, promotion, endorsement, seconding, patronage, sponsorship, finance, funds, grant, subsidy.

backlash *n* reaction, response, repercussion, reprisal, retaliation, recoil, kickback, backfire, boomerang.

backlog *n* accumulation, stock,

supply, resources, reserve, reserves, excess.

backsliding *n* lapse, relapse, apostasy, defection, desertion, defaulting.

backward *adj* 1 *a backward step*: rétrograde, retrogressive, regressive. 2 SHY, bashful, reluctant, unwilling, hesitant, hesitating, wavering, slow, behind, behindhand, late, immature, underdeveloped, retarded, subnormal, stupid.

F₃ 1 forward. 2 precocious.

bacteria *n* germs, bugs (*infml*), viruses, microbes, micro-organisms, bacilli.

bad *adj* 1 UNPLEASANT, disagreeable, nasty, undesirable, unfortunate, distressing, adverse, detrimental, harmful, damaging, injurious, serious, grave, severe, harsh. 2 EVIL, wicked, sinful, criminal, corrupt, immoral, vile. 3 *bad workmanship*: poor, inferior, substandard, imperfect, faulty, defective, deficient, unsatisfactory, useless. 4 ROTTEN, mouldy, decayed, spoilt, putrid, rancid, sour, off, tainted, contaminated. 5 *a bad child*: naughty, mischievous, ill-behaved, disobedient.

F₃ 1 good, pleasant, mild, slight. 2 virtuous. 3 skilled. 4 fresh. 5 well-behaved.

badge *n* identification, emblem, device, insignia, sign, mark, token, stamp, brand, trademark, logo.

badly *adv* 1 GREATLY, extremely, exceedingly, intensely, deeply, acutely, bitterly, painfully, seriously, desperately, severely, critically, crucially. 2 WICKEDLY, criminally, immorally, shamefully, unfairly. 3 WRONG, wrongly, incorrectly, improperly, defectively, faultily, imperfectly, inadequately, unsatisfactorily, poorly, incompetently, negligently, carelessly. 4 UNFAVOURABLY, adversely, unfortunately, unsuccessfully.

E3 3 well.

bad-tempered adj. irritable, cross, crotchety, crabbed, crabby, snappy, grumpy, querulous, petulant, fractious, stroppy (infml).

E3 good-tempered, genial, equable.

baffle v puzzle, perplex, mystify, bemuse, bewilder, confuse, confound, bamboozle (infml), flummox (infml), daze, upset, disconcert, foil, thwart, frustrate, hinder, check, defeat, stump (infml).

E3 enlighten, help.

bag v 1 CATCH, capture, trap, land, kill, shoot. 2 OBTAIN, acquire, get, gain, corner, take, grab, appropriate, commandeer, reserve.

n container, sack, case, suitcase, grip, carrier, hold-all, handbag, shoulder-bag, satchel, rucksack, haversack, pack.

baggage n luggage, suitcases, bags, belongings, things, equipment, gear, paraphernalia, impedimenta (fml).

baggy adj loose, slack, roomy, ill-fitting, billowing, bulging, floppy, sagging, droopy.

E3 tight, firm.

bail n security, surety, pledge, bond, guarantee, warranty.

bail out¹ help, aid, assist, relieve, rescue, finance.

bail out², bale out withdraw, retreat, quit, back out, cop out (sl), escape.

bait n lure, incentive, inducement, bribe, temptation, enticement, allurement, attraction.

E3 disincentive.

v tease, provoke, goad, irritate, annoy, irk, needle (infml), harass, persecute, torment.

balance v 1 STEADY, poise, stabilize, level, square, equalize, equate, match, counterbalance, counteract, neutralize, offset, adjust. 2 COMPARE, consider, weigh, estimate.

E3 1 unbalance, overbalance.

n 1 EQUILIBRIUM, steadiness, stability, evenness, symmetry, equality, parity, equity, equivalence, correspondence. 2 COMPOSURE, self-possession, poise, equanimity. 3 REMAINDER, rest, residue, surplus, difference.

E3 imbalance, instability.

balcony n terrace, veranda, gallery, upper circle, gods.

bald adj 1 BALD-HEADED, hairless, smooth, uncovered. 2 BARE, naked, unadorned, plain, simple, severe, stark, barren, treeless. 3 a bald statement: forthright, direct, straight, outright, downright, straightforward.

E3 1 hairy, hirsute. 2 adorned.

bale n bundle, truss, pack, package, parcel.

bale out see bail out².

balk, baulk v 1 FLINCH, recoil, shrink, jib, boggle, hesitate, refuse, resist, dodge, evade, shirk. 2 THWART, frustrate, foil, forestall, disconcert, baffle, hinder, obstruct, check, stall, bar, prevent, defeat, counteract.

ball¹ n sphere, globe, orb, globule, drop, conglomeration, pellet, pill, shot, bullet, slug (infml).

ball² n dance, dinner-dance, party, soirée, masquerade, carnival, assembly.

ballad n poem, song, folk-song, shanty, carol, ditty.

ballet

Terms used in ballet include: à pointe, arabesque, attitude, ballerina, prima ballerina, ballon, barre, battement, batterie, battu, bourrée, capriole, chassé, choreography, ciseaux, company, corps de ballet, coryphée, divertissement, écarté, élévation, entrechat, fish dive, five positions, fouetté, fouetté en tournant, glissade, jeté, grand jeté, leotard, pas de deux, pas de seul, pirouette, plié, pointes, sur les pointes, port de bras, principal male dancer, régisseur, répétiteur, ballet shoe, point shoe, splits, stulchak, tutu.

ballot n poll, polling, vote, voting, election, referendum, plebiscite.

ban v forbid, prohibit, disallow, proscribe, bar, exclude, ostracize, outlaw, banish, suppress, restrict.
☒ allow, permit, authorize.
n prohibition, embargo, veto, boycott, stoppage, restriction, suppression, censorship, outlawry, proscription, condemnation, denunciation, curse, taboo.
☒ permission, dispensation.

banal adj trite, commonplace, ordinary, everyday, humdrum, boring, unimaginative, hackneyed, clichéed, stock, stereotyped, corny (infml), stale, threadbare, tired, empty.
☒ original, fresh, imaginative.

band¹ n strip, belt, ribbon, tape, bandage, binding, tie, ligature, bond, strap, cord, chain.

band² n 1 TROOP, gang, crew, group, herd, flock, party, body, association, company, society, club, clique. 2 the band played on: group, orchestra, ensemble.
v group, gather, join, unite, ally, collaborate, consolidate, amalgamate, merge, affiliate, federate.
☒ disband, disperse.

bandage n dressing, plaster, compress, ligature, tourniquet, swathe, swaddle.
v bind, dress, cover, swathe, swaddle.

bandit n robber, thief, brigand, marauder, outlaw, highwayman, pirate, buccaneer, hijacker, cowboy, gunman, desperado, gangster.

bandy¹ v exchange, swap, trade, barter, interchange, reciprocate, pass, toss, throw.

bandy² adj bandy-legged, bow-

legged, curved, bowed, bent, crooked.

bang n 1 BLOW, hit, knock, bump, crash, collision, smack, punch, thump, wallop (infml), stroke, whack (infml). 2 a loud bang: explosion, detonation, pop, boom, clap, peal, clang, clash, thud, thump, slam, noise, report, shot.
v 1 STRIKE, hit, bash, knock, bump, rap, drum, hammer, pound, thump, stamp. 2 EXPLODE, burst, detonate, boom, echo, resound, crash, slam, clatter, clang, peal, thunder.
adv straight, directly, headlong, right, precisely, slap, smack, hard, noisily, suddenly, abruptly.

banish v expel, eject, evict, deport, transport, exile, outlaw, ban, bar, debar, exclude, shut out, ostracize, excommunicate, dismiss, oust, dislodge, remove, get rid of, discard, dispel, eliminate, eradicate.
☒ recall, welcome.

banishment n expulsion, eviction, deportation, expatriation, transportation, exile, outlawry, ostracism, excommunication.
☒ return, recall, welcome.

bank¹ n accumulation, fund, pool, reservoir, depository, repository, treasury, savings, reserve, store, stock, stockpile, hoard, cache.
v deposit, save, keep, store, accumulate, stockpile.
☒ spend.

bank² n heap, pile, mass, mound, earthwork, ridge, rampart, embankment, side, slope, tilt, edge, shore.
v 1 HEAP, pile, stack, mass, amass, accumulate, mound, drift. 2 SLOPE, incline, pitch, slant, tilt, tip.

bank³ n array, panel, bench, group, tier, rank, line, row, series, succession, sequence, train.

bankrupt adj insolvent, in liquidation, ruined, failed, beggared, destitute, impoverished, broke (*infml*), spent, exhausted, depleted, lacking.

☒ solvent, wealthy.

n insolvent, debtor, pauper.

banner *n* flag, standard, colours, ensign, pennant, streamer.

banquet *n* feast, dinner, meal, repast (*fml*), treat.

banter *n* joking, jesting, pleasantry, badinage, repartee, word play, chaff, chaffing, kidding (*infml*), ribbing (*sl*), derision, mockery, ridicule.

baptism *n* christening, dedication, beginning, initiation, introduction, debut, launch, launching, immersion, sprinkling, purification.

baptize *v* christen, name, call, term, style, title, introduce, initiate, enrol, recruit, immerse, sprinkle, purify, cleanse.

bar *n* **1** PUBLIC HOUSE, pub (*infml*), inn, tavern, saloon, lounge, counter. **2** SLAB, block, lump, chunk, wedge, ingot, nugget. **3** ROD, stick, shaft, pole, stake, stanchion, batten, crosspiece, rail, railing, paling, barricade. **4** OBSTACLE, impediment, hindrance, obstruction, barrier, stop, check, deterrent.

v **1** EXCLUDE, debar, ban, forbid, prohibit, prevent, preclude, hinder, obstruct, restrain. **2** *bar the door*: barricade, lock, bolt, latch, fasten, secure.

barbarian *n* savage, brute, ruffian, hooligan, vandal, lout, oaf, boor, philistine, ignoramus, illiterate.

barbaric *adj* barbarous, primitive, wild, savage, fierce, ferocious, cruel, inhuman, brutal, brutish, uncivilized, uncouth, vulgar, coarse, crude, rude.

☒ humane, civilized, gracious.

barbarity *n* barbarousness, wildness, savagery, ferocity, viciousness, cruelty, inhumanity, brutality, brutishness, rudeness.

☒ civilization, humanity, civility.

barbed *adj* **1** PRICKLY, spiny, thorny, spiked, pronged, hooked,

jagged, toothed, pointed. **2** *a barbed remark*: cutting, caustic, acid, hurtful, unkind, nasty, snide, hostile, critical.

bare *adj* **1** NAKED, nude, unclothed, undressed, stripped, denuded, uncovered, exposed. **2** PLAIN, simple, unadorned, unfurnished, empty, barren, bald, stark, basic, essential.

☒ **1** clothed. **2** decorated, detailed.

barely *adv* hardly, scarcely, only just, just, almost.

bargain *n* **1** DEAL, transaction, contract, treaty, pact, pledge, promise, agreement, understanding, arrangement, negotiation. **2** DISCOUNT, reduction, snip, giveaway, special offer.

v negotiate, haggle, deal, trade, traffic, barter, buy, sell, transact, contract, covenant, promise, agree.

bargain for expect, anticipate, plan for, include, reckon on, look for, foresee, imagine, contemplate, consider.

barge *v* bump, hit, collide, impinge, shove, elbow, push (in), muscle in, butt in, interrupt, gatecrash, intrude, interfere.

n canal-boat, flatboat, narrow-boat, houseboat, lighter.

bark *n* yap, woof, yelp, snap, snarl, growl, bay, howl.

v yap, woof, yelp, snap, snarl, growl, bay, howl.

baroque *adj* elaborate, ornate, rococo, florid, flamboyant, exuberant, vigorous, bold, convoluted, overdecorated, overwrought, extravagant, fanciful, fantastic, grotesque.

☒ plain, simple.

barracks *n* garrison, camp, encampment, guardhouse, quarters, billet, lodging, accommodation.

barrage *n* bombardment, shelling, gunfire, cannonade, broadside, volley, salvo, burst, assault, attack, onset, onslaught, deluge, torrent, stream, storm, hail, rain, shower, mass, profusion.

barrel n cask, keg, tun, butt, water-butt.

barren adj **1** ARID, dry, desert, desolate, waste, empty, flat, dull, uninteresting, uninspiring, uninformative, uninstructive, unrewarding, unproductive, profitless, unfruitful, fruitless, pointless, useless, boring. **2** INFERTILE, sterile, childless, unprolific, unbearing.
E3 1 productive, fruitful, useful. **2** fertile.

barricade n blockade, obstruction, barrier, fence, stockade, bulwark, rampart, protection.
v block, obstruct, bar, fortify, defend, protect.

barrier n **1** WALL, fence, railing, barricade, blockade, boom, rampart, fortification, ditch, frontier, boundary, bar, check. **2** a barrier to success: obstacle, hurdle, stumbling-block, impediment, obstruction, hindrance, handicap, limitation, restriction, drawback, difficulty.

bartender n barman, barmaid, barkeeper, publican.

barter v exchange, swap, trade, traffic, deal, negotiate, bargain, haggle.

base n **1** the base of the statue: bottom, foot, pedestal, plinth, stand, rest, support, foundation, bed, groundwork. **2** BASIS, fundamental, essential, principal, key, heart, core, essence, root, origin, source. **3** HEADQUARTERS, centre, post, station, camp, settlement, home, starting point.
v establish, found, ground, locate, station, build, construct, derive, depend, hinge.

baseless adj groundless, unfounded, unsupported, unsubstantiated, unauthenticated, unconfirmed, unjustified, uncalled-for, gratuitous.
E3 justifiable.

bashful adj shy, retiring, backward, reticent, reserved, unforthcoming, hesitant, shrinking, nervous, timid, coy, diffident, modest, inhibited, self-conscious, embarrassed, blushing, abashed, shamefaced, sheepish.
E3 bold, confident, aggressive.

basic adj fundamental, elementary, primary, root, underlying, key, central, inherent, intrinsic, essential, indispensable, vital, necessary, important.
E3 inessential, minor, peripheral.

basically adv fundamentally, at bottom, at heart, inherently, intrinsically, essentially, principally, primarily.

basics n fundamentals, rudiments, principles, essentials, necessaries, practicalities, brass tacks (infml), grass roots, bedrock, rock bottom, core, facts.

basin n bowl, dish, sink, crater, cavity, hollow, depression, dip.

basis n base, bottom, footing, support, foundation, ground, groundwork, fundamental, premise, principle, essential, heart, core, thrust.

bask v sunbathe, lie, lounge, relax, laze, wallow, revel, delight in, enjoy, relish, savour.

basket n hamper, creel, pannier, punnet, bassinet.

bass adj deep, low, low-toned, grave, resonant.

bastion n stronghold, citadel, fortress, defence, bulwark, mainstay, support, prop, pillar, rock.

batch n lot, consignment, parcel, pack, bunch, set, assortment, collection, assemblage, group, contingent, amount, quantity.

bath n wash, scrub, soak, shower, douche, tub, Jacuzzi®.
v bathe, wash, clean, soak, shower.

bathe v swim, wet, moisten, immerse, wash, cleanse, rinse, soak, steep, flood, cover, suffuse.
n swim, dip, paddle, wash, rinse, soak.

battalion n army, force, brigade, regiment, squadron, company, platoon, division, contingent, legion, horde, multitude, throng, host, mass, herd.

batter v beat, pound, pummel, buffet, smash, dash, pelt, lash, thrash, wallop (infml), abuse, maltreat, ill-treat, manhandle, maul, assault, hurt, injure, bruise, disfigure, mangle, distress, crush, demolish, destroy, ruin, shatter.

battered adj beaten, abused, ill-treated, injured, bruised, weather-beaten, dilapidated, tumbledown, ramshackle, crumbling, damaged, crushed.

battle n war, warfare, hostilities, action, conflict, strife, combat, fight, engagement, encounter, attack, fray, skirmish, clash, struggle, contest, campaign, crusade, row, disagreement, dispute, debate, controversy.
v fight, combat, war, feud, contend, struggle, strive, campaign, crusade, agitate, clamour, contest, argue, dispute.

battle-cry n war cry, war song, slogan, motto, watchword, catchword.

baulk see **balk**.

bay[1] n gulf, bight, arm, inlet, cove.

bay[2] n recess, alcove, niche, nook, opening, compartment, cubicle, booth, stall, carrel.

bay[3] v howl, roar, bellow, bell, bawl, cry, holler (infml), bark.

bazaar n market, marketplace, mart, exchange, sale, fair, fête, bring-and-buy.

be v 1 EXIST, breathe, live, inhabit, reside, dwell. 2 STAY, remain, abide, last, endure, persist, continue, survive, stand, prevail, obtain. 3 HAPPEN, occur, arise, come about, take place, come to pass, befall, develop.

beach n sand, sands, shingle, shore, strand, seashore, seaside, water's edge, coast, seaboard.

beacon n signal, fire, watch fire, bonfire, light, beam, lighthouse, flare, rocket, sign.

bead n drop, droplet, drip, globule, glob (infml), blob, dot, bubble, pearl, jewel, pellet.

beaker n glass, tumbler, jar, cup, mug, tankard.

beam n 1 a beam of light: ray, shaft, gleam, glint, glimmer, glow. 2 PLANK, board, timber, rafter, joist, girder, spar, boom, bar, support.
v 1 EMIT, broadcast, transmit, radiate, shine, glare, glitter, glow, glimmer. 2 SMILE, grin.

bear v 1 CARRY, convey, transport, move, take, bring. 2 HOLD, support, shoulder, uphold, sustain, maintain, harbour, cherish. 3 bear children: give birth to, breed, propagate, beget, engender, produce, generate, develop, yield, bring forth, give up. 4 TOLERATE, stand, put up with, endure, abide, suffer, permit, allow, admit.

bear on refer to, relate to, affect, concern, involve.

bear out confirm, endorse, support, uphold, prove, demonstrate, corroborate, substantiate, vindicate, justify.

bear up persevere, soldier on, carry on, suffer, endure, survive, withstand.

bear with tolerate, put up with, endure, suffer, forbear, be patient with, make allowances for.

bearable adj tolerable, endurable, sufferable, supportable, sustainable, acceptable, manageable.
E3 unbearable, intolerable.

bearded adj unshaven, bristly, whiskered, tufted, hairy, hirsute,

shaggy, bushy.
🔁 beardless, clean-shaven, smooth.

bearer n carrier, conveyor, porter, courier, messenger, runner, holder, possessor.

bearing n 1 *have no bearing on the matter*: relevance, significance, connection, relation, reference. 2 DEMEANOUR, manner, mien, air, aspect, attitude, behaviour, comportment, poise, deportment, carriage, posture.

bearings n orientation, position, situation, location, whereabouts, course, track, way, direction, aim.

beast n animal, creature, brute, monster, savage, barbarian, pig, swine, devil, fiend.

beat v 1 WHIP, flog, lash, tan (*infml*), cane, strap, thrash, lay into, hit, punch, strike, swipe, knock, bang, wham, bash, pound, hammer, batter, buffet, pelt, bruise.
2 PULSATE, pulse, throb, thump, race, palpitate, flutter, vibrate, quiver, tremble, shake, quake.
3 DEFEAT, trounce, best, worst, hammer (*infml*), slaughter (*sl*), conquer, overcome, overwhelm, vanquish, subdue, surpass, excel, outdo, outstrip, outrun.
n 1 PULSATION, pulse, stroke, throb, thump, palpitation, flutter.
2 RHYTHM, time, tempo, metre, measure, rhyme, stress, accent. 3 *a policeman's beat*: round, rounds, territory, circuit, course, journey, way, path, route.

beat up (*infml*) attack, assault, knock about, knock around, batter, do over (*infml*).

beaten adj 1 HAMMERED, stamped, forged, wrought, worked, formed, shaped, fashioned. 2 WHISKED, whipped, mixed, blended, frothy, foamy.

beating n 1 CORPORAL PUNISHMENT, chastisement, whipping, flogging, caning,

thrashing. 2 DEFEAT, conquest, rout, ruin, downfall.

beautiful adj attractive, fair, pretty, lovely, good-looking, handsome, gorgeous, radiant, ravishing, stunning (*infml*), pleasing, appealing, alluring, charming, delightful, fine, exquisite.
🔁 ugly, plain, hideous.

beautify v embellish, enhance, improve, grace, gild, garnish, decorate, ornament, deck, bedeck, adorn, array, glamorize, titivate (*infml*), tart up (*sl*).
🔁 disfigure, spoil.

beauty n attractiveness, fairness, prettiness, loveliness, (good) looks, handsomeness, glamour, appeal, allure, charm, grace, elegance, symmetry, excellence.
🔁 ugliness, repulsiveness.

because conj as, for, since, owing to, on account of, by reason of, thanks to.

beckon v summon, motion, gesture, signal, nod, wave, gesticulate, call, invite, attract, pull, draw, lure, allure, entice, tempt, coax.

become v 1 *become old-fashioned*: turn, grow, get, change into, develop into. 2 SUIT, befit, flatter, enhance, grace, embellish, ornament, set off, harmonize.

bed n 1 divan, couch, bunk, berth, cot, mattress, pallet, sack (*sl*).
2 LAYER, stratum, substratum, matrix, base, bottom, foundation, groundwork, watercourse, channel.
3 *bed of flowers*: garden, border, patch, plot.

bedclothes n bedding, bed-linen, sheets, pillowcases, pillowslips, covers, blankets, bedspreads, coverlets, quilts, eiderdowns, pillows.

bedraggled adj untidy, unkempt, dishevelled, disordered, scruffy, slovenly, messy, dirty, muddy, muddied, soiled, wet, sodden, drenched.

before

◻ neat, tidy, clean.

before *adv* ahead, in front, in advance, sooner, earlier, formerly, previously.
◻ after, later.

beforehand *adv* in advance, preliminarily, already, before, previously, earlier, sooner.

befriend *v* help, aid, assist, succour, back, support, stand by, uphold, sustain, comfort, encourage, welcome, favour, benefit, take under one's wing, make friends with, get to know.
◻ neglect, oppose.

beg *v* request, require, desire, crave, beseech, plead, entreat, implore, pray, supplicate, petition, solicit, cadge, scrounge, sponge.

beggar *n* mendicant, supplicant, pauper, down-and-out, tramp, vagrant, cadger, scrounger, sponger.

begin *v* start, commence, set about, embark on, set in motion, activate, originate, initiate, introduce, found, institute, instigate, arise, spring, emerge, appear.
◻ end, finish, cease.

beginner *n* novice, tiro, starter, learner, trainee, apprentice, student, freshman, fresher, recruit, cub, tenderfoot, fledgling.
◻ veteran, old hand, expert.

beginning *n* start, commencement, onset, outset, opening, preface, prelude, introduction, initiation, establishment, inauguration, inception, starting point, birth, dawn, origin, source, fountainhead, root, seed, emergence, rise.
◻ end, finish.

begrudge *v* resent, grudge, mind, object to, envy, covet, stint.
◻ allow.

beguile *v* **1** CHARM, enchant, bewitch, captivate, amuse, entertain, divert, distract, occupy, engross. **2** DECEIVE, fool, hoodwink, dupe, trick, cheat, delude, mislead.

behalf *n* sake, account, good, interest, benefit, advantage, profit, name, authority, side, support.

behave *v* act, react, respond, work, function, run, operate, perform, conduct oneself, acquit oneself, comport oneself (*fml*).

behaviour *n* conduct, comportment (*fml*), manner, manners, actions, doings, dealings, ways, habits, action, reaction, response, functioning, operation, performance.

behead *v* decapitate, execute, guillotine.

behind *prep* **1** FOLLOWING, after, later than, causing, responsible for, instigating, initiating. SUPPORTING, backing, for.
adv after, following, next, subsequently, behindhand, late, overdue, in arrears, in debt.
n rump, rear, posterior (*infml*), buttocks, seat, bottom, backside (*infml*), bum (*sl*), butt (*US infml*), tail (*infml*).

beige *adj* buff, fawn, mushroom, camel, sandy, khaki, coffee, neutral.

being *n* **1** EXISTENCE, actuality, reality, life, animation, essence, substance, nature, soul, spirit. **2** CREATURE, animal, beast, human being, mortal, person, individual, thing, entity.

belated *adj* late, tardy, overdue, delayed, behindhand, unpunctual.
◻ punctual, timely.

belch *v* burp (*infml*), hiccup, emit, discharge, disgorge, spew.
n burp (*infml*), hiccup.

beleaguered *adj* harassed, pestered, badgered, bothered, worried, vexed, plagued, persecuted, surrounded, beset, besieged.

belief *n* **1** CONVICTION, persuasion, credit, trust, reliance, confidence, assurance, certainty, sureness, presumption, expectation, feeling, intuition, impression, notion, theory, view, opinion, judgement.

2 IDEOLOGY, faith, creed, doctrine, dogma, tenet, principle.
■ **1** disbelief.

believable *adj* credible, imaginable, conceivable, acceptable, plausible, possible, likely, probable, authoritative, reliable, trustworthy.
■ unbelievable, incredible, unconvincing.

believe *v* accept, wear (*infml*), swallow (*infml*), credit, trust, count on, depend on, rely on, swear by, hold, maintain, postulate, assume, presume, gather, speculate, conjecture, guess, imagine, think, consider, reckon, suppose, deem, judge.
■ disbelieve, doubt.

believer *n* convert, proselyte, disciple, follower, adherent, devotee, zealot, supporter, upholder.
■ unbeliever, sceptic.

belittle *v* minimize, play down, dismiss, underrate, undervalue, underestimate, lessen, diminish, detract from, deprecate, decry, disparage, run down, deride, scorn, ridicule.
■ exaggerate, praise.

belligerent *adj* aggressive, militant, argumentative, quarrelsome, contentious, combative, pugnacious, violent, bullying, antagonistic, warring, warlike, bellicose.
■ peaceable.

bellow *v* roar, yell, shout, bawl, cry, scream, shriek, howl, clamour.

belong *v* fit, go with, be part of, attach to, link up with, tie up with, be connected with, relate to.

belongings *n* possessions, property, chattels, goods, effects, things, stuff (*infml*), gear (*infml*), paraphernalia.

beloved *adj* loved, adored, cherished, treasured, prized, precious, pet, favourite, dearest, dear, darling, admired, revered.

below *adv* beneath, under, underneath, down, lower, lower

down.
■ above.
prep **1** UNDER, underneath, beneath.
2 INFERIOR TO, lesser than, subordinate to, subject to.
■ above.

belt *n* **1** SASH, girdle, waistband, girth, strap. **2** STRIP, band, swathe, stretch, tract, area, region, district, zone, layer.

bemused *adj* confused, muddled, bewildered, puzzled, perplexed, dazed, befuddled, stupefied.
■ clear-headed, clear, lucid.

bench *n* **1** SEAT, form, settle, pew, ledge, counter, table, stall, workbench, worktable. **2** COURT, courtroom, tribunal, judiciary, judicature, judge, magistrate.

bend *v* curve, turn, deflect, swerve, veer, diverge, twist, contort, flex, shape, mould, buckle, bow, incline, lean, stoop, crouch.
■ straighten.
n curvature, curve, arc, bow, loop, hook, crook, elbow, angle, corner, turn, twist, zigzag.

beneath *adv* below, under, underneath, lower, lower down.
prep **1** UNDER, underneath, below, lower than. **2** UNWORTHY OF, unbefitting.

benefactor *n* philanthropist, patron, sponsor, angel (*infml*), backer, supporter, promoter, donor, contributor, subscriber, provider, helper, friend, well-wisher.
■ opponent, persecutor.

beneficial *adj* advantageous, favourable, useful, helpful, profitable, rewarding, valuable, improving, edifying, wholesome.
■ harmful, detrimental, useless.

beneficiary *n* payee, receiver, recipient, inheritor, legatee, heir, heiress, successor.

benefit *n* advantage, good, welfare, interest, favour, help, aid, assistance, service, use, avail, gain, profit, asset, blessing.

≢ disadvantage, harm, damage.

v help, aid, assist, serve, avail, advantage, profit, improve, enhance, better, further, advance, promote.

≢ mean, selfish, malevolent.

benevolent *adj* philanthropic, humanitarian, charitable, generous, liberal, munificent, altruistic, benign, humane, kind, kindly, well-disposed, compassionate, caring, considerate.

≢ mean, selfish, malevolent.

benign *adj* **1** BENEVOLENT, good, gracious, gentle, kind, obliging, friendly, amiable, genial, sympathetic. **2** *a benign tumour*: curable, harmless. **3** FAVOURABLE, propitious, beneficial, temperate, mild, warm, refreshing, restorative, wholesome.

≢ **1** hostile. **2** malignant. **3** harmful, unpleasant.

bent *adj* **1** ANGLED, curved, bowed, arched, folded, doubled, twisted, hunched, stooped. **2** (*infml*) DISHONEST, crooked (*infml*), illegal, criminal, corrupt, untrustworthy.

≢ **1** straight, upright. **2** honest.

n tendency, inclination, leaning, preference, ability, capacity, faculty, aptitude, facility, gift, talent, knack, flair, forte.

bent on determined, resolved, set, fixed, inclined, disposed.

bequeath *v* will, leave, bestow, gift, endow, grant, settle, hand down, pass on, impart, transmit, assign, entrust, commit.

bequest *n* legacy, inheritance, heritage, trust, bestowal, endowment, gift, donation, estate, devisal, settlement.

bereavement *n* loss, deprivation, dispossession, death.

bereft *adj* deprived, robbed, stripped, destitute, devoid, lacking, wanting, minus.

berserk *adj* mad, crazy, demented, insane, deranged, frantic, frenzied,

wild, raging, furious, violent, rabid, raving.

≢ sane, calm.

berth *n* **1** BED, bunk, hammock, billet. **2** MOORING, anchorage, quay, wharf, dock, harbour, port.

beside *prep* alongside, abreast of, next to, adjacent, abutting, bordering, neighbouring, next door to, close to, near, overlooking.

besides *adv* also, as well, too, in addition, additionally, further, furthermore, moreover.

prep apart from, other than, in addition to, over and above.

besiege *v* **1** LAY SIEGE TO, blockade, surround, encircle, confine. **2** TROUBLE, bother, importune, assail, beset, beleaguer, harass, pester, badger, nag, hound, plague.

besotted *adj* infatuated, doting, obsessed, smitten, hypnotized, spellbound, intoxicated.

≢ indifferent, disenchanted.

best *adj* optimum, optimal, first, foremost, leading, unequalled, unsurpassed, matchless, incomparable, supreme, greatest, highest, largest, finest, excellent, outstanding, superlative, first-rate, first-class, perfect.

≢ worst.

adv greatly, extremely, exceptionally, excellently, superlatively.

≢ worst.

n finest, cream, prime, élite, top, first, pick, choice, favourite.

≢ worst.

bestow *v* award, present, grant, confer, endow, bequeath, commit, entrust, impart, transmit, allot, apportion, accord, give, donate, lavish.

≢ withhold, deprive.

bet *n* wager, flutter (*infml*), gamble, speculation, risk, venture, stake, ante, bid, pledge.

v wager, gamble, punt, speculate, risk, hazard, chance, venture, lay, stake, bid, pledge.

betray v 1 *betray a friend*: inform on, shop (*sl*), sell (out), double-cross, desert, abandon, forsake.
2 DISCLOSE, give away, tell, divulge, expose, reveal, show, manifest.
🔁 1 defend, protect. 2 conceal, hide.

betrayal n treachery, treason, sell-out, disloyalty, unfaithfulness, double-dealing, duplicity, deception, trickery, falseness.
🔁 loyalty, protection.

betrayer n traitor, Judas, informer, grass (*sl*), supergrass (*sl*), double-crosser, deceiver, conspirator, renegade, apostate.
🔁 protector, supporter.

better adj 1 SUPERIOR, bigger, larger, longer, greater, worthier, finer, surpassing, preferable.
2 IMPROVING, progressing, on the mend, recovering, fitter, healthier, stronger, recovered, restored.
🔁 1 inferior. 2 worse.
v 1 IMPROVE, ameliorate, enhance, raise, further, promote, forward, reform, mend, correct. 2 SURPASS, top, beat, outdo, outstrip, overtake.
🔁 1 worsen, deteriorate.

between prep mid, amid, amidst, among, amongst.

beverage n drink, draught, liquor, liquid, refreshment.

bevy n gathering, band, company, troupe, group, flock, gaggle, pack, bunch, crowd, throng.

beware v watch out, look out, mind, take heed, steer clear of, avoid, shun, guard against.

bewilder v confuse, muddle, disconcert, confound, bamboozle (*infml*), baffle, puzzle, perplex, mystify, daze, stupefy, disorient.

bewildered adj confused, muddled, uncertain, disoriented, nonplussed, bamboozled (*infml*), baffled, puzzled, perplexed, mystified, bemused, surprised, stunned.
🔁 unperturbed, collected.

bewitch v charm, enchant, allure, beguile, spellbind, possess, captivate, enrapture, obsess, fascinate, entrance, hypnotize.

beyond prep past, further than, apart from, away from, remote from, out of range of, out of reach of, above, over, superior to.

bias n slant, angle, distortion, bent, leaning, inclination, tendency, propensity, partiality, favouritism, prejudice, one-sidedness, unfairness, bigotry, intolerance.
🔁 impartiality, fairness.

biased adj slanted, angled, distorted, warped, twisted, loaded, weighted, influenced, swayed, partial, predisposed, prejudiced, one-sided, unfair, bigoted, blinkered, jaundiced.
🔁 impartial, fair.

bicker v squabble, row, quarrel, wrangle, argue, scrap, spar, fight, clash, disagree, dispute.
🔁 agree.

bicycle n cycle, bike (*infml*), two-wheeler, push-bike, racer, mountain-bike, tandem, penny-farthing.

bid v 1 ASK, request, desire, instruct, direct, command, enjoin, require, charge, call, summon, invite, solicit.
2 *he bid more than the painting was worth*: offer, proffer, tender, submit, propose.
n 1 OFFER, tender, sum, amount, price, advance, submission, proposal.
2 ATTEMPT, effort, try, go (*infml*), endeavour, venture.

big adj 1 LARGE, great, sizable, considerable, substantial, huge, enormous, immense, massive, colossal, gigantic, mammoth, burly, bulky, extensive, spacious, vast, voluminous. 2 IMPORTANT, significant, momentous, serious, main, principal, eminent, prominent, influential. 3 *that's big of you*: generous, magnanimous, gracious, unselfish.
🔁 1 small, little. 2 insignificant,

unknown.

bigot *n* chauvinist, sectarian, racist, sexist, dogmatist, fanatic, zealot.
ᴇᴈ liberal, humanitarian.

bigoted *adj* prejudiced, biased, intolerant, illiberal, narrow-minded, narrow, blinkered, closed, dogmatic, opinionated, obstinate.
ᴇᴈ tolerant, liberal, broad-minded, enlightened.

bigotry *n* prejudice, discrimination, bias, injustice, unfairness, intolerance, narrow-mindedness, chauvinism, jingoism, sectarianism, racism, racialism, sexism, dogmatism, fanaticism.
ᴇᴈ tolerance.

bilious *adj* **1** IRRITABLE, choleric, cross, grumpy, crotchety, testy, grouchy, peevish. **2** SICK, queasy, nauseated, sickly, out of sorts (*infml*).

bill *n* **1** INVOICE, statement, account, charges, reckoning, tally, score. **2** CIRCULAR, leaflet, handout, bulletin, handbill, broadsheet, advertisement, notice, poster, placard, playbill, programme. **3** *parliamentary bill*: proposal, measure, legislation.
v invoice, charge, debit.

billet *n* **1** ACCOMMODATION, quarters, barracks, lodging, housing, berth. **2** EMPLOYMENT, post, occupation.

billow *v* swell, expand, bulge, puff out, fill out, balloon, rise, heave, surge, roll, undulate.

bind *v* **1** ATTACH, fasten, secure, clamp, stick, tie, lash, truss, strap, bandage, cover, dress, wrap. **2** OBLIGE, force, compel, constrain, necessitate, restrict, confine, restrain, hamper.

binding *adj* obligatory, compulsory, mandatory, necessary, requisite, permanent, conclusive, irrevocable, unalterable, indissoluble, unbreakable, strict.

n border, edging, trimming, tape, bandage, covering, wrapping.

biography *n* life story, life, history, autobiography, memoirs, recollections, curriculum vitae, account, record.

biology

Biological terms include: bacteriology, biochemistry, biology, bionics, botany, cybernetics, cytology, Darwinism, neo-Darwinism, ecology, embryology, endocrinology, evolution, Haeckel's law, genetics, Mendelism, Lamarckism, marine biology, natural history, palaeontology, pathology, physiology, systematics, taxonomy, zoology; amino acid, anatomy, animal behaviour, animal kingdom, bacillus, bacteria, biologist, botanist, cell, chromosome, class, coccus, conservation, corpuscle, cultivar, cytoplasm, deoxyribonucleic acid (DNA), diffusion, ecosystem, ectoplasm, embryo, endoplasmic reticulum (ER), enzyme, evolution, excretion, extinction, flora and fauna, food chain, fossil, gene, genetic engineering, genetic fingerprinting, population genetics, germ, Golgi apparatus, hereditary factor, homeostasis, living world, meiosis, membrane, metabolism, micro-organism, microbe, mitosis, molecule, mutation, natural selection, nuclear membrane, nucleus, nutrition, order, organism, osmosis, parasitism, photosynthesis, pollution, protein, protoplasm, reproduction, respiration, reticulum, ribonucleic acid (RNA), ribosome, secretion, survival of the fittest, symbiosis, virus.

bird

Birds include: sparrow, thrush, starling, blackbird, bluetit, chaffinch, greenfinch, bullfinch, dunnock, robin, wagtail, swallow, tit, wren, martin, swift, crow, magpie, dove, pigeon, skylark, nightingale, linnet, warbler, jay, jackdaw, rook, raven, cuckoo, woodpecker, yellowhammer; duck, mallard, eider, teal, swan, goose, heron, stork, flamingo, pelican, kingfisher, moorhen, coot, lapwing, peewit, plover, curlew, snipe, avocet, seagull, guillemot, tern, petrel, crane, bittern, petrel, albatross, gannet, cormorant, auk, puffin, dipper; eagle, owl, hawk, sparrowhawk, falcon, kestrel, osprey, buzzard, vulture, condor; emu, ostrich, kiwi, peacock, penguin; chicken, grouse, partridge, pheasant, quail, turkey; canary, budgerigar, budgie (*infml*), cockatiel, cockatoo, lovebird, parakeet, parrot, macaw, toucan, myna bird, mockingbird, kookaburra, bird of paradise.

birth *n* **1** CHILDBIRTH, parturition, confinement, delivery, nativity. **2** *of noble birth*: ancestry, family, parentage, descent, line, lineage, genealogy, blood, stock, race, extraction, background, breeding. **3** BEGINNING, rise, emergence, origin, source, derivation.

birthplace *n* place of origin, native town, native country, fatherland, mother country, roots, provenance, source, fount.

bisect *v* halve, divide, separate, split, intersect, cross, fork, bifurcate.

bit *n* fragment, part, segment, piece, slice, crumb, morsel, scrap, atom, mite, whit, jot, iota, grain, speck.
bit by bit gradually, little by little, step by step, piecemeal.
🖛 wholesale.

bitchy *adj* catty, snide, nasty, mean, spiteful, malicious, vindictive, backbiting, venomous, cruel, vicious.
🖛 kind.

bite *v* **1** CHEW, masticate, munch,

gnaw, nibble, champ, crunch, crush. **2** *the dog bit her hand*: nip, pierce, wound, tear, rend. **3** SMART, sting, tingle. **4** GRIP, hold, seize, pinch, take effect.

n **1** NIP, wound, sting, smarting, pinch. **2** *a bite to eat*: snack, refreshment, mouthful, morsel, taste. **3** PUNGENCY, piquancy, kick (*infml*), punch.

biting *adj* **1** COLD, freezing, bitter, harsh, severe. **2** CUTTING, incisive, piercing, penetrating, raw, stinging, sharp, tart, caustic, scathing, cynical, hurtful.
🖛 **1** mild. **2** bland.

bitter *adj* **1** SOUR, tart, sharp, acid, acid, vinegary, unsweetened. **2** RESENTFUL, embittered, jaundiced, cynical, rancorous, acrimonious, acerbic, hostile. **3** INTENSE, severe, harsh, fierce, cruel, savage, merciless, painful, stinging, biting, freezing, raw.
🖛 **1** sweet. **2** contented. **3** mild.

bizarre *adj* strange, odd, queer, curious, weird, peculiar, eccentric, way-out (*infml*), outlandish, ludicrous, ridiculous, fantastic, extravagant, grotesque, freakish, abnormal, deviant, unusual, extraordinary.
🖛 normal, ordinary.

black *adj* **1** JET-BLACK, coal-black, jet, ebony, sable, inky, sooty, dusky, swarthy. **2** DARK, unlit, moonless, starless, overcast, dingy, gloomy, sombre, funereal. **3** FILTHY, dirty, soiled, grimy, grubby.
🖛 **1** white. **2** bright. **3** clean.
v boycott, blacklist, ban, bar, taboo

black out 1 FAINT, pass out, collapse, flake out (*infml*). **2** DARKEN, eclipse, cover up, conceal, suppress, withhold, censor, gag.

blacken *v* **1** DARKEN, dirty, soil, smudge, cloud. **2** DEFAME, malign, slander, libel, vilify, revile, denigrate, detract, smear, besmirch, sully, stain,

tarnish, taint, defile, discredit, dishonour.
⊟ 2 praise, enhance.

blackmail *n* extortion, chantage, hush money (*infml*), intimidation, protection, pay-off, ransom.
v extort, bleed, milk, squeeze, hold to ransom, threaten, lean on (*infml*), force, compel, coerce, demand.

blackout *n* **1** *a news blackout*: suppression, censorship, cover-up (*infml*), concealment, secrecy. **2** FAINT, coma, unconsciousness, oblivion. **3** power failure, power cut.

blade *n* edge, knife, dagger, sword, scalpel, razor, vane.

blame *n* censure, criticism, stick (*sl*), reprimand, reproof, reproach, recrimination, condemnation, accusation, charge, rap (*sl*), incrimination, guilt, culpability, fault, responsibility, accountability, liability, onus.
v accuse, charge, tax, reprimand, chide, reprove, upbraid, reprehend, admonish, rebuke, reproach, censure, criticize, find fault with, disapprove, condemn.
⊟ exonerate, vindicate.

blameless *adj* innocent, guiltless, clear, faultless, perfect, unblemished, stainless, virtuous, sinless, upright, above reproach, irreproachable, unblamable, unimpeachable.
⊟ guilty, blameworthy.

blanch *v* blench, whiten, pale, fade, bleach.
⊟ colour, blush, redden.

bland *adv* boring, monotonous, humdrum, tedious, dull, uninspiring, uninteresting, unexciting, nondescript, characterless, flat, insipid, tasteless, weak, mild, smooth, soft, gentle, non-irritant.
⊟ lively, stimulating, sharp.

blank *adj* **1** *a blank page*: empty, unfilled, void, clear, bare, unmarked, plain, clean, white.
2 EXPRESSIONLESS, deadpan, poker-

faced, impassive, apathetic, glazed, vacant, uncomprehending.
n space, gap, break, void, emptiness, vacancy, vacuity, nothingness, vacuum.

blanket *n* covering, coating, coat, layer, film, carpet, rug, cloak, mantle, cover, sheet, envelope, wrapper, wrapping.
v cover, coat, eclipse, hide, conceal, mask, cloak, surround, muffle, deaden, obscure, cloud.

blare *v* trumpet, clamour, roar, blast, boom, resound, ring, peal, clang, hoot, toot, honk.

blasé *adj* nonchalant, offhand, unimpressed, unmoved, unexcited, jaded, weary, bored, uninterested, uninspired, apathetic, indifferent, cool, unconcerned.
⊟ excited, enthusiastic.

blaspheme *v* profane, desecrate, swear, curse, imprecate, damn, execrate, revile, abuse.

blasphemous *adj* profane, impious, sacrilegious, imprecatory, godless, ungodly, irreligious, irreverent.

blasphemy *n* profanity, curse, expletive, imprecation, cursing, swearing, execration, impiety, irreverence, sacrilege, desecration, violation, outrage.

blast *n* **1** EXPLOSION, detonation, bang, crash, clap, crack, volley, burst, outburst, discharge. **2** *a blast of cold air*: draught, gust, gale, squall, storm, tempest. **3** SOUND, blow, blare, roar, boom, peal, hoot, wail, scream, shriek.
v **1** EXPLODE, blow up, burst, shatter, destroy, demolish, ruin, assail, attack. **2** SOUND, blare, roar, boom, peal, hoot, wail, scream, shriek.

blatant *adj* flagrant, brazen, barefaced, arrant, open, overt, undisguised, ostentatious, glaring, conspicuous, obtrusive, prominent, pronounced, obvious, sheer, outright, unmitigated.

bliss

blaze n fire, flames, conflagration, bonfire, flare-up, explosion, blast, burst, outburst, radiance, brilliance, glare, flash, gleam, glitter, glow, light, flame.
v burn, flame, flare (up), erupt, explode, burst, fire, flash, gleam, glare, beam, shine, glow.

bleach v whiten, blanch, decolorize, fade, pale, lighten.

bleak adj 1 GLOOMY, sombre, leaden, grim, dreary, dismal, depressing, joyless, cheerless, comfortless, hopeless, discouraging, disheartening. 2 COLD, chilly, raw, weather-beaten, unsheltered, windy, windswept, exposed, open, barren, bare, empty, desolate, gaunt.
F3 1 bright, cheerful.

bleed v 1 HAEMORRHAGE, gush, spurt, flow, run, exude, weep, ooze, seep, trickle. 2 DRAIN, suck dry, exhaust, squeeze, milk, sap, reduce, deplete.

blemish n flaw, imperfection, defect, fault, deformity, disfigurement, birthmark, naevus, spot, mark, speck, smudge, blotch, blot, stain, taint, disgrace, dishonour.
v flaw, deface, disfigure, spoil, mar, damage, impair, spot, mark, blot, blotch, stain, sully, taint, tarnish.

blend v 1 MERGE, amalgamate, coalesce, compound, synthesize, fuse, unite, combine, mix, mingle.
2 HARMONIZE, complement, fit, match.
F3 1 separate.
n compound, composite, alloy, amalgam, amalgamation, synthesis, fusion, combination, union, mix, mixture, concoction.

bless v 1 ANOINT, sanctify, consecrate, hallow, dedicate, ordain.
2 PRAISE, extol, magnify, glorify, exalt, thank. 3 APPROVE, countenance, favour, grace, bestow, endow, provide.
F3 1 curse. 2 condemn.

blessed adj 1 HOLY, sacred, hallowed, sanctified, revered, adored, divine. 2 HAPPY, contented, glad, joyful, joyous, lucky, fortunate, prosperous, favoured, endowed.
F3 1 cursed.

blessing n 1 CONSECRATION, dedication, benediction, grace, thanksgiving, invocation. 2 BENEFIT, advantage, favour, godsend, windfall, gift, gain, profit, help, service. 3 give a proposal one's blessing: approval, concurrence, backing, support, authority, sanction, consent, permission, leave.
F3 2 curse, blight. 3 condemnation.

blight n curse, bane, evil, scourge, affliction, disease, cancer, canker, fungus, mildew, rot, decay, pollution, contamination, corruption, infestation.
F3 blessing, boon.
v spoil, mar, injure, undermine, ruin, wreck, crush, shatter, destroy, annihilate, blast, wither, shrivel, frustrate, disappoint.
F3 bless.

blind adj 1 SIGHTLESS, unsighted, unseeing, eyeless, purblind, partially sighted. 2 IMPETUOUS, impulsive, hasty, rash, reckless, wild, mad, indiscriminate, careless, heedless, mindless, unthinking, unreasoning, irrational. 3 blind to their needs: ignorant, oblivious, unaware, unconscious, unobservant, inattentive, neglectful, indifferent, insensitive, thoughtless, inconsiderate. 4 CLOSED, obstructed, hidden, concealed, obscured.
F3 1 sighted. 2 careful, cautious.
3 aware, sensitive.
n screen, cover, cloak, mask, camouflage, masquerade, front, façade, distraction, smokescreen, cover-up (infml).

bliss n blissfulness, ecstasy, euphoria, rapture, joy, happiness, gladness, blessedness, paradise, heaven.

▣ misery, hell, damnation.

blissful *adj* ecstatic, euphoric, elated, enraptured, rapturous, delighted, enchanted, joyful, joyous, happy.

▣ miserable, wretched.

blister *n* sore, swelling, cyst, boil, abscess, ulcer, pustule, pimple, carbuncle.

blizzard *n* snowstorm, squall, storm, tempest.

bloated *adj* swollen, puffy, blown up, inflated, distended, dilated, expanded, enlarged, turgid, bombastic.

▣ thin, shrunken, shrivelled.

blob *n* drop, droplet, globule, glob (*infml*), bead, pearl, bubble, dab, spot, gob, lump, mass, ball, pellet, pill.

block *n* **1** *a block of stone*: piece, lump, mass, chunk, hunk, square, cube, brick, bar. **2** OBSTACLE, barrier, bar, jam, blockage, stoppage, resistance, obstruction, impediment, hindrance, let, delay.
v choke, clog, plug, stop up, dam up, close, bar, obstruct, impede, hinder, stonewall, stop, check, arrest, halt, thwart, scotch, deter.

blockade *n* barrier, barricade, siege, obstruction, restriction, stoppage, closure.

blockage *n* blocking, obstruction, stoppage, occlusion, block, clot, jam, log-jam, congestion, hindrance, impediment.

blond, blonde *adj* fair, flaxen, golden, fair-haired, golden-haired, light-coloured, bleached.

blood *n* extraction, birth, descent, lineage, family, kindred, relations, ancestry, descendants, kinship, relationship.

bloodcurdling *adj* horrifying, chilling, spine-chilling, hair-raising, terrifying, frightening, scary, dreadful, fearful, horrible, horrid,

horrendous.

bloodshed *n* killing, murder, slaughter, massacre, blood-bath, butchery, carnage, gore, bloodletting.

bloodthirsty *adj* murderous, homicidal, warlike, savage, barbaric, barbarous, brutal, ferocious, vicious, cruel, inhuman, ruthless.

bloody *adj* bleeding, bloodstained, gory, sanguinary, murderous, savage, brutal, ferocious, fierce, cruel.

bloom *n* **1** BLOSSOM, flower, bud. **2** PRIME, heyday, perfection, blush, flush, glow, rosiness, beauty, radiance, lustre, health, vigour, freshness.
v bud, sprout, grow, wax, develop, mature, blossom, flower, blow, open.

▣ fade, wither.

blossom *n* bloom, flower, bud.
v develop, mature, bloom, flower, blow, flourish, thrive, prosper, succeed.

▣ fade, wither.

blot *n* spot, stain, smudge, blotch, smear, mark, speck, blemish, flaw, fault, defect, taint, disgrace.
v spot, mark, stain, smudge, blur, sully, taint, tarnish, spoil, mar, disfigure, disgrace.

blot out obliterate, cancel, delete, erase, expunge, darken, obscure, shadow, eclipse.

blotch *n* patch, splodge, splotch, splash, smudge, blot, spot, mark, stain, blemish.

blotchy *adj* spotty, spotted, patchy, uneven, smeary, blemished, reddened, inflamed.

blow¹ *v* **1** BREATHE, exhale, pant, puff, waft, fan, flutter, float, flow, stream, rush, whirl, whisk, sweep, fling, buffet, drive, blast. **2** *blow a horn*: play, sound, pipe, trumpet, toot, blare.
n puff, draught, flurry, gust, blast, wind, gale, squall, tempest.

blow over die down, subside, end, finish, cease, pass, vanish, disappear, dissipate, fizzle out, peter out.

blow up 1 EXPLODE, go off, detonate, burst, blast, bomb. **2** LOSE ONE'S TEMPER, blow one's top (*infml*), erupt, hit the roof (*infml*), rage, go mad (*infml*). **3** INFLATE, pump up, swell, fill (out), puff up, bloat, distend, dilate, expand, enlarge, magnify, exaggerate, overstate.

blow² *n* **1** *a blow on the head*: concussion, box, cuff, clip, clout, swipe, biff (*infml*), bash, slap, smack, whack (*infml*), wallop (*infml*), belt (*infml*), buffet, bang, clap, knock, rap, stroke, thump, punch.
2 MISFORTUNE, affliction, reverse, setback, comedown, disappointment, upset, jolt, shock, bombshell, calamity, catastrophe, disaster.

blowy *adj* breezy, windy, fresh, blustery, gusty, squally, stormy.

bludgeon *v* **1** BEAT, strike, club, batter, cosh (*sl*) cudgel. **2** FORCE, coerce, bulldoze, badger, hector, harass, browbeat, bully, terrorize, intimidate.

blue *adj* **1** AZURE, sapphire, cobalt, ultramarine, navy, indigo, aquamarine, turquoise, cyan.
2 DEPRESSED, low, down in the dumps (*infml*), dejected, downcast, dispirited, down-hearted, despondent, gloomy, glum, dismal, sad, unhappy, miserable, melancholy, morose, fed up (*infml*). **3** *a blue joke*: obscene, offensive, indecent, improper, coarse, vulgar, lewd, dirty, pornographic, bawdy, smutty, near the bone, near the knuckle, risqué.
ᴇᴁ 2 cheerful, happy. **3** decent, clean.

blueprint *n* archetype, prototype, model, pattern, design, outline, draft, sketch, pilot, guide, plan, scheme, project.

bluff *v* lie, pretend, feign, sham, fake, deceive, delude, mislead, hoodwink, blind, bamboozle (*infml*), fool.
n lie, idle boast, bravado, humbug, pretence, show, sham, fake, fraud,

trick, subterfuge, deceit, deception.

blunder *n* mistake, error, solecism, howler (*infml*), bloomer (*infml*), clanger (*infml*), inaccuracy, slip, boob (*infml*), indiscretion, gaffe, faux pas, slip-up (*infml*), oversight, fault, cock-up (*sl*).
v stumble, flounder, bumble, err, slip up (*infml*), miscalculate, misjudge, bungle, botch, fluff (*infml*), mismanage, cock up (*sl*).

blunt *adj* **1** UNSHARPENED, dull, worn, pointless, rounded, stubbed.
2 FRANK, candid, direct, forthright, unceremonious, explicit, plain-spoken, honest, downright, outspoken, tactless, insensitive, rude, impolite, uncivil, brusque, curt, abrupt.
ᴇᴁ 1 sharp, pointed. **2** subtle, tactful.
v dull, take the edge off, dampen, soften, deaden, numb, anaesthetize, alleviate, allay, abate, weaken.
ᴇᴁ sharpen, intensify.

blur *v* smear, smudge, mist, fog, befog, cloud, becloud, blear, dim, darken, obscure, mask, conceal, soften.
n smear, smudge, blotch, haze, mist, fog, cloudiness, fuzziness, indistinctness, muddle, confusion, dimness, obscurity.

blurred *adj* out of focus, fuzzy, unclear, indistinct, vague, ill-defined, faint, hazy, misty, foggy, cloudy, bleary, dim, obscure, confused.
ᴇᴁ clear, distinct.

blurt out *v* exclaim, cry, gush, spout, utter, tell, reveal, disclose, divulge, blab (*infml*), let out, leak, let slip, spill the beans (*infml*).
ᴇᴁ bottle up, hush up.

blush *v* flush, redden, colour, glow.
ᴇᴁ blanch.
n flush, reddening, rosiness, ruddiness, colour, glow.

blushing *adj* flushed, red, rosy, glowing, confused, embarrassed, ashamed, modest.

◳ pale, white, composed.

bluster v boast, brag, crow, talk big (*infml*), swagger, strut, vaunt, show off, rant, roar, storm, bully, hector.
n boasting, crowing, bravado, bluff, swagger.

blustery adj windy, gusty, squally, stormy, tempestuous, violent, wild, boisterous.

◳ calm.

board n **1** *a wooden board*: sheet, panel, slab, plank, beam, timber, slat. **2** COMMITTEE, council, panel, jury, commission, directorate, directors, trustees, advisers. **3** MEALS, food, provisions, rations.
v get on, embark, mount, enter, catch.

boast v brag, crow, swank (*infml*), claim, exaggerate, talk big (*infml*), bluster, trumpet, vaunt, strut, swagger, show off, exhibit, possess.

◳ belittle, deprecate.

n brag, swank (*infml*), claim, vaunt, pride, joy, gem, treasure.

boastful adj proud, conceited, vain, swollen-headed, big-headed (*infml*), puffed up, bragging, crowing, swanky (*infml*), cocky, swaggering.

◳ modest, self-effacing, humble.

boats and ships

Types of boat or ship include: canoe, dinghy, lifeboat, rowing-boat, kayak, coracle, skiff, punt, sampan, dhow, gondola, pedalo, catamaran, trimaran, yacht; cabin-cruiser, motor-boat, motor-launch, speedboat, trawler, barge, narrow boat, houseboat, dredger, junk, smack, lugger; hovercraft, hydrofoil; clipper, cutter, ketch, packet, brig, schooner, square-rigger, galleon; ferry, paddle-steamer, tug, freighter, liner, container-ship, tanker; warship, battleship, destroyer, submarine, U-boat, frigate, aircraft-carrier, cruiser, dreadnought, corvette, minesweeper, man-of-war.

bob v bounce, hop, skip, spring, jump, leap, twitch, jerk, jolt, shake, quiver, wobble, oscillate, nod, bow, curtsy.

bob up appear, emerge, arrive, show up (*infml*), materialize, rise, surface, pop up, spring up, crop up, arise.

bodily adj physical, corporeal, carnal, fleshly, real, actual, tangible, substantial, concrete, material.

◳ spiritual.

adv altogether, en masse, collectively, as a whole, completely, fully, wholly, entirely, totally, in toto.

◳ piecemeal.

body n **1** ANATOMY, physique, build, figure, trunk, torso. **2** CORPSE, cadaver, carcase, stiff (*sl*). **3** COMPANY, association, society, corporation, confederation, bloc, cartel, syndicate, congress, collection, group, band, crowd, throng, multitude, mob, mass. **4** CONSISTENCY, density, solidity, firmness, bulk, mass, substance, essence, fullness, richness.

bodyguard n guard, protector, minder (*infml*).

bog n marsh, swamp, fen, mire, quagmire, quag, slough, morass, quicksands, marshland, swampland, wetlands.

bog down encumber, hinder, impede, overwhelm, deluge, sink, stick, slow down, slow up, delay, retard, halt, stall.

bogus adj false, fake, counterfeit, forged, fraudulent, phoney (*infml*), spurious, sham, pseudo, artificial, imitation, dummy.

◳ genuine, true, real, valid.

bohemian adj artistic, arty (*infml*), unconventional, unorthodox, nonconformist, alternative, eccentric, offbeat, way-out (*sl*), bizarre, exotic.

◳ bourgeois, conventional, orthodox.

n beatnik, hippie, drop-out, nonconformist.

◳ bourgeois, conformist.

boil¹ v **1** SIMMER, stew, seethe, brew,

gurgle, bubble, fizz, effervesce, froth, foam, steam. **2** *boil with anger*: erupt, explode, rage, rave, storm, fulminate, fume.

boil down reduce, concentrate, distil, condense, digest, abstract, summarize, abridge.

boil² *n* pustule, abscess, gumboil, ulcer, tumour, pimple, carbuncle, blister, inflammation.

boiling *adj* **1** *boiling water*: turbulent, gurgling, bubbling, steaming. **2** HOT, baking, roasting, scorching, blistering. **3** ANGRY, indignant, incensed, infuriated, enraged, furious, fuming, flaming.

boisterous *adj* exuberant, rumbustious (*infml*), rollicking, bouncy, turbulent, tumultuous, loud, noisy, clamorous, rowdy, rough, disorderly, riotous, wild, unrestrained, unruly, obstreperous.
F3 quiet, calm, restrained.

bold *adj* **1** FEARLESS, dauntless, daring, audacious, brave, courageous, valiant, heroic, gallant, intrepid, adventurous, venturesome, enterprising, plucky, spirited, confident, outgoing. **2** EYE-CATCHING, striking, conspicuous, prominent, strong, pronounced, bright, vivid, colourful, loud, flashy, showy, flamboyant. **3** BRAZEN, brash, forward, shameless, unabashed, cheeky (*infml*), impudent, insolent.
F3 **1** cautious, timid, shy. **2** faint, restrained.

bolt *n* bar, rod, shaft, pin, peg, rivet, fastener, latch, catch, lock.
v **1** FASTEN, secure, bar, latch, lock. **2** ABSCOND, escape, flee, fly, run, sprint, rush, dash, hurtle. **3** *bolt one's food*: gulp, wolf, gobble, gorge, devour, cram, stuff.

bomb *n* atom bomb, petrol bomb, shell, bombshell, explosive, charge, grenade, mine, torpedo, rocket, missile, projectile.

v bombard, shell, torpedo, attack, blow up, destroy.

bombard *v* attack, assault, assail, pelt, pound, strafe, blast, bomb, shell, blitz, besiege, hound, harass, pester.

bombardment *n* attack, assault, air-raid, bombing, shelling, blitz, barrage, cannonade, fusillade, salvo, fire, flak.

bombastic *adj* grandiloquent, magniloquent, grandiose, pompous, high-flown, inflated, bloated, windy, wordy, verbose.

bond *n* **1** CONNECTION, relation, link, tie, union, affiliation, attachment, affinity. **2** CONTRACT, covenant, agreement, pledge, promise, word, obligation. **3** FETTER, shackle, manacle, chain, cord, band, binding.
v connect, fasten, bind, unite, fuse, glue, gum, paste, stick, seal.

bondage *n* imprisonment, incarceration, captivity, confinement, restraint, slavery, enslavement, serfdom, servitude, subservience, subjection, subjugation, yoke.
F3 freedom, independence.

bone

Human bones include: clavicle, coccyx, collar-bone, femur, fibula, hip-bone, humerus, ilium, ischium, mandible, maxilla, metacarpal, metatarsal, patella, pelvic girdle, pelvis, pubis, radius, rib, scapula, shoulder-blade, skull, sternum, stirrup-bone, temporal, thigh-bone, tibia, ulna, vertebra.

bonus *n* advantage, benefit, plus (*infml*), extra, perk (*infml*), perquisite, commission, dividend, premium, prize, reward, honorarium, tip, gratuity, gift, handout.
F3 disadvantage, disincentive.

bony *adj* thin, lean, angular, lanky, gawky, gangling, skinny, scrawny,

emaciated, rawboned, gaunt, drawn.
Ea fat, plump.

book *n* volume, tome, publication, work, booklet, tract.

> *Types of book include*: hardback, paperback, bestseller; fiction, novel, story, thriller, romantic novel; children's book, primer, picture-book, annual; reference book, encyclopedia, dictionary, lexicon, thesaurus, concordance, anthology, compendium, omnibus, atlas, guidebook, gazetteer, directory, anthology, pocket companion, handbook, manual, cookbook, yearbook, almanac, catalogue; notebook, exercise book, textbook, scrapbook, album, sketchbook, diary, jotter, pad, ledger; libretto, manuscript, hymn-book, hymnal, prayer-book, psalter, missal, lectionary. *see also* **literature**.

v reserve, bag (*infml*), engage, charter, procure, order, arrange, organize, schedule, programme.
Ea cancel.

boom *v* 1 BANG, crash, roar, thunder, roll, rumble, resound, reverberate, blast, explode.
2 FLOURISH, thrive, prosper, succeed, develop, grow, increase, gain, expand, swell, escalate, intensify, strengthen, explode.
Ea 2 fail, collapse, slump.
n 1 BANG, clap, crash, roar, thunder, rumble, reverberation, blast, explosion, burst. 2 INCREASE, growth, expansion, gain, upsurge, jump, spurt, boost, upturn, improvement, advance, escalation, explosion.
Ea 2 failure, collapse, slump, recession, depression.

boon *n* blessing, advantage, benefit, godsend, windfall, favour, kindness, gift, present, grant, gratuity.
Ea disadvantage, blight.

boorish *adj* uncouth, oafish, loutish, ill-mannered, rude, coarse, crude, vulgar, unrefined, uncivilized, uneducated, ignorant.
Ea polite, refined, cultured.

boost *n* improvement, enhancement, expansion, increase, rise, jump, increment, addition, supplement, booster, lift, hoist, heave, push, thrust, help, advancement, promotion, praise, encouragement, fillip, ego-trip (*sl*).
Ea setback, blow.
v raise, elevate, improve, enhance, develop, enlarge, expand, amplify, increase, augment, heighten, lift, hoist, jack up, heave, push, thrust, help, aid, assist, advance, further, promote, advertise, plug (*infml*), praise, inspire, encourage, foster, support, sustain, bolster, supplement.
Ea hinder, undermine.

boot *n* gumboot, wellington, welly (*infml*), galosh, overshoe, walking-boot, riding-boot, top-boot.

booth *n* kiosk, stall, stand, hut, box, compartment, cubicle, carrel.

booty *n* loot, plunder, pillage, spoils, swag (*sl*), haul, gains, takings, pickings, winnings.

border *n* 1 BOUNDARY, frontier, bound, bounds, confine, confines, limit, demarcation, borderline, margin, fringe, periphery, surround, perimeter, circumference, edge, rim, brim, verge, brink. 2 TRIMMING, frill, valance, skirt, hem, frieze.
border on 1 ADJOIN, abut, touch, impinge, join, connect, communicate with. 2 RESEMBLE, approximate, approach, verge on.

bore¹ *v* drill, mine, pierce, perforate, penetrate, sink, burrow, tunnel, undermine, sap.

bore² *v* tire, weary, fatigue, jade, trouble, bother, worry, irritate, annoy, vex, irk.
Ea interest, excite.
n (*infml*) nuisance, bother, bind

(*infml*), drag (*infml*), pain (*infml*), headache (*infml*).

F3 pleasure, delight.

boredom *n* tedium, tediousness, monotony, dullness, apathy, listlessness, weariness, world-weariness.

F3 interest, excitement.

boring *adj* tedious, monotonous, routine, repetitious, uninteresting, unexciting, uneventful, dull, dreary, humdrum, commonplace, trite, unimaginative, uninspired, dry, stale, flat, insipid.

F3 interesting, exciting, stimulating, original.

borrow *v* steal, pilfer, filch, lift, plagiarize, crib, copy, imitate, mimic, echo, take, draw, derive, obtain, adopt, use, scrounge, cadge, sponge, appropriate, usurp.

F3 lend.

bosom *n* **1** BUST, breasts, chest, breast. **2** HEART, core, centre, midst, protection, shelter, sanctuary.

boss *n* employer, governor, master, owner, captain, head, chief, leader, supremo, administrator, executive, director, manager, foreman, gaffer, superintendent, overseer, supervisor.

boss around order around, order about, domineer, tyrannize, bully, bulldoze, browbeat, push around, dominate.

bossy *adj* authoritarian, autocratic, tyrannical, despotic, dictatorial, domineering, overbearing, oppressive, lordly, high-handed, imperious, insistent, assertive, demanding, exacting.

F3 unassertive.

bother *v* disturb, inconvenience, harass, hassle (*infml*), pester, plague, nag, annoy, irritate, irk, molest, trouble, worry, concern, alarm, dismay, distress, upset, vex.

n inconvenience, trouble, problem, difficulty, hassle (*infml*), fuss, bustle, flurry, nuisance, pest, annoyance,

irritation, aggravation (*infml*), vexation, worry, strain.

bottle *n* phial, flask, carafe, decanter, flagon, demijohn.

bottle up hide, conceal, restrain, curb, hold back, suppress, inhibit, restrict, enclose, contain.

F3 unbosom, unburden.

bottle-neck *n* hold-up, traffic jam, snarl-up, congestion, clogging, blockage, obstruction, block, obstacle.

bottom *n* **1** UNDERSIDE, underneath, sole, base, foot, plinth, pedestal, support, foundation, substructure, ground, floor, bed, depths, nadir. **2** RUMP, rear, behind, posterior (*infml*), buttocks, seat, backside (*infml*), bum (*sl*), butt (*US infml*), tail (*infml*).

F3 1 top.

bottomless *adj* deep, profound, fathomless, unfathomed, unplumbed, immeasurable, measureless, infinite, boundless, limitless, unlimited, inexhaustible.

F3 shallow, limited.

bounce *v* spring, jump, leap, bound, bob, ricochet, rebound, recoil.

n **1** SPRING, bound, springiness, elasticity, give, resilience, rebound, recoil. **2** EBULLIENCE, exuberance, vitality, vivacity, energy, vigour, go (*infml*), zip (*infml*), animation, liveliness.

bound[1] *adj* **1** FASTENED, secured, fixed, tied (up), chained, held, restricted, bandaged. **2** LIABLE, committed, duty-bound, obliged, required, forced, compelled, constrained, destined, fated, doomed, sure, certain.

bound[2] *v* jump, leap, vault, hurdle, spring, bounce, bob, hop, skip, frisk, gambol, frolic, caper, prance.

n jump, leap, vault, spring, bounce, bob, hop, skip, gambol, frolic, caper, dance, prance.

boundary *n* border, frontier,

barrier, line, borderline, demarcation, bounds, confines, limits, margin, fringe, verge, brink, edge, perimeter, extremity, termination.

boundless *adj* unbounded, limitless, unlimited, unconfined, countless, untold, incalculable, vast, immense, measureless, immeasurable, infinite, endless, unending, interminable, inexhaustible, unflagging, indefatigable.
F3 limited, restricted.

bounds *n* confines, limits, borders, marches, margins, fringes, periphery, circumference, edges, extremities.

bounty *n* **1** GENEROSITY, liberality, munificence, largesse, almsgiving, charity, philanthropy, beneficence, kindness. **2** REWARD, recompense, premium, bonus, gratuity, gift, present, donation, grant, allowance.

bouquet *n* **1** *bouquet of flowers*: bunch, posy, nosegay, spray, corsage, buttonhole, wreath, garland. **2** AROMA, smell, odour, scent, perfume, fragrance.

bourgeois *adj* middle-class, materialistic, conservative, traditional, conformist, conventional, hide-bound, unadventurous, dull, humdrum, banal, commonplace, trite, unoriginal, unimaginative.
F3 bohemian, unconventional, original.

bout *n* **1** FIGHT, battle, engagement, encounter, struggle, set-to, match, contest, competition, round, heat. **2** PERIOD, spell, time, stint, turn, go (*infml*), term, stretch, run, course, session, spree, attack, fit.

bow *v* **1** *bow one's head*: incline, bend, nod, bob, curtsy, genuflect (*fml*), kowtow, salaam, stoop. **2** YIELD, give in, consent, surrender, capitulate, submit, acquiesce, concede, accept, comply, defer. **3** SUBDUE, overpower, conquer, vanquish, crush, subjugate.

n inclination, bending, nod, bob, curtsy, genuflexion (*fml*), kowtow, salaam, obeisance (*fml*), salutation, acknowledgement.
bow out withdraw, pull out, desert, abandon, defect, back out, chicken out (*infml*), retire, resign, quit, stand down, step down, give up.

bowels *n* **1** INTESTINES, viscera, entrails, guts, insides, innards (*infml*). **2** DEPTHS, interior, inside, middle, centre, core, heart.

bowl[1] *n* receptacle, container, vessel, dish, basin, sink.

bowl[2] *v* throw, hurl, fling, pitch, roll, spin, whirl, rotate, revolve.
bowl over surprise, amaze, astound, astonish, stagger, stun, dumbfound, flabbergast (*infml*), floor (*infml*).

box[1] *n* container, receptacle, case, crate, carton, packet, pack, package, present, chest, coffer, trunk, coffin. *v* case, encase, package, pack, wrap.
box in enclose, surround, circumscribe, cordon off, hem in, corner, trap, confine, restrict, imprison, cage, coop up, contain.

box[2] *v* fight, spar, punch, hit, strike, slap, buffet, cuff, clout, sock (*sl*), wallop (*infml*), whack (*infml*).

boxer *n* pugilist, fighter, prizefighter, sparring partner, flyweight, featherweight, lightweight, welterweight, middleweight, heavyweight.

boxing *n* pugilism, prizefighting, fisticuffs, sparring.

boy *n* son, lad, youngster, kid (*infml*), nipper (*infml*), stripling, youth, fellow.

boycott *v* refuse, reject, embargo, black, ban, prohibit, disallow, bar, exclude, blacklist, outlaw, ostracize, cold-shoulder, ignore, spurn.
F3 encourage, support.

boyfriend *n* young man, man, fellow (*infml*), bloke (*infml*), admirer, date, sweetheart, lover, fiancé.

brace *n* pair, couple, twosome, duo,

v strengthen, reinforce, fortify, bolster, buttress, prop, shore (up), support, steady, tighten, fasten, tie, strap, bind, bandage.

bracing *adj* fresh, crisp, refreshing, reviving, strengthening, fortifying, tonic, rousing, stimulating, exhilarating, invigorating, enlivening, energizing, brisk, energetic, vigorous.
☒ weakening, debilitating.

braid *v* plait, interweave, interlace, intertwine, weave, lace, twine, entwine, ravel, twist, wind.
☒ undo, unravel.

brain *n* **1** CEREBRUM, grey matter, head, mind, intellect, nous, brains (*infml*), intelligence, wit, reason, sense, common sense, shrewdness, understanding. **2** MASTERMIND, intellectual, highbrow, egghead (*infml*), scholar, expert, boffin, genius, prodigy.
☒ **2** simpleton.

Parts of the brain include: brainstem, cerebellum, cerebral cortex (grey matter), cerebrum, corpus callosum, forebrain, frontal lobe, hindbrain, hypothalamus, medulla oblongata, mesencephalon, midbrain, occipital lobe, optic thalamus, parietal lobe, pineal body, pituitary gland, pons, spinal cord, temporal lobe, thalamus.

brainy (*infml*) *adj* intellectual, intelligent, clever, smart, bright, brilliant.
☒ dull.

brake *n* check, curb, rein, restraint, control, restriction, constraint, drag.
v slow, decelerate, retard, drag, slacken, moderate, check, halt, stop, pull up.
☒ accelerate.

branch *n* **1** BOUGH, limb, sprig, shoot, offshoot, arm, wing, prong. **2** *a different branch of the company*: department, office, part, section, division, subsection, subdivision.
branch out diversify, vary, develop, expand, enlarge, extend, broaden out, increase, multiply, proliferate, ramify.

brand *n* make, brand-name, tradename, trademark, logo, mark, symbol, sign, emblem, label, stamp, hallmark, grade, quality, class, kind, type, sort, line, variety, species.
v mark, stamp, label, type, stigmatize, burn, scar, stain, taint, disgrace, discredit, denounce, censure.

brandish *v* wave, flourish, shake, raise, swing, wield, flash, flaunt, exhibit, display, parade.

brash *adj* **1** BRAZEN, forward, impertinent, impudent, insolent, rude, cocky, assured, bold, audacious. **2** RECKLESS, rash, impetuous, impulsive, hasty, precipitate, foolhardy, incautious, indiscreet.
☒ **1** reserved. **2** cautious.

bravado *n* swagger, boasting, bragging, bluster, bombast, talk, boast, vaunting, showing off, parade, show, pretence.
☒ modesty, restraint.

brave *adj* courageous, plucky, unafraid, fearless, dauntless, undaunted, bold, audacious, daring, intrepid, stalwart, hardy, stoical, resolute, stout-hearted, valiant, gallant, heroic, indomitable.
☒ cowardly, afraid, timid.
v face, confront, defy, challenge, dare, stand up to, face up to, suffer, endure, bear, withstand.
☒ capitulate.

bravery *n* courage, pluck, guts (*infml*), fearlessness, dauntlessness, boldness, audacity, daring, intrepidity, stalwartness, hardiness, fortitude, resolution, stout-heartedness, valiance, valour, gallantry, heroism, indomitability, grit, mettle, spirit.
☒ cowardice, faint-heartedness, timidity.

brawl n fight, punch-up (infml),
scrap, scuffle, dust-up (infml), mêlée,
free-for-all, fray, affray, broil, fracas,
rumpus, disorder, row, argument,
quarrel, squabble, altercation,
dispute, clash.
  v fight, scrap, scuffle, wrestle, tussle,
row, argue, quarrel, squabble, wrangle,
dispute.

brawny adj muscular, sinewy,
athletic, well-built, burly, beefy,
hefty, solid, bulky, hulking, massive,
strapping, strong, powerful,
vigorous, sturdy, robust, hardy,
stalwart.
  ◪ slight, frail.

brazen adj blatant, flagrant, brash,
brassy, bold, forward, saucy, pert,
barefaced, impudent, insolent,
defiant, shameless, unashamed,
unabashed, immodest.
  ◪ shy, shamefaced, modest.

breach n 1 a breach of the rules:
violation, contravention,
infringement, trespass, disobedience,
offence, transgression, lapse,
disruption. 2 QUARREL,
disagreement, dissension, difference,
variance, schism, rift, rupture, split,
division, separation, parting,
estrangement, alienation,
disaffection, dissociation. 3 BREAK,
crack, rift, rupture, fissure, cleft,
crevice, opening, aperture, gap,
space, hole, chasm.

bread n loaf, roll, food, provisions,
diet, fare, nourishment, nutriment,
sustenance, subsistence, necessities.

breadth n width, broadness,
wideness, latitude, thickness, size,
magnitude, measure, scale, range,
reach, scope, compass, span, sweep,
extent, expanse, spread,
comprehensiveness, extensiveness,
vastness.

break v 1 FRACTURE, crack, snap,
split, sever, separate, divide, rend,
smash, disintegrate, splinter, shiver,
shatter, ruin, destroy, demolish.

2 break the law: violate, contravene,
infringe, breach, disobey, flout.
3 PAUSE, halt, stop, discontinue,
interrupt, suspend, rest. 4 SUBDUE,
tame, weaken, enfeeble, impair,
undermine, demoralize. 5 break the
news: tell, inform, impart, divulge,
disclose, reveal, announce. 6 break a
record: exceed, beat, better, excel,
surpass, outdo, outstrip.
  ◪ 1 mend. 2 keep, observe, abide by.
4 strengthen.
  n 1 FRACTURE, crack, split, rift,
rupture, schism, separation, tear,
gash, fissure, cleft, crevice, opening,
gap, hole, breach. 2 INTERVAL,
intermission, interlude, interruption,
pause, halt, lull, let-up (infml), respite,
rest, breather (infml), time out,
holiday. 3 OPPORTUNITY, chance,
advantage, fortune, luck.

break away separate, split, part
company, detach, secede, leave,
depart, quit, run away, escape, flee, fly.

break down 1 the van broke down: fail,
stop, pack up (infml), conk out (sl), seize
up, give way, collapse, crack up (infml).
2 ANALYSE, dissect, separate, itemize,
detail.

break in 1 INTERRUPT, butt in,
interpose, interject, intervene, intrude,
encroach, impinge. 2 BURGLE, rob,
raid, invade.

break off 1 DETACH, snap off, sever,
separate, part, divide, disconnect.
2 PAUSE, interrupt, suspend,
discontinue, halt, stop, cease, end,
finish, terminate.

break out 1 START, begin, commence,
arise, emerge, happen, occur, erupt,
flare up, burst out. 2 ESCAPE, abscond,
bolt, flee.

break up 1 DISMANTLE, take apart,
demolish, destroy, disintegrate,
splinter, sever, divide, split, part,
separate, divorce. 2 DISBAND,
disperse, dissolve, adjourn, suspend,
stop, finish, terminate.

breakable adj brittle, fragile,

delicate, flimsy, insubstantial, frail.
Ea unbreakable, durable, sturdy.

breakdown *n* **1** FAILURE, collapse, disintegration, malfunction, interruption, stoppage. **2** ANALYSIS, dissection, itemization, classification, categorization.

break-in *n* burglary, house-breaking, robbery, raid, invasion, intrusion, trespass.

breakthrough *n* discovery, find, finding, invention, innovation, advance, progress, headway, step, leap, development, improvement.

break-up *n* divorce, separation, parting, split, rift, finish, termination, dissolution, dispersal, disintegration, crumbling.

breakwater *n* groyne, mole, jetty, pier, quay, wharf, dock.

breath *n* **1** AIR, breathing, respiration, inhalation, exhalation, sigh, gasp, pant, gulp. **2** BREEZE, puff, waft, gust. **3** AROMA, smell, odour, whiff. **4** HINT, suggestion, suspicion, undertone, whisper, murmur.

breathe *v* **1** RESPIRE, inhale, exhale, expire, sigh, gasp, pant, puff. **2** SAY, utter, express, voice, articulate, murmur, whisper, impart, tell. **3** INSTIL, imbue, infuse, inject, inspire.

breathless *adj* **1** SHORT-WINDED, out of breath, panting, puffing, puffed (out), exhausted, winded, gasping, wheezing, choking. **2** *breathless anticipation*: expectant, impatient, eager, agog, excited, feverish, anxious.

breathtaking *adj* awe-inspiring, impressive, magnificent, overwhelming, amazing, astonishing, stunning, exciting, thrilling, stirring, moving.

breed *v* **1** REPRODUCE, procreate, multiply, propagate, hatch, bear, bring forth, rear, raise, bring up, educate, train, instruct. **2** PRODUCE,

create, originate, arouse, cause, occasion, engender, generate, make, foster, nurture, nourish, cultivate, develop.
n species, strain, variety, family, ilk, sort, kind, type, stamp, stock, race, progeny, line, lineage, pedigree.

breeding *n* **1** REPRODUCTION, procreation, nurture, development, rearing, raising, upbringing, education, training, background, ancestry, lineage, stock. **2** MANNERS, politeness, civility, gentility, urbanity, refinement, culture, polish.
Ea 2 vulgarity.

breeze *n* wind, gust, flurry, waft, puff, breath, draught, air.

breezy *adj* **1** WINDY, blowing, fresh, airy, gusty, blustery, squally. **2** ANIMATED, lively, vivacious, jaunty, buoyant, blithe, debonair, carefree, cheerful, easy-going (*infml*), casual, informal, light, bright, exhilarating.
Ea 1 still. **2** staid, serious.

brevity *n* briefness, shortness, terseness, conciseness, succinctness, pithiness, crispness, incisiveness, abruptness, curtness, impermanence, ephemerality, transience, transitoriness.
Ea verbosity, permanence, longevity.

brew *v* **1** INFUSE, stew, boil, seethe, ferment, prepare, soak, steep, mix, cook. **2** PLOT, scheme, plan, project, devise, contrive, concoct, hatch, excite, foment, build up, gather, develop.
n infusion, drink, beverage, liquor, potion, broth, gruel, stew, mixture, blend, concoction, preparation, fermentation, distillation.

bribe *n* incentive, inducement, allurement, enticement, back-hander (*infml*), kickback, payola, refresher (*infml*), sweetener (*infml*), hush money (*infml*), protection money.
v corrupt, suborn, buy off, reward.

bribery *n* corruption, graft (*sl*),

palm-greasing, inducement, lubrication.

bric-à-brac n knick-knacks, ornaments, curios, antiques, trinkets, baubles.

bridal adj wedding, nuptial, marriage, matrimonial, marital, conjugal.

bridge n arch, span, causeway, link, connection, bond, tie.

> *Types of bridge include*: suspension bridge, arch bridge, cantilever bridge, flying bridge, flyover, overpass, footbridge, railway bridge, viaduct, aqueduct, humpback bridge, toll bridge, pontoon bridge, Bailey bridge, rope bridge, drawbridge, swing bridge.

v span, cross, traverse, fill, link, connect, couple, join, unite, bind.

bridle v check, curb, restrain, control, govern, master, subdue, moderate, repress, contain.

brief adj **1** SHORT, terse, succinct, concise, pithy, crisp, compressed, thumbnail, laconic, abrupt, sharp, brusque, blunt, curt, surly. **2** SHORT-LIVED, momentary, ephemeral, transient, fleeting, passing, transitory, temporary, limited, cursory, hasty, quick, swift, fast.
E3 1 long. **2** lengthy.
n **1** ORDERS, instructions, directions, remit, mandate, directive, advice, briefing, data, information.
2 OUTLINE, summary, précis, dossier, case, defence, argument.
v instruct, direct, explain, guide, advise, prepare, prime, inform, fill in (*infml*), gen up (*sl*).

briefing n meeting, conference, preparation, priming, filling-in (*infml*), gen (*sl*), low-down (*sl*), information, advice, guidance, directions, instructions, orders.

bright adj **1** LUMINOUS, illuminated, radiant, shining, beaming, flashing, gleaming, glistening, glittering, sparkling, twinkling, shimmering, glowing, brilliant, resplendent, glorious, splendid, dazzling, glaring, blazing, intense, vivid. **2** HAPPY, cheerful, glad, joyful, merry, jolly, lively, vivacious. **3** *the future looks bright*: promising, propitious, auspicious, favourable, rosy, optimistic, hopeful, encouraging. **4** CLEVER, brainy (*infml*), smart, intelligent, quick-witted, quick, sharp, acute, keen, astute, perceptive. **5** CLEAR, transparent, translucent, lucid. **6** *a bright day*: fine, sunny, cloudless, unclouded.
E3 1 dull. **2** sad. **3** depressing. **4** stupid. **5** muddy. **6** dark.

brighten v **1** LIGHT UP, illuminate, lighten, clear up. **2** POLISH, burnish, rub up, shine, gleam, glow. **3** CHEER UP, gladden, hearten, encourage, enliven, perk up.
E3 1 darken. **2** dull, tarnish.

brilliance n **1** TALENT, virtuosity, genius, greatness, distinction, excellence, aptitude, cleverness. **2** RADIANCE, brightness, sparkle, dazzle, intensity, vividness, gloss, lustre, sheen, glamour, glory, magnificence, splendour.

brilliant adj **1** *a brilliant pianist*: gifted, talented, accomplished, expert, skilful, masterly, exceptional, outstanding, superb, illustrious, famous, celebrated. **2** SPARKLING, glittering, scintillating, dazzling, glaring, blazing, intense, vivid, bright, shining, glossy, showy, glorious, magnificent, splendid. **3** CLEVER, brainy (*infml*), intelligent, quick, astute.
E3 1 undistinguished. **2** dull. **3** stupid.

brim n rim, perimeter, circumference, lip, edge, margin, border, brink, verge, top, limit.

bring v **1** CARRY, bear, convey, transport, fetch, take, deliver, escort, accompany, usher, guide, conduct, lead. **2** CAUSE, produce, engender, create, prompt, provoke, force, attract, draw.

bring about cause, occasion, create, produce, generate, effect, accomplish, achieve, fulfil, realize, manage, engineer, manoeuvre, manipulate.

bring in earn, net, gross, produce, yield, fetch, return, accrue, realize.

bring off achieve, accomplish, fulfil, execute, discharge, perform, succeed, win.

bring on cause, occasion, induce, lead to, give rise to, generate, inspire, prompt, provoke, precipitate, expedite, accelerate, advance.

F3 inhibit.

bring out 1 EMPHASIZE, stress, highlight, enhance, draw out.
2 PUBLISH, print, issue, launch, introduce.

bring up 1 REAR, raise, foster, nurture, educate, teach, train, form. **2** *bring up a subject*: introduce, broach, mention, submit, propose. **3** VOMIT, regurgitate, throw up (*infml*).

brink *n* verge, threshold, edge, margin, fringe, border, boundary, limit, extremity, lip, rim, brim, bank.

brisk *adj* **1** ENERGETIC, vigorous, quick, snappy, lively, spirited, active, busy, bustling, agile, nimble, alert.
2 INVIGORATING, exhilarating, stimulating, bracing, refreshing, fresh, crisp.

F3 **1** lazy, sluggish.

bristle *n* hair, whisker, stubble, spine, prickle, barb, thorn.

bristly *adj* hairy, whiskered, bearded, unshaven, stubbly, rough, spiny, prickly, spiky, thorny.

F3 clean-shaven, smooth.

brittle *adj* breakable, fragile, delicate, frail, crisp, crumbly, crumbling, friable, shattery, shivery.

F3 durable, resilient.

broad *adj* **1** WIDE, large, vast, roomy, spacious, capacious, ample, extensive, widespread. **2** WIDE-RANGING, far-reaching, encyclopedic, catholic, eclectic, all-embracing, inclusive, comprehensive, general, sweeping, universal, unlimited.

F3 **1** narrow. **2** restricted.

broadcast *v* air, show, transmit, beam, relay, televise, report, announce, publicize, advertise, publish, circulate, promulgate, disseminate, spread.

n transmission, programme, show.

broaden *v* widen, thicken, swell, spread, enlarge, expand, extend, stretch, increase, augment, develop, open up, branch out, diversify.

broadminded *adj* liberal, tolerant, permissive, enlightened, free-thinking, open-minded, receptive, unbiased, unprejudiced.

F3 narrow-minded, intolerant, biased.

brochure *n* leaflet, booklet, pamphlet, prospectus, broadsheet, handbill, circular, handout, folder.

broke (*infml*) *adj* insolvent, penniless, bankrupt, bust, ruined, impoverished, destitute.

F3 solvent, rich, affluent.

broken *adj* **1** FRACTURED, burst, ruptured, severed, separated, faulty, defective, out of order, shattered, destroyed, demolished.
2 DISJOINTED, disconnected, fragmentary, discontinuous, interrupted, intermittent, spasmodic, erratic, hesitating, stammering, halting, imperfect. **3** *a broken man*: beaten, defeated, crushed, demoralized, down, weak, feeble, exhausted, tamed, subdued, oppressed.

F3 **1** mended. **2** fluent.

broken-down *adj* dilapidated, worn-out, ruined, collapsed, decayed, inoperative, out of order.

broken-hearted *adj* heartbroken, inconsolable, devastated, grief-stricken, desolate, despairing, miserable, wretched, mournful, sorrowful, sad, unhappy, dejected, despondent, crestfallen, disappointed.

brooch *n* badge, pin, clip, clasp.

brood *v* ponder, ruminate, meditate, muse, mull over, go over, rehearse, dwell on, agonize, fret, mope.
n clutch, chicks, hatch, litter, young, offspring, issue, progeny, children, family.

brook *n* stream, rivulet, beck, burn, watercourse, channel.

brother *n* sibling, relation, relative, comrade, friend, mate, partner, colleague, associate, fellow, companion, monk, friar.

brotherhood *n* fraternity, association, society, league, confederation, confederacy, alliance, union, guild, fellowship, community, clique.

browbeat *v* bully, coerce, dragoon, bulldoze, awe, cow, intimidate, threaten, tyrannize, domineer, overbear, oppress, hound.
E3 coax.

brown *adj* mahogany, chocolate, coffee, hazel, bay, chestnut, umber, sepia, tan, tawny, russet, rust, rusty, brunette, dark, dusky, sunburnt, tanned, bronzed, browned, toasted.

browse *v* 1 LEAF THROUGH, flick through, dip into, skim, survey, scan, peruse. 2 GRAZE, pasture, feed, eat, nibble.

bruise *v* discolour, blacken, mark, blemish, pound, pulverize, crush, hurt, injure, insult, offend, grieve.
n contusion, discoloration, black eye, shiner (*sl*), mark, blemish, injury.

brush[1] *n* broom, sweeper, besom.
v 1 CLEAN, sweep, flick, burnish, polish, shine. 2 TOUCH, contact, graze, kiss, stroke, rub, scrape.
brush aside dismiss, pooh-pooh, belittle, disregard, ignore, flout, override.
brush off disregard, ignore, slight, snub, cold-shoulder, rebuff, dismiss, spurn, reject, repulse, disown,

repudiate.
brush up 1 REVISE, relearn, improve, polish up, study, read up, swot (*infml*). 2 REFRESH, freshen up, clean, tidy.

brush[2] *n* scrub, thicket, bushes, shrubs, brushwood, undergrowth, ground cover.

brush[3] *n* confrontation, encounter, clash, conflict, fight, scrap, skirmish, set-to, tussle, dust-up (*infml*), fracas.

brusque *adj* abrupt, sharp, short, terse, curt, gruff, surly, discourteous, impolite, uncivil, blunt, tactless, undiplomatic.
E3 courteous, polite, tactful.

brutal *adj* animal, bestial, beastly, brutish, inhuman, savage, bloodthirsty, vicious, ferocious, cruel, inhumane, remorseless, pitiless, merciless, ruthless, callous, insensitive, unfeeling, heartless, harsh, gruff, rough, coarse, crude, rude, uncivilized, barbarous.
E3 kindly, humane, civilized.

brutality *n* savagery, bloodthirstiness, viciousness, ferocity, cruelty, inhumanity, violence, atrocity, ruthlessness, callousness, roughness, coarseness, barbarism, barbarity.
E3 gentleness, kindness.

brute *n* animal, beast, swine, creature, monster, ogre, devil, fiend, savage, sadist, bully, lout.

bubble *n* blister, vesicle, globule, ball, drop, droplet, bead.
v effervesce, fizz, sparkle, froth, foam, seethe, boil, burble, gurgle.

bubbly *adj* 1 EFFERVESCENT, fizzy, sparkling, carbonated, frothy, foaming, sudsy. 2 LIVELY, bouncy, happy, merry, elated, excited.
E3 1 flat, still. 2 lethargic.

bucket *n* pail, can, bail, scuttle, vessel.

buckle *n* clasp, clip, catch, fastener.
v 1 *buckle one's belt*: fasten, clasp, catch, hook, hitch, connect, close, secure. 2 BEND, warp, twist, distort,

bulge, cave in, fold, wrinkle, crumple, collapse.

bud *n* shoot, sprout, germ, embryo.
v shoot, sprout, burgeon, develop, grow.
 ☒ wither, waste away.

budding *adj* potential, promising, embryonic, burgeoning, developing, growing, flowering.

budge *v* move, stir, shift, remove, dislodge, push, roll, slide, propel, sway, influence, persuade, convince, change, bend, yield, give (way).

budget *n* finances, funds, resources, means, allowance, allotment, allocation, estimate.
v plan, estimate, alow, allot, allocate, apportion, ration.

buff[1] *adj* yellowish-brown, straw, sandy, fawn, khaki.
v polish, burnish, shine, smooth, rub, brush.

buff[2] (*infml*) *n* expert, connoisseur, enthusiast, fan, admirer, devotee, addict, fiend, freak.

buffer *n* shock-absorber, bumper, fender, pad, cushion, pillow, intermediary, screen, shield.

buffet[1] *n* snack-bar, counter, café, cafeteria.

buffet[2] *v* batter, hit, strike, knock, bang, bump, push, shove, pound, pummel, beat, thump, box, cuff, clout, slap.
n blow, knock, bang, bump, jar, jolt, push, shove, thump, box, cuff, clout, slap, smack.

bug *n* **1** VIRUS, bacterium, germ, microbe, micro-organism, infection, disease. **2** FAULT, defect, flaw, blemish, imperfection, failing, error, gremlin (*infml*).
v (*infml*) annoy, irritate, vex, irk, needle (*infml*), bother, disturb, harass, badger.

build *v* **1** ERECT, raise, construct, fabricate, make, form, constitute, assemble, knock together, develop, enlarge, extend, increase, augment,

escalate, intensify. **2** BASE, found, establish, institute, inaugurate, initiate, begin.
 ☒ **1** destroy, demolish, knock down, lessen.
n physique, figure, body, form, shape, size, frame, structure.

build up strengthen, reinforce, fortify, extend, expand, develop, amplify, increase, escalate, intensify, heighten, boost, improve, enhance, publicize, advertise, promote, plug (*infml*), hype (*sl*).
 ☒ weaken, lessen.

building *n* edifice, dwelling, erection, construction, fabrication, structure, architecture.

Types of building include: house, bungalow, cottage, block of flats, cabin, farmhouse, villa, mansion, chateau, castle, palace; church, chapel, cathedral, abbey, monastery, temple, pagoda, mosque, synagogue; shop, store, garage, factory, warehouse, silo, office block, tower block, skyscraper, theatre, cinema, gymnasium, sports hall, restaurant, café, hotel, pub (*infml*), public house, inn, school, college, museum, library, hospital, prison, power station, observatory; barracks, fort, fortress, monument, mausoleum; shed, barn, outhouse, stable, mill, lighthouse, pier, pavilion, boat-house, beach-hut, summerhouse, gazebo, dovecote, windmill. *see also* **house**; **shop**.

build-up *n* **1** ENLARGEMENT, expansion, development, increase, gain, growth, escalation, publicity, promotion, plug (*infml*), hype (*sl*). **2** ACCUMULATION, mass, load, heap, stack, store, stockpile.
 ☒ **1** reduction, decrease.

bulbs and corms

Plants grown from bulbs and corms include: acidanthera, allium,

bulge

amaryllis, anemone, bluebell
(endymion), chincherinchee,
chionodoxa, crocosmia, crocus,
autumn crocus (colchicum),
cyclamen, daffodil, crown imperial
(fritillaria), galtonia, garlic, gladiolus,
grape hyacinth (muscari), hyacinth,
iris, ixia, jonquil, lily, montbretia,
narcissus, nerine, ranunculus, scilla,
snowdrop (galanthus), sparaxis, tulip,
winter aconite.

bulge n **1** SWELLING, bump, lump,
hump, distension, protuberance,
projection. **2** RISE, increase, surge,
upsurge, intensification.
v swell, puff out, bulb, hump, dilate,
expand, enlarge, distend, protrude,
project.

bulk n size, magnitude, dimensions,
extent, amplitude, bigness, largeness,
immensity, volume, mass, weight,
substance, body, preponderance,
majority, most.

bulky adj substantial, big, large,
huge, enormous, immense,
mammoth, massive, colossal,
hulking, hefty, heavy, weighty,
unmanageable, unwieldy, awkward,
cumbersome.
F3 insubstantial, small, handy.

bullet n shot, pellet, ball, slug
(infml), missile, projectile.

bulletin n report, newsflash,
dispatch, communiqué, statement,
announcement, notification,
communication, message.

bully n persecutor, tormentor,
browbeater, intimidator, bully-boy,
heavy (sl), ruffian, tough.
v persecute, torment, terrorize,
bulldoze, coerce, browbeat, bullyrag,
intimidate, cow, tyrannize, domineer,
overbear, oppress, push around.

bump v **1** HIT, strike, knock, bang,
crash, collide (with). **2** JOLT, jerk,
jar, jostle, rattle, shake, bounce.
n **1** BLOW, hit, knock, bang, thump,
thud, smash, crash, collision, impact,

jolt, jar, shock. **2** LUMP, swelling,
bulge, hump, protuberance.

bump into meet, encounter, run into,
chance upon, come across.

bump off (infml) kill, murder,
assassinate, eliminate (sl), liquidate
(sl), do in (sl), top (sl).

bumper adj plentiful, abundant,
large, great, enormous, massive,
excellent, exceptional.
F3 small.

bumptious adj self-important,
pompous, officious, overbearing,
pushy, assertive, over-confident,
presumptuous, forward, impudent,
arrogant, cocky, conceited,
swaggering, boastful, full of oneself,
egotistic.
F3 humble, modest.

bumpy adj jerky, jolting, bouncy,
choppy, rough, lumpy, knobbly,
knobby, uneven, irregular.
F3 smooth, even.

bunch n **1** BUNDLE, sheaf, tuft,
clump, cluster, batch, lot, heap, pile,
stack, mass, number, quantity,
collection, assortment. **2** bunch of
flowers: bouquet, posy, spray. **3**
GANG, band, troop, crew, team,
party, gathering, flock, swarm,
crowd, mob, multitude.
v group, bundle, cluster, collect,
assemble, congregate, gather, flock,
herd, crowd, mass, pack, huddle.
F3 disperse, scatter, spread out.

bundle n bunch, sheaf, roll, bale,
truss, parcel, package, packet,
carton, box, bag, pack, batch,
consignment, group, set, collection,
assortment, quantity, mass,
accumulation, pile, stack, heap.
v pack, wrap, bale, truss, bind, tie,
fasten.

bungle v mismanage, cock up (sl),
screw up (sl), foul up (infml), mess
up (infml), ruin, spoil, mar, botch,
fudge, blunder.

buoy n float, marker, signal, beacon.
buoy up support, sustain, raise, lift,

boost, encourage, cheer, hearten.
🔁 depress, discourage.

buoyant *adj* **1** *in buoyant mood*:
light-hearted, carefree, bright,
cheerful, happy, joyful, lively,
animated, bouncy. **2** FLOATABLE,
floating, afloat, light, weightless.
🔁 **1** depressed, despairing. **2** heavy.

burden *n* cargo, load, weight, dead-
weight, encumbrance, millstone,
onus, responsibility, obligation, duty,
strain, stress, worry, anxiety, care,
trouble, trial, affliction, sorrow.
v load, weigh down, encumber,
handicap, bother, worry, tax, strain,
overload, lie heavy on, oppress,
overwhelm.
🔁 unburden, relieve.

bureau *n* service, agency, office,
branch, department, division,
counter, desk.

bureaucracy *n* administration,
government, ministry, civil service,
the authorities, the system,
officialdom, red tape, regulations.

burglar *n* housebreaker, robber,
thief, pilferer, trespasser.

burglary *n* housebreaking, break-in,
robbery, theft, stealing, trespass.

burial *n* burying, interment,
entombment, funeral, obsequies.

burly *adj* big, well-built, hulking,
hefty, heavy, stocky, sturdy, brawny,
beefy, muscular, athletic, strapping,
strong, powerful.
🔁 small, puny, thin, slim.

burn *v* **1** FLAME, blaze, flare, flash,
glow, flicker, smoulder, smoke, fume,
simmer, seethe. **2** IGNITE, light,
kindle, incinerate, cremate, consume,
corrode. **3** SCALD, scorch, parch,
shrivel, singe, char, toast, brand,
sear, smart, sting, bite, hurt, tingle.

burning *adj* **1** ABLAZE, aflame,
afire, fiery, flaming, blazing,
flashing, gleaming, glowing,
smouldering, alight, lit, illuminated.
2 HOT, scalding, scorching, searing,
piercing, acute, smarting, stinging,

prickling, tingling, biting, caustic,
pungent. **3** *burning desire*: ardent,
fervent, eager, earnest, intense,
vehement, passionate, impassioned,
frantic, frenzied, consuming.
4 *burning issue*: urgent, pressing,
important, significant, crucial,
essential, vital.
🔁 **2** cold. **3** apathetic. **4** unimportant.

burrow *n* warren, hole, earth, set,
den, lair, retreat, shelter, tunnel.
v tunnel, dig, delve, excavate, mine,
undermine.

burst *v* puncture, rupture, tear, split,
crack, break, fragment, shatter,
shiver, disintegrate, explode, blow
up, erupt, gush, spout, rush, run.
n **1** PUNCTURE, blow-out (*infml*),
rupture, split, crack, break, breach,
explosion, blast, bang, eruption. **2**
DISCHARGE, gush, spurt, surge, rush,
spate, torrent, outpouring, outburst,
outbreak, fit.

bury *v* **1** *bury the dead*: inter,
entomb, lay to rest, shroud. **2** SINK,
submerge, immerse, plant, implant,
embed, conceal, hide, cover,
enshroud, engulf, enclose, engross,
occupy, engage, absorb.
🔁 **1** disinter, exhume. **2** uncover.

bush *n* **1** SHRUB, hedge, thicket. **2**
SCRUB, brush, scrubland,
backwoods, wilds.

business *n* **1** TRADE, commerce,
industry, manufacturing, dealings,
transactions, bargaining, trading,
buying, selling. **2** COMPANY, firm,
corporation, establishment,
organization, concern, enterprise,
venture. **3** JOB, occupation, work,
employment, trade, profession, line,
calling, career, vocation, duty, task,
responsibility. **4** AFFAIR, matter,
issue, subject, topic, question,
problem, point.

businesslike *adj* professional,
efficient, thorough, systematic,
methodical, organized, orderly, well-
ordered, practical, matter-of-fact,

precise, correct, formal, impersonal.
F3 inefficient, disorganized.

businesswoman *n*
entrepreneur, industrialist, trader,
merchant, tycoon, magnate,
capitalist, financier, employer,
executive.

bust *n* **1** SCULPTURE, head, torso,
statue. **2** BOSOM, beasts, chest, breast.

bustle *v* dash, rush, scamper, scurry,
hurry, hasten, scramble, fuss.
n activity, stir, commotion, tumult,
agitation, excitement, fuss, ado, flurry,
hurry, haste.

busy *adj* occupied, engaged, tied up
(*infml*), employed, working, slaving,
stirring, restless, tireless, diligent,
industrious, active, lively, energetic,
strenuous, tiring, full, crowded,
swarming, teeming, bustling, hectic,
eventful.
F3 idle, lazy, quiet.
v occupy, engage, employ, engross,
absorb, immerse, interest, concern,
bother.

busybody *n* meddler, nosey parker
(*infml*), intruder, pry, gossip,
eavesdropper, snoop, snooper,
troublemaker.

butt¹ *n* stub, end, tip, tail, base, foot,
shaft, stock, handle, haft.

butt² *n* target, mark, object, subject,
victim, laughing-stock, dupe.

butt³ *v, n* hit, bump, knock, buffet,
push, shove, ram, thrust, punch, jab,
prod, poke.

butt in interrupt, cut in, interpose,
intrude, meddle, interfere.

butterflies and moths

Types of butterfly include: red
admiral, white admiral, apollo,
cabbage white, chalkhill blue,
common blue, brimstone, meadow
brown, Camberwell beauty, clouded
yellow, comma, large copper, small
copper, fritillary, Duke of Burgundy
fritillary, heath fritillary, gatekeeper,
grayling, hairstreak, purple

hairstreak, white letter hairstreak,
hermit, monarch, orange-tip, painted
lady, peacock, purple emperor,
ringlet, grizzled skipper, swallowtail,
tortoiseshell.
Types of moth include: brown-tail,
buff-tip, burnet, six-spot, carpet,
cinnabar, clothes, emperor, garden
tiger, gypsy, death's head hawkmoth,
privet hawkmoth, Kentish glory,
lackey, lappet, leopard, lobster,
magpie, oak hook-tip, pale tussock,
peach blossom, peppered, puss, red
underwing, silkworm, silver-Y,
swallowtail, turnip, wax, winter.

buttocks *n* rump, hindquarters, rear,
posterior (*infml*), seat, bottom,
behind, backside (*infml*), arse (*sl*).

buttonhole *v* accost, waylay, catch,
grab, nab, detain, importune.

buttress *n* support, prop, shore,
stay, brace, pier, strut, stanchion,
mainstay, reinforcement.
v support, prop up, shore up, hold
up, brace, strengthen, reinforce,
bolster up, sustain.
F3 undermine, weaken.

buy *v* purchase, invest in (*infml*), pay
for, procure, acquire, obtain, get.
F3 sell.
n purchase, acquisition, bargain, deal.

buyer *n* purchaser, shopper,
consumer, customer, vendee, emptor.
F3 seller, vendor.

by *prep* near, next to, beside, along,
over, through, via, past.
adv near, close, handy, at hand, past,
beyond, away, aside.

bypass *v* avoid, dodge, sidestep,
skirt, circumvent, ignore, neglect,
omit.
n ring road, detour, diversion.

by-product *n* consequence, result,
side-effect, fallout (*infml*),
repercussion, after-effect.

bystander *n* spectator, onlooker,
looker-on, watcher, observer,
witness, eye-witness, passer-by.

C

cabin *n* **1** BERTH, quarters, compartment, room. **2** HUT, shack, shanty, lodge, chalet, cottage, shed, shelter.

cabinet *n* cupboard, closet, dresser, case, locker.

cable *n* line, rope, cord, chain, wire, flex, lead.

cadge *v* scrounge, sponge, beg, hitch.

café *n* coffee shop, tea shop, tea room, coffee bar, cafeteria, snackbar, bistro, brasserie, restaurant.

cage *v* encage, coop up, shut up, confine, restrain, fence in, imprison, impound, incarcerate, lock up.
◪ release, let out, free.
n aviary, coop, hutch, enclosure, pen, pound, corral.

cajole *v* coax, persuade, wheedle, flatter, sweet-talk (*infml*), butter up (*infml*), tempt, lure, seduce, entice, beguile, mislead, dupe.
◪ bully, force, compel.

cake *v* coat, cover, encrust, dry, harden, solidify, consolidate, coagulate, congeal, thicken.
n **1** *tea and cakes*: gâteau, fancy, madeleine, bun, pie, flan. **2** LUMP, mass, bar, slab, block, loaf.

calamitous *adj* disastrous, catastrophic, ruinous, devastating, deadly, fatal, dire, ghastly, dreadful, tragic, woeful, grievous.
◪ good, fortunate, happy.

calamity disaster, catastrophe, mishap, misadventure, mischance, misfortune, adversity, reverse, trial, tribulation, affliction, distress, tragedy, ruin, downfall.
◪ blessing, godsend.

calculate *v* compute, work out, count, enumerate, reckon, figure, determine, weigh, rate, value, estimate, gauge, judge, consider, plan, intend, aim.

calculating *adj* crafty, cunning, sly, devious, scheming, designing, contriving, sharp, shrewd.
◪ artless, naïve.

calculation *n* sum, computation, answer, result, reckoning, figuring, estimate, forecast, judgement, planning, deliberation.

calibre *n* **1** DIAMETER, bore, gauge, size, measure. **2** *candidates of the right calibre*: talent, gifts, strength, worth, merit, quality, character, ability, capacity, faculty, stature, distinction.

call *v* **1** NAME, christen, baptize, title, entitle, dub, style, term, label, designate. **2** SHOUT, yell, exclaim, cry. **3** SUMMON, invite, bid, convene, assemble. **4** TELEPHONE, phone, ring (up), contact.
n **1** CRY, exclamation, shout, yell, scream. **2** VISIT, ring, summons, invitation. **3** *there's no call for it*: demand, need, occasion, cause, excuse, justification, reason, grounds, right. **4** APPEAL, request, plea, order, command, claim, announcement, signal.

call for 1 DEMAND, require, need, necessitate, involve, entail, occasion, suggest. **2** FETCH, collect, pick up.

call off cancel, drop, abandon, discontinue, break off, withdraw.

calling *n* mission, vocation, career, profession, occupation, job, trade, business, line, work, employment, field, province, pursuit.

callous *adj* heartless, hard-hearted,

cold, indifferent, uncaring, unsympathetic, unmoved, unfeeling, insensitive, hardened, thick-skinned.
⊞ kind, caring, sympathetic, sensitive.

calm *adj* **1** COMPOSED, self-possessed, collected, cool, dispassionate, unemotional, impassive, unmoved, placid, sedate, imperturbable, unflappable, unexcitable, laid back (*sl*), relaxed, unexcited, unruffled, unflustered, unperturbed, undisturbed, untroubled, unapprehensive. **2** *calm waters*: smooth, still, windless, unclouded, mild, tranquil, serene, peaceful, quiet, uneventful, restful.
⊞ **1** excitable, worried, anxious. **2** rough, wild, stormy.
v compose, soothe, relax, sedate, tranquillize, hush, quieten, placate, pacify.
⊞ excite, worry.
n calmness, stillness, tranquillity, serenity, peacefulness, peace, quiet, hush, repose.
⊞ storminess, restlessness.

camera

Types of camera include:
automatic, bellows, binocular, box Brownie®, camcorder, camera obscura, cine, cinematographic, compact, daguerreotype, disc, disposable, film, Instamatic®, large-format, miniature, subminiature, panoramic, plate, dry-plate, half-plate, quarter-plate, wet-plate, point-and-press, Polaroid®, press, reflex, folding reflex, single-lens reflex (SLR), twin-lens reflex (TLR), security, sliding box, sound, still, stereo, Super 8®, TV, video.

camouflage *n* disguise, guise, masquerade, mask, cloak, screen, blind, front, cover, concealment, deception.
v disguise, mask, cloak, veil, screen,

cover, conceal, hide, obscure.
⊞ uncover, reveal.

campaign *n* crusade, movement, promotion, drive, push, offensive, attack, battle, expedition, operation.
v crusade, promote, push, advocate, fight, battle.

cancel *v* call off, abort, abandon, drop, abolish, annul, quash, rescind, revoke, repeal, countermand, delete, erase, obliterate, eliminate, offset, compensate, redeem, neutralize, nullify.

cancer *n* **1** EVIL, blight, canker, pestilence, sickness, corruption, rot. **2** TUMOUR, growth, malignancy, carcinoma.

candid *adj* frank, open, truthful, honest, sincere, forthright, straightforward, ingenuous, guileless, simple, plain, clear, unequivocal, blunt, outspoken.
⊞ guarded, evasive, devious.

candidate *n* applicant, aspirant, contender, contestant, competitor, entrant, runner, possibility, nominee, claimant, pretender, suitor.

candour *n* frankness, openness, truthfulness, honesty, plain-dealing, sincerity, straightforwardness, directness, ingenuousness, guilelessness, naïvety, artlessness, simplicity, plainness, bluntness, unequivocalness, outspokenness.
⊞ evasiveness, deviousness.

canonical hours

Names of canonical hours include:
compline, lauds, matins, none, prime, sext, terce, vespers.

canopy *n* awning, covering, shade, shelter, sunshade, umbrella.

cantankerous *adj* irritable, irascible, grumpy, grouchy, crusty, crotchety, crabbed, crabby, testy, bad-tempered, ill-humoured, cross, peevish, difficult, perverse, contrary, quarrelsome.

🖪 good-natured, easy-going (*infml*).

canvass *v* **1** ELECTIONEER, agitate, campaign, solicit, ask for, seek, poll. **2** EXAMINE, inspect, scrutinize, study, scan, investigate, analyse, sift, discuss, debate.
n poll, survey, examination, scrutiny, investigation, inquiry.

canyon *n* gorge, ravine, gully, valley.

cap *v* exceed, surpass, transcend, better, beat, outdo, outstrip, eclipse, complete, finish, crown, top, cover.
n **1** HAT, skullcap, beret, tam-o'-shanter. **2** LID, top, cover.

capability *n* ability, capacity, faculty, power, potential, means, facility, competence, qualification, skill, proficiency, talent.
🖪 inability, incompetence.

capable *adj* able, competent, efficient, qualified, experienced, accomplished, skilful, proficient, gifted, talented, masterly, clever, intelligent, fitted, suited, apt, liable, disposed.
🖪 incapable, incompetent, useless.

capacity *n* **1** VOLUME, space, room, size, dimensions, magnitude, extent, compass, range, scope. **2** CAPABILITY, ability, faculty, power, potential, competence, efficiency, skill, gift, talent, genius, cleverness, intelligence, aptitude, readiness. **3** *in her capacity as president*: role, function, position, office, post, appointment, job.

cape¹ *n* headland, head, promontory, point, ness, peninsula.

cape² *n* cloak, shawl, wrap, robe, poncho, coat.

capital *n* funds, finance, principal, money, cash, savings, investment(s), wealth, means, wherewithal, resources, assets, property, stock.

capitalize on *v* profit from, take advantage of, exploit, cash in on.

capitulate *v* surrender, throw in the towel, yield, give in, relent, submit,

succumb.
🖪 fight on.

capsize *v* overturn, turn over, turn turtle, invert, keel over, upset.

capsule *n* pill, tablet, lozenge, receptacle, shell, sheath, pod, module.

captain *n* commander, master, skipper, pilot, head, chief, leader, boss, officer.

captivate *v* charm, enchant, bewitch, beguile, fascinate, enthral, hypnotize, mesmerize, lure, allure, seduce, win, attract, enamour, infatuate, enrapture, dazzle.
🖪 repel, disgust, appal.

captive *n* prisoner, hostage, slave, detainee, internee, convict.
adj imprisoned, caged, confined, restricted, secure, locked up, enchained, enslaved, ensnared.
🖪 free.

captivity *n* custody, detention, imprisonment, incarceration, internment, confinement, restraint, bondage, duress, slavery, servitude.
🖪 freedom.

capture *v* catch, trap, snare, take, seize, arrest, apprehend, imprison, secure.
n catching, trapping, taking, seizure, arrest, imprisonment.

car *n* automobile, motor car, motor, vehicle.

Types of car include: saloon, hatchback, fastback, estate, sports car, cabriolet, convertible, limousine, limo (*infml*), wheels (*sl*), banger (*infml*), Mini, bubble-car, coupé, station wagon, shooting brake, veteran car, vintage car, Beetle (*infml*), four-wheel drive, Jeep®, buggy, Land Rover, Range Rover, panda car, patrol car, taxi, cab.

carcase *n* body, corpse, cadaver, remains, relics, skeleton, shell, structure, framework, hulk.

care *n* **1** WORRY, anxiety, stress,

strain, pressure, concern, trouble, distress, affliction, tribulation, vexation. **2** CAREFULNESS, caution, prudence, forethought, vigilance, watchfulness, pains, meticulousness, attention, heed, regard, consideration, interest. **3** *in their care*: keeping, custody, guardianship, protection, ward, charge, responsibility, control, supervision.
≠ **2** carelessness, thoughtlessness, inattention, neglect.
v worry, mind, bother.
care for 1 LOOK AFTER, nurse, tend, mind, watch over, protect, minister to, attend. **2** LIKE, be fond of, love, be keen on, enjoy, delight in, want, desire.

career *n* vocation, calling, life-work, occupation, pursuit, profession, trade, job, employment, livelihood.
v rush, dash, tear, hurtle, race, run, gallop, speed, shoot, bolt.

carefree *adj* unworried, untroubled, unconcerned, blithe, breezy, happy-go-lucky, cheery, light-hearted, cheerful, happy, easy-going (*infml*), laid back (*infml*).
≠ worried, anxious, despondent.

careful *adj* **1** CAUTIOUS, prudent, circumspect, judicious, wary, chary, vigilant, watchful, alert, attentive, mindful. **2** METICULOUS, painstaking, conscientious, scrupulous, thorough, detailed, punctilious, particular, accurate, precise, thoughtful.
≠ **1** careless, inattentive, thoughtless, reckless. **2** careless.

careless *adj* **1** UNTHINKING, thoughtless, inconsiderate, uncaring, unconcerned, heedless, unmindful, forgetful, remiss, negligent, irresponsible, unguarded. **2** *careless work*: inaccurate, messy, untidy, disorderly, sloppy, neglectful, slipshod, slap-dash, hasty, cursory, offhand, casual.
≠ **1** thoughtful, prudent. **2** careful, accurate, meticulous.

caress *v* stroke, pet, fondle, cuddle, hug, embrace, kiss, touch, rub.
n stroke, pat, fondle, cuddle, hug, embrace, kiss.

caretaker *n* janitor, porter, watchman, keeper, custodian, curator, warden, superintendent.

cargo *n* freight, load, pay-load, lading, tonnage, shipment, consignment, contents, goods, merchandise, baggage.

caricature *n* cartoon, parody, lampoon, burlesque, satire, send-up, take-off, imitation, representation, distortion, travesty.
v parody, mock, ridicule, satirize, send up, take off, mimic, distort, exaggerate.

carnage *n* bloodshed, blood-bath, butchery, slaughter, killing, murder, massacre, holocaust.

carnival *n* festival, fiesta, gala, jamboree, fête, fair, holiday, jubilee, celebration, merrymaking, revelry.

carriage *n* **1** COACH, wagon, car, vehicle. **2** DEPORTMENT, posture, bearing, air, manner, mien, demeanour, behaviour, conduct. **3** CARRYING, conveyance, transport, transportation, delivery, postage.

carry *v* **1** BRING, convey, transport, haul, move, transfer, relay, release, conduct, take, fetch. **2** BEAR, shoulder, support, underpin, maintain, uphold, sustain, suffer, stand.
carry on 1 CONTINUE, proceed, last, endure, maintain, keep on, persist, persevere. **2** *carry on a business*: operate, run, manage, administer.
≠ **1** stop, finish.
carry out do, perform, undertake, discharge, conduct, execute, implement, fulfil, accomplish, achieve, realize, bring off.

cart *n* barrow, handcart, wheel-barrow, wagon, truck.
v move, convey, transport, haul, lug (*infml*), hump (*infml*), bear, carry.

carton *n* box, packet, pack, case, container, package, parcel.

cartoon *n* comic strip, animation, sketch, drawing, caricature, parody.

cartridge *n* cassette, canister, cylinder, tube, container, case, capsule, shell, magazine, round, charge.

carve *v* cut, slice, hack, hew, chisel, chip, sculpt, sculpture, shape, form, fashion, mould, etch, engrave, incise, indent.

cascade *n* rush, gush, outpouring, flood, deluge, torrent, avalanche, cataract, waterfall, falls, fountain, shower.
 F3 trickle.
 v rush, gush, surge, flood, overflow, spill, tumble, fall, descend, shower, pour, plunge, pitch.

case[1] *n* container, receptacle, holder, suitcase, trunk, crate, box, carton, casket, chest, cabinet, showcase, casing, cartridge, shell, capsule, sheath, cover, jacket, wrapper.

case[2] *n* **1** CIRCUMSTANCES, context, state, condition, position, situation, contingency, occurrence, occasion, event, specimen, example, instance, illustration, point.
 2 LAWSUIT, suit, trial, proceedings, action, process, cause, argument, dispute.

cash *n* money, hard money, ready money, bank-notes, notes, coins, change, legal tender, currency, hard currency, bullion, funds, resources, wherewithal.
 v encash, exchange, realize, liquidate.

cashier *n* clerk, teller, treasurer, bursar, purser, banker, accountant.

cask *n* barrel, tun, hogshead, firkin, vat, tub, butt.

cast *v* **1** THROW, hurl, lob, pitch, fling, toss, sling, shy, launch, impel, drive, direct, project, shed, emit, diffuse, spread, scatter. **2** MOULD, shape, form, model, found.

n **1** COMPANY, troupe, actors, players, performers, entertainers, characters, dramatis personae.
 2 CASTING, mould, shape, form.

cast down depress, discourage, dishearten, deject, sadden, crush, desolate.
 F3 cheer up, encourage.

castle *n* stronghold, fortress, citadel, keep, tower, château, palace, mansion, stately home, country house.

Parts of a castle include: approach, bailey, barbican, bartizan, bastion, battlements, brattice, buttress, chapel, corbel, courtyard, crenel, crenellation, curtain wall, ditch, donjon, drawbridge, dungeon, embrasure, enclosure wall, fosse, gatehouse, inner wall, keep, merlon, moat, motte, mound, outer bailey, parapet, portcullis, postern, rampart, scarp, stockade, tower, lookout tower, turret, ward, watchtower.

---

casual *adj* **1** *a casual meeting*: chance, fortuitous, accidental, unintentional, unpremeditated, unexpected, unforeseen, irregular, random, occasional, incidental, superficial, cursory.
 2 NONCHALANT, blasé, lackadaisical, negligent, couldn't-care-less (*infml*), apathetic, indifferent, unconcerned, informal, offhand, relaxed, laid back (*infml*).
 F3 **1** deliberate, planned. **2** formal.

casualty *n* injury, loss, death, fatality, victim, sufferer, injured person, wounded, dead person.

cat

Breeds of cat include: Abyssinian, American shorthair, Balinese, Birman, Bombay, British shorthair, British longhair, Burmese, Carthusian, chinchilla, Cornish rex, Cymric, Devon rex, domestic tabby,

Egyptian Mau, Exotic shorthair,
Foreign Blue, Foreign spotted
shorthair, Foreign White, Havana,
Himalayan, Japanese Bobtail, Korat,
Maine Coon, Manx, Norwegian
Forest, Persian, rag-doll, rex,
Russian Blue, Scottish Fold, Siamese,
silver tabby, Singapura, Somali,
Tiffany, Tonkinese, Tortoiseshell,
Turkish Angora, Turkish Van.

catalogue n list, inventory, roll,
register, roster, schedule, record,
table, index, directory, gazetteer,
brochure, prospectus.
v list, register, record, index, classify,
alphabetize, file.

catapult v hurl, fling, throw, pitch,
toss, sling, launch, propel, shoot, fire.

cataract n waterfall, falls, rapids,
force, cascade, downpour, torrent,
deluge.

catastrophe n disaster, calamity,
cataclysm, debacle, fiasco, failure,
ruin, devastation, tragedy, blow,
reverse, mischance, misfortune,
adversity, affliction, trouble,
upheaval.

catch v 1 SEIZE, grab, take, hold,
grasp, grip, clutch, capture, trap,
entrap, snare, ensnare, hook, net,
arrest, apprehend. 2 HEAR,
understand, perceive, recognize. 3
SURPRISE, expose, unmask, find
(out), discover, detect, discern.
4 catch a cold: contract, get, develop,
go down with.
🔁 1 drop, release, free. 2 miss.
n 1 FASTENER, clip, hook, clasp,
hasp, latch, bolt. 2 DISADVANTAGE,
drawback, snag, hitch, obstacle,
problem.

catch up gain on, draw level with,
overtake.

catching adj infectious, contagious,
communicable, transmittable.

catchword n catch-phrase, slogan,
motto, watchword, byword,
password.

catchy adj memorable, haunting,
popular, melodic, tuneful, attractive,
captivating.
🔁 dull, boring.

categorical adj absolute, total,
utter, unqualified, unreserved,
unconditional, downright, positive,
definite, emphatic, unequivocal,
clear, explicit, express, direct.
🔁 tentative, qualified, vague.

categorize v class, classify, group,
sort, grade, rank, order, list.

category n class, classification,
group, grouping, sort, type, section,
division, department, chapter, head,
heading, grade, rank, order, list.

cater v provision, victual, provide,
supply, furnish, serve, indulge,
pander.

catholic adj broad, wide, wide-
ranging, universal, global, general,
comprehensive, inclusive, all-
inclusive, all-embracing, liberal,
tolerant, broad-minded.
🔁 narrow, limited, narrow-minded.

cattle n cows, bulls, oxen, livestock,
stock, beasts.

Breeds of cattle include: Aberdeen
Angus, Africander, Alderney, Ankole,
Ayrshire, Blonde d'Aquitaine,
Brahman, Brown Swiss, cattabu,
cattalo, Charolais, Chillingham,
Devon, dexter, Durham, Friesian,
Galloway, Guernsey, Hereford,
Highland, Holstein, Jersey, Latvian,
Limousin, Longhorn, Luing, Red Poll,
Romagnola, Santa Gertrudis,
Shetland, Shorthorn, Simmenthaler,
Teeswater, Ukrainian, Welsh Black.

cause n 1 SOURCE, origin,
beginning, root, basis, spring,
originator, creator, producer, maker,
agent, agency. 2 REASON, motive,
grounds, motivation, stimulus,
incentive, inducement, impulse. 3 a
worthy cause: object, purpose, end,
ideal, belief, conviction, movement,

undertaking, enterprise.

₤ 1 effect, result, consequence.

v begin, give rise to, lead to, result in, occasion, bring about, effect, produce, generate, create, precipitate, motivate, stimulate, provoke, incite, induce, force, compel.

₤ stop, prevent.

caustic *adj* corrosive, acid, burning, stinging, biting, cutting, mordant, trenchant, keen, pungent, bitter, acrimonious, sarcastic, scathing, virulent, severe.

₤ soothing, mild.

caution *n* 1 CARE, carefulness, prudence, vigilance, watchfulness, alertness, heed, discretion, forethought, deliberation, wariness. 2 WARNING, caveat, injunction, admonition, advice, counsel.

₤ 1 carelessness, recklessness.

v warn, admonish, advise, urge.

cautious *adj* careful, prudent, circumspect, judicious, vigilant, watchful, alert, heedful, discreet, tactful, chary, wary, cagey (*infml*), guarded, tentative, softly-softly, unadventurous.

₤ incautious, imprudent, heedless, reckless.

cavalcade *n* procession, parade, march-past, troop, array, retinue, train.

cavalier *n* horseman, equestrian, knight, gentleman, gallant, escort, partner.

adj supercilious, condescending, lordly, haughty, lofty, arrogant, swaggering, insolent, scornful, disdainful, curt, offhand, free-and-easy.

cave *n* cavern, grotto, hole, pothole, hollow, cavity.

cave in collapse, subside, give way, yield, fall, slip.

cavernous *adj* hollow, concave, gaping, yawning, echoing, resonant, deep, sunken.

cavity *n* hole, gap, dent, hollow, crater, pit, well, sinus, ventricle.

cavort *v* caper, frolic, gambol, prance, skip, dance, frisk, sport, romp.

cease *v* stop, desist, refrain, pack in (*sl*), halt, call a halt, break off, discontinue, finish, end, conclude, terminate, fail, die.

₤ begin, start, commence.

ceaseless *adj* endless, unending, never-ending, eternal, everlasting, continuous, non-stop, incessant, interminable, constant, perpetual, continual, persistent, untiring, unremitting.

₤ occasional, irregular.

cede *v* surrender, give up, resign, abdicate, renounce, abandon, yield, relinquish, convey, transfer, hand over, grant, allow, concede.

celebrate *v* commemorate, remember, observe, keep, rejoice, toast, drink to, honour, exalt, glorify, praise, extol, eulogize, commend, bless, solemnize.

celebrated *adj* famous, well-known, famed, renowned, illustrious, glorious, eminent, distinguished, notable, prominent, outstanding, popular, acclaimed, exalted, revered.

₤ unknown, obscure, forgotten.

celebration *n* commemoration, remembrance, observance, anniversary, jubilee, festival, gala, merrymaking, jollification, revelry, festivity, party, rave-up (*infml*).

Celebrations include: anniversary, banquet, baptism, bar mitzvah, birthday, centenary, christening, coming-of-age, commemoration, feast, fête, festival, gala, graduation, harvest festival, homecoming, Independence Day, jubilee, marriage, May Day, name-day, party, reception, remembrance, retirement, reunion, saint's day, thanksgiving, tribute, wedding. *see also* **anniversary**; **party**.

celebrity n personage, dignitary, VIP (*infml*), luminary, worthy, personality, name, big name, star, superstar.
ЕЗ nobody, nonentity.

celibacy n singleness, bachelorhood, spinsterhood, virginity, chastity, purity, abstinence, continence.

cell n dungeon, prison, room, cubicle, chamber, compartment, cavity, unit.

cellar n basement, crypt, vault, storeroom, wine cellar.

cement v stick, bond, weld, solder, join, unite, bind, combine.
n plaster, mortar, concrete.

cemetery n burial-ground, graveyard, churchyard.

censor v cut, edit, blue-pencil, bowdlerize, expurgate.

censorious adj condemnatory, disapproving, disparaging, fault-finding, carping, cavilling, critical, hypercritical, severe.
ЕЗ complimentary, approving.

censure n condemnation, blame, disapproval, criticism, admonishment, admonition, reprehension, reproof, reproach, rebuke, reprimand, telling-off (*infml*).
ЕЗ praise, compliments, approval.
v condemn, denounce, blame, criticize, castigate, admonish, reprehend, reprove, upbraid, reproach, rebuke, reprimand, scold, tell off (*infml*).
ЕЗ praise, compliment, approve.

central adj middle, mid, inner, interior, focal, main, chief, key, principal, primary, fundamental, vital, essential, important.
ЕЗ peripheral, minor, secondary.

centre n middle, mid-point, bull's-eye, heart, core, nucleus, pivot, hub, focus, crux.
ЕЗ edge, periphery, outskirts.
v focus, concentrate, converge, gravitate, revolve, pivot, hinge.

ceremonial adj formal, official, stately, solemn, ritual, ritualistic.
ЕЗ informal, casual.
n ceremony, formality, protocol, solemnity, ritual, rite.

ceremonious adj stately, dignified, grand, solemn, ritual, civil, polite, courteous, deferential, courtly, formal, stiff, starchy, exact, precise, punctilious.
ЕЗ unceremonious, informal, relaxed.

ceremony n **1** *wedding ceremony*: service, rite, commemoration, observance, celebration, function, parade. **2** ETIQUETTE, protocol, decorum, propriety, formality, form, niceties, ceremonial, ritual, pomp, show.

certain adj **1** SURE, positive, assured, confident, convinced, undoubted, indubitable, unquestionable, incontrovertible, undeniable, irrefutable, plain, conclusive, absolute, convincing, true. **2** INEVITABLE, unavoidable, bound, destined, fated. **3** SPECIFIC, special, particular, individual, precise, express, fixed, established, settled, decided, definite. **4** DEPENDABLE, reliable, trustworthy, constant, steady, stable.
ЕЗ 1 uncertain, unsure, hesitant, doubtful. **2** unlikely. **4** unreliable.

certainly adv of course, naturally, definitely, for sure, undoubtedly, doubtlessly.

certainty n sureness, positiveness, assurance, confidence, conviction, faith, trust, truth, validity, fact, reality, inevitability.
ЕЗ uncertainty, doubt, hesitation.

certificate n document, award, diploma, qualification, credentials, testimonial, guarantee, endorsement, warrant, licence, authorization, pass, voucher.

certify v declare, attest, aver, assure, guarantee, endorse, corroborate, confirm, vouch, testify, witness, verify, authenticate, validate, authorize, license.

chain n **1** FETTER, manacle, restraint, bond, link, coupling, union. **2** *chain of events*: sequence, succession, progression, string, train, series, set.

v tether, fasten, secure, bind, restrain, confine, fetter, shackle, manacle, handcuff, enslave.

🔁 release, free.

chairman, chairwoman n chairperson, chair, president, convenor, organizer, director, master of ceremonies, MC, toastmaster, speaker.

challenge v **1** DARE, defy, throw down the gauntlet, confront, brave, accost, provoke, test, tax, try. **2** DISPUTE, question, query, protest, object to.

n dare, defiance, confrontation, provocation, test, trial, hurdle, obstacle, question, ultimatum.

champion n winner, victor, conqueror, hero, guardian, protector, defender, vindicator, patron, backer, supporter, upholder, advocate.

v defend, stand up for, back, support, maintain, uphold, espouse, advocate, promote.

chance n **1** ACCIDENT, fortuity, coincidence, fluke (*infml*), luck, fortune, providence, fate, destiny, risk, gamble, speculation, possibility, prospect, probability, likelihood, odds. **2** *a second chance*: opportunity, opening, occasion, time.

🔁 **1** certainty.

v **1** RISK, hazard, gamble, wager, stake, try, venture. **2** HAPPEN, occur.

adj fortuitous, casual, accidental, inadvertent, unintentional, unintended, unforeseen, unlooked-for, random, haphazard, incidental.

🔁 deliberate, intentional, foreseen, certain.

change v alter, modify, convert, reorganize, reform, remodel, restyle,

transform, transfigure, metamorphose, mutate, vary, fluctuate, vacillate, shift, displace, swap, exchange, trade, switch, transpose, substitute, replace, alternate, interchange.

n alteration, modification, conversion, transformation, metamorphosis, mutation, variation, fluctuation, shift, exchange, transposition, substitution, interchange, difference, diversion, novelty, innovation, variety, transition, revolution, upheaval.

changeable adj variable, mutable, fluid, kaleidoscopic, shifting, mobile, unsettled, uncertain, unpredictable, unreliable, erratic, irregular, inconstant, fickle, capricious, volatile, unstable, unsteady, wavering, vacillating.

🔁 constant, reliable.

channel n **1** DUCT, conduit, main, groove, furrow, trough, gutter, canal, flume, watercourse, waterway, strait, sound. **2** *channel of communication*: route, course, path, avenue, way, means, medium, approach, passage.

v direct, guide, conduct, convey, send, transmit, force.

chant n plainsong, psalm, song, melody, chorus, refrain, slogan, war cry.

v recite, intone, sing, chorus.

chaos n disorder, confusion, disorganization, anarchy, lawlessness, tumult, pandemonium, bedlam.

🔁 order.

chaotic adj disordered, confused, disorganized, topsy-turvy, deranged, anarchic, lawless, riotous, tumultuous, unruly, uncontrolled.

🔁 ordered, organized.

chap (*infml*) n fellow, bloke (*infml*), guy (*infml*), man, boy, person, individual, character, sort, type.

chapter n part, section, division, clause, topic, episode, period, phase, stage.

character n 1 PERSONALITY,
nature, disposition, temperament,
temper, constitution, make-up,
individuality, peculiarity, feature,
attributes, quality, type, stamp,
calibre, reputation, status, position,
trait. 2 LETTER, figure, symbol, sign,
mark, type, cipher, rune, hieroglyph,
ideograph. 3 INDIVIDUAL, person,
sort, type, role, part.

characteristic adj distinctive,
distinguishing, individual,
idiosyncratic, peculiar, specific,
special, typical, representative,
symbolic, symptomatic.
≠ uncharacteristic, untypical.
n peculiarity, idiosyncrasy,
mannerism, feature, trait, attribute,
property, quality, hallmark, mark,
symptom.

characterize v typify, mark, stamp,
brand, identify, distinguish, indicate,
represent, portray.

charge v 1 charge a high price: ask,
demand, levy, exact, debit.
2 ACCUSE, indict, impeach,
incriminate, blame. 3 ATTACK,
assail, storm, rush.
n 1 PRICE, cost, fee, rate, amount,
expense, expenditure, outlay, payment.
2 ACCUSATION, indictment,
allegation, imputation. 3 ATTACK,
assault, onslaught, sortie, rush. 4 in
your charge: custody, keeping, care,
safekeeping, guardianship, ward,
trust, responsibility, duty.

charitable adj philanthropic,
humanitarian, benevolent, benign,
kind, compassionate, sympathetic,
understanding, considerate,
generous, magnanimous, liberal,
tolerant, broad-minded, lenient,
forgiving, indulgent, gracious.
≠ uncharitable, inconsiderate,
unforgiving.

charity n 1 GENEROSITY,
bountifulness, alms-giving,
beneficence, philanthropy,

unselfishness, altruism, benevolence,
benignness, kindness, goodness,
humanity, compassion, tender-
heartedness, love, affection,
clemency, indulgence. 2 ALMS, gift,
handout, aid, relief, assistance.
≠ 1 selfishness, malice.

charm v please, delight, enrapture,
captivate, fascinate, beguile, enchant,
bewitch, mesmerize, attract, allure,
cajole, win, enamour.
≠ repel.
n 1 ATTRACTION, allure,
magnetism, appeal, desirability,
fascination, enchantment, spell,
sorcery, magic. 2 lucky charm: trinket,
talisman, amulet, fetish, idol.

charming adj pleasing, delightful,
pleasant, lovely, captivating,
enchanting, attractive, fetching,
appealing, sweet, winsome, seductive,
winning, irresistible.
≠ ugly, unattractive, repulsive.

chart n diagram, table, graph, map,
plan, blueprint.
v map, map out, sketch, draw, draft,
outline, delineate, mark, plot, place.

charter n right, privilege,
prerogative, authorization, permit,
licence, franchise, concession,
contract, indenture, deed, bond,
document.
v hire, rent, lease, commission,
engage, employ, authorize, sanction,
license.

chase v pursue, follow, hunt, track,
drive, expel, rush, hurry.

chasm n gap, opening, gulf, abyss,
void, hollow, cavity, crater, breach,
rift, split, cleft, fissure, crevasse,
canyon, gorge, ravine.

chaste adj pure, virginal, unsullied,
undefiled, immaculate, abstinent,
continent, celibate, virtuous, moral,
innocent, wholesome, modest,
decent, plain, simple, austere.
≠ corrupt, lewd, vulgar, indecorous.

chasten v humble, humiliate, tame,
subdue, repress, curb, moderate,

soften, discipline, punish, correct, chastise, castigate, reprove.

chastise v punish, discipline, correct, beat, flog, whip, lash, scourge, smack, spank, castigate, reprove, admonish, scold, upbraid, berate, censure.

chat n talk, conversation, natter (infml), gossip, chinwag (infml), tête-à-tête, heart-to-heart.
v talk, crack, natter (infml), gossip, chatter, gab (on) (infml).

chatter v, n prattle, babble, chat, natter (infml), gossip, tattle.

chatty adj talkative, gossipy, newsy, friendly, informal, colloquial, familiar.
☒ quiet.

cheap adj 1 INEXPENSIVE, reasonable, dirt-cheap, bargain, reduced, cut-price, knock-down, budget, economy, economical.
2 TAWDRY, tatty, cheapo (sl), shoddy, inferior, second-rate, worthless, vulgar, common, poor, paltry, mean, contemptible, despicable, low.
☒ 1 expensive, costly. 2 superior, noble, admirable.

cheapen v devalue, degrade, lower, demean, depreciate, belittle, disparage, denigrate, downgrade.

cheat v defraud, swindle, diddle, short-change, do (infml), rip off (sl), fleece, con (infml), double-cross, mislead, deceive, dupe, fool, trick, hoodwink, bamboozle (infml), beguile.
n cheater, dodger, fraud, swindler, shark (infml), con man (infml), extortioner, double-crosser, impostor, charlatan, deceiver, trickster, rogue.

check v 1 EXAMINE, inspect, scrutinize, give the once-over (infml), investigate, probe, test, monitor, study, research, compare, cross-check, confirm, verify. 2 check an impulse: curb, bridle, restrain, control, limit, repress, inhibit, damp,

thwart, hinder, impede, obstruct, bar, retard, delay, stop, arrest, halt.
n 1 EXAMINATION, inspection, scrutiny, once-over (infml), check-up, investigation, audit, test, research.
2 CURB, restraint, control, limitation, constraint, inhibition, damper, blow, disappointment, reverse, setback, frustration, hindrance, impediment, obstruction, stoppage.

cheek (infml) n impertinence, impudence, insolence, disrespect, effrontery, brazenness, temerity, audacity, nerve (infml), gall.

cheeky (infml) adj impertinent, impudent, insolent, disrespectful, forward, brazen, pert, saucy (infml), audacious.
☒ respectful, polite.

cheer v 1 ACCLAIM, hail, clap, applaud. 2 COMFORT, console, brighten, gladden, warm, uplift, elate, exhilarate, encourage, hearten.
☒ 1 boo, jeer. 2 dishearten.
n acclamation, hurrah, bravo, applause, ovation.

cheer up encourage, hearten, take heart, rally, buck up (infml), perk up (infml).

cheerful adj happy, glad, contented, joyful, joyous, blithe, carefree, light-hearted, cheery, good-humoured, sunny, optimistic, enthusiastic, hearty, genial, jovial, jolly, merry, lively, animated, bright, chirpy, breezy, jaunty, buoyant, sparkling.
☒ sad, dejected, depressed.

cheese

Varieties of cheese include: Amsterdam, Bel Paese, Bleu d'Auvergne, Blue Cheshire, Blue Vinny, Boursin, Brie, Caboc, Caerphilly, Camembert, Carré, Cheddar, Cheshire, Churnton, cottage cheese, cream cheese, Crowdie, curd cheese, Danish blue, Derby, Dolcelatte, Dorset Blue, Double Gloucester, Dunlop, Edam, Emmental,

Emmentaler, ewe-cheese, Feta, fromage frais, Gloucester, Gorgonzola, Gouda, Gruyère, Huntsman, Jarlsberg, Killarney, Lancashire, Leicester, Limburg(er), Lymeswold, mascarpone, mouse-trap, mozzarella, Neufchâtel, Orkney, Parmesan, Petit Suisse, Pont-l'Eveque, Port Salut, processed cheese, quark, Red Leicester, Red Windsor, ricotta, Roquefort, sage Derby, Saint-Paulin, Stilton, stracchino, vegetarian cheese, Vacherin, Wensleydale.

chemical elements

The chemical elements (with their symbols) are: actinium (Ac), aluminium (Al), americium (Am), antimony (Sb), argon (Ar), arsenic (As), astatine (At), barium (Ba), berkelium (Bk), beryllium (Be), bismuth (Bi), boron (B), bromine (Br), cadmium (Cd), caesium (Cs), calcium (Ca), californium (Cf), carbon (C), cerium (Ce), chlorine (Cl), chromium (Cr), cobalt (Co), copper (Cu), curium (Cm), dysprosium (Dy), einsteinium (Es), erbium (Er), europium (Eu), fermium (Fm), fluorine (F), francium (Fr), gadolinium (Gd), gallium (Ga), germanium (Ge), gold (Au), hafnium (Hf), hahnium (Ha), helium (He), holmium (Ho), hydrogen (H), indium (In), iodine (I), iridium (Ir), iron (Fe), krypton (Kr), lanthanum (La), lawrencium (Lr), lead (Pb), lithium (Li), lutetium (Lu), magnesium (Mg), manganese (Mn), mendelevium (Md), mercury (Hg), molybdenum (Mo), neodymium (Nd), neon (Ne), neptunium (Np), nickel (Ni), niobium (Nb), nitrogen (N), nobelium (No), osmium (Os), oxygen (O), palladium (Pd), phosphorus (P), platinum (Pt), plutonium (Pu), polonium (Po), potassium (K), praseodymium (Pr), promethium (Pm), protactinium (Pa),

radium (Ra), radon (Rn), rhenium (Re), rhodium (Rh), rubidium (Rb), ruthenium (Ru), rutherfordium (Rf), samarium (Sm), scandium (Sc), selenium (Se), silicon (Si), silver (Ag), sodium (Na), strontium (Sr), sulphur (S), tantalum (Ta), technetium (Tc), tellurium (Te), terbium (Tb), thallium (Tl), thorium (Th), thulium (Tm), tin (Sn), titanium (Ti), tungsten (W), uranium (U), vanadium (V), xenon (Xe), ytterbium (Yb), yttrium (Y), zinc (Zn), zirconium (Zr).

chemistry

Terms used in chemistry include: analytical chemistry, biochemistry, inorganic chemistry, organic chemistry, physical chemistry; acid, alkali, analysis, atom, atomic number, atomic structure, subatomic particles, base, bond, buffer, catalysis, catalyst, chain reaction, chemical bond, chemical compound, chemical element, chemical equation, chemical reaction, chemist, chlorination, combustion, compound, corrosion, covalent bond, crystal, cycle, decomposition, diffusion, dissociation, distillation, electrochemical cell, electrode, electron, electrolysis, emulsion, fermentation, fixation, formula, free radical, gas, halogen, hydrolysis, immiscible, indicator, inert gas, ion, ionic bond, isomer, isotope, lipid, liquid, litmus paper, litmus test, mass, matter, metallic bond, mixture, mole, molecule, neutron, noble gas, nucleus, oxidation, periodic table, pH, polymer, proton, radioactivity, reaction, reduction, respiration, salt, solids, solution, solvent, substance, suspension, symbol, synthesis, valency, zwitterion.

cherish *v* foster, care for, look after, nurse, nurture, nourish, sustain, support, harbour, shelter, entertain, hold dear, value, prize, treasure.

chest n trunk, crate, box, case, casket, coffer, strongbox.

chew v masticate, gnaw, munch, champ, crunch, grind.

chief adj leading, foremost, uppermost, highest, supreme, grand, arch, premier, principal, main, key, central, prime, prevailing, predominant, pre-eminent, outstanding, vital, essential, primary, major.

☒ minor, unimportant.

n ruler, chieftain, lord, master, supremo, head, principal, leader, commander, captain, governor, boss, director, manager, superintendent, superior, ringleader.

chiefly adv mainly, mostly, for the most part, predominantly, principally, primarily, essentially, especially, generally, usually.

child n youngster, kid (infml), nipper (infml), brat (infml), baby, infant, toddler, tot (infml), minor, juvenile, offspring, issue, progeny, descendant.

childhood n babyhood, infancy, boyhood, girlhood, schooldays, youth, adolescence, minority, immaturity.

childish adj babyish, boyish, girlish, infantile, puerile, juvenile, immature, silly, foolish, frivolous.

☒ mature, sensible.

childlike adj innocent, naïve, ingenuous, artless, guileless, credulous, trusting, trustful, simple, natural.

chill v 1 COOL, refrigerate, freeze, ice. 2 FRIGHTEN, terrify, dismay, dishearten, discourage, depress, dampen.

☒ 1 warm, heat.

n coolness, cold, coldness, frigidity, rawness, bite, nip, crispness.

☒ warmth.

chilly adj 1 chilly weather: cold, fresh, brisk, crisp, nippy (infml),

wintry. 2 a chilly response: cool, frigid, unsympathetic, unwelcoming, aloof, stony, unfriendly, hostile.

☒ 1 warm. 2 friendly.

chime v sound, strike, toll, ring, peal, clang, dong, jingle, tinkle.

china adj porcelain, ceramic, pottery, earthenware, terracotta.

Chinese calendar

The animals representing the years in which people are born: rat, buffalo, tiger, rabbit (or hare), dragon, snake, horse, goat (or sheep), monkey, rooster, dog, pig.

chink n crack, rift, cleft, fissure, crevice, slot, opening, aperture, gap, space.

chip n 1 NOTCH, nick, scratch, dent, flaw. 2 FRAGMENT, scrap, wafer, sliver, flake, shaving, paring.

v chisel, whittle, nick, notch, gash, damage.

chirp v, n chirrup, tweet, cheep, peep, twitter, warble, sing, pipe, whistle.

chivalrous adj gentlemanly, polite, courteous, gallant, heroic, valiant, brave, courageous, bold, noble, honourable.

☒ ungallant, cowardly.

chivalry n gentlemanliness, politeness, courtesy, gallantry, bravery, courage, boldness.

choice n option, alternative, selection, variety, pick, preference, say, decision, dilemma, election, discrimination, choosing, opting.

adj best, superior, prime, plum, excellent, fine, exquisite, exclusive, select, hand-picked, special, prize, valuable, precious.

☒ inferior, poor.

choke v 1 THROTTLE, strangle, asphyxiate, suffocate, stifle, smother, suppress. 2 OBSTRUCT, constrict, congest, clog, block, dam, bar, close, stop. 3 COUGH, gag, retch.

choose v pick, select, single out, designate, predestine, opt for, plump for, vote for, settle on, fix on, adopt, elect, prefer, wish, desire, see fit.

choosy (infml) adj selective, discriminating, picky (infml), fussy, particular, finicky, fastidious, exacting.
Ⓔ undemanding.

chop v cut, hack, hew, lop, sever, truncate, cleave, divide, split, slash.
chop up cut (up), slice (up), divide, cube, dice, mince.

choppy adj rough, turbulent, tempestuous, stormy, squally, ruffled, wavy, uneven, broken.
Ⓔ calm, still.

chore n task, job, errand, duty, burden.

chorus n 1 REFRAIN, burden, response, call, shout. 2 CHOIR, choristers, singers, vocalists, ensemble.

christen v baptize, name, call, dub, title, style, term, designate, inaugurate, use.

Christmas n Xmas, Noel, Yule, Yuletide.

chronic adj 1 INCURABLE, deep-seated, recurring, incessant, persistent, inveterate, confirmed, habitual, ingrained, deep-rooted.
2 (infml) a chronic film: awful, terrible, dreadful, appalling, atrocious.
Ⓔ 1 acute, temporary.

chronological adj historical, consecutive, sequential, progressive, ordered.

chubby adj plump, podgy, fleshy, flabby, stout, portly, rotund, round, tubby, paunchy.
Ⓔ slim, skinny.

chuckle v laugh, giggle, titter, snigger, chortle, snort, crow.

chunk n lump, hunk, mass, wodge (infml), wedge, block, slab, piece, portion.

church n chapel, house of God, cathedral, minster, abbey, temple.

> *Names of church services include*: baptism, christening, Christingle, communion, Holy Communion, confirmation, dedication, Eucharist, evening service, evensong, funeral, Lord's Supper, marriage, Mass, High Mass, Midnight Mass, nuptial Mass, Requiem Mass, Holy Matrimony, memorial service, morning prayers, morning service. *see also* **canonical hours**.

cinema n 1 films, pictures, movies (infml), flicks (sl), big screen.
2 picture-house, picture-palace, fleapit (infml).

circle n 1 RING, hoop, loop, round, disc, sphere, globe, orb, cycle, turn, revolution, circuit, orbit, circumference, perimeter, coil, spiral.
2 circle of friends: group, band, company, crowd, set, clique, coterie, club, society, fellowship, fraternity.
v 1 RING, loop, encircle, surround, gird, encompass, enclose, hem in, circumscribe, circumnavigate.
2 ROTATE, revolve, pivot, gyrate, whirl, turn, coil, wind.

> *Types of circle include*: annulus, ball, band, belt, circuit, circumference, coil, cordon, coronet, crown, curl, cycle, disc, discus, ellipse, girdle, globe, halo, hoop, lap, loop, orb, orbit, oval, perimeter, plate, revolution, ring, rotation, round, saucer, sphere, spiral, turn, tyre, wheel, wreath.

circuit n lap, orbit, revolution, tour, journey, course, route, track, round, beat, district, area, region, circumference, boundary, bounds, limit, range, compass, ambit.

circuitous adj roundabout, periphrastic, indirect, oblique, devious, tortuous, winding,

meandering, rambling, labyrinthine.
Ea direct, straight.

circular *adj* round, annular, ring-shaped, hoop-shaped, disc-shaped.
n handbill, leaflet, pamphlet, notice, announcement, advertisement, letter.

circulate *v* **1** *circulate information*: spread, diffuse, broadcast, publicize, publish, issue, propagate, pass round, distribute. **2** GO ROUND, rotate, revolve, gyrate, whirl, swirl, flow.

circulation *n* **1** BLOOD-FLOW, flow, motion, rotation, circling. **2** SPREAD, transmission, publication, dissemination, distribution.

circumference *n* circuit, perimeter, rim, edge, outline, boundary, border, bounds, limits, extremity, margin, verge, fringe, periphery.

circumstances *n* details, particulars, facts, items, elements, factors, conditions, state, state of affairs, situation, position, status, lifestyle, means, resources.

cistern *n* tank, reservoir, sink, basin, vat.

citadel *n* fortress, stronghold, bastion, castle, keep, tower, fortification, acropolis.

cite *v* quote, adduce, name, specify, enumerate, mention, refer to, advance, bring up.

citizen *n* city-dweller, townsman, townswoman, inhabitant, denizen, resident, householder, taxpayer, subject.

city *n* metropolis, town, municipality, conurbation.

civic *adj* city, urban, municipal, borough, community, local, public, communal.

civil *adj* **1** POLITE, courteous, well-mannered, well-bred, courtly, refined, civilized, polished, urbane, affable, complaisant, obliging, accommodating. **2** *civil affairs*: domestic, home, national, internal, interior, state, municipal, civic.
Ea **1** uncivil, discourteous, rude.

2 international, military.

civility *n* politeness, courteousness, courtesy, breeding, refinement, urbanity, graciousness, affability, amenity.
Ea discourtesy, rudeness.

civilization *n* progress, advancement, development, education, enlightenment, cultivation, culture, refinement, sophistication, urbanity.
Ea barbarity, primitiveness.

civilize *v* tame, humanize, educate, enlighten, cultivate, refine, polish, sophisticate, improve, perfect.

civilized *adj* advanced, developed, educated, enlightened, cultured, refined, sophisticated, urbane, polite, sociable.
Ea uncivilized, barbarous, primitive.

claim *v* **1** ALLEGE, pretend, profess, state, affirm, assert, maintain, contend, hold, insist. **2** *claim a refund*: ask, request, require, need, demand, exact, take, collect.
n **1** ALLEGATION, pretension, affirmation, assertion, contention, insistence. **2** APPLICATION, petition, request, requirement, demand, call, right, privilege.

clairvoyant *adj* psychic, prophetic, visionary, telepathic, extra-sensory.
n psychic, fortune-teller, prophet, prophetess, visionary, seer, soothsayer, augur, oracle, diviner, telepath.

clammy *adj* damp, moist, sweaty, sweating, sticky, slimy, dank, muggy, heavy, close.

clamp *n* vice, grip, press, brace, bracket, fastener.
v fasten, secure, fix, clinch, grip, brace.

clan *n* tribe, family, house, race, society, brotherhood, fraternity, confraternity, sect, faction, group, band, set, clique, coterie.

clap *v* **1** APPLAUD, acclaim, cheer.
2 SLAP, smack, pat, wallop (*infml*), whack (*infml*), bang.

clarify v 1 EXPLAIN, throw light on, illuminate, elucidate, gloss, define, simplify, resolve, clear up. 2 REFINE, purify, filter, clear.
E3 1 obscure, confuse. 2 cloud.

clarity n clearness, transparency, lucidity, simplicity, intelligibility, comprehensibility, explicitness, unambiguousness, obviousness, definition, precision.
E3 obscurity, vagueness, imprecision.

clash v 1 CRASH, bang, clank, clang, jangle, clatter, rattle, jar.
2 CONFLICT, disagree, quarrel, wrangle, grapple, fight, feud, war.
n 1 CRASH, bang, jangle, clatter, noise. 2 *a clash with the police*: confrontation, showdown, conflict, disagreement, fight, brush.

clasp n 1 FASTENER, buckle, clip, pin, hasp, hook, catch. 2 HOLD, grip, grasp, embrace, hug.
v 1 HOLD, grip, grasp, clutch, embrace, enfold, hug, squeeze, press.
2 FASTEN, connect, attach, grapple, hook, clip, pin.

class n 1 CATEGORY, classification, group, set, section, division, department, sphere, grouping, order, league, rank, status, caste, quality, grade, type, genre, sort, kind, species, genus, style. 2 *a French class*: lesson, lecture, seminar, tutorial, course.

> *Social classes/groups include*:
> aristocracy, nobility, gentry, landed
> gentry, gentlefolk, élite, nob (*sl*), high
> society, top drawer (*infml*), upper
> class, Sloane Ranger (*sl*), ruling class,
> jet set, middle class, lower class,
> working class, bourgeoisie, proletariat,
> hoi-polloi, commoner, serf, plebeian,
> pleb (*infml*).

v categorize, classify, group, sort, rank, grade, rate, designate, brand.

classic adj typical, characteristic, standard, regular, usual, traditional, time-honoured, established,
archetypal, model, exemplary, ideal, best, finest, first-rate, consummate, definitive, masterly, excellent, ageless, immortal, undying, lasting, enduring, abiding.
E3 unrepresentative, second-rate.
n standard, model, prototype, exemplar, masterwork, masterpiece, pièce de résistance.

classical adj elegant, refined, pure, traditional, excellent, well-proportioned, symmetrical, harmonious, restrained.
E3 modern, inferior.

classification n categorization, taxonomy, sorting, grading, arrangement, systematization, codification, tabulation, cataloguing.

classify v categorize, class, group, pigeonhole, sort, grade, rank, arrange, dispose, distribute, systematize, codify, tabulate, file, catalogue.

clause n article, item, part, section, subsection, paragraph, heading, chapter, passage, condition, proviso, provision, specification, point.

claw n talon, nail, pincer, nipper, gripper.
v scratch, scrabble, scrape, graze, tear, rip, lacerate, maul, mangle.

clean adj 1 WASHED, laundered, sterile, aseptic, antiseptic, hygienic, sanitary, sterilized, decontaminated, purified, pure, unadulterated, fresh, unpolluted, uncontaminated, immaculate, spotless, unspotted, unstained, unsoiled, unsullied, perfect, faultless, flawless, unblemished. 2 *a clean life*: innocent, guiltless, virtuous, upright, moral, honest, honourable, respectable, decent, chaste. 3 SMOOTH, regular, straight, neat, tidy.
E3 1 dirty, polluted. 2 dishonourable, indecent. 3 rough.
v wash, bath, launder, rinse, wipe, sponge, scrub, scour, mop, swab, sweep, vacuum, dust, freshen,

clip

deodorize, cleanse, purge, purify, decontaminate, disinfect, sanitize, sterilize, clear, filter.
⊟ dirty, defile.

cleanser *n* soap, soap powder, detergent, cleaner, solvent, scourer, scouring powder, purifier, disinfectant.

clear *adj* **1** PLAIN, distinct, comprehensible, intelligible, coherent, lucid, explicit, precise, unambiguous, well-defined, apparent, evident, patent, obvious, manifest, conspicuous, unmistakable, unquestionable. **2** SURE, certain, positive, definite, convinced. **3** *clear water*: transparent, limpid, crystalline, glassy, see-through, clean, unclouded, colourless. **4** *a clear day*: cloudless, unclouded, fine, bright, sunny, light, luminous, undimmed. **5** UNOBSTRUCTED, unblocked, open, free, empty, unhindered, unimpeded. **6** AUDIBLE, perceptible, pronounced, distinct, recognizable.
⊟ **1** unclear, vague, ambiguous, confusing. **2** unsure, muddled. **3** opaque, cloudy. **4** dull. **5** blocked. **6** inaudible, indistinct.
v **1** UNBLOCK, unclog, decongest, free, rid, extricate, disentangle, loosen. **2** CLEAN, wipe, erase, cleanse, refine, filter, tidy, empty, unload. **3** ACQUIT, exculpate, exonerate, absolve, vindicate, excuse, justify, free, liberate, release, let go.
⊟ **1** block. **2** dirty, defile. **3** condemn.

clear up 1 EXPLAIN, clarify, elucidate, unravel, solve, resolve, answer.
2 TIDY, order, sort, rearrange, remove.

clearance *n* **1** AUTHORIZATION, sanction, endorsement, permission, consent, leave, OK (*infml*), go-ahead, green light (*infml*). **2** SPACE, gap, headroom, margin, allowance.

clearing *n* space, gap, opening, glade, dell.

clergy *n* clergymen, churchmen,

clerics, the church, the cloth, ministry, priesthood.

clergyman *n* churchman, cleric, ecclesiastic, divine, man of God, minister, priest, reverend, father, vicar, pastor, padre, parson, rector, canon, dean, deacon, chaplain, curate, presbyter, rabbi.

clerical *adj* **1** OFFICE, secretarial, white-collar, official, administrative. **2** ECCLESIASTIC(AL), pastoral, ministerial, priestly, episcopal, canonical, sacerdotal.

clever *adj* intelligent, brainy (*infml*), bright, smart, witty, gifted, expert, knowledgeable, adroit, apt, able, capable, quick, quick-witted, sharp, keen, shrewd, knowing, discerning, cunning, ingenious, inventive, resourceful, sensible, rational.
⊟ foolish, stupid, senseless, ignorant.

cliché *n* platitude, commonplace, banality, truism, bromide, chestnut, stereotype.

client *n* customer, patron, regular, buyer, shopper, consumer, user, patient, applicant.

cliff *n* bluff, face, rock-face, scar, scarp, escarpment, crag, overhang, precipice.

climate *n* weather, temperature, setting, milieu, environment, ambience, atmosphere, feeling, mood, temper, disposition, tendency, trend.

climax *n* culmination, height, high point, highlight, acme, zenith, peak, summit, top, head.
⊟ nadir.

climb *v* ascend, scale, shin up, clamber, mount, rise, soar, top.
climb down retract, eat one's words, back down, retreat.

cling *v* clasp, clutch, grasp, grip, stick, adhere, cleave, fasten, embrace, hug.

clip[1] *v* trim, snip, cut, prune, pare, shear, crop, dock, poll, truncate, curtail, shorten, abbreviate.

clip² *v* pin, staple, fasten, attach, fix, hold.

clipping *n* cutting, snippet, quotation, citation, passage, section, excerpt, extract, clip.

clique *n* circle, set, coterie, group, bunch, pack, gang, crowd, faction, clan.

cloak *n* cape, mantle, robe, wrap, coat, cover, shield, mask, front, pretext.
v cover, veil, mask, screen, hide, conceal, obscure, disguise, camouflage.

clocks and watches

Types of clock or watch include: alarm-clock, digital clock, mantel clock, bracket clock, carriage clock, cuckoo-clock, longcase clock, grandfather clock, grandmother clock, speaking clock, Tim (*infml*); wrist-watch, fob-watch, repeating watch, chronograph, pendant watch, ring-watch, stop-watch; chronometer, sundial.

clog *v* block, choke, stop up, bung up, dam, congest, jam, obstruct, impede, hinder, hamper, burden.
E3 unblock.

close¹ *v* **1** SHUT, fasten, secure, lock, bar, obstruct, block, clog, plug, cork, stop up, fill, seal, fuse, join, unite. **2** END, finish, complete, conclude, terminate, wind up, stop, cease.
E3 1 open, separate. **2** start.
n end, finish, completion, conclusion, culmination, ending, finale, dénouement, termination, cessation, stop, pause.

close² *adj* **1** NEAR, nearby, at hand, neighbouring, adjacent, adjoining, impending, imminent. **2** INTIMATE, dear, familiar, attached, devoted, loving. **3** OPPRESSIVE, heavy, muggy, humid, sultry, sweltering, airless, stifling, suffocating, stuffy,

unventilated. **4** MISERLY, mean, parsimonious, tight (*infml*), stingy, niggardly. **5** SECRETIVE, uncommunicative, taciturn, private, secret, confidential. **6** *a close translation*: exact, precise, accurate, strict, literal, faithful. **7** *pay close attention*: fixed, concentrated, intense, keen. **8** DENSE, solid, packed, cramped.
E3 1 far, distant. **2** cool, unfriendly. **3** fresh, airy. **4** generous. **5** open. **6** rough.

clot *n* lump, mass, thrombus, thrombosis, clotting, coagulation.
v coalesce, curdle, coagulate, congeal, thicken, solidify, set, gel.

cloth *n* **1** FABRIC, material, stuff, textile. **2** RAG, face-cloth, flannel, dish-cloth, floorcloth, duster, towel.

clothe *v* dress, put on, robe, attire, deck, outfit, rig, vest, invest, drape, cover.
E3 undress, strip, disrobe.

clothes *n* clothing, garments, wear, attire, garb, gear (*infml*), togs (*infml*), outfit, get-up (*infml*), dress, costume, wardrobe.

Clothes include: suit, trouser suit, dress suit, catsuit, jumpsuit, tracksuit, shell suit, wet suit; dress, frock, evening-dress, shirtwaister, caftan, kimono, sari; skirt, mini skirt, dirndl, pencil-skirt, pinafore-skirt, divided-skirt, culottes, kilt, sarong; cardigan, jumper, jersey, sweater, polo-neck, turtle-neck, guernsey, pullover, twin-set, shirt, dress-shirt, sweat-shirt, tee-shirt, T-shirt, waistcoat, blouse, smock, tabard, tunic; trousers, jeans, Levis®, denims, slacks, cords, flannels, drainpipes, bell-bottoms, dungarees, leggings, pedal-pushers, breeches, plus-fours, jodhpurs, Bermuda shorts, hot pants, shorts; bra, brassière, body stocking, camisole, liberty bodice, corset, girdle, garter, suspender belt, suspenders, shift, slip, petticoat, teddy, basque, briefs, pants, panties, French knickers, camiknickers, pantihose, tights, stockings, underpants, boxer-shorts, Y-fronts, vest, string vest, singlet; swimsuit, bathing-costume, bikini, swimming costume, swimming trunks, leotard, salopette; nightdress, nightie (*infml*), pyjamas, bed-jacket, bedsocks, dressing-gown, housecoat, negligee; scarf, glove, mitten, muffler, earmuffs, leg-warmers, sock, tie, bow-tie, cravat, stole, shawl, belt, braces, cummerbund, veil, yashmak. *see also* **coat**; **footwear**; **hat**.

cloud *n* vapour, haze, mist, fog, gloom, darkness, obscurity.
  v mist, fog, blur, dull, dim, darken, shade, shadow, overshadow, eclipse, veil, shroud, obscure, muddle, confuse, obfuscate.
  ▣ clear.

Types of cloud include: cirrus, cirrostratus, cirrocumulus, altocumulus, altostratus, cumulus, stratocumulus, nimbostratus, fractostratus, fractocumulus, cumulonimbus, stratus.

cloudy *adj* nebulous, hazy, misty, foggy, blurred, blurry, opaque, milky, muddy, dim, indistinct, obscure, dark, murky, sombre, leaden, lowering, overcast, dull, sunless.
  ▣ clear, bright, sunny, cloudless.
clown *n* buffoon, comic, comedian, joker, jester, fool, harlequin, pierrot.
club *n* **1** ASSOCIATION, society, company, league, guild, order, union, fraternity, group, set, circle, clique.
  2 BAT, stick, mace, bludgeon, truncheon, cosh (*sl*), cudgel.
  v hit, strike, beat, bash, clout, clobber (*sl*), bludgeon, cosh (*sl*), batter,

pummel.
clue *n* hint, tip, suggestion, idea, notion, lead, tip-off, pointer, sign, indication, evidence, trace, suspicion, inkling, intimation.
clump *n* cluster, bundle, bunch, mass, tuft, thicket.
  v tramp, clomp, stamp, stomp, plod, lumber, thump, thud.
clumsy *adj* bungling, ham-fisted, unhandy, unskilful, inept, bumbling, blundering, lumbering, gauche, ungainly, gawky (*infml*), unco-ordinated, awkward, ungraceful, uncouth, rough, crude, ill-made, shapeless, unwieldy, heavy, bulky, cumbersome.
  ▣ careful, graceful, elegant.
cluster *n* bunch, clump, batch, group, knot, mass, crowd, gathering, collection, assembly.
  v bunch, group, gather, collect, assemble, flock.
clutch *v* hold, clasp, grip, hang on to, grasp, seize, snatch, grab, catch, grapple, embrace.
clutter *n* litter, mess, jumble, untidiness, disorder, disarray, muddle, confusion.
  v litter, encumber, fill, cover, strew, scatter.
coach *n* trainer, instructor, tutor, teacher.
  v train, drill, instruct, teach, tutor, cram, prepare.
coagulate *v* clot, curdle, congeal, thicken, solidify, gel.
  ▣ melt.
coalition *n* merger, amalgamation, combination, integration, fusion, alliance, league, bloc, compact, federation, confederation, confederacy, association, affiliation, union.
coarse *adj* **1** ROUGH, unpolished, unfinished, uneven, lumpy, unpurified, unrefined, unprocessed.
  2 *coarse humour*: bawdy, ribald, earthy, smutty, vulgar, crude,

offensive, foul-mouthed, boorish, loutish, rude, impolite, indelicate, improper, indecent, immodest.

Ⅲ 1 smooth, fine. **2** refined, sophisticated, polite.

coast *n* coastline, seaboard, shore, beach, seaside.
v free-wheel, glide, slide, sail, cruise, drift.

coat *n* **1** FUR, hair, fleece, pelt, hide, skin. **2** LAYER, coating, covering.

> *Types of coat include:* overcoat, greatcoat, car-coat, duffel coat, Afghan, blanket, frock-coat, tail-coat, jacket, bomber jacket, dinner-jacket, donkey-jacket, hacking-jacket, reefer, pea-jacket, shooting-jacket, safari jacket, Eton jacket, matinee jacket, tuxedo, blazer, raincoat, trench-coat, mackintosh, mac (*infml*), Burberry, parka, anorak, cagoul, windcheater, jerkin, blouson, cape, cloak, poncho.

v cover, paint, spread, smear, plaster.

coating *n* covering, layer, dusting, wash, coat, blanket, sheet, membrane, film, glaze, varnish, finish, veneer, lamination, overlay.

coax *v* persuade, cajole, wheedle, sweet-talk (*infml*), soft-soap, flatter, beguile, allure, entice, tempt.

cocky *adj* arrogant, bumptious, self-important, conceited, vain, swollen-headed, egotistical, swaggering, brash, cocksure, self-assured, self-confident, overconfident.
Ⅲ humble, modest, shy.

code *n* **1** ETHICS, rules, regulations, principles, system, custom, convention, etiquette, manners. **2** *written in code:* cipher, secret language.

coerce *v* force, drive, compel, constrain, pressurize, bully, intimidate, browbeat, bludgeon, bulldoze, dragoon, press-gang.

coercion *n* force, duress, compulsion, constraint, pressure,

bullying, intimidation, threats, browbeating.

coffer *n* casket, case, box, chest, trunk, strongbox, treasury, repository.

cognition *n* perception, awareness, knowledge, apprehension, discernment, insight, comprehension, understanding, intelligence, reasoning.

cohere *v* **1** STICK, adhere, cling, fuse, unite, bind, combine, coalesce, consolidate. **2** *the argument does not cohere:* agree, square, correspond, harmonize, hold, hang together.
Ⅲ 1 separate.

coherent *adj* articulate, intelligible, comprehensible, meaningful, lucid, consistent, logical, reasoned, rational, sensible, orderly, systematic, organized.
Ⅲ incoherent, unintelligible, meaningless.

coil *v* wind, spiral, convolute, curl, loop, twist, writhe, snake, wreathe, twine, entwine.
n roll, curl, loop, ring, convolution, spiral, corkscrew, helix, twist.

coin *v* invent, make up, think up, conceive, devise, formulate, originate, create, fabricate, produce, mint, forge.
n piece, bit, money, cash, change, small change, loose change, silver, copper.

coincide *v* coexist, synchronize, agree, concur, correspond, square, tally, accord, harmonize, match.

coincidence *n* **1** CHANCE, accident, eventuality, fluke (*infml*), luck, fortuity. **2** COEXISTENCE, conjunction, concurrence, correspondence, correlation.

coincidental *adj* **1** CHANCE, accidental, casual, unintentional, unplanned, flukey (*infml*), lucky, fortuitous. **2** COINCIDENT, coexistent, concurrent, simultaneous, synchronous.

1 deliberate, planned.

cold adj **1** UNHEATED, cool, chilled, chilly, chill, shivery, nippy, parky (infml), raw, biting, bitter, wintry, frosty, icy, glacial, freezing, frozen, arctic, polar. **2** UNSYMPATHETIC, unmoved, unfeeling, stony, frigid, unfriendly, distant, aloof, standoffish, reserved, undemonstrative, unresponsive, indifferent, lukewarm.

1 hot, warm. **2** friendly, responsive.

n coldness, chill, chilliness, coolness, frigidity, iciness.

warmth.

cold-blooded adj cruel, inhuman, brutal, savage, barbaric, barbarous, merciless, pitiless, callous, unfeeling, heartless.

compassionate, merciful.

collaborate v conspire, collude, work together, co-operate, join forces, team up, participate.

collaboration n conspiring, collusion, association, alliance, partnership, teamwork, co-operation.

collaborator n co-worker, associate, partner, team-mate, colleague, assistant, accomplice, traitor, turncoat.

collapse v **1** collapse with exhaustion: faint, pass out, crumple. **2** FALL, sink, founder, fail, fold (infml), fall apart, disintegrate, crumble, subside, cave in.

n failure, breakdown, flop, debacle, downfall, ruin, disintegration, subsidence, cave-in, faint, exhaustion.

colleague n workmate, co-worker, team-mate, partner, collaborator, ally, associate, confederate, confrère, comrade, companion, aide, helper, assistant, auxiliary.

collect v gather, assemble, congregate, convene, muster, rally, converge, cluster, aggregate, accumulate, amass, heap, hoard, stockpile, save, acquire, obtain, secure.

disperse, scatter.

collected adj composed, self-possessed, placid, serene, calm, unruffled, unperturbed, imperturbable, cool.

anxious, worried, agitated.

collection n **1** GATHERING, assembly, convocation, congregation, crowd, group, cluster, accumulation, conglomeration, mass, heap, pile, hoard, stockpile, store. **2** SET, assemblage, assortment, job-lot, anthology, compilation.

collective adj united, combined, concerted, co-operative, joint, common, shared, corporate, democratic, composite, aggregate, cumulative.

individual.

collective nouns

Collective nouns (by animal) include: shrewdness of *apes*, cete of *badgers*, sloth of *bears*, swarm of *bees*, obstinacy of *buffaloes*, clowder of *cats*, drove of *cattle*, brood of *chickens*, bask of *crocodiles*, murder of *crows*, herd of *deer*, pack of *dogs*, school of *dolphins*, dole of *doves*, team of *ducks*, parade of *elephants*, busyness of *ferrets*, charm of *finches*, shoal of *fish*, skulk of *foxes*, army of *frogs*, gaggle/skein of *geese*, tribe of *goats*, husk of *hares*, cast of *hawks*, brood of *hens*, bloat of *hippopotamuses*, string of *horses*, pack of *hounds*, troop of *kangaroos*, kindle of *kittens*, exaltation of *larks*, leap of *leopards*, pride of *lions*, swarm of *locusts*, tittering of *magpies*, troop of *monkeys*, watch of *nightingales*, family of *otters*, parliament of *owls*, pandemonium of *parrots*, covey of *partridges*, muster of *peacocks*, rookery of *penguins*, nye of *pheasants*, litter of *pigs*, school of *porpoises*, bury of *rabbits*, colony of *rats*, unkindness of *ravens*, crash of *rhinoceroses*, building of *rooks*, pod *of seals*, flock *of sheep*, murmuration *of starlings*, ambush *of tigers*, rafter *of turkeys*, turn *of turtles*, descent *of woodpeckers*, gam *of whales*, rout *of wolves*, zeal *of zebras*.

collectors and enthusiasts

Names of collectors and enthusiasts include: zoophile (*animals*), antiquary (*antiques*), tegestollogist (*beer mats*), campanologist (*bell-ringing*), ornithologist (*birds*), bibliophile (*books*), audiophile (*broadcast and recorded sound*), lepidopterist (*butterflies*), cartophilist (*cigarette cards*), numismatist (*coins/medals*), conservationist (*countryside*), environmentalist (*the environment*), xenophile (*foreigners*), gourmet (*good food*), gastronome (*good-living*), discophile (*gramophone records*), chirographist (*hand-writing*), hippophile (*horses*), entomologist (*insects*), phillumenist (*matches/matchboxes*), monarchist (*the monarchy*), deltiologist (*postcards*), arachnologist (*spiders/arachnids*), philatelist (*stamps*), arctophile (*teddy bears*), etymologist (*words*).

collide *v* crash, bump, smash, clash, conflict, confront, meet.

collision *n* impact, crash, bump, smash, accident, pile-up, clash, conflict, confrontation, opposition.

colloquial *adj* conversational, informal, familiar, everyday, vernacular, idiomatic.
🔁 formal.

collude *v* conspire, plot, connive, collaborate, scheme, machinate, intrigue.

colonist *n* colonial, settler, immigrant, emigrant, pioneer.

colonize *v* settle, occupy, people, populate.

colony *n* settlement, outpost,

dependency, dominion, possession, territory, province.

colossal *adj* huge, enormous, immense, vast, massive, gigantic, mammoth, monstrous, monumental.
🔁 tiny, minute.

colour *n* 1 HUE, shade, tinge, tone, tincture, tint, dye, paint, wash, pigment, pigmentation, coloration, complexion. 2 VIVIDNESS, brilliance, rosiness, ruddiness, glow, liveliness, animation.

The range of colours includes: red, crimson, scarlet, vermilion, cherry, cerise, magenta, maroon, burgundy, ruby, orange, tangerine, apricot, coral, salmon, peach, amber, brown, chestnut, mahogany, bronze, auburn, rust, copper, cinnamon, chocolate, tan, sepia, taupe, beige, fawn, yellow, lemon, canary, ochre, saffron, topaz, gold, chartreuse, green, eau de nil, emerald, jade, bottle, avocado, sage, khaki, turquoise, aquamarine, cobalt, blue, sapphire, gentian, indigo, navy, violet, purple, mauve, plum, lavender, lilac, pink, rose, magnolia, cream, ecru, milky, white, grey, silver, charcoal, ebony, jet, black.

v 1 PAINT, crayon, dye, tint, stain, tinge. 2 BLUSH, flush, redden. 3 *colour one's judgement*: affect, bias, prejudice, distort, pervert, exaggerate, falsify.

colourful *adj* 1 MULTICOLOURED, kaleidoscopic, variegated, parti-coloured, vivid, bright, brilliant, rich, intense. 2 *a colourful description*: vivid, graphic, picturesque, lively, stimulating, exciting, interesting.
🔁 1 colourless, drab.

colourless *adj* 1 TRANSPARENT, neutral, bleached, washed out, faded, pale, ashen, sickly, anaemic.
2 INSIPID, lacklustre, dull, dreary, drab, plain, characterless, unmemorable, uninteresting, tame.

⊞ **1** colourful. **2** bright, exciting.

column n **1** PILLAR, post, shaft, upright, support, obelisk. **2** LIST, line, row, rank, file, procession, queue, string.

comb v **1** *comb one's hair*: groom, neaten, tidy, untangle. **2** SEARCH, hunt, scour, sweep, sift, screen, rake, rummage, ransack.

combat n war, warfare, hostilities, action, battle, fight, skirmish, struggle, conflict, clash, encounter, engagement, contest, bout, duel. v fight, battle, strive, struggle, contend, contest, oppose, resist, withstand, defy.

combination n **1** BLEND, mix, mixture, composite, amalgam, synthesis, compound. **2** MERGER, amalgamation, unification, alliance, coalition, association, federation, confederation, confederacy, combine, consortium, syndicate, union, integration, fusion, coalescence, connection.

combine v merge, amalgamate, unify, blend, mix, integrate, incorporate, synthesize, compound, fuse, bond, bind, join, connect, link, marry, unite, pool, associate, co-operate.

⊞ divide, separate, detach.

come v advance, move towards, approach, near, draw near, reach, attain, arrive, enter, appear, materialize, happen, occur.

⊞ go, depart, leave.

come about happen, occur, come to pass, transpire, result, arise.

come across find, discover, chance upon, happen upon, bump into, meet, encounter, notice.

come along arrive, happen, develop, improve, progress, rally, mend, recover, recuperate.

come apart disintegrate, fall to bits, break, separate, split, tear.

come between separate, part, divide, split up, disunite, estrange, alienate.

come down descend, fall, reduce, decline, deteriorate, worsen, degenerate.

come in enter, appear, show up (*infml*), arrive, finish.

come off happen, occur, take place, succeed.

come on begin, appear, advance, proceed, progress, develop, improve, thrive, succeed.

come out result, end, conclude, terminate.

come out with say, state, affirm, declare, exclaim, disclose, divulge.

come round 1 *come round from the anaesthetic*: recover, wake, awake. **2** YIELD, relent, concede, allow, grant, accede.

come through endure, withstand, survive, prevail, triumph, succeed, accomplish, achieve.

come up rise, arise, happen, occur, crop up.

comeback n return, reappearance, resurgence, revival, recovery.

comedian n comic, clown, humorist, wit, joker, wag.

comedown n anticlimax, let-down, disappointment, deflation, blow, reverse, decline, descent, demotion, humiliation, degradation.

comedy n farce, slapstick, clowning, hilarity, drollery, humour, wit, joking, jesting, facetiousness.

comfort v ease, soothe, relieve, alleviate, assuage, console, cheer, gladden, reassure, hearten, encourage, invigorate, strengthen, enliven, refresh.

n **1** CONSOLATION, compensation, cheer, reassurance, encouragement, alleviation, relief, help, aid, support. **2** EASE, relaxation, luxury, snugness, cosiness, wellbeing, satisfaction, contentment, enjoyment.

⊞ **1** distress. **2** discomfort.

comfortable adj **1** SNUG, cosy, comfy (*infml*), relaxing, restful, easy, convenient, pleasant, agreeable, enjoyable, delightful. **2** AT EASE, relaxed, contented, happy. **3** AFFLUENT, well-off, well-to-do, prosperous.

≢ 1 uncomfortable, unpleasant. **2** uneasy, nervous. **3** poor.

comic *adj* funny, hilarious, side-splitting, comical, droll, humorous, witty, amusing, entertaining, diverting, joking, facetious, light, farcical, ridiculous, ludicrous, absurd, laughable, priceless (*infml*), rich (*infml*).

≢ tragic, serious.

n comedian, gagster (*infml*), joker, jester, clown, buffoon, humorist, wit, wag.

coming *adj* next, forthcoming, impending, imminent, due, approaching, near, future, aspiring, rising, up-and-coming.

n advent, approach, arrival, accession.

command *v* **1** ORDER, bid, charge, enjoin, direct, instruct, require, demand, compel. **2** LEAD, head, rule, reign, govern, control, dominate, manage, supervise.

n **1** COMMANDMENT, decree, edict, precept, mandate, order, bidding, charge, injunction, directive, direction, instruction, requirement. **2** *be in command*: power, authority, leadership, control, domination, dominion, rule, sway, government, management.

commander *n* leader, head, chief, boss, commander-in-chief, general, admiral, captain, commanding officer, officer.

commemorate *v* celebrate, solemnize, remember, memorialize, mark, honour, salute, immortalize, observe, keep.

commemoration *n* celebration, observance, remembrance, tribute, honouring, ceremony.

commence *v* begin, start, embark on, originate, initiate, inaugurate,

open, launch.

≢ finish, end, cease.

commend *v* **1** PRAISE, compliment, acclaim, extol, applaud, approve, recommend. **2** COMMIT, entrust, confide, consign, deliver, yield.

≢ 1 criticize, censure.

comment *v* say, mention, interpose, interject, remark, observe, note, annotate, interpret, explain, elucidate, criticize.

n statement, remark, observation, note, annotation, footnote, marginal note, explanation, elucidation, illustration, exposition, commentary, criticism.

commentary *n* narration, voice-over, analysis, description, review, critique, explanation, notes, treatise.

commentator *n* sportscaster, broadcaster, reporter, narrator, commenter, critic, annotator, interpreter.

commerce *n* trade, traffic, business, dealings, relations, dealing, trafficking, exchange, marketing, merchandising.

commercial *adj* trade, trading, business, sales, profit-making, profitable, sellable, saleable, popular, monetary, financial, mercenary, venal.

commission *n* **1** ASSIGNMENT, mission, errand, task, job, duty, function, appointment, employment, mandate, warrant, authority, charge, trust. **2** COMMITTEE, board, delegation, deputation, representative. **3** *commission on a sale*: percentage, cut (*infml*), rake-off (*infml*), allowance, fee.

v nominate, select, appoint, engage, employ, authorize, empower, delegate, depute, send, order, request, ask for.

commit *v* **1** *commit a crime*: do, perform, execute, enact, perpetrate. **2** ENTRUST, confide, commend, consign, deliver, hand over, give, deposit. **3** BIND, obligate, pledge, engage, involve.

commit oneself decide, undertake, promise, pledge, bind oneself.

commitment n undertaking, guarantee, assurance, promise, word, pledge, vow, engagement, involvement, dedication, devotion, adherence, loyalty, tie, obligation, duty, responsibility, liability.
F∃ vacillation, wavering.

committee n council, board, panel, jury, commission, advisory group, think-tank, working party, task force.

common adj **1** FAMILIAR, customary, habitual, usual, daily, everyday, routine, regular, frequent, widespread, prevalent, general, universal, standard, average, ordinary, plain, simple, workaday, run-of-the-mill, undistinguished, unexceptional, conventional, accepted, popular, commonplace. **2** VULGAR, coarse, unrefined, crude, inferior, low, ill-bred, loutish, plebeian. **3** COMMUNAL, public, shared, mutual, joint, collective.
F∃ 1 uncommon, unusual, rare, noteworthy. **2** tasteful, refined.

commonplace adj ordinary, everyday, common, humdrum, pedestrian, banal, trite, widespread, frequent, hackneyed, stock, stale, obvious, worn out, boring, uninteresting, threadbare.
F∃ memorable, exceptional.

commonsense adj commonsensical, matter-of-fact, sensible, level-headed, sane, sound, reasonable, practical, down-to-earth, pragmatic, hard-headed, realistic, shrewd, astute, prudent, judicious.
F∃ foolish, unreasonable, unrealistic.

commotion n agitation, hurly-burly, turmoil, tumult, excitement, ferment, fuss, bustle, ado, to-do (infml), uproar, furore, ballyhoo (infml), hullabaloo (infml), racket, hubbub, rumpus, fracas, disturbance, bust-up

(infml), disorder, riot.

communal adj public, community, shared, joint, collective, general, common.
F∃ private, personal.

commune n collective, co-operative, kibbutz, community, fellowship, colony, settlement.
v converse, discourse, communicate, make contact.

communicate v **1** ANNOUNCE, declare, proclaim, report, reveal, disclose, divulge, impart, inform, acquaint, intimate, notify, publish, disseminate, spread, diffuse, transmit, convey. **2** TALK, converse, commune, correspond, write, phone, telephone, contact.

communication n information, intelligence, intimation, disclosure, contact, connection, transmission, dissemination.

> *Forms of communication include:*
> broadcasting, radio, wireless,
> television, TV, cable TV, satellite, video,
> teletext; newspaper, press, news,
> newsflash, magazine, journal,
> advertising, publicity, poster, leaflet,
> pamphlet, brochure, catalogue; post,
> dispatch, correspondence, letter,
> postcard, aerogram, telegram, cable,
> wire (infml), chain letter, junk mail,
> mailshot; conversation, word,
> message, dialogue, speech, gossip,
> grapevine (infml); notice, bulletin,
> announcement, communiqué, circular,
> memo, note, report; telephone,
> intercom, answering machine, walkie-
> talkie, bleeper, tannoy, telex,
> teleprinter, facsimile, fax, computer,
> word processor, typewriter,
> dictaphone, megaphone, loud-hailer;
> radar, Morse code, semaphore,
> Braille, sign language.

communicative adj talkative, voluble, expansive, informative, chatty, sociable, friendly,

forthcoming, outgoing, extrovert,
unreserved, free, open, frank, candid.
F3 quiet, reserved, reticent, secretive.

community n district, locality,
population, people, populace, public,
residents, nation, state, colony,
commune, kibbutz, society,
association, fellowship, brotherhood,
fraternity.

commute v **1** REDUCE, decrease,
shorten, curtail, lighten, soften,
mitigate, remit, adjust, modify, alter,
change, exchange, alternate.
2 *commute by train*: travel, journey.

compact adj small, short, brief,
terse, succinct, concise, condensed,
compressed, close, dense,
impenetrable, solid, firm.
F3 large, rambling, diffuse.

companion n fellow, comrade,
friend, buddy (*infml*), crony (*infml*),
intimate, confidant(e), ally,
confederate, colleague, associate,
partner, mate, consort, escort,
chaperon, attendant, aide, assistant,
accomplice, follower.

companionship n fellowship,
comradeship, camaraderie, esprit de
corps, support, friendship, company,
togetherness, conviviality, sympathy,
rapport.

company n **1** *a manufacturing
company*: firm, business, concern,
association, corporation,
establishment, house, partnership,
syndicate, cartel, consortium.
2 TROUPE, group, band, ensemble,
set, circle, crowd, throng, body,
troop, crew, party, assembly,
gathering, community, society.
3 GUESTS, visitors, callers, society,
companionship, fellowship, support,
attendance, presence.

comparable adj similar, alike,
related, akin, cognate,
corresponding, analogous,
equivalent, tantamount,
proportionate, commensurate,
parallel, equal.

F3 dissimilar, unlike, unequal.

compare v liken, equate, contrast,
juxtapose, balance, weigh, correlate,
resemble, match, equal, parallel.

comparison n juxtaposition,
analogy, parallel, correlation,
relationship, likeness, resemblance,
similarity, comparability, contrast,
distinction.

compartment n section, division,
subdivision, category, pigeonhole,
cubbyhole, niche, alcove, bay, area,
stall, booth, cubicle, locker, carrel,
cell, chamber, berth, carriage.

compassion n kindness, tenderness,
fellow-feeling, humanity, mercy, pity,
sympathy, commiseration,
condolence, sorrow, concern, care.
F3 cruelty, indifference.

compassionate adj kind-hearted,
kindly, tender-hearted, tender,
caring, warm-hearted, benevolent,
humanitarian, humane, merciful,
clement, lenient, pitying,
sympathetic, understanding,
supportive.
F3 cruel, indifferent.

compatible adj harmonious,
consistent, congruous, matching,
consonant, accordant, suitable,
reconcilable, adaptable, conformable,
sympathetic, like-minded, well-
matched, similar.
F3 incompatible, antagonistic,
contradictory.

compel v force, make, constrain,
oblige, necessitate, drive, urge, impel,
coerce, pressurize, hustle, browbeat,
bully, strongarm, bulldoze, press-
gang, dragoon.

compelling adj forceful, coercive,
imperative, urgent, pressing,
irresistible, overriding, powerful,
cogent, persuasive, convincing,
conclusive, incontrovertible,
irrefutable, gripping, enthralling,
spellbinding, mesmeric, compulsive.
F3 weak, unconvincing, boring.

compensate v balance,

counterbalance, cancel, neutralize, counteract, offset, redress, satisfy, requite, repay, refund, reimburse, indemnify, recompense, reward, remunerate, atone, redeem, make good, restore.

compensation n amends, redress, satisfaction, requital, repayment, refund, reimbursement, indemnification, indemnity, damages, reparation, recompense, reward, payment, remuneration, return, restoration, restitution, consolation, comfort.

compete v vie, contest, fight, battle, struggle, strive, oppose, challenge, rival, emulate, contend, participate, take part.

competent adj capable, able, adept, efficient, trained, qualified, well-qualified, skilled, experienced, proficient, expert, masterly, equal, fit, suitable, appropriate, satisfactory, adequate, sufficient.
🖃 incompetent, incapable, unable, inefficient.

competition n 1 CONTEST, championship, tournament, cup, event, race, match, game, quiz.
2 RIVALRY, opposition, challenge, contention, conflict, struggle, strife, competitiveness, combativeness.
3 COMPETITORS, rivals, opponents, challengers, field.

competitive adj combative, contentious, antagonistic, aggressive, pushy, ambitious, keen, cut-throat.

competitor n contestant, contender, entrant, candidate, challenger, opponent, adversary, antagonist, rival, emulator, competition, opposition.

compile v compose, put together, collect, gather, garner, cull, accumulate, amass, assemble, marshal, organize, arrange.

complacent adj smug, self-satisfied, gloating, triumphant, proud, self-righteous, unconcerned, serene, self-

assured, pleased, gratified, contented, satisfied.
🖃 diffident, concerned, discontented.

complain v protest, grumble, grouse, gripe, beef, carp, fuss, lament, bemoan, bewail, moan, whine, groan, growl.

complaint n 1 PROTEST, objection, grumble, grouse, gripe, beef, moan, grievance, dissatisfaction, annoyance, fault-finding, criticism, censure, accusation, charge. 2 a chest complaint: ailment, illness, sickness, disease, malady, malaise, indisposition, affliction, disorder, trouble, upset.

complementary adj reciprocal, interdependent, correlative, interrelated, corresponding, matching, twin, fellow, companion.
🖃 contradictory, incompatible.

complete adj 1 UTTER, total, absolute, downright, out-and-out, thorough, perfect. 2 FINISHED, ended, concluded, over, done, accomplished, achieved.
3 UNABRIDGED, unabbreviated, unedited, unexpurgated, integral, whole, entire, full, undivided, intact.
🖃 1 partial. 2 incomplete. 3 abridged.
v finish, end, close, conclude, wind up, terminate, finalize, settle, clinch, perform, discharge, execute, fulfil, realize, accomplish, achieve, consummate, crown, perfect.

completion n finish, end, close, conclusion, termination, finalization, settlement, discharge, fulfilment, realization, accomplishment, achievement, attainment, fruition, culmination, consummation, perfection.

complex adj complicated, intricate, elaborate, involved, convoluted, circuitous, tortuous, devious, mixed, varied, diverse, multiple, composite, compound, ramified.
🖃 simple, easy.
n 1 NETWORK, structure, system,

scheme, organization, establishment, institute, development. **2** FIXATION, obsession, preoccupation, hang-up (*infml*), phobia.

complexion *n* **1** skin, colour, colouring, pigmentation. **2** look, appearance, aspect, light, character, nature, type, kind.

complicate *v* compound, elaborate, involve, muddle, mix up, confuse, tangle, entangle.
ᴇꜰ simplify.

complicated *adj* complex, intricate, elaborate, involved, convoluted, tortuous, difficult, problematic, puzzling, perplexing.
ᴇꜰ simple, easy.

complication *n* difficulty, drawback, snag, obstacle, problem, ramification, repercussion, complexity, intricacy, elaboration, convolution, tangle, web, confusion, mixture.

compliment *n* flattery, admiration, favour, approval, congratulations, tribute, honour, accolade, bouquet, commendation, praise, eulogy.
ᴇꜰ insult, criticism.
v flatter, admire, commend, praise, extol, congratulate, applaud, salute.
ᴇꜰ insult, condemn.

complimentary *adj* **1** FLATTERING, admiring, favourable, approving, appreciative, congratulatory, commendatory, eulogistic.
2 *complimentary ticket*: free, gratis, honorary, courtesy.
ᴇꜰ 1 insulting, unflattering, critical.

comply *v* agree, consent, assent, accede, yield, submit, defer, respect, observe, obey, fall in, conform, follow, perform, discharge, fulfil, satisfy, meet, oblige, accommodate.
ᴇꜰ defy, disobey.

component *n* part, constituent, ingredient, element, factor, item, unit, piece, bit, spare part.

compose *v* **1** CONSTITUTE, make up, form. **2** CREATE, invent, devise,

write, arrange, produce, make, form, fashion, build, construct, frame.
3 CALM, soothe, quiet, still, tranquillize, quell, pacify, control, regulate.

composed *adj* calm, tranquil, serene, relaxed, unworried, unruffled, level-headed, cool, collected, self-possessed, confident, imperturbable, unflappable, placid.
ᴇꜰ agitated, worried, troubled.

composition *n* **1** MAKING, production, formation, creation, invention, design, formulation, writing, compilation, proportion. **2** CONSTITUTION, make-up, combination, mixture, form, structure, configuration, layout, arrangement, organization, harmony, consonance, balance, symmetry. **3** *a musical composition*: work, opus, piece, study, exercise.

composure *n* calm, tranquillity, serenity, ease, coolness, self-possession, confidence, assurance, self-assurance, aplomb, poise, dignity, imperturbability, placidity, equanimity, dispassion, impassivity.
ᴇꜰ agitation, nervousness, discomposure.

compound *v* **1** COMBINE, amalgamate, unite, fuse, coalesce, synthesize, alloy, blend, mix, mingle, intermingle. **2** WORSEN, exacerbate, aggravate, complicate, intensify, heighten, magnify, increase, augment.
n alloy, blend, mixture, medley, composite, amalgam, synthesis, fusion, composition, amalgamation, combination.
adj composite, mixed, multiple, complex, complicated, intricate.

comprehend *v* **1** UNDERSTAND, conceive, see, grasp, fathom, penetrate, tumble to (*infml*), realize, appreciate, know, apprehend, perceive, discern, take in, assimilate.
2 INCLUDE, comprise, encompass,

embrace, cover.

Ⓕ 1 misunderstand.

comprehensible *adj*
understandable, intelligible, coherent,
explicit, clear, lucid, plain, simple,
straightforward.

Ⓕ incomprehensible, obscure.

comprehension *n* understanding,
conception, grasp, realization,
appreciation, knowledge,
apprehension, perception,
discernment, judgement, sense,
intelligence.

Ⓕ incomprehension, unawareness.

comprehensive *adj* thorough,
exhaustive, full, complete,
encyclopedic, compendious, broad,
wide, extensive, sweeping, general,
blanket, inclusive, all-inclusive, all-
embracing, across-the-board.

Ⓕ partial, incomplete, selective.

compress *v* press, squeeze, crush,
squash, flatten, jam, wedge, cram,
stuff, compact, concentrate,
condense, contract, telescope,
shorten, abbreviate, summarize.

Ⓕ expand, diffuse.

comprise *v* consist of, include,
contain, incorporate, embody,
involve, encompass, embrace, cover.

compromise *v* **1** NEGOTIATE,
bargain, arbitrate, settle, agree,
concede, make concessions, meet
halfway, adapt, adjust. **2** *compromise
one's principles*: weaken, undermine,
expose, endanger, imperil,
jeopardize, risk, prejudice.

3 DISHONOUR, discredit, embarrass,
involve, implicate.

n bargain, trade-off, settlement,
agreement, concession, give and take,
co-operation, accommodation,
adjustment.

Ⓕ disagreement, intransigence.

compulsive *adj* **1** IRRESISTIBLE,
overwhelming, overpowering,
uncontrollable, compelling, driving,
urgent. **2** *a compulsive gambler*:
obsessive, hardened, incorrigible,

irredeemable, incurable, hopeless.

compulsory *adj* obligatory,
mandatory, imperative, forced,
required, requisite, set, stipulated,
binding, contractual.

Ⓕ optional, voluntary, discretionary.

computer *n* personal computer, PC,
mainframe, processor, word-
processor, data processor, calculator,
adding machine.

Computing terms include:
mainframe, microcomputer,
minicomputer, PC (personal
computer), Applemac®; hardware,
CPU (central processing unit), disk
drive, joystick, keyboard, lap-top,
light pen, microprocessor, modem,
monitor, mouse, mouse mat,
notebook computer, printer,
bubblejet printer, daisywheel printer,
dot-matrix printer, ink-jet printer,
laser printer, screen, VDU (visual
display unit); software, program,
Windows®, WordPerfect®,
Wordstar®; disk, magnetic disk,
floppy disk, hard disk, optical disk,
magnetic tape; programming
language, BASIC, COBOL,
FORTRAN; memory, backing
storage, external memory, immediate
access memory, internal memory,
RAM (Random Access Memory),
ROM (Read Only Memory), CD-
ROM (Compact Disc Read Only
Memory); access, ASCII, backup, bit,
boot, buffer, byte, kilobyte, megabyte,
character, chip, silicon chip, computer
game, computer graphics, computer
literate, computer simulation,
computer terminal, cursor, data,
databank, database, default, desktop
publishing (DTP), digitizer, directory,
DOS (disk operating system),
electronic mail, E-mail, format,
function, grammar checker, graphics,
hacking, interface, macro, menu,
MSDOS (Microsoft® disk operating
system), network, peripheral, pixel,

scrolling, spellchecker, spreadsheet, template, toggle, toolbar, user-friendly, user interface, video game, virtual reality, virus, window, word-processing, work station, WYSIWYG (what you see is what you get).

con (*infml*) *v* trick, hoax, dupe, deceive, mislead, inveigle, hoodwink, bamboozle (*infml*), cheat, double-cross, swindle, defraud, rip off (*sl*), rook.
n confidence trick, trick, bluff, deception, swindle, fraud.

concave *adj* hollow, hollowed, cupped, scooped, excavated, sunken, depressed.
🔁 convex.

conceal *v* hide, obscure, disguise, camouflage, mask, screen, veil, cloak, cover, bury, submerge, smother, suppress, keep dark, keep quiet, hush up (*infml*).
🔁 reveal, disclose, uncover.

concede *v* 1 ADMIT, confess, acknowledge, recognize, own, grant, allow, accept. 2 YIELD, give up, surrender, relinquish, forfeit, sacrifice.
🔁 1 deny.

conceit *n* conceitedness, vanity, boastfulness, swagger, egotism, self-love, self-importance, cockiness, self-satisfaction, complacency, pride, arrogance.
🔁 modesty, diffidence.

conceited *adj* vain, boastful, swollen-headed, bigheaded (*infml*), egotistical, self-important, cocky, self-satisfied, complacent, smug, proud, arrogant, stuck-up (*infml*), toffee-nosed (*infml*).
🔁 modest, self-effacing, diffident, humble.

conceivable *adj* imaginable, credible, believable, thinkable, tenable, possible, likely, probable.
🔁 inconceivable, unimaginable.

conceive *v* 1 IMAGINE, envisage,

visualize, see, grasp, understand, comprehend, realize, appreciate, believe, think, suppose. 2 INVENT, design, devise, formulate, create, originate, form, produce, develop.

concentrate *v* 1 FOCUS, converge, centre, cluster, crowd, congregate, gather, collect, accumulate. 2 APPLY ONESELF, think, pay attention, attend. 3 CONDENSE, evaporate, reduce, thicken, intensify.
🔁 1 disperse. 3 dilute.

concentrated *adj* 1 *concentrated liquid*: condensed, evaporated, reduced, thickened, dense, rich, strong, undiluted. 2 INTENSE, intensive, all-out, concerted, hard, deep.
🔁 1 diluted. 2 half-hearted.

concentration *n* 1 CONVERGENCE, centralization, cluster, crowd, grouping, collection, accumulation, agglomeration, conglomeration. 2 ATTENTION, heed, absorption, application, single-mindedness, intensity. 3 COMPRESSION, reduction, consolidation, denseness, thickness.
🔁 1 dispersal. 2 distraction. 3 dilution.

concept *n* idea, notion, plan, theory, hyphothesis, thought, abstraction, conception, conceptualization, visualization, image, picture, impression.

conception *n* 1 CONCEPT, idea, notion, thought. 2 KNOWLEDGE, understanding, appreciation, perception, visualization, image, picture, impression, inkling, clue. 3 INVENTION, design, birth, beginning, origin, outset, initiation, inauguration, formation. 4 *from conception to birth*: impregnation, insemination, fertilization.

concern *v* 1 UPSET, distress, trouble, disturb, bother, worry. 2 RELATE TO, refer to, regard, involve, interest, affect, touch.

n **1** *a cause for concern*: anxiety, worry, unease, disquiet, care, sorrow, distress. **2** REGARD, consideration, attention, heed, thought. **3** *it's not my concern*: duty, responsibility, charge, job, task, field, business, affair, matter, problem, interest, involvement. **4** COMPANY, firm, business, corporation, establishment, enterprise, organization.
F3 1 joy. 2 indifference.

concerned *adj* **1** ANXIOUS, worried, uneasy, apprehensive, upset, unhappy, distressed, troubled, disturbed, bothered, attentive, caring. **2** CONNECTED, related, involved, implicated, interested, affected.
F3 1 unconcerned, indifferent, apathetic.

concerning *prep* about, regarding, with regard to, as regards, respecting, with reference to, relating to, in the matter of.

concerted *adj* combined, united, joint, collective, shared, collaborative, co-ordinated, organized, prearranged, planned.
F3 separate, unco-ordinated, disorganized.

concession *n* compromise, adjustment, grant, allowance, exception, privilege, favour, indulgence, permit, admission, acknowledgement.

concise *adj* short, brief, terse, succinct, pithy, compendious, compact, compressed, condensed, abridged, abbreviated, summary, synoptic.
F3 diffuse, wordy.

conclude *v* **1** INFER, deduce, assume, surmise, suppose, reckon, judge. **2** END, close, finish, complete, consummate, cease, terminate, culminate. **3** SETTLE, resolve, decide, establish, determine, clinch.
F3 2 start, commence.

conclusion *n* **1** INFERENCE,

deduction, assumption, opinion, conviction, judgement, verdict, decision, resolution, settlement, result, consequence, outcome, upshot, answer, solution. **2** END, close, finish, completion, consummation, termination, culmination, finale.

conclusive *adj* final, ultimate, definitive, decisive, clear, convincing, definite, undeniable, irrefutable, indisputable, incontrovertible, unarguable, unanswerable, clinching.
F3 inconclusive, questionable.

concoct *v* fabricate, invent, devise, contrive, formulate, plan, plot, hatch, brew, prepare, develop.

concoction *n* brew, potion, preparation, mixture, blend, compound, creation, contrivance.

concrete *adj* real, actual, factual, solid, physical, material, substantial, tangible, touchable, perceptible, visible, firm, definite, specific, explicit.
F3 abstract, vague.

concurrent *adj* simultaneous, synchronous, contemporaneous, coinciding, coincident, concomitant, coexisting, coexistent.

condemn *v* disapprove, reprehend, reprove, upbraid, reproach, castigate, blame, disparage, revile, denounce, censure, slam (*infml*), slate (*infml*), damn, doom, convict.
F3 praise, approve.

condemnation *n* disapproval, reproof, reproach, castigation, blame, disparagement, denunciation, censure, thumbs-down (*infml*), damnation, conviction, sentence, judgement.
F3 praise, approval.

condensation *n* **1** *condensation of liquid*: distillation, liquefaction, precipitation, concentration, evaporation, reduction, consolidation. **2** ABRIDGEMENT, précis, synopsis, digest, contraction,

condense 106

compression, curtailment.
condense v 1 *condense a book*:
shorten, curtail, abbreviate, abridge,
précis, summarize, encapsulate,
contract, compress, compact.
2 DISTIL, precipitate, concentrate,
evaporate, reduce, thicken, solidify,
coagulate.
🔁 1 expand. 2 dilute.
condescend v deign, see fit, stoop,
bend, lower oneself, patronize, talk
down.
condescending adj patronizing,
disdainful, supercilious, snooty,
snobbish, haughty, lofty, superior,
lordly, imperious.
🔁 gracious, humble.
condition n 1 CASE, state,
circumstances, position, situation,
predicament, plight.
2 REQUIREMENT, obligation,
prerequisite, terms, stipulation,
proviso, qualification, limitation,
restriction, rule. 3 *a heart condition*:
disorder, defect, weakness, infirmity,
problem, complaint, disease. 4 *out of
condition*: fitness, health, state,
shape, form, fettle, nick (*sl*).
v indoctrinate, brainwash, influence,
mould, educate, train, groom, equip,
prepare, prime, accustom, season,
temper, adapt, adjust, tune.
conditional adj provisional,
qualified, limited, restricted, tied,
relative, dependent, contingent.
🔁 unconditional, absolute.
conditions n surroundings,
environment, milieu, setting,
atmosphere, background, context,
circumstances, situation, state.
condom n sheath, French letter (*sl*),
johnnie (*sl*), rubber (*sl*), protective.
condone v forgive, pardon, excuse,
overlook, ignore, disregard, tolerate,
brook, allow.
🔁 condemn, censure.
conducive adj leading, tending,
contributory, productive,
advantageous, beneficial, favourable,

helpful, encouraging.
🔁 detrimental, adverse, unfavourable.
conduct n 1 *good conduct*:
behaviour, comportment, actions,
ways, manners, bearing, attitude. 2
ADMINISTRATION, management,
direction, running, organization,
operation, control, supervision,
leadership, guidance.
v 1 ADMINISTER, manage, run,
organize, orchestrate, chair, control,
handle, regulate. 2 ACCOMPANY,
escort, usher, lead, guide, direct,
pilot, steer. 3 *conduct heat*: convey,
carry, bear, transmit. 4 *conduct
oneself*: behave, acquit, comport, act.
confer v 1 DISCUSS, debate,
deliberate, consult, talk, converse.
2 BESTOW, award, present, give,
grant, accord, impart, lend.
conference n meeting, convention,
congress, convocation, symposium,
forum, discussion, debate,
consultation.
confess v admit, confide, own (up),
come clean (*infml*), grant, concede,
acknowledge, recognize, affirm,
assert, profess, declare, disclose,
divulge, expose.
🔁 deny, conceal.
confession n admission,
acknowledgement, affirmation,
assertion, profession, declaration,
disclosure, divulgence, revelation,
unburdening.
🔁 denial, concealment.
confide v confess, admit, reveal,
disclose, divulge, whisper, breathe,
tell, impart, unburden.
🔁 hide, suppress.
confidence n certainty, faith,
credence, trust, reliance, dependence,
assurance, composure, calmness, self-
possession, self-confidence, self-
reliance, self-assurance, boldness,
courage.
🔁 distrust, diffidence.
confident adj sure, certain, positive,
convinced, assured, composed, self-

possessed, cool, self-confident, self-reliant, self-assured, unselfconscious, bold, fearless, dauntless, unabashed.

⊟ doubtful, diffident.

confidential *adj* secret, top secret, classified, restricted, hush-hush (*infml*), off-the-record, private, personal, intimate, privy.

confine *v* enclose, circumscribe, bound, limit, restrict, cramp, constrain, imprison, incarcerate, intern, cage, shut up, immure, bind, shackle, trammel, restrain, repress, inhibit.

⊟ free.

confinement *n* **1** IMPRISONMENT, incarceration, internment, custody, detention, house arrest.
2 CHILDBIRTH, birth, labour, delivery.

⊟ 1 freedom, liberty.

confines *n* limits, bounds, border, boundary, frontier, circumference, perimeter, edge.

confirm *v* **1** ENDORSE, back, support, reinforce, strengthen, fortify, validate, authenticate, corroborate, substantiate, verify, prove, evidence. **2** ESTABLISH, fix, settle, clinch, ratify, sanction, approve.

⊟ 1 refute, deny.

confirmation *n* ratification, sanction, approval, assent, acceptance, agreement, endorsement, backing, support, validation, authentication, corroboration, substantiation, verification, proof, evidence, testimony.

⊟ denial.

confirmed *adj* inveterate, entrenched, dyed-in-the-wool, rooted, established, long-established, long-standing, habitual, chronic, seasoned, hardened, incorrigible, incurable.

confiscate *v* seize, appropriate, expropriate, remove, take away, impound, sequester, commandeer.

⊟ return, restore.

conflict *n* **1** DIFFERENCE, variance, discord, contention, disagreement, dissension, dispute, opposition, antagonism, hostility, friction, strife, unrest, confrontation. **2** BATTLE, war, warfare, combat, fight, contest, engagement, skirmish, set-to, fracas, brawl, quarrel, feud, encounter, clash.

⊟ 1 agreement, harmony, concord.
v differ, clash, collide, disagree, contradict, oppose, contest, fight, combat, battle, war, strive, struggle, contend.

⊟ agree, harmonize.

conform *v* agree, accord, harmonize, match, correspond, tally, square, adapt, adjust, accommodate, comply, obey, follow.

⊟ differ, conflict, rebel.

conformity *n* conventionality, orthodoxy, traditionalism, compliance, observance, allegiance, affinity, agreement, consonance, harmony, correspondence, congruity, likeness, similarity, resemblance.

⊟ nonconformity, rebellion, difference.

confound *v* **1** CONFUSE, bewilder, baffle, perplex, mystify, bamboozle (*infml*), nonplus, surprise, amaze, astonish, astound, flabbergast (*infml*), dumbfound, stupefy.
2 *confound their plans*: thwart, upset, defeat, overwhelm, overthrow, destroy, demolish, ruin.

confront *v* face, meet, encounter, accost, address, oppose, challenge, defy, brave, beard.

⊟ evade.

confrontation *n* encounter, clash, collision, showdown, conflict, disagreement, fight, battle, quarrel, set-to, engagement, contest.

confuse *v* **1** PUZZLE, baffle, perplex, mystify, confound, bewilder, disorient, disconcert, fluster, discompose, upset, embarrass, mortify. **2** MUDDLE, mix up, mistake, jumble, disarrange, disorder, tangle, entangle, involve, mingle.

≢ 1 enlighten, clarify.

confused adj **1** MUDDLED, jumbled, disarranged, disordered, untidy, disorderly, higgledy-piggledy (infml), chaotic, disorganized. **2** PUZZLED, baffled, perplexed, flummoxed (infml), nonplussed, bewildered, disorientated.

≢ 1 orderly.

confusion n **1** DISORDER, disarray, untidiness, mess, clutter, jumble, muddle, mix-up, disorganization, chaos, turmoil, commotion, upheaval. **2** MISUNDERSTANDING, puzzlement, perplexity, mystification, bewilderment.

≢ 1 order. **2** clarity.

congeal v clot, curdle, coalesce, coagulate, thicken, stiffen, harden, solidify, set, gel, freeze.

≢ dissolve, melt.

congested adj clogged, blocked, jammed, packed, stuffed, crammed, full, crowded, overcrowded, overflowing, teeming.

≢ clear.

congestion n clogging, blockage, overcrowding, jam, traffic jam, snarl-up, gridlock, bottle-neck.

conglomeration n mass, agglomeration, aggregation, accumulation, collection, assemblage, composite, medley, hotchpotch.

congratulate v praise, felicitate, compliment, wish well.

≢ commiserate.

congregate v gather, assemble, collect, muster, rally, rendezvous, meet, convene, converge, flock, crowd, throng, mass, accumulate, cluster, clump, conglomerate.

≢ disperse.

congregation n assembly, crowd, throng, multitude, host, flock, parishioners, parish, laity, fellowship.

conical adj cone-shaped, pyramidal, tapering, tapered, pointed.

conjecture v speculate, theorize, hypothesize, guess, estimate, reckon, suppose, surmise, assume, infer, imagine, suspect.
n speculation, theory, hypothesis, notion, guesswork, guess, estimate, supposition, surmise, assumption, presumption, conclusion, inference, extrapolation, projection.

conjure v summon, invoke, rouse, raise, bewitch, charm, fascinate, compel.

conjure up evoke, create, produce, excite, awaken, recollect, recall.

connect v join, link, unite, couple, combine, fasten, affix, attach, relate, associate, ally.

≢ disconnect, cut off, detach.

connected adj joined, linked, united, coupled, combined, related, akin, associated, affiliated, allied.

≢ disconnected, unconnected.

connection n junction, coupling, fastening, attachment, bond, tie, link, association, alliance, relation, relationship, interrelation, contact, communication, correlation, correspondence, relevance.

≢ disconnection.

connoisseur n authority, specialist, expert, judge, devotee, buff (infml), gourmet, epicure.

connotation n implication, suggestion, hint, nuance, undertone, overtone, colouring, association.

conquer v **1** DEFEAT, beat, overthrow, vanquish, rout, overrun, best, worst, get the better of, overcome, surmount, win, succeed, triumph, prevail, overpower, master, crush, subdue, quell, subjugate, humble. **2** SEIZE, take, annex, occupy, possess, acquire, obtain.

≢ 1 surrender, yield, give in.

conqueror n victor, winner, champion, champ (infml), hero, vanquisher, master, lord.

conquest n victory, triumph, defeat, overthrow, coup, rout, mastery, subjugation, subjection, invasion, occupation, capture, appropriation, annexation, acquisition.

conscience n principles, standards, morals, ethics, scruples, qualms.

conscientious adj diligent, hard-working, scrupulous, painstaking, thorough, meticulous, punctilious, particular, careful, attentive, responsible, upright, honest, faithful, dutiful.
🔁 careless, irresponsible, unreliable.

conscious adj 1 AWAKE, alive, responsive, sentient, sensible, rational, reasoning, alert. 2 AWARE, self-conscious, heedful, mindful, knowing, deliberate, intentional, calculated, premeditated, studied, wilful, voluntary.
🔁 1 unconscious. 2 unaware.

consciousness n awareness, sentience, sensibility, knowledge, intuition, realization, recognition.
🔁 unconsciousness.

consecrate v sanctify, hallow, bless, dedicate, devote, ordain, venerate, revere, exalt.

consecutive adj sequential, successive, continuous, unbroken, uninterrupted, following, succeeding, running.
🔁 discontinuous.

consent v agree, concur, accede, assent, approve, permit, allow, grant, admit, concede, acquiesce, yield, comply.
🔁 refuse, decline, oppose.
n agreement, concurrence, assent, approval, permission, go-ahead, green light (infml), sanction, concession, acquiescence, compliance.
🔁 disagreement, refusal, opposition.

consequence n 1 RESULT, outcome, issue, end, upshot, effect, side effect, repercussion. 2 of no consequence: importance, significance, concern, value, weight, note, eminence, distinction.
🔁 1 cause. 2 unimportance, insignificance.

consequent adj resultant, resulting, ensuing, subsequent, following, successive, sequential.

conservation n keeping, safe-keeping, custody, saving, economy, husbandry, maintenance, upkeep, preservation, protection, safeguarding, ecology, environmentalism.
🔁 destruction.

conservative adj Tory, right-wing, hidebound, die-hard, reactionary, establishmentarian, unprogressive, conventional, traditional, moderate, middle-of-the-road, cautious, guarded, sober.
🔁 left-wing, radical, innovative.
n Tory, right-winger, die-hard, stick-in-the-mud, reactionary, traditionalist, moderate.
🔁 left-winger, radical.

conservatory n greenhouse, glasshouse, hothouse.

conserve v keep, save, store up, hoard, maintain, preserve, protect, guard, safeguard.
🔁 use, waste, squander.

consider v 1 PONDER, deliberate, reflect, contemplate, meditate, muse, mull over, chew over, examine, study, weigh, respect, remember, take into account. 2 consider it an honour: regard, deem, think, believe, judge, rate, count.

considerable adj great, large, big, sizable, substantial, tidy (infml), ample, plentiful, abundant, lavish, marked, noticeable, perceptible, appreciable, reasonable, tolerable, respectable, important, significant, noteworthy, distinguished, influential.
🔁 small, slight, insignificant, unremarkable.

considerate adj kind, thoughtful,

caring, attentive, obliging, helpful,
charitable, unselfish, altruistic,
gracious, sensitive, tactful, discreet.
🔁 inconsiderate, thoughtless, selfish.

consideration n 1 THOUGHT,
deliberation, reflection,
contemplation, meditation,
examination, analysis, scrutiny,
review, attention, notice, regard.
2 KINDNESS, thoughtfulness, care,
attention, regard, respect.
🔁 1 disregard. 2 thoughtlessness.

consign v entrust, commit, devote,
hand over, transfer, deliver, convey,
ship, banish, relegate.

consignment n cargo, shipment,
load, batch, delivery, goods.

consist of comprise, be composed of,
contain, include, incorporate,
embody, embrace, involve, amount
to.

consistency n 1 of the consistency
of porridge: viscosity, thickness,
density, firmness. 2 STEADINESS,
regularity, evenness, uniformity,
sameness, identity, constancy,
steadfastness. 3 AGREEMENT,
accordance, correspondence,
congruity, compatibility, harmony.
🔁 3 inconsistency.

consistent adj 1 STEADY, stable,
regular, uniform, unchanging,
undeviating, constant, persistent,
unfailing, dependable. 2 AGREEING,
accordant, consonant, congruous,
compatible, harmonious, logical.
🔁 1 irregular, erratic. 2 inconsistent.

console v comfort, cheer, hearten,
encourage, relieve, soothe, calm.
🔁 upset, agitate.

consolidate v reinforce, strengthen,
secure, stabilize, unify, unite, join,
combine, amalgamate, fuse, cement,
compact, condense, thicken, harden,
solidify.

conspicuous adj apparent, visible,
noticeable, marked, clear, obvious,
evident, patent, manifest, prominent,
striking, blatant, flagrant, glaring,
ostentatious, showy, flashy, garish.
🔁 inconspicuous, concealed, hidden.

conspiracy n plot, scheme, intrigue,
machination, fix (infml), frame-up
(infml), collusion, league, treason.

conspirator n conspirer, plotter,
schemer, intriguer, traitor.

conspire v plot, scheme, intrigue,
manoeuvre, connive, collude, hatch,
devise.

constancy n 1 STABILITY,
steadiness, permanence, firmness,
regularity, uniformity, resolution,
perseverance, tenacity. 2 LOYALTY,
faithfulness, fidelity, devotion.
🔁 1 change, irregularity. 2 fickleness.

constant adj 1 CONTINUOUS,
unbroken, never-ending, non-stop,
endless, interminable, ceaseless,
incessant, eternal, everlasting,
perpetual, continual, unremitting,
relentless, persistent, resolute,
persevering, unflagging, unwavering,
stable, steady, unchanging,
unvarying, changeless, immutable,
invariable, unalterable, fixed,
permanent, firm, even, regular,
uniform. 2 a constant friend: loyal,
faithful, staunch, steadfast,
dependable, trustworthy, true,
devoted.
🔁 1 variable, irregular, fitful,
occasional. 2 disloyal, fickle.

constituent adj component,
integral, essential, basic, intrinsic,
inherent.
n ingredient, element, factor,
principle, component, part, bit,
section, unit.
🔁 whole.

constitute v represent, make up,
compose, comprise, form, create,
establish, set up, found.

constrain v 1 FORCE, compel,
oblige, necessitate, drive, impel, urge.
2 limit, confine, constrict, restrain,
check, curb, bind.

constrained adj uneasy,
embarrassed, inhibited, reticent,

reserved, guarded, stiff, forced, unnatural.
▣ relaxed, free.

constraint n **1** FORCE, duress, compulsion, coercion, pressure, necessity, deterrent. **2** RESTRICTION, limitation, hindrance, restraint, check, curb, damper.

constrict v squeeze, compress, pinch, cramp, narrow, tighten, contract, shrink, choke, strangle, inhibit, limit, restrict.
▣ expand.

construct v build, erect, raise, elevate, make, manufacture, fabricate, assemble, put together, compose, form, shape, fashion, model, design, engineer, create, found, establish, formulate.
▣ demolish, destroy.

construction n building, edifice, erection, structure, fabric, form, shape, figure, model, manufacture, fabrication, assembly, composition, constitution, formation, creation.
▣ destruction.

constructive adj practical, productive, positive, helpful, useful, valuable, beneficial, advantageous.
▣ destructive, negative, unhelpful.

consult v refer to, ask, question, interrogate, confer, discuss, debate, deliberate.

consultant n adviser, expert, authority, specialist.

consultation n discussion, deliberation, dialogue, conference, meeting, hearing, interview, examination, appointment, session.

consume v **1** EAT, drink, swallow, devour, gobble. **2** USE, absorb, spend, expend, deplete, drain, exhaust, use up, dissipate, squander, waste. **3** DESTROY, demolish, annihilate, devastate, ravage.

consumer n user, end-user, customer, buyer, purchaser, shopper.

consumption n use, utilization, spending, expenditure, depletion, exhaustion, waste.

contact n touch, impact, juxtaposition, contiguity, communication, meeting, junction, union, connection, association.
v approach, apply to, reach, get hold of, get in touch with, telephone, phone, ring, call, notify.

contagious adj infectious, catching, communicable, transmissible, spreading, epidemic.

contain v **1** INCLUDE, comprise, incorporate, embody, involve, embrace, enclose, hold, accommodate, seat. **2** *contain one's feelings*: repress, stifle, restrain, control, check, curb, limit.
▣ 1 exclude.

container n receptacle, vessel, holder.

contaminate v infect, pollute, adulterate, taint, soil, sully, defile, corrupt, deprave, debase, stain, tarnish.
▣ purify.

contemplate v **1** MEDITATE, reflect on, ponder, mull over, deliberate, consider, regard, view, survey, observe, study, examine, inspect, scrutinize. **2** EXPECT, foresee, envisage, plan, design, propose, intend, mean.

contemporary adj **1** MODERN, current, present, present-day, recent, latest, up-to-date, fashionable, up-to-the-minute, ultra-modern.
2 CONTEMPORANEOUS, coexistent, concurrent, synchronous, simultaneous.
▣ 1 out-of-date, old-fashioned.

contempt n scorn, disdain, condescension, derision, ridicule, mockery, disrespect, dishonour, disregard, neglect, dislike, loathing, detestation.
▣ admiration, regard.

contemptible adj despicable, shameful, ignominious, low, mean, vile, detestable, loathsome, abject,

wretched, pitiful, paltry, worthless.
Ea admirable, honourable.

contemptuous *adj* scornful,
disdainful, sneering, supercilious,
condescending, arrogant, haughty,
high and mighty, cynical, derisive,
insulting, disrespectful, insolent.
Ea humble, respectful.

contend *v* **1** MAINTAIN, hold, argue,
allege, assert, declare, affirm.
2 COMPETE, vie, contest, dispute,
clash, wrestle, grapple, struggle,
strive, cope.

content *v* satisfy, humour, indulge,
gratify, please, delight, appease,
pacify, placate.
Ea displease.
n **1** SUBSTANCE, matter, essence,
gist, meaning, significance, text,
subject matter, ideas, contents, load,
burden. **2** CAPACITY, volume, size,
measure.
adj satisfied, fulfilled, contented,
untroubled, pleased, happy, willing.
Ea dissatisfied, troubled.

contented *adj* happy, glad, pleased,
cheerful, comfortable, relaxed,
content, satisfied.
Ea discontented, unhappy, annoyed.

contentment *n* contentedness,
happiness, gladness, pleasure,
gratification, comfort, ease,
complacency, peace, peacefulness,
serenity, equanimity, content,
satisfaction, fulfilment.
Ea unhappiness, discontent,
dissatisfaction.

contents *n* **1** *the contents of the
package*: constituents, parts,
elements, ingredients, content, load,
items. **2** CHAPTERS, divisions,
subjects, topics, themes.

contest *n* competition, game, match,
tournament, encounter, fight, battle,
set-to, combat, conflict, struggle,
dispute, debate, controversy.
v **1** DISPUTE, debate, question,
doubt, challenge, oppose, argue
against, litigate, deny, refute.

2 COMPETE, vie, contend, strive,
fight.
Ea **1** accept.

contestant *n* competitor, contender,
player, participant, entrant,
candidate, aspirant, rival, opponent.

context *n* background, setting,
surroundings, framework, frame of
reference, situation, position,
circumstances, conditions.

contingent *n* body, company,
deputation, delegation, detachment,
section, group, set, batch, quota,
complement.

continual *adj* constant, perpetual,
incessant, interminable, eternal,
everlasting, regular, frequent,
recurrent, repeated.
Ea occasional, intermittent,
temporary.

continuation *n* resumption,
maintenance, prolongation,
extension, development, furtherance,
addition, supplement.
Ea cessation, termination.

continue *v* resume, recommence,
carry on, go on, proceed, persevere,
stick at, persist, last, endure, survive,
remain, abide, stay, rest, pursue,
sustain, maintain, lengthen, prolong,
extend, project.
Ea discontinue, stop.

continuity *n* flow, progression,
succession, sequence, linkage,
interrelationship, connection,
cohesion.
Ea discontinuity.

continuous *adj* unbroken,
uninterrupted, consecutive, non-stop,
endless, ceaseless, unending,
unceasing, constant, unremitting,
prolonged, extended, continued,
lasting.
Ea discontinuous, broken, sporadic.

contort *v* twist, distort, warp,
wrench, disfigure, deform, misshape,
convolute, gnarl, knot, writhe,
squirm, wriggle.

contour *n* outline, silhouette, shape,

form, figure, curve, relief, profile, character, aspect.

contract v 1 SHRINK, lessen, diminish, reduce, shorten, curtail, abbreviate, abridge, condense, compress, constrict, narrow, tighten, tense, shrivel, wrinkle. 2 *contract pneumonia*: catch, get, go down with, develop. 3 PLEDGE, promise, undertake, agree, stipulate, arrange, negotiate, bargain.

🔁 1 expand, enlarge, lengthen.

n bond, commitment, engagement, covenant, treaty, convention, pact, compact, agreement, transaction, deal, bargain, settlement, arrangement, understanding.

contradict v deny, disaffirm, confute, challenge, oppose, impugn, dispute, counter, negate, gainsay.

🔁 agree, confirm, corroborate.

contradictory adj contrary, opposite, paradoxical, conflicting, discrepant, inconsistent, incompatible, antagonistic, irreconcilable, opposed, repugnant.

🔁 consistent.

contraption n contrivance, device, gadget, apparatus, rig, machine, mechanism.

contrary adj 1 OPPOSITE, counter, reverse, conflicting, antagonistic, opposed, adverse, hostile. 2 PERVERSE, awkward, disobliging, difficult, wayward, obstinate, intractable, cantankerous, stroppy (*infml*).

🔁 1 like. 2 obliging.

n opposite, converse, reverse.

contrast n difference, dissimilarity, disparity, divergence, distinction, differentiation, comparison, foil, antithesis, opposition.

🔁 similarity.

v compare, differentiate, distinguish, discriminate, differ, oppose, clash, conflict.

contravene v infringe, violate, break, breach, disobey, defy, flout,

transgress.

🔁 uphold, observe, obey.

contribute v donate, subscribe, chip in (*infml*), add, give, bestow, provide, supply, furnish, help, lead, conduce.

🔁 withhold.

contribution n donation, subscription, gift, gratuity, handout, grant, offering, input, addition.

contributor n 1 DONOR, subscriber, giver, patron, benefactor, sponsor, backer, supporter. 2 WRITER, journalist, reporter, correspondent, freelance.

contrite adj sorry, regretful, remorseful, repentant, penitent, conscience-stricken, chastened, humble, ashamed.

contrivance n 1 INVENTION, device, contraption, gadget, implement, appliance, machine, mechanism, apparatus, equipment, gear. 2 STRATAGEM, ploy, trick, dodge, ruse, expedient, plan, design, project, scheme, plot, intrigue, machination.

contrived adj unnatural, artificial, false, forced, strained, laboured, mannered, elaborate, overdone.

🔁 natural, genuine.

control v 1 LEAD, govern, rule, command, direct, manage, oversee, supervise, superintend, run, operate. 2 *control the temperature*: regulate, adjust, monitor, verify. 3 *control one's temper*: restrain, check, curb, subdue, repress, hold back, contain.

n 1 POWER, charge, authority, command, mastery, government, rule, direction, management, oversight, supervision, superintendence, discipline, guidance. 2 RESTRAINT, check, curb, repression.

3 INSTRUMENT, dial, switch, button, knob, lever.

controversial adj contentious, polemical, disputed, doubtful, questionable, debatable, disputable.

controversy n debate, discussion,

war of words, polemic, dispute, disagreement, argument, quarrel, squabble, wrangle, strife, contention, dissension.
≢ accord, agreement.

convenience n 1 ACCESSIBILITY, availability, handiness, usefulness, use, utility, serviceability, service, benefit, advantage, help, suitability, fitness. 2 *all modern conveniences*: facility, amenity, appliance.
≢ 1 inconvenience.

convenient adj nearby, at hand, accessible, available, handy, useful, commodious, beneficial, helpful, labour-saving, adapted, fitted, suited, suitable, fit, appropriate, opportune, timely, well-timed.
≢ inconvenient, awkward.

convention n 1 CUSTOM, tradition, practice, usage, protocol, etiquette, formality, matter of form, code. 2 ASSEMBLY, congress, conference, meeting, council, delegates, representatives.

conventional adj traditional, orthodox, formal, correct, proper, prevalent, prevailing, accepted, received, expected, unoriginal, ritual, routine, usual, customary, regular, standard, normal, ordinary, straight, stereotyped, hidebound, pedestrian, commonplace, common, run-of-the-mill.
≢ unconventional, unusual, exotic.

converge v focus, concentrate, approach, merge, coincide, meet, join, combine, gather.
≢ diverge, disperse.

convergence n concentration, approach, merging, confluence, blending, meeting, coincidence, junction, intersection, union.
≢ divergence, separation.

conversation n talk, chat, gossip, discussion, discourse, dialogue, exchange, communication.

converse n opposite, reverse, contrary, antithesis, obverse.

adj opposite, reverse, counter, contrary, reversed, transposed.

conversion n alteration, change, transformation, adaptation, modification, remodelling, reconstruction, reorganization, reformation, regeneration, rebirth.

convert v 1 ALTER, change, turn, transform, adapt, modify, remodel, restyle, revise, reorganize. 2 WIN OVER, convince, persuade, reform, proselytize.

convex adj rounded, bulging, protuberant.
≢ concave.

convey v carry, bear, bring, fetch, move, transport, send, forward, deliver, transfer, conduct, guide, transmit, communicate, impart, tell, relate, reveal.

convict v condemn, sentence, imprison.
n criminal, felon, culprit, prisoner.

conviction n assurance, confidence, fervour, earnestness, certainty, firmness, persuasion, view, opinion, belief, faith, creed, tenet, principle.

convince v assure, persuade, sway, win over, bring round, reassure, satisfy.

convincing adj persuasive, cogent, powerful, telling, impressive, credible, plausible, likely, probable, conclusive, incontrovertible.
≢ unconvincing, improbable.

convoluted adj twisting, winding, meandering, tortuous, involved, complicated, complex, tangled.
≢ straight, straightforward.

convoy n fleet, escort, guard, protection, attendance, train.

convulsion n 1 FIT, seizure, paroxysm, spasm, cramp, contraction, tic, tremor. 2 ERUPTION, outburst, furore, disturbance, commotion, tumult, agitation, turbulence, upheaval.

convulsive adj jerky, spasmodic, fitful, sporadic, uncontrolled, violent.

cook

Ways of cooking include: bake, barbecue, boil, braise, broil, casserole, coddle, deep-fry, fry, grill, microwave, poach, pot-roast, roast, sauté, scramble, simmer, spit-roast, steam, stew, stir-fry, toast; prepare, heat.

cook up concoct, prepare, brew, invent, fabricate, contrive, devise, plan, plot, scheme.

cool *adj* **1** CHILLY, fresh, breezy, nippy, cold, chilled, iced, refreshing. **2** CALM, unruffled, unexcited, composed, self-possessed, level-headed, unemotional, quiet, relaxed, laid-back (*infml*). **3** *a cool reception*: unfriendly, unwelcoming, cold, frigid, lukewarm, half-hearted, unenthusiastic, apathetic, uninterested, unresponsive, uncommunicative, reserved, distant, aloof, standoffish.
E3 **1** warm, hot. **2** excited, angry. **3** friendly, welcoming.
v **1** CHILL, refrigerate, ice, freeze, fan. **2** MODERATE, lessen, temper, dampen, quiet, abate, calm, allay, assuage.
E3 **1** warm, heat. **2** excite.
n coolness, calmness, collectedness, composure, poise, self-possession, self-discipline, self-control, control, temper.

co-operate *v* collaborate, work together, play ball (*infml*), help, assist, aid, contribute, participate, combine, unite, conspire.

co-operation *n* helpfulness, assistance, participation, collaboration, teamwork, unity, co-ordination, give-and-take.
E3 opposition, rivalry, competition.

co-operative *adj* **1** HELPFUL, supportive, obliging, accommodating, willing.
2 COLLECTIVE, joint, shared, combined, united, concerted, co-ordinated.
E3 **1** unco-operative, rebellious.

co-ordinate *v* organize, arrange, systematize, tabulate, integrate, mesh, synchronize, harmonize, match, correlate, regulate.

cope *v* manage, carry on, survive, get by, make do.
cope with deal with, encounter, contend with, struggle with, grapple with, wrestle with, handle, manage, weather.

copious *adj* abundant, plentiful, inexhaustible, overflowing, profuse, rich, lavish, bountiful, liberal, full, ample, generous, extensive, great, huge.
E3 scarce, meagre.

copy *n* duplicate, carbon copy, photocopy, Photostat®, Xerox®, facsimile, reproduction, print, tracing, transcript, transcription, replica, model, pattern, archetype, representation, image, likeness, counterfeit, forgery, fake, imitation, borrowing, plagiarism, crib.
E3 original.
v duplicate, photocopy, reproduce, print, trace, transcribe, forge, counterfeit, simulate, imitate, impersonate, mimic, ape, parrot, repeat, echo, mirror, follow, emulate, borrow, plagiarize, crib.

cord *n* string, twine, rope, line, cable, flex, connection, link, bond, tie.

core *n* kernel, nucleus, heart, centre, middle, nub, crux, essence, gist, nitty-gritty (*infml*).
E3 surface, exterior.

corner *n* **1** *round the corner*: angle, joint, crook, bend, turning. **2** NOOK, cranny, niche, recess, cavity, hole, hideout, hide-away, retreat.

corporation *n* council, authorities, association, society, organization, company, firm, combine, conglomerate.

corpse *n* body, stiff (*sl*), carcase,

skeleton, remains.

correct v **1** *correct an error*: rectify, put right, right, emend, remedy, cure, debug, redress, adjust, regulate, improve, amend. **2** PUNISH, discipline, reprimand, reprove, reform.
adj **1** *the correct answer*: right, accurate, precise, exact, strict, true, truthful, word-perfect, faultless, flawless. **2** PROPER, acceptable, OK (*infml*), standard, regular, just, appropriate, fitting.
F∃ 1 incorrect, wrong, inaccurate.

correction n rectification, emendation, adjustment, alteration, modification, amendment, improvement.

correspond v **1** MATCH, fit, answer, conform, tally, square, agree, concur, coincide, correlate, accord, harmonize, dovetail, complement. **2** COMMUNICATE, write.

correspondence n **1** COMMUNICATION, writing, letters, post, mail. **2** CONFORMITY, agreement, concurrence, coincidence, correlation, relation, analogy, comparison, comparability, similarity, resemblance, congruity, equivalence, harmony, match.
F∃ 2 divergence, incongruity.

correspondent n journalist, reporter, contributor, writer.

corresponding adj matching, complementary, reciprocal, interrelated, analogous, equivalent, similar, identical.

corridor n aisle, passageway, passage, hallway, hall, lobby.

corroborate v confirm, prove, bear out, support, endorse, ratify, substantiate, validate, authenticate, document, underpin, sustain.
F∃ contradict.

corrode v erode, wear away, eat away, consume, waste, rust, oxidize, tarnish, impair, deteriorate, crumble, disintegrate.

corrosive adj corroding, acid, caustic, cutting, abrasive, erosive, wearing, consuming, wasting.

corrugated adj ridged, fluted, grooved, channelled, furrowed, wrinkled, crinkled, rumpled, creased.

corrupt adj rotten, unscrupulous, unprincipled, unethical, immoral, fraudulent, shady (*infml*), dishonest, bent (*infml*), crooked (*infml*), untrustworthy, depraved, degenerate, dissolute.
F∃ ethical, virtuous, upright, honest, trustworthy.
v contaminate, pollute, adulterate, taint, defile, debase, pervert, deprave, lead astray, lure, bribe, suborn.
F∃ purify.

corruption n unscrupulousness, immorality, impurity, depravity, degeneration, degradation, perversion, distortion, dishonesty, crookedness (*infml*), fraud, shadiness (*infml*), bribery; extortion, vice, wickedness, iniquity, evil.
F∃ honesty, virtue.

cosmetic adj superficial, surface.
F∃ essential.

cosmetics n make-up, grease paint.

Types of cosmetics include: blusher, cleanser, eyebrow pencil, eyelash dye, eyeliner, eye shadow, face cream, face mask, face pack, face powder, false eyelashes, foundation, kohl pencil, lip gloss, lip liner, lipstick, loose powder, mascara, moisturizer, nail polish, nail varnish, Pan-cake®, pressed powder, rouge, toner.

cosmopolitan adj worldly, worldly-wise, well-travelled, sophisticated, urbane, international, universal.
F∃ insular, parochial, rustic.

cosset v coddle, mollycoddle, baby, pamper, indulge, spoil, pet, fondle, cuddle, cherish.

cost n **1** EXPENSE, outlay, payment, disbursement, expenditure, charge, price, rate, amount, figure, worth. **2** DETRIMENT, harm, injury, hurt, loss, deprivation, sacrifice, penalty, price.

costly adj **1** EXPENSIVE, dear, pricey (*infml*), exorbitant, excessive, lavish, rich, splendid, valuable, precious, priceless. **2** HARMFUL, damaging, disastrous, catastrophic, loss-making. **E3** cheap, inexpensive.

costume n outfit, uniform, livery, robes, vestments, dress, clothing, get-up (*infml*), fancy dress.

cosy adj snug, comfortable, comfy (*infml*), warm, sheltered, secure, homely, intimate. **E3** uncomfortable, cold.

cottage n lodge, chalet, bungalow, hut, cabin, shack.

couch n sofa, settee, chesterfield, chaise-longue, ottoman, divan, bed.

council n committee, panel, board, cabinet, ministry, parliament, congress, assembly, convention, conference.

counsel n **1** ADVICE, suggestion, recommendation, guidance, direction, information, consultation, deliberation, consideration, forethought. **2** *counsel for the defence*: lawyer, advocate, solicitor, attorney, barrister. v advise, warn, caution, suggest, recommend, advocate, urge, exhort, guide, direct, instruct.

count v **1** NUMBER, enumerate, list, include, reckon, calculate, compute, tell, check, add, total, tot up, score. **2** MATTER, signify, qualify. **3** *count yourself lucky*: consider, regard, deem, judge, think, reckon, hold. n numbering, enumeration, poll, reckoning, calculation, computation, sum, total, tally.

count on depend on, rely on, bank on, reckon on, expect, believe, trust.

counter adv against, in opposition, conversely. adj contrary, opposite, opposing, conflicting, contradictory, contrasting, opposed, against, adverse. v parry, resist, offset, answer, respond, retaliate, retort, return, meet.

counteract v neutralize, counterbalance, offset, countervail, act against, oppose, resist, hinder, check, thwart, frustrate, foil, defeat, undo, negate, annul, invalidate. **E3** support, assist.

counterfeit v fake, forge, fabricate, copy, imitate, impersonate, pretend, feign, simulate, sham. adj fake, false, phoney (*infml*), forged, copied, fraudulent, bogus, pseudo, sham, spurious, imitation, artificial, simulated, feigned, pretended. **E3** genuine, authentic, real. n fake, forgery, copy, reproduction, imitation, fraud, sham.

counterpart n equivalent, opposite number, complement, supplement, match, fellow, mate, twin, duplicate, copy.

countless adj innumerable, myriad, numberless, unnumbered, untold, incalculable, infinite, endless, immeasurable, measureless, limitless. **E3** finite, limited.

country n **1** STATE, nation, people, kingdom, realm, principality. **2** COUNTRYSIDE, green belt, farmland, provinces, sticks (*infml*), backwoods, wilds. **3** TERRAIN, land, territory, region, area, district. **E3** **2** town, city. adj rural, provincial, agrarian, agricultural, pastoral, rustic, bucolic, landed. **E3** urban.

countryside n landscape, scenery, country, green belt, farmland, outdoors.

county n shire, province, region, area, district.

couple n pair, brace, twosome, duo. v pair, match, marry, wed, unite, join, link, connect, fasten, hitch, clasp, buckle, yoke.

coupon n voucher, token, slip, check, ticket, certificate.

courage n bravery, pluck, guts (*infml*), fearlessness, dauntlessness, heroism, gallantry, valour, boldness, audacity, nerve, daring, resolution, fortitude, spirit, mettle.

🔁 cowardice, fear.

courageous adj brave, plucky, fearless, dauntless, indomitable, heroic, gallant, valiant, lion-hearted, hardy, bold, audacious, daring, intrepid, resolute.

🔁 cowardly, afraid.

course n 1 CURRICULUM, syllabus, classes, lessons, lectures, studies. 2 FLOW, movement, advance, progress, development, furtherance, order, sequence, series, succession, progression. 3 DURATION, time, period, term, passage. 4 DIRECTION, way, path, track, road, route, channel, trail, line, circuit, orbit, trajectory, flight path. 5 *course of action*: plan, schedule, programme, policy, procedure, method, mode.

court n 1 LAW-COURT, bench, bar, tribunal, trial, session. 2 COURTYARD, yard, quadrangle, square, cloister, forecourt, enclosure. 3 ENTOURAGE, attendants, retinue, suite, train, cortège.

courteous adj polite, civil, respectful, well-mannered, well-bred, ladylike, gentlemanly, gracious, obliging, considerate, attentive, gallant, courtly, urbane, debonair, refined, polished.

🔁 discourteous, impolite, rude.

courtesy n politeness, civility, respect, manners, breeding, graciousness, consideration, attention, gallantry, urbanity.

🔁 discourtesy, rudeness.

courtier n noble, nobleman, lord, lady, steward, page, attendant, follower, flatterer, sycophant, toady.

courtyard n yard, quadrangle, quad

(*infml*), area, enclosure, court.

cove n bay, bight, inlet, estuary, firth, fiord, creek.

cover v 1 HIDE, conceal, obscure, shroud, veil, screen, mask, disguise, camouflage. 2 *covered with mud*: coat, spread, daub, plaster, encase, wrap, envelop, clothe, dress. 3 SHELTER, protect, shield, guard, defend. 4 *cover a topic*: deal with, treat, consider, examine, investigate, encompass, embrace, incorporate, embody, involve, include, contain, comprise.

🔁 1 uncover. 2 strip. 3 expose. 4 exclude.

n 1 COATING, covering, top, lid, cup, veil, screen, mask, front, façade, jacket, wrapper, case, envelope, clothing, dress, bedspread, canopy. 2 SHELTER, refuge, protection, shield, guard, defence, concealment, disguise, camouflage.

cover up (*infml*) conceal, hide, whitewash, dissemble, suppress, hush up, keep dark, repress.

🔁 disclose, reveal.

covering n layer, coat, coating, blanket, film, veneer, skin, crust, shell, casing, housing, wrapping, clothing, protection, mask, overlay, cover, top, shelter, roof.

cover-up (*infml*) n concealment, whitewash, smokescreen, front, façade, pretence, conspiracy, complicity.

covet v envy, begrudge, crave, long for, yearn for, hanker for, want, desire, fancy (*infml*), lust after.

coward n craven, faint-heart, chicken (*infml*), scaredy-cat, yellow-belly (*sl*), wimp (*infml*), renegade, deserter.

🔁 hero.

cowardice n cowardliness, faint-heartedness, timorousness, spinelessness.

🔁 courage, valour.

cowardly adj faint-hearted, craven,

fearful, timorous, scared, unheroic, chicken-hearted, chicken-livered, chicken (*infml*), yellow-bellied (*sl*), yellow (*sl*), spineless, weak, weak-kneed, soft.

⟫ brave, courageous, bold.

cower v crouch, grovel, skulk, shrink, flinch, cringe, quail, tremble, shake, shiver.

coy adj modest, demure, prudish, diffident, shy, bashful, timid, shrinking, backward, retiring, self-effacing, reserved, evasive, arch, flirtatious, coquettish, skittish, kittenish.

⟫ bold, forward.

crack v 1 SPLIT, burst, fracture, break, snap, shatter, splinter, chip. 2 EXPLODE, burst, pop, crackle, snap, crash, clap, slap, whack (*infml*). 3 *crack a code*: decipher, work out, solve.

n 1 BREAK, fracture, split, rift, gap, crevice, fissure, chink, line, flaw, chip. 2 EXPLOSION, burst, pop, snap, crash, clap, blow, smack, slap, whack (*infml*). 3 JOKE, quip, witticism, gag (*infml*), wisecrack, gibe, dig.

adj (*infml*) first-class, first-rate, top-notch (*infml*), excellent, superior, choice, hand-picked.

crack down on clamp down on, end, stop, put a stop to, crush, suppress, check, repress, act against.

crack up go mad, go to pieces, break down, collapse.

cradle n 1 COT, crib, bed. 2 SOURCE, origin, spring, wellspring, fount, fountain-head, birthplace, beginning.

v hold, support, rock, lull, nurse, nurture, tend.

craft n 1 SKILL, expertise, mastery, talent, knack, ability, aptitude, dexterity, cleverness, art, handicraft, handiwork. 2 TRADE, business, calling, vocation, job, occupation, work, employment. 3 VESSEL, boat, ship, aircraft, spacecraft, spaceship.

craftsman, craftswoman n artisan, technician, master, maker, wright, smith.

craftsmanship n artistry, workmanship, technique, dexterity, expertise, mastery.

crafty adj sly, cunning, artful, wily, devious, subtle, scheming, calculating, designing, deceitful, fraudulent, sharp, shrewd, astute, canny.

⟫ artless, naïve.

cram v stuff, jam, ram, force, press, squeeze, crush, compress, pack, crowd, overfill, glut, gorge.

cramp[1] v hinder, hamper, obstruct, impede, inhibit, handicap, thwart, frustrate, check, restrict, confine, shackle, tie.

cramp[2] n pain, ache, twinge, pang, contraction, convulsion, spasm, crick, stitch, pins and needles, stiffness.

cramped adj narrow, tight, uncomfortable, restricted, confined, crowded, packed, squashed, squeezed, overcrowded, jam-packed, congested.

⟫ spacious.

crash n 1 *car crash*: accident, collision, bump, smash, pile-up, smash-up (*infml*), wreck. 2 BANG, clash, clatter, clang, thud, thump, boom, thunder, racket, din. 3 *stock-market crash*: collapse, failure, ruin, downfall, bankruptcy, depression.

v 1 COLLIDE, hit, knock, bump, bang. 2 BREAK, fracture, smash, dash, shatter, splinter, shiver, fragment, disintegrate. 3 FALL, topple, pitch, plunge, collapse, fail, fold (up), go under, go bust (*infml*).

crate n container, box, case, tea-chest, packing-box, packing-case.

crave v hunger for, thirst for, long for, yearn for, pine for, hanker after, fancy (*infml*), desire, want, need, require.

⟫ dislike.

craving *n* appetite, hunger, thirst, longing, yearning, hankering, lust, desire, urge.
🔁 dislike, distaste.

crawl *v* **1** CREEP, inch, edge, slither, wriggle. **2** GROVEL, cringe, toady, fawn, flatter, suck up (*sl*).

craze *n* fad, novelty, fashion, vogue, mode, trend, rage (*infml*), thing (*infml*), obsession, preoccupation, mania, frenzy, passion, infatuation, enthusiasm.

crazy *adj* **1** MAD, insane, lunatic, unbalanced, deranged, demented, crazed, potty (*infml*), barmy (*infml*), daft (*infml*), silly, foolish, idiotic, senseless, unwise, imprudent, nonsensical, absurd, ludicrous, ridiculous, preposterous, outrageous, half-baked, impracticable, irresponsible, wild, berserk. **2** (*infml*) *crazy about golf*: enthusiastic, fanatical, zealous, ardent, passionate, infatuated, enamoured, smitten, mad, wild.
🔁 **1** sane, sensible. **2** indifferent.

creak *v* squeak, groan, grate, scrape, rasp, scratch, grind, squeal, screech.

cream *n* **1** PASTE, emulsion, oil, lotion, ointment, salve, cosmetic. **2** BEST, pick, élite, prime.

creamy *adj* **1** CREAM-COLOURED, off-white, yellowish-white. **2** MILKY, buttery, oily, smooth, velvety, rich, thick.

crease *v* fold, pleat, wrinkle, pucker, crumple, rumple, crinkle, crimp, corrugate, ridge.
n fold, line, pleat, tuck, wrinkle, pucker, ruck, crinkle, corrugation, ridge, groove.

create *v* invent, coin, formulate, compose, design, devise, concoct, hatch, originate, initiate, found, establish, set up, institute, cause, occasion, produce, generate, engender, make, form, appoint, install, invest, ordain.
🔁 destroy.

creation *n* **1** MAKING, formation, constitution, invention, concoction, origination, foundation, establishment, institution, production, generation, procreation, conception, birth. **2** INVENTION, brainchild, concept, product, handiwork, chef d'oeuvre, achievement.
🔁 **1** destruction.

creative *adj* artistic, inventive, original, imaginative, inspired, visionary, talented, gifted, clever, ingenious, resourceful, fertile, productive.
🔁 unimaginative.

creator *n* maker, inventor, designer, architect, author, originator, initiator.

creature *n* animal, beast, bird, fish, organism, being, mortal, individual, person, man, woman, body, soul.

credentials *n* diploma, certificate, reference, testimonial, recommendation, accreditation, authorization, warrant, licence, permit, passport, identity card, papers, documents, deed, title.

credibility *n* integrity, reliability, trustworthiness, plausibility, probability.
🔁 implausibility.

credible *adj* believable, imaginable, conceivable, thinkable, tenable, plausible, likely, probable, possible, reasonable, persuasive, convincing, sincere, honest, trustworthy, reliable, dependable.
🔁 incredible, unbelievable, implausible, unreliable.

credit *n* acknowledgement, recognition, thanks, approval, commendation, praise, acclaim, tribute, glory, fame, prestige, distinction, honour, reputation, esteem, estimation.
🔁 discredit, shame.
v believe, swallow (*infml*), accept, subscribe to, trust, rely on.

⊠ disbelieve.

creditable *adj* honourable, reputable, respectable, estimable, admirable, commendable, praiseworthy, good, excellent, exemplary, worthy, deserving.
⊠ shameful, blameworthy.

credulous *adj* naïve, gullible, wide-eyed, trusting, unsuspecting, uncritical.
⊠ sceptical, suspicious.

creed *n* belief, faith, persuasion, credo, catechism, doctrine, principles, tenets, articles, canon, dogma.

creek *n* inlet, estuary, cove, bay, bight.

creep *v* inch, edge, tiptoe, steal, sneak, slink, crawl, slither, worm, wriggle, squirm, grovel, writhe.

creepy *adj* eerie, spooky, sinister, threatening, frightening, scary, terrifying, hair-raising, nightmarish, macabre, gruesome, horrible, unpleasant, disturbing.

crest *n* **1** *the crest of the hill*: ridge, crown, top, peak, summit, pinnacle, apex, head. **2** TUFT, tassel, plume, comb, mane. **3** INSIGNIA, device, symbol, emblem, badge.

crevice *n* crack, fissure, split, rift, cleft, slit, chink, cranny, gap, hole, opening, break.

crew *n* team, party, squad, troop, corps, company, gang, band, bunch, crowd, mob, set, lot.

crime *n* law-breaking, lawlessness, delinquency, offence, felony, misdemeanour, misdeed, wrongdoing, misconduct, transgression, violation, sin, iniquity, vice, villainy, wickedness, atrocity, outrage.

Crimes include: theft, robbery, burglary, larceny, pilfering, mugging, poaching; assault, rape, grievous bodily harm, GBH (*infml*), battery, manslaughter, homicide, murder, assassination; fraud, bribery, corruption, embezzlement, extortion, blackmail; arson, treason, terrorism, hijack, piracy, kidnapping, sabotage, vandalism, hooliganism, drug-smuggling, forgery, counterfeiting, perjury, joy-riding, drink-driving, drunk and disorderly.

criminal *n* law-breaker, crook, felon, delinquent, offender, wrongdoer, miscreant, culprit, convict, prisoner.
adj illegal, unlawful, illicit, lawless, wrong, culpable, indictable, crooked (*infml*), bent (*infml*), dishonest, corrupt, wicked, scandalous, deplorable.
⊠ legal, lawful, honest, upright.

cringe *v* shrink, recoil, shy, start, flinch, wince, quail, tremble, quiver, cower, crouch, bend, bow, stoop, grovel, crawl, creep.

cripple *v* lame, paralyse, disable, handicap, injure, maim, mutilate, damage, impair, spoil, ruin, destroy, sabotage, incapacitate, weaken, debilitate.

crippled *adj* lame, paralysed, disabled, handicapped, incapacitated.

crisis *n* emergency, extremity, crunch (*infml*), catastrophe, disaster, calamity, dilemma, quandary, predicament, difficulty, trouble, problem.

crisp *adj* **1** *a crisp biscuit*: crispy, crunchy, brittle, crumbly, firm, hard. **2** BRACING, invigorating, refreshing, fresh, brisk. **3** TERSE, pithy, snappy, brief, short, clear, incisive.
⊠ 1 soggy, limp, flabby. **2** muggy. **3** wordy, vague.

criterion *n* standard, norm, touchstone, benchmark, yardstick, measure, gauge, rule, principle, canon, test.

critic *n* reviewer, commentator, analyst, pundit, authority, expert, judge, censor, carper, fault-finder, attacker, knocker (*infml*).

critical *adj* **1** *at the critical moment*: crucial, vital, essential, all-important, momentous, decisive, urgent, pressing, serious, grave, dangerous, perilous. **2** ANALYTICAL, diagnostic, penetrating, probing, discerning, perceptive. **3** UNCOMPLIMENTARY, derogatory, disparaging, disapproving, censorious, carping, fault-finding, cavilling, nit-picking (*infml*).
F3 **1** unimportant. **3** complimentary, appreciative.

criticism *n* **1** CONDEMNATION, disapproval, disparagement, fault-finding, censure, blame, brickbat, flak (*infml*). **2** REVIEW, critique, assessment, evaluation, appraisal, judgement, analysis, commentary, appreciation.
F3 **1** praise, commendation.

criticize *v* **1** CONDEMN, slate (*infml*), slam (*infml*), knock (*infml*), disparage, carp, find fault, censure, blame. **2** REVIEW, assess, evaluate, appraise, judge, analyse.
F3 **1** praise, commend.

crockery *n* dishes, tableware, china, porcelain, earthenware, stoneware, pottery.

Items of crockery include: cup, saucer, coffee cup, mug, beaker, plate, side plate, dinner plate, bowl, cereal bowl, soup bowl, salad-bowl, sugar bowl, jug, milk-jug, basin, pot, teapot, coffee pot, percolator, cafétière, cakestand, meat dish, butter-dish, tureen, gravy boat, cruet, teaset, dinner service.

crook *n* criminal, thief, robber, swindler, cheat, shark (*infml*), rogue, villain.

crooked *adj* **1** ASKEW, skew-whiff (*infml*), awry, lopsided, asymmetric, irregular, uneven, off-centre, tilted, slanting, bent, angled, hooked,

curved, bowed, warped, distorted, misshapen, deformed, twisted, tortuous, winding, zigzag. **2** (*infml*) ILLEGAL, unlawful, illicit, criminal, nefarious, dishonest, deceitful, bent (*infml*), corrupt, fraudulent, shady (*infml*), shifty, underhand, treacherous, unscrupulous, unprincipled, unethical.
F3 **1** straight. **2** honest.

crop *n* growth, yield, produce, fruits, harvest, vintage, gathering.
v cut, snip, clip, shear, trim, pare, prune, lop, shorten, curtail.

crop up arise, emerge, appear, arrive, occur, happen.

cross *adj* **1** IRRITABLE, annoyed, angry, vexed, shirty (*infml*), bad-tempered, ill-tempered, crotchety, grumpy, grouchy, irascible, crabby, short, snappy, snappish, surly, sullen, fractious, fretful, impatient.
2 TRANSVERSE, crosswise, oblique, diagonal, intersecting, opposite, reciprocal.
F3 **1** placid, pleasant.
v **1** *cross the river*: go across, traverse, ford, bridge, span. **2** INTERSECT, meet, criss-cross, lace, intertwine.
3 CROSSBREED, interbreed, mongrelize, hybridize, cross-fertilize, cross-pollinate, blend, mix.
4 THWART, frustrate, foil, hinder, impede, obstruct, block, oppose.
n **1** BURDEN, load, affliction, misfortune, trouble, worry, trial, tribulation, grief, misery, woe.
2 CROSSBREED, hybrid, mongrel, blend, mixture, amalgam, combination. **3** crucifix.

crouch *v* squat, kneel, stoop, bend, bow, hunch, duck, cower, cringe.

crowd *n* **1** THRONG, multitude, host, mob, masses, populace, people, public, riff-raff, rabble, horde, swarm, flock, herd, pack, press, crush, squash, assembly, company, group, bunch, lot, set, circle, clique.
2 SPECTATORS, gate, attendance,

audience.

v gather, congregate, muster, huddle, mass, throng, swarm, flock, surge, stream, push, shove, elbow, jostle, press, squeeze, bundle, pile, pack, congest, cram, compress.

crowded *adj* full, filled, packed, jammed, jam-packed, congested, cramped, overcrowded, overpopulated, busy, teeming, swarming, overflowing.

🖃 empty, deserted.

crown *n* **1** CORONET, diadem, tiara, circlet, wreath, garland. **2** PRIZE, trophy, reward, honour, laurels. **3** SOVEREIGN, monarch, king, queen, ruler, sovereignty, monarchy, royalty. **4** TOP, tip, apex, crest, summit, pinnacle, peak, acme.

v **1** ENTHRONE, anoint, adorn, festoon, honour, dignify, reward. **2** TOP, cap, complete, fulfil, consummate, perfect.

crucial *adj* urgent, pressing, vital, essential, key, pivotal, central, important, momentous, decisive, critical, trying, testing, searching.

🖃 unimportant, trivial.

crude *adj* **1** RAW, unprocessed, unrefined, rough, unfinished, unpolished, natural, primitive. **2** *a crude remark*: VULGAR, coarse, rude, indecent, obscene, gross, dirty, lewd.

🖃 **1** refined, finished. **2** polite, decent.

cruel *adj* fierce, ferocious, vicious, savage, barbarous, bloodthirsty, murderous, cold-blooded, sadistic, brutal, inhuman, inhumane, unkind, malevolent, spiteful, callous, heartless, unfeeling, merciless, pitiless, flinty, hard-hearted, stony-hearted, implacable, ruthless, remorseless, relentless, unrelenting, inexorable, grim, hellish, atrocious, bitter, harsh, severe, cutting, painful, excruciating.

🖃 kind, compassionate, merciful.

cruelty *n* ferocity, viciousness, savagery, barbarity, bloodthirstiness,

murderousness, violence, sadism, brutality, bestiality, inhumanity, spite, venom, callousness, heartlessness, hard-heartedness, mercilessness, ruthlessness, tyranny, harshness, severity.

🖃 kindness, compassion, mercy.

crumble *v* fragment, break up, decompose, disintegrate, decay, degenerate, deteriorate, collapse, crush, pound, grind, powder, pulverize.

crumple *v* crush, wrinkle, pucker, crinkle, rumple, crease, fold, collapse.

crunch *v* munch, chomp, champ, masticate, grind, crush.

crusade *n* campaign, drive, push, movement, cause, undertaking, expedition, holy war, jihad.

crush *v* **1** SQUASH, compress, squeeze, press, pulp, break, smash, pound, pulverize, grind, crumble, crumple, wrinkle. **2** *the rebels were crushed*: conquer, vanquish, demolish, devastate, overpower, overwhelm, overcome, quash, quell, subdue, put down, humiliate, shame, abash.

crust *n* surface, exterior, outside, covering, coat, coating, layer, film, skin, rind, shell, scab, incrustation, caking, concretion.

crux *n* nub, heart, core, essence.

cry *v* **1** WEEP, sob, blubber, wail, bawl, whimper, snivel. **2** SHOUT, call, exclaim, roar, bellow, yell, scream, shriek, screech.

n **1** WEEP, sob, blubber, wail, bawl, whimper, snivel. **2** SHOUT, call, plea, exclamation, roar, bellow, yell, scream, shriek.

cryptic *adj* enigmatic, ambiguous, equivocal, puzzling, perplexing, mysterious, strange, bizarre, secret, hidden, veiled, obscure, abstruse, esoteric, dark, occult.

🖃 straightforward, clear, obvious.

cuddle *v* hug, embrace, clasp, hold,

nurse, nestle, snuggle, pet, fondle, caress.

cuddly *adj* cuddlesome, lovable, huggable, plump, soft, warm, cosy.

cue *n* signal, sign, nod, hint, suggestion, reminder, prompt, incentive, stimulus.

cuff *v* hit, thump, box, clip, knock, biff (*infml*), buffet, slap, smack, strike, clout, clobber (*sl*), belt (*infml*), beat, whack (*infml*).

culminate *v* climax, end (up), terminate, close, conclude, finish, consummate.
  🔁 start, begin.

culmination *n* climax, height, peak, pinnacle, summit, top, crown, perfection, consummation, finale, conclusion, completion.
  🔁 start, beginning.

culprit *n* guilty party, offender, wrongdoer, miscreant, law-breaker, criminal, felon, delinquent.

cult *n* 1 SECT, denomination, school, movement, party, faction. 2 CRAZE, fad, fashion, vogue, trend.

cultivate *v* 1 FARM, till, work, plough, grow, sow, plant, tend, harvest. 2 FOSTER, nurture, cherish, help, aid, support, encourage, promote, further, work on, develop, train, prepare, polish, refine, improve, enrich.
  🔁 neglect.

cultural *adj* artistic, aesthetic, liberal, civilizing, humanizing, enlightening, educational, edifying, improving, enriching, elevating.

culture *n* 1 CIVILIZATION, society, lifestyle, way of life, customs, mores, the arts. 2 CULTIVATION, taste, education, enlightenment, breeding, gentility, refinement, politeness, urbanity.

cultured *adj* cultivated, civilized, advanced, enlightened, educated, well-read, well-informed, scholarly, highbrow, well-bred, refined, polished, genteel, urbane.

🔁 uncultured, uneducated, ignorant.

cumbersome *adj* awkward, inconvenient, bulky, unwieldy, unmanageable, burdensome, onerous, heavy, weighty.
  🔁 convenient, manageable.

cunning *adj* crafty, sly, artful, wily, tricky, devious, subtle, deceitful, guileful, sharp, shrewd, astute, canny, knowing, deep, imaginative, ingenious, skilful, deft, dexterous.
  🔁 naïve, ingenuous, gullible.
  n craftiness, slyness, artfulness, trickery, deviousness, subtlety, deceitfulness, guile, sharpness, shrewdness, astuteness, ingenuity, cleverness, adroitness.

cup *n* mug, tankard, beaker, goblet, chalice, trophy.

cupboard *n* cabinet, locker, closet, wardrobe.

curb *v* restrain, constrain, restrict, contain, control, check, moderate, bridle, muzzle, suppress, subdue, repress, inhibit, hinder, impede, hamper, retard.
  🔁 encourage, foster.

curdle *v* coagulate, congeal, clot, thicken, turn, sour, ferment.

cure *v* 1 HEAL, remedy, correct, restore, repair, mend, relieve, ease, alleviate, help. 2 PRESERVE, dry, smoke, salt, pickle, kipper.
  n remedy, antidote, panacea, medicine, specific, corrective, restorative, healing, treatment, therapy, alleviation, recovery.

curiosity *n* 1 INQUISITIVENESS, nosiness, prying, snooping, interest. 2 CURIO, objet d'art, antique, bygone, novelty, trinket, knick-knack. 3 ODDITY, rarity, freak, phenomenon, spectacle.

curious *adj* 1 INQUISITIVE, nosey, prying, meddlesome, questioning, inquiring, interested. 2 *a curious sight*: ODD, queer, funny (*infml*), strange, peculiar, bizarre, mysterious, puzzling, extraordinary, unusual,

rare, unique, novel, exotic, unconventional, unorthodox, quaint.
Ǝ 1 uninterested, indifferent.
2 ordinary, usual, normal.

curl *v* crimp, frizz, wave, ripple, bend, curve, meander, loop, turn, twist, wind, wreathe, twine, coil, spiral, corkscrew, scroll.
Ǝ uncurl.
n wave, kink, swirl, twist, ringlet, coil, spiral, whorl.

curly *adj* wavy, kinky, curling, spiralled, corkscrew, curled, crimped, permed, frizzy, fuzzy.
Ǝ straight.

currency *n* **1** MONEY, legal tender, coinage, coins, notes, bills.
2 ACCEPTANCE, publicity, popularity, vogue, circulation, prevalence, exposure.

Currencies of the world include: baht (Thailand), bolivar (Venezuela), cent (US, Canada, Australia, NZ, S Africa, etc), centavo (Portugal, Brazil, Mexico, etc), centime (France, Belgium, Algeria, etc), cruzeiro (Brazil), dinar (Iraq, Jordan, etc), dirham (Morocco), dollar (US, Canada, Australia, NZ, etc), dong (Vietnam), drachma (Greece), ecu (EC), escudo (Portugal), fils (Iraq, Jordan, etc), guilder (Netherlands), franc (France, Belgium, Switzerland, etc), karbovanets (Ukraine), kopeck (Russia), koruna (Czech Republic, Slovakia), krona (Sweden), króna (Iceland), krone (Denmark, Norway), kyat (Myanmar), lek (Albania), leu (Romania), lev (Bulgaria), lira (Italy), mark (Germany), pence (UK), peseta (Spain), peso (Mexico, Chile, etc), pfennig (Germany), piastre (Egypt, Syria, etc), pound (UK, Egypt, etc), punt (Ireland), rand (S Africa), rial (Iran), riyal (Saudi Arabia), rouble (Russia), rupee (India, Pakistan, etc), schilling (Austria), shekel (Israel), shilling (Kenya, Uganda, etc), som (Uzbekistan), sterling (UK), sucre (Ecuador), tolar (Slovenia), won (N Korea, S Korea), yen (Japan), yuan (China), zaïre (Zaire), zloty (Poland).

current *adj* present, on-going, existing, contemporary, present-day, modern, fashionable, up-to-date, up-to-the-minute, trendy (*infml*), popular, widespread, prevalent, common, general, prevailing, reigning, accepted.
Ǝ obsolete, old-fashioned.
n draught, stream, jet, flow, drift, tide, course, trend, tendency, undercurrent, mood, feeling.

curse *n* **1** SWEAR-WORD, oath, expletive, obscenity, profanity, blasphemy. **2** JINX, anathema, bane, evil, plague, scourge, affliction, trouble, torment, ordeal, calamity, disaster.
Ǝ 2 blessing, advantage.
v **1** SWEAR, blaspheme, damn, condemn, denounce, fulminate.
2 BLIGHT, plague, scourge, afflict, trouble, torment.
Ǝ 2 bless.

curtail *v* shorten, truncate, cut, trim, abridge, abbreviate, lessen, decrease, reduce, restrict.
Ǝ lengthen, extend, prolong.

curtain *n* blind, screen, backdrop, hanging, drapery, tapestry.

curve *v* bend, arch, arc, bow, bulge, hook, crook, turn, wind, twist, spiral, coil.
n bend, turn, arc, trajectory, loop, camber, curvature.

curved *adj* bent, arched, bowed, rounded, humped, convex, concave, crooked, twisted, sweeping, sinuous, serpentine.
Ǝ straight.

cushion *n* pad, buffer, shock absorber, bolster, pillow, headrest, hassock.
v soften, deaden, dampen, absorb, muffle, stifle, suppress, lessen,

mitigate, protect, bolster, buttress, support.

custody n **1** KEEPING, possession, charge, care, safe-keeping, protection, preservation, custodianship, trusteeship, guardianship, supervision. **2** DETENTION, confinement, imprisonment, incarceration.

custom n tradition, usage, use, habit, routine, procedure, practice, policy, way, manner, style, form, convention, etiquette, formality, observance, ritual.

customary adj traditional, conventional, accepted, established, habitual, routine, regular, usual, normal, ordinary, everyday, familiar, common, general, popular, fashionable, prevailing.

F3 unusual, rare.

customer n client, patron, regular, punter (infml), consumer, shopper, buyer, purchaser, prospect.

cut v **1** CLIP, trim, crop, shear, mow, shave, pare, chop, hack, hew, slice, carve, divide, part, split, bisect, dock, lop, sever, prune, excise, incise, penetrate, pierce, stab, wound, nick, gash, slit, slash, lacerate, score, engrave, chisel, sculpt. **2** REDUCE, decrease, lower, shorten, curtail, abbreviate, abridge, condense, précis, edit, delete. **3** IGNORE, cold-shoulder, spurn, avoid, snub, slight, rebuff, insult.

n **1** INCISION, wound, nick, gash, slit, slash, rip, laceration. **2** spending cuts: REDUCTION, decrease, lowering, cutback, saving, economy.

cut down 1 cut down a tree: fell, hew, lop, level, raze. **2** REDUCE, decrease, lower, lessen, diminish.

cut in interrupt, butt in, interject, interpose, intervene, intrude.

cut off 1 SEVER, amputate, separate, isolate, disconnect, block, obstruct, intercept. **2** STOP, end, halt, suspend, discontinue, disown, disinherit.

cut out excise, extract, remove, delete, eliminate, exclude, debar, stop, cease.

cut up chop, dice, mince, dissect, divide, carve, slice, slash.

cutback n cut, saving, economy, retrenchment, reduction, decrease, lowering, lessening.

cutlery

Items of cutlery include: knife, butter-knife, carving-knife, fish knife, steak knife, cheese knife, breadknife, vegetable knife, fork, fish fork, carving fork, spoon, dessert-spoon, tablespoon, teaspoon, soup-spoon, caddy spoon, salt spoon, apostle spoon, ladle, salad servers, fish slice, cake server, sugar tongs, chopsticks, canteen of cutlery.

---

cut-price adj reduced, sale, discount, bargain, cheap, low-priced.

cutter

Types of cutter include: axe, billhook, blade, chisel, chopper, clippers, guillotine, hedgetrimmer, knife, flick knife, penknife, pocket knife, Stanley knife®, Swiss army knife, lopper, machete, mower, lawnmower, plane, razor, saw, chainsaw, fretsaw, hacksaw, jigsaw, scalpel, scissors, scythe, secateurs, shears, pinking shears, sickle, Strimmer®, sword.

---

cutting adj sharp, keen, pointed, trenchant, incisive, penetrating, piercing, wounding, stinging, biting, mordant, caustic, acid, scathing, sarcastic, malicious, bitter, raw, chill. n clipping, extract, piece.

cycle n circle, round, rotation, revolution, series, sequence, phase, period, era, age, epoch, aeon.

cylinder n column, barrel, drum, reel, bobbin, spool, spindle.

cynic n sceptic, doubter, pessimist, killjoy, spoilsport (infml), scoffer, knocker (*infml*).

cynical *adj* sceptical, doubtful, distrustful, pessimistic, negative, scornful, derisive, contemptuous, sneering, scoffing, mocking, sarcastic, sardonic, ironic.

cynicism *n* scepticism, doubt, disbelief, distrust, pessimism, scorn, sarcasm, irony.

D

dab *v* pat, tap, daub, swab, wipe. *n* **1** BIT, dollop (*infml*), drop, speck, spot, trace, smear, smudge, fleck. **2** TOUCH, pat, stroke, tap.

dabble *v* **1** TRIFLE, tinker, toy, dally, potter. **2** PADDLE, moisten, wet, sprinkle, splash.

dabbler *n* amateur, dilettante, trifler.
F3 professional, expert.

daft *adj* **1** FOOLISH, crazy, silly, stupid, absurd, dotty (*infml*), idiotic, inane. **2** INSANE, mad, lunatic, simple, crazy, mental. **3** (*infml*) INFATUATED.
F3 **1** sensible. **2** sane.

daily *adj* **1** REGULAR, routine, everyday, customary, common, commonplace, ordinary. **2** EVERYDAY, diurnal (*fml*).

dainty *adj* **1** DELICATE, elegant, exquisite, refined, fine, graceful, neat, charming, delectable. **2** FASTIDIOUS, fussy, particular, scrupulous, nice (*fml*).
F3 **1** gross, clumsy.

dam *n* barrier, barrage, embankment, blockage, obstruction, hindrance.
v block, confine, restrict, check, barricade, staunch, stem, obstruct.

damage *n* harm, injury, hurt, destruction, devastation, loss, suffering, mischief, mutilation, impairment, detriment.
F3 repair.
v harm, injure, hurt, spoil, ruin, impair, mar, wreck, deface, mutilate,
weaken, tamper with, play havoc with, incapacitate.
F3 mend, repair, fix.

damn *v* **1** CURSE, swear, blast, imprecate, blaspheme. **2** ABUSE, revile, denounce, criticise, censure, slate (*infml*), denunciate, execrate, castigate, slam (*infml*). **3** CONDEMN, doom, sentence.
F3 bless.

damnation *n* condemnation, doom, denunciation, perdition, excommunication, anathema.

damp *n* dampness, moisture, clamminess, dankness, humidity, wet, dew, drizzle, fog, mist, vapour.
F3 dryness.
adj moist, wet, clammy, dank, humid, dewy, muggy, drizzly, misty, soggy.
F3 dry, arid.

dampen *v* **1** MOISTEN, wet, spray. **2** DISCOURAGE, dishearten, deter, dash, dull, deaden, restrain, check, depress, dismay, reduce, lessen, moderate, decrease, diminish, muffle, stifle, smother.
F3 **1** dry. **2** encourage.

dance *n* ball, hop (*infml*), knees-up (*infml*), social, shindig (*infml*).

Dances include: waltz, quickstep, foxtrot, tango, polka, one-step, military two-step, valeta, Lancers, rumba, samba, mambo, bossanova, beguine, fandango, flamenco, mazurka, bolero, paso doble, can-can, rock 'n' roll, jive, twist, stomp, bop, jitterbug, mashed potato; black bottom, Charleston, cha-cha, turkey-trot; Circassian circle, Paul Jones, jig, reel, quadrille, Highland fling, morris-dance, clog dance, hoe-down, hokey-cokey, Lambeth Walk, conga, belly-dance; galliard, gavotte, minuet.

Types of dancing include: ballet, tap, ballroom, old-time, disco, folk, country, Irish, Highland, Latin-American, flamenco, clog-dancing, morris dancing, limbo-dancing, break-dancing, robotics.

Dance functions include: disco, dance, social, tea dance, barn dance, ball, fancy dress ball, charity ball, hunt ball, hop (*infml*), knees-up (*sl*), shindig (*infml*), rave (*infml*), prom (*US*), ceilidh.

danger n 1 *in danger of falling*: insecurity, endangerment, jeopardy, precariousness, liability, vulnerability. 2 *the dangers of smoking*: risk, threat, peril, hazard, menace.
E3 1 safety, security. 2 safety.

dangerous adj unsafe, insecure, risky, threatening, breakneck, hairy (*infml*), hazardous, perilous, precarious, reckless, treacherous, vulnerable, menacing, exposed, alarming, critical, severe, serious, grave, daring, nasty.
E3 safe, secure, harmless.

dangle v 1 HANG, droop, swing, sway, flap, trail. 2 TEMPT, entice, flaunt, flourish, lure, tantalize.

dank adj damp, moist, clammy, dewy, slimy, soggy.
E3 dry.

dappled adj speckled, mottled, spotted, stippled, dotted, flecked, freckled, variegated, bespeckled, piebald, checkered.

dare v 1 RISK, venture, brave, hazard, adventure, endanger, stake, gamble. 2 CHALLENGE, goad, provoke, taunt. 3 DEFY, presume.
n challenge, provocation, taunt, gauntlet.

daredevil n adventurer, desperado, madcap.
E3 coward.

daring adj bold, adventurous, intrepid, fearless, brave, plucky, audacious, dauntless, reckless, rash, impulsive, valiant.
E3 cautious, timid, afraid.
n boldness, fearlessness, courage, bravery, nerve, audacity, guts (*infml*), intrepidity, defiance, pluck, rashness, spirit, grit, gall, prowess.
E3 caution, timidity, cowardice.

dark adj 1 *a dark room*: unlit, overcast, black, dim, unilluminated, shadowy, murky, cloudy, dusky, dingy. 2 *a dark manner*: gloomy, grim, cheerless, dismal, bleak, forbidding, sombre, sinister, mournful, ominous, menacing, drab. 3 *dark secrets*: hidden, mysterious, obscure, secret, unintelligible, enigmatic, cryptic, abstruse.
E3 1 light. 2 bright, cheerful.
3 comprehensible.
n 1 DARKNESS, dimness, night, night-time, nightfall, gloom, dusk, twilight, murkiness.
2 CONCEALMENT, secrecy, obscurity.
E3 1 light. 2 openness.

darken v 1 DIM, obscure, blacken, cloud (over), shadow, overshadow, eclipse. 2 DEPRESS, sadden.
E3 1 lighten. 2 brighten.

darling n beloved, dear, dearest, favourite, sweetheart, love, pet.
adj dear, beloved, adored, cherished, precious, treasured.

dart v 1 DASH, bound, sprint, flit, flash, fly, rush, run, race, spring, tear. 2 THROW, hurl, fling, shoot, sling, launch, propel, send.
n bolt, arrow, barb, shaft.

dash v **1** RUSH, dart, hurry, race, sprint, run, bolt, tear. **2** FLING, throw, crash, hurl. **3** DISCOURAGE, disappoint, dampen, confound, blight, ruin, destroy, spoil, frustrate, smash, shatter.
n **1** DROP, pinch, touch, flavour, soupçon, suggestion, hint, bit, little. **2** SPRINT, dart, bolt, rush, spurt, race, run.

dashing adj **1** LIVELY, vigorous, spirited, gallant, daring, bold, plucky, exuberant. **2** SMART, stylish, elegant, debonair, showy, flamboyant.
1 lethargic. **2** dowdy.

data n information, documents, facts, input, statistics, figures, details, materials.

date n **1** TIME, age, period, era, stage, epoch. **2** APPOINTMENT, engagement, assignation, meeting, rendezvous. **3** ESCORT, steady (infml), partner, friend.

out-of-date adj old-fashioned, unfashionable, outdated, obsolete, dated, outmoded, antiquated, passé.
1 fashionable, modern.

up-to-date adj fashionable, modern, current, contemporary.
old-fashioned, dated.

daunt v **1** DISCOURAGE, dishearten, put off, dispirit, deter.
2 INTIMIDATE, overawe, unnerve, alarm, dismay, frighten, scare.
1 encourage.

dauntless adj fearless, undaunted, resolute, brave, courageous, bold, intrepid, daring, plucky, valiant.
discouraged, disheartened.

dawdle v delay, loiter, lag, hang about, dally, trail, potter, dilly-dally (infml).
hurry.

dawn n **1** SUNRISE, daybreak, morning, daylight. **2** BEGINNING, start, emergence, onset, origin, birth, advent.
1 dusk. **2** end.

v **1** BREAK, brighten, lighten, gleam, glimmer. **2** BEGIN, appear, emerge, open, develop, originate, rise.

day n **1** DAYTIME, daylight. **2** AGE, period, time, date, era, generation, epoch.
1 night.

day after day regularly, continually, endlessly, persistently, monotonously, perpetually, relentlessly.

day by day gradually, progressively, slowly but surely, steadily.

daydream n fantasy, imagining, reverie, castles in the air, pipe dream, vision, musing, wish, dream, figment.
v fantasize, imagine, muse, fancy, dream.

daze v **1** STUN, stupefy, shock. **2** DAZZLE, bewilder, blind, confuse, baffle, dumbfound, amaze, surprise, startle, perplex, astonish, flabbergast (infml), astound, stagger.
n bewilderment, confusion, stupor, trance, shock, distraction.

dazzle v **1** DAZE, blind, confuse, blur. **2** SPARKLE, fascinate, impress, overwhelm, awe, overawe, scintillate, bedazzle, amaze, astonish, bewitch, stupefy.
n sparkle, brilliance, magnificence, splendour, scintillation, glitter, glare.

dead adj **1** LIFELESS, deceased, inanimate, defunct, departed, late, gone. **2** UNRESPONSIVE, apathetic, dull, indifferent, insensitive, numb, cold, frigid, lukewarm, torpid.
3 EXHAUSTED, tired, worn out, dead-beat (infml). **4** EXACT, absolute, perfect, unqualified, utter, outright, complete, entire, total, downright.
1 alive. **2** lively. **3** refreshed.

deaden v reduce, blunt, muffle, lessen, quieten, suppress, weaken, numb, diminish, stifle, alleviate, anaesthetize, desensitize, smother, check, abate, allay, dampen, hush, mute, paralyse.
heighten.

deadlock *n* standstill, stalemate, impasse, halt.

deadly *adj* **1** *deadly poison*: lethal, fatal, dangerous, venomous, destructive, pernicious, malignant, murderous, mortal. **2** *a deadly lecture*: dull, boring, uninteresting, tedious, monotonous. **3** *deadly aim*: unerring, effective, true.
ⓔ **1** harmless. **2** exciting.

deaf *adj* **1** HARD OF HEARING, stone-deaf. **2** UNCONCERNED, indifferent, unmoved, oblivious, heedless, unmindful.
ⓔ **2** aware, conscious.

deafening *adj* piercing, ear-splitting, booming, resounding, thunderous, ringing, roaring.
ⓔ quiet.

deal *v* **1** APPORTION, distribute, share, dole out, divide, allot, dispense, assign, mete out, give, bestow. **2** TRADE, negotiate, traffic, bargain, treat.
n **1** QUANTITY, amount, extent, degree, portion, share.
2 AGREEMENT, contract, understanding, pact, transaction, bargain, buy. **3** ROUND, hand, distribution.
deal with attend to, concern, see to, manage, handle, cope with, treat, consider, oversee.

dealer *n* trader, merchant, wholesaler, marketer, merchandizer.

dear *adj* **1** LOVED, beloved, treasured, valued, cherished, precious, favourite, esteemed, intimate, close, darling, familiar. **2** EXPENSIVE, high-priced, costly, overpriced, pric(e)y (*infml*).
ⓔ **1** disliked, hated. **2** cheap.
n beloved, loved one, precious, darling, treasure.

dearly *adv* **1** *he loves her dearly*: fondly, affectionately, lovingly, devotedly, tenderly. **2** *I wish it dearly*: greatly, extremely, profoundly.

dearth *n* scarcity, shortage, insufficiency, inadequacy, deficiency, lack, want, absence, scantiness, sparsity, need, paucity, poverty, famine.
ⓔ excess, abundance.

death *n* **1** DECEASE, end, finish, loss, demise, departure, fatality, cessation, passing, expiration, dissolution. **2** DESTRUCTION, ruin, undoing, annihilation, downfall, extermination, extinction, obliteration, eradication.
ⓔ **1** life, birth.

deathly *adj* **1** ASHEN, grim, haggard, pale, pallid, ghastly, wan. **2** FATAL, deadly, mortal, intense.

debase *v* **1** DEGRADE, demean, devalue, disgrace, dishonour, shame, humble, humiliate, lower, reduce, abase, defile. **2** CONTAMINATE, pollute, corrupt, adulterate, taint.
ⓔ **1** elevate. **2** purify.

debatable *adj* questionable, uncertain, disputable, contestable, controversial, arguable, open to question, doubtful, contentious, undecided, unsettled, problematical, dubious, moot.
ⓔ unquestionable, certain, incontrovertible.

debate *v* **1** DISPUTE, argue, discuss, contend, wrangle. **2** CONSIDER, deliberate, ponder, reflect, meditate on, mull over, weigh.
n discussion, argument, controversy, disputation, deliberation, consideration, contention, dispute, reflection, polemic.

debauchery *n* depravity, intemperance, overindulgence, dissipation, licentiousness, dissoluteness, excess, decadence, wantonness, lewdness, carousal, orgy, revel, lust, riot.
ⓔ restraint, temperance.

debilitate *v* weaken, enervate, undermine, sap, incapacitate, wear out, exhaust, impair.

strengthen, invigorate, energize.

debris n remains, ruins, rubbish, waste, wreck, wreckage, litter, fragments, rubble, trash, pieces, bits, sweepings, drift.

debt n indebtedness, obligation, debit, arrears, due, liability, duty, bill, commitment, claim, score.
credit, asset.

debtor n borrower, bankrupt, insolvent, defaulter, mortgagor.
creditor.

debunk v expose, deflate, show up, ridicule, mock, explode, lampoon.

debut n introduction, launching, beginning, entrance, presentation, inauguration, première, appearance, initiation.

decadent adj **1** CORRUPT, debased, debauched, depraved, dissolute, immoral, degenerate, degraded, self-indulgent. **2** DECAYING, declining.
1 moral.

decay v **1** ROT, go bad, putrefy, decompose, spoil, perish, mortify. **2** DECLINE, deteriorate, disintegrate, corrode, crumble, waste away, degenerate, wear away, dwindle, shrivel, wither, sink.
2 flourish, grow.
n **1** ROT, decomposition, rotting, perishing. **2** DECLINE, deterioration, disintegration, degeneration, collapse, decadence, wasting, failing, withering, fading.

decease n death, dying, demise, departure, passing, dissolution.

deceased adj dead, departed, former, late, lost, defunct, expired, gone, finished, extinct.
n dead, departed.

deceit n deception, pretence, cheating, misrepresentation, fraud, duplicity, trickery, fraudulence, double-dealing, underhandedness, fake, guile, sham, subterfuge, swindle, treachery, hypocrisy, artifice, ruse, cunning, slyness, craftiness, stratagem, wile,

imposition, feint, shift, abuse.
honesty, openness, frankness.

deceitful adj dishonest, deceptive, deceiving, false, insincere, untrustworthy, double-dealing, fraudulent, two-faced (infml), treacherous, duplicitous, guileful, tricky (infml), underhand, sneaky, counterfeit, crafty, hypocritical, designing, illusory, knavish.
honest, open.

deceive v mislead, delude, cheat, betray, fool, take in (infml), trick, dissemble, hoax, con (infml), have on (infml), take for a ride (infml), double-cross (infml), dupe, kid (infml), swindle, impose upon, bamboozle (infml), two-time (infml), lead on, outwit, hoodwink, beguile, ensnare, camouflage, abuse, befool, gull.

decency n propriety, courtesy, modesty, decorum, respectability, civility, correctness, fitness, etiquette, helpfulness.
impropriety, discourtesy.

decent adj **1** RESPECTABLE, proper, fitting, decorous, chaste, seemly, suitable, modest, appropriate, presentable, pure, fit, becoming, befitting, nice. **2** KIND, obliging, courteous, helpful, generous, polite, gracious. **3** ADEQUATE, acceptable, satisfactory, reasonable, sufficient, tolerable, competent.
1 indecent. **2** disobliging.

deception n deceit, pretence, trick, cheat, fraud, imposture, lie, dissembling, deceptiveness, insincerity, con (infml), sham, subterfuge, artifice, hypocrisy, bluff, treachery, hoax, fraudulence, duplicity, ruse, snare, stratagem, leg-pull (infml), illusion, wile, guile, craftiness, cunning.
openness, honesty.

deceptive adj dishonest, false, fraudulent, misleading, unreliable, illusive, fake, illusory, spurious,

decide

mock, fallacious, ambiguous, specious.

Ea genuine, artless, open.

decide v choose, determine, resolve, reach a decision, settle, elect, opt, judge, adjudicate, conclude, fix, purpose, decree.

decided adj **1** DEFINITE, certain, undeniable, indisputable, absolute, clear-cut, undisputed, unmistakable, unquestionable, positive, unambiguous, categorical, distinct, emphatic. **2** RESOLUTE, decisive, determined, firm, unhesitating, deliberate, forthright.

Ea 1 inconclusive. **2** irresolute.

decipher v decode, unscramble, crack, construe, interpret, make out (*infml*), figure out (*infml*), understand, transliterate.

Ea encode.

decision n **1** RESULT, conclusion, outcome, verdict, finding, settlement, judgement, arbitration, ruling. **2** DETERMINATION, decisiveness, firmness, resolve, purpose.

decisive adj **1** CONCLUSIVE, definite, definitive, absolute, final. **2** DETERMINED, resolute, decided, positive, firm, forceful, forthright, strong-minded. **3** SIGNIFICANT, critical, crucial, influential, momentous, fateful.

Ea 1 inconclusive. **2** indecisive. **3** insignificant.

declaration n **1** AFFIRMATION, acknowledgement, assertion, statement, testimony, attestation, disclosure, profession, revelation. **2** ANNOUNCEMENT, notification, pronouncement, proclamation, edict, manifesto, promulgation.

declare v **1** AFFIRM, assert, claim, profess, maintain, state, attest, certify, confess, confirm, disclose, reveal, show, aver, swear, testify, witness, validate. **2** ANNOUNCE, proclaim, pronounce, decree, broadcast.

decline v **1** REFUSE, reject, deny, forgo, avoid, balk. **2** DIMINISH, decrease, dwindle, lessen, fall, sink, wane. **3** DECAY, deteriorate, worsen, degenerate. **4** DESCEND, sink, slope, dip, slant.

Ea 3 improve. **4** rise.

n **1** DETERIORATION, dwindling, lessening, decay, degeneration, weakening, worsening, failing, downturn, diminution, falling-off, recession, slump, abatement. **2** DESCENT, dip, declivity, declination, hill, slope, incline, divergence, deviation.

Ea 1 improvement. **2** rise.

decode v decipher, interpret, unscramble, translate, transliterate, uncipher.

Ea encode.

decompose v disintegrate, rot, decay, putrefy, break down, break up, crumble, spoil, dissolve, separate, fester.

décor n decoration, furnishings, colour scheme, ornamentation, scenery.

decorate v **1** ORNAMENT, adorn, beautify, embellish, trim, deck, tart up (*sl*), grace, enrich, prettify, trick out. **2** RENOVATE, do up (*infml*), paint, paper, colour, refurbish. **3** HONOUR, crown, cite, garland, bemedal.

decoration n **1** ORNAMENT, adornment, ornamentation, trimming, embellishment, beautification, garnish, flourish, enrichment, elaboration, frill, scroll, bauble. **2** AWARD, medal, order, badge, garland, crown, colours, ribbon, laurel, star, emblem.

decorative adj ornamental, fancy, adorning, beautifying, embellishing, non-functional, pretty, ornate, enhancing.

Ea plain.

decorum n propriety, seemliness, etiquette, good manners, respectability, protocol, behaviour, decency, dignity, deportment, restraint, politeness, modesty, grace, breeding.

🔁 impropriety, indecorum, bad manners.

decoy n lure, trap, enticement, inducement, ensnarement, pretence, attraction, bait.

v bait, lure, entrap, entice, ensnare, allure, tempt, deceive, attract, seduce, lead, draw.

decrease v lessen, lower, diminish, dwindle, decline, fall off, reduce, subside, abate, cut down, contract, drop, ease, shrink, taper, wane, slim, slacken, peter out, curtail.

🔁 increase.

n lessening, reduction, decline, falling-off, dwindling, loss, diminution, abatement, cutback, contraction, downturn, ebb, shrinkage, subsidence, step-down.

🔁 increase.

decree n order, command, law, ordinance, regulation, ruling, statute, act, enactment, edict, proclamation, mandate, precept, interlocution.

v order, command, rule, lay down, dictate, decide, determine, ordain, prescribe, proclaim, pronounce, enact.

decrepit adj dilapidated, run-down, rickety, broken-down, worn-out, tumble-down.

dedicate v **1** DEVOTE, commit, assign, give over to, pledge, present, offer, sacrifice, surrender. **2** CONSECRATE, bless, sanctify, set apart, hallow. **3** dedicate a book: inscribe, address.

dedicated adj devoted, committed, enthusiastic, single-minded, whole-hearted, single-hearted, zealous, given over to, purposeful.

🔁 uncommitted, apathetic.

dedication n **1** COMMITMENT, devotion, single-mindedness, whole-heartedness, allegiance, attachment,

adherence, faithfulness, loyalty, self-sacrifice. **2** CONSECRATION, hallowing, presentation. **3** INSCRIPTION, address.

🔁 **1** apathy.

deduce v derive, infer, gather, conclude, reason, surmise, understand, draw, glean.

deduct v subtract, take away, remove, reduce by, decrease by, knock off (infml), withdraw.

🔁 add.

deduction n **1** INFERENCE, reasoning, finding, conclusion, corollary, assumption, result. **2** SUBTRACTION, reduction, decrease, diminution, abatement, withdrawal, discount, allowance.

🔁 **2** addition, increase.

deed n **1** ACTION, act, achievement, performance, exploit, feat, fact, truth, reality. **2** DOCUMENT, contract, record, title, transaction, indenture (fml).

deep adj **1** PROFOUND, bottomless, unplumbed, fathomless, yawning, immersed. **2** OBSCURE, mysterious, difficult, recondite, abstruse, esoteric. **3** WISE, perceptive, discerning, profound, learned, astute. **4** INTENSE, serious, earnest, extreme. **5** LOW, bass, resonant, booming.

🔁 **1** shallow, open. **2** clear, plain, open. **3** superficial. **4** light. **5** high.

deepen v **1** INTENSIFY, grow, increase, strengthen, reinforce, magnify. **2** HOLLOW, scoop out.

deep-seated adj ingrained, entrenched, deep-rooted, fixed, confirmed, deep, settled.

🔁 eradicable, temporary.

deface v damage, spoil, disfigure, blemish, impair, mutilate, mar, sully, tarnish, vandalize, deform, obliterate, injure, destroy.

🔁 repair.

defamation (fml) n vilification, aspersion (fml), slander, libel, disparagement, slur, smear, innuendo, scandal.

🔁 commendation, praise.

defamatory (*fml*) *adj* vilifying, slanderous, libellous, denigrating, disparaging, pejorative, insulting, injurious, derogatory.

🔁 complimentary, appreciative.

default *n* failure, absence, neglect, non-payment, omission, deficiency, lapse, fault, want, lack, defect.

v fail, evade, defraud, neglect, dodge, swindle, backslide.

defaulter *n* non-payer, offender.

defeat *v* 1 CONQUER, beat, overpower, subdue, overthrow, worst, repel, subjugate, overwhelm, rout, ruin, thump (*infml*), quell, vanquish (*fml*). 2 FRUSTRATE, confound, balk, get the better of, disappoint, foil, thwart, baffle, checkmate.

n 1 CONQUEST, beating, overthrow, rout, subjugation, vanquishment (*fml*). 2 FRUSTRATION, failure, setback, reverse, disappointment, checkmate.

defeatist *n* pessimist, quitter, prophet of doom.

🔁 optimist.

adj pessimistic, resigned, fatalistic, despondent, helpless, hopeless, despairing, gloomy.

🔁 optimistic.

defect *n* imperfection, fault, flaw, deficiency, failing, mistake, inadequacy, blemish, error, bug (*infml*), shortcoming, want, weakness, frailty, lack, spot, absence, taint.

v desert, break faith, rebel, apostatize (*fml*), revolt, renegue.

defective *adj* faulty, imperfect, out of order, flawed, deficient, broken, abnormal.

🔁 in order, operative.

defence *n* 1 PROTECTION, resistance, security, fortification, cover, safeguard, shelter, guard, shield, deterrence, barricade, bastion, immunity, bulwark, rampart,

buttress. 2 JUSTIFICATION, explanation, excuse, argument, exoneration, plea, vindication, apologia (*fml*), pleading, alibi, case.

🔁 1 attack, assault. 2 accusation.

defenceless *adj* unprotected, undefended, unarmed, unguarded, vulnerable, exposed, helpless, powerless.

🔁 protected, guarded.

defend *v* 1 PROTECT, guard, safeguard, shelter, fortify, secure, shield, screen, cover, contest. 2 SUPPORT, stand up for, stand by, uphold, endorse, vindicate, champion, argue for, speak up for, justify, plead.

🔁 1 attack. 2 accuse.

defendant *n* accused, offender, prisoner, respondent.

defender *n* 1 PROTECTOR, guard, bodyguard. 2 SUPPORTER, advocate, vindicator, champion, patron, sponsor, counsel.

🔁 1 attacker. 2 accuser.

defensive *adj* 1 PROTECTIVE, defending, safeguarding, wary, opposing, cautious, watchful. 2 SELF-JUSTIFYING, apologetic.

defer[1] *v* delay, postpone, put off, adjourn, hold over, shelve, suspend, procrastinate, prorogue (*fml*), protract, waive.

defer[2] *v* yield, give way, comply, submit, accede, capitulate, respect, bow.

deference *n* 1 SUBMISSION, submissiveness, compliance, acquiescence, obedience, yielding. 2 RESPECT, regard, honour, esteem, reverence, courtesy, civility, politeness, consideration.

🔁 1 resistance. 2 contempt.

defiance *n* opposition, confrontation, resistance, challenge, disobedience, rebelliousness, contempt, insubordination, disregard, insolence.

🔁 compliance, acquiescence,

submissiveness.

defiant *adj* challenging, resistant, antagonistic, aggressive, rebellious, insubordinate, disobedient, intransigent, bold, contumacious (*fml*) insolent, obstinate, unco-operative, provocative.
🔁 compliant, acquiescent, submissive.

deficiency *n* **1** SHORTAGE, lack, inadequacy, scarcity, insufficiency, dearth, want, scantiness, absence, deficit. **2** IMPERFECTION, shortcoming, weakness, fault, defect, flaw, failing, frailty.
🔁 **1** excess, surfeit. **2** perfection.

deficient *adj* **1** INADEQUATE, insufficient, scarce, short, lacking, wanting, meagre, scanty, skimpy, incomplete. **2** IMPERFECT, impaired, flawed, faulty, defective, unsatisfactory, inferior, weak.
🔁 **1** excessive. **2** perfect.

deficit *n* shortage, shortfall, deficiency, loss, arrears, lack, default.
🔁 excess.

defile *v* pollute, violate, contaminate, degrade, dishonour, desecrate, debase, soil, stain, sully, tarnish, taint, profane, corrupt, disgrace.

define *v* **1** *define the boundaries*: bound, limit, delimit, demarcate, mark out. **2** *define the meaning*: explain, characterize, describe, interpret, expound, determine, designate, specify, spell out, detail.

definite *adj* **1** CERTAIN, settled, sure, positive, fixed, decided, determined, assured, guaranteed. **2** CLEAR, clear-cut, exact, precise, specific, explicit, particular, obvious, marked.
🔁 **1** indefinite. **2** vague.

definitely *adv* positively, surely, unquestionably, absolutely, certainly, categorically, undeniably, clearly, doubtless, unmistakably, plainly, obviously, indeed, easily.

definition *n* **1** DELINEATION,

demarcation, delimitation. **2** EXPLANATION, description, interpretation, exposition, clarification, elucidation, determination. **3** DISTINCTNESS, clarity, precision, clearness, focus, contrast, sharpness.

definitive *adj* decisive, conclusive, final, authoritative, standard, correct, ultimate, reliable, exhaustive, perfect, exact, absolute, complete.
🔁 interim.

deflate *v* **1** FLATTEN, puncture, collapse, exhaust, squash, empty, contract, void, shrink, squeeze. **2** DEBUNK, humiliate, put down (*infml*), dash, dispirit, humble, mortify, disconcert. **3** DECREASE, devalue, reduce, lessen, lower, diminish, depreciate, depress.
🔁 **1** inflate. **2** boost. **3** increase.

deflect *v* deviate, diverge, turn (aside), swerve, veer, sidetrack, twist, avert, wind, glance off, bend, ricochet.

deform *v* distort, contort, disfigure, warp, mar, pervert, ruin, spoil, twist.

deformed *adj* distorted, misshapen, contorted, disfigured, crippled, crooked, bent, twisted, warped, buckled, defaced, mangled, maimed, marred, ruined, mutilated, perverted, corrupted.

deformity *n* distortion, misshapenness, malformation, disfigurement, abnormality, irregularity, misproportion, defect, ugliness, monstrosity, corruption.

defraud *v* cheat, swindle, dupe, fleece, sting (*infml*), rip off (*infml*), do (*infml*), diddle (*infml*), rob, trick, con (*infml*), rook, deceive, delude, embezzle, beguile.

deft *adj* adept, handy, dexterous, nimble, skilful, adroit, agile, expert, nifty, proficient, able, neat, clever.
🔁 clumsy, awkward.

defunct *adj* **1** DEAD, deceased, departed, gone, expired, extinct.

2 OBSOLETE, invalid, inoperative, expired.

☷ 1 alive, live. 2 operative.

defy v 1 *defy the authorities*: challenge, confront, resist, dare, brave, face, repel, spurn, beard, flout, withstand, disregard, scorn, despise, defeat, provoke, thwart. 2 *her writings defy categorization*: elude, frustrate, baffle, foil.

☷ 1 obey. 2 permit.

degenerate adj dissolute, debauched, depraved, degraded, debased, base, low, decadent, corrupt, fallen, immoral, mean, degenerated, perverted, deteriorated.

☷ moral, upright.

v decline, deteriorate, sink, decay, rot, slip, worsen, regress, fall off, lapse, decrease.

☷ improve.

degradation n 1 DETERIORATION, degeneration, decline, downgrading, demotion. 2 ABASEMENT, humiliation, mortification, dishonour, disgrace, shame, ignominy, decadence.

☷ 1 virtue. 2 enhancement.

degrade v 1 DISHONOUR, disgrace, debase, abase, shame, humiliate, humble, discredit, demean, lower, weaken, impair, deteriorate, cheapen, adulterate, corrupt. 2 DEMOTE, depose, downgrade, deprive, cashier.

☷ 1 exalt. 2 promote.

degree n 1 GRADE, class, rank, order, position, standing, status. 2 EXTENT, measure, range, stage, step, level, intensity, standard. 3 LEVEL, limit, unit, mark.

deify v exalt, elevate, worship, glorify, idolize, extol, venerate, immortalize, ennoble, idealize.

deign v condescend, stoop, lower oneself, consent, demean oneself.

deity n god, goddess, divinity, godhead, idol, demigod, demigoddess, power, immortal.

dejected adj downcast, despondent, depressed, downhearted, disheartened, down, low, melancholy, disconsolate, sad, miserable, cast down, gloomy, glum, crestfallen, dismal, wretched, doleful, morose, spiritless.

☷ cheerful, high-spirited, happy.

delay v 1 OBSTRUCT, hinder, impede, hold up, check, hold back, set back, stop, halt, detain. 2 DEFER, put off, postpone, procrastinate, suspend, shelve, hold over, stall. 3 DAWDLE, linger, lag, loiter, dilly-dally (*infml*), tarry.

☷ 1 accelerate. 2 bring forward. 3 hurry.

n 1 OBSTRUCTION, hindrance, impediment, hold-up, check, setback, stay, stoppage. 2 DEFERMENT, postponement, procrastination, suspension. 3 DAWDLING, lingering, tarrying. 4 INTERRUPTION, lull, interval, wait.

☷ 1 hastening. 3 hurry. 4 continuation.

delegate n representative, agent, envoy, messenger, deputy, ambassador, commissioner.

v authorize, appoint, depute, charge, commission, assign, empower, entrust, devolve, consign, designate, nominate, name, hand over.

delegation n 1 DEPUTATION, commission, legation, mission, contingent, embassy. 2 AUTHORIZATION, commissioning, assignment.

delete v erase, remove, cross out, cancel, rub out, strike (out), obliterate, edit (out), blot out, efface.

☷ add, insert.

deliberate v consider, ponder, reflect, think, cogitate, meditate, mull over, debate, discuss, weigh, consult.

adj 1 INTENTIONAL, planned, calculated, prearranged, premeditated, willed, conscious, designed, considered, advised. 2

CAREFUL, unhurried, thoughtful, methodical, cautious, circumspect, studied, prudent, slow, ponderous, measured, heedful.
F3 1 unintentional, accidental. 2 hasty.

deliberation n 1 CONSIDERATION, reflection, thought, calculation, forethought, meditation, rumination, study, debate, discussion, consultation, speculation. 2 CARE, carefulness, caution, circumspection, prudence.

delicacy n 1 DAINTINESS, fineness, elegance, exquisiteness, lightness, precision. 2 REFINEMENT, sensitivity, subtlety, finesse, discrimination, tact, niceness. 3 TITBIT, dainty, taste, sweetmeat, savoury, relish.
F3 1 coarseness, roughness.
2 tactlessness.

delicate adj 1 FINE, fragile, dainty, exquisite, flimsy, elegant, graceful. 2 FRAIL, weak, ailing, faint.
3 SENSITIVE, scrupulous, discriminating, careful, accurate, precise. 4 SUBTLE, muted, pastel, soft.
F3 1 coarse, clumsy. 2 healthy.

delicious adj 1 ENJOYABLE, pleasant, agreeable, delightful.
2 APPETIZING, palatable, tasty, delectable, scrumptious (infml), mouth-watering, succulent, savoury.
F3 1 unpleasant. 2 unpalatable.

delight n bliss, happiness, joy, pleasure, ecstasy, enjoyment, gladness, rapture, transport, gratification, jubilation.
F3 disgust, displeasure.
v please, charm, gratify, enchant, tickle, thrill, ravish.
F3 displease, dismay.

delight in enjoy, relish, like, love, appreciate, revel in, take pride in, glory in, savour.
F3 dislike, hate.

delighted adj charmed, elated, happy, pleased, enchanted, captivated, ecstatic, thrilled,

overjoyed, jubilant, joyous.
F3 disappointed, dismayed.

delightful adj charming, enchanting, captivating, enjoyable, pleasant, thrilling, agreeable, pleasurable, engaging, attractive, pleasing, gratifying, entertaining, fascinating.
F3 nasty, unpleasant.

delinquency n crime, offence, wrong-doing, misbehaviour, misconduct, law-breaking, misdemeanour, criminality.

delinquent n offender, criminal, wrong-doer, law-breaker, hooligan, culprit, miscreant (fml).

delirious adj demented, raving, incoherent, beside oneself, deranged, frenzied, light-headed, wild, mad, frantic, insane, crazy, ecstatic.
F3 sane.

deliver v 1 deliver a parcel: convey, bring, send, give, carry, supply.
2 SURRENDER, hand over, relinquish, yield, transfer, grant, entrust, commit. 3 UTTER, speak, proclaim, pronounce.
4 ADMINISTER, inflict, direct. 5 SET FREE, liberate, release, emancipate.

delivery n 1 CONVEYANCE, consignment, dispatch, transmission, transfer, surrender.
2 ARTICULATION, enunciation, speech, utterance, intonation, elocution. 3 CHILDBIRTH, labour, confinement.

delude v deceive, mislead, beguile, dupe, take in, trick, hoodwink, hoax, cheat, misinform.

deluge n flood, inundation, downpour, torrent, spate, rush.
v flood, inundate, drench, drown, overwhelm, soak, swamp, engulf, submerge.

delusion n illusion, hallucination, fancy, misconception, misapprehension, deception, misbelief, fallacy.

demand v 1 ASK, request, call for, insist on, solicit, claim, exact, inquire, question, interrogate. **2** NECESSITATE, need, require, involve. n **1** REQUEST, question, claim, order, inquiry, desire, interrogation. **2** NEED, necessity, call.

demanding adj hard, difficult, challenging, exacting, taxing, tough, exhausting, wearing, back-breaking, insistent, pressing, urgent, trying.
ⓔ easy, undemanding, easy-going.

demean v lower, humble, degrade, humiliate, debase, abase, descend, stoop, condescend.
ⓔ exalt, enhance.

demeanour n bearing, manner, deportment, conduct, behaviour, air.

demented adj mad, insane, lunatic, out of one's mind, crazy, loony (sl), deranged, unbalanced, frenzied.
ⓔ sane.

demise n **1** DEATH, decease, end, passing, departure, termination, expiration. **2** DOWNFALL, fall, collapse, failure, ruin. **3** TRANSFER, conveyance, inheritance, transmission, alienation.

democracy n self-government, commonwealth, autonomy, republic.

democratic adj self-governing, representative, egalitarian, autonomous, popular, populist, republican.

demolish v **1** DESTROY, dismantle, knock down, pull down, flatten, bulldoze, raze, tear down, level. **2** RUIN, defeat, destroy, annihilate, wreck, overturn, overthrow.
ⓔ 1 build up.

demolition n destruction, dismantling, levelling, razing.

demon n **1** DEVIL, fiend, evil spirit, fallen angel, imp. **2** VILLAIN, devil, rogue, monster.

demonstrable adj verifiable, provable, arguable, attestable, self-evident, obvious, evident, certain, clear, positive.
ⓔ unverifiable.

demonstrate v **1** SHOW, display,

prove, establish, exhibit, substantiate, manifest, testify to, indicate. **2** EXPLAIN, illustrate, describe, teach. **3** PROTEST, march, parade, rally, picket, sit in.

demonstration n **1** DISPLAY, exhibition, manifestation, proof, confirmation, affirmation, substantiation, validation, evidence, testimony, expression. **2** EXPLANATION, illustration, description, exposition, presentation, test, trial. **3** PROTEST, march, demo (infml), rally, picket, sit-in, parade.

demonstrative adj affectionate, expressive, expansive, emotional, open, loving.
ⓔ reserved, cold, restrained.

demoralize v **1** DISCOURAGE, dishearten, dispirit, undermine, depress, deject, crush, lower, disconcert. **2** CORRUPT, deprave, debase.
ⓔ 1 encourage. 2 improve.

demote v downgrade, degrade, relegate, reduce, cashier.
ⓔ promote, upgrade.

demur v disagree, dissent, object, take exception, refuse, protest, dispute, balk, scruple, doubt, hesitate.

demure adj modest, reserved, reticent, prim, coy, shy, retiring, prissy, grave, prudish, sober, strait-laced, staid.
ⓔ wanton, forward.

den n lair, hide-out, hole, retreat, study, hide-away, shelter, sanctuary, haunt.

denial n **1** CONTRADICTION, negation, dissent, repudiation, disavowal, disclaimer, dismissal, renunciation. **2** REFUSAL, rebuff, rejection, prohibition, veto.

denigrate v disparage, run down, slander, revile, defame, malign, vilify, decry, besmirch, impugn, belittle, abuse, assail, criticize.
ⓔ praise, acclaim.

denomination n 1
CLASSIFICATION, category, class,
kind, sort. 2 RELIGION, persuasion,
sect, belief, faith, creed, communion,
school.

denote v indicate, stand for, signify,
represent, symbolize, mean, express,
designate, typify, mark, show, imply.

dénouement n climax, culmination,
conclusion, outcome, upshot, pay-off
(*infml*), finale, resolution, finish,
solution, close.

denounce v condemn, censure,
accuse, revile, decry, attack, inform
against, betray, impugn, vilify,
fulminate.
🔁 acclaim, praise.

dense adj 1 COMPACT, thick,
compressed, condensed, close, close-
knit, heavy, solid, opaque,
impenetrable, packed, crowded.
2 STUPID, thick (*infml*), crass, dull,
slow, slow-witted.
🔁 1 thin, sparse. 2 quick-witted,
clever.

dent n hollow, depression, dip,
concavity, indentation, crater,
dimple, dint, pit.
v depress, gouge, push in, indent.

denude v strip, divest, expose,
uncover, bare, deforest.
🔁 cover, clothe.

denunciation n condemnation,
denouncement, censure, accusation,
incrimination, invective, criticism.
🔁 praise.

deny v 1 *deny God's existence*:
contradict, oppose, refute, disagree
with, disaffirm, disprove. 2 *deny
one's parentage*: disown, disclaim,
renounce, repudiate, recant. 3 *deny
their human rights*: refuse, turn
down, forbid, reject, withhold,
rebuff, veto.
🔁 1 admit. 3 allow.

depart v 1 GO, leave, withdraw, exit,
make off, quit, decamp, take one's
leave, absent oneself, set off, remove,
retreat, migrate, escape, disappear,
retire, vanish. 2 DEVIATE, digress,
differ, diverge, swerve, veer.
🔁 1 arrive, return. 2 keep to.

departed adj dead, deceased, gone,
late, expired.

department n 1 DIVISION, branch,
subdivision, section, sector, office,
station, unit, region, district.
2 SPHERE, realm, province, domain,
field, area, concern, responsibility,
speciality, line.

departure n 1 EXIT, going, leave-
taking, removal, withdrawal,
retirement, exodus. 2 DEVIATION,
digression, divergence, variation,
innovation, branching (out),
difference, change, shift, veering.
🔁 1 arrival, return.

depend on 1 RELY UPON, count on,
bank on (*infml*), calculate on, reckon
on (*infml*), build upon, trust in, lean
on, expect. 2 HINGE ON, rest on,
revolve around, be contingent upon,
hang on.

dependable adj reliable,
trustworthy, steady, trusty,
responsible, faithful, unfailing, sure,
honest, conscientious, certain.
🔁 unreliable, fickle.

dependence n 1 RELIANCE,
confidence, faith, trust, need,
expectation. 2 SUBORDINATION,
attachment, subservience,
helplessness, addiction.
🔁 2 independence.

dependent adj 1 RELIANT, helpless,
weak, immature, subject,
subordinate, vulnerable.
2 CONTINGENT, conditional,
determined by, relative.
🔁 1 independent.

depict v portray, illustrate,
delineate, sketch, outline, draw,
picture, paint, trace, describe,
characterize, detail.

deplete v empty, drain, exhaust,
evacuate, use up, expend, run down,
reduce, lessen, decrease.

deplorable adj 1 GRIEVOUS,

lamentable, pitiable, regrettable, unfortunate, wretched, distressing, sad, miserable, heartbreaking, melancholy, disastrous, dire, appalling. **2** REPREHENSIBLE, disgraceful, scandalous, shameful, dishonourable, disreputable.
F3 1 excellent. **2** commendable.

deplore v **1** GRIEVE FOR, lament, mourn, regret, bemoan, rue.
2 CENSURE, condemn, denounce, deprecate.
F3 2 extol.

deploy v dispose, arrange, position, station, use, utilize, distribute.

deport v expel, banish, exile, extradite, transport, expatriate, oust, ostracize.

depose v demote, dethrone, downgrade, dismiss, unseat, topple, disestablish, displace, oust.

deposit v **1** LAY, drop, place, put, settle, dump (infml), park, precipitate, sit, locate. **2** SAVE, store, hoard, bank, amass, consign, entrust, lodge, file.
n **1** SEDIMENT, accumulation, dregs, precipitate, lees, silt. **2** SECURITY, stake, down payment, pledge, retainer, instalment, part payment, money.

depot n **1** military depot: storehouse, store, warehouse, depository, repository, arsenal. **2** bus depot: station, garage, terminus.

deprave v corrupt, debauch, debase, degrade, pervert, subvert, infect, demoralize, seduce.
F3 improve, reform.

depraved adj corrupt, debauched, degenerate, perverted, debased, dissolute, immoral, base, shameless, licentious, wicked, sinful, vile, evil.
F3 upright, moral.

deprecate (fml) v deplore, condemn, censure, disapprove of, object to, protest at, reject.
F3 approve, commend.

depreciate v **1** DEVALUE, deflate, downgrade, decrease, reduce, lower,

drop, fall, lessen, decline, slump. **2** DISPARAGE, belittle, undervalue, underestimate, underrate, slight.
F3 1 appreciate. **2** overrate.

depreciation n **1** DEVALUATION, deflation, depression, slump, fall.
2 DISPARAGEMENT, belittlement, underestimation.

depress v **1** DEJECT, sadden, dishearten, discourage, oppress, upset, daunt, burden, overburden. **2** WEAKEN, undermine, sap, tire, drain, exhaust, weary, impair, reduce, lessen, press, lower, level.
3 DEVALUE, bring down, lower.
F3 1 cheer. **2** fortify. **3** increase, raise.

depressed adj **1** DEJECTED, low-spirited, melancholy, dispirited, sad, unhappy, low, down, downcast, disheartened, fed up (infml), miserable, moody, cast down, discouraged, glum, downhearted, distressed, despondent, morose, crestfallen, pessimistic. **2** POOR, disadvantaged, deprived, destitute. **3** SUNKEN, recessed, concave, hollow, indented, dented.
F3 1 cheerful. **2** affluent. **3** convex, protuberant.

depressing adj dejecting, dismal, bleak, gloomy, saddening, cheerless, dreary, disheartening, sad, melancholy, sombre, grey, black, daunting, discouraging, heartbreaking, distressing, hopeless.
F3 cheerful, encouraging.

depression n **1** DEJECTION, despair, despondency, melancholy, low spirits, sadness, gloominess, doldrums, blues (infml), glumness, dumps (infml), hopelessness.
2 RECESSION, slump, stagnation, hard times, decline, inactivity. **3** INDENTATION, hollow, dip, concavity, dent, dimple, valley, pit, sink, dint, bowl, cavity, basin, impression, dish, excavation.
F3 1 cheerfulness. **2** prosperity, boom.
3 convexity, protuberance.

deprive v **1** DISPOSSESS, strip, divest, denude, bereave, expropriate, rob. **2** DENY, withhold, refuse.
E **1** endow. **2** provide.

deprived adj poor, needy, underprivileged, disadvantaged, impoverished, destitute, lacking, bereft.
E prosperous.

depth n **1** DEEPNESS, profoundness, extent, measure, drop. **2** MIDDLE, midst, abyss, deep, gulf. **3** WISDOM, insight, discernment, penetration. **4** INTENSITY, strength.
E **1** shallowness. **2** surface.

deputation n commission, delegation, embassy, mission, representatives, legation.

deputise v **1** REPRESENT, stand in for, substitute, replace, understudy, double. **2** DELEGATE, commission.

deputy n representative, agent, delegate, proxy, substitute, second-in-command, ambassador, commissioner, lieutenant, surrogate, subordinate, assistant, locum.

deranged adj disordered, demented, crazy, mad, lunatic, insane, unbalanced, disturbed, confused, frantic, delirious, distraught, berserk.
E sane, calm.

derelict adj abandoned, neglected, deserted, forsaken, desolate, discarded, dilapidated, ruined.

deride v ridicule, mock, scoff, scorn, jeer, sneer, satirize, knock (infml), gibe, disparage, insult, belittle, disdain, taunt.
E respect, praise.

derision n ridicule, mockery, scorn, contempt, scoffing, satire, sneering, disrespect, insult, disparagement, disdain.
E respect, praise.

derisive adj mocking, scornful, contemptuous, disrespectful, irreverent, jeering, disdainful, taunting.
E respectful, flattering.

derivation n source, origin, root, beginning, etymology, extraction, foundation, genealogy, ancestry, basis, descent, deduction, inference.

derivative adj unoriginal, acquired, copied, borrowed, derived, imitative, obtained, second-hand, secondary, plagiarized, cribbed (infml), hackneyed, trite.
n derivation, offshoot, by-product, development, branch, outgrowth, spin-off, product, descendant.

derive v **1** GAIN, obtain, get, draw, extract, receive, procure, acquire, borrow. **2** ORIGINATE, arise, spring, flow, emanate, descend, proceed, stem, issue, follow, develop. **3** INFER, deduce, trace, gather, glean.

derogatory adj insulting, pejorative, offensive, disparaging, depreciative, critical, defamatory, injurious.
E flattering.

descend v **1** DROP, go down, fall, plummet, plunge, tumble, swoop, sink, arrive, alight, dismount, dip, slope, subside. **2** DEGENERATE, deteriorate. **3** CONDESCEND, deign, stoop. **4** ORIGINATE, proceed, spring, stem.
E ascend, rise.

descendants n offspring, children, issue, progeny, successors, lineage, line, seed (fml).

descent n **1** FALL, drop, plunge, dip, decline, incline, slope. **2** COMEDOWN, debasement, degradation. **3** ANCESTRY, parentage, heredity, family tree, genealogy, lineage, extraction, origin.
E **1** ascent, rise.

describe v portray, depict, delineate, illustrate, characterize, specify, draw, define, detail, explain, express, tell, narrate, outline, relate, recount, present, report, sketch, mark out, trace.

description n **1** PORTRAYAL, representation, characterization, account, delineation, depiction,

sketch, presentation, report, outline, explanation, exposition, narration.
2 SORT, type, kind, variety, specification, order.

descriptive *adj* illustrative, explanatory, expressive, detailed, graphic, colourful, pictorial, vivid.

desert[1] *n* wasteland, wilderness, wilds, void.
adj bare, barren, waste, wild, uninhabited, uncultivated, dry, arid, infertile, desolate, sterile, solitary.

desert[2] *v* abandon, forsake, leave, maroon, strand, decamp, defect, give up, renounce, relinquish, jilt, abscond, quit.
⧏ stand by, support.

desert[3] *n* **1** DUE, right, reward, deserts, return, retribution, come-uppance (*infml*), payment, recompense, remuneration.
2 WORTH, merit, virtue.

deserted *adj* abandoned, forsaken, empty, derelict, desolate, godforsaken, neglected, underpopulated, stranded, isolated, bereft, vacant, betrayed, lonely, solitary, unoccupied.
⧏ populous.

deserter *n* runaway, absconder, escapee, truant, renegade, defector, rat (*infml*), traitor, fugitive, betrayer, apostate, backslider, delinquent.

deserve *v* earn, be worthy of, merit, be entitled to, warrant, justify, win, rate, incur.

deserved *adj* due, earned, merited, justifiable, warranted, right, rightful, well-earned, suitable, proper, fitting, fair, just, apposite, meet (*fml*).
⧏ gratuitous, undeserved.

deserving *adj* worthy, estimable, exemplary, praiseworthy, admirable, commendable, laudable, righteous.
⧏ undeserving, unworthy.

design *n* **1** BLUEPRINT, draft, pattern, plan, prototype, sketch, drawing, outline, model, guide.

2 STYLE, shape, form, figure, structure, organization, arrangement, composition, construction, motif.
3 AIM, intention, goal, purpose, plan, end, object, objective, scheme, plot, project, meaning, target, undertaking.
v **1** PLAN, plot, intend, devise, purpose, aim, scheme, shape, project, propose, tailor, mean. **2** SKETCH, draft, outline, draw (up). **3** INVENT, originate, conceive, create, think up, develop, construct, fashion, form, model, fabricate, make.

designation *n* **1** NAME, title, label, epithet, nickname. **2** INDICATION, specification, description, definition, classification, category.
3 NOMINATION, appointment, selection.

designer *n* deviser, originator, maker, stylist, inventor, creator, contriver, fashioner, architect, author.

designing *adj* artful, crafty, scheming, conspiring, devious, intriguing, plotting, tricky, wily, sly, deceitful, cunning, guileful, underhand, sharp, shrewd.
⧏ artless, naïve.

desirable *adj* **1** ADVANTAGEOUS, profitable, worthwhile, advisable, appropriate, expedient, beneficial, preferable, sensible, eligible, good, pleasing. **2** ATTRACTIVE, alluring, sexy (*infml*), seductive, fetching, tempting.
⧏ 1 undesirable. **2** unattractive.

desire *v* **1** ASK, request, petition, solicit. **2** WANT, wish for, covet, long for, need, crave, hunger for, yearn for, fancy (*infml*), hanker after.
n **1** WANT, longing, wish, need, yearning, craving, hankering, appetite, aspiration. **2** LUST, passion, concupiscence (*fml*), ardour.
3 REQUEST, petition, appeal, supplication.

desist *v* stop, cease, leave off,

refrain, discontinue, end, break off, give up, halt, abstain, suspend, pause, peter out, remit, forbear (*fml*).
⊟ continue, resume.

desolate *adj* 1 DESERTED, uninhabited, abandoned, unfrequented, barren, bare, arid, bleak, gloomy, dismal, dreary, lonely, god-forsaken, forsaken, waste, depressing. 2 FORLORN, bereft, depressed, dejected, forsaken, despondent, distressed, melancholy, miserable, lonely, gloomy, disheartened, dismal, downcast, solitary, wretched.
⊟ 1 populous. 2 cheerful.
v devastate, lay waste, destroy, despoil, spoil, wreck, denude, depopulate, ruin, waste, ravage, plunder, pillage.

desolation *n* 1 DESTRUCTION, ruin, devastation, ravages. 2 DEJECTION, despair, despondency, gloom, misery, sadness, melancholy, sorrow, unhappiness, anguish, grief, distress, wretchedness. 3 BARRENNESS, bleakness, emptiness, forlornness, loneliness, isolation, solitude, wildness.

despair *v* lose heart, lose hope, give up, give in, collapse, surrender.
⊟ hope.
n despondency, gloom, hopelessness, desperation, anguish, inconsolableness, melancholy, misery, wretchedness.
⊟ cheerfulness, resilience.

despairing *adj* despondent, distraught, inconsolable, desolate, desperate, heart-broken, suicidal, grief-stricken, hopeless, disheartened, dejected, miserable, wretched, sorrowful, dismayed, downcast.
⊟ cheerful, hopeful.

despatch *see* dispatch.

desperado *n* bandit, criminal, brigand, gangster, hoodlum (*infml*), outlaw, ruffian, thug, cut-throat, law-breaker.

desperate *adj* 1 HOPELESS, inconsolable, wretched, despondent, abandoned. 2 RECKLESS, rash, impetuous, audacious, daring, dangerous, do-or-die, foolhardy, risky, hazardous, hasty, precipitate, wild, violent, frantic, frenzied, determined. 3 CRITICAL, acute, serious, severe, extreme, urgent.
⊟ 1 hopeful. 2 cautious.

desperately *adv* dangerously, critically, gravely, hopelessly, seriously, severely, badly, dreadfully, fearfully, frightfully.

desperation *n* 1 DESPAIR, despondency, anguish, hopelessness, misery, agony, distress, pain, sorrow, trouble, worry, anxiety. 2 RECKLESSNESS, rashness, frenzy, madness, hastiness.

despicable *adj* contemptible, vile, worthless, detestable, disgusting, mean, wretched, disgraceful, disreputable, shameful, reprobate.
⊟ admirable, noble.

despise *v* scorn, deride, look down on, disdain, condemn, spurn, undervalue, slight, revile, deplore, dislike, detest, loathe.
⊟ admire.

despite *prep* in spite of, notwithstanding, regardless of, in the face of, undeterred by, against, defying.

despondent *adj* depressed, dejected, disheartened, downcast, down, low, gloomy, glum, discouraged, miserable, melancholy, sad, sorrowful, doleful, despairing, heart-broken, inconsolable, mournful, wretched.
⊟ cheerful, heartened, hopeful.

despot *n* autocrat, tyrant, dictator, oppressor, absolutist, boss.

despotic *adj* autocratic, tyrannical, imperious, oppressive, dictatorial, authoritarian, domineering, absolute, overbearing, arbitrary, arrogant.
⊟ democratic, egalitarian, liberal,

tolerant.

despotism *n* autocracy, totalitarianism, tyranny, dictatorship, absolutism, oppression, repression.

F3 democracy, egalitarianism, liberalism, tolerance.

destination *n* **1** GOAL, aim, objective, object, purpose, target, end, intention, aspiration, design, ambition. **2** JOURNEY'S END, terminus, station, stop.

destined *adj* **1** FATED, doomed, inevitable, predetermined, ordained, certain, foreordained, meant, unavoidable, inescapable, intended, designed, appointed. **2** BOUND, directed, en route, headed, heading, scheduled, assigned, booked.

destiny *n* fate, doom, fortune, karma, lot (*fml*), portion (*fml*), predestiny, kismet.

destitute *adj* **1** LACKING, needy, wanting, devoid of, bereft, innocent of, deprived, deficient, depleted. **2** POOR, penniless, poverty-stricken, impoverished, down and out (*infml*), distressed, bankrupt.

F3 2 prosperous, rich.

destroy *v* **1** DEMOLISH, ruin, shatter, wreck, devastate, smash, break, crush, overthrow, sabotage, undo, dismantle, thwart, undermine, waste, gut, level, ravage, raze, torpedo, unshape. **2** KILL, annihilate, eliminate, extinguish, eradicate, dispatch, slay (*fml*), nullify.

F3 1 build up. **2** create.

destruction *n* **1** RUIN, devastation, shattering, crushing, wreckage, demolition, defeat, downfall, overthrow, ruination, desolation, undoing, wastage, havoc, ravagement. **2** ANNIHILATION, extermination, eradication, elimination, extinction, slaughter, massacre, end, liquidation, nullification.

F3 2 creation.

destructive *adj* **1** *destructive storms*: devastating, damaging, catastrophic, disastrous, deadly, harmful, fatal, disruptive, lethal, ruinous, detrimental, hurtful, malignant, mischievous, nullifying, slaughterous. **2** *destructive criticism*: adverse, hostile, negative, discouraging, disparaging, contrary, undermining, subversive, vicious.

F3 1 creative. **2** constructive.

desultory *adj* random, erratic, aimless, disorderly, haphazard, irregular, spasmodic, inconsistent, undirected, unco-ordinated, unsystematic, unmethodical, fitful, disconnected, loose, capricious.

F3 systematic, methodical.

detach *v* separate, disconnect, unfasten, disjoin, cut off, disengage, remove, undo, uncouple, sever, dissociate, isolate, loosen, free, unfix, unhitch, segregate, divide, disentangle, estrange.

F3 attach.

detached *adj* **1** SEPARATE, disconnected, dissociated, severed, free, loose, divided, discrete. **2** ALOOF, dispassionate, impersonal, neutral, impartial, independent, disinterested, objective.

F3 1 connected. **2** involved.

detachment *n* **1** ALOOFNESS, remoteness, coolness, unconcern, indifference, impassivity, disinterestedness, neutrality, impartiality, objectivity, fairness. **2** SEPARATION, disconnection, disunion, disengagement. **3** SQUAD, unit, force, corps, brigade, patrol, task force.

detail *n* particular, item, factor, element, aspect, component, feature, point, specific, ingredient, attribute, count, respect, technicality, complication, intricacy, triviality, fact, thoroughness, elaboration, meticulousness, refinement, nicety.

v 1 LIST, enumerate, itemize, specify, catalogue, recount, relate. 2 ASSIGN, appoint, charge, delegate, commission.

detailed *adj* comprehensive, exhaustive, full, blow-by-blow (*infml*), thorough, minute, exact, specific, particular, itemized, intricate, elaborate, complex, complicated, meticulous, descriptive.
￡ cursory, general.

detain *v* 1 DELAY, hold (up), hinder, impede, check, retard, slow, stay, stop. 2 CONFINE, arrest, intern, hold, restrain, keep.
￡ 2 release.

detect *v* 1 NOTICE, ascertain, note, observe, perceive, recognize, discern, distinguish, identify, sight, spot, spy. 2 UNCOVER, catch, discover, disclose, expose, find, track down, unmask, reveal.

detective *n* investigator, private eye (*infml*), sleuth (*infml*), sleuth-hound (*infml*).

detention *n* 1 DETAINMENT, custody, confinement, imprisonment, restraint, incarceration, constraint, quarantine. 2 DELAY, hindrance, holding back.
￡ release.

deter *v* discourage, put off, inhibit, intimidate, dissuade, daunt, turn off (*infml*), check, caution, warn, restrain, hinder, frighten, disincline, prevent, prohibit, stop.
￡ encourage.

deteriorate *v* 1 WORSEN, decline, degenerate, depreciate, go downhill (*infml*), fail, fall off, lapse, slide, relapse, slip. 2 DECAY, disintegrate, decompose, weaken, fade.
￡ improve. 2 progress.

determination *n* 1 RESOLUTENESS, tenacity, firmness, will-power, perseverance, persistence, purpose, backbone, guts (*infml*), grit (*infml*), steadfastness, single-mindedness, will, insistence, conviction,

dedication, drive, fortitude. 2 DECISION, judgement, settlement, resolution, conclusion.
￡ 1 irresolution.

determine *v* 1 DECIDE, settle, resolve, make up one's mind, choose, conclude, fix on, elect, clinch, finish. 2 DISCOVER, establish, find out, ascertain, identify, check, detect, verify. 3 AFFECT, influence, govern, control, dictate, direct, guide, regulate, ordain.

determined *adj* resolute, firm, purposeful, strong-willed, single-minded, persevering, persistent, strong-minded, steadfast, tenacious, dogged, insistent, intent, fixed, convinced, decided, unflinching.
￡ irresolute, wavering.

deterrent *n* hindrance, impediment, obstacle, repellent, check, bar, discouragement, obstruction, curb, restraint, difficulty.
￡ incentive, encouragement.

detest *v* hate, abhor, loathe, abominate, execrate (*fml*), dislike, recoil from, deplore, despise.
￡ adore, love.

detestable *adj* hateful, loathsome, abhorrent, abominable, repellent, obnoxious, execrable (*fml*), despicable, revolting, repulsive, repugnant, offensive, vile, disgusting, accursed (*fml*), heinous, shocking, sordid.
￡ adorable, admirable.

detour *n* deviation, diversion, indirect route, circuitous route, roundabout route, digression, byroad, byway, bypath, bypass.

detract (from) *v* diminish, subtract from, take away from, reduce, lessen, lower, devaluate, depreciate, belittle, disparage.
￡ add to, enhance, praise.

detriment *n* damage, harm, hurt, disadvantage, loss, ill, injury, disservice, evil, mischief, prejudice.
￡ advantage, benefit.

detrimental *adj* damaging, harmful, hurtful, adverse, disadvantageous, injurious, prejudicial, mischievous, destructive.
E3 advantageous, favourable, beneficial.

devastate *v* **1** DESTROY, desolate, lay waste, demolish, spoil, despoil, wreck, ruin, ravage, waste, ransack, plunder, level, raze, pillage, sack. **2** DISCONCERT, overwhelm, take aback, confound, shatter (*infml*), floor (*infml*), nonplus, discomfit.

devastating *adj* **1** *devastating storms*: destructive, disastrous. **2** *a devastating argument*: effective, incisive, overwhelming, stunning.

devastation *n* destruction, desolation, havoc, ruin, wreckage, ravages, demolition, annihilation, pillage, plunder, spoliation.

develop *v* **1** ADVANCE, evolve, expand, progress, foster, flourish, mature, prosper, branch out. **2** ELABORATE, amplify, argument, enhance, unfold. **3** ACQUIRE, contract, begin, generate, create, invent. **4** RESULT, come about, grow, ensue, arise, follow, happen.

development *n* **1** GROWTH, evolution, advance, blossoming, elaboration, furtherance, progress, unfolding, expansion, extension, spread, increase, improvement, maturity, promotion, refinement, issue. **2** OCCURRENCE, happening, event, change, outcome, situation, result, phenomenon.

deviate *v* diverge, veer, turn (aside), digress, swerve, vary, differ, depart, stray, yaw, wander, err, go astray, go off the rails (*infml*), drift, part.

deviation *n* divergence, aberration, departure, abnormality, irregularity, variance, variation, digression, eccentricity, anomaly, deflection, alteration, disparity, discrepancy, detour, fluctuation, change, quirk, shift, freak.

E3 conformity, regularity.

device *n* **1** TOOL, implement, appliance, gadget, contrivance, contraption (*infml*), apparatus, utensil, instrument, machine. **2** SCHEME, ruse, strategy, plan, plot, gambit, manoeuvre, wile, trick, dodge (*infml*), machination. **3** EMBLEM, symbol, motif, logo (*infml*), design, insignia, crest, badge, shield.

devil *n* **1** DEMON, Satan, fiend, evil spirit, arch-fiend, Lucifer, imp, Evil One, Prince of Darkness, Adversary, Beelzebub, Mephistopheles, Old Nick (*infml*), Old Harry (*infml*). **2** BRUTE, rogue, monster, ogre.

devious *adj* **1** UNDERHAND, deceitful, dishonest, disingenuous, double-dealing, scheming, tricky (*infml*), insidious, insincere, calculating, cunning, evasive, wily, sly, slippery (*infml*), surreptitious, treacherous, misleading. **2** INDIRECT, circuitous, rambling, roundabout, wandering, winding, tortuous, erratic.
E3 straightforward.

devise *v* invent, contrive, plan, plot, design, conceive, arrange, formulate, imagine, scheme, construct, concoct, forge, frame, project, shape, form.

devoid *adj* lacking, wanting, without, free, bereft, destitute, deficient, deprived, barren, empty, vacant, void.
E3 endowed.

devote *v* dedicate, consecrate, commit, give oneself, set apart, set aside, reserve, apply, allocate, allot, sacrifice, enshrine, assign, appropriate, surrender, pledge.

devoted *adj* dedicated, ardent, committed, loyal, faithful, devout, loving, staunch, steadfast, true, constant, fond, unswerving, tireless, concerned, attentive, caring.
E3 indifferent, disloyal.

devotee *n* enthusiast, fan (*infml*), fanatic, addict, aficionado, follower, supporter, zealot, adherent, admirer, disciple, buff (*infml*), freak (*infml*), merchant (*infml*), fiend (*infml*), hound.

devotion *n* **1** DEDICATION, commitment, consecration, ardour, loyalty, allegiance, adherence, zeal, support, love, passion, fervour, fondness, attachment, adoration, affection, faithfulness, reverence, steadfastness, regard, earnestness. **2** DEVOUTNESS, piety, godliness, faith, holiness, spirituality. **3** PRAYER, worship.
E3 **1** inconstancy. **2** irreverence.

devour *v* **1** EAT, consume, guzzle, gulp, gorge, gobble, bolt, wolf down, swallow, stuff (*infml*), cram, polish off (*infml*), gormandize, feast on, relish, revel in. **2** DESTROY, consume, absorb, engulf, ravage, dispatch.

devout *adj* **1** SINCERE, earnest, devoted, fervent, genuine, staunch, steadfast, ardent, passionate, serious, whole-hearted, constant, faithful, intense, heartfelt, zealous, unswerving, deep, profound. **2** PIOUS, godly, religious, reverent, prayerful, saintly, holy, orthodox.
E3 **1** insincere. **2** irreligious.

dexterous *adj* deft, adroit, agile, able, nimble, proficient, skilful, clever, expert, nifty, nippy, handy, facile, nimble-fingered, neat-handed.
E3 clumsy, inept, awkward.

diabolical *adj* devilish, fiendish, demonic, hellish, damnable, evil, infernal, wicked, vile, dreadful, outrageous, shocking, disastrous, excruciating, atrocious.

diagnose *v* identify, determine, recognize, pinpoint, distinguish, analyse, explain, isolate, interpret, investigate.

diagnosis *n* identification, verdict, explanation, conclusion, answer, interpretation, analysis, opinion, investigation, examination, scrutiny.

diagonal *adj* oblique, slanting,

cross, crosswise, sloping, crooked, angled, cornerways.

diagram *n* plan, sketch, chart, drawing, figure, representation, schema, illustration, outline, graph, picture, layout, table.

dial *n* circle, disc, face, clock, control.
v phone, ring, call (up).

dialect *n* idiom, language, regionalism, patois, provincialism, vernacular, argot, jargon, accent, lingo (*infml*), speech, diction.

dialectic *adj* dialectical, logical, rational, argumentative, analytical, rationalistic, logistic, polemical, inductive, deductive.
n dialectics, logic, reasoning, rationale, disputation, analysis, debate, argumentation, contention, discussion, polemics, induction, deduction.

dialogue *n* **1** CONVERSATION, interchange, discourse, communication, talk, exchange, discussion, converse, debate, conference. **2** LINES, script.

diametric *adj* diametrical, opposed, opposite, contrary, counter, contrasting, antithetical.

diary *n* journal, day-book, logbook, chronicle, year-book, appointment book, engagement book.

diatribe *n* tirade, invective, abuse, harangue, attack, onslaught, denunciation, criticism, insult, reviling, upbraiding.
E3 praise, eulogy.

dicey (*infml*) *adj* risky, chancy, unpredictable, tricky, problematic, dangerous, difficult, iffy (*infml*), dubious, hairy (*infml*).
E3 certain.

dictate *v* **1** SAY, speak, utter, announce, pronounce, transmit. **2** COMMAND, order, direct, decree, instruct, rule.
n command, decree, precept, principle, rule, direction, injunction,

edict, order, ruling, statute, requirement, ordinance, law, bidding, mandate, ultimatum, word.

dictator n despot, autocrat, tyrant, supremo (*infml*), Big Brother (*infml*).

dictatorial adj tyrannical, despotic, totalitarian, authoritarian, autocratic, oppressive, imperious, domineering, bossy (*infml*), absolute, repressive, overbearing, arbitrary, dogmatic.

F3 democratic, egalitarian, liberal.

diction n speech, articulation, language, elocution, enunciation, intonation, pronunciation, inflection, fluency, delivery, expression, phrasing.

dictionary n lexicon, glossary, thesaurus, vocabulary, wordbook, encyclopaedia, concordance.

dictum n pronouncement, ruling, maxim, decree, dictate, edict, fiat (*fml*), precept, axiom, command, order, utterance.

didactic adj instructive, educational, educative, pedagogic, prescriptive, pedantic, moralizing, moral.

die v 1 DECEASE, perish, pass away, expire, depart, breathe one's last, peg out (*infml*), snuff it (*sl*), bite the dust (*infml*), kick the bucket (*sl*). 2 DWINDLE, fade, ebb, sink, wane, wilt, wither, peter out, decline, decay, finish, lapse, end, disappear, vanish, subside. 3 LONG FOR, pine for, yearn, desire.

F3 1 live.

die-hard n reactionary, intransigent, hardliner, blimp (*infml*), ultra-conservative, old fogey (*infml*), stick-in-the-mud (*infml*), rightist, fanatic.

diet n 1 FOOD, nutrition, provisions, sustenance, rations, foodstuffs, subsistence. 2 FAST, abstinence, regimen.

v lose weight, slim, fast, reduce, abstain, weight-watch (*infml*).

differ v 1 VARY, diverge, deviate, depart from, contradict, contrast.

2 DISAGREE, argue, conflict, oppose, dispute, dissent, be at odds with, clash, quarrel, fall out, debate, contend, take issue.

F3 1 conform. 2 agree.

difference n 1 DISSIMILARITY, unlikeness, discrepancy, divergence, diversity, variation, variety, distinctness, distinction, deviation, differentiation, contrast, disparity, singularity, exception. 2 DISAGREEMENT, clash, dispute, conflict, contention, controversy. 3 REMAINDER, rest.

F3 1 conformity. 2 agreement.

different adj 1 DISSIMILAR, unlike, contrasting, divergent, inconsistent, deviating, at odds, clashing, opposed. 2 VARIED, various, diverse, miscellaneous, assorted, disparate, many, numerous, several, sundry, other. 3 UNUSUAL, unconventional, unique, distinct, distinctive, extraordinary, individual, original, special, strange, separate, peculiar, rare, bizarre, anomalous.

F3 1 similar. 2 same. 3 conventional.

differentiate v distinguish, tell apart, discriminate, contrast, separate, mark off, individualize, particularize.

difficult adj 1 HARD, laborious, demanding, arduous, strenuous, tough, wearisome, uphill, formidable. 2 COMPLEX, complicated, intricate, involved, abstruse, obscure, dark, knotty, thorny, problematical, perplexing, abstract, baffling, intractable. 3 UNMANAGEABLE, perverse, troublesome, trying, unco-operative, tiresome, stubborn, obstinate, intractable.

F3 1 easy. 2 straightforward. 3 manageable.

difficulty n 1 HARDSHIP, trouble, labour, arduousness, painfulness, trial, tribulation, awkwardness. 2 PROBLEM, predicament, dilemma, quandary, perplexity, embarrassment, plight, distress, fix (*infml*), mess (*infml*), jam (*infml*), spot (*infml*), hiccup (*infml*), hang-up. **3** OBSTACLE, hindrance, hurdle, impediment, objection, opposition, block, complication, pitfall, protest, stumbling-block.

☒ 1 ease.

diffidence *n* unassertiveness, modesty, shyness, self-consciousness, self-effacement, timidity, insecurity, reserve, bashfulness, humility, inhibition, meekness, self-distrust, self-doubt, hesitancy, reluctance, backwardness.

☒ confidence.

diffident *adj* unassertive, modest, shy, timid, self-conscious, self-effacing, insecure, bashful, abashed, meek, reserved, withdrawn, tentative, shrinking, inhibited, hesitant, reluctant, unsure, shamefaced.

☒ assertive, confident.

diffuse *adj* **1** *diffuse outbreaks of rain*: scattered, unconcentrated, diffused, dispersed, disconnected. **2** *a diffuse prose style*: verbose, imprecise, wordy, rambling, long-winded, waffling (*infml*), vague, discursive.

☒ 1 concentrated. **2** succinct.

v spread, scatter, disperse, distribute, propagate, dispense, disseminate, circulate, dissipate.

☒ concentrate.

dig *v* **1** EXCAVATE, penetrate, burrow, mine, quarry, scoop, tunnel, till, gouge, delve, pierce. **2** POKE, prod. **3** INVESTIGATE, probe, go into, research, search.

n gibe, jeer, sneer, taunt, crack, insinuation, insult, wisecrack.

☒ compliment.

dig up discover, unearth, uncover, disinter, expose, extricate, exhume, find, retrieve, track down.

☒ bury, obscure.

digest *v* **1** ABSORB, assimilate, incorporate, process, dissolve.

2 TAKE IN, absorb, understand, assimilate, grasp, study, consider, contemplate, meditate, ponder. **3** SHORTEN, summarize, condense, compress, reduce.

n summary, abridgement, abstract, précis, synopsis, résumé, reduction, abbreviation, compression, compendium.

dignified *adj* stately, solemn, imposing, majestic, noble, august, lordly, lofty, exalted, formal, distinguished, grave, impressive, reserved, honourable.

☒ undignified, lowly.

dignitary *n* worthy, notable, VIP (*infml*), high-up, personage, bigwig (*infml*).

dignity *n* stateliness, propriety, solemnity, decorum, courtliness, grandeur, loftiness, majesty, honour, eminence, importance, nobility, self-respect, self-esteem, standing, poise, respectability, greatness, status, pride.

digress *v* diverge, deviate, stray, wander, go off at a tangent, drift, depart, ramble.

dilapidated *adj* ramshackle, shabby, broken-down, neglected, tumble-down, uncared-for, rickety, decrepit, crumbling, run-down, worn-out, ruined, decayed, decaying.

dilate *v* distend, enlarge, expand, spread, broaden, widen, increase, extend, stretch, swell.

☒ contract.

dilatory *adj* delaying, procrastinating, slow, tardy, tarrying, sluggish, lingering, lackadaisical, slack.

☒ prompt.

dilemma *n* quandary, conflict, predicament, problem, catch-22 (*infml*), difficulty, puzzle, embarrassment, perplexity, plight.

diligent *adj* assiduous, industrious, hard-working, conscientious, painstaking, busy, attentive, tireless,

dilute

careful, meticulous, persevering, persistent, studious.
☒ negligent, lazy.

dilute v adulterate, water down, thin (out), attenuate, weaken, diffuse, diminish, decrease, lessen, reduce, temper, mitigate.
☒ concentrate.

dim adj 1 DARK, dull, dusky, cloudy, shadowy, gloomy, sombre, dingy, lack-lustre, feeble, imperfect. 2 INDISTINCT, blurred, hazy, ill-defined, obscure, misty, unclear, foggy, fuzzy, vague, faint, weak. 3 STUPID, dense, obtuse, thick (infml), doltish.
☒ 1 bright. 2 distinct. 3 bright, intelligent.
v darken, dull, obscure, cloud, blur, fade, tarnish, shade.
☒ brighten, illuminate.

dimension(s) n extent, measurement, measure, size, scope, magnitude, largeness, capacity, mass, scale, range, bulk, importance, greatness.

diminish v 1 DECREASE, lessen, reduce, lower, contract, decline, dwindle, shrink, recede, taper off, wane, weaken, abate, fade, sink, subside, ebb, slacken, cut. 2 BELITTLE, disparage, deprecate, devalue.
☒ 1 increase. 2 exaggerate.

diminutive adj undersized, small, tiny, little, miniature, minute, infinitesimal, wee, petite, midget, mini (infml), teeny (infml), teeny-weeny (infml), Lilliputian, dinky (infml), pint-size(d) (infml), pocket(-sized), pygmy.
☒ big, large, oversized.

din n noise, row, racket, clash, clatter, clamour, pandemonium, uproar, commotion, crash, hullabaloo (infml), hubbub, outcry, shout, babble.
☒ quiet, calm.

dine v eat, feast, sup, lunch,

banquet, feed.

dingy adj dark, drab, grimy, murky, faded, dull, dim, shabby, soiled, discoloured, dirty, dreary, gloomy, seedy, sombre, obscure, run-down, colourless, dusky, worn.
☒ bright, clean.

dinner n meal, supper, tea (infml), banquet, feast, spread, repast (fml).

dinosaur

> *Dinosaurs include*: Ornithischia, Saurischia; Allosaurus, Ankylosaurus, Apatosaurus, Barosaurus, Brachiosaurus, Brontosaurus, Camptosaurus, Coelophysis, Compsognathus, Corythosaurus, Deinonychus, Diplodocus, Heterodontosaurus, Iguanodon, Ophiacodon, Ornithomimus, Pachycephalosaurus, Parasaurolophus, Plateosaurus, Stegosaurus, Styracosaurus, Triceratops, Tyrannosaurus.

dip v 1 PLUNGE, immerse, submerge, duck, dunk, bathe, douse, sink. 2 DESCEND, decline, drop, fall, subside, slump, sink, lower.
n 1 HOLLOW, basin, decline, hole, concavity, incline, depression, fall, slope, slump, lowering. 2 BATHE, immersion, plunge, soaking, ducking, swim, drenching, infusion, dive.

diplomacy n 1 TACT, tactfulness, finesse, delicacy, discretion, savoir-faire, subtlety, skill, craft. 2 STATECRAFT, statesmanship, politics, negotiation, manoeuvring.

diplomat n go-between, mediator, negotiator, ambassador, envoy, conciliator, peacemaker, moderator, politician.

diplomatic adj tactful, politic, discreet, judicious, subtle, sensitive, prudent, discreet.
☒ tactless.

dire adj 1 DISASTROUS, dreadful, awful, appalling, calamitous, catastrophic. **2** DESPERATE, urgent, grave, drastic, crucial, extreme, alarming, ominous.

direct v **1** CONTROL, manage, run, administer, organize, lead, govern, regulate, superintend, supervise. **2** INSTRUCT, command, order, charge. **3** GUIDE, lead, conduct, point. **4** AIM, point, focus, turn.
adj **1** STRAIGHT, undeviating, through, uninterrupted.
2 STRAIGHTFORWARD, outspoken, blunt, frank, unequivocal, sincere, candid, honest, explicit.
3 IMMEDIATE, first-hand, face-to-face, personal.
☒ 1 circuitous. **2** equivocal. **3** indirect.

direction n **1** CONTROL, administration, management, government, supervision, guidance, leadership. **2** ROUTE, way, line, road.

directions n instructions, guidelines, orders, briefing, guidance, recommendations, indication, plan.

directive n command, instruction, order, regulation, ruling, imperative, dictate, decree, charge, mandate, injunction, ordinance, edict, fiat, notice.

directly adv **1** IMMEDIATELY, instantly, promptly, right away, speedily, forthwith, instantaneously, quickly, soon, presently, straightaway, straight. **2** FRANKLY, bluntly, candidly, honestly.

director n manager, head, boss, chief, controller, executive, principal, governor, leader, organizer, supervisor, administrator, producer, conductor.

dirt n **1** EARTH, soil, clay, dust, mud. **2** FILTH, grime, muck, mire, excrement, stain, smudge, slime, tarnish. **3** INDECENCY, impurity, obscenity, pornography.

dirty adj **1** FILTHY, grimy, grubby, mucky, soiled, unwashed, foul, messy, muddy, polluted, squalid, dull, miry, scruffy, shabby, sullied, clouded, dark. **2** INDECENT, obscene, filthy, smutty, sordid, salacious, vulgar, pornographic, corrupt.
☒ 1 clean. **2** decent.
v pollute, soil, stain, foul, mess up, defile, smear, smirch, spoil, smudge, sully, muddy, blacken.
☒ clean, cleanse.

disability n handicap, impairment, disablement, disorder, inability, incapacity, infirmity, defect, unfitness, disqualification, affliction, ailment, complaint, weakness.

disable v cripple, lame, incapacitate, damage, handicap, impair, debilitate, disqualify, weaken, immobilize, invalidate, paralyse, prostrate.

disabled adj handicapped, incapacitated, impaired, infirm, crippled, lame, immobilized, maimed, weak, weakened, paralysed, wrecked.
☒ able, able-bodied.

disadvantage n **1** HARM, damage, detriment, hurt, injury, loss, prejudice. **2** DRAWBACK, snag, hindrance, handicap, impediment, inconvenience, flaw, nuisance, weakness, trouble.
☒ 2 advantage, benefit.

disadvantaged adj deprived, underprivileged, poor, handicapped, impoverished, struggling.
☒ privileged.

disadvantageous adj harmful, detrimental, inopportune, unfavourable, prejudicial, adverse, damaging, hurtful, injurious, inconvenient, ill-timed.
☒ advantageous, auspicious.

disaffected adj disloyal, hostile, estranged, alienated, antagonistic, rebellious, dissatisfied, disgruntled, discontented.
☒ loyal.

disaffection n disloyalty, hostility, alienation, discontentment, resentment, ill-will, dissatisfaction, animosity, coolness, unfriendliness,

antagonism, disharmony, discord, disagreement, aversion, dislike.
F3 loyalty, contentment.

disagree v **1** DISSENT, oppose, quarrel, argue, bicker, fall out (*infml*), wrangle, fight, squabble, contend, dispute, contest, object. **2** CONFLICT, clash, diverge, contradict, counter, differ, deviate, depart, run counter to, vary.
F3 1 agree. **2** correspond.

disagreeable adj **1** *a disagreeable old man*: bad-tempered, ill-humoured, difficult, peevish, rude, surly, churlish, irritable, contrary, cross, brusque. **2** *a disagreeable taste*: disgusting, offensive, repulsive, repellent, obnoxious, unsavoury, objectionable, nasty.
F3 1 amiable, pleasant. **2** agreeable.

disagreement n **1** DISPUTE, argument, conflict, altercation (*fml*), quarrel, clash, dissent, falling-out, contention, strife, misunderstanding, squabble, tiff (*infml*), wrangle. **2** DIFFERENCE, variance, unlikeness, disparity, discrepancy, deviation, discord, dissimilarity, incompatibility, divergence, diversity, incongruity.
F3 1 agreement, harmony. **2** similarity.

disappear v **1** VANISH, wane, recede, fade, evaporate, dissolve, ebb. **2** GO, depart, withdraw, retire, flee, fly, escape, scarper (*infml*), hide. **3** END, expire, perish, pass.
F3 1 appear. **3** emerge.

disappearance n vanishing, fading, evaporation, departure, loss, going, passing, melting, desertion, flight.
F3 appearance, manifestation.

disappoint v fail, dissatisfy, let down, disillusion, dash, dismay, disenchant, sadden, thwart, vex, frustrate, foil, dishearten, disgruntle, disconcert, hamper, hinder, deceive, defeat, delude.
F3 satisfy, please, delight.

disappointed adj let down,

frustrated, thwarted, disillusioned, dissatisfied, miffed (*infml*), upset, discouraged, disgruntled, disheartened, distressed, down-hearted, saddened, despondent, depressed.
F3 pleased, satisfied.

disappointment n **1** FRUSTRATION, dissatisfaction, failure, disenchantment, disillusionment, displeasure, discouragement, distress, regret. **2** FAILURE, let-down, setback, comedown, blow, misfortune, fiasco, disaster, calamity, washout (*infml*), damp squib (*infml*), swiz (*infml*), swizzle (*infml*).
F3 1 pleasure, satisfaction, delight. **2** success.

disapproval n censure, disapprobation (*fml*), condemnation, criticism, displeasure, reproach, objection, dissatisfaction, denunciation, dislike.
F3 approbation (*fml*), approval.

disapprove of censure, condemn, blame, take exception to, object to, deplore, denounce, disparage, dislike, reject, spurn.
F3 approve of.

disarm v **1** DISABLE, unarm, demilitarize, demobilize, deactivate, disband. **2** APPEASE, conciliate, win, mollify, persuade.
F3 1 arm.

disarray n disorder, confusion, chaos, mess, muddle, shambles (*infml*), disorganization, clutter, untidiness, unruliness, jumble, indiscipline, tangle, upset.
F3 order.

disaster n calamity, catastrophe, misfortune, reverse, tragedy, blow, accident, act of God, cataclysm, debacle, mishap, failure, flop (*infml*), fiasco, ruin, stroke, trouble, mischance, ruination.
F3 success, triumph.

disastrous adj calamitous,

catastrophic, cataclysmic, devastating, ruinous, tragic, unfortunate, dreadful, dire, terrible, destructive, ill-fated, fatal, miserable.
🔁 successful, auspicious.

disband v disperse, break up, scatter, dismiss, demobilize, part company, separate, dissolve.
🔁 assemble, muster.

disbelief n unbelief, incredulity, doubt, scepticism, suspicion, distrust, mistrust, rejection.
🔁 belief.

disbelieve v discount, discredit, repudiate, reject, mistrust, suspect.
🔁 believe, trust.

disc n 1 CIRCLE, face, plate, ring. 2 RECORD, album, LP, CD. 3 DISK, diskette, hard disk, floppy disk, CD-ROM.

discard v reject, abandon, dispose of, get rid of, jettison, dispense with, cast aside, ditch (infml), dump (infml), drop, scrap, shed, remove, relinquish.
🔁 retain, adopt.

discern v 1 PERCEIVE, make out, observe, detect, recognize, see, ascertain, notice, determine, discover, descry. 2 DISCRIMINATE, distinguish, differentiate, judge.

discernible adj perceptible, noticeable, detectable, appreciable, distinct, observable, recognizable, visible, apparent, clear, obvious, plain, patent, manifest, discoverable.
🔁 imperceptible.

discerning adj discriminating, perceptive, astute, clear-sighted, sensitive, shrewd, wise, sharp, subtle, sagacious, penetrating, acute, piercing, critical, eagle-eyed.
🔁 dull, obtuse.

discharge v 1 LIBERATE, free, pardon, release, clear, absolve, exonerate, acquit, relieve, dismiss. 2 EXECUTE, carry out, perform, fulfil, dispense. 3 FIRE, shoot, let off, detonate, explode. 4 EMIT, sack

(infml), remove, fire (infml), expel, oust, eject.
🔁 1 detain. 2 neglect. 4 appoint.
n 1 LIBERATION, release, acquittal, exoneration. 2 EMISSION, secretion, ejection. 3 EXECUTION, accomplishment, fulfilment.
🔁 1 confinement, detention. 2 absorption. 3 neglect.

disciple n follower, convert, proselyte, adherent, believer, devotee, supporter, learner, pupil, student.

disciplinarian n authoritarian, taskmaster, autocrat, stickler, despot, tyrant.

discipline n 1 TRAINING, exercise, drill, practice. 2 PUNISHMENT, chastisement, correction. 3 STRICTNESS, restraint, regulation, self-control, orderliness.
🔁 3 indiscipline.
v 1 TRAIN, instruct, drill, educate, exercise, break in. 2 CHECK, control, correct, restrain, govern. 3 PUNISH, chastize, chasten, penalize, reprimand, castigate.

disclaim v deny, disown, repudiate, abandon, renounce, reject, abjure (fml).
🔁 accept, confess.

disclose v 1 DIVULGE, make known, reveal, tell, confess, let slip, relate, publish, communicate, impart, leak (infml). 2 EXPOSE, reveal, uncover, lay bare, unveil, discover.
🔁 conceal.

disclosure n divulgence, exposure, exposé, revelation, uncovering, publication, leak (infml), discovery, admission, acknowledgement, announcement, declaration.

discomfort n ache, pain, uneasiness, malaise, trouble, distress, disquiet, hardship, vexation, irritation, annoyance.
🔁 comfort, ease.

disconcerting adj disturbing, confusing, upsetting, unnerving, alarming, bewildering, off-putting (*infml*), distracting, embarrassing, awkward, baffling, perplexing, dismaying, bothersome.

disconnect *v* cut off, disengage, uncouple, sever, separate, detach, unplug, unhook, part, divide.
E3 attach, connect.

disconnected *adj* confused, incoherent, rambling, unco-ordinated, unintelligible, loose, irrational, disjointed, illogical, jumbled.
E3 coherent, connected.

disconsolate *adj* desolate, dejected, dispirited, sad, melancholy, unhappy, wretched, miserable, gloomy, forlorn, inconsolable, crushed, heavy-hearted, hopeless.
E3 cheerful, joyful.

discontent *n* uneasiness, dissatisfaction, disquiet, restlessness, fretfulness, unrest, impatience, vexation, regret.
E3 content.

discontented *adj* dissatisfied, fed up (*infml*), disgruntled, unhappy, browned off (*infml*), cheesed off (*infml*), disaffected, miserable, exasperated, complaining.
E3 contented, satisfied.

discontinue *v* stop, end, finish, cease, break off, terminate, halt, drop, suspend, abandon, cancel, interrupt.
E3 continue.

discord *n* **1** DISSENSION, disagreement, discordance, clashing, disunity, incompatibility, conflict, difference, dispute, contention, friction, division, opposition, strife, split, wrangling. **2** DISSONANCE, disharmony, cacophony (*fml*), jangle, jarring, harshness.
E3 1 concord, agreement. **2** harmony.

discordant *adj* **1** DISAGREEING, conflicting, at odds, clashing, contradictory, incongruous, incompatible, inconsistent.

2 DISSONANT, cacophonous (*fml*), grating, jangling, jarring, harsh.
E3 1 harmonious. **2** harmonious.

discount[1] *v* **1** DISREGARD, ignore, overlook, disbelieve, gloss over. **2** REDUCE, deduct, mark down, knock off (*infml*).

discount[2] *n* reduction, rebate, allowance, cut, concession, deduction, mark-down.

discourage *v* **1** DISHEARTEN, dampen, dispirit, depress, demoralize, dismay, unnerve, deject, disappoint. **2** DETER, dissuade, hinder, put off, restrain, prevent.
E3 1 hearten. **2** encourage.

discouragement *n*
1 DOWNHEARTEDNESS, despondency, pessimism, dismay, depression, dejection, despair, disappointment. **2** DETERRENT, damper, setback, impediment, obstacle, opposition, hindrance, restraint, rebuff.
E3 1 encouragement. **2** incentive.

discourse *n* **1** CONVERSATION, dialogue, chat, communication, talk, converse, discussion. **2** SPEECH, address, oration (*fml*), lecture, sermon, essay, treatise, dissertation, homily.
v converse, talk, discuss, debate, confer, lecture.

discourteous *adj* rude, bad-mannered, ill-mannered, impolite, boorish, disrespectful, ill-bred, uncivil, unceremonious, insolent, offhand, curt, brusque, abrupt.
E3 courteous, polite.

discover *v* **1** FIND, uncover, unearth, dig up, disclose, reveal, light on, locate. **2** ASCERTAIN, determine, realize, notice, recognize, perceive, see, find out, spot, discern, learn, detect. **3** ORIGINATE, invent, pioneer.
E3 1 miss. **2** conceal, cover (up).

discovery *n* **1** BREAKTHROUGH, find, origination, introduction,

disengage

innovation, invention, exploration.
2 DISCLOSURE, detection, revelation,
location.

discredit v 1 DISBELIEVE, distrust,
doubt, question, mistrust, challenge.
2 DISPARAGE, dishonour, degrade,
defame, disgrace, slander, slur,
smear, reproach, vilify.
F3 1 believe. 2 honour.
n 1 DISBELIEF, distrust, doubt,
mistrust, scepticism, suspicion.
2 DISHONOUR, disrepute, censure,
aspersion, disgrace, blame, shame,
reproach, slur, smear, scandal.
F3 1 belief. 2 credit.

discreditable adj dishonourable,
disreputable, disgraceful,
reprehensible, scandalous,
blameworthy, shameful, infamous,
degrading, improper.
F3 creditable.

discreet adj tactful, careful,
diplomatic, politic, prudent,
cautious, delicate, judicious,
reserved, wary, sensible.
F3 tactless, indiscreet.

discrepancy n difference, disparity,
variance, variation, inconsistency,
dissimilarity, discordance,
divergence, disagreement, conflict,
inequality.

discretion n 1 TACT, diplomacy,
judiciousness, caution, prudence,
wisdom, circumspection,
discernment, judgement, care,
carefulness, consideration, wariness.
2 CHOICE, freedom, preference, will,
wish.
F3 1 indiscretion.

discriminate v distinguish,
differentiate, discern, tell apart, make
a distinction, segregate, separate.
F3 confuse, confound.
  discriminate (against) be prejudiced,
  be biased, victimize.

discriminating adj discerning,
fastidious, selective, critical,
perceptive, particular, tasteful,
astute, sensitive, cultivated.

discrimination n 1 BIAS, prejudice,
intolerance, unfairness, bigotry,
favouritism, inequity, racism, sexism.
2 DISCERNMENT, judgement,
acumen, perception, acuteness,
insight, penetration, subtlety,
keenness, refinement, taste.

discursive adj rambling, digressing,
wandering, long-winded,
meandering, wide-ranging,
circuitous.
F3 terse.

discuss v debate, talk about, confer,
argue, consider, deliberate, converse,
consult, examine.

discussion n debate, conference,
argument, conversation, dialogue,
exchange, consultation, discourse,
deliberation, consideration, analysis,
review, examination, scrutiny,
seminar, symposium.

disdain n scorn, contempt,
arrogance, haughtiness, derision,
sneering, dislike, snobbishness.
F3 admiration, respect.

disdainful adj scornful,
contemptuous, derisive, haughty,
aloof, arrogant, supercilious,
sneering, superior, proud, insolent.
F3 respectful.

disease n illness, sickness, ill-
health, infirmity, complaint,
disorder, ailment, indisposition,
malady, condition, affliction,
infection, epidemic.
F3 health.

diseased adj sick, ill, unhealthy,
ailing, unsound, contaminated,
infected.
F3 healthy.

disembark v land, arrive, alight,
debark.
F3 embark.

disembodied adj bodiless,
incorporeal (fml), ghostly, phantom,
spiritual, immaterial, intangible.

disengage v disconnect, detach,
loosen, free, extricate, undo, release,
liberate, separate, disentangle, untie,

withdraw.

☒ connect, engage.

disentangle v **1** LOOSE, free, extricate, disconnect, untangle, disengage, detach, unravel, separate, unfold. **2** RESOLVE, clarify, simplify.

☒ **1** entangle.

disfigure v deface, blemish, mutilate, scar, mar, deform, distort, damage, spoil.

☒ adorn, embellish.

disgrace n shame, ignominy, disrepute, dishonour, disfavour, humiliation, defamation, discredit, scandal, reproach, slur, stain.

☒ honour, esteem.

v shame, dishonour, abase, defame, humiliate, disfavour, stain, discredit, reproach, slur, sully, taint, stigmatize.

☒ honour, respect.

disgraceful adj shameful, dishonourable, disreputable, ignominious, scandalous, shocking, unworthy, dreadful, appalling.

☒ honourable, respectable.

disguise v **1** CONCEAL, cover, camouflage, mask, hide, dress up, cloak, screen, veil, shroud. **2** FALSIFY, deceive, dissemble, misrepresent, fake, fudge.

☒ **1** reveal, expose.

n concealment, camouflage, cloak, cover, costume, mask, front, façade, masquerade, deception, pretence, travesty, screen, veil.

disgust v offend, displease, nauseate, revolt, sicken, repel, outrage, put off.

☒ delight, please.

n revulsion, repulsion, repugnance, distaste, aversion, abhorrence, nausea, loathing, detestation, hatred.

disgusted adj repelled, repulsed, revolted, offended, appalled, outraged.

☒ attracted, delighted.

disgusting adj repugnant, repellent, revolting, offensive, sickening, nauseating, odious, foul,

unappetizing, unpleasant, vile, obscene, abominable, detestable, objectionable, nasty.

☒ delightful, pleasant.

dish n plate, bowl, platter, food, recipe.

dish out distribute, give out, hand out, hand round, dole out, allocate, mete out, inflict.

dish up serve, present, ladle, spoon, dispense, scoop.

dishearten v discourage, dispirit, dampen, cast down, depress, dismay, dash, disappoint, deject, daunt, crush, deter.

☒ encourage, hearten.

dishevelled adj tousled, unkempt, uncombed, untidy, bedraggled, messy, ruffled, slovenly, disordered.

☒ neat, tidy.

dishonest adj untruthful, fraudulent, deceitful, false, lying, deceptive, double-dealing, cheating, crooked (*infml*), treacherous, unprincipled, swindling, shady (*infml*), corrupt, disreputable.

☒ honest, trustworthy, scrupulous.

dishonesty n deceit, falsehood, falsity, fraudulence, fraud, criminality, insincerity, treachery, cheating, crookedness (*infml*), corruption, unscrupulousness, trickery.

☒ honesty, truthfulness.

dishonour v disgrace, shame, humiliate, debase, defile, degrade, defame, discredit, demean, debauch.

☒ honour.

n disgrace, abasement, humiliation, shame, degradation, discredit, disrepute, indignity, ignominy, reproach, slight, slur, scandal, insult, disfavour, outrage, aspersion, abuse, discourtesy.

☒ honour.

disillusioned adj disenchanted, disabused, undeceived, disappointed.

disinclined adj averse, reluctant, resistant, indisposed, loath, opposed,

hesitant.
🖅 inclined, willing.

disinfect v sterilize, fumigate, sanitize, decontaminate, cleanse, purify, purge, clean.
🖅 contaminate, infect.

disinfectant n sterilizer, antiseptic, sanitizer.

disintegrate v break up, decompose, fall apart, crumble, rot, moulder, separate, splinter.

disinterest n disinterestedness, impartiality, neutrality, detachment, unbiasedness, dispassionateness, fairness.

disinterested adj unbiased, neutral, impartial, unprejudiced, dispassionate, detached, uninvolved, open-minded, equitable, even-handed, unselfish.
🖅 biased, concerned.

disjointed adj **1** DISCONNECTED, dislocated, divided, separated, disunited, displaced, broken, fitful, split, disarticulated. **2** INCOHERENT, aimless, confused, disordered, loose, unconnected, bitty, rambling, spasmodic.
🖅 **2** coherent.

dislike n aversion, hatred, repugnance, hostility, distaste, disinclination, disapproval, disapprobation, displeasure, animosity, antagonism, enmity, detestation, disgust, loathing.
🖅 liking, predilection.
v hate, detest, object to, loathe, abhor, abominate, disapprove, shun, despise, scorn.
🖅 like, favour.

dislocate v disjoint, displace, misplace, disengage, put out (infml), disorder, shift, disconnect, disrupt, disunite.

dislodge v displace, eject, remove, oust, extricate, shift, move, uproot.

disloyal adj treacherous, faithless, false, traitorous, two-faced (infml), unfaithful, apostate, unpatriotic.

🖅 loyal, trustworthy.

dismal adj dreary, gloomy, depressing, bleak, cheerless, dull, drab, low-spirited, melancholy, sad, sombre, lugubrious, forlorn, despondent, dark, sorrowful, long-faced (infml), hopeless, discouraging.
🖅 cheerful, bright.

dismantle v demolish, take apart, disassemble, strip.
🖅 assemble, put together.

dismay v alarm, daunt, frighten, unnerve, unsettle, scare, put off, dispirit, distress, disconcert, dishearten, discourage, disillusion, depress, horrify, disappoint.
🖅 encourage, hearten.
n consternation, alarm, distress, apprehension, dread, fear, trepidation, fright, horror, terror, discouragement, disappointment.
🖅 boldness, encouragement.

dismember v disjoint, amputate, dissect, dislocate, divide, mutilate, sever.
🖅 assemble, join.

dismiss v **1** the class was dismissed: discharge, free, let go, release, send away, remove, drop, discord, banish. **2** dismiss employees: sack (infml), make redundant, lay off, fire (infml), relegate. **3** dismiss it from your mind: discount, disregard, reject, repudiate, set aside, shelve, spurn.
🖅 **1** retain. **2** appoint. **3** accept.

disobey v contravene, infringe, violate, transgress, flout, disregard, defy, ignore, resist, rebel.
🖅 obey.

disorder n **1** CONFUSION, chaos, muddle, disarray, mess, untidiness, shambles (infml), clutter, disorganization, jumble. **2** DISTURBANCE, tumult, riot, confusion, commotion, uproar, fracas, brawl, fight, clamour, quarrel. **3** ILLNESS, complaint, disease, sickness, disability, ailment, malady, affliction.

≡ 1 neatness, order. 2 law and order, peace.

v disturb, mess up, disarrange, mix up, muddle, upset, disorganize, confuse, confound, clutter, jumble, discompose, scatter, unsettle.

≡ arrange, organize.

disorderly *adj* 1 DISORGANIZED, confused, chaotic, irregular, messy, untidy. 2 UNRULY, undisciplined, unmanageable, obstreperous, rowdy, turbulent, rebellious, lawless.

≡ 1 neat, tidy. 2 well-behaved.

disorganize *v* disorder, disrupt, disturb, disarrange, muddle, upset, confuse, discompose, jumble, play havoc with, unsettle, break up, destroy.

≡ organize.

disown *v* repudiate, renounce, disclaim, deny, cast off, disallow, reject, abandon.

≡ accept, acknowledge.

disparaging *adj* derisive, derogatory, mocking, scornful, critical, insulting, snide (*infml*).

≡ flattering, praising.

dispassionate *adj* detached, objective, impartial, neutral, disinterested, impersonal, fair, cool, calm, composed.

≡ biased, emotional.

dispatch, despatch *v* 1 SEND, express, transmit, forward, consign, expedite, accelerate. 2 DISPOSE OF, finish, perform, discharge, conclude. 3 KILL, murder, execute.

≡ 1 receive.

n 1 COMMUNICATION, message, report, bulletin, communiqué, news, letter, account. 2 PROMPTNESS, speed, alacrity, expedition, celerity, haste, rapidity, swiftness.

≡ 2 slowness.

dispense *v* 1 DISTRIBUTE, give out, apportion, allot, allocate, assign, share, mete out. 2 ADMINISTER, apply, implement, enforce, discharge, execute, operate.

dispense with dispose of, get rid of, abolish, discard, omit, disregard, cancel, forgo, ignore, waive.

disperse *v* scatter, dispel, spread, distribute, diffuse, dissolve, break up, dismiss, separate.

≡ gather.

displace *v* 1 DISLODGE, move, shift, misplace, disturb, dislocate. 2 DEPOSE, oust, remove, replace, dismiss, discharge, supplant, eject, evict, succeed, supersede.

display *v* 1 SHOW, present, demonstrate, exhibit. 2 BETRAY, disclose, reveal, show, expose. 3 SHOW OFF, flourish, parade, flaunt.

≡ 1 conceal. 2 disguise.

n show, exhibition, demonstration, presentation, parade, spectacle, revelation.

displease *v* offend, annoy, irritate, anger, upset, put out (*infml*), infuriate, exasperate, incense.

≡ please.

displeasure *n* offence, annoyance, disapproval, irritation, resentment, disfavour, anger, indignation, wrath.

≡ pleasure.

disposal *n* 1 ARRANGEMENT, grouping, order. 2 CONTROL, direction, command. 3 REMOVAL, riddance, discarding, jettisoning.

dispose of 1 DEAL WITH, decide, settle. 2 GET RID OF, discard, scrap, destroy, dump (*infml*), jettison.

≡ 2 keep.

disposed *adj* liable, inclined, predisposed, prone, likely, apt, minded, subject, ready, willing.

≡ disinclined.

disposition *n* character, nature, temperament, inclination, make-up, bent, leaning, predisposition, constitution, habit, spirit, tendency, proneness.

disproportionate *adj* unequal, uneven, incommensurate, excessive, unreasonable.

☞ balanced.

disprove *v* refute, rebut, confute, discredit, invalidate, contradict, expose.
☞ confirm, prove.

dispute *v* argue, debate, question, contend, challenge, discuss, doubt, contest, contradict, deny, quarrel, clash, wrangle, squabble.
☞ agree.
n argument, debate, disagreement, controversy, conflict, contention, quarrel, wrangle, feud, strife, squabble.
☞ agreement, settlement.

disqualify *v* **1** INCAPACITATE, disable, invalidate. **2** DEBAR, preclude, rule out, disentitle, eliminate, prohibit.
☞ 2 qualify, accept.

disquiet *n* anxiety, worry, concern, nervousness, uneasiness, restlessness, alarm, distress, fretfulness, fear, disturbance, trouble.
☞ calm, reassurance.

disregard *v* **1** IGNORE, overlook, discount, neglect, pass over, disobey, make light of, turn a blind eye to (*infml*), brush aside. **2** SLIGHT, snub, despise, disdain, disparage.
☞ 1 heed, pay attention to. **2** respect.
n neglect, negligence, inattention, oversight, indifference, disrespect, contempt, disdain, brush-off (*infml*).
☞ attention, heed.

disrepair *n* dilapidation, deterioration, decay, collapse, ruin, shabbiness.
☞ good repair.

disreputable *adj* **1** DISGRACEFUL, discreditable, dishonourable, unrespectable, notorious, scandalous, shameful, shady, base, contemptible, low, mean, shocking. **2** SCRUFFY, shabby, seedy, unkempt.
☞ 1 respectable. **2** smart.

disrespectful *adj* rude, discourteous, impertinent, impolite, impudent, insolent, uncivil,
unmannerly, cheeky, insulting, irreverent, contemptuous.
☞ polite, respectful.

disrupt *v* disturb, disorganize, confuse, interrupt, break up, unsettle, intrude, upset.

dissatisfaction *n* discontent, displeasure, dislike, discomfort, disappointment, frustration, annoyance, irritation, exasperation, regret, resentment.
☞ satisfaction.

dissect *v* **1** DISMEMBER, anatomize. **2** ANALYSE, investigate, scrutinize, examine, inspect, pore over.

dissension *n* disagreement, discord, dissent, dispute, contention, conflict, strife, friction, quarrel.
☞ agreement.

dissent *v* disagree, differ, protest, object, refuse, quibble.
☞ assent.
n disagreement, difference, dissension, discord, resistance, opposition, objection.
☞ agreement, conformity.

disservice *n* disfavour, injury, wrong, bad turn, harm, unkindness, injustice.
☞ favour.

dissident *adj* disagreeing, differing, dissenting, discordant, nonconformist, heterodox (*fml*).
☞ acquiescent, orthodox.
n dissenter, protestor, noncomformist, rebel, agitator, revolutionary, schismatic, recusant.
☞ assenter.

dissimilar *adj* unlike, different, divergent, disparate, unrelated, incompatible, mismatched, diverse, various, heterogeneous.
☞ similar, like.

dissipate *v* **1** *he dissipated his inheritance*: spend, waste, squander, expend, consume, deplete, fritter away, burn up. **2** *the clouds dissipated*: disperse, vanish, disappear, dispel, diffuse, evaporate,

dissociate 160

dissolve.
➟ 1 accumulate. **2** appear.

dissociate v separate, detach, break off, disunite, disengage, disconnect, cut off, disband, divorce, disrupt, isolate, segregate.
➟ associate, join.

dissolute adj dissipated, debauched, degenerate, depraved, wanton, abandoned, corrupt, immoral, licentious, lewd, wild.
➟ restrained, virtuous.

dissolution n **1** DISINTEGRATION, decomposition, separation, resolution, division. **2** ENDING, termination, conclusion, finish, discontinuation, divorce, dismissal, dispersal, destruction, overthrow. **3** EVAPORATION, disappearance.

dissolve v **1** EVAPORATE, disintegrate, liquefy, melt. **2** DECOMPOSE, disintegrate, disperse, break up, disappear, crumble. **3** END, terminate, separate, sever, divorce.

dissuade v deter, discourage, put off, disincline.
➟ persuade.

distance n **1** SPACE, interval, gap, extent, range, reach, length, width. **2** ALOOFNESS, reserve, coolness, coldness, remoteness.
➟ 1 closeness. **2** approachability.

distant adj **1** FAR, faraway, far-flung, out-of-the-way, remote, outlying, abroad, dispersed. **2** ALOOF, cool, reserved, stand-offish (infml), formal, cold, restrained, stiff.
➟ 1 close. **2** approachable.

distaste n dislike, aversion, repugnance, disgust, revulsion, loathing, abhorrence.
➟ liking.

distasteful adj disagreeable, offensive, unpleasant, objectionable, repulsive, obnoxious, repugnant, unsavoury, loathsome, abhorrent.
➟ pleasing.

distinct adj **1** SEPARATE, different, detached, individual, dissimilar.

2 CLEAR, plain, evident, obvious, apparent, marked, definite, noticeable, recognizable.
➟ 2 indistinct, vague.

distinction n **1** DIFFERENTIATION, discrimination, discernment, separation, difference, dissimilarity, contrast. **2** CHARACTERISTIC, peculiarity, individuality, feature, quality, mark. **3** RENOWN, fame, celebrity, prominence, eminence, importance, reputation, greatness, honour, prestige, repute, superiority, worth, merit, excellence, quality.
➟ 3 unimportance, obscurity.

distinctive adj characteristic, distinguishing, individual, peculiar, different, unique, singular, special, original, extraordinary, idiosyncratic.
➟ ordinary, common.

distinguish v **1** DIFFERENTIATE, tell apart, discriminate, determine, categorize, characterize, classify. **2** DISCERN, perceive, identify, ascertain, make out, recognize, see, discriminate.

distinguished adj famous, eminent, celebrated, well-known, acclaimed, illustrious, notable, noted, renowned, famed, honoured, outstanding, striking, marked, extraordinary, conspicuous.
➟ insignificant, obscure, unimpressive.

distort v **1** DEFORM, contort, bend, misshape, disfigure, twist, warp. **2** FALSIFY, misrepresent, pervert, slant, colour, garble.

distract v **1** DIVERT, sidetrack, deflect. **2** CONFUSE, disconcert, bewilder, confound, disturb, perplex, puzzle. **3** AMUSE, occupy, divert, engross.

distraught adj agitated, anxious, overwrought, upset, distressed, distracted, beside oneself, worked up, frantic, hysterical, raving, mad, wild, crazy.
➟ calm, untroubled.

distress n **1** ANGUISH, grief, misery, sorrow, heartache, affliction, suffering, torment, wretchedness, sadness, worry, anxiety, desolation, pain, agony. **2** ADVERSITY, hardship, poverty, need, privation, destitution, misfortune, trouble, difficulties, trial.
🔁 **1** content. **2** comfort, ease.
v upset, afflict, grieve, disturb, trouble, sadden, worry, torment, harass, harrow, pain, agonize, bother.
🔁 comfort.

distribute v **1** DISPENSE, allocate, dole out, dish out, share, deal, divide, apportion. **2** DELIVER, hand out, spread, issue, circulate, diffuse, disperse, scatter.
🔁 **2** collect.

distribution n **1** ALLOCATION, apportionment, division, sharing. **2** CIRCULATION, spreading, scattering, delivery, dissemination, supply, dealing, handling. **3** ARRANGEMENT, grouping, classification, organization.
🔁 **2** collection.

district n region, area, quarter, neighbourhood, locality, sector, precinct, parish, locale, community, vicinity, ward.

distrust v mistrust, doubt, disbelieve, suspect, question.
🔁 trust.
n mistrust, doubt, disbelief, suspicion, misgiving, wariness, scepticism, question, qualm.
🔁 trust.

disturb v **1** DISRUPT, interrupt, distract. **2** AGITATE, unsettle, upset, distress, worry, fluster, annoy, bother. **3** DISARRANGE, disorder, confuse, upset.
🔁 **2** reassure. **3** order.

disturbance n **1** DISRUPTION, agitation, interruption, intrusion, upheaval, upset, confusion, annoyance, bother, trouble, hindrance. **2** DISORDER, uproar, commotion, tumult, turmoil, fracas, fray, brawl, riot.
🔁 **1** peace. **2** order.

disuse n neglect, desuetude (*fml*), abandonment, discontinuance, decay.
🔁 use.

ditch n trench, dyke, channel, gully, furrow, moat, drain, level, watercourse.

dither v hesitate, shilly-shally (*infml*), waver, vacillate.

dive v plunge, plummet, dip, submerge, jump, leap, nose-dive, fall, drop, swoop, descend, pitch.
n **1** PLUNGE, lunge, header, jump, leap, nose-dive, swoop, dash, spring. **2** (*infml*) BAR, club, saloon.

diverge v **1** DIVIDE, branch, fork, separate, spread, split. **2** DEVIATE, digress, stray, wander. **3** DIFFER, vary, disagree, dissent, conflict.
🔁 **1** converge. **3** agree.

diverse adj various, varied, varying, sundry, different, differing, assorted, dissimilar, miscellaneous, discrete, separate, several, distinct.
🔁 similar, identical.

diversify v vary, change, expand, branch out, spread out, alter, mix, assort.

diversion n **1** DEVIATION, detour. **2** AMUSEMENT, entertainment, distraction, pastime, recreation, relaxation, play, game. **3** ALTERATION, change.

diversity n variety, dissimilarity, difference, variance, assortment, range, medley.
🔁 similarity, likeness.

divert v **1** DEFLECT, redirect, reroute, side-track, avert, distract, switch. **2** AMUSE, entertain, occupy, distract, interest.

divide v **1** SPLIT, separate, part, cut, break up, detach, bisect, disconnect. **2** DISTRIBUTE, share, allocate, deal out, allot, apportion. **3** DISUNITE, separate, estrange, alienate. **4** CLASSIFY, group, sort, grade, segregate.

1 join. **2** collect. **3** unite.

divine *adj* **1** GODLIKE, superhuman, supernatural, celestial, heavenly, angelic, spiritual. **2** HOLY, sacred, sanctified, consecrated, transcendent, exalted, glorious, religious, supreme.
1 human. **2** mundane.

divinity *n* god, goddess, deity, godliness, holiness, sanctity, godhead, spirit.

division *n* **1** SEPARATION, detaching, parting, cutting, disunion. **2** BREACH, rupture, split, schism, disunion, estrangement, disagreement, feud. **3** DISTRIBUTION, sharing, allotment, apportionment. **4** SECTION, sector, segment, part, department, category, class, compartment, branch.
1 union. **2** unity. **3** collection. **4** whole.

divorce *n* dissolution, annulment, break-up, split-up, rupture, separation, breach, disunion.
v separate, part, annul, split up, sever, dissolve, divide, dissociate.
marry, unite.

divulge *v* disclose, reveal, communicate, tell, leak (*infml*), impart, confess, betray, uncover, let slip, expose, publish, proclaim.

dizzy *adj* **1** GIDDY, faint, light-headed, woozy (*infml*), shaky, reeling. **2** CONFUSED, bewildered, dazed, muddled.

do *v* **1** PERFORM, carry out, execute, accomplish, achieve, fulfil, implement, complete, undertake, work, put on, present, conclude, end, finish. **2** BEHAVE, act, conduct oneself. **3** FIX, prepare, organize, arrange, deal with, look after, manage, produce, make, create, cause, proceed. **4** SUFFICE, satisfy, serve.
n(*infml*) function, affair, event, gathering, party, occasion.

do away with get rid of, dispose of, exterminate, eliminate, abolish, discontinue, remove, destroy, discard, kill, murder.

do up 1 FASTEN, tie, lace, pack. **2** RENOVATE, restore, decorate, redecorate, modernize, repair.

do without dispense with, abstain from, forgo, give up, relinquish.

docile *adj* tractable, co-operative, manageable, submissive, obedient, amenable, controlled, obliging.
truculent, unco-operative.

dock[1] *n* harbour, wharf, quay, boat-yard, pier, waterfront, marina.
v anchor, moor, drop anchor, land, berth, put in, tie up.

dock[2] *v* crop, clip, cut, shorten, curtail, deduct, reduce, lessen, withhold, decrease, subtract, diminish.

doctor *n* physician, general practitioner, GP, medic (*infml*), medical officer, consultant, clinician.

> *Types of medical doctor include*: general practitioner, GP, family doctor, family practitioner, locum, hospital doctor, houseman, intern, resident, registrar, consultant, medical officer (MO), doc (*infml*), bones (*infml*), quack (*infml*), dentist, veterinary surgeon, vet (*infml*).

v **1** ALTER, tamper with, falsify, misrepresent, pervert, adulterate, change, disguise, dilute. **2** REPAIR, fix, patch up.

doctrine *n* dogma, creed, belief, tenet, principle, teaching, precept, conviction, opinion, canon.

document *n* paper, certificate, deed, record, report, form, instrument (*fml*).
v **1** RECORD, report, chronicle, list, detail, cite. **2** SUPPORT, prove, corroborate, verify.

dodge *v* avoid, elude, evade, swerve, side-step, shirk, shift.
n trick, ruse, ploy, wile, scheme, stratagem, machination, manoeuvre.

dog n hound, cur, mongrel, canine, puppy, pup, bitch, mutt (*infml*), pooch (*infml*).

> *Breeds of dog include*: Afghan hound, alsatian, basset-hound, beagle, Border collie, borzoi, bull-mastiff, bulldog, bull-terrier, cairn terrier, chihuahua, chow, cocker spaniel, collie, corgi, dachshund, Dalmatian, Doberman pinscher, foxhound, fox-terrier, German Shepherd, golden retriever, Great Dane, greyhound, husky, Irish wolfhound, Jack Russell, King Charles spaniel, Labrador, lhasa apso, lurcher, Maltese, Old English sheepdog, Pekingese, pit bull terrier, pointer, poodle, pug, Rottweiler, saluki, sausage-dog (*infml*), schnauzer, Scottie (*infml*), Scottish-terrier, Sealyham, setter, sheltie, shih tzu, springer spaniel, St Bernard, terrier, whippet, West Highland terrier, Westie (*infml*), wolf-hound, Yorkshire terrier.

v pursue, follow, trail, track, tail, hound, shadow, plague, harry, haunt, trouble, worry.

dogged adj determined, resolute, persistent, persevering, intent, tenacious, firm, steadfast, staunch, single-minded, indefatigable, steady, unshakable, stubborn, obstinate, relentless, unyielding.
🔁 irresolute, apathetic.

dogma n doctrine, creed, belief, precept, principle, article (of faith), credo, tenet, conviction, teaching, opinion.

dogmatic adj opinionated, assertive, authoritative, positive, doctrinaire, dictatorial, doctrinal, categorical, emphatic, overbearing, arbitrary.

dole out v distribute, allocate, hand out, dish out, apportion, allot, mete out, share, divide, deal, issue, ration, dispense, administer, assign.

domain n **1** DOMINION, kingdom, realm, territory, region, empire, lands, province. **2** FIELD, area, speciality, concern, department, sphere, discipline, jurisdiction.

domestic adj **1** HOME, family, household, home-loving, stay-at-home, homely, house-trained, tame, pet, private. **2** INTERNAL, indigenous, native.
n servant, maid, charwoman, char, daily help, daily, au pair.

domesticate v tame, house-train, break, train, accustom, familiarize.

dominant adj **1** AUTHORITATIVE, controlling, governing, ruling, powerful, assertive, influential. **2** PRINCIPAL, main, outstanding, chief, important, predominant, primary, prominent, leading, pre-eminent, prevailing, prevalent, commanding.
🔁 **1** submissive. **2** subordinate.

dominate v **1** CONTROL, domineer, govern, rule, direct, monopolize, master, lead, overrule, prevail, overbear, tyrannize. **2** OVERSHADOW, eclipse, dwarf.

domineering adj overbearing, authoritarian, imperious, autocratic, bossy (*infml*), dictatorial, despotic, masterful, high-handed, oppressive, tyrannical, arrogant.
🔁 meek, servile.

dominion n **1** POWER, authority, domination, command, control, rule, sway, jurisdiction, government, lordship, mastery, supremacy, sovereignty. **2** DOMAIN, country, territory, province, colony, realm, kingdom, empire.

donate v give, contribute, present, bequeath, cough up (*infml*), fork out (*infml*), bestow (*fml*), confer (*fml*), subscribe.
🔁 receive.

donation n gift, present, offering, grant, gratuity, largess(e), contribution, presentation, subscription, alms, benefaction (*fml*), bequest.

done *adj* 1 FINISHED, over, accomplished, completed, ended, concluded, settled, realized, executed. 2 CONVENTIONAL, acceptable, proper. 3 COOKED, ready.

donor *n* giver, donator, benefactor, contributor, philanthropist, provider, fairy godmother (*infml*).
✗ beneficiary.

doom *n* 1 FATE, fortune, destiny, portion, lot. 2 DESTRUCTION, catastrophe, downfall, ruin, death, death-knell. 3 CONDEMNATION, judgement, sentence, verdict.
v condemn, damn, consign, judge, sentence, destine.

doomed *adj* condemned, damned, fated, ill-fated, ill-omened, cursed, destined, hopeless, luckless, ill-starred.

door *n* opening, entrance, entry, exit, doorway, portal, hatch.

dope (*infml*) *n* 1 NARCOTIC, drugs, marijuana, cannabis, opiate, hallucinogen. 2 FOOL, dolt, idiot, half-wit (*infml*), dimwit (*infml*), dunce, simpleton, clot (*infml*), blockhead. 3 INFORMATION, facts, low-down (*infml*), details.
v drug, sedate, anaesthetize, stupefy, medicate, narcotize, inject, doctor.

dormant *adj* 1 INACTIVE, asleep, sleeping, inert, resting, slumbering, sluggish, torpid, hibernating, fallow, comatose. 2 LATENT, unrealized, potential, undeveloped, undisclosed.
✗ 1 active, awake. 2 realized, developed.

dose *n* measure, dosage, amount, portion, quantity, draught, potion, prescription, shot.
v medicate, administer, prescribe, dispense, treat.

dot *n* point, spot, speck, mark, fleck, circle, pin-point, atom, decimal point, full stop, iota, jot.
v spot, sprinkle, stud, dab, punctuate.

dote on adore, idolize, treasure, admire, indulge.

double *adj* dual, twofold; twice, duplicate, twin, paired, doubled, coupled.
✗ single, half.
v duplicate, enlarge, increase, repeat, multiply, fold, magnify.
n twin, duplicate, copy, clone, replica, doppelgänger, lookalike, spitting image (*infml*), ringer (*infml*), image, counterpart, impersonator.
at the double immediately, at once, quickly, without delay.

double-cross *v* cheat, swindle, defraud, trick, con (*infml*), hoodwink, betray, two-time (*infml*), mislead.

doubt *v* 1 DISTRUST, mistrust, query, question, suspect, fear. 2 BE UNCERTAIN, be dubious, hesitate, vacillate, waver.
✗ 1 believe, trust.
n 1 DISTRUST, suspicion, mistrust, scepticism, reservation, misgiving, incredulity, apprehension, hesitation. 2 UNCERTAINTY, difficulty, confusion, ambiguity, problem, indecision, perplexity, dilemma, quandary.
✗ 1 trust, faith. 2 certainty, belief.

doubtful *adj* 1 *doubtful about his future*: uncertain, unsure, undecided, suspicious, irresolute, wavering, hesitant, vacillating, tentative, sceptical. 2 *writing of doubtful origin*: dubious, questionable, unclear, ambiguous, vague, obscure, debatable.
✗ 1 certain, decided. 2 definite, settled.

doubtless *adv* 1 CERTAINLY, without doubt, undoubtedly, unquestionably, indisputably, no doubt, clearly, surely, of course, truly, precisely. 2 PROBABLY, presumably, most likely, seemingly, supposedly.

dour *adj* 1 GLOOMY, dismal,

forbidding, grim, morose, unfriendly, dreary, austere, sour, sullen. **2** HARD, inflexible, unyielding, rigid, severe, rigorous, strict, obstinate.
☒ 1 cheerful, bright. **2** easy-going.

douse, dowse v **1** SOAK, saturate, steep, submerge, immerse, immerge, dip, duck, drench, dunk, plunge. **2** EXTINGUISH, put out, blow out, smother, snuff.

dowdy adj unfashionable, ill-dressed, frumpish, drab, shabby, tatty (infml), frowsy, tacky (infml), dingy, old-fashioned, slovenly.
☒ fashionable, smart.

down v **1** KNOCK DOWN, fell, floor, prostrate, throw, topple.
2 SWALLOW, drink, gulp, swig (infml), knock back (infml).
down and out destitute, impoverished, penniless, derelict, ruined.

downcast adj dejected, depressed, despondent, sad, unhappy, miserable, down, low, disheartened, dispirited, blue (infml), fed up (infml), discouraged, disappointed, crestfallen, dismayed.
☒ cheerful, happy, elated.

downfall n fall, ruin, failure, collapse, destruction, disgrace, debacle, undoing, overthrow.

downgrade v **1** DEGRADE, demote, lower, humble. **2** DISPARAGE, denigrate, belittle, run down, decry.
☒ 1 upgrade, improve. **2** praise.

downhearted adj depressed, dejected, despondent, sad, downcast, discouraged, disheartened, low-spirited, unhappy, gloomy, glum, dismayed.
☒ cheerful, enthusiastic.

downpour n cloudburst, deluge, rainstorm, flood, inundation, torrent.

downright adj, adv absolute(ly), outright, plain(ly), utter(ly), clear(ly), complete(ly), out-and-out, frank(ly), explicit(ly).

down-trodden adj oppressed, subjugated, subservient, exploited, trampled on, abused, tyrannized, victimized, helpless.

downward adj descending, declining, downhill, sliding, slipping.
☒ upward.

dowse see **douse**.

doze v sleep, nod off, drop off, snooze (infml), kip (infml), zizz (sl).
n nap, catnap, siesta, snooze (infml), forty winks (infml), kip (infml), shut-eye (infml), zizz (sl).

drab adj dull, dingy, dreary, dismal, gloomy, flat, grey, lacklustre, cheerless, sombre, shabby.
☒ bright, cheerful.

draft[1] v draw (up), outline, sketch, plan, design, formulate, compose.
n outline, sketch, plan, delineation, abstract, rough, blueprint, protocol (fml).

draft[2] n bill of exchange, cheque, money order, letter of credit, postal order.

drag v **1** DRAW, pull, haul, lug, tug, trail, tow. **2** GO SLOWLY, creep, crawl, lag.
n (infml) bore, annoyance, nuisance, pain (infml), bother.

drain v **1** EMPTY, remove, evacuate, draw off, strain, dry, milk, bleed.
2 DISCHARGE, trickle, flow out, leak, ooze. **3** EXHAUST, consume, sap, use up, deplete, drink up, swallow.
☒ fill.
n **1** CHANNEL, conduit, culvert, duct, outlet, trench, ditch, pipe, sewer.
2 DEPLETION, exhaustion, sap, strain.

drama n **1** PLAY, acting, theatre, show, spectacle, stage-craft, scene, melodrama. **2** EXCITEMENT, crisis, turmoil.

dramatic adj **1** EXCITING, striking, stirring, thrilling, marked, significant, expressive, impressive.
2 HISTRIONIC, exaggerated, melodramatic, flamboyant.

dramatize v **1** STAGE, put on, adapt. **2** ACT, play-act, exaggerate, overdo, overstate.

drape v cover, wrap, hang, fold, drop, suspend.

drastic adj extreme, radical, strong, forceful, severe, harsh, far-reaching, desperate, dire.
F3 moderate, cautious.

draught n **1** PUFF, current, influx, flow. **2** DRINK, potion, quantity. **3** PULLING, traction.

draw v **1** ATTRACT, allure, entice, bring in, influence, persuade, elicit. **2** PULL, drag, haul, tow, tug. **3** DELINEATE, map out, sketch, portray, trace, pencil, depict, design. **4** TIE, be equal, be even.
F3 1 repel. **2** push.
n **1** ATTRACTION, enticement, lure, appeal, bait, interest. **2** TIE, stalemate, dead-heat.

draw out protract, extend, prolong, drag out, spin out, elongate, stretch, lengthen, string out.
F3 shorten.

draw up 1 DRAFT, compose, formulate, prepare, frame, write out. **2** PULL UP, stop, halt, run in.

drawback n disadvantage, snag, hitch, obstacle, impediment, hindrance, difficulty, flaw, fault, fly in the ointment (infml), catch, stumbling block, nuisance, trouble, defect, handicap, deficiency, imperfection.
F3 advantage, benefit.

drawing n sketch, picture, outline, representation, delineation, portrayal, illustration, cartoon, graphic, portrait.

dread v fear, shrink from, quail, cringe at, flinch, shy, shudder, tremble.
n fear, apprehension, misgiving, trepidation, dismay, alarm, horror, terror, fright, disquiet, worry, quietly, qualm.
F3 confidence, security.

dreadful adj awful, terrible, frightful, horrible, appalling, dire,

shocking, ghastly, horrendous, tragic, grievous, hideous, tremendous.
F3 wonderful, comforting.

dream n **1** VISION, illusion, reverie, trance, fantasy, daydream, nightmare, hallucination, delusion, imagination. **2** ASPIRATION, wish, hope, ambition, desire, pipe-dream, ideal, goal, design, speculation.
v imagine, envisage, fancy, fantasize, daydream, hallucinate, conceive, visualize, conjure up, muse.

dream up invent, devise, conceive, think up, imagine, concoct, hatch, create, spin, contrive.

dreamer n idealist, visionary, fantasizes, romancer, daydreamer, star-gazer, theorizer.
F3 realist, pragmatist.

dreamy adj **1** FANTASTIC, unreal, imaginary, shadowy, vague, misty. **2** IMPRACTICAL, fanciful, daydreaming, romantic, visionary, faraway, absent, musing, pensive.
F3 1 real. **2** practical, down-to-earth.

dreary adj **1** a dreary job: boring, tedious, uneventful, dull, humdrum, routine, monotonous, wearisome, commonplace, colourless, lifeless. **2** a dreary landscape: gloomy, depressing, drab, dismal, bleak, sombre, sad, mournful.
F3 1 interesting. **2** cheerful.

dregs n **1** SEDIMENT, deposit, residue, lees, grounds, scum, dross, trash, waste. **2** OUTCASTS, rabble, riff-raff, scum, down-and-outs.

drench v soak, saturate, steep, wet, douse, souse, immerse, inundate, duck, flood, imbue, drown.

dress n **1** FROCK, gown, robe. **2** CLOTHES, clothing, garment(s), outfit, costume, garb, get-up (infml), gear (infml), togs (infml).
v **1** CLOTHE, put on, garb, rig, robe, wear, don, decorate, deck, garnish, trim, adorn, fit, drape. **2** ARRANGE, adjust, dispose, prepare, groom, straighten. **3** BANDAGE, tend, treat.

1 strip, undress.

dress up beautify, adorn, embellish, improve, deck, doll up, tart up (*infml*), gild, disguise.

dribble v **1** TRICKLE, drip, leak, run, seep, drop, ooze. **2** DROOL, slaver, slobber, drivel.

drift v **1** WANDER, waft, stray, float, freewheel, coast. **2** GATHER, accumulate, pile up, drive.
n **1** ACCUMULATION, mound, pile, bank, mass, heap. **2** TREND, tendency, course, direction, flow, movement, current, rush, sweep.
3 MEANING, intention, implication, gist, tenor, thrust, significance, aim, design, scope.

drill v **1** TEACH, train, instruct, coach, practise, school, rehearse, exercise, discipline. **2** BORE, pierce, penetrate, puncture, perforate.
n **1** INSTRUCTION, training, practice, coaching, exercise, repetition, tuition, preparation, discipline. **2** BORER, awl, bit, gimlet.

drink v **1** IMBIBE, swallow, sip, drain, down, gulp, swig (*infml*), knock back (*infml*), sup, quaff, absorb, guzzle, partake of (*fml*), swill. **2** GET DRUNK, booze (*infml*), tipple (*infml*), indulge, carouse, revel, tank up (*infml*).
n **1** BEVERAGE, liquid, refreshment, draught, sip, swallow, swig (*infml*), gulp. **2** ALCOHOL, spirits, booze (*infml*), liquor, tipple (*infml*), tot, the bottle (*infml*), stiffener (*infml*).

> *Alcoholic drinks include*: ale, beer, cider, lager, shandy, stout, Guinness®; aquavit, Armagnac, bourbon, brandy, Calvados, Cognac, gin, gin-and-tonic, pink gin, sloe gin, rum, grog, rye, vodka, whisky, Scotch and soda, hot toddy; wine, red wine, vin rouge, white wine, vin blanc, Beaujolais, Beaune, Bordeaux, burgundy, claret, mulled wine, muscatel, Chianti, Graves, Rioja,

> Chablis, champagne, bubbly (*infml*), hock, Moselle, Riesling, Sauterne, mead, perry, vino (*infml*), plonk (*infml*); absinthe, advocaat, Benedictine, Chartreuse, black velvet, bloody Mary, Buck's fizz, Campari, cherry brandy, cocktail, Cointreau®, crème de menthe, daiquiri, eggnog, ginger wine, kirsch, Marsala, Martini®, ouzo, Pernod®, piña colada, port, punch, retsina, sake, sangria, schnapps, sherry, snowball, tequila, Tom Collins, vermouth.

drip v drop, dribble, trickle, plop, perculate, drizzle, splash, sprinkle, weep.
n **1** DROP, trickle, dribble, leak, bead, tear. **2** (*infml*) WEAKLING, wimp (*infml*), softy (*infml*), bore, wet (*infml*), ninny (*infml*).

drive v **1** DIRECT, control, manage, operate, run, handle, motivate.
2 FORCE, compel, impel, coerce, constrain, press, push, urge, dragoon, gpad, guide, oblige. **3** STEER, motor, propel, ride, travel.
n **1** ENERGY, enterprise, ambition, initiative, get-up-and-go (*infml*), vigour, motivation, determination.
2 CAMPAIGN, crusade, appeal, effort, action. **3** EXCURSION, outing, journey, ride, spin, trip, jaunt.
4 URGE, instinct, impulse, need, desire.

drive at imply, allude to, intimate, mean, suggest, hint, get at, intend, refer to, signify, insinuate, indicate.

driving adj compelling, forceful, vigorous, dynamic, energetic, forthright, heavy, violent, sweeping.

drizzle n mist, mizzle, rain, spray, shower.
v spit, spray, sprinkle, rain, spot, shower.

droop v **1** HANG (DOWN), dangle, sag, bend. **2** LANGUISH, decline, flag, falter, slump, lose heart, wilt, wither, drop, faint, fall down, fade, slouch. **3** sink.

◨ 1 straighten. **2** flourish, rise.

drop *n* **1** DROPLET, bead, lear, drip, bubble, globule, trickle. **2** DASH, pinch, spot, sip, trace, dab. **3** FALL, decline, falling-off, lowering, downturn, decrease, reduction, slump, plunge, deterioration.
4 DESCENT, precipice, slope, chasm, abyss.

v **1** FALL, sink, decline, plunge, plummet, tumble, dive, descend, lower, droop, depress, diminish.
2 ABANDON, forsake, desert, give up, relinquish, reject, jilt, leave, renounce, throw over, repudiate, cease, discontinue, quit.

◨ 1 rise.

drop off 1 NOD OFF, doze, snooze (*infml*), have forty winks (*infml*).
2 DECLINE, fall off, decrease, dwindle, lessen, diminish, slacken. **3** DELIVER, set down, leave.

◨ 1 wake up. **2** increase. **3** pick up.

drop out back out, abandon, cry off, withdraw, forsake, leave, quit.

drought *n* dryness, aridity, parchedness, dehydration, desiccation, shortage, want.

drove *n* herd, horde, gathering, crowd, multitude, swarm, throng, flock, company, mob, press.

drown *v* **1** SUBMERGE, immerse, inundate, go under, flood, sink, deluge, engulf, drench.
2 OVERWHELM, overpower, overcome, swamp, wipe out, extinguish.

drowsy *adj* sleepy, tired, lethargic, nodding, dreamy, dozy, somnolent (*fml*).

◨ alert, awake.

drudge *n* toiler, menial, dogsbody (*infml*), hack, servant, slave, factotum, worker, skivvy (*infml*), galley-slave, lackey.

v plod, toil, work, slave, plug away (*infml*), grind (*infml*), labour, beaver (*infml*).

◨ idle, laze.

drudgery *n* labour, donkey-work (*infml*), hack-work, slog (*infml*), grind (*infml*), slavery, sweat, sweated labour, toil, skivvying, chore.

drug *n* medication, medicine, remedy, potion.

> *Types of drug include*: anaesthetic, analgesic, antibiotic, antidepressant, antihistamine, barbiturate, narcotic, opiate, hallucinogenic, sedative, steroid, stimulant, tranquillizer; chloroform, aspirin, codeine, paracetamol, morphine, penicillin, diazepam, Valium®, cortisone, insulin, digitalis, laudanum, quinine, progesterone, oestrogen, cannabis, marijuana, smack, LSD, acid, ecstasy, E (*sl*), heroin, opium, cocaine, crack, dope (*infml*). *see also* **medicine**.

v medicate, sedate, tranquillize, dope (*infml*), anaesthetize, dose, knock out (*infml*), stupefy, deaden, numb.

drum *v* beat, pulsate, tap, throb, thrum, tattoo, reverberate, rap.
drum up obtain, round up, collect, gather, solicit, canvass, petition, attract.

drunk *adj* inebriated, intoxicated, under the influence, drunken, stoned (*sl*), legless (*sl*), paralytic (*infml*), sloshed (*infml*), merry (*infml*), tight (*infml*), tipsy (*infml*), tanked up (*infml*), tiddly (*infml*), plastered (*infml*), loaded (*infml*), lit up (*infml*), sozzled (*infml*), well-oiled (*infml*), canned (*sl*), blotto (*sl*).

◨ sober, temperate, abstinent, teetotal.

drunkard *n* drunk, inebriate, alcoholic, dipsomaniac, boozer (*infml*), wino (*infml*), tippler (*infml*), soak (*infml*), sot (*infml*).

dry *adj* **1** ARID, parched, thirsty, dehydrated, desiccated, barren.
2 BORING, dull, dreary, tedious,

monotonous. **3** *dry humour*: ironic, cynical, droll, deadpan, sarcastic, cutting.

⊟ 1 wet. **2** interesting.

v dehydrate, parch, desiccate, drain, shrivel, wither.

⊟ soak.

dual *adj* double, twofold, duplicate, duplex, binary, combined, paired, twin, matched.

dubious *adj* **1** DOUBTFUL, uncertain, undecided, unsure, wavering, unsettled, suspicious, sceptical, hesitant. **2** QUESTIONABLE, debatable, unreliable, ambiguous, suspect, obscure, fishy (*infml*), shady (*infml*).

⊟ 1 certain. **2** trustworthy.

duck *v* **1** CROUCH, stoop, bob, bend. **2** AVOID, dodge, evade, shirk, sidestep. **3** DIP, immerse, plunge, dunk, dive, submerge, douse, souse, wet, lower.

due *adj* **1** OWED, owing, payable, unpaid, outstanding, in arrears. **2** RIGHTFUL, fitting, appropriate, proper, merited, deserved, justified, suitable. **3** ADEQUATE, enough, sufficient, ample, plenty of. **4** EXPECTED, scheduled.

⊟ 1 paid. **3** inadequate.

adv exactly, direct(ly), precisely, straight, dead (*infml*).

duel *n* affair of honour, combat, contest, fight, clash, competition, rivalry, encounter.

dull *adj* **1** BORING, uninteresting, unexciting, flat, dreary, monotonous, tedious, uneventful, humdrum, unimaginative, dismal, lifeless, plain, insipid, heavy. **2** DARK, gloomy, drab, murky, indistinct, grey, cloudy, lack-lustre, opaque, dim, overcast. **3** UNINTELLIGENT, dense, dim, dimwitted (*infml*), thick (*infml*), stupid, slow.

⊟ 1 interesting, exciting. **2** bright. **3** intelligent, clever.

v **1** BLUNT, alleviate, mitigate, moderate, lessen, relieve, soften. **2** DEADEN, numb, paralyse. **3** DISCOURAGE, dampen, subdue, sadden. **4** DIM, obscure, fade.

dumb *adj* silent, mute, soundless, speechless, tongue-tied, inarticulate, mum (*infml*).

dumbfounded *adj* astonished, amazed, astounded, overwhelmed, speechless, taken aback, thrown (*infml*), startled, overcome, confounded, flabbergasted (*infml*), staggered, confused, bowled over, dumb, floored (*infml*), paralysed.

dummy *n* **1** COPY, duplicate, imitation, counterfeit, substitute. **2** MODEL, lay-figure, mannequin, figure, form. **3** TEAT, pacifier.

adj **1** ARTIFICIAL, fake, imitation, false, bogus, mock, sham, phoney. **2** SIMULATED, practice, trial.

dump *v* **1** DEPOSIT, drop, offload, throw down, let fall, unload, empty out, discharge, park. **2** GET RID OF, scrap, throw away, dispose of, ditch, tip, jettison.

n **1** RUBBISH-TIP, junk-yard, rubbish-heap, tip. **2** HOVEL, slum, shack, shanty, hole (*infml*), joint (*infml*), pigsty, mess.

dungeon *n* cell, prison, jail, gaol, cage, lock-up, keep, oubliette, vault.

dupe *n* victim, sucker (*infml*), fool, gull, mug (*infml*), push-over (*infml*), fall guy (*infml*), pawn, puppet, instrument, stooge (*infml*), simpleton.

v deceive, delude, fool, trick, outwit, con (*infml*), cheat, hoax, swindle, rip off (*infml*), take in, hoodwink, defraud, bamboozle (*infml*).

duplicate *adj* identical, matching, twin, twofold, corresponding, matched.

n copy, replica, reproduction, photocopy, carbon (copy), match, facsimile.

v copy, reproduce, repeat, photocopy, double, clone, echo.

durable *adj* lasting, enduring, long-lasting, abiding, hard-wearing, strong, sturdy, tough, unfading, substantial, sound, reliable, dependable, stable, resistant, persistent, constant, permanent, firm, fixed, fast.

Fe perishable, weak, fragile.

duress *n* constraint, coercion, compulsion, pressure, restraint, threat, force.

dusk *n* twilight, sunset, nightfall, evening, sundown, gloaming, darkness, dark, gloom, shadows, shade.

Fe dawn, brightness.

dust *n* powder, particles, dirt, earth, soil, ground, grit, grime.

dusty *adj* **1** DIRTY, grubby, filthy. **2** POWDERY, granular, crumbly, chalky, sandy.

Fe **1** clean. **2** solid, hard.

dutiful *adj* obedient, respectful, conscientious, devoted, filial, reverential, submissive.

duty *n* **1** OBLIGATION, responsibility, assignment, calling, charge, role, task, job, business, function, work, office, service. **2** OBEDIENCE, respect, loyalty. **3** TAX, toll, tariff, levy, customs, excise.

on duty at work, engaged, busy.

dwarf *n* **1** PERSON OF RESTRICTED GROWTH, midget, pygmy, Tom Thumb, Lilliputian. **2** GNOME, goblin.

adj miniature, small, tiny, pocket, mini (*infml*), diminutive, petite, Lilliputian, baby.

Fe large.

v **1** STUNT, retard, check. **2** OVERSHADOW, tower over, dominate.

dwell *v* live, inhabit, reside, stay, settle, populate, people, lodge, rest, abide (*fml*).

dwindle *v* diminish, decrease, decline, lessen, subside, ebb, fade, weaken, taper off, tail off, shrink, peter out, fall, wane, waste away, die out, wither, shrivel, disappear.

Fe increase, grow.

dye *n* colour, colouring, stain, pigment, tint, tinge.

v colour, tint, stain, pigment, tinge, imbue.

dying *adj* moribund, passing, final, going, mortal, not long for this world, perishing, failing, fading, vanishing.

Fe reviving.

dynamic *adj* forceful, powerful, energetic, vigorous, go-ahead, high-powered, driving, self-starting, spirited, vital, lively, active.

Fe inactive, apathetic.

dynasty *n* house, line, succession, dominion, regime, government, rule, empire, sovereignty.

E

eager *adj* **1** KEEN, enthusiastic, fervent, intent, earnest, zealous. **2** LONGING, yearning.

Fe **1** unenthusiastic, indifferent.

ear *n* **1** ATTENTION, heed, notice, regard. **2** *an ear for language*: perception, sensitivity, discrimination, appreciation, hearing, skill, ability.

Parts of the ear include: anvil (incus), auditory canal, auditory nerve, auricle, cochlea, concha, eardrum, eustachian tube, hammer (malleus), helix, labyrinth, lobe, oval window, pinna, round window,

semicircular canal, stirrup (stapes),
tragus, tympanum, vestibular nerve,
vestibule.

early adj **1** *early symptoms*: forward,
advanced, premature, untimely,
undeveloped. **2** *early theatre*:
primitive, ancient, primeval.
adv ahead of time, in good time,
beforehand, in advance, prematurely.
🔁 late.

earn v **1** *earn a good salary*: receive,
obtain, make, get, draw, bring in
(*infml*), gain, realize, gross, reap.
2 *earn one's reputation*: deserve,
merit, warrant, win, rate.
🔁 **1** spend, lose.

earnest adj **1** RESOLUTE, devoted,
ardent, conscientious, intent, keen,
fervent, firm, fixed, eager,
enthusiastic, steady. **2** SERIOUS,
sincere, solemn, grave, heartfelt.
🔁 **1** apathetic. **2** frivolous, flippant.

earnings n pay, income, salary,
wages, profits, gain, proceeds,
reward, receipts, return, revenue,
remuneration, stipend.
🔁 expenditure, outgoings.

earth n **1** WORLD, planet, globe,
sphere. **2** LAND, ground, soil, clay,
loam, sod, humus.

earthenware n pottery, ceramics,
crockery, pots.

earthly adj **1** *our earthly life*:
material, physical, human, worldly,
mortal, mundane, fleshly, secular,
sensual, profane, temporal. **2** *no
earthly explanation*: possible, likely,
conceivable, slightest.
🔁 **1** spiritual, heavenly.

earthy adj crude, coarse, vulgar,
bawdy, rough, raunchy (*infml*),
down-to-earth, ribald, robust.
🔁 refined, modest.

ease n **1** FACILITY, effortlessness,
skilfulness, deftness, dexterity,
naturalness, cleverness. **2** COMFORT,
contentment, peace, affluence,
repose, leisure, relaxation, rest, quiet,

happiness.
🔁 **1** difficulty. **2** discomfort.
v **1** *ease the pain*: alleviate, moderate,
lessen, lighten, relieve, mitigate, abate,
relent, allay, assuage, relax, comfort,
calm, soothe, facilitate, smooth.
2 *ease it into position*: inch, steer,
slide, still.
🔁 **1** aggravate, intensify, worsen.

easily adv **1** EFFORTLESSLY,
comfortably, readily, simply. **2** BY
FAR, undoubtedly, indisputably,
definitely, certainly, doubtlessly,
clearly, far and away, undeniably,
simply, surely, probably, well.
🔁 **1** laboriously.

easy adj **1** EFFORTLESS, simple,
uncomplicated, undemanding,
straightforward, manageable, cushy
(*infml*). **2** RELAXED, carefree, easy-
going, comfortable, informal, calm,
natural, leisurely.
🔁 **1** difficult, demanding, exacting.
2 tense, uneasy.

easy-going adj relaxed, tolerant,
laid-back (*infml*), amenable, happy-
go-lucky (*infml*), carefree, calm,
even-tempered, serene.
🔁 strict, intolerant, critical.

eat v **1** CONSUME, feed, swallow,
devour, chew, scoff (*infml*), munch,
dine. **2** CORRODE, erode, wear away,
decay, rot, crumble, dissolve.

eatable adj edible, palatable, good,
wholesome, digestible, comestible
(*fml*), harmless.
🔁 inedible, unpalatable.

eavesdrop v listen in, spy,
overhear, snoop (*infml*), tap (*infml*),
bug (*infml*), monitor.

eccentric adj odd, peculiar,
abnormal, unconventional, strange,
quirky, weird, way-out (*infml*),
queer, outlandish, idiosyncratic,
bizarre, freakish, erratic, singular,
dotty.
🔁 conventional, orthodox, normal.
n nonconformist, oddball (*infml*),
oddity, crank (*infml*), freak (*infml*),

character (*infml*).

eccentricity *n*
UNCONVENTIONALITY, strangeness, peculiarity, nonconformity, abnormality, oddity, weirdness, idiosyncrasy, singularity, quirk, freakishness, aberration, anomaly, capriciousness.
🔁 conventionality, ordinariness.

ecclesiastical *adj* church, churchly, religious, clerical, priestly, divine, spiritual.

echo *v* 1 REVERBERATE, resound, repeat, reflect, reiterate, ring.
2 IMITATE, copy, reproduce, mirror, resemble, mimic.
n 1 REVERBERATION, reiteration, repetition, reflection. 2 IMITATION, copy, reproduction, mirror image, image, parallel.

eclipse *v* 1 BLOT OUT, obscure, cloud, veil, darken, dim. 2 OUTDO, overshadow, outshine, surpass, transcend.
n 1 OBSCURATION, overshadowing, darkening, shading, dimming.
2 DECLINE, failure, fall, loss.

economic *adj* 1 COMMERCIAL, business, industrial. 2 FINANCIAL, budgetary, fiscal, monetary.
3 PROFITABLE, profit-making, money-making, productive, cost-effective, viable.

economical *adj* 1 THRIFTY, careful, prudent, saving, sparing, frugal.
2 CHEAP, inexpensive, low-priced, reasonable, cost-effective, modest, efficient.
🔁 1 wasteful. 2 expensive, uneconomical.

economize *v* save, cut back, tighten one's belt (*infml*), cut costs.
🔁 waste, squander.

economy *n* thrift, saving, restraint, prudence, frugality, parsimony, providence, husbandry.
🔁 extravagance.

ecstasy *n* delight, rapture, bliss, elation, joy, euphoria, frenzy,

exaltation, fervour.
🔁 misery, torment.

ecstatic *adj* elated, blissful, joyful, rapturous, overjoyed, euphoric, delirious, frenzied, fervent.
🔁 downcast.

eddy *n* whirlpool, swirl, vortex, twist.
v swirl, whirl.

edge *n* 1 BORDER, rim, boundary, limit, brim, threshold, brink, fringe, margin, outline, side, verge, line, perimeter, periphery, lip.
2 ADVANTAGE, superiority, force.
3 SHARPNESS, acuteness, keenness, incisiveness, pungency, zest.
v creep, inch, ease, sidle.

edgy *adj* on edge, nervous, tense, anxious, ill at ease, keyed-up, touchy, irritable.
🔁 calm.

edible *adj* eatable, palatable, digestible, wholesome, good, harmless.
🔁 inedible.

edict *n* command, order, proclamation, law, decree, regulation, pronouncement, ruling, mandate, statute, injunction, manifesto.

edifice *n* building, construction, structure, erection.

edify *v* instruct, improve, enlighten, inform, guide, educate, nurture, teach.

edit *v* correct, emend, revise, rewrite, reorder, rearrange, adapt, check, compile, rephrase, select, polish, annotate, censor.

edition *n* copy, volume, impression, printing, issue, version, number.

educate *v* teach, train, instruct, tutor, coach, school, inform, cultivate, edify, drill, improve, discipline, develop.

educated *adj* learned, taught, schooled, trained, knowledgeable, informed, instructed, lettered, cultured, civilized, tutored, refined, well-bred.

🇪🇸 uneducated, uncultured.

education *n* teaching, training, schooling, tuition, tutoring, coaching, guidance, instruction, cultivation, culture, scholarship, improvement, enlightenment, knowledge, nurture, development.

Educational establishments include: kindergarten, nursery school, infant school, primary school, middle school, combined school, secondary school, secondary modern, upper school, high school, grammar school, grant-maintained school, preparatory school, public school, private school, boarding-school, college, sixth-form college, polytechnic, poly, city technical college, CTC, technical college, university, adult-education centre, academy, seminary, finishing school, business school, secretarial college, Sunday school, convent school, summer-school.

Educational terms include: adult education, assisted places scheme, A-level, baccalaureate, board of governors, break time, bursar, campus, catchment area, certificate, classroom, coeducation, common entrance, course, curriculum, degree, diploma, double-first, eleven-plus, enrolment, examination, exercise book, final exam, finals, further education, GCSE (General Certificate of Secondary Education), governor, graduation, half-term, head boy, head girl, head teacher, higher education, homework, intake, invigilator, lecture, literacy, matriculation, matron, mixed-ability teaching, modular course, national curriculum, NVQ (national vocational qualification), numeracy, O-level, opting out, parent governor, PTA (parent teacher association), playground, playtime, prefect, primary education, proctor, professor, pupil, quadrangle, qualification, refresher course, register, report, scholarship, school term, secondary education, special education, statemented, streaming, student, student grant, student loan, study, subject, syllabus, teacher, teacher training, test paper, textbook, thesis, timetable, truancy, university entrance, work experience, YTS (Youth Training Scheme).

---

eerie *adj* weird, strange, uncanny, spooky (*infml*), creepy, frightening, scary, spine-chilling.

effect *n* **1** OUTCOME, result, conclusion, consequence, upshot, aftermath, issue. **2** POWER, force, impact, efficacy, impression, strength. **3** MEANING, significance, import.

v cause, execute, create, achieve, accomplish, perform, produce, make, initiate, fulfil, complete.

in effect in fact, actually, really, in reality, to all intents and purposes, for all practical purposes, essentially, effectively, virtually.

take effect be effective, become operative, come into force, come into operation, be implemented, begin, work.

effective *adj* **1** EFFICIENT, efficacious, productive, adequate, capable, useful. **2** OPERATIVE, in force, functioning, current, active. **3** STRIKING, impressive, forceful, cogent, powerful, persuasive, convincing, telling.

🇪🇸 **1** ineffective, powerless.

effects *n* belongings, possessions, property, goods, gear (*infml*), movables, chattels (*fml*), things, trappings.

effeminate *adj* unmanly, womanly, womanish, feminine, sissy (*infml*), delicate.

◨ manly.

effervescent *adj* **1** BUBBLY, sparkling, fizzy, frothy, carbonated, foaming. **2** LIVELY, ebullient, vivacious, animated, buoyant, exhilarated, enthusiastic, exuberant, excited, vital.

◨ 1 flat. 2 dull.

efficiency *n* effectiveness, competence, proficiency, skill, expertise, skilfulness, capability, ability, productivity.

◨ inefficiency, incompetence.

efficient *adj* effective, competent, proficient, skilful, capable, able, productive, well-organized, businesslike, powerful, well-conducted.

◨ inefficient, incompetent.

effort *n* **1** EXERTION, strain, application, struggle, trouble, energy, toil, striving, pains, travail (*fml*). **2** ATTEMPT, try, go (*infml*), endeavour, shot, stab. **3** ACHIEVEMENT, accomplishment, feat, exploit, production, creation, deed, product, work.

effortless *adj* easy, simple, undemanding, facile, painless, smooth.

◨ difficult.

effrontery *n* audacity, impertinence, insolence, cheek (*infml*), impudence, temerity, boldness, brazenness, cheekiness, gall, nerve, presumption, disrespect, arrogance, brashness.

◨ respect, timidity.

effusive *adj* fulsome, gushing, unrestrained, expansive, ebullient, demonstrative, profuse, overflowing, enthusiastic, exuberant, extravagant, lavish, talkative, voluble.

◨ reserved, restrained.

egotism *n* egoism, egomania, self-centredness, self-importance, conceitedness, self-regard, self-love, self-conceit, narcissism, self-admiration, vanity, bigheadedness (*infml*).

◨ humility.

egotistic *adj* egoistic, egocentric, self-centred, self-important, conceited, vain, swollen-headed (*infml*), bigheaded (*infml*), boasting, bragging.

◨ humble.

ejaculate *v* **1** DISCHARGE, eject, spurt, emit. **2** EXCLAIM, call, cry (out), cry, shout, yell, utter, scream.

eject *v* **1** EMIT, expel, discharge, spout, spew, evacuate, vomit. **2** OUST, evict, throw out, drive out, turn out, expel, remove, banish, deport, dismiss, exile, kick out, fire (*infml*), sack (*infml*).

elaborate *adj* **1** *elaborate plans*: detailed, careful, thorough, exact, extensive, painstaking, precise, perfected, minute, laboured, studied. **2** *elaborate design*: intricate, complex, complicated, involved, ornamental, ornate, fancy, decorated, ostentatious, showy, fussy.

◨ 2 simple, plain.

v amplify, develop, enlarge, expand, flesh out, polish, improve, refine, devise, explain.

◨ précis, simplify.

elapse *v* pass, lapse, go by, slip away.

elastic *adj* **1** PLIABLE, flexible, stretchable, supple, resilient, yielding, springy, rubbery, pliant, plastic, bouncy, buoyant. **2** ADAPTABLE, accommodating, flexible, tolerant, adjustable.

◨ 1 rigid. 2 inflexible.

elasticity *n* **1** PLIABILITY, flexibility, resilience, stretch, springiness, suppleness, give, plasticity, bounce, buoyancy. **2** ADAPTABILITY, flexibility, tolerance, adjustability.

◨ 1 rigidity. 2 inflexibility.

elated *adj* exhilarated, excited, euphoric, ecstatic, exultant, jubilant, overjoyed, joyful.

E3 despondent, downcast.

elbow v jostle, nudge, push, shove, bump, crowd, knock, shoulder.

elder adj older, senior, first-born, ancient.
E3 younger.

elderly adj aging, aged, old, hoary, senile.
E3 young, youthful.

elect v choose, pick, opt for, select, vote for, prefer, adopt, designate, appoint, determine.
adj choice, elite, chosen, designated, designate, picked, prospective, selected, to be, preferred, hand-picked.

election n choice, selection, voting, ballot, poll, appointment, determination, decision, preference.

elector n selector, voter, constituent.

electric adj electrifying, exciting, stimulating, thrilling, charged, dynamic, stirring, tense, rousing.
E3 unexciting, flat.

electrify v thrill, excite, shock, invigorate, animate, stimulate, stir, rouse, fire, jolt, galvanize, amaze, astonish, astound, stagger.
E3 bore.

elegant adj stylish, chic, fashionable, modish, smart, refined, polished, genteel, smooth, tasteful, fine, exquisite, beautiful, graceful, handsome, delicate, neat, artistic.
E3 inelegant, unrefined, unfashionable.

elegy n dirge, lament, requiem, plaint.

element n factor, component, constituent, ingredient, member, part, piece, fragment, feature, trace.
E3 whole.

elementary adj basic, fundamental, rudimentary, principal, primary, clear, easy, introductory, straightforward, uncomplicated, simple.
E3 advanced.

elements n basics, fundamentals,

foundations, principles, rudiments, essentials.

elevate v **1** LIFT, raise, hoist, heighten, intensify, magnify. **2** EXALT, advance, promote, aggrandize, upgrade. **3** UPLIFT, rouse, boost, brighten.
E3 **1** lower. **2** downgrade.

elevated adj raised, lofty, exalted, high, grand, noble, dignified, sublime.
E3 base.

elevation n **1** RISE, promotion, advancement, preferment, aggrandizement. **2** EXALTATION, loftiness, grandeur, eminence, nobility. **3** HEIGHT, altitude, hill, rise.
E3 **1** demotion. **2** dip.

elicit v evoke, draw out, derive, extract, obtain, exact, extort, cause.

eligible adj qualified, fit, appropriate, suitable, acceptable, worthy, proper, desirable.
E3 ineligible.

eliminate v remove, get rid of, cut out, take out, exclude, delete, dispense with, rub out, omit, reject, disregard, dispose of, drop, do away with, eradicate, expel, extinguish, stamp out, exterminate, knock out, kill, murder.
E3 include, accept.

elite n best, elect, aristocracy, upper classes, nobility, gentry, crème de la crème, establishment, high society.
adj choice, best, exclusive, selected, first-class, aristocratic, noble, upper-class.

elocution n delivery, articulation, diction, enunciation, pronunciation, oratory, rhetoric, speech, utterance.

elongated adj lengthened, extended, prolonged, protracted, stretched, long.

elope v run off, run away, decamp, bolt, abscond, do a bunk (infml), escape, steal away, leave, disappear.

eloquent adj articulate, fluent, well-

expressed, glib, expressive, vocal, voluble, persuasive, moving, forceful, graceful, plausible, stirring, vivid.
☒ inarticulate, tongue-tied.

elucidate v explain, clarify, clear up, interpret, spell out, illustrate, unfold.
☒ confuse.

elude v 1 AVOID, escape, evade, dodge, shirk, duck (*infml*), flee. 2 PUZZLE, frustrate, baffle, confound, thwart, stump, foil.

elusive adj 1 INDEFINABLE, intangible, unanalysable, subtle, puzzling, baffling, transient, transitory. 2 EVASIVE, shifty, slippery, tricky.

emaciated adj thin, gaunt, lean, haggard, wasted, scrawny, skeletal, pinched, attenuated, meagre, lank.
☒ plump, well-fed.

emanate v 1 ORIGINATE, proceed, arise, derive, issue, spring, stem, flow, come, emerge. 2 DISCHARGE, send out, emit, give out, give off, radiate.

emancipate v free, liberate, release, set free, enfranchise, deliver, discharge, loose, unchain, unshackle, unfetter.
☒ enslave.

embankment n causeway, dam, rampart, levee, earthwork.

embargo n restriction, ban, prohibition, restraint, proscription, bar, barrier, interdiction (*fml*), impediment, check, hindrance, blockage, stoppage, seizure.

embark v board (ship), go aboard, take ship.
☒ disembark.

embark on begin, start, commence, set about, launch, undertake, enter, initiate, engage.
☒ complete, finish.

embarrass v disconcert, mortify, show up, discompose, fluster, humiliate, shame, distress.

embarrassment n

1 DISCOMPOSURE, self-consciousness, chagrin, mortification, humiliation, shame, awkwardness, confusion, bashfulness. 2 DIFFICULTY, constraint, predicament, distress, discomfort.

embellish v adorn, ornament, decorate, deck, dress up, beautify, gild, garnish, festoon, elaborate, embroider, enrich, exaggerate, enhance, varnish, grace.
☒ simplify, denude.

embellishment n adornment, ornament, ornamentation, decoration, elaboration, garnish, trimming, gilding, enrichment, enhancement, embroidery, exaggeration.

embezzle v appropriate, misappropriate, steal, pilfer, filch, pinch (*infml*).

embezzlement n appropriation, misappropriation, pilfering, fraud, stealing, theft, filching.

embittered adj bitter, disaffected, sour, disillusioned.

emblem n symbol, sign, token, representation, logo, insignia, device, crest, mark, badge, figure.

embodiment n incarnation, personification, exemplification, expression, epitome, example, incorporation, realization, representation, manifestation, concentration.

embody v 1 PERSONIFY, exemplify, represent, stand for, symbolize, incorporate, express, manifest. 2 INCLUDE, contain, integrate.

embrace v 1 HUG, clasp, cuddle, hold, grasp, squeeze. 2 INCLUDE, encompass, incorporate, contain, comprise, cover, involve. 3 ACCEPT, take up, welcome.
n hug, cuddle, clasp, clinch (*infml*).

embroil v involve, implicate, entangle, enmesh, mix up, incriminate.

embryo n nucleus, germ, beginning,

root.

embryonic *adj* undeveloped, rudimentary, immature, early, germinal, primary.

⊟ developed.

emerge *v* **1** ARISE, rise, surface, appear, develop, crop up (*infml*), transpire, turn up, materialize.
2 EMANATE, issue, proceed.

⊟ 1 disappear.

emergence *n* appearance, rise, advent, coming, dawn, development, arrival, disclosure, issue.

⊟ disappearance.

emergency *n* crisis, danger, difficulty, exigency (*fml*), predicament, plight, pinch, strait, quandary.

emigrate *n* migrate, relocate, move, depart.

eminence *n* distinction, fame, pre-eminence, prominence, renown, reputation, greatness, importance, esteem, note, prestige, rank.

eminent *adj* distinguished, famous, prominent, illustrious, outstanding, notable, pre-eminent, prestigious, celebrated, renowned, noteworthy, conspicuous, esteemed, important, well-known, elevated, respected, great, high-ranking, grand, superior.

⊟ unknown, obscure, unimportant.

emissary *n* ambassador, agent, envoy, messenger, delegate, herald, courier, representative, scout, deputy, spy.

emission *n* discharge, issue, ejection, emanation, ejaculation, diffusion, transmission, exhalation, radiation, release, exudation, vent.

emit *v* discharge, issue, eject, emanate, exude, give out, give off, diffuse, radiate, release, shed, vent.

⊟ absorb.

emotion *n* feeling, passion, sensation, sentiment, ardour, fervour, warmth, reaction, vehemence, excitement.

emotional *adj* **1** FEELING, passionate, sensitive, responsive, ardent, tender, warm, roused, demonstrative, excitable, enthusiastic, fervent, impassioned, moved, sentimental, zealous, hot-blooded, heated, tempestuous, overcharged, temperamental, fiery.
2 EMOTIVE, moving, poignant, thrilling, touching, stirring, heart-warming, exciting, pathetic.

⊟ 1 unemotional, cold, detached, calm.

emphasis *n* stress, weight, significance, importance, priority, underscoring, accent, force, power, prominence, pre-eminence, attention, intensity, strength, urgency, positiveness, insistence, mark, moment.

emphasize *v* stress, accentuate, underline, highlight, accent, feature, dwell on, weight, point up, spotlight, play up, insist on, press home, intensify, strengthen, punctuate.

⊟ play down, understate.

emphatic *adj* forceful, positive, insistent, certain, definite, decided, unequivocal, absolute, categorical, earnest, marked, pronounced, significant, strong, striking, vigorous, distinct, energetic, forcible, important, impressive, momentous, powerful, punctuated, telling, vivid, graphic, direct.

⊟ tentative, hesitant, understated.

empire *n* **1** SUPREMACY, sovereignty, rule, authority, command, government, jurisdiction, control, power, sway. **2** DOMAIN, dominion, kingdom, realm, commonwealth, territory.

employ *v* **1** ENGAGE, hire, take on, recruit, enlist, commission, retain, fill, occupy, take up. **2** USE, utilize, make use of, apply, bring to bear, ply, exercise.

employee *n* worker, member of staff, job-holder, hand, wage-earner.

employer *n* boss, proprietor, owner,

manager, gaffer (*infml*),
management, company, firm,
business, establishment.

employment *n* **1** JOB, work,
occupation, situation, business,
calling, profession, line (*infml*),
vocation, trade, pursuit, craft.
2 ENLISTMENT, employ,
engagement, hire.
☒ 1 unemployment.

empower *v* authorize, warrant,
enable, license, sanction, permit,
entitle, commission, delegate,
qualify.

emptiness *n* **1** VACUUM,
vacantness, void, hollowness, hunger,
bareness, barrenness, desolation.
2 FUTILITY, meaninglessness,
worthlessness, aimlessness,
ineffectiveness, unreality.
☒ 1 fullness.

empty *adj* **1** VACANT, void,
unoccupied, uninhabited, unfilled,
deserted, bare, hollow, desolate,
blank, clear. **2** FUTILE, aimless,
meaningless, senseless, trivial, vain,
worthless, useless, insubstantial,
ineffective, insincere. **3** VACUOUS,
inane, expressionless, blank, vacant.
☒ 1 full. **2** meaningful.
v drain, exhaust, discharge, clear,
evacuate, vacate, pour out, unload,
void, gut.
☒ fill.

empty-headed *adj* inane, silly,
frivolous, scatter-brained (*infml*),
feather-brained (*infml*).

emulate *v* match, copy, mimic,
follow, imitate, echo, compete with,
contend with, rival, vie with.

enable *v* equip, qualify, empower,
authorize, sanction, warrant, allow,
permit, prepare, fit, facilitate, license,
commission, endue.
☒ prevent, inhibit, forbid.

enact *v* **1** DECREE, ordain, order,
authorize, command, legislate,
sanction, ratify, pass, establish.
2 ACT (OUT), perform, play,

portray, represent, depict.
☒ 1 repeal, rescind.

enamoured *adj* charmed,
infatuated, in love with, enchanted,
captivated, entranced, smitten, keen,
taken, fascinated, fond.

enchant *v* **1** CAPTIVATE, charm,
fascinate, enrapture, attract, allure,
appeal, delight, thrill. **2** ENTRANCE,
enthral, bewitch, spellbind,
hypnotize, mesmerize.
☒ 1 repel.

enclose *v* encircle, encompass,
surround, fence, hedge, hem in,
bound, encase, embrace, envelop,
confine, hold, shut in, wrap, pen,
cover, circumscribe, incorporate,
include, insert, contain, comprehend.

enclosure *n* pen, pound,
compound, paddock, fold, stockade,
sty, arena, corral, court, ring,
cloister.

encompass *v* **1** ENCIRCLE, circle,
ring, surround, gird, envelop,
circumscribe, hem in, enclose, hold.
2 INCLUDE, cover, embrace, contain,
comprise, admit, incorporate,
involve, embody, comprehend.

encounter *v* **1** MEET, come across,
run into (*infml*), happen on, chance
upon, run across, confront, face,
experience. **2** FIGHT, clash with,
combat, cross swords with (*infml*),
engage, grapple with, struggle, strive,
contend.
n **1** MEETING, brush, confrontation.
2 CLASH, fight, combat, conflict,
contest, battle, set-to (*infml*), dispute,
engagement, action, skirmish, run-in,
collision.

encourage *v* **1** HEARTEN, exhort,
stimulate, spur, reassure, rally,
inspire, incite, egg on (*infml*), buoy
up, cheer, urge, rouse, comfort,
console. **2** PROMOTE, advance, aid,
boost, forward, further, foster,
support, help, strengthen.
☒ 1 discourage, depress. **2** discourage.

encouragement *n* **1**

REASSURANCE, inspiration, cheer, exhortation, incitement, pep talk (*infml*), urging, stimulation, consolation, succour (*fml*), stimulus.
2 PROMOTION, help, aid, boost, shot in the arm (*infml*), incentive, support, stimulus.
Ɛ₃ 1 discouragement, disapproval.

encouraging *adj* heartening, promising, hopeful, reassuring, stimulating, uplifting, auspicious, cheering, comforting, bright, rosy, cheerful, satisfactory.
Ɛ₃ discouraging.

encroach *v* intrude, invade, impinge, trespass, infringe, usurp, overstep, make inroads, muscle in (*infml*).

encumber *v* burden, overload, weigh down, saddle, oppress, handicap, hamper, hinder, impede, slow down, obstruct, inconvenience, prevent, retard, cramp.

encumbrance *n* burden, cumbrance, load, cross, millstone, albatross, difficulty, handicap, impediment, obstruction, obstacle, inconvenience, hindrance, liability.

end *n* **1** FINISH, conclusion, termination, close, completion, cessation, culmination, dénouement. **2** EXTREMITY, boundary, edge, limit, tip. **3** REMAINDER, tip, butt, left-over, remnant, stub, scrap, fragment. **4** AIM, object, objective, purpose, intention, goal, point, reason, design. **5** RESULT, outcome, consequence, upshot. **6** DEATH, demise, destruction, extermination, downfall, doom, ruin, dissolution.
Ɛ₃ 1 beginning, start. **6** birth.
v **1** FINISH, close, cease, conclude, stop, terminate, complete, culminate, wind up. **2** DESTROY, annihilate, exterminate, extinguish, ruin, abolish, dissolve.
Ɛ₃ 1 begin, start.

endanger *v* imperil, hazard, jeopardize, risk, expose, threaten, compromise.
Ɛ₃ protect.

endearing *adj* lovable, charming, appealing, attractive, winsome, delightful, enchanting.

endeavour *n* attempt, effort, go (*infml*), try, shot (*infml*), stab (*infml*), undertaking, enterprise, aim, venture.
v attempt, try, strive, aim, aspire, undertake, venture, struggle, labour, take pains.

ending *n* end, close, finish, completion, termination, conclusion, culmination, climax, resolution, consummation, dénouement, finale, epilogue.
Ɛ₃ beginning, start.

endless *adj* **1** INFINITE, boundless, unlimited, measureless.
2 EVERLASTING, ceaseless, perpetual, constant, continual, continuous, undying, eternal, interminable, monotonous.
Ɛ₃ 1 finite, limited. **2** temporary.

endorse *v* **1** APPROVE, sanction, authorize, support, back, affirm, ratify, confirm, vouch for, advocate, warrant, recommend, subscribe to, sustain, adopt. **2** SIGN, countersign.

endorsement *n* **1** APPROVAL, sanction, authorization, support, backing, affirmation, ratification, confirmation, advocacy, warrant, recommendation, commendation, seal of approval, testimonial, OK (*infml*). **2** SIGNATURE, countersignature.

endow *v* bestow, bequeath, leave, will, give, donate, endue (*fml*), confer, grant, present, award, finance, fund, support, make over, furnish, provide, supply.

endowment *n* **1** BEQUEST, legacy, award, grant, fund, gift, provision, settlement, donation, bestowal, benefaction, dowry, income, revenue.
2 TALENT, attribute, faculty, gift, ability, quality, flair, genius, qualification.

endurance *n* fortitude, patience, staying power, stamina, resignation, stoicism, tenacity, perseverance, resolution, stability, persistence, strength, toleration.

endure *v* **1** *endure hardship*: bear, stand, put up with, tolerate, weather, brave, cope with, face, go through, experience, submit to, suffer, sustain, swallow, undergo, withstand, stick, stomach, allow, permit, support. **2** *a peace that will endure for ever*: last, abide (*fml*), remain, live, survive, stay, persist, hold, prevail.

enemy *n* adversary, opponent, foe (*fml*), rival, antagonist, the opposition, competitor, opposer, other side.
F3 friend, ally.

energetic *adj* lively, vigorous, active, animated, dynamic, spirited, tireless, zestful, brisk, strong, forceful, potent, powerful, strenuous, high-powered.
F3 lethargic, sluggish, inactive, idle.

energy *n* liveliness, vigour, activity, animation, drive, dynamism, get-up-and-go (*infml*), life, spirit, verve, vivacity, vitality, zest, zeal, ardour, fire, efficiency, force, forcefulness, zip (*infml*), strength, power, intensity, exertion, stamina.
F3 lethargy, inertia, weakness.

enforce *v* impose, administer, implement, apply, execute, discharge, insist on, compel, oblige, urge, carry out, constrain, require, coerce, prosecute, reinforce.

engage *v* **1** PARTICIPATE, take part, embark on, take up, practise, involve. **2** ATTRACT, allure, draw, captivate, charm, catch. **3** OCCUPY, engross, absorb, busy, tie up, grip. **4** EMPLOY, hire, appoint, take on, enlist, enrol, commission, recruit, contract. **5** INTERLOCK, mesh, interconnect, join, interact, attach. **6** FIGHT, battle with, attack, take on, encounter, assail, combat.

F3 2 repel. **4** dismiss, discharge. **5** disengage.

engaged *adj* **1** *engaged in his work*: occupied, busy, engrossed, immersed, absorbed, preoccupied, involved, employed. **2** *engaged to be married*: promised, betrothed (*fml*), pledged, spoken for, committed. **3** *the phone is engaged*: busy, tied up, unavailable.

engagement *n* **1** APPOINTMENT, meeting, date, arrangement, assignation, fixture, rendezvous. **2** PROMISE, pledge, betrothal (*fml*), commitment, obligation, assurance, vow, troth (*fml*). **3** FIGHT, battle, combat, conflict, action, encounter, confrontation, contest.

engaging *adj* charming, attractive, appealing, captivating, pleasing, delightful, winsome, lovable, likable, pleasant, fetching, fascinating, agreeable.
F3 repulsive, repellant.

engine *n* motor, machine, mechanism, appliance, contraption, apparatus, device, instrument, tool, locomotive, dynamo.

Types of engine include: diesel, donkey, fuel-injection, internal-combustion, jet, petrol, steam, turbine, turbojet, turboprop, V-engine.

engineer *n* **1** MECHANIC, technician, engine driver. **2** DESIGNER, originator, planner, inventor, deviser, mastermind, architect.
v plan, contrive, devise, manoeuvre, cause, manipulate, control, bring about, mastermind, originate, orchestrate, effect, plot, scheme, manage, create, rig.

engrave *v* **1** INSCRIBE, cut, carve, chisel, etch, chase. **2** *engraved on her mind*: imprint, impress, fix, stamp, lodge, ingrain.

engraving *n* print, impression, inscription, carving, etching, woodcut, plate, block, cutting, chiselling, mark.

engross v absorb, occupy, engage, grip, hold, preoccupy, rivet, fascinate, captivate, enthral, arrest, involve, intrigue.
🔢 bore.

enhance v heighten, intensify, increase, improve, elevate, magnify, swell, exalt, raise, lift, boost, strengthen, reinforce, embellish.
🔢 reduce, minimize.

enigma n mystery, riddle, puzzle, conundrum, problem, poser (*infml*), brain-teaser.

enigmatic adj mysterious, puzzling, cryptic, obscure, strange, perplexing.
🔢 simple, straightforward.

enjoy v take pleasure in, delight in, appreciate, like, relish, revel in, rejoice in, savour.
🔢 dislike, hate.

enjoy oneself have a good time, have fun, make merry.

enjoyable adj pleasant, agreeable, delightful, pleasing, gratifying, entertaining, amusing, fun, delicious, good, satisfying.
🔢 disagreeable.

enjoyment n 1 PLEASURE, delight, amusement, gratification, entertainment, relish, joy, fun, happiness, diversion, indulgence, recreation, zest, satisfaction.
2 POSSESSION, use, advantage, benefit.
🔢 displeasure.

enlarge v increase, expand, augment, add to, grow, extend, magnify, inflate, swell, wax, stretch, multiply, develop, amplify, blow up, widen, broaden, lengthen, heighten, elaborate.
🔢 diminish, shrink.

enlighten v instruct, edify, educate, inform, illuminate, teach, counsel, apprise, advise.
🔢 confuse.

enlightened adj informed, aware,

knowledgeable, educated, civilized, cultivated, refined, sophisticated, conversant, wise, reasonable, liberal, open-minded, literate.
🔢 ignorant, confused.

enlist v engage, enrol, register, sign up, recruit, conscript, employ, volunteer, join (up), gather, muster, secure, obtain, procure, enter.

enmity n animosity, hostility, antagonism, discord, strife, feud, antipathy, acrimony, bitterness, hatred, aversion, ill-will, bad blood, rancour, malevolence, malice, venom.
🔢 friendship.

enormity n atrocity, outrage, iniquity, horror, evil, crime, abomination, monstrosity, wickedness, vileness, depravity, atrociousness, viciousness.

enormous adj huge, immense, vast, gigantic, massive, colossal, gross, gargantuan, monstrous, mammoth, jumbo (*infml*), tremendous, prodigious.
🔢 small, tiny.

enough adj sufficient, adequate, ample, plenty, abundant.
n sufficiency, adequacy, plenty, abundance.
adv sufficiently, adequately, reasonably, tolerably, passably, moderately, fairly, satisfactorily, amply.

enquire *see* **inquire**.

enquiry *see* **inquiry**.

enrage v incense, infuriate, anger, madden, provoke, incite, inflame, exasperate, irritate, rile.
🔢 calm, placate.

enrich v 1 ENDOW, enhance, improve, refine, develop, cultivate, augment. **2** ADORN, ornament, beautify, embellish, decorate, grace.
🔢 1 impoverish.

enrol v 1 REGISTER, enlist, sign on, sign up, join up, recruit, engage, admit. **2** RECORD, list, note, inscribe.

enrolment n registration,

recruitment, enlistment, admission, acceptance.

ensemble *n* **1** WHOLE, total, entirety, sum, aggregate, set, collection. **2** OUTFIT, costume, get-up (*infml*), rig-out (*infml*). **3** GROUP, band, company, troupe, chorus.

ensign *n* banner, standard, flag, colours, pennant, jack, badge.

enslave *v* subjugate, subject, dominate, bind, enchain, yoke.
🔳 free, emancipate.

ensue *v* follow, issue, proceed, succeed, result, arise, happen, turn out, befall, flow, derive, stem.
🔳 precede.

ensure *v* **1** CERTIFY, guarantee, warrant. **2** PROTECT, guard, safeguard, secure.

entail *v* involve, necessitate, occasion, require, demand, cause, give rise to, lead to, result in.

entangle *v* enmesh, ensnare, embroil, involve, implicate, snare, tangle, entrap, trap, catch, mix up, knot, ravel, muddle.
🔳 disentangle.

enter *v* **1** COME IN, go in, arrive, insert, introduce, board, penetrate. **2** RECORD, log, note, register, take down, inscribe. **3** JOIN, embark upon, enrol, enlist, set about, sign up, participate, commence, start, begin.
🔳 **1** depart. **2** delete.

enterprise *n* **1** UNDERTAKING, venture, project, plan, effort, operation, programme, endeavour. **2** INITIATIVE, resourcefulness, drive, adventurousness, boldness, get-up-and-go (*infml*), push, energy, enthusiasm, spirit. **3** BUSINESS, company, firm, establishment, concern.
🔳 **2** apathy.

enterprising *adj* venturesome, adventurous, bold, daring, go-ahead, imaginative, resourceful, self-reliant, enthusiastic, energetic, keen,

ambitious, aspiring, spirited, active.
🔳 unenterprising, lethargic.

entertain *v* **1** AMUSE, divert, please, delight, cheer. **2** RECEIVE, have guests, accommodate, put up, treat. **3** HARBOUR, countenance, contemplate, consider, imagine, conceive.
🔳 **1** bore. **3** reject.

entertainer

> *Entertainers include*: acrobat, actor, actress, busker, chat-show host, clown, comedian, comic, conjuror, dancer, disc jockey, DJ (*infml*), escapologist, game-show host, hypnotist, ice-skater, impressionist, jester, juggler, magician, mimic, mind-reader, minstrel, musician, presenter, singer, song-and-dance act, stand-up comic, striptease-artist, stripper (*infml*), trapeze-artist, tight-rope walker, ventriloquist; performer, artiste. *see also* **musician**; **singer**.

entertaining *adj* amusing, diverting, fun, delightful, interesting, pleasant, pleasing, humorous, witty.
🔳 boring.

entertainment *n* **1** AMUSEMENT, diversion, recreation, enjoyment, play, pastime, fun, sport, distraction, pleasure. **2** SHOW, spectacle, performance, extravaganza.

> *Forms of entertainment include*: cinema, cartoon show, video, radio, television, theatre, pantomime; dance, disco, discothèque, concert, recital, musical, opera, variety show, music hall, revue, karaoke, cabaret, night-club, casino; magic-show, puppet show, Punch-and-Judy show, circus, gymkhana, waxworks, laser-light show, zoo, rodeo, carnival, pageant, fête, festival, firework party, barbecue.

enthral *v* captivate, entrance, enchant, fascinate, charm, beguile,

thrill, intrigue, hypnotize, mesmerize, engross.
Ea bore.

enthusiasm *n* zeal, ardour, fervour, passion, keenness, eagerness, vehemence, warmth, frenzy, excitement, earnestness, relish, spirit, devotion, craze, mania, rage.
Ea apathy.

enthusiast *n* devotee, zealot, admirer, fan (*infml*), supporter, follower, buff (*infml*), freak (*infml*), fanatic, fiend (*infml*), lover.

enthusiastic *adj* keen, ardent, eager, fervent, vehement, passionate, warm, whole-hearted, zealous, vigorous, spirited, earnest, devoted, avid, excited, exuberant.
Ea unenthusiastic, apathetic.

entice *v* tempt, lure, attract, seduce, lead on, draw, coax, persuade, induce, sweet-talk (*infml*).

entire *adj* complete, whole, total, full, intact, perfect.
Ea incomplete, partial.

entirely *adv* completely, wholly, totally, fully, utterly, unreservedly, absolutely, in toto, thoroughly, altogether, perfectly, solely, exclusively, every inch.
Ea partially.

entitle *v* **1** AUTHORIZE, qualify, empower, enable, allow, permit, license, warrant. **2** NAME, call, term, title, style, christen, dub, label, designate.

entity *n* being, existence, thing, body, creature, individual, organism, substance.

entrance[1] *n* **1** ACCESS, admission, admittance, entry, entrée.
2 ARRIVAL, appearance, debut, initiation, introduction, start.
3 OPENING, way in, door, doorway, gate.
Ea 2 departure. **3** exit.

entrance[2] *v* charm, enchant, enrapture, captivate, bewitch, spellbind, fascinate, delight, ravish,

transport, hypnotize, mesmerize.
Ea repel.

entrant *n* **1** NOVICE, beginner, newcomer, initiate, convert, probationer. **2** COMPETITOR, candidate, contestant, contender, entry, participant, player.

entreat *v* beg, implore, plead with, beseech, crave, supplicate, pray, invoke, ask, petition, request, appeal to.

entreaty *n* appeal, plea, prayer, petition, supplication, suit, invocation, cry, solicitation, request.

entrench *v* establish, fix, embed, dig in, ensconce, install, lodge, root, ingrain, settle, seat, plant, anchor, set.
Ea dislodge.

entrust *v* trust, commit, confide, consign, authorize, charge, assign, turn over, commend, depute, invest, delegate, deliver.

entry *n* **1** ENTRANCE, appearance, admittance, admission, access, entrée, introduction. **2** OPENING, entrance, door, doorway, access, threshold, way in, passage, gate.
3 RECORD, item, minute, note, memorandum, statement, account.
4 ENTRANT, competitor, contestant, candidate, participant, player.
Ea 2 exit.

enumerate *v* list, name, itemize, cite, detail, specify, count, number, relate, recount, spell out, tell, mention, calculate, quote, recite, reckon.

enunciate *v* **1** ARTICULATE, pronounce, vocalize, voice, express, say, speak, utter, sound. **2** STATE, declare, proclaim, announce, propound.

envelop *v* wrap, enfold, enwrap, encase, cover, swathe, shroud, engulf, enclose, encircle, encompass, surround, cloak, veil, blanket, conceal, obscure, hide.

envelope *n* wrapper, wrapping,

cover, case, casing, sheath, covering, shell, skin, jacket, coating.

enviable *adj* desirable, privileged, favoured, blessed, fortunate, lucky, advantageous, sought-after, excellent, fine.
⊟ unenviable.

envious *adj* covetous, jealous, resentful, green (with envy), dissatisfied, grudging, jaundiced, green-eyed (*infml*).

environment *n* surroundings, conditions, circumstances, milieu, atmosphere, habitat, situation, element, medium, background, ambience, setting, context, territory, domain.

envisage *v* visualize, imagine, picture, envision, conceive of, preconceive, predict, anticipate, foresee, image, see, contemplate.

envoy *n* agent, representative, ambassador, diplomat, messenger, legate, emissary, minister, delegate, deputy, courier, intermediary.

envy *n* covetousness, jealousy, resentfulness, resentment, dissatisfaction, grudge, ill-will, malice, spite.
v covet, resent, begrudge, grudge, crave.

epidemic *adj* widespread, prevalent, rife, rampant, pandemic, sweeping, wide-ranging, prevailing.
n plague, outbreak, spread, rash, upsurge, wave.

epilogue *n* afterword, postscript, coda, conclusion.
⊟ foreword, prologue, preface.

episode *n* **1** INCIDENT, event, occurrence, happening, occasion, circumstance, experience, adventure, matter, business. **2** INSTALMENT, part, chapter, passage, section, scene.

epitome *n* **1** PERSONIFICATION, embodiment, representation, model, archetype, type, essence. **2** SUMMARY, abstract, abridgement, digest.

epoch *n* age, era, period, time, date.

equable *adj* **1** *an equable person*: even-tempered, placid, calm, serene, unexcitable, tranquil, unflappable, composed, level-headed, easy-going. **2** *an equable climate*: uniform, even, consistent, constant, regular, temperate, unvarying, steady, stable, smooth.
⊟ **1** excitable. **2** variable.

equal *adj* **1** IDENTICAL, the same, alike, like, equivalent, corresponding, commensurate, comparable. **2** EVEN, uniform, regular, unvarying, balanced, matched. **3** COMPETENT, able, adequate, fit, capable, suitable.
⊟ **1** different. **2** unequal. **3** unsuitable.
n peer, counterpart, equivalent, coequal, match, parallel, twin, fellow.
v match, parallel, correspond to, balance, square with, tally with, equalize, equate, rival, level, even.

equality *n* **1** UNIFORMITY, evenness, equivalence, correspondence, balance, parity, par, symmetry, proportion, identity, sameness, likeness. **2** IMPARTIALITY, fairness, justice, egalitarianism.
⊟ **2** inequality.

equalize *v* level, even up, match, equal, equate, draw level, balance, square, standardize, compensate, smooth.

equate *v* compare, liken, match, pair, correspond to, correspond with, balance, parallel, equalize, offset, square, agree, tally, juxtapose.

equation *n* equality, correspondence, equivalence, balancing, agreement, parallel, pairing, comparison, match, likeness, juxtaposition.

equilibrium *n* **1** BALANCE, poise, symmetry, evenness, stability. **2** EQUANIMITY, self-possession, composure, calmness, coolness, serenity.
⊟ **1** imbalance.

equip *v* provide, fit out, supply,

furnish, prepare, arm, fit up, kit out, stock, endow, rig, dress, array, deck out.

equipment n apparatus, gear, supplies, tackle, rig-out (*infml*), tools, material, furnishings, baggage, outfit, paraphernalia, stuff, things, accessories, furniture.

equivalence n identity, parity, correspondence, agreement, likeness, interchangeability, similarity, substitutability, correlation, parallel, conformity, sameness.

🖛 unlikeness, dissimilarity.

equivalent adj equal, same, similar, substitutable, corresponding, alike, comparable, interchangeable, even, tantamount, twin.

🖛 unlike, different.

equivocal adj ambiguous, uncertain, obscure, vague, evasive, oblique, misleading, dubious, confusing, indefinite.

🖛 unequivocal, clear.

equivocate v prevaricate, evade, dodge, fence, beat about the bush (*infml*), hedge, mislead.

era n age, epoch, period, date, day, days, time, aeon, stage, century.

eradicate v eliminate, annihilate, get rid of, remove, root out, suppress, destroy, exterminate, extinguish, weed out, stamp out, abolish, erase, obliterate.

erase v obliterate, rub out, expunge (*fml*), delete, blot out, cancel, efface, get rid of, remove, eradicate.

erect adj upright, straight, vertical, upstanding, standing, raised, rigid, stiff.

v build, construct, put up, establish, set up, elevate, assemble, found, form, institute, initiate, raise, rear, lift, mount, pitch, create.

erode v wear away, eat away, wear down, corrode, abrade, consume, grind down, disintegrate, deteriorate, spoil.

erosion n wear, corrosion, abrasion,

attrition, denudation, disintegration, deterioration, destruction, undermining.

erotic adj aphrodisiac, seductive, sexy, sensual, titillating, pornographic, lascivious, stimulating, suggestive, amorous, amatory, venereal, carnal, lustful, voluptuous.

err v **1** MAKE A MISTAKE, be wrong, miscalculate, mistake, misjudge, slip up, blunder, misunderstand. **2** DO WRONG, sin, misbehave, go astray, offend, transgress, deviate.

errand n commission, charge, mission, assignment, message, task, job, duty.

erratic adj changeable, variable, fitful, fluctuating, inconsistent, irregular, unstable, shifting, inconstant, unpredictable, unreliable, aberrant, abnormal, eccentric, desultory, meandering.

🖛 steady, consistent, stable.

erroneous adj incorrect, wrong, mistaken, false, untrue, inaccurate, inexact, invalid, illogical, unfounded, faulty, flawed.

🖛 correct, right.

error n mistake, inaccuracy, slip, slip-up, blunder, howler (*infml*), gaffe, faux pas, solecism, lapse, miscalculation, misunderstanding, misconception, misapprehension, misprint, oversight, omission, fallacy, flaw, fault, wrong.

erudite adj learned, scholarly, well-educated, knowledgeable, lettered, educated, well-read, literate, academic, cultured, wise, highbrow, profound.

🖛 illiterate, ignorant.

erupt v break out, explode, belch, discharge, burst, gush, spew, spout, eject, expel, emit, flare up, vomit, break.

eruption n **1** OUTBURST, discharge, ejection, emission, explosion, flare-up. **2** RASH, outbreak, inflammation.

escalate v increase, intensify, grow,

accelerate, rise, step up, heighten, raise, spiral, magnify, enlarge, expand, extend, mount, ascend, climb, amplify.

ⓕ decrease, diminish.

escapade n adventure, exploit, fling, prank, caper, romp, spree, lark (*infml*), antic, stunt, trick.

escape v 1 GET AWAY, break free, run away, bolt, abscond, flee, fly, decamp, break loose, break out, do a bunk (*infml*), flit, slip away, shake off, slip. 2 AVOID, evade, elude, dodge, skip, shun. 3 LEAK, seep, flow, drain, gush, issue, discharge, ooze, trickle, pour forth, pass.

n 1 GETAWAY, flight, bolt, flit, break-out, decampment, jail-break. 2 AVOIDANCE, evasion. 3 LEAK, seepage, leakage, outflow, gush, drain, discharge, emission, spurt, outpour, emanation. 4 ESCAPISM, diversion, distraction, recreation, relaxation, pastime, safety-valve.

escapist n dreamer, daydreamer, fantasizer, wishful thinker, non-realist, ostrich (*infml*).

ⓕ realist.

escort n 1 COMPANION, chaperon(e), partner, attendant, aide, squire, guide, bodyguard, protector. 2 ENTOURAGE, company, retinue, suite, train, guard, convoy, cortège.

v accompany, partner, chaperon(e), guide, lead, usher, conduct, guard, protect.

esoteric adj recondite, obscure, abstruse, cryptic, inscrutable, mysterious, mystic, mystical, occult, hidden, secret, confidential, private, inside.

ⓕ well-known, familiar.

especially adv 1 CHIEFLY, mainly, principally, primarily, pre-eminently, above all. 2 PARTICULARLY, specially, markedly, notably, exceptionally, outstandingly, expressly, supremely, uniquely, unusually, strikingly, very.

essay n composition, dissertation, paper, article, assignment, thesis, piece, commentary, critique, discourse, treatise, review, leader, tract.

essence n 1 NATURE, being, quintessence, substance, soul, spirit, core, centre, heart, meaning, quality, significance, life, entity, crux, kernel, marrow, pith, character, characteristics, attributes, principle. 2 CONCENTRATE, extract, distillation, spirits.

essential adj 1 FUNDAMENTAL, basic, intrinsic, inherent, principal, main, key, characteristic, definitive, typical, constituent. 2 CRUCIAL, indispensable, necessary, vital, requisite, required, needed, important.

ⓕ 1 incidental. 2 dispensable, inessential.

n necessity, prerequisite, must, requisite, sine qua non (*fml*), requirement, basic, fundamental, necessary, principle.

ⓕ inessential.

establish v 1 SET UP, found, start, form, institute, create, organize, inaugurate, introduce, install, plant, settle, secure, lodge, base. 2 PROVE, substantiate, demonstrate, authenticate, ratify, verify, validate, certify, confirm, affirm.

ⓕ 1 uproot. 2 refute.

establishment n 1 FORMATION, setting up, founding, creation, foundation, installation, institution, inauguration. 2 BUSINESS, company, firm, institute, organization, concern, institution, enterprise. 3 RULING CLASS, the system, the authorities, the powers that be.

estate n 1 POSSESSIONS, effects, assets, belongings, holdings, property, goods, lands. 2 AREA, development, land, manor. 3 (*fml*) STATUS, standing, situation, position, class, place, condition, state, rank.

estimate *v* assess, reckon, evaluate, calculate, gauge, guess, value, conjecture, consider, judge, think, number, count, compute, believe. *n* reckoning, valuation, judgement, guess, approximation, assessment, estimation, evaluation, computation, opinion.

estimation *n* **1** JUDGEMENT, opinion, belief, consideration, estimate, view, evaluation, assessment, reckoning, conception, calculation, computation. **2** RESPECT, regard, appreciation, esteem, credit.

estranged *adj* divided, separate, alienated, disaffected, antagonized. ⊞ reconciled, united.

estuary *n* inlet, mouth, firth, fjord, creek, arm, sea-loch.

eternal *adj* **1** *eternal bliss*: unending, endless, ceaseless, everlasting, never-ending, infinite, limitless, immortal, undying, imperishable. **2** *eternal truths*: unchanging, timeless, enduring, lasting, perennial, abiding. **3** (*infml*) *eternal quarrelling*: constant, continuous, perpetual, incessant, interminable. ⊞ **1** ephemeral, temporary. **2** changeable.

eternity *n* **1** EVERLASTINGNESS, endlessness, everlasting, imperishability, infinity, timelessness, perpetuity, immutability, ages, age, aeon. **2** AFTER-LIFE, hereafter, immortality, heaven, paradise, next world, world to come.

ethical *adj* moral, principled, just, right, proper, virtuous, honourable, fair, upright, righteous, seemly, honest, good, correct, commendable, fitting, noble, meet (*fml*). ⊞ unethical.

ethics *n* moral values, morality, principles, standards, code, moral philosophy, rules, beliefs, propriety, conscience, equity.

ethnic *adj* racial, native, indigenous, traditional, tribal, folk, cultural, national, aboriginal.

ethos *n* attitude, beliefs, standards, manners, ethics, morality, code, principles, spirit, tenor, rationale, character, disposition.

etiquette *n* code, formalities, standards, correctness, conventions, customs, protocol (*fml*), rules, manners, politeness, courtesy, civility, decorum, ceremony, decency.

euphemism *n* evasion, polite term, substitution, genteelism, politeness, understatement.

euphoria *n* elation, ecstasy, bliss, rapture, high spirits, well-being, high (*infml*), exhilaration, exultation, joy, intoxication, jubilation, transport, glee, exaltation, enthusiasm, cheerfulness. ⊞ depression, despondency.

evacuate *v* **1** LEAVE, depart, withdraw, quit, remove, retire from, clear (out) (*infml*), abandon, desert, forsake, vacate, decamp, relinquish. **2** EMPTY, eject, void, expel, discharge, eliminate, defecate, purge.

evacuation *n* **1** DEPARTURE, withdrawal, retreat, exodus, removal, quitting, desertion, abandonment, clearance, relinquishment, retirement, vacation. **2** EMPTYING, expulsion, ejection, discharge, elimination, defecation, urination.

evade *v* **1** *evade one's duties*: elude, avoid, escape, dodge, shirk, steer clear of, shun, sidestep, duck (*infml*), balk, skive (*infml*), fend off, chicken out (*infml*), cop out (*infml*). **2** *evade a question*: prevaricate, equivocate, fence, fudge, parry, quibble, hedge. ⊞ **1** confront, face.

evaluate *v* value, assess, appraise, estimate, reckon, calculate, gauge, judge, rate, size up, weigh, compute, rank.

evaluation *n* valuation, appraisal, assessment, estimation, estimate, judgement, reckoning, calculation, opinion, computation.

evaporate v **1** DISAPPEAR, dematerialize, vanish, melt (away), dissolve, disperse, dispel, dissipate, fade. **2** VAPORIZE, dry, dehydrate, exhale.

evasion n avoidance, escape, dodge, equivocation, excuse, prevarication, put-off, trickery, subterfuge, shirking.
Ⓔ frankness, directness.

evasive adj equivocating, indirect, prevaricating, devious, shifty (infml), unforthcoming, slippery (infml), misleading, deceitful, deceptive, cagey (infml), oblique, secretive, tricky, cunning.
Ⓔ direct, frank.

eve n day before, verge, brink, edge, threshold.

even adj **1** LEVEL, flat, smooth, horizontal, flush, parallel, plane. **2** STEADY, unvarying, constant, regular, uniform. **3** EQUAL, balanced, matching, same, similar, like, symmetrical, fifty-fifty, level, side by side, neck and neck (infml). **4** EVEN-TEMPERED, calm, placid, serene, tranquil, composed, unruffled. **5** EVEN-HANDED, balanced, equitable, fair, impartial.
Ⓔ 1 uneven. 3 unequal.
v smooth, flatten, level, match, regularize, balance, equalize, align, square, stabilize, steady, straighten.

evening n nightfall, dusk, eve, eventide, twilight, sunset, sundown.

event n **1** HAPPENING, occurrence, incident, occasion, affair, circumstance, episode, eventuality, experience, matter, case, adventure, business, fact, possibility, milestone. **2** CONSEQUENCE, result, outcome, conclusion, end, effect, issue, termination. **3** GAME, match, competition, contest, tournament, engagement.

even-tempered adj calm, level-headed, placid, stable, tranquil, serene, composed, cool, steady, peaceful, peaceable.
Ⓔ excitable, erratic.

eventful adj busy, exciting, lively, active, full, interesting, remarkable, significant, memorable, momentous, notable, noteworthy, unforgettable.
Ⓔ dull, ordinary.

eventual adj final, ultimate, resulting, concluding, ensuing, future, later, subsequent, prospective, projected, planned, impending.

eventually adv finally, ultimately, at last, in the end, at length, subsequently, after all, sooner or later.

ever adv **1** ALWAYS, evermore, for ever, perpetually, constantly, at all times, continually, endlessly. **2** AT ANY TIME, in any case, in any circumstances, at all, on any account.
Ⓔ 1 never.

everlasting adj eternal, undying, never-ending, endless, immortal, infinite, imperishable, constant, permanent, perpetual, indestructible, timeless.
Ⓔ temporary, transient.

everyday adj ordinary, common, commonplace, day-to-day, familiar, run-of-the-mill, regular, plain, routine, usual, workaday, common-or-garden (infml), normal, customary, stock, accustomed, conventional, daily, habitual, monotonous, frequent, simple, informal.
Ⓔ unusual, exceptional, special.

everyone n everybody, one and all, each one, all and sundry, the whole world.

everywhere adv all around, all over, throughout, far and near, far and wide, high and low, ubiquitous, left, right and centre (infml).

evict v expel, eject, dispossess, put out, turn out, turf out (infml), kick out (infml), force out, remove, cast out, chuck out (*infml*), oust, dislodge, expropriate.

evidence *n* **1** PROOF, verification, confirmation, affirmation, grounds, substantiation, documentation, data. **2** TESTIMONY, declaration. **3** INDICATION, manifestation, suggestion, sign, mark, hint, demonstration, token.

evident *adj* clear, obvious, manifest, apparent, plain, patent, visible, conspicuous, noticeable, clear-cut, unmistakable, perceptible, distinct, discernible, tangible, incontestable, indisputable, incontrovertible.

evidently *adv* clearly, apparently, plainly, patently, manifestly, obviously, seemingly, undoubtedly, doubtless(ly), indisputably.

evil *adj* **1** WICKED, wrong, sinful, bad, immoral, vicious, vile, malevolent, iniquitous, cruel, base, corrupt, heinous, malicious, malignant, devilish, depraved, mischievous. **2** HARMFUL, pernicious, destructive, deadly, detrimental, hurtful, poisonous. **3** DISASTROUS, ruinous, calamitous, catastrophic, adverse, dire, inauspicious. **4** OFFENSIVE, noxious, foul.
n **1** WICKEDNESS, wrong-doing, wrong, immorality, badness, sin, sinfulness, vice, viciousness, iniquity, depravity, baseness, corruption, malignity, mischief, heinousness. **2** ADVERSITY, affliction, calamity, disaster, misfortune, suffering, sorrow, ruin, catastrophe, blow, curse, distress, hurt, harm, ill, injury, misery, woe.

evoke *v* summon (up), call, elicit, invoke, arouse, stir, raise, stimulate, call forth, call up, conjure up, awaken, provoke, excite, recall.
ᴇᴁ suppress.

evolution *n* development, growth, progression, progress, expansion, increase, ripening, derivation, descent.

evolve *v* develop, grow, increase, mature, progress, unravel, expand, enlarge, emerge, descend, derive, result, elaborate.

exact *adj* **1** PRECISE, accurate, correct, faithful, literal, flawless, faultless, right, true, veracious, definite, explicit, detailed, specific, strict, unerring, close, factual, identical, express, word-perfect, blow-by-blow (*infml*). **2** CAREFUL, scrupulous, particular, rigorous, methodical, meticulous, orderly, painstaking.
ᴇᴁ inexact, imprecise.
v extort, extract, claim, insist on, wrest, wring, compel, demand, command, force, impose, require, squeeze, milk (*infml*).

exacting *adj* demanding, difficult, hard, laborious, arduous, rigorous, taxing, tough, harsh, painstaking, severe, strict, unsparing.
ᴇᴁ easy.

exactly *adv* **1** PRECISELY, accurately, literally, faithfully, correctly, specifically, rigorously, scrupulously, veraciously, verbatim, carefully, faultlessly, unerringly, strictly, to the letter, particularly, methodically, explicitly, expressly, dead (*infml*). **2** ABSOLUTELY, definitely, precisely, indeed, certainly, truly, quite, just, unequivocally.
ᴇᴁ 1 inaccurately, roughly.

exaggerate *v* overstate, overdo, magnify, overemphasize, emphasize, embellish, embroider, enlarge, amplify, oversell, pile it on (*infml*).
ᴇᴁ understate.

examination *n* **1** INSPECTION, enquiry, scrutiny, study, survey, search, analysis, exploration, investigation, probe, appraisal, observation, research, review, scan, once-over (*infml*), perusal, check, check-up, audit, critique. **2** TEST, exam, quiz, questioning, cross-

examine

examination, cross-questioning, trial, inquisition, interrogation, viva.

examine v **1** INSPECT, investigate, scrutinize, study, survey, analyse, explore, enquire, consider, probe, review, scan, check (out), ponder, pore over, sift, vet, weigh up, appraise, assay, audit, peruse, case (sl). **2** TEST, quiz, question, cross-examine, cross-question, interrogate, grill (infml), catechize (fml).

example n instance, case, case in point, illustration, exemplification, sample, specimen, model, pattern, ideal, archetype, prototype, standard, type, lesson, citation.

exasperate v infuriate, annoy, anger, incense, irritate, madden, provoke, get on someone's nerves, enrage, irk, rile, rankle, rouse, get to (infml), goad, vex.
≠ appease, pacify.

excavate v dig (out), dig up, hollow, burrow, tunnel, delve, unearth, mine, quarry, disinter, gouge, scoop, exhume, uncover.

excavation n hole, hollow, pit, quarry, mine, dugout, dig, diggings, burrow, cavity, crater, trench, trough, shaft, ditch, cutting.

exceed v surpass, outdo, outstrip, beat, better, pass, overtake, top, outshine, eclipse, outreach, outrun, transcend, cap, overdo, overstep.

excel v **1** SURPASS, outdo, beat, outclass, outperform, outrank, eclipse, better. **2** BE EXCELLENT, succeed, shine, stand out, predominate.

excellence n superiority, pre-eminence, distinction, merit, supremacy, quality, worth, fineness, eminence, goodness, greatness, virtue, perfection, purity.

excellent adj superior, first-class, first-rate, prime, superlative, unequalled, outstanding, surpassing, remarkable, distinguished, great, good, exemplary, select, superb,

admirable, commendable, top-notch (infml), splendid, noteworthy, notable, fine, wonderful, worthy.
≠ inferior, second-rate.

except prep excepting, but, apart from, other than, save, omitting, not counting, leaving out, excluding, except for, besides, bar, minus, less. v leave out, omit, bar, exclude, reject, rule out.

exception n oddity, anomaly, deviation, abnormality, irregularity, peculiarity, inconsistency, rarity, special case, quirk.

exceptional adj **1** ABNORMAL, unusual, anomalous, strange, odd, irregular, extraordinary, peculiar, special, rare, uncommon. **2** OUTSTANDING, remarkable, phenomenal, prodigious, notable, noteworthy, superior, unequalled, marvellous.
≠ **1** normal. **2** mediocre.

excerpt n extract, passage, portion, section, selection, quote, quotation, part, citation, scrap, fragment.

excess n **1** SURFEIT, overabundance, glut, plethora, superfluity, superabundance, surplus, overflow, overkill, remainder, left-over. **2** OVERINDULGENCE, dissipation, immoderateness, intemperance, extravagance, unrestraint, debauchery.
≠ **1** deficiency. **2** restraint.
adj extra, surplus, spare, redundant, remaining, residual, left-over, additional, superfluous, supernumerary.
≠ inadequate.

excessive adj immoderate, inordinate, extreme, undue, uncalled-for, disproportionate, unnecessary, unneeded, superfluous, unreasonable, exorbitant, extravagant, steep (infml).
≠ insufficient.

exchange v barter, change, trade, swap, switch, replace, interchange,

convert, commute, substitute, reciprocate, bargain, bandy.
n **1** CONVERSATION, discussion, chat. **2** TRADE, commerce, dealing, market, traffic, barter, bargain. **3** INTERCHANGE, swap, switch, replacement, substitution, reciprocity.

excitable *adj* temperamental, volatile, passionate, emotional, highly-strung, fiery, hot-headed, hasty, nervous, hot-tempered, irascible, quick-tempered, sensitive, susceptible.
ε₃ calm, stable.

excite *v* **1** MOVE, agitate, disturb, upset, touch, stir up, thrill, elate, turn on (*infml*), impress. **2** AROUSE, rouse, animate, awaken, fire, inflame, kindle, motivate, stimulate, engender, inspire, instigate, incite, induce, ignite, galvanize, generate, provoke, sway, quicken, evoke.
ε₃ **1** calm.

excited *adj* aroused, roused, stimulated, stirred, thrilled, elated, enthusiastic, eager, moved, high (*infml*), worked up, wrought-up, overwrought, restless, frantic, frenzied, wild.
ε₃ calm, apathetic.

excitement *n* **1** UNREST, ado, action, activity, commotion, fuss, tumult, flurry, furore, adventure. **2** DISCOMPOSURE, agitation, passion, thrill, animation, elation, enthusiasm, restlessness, kicks (*infml*), ferment, fever, eagerness, stimulation.
ε₃ **1** calm. **2** apathy.

exciting *adj* stimulating, stirring, intoxicating, exhilarating, thrilling, rousing, moving, enthralling, electrifying, nail-biting (*infml*), cliff-hanging (*infml*), striking, sensational, provocative, inspiring, interesting.
ε₃ dull, unexciting.

exclaim *v* cry (out), declare, blurt (out), call, yell, shout, proclaim, utter.

exclamation *n* cry, call, yell, shout,
expletive, interjection, ejaculation, outcry, utterance.

exclude *v* **1** BAN, bar, prohibit, disallow, veto, proscribe, forbid, blacklist. **2** OMIT, leave out, keep out, refuse, reject, ignore, shut out, rule out, ostracize, eliminate. **3** EXPEL, eject, evict, excommunicate.
ε₃ **1** admit. **2** include.

exclusive *adj* **1** SOLE, single, unique, only, undivided, unshared, whole, total, peculiar.
2 RESTRICTED, limited, closed, private, narrow, restrictive, choice, select, discriminative, cliquey, chic, classy (*infml*), elegant, fashionable, posh (*infml*), snobbish.

excruciating *adj* agonizing, painful, severe, tormenting, unbearable, insufferable, acute, intolerable, intense, sharp, piercing, extreme, atrocious, racking, harrowing, savage, burning, bitter.

excursion *n* outing, trip, jaunt, expedition, day trip, journey, tour, airing, breather, junket (*infml*), ride, drive, walk, ramble.

excuse *v* **1** FORGIVE, pardon, overlook, absolve, acquit, exonerate, tolerate, ignore, indulge. **2** RELEASE, free, discharge, liberate, let off, relieve, spare, exempt. **3** CONDONE, explain, mitigate, justify, vindicate, defend, apologize for.
ε₃ **1** criticize. **2** punish.
n justification, explanation, grounds, defence, plea, alibi, reason, apology, pretext, pretence, exoneration, evasion, cop-out (*infml*), shift, substitute.

execute *v* **1** PUT TO DEATH, kill, liquidate, hang, electrocute, shoot, guillotine, decapitate, behead. **2** CARRY OUT, perform, do, accomplish, achieve, fulfil, complete, discharge, effect, deliver, enforce, finish, implement, administer, consummate, realize, dispatch, expedite, validate, serve, render, sign.

execution n **1** DEATH PENALTY, capital punishment, killing, hanging, electrocution, firing squad, shooting, guillotining, decapitation, beheading. **2** ACCOMPLISHMENT, operation, performance, completion, achievement, administration, effect, enactment, implementation, realization, discharge, dispatch, consummation, enforcement. **3** STYLE, technique, rendition, delivery, performance, manner, mode.

executive n **1** ADMINISTRATION, management, government, leadership, hierarchy. **2** ADMINISTRATOR, manager, organizer, leader, controller, director, governor, official. adj administrative, managerial, controlling, supervisory, regulating, decision-making, governing, organizing, directing, directorial, organizational, leading, guiding.

exemplary adj **1** MODEL, ideal, perfect, admirable, excellent, faultless, flawless, correct, good, commendable, praiseworthy, worthy, laudable, estimable, honourable. **2** CAUTIONARY, warning.
🗗 **1** imperfect, unworthy.

exemplify v illustrate, demonstrate, show, instance, represent, typify, manifest, embody, epitomize, exhibit, depict, display.

exempt v excuse, release, relieve, let off, free, absolve, discharge, dismiss, liberate, spare. adj excused, not liable, immune, released, spared, absolved, discharged, excluded, free, liberated, clear.
🗗 liable.

exercise v **1** USE, utilize, employ, apply, exert, practise, wield, try, discharge. **2** TRAIN, drill, practise, work out (infml), keep fit. **3** WORRY, disturb, trouble, upset, burden,

distress, vex, annoy, agitate, afflict.
n **1** TRAINING, drill, practice, effort, exertion, task, lesson, work, discipline, activity, physical jerks (infml), work-out (infml), aerobics, labour. **2** USE, utilization, employment, application, implementation, practice, operation, discharge, assignment, fulfilment, accomplishment.

exert v use, utilize, employ, apply, exercise, bring to bear, wield, expend.
exert oneself strive, struggle, strain, make every effort, take pains, toil, labour, work, sweat (infml), endeavour, apply oneself.

exertion n **1** EFFORT, industry, labour, toil, work, struggle, diligence, assiduousness, perseverance, pains, endeavour, attempt, strain, travail (fml), trial. **2** USE, utilization, employment, application, exercise, operation, action.
🗗 **1** idleness, rest.

exhaust v **1** CONSUME, empty, deplete, drain, sap, spend, waste, squander, dissipate, impoverish, use up, finish, dry, bankrupt. **2** TIRE (OUT), weary, fatigue, tax, strain, weaken, overwork, wear out.
🗗 **1** renew. **2** refresh.
n emission, exhalation, discharge, fumes.

exhausted adj **1** EMPTY, finished, depleted, spent, used up, drained, dry, worn out, void. **2** TIRED (OUT), dead tired, dead-beat (infml), all in (infml), done (in) (infml), fatigued, weak, washed-out, whacked (infml), knackered (infml), jaded.
🗗 **1** fresh. **2** vigorous.

exhausting adj tiring, strenuous, taxing, gruelling, arduous, hard, laborious, backbreaking, draining, severe, testing, punishing, formidable, debilitating.
🗗 refreshing.

exhaustion n fatigue, tiredness, weariness, debility, feebleness, jetlag.

◪ freshness, liveliness.

exhaustive *adj* comprehensive, all-embracing, all-inclusive, far-reaching, complete, extensive, encyclopedic, full-scale, thorough, full, in-depth, intensive, detailed, definitive, all-out, sweeping.

◪ incomplete, restricted.

exhibit *v* display, show, present, demonstrate, manifest, expose, parade, reveal, express, disclose, indicate, air, flaunt, offer.

◪ conceal.

n display, exhibition, show, illustration, model.

exhibition *n* display, show, demonstration, exhibit, presentation, manifestation, spectacle, exposition, expo (*infml*), showing, fair, performance, airing, representation, showcase.

exhilarate *v* thrill, excite, elate, animate, enliven, invigorate, vitalize, stimulate.

◪ bore.

exile *n* 1 BANISHMENT, deportation, expatriation, expulsion, ostracism, transportation. 2 EXPATRIATE, refugee, émigré, deportee, outcast.

v banish, expel, deport, expatriate, drive out, ostracize, oust.

exist *v* 1 BE, live, abide, continue, endure, have one's being, breathe, prevail. 2 SUBSIST, survive. 3 BE PRESENT, occur, happen, be available, remain.

existence *n* 1 BEING, life, reality, actuality, continuance, continuation, endurance, survival, breath, subsistence. 2 CREATION, the world. 3 (*fml*) ENTITY, creature, thing.

◪ 1 death, non-existence.

exit *n* 1 DEPARTURE, going, retreat, withdrawal, leave-taking, retirement, farewell, exodus. 2 DOOR, way out, doorway, gate, vent.

◪ 1 entrance, arrival. 2 entrance.

v depart, leave, go, retire, withdraw,

take one's leave, retreat, issue.

◪ arrive, enter.

exonerate *v* 1 ABSOLVE, acquit, clear, vindicate, exculpate (*fml*), justify, pardon, discharge. 2 EXEMPT, excuse, spare, let off, release, relieve.

◪ 1 incriminate.

exorbitant *adj* excessive, unreasonable, unwarranted, undue, inordinate, immoderate, extravagant, extortionate, enormous, preposterous.

◪ reasonable, moderate.

exotic *adj* 1 FOREIGN, alien, imported, introduced. 2 UNUSUAL, striking, different, unfamiliar, extraordinary, bizarre, curious, strange, fascinating, colourful, peculiar, outlandish.

◪ 1 native. 2 ordinary.

expand *v* 1 STRETCH, swell, widen, lengthen, thicken, magnify, multiply, inflate, broaden, blow up, open out, fill out, fatten. 2 INCREASE, grow, extend, enlarge, develop, amplify, spread, branch out, diversify, elaborate.

◪ 1 contract.

expanse *n* extent, space, area, breadth, range, stretch, sweep, field, plain, tract.

expansive *adj* 1 FRIENDLY, genial, outgoing, open, affable, sociable, talkative, warm, communicative, effusive. 2 EXTENSIVE, broad, comprehensive, wide-ranging, all-embracing, thorough.

◪ 1 reserved, cold. 2 restricted, narrow.

expect *v* 1 *expect the money soon*: anticipate, await, look forward to, hope for, look for, bank on, bargain for, envisage, predict, forecast, contemplate, project, foresee. 2 *expect you to comply*: require, want, wish, insist on, demand, rely on, count on. 3 *expect you're right*: suppose, surmise, assume, believe, think, presume, imagine, reckon, guess (*infml*), trust.

expectant *adj* **1** AWAITING, anticipating, hopeful, in suspense, ready, apprehensive, anxious, watchful, eager, curious. **2** PREGNANT, expecting (*infml*), with child (*fml*).

expedition *n* **1** JOURNEY, excursion, trip, voyage, tour, exploration, trek, safari, hike, sail, ramble, raid, quest, pilgrimage, mission, crusade. **2** (*fml*) PROMPTNESS, speed, alacrity, haste.

expel *v* **1** DRIVE OUT, eject, evict, banish, throw out, ban, bar, oust, exile, expatriate. **2** DISCHARGE, evacuate, void, cast out.
≡ 1 welcome.

expend *v* **1** SPEND, pay, disburse (*fml*), fork out (*infml*). **2** CONSUME, use (up), dissipate, exhaust, employ.
≡ 1 save. 2 conserve.

expenditure *n* spending, expense, outlay, outgoings, disbursement (*fml*), payment, output.
≡ income.

expense *n* spending, expenditure, disbursement (*fml*), outlay, payment, loss, cost, charge.

expensive *adj* dear, high-priced, costly, exorbitant, extortionate, steep (*infml*), extravagant, lavish.
≡ cheap, inexpensive.

experience *n* **1** KNOWLEDGE, familiarity, know-how, involvement, participation, practice, understanding. **2** INCIDENT, event, episode, happening, encounter, occurrence, adventure.
≡ 1 inexperience.
v undergo, go through, live through, suffer, feel, endure, encounter, face, meet, know, try, perceive, sustain.

experienced *adj* **1** PRACTISED, knowledgeable, familiar, capable, competent, well-versed, expert, accomplished, qualified, skilled, tried, trained, professional. **2** MATURE, seasoned, wise, veteran.

≡ 1 inexperienced, unskilled.

experiment *n* trial, test, investigation, experimentation, research, examination, trial run, venture, trial and error, attempt, procedure, proof.
v try, test, investigate, examine, research, sample, verify.

experimental *adj* trial, test, exploratory, empirical (*fml*), tentative, provisional, speculative, pilot, preliminary, trial-and-error.

expert *n* specialist, connoisseur, authority, professional, pro (*infml*), dab hand (*infml*), maestro, virtuoso. *adj* proficient, adept, skilled, skilful, knowledgeable, experienced, able, practised, professional, masterly, specialist, qualified, virtuoso.
≡ amateurish, novice.

expertise *n* expertness, proficiency, skill, skilfulness, know-how, knack (*infml*), knowledge, mastery, dexterity, virtuosity.
≡ inexperience.

expire *v* end, cease, finish, stop, terminate, close, conclude, discontinue, run out, lapse, die, depart, decease, perish.
≡ begin.

explain *v* **1** INTERPRET, clarify, describe, define, make clear, elucidate, simplify, resolve, solve, spell out, translate, unfold, unravel, untangle, illustrate, demonstrate, disclose, expound, teach. **2** JUSTIFY, excuse, account for, rationalize.
≡ 1 obscure, confound.

explanation *n* **1** INTERPRETATION, clarification, definition, elucidation, illustration, demonstration, account, description, exegesis (*fml*). **2** JUSTIFICATION, excuse, warrant, rationalization. **3** ANSWER, meaning, motive, reason, key, sense, significance.

explanatory *adj* descriptive, interpretive, explicative, demonstrative, expository (*fml*), justifying.

explicit adj **1** CLEAR, distinct, exact, categorical, absolute, certain, positive, precise, specific, unambiguous, express, definite, declared, detailed, stated. **2** OPEN, direct, frank, outspoken, straightforward, unreserved, plain.
🖃 **1** implicit, unspoken, vague.

explode v **1** BLOW UP, burst, go off, set off, detonate, discharge, blast, erupt. **2** DISCREDIT, disprove, give the lie to, debunk, invalidate, refute, rebut, repudiate.
🖃 **2** prove, confirm.

exploit n deed, feat, adventure, achievement, accomplishment, attainment, stunt.
v **1** USE, utilize, capitalize on, profit by, turn to account, take advantage of, cash in on, make capital out of.
2 MISUSE, abuse, oppress, ill-treat, impose on, manipulate, rip off (infml), fleece (infml).

exploration n **1** INVESTIGATION, examination, enquiry, research, scrutiny, study, inspection, analysis, probe. **2** EXPEDITION, survey, reconnaissance, search, trip, tour, voyage, travel, safari.

explore v **1** INVESTIGATE, examine, inspect, research, scrutinize, probe, analyse. **2** TRAVEL, tour, search, reconnoitre, prospect, scout, survey.

explosion n detonation, blast, burst, outburst, discharge, eruption, bang, outbreak, clap, crack, fit, report.

explosive adj unstable, volatile, sensitive, tense, fraught, charged, touchy, overwrought, dangerous, hazardous, perilous, stormy.
🖃 stable, calm.

expose v **1** REVEAL, show, exhibit, display, disclose, uncover, bring to light, present, manifest, detect, divulge, unveil, unmask, denounce. **2** ENDANGER, jeopardize, imperil, risk, hazard.

🖃 **1** conceal. **2** cover up.

exposed adj bare, open, revealed, laid bare, unprotected, vulnerable, exhibited, on display, on show, on view, shown, susceptible.
🖃 covered, sheltered.

exposure n **1** REVELATION, uncovering, disclosure, exposé, showing, unmasking, unveiling, display, airing, exhibition, presentation, publicity, manifestation, discovery, divulgence. **2** FAMILIARITY, experience, knowledge, contact. **3** JEOPARDY, danger, hazard, risk, vulnerability.

express v **1** ARTICULATE, verbalize, utter, voice, say, speak, state, communicate, pronounce, tell, assert, declare, put across, formulate, intimate, testify, convey. **2** SHOW, manifest, exhibit, disclose, divulge, reveal, indicate, denote, depict, embody. **3** SYMBOLIZE, stand for, represent, signify, designate.
adj **1** SPECIFIC, explicit, exact, definite, clear, categorical, precise, distinct, clear-cut, certain, plain, manifest, particular, stated, unambiguous. **2** FAST, speedy, rapid, quick, high-speed, non-stop.
🖃 vague.

expression n **1** LOOK, air, aspect, countenance, appearance, mien (fml). **2** REPRESENTATION, manifestation, demonstration, indication, exhibition, embodiment, show, sign, symbol, style. **3** UTTERANCE, verbalization, communication, articulation, statement, assertion, announcement, declaration, pronouncement, speech. **4** TONE, intonation, delivery, diction, enunciation, modulation, wording. **5** PHRASE, term, turn of phrase, saying, set phrase, idiom.

expressionless adj dull, blank, dead-pan, impassive, straight-faced, poker-faced (infml), inscrutable, empty, vacuous, glassy.

☒ expressive.

expressive *adj* eloquent, meaningful, forceful, telling, revealing, informative, indicative, communicative, demonstrative, emphatic, moving, poignant, lively, striking, suggestive, significant, thoughtful, vivid, sympathetic.

expulsion *n* ejection, eviction, exile, banishment, removal, discharge, exclusion, dismissal.

exquisite *adj* **1** BEAUTIFUL, attractive, dainty, delicate, charming, elegant, delightful, lovely, pleasing. **2** PERFECT, flawless, fine, excellent, choice, precious, rare, outstanding. **3** REFINED, discriminating, meticulous, sensitive, impeccable. **4** INTENSE, keen, sharp, poignant.
☒ **1** ugly. **2** flawed. **3** unrefined.

extend *v* **1** SPREAD, stretch, reach, continue. **2** ENLARGE, increase, expand, develop, amplify, lengthen, widen, elongate, draw out, protract, prolong, spin out, unwind. **3** OFFER, give, grant, hold out, impart, present, bestow, confer.
☒ **2** contract, shorten. **3** withhold.

extension *n* **1** ENLARGEMENT, increase, stretching, broadening, widening, lengthening, expansion, elongation, development, enhancement, protraction, continuation. **2** ADDITION, supplement, appendix, annexe, addendum (*fml*). **3** DELAY, postponement.

extensive *adj* **1** BROAD, comprehensive, far-reaching, large-scale, thorough, widespread, universal, extended, all-inclusive, general, pervasive, prevalent. **2** LARGE, huge, roomy, spacious, vast, voluminous, long, lengthy, wide.
☒ **1** restricted, narrow. **2** small.

extent *n* **1** DIMENSION(S), amount, magnitude, expanse, size, area, bulk, degree, breadth, quantity, spread, stretch, volume, width, measure, duration, term, time. **2** LIMIT, bounds, lengths, range, reach, scope, compass, sphere, play, sweep.

exterior *n* outside, surface, covering, coating, face, façade, shell, skin, finish, externals, appearance.
☒ inside, interior.
adj outer, outside, outermost, surface, external, superficial, surrounding, outward, peripheral, extrinsic.
☒ inside, interior.

exterminate *v* annihilate, eradicate, destroy, eliminate, massacre, abolish, wipe out.

external *adj* outer, surface, outside, exterior, superficial, outward, outermost, apparent, visible, extraneous, extrinsic, extramural, independent.
☒ internal.

extinct *adj* **1** DEFUNCT, dead, gone, obsolete, ended, exterminated, terminated, vanished, lost, abolished. **2** EXTINGUISHED, quenched, inactive, out.
☒ **1** living.

extinction *n* annihilation, extermination, death, eradication, obliteration, destruction, abolition, excision.

extinguish *v* **1** PUT OUT, blow out, snuff out, stifle, smother, douse, quench. **2** ANNIHILATE, exterminate, eliminate, destroy, kill, eradicate, erase, expunge, abolish, remove, end, suppress.

extort *v* extract, wring, exact, coerce, force, milk (*infml*), blackmail, squeeze, bleed (*infml*), bully.

extortionate *adj* exorbitant, excessive, grasping, exacting, immoderate, rapacious, unreasonable, oppressive, blood-sucking (*infml*), rigorous, severe, hard, harsh, inordinate.

extra *adj* **1** ADDITIONAL, added, auxiliary, supplementary, new, more,

further, ancillary, fresh, other. **2**
EXCESS, spare, superfluous,
supernumerary, surplus, unused,
unneeded, leftover, reserve,
redundant.

🖻 **1** integral. **2** essential.

n addition, supplement, extension,
accessory, appendage, bonus,
complement, adjunct, addendum
(*fml*), attachment.

adv especially, exceptionally,
extraordinarily, particularly, unusually,
remarkably, extremely.

extract *v* **1** REMOVE, take out, draw
out, exact, uproot, withdraw.
2 DERIVE, draw, distil, obtain, get,
gather, glean, wrest, wring, elicit.
3 CHOOSE, select, cull, abstract, cite,
quote.

🖻 **1** insert.

n **1** DISTILLATION, essence, juice. **2**
EXCERPT, passage, selection, clip,
cutting, quotation, abstract, citation.

extraordinary *adj* remarkable,
unusual, exceptional, notable,
noteworthy, outstanding, unique,
special, strange, peculiar, rare,
surprising, amazing, wonderful,
unprecedented, marvellous, fantastic,
significant, particular.

🖻 commonplace, ordinary.

extravagance *n* **1** OVERSPENDING,
profligacy, squandering, waste.
2 EXCESS, immoderation,
recklessness, profusion,
outrageousness, folly.

🖻 **1** thrift. **2** moderation.

extravagant *adj* **1** PROFLIGATE,
prodigal, spendthrift, thriftless,
wasteful, reckless. **2** IMMODERATE,
flamboyant, preposterous,
outrageous, ostentatious, pretentious,
lavish, ornate, flashy (*infml*),
fanciful, fantastic, wild. **3**
OVERPRICED, exorbitant, expensive,
excessive, costly.

🖻 **1** thrifty. **2** moderate. **3** reasonable.

extreme *adj* **1** INTENSE, great,
immoderate, inordinate, utmost,

utter, out-and-out, maximum, acute,
downright, extraordinary,
exceptional, greatest, highest,
unreasonable, remarkable.
2 FARTHEST, far-off, faraway,
distant, endmost, outermost,
remotest, uttermost, final, last,
terminal, ultimate. **3** RADICAL,
zealous, extremist, fanatical.
4 DRASTIC, dire, uncompromising,
stern, strict, rigid, severe, harsh.

🖻 **1** mild. **3** moderate.

n extremity, limit, maximum,
ultimate, utmost, excess, top,
pinnacle, peak, height, end, climax,
depth, edge, termination.

extremity *n* **1** EXTREME, limit,
boundary, brink, verge, bound,
border, apex, height, tip, top, edge,
excess, end, acme, termination, peak,
pinnacle, margin, terminal, terminus,
ultimate, pole, maximum, minimum,
frontier, depth. **2** CRISIS, danger,
emergency, plight, hardship.

extricate *v* disentangle, clear,
disengage, free, deliver, liberate,
release, rescue, relieve, remove,
withdraw.

🖻 involve.

extroverted *adj* outgoing, friendly,
sociable, amicable, amiable,
exuberant.

🖻 introverted.

exuberant *adj* **1** LIVELY, vivacious,
spirited, zestful, high-spirited,
effervescent, ebullient, enthusiastic,
sparkling, excited, exhilarated,
effusive, cheerful, fulsome. **2**
PLENTIFUL, lavish, overflowing,
plenteous.

🖻 **1** apathetic. **2** scarce.

exult *v* rejoice, revel, delight, glory,
celebrate, relish, crow, gloat,
triumph.

eye *n* **1** APPRECIATION,
discrimination, discernment,
perception, recognition.
2 VIEWPOINT, opinion, judgement,
mind. **3** WATCH, observation,

lookout.

Parts of the eye include: anterior chamber, aqueous humour, blind spot, choroid, ciliary body, cone, conjunctiva, cornea, eyelash, fovea, iris, lacrimal duct, lens, lower eyelid, ocular muscle, optic nerve, papilla, pupil, posterior chamber, retina, rod, sclera, suspension ligament, upper eyelid, vitreous humour.

v look at, watch, regard, observe, stare at, gaze at, glance at, view, scrutinize, scan, examine, peruse, study, survey, inspect, contemplate.

eyesight *n* vision, sight, perception, observation, view.

eyesore *n* ugliness, blemish, monstrosity, blot on the landscape, disfigurement, horror, blight, atrocity, mess.

eye-witness *n* witness, observer, spectator, looker-on, onlooker, bystander, viewer, passer-by.

F

fable *n* allegory, parable, story, tale, yarn, myth, legend, fiction, fabrication, invention, lie, untruth, falsehood, tall story, old wives' tale.

fabric *n* **1** CLOTH, material, textile, stuff, web, texture. **2** STRUCTURE, framework, construction, make-up, constitution, organization, infrastructure, foundations.

Fabrics include: alpaca, angora, astrakhan, barathea, bouclé, cashmere, chenille, duffel, felt, flannel, fleece, Harris tweed®, mohair, paisley, serge, sheepskin, Shetland wool, tweed, vicuña, wool, worsted; brocade, buckram, calico, cambric, candlewick, canvas, chambray, cheesecloth, chino, chintz, cord, corduroy, cotton, crepe, denim, drill, jean, flannelette, gaberdine, gingham, jersey, lawn, linen, lisle, madras, moleskin, muslin, needlecord, piqué, poplin, sateen, seersucker, terry towelling, ticking, Viyella®, webbing, winceyette; brocade, grosgrain, damask, Brussels lace, chiffon, georgette, gossamer, voile, organza, organdie, tulle, net, crepe de Chine, silk, taffeta, shantung, velvet, velour; polycotton, polyester, rayon, nylon, Crimplene®, Terylene®, Lurex®, lamé; hessian, horsehair, chamois, kid, leather, leather-cloth, sharkskin, suede.

fabricate *v* **1** FAKE, falsify, forge, invent, make up, trump up, concoct. **2** MAKE, manufacture, construct, assemble, build, erect, form, shape, fashion, create, devise.
Ea 2 demolish, destroy.

fabulous *adj* **1** WONDERFUL, marvellous, fantastic, superb, breathtaking, spectacular, phenomenal, amazing, astounding, unbelievable, incredible, inconceivable. **2** *a fabulous beast*: mythical, legendary, fabled, fantastic, fictitious, invented, imaginary.
Ea 2 real.

face *n* **1** FEATURES, countenance, visage, physiognomy. **2** EXPRESSION, look, appearance, air. **3** *pull a face*: grimace, frown, scowl, pout. **4** EXTERIOR, outside, surface, cover, front, façade, aspect, side.
v **1** BE OPPOSITE, give on to, front, overlook. **2** CONFRONT, face up to, deal with, cope with, tackle, brave,

defy, oppose, encounter, meet, experience. **3** COVER, coat, dress, clad, overlay, veneer.

face to face opposite, eye to eye, eyeball to eyeball, in confrontation.

face up to accept, come to terms with, acknowledge, recognize, cope with, deal with, confront, meet head-on, stand up to.

facet n surface, plane, side, face, aspect, angle, point, feature, characteristic.

facetious adj flippant, frivolous, playful, jocular, jesting, tongue-in-cheek, funny, amusing, humorous, comical, witty.
☒ serious.

facile adj easy, simple, simplistic, ready, quick, hasty, glib, fluent, smooth, slick, plausible, shallow, superficial.
☒ complicated, profound.

facilitate v ease, help, assist, further, promote, forward, expedite, speed up.

facilities n amenities, services, conveniences, resources, prerequisites, equipment, mod cons (infml), means, opportunities.

facility n ease, effortlessness, readiness, quickness, fluency, proficiency, skill, skilfulness, talent, gift, knack, ability.

fact n **1** facts and figures: information, datum, detail, particular, specific, point, item, circumstance, event, incident, occurrence, happening, act, deed, fait accompli. **2** REALITY, actuality, truth.
☒ **2** fiction.

in fact actually, in actual fact, in point of fact, as a matter of fact, in reality, really, indeed.

faction n splinter group, ginger group, minority, division, section, contingent, party, camp, set, clique, coterie, cabal, junta, lobby, pressure group.

factor n cause, influence, circumstance, contingency, consideration, element, ingredient, component, part, point, aspect, fact, item, detail.

factory n works, plant, mill, shop floor, assembly line, manufactory.

factual adj true, historical, actual, real, genuine, authentic, correct, accurate, precise, exact, literal, faithful, close, detailed, unbiased, objective.
☒ false, fictitious, imaginary, fictional.

faculties n wits, senses, intelligence, reason, powers, capabilities.

faculty n ability, capability, capacity, power, facility, knack, gift, talent, skill, aptitude, bent.

fad n craze, rage (infml), mania, fashion, mode, vogue, trend, whim, fancy, affectation.

fade v **1** DISCOLOUR, bleach, blanch, blench, pale, whiten, dim, dull. **2** DECLINE, fall, diminish, dwindle, ebb, wane, disappear, vanish, flag, weaken, droop, wilt, wither, shrivel, perish, die.

fail v **1** GO WRONG, miscarry, misfire, flop, miss, flunk (sl), fall through, come to grief, collapse, fold (infml), go bankrupt, go bust, go under, founder, sink, decline, fall, weaken, dwindle, fade, wane, peter out, cease, die. **2** fail to pay a bill: omit, neglect, forget. **3** LET DOWN, disappoint, leave, desert, abandon, forsake.
☒ **1** succeed, prosper.

failing n weakness, foible, fault, defect, imperfection, flaw, blemish, drawback, deficiency, shortcoming, failure, lapse, error.
☒ strength, advantage.

failure n **1** MISCARRIAGE, flop, wash-out (infml), fiasco, disappointment, loss, defeat, downfall, decline, decay, deterioration, ruin, bankruptcy, crash, collapse, breakdown, stoppage. **2** OMISSION, slip-up (*infml*), neglect, negligence, failing, shortcoming, deficiency.

☒ **1** success, prosperity.

faint *adj* **1** SLIGHT, weak, feeble, soft, low, hushed, muffled, subdued, faded, bleached, light, pale, dull, dim, hazy, indistinct, vague. **2** *I feel faint*: dizzy, giddy, woozy (*infml*), light-headed, weak, feeble, exhausted.

☒ **1** strong, clear.

v black out, pass out, swoon, collapse, flake out (*infml*), keel over (*infml*), drop.

n blackout, swoon, collapse, unconsciousness.

fair[1] *adj* **1** JUST, equitable, square, even-handed, dispassionate, impartial, objective, disinterested, unbiased, unprejudiced, right, proper, lawful, legitimate, honest, trustworthy, upright, honourable. **2** FAIR-HAIRED, fair-headed, blond(e), light. **3** *fair weather*: fine, dry, sunny, bright, clear, cloudless, unclouded. **4** AVERAGE, moderate, middling, not bad, all right, OK (*infml*), satisfactory, adequate, acceptable, tolerable, reasonable, passable, mediocre, so-so (*infml*).

☒ **1** unfair. **2** dark. **3** inclement, cloudy. **4** excellent, poor.

fair[2] *n* show, exhibition, exposition, expo (*infml*), market, bazaar, fête, festival, carnival, gala.

faith *n* **1** BELIEF, credit, trust, reliance, dependence, conviction, confidence, assurance. **2** RELIGION, denomination, persuasion, church, creed, dogma. **3** FAITHFULNESS, fidelity, loyalty, allegiance, honour, sincerity, honesty, truthfulness.

☒ **1** mistrust. **3** unfaithfulness, treachery.

faithful *adj* **1** LOYAL, devoted, staunch, steadfast, constant, trusty, reliable, dependable, true. **2** *a faithful*

description: accurate, precise, exact, strict, close, true, truthful.

☒ **1** disloyal, treacherous. **2** inaccurate, vague.

fake *v* forge, fabricate, counterfeit, copy, imitate, simulate, feign, sham, pretend, put on, affect, assume.

n forgery, copy, reproduction, replica, imitation, simulation, sham, hoax, fraud, phoney (*infml*), impostor, charlatan.

adj forged, counterfeit, false, spurious, phoney (*infml*), pseudo, bogus, assumed, affected, sham, artificial, simulated, mock, imitation, reproduction.

☒ genuine.

fall *v* **1** TUMBLE, stumble, trip, topple, keel over, collapse, slump, crash. **2** DESCEND, go down, drop, slope, incline, slide, sink, dive, plunge, plummet, nose-dive, pitch. **3** DECREASE, lessen, decline, diminish, dwindle, fall off, subside.

☒ **2** rise. **3** increase.

n **1** TUMBLE, descent, slope, incline, dive, plunge, decrease, reduction, lessening, drop, decline, dwindling, slump, crash. **2** *the fall of Rome*: defeat, conquest, overthrow, downfall, collapse, surrender, capitulation.

fall apart break, go to pieces, shatter, disintegrate, crumble, decompose, decay, rot.

fall asleep drop off, doze off, nod off (*infml*).

fall back on resort to, have recourse to, use, turn to, look to.

fall behind lag, trail, drop back.

fall in cave in, come down, collapse, give way, subside, sink.

fall in with agree with, assent to, go along with, accept, comply with, co-operate with.

fall off decrease, lessen, drop, slump, decline, deteriorate, worsen, slow, slacken.

fall out quarrel, argue, squabble, bicker, fight, clash, disagree, differ.

agree.

fall through come to nothing, fail,
miscarry, founder, collapse.
come off, succeed.

fallacy n misconception, delusion,
mistake, error, flaw, inconsistency,
falsehood.
truth.

fallow adj uncultivated, unplanted,
unsown, undeveloped, unused, idle,
inactive, dormant, resting.

false adj **1** wrong, incorrect,
mistaken, erroneous, inaccurate,
inexact, misleading, faulty,
fallacious, invalid. **2** UNREAL,
artificial, synthetic, imitation,
simulated, mock, fake, counterfeit,
forged, feigned, pretended, sham,
bogus, assumed, fictitious. **3** *false
friends*: disloyal, unfaithful, faithless,
lying, deceitful, insincere,
hypocritical, two-faced, double-
dealing, treacherous, unreliable.
1 true, right. **2** real, genuine.
3 faithful, reliable.

falsehood n untruth, lie, fib, story,
fiction, fabrication, perjury,
untruthfulness, deceit, deception,
dishonesty.
truth, truthfulness.

falsify v alter, cook (*infml*), tamper
with, doctor, distort, pervert,
misrepresent, misstate, forge,
counterfeit, fake.

falter v totter, stumble, stammer,
stutter, hesitate, waver, vacillate,
flinch, quail, shake, tremble, flag,
fail.

fame n renown, celebrity, stardom,
prominence, eminence,
illustriousness, glory, honour,
esteem, reputation, name.

familiar adj **1** EVERYDAY, routine,
household, common, ordinary, well-
known, recognizable. **2** INTIMATE,
close, confidential, friendly, informal,
free, free-and-easy, relaxed.
3 *familiar with the procedure*: aware,
acquainted, abreast, knowledgeable,

versed, conversant.
1 unfamiliar, strange. **2** formal,
reserved. **3** unfamiliar, ignorant.

familiarity n **1** INTIMACY, liberty,
closeness, friendliness, sociability,
openness, naturalness, informality.
2 AWARENESS, acquaintance,
experience, knowledge,
understanding, grasp.

familiarize v accustom, acclimatize,
school, train, coach, instruct, prime,
brief.

family n **1** RELATIVES, relations,
kin, kindred, kinsmen, people, folk
(*infml*), ancestors, forebears,
children, offspring, issue, progeny,
descendants. **2** CLAN, tribe, race,
dynasty, house, pedigree, ancestry,
parentage, descent, line, lineage,
extraction, blood, stock, birth.
3 CLASS, group, classification.

Members of a family include:
ancestor, forebear, forefather,
descendant, offspring, heir; husband,
wife, spouse, parent, father, dad
(*infml*), daddy (*infml*), old man
(*infml*), mother, mum (*infml*), mummy
(*infml*), mom (*US infml*), grandparent,
grandfather, grandmother, granny
(*infml*), nanny (*infml*), grandchild,
son, daughter, brother, half-brother,
sister, half-sister, sibling, uncle, aunt,
nephew, niece, cousin, godfather,
godmother, godchild, stepfather,
stepmother, foster-parent, foster-child.

family tree ancestry, pedigree,
genealogy, line, lineage, extraction.

famine n starvation, hunger,
destitution, want, scarcity, death.
plenty.

famous adj well-known, famed,
renowned, celebrated, noted, great,
distinguished, illustrious, eminent,
honoured, acclaimed, glorious,
legendary, remarkable, notable,
prominent, signal.
unheard-of, unknown, obscure.

fan[1] v 1 COOL, ventilate, air, air-condition, air-cool, blow, refresh.
2 INCREASE, provoke, stimulate, rouse, arouse, excite, agitate, stir up, work up, whip up.
n extractor fan, ventilator, air-conditioner, blower, propeller, vane.

fan[2] n enthusiast, admirer, supporter, follower, adherent, devotee, lover, buff (infml), fiend, freak.

fanatic n zealot, devotee, enthusiast, addict, fiend, freak, maniac, visionary, bigot, extremist, militant, activist.

fanatical adj overenthusiastic, extreme, passionate, zealous, fervent, burning, mad, wild, frenzied, rabid, obsessive, single-minded, bigoted, visionary.
F∃ moderate, unenthusiastic.

fanaticism n extremism, monomania, single-mindedness, obsessiveness, madness, infatuation, bigotry, zeal, fervour, enthusiasm, dedication.
F∃ moderation.

fanciful adj imaginary, mythical, fabulous, fantastic, visionary, romantic, fairy-tale, airy-fairy, vaporous, whimsical, wild, extravagant, curious.
F∃ real, ordinary.

fancy v 1 LIKE, be attracted to, take a liking to, take to, go for, prefer, favour, desire, wish for, long for, yearn for. 2 THINK, conceive, imagine, dream of, picture, conjecture, believe, suppose, reckon, guess.
F∃ 1 dislike.
n 1 DESIRE, craving, hankering, urge, liking, fondness, inclination, preference. 2 NOTION, thought, impression, imagination, dream, fantasy.
F∃ 1 dislike, aversion. 2 fact, reality.
adj elaborate, ornate, decorated, ornamented, rococo, baroque, elegant, extravagant, fantastic, fanciful, far-fetched.
F∃ plain.

fantastic adj 1 WONDERFUL, marvellous, sensational, superb, excellent, first-rate, tremendous, terrific, great, incredible, unbelievable, overwhelming, enormous, extreme.
2 STRANGE, weird, odd, exotic, outlandish, fanciful, fabulous, imaginative, visionary.
F∃ 1 ordinary. 2 real.

fantasy n dream, daydream, reverie, pipe-dream, nightmare, vision, hallucination, illusion, mirage, apparition, invention, fancy, flight of fancy, delusion, misconception, imagination, unreality.
F∃ reality.

far adv a long way, a good way, miles (infml), much, greatly, considerably, extremely, decidedly, incomparably.
F∃ near, close.
adj distant, far-off, faraway, far-flung, outlying, remote, out-of-the-way, god-forsaken, removed, far-removed, further, opposite, other.
F∃ nearby, close.

farce n 1 COMEDY, slapstick, buffoonery, satire, burlesque.
2 TRAVESTY, sham, parody, joke, mockery, ridiculousness, absurdity, nonsense.

fare n 1 pay one's fare: charge, cost, price, fee, passage. 2 FOOD, eatables (infml), provisions, rations, sustenance, meals, diet, menu, board, table.

far-fetched adj implausible, improbable, unlikely, dubious, incredible, unbelievable, fantastic, preposterous, crazy, unrealistic.
F∃ plausible.

farm n ranch, farmstead, grange, homestead, station, land, holding, acreage, acres.

Types of farm include: arable farm, cattle ranch, dairy farm, fish farm, mixed farm, organic farm, pig farm, sheep station, croft, smallholding, estate, plantation.

v cultivate, till, work the land, plant, operate.

farmer *n* agriculturist, crofter, smallholder, husbandman, yeoman.

farming *n* agriculture, cultivation, husbandry, crofting.

far-reaching *adj* broad, extensive, widespread, sweeping, important, significant, momentous.
Ⓔ insignificant.

fascinate *v* absorb, engross, intrigue, delight, charm, captivate, spellbind, enthral, rivet, transfix, hypnotize, mesmerize.
Ⓔ bore, repel.

fascination *n* interest, attraction, lure, magnetism, pull, charm, enchantment, spell, sorcery, magic.
Ⓔ boredom, repulsion.

fashion *n* 1 MANNER, way, method, mode, style, shape, form, pattern, line, cut, look, appearance, type, sort, kind. 2 VOGUE, trend, mode, style, fad, craze, rage (*infml*), latest (*infml*), custom, convention.
v create, form, shape, mould, model, design, fit, tailor, alter, adjust, adapt, suit.

fashionable *adj* chic, smart, elegant, stylish, modish, à la mode, in vogue, trendy (*infml*), in, all the rage (*infml*), popular, prevailing, current, latest, up-to-the-minute, contemporary, modern, up-to-date.
Ⓔ unfashionable.

fast¹ *adj* 1 QUICK, swift, rapid, brisk, accelerated, speedy, nippy (*infml*), hasty, hurried, flying. 2 FASTENED, secure, fixed, immovable, immobile, firm, tight.
Ⓔ 1 slow, unhurried. 2 loose.
adv quickly, swiftly, rapidly, speedily, like a flash, like a shot, hastily,

hurriedly, apace, presto.
Ⓔ slowly, gradually.

fast² *v* go hungry, diet, starve, abstain.
n fasting, diet, starvation, abstinence.
Ⓔ gluttony, self-indulgence.

fasten *v* fix, attach, clamp, grip, anchor, rivet, nail, seal, close, shut, lock, bolt, secure, tie, bind, chain, link, interlock, connect, join, unite, do up, button, lace, buckle.
Ⓔ unfasten, untie.

fat *adj* plump, obese, tubby, stout, corpulent, portly, round, rotund, paunchy, pot-bellied, overweight, heavy, beefy, solid, chubby, podgy, fleshy, flabby, gross.
Ⓔ thin, slim, poor.
n fatness, obesity, overweight, corpulence, paunch, pot (belly), blubber, flab (*infml*).

fatal *adj* deadly, lethal, mortal, killing, incurable, malignant, terminal, final, destructive, calamitous, catastrophic, disastrous.
Ⓔ harmless.

fatality *n* death, mortality, loss, casualty, deadliness, lethality, disaster.

fate *n* destiny, providence, chance, future, fortune, horoscope, stars, lot, doom, end, outcome, ruin, destruction, death.

fated *adj* destined, predestined, preordained, foreordained, doomed, unavoidable, inevitable, inescapable, certain, sure.
Ⓔ avoidable.

fateful *adj* crucial, critical, decisive, important, momentous, significant, fatal, lethal, disastrous.
Ⓔ unimportant.

father *n* 1 PARENT, begetter, procreator, progenitor, sire (*fml*), papa, dad (*infml*), daddy (*infml*), old man (*infml*), patriarch, elder, forefather, ancestor, forebear, predecessor. 2 FOUNDER, creator,

originator, inventor, maker,
architect, author, patron, leader,
prime mover. **3** PRIEST, padre, abbé,
curé.

v beget, procreate, sire, produce.

fathom *v* **1** MEASURE, gauge, plumb,
sound, probe, penetrate.
2 UNDERSTAND, comprehend, grasp,
see, work out, get to the bottom of,
interpret.

fatigue *n* tiredness, weariness,
exhaustion, lethargy, listlessness,
lassitude, weakness, debility.

🔁 energy.

v tire, wear out, weary, exhaust,
drain, weaken, debilitate.

fatten *v* feed, nourish, build up,
overfeed, cram, stuff, bloat, swell, fill
out, spread, expand, thicken.

fatty *adj* fat, greasy, oily.

fault *n* **1** DEFECT, flaw, blemish,
imperfection, deficiency,
shortcoming, weakness, failing,
foible, negligence, omission,
oversight. **2** ERROR, mistake,
blunder, slip-up (*infml*), slip, lapse,
misdeed, offence, wrong, sin. **3** *it's
your fault*: responsibility,
accountability, liability, culpability.

v find fault with, pick holes in,
criticize, knock (*infml*), impugn,
censure, blame, call to account.

🔁 praise.

at fault (in) wrong, blameworthy,
to blame, responsible, guilty, culpable.

faultless *adj* perfect, flawless,
unblemished, spotless, immaculate,
unsullied, pure, blameless,
exemplary, model, correct, accurate.

🔁 faulty, imperfect, flawed.

faulty *adj* imperfect, defective,
flawed, blemished, damaged,
impaired, out of order, broken,
wrong.

🔁 faultless.

favour *n* **1** APPROVAL, esteem,
support, backing, sympathy,
goodwill, patronage, favouritism,
preference, partiality. **2** *he did me a*

favour: kindness, service, good turn,
courtesy.

🔁 **1** disapproval.

v **1** PREFER, choose, opt for, like,
approve, support, back, advocate,
champion. **2** HELP, assist, aid,
benefit, promote, encourage, pamper,
spoil.

🔁 **1** dislike. **2** mistreat.

in favour of for, supporting, on the side
of.

🔁 against.

favourable *adj* beneficial,
advantageous, helpful, fit, suitable,
convenient, timely, opportune, good,
fair, promising, auspicious, hopeful,
positive, encouraging,
complimentary, enthusiastic,
friendly, amicable, well-disposed,
kind, sympathetic, understanding,
reassuring.

🔁 unfavourable, unhelpful, negative.

favourite *adj* preferred, favoured,
pet, best-loved, dearest, beloved,
esteemed, chosen.

🔁 hated.

n preference, choice, pick, pet, blue-
eyed boy, teacher's pet, the apple of
one's eye, darling, idol.

🔁 bête noire, pet hate.

favouritism *n* nepotism, preferential
treatment, preference, partiality, one-
sidedness, partisanship, bias,
injustice.

🔁 impartiality.

fear *n* alarm, fright, terror, horror,
panic, agitation, worry, anxiety,
consternation, concern, dismay,
distress, uneasiness, qualms,
misgivings, apprehension,
trepidation, dread, foreboding, awe,
phobia, nightmare.

🔁 courage, bravery, confidence.

v take fright, shrink from, dread,
shudder at, tremble, worry, suspect,
anticipate, expect, foresee, respect,
venerate.

fearful *adj* **1** FRIGHTENED, afraid,
scared, alarmed, nervous, anxious,

tense, uneasy, apprehensive, hesitant, nervy, panicky. **2** TERRIBLE, fearsome (*fml*), dreadful, awful, frightful, atrocious, shocking, appalling, monstrous, gruesome, hideous, ghastly, horrible.
Ea 1 brave, courageous, fearless.
2 wonderful, delightful.

feasible *adj* practicable, practical, workable, achievable, attainable, realizable, viable, reasonable, possible, likely.
Ea impossible.

feast *n* **1** BANQUET, dinner, spread, blow-out (*sl*), binge (*infml*), beano (*infml*), junket. **2** FESTIVAL, holiday, gala, fête, celebration, revels.
v gorge, eat one's fill, wine and dine, treat, entertain.

feat *n* exploit, deed, act, accomplishment, achievement, attainment, performance.

feature *n* **1** ASPECT, facet, point, factor, attribute, quality, property, trait, lineament, characteristic, peculiarity, mark, hallmark, speciality, highlight. **2** *a magazine feature*: column, article, report, story, piece, item, comment.
v **1** EMPHASIZE, highlight, spotlight, play up, promote, show, present.
2 APPEAR, figure, participate, act, perform, star.

fee *n* charge, terms, bill, account, pay, remuneration, payment, retainer, subscription, reward, recompense, hire, toll.

feeble *adj* **1** WEAK, faint, exhausted, frail, delicate, puny, sickly, infirm, powerless, helpless. **2** INADEQUATE, lame, poor, thin, flimsy, ineffective, incompetent, indecisive.
Ea 1 strong, powerful.

feed *v* nourish, cater for, provide for, supply, sustain, suckle, nurture, foster, strengthen, fuel, graze, pasture, eat, dine.
n food, fodder, forage, pasture, silage.

feed on eat, consume, devour, live on, exist on.

feel *v* **1** EXPERIENCE, go through, undergo, suffer, endure, enjoy.
2 TOUCH, finger, handle, manipulate, hold, stroke, caress, fondle, paw, fumble, grope. **3** *feel soft*: seem, appear. **4** THINK, believe, consider, reckon, judge. **5** SENSE, perceive, notice, observe, know.
n texture, surface, finish, touch, knack, sense, impression, feeling, quality.

feel for pity, sympathize (with), commiserate (with), be sorry for.

feel like fancy, want, desire.

feeling *n* **1** SENSATION, perception, sense, instinct, hunch, suspicion, inkling, impression, idea, notion, opinion, view, point of view.
2 EMOTION, passion, intensity, warmth, compassion, sympathy, understanding, hold, concern, affection, fondness, sentiment, sentimentality, susceptibility, sensibility, sensitivity, appreciation.
3 AIR, aura, atmosphere, mood, quality.

fell *v* cut down, hew, knock down, strike down, floor, level, flatten, raze, demolish.

fellow *n* **1** PERSON, man, boy, chap (*infml*), bloke (*infml*), guy (*infml*), individual, character. **2** PEER, compeer, equal, partner, associate, colleague, co-worker, companion, comrade, friend, counterpart, match, mate, twin, double.
adj co-, associate, associated, related, like, similar.

fellowship *n* **1** COMPANIONSHIP, camaraderie, communion, familiarity, intimacy.
2 ASSOCIATION, league, guild, society, club, fraternity, brotherhood, sisterhood, order.

female *adj* feminine, she-, girlish, womanly.
Ea male.

Female terms include: girl, lass, maiden, woman, lady, daughter, sister, girlfriend, fiancée, bride, wife, mother, aunt, niece, grandmother, matriarch, godmother, widow, dowager, dame, madam, mistress, virgin, spinster, old-maid, bird (*sl*), chick (*sl*), lesbian, bitch (*sl*), prostitute, whore, harlot; cow, heifer, bitch, doe, ewe, hen, mare, filly, nanny-goat, sow, tigress, vixen.

feminine *adj* **1** FEMALE, womanly, ladylike, graceful, gentle, tender. **2** EFFEMINATE, unmanly, womanish, girlish, sissy.
E3 1 masculine. **2** manly.

feminism *n* women's movement, women's lib(eration), female emancipation, women's rights.

fence *n* barrier, railing, paling, wall, hedge, windbreak, guard, defence, barricade, stockade, rampart.
v **1** SURROUND, encircle, bound, hedge, wall, enclose, pen, coop, confine, restrict, separate, protect, guard, defend, fortify. **2** PARRY, dodge, evade, hedge, equivocate, quibble, pussyfoot, stonewall.

fencing

Fencing terms include: appel, attack, balestra, barrage, coquille, disengage, en garde, épée, feint, flèche, foible, foil, forte, hit, lunge, on guard, parry, counter-parry, pink, piste, plastron, remise, reprise, riposte, counter-riposte, sabre, tac-au-tac, thrust, touch, touché, volt.

fend for look after, take care of, shift for, support, maintain, sustain, provide for.
fend off ward off, beat off, parry, deflect, avert, resist, repel, repulse, hold at bay, keep off, shut out.
ferment *v* **1** BUBBLE, effervesce, froth, foam, boil, seethe, smoulder, fester, brew, rise. **2** ROUSE, stir up,

excite, work up, agitate, foment, incite, provoke, inflame, heat.
n unrest, agitation, turbulence, stir, excitement, turmoil, disruption, commotion, tumult, hubbub, uproar, furore, frenzy, fever, glow.
E3 calm.

ferocious *adj* vicious, savage, fierce, wild, barbarous, barbaric, brutal, inhuman, cruel, sadistic, murderous, bloodthirsty, violent, merciless, pitiless, ruthless.
E3 gentle, mild, tame.

ferocity *n* viciousness, savagery, fierceness, wildness, barbarity, brutality, inhumanity, cruelty, sadism, bloodthirstiness, violence, ruthlessness.
E3 gentleness, mildness.

ferry *n* ferry-boat, car ferry, ship, boat, vessel.
v transport, ship, convey, carry, take, shuttle, taxi, drive, run, move, shift.

fertile *adj* fruitful, productive, generative, yielding, prolific, teeming, abundant, plentiful, rich, lush, luxuriant, fat.
E3 infertile, barren, sterile, unproductive.

fertilize *v* **1** IMPREGNATE, inseminate, pollinate. **2** *fertilize land*: enrich, feed, dress, compost, manure, dung.

fertilizer *n* dressing, compost, manure, dung.

fervent *adj* ardent, earnest, eager, enthusiastic, whole-hearted, excited, energetic, vigorous, fiery, spirited, intense, vehement, passionate, full-blooded, zealous, devout, heartfelt, impassioned, emotional, warm.
E3 cool, indifferent, apathetic.

fervour *n* ardour, eagerness, enthusiasm, excitement, animation, energy, vigour, spirit, verve, intensity, vehemence, passion, zeal, warmth.
E3 apathy.

fester *v* ulcerate, gather, suppurate,

discharge, putrefy, rot, decay, rankle, smoulder.

festival *n* celebration, commemoration, anniversary, jubilee, holiday, feast, gala, fête, carnival, fiesta, party, merrymaking, entertainment, festivities.

festive *adj* celebratory, festal, holiday, gala, carnival, happy, joyful, merry, hearty, cheery, jolly, jovial, cordial, convivial.
� gloomy, sombre, sober.

festivity *n* celebration, jubilation, feasting, banqueting, fun, enjoyment, pleasure, entertainment, sport, amusement, merriment, merrymaking, revelry, jollity, joviality, conviviality.

festoon *v* adorn, deck, bedeck, garland, wreathe, drape, hang, swathe, decorate, garnish.

fetch *v* **1** *fetch a bucket*: get, collect, bring, carry, transport, deliver, escort. **2** SELL FOR, go for, bring in, yield, realize, make, earn.

fetching *adj* attractive, pretty, sweet, cute, charming, enchanting, fascinating, captivating.
� repellent.

fête *n* fair, bazaar, sale of work, garden party, gala, carnival, festival. *v* entertain, treat, regale, welcome, honour, lionize.

feud *n* vendetta, quarrel, row, argument, disagreement, dispute, conflict, strife, discord, animosity, ill will, bitterness, enmity, hostility, antagonism, rivalry.
� agreement, peace.

fever *n* **1** FEVERISHNESS, (high) temperature, delirium. **2** EXCITEMENT, agitation, turmoil, unrest, restlessness, heat, passion, ecstasy.

feverish *adj* **1** DELIRIOUS, hot, burning, flushed. **2** EXCITED, impatient, agitated, restless, nervous, overwrought, frenzied, frantic, hectic, hasty, hurried.

✓ **1** cool. **2** calm.

few *adj* scarce, rare, uncommon, sporadic, infrequent, sparse, thin, scant, scanty, meagre, inconsiderable, inadequate, insufficient, in short supply.
� many.
pron not many, hardly any, one or two, a couple, scattering, sprinkling, handful, some.
� many.

fibre *n* **1** FILAMENT, strand, thread, nerve, sinew, pile, texture. **2** *moral fibre*: character, calibre, backbone, strength, stamina, toughness, courage, resolution, determination.

fickle *adj* inconstant, disloyal, unfaithful, faithless, treacherous, unreliable, unpredictable, changeable, capricious, mercurial, irresolute, vacillating.
� constant, steady, stable.

fiction *n* **1** FANTASY, fancy, imagination, figment, invention, fabrication, concoction, improvisation, story-telling. **2** NOVEL, romance, story, tale, yarn, fable, parable, legend, myth, lie.
� **2** non-fiction, fact, truth.

fictional *adj* literary, invented, made-up, imaginary, make-believe, legendary, mythical, mythological, fabulous, non-existent, unreal.
� factual, real.

fictitious *adj* false, untrue, invented, made-up, fabricated, apocryphal, imaginary, non-existent, bogus, counterfeit, spurious, assumed, supposed.
� true, genuine.

fiddle *v* **1** *fiddling with her necklace*: play, tinker, toy, trifle, tamper, mess around, meddle, interfere, fidget. **2** CHEAT, swindle, diddle, cook the books (*infml*), juggle, manoeuvre, racketeer, graft (*sl*).
n swindle, con (*infml*), rip-off (*sl*), fraud, racket, sharp practice, graft (*sl*).

fiddling *adj* trifling, petty, trivial,

insignificant, negligible, paltry.

E3 important, significant.

fidelity n **1** FAITHFULNESS, loyalty, allegiance, devotion, constancy, reliability. **2** ACCURACY, exactness, precision, closeness, adherence.

E3 1 infidelity, inconstancy, treachery. **2** inaccuracy.

fidget v squirm, wriggle, shuffle, twitch, jerk, jump, fret, fuss, bustle, fiddle, mess about, play around.

fidgety adj restless, impatient, uneasy, nervous, agitated, jittery, jumpy, twitchy, on edge.

E3 still.

field n **1** GRASSLAND, meadow, pasture, paddock, playing-field, ground, pitch, green, lawn. **2** RANGE, scope, bounds, limits, confines, territory, area, province, domain, sphere, environment, department, discipline, speciality, line, forte. **3** PARTICIPANTS, entrants, contestants, competitors, contenders, runners, candidates, applicants, opponents, opposition, competition.

fiend n **1** EVIL SPIRIT, demon, devil, monster. **2** a health fiend: enthusiast, fanatic, addict, devotee, freak (infml), nut (infml).

fiendish adj devilish, diabolical, infernal, wicked, malevolent, cunning, cruel, inhuman, savage, monstrous, unspeakable.

fierce adj ferocious, vicious, savage, cruel, brutal, merciless, aggressive, dangerous, murderous, frightening, menacing, threatening, stern, grim, relentless, raging, wild, passionate, intense, strong, powerful.

E3 gentle, kind, calm.

fiery adj **1** BURNING, afire, flaming, aflame, blazing, ablaze, red-hot, glowing, aglow, flushed, hot, torrid, sultry. **2** PASSIONATE, inflamed, ardent, fervent, impatient, excitable, impetuous, impulsive, hot-headed, fierce, violent, heated.

E3 1 cold. **2** impassive.

fight v **1** WRESTLE, box, fence, joust, brawl, scrap, scuffle, tussle, skirmish, combat, battle, do battle, war, wage war, clash, cross swords, engage, grapple, struggle, strive, contend. **2** QUARREL, argue, dispute, squabble, bicker, wrangle. **3** OPPOSE, contest, campaign against, resist, withstand, defy, stand up to.

n **1** BOUT, contest, duel, combat, action, battle, war, hostilities, brawl, scrap, scuffle, tussle, struggle, skirmish, set-to, clash, engagement, brush, encounter, conflict, fray, free-for-all, fracas, riot. **2** QUARREL, row, argument, dispute, dissension.

fight back 1 RETALIATE, defend oneself, resist, put up a fight, retort, reply. **2** fight back the tears: hold back, restrain, curb, control, repress, bottle up, contain, suppress.

fight off hold off, keep at bay, ward off, stave off, resist, repel, rebuff, beat off, rout, put to flight.

fighter n combatant, contestant, contender, disputant, boxer, wrestler, pugilist, prizefighter, soldier, trouper, mercenary, warrior, man-at-arms, swordsman, gladiator.

figurative adj metaphorical, symbolic, emblematic, representative, allegorical, parabolic, descriptive, pictorial.

E3 literal.

figure n **1** NUMBER, numeral, digit, integer, sum, amount. **2** SHAPE, form, outline, silhouette, body, frame, build, physique. **3** public figure: dignitary, celebrity, personality, character, person. **4** DIAGRAM, illustration, picture, drawing, sketch, image, representation, symbol.

v **1** RECKON, guess, estimate, judge, think, believe. **2** FEATURE, appear, crop up.

figure out work out, calculate, compute, reckon, puzzle out, resolve, fathom, understand, see, make out, decipher.

figurehead n mouthpiece, front man, name, dummy, puppet.

filament n fibre, strand, thread, hair, whisker, wire, string, pile.

file¹ v rub (down), sand, abrade, scour, scrape, grate, rasp, hone, whet, shave, plane, smooth, polish.

file² n folder, dossier, portfolio, binder, case, record, documents, data, information.
v record, register, note, enter, process, store, classify, categorize, pigeonhole, catalogue.

file³ n line, queue, column, row, procession, cortège, train, string, stream, trail.
v march, troop, parade, stream, trail.

fill v 1 REPLENISH, stock, supply, furnish, satisfy, pack, crowd, cram, stuff, congest, block, clog, plug, bung, cork, stop, close, seal. 2 PERVADE, imbue, permeate, soak, impregnate. 3 *fill a post:* take up, hold, occupy, discharge, fulfil.
🔁 1 empty, drain.

fill in 1 *fill in a form:* complete, fill out, answer. 2 (*infml*) STAND IN, deputize, understudy, substitute, replace, represent, act for. 3 (*infml*) BRIEF, inform, advise, acquaint, bring up to date.

filling n contents, inside, stuffing, padding, wadding, filler.
adj satisfying, nutritious, square, solid, substantial, heavy, large, big, generous, ample.
🔁 insubstantial.

film n 1 MOTION PICTURE, picture, movie (*infml*), video, feature film, short, documentary. 2 LAYER, covering, dusting, coat, coating, glaze, skin, membrane, tissue, sheet, veil, screen, cloud, mist, haze.
v photograph, shoot, video, videotape.

filter v strain, sieve, sift, screen, refine, purify, clarify, percolate, ooze, seep, leak, trickle, dribble.

n strainer, sieve, sifter, colander, mesh, gauze, membrane.

filth n 1 DIRT, grime, muck, dung, excrement, faeces, sewage, refuse, rubbish, garbage, trash, slime, sludge, effluent, pollution, contamination, corruption, impurity, uncleanness, foulness, sordidness, squalor. 2 OBSCENITY, pornography, smut, indecency, vulgarity, coarseness.
🔁 1 cleanness, cleanliness, purity.

filthy adj 1 DIRTY, soiled, unwashed, grimy, grubby, mucky, muddy, slimy, sooty, unclean, impure, foul, gross, sordid, squalid, vile, low, mean, base, contemptible, despicable. 2 OBSCENE, pornographic, smutty, bawdy, suggestive, indecent, offensive, foul-mouthed, vulgar, coarse, corrupt, depraved.
🔁 1 clean, pure. 2 decent.

final adj last, latest, closing, concluding, finishing, end, ultimate, terminal, dying, last-minute, eventual, conclusive, definitive, decisive, definite, incontrovertible.
🔁 first, initial.

finale n climax, dénouement, culmination, crowning glory, end, conclusion, close, curtain, epilogue.

finalize v conclude, finish, complete, round off, resolve, settle, agree, decide, close, clinch, sew up (*infml*), wrap up (*infml*).

finally adv lastly, in conclusion, ultimately, eventually, at last, at length, in the end, conclusively, once and for all, for ever, irreversibly, irrevocably, definitely.

finance n economics, money management, accounting, banking, investment, stock market, business, commerce, trade, money, funding, sponsorship, subsidy.
v pay for, fund, sponsor, back, support, underwrite, guarantee, subsidize, capitalize, float, set up.

finances n accounts, affairs, budget,

bank account, income, revenue, liquidity, resources, assets, capital, wealth, money, cash, funds, wherewithal.

financial *adj* monetary, money, pecuniary, economic, fiscal, budgetary, commercial.

financier *n* financialist, banker, stockbroker, money-maker, investor, speculator.

find *v* 1 DISCOVER, locate, track down, trace, retrieve, recover, unearth, uncover, expose, reveal, come across, chance on, stumble on, meet, encounter, detect, recognize, notice, observe, perceive, realize, learn. 2 ATTAIN, achieve, win, reach, gain, obtain, get. 3 *find it difficult*: consider, think, judge, declare.
F3 1 lose.

find out 1 LEARN, ascertain, discover, detect, note, observe, perceive, realize. 2 UNMASK, expose, show up, uncover, reveal, disclose, catch, suss out (*sl*), rumble (*sl*), tumble to (*infml*).

finding *n* 1 FIND, discovery, breakthrough. 2 DECISION, conclusion, judgement, verdict, pronouncement, decree, recommendation, award.

fine¹ *adj* 1 EXCELLENT, outstanding, exceptional, superior, exquisite, splendid, magnificent, brilliant, beautiful, handsome, attractive, elegant, lovely, nice, good. 2 THIN, slender, sheer, gauzy, powdery, flimsy, fragile, delicate, dainty. 3 SATISFACTORY, acceptable, all right, OK (*infml*). 4 *fine weather*: bright, sunny, clear, cloudless, dry, fair.
F3 1 mediocre. 2 thick, coarse. 4 cloudy.

fine² *n* penalty, punishment, forfeit, forfeiture, damages.

finger *v* touch, handle, manipulate, feel, stroke, caress, fondle, paw, fiddle with, toy with, play about with, meddle with.

finicky *adj* 1 PARTICULAR, finickety, pernickety, fussy, choosy (*infml*), fastidious, meticulous, scrupulous, critical, hypercritical, nit-picking. 2 FIDDLY, intricate, tricky, difficult, delicate.
F3 1 easy-going. 2 easy.

finish *v* 1 END, terminate, stop, cease, complete, accomplish, achieve, fulfil, discharge, deal with, do, conclude, close, wind up, settle, round off, culminate, perfect. 2 DESTROY, ruin, exterminate, get rid of, annihilate, defeat, overcome, rout, overthrow. 3 USE (UP), consume, devour, eat, drink, exhaust, drain, empty.
F3 1 begin, start.
n 1 END, termination, completion, conclusion, close, ending, finale, culmination. 2 SURFACE, appearance, texture, grain, polish, shine, gloss, lustre, smoothness.
F3 1 beginning, start, commencement.

finite *adj* limited, restricted, bounded, demarcated, terminable, definable, fixed, measurable, calculable, countable, numbered.
F3 infinite.

fire *n* 1 FLAMES, blaze, bonfire, conflagration, inferno, burning, combustion. 2 PASSION, feeling, excitement, enthusiasm, spirit, intensity, heat, radiance, sparkle.
v 1 IGNITE, light, kindle, set fire to, set on fire, set alight. 2 *fire a missile*: shoot, launch, set off, let off, detonate, explode. 3 DISMISS, discharge, sack (*infml*), eject. 4 EXCITE, whet, enliven, galvanize, electrify, stir, arouse, rouse, stimulate, inspire, incite, spark off, trigger off.

on fire burning, alight, ignited, flaming, in flames, aflame, blazing, ablaze, fiery.

firm¹ *adj* 1 *firm ground*: dense, compressed, compact, concentrated, set, solid, hard, unyielding, stiff, rigid, inflexible. 2 FIXED, embedded, fast, tight, secure, fastened, anchored, immovable, motionless, stationary, steady, stable, sturdy, strong. **3** ADAMANT, unshakable, resolute, determined, dogged, unwavering, strict, constant, steadfast, staunch, dependable, true, sure, convinced, definite, settled, committed.

F3 1 soft, flabby. **2** unsteady. **3** hesitant.

firm² n company, corporation, business, enterprise, concern, house, establishment, institution, organization, association, partnership, syndicate, conglomerate.

first adj **1** INITIAL, opening, introductory, preliminary, elementary, primary, basic, fundamental. **2** ORIGINAL, earliest, earlier, prior, primitive, primeval, oldest, eldest, senior. **3** CHIEF, main, key, cardinal, principal, head, leading, ruling, sovereign, highest, uppermost, paramount, prime, predominant, pre-eminent.

F3 last, final.

adv initially, to begin with, to start with, at the outset, beforehand, originally, in preference, rather, sooner.

first name forename, Christian name, baptismal name, given name.

first-rate adj first-class, A1, second-to-none, matchless, peerless, top, top-notch (infml), top-flight, leading, supreme, superior, prime, excellent, outstanding, superlative, exceptional, splendid, superb, fine, admirable.

F3 inferior.

fish

Types of fish include: bloater, brisling, cod, coley, Dover sole, haddock, hake, halibut, herring, jellied eel, kipper, mackerel, pilchard, plaice, rainbow trout, salmon, sardine, sole, sprat, trout, tuna, turbot, whitebait; bass, Bombay duck, bream, brill, carp, catfish, chub, conger eel, cuttlefish, dab, dace, dogfish, dory, eel, goldfish, guppy, marlin, minnow, monkfish, mullet, octopus, perch, pike, piranha, roach, shark, skate, snapper, squid, stickleback, stingray, sturgeon, swordfish, tench, whiting; clam, cockle, crab, crayfish, crawfish (US), kingprawn, lobster, mussel, oyster, prawn, scallop, shrimp, whelk.

v angle, trawl, delve, hunt, seek, invite, solicit.

fish out produce, take out, extract, find, come up with, dredge up, haul up.

fishing n angling, trawling.

fit¹ adj **1** SUITABLE, appropriate, apt, fitting, correct, right, proper, ready, prepared, able, capable, competent, qualified, eligible, worthy. **2** HEALTHY, well, able-bodied, in good form, in good shape, sound, sturdy, strong, robust, hale and hearty.

F3 1 unsuitable, unworthy. **2** unfit.

v **1** MATCH, correspond, conform, follow, agree, concur, tally, suit, harmonize, go, belong, dovetail, interlock, join, meet, arrange, place, position, accommodate. **2** ALTER, modify, change, adjust, adapt, tailor, shape, fashion.

fit out equip, rig out, kit out, outfit, provide, supply, furnish, prepare, arm.

fit² n seizure, convulsion, spasm, paroxysm, attack, outbreak, bout, spell, burst, surge, outburst, eruption, explosion.

fitful adj sporadic, intermittent, occasional, spasmodic, erratic, irregular, uneven, broken, disturbed.

F3 steady, regular.

fitted adj **1** fitted wardrobe: built-in, permanent. **2** EQUIPPED, rigged out, provided, furnished, appointed, prepared, armed. **3** SUITED, right, suitable, fit, qualified.

fitting adj apt, appropriate, suitable, fit, correct, right, proper, seemly,

meet (*fml*), desirable, deserved.
F3 unsuitable, improper.
n connection, attachment, accessory, part, component, piece, unit, fitment.

fittings *n* equipment, furnishings, furniture, fixtures, installations, fitments, accessories, extras.

fix *v* **1** FASTEN, secure, tie, bind, attach, join, connect, link, couple, anchor, pin, nail, rivet, stick, glue, cement, set, harden, solidify, stiffen, stabilize, plant, root, implant, embed, establish, install, place, locate, position. **2** *fix a date*: arrange, set, specify, define, agree on, decide, determine, settle, resolve, finalize. **3** MEND, repair, correct, rectify, adjust, restore.
F3 1 move, shift. 3 damage.
n (*infml*) dilemma, quandary, predicament, plight, difficulty, hole (*infml*), corner, spot (*infml*), mess, muddle.

fix up arrange, organize, plan, lay on, provide, supply, furnish, equip, settle, sort out, produce, bring about.

fixation *n* preoccupation, obsession, mania, fetish, thing (*infml*), infatuation, compulsion, hang-up (*infml*), complex.

fixed *adj* decided, settled, established, definite, arranged, planned, set, firm, rigid, inflexible, steady, secure, fast, rooted, permanent.
F3 variable.

fizz *v* effervesce, sparkle, bubble, froth, foam, fizzle, hiss, sizzle, sputter, spit.

fizzy *adj* effervescent, sparkling, aerated, carbonated, gassy, bubbly, bubbling, frothy, foaming.

flabbergasted (*infml*) *adj* amazed, confounded, astonished, astounded, staggered, dumbfounded, speechless, stunned, dazed, overcome, overwhelmed, bowled over.

flabby *adj* fleshy, soft, yielding, flaccid, limp, floppy, drooping,

hanging, sagging, slack, loose, lax, weak, feeble.
F3 firm, strong.

flag¹ *v* lessen, diminish, decline, fall (off), abate, subside, sink, slump, dwindle, peter out, fade, fail, weaken, slow, falter, tire, weary, wilt, droop, sag, flop, faint, die.
F3 revive.

flag² *n* ensign, jack, pennant, colours, standard, banner, streamer.

Types of flag include: banner, bunting, burgee, colours, cornet, gonfalon, jack, oriflamme, pennant, pilot flag, signal flag, standard, streamer, swallow tail.
Names of flag include: Blue Ensign, Blue Peter, Crescent, Hammer and Sickle, Jolly Roger, Old Glory, Olympic Flag, Red Ensign, Rising Sun, Skull and Crossbones, Star Spangled Banner, Stars and Stripes, Tricolour, Union Jack, White Ensign, Yellow Jack.

v **1** SIGNAL, wave, salute, motion. **2** MARK, indicate, label, tag, note.

flail *v* thresh, thrash, beat, whip.

flair *n* skill, ability, aptitude, faculty, gift, talent, facility, knack, mastery, genius, feel, taste, discernment, acumen, style, elegance, stylishness, panache.
F3 inability, ineptitude.

flake *n* scale, peeling, paring, shaving, sliver, wafer, chip, splinter.
v scale, peel, chip, splinter.

flamboyant *adj* showy, ostentatious, flashy, gaudy, colourful, brilliant, dazzling, striking, extravagant, rich, elaborate, ornate, florid.
F3 modest, restrained.

flame *v* burn, flare, blaze, glare, flash, beam, shine, glow, radiate.
n **1** FIRE, blaze, light, brightness, heat, warmth. **2** PASSION, ardour, fervour, enthusiasm, zeal, intensity, radiance.

flaming *adj* **1** *a flaming torch*: burning, alight, aflame, blazing, fiery, brilliant, scintillating, red-hot, glowing, smouldering. **2** INTENSE, vivid, aroused, impassioned, hot, raging, frenzied.

flammable *adj* inflammable, ignitable, combustible.
ⅎ non-flammable, incombustible, flameproof, fire-resistant.

flank *n* side, edge, quarter, wing, loin, hip, thigh.
v edge, fringe, skirt, line, border, bound, confine, wall, screen.

flap *v* flutter, vibrate, wave, agitate, shake, wag, swing, swish, thrash, beat.
n **1** FOLD, fly, lapel, tab, lug, tag, tail, skirt, aileron. **2** (*infml*) PANIC, state (*infml*), fuss, commotion, fluster, agitation, flutter, dither, tizzy (*infml*).

flare *v* **1** FLAME, burn, blaze, glare, flash, flicker, burst, explode, erupt. **2** BROADEN, widen, flare out, spread out, splay.
n **1** FLAME, blaze, glare, flash, flicker, burst. **2** BROADENING, widening, splay.
flare up erupt, break out, explode, blow up.

flash *v* **1** BEAM, shine, light up, flare, blaze, glare, gleam, glint, flicker, twinkle, sparkle, glitter, shimmer. **2** *the train flashed past*: streak, fly, dart, race, dash.
n beam, ray, shaft, spark, blaze, flare, burst, streak, gleam, glint, flicker, twinkle, sparkle, shimmer.

flashy *adj* showy, ostentatious, flamboyant, glamorous, bold, loud, garish, gaudy, jazzy, flash, tawdry, cheap, vulgar, tasteless.
ⅎ plain, tasteful.

flat¹ *adj* **1** LEVEL, plane, even, smooth, uniform, unbroken, horizontal, outstretched, prostrate, prone, recumbent, reclining, low. **2** DULL, boring, monotonous, tedious, uninteresting, unexciting,

stale, lifeless, dead, spiritless, lacklustre, vapid, insipid, weak, watery, empty, pointless. **3** *a flat refusal*: absolute, utter, total, unequivocal, categorical, positive, unconditional, unqualified, point-blank, direct, straight, explicit, plain, final. **4** *a flat tyre*: punctured, burst, deflated, collapsed.
ⅎ 1 bumpy, vertical. **2** exciting, full. **3** equivocal.
flat out at top speed, at full speed, all out, for all one is worth.

flat² *n* apartment, penthouse, maisonnette, tenement, flatlet, rooms, suite, bed-sit(ter).

flatten *v* **1** SMOOTH, iron, press, roll, crush, squash, compress, level, even out. **2** KNOCK DOWN, prostrate, floor, fell, demolish, raze, overwhelm, subdue.

flatter *v* praise, compliment, sweet-talk (*infml*), adulate, fawn, butter up (*infml*), wheedle, humour, play up to, court, curry favour with.
ⅎ criticize.

flattery *n* adulation, eulogy, sweet talk (*infml*), soft soap (*infml*), flannel (*infml*), blarney, cajolery, fawning, toadyism, sycophancy, ingratiation, servility.
ⅎ criticism.

flavour *n* **1** TASTE, tang, smack, savour, relish, zest, zing (*infml*), aroma, odour. **2** QUALITY, property, character, style, aspect, feeling, feel, atmosphere. **3** HINT, suggestion, touch, tinge, tone.
v season, spice, ginger up, infuse, imbue.

flavouring *n* seasoning, zest, essence, extract, additive.

flaw *n* defect, imperfection, fault, blemish, spot, mark, speck, crack, crevice, fissure, cleft, split, rift, break, fracture, weakness, shortcoming, failing, fallacy, lapse, slip, error, mistake.

flawed *adj* imperfect, defective,

flawless 214

faulty, blemished, marked, damaged, spoilt, marred, cracked, chipped, broken, unsound, fallacious, erroneous.
€3 flawless, perfect.

flawless *adj* perfect, faultless, unblemished, spotless, immaculate, stainless, sound, intact, whole, unbroken, undamaged.
€3 flawed, imperfect.

fleck *v* dot, spot, mark, speckle, dapple, mottle, streak, sprinkle, dust.
n dot, point, spot, mark, speck, speckle, streak.

flee *v* run away, bolt, fly, take flight, take off, make off, cut and run, escape, get away, decamp, abscond, leave, depart, withdraw, retreat, vanish, disappear.
€3 stay.

fleet *n* flotilla, armada, navy, task force, squadron.

fleeting *adj* short, brief, flying, short-lived, momentary, ephemeral, transient, transitory, passing, temporary.
€3 lasting, permanent.

flesh *n* body, tissue, fat, muscle, brawn, skin, meat, pulp, substance, matter, physicality.

flex *v* bend, bow, curve, angle, ply, double up, tighten, contract.
€3 straighten, extend.
n cable, wire, lead, cord.

flexible *adj* 1 BENDABLE, bendy (*infml*), pliable, pliant, plastic, malleable, mouldable, elastic, stretchy, springy, yielding, supple, lithe, limber, double-jointed, mobile. 2 ADAPTABLE, adjustable, amenable, accommodating, variable, open.
€3 1 inflexible, rigid.

flick *v* hit, strike, rap, tap, touch, dab, flip, jerk, whip, lash.
n rap, tap, touch, dab, flip, jerk, click.
flick through flip through, thumb through, leaf through, glance at, skim, scan.

flicker *v* flash, blink, wink, twinkle, sparkle, glimmer, shimmer, gutter, flutter, vibrate, quiver, waver.
n flash, gleam, glint, twinkle, glimmer, spark, trace, drop, iota, atom, indication.

flight[1] *n* 1 FLYING, aviation, aeronautics, air transport, air travel. 2 JOURNEY, trip, voyage.

flight[2] *n* fleeing, escape, getaway, breakaway, exit, departure, exodus, retreat.

flimsy *adj* thin, fine, light, slight, insubstantial, ethereal, fragile, delicate, shaky, rickety, makeshift, weak, feeble, meagre, inadequate, shallow, superficial, trivial, poor, unconvincing, implausible.
€3 sturdy.

flinch *v* wince, start, cringe, cower, quail, tremble, shake, quake, shudder, shiver, shrink, recoil, draw back, balk, shy away, duck, shirk, withdraw, retreat, flee.

fling *v* throw, hurl, pitch, lob, toss, chuck (*infml*), cast, sling, catapult, launch, propel, send, let fly, heave, jerk.

flip *v* flick, spin, twirl, twist, turn, toss, throw, cast, pitch, jerk, flap.
n flick, spin, twirl, twist, turn, toss, jerk, flap.

flippant *adj* facetious, light-hearted, frivolous, superficial, offhand, flip, glib, pert, saucy (*infml*), cheeky (*infml*), impudent, impertinent, rude, disrespectful, irreverent.
€3 serious, respectful.

flirt *v* chat up, make up to, lead on, philander, dally.
flirt with consider, entertain, toy with, play with, trifle with, dabble in, try.

flit *v* dart, speed, flash, fly, wing, flutter, whisk, skim, slip, pass, bob, dance.

float *v* 1 GLIDE, sail, swim, bob, drift, waft, hover, hang. 2 LAUNCH, initiate, set up, promote.

◨ 1 sink.

floating *adj* **1** AFLOAT, buoyant, unsinkable, sailing, swimming, bobbing, drifting. **2** VARIABLE, fluctuating, movable, migratory, transitory, wandering, unattached, free, uncommitted.

◨ 1 sinking. **2** fixed.

flock *n* herd, swarm, troop, converge, mass, bunch, cluster, huddle, crowd, throng, group, gather, collect, congregate.
n herd, pack, crowd, throng, multitude, mass, bunch, cluster, group, gathering, assembly, congregation.

flog *v* beat, whip, lash, flagellate, scourge, birch, cane, flay, drub, thrash, whack (*infml*), chastise, punish.

flogging *n* beating, whipping, lashing, flagellation, scourging, birching, caning, flaying, thrashing, hiding.

flood *v* **1** DELUGE, inundate, soak, drench, saturate, fill, overflow, immerse, submerge, engulf, swamp, overwhelm, drown. **2** FLOW, pour, stream, rush, surge, gush.
n deluge, inundation, downpour, torrent, flow, tide, stream, rush, spate, outpouring, overflow, glut, excess, abundance, profusion.

◨ drought, trickle, dearth.

floor *n* **1** FLOORING, ground, base, basis. **2** *on the third floor*: storey, level, stage, landing, deck, tier.
v (*infml*) defeat, overwhelm, beat, stump (*infml*), frustrate, confound, perplex, baffle, puzzle, bewilder, disconcert, throw.

flop *v* **1** DROOP, hang, dangle, sag, drop, fall, topple, tumble, slump, collapse. **2** FAIL, misfire, fall flat, founder, fold.
n failure, non-starter, fiasco, debacle, wash-out (*infml*), disaster.

floppy *adj* droopy, hanging, dangling, sagging, limp, loose, baggy, soft,

flabby.

◨ firm.

florid *adj* **1** FLOWERY, ornate, elaborate, fussy, overelaborate, baroque, rococo, flamboyant, grandiloquent. **2** *a florid complexion*: ruddy, red, purple.

◨ 1 plain, simple. **2** pale.

flotsam *n* jetsam, wreckage, debris, rubbish, junk, oddments.

flounder *v* wallow, struggle, grope, fumble, blunder, stagger, stumble, falter.

flourish *v* **1** THRIVE, grow, wax, increase, flower, blossom, bloom, develop, progress, get on, do well, prosper, succeed, boom.
2 BRANDISH, wave, shake, twirl, swing, display, wield, flaunt, parade, vaunt.

◨ 1 decline, languish, fail.
n display, parade, show, gesture, wave, sweep, fanfare, ornament, decoration, panache, pizzazz (*infml*).

flourishing *adj* thriving, blooming, prosperous, successful, booming.

flout *v* defy, disobey, violate, break, disregard, spurn, reject, scorn, jeer at, scoff at, mock, ridicule.

◨ obey, respect, regard.

flow *v* **1** CIRCULATE, ooze, trickle, ripple, bubble, well, spurt, squirt, gush, spill, run, pour, cascade, rush, stream, teem, flood, overflow, surge, sweep, move, drift, slip, slide, glide, roll, swirl. **2** ORIGINATE, derive, arise, spring, emerge, issue, result, proceed, emanate.
n course, flux, tide, current, drift, outpouring, stream, deluge, cascade, spurt, gush, flood, spate, abundance, plenty.

flower *n* **1** BLOOM, blossom, bud, floret.

Flowers include: African violet, alyssum, anemone, aster, aubrietia, azalea, begonia, bluebell, busy lizzie (impatiens), calendula, candytuft, carnation, chrysanthemum, cornflower, cowslip, crocus, cyclamen, daffodil, dahlia, daisy, delphinium, forget-me-not, foxglove (digitalis), freesia, fuchsia, gardenia, geranium, gladioli, hollyhock, hyacinth, iris (flag), lily, lily-of-the-valley, lobelia, lupin, marigold, narcissus, nasturtium, nemesia, nicotiana, night-scented stock, orchid, pansy, petunia, pink (dianthus), phlox, poinsettia, polyanthus, poppy, primrose, primula, rose, salvia, snapdragon (antirrhinum), snowdrop, stock, sunflower, sweet pea, sweet william, tulip, verbena, viola, violet, wallflower, zinnia. *see also* **plant**; **shrub**.

Parts of a flower include: anther, calyx, capitulum, carpel, corolla, corymb, dichasium, filament, gynoecium, monochasium, nectary, ovary, ovule, panicle, pedicel, petal, pistil, raceme, receptacle, sepal, spadix, spike, stalk, stamen, stigma, style, thalamus, torus, umbel.

2 BEST, cream, pick, choice, élite.
v bud, burgeon, bloom, blossom, open, come out.

flowery *adj* florid, ornate, elaborate, fancy, baroque, rhetorical.
🔁 plain, simple.

fluctuate *v* vary, change, alter, shift, rise and fall, seesaw, ebb and flow, alternate, swing, sway, oscillate, vacillate, waver.

fluent *adj* flowing, smooth, easy, effortless, articulate, eloquent, voluble, glib, ready.
🔁 broken, inarticulate, tongue-tied.

fluff *n* down, nap, pile, fuzz, floss, lint, dust.

fluffy *adj* furry, fuzzy, downy, feathery, fleecy, woolly, hairy, shaggy, velvety, silky, soft.

fluid *adj* 1 LIQUID, liquefied,

aqueous, watery, running, runny, melted, molten. 2 *a fluid situation*: variable, changeable, unstable, inconstant, shifting, mobile, adjustable, adaptable, flexible, open. 3 *fluid movements*: flowing, smooth, graceful.
🔁 1 solid. 2 stable.
n liquid, solution, liquor, juice, gas, vapour.

flurry *n* 1 BURST, outbreak, spell, spurt, gust, blast, squall. 2 BUSTLE, hurry, fluster, fuss, to-do, commotion, tumult, whirl, disturbance, stir, flap (*infml*).

flush[1] *v* 1 BLUSH, go red, redden, crimson, colour, burn, glow, suffuse. 2 CLEANSE, wash, rinse, hose, swab, clear, empty, evacuate.
adj 1 ABUNDANT, lavish, generous, full, overflowing, rich, wealthy, moneyed, prosperous, well-off, well-heeled, well-to-do. 2 LEVEL, even, smooth, flat, plane, square, true.

flush[2] *v* start, rouse, disturb, drive out, force out, expel, eject, run to earth, discover, uncover.

fluster *v* bother, upset, embarrass, disturb, perturb, agitate, ruffle, discompose, confuse, confound, unnerve, disconcert, rattle (*infml*), put off, distract.
🔁 calm.
n flurry, bustle, commotion, disturbance, turmoil, state (*infml*), agitation, embarrassment, flap (*infml*), dither, tizzy (*infml*).
🔁 calm.

fluted *adj* grooved, furrowed, channelled, corrugated, ribbed, ridged.

flutter *v* flap, wave, beat, bat, flicker, vibrate, palpitate, agitate, shake, tremble, quiver, shiver, ruffle, ripple, twitch, toss, waver, fluctuate.
n flapping, beat, flicker, vibration, palpitation, tremble, tremor, quiver, shiver, shudder, twitch.

flux *n* fluctuation, instability,

change, alteration, modification, fluidity, flow, movement, motion, transition, development.

Ⅎ stability, rest.

fly v **1** TAKE OFF, rise, ascend, mount, soar, glide, float, hover, flit, wing. **2** RACE, sprint, dash, tear, rush, hurry, speed, zoom, shoot, dart, career.

fly at attack, go for, fall upon.

foam n froth, lather, suds, head, bubbles, effervescence.

v froth, lather, bubble, effervesce, fizz, boil, seethe.

fob off foist, pass off, palm off (*infml*), get rid of, dump, unload, inflict, impose, deceive, put off.

focus n focal point, target, centre, heart, core, nucleus, kernel, crux, hub, axis, linchpin, pivot, hinge.

v converge, meet, join, centre, concentrate, aim, direct, fix, spotlight, home in, zoom in, zero in (*infml*).

fog n **1** MIST, haze, cloud, gloom, murkiness, smog, pea-souper. **2** PERPLEXITY, puzzlement, confusion, bewilderment, daze, trance, vagueness, obscurity.

v mist, steam up, cloud, dull, dim, darken, obscure, blur, confuse, muddle.

foggy adj misty, hazy, smoggy, cloudy, murky, dark, shadowy, dim, indistinct, obscure.

Ⅎ clear.

foil[1] v defeat, outwit, frustrate, thwart, baffle, counter, nullify, stop, check, obstruct, block, circumvent, elude.

Ⅎ abet.

foil[2] n setting, background, relief, contrast, complement, balance.

fold v **1** BEND, ply, double, overlap, tuck, pleat, crease, crumple, crimp, crinkle. **2** (*infml*) *the business folded*: fail, go bust, shut down, collapse, crash. **3** ENFOLD, embrace, hug, clasp, envelop, wrap (up), enclose, entwine, intertwine.

n bend, turn, layer, ply, overlap, tuck, pleat, crease, knife-edge, line, wrinkle, furrow, corrugation.

folder n file, binder, folio, portfolio, envelope, holder.

folk n people, society, nation, race, tribe, clan, family, kin, kindred.

adj ethnic, national, traditional, native, indigenous, tribal, ancestral.

follow v **1** *night follows day*: come after, succeed, come next, replace, supersede, supplant. **2** CHASE, pursue, go after, hunt, track, trail, shadow, tail, hound, catch.

3 ACCOMPANY, go (along) with, escort, attend. **4** RESULT, ensue, develop, emanate, arise. **5** OBEY, comply with, adhere to, heed, mind, observe, conform to, carry out, practise. **6** GRASP, understand, comprehend, fathom.

Ⅎ **1** precede. **3** abandon, desert. **5** disobey.

follow through continue, pursue, see through, finish, complete, conclude, fulfil, implement.

follow up investigate, check out, continue, pursue, reinforce, consolidate.

follower n attendant, retainer, helper, companion, sidekick (*infml*), apostle, disciple, pupil, imitator, emulator, adherent, hanger-on, believer, convert, backer, supporter, admirer, fan, devotee, freak (*infml*), buff (*infml*).

Ⅎ leader, opponent.

following adj subsequent, next, succeeding, successive, resulting, ensuing, consequent, later.

Ⅎ previous.

n followers, suite, retinue, entourage, circle, fans, supporters, support, backing, patronage, clientele, audience, public.

folly n foolishness, stupidity, senselessness, rashness, recklessness, irresponsibility, indiscretion, craziness, madness, lunacy, insanity, idiocy, imbecility, silliness, absurdity, nonsense.

ᴇ wisdom, prudence, sanity.

fond *adj* affectionate, warm, tender, caring, loving, adoring, devoted, doting, indulgent.

fond of partial to, attached to, enamoured of, keen on, addicted to, hooked on.

fondle *v* caress, stroke, pat, pet, cuddle.

food *n* foodstuffs, comestibles, eatables (*infml*), provisions, stores, rations, eats (*infml*), grub (*sl*), nosh (*sl*), refreshment, sustenance, nourishment, nutrition, nutriment, subsistence, feed, fodder, diet, fare, cooking, cuisine, menu, board, table, larder.

Kinds of food include: soup, broth, minestrone, bouillabaisse, borsch, cockaleekie, consommé, gazpacho, goulash, vichyssoise; chips, French fries, ratatouille, sauerkraut, bubble-and-squeak, nut cutlet, cauliflower cheese, chilladas, hummus, macaroni cheese; pasta, cannelloni, fettuccine, ravioli, spaghetti bolognese, tortellini, lasagne; fish and chips, fishcake, fish-finger, fisherman's pie, kedgeree, gefilte fish, kipper, pickled herring, scampi, calamari, prawn cocktail, caviar; meat, casserole, cassoulet, hotpot, shepherd's pie, cottage pie, chilli con carne, biriyani, chop suey, moussaka, paella, samosa, pizza, ragout, risotto, tandoori, vindaloo, Wiener schnitzel, smöga[an]sbord, stroganoff, Scotch woodcock, welsh rarebit, faggot, haggis, sausage, frankfurter, hot dog, fritter, hamburger, McDonald's®, Big Mac®, Wimpy®, bacon, egg, omelette, quiche, tofu, Quorn®, Yorkshire pudding, toad-in-the-hole; ice cream, charlotte russe, egg custard, fruit salad, fruit cocktail, gateau, millefeuilles, pavlova,

profiterole, Sachertorte, soufflé, summer pudding, Bakewell tart, trifle, yogurt, sundae, syllabub, queen of puddings, Christmas pudding, tapioca, rice pudding, roly-poly pudding, spotted dick, zabaglione; doughnut, Chelsea bun, Eccles cake, éclair, flapjack, fruitcake, Danish pastry, Genoa cake, Battenburg cake, Madeira cake, lardy cake, hot-cross-bun, ginger nut, gingerbread, shortbread, ginger snap, macaroon, Garibaldi biscuit; bread, French bread, French toast, pumpernickel, cottage loaf, croissant; gravy, fondue, salad cream, mayonnaise, French dressing; sauces: tartare, Worcestershire, bechamel, white, barbecue, tomato ketchup, hollandaise, Tabasco®, apple, mint, cranberry, horseradish, pesto. *see also* **cheese**; **fish**; **fruit**; **meat**; **nut**; **sweets**; **vegetable**.

fool *n* blockhead, fat-head, nincompoop (*infml*), ass (*infml*), chump (*infml*), ninny (*infml*), clot (*infml*), dope (*infml*), wally (*sl*), twit (*infml*), nitwit (*infml*), nit (*infml*), dunce, dimwit, simpleton, halfwit, idiot, imbecile, moron, dupe, sucker (*infml*), mug (*infml*), stooge, clown, buffoon, jester.

v deceive, take in, delude, mislead, dupe, gull, hoodwink, put one over on, trick, hoax, con (*infml*), cheat, swindle, diddle (*infml*), string along (*infml*), have on (*infml*), kid (*infml*), tease, joke, jest.

fool about lark about, horse around (*sl*), play about, mess about (*infml*), mess around (*infml*).

foolhardy *adj* rash, reckless, imprudent, ill-advised, irresponsible.

ᴇ cautious, prudent.

foolish *adj* stupid, senseless, unwise, ill-advised, ill-considered, short-sighted, half-baked, daft (*infml*), crazy, mad, insane, idiotic, moronic,

hare-brained, half-witted, simple-minded, simple, unintelligent, inept, inane, silly, absurd, ludicrous, nonsensical.
◪ wise, prudent.

foolproof *adj* idiot-proof, infallible, fail-safe, sure, certain, sure-fire (*infml*), guaranteed.
◪ unreliable.

footing *n* base, foundation, basis, ground, relations, relationship, terms, conditions, state, standing, status, grade, rank, position, balance, foothold, purchase.

footprint *n* footmark, track, trail, trace, vestige.

footwear

Types of footwear include: shoe, court-shoe, brogue, casual, lace-up (*infml*), slip-on (*infml*), slingback, sandal, espadrille, stiletto heel, platform heel, moccasin, Doc Martens®, slipper, flip-flop (*infml*), boot, bootee, wellington boot, welly (*infml*), galosh, gumboot, football boot, rugby boot, tennis shoe, plimsoll, pump, sneaker, trainer, ballet shoe, clog, sabot, snow-shoe, beetle-crushers (*sl*), brothel-creepers (*sl*).

forage *n* fodder, pasturage, feed, food, foodstuffs.
v rummage, search, cast about, scour, hunt, scavenge, ransack, plunder, raid.

forbid *v* prohibit, disallow, ban, proscribe, interdict, veto, refuse, deny, outlaw, debar, exclude, rule out, preclude, prevent, block, hinder, inhibit.
◪ allow, permit, approve.

forbidden *adj* prohibited, banned, proscribed, taboo, vetoed, outlawed, out of bounds.

forbidding *adj* stern, formidable, awesome, daunting, off-putting, uninviting, menacing, threatening,

ominous, sinister, frightening.
◪ approachable, congenial.

force *n* **1** COMPULSION, impulse, influence, coercion, constraint, pressure, duress, violence, aggression. **2** POWER, might, strength, intensity, effort, energy, vigour, drive, dynamism, stress, emphasis. **3** ARMY, troop, body, corps, regiment, squadron, battalion, division, unit, detachment, patrol.
◪ **2** weakness.
v **1** COMPEL, make, oblige, necessitate, urge, coerce, constrain, press, pressurize, lean on (*infml*), press-gang, bulldoze, drive, propel, push, thrust. **2** PRISE, wrench, wrest, extort, exact, wring.

forced *adj* unnatural, stiff, wooden, stilted, laboured, strained, false, artificial, contrived, feigned, affected, insincere.
◪ spontaneous, sincere.

forceful *adj* strong, mighty, powerful, potent, effective, compelling, convincing, persuasive, cogent, telling, weighty, urgent, emphatic, vehement, forcible, dynamic, energetic, vigorous.
◪ weak, feeble.

forebear *n* ancestor, forefather, father, predecessor, forerunner, antecedent.
◪ descendant.

foreboding *n* misgiving, anxiety, worry, apprehension, dread, fear, omen, sign, token, premonition, warning, prediction, prognostication, intuition, feeling.

forecast *v* predict, prophesy, foretell, foresee, anticipate, expect, estimate, calculate.
n prediction, prophecy, expectation, prognosis, outlook, projection, guess, guesstimate (*infml*).

forefront *n* front, front line, firing line, van, vanguard, lead, fore, avant-garde.
◪ rear.

foregoing *adj* preceding, antecedent, above, previous, earlier, former, prior.
☒ following.

foreign *adj* alien, immigrant, imported, international, external, outside, overseas, exotic, faraway, distant, remote, strange, unfamiliar, unknown, uncharacteristic, incongruous, extraneous, borrowed.
☒ native, indigenous.

foreigner *n* alien, immigrant, incomer, stranger, newcomer, visitor.
☒ native.

foremost *adj* first, leading, front, chief, main, principal, primary, cardinal, paramount, central, highest, uppermost, supreme, prime, pre-eminent.

forerunner *n* predecessor, ancestor, antecedent, precursor, harbinger, herald, envoy, sign, token.
☒ successor, follower.

foresee *v* envisage, anticipate, expect, forecast, predict, prophesy, prognosticate, foretell, forebode, divine.

foreshadow *v* prefigure, presage, augur, predict, prophesy, signal, indicate, promise.

foresight *n* anticipation, planning, forethought, far-sightedness, vision, caution, prudence, circumspection, care, readiness, preparedness, provision, precaution.
☒ improvidence.

forestall *v* pre-empt, anticipate, preclude, obviate, avert, head off, ward off, parry, balk, frustrate, thwart, hinder, prevent.

foretaste *n* preview, trailer, sample, specimen, example, whiff, indication, warning, premonition.

foretell *v* prophesy, forecast, predict, prognosticate, augur, presage, signify, foreshadow, forewarn.

forethought *n* preparation, planning, forward planning,

provision, precaution, anticipation, foresight, far-sightedness, circumspection, prudence, caution.
☒ improvidence, carelessness.

forever *adv* continually, constantly, persistently, incessantly, perpetually, endlessly, eternally, always, evermore, for all time, permanently.

foreword *n* preface, introduction, prologue.
☒ appendix, postscript, epilogue.

forfeit *n* loss, surrender, confiscation, sequestration, penalty, fine, damages.
v lose, give up, surrender, relinquish, sacrifice, forgo, renounce, abandon.

forge *v* 1 MAKE, mould, cast, shape, form, fashion, beat out, hammer out, work, create, invent. 2 *forge a document*: fake, counterfeit, falsify, copy, imitate, simulate, feign.

forgery *n* fake, counterfeit, copy, replica, reproduction, imitation, dud (*infml*), phoney (*infml*), sham, fraud.
☒ original.

forget *v* omit, fail, neglect, let slip, overlook, disregard, ignore, lose sight of, dismiss, think no more of, unlearn.
☒ remember, recall, recollect.

forgetful *adj* absent-minded, dreamy, inattentive, oblivious, negligent, lax, heedless.
☒ attentive, heedful.

forgive *v* pardon, absolve, excuse, exonerate, exculpate, acquit, remit, let off, overlook, condone.
☒ punish, censure.

forgiveness *n* pardon, absolution, exoneration, acquittal, remission, amnesty, mercy, clemency, leniency.
☒ punishment, censure, blame.

forgiving *adj* merciful, clement, lenient, tolerant, forbearing, indulgent, kind, humane, compassionate, soft-hearted, mild.
☒ merciless, censorious, harsh.

forgo *v* give up, yield, surrender, relinquish, sacrifice, forfeit, waive,

renounce, abandon, resign, pass up, do without, abstain from, refrain from.
F3 claim, indulge in.

fork v split, divide, part, separate, diverge, branch (off).

forlorn adj deserted, abandoned, forsaken, forgotten, bereft, friendless, lonely, lost, homeless, destitute, desolate, hopeless, unhappy, miserable, wretched, helpless, pathetic, pitiable.
F3 cheerful.

form v 1 SHAPE, mould, model, fashion, make, manufacture, produce, create, found, establish, build, construct, assemble, put together, arrange, organize.
2 COMPRISE, constitute, make up, compose. 3 APPEAR, take shape, materialize, crystallize, grow, develop.
n 1 APPEARANCE, shape, mould, cast, cut, outline, silhouette, figure, build, frame, structure, format, model, pattern, design, arrangement, organization, system. 2 *a form of punishment*: type, kind, sort, order, species, variety, genre, style, manner, nature, character, description.
3 CLASS, year, grade, stream. 4 *on top form*: health, fitness, fettle, condition, spirits. 5 ETIQUETTE, protocol, custom, convention, ritual, behaviour, manners. 6 QUESTIONNAIRE, document, paper, sheet.

formal adj 1 OFFICIAL, ceremonial, stately, solemn, conventional, orthodox, correct, fixed, set, regular.
2 PRIM, starchy, stiff, strict, rigid, precise, exact, punctilious, ceremonious, stilted, reserved.
F3 informal, casual.

formality n custom, convention, ceremony, ritual, procedure, matter of form, bureaucracy, red tape, protocol, etiquette, form, correctness, propriety, decorum, politeness.
F3 informality.

formation n 1 STRUCTURE, construction, composition, constitution, configuration, format, organization, arrangement, grouping, pattern, design, figure. 2 CREATION, generation, production, manufacture, appearance, development, establishment.

former adj past, ex-, one-time, sometime, late, departed, old, old-time, ancient, bygone, earlier, prior, previous, preceding, antecedent, foregoing, above.
F3 current, present, future, following.

formerly adv once, previously, earlier, before, at one time, lately.
F3 currently, now, later.

formidable adj daunting, challenging, intimidating, threatening, frightening, terrifying, terrific, frightful, fearful, great, huge, tremendous, prodigious, impressive, awesome, overwhelming, staggering.

formula n recipe, prescription, proposal, blueprint, code, wording, rubric, rule, principle, form, procedure, technique, method, way.

formulate v create, invent, originate, found, form, devise, work out, plan, design, draw up, frame, define, express, state, specify, detail, develop, evolve.

forsake v desert, abandon, jilt, throw over, discard, jettison, reject, disown, leave, quit, give up, surrender, relinquish, renounce, forgo.

fort n fortress, castle, tower, citadel, stronghold, fortification, garrison, station, camp.

forthcoming adj 1 *their forthcoming wedding*: impending, imminent, approaching, coming, future, prospective, projected, expected.
2 COMMUNICATIVE, talkative, chatty, conversational, sociable, informative, expansive, open, frank, direct.
F3 2 reticent, reserved.

forthright *adj* direct, straightforward, blunt, frank, candid, plain, open, bold, outspoken.
✏ devious, secretive.

fortify *v* **1** STRENGTHEN, reinforce, brace, shore up, buttress, garrison, defend, protect, secure. **2** INVIGORATE, sustain, support, boost, encourage, hearten, cheer, reassure.
✏ **1** weaken.

fortitude *n* courage, bravery, valour, grit, pluck, resolution, determination, perseverance, firmness, strength of mind, willpower, hardihood, endurance, stoicism.
✏ cowardice, fear.

fortuitous *adj* accidental, chance, random, arbitrary, casual, incidental, unforeseen, lucky, fortunate, providential.
✏ intentional, planned.

fortunate *adj* lucky, providential, happy, felicitous, prosperous, successful, well-off, timely, well-timed, opportune, convenient, propitious, advantageous, favourable, auspicious.
✏ unlucky, unfortunate, unhappy.

fortune *n* **1** WEALTH, riches, treasure, mint (*infml*), pile (*infml*), income, means, assets, estate, property, possessions, affluence, prosperity, success. **2** LUCK, chance, accident, providence, fate, destiny, doom, lot, portion, life, history, future.

forward *adj* **1** FIRST, head, front, fore, foremost, leading, onward, progressive, go-ahead, forward-looking, enterprising. **2** CONFIDENT, assertive, pushy, bold, audacious, brazen, brash, barefaced, cheeky (*infml*), impudent, impertinent, fresh (*sl*), familiar, presumptuous. **3** EARLY, advance, precocious, premature, advanced, well-advanced, well-developed.
✏ **1** backward, retrograde. **2** shy, modest. **3** late, retarded.

adv forwards, ahead, on, onward, out, into view.

v advance, promote, further, foster, encourage, support, back, favour, help, assist, aid, facilitate, accelerate, speed, hurry, hasten, expedite, dispatch, send (on), post, transport, ship.
✏ impede, obstruct, hinder, slow.

foster *v* raise, rear, bring up, nurse, care for, take care of, nourish, feed, sustain, support, promote, advance, encourage, stimulate, cultivate, nurture, cherish, entertain, harbour.
✏ neglect, discourage.

foul *adj* **1** DIRTY, filthy, unclean, tainted, polluted, contaminated, rank, fetid, stinking, smelly, putrid, rotten, nauseating, offensive, repulsive, revolting, disgusting, squalid. **2** *foul language*: obscene, lewd, smutty, indecent, coarse, vulgar, gross, blasphemous, abusive. **3** NASTY, disagreeable, wicked, vicious, vile, base, abhorrent, disgraceful, shameful. **4** *foul weather*: bad, unpleasant, rainy, wet, stormy, rough.
✏ **1** clean. **4** fine.

v **1** DIRTY, soil, stain, sully, defile, taint, pollute, contaminate. **2** BLOCK, obstruct, clog, choke, foul up. **3** ENTANGLE, catch, snarl, twist, ensnare.
✏ **1** clean. **2** clear. **3** disentangle.

found *v* **1** START, originate, create, initiate, institute, inaugurate, set up, establish, endow, organize. **2** BASE, ground, bottom, rest, settle, fix, plant, raise, build, erect, construct.

foundation *n* **1** BASE, foot, bottom, ground, bedrock, substance, basis, footing. **2** SETTING UP, establishment, institution, inauguration, endowment, organization, groundwork.

founder[1] *n* originator, initiator, father, mother, benefactor, creator, author, architect, designer, inventor, maker, builder, constructor, organizer.

founder² v sink, go down, submerge, subside, collapse, break down, fall, come to grief, fail, misfire, miscarry, abort, fall through, come to nothing.

fountain n 1 SPRAY, jet, spout, spring, well, wellspring, reservoir, waterworks. 2 SOURCE, origin, fount, font, fountain-head, wellhead.

fracture n break, crack, fissure, cleft, rupture, split, rift, rent, schism, breach, gap, opening.
v break, crack, rupture, split, splinter, chip.
🖅 join.

fragile adj brittle, breakable, frail, delicate, flimsy, dainty, fine, slight, insubstantial, weak, feeble, infirm.
🖅 robust, tough, durable.

fragment n piece, bit, part, portion, fraction, particle, crumb, morsel, scrap, remnant, shred, chip, splinter, shiver, sliver, shard.
v break, shatter, splinter, shiver, crumble, disintegrate, come to pieces, come apart, break up, divide, split (up), disunite.
🖅 hold together, join.

fragmentary adj bitty, piecemeal, scrappy, broken, disjointed, disconnected, separate, scattered, sketchy, partial, incomplete.
🖅 whole, complete.

fragrance n perfume, scent, smell, odour, aroma, bouquet.

fragrant adj perfumed, scented, sweet-smelling, sweet, balmy, aromatic, odorous.
🖅 unscented.

frail adj delicate, brittle, breakable, fragile, flimsy, insubstantial, slight, puny, weak, feeble, infirm, vulnerable.
🖅 robust, tough, strong.

frailty n weakness, foible, failing, deficiency, shortcoming, fault, defect, flaw, blemish, imperfection,

fallibility, susceptibility.
🖅 strength, robustness, toughness.

frame v 1 COMPOSE, formulate, conceive, devise, contrive, concoct, cook up, plan, map out, sketch, draw up, draft, shape, form, model, fashion, mould, forge, assemble, put together, build, construct, fabricate, make. 2 SURROUND, enclose, box in, case, mount. 3 I've been framed: set up, fit up (sl), trap.
n 1 STRUCTURE, fabric, framework, skeleton, carcase, shell, casing, chassis, construction, bodywork, body, build, form. 2 MOUNT, mounting, setting, surround, border, edge.

frame of mind state of mind, mood, humour, temper, disposition, spirit, outlook, attitude.

framework n structure, fabric, bare bones, skeleton, shell, frame, outline, plan, foundation, groundwork.

franchise n concession, licence, charter, authorization, privilege, right, suffrage, liberty, freedom, immunity, exemption.

frank adj honest, truthful, sincere, candid, blunt, open, free, plain, direct, forthright, straight, straightforward, downright, outspoken.
🖅 insincere, evasive.

frankly adv to be frank, to be honest, in truth, honestly, candidly, bluntly, openly, freely, plainly, directly, straight.
🖅 insincerely, evasively.

frantic adj agitated, overwrought, fraught, desperate, beside oneself, furious, raging, mad, wild, raving, frenzied, berserk, hectic.
🖅 calm, composed.

fraternize v mix, mingle, socialize, consort, associate, affiliate, unite, sympathize.
🖅 shun, ignore.

fraud n 1 DECEIT, deception, guile, cheating, swindling, double-dealing, sharp practice, fake, counterfeit, forgery, sham, hoax, trick. **2** (*infml*) CHARLATAN, impostor, pretender, phoney (*infml*), bluffer, hoaxer, cheat, swindler, double-dealer, con man (*infml*).

fraudulent *adj* dishonest, crooked (*infml*), criminal, deceitful, deceptive, false, bogus, phoney (*infml*), sham, counterfeit, swindling, double-dealing.

■ honest, genuine.

fray *n* brawl, scuffle, dust-up (*infml*), free-for-all, set-to, clash, conflict, fight, combat, battle, quarrel, row, rumpus, disturbance, riot.

frayed *adj* ragged, tattered, worn, threadbare, unravelled.

freak *n* **1** MONSTER, mutant, monstrosity, malformation, deformity, irregularity, anomaly, abnormality, aberration, oddity, curiosity, quirk, caprice, vagary, twist, turn. **2** ENTHUSIAST, fanatic, addict, devotee, fan, buff (*infml*), fiend (*infml*), nut (*infml*).
adj abnormal, atypical, unusual, exceptional, odd, queer, bizarre, aberrant, capricious, erratic, unpredictable, unexpected, surprise, chance, fortuitous, flukey.

■ normal, common.

free *adj* **1** AT LIBERTY, at large, loose, unattached, unrestrained, liberated, emancipated, independent, democratic, self-governing. **2** *free time*: spare, available, idle, unemployed, unoccupied, vacant, empty. **3** *free tickets*: gratis, without charge, free of charge, complimentary, on the house. **4** CLEAR, unobstructed, unimpeded, open. **5** GENEROUS, liberal, open-handed, lavish, charitable, hospitable.

■ imprisoned, confined, restricted. **2** busy, occupied.

v release, let go, loose, turn loose, set free, untie, unbind, unchain, unleash,

liberate, emancipate, rescue, deliver, save, ransom, disentangle, disengage, extricate, clear, rid, relieve, unburden, exempt, absolve, acquit.

■ imprison, confine.

free of lacking, devoid of, without, unaffected by, immune to, exempt from, safe from.

freedom *n* **1** LIBERTY, emancipation, deliverance, release, exemption, immunity, impunity. **2** INDEPENDENCE, autonomy, self-government, home rule. **3** RANGE, scope, play, leeway, latitude, licence, privilege, power, free rein, free hand, opportunity, informality.

■ **1** captivity, confinement. **3** restriction.

freely *adv* **1** READILY, willingly, voluntarily, spontaneously, easily. **2** *give freely*: generously, liberally, lavishly, extravagantly, amply, abundantly. **3** *speak freely*: frankly, candidly, unreservedly, openly, plainly.

■ **2** grudgingly. **3** evasively, cautiously.

freeze *v* **1** ICE OVER, ice up, glaciate, congeal, solidify, harden, stiffen. **2** DEEP-FREEZE, ice, refrigerate, chill, cool. **3** STOP, suspend, fix, immobilize, hold.
n **1** FROST, freeze-up. **2** STOPPAGE, halt, standstill, shutdown, suspension, interruption, postponement, stay, embargo, moratorium.

freezing *adj* icy, frosty, glacial, arctic, polar, Siberian, wintry, raw, bitter, biting, cutting, penetrating, numbing, cold, chilly.

■ hot, warm.

freight *n* cargo, load, lading, pay-load, contents, goods, merchandise, consignment, shipment, transportation, conveyance, carriage, haulage.

frenzied *adj* frantic, frenetic, hectic, feverish, desperate, furious, wild, uncontrolled, mad, demented, hysterical.

EX calm, composed.

frenzy n 1 TURMOIL, agitation, distraction, derangement, madness, lunacy, mania, hysteria, delirium, fever. 2 BURST, fit, spasm, paroxysm, convulsion, seizure, outburst, transport, passion, rage, fury. **EX** 1 calm, composure.

frequent adj 1 NUMEROUS, countless, incessant, constant, continual, persistent, repeated, recurring, regular. 2 COMMON, commonplace, everyday, familiar, usual, customary. **EX** 1 infrequent.
v visit, patronize, attend, haunt, hang out at (infml), associate with, hang about with (infml), hang out with (infml).

fresh adj 1 ADDITIONAL, supplementary, extra, more, further, other. 2 NEW, novel, innovative, original, different, unconventional, modern, up-to-date, recent, latest. 3 REFRESHING, bracing, invigorating, brisk, crisp, keen, cool, fair, bright, clear, pure. 4 fresh fruit: raw, natural, unprocessed, crude. 5 REFRESHED, revived, restored, renewed, rested, invigorated, energetic, vigorous, lively, alert. 6 PERT, saucy (infml), cheeky (infml), disrespectful, impudent, insolent, bold, brazen, forward, familiar, presumptuous. **EX** 2 old, hackneyed. 3 stale. 4 processed. 5 tired.

freshen v 1 AIR, ventilate, purify. 2 REFRESH, restore, revitalize, reinvigorate, liven, enliven, spruce up, tart up (infml). **EX** tire.

fret v 1 WORRY, agonize, brood, pine. 2 VEX, irritate, nettle, bother, trouble, torment.

friction n 1 DISAGREEMENT, dissension, dispute, disharmony, conflict, antagonism, hostility, opposition, rivalry, animosity, ill feeling, bad blood, resentment. 2 RUBBING, chafing, irritation, abrasion, scraping, grating, rasping, erosion, wearing away, resistance.

friend n mate (infml), pal (infml), chum (infml), buddy (infml), crony (infml), intimate, confidant(e), bosom friend, soul mate, comrade, ally, partner, associate, companion, playmate, pen-friend, acquaintance, well-wisher, supporter. **EX** enemy, opponent.

friendly adj 1 AMIABLE, affable, genial, kind, kindly, neighbourly, helpful, sympathetic, fond, affectionate, familiar, intimate, close, matey (infml), pally (infml), chummy (infml), companionable, sociable, outgoing, approachable, receptive, comradely, amicable, peaceable, well-disposed, favourable. 2 a friendly atmosphere: convivial, congenial, cordial, welcoming, warm. **EX** 1 hostile, unsociable. 2 cold.

friendship n closeness, intimacy, familiarity, affinity, rapport, attachment, affection, fondness, love, harmony, concord, goodwill, friendliness, alliance, fellowship, comradeship. **EX** enmity, animosity.

fright n shock, scare, alarm, consternation, dismay, dread, apprehension, trepidation, fear, terror, horror, panic.

frighten v alarm, daunt, unnerve, dismay, intimidate, terrorize, scare, startle, scare stiff, terrify, petrify, horrify, appal, shock. **EX** reassure, calm.

frightening adj alarming, daunting, formidable, fearsome, scary, terrifying, hair-raising, bloodcurdling, spine-chilling, petrifying, traumatic.

frightful adj unpleasant, disagreeable, awful, dreadful, fearful, terrible, appalling, shocking, harrowing, unspeakable, dire, grim, ghastly, hideous, horrible, horrid, grisly, macabre, gruesome.

🡢 pleasant, agreeable.

frigid adj **1** UNFEELING, unresponsive, passionless, unloving, cool, aloof, passive, lifeless. **2** FROZEN, icy, frosty, glacial, arctic, cold, chill, chilly, wintry.

🡢 **1** responsive. **2** hot.

frilly adj ruffled, crimped, gathered, frilled, trimmed, lacy, fancy, ornate.

🡢 plain.

fringe n **1** MARGIN, periphery, outskirts, edge, perimeter, limits, borderline. **2** BORDER, edging, trimming, tassel, frill, valance.

adj unconventional, unorthodox, unofficial, alternative, avant-garde.

🡢 conventional, mainstream.

frisk v jump, leap, skip, hop, bounce, caper, dance, gambol, frolic, romp, play, sport.

frisky adj lively, spirited, high-spirited, frolicsome, playful, romping, rollicking, bouncy.

🡢 quiet.

fritter v waste, squander, dissipate, idle, misspend, blow (sl).

frivolity n fun, gaiety, flippancy, facetiousness, jest, light-heartedness, levity, triviality, superficiality, silliness, folly, nonsense.

🡢 seriousness.

frivolous adj trifling, trivial, unimportant, shallow, superficial, light, flippant, jocular, light-hearted, juvenile, puerile, foolish, silly, idle, vain, pointless.

🡢 serious, sensible.

frolic v gambol, caper, romp, play, lark around, rollick, make merry, frisk, prance, cavort, dance.

n fun, amusement, sport, gaiety, jollity, merriment, revel, romp, prank, lark, caper, high jinks, antics.

front n **1** at the front: face, aspect, frontage, façade, outside, exterior, facing, cover, obverse, top, head, lead, vanguard, forefront, front line, foreground, forepart, bow. **2** PRETENCE, show, air, appearance, look, expression, manner, façade, cover, mask, disguise, pretext, cover-up.

🡢 **1** back, rear.

adj fore, leading, foremost, head, first.

🡢 back, rear, last.

in front ahead, leading, first, in advance, before, preceding.

🡢 behind.

frontier n border, boundary, borderline, limit, edge, perimeter, confines, marches, bounds, verge.

frosty adj **1** ICY, frozen, freezing, frigid, wintry, cold, chilly. **2** UNFRIENDLY, unwelcoming, cool, aloof, standoffish, stiff, discouraging.

🡢 warm.

froth n bubbles, effervescence, foam, lather, suds, head, scum.

v foam, lather, ferment, fizz, effervesce, bubble.

frown v scowl, glower, lour, glare, grimace.

n scowl, glower, dirty look (infml), glare, grimace.

frown on disapprove of, object to, dislike, discourage.

🡢 approve of.

frozen adj iced, chilled, icy, icebound, ice-covered, arctic, ice-cold, frigid, freezing, numb, solidified, stiff, rigid, fixed.

🡢 warm.

frugal adj thrifty, penny-wise, parsimonious, careful, provident, saving, economical, sparing, meagre.

🡢 wasteful, generous.

fruit

Varieties of fruit include: apple, Bramley, Cox's Orange Pippin, Golden Delicious, Granny Smith, crab apple; pear, William, Conference; orange, Jaffa, mandarin, mineola, clementine, satsuma, tangerine,

Seville; apricot, peach, plum, nectarine, cherry, sloe, damson, greengage, grape, gooseberry, goosegog (*infml*), rhubarb, tomato; banana, pineapple, olive, lemon, lime, ugli fruit, star fruit, lychee, date, fig, grapefruit, kiwi fruit, mango, avocado; melon, honeydew, cantaloupe, watermelon; strawberry, raspberry, blackberry, bilberry, loganberry, elderberry, blueberry, boysenberry, cranberry; redcurrant, blackcurrant.

fruitful *adj* **1** FERTILE, rich, teeming, plentiful, abundant, prolific, productive. **2** REWARDING, profitable, advantageous, beneficial, worthwhile, well-spent, useful, successful.

🔁 **1** barren. **2** fruitless.

fruition *n* realization, fulfilment, attainment, achievement, completion, maturity, ripeness, consummation, perfection, success, enjoyment.

fruitless *adj* unsuccessful, abortive, useless, futile, pointless, vain, idle, hopeless, barren, sterile.

🔁 fruitful, successful, profitable.

frustrate *v* **1** THWART, foil, balk, baffle, block, check, spike, defeat, circumvent, forestall, counter, nullify, neutralize, inhibit. **2** DISAPPOINT, discourage, dishearten, depress.

🔁 **1** further, promote. **2** encourage.

fuel *n* **1** *a tax on fuel*: combustible, propellant, motive power. **2** PROVOCATION, incitement, encouragement, ammunition, material.

Fuels include: gas, calor gas®, propane, butane, methane, acetylene, electricity, coal, coke, anthracite, charcoal, oil, petrol, gasoline, diesel, derv, paraffin, kerosine, methylated spirit, wood, logs, peat, nuclear power.

v incite, inflame, fire, encourage, fan, feed, nourish, sustain, stoke up.

🔁 discourage, damp down.

fugitive *n* escapee, runaway, deserter, refugee. *adj* fleeting, transient, transitory, passing, short, brief, flying, temporary, ephemeral, elusive.

🔁 permanent.

fulfil *v* complete, finish, conclude, consummate, perfect, realize, achieve, accomplish, perform, execute, discharge, implement, carry out, comply with, observe, keep, obey, conform to, satisfy, fill, answer.

🔁 fail, break.

fulfilment *n* completion, perfection, consummation, realization, achievement, accomplishment, success, performance, execution, discharge, implementation, observance, satisfaction.

🔁 failure.

full *adj* **1** FILLED, loaded, packed, crowded, crammed, stuffed, jammed. **2** ENTIRE, whole, intact, total, complete, unabridged, unexpurgated. **3** THOROUGH, comprehensive, exhaustive, all-inclusive, broad, vast, extensive, ample, generous, abundant, plentiful, copious, profuse. **4** *a full sound*: rich, resonant, loud, deep, clear, distinct. **5** *at full speed*: maximum, top, highest, greatest, utmost.

🔁 **1** empty. **2** partial, incomplete. **3** superficial.

full-grown *adj* adult, grown-up, of age, mature, ripe, developed, full-blown, full-scale.

🔁 young, undeveloped.

fully *adv* completely, totally, utterly, wholly, entirely, thoroughly, altogether, quite, positively, without reserve, perfectly.

🔁 partly.

fumble *v* grope, feel, bungle, botch, mishandle, mismanage.

fume v 1 SMOKE, smoulder, boil, steam. 2 RAGE, storm, rant, rave, seethe.

fumes n exhaust, smoke, gas, vapour, haze, fog, smog, pollution.

fumigate v deodorize, disinfect, sterilize, purify, cleanse.

fun n enjoyment, pleasure, amusement, entertainment, diversion, distraction, recreation, play, sport, game, foolery, tomfoolery, horseplay, skylarking, romp, merrymaking, mirth, jollity, jocularity, joking, jesting.

make fun of rag, jeer at, ridicule, laugh at, mock, taunt, tease, rib (sl).

function n 1 ROLE, part, office, duty, charge, responsibility, concern, job, task, occupation, business, activity, purpose, use. 2 RECEPTION, party, gathering, affair, do (infml), dinner, luncheon.

v work, operate, run, go, serve, act, perform, behave.

functional adj working, operational, practical, useful, utilitarian, utility, plain, hard-wearing.

🖅 useless, decorative.

fund n pool, kitty, treasury, repository, storehouse, store, reserve, stock, hoard, cache, stack, mine, well, source, supply.

v finance, capitalize, endow, subsidize, underwrite, sponsor, back, support, promote, float.

fundamental adj basic, primary, first, rudimentary, elementary, underlying, integral, central, principal, cardinal, prime, main, key, essential, indispensable, vital, necessary, crucial, important.

funds n money, finance, backing, capital, resources, savings, wealth, cash.

funeral n burial, interment, entombment, cremation, obsequies, wake.

fungus

Types of fungus include: black spot, blight, botritis, brown rot, candida, downy mildew, ergot, grey mould, mushroom, orange-peel fungus, penicillium, potato blight, powdery mildew, rust, scab, smut, sooty mould, toadstool, yeast, brewer's yeast. *see also* **mushrooms and toadstools**.

funnel v channel, direct, convey, move, transfer, pass, pour, siphon, filter.

funny adj 1 HUMOROUS, amusing, entertaining, comic, comical, hilarious, witty, facetious, droll, farcical, laughable, ridiculous, absurd, silly. 2 ODD, strange, peculiar, curious, queer, weird, unusual, remarkable, puzzling, perplexing, mysterious, suspicious, dubious.

🖅 1 serious, solemn, sad. 2 normal, ordinary, usual.

furious adj 1 ANGRY, mad (infml), up in arms (infml), livid, enraged, infuriated, incensed, raging, fuming, boiling. 2 VIOLENT, wild, fierce, intense, vigorous, frantic, boisterous, stormy, tempestuous.

🖅 1 calm, pleased.

furnish v equip, fit out, decorate, rig, stock, provide, supply, afford, grant, give, offer, present.

🖅 divest.

furniture n equipment, appliances, furnishings, fittings, fitments, household goods, movables, possessions, effects, things.

Types of furniture include: table, dining-table, gateleg table, refectory table, lowboy, side-table, coffee-table, card table; chair, easy chair, armchair, rocking-chair, recliner, dining-chair, carver, kitchen chair, stool, swivel-chair, high-chair, suite, settee, sofa, couch, studio couch, chesterfield, pouffe, footstool, bean-bag; bed, four-poster, chaise-longue, daybed, bed-settee, divan, camp-bed, bunk, water-bed, cot, cradle; desk, bureau, secretaire, bookcase, cupboard, cabinet, china cabinet, Welsh dresser, sideboard, buffet, dumb-waiter, fireplace, overmantel, fender, firescreen, hallstand, umbrella-stand, mirror, magazine rack; wardrobe, armoire, dressing-table, vanity unit, washstand, chest-of-drawers, tallboy, chiffonier, commode, ottoman, chest, coffer, blanket box.

furrow n groove, channel, trench, hollow, rut, track, line, crease, wrinkle.
v seam, flute, corrugate, groove, crease, wrinkle, draw together, knit.

further adj more, additional, supplementary, extra, fresh, new, other.
v advance, forward, promote, champion, push, encourage, foster, help, aid, assist, ease, facilitate, speed, hasten, accelerate, expedite.
E3 stop, frustrate.

furthermore adv moreover, what's more, in addition, further, besides, also, too, as well, additionally.

furthest adj farthest, furthermost, remotest, outermost, outmost, extreme, ultimate, utmost, uttermost.
E3 nearest.

furtive adj surreptitious, sly, stealthy, secretive, underhand, hidden, covert, secret.
E3 open.

fury n anger, rage, wrath, frenzy, madness, passion, vehemence, fierceness, ferocity, violence, wildness, turbulence, power.
E3 calm, peacefulness.

fusion n melting, smelting, welding, union, synthesis, blending, coalescence, amalgamation, integration, merger, federation.

fuss n bother, trouble, hassle (infml), palaver, to-do (infml), hoo-ha (infml), furore, squabble, row, commotion, stir, fluster, confusion, upset, worry, agitation, flap (infml), excitement, bustle, flurry, hurry.
E3 calm.
v complain, grumble, fret, worry, flap (infml), take pains, bother, bustle, fidget.

fussy adj 1 PARTICULAR, fastidious, scrupulous, finicky, pernickety, difficult, hard to please, choosy (infml), discriminating.
2 FANCY, elaborate, ornate, cluttered.
E3 1 casual, uncritical. 2 plain.

futile adj pointless, useless, worthless, vain, idle, wasted, fruitless, profitless, unavailing, unsuccessful, abortive, unprofitable, unproductive, barren, empty, hollow, forlorn.
E3 fruitful, profitable.

futility n pointlessness, uselessness, worthlessness, vanity, emptiness, hollowness, aimlessness.
E3 use, purpose.

future n hereafter, tomorrow, outlook, prospects, expectations.
E3 past.
adj prospective, designate, to be, fated, destined, to come, forthcoming, in the offing, impending, coming, approaching, expected, planned, unborn, later, subsequent, eventual.
E3 past.

fuzzy adj 1 FRIZZY, fluffy, furry, woolly, fleecy, downy, velvety, napped. 2 BLURRED, unfocused, ill-defined, unclear, vague, faint, hazy, shadowy, woolly, muffled, distorted.
E3 2 clear, distinct.

G

gadget *n* tool, appliance, device, contrivance, contraption, thing, thingumajig (*infml*), invention, novelty, gimmick.

gag[1] mufle, muzzle, silence, quiet, stifle, throttle, suppress, curb, check, still.

gag[2] (*infml*) joke, jest, quip, crack, wisecrack, one-liner, pun, witticism, funny (*infml*).

gaiety *n* happiness, glee, cheerfulness, joie de vivre, jollity, merriment, mirth, hilarity, fun, merrymaking, revelry, festivity, celebration, joviality, good humour, high spirits, light-heartedness, liveliness, brightness, brilliance, sparkle, colour, colourfulness, show, showiness.
F3 sadness, drabness.

gaily *adv* happily, joyfully, merrily, blithely, brightly, brilliantly, colourfully, flamboyantly.
F3 sadly, dully.

gain *v* **1** EARN, make, produce, gross, net, clear, profit, yield, bring in, reap, harvest, win, capture, secure, net, obtain, acquire, procure. **2** REACH, arrive at, come to, get to, attain, achieve, realize. **3** *gain speed*: increase, pick up, gather, collect, advance, progress, improve.
F3 1 lose. 3 lose.
n earnings, proceeds, income, revenue, winnings, profit, return, yield, dividend, growth, increase, increment, rise, advance, progress, headway, improvement, advantage, benefit, attainment, achievement, acquisition.
F3 loss.

gain on close with, narrow the gap, approach, catch up, level with, overtake, outdistance, leave behind.

gala *n* festivity, celebration, festival, carnival, jubilee, jamboree, fête, fair, pageant, procession.

gale *n* **1** WIND, squall, storm, hurricane, tornado, typhoon, cyclone. **2** BURST, outburst, outbreak, fit, eruption, explosion, blast.

gallant *adj* chivalrous, gentlemanly, courteous, polite, gracious, courtly, noble, dashing, heroic, valiant, brave, courageous, fearless, dauntless, bold, daring.
F3 ungentlemanly, cowardly.

gallery *n* art gallery, museum, arcade, passage, walk, balcony, circle, gods (*infml*), spectators.

gallop *v* bolt, run, sprint, race, career, fly, dash, tear, speed, zoom, shoot, dart, rush, hurry, hasten.
F3 amble.

galvanize *v* electrify, shock, jolt, prod, spur, provoke, stimulate, stir, move, arouse, excite, fire, invigorate, vitalize.

gamble *v* bet, wager, have a flutter (*infml*), try one's luck, punt, play, game, stake, chance, take a chance, risk, hazard, venture, speculate, back.
n bet, wager, flutter (*infml*), punt, lottery, chance, risk, venture, speculation.

gambler *n* better, punter.

gambol *v* caper, frolic, frisk, skip, jump, bound, hop, bounce.

game[1] *n* **1** RECREATION, play, sport, pastime, diversion, distraction, entertainment, amusement, fun, frolic, romp, joke, jest.

garments

Types of indoor game include:
board game, backgammon, checkers
(*North Amer.*), chess, Cluedo®,
draughts, halma, ludo, mah-jong,
Monopoly®, nine men's morris,
Scrabble®, snakes and ladders, Trivial
Pursuit®; card game, baccarat,
beggar-my-neighbour, bezique,
blackjack, brag, bridge, canasta,
chemin de fer, crib (*infml*), cribbage,
faro, gin rummy, rummy, happy
families, nap (*infml*), napoleon,
newmarket, old maid, patience,
Pelmanism, picquet, poker, draw
poker, stud poker, pontoon, vingt-et-
un, snap, solitaire, twenty-one, whist,
partner whist, solo whist; bagatelle,
pinball, billiards, pool, snooker,
bowling, ten-pin bowling, bowls, darts,
dice, craps, dominoes, roulette, shove
ha'penny, table tennis, ping pong.

Types of children's games include:
battleships, blind man's buff,
charades, Chinese whispers,
consequences, fivestones, forfeits,
hangman, hide-and-seek, I-spy, jacks,
jackstraws, musical chairs, noughts
and crosses, pass the parcel, piggy-
in-the-middle, pin the tail on the donkey,
postman's knock, sardines, Simon
says, spillikins, spin the bottle,
tiddlywinks.

2 COMPETITION, contest, match,
round, tournament, event, meeting.
3 GAME BIRDS, animals, meat, flesh,
prey, quarry, bag, spoils.

*Types of game (killed for
sport) include*: antelope, badger,
bear, blackcock, boar, wild boar,
caribou, deer, fallow deer, red deer,
roe deer, duck, elk, fox, grouse, hazel
grouse, wood grouse, hare, lion,
moose, mountain lion, partridge,
pheasant, quail, rabbit, snipe,
squirrel, stag, tiger, waterfowl.

game² *adj* (*infml*) **1** *game for
anything*: willing, inclined, ready,
prepared, eager. **2** BOLD, daring,
intrepid, brave, courageous, fearless,
resolute, spirited.
⊟ 1 unwilling. **2** cowardly.

gamut *n* scale, series, range, sweep,
scope, compass, spectrum, field, area.

gang *n* group, band, ring, pack,
herd, mob, crowd, circle, clique,
coterie, set, lot, team, crew, squad,
shift, party.

gangster *n* mobster, desperado,
hoodlum, ruffian, rough, tough,
thug, heavy (*sl*), racketeer, bandit,
brigand, robber, criminal, crook
(*infml*).

gaol *see* **jail**.

gaoler *see* **jailer**.

gap *n* **1** SPACE, blank, void, hole,
opening, crack, chink, crevice, cleft,
breach, rift, divide, divergence,
difference. **2** INTERRUPTION, break,
recess, pause, lull, interlude,
intermission, interval.

gape *v* **1** STARE, gaze, gawp (*infml*),
goggle, gawk (*infml*). **2** OPEN, yawn,
part, split, crack.

gaping *adj* open, yawning, broad,
wide, vast, cavernous.
⊟ tiny.

garage *n* lock-up, petrol station,
service station.

garble *v* confuse, muddle, jumble,
scramble, mix up, twist, distort,
pervert, slant, misrepresent, falsify.
⊟ decipher.

garden *n* yard, backyard, plot,
allotment, orchard, park.

garish *adj* gaudy, lurid, loud,
glaring, flashy, showy, tawdry,
vulgar, tasteless.
⊟ quiet, tasteful.

garland *n* wreath, festoon,
decoration, flowers, laurels, honours.
v wreathe, festoon, deck, adorn,
crown.

garments *n* clothes, clothing, wear,
attire, gear (*infml*), togs (*infml*),

outfit, get-up (*infml*), dress, costume, uniform.

garnish v decorate, adorn, ornament, trim, embellish, enhance, grace, set off.
Fa divest.
n decoration, ornament, trimming, embellishment, enhancement, relish.

gash v cut, wound, slash, slit, incise, lacerate, tear, rend, split, score, gouge.
n cut, wound, slash, slit, incision, laceration, tear, rent, split, score, gouge.

gasp v pant, puff, blow, breathe, wheeze, choke, gulp.
n pant, puff, blow, breath, gulp, exclamation.

gate n barrier, door, doorway, gateway, opening, entrance, exit, access, passage.

gather v **1** CONGREGATE, convene, muster, rally, round up, assemble, collect, group, amass, accumulate, hoard, stockpile, heap, pile up, build. **2** INFER, deduce, conclude, surmise, assume, understand, learn, hear. **3** FOLD, pleat, tuck, pucker. **4** *gather flowers*: pick, pluck, cull, select, reap, harvest, glean.
Fa 1 scatter, dissipate.

gathering n assembly, convocation, convention, meeting, round-up, rally, get-together, jamboree, party, group, company, congregation, mass, crowd, throng, turnout.

gaudy adj bright, brilliant, glaring, garish, loud, flashy, showy, ostentatious, tinselly, glitzy (*infml*), tawdry, vulgar, tasteless.
Fa drab, plain.

gauge v estimate, guess, judge, assess, evaluate, value, rate, reckon, figure, calculate, compute, count, measure, weigh, determine, ascertain.
n **1** STANDARD, norm, criterion, benchmark, yardstick, rule, guideline, indicator, measure, meter, test, sample, example, model, pattern.

2 SIZE, magnitude, measure, capacity, bore, calibre, thickness, width, span, extent, scope, height, depth, degree.

gaunt adj **1** HAGGARD, hollow-eyed, angular, bony, thin, lean, lank, skinny, scraggy, scrawny, skeletal, emaciated, wasted. **2** BLEAK, stark, bare, desolate, forlorn, dismal, dreary, grim, harsh.
Fa 1 plump.

gawky adj awkward, clumsy, maladroit, gauche, inept, oafish, ungainly, gangling, unco-ordinated, graceless.
Fa graceful.

gay adj **1** HAPPY, joyful, jolly, merry, cheerful, blithe, sunny, carefree, debonair, fun-loving, pleasure-seeking, vivacious, lively, animated, playful, light-hearted. **2** *gay colours*: vivid, rich, bright, brilliant, sparkling, festive, colourful, gaudy, garish, flashy, showy, flamboyant. **3** HOMOSEXUAL, lesbian, queer (*sl*).
Fa 1 sad, gloomy. 3 heterosexual, straight (*sl*).
n homosexual, queer (*sl*), poof (*sl*), lesbian, dike (*sl*).
Fa heterosexual.

gaze v stare, contemplate, regard, watch, view, look, gape, wonder.
n stare, look.

gear n **1** EQUIPMENT, kit, outfit, tackle, apparatus, tools, instruments, accessories. **2** GEARWHEEL, cogwheel, cog, gearing, mechanism, machinery, works. **3** (*infml*) BELONGINGS, possessions, things, stuff, baggage, luggage, paraphernalia. **4** (*infml*) CLOTHES, clothing, garments, attire, dress, garb (*infml*), togs (*infml*), get-up (*infml*).

gel, jell v set, congeal, coagulate, crystallize, harden, thicken, solidify, materialize, come together, finalize, form, take shape.

gelatinous adj jelly-like, jellied, congealed, rubbery, glutinous, gummy, gluey, gooey (*infml*), sticky, viscous.

gem *n* gemstone, precious stone, stone, jewel, treasure, prize, masterpiece, pièce de résistance.

> *Gems and gemstones include:* diamond, white sapphire, zircon, cubic zirconia, marcasite, rhinestone, pearl, moonstone, onyx, opal, mother-of-pearl, amber, citrine, fire opal, topaz, agate, tiger's eye, jasper, morganite, ruby, garnet, rose quartz, beryl, cornelian, coral, amethyst, sapphire, turquoise, lapis lazuli, emerald, aquamarine, bloodstone, jade, peridot, tourmaline, jet.

genealogy *n* family tree, pedigree, lineage, ancestry, descent, derivation, extraction, family, line.

general *adj* **1** *a general statement*: broad, sweeping, blanket, all-inclusive, comprehensive, universal, global, total, across-the-board, widespread, prevalent, extensive, overall, panoramic. **2** VAGUE, ill-defined, indefinite, imprecise, inexact, approximate, loose, unspecific. **3** USUAL, regular, normal, typical, ordinary, everyday, customary, conventional, common, public. **1** particular, limited. **2** specific. **3** rare.

generally *adv* usually, normally, as a rule, by and large, on the whole, mostly, mainly, chiefly, broadly, commonly, universally.

generate *v* produce, engender, whip up, arouse, cause, bring about, give rise to, create, originate, initiate, make, form, breed, propagate. **prevent.**

generation *n* **1** AGE GROUP, age, era, epoch, period, time. **2** PRODUCTION, creation, origination, formation, genesis, procreation, reproduction, propagation, breeding.

generosity *n* liberality, munificence, open-handedness, bounty, charity, magnanimity, philanthropy, kindness, big-heartedness, benevolence, goodness. **meanness, selfishness.**

generous *adj* **1** LIBERAL, free, bountiful, open-handed, unstinting, unsparing, lavish. **2** MAGNANIMOUS, charitable, philanthropic, public-spirited, unselfish, kind, big-hearted, benevolent, good, high-minded, noble. **3** AMPLE, full, plentiful, abundant, copious, overflowing. **1** mean, miserly. **2** selfish. **3** meagre.

genial *adj* affable, amiable, friendly, convivial, cordial, kindly, kind, warm-hearted, warm, hearty, jovial, jolly, cheerful, happy, good-natured, easy-going (*infml*), agreeable, pleasant. **cold.**

genius *n* **1** VIRTUOSO, maestro, master, past master, expert, adept, egghead (*infml*), intellectual, mastermind, brain, intellect. **2** INTELLIGENCE, brightness, brilliance, ability, aptitude, gift, talent, flair, knack, bent, inclination, propensity, capacity, faculty.

gentle *adj* **1** KIND, kindly, amiable, tender, soft-hearted, compassionate, sympathetic, merciful, mild, placid, calm, tranquil. **2** *a gentle slope*: gradual, slow, easy, smooth, moderate, slight, light, imperceptible. **3** SOOTHING, peaceful, serene, quiet, soft, balmy. **1** unkind, rough, harsh, wild.

genuine *adj* real, actual, natural, pure, original, authentic, veritable, true, bona fide, legitimate, honest, sincere, frank, candid, earnest. **artificial, false, insincere.**

germ *n* **1** MICRO-ORGANISM, microbe, bacterium, bacillus, virus, bug (*infml*). **2** BEGINNING, start, origin, source, cause, spark, rudiment, nucleus, root, seed, embryo, bud, sprout.

germinate *v* bud, sprout, shoot, develop, grow, swell.

gesticulate *v* wave, signal, gesture, indicate, sign.

gesture *n* act, action, movement, motion, indication, sign, signal, wave, gesticulation.
v indicate, sign, motion, beckon, point, signal, wave, gesticulate.

get *v* **1** OBTAIN, acquire, procure, come by, receive, earn, gain, win, secure, achieve, realize. **2** *it's getting dark*: become, turn, go, grow. **3** *get him to help*: persuade, coax, induce, urge, influence, sway. **4** MOVE, go, come, reach, arrive. **5** FETCH, collect, pick up, take, catch, capture, seize, grab. **6** CONTRACT, catch, pick up, develop, come down with.
F3 **1** lose. **4** leave.

get across communicate, transmit, convey, impart, put across, bring home to.

get ahead advance, progress, get on, go places (*infml*), thrive, flourish, prosper, succeed, make good, make it, get there (*infml*).
F3 fall behind, fail.

get along 1 COPE, manage, get by, survive, fare, progress, develop.
2 AGREE, harmonize, get on, hit it off.

get at 1 REACH, attain, find, discover.
2 (*infml*) BRIBE, suborn, corrupt, influence. **3** (*infml*) MEAN, intend, imply, insinuate, hint, suggest.
4 (*infml*) CRITICIZE, find fault with, pick on, attack, make fun of.

get away escape, get out, break out, break away, run away, flee, depart, leave.

get back recover, regain, recoup, repossess, retrieve.

get down 1 DEPRESS, sadden, dishearten, dispirit. **2** DESCEND, dismount, disembark, alight, get off.
F3 **1** encourage. **2** board.

get in enter, penetrate, infiltrate, arrive, come, land, embark.

get off 1 *get off a train*: alight, disembark, dismount, descend.
2 REMOVE, detach, separate, shed, get down.
F3 **1** get on. **2** put on.

get on 1 BOARD, embark, mount, ascend. **2** COPE, manage, fare, get along, make out, prosper, succeed.
3 CONTINUE, proceed, press on, advance, progress.
F3 **1** get off.

get out 1 ESCAPE, flee, break out, extricate oneself, free oneself, leave, quit, vacate, evacuate, clear out, clear off (*infml*). **2** *she got out a pen*: take out, produce.

get over 1 RECOVER FROM, shake off, survive. **2** SURMOUNT, overcome, defeat, deal with. **3** COMMUNICATE, get across, convey, put over, impart, explain.

get round 1 CIRCUMVENT, bypass, evade, avoid. **2** PERSUADE, win over, talk round, coax, prevail upon.

get together assemble, collect, gather, congregate, rally, meet, join, unite, collaborate.

get up stand (up), arise, rise, ascend, climb, mount, scale.

ghastly *adj* awful, dreadful, frightful, terrible, grim, gruesome, hideous, horrible, horrid, loathsome, repellent, shocking, appalling.
F3 delightful, attractive.

ghost *n* spectre, phantom, spook (*infml*), apparition, visitant, spirit, wraith, soul, shade, shadow.

ghostly *adj* eerie, spooky (*infml*), creepy, supernatural, unearthly, ghostlike, spectral, wraith-like, phantom, illusory.

giant *n* monster, titan, colossus, Goliath, Hercules.
adj gigantic, colossal, titanic, mammoth, jumbo (*infml*), king-size, huge, enormous, immense, vast, large.

gibe, jibe *n* jeer, sneer, mockery,

ridicule, taunt, derision, scoff, dig (*infml*), crack (*infml*), poke, quip.

giddy *adj* **1** DIZZY, faint, light-headed, unsteady, reeling, vertiginous. **2** SILLY, flighty, wild.

gift *n* **1** PRESENT, offering, donation, contribution, bounty, largess, gratuity, tip, bonus, freebie (*sl*), legacy, bequest, endowment. **2** TALENT, genius, flair, aptitude, bent, knack, power, faculty, attribute, ability, capability, capacity.

gifted *adj* talented, adept, skilful, expert, masterly, skilled, accomplished, able, capable, clever, intelligent, bright, brilliant.

gigantic *adj* huge, enormous, immense, vast, giant, colossal, titanic, mammoth, gargantuan, Brobdingnagian.
☒ tiny, Lilliputian.

giggle *v, n* titter, snigger, chuckle, chortle, laugh.

gilded *adj* gilt, gold, golden, gold-plated.

gimmick *n* attraction, ploy, stratagem, ruse, scheme, trick, stunt, dodge, device, contrivance, gadget.

gingerly *adv* tentatively, hesitantly, warily, cautiously, carefully, delicately.
☒ boldly, carelessly.

gipsy *see* **gypsy**.

girdle *n* belt, sash, band, waistband, corset.

girl *n* lass, young woman, girlfriend, sweetheart, daughter.

girth *n* circumference, perimeter, measure, size, bulk, strap, band.

gist *n* pith, essence, marrow, substance, matter, meaning, significance, import, sense, idea, drift, direction, point, nub, core, quintessence.

give *v* **1** PRESENT, award, confer, offer, lend, donate, contribute, provide, supply, furnish, grant, bestow, endow, gift, make over, hand

over, deliver, entrust, commit, devote. **2** *give news*: communicate, transmit, impart, utter, announce, declare, pronounce, publish, set forth. **3** CONCEDE, allow, admit, yield, give way, surrender. **4** *give trouble*: cause, occasion, make, produce, do, perform. **5** SINK, yield, bend, give way, break, collapse, fall.
☒ **1** take, withhold. **5** withstand.

give away betray, inform on, expose, uncover, divulge, let slip, disclose, reveal, leak, let out.

give in surrender, capitulate, submit, yield, give way, concede, give up, quit.
☒ hold out.

give off emit, discharge, release, give out, send out, throw out, pour out, exhale, exude, produce.

give out 1 DISTRIBUTE, hand out, dole out, deal. **2** ANNOUNCE, declare, broadcast, publish, disseminate, communicate, transmit, impart, notify, advertise.

give up 1 STOP, cease, quit, resign, abandon, renounce, relinquish, waive. **2** SURRENDER, capitulate, give in.
☒ **1** start. **2** hold out.

given *adj* **1** *a given number*: specified, particular, definite. **2** INCLINED, disposed, likely, liable, prone.

glad *adj* **1** PLEASED, delighted, gratified, contented, happy, joyful, merry, cheerful, cheery, bright. **2** WILLING, eager, keen, ready, inclined, disposed.
☒ **1** sad, unhappy. **2** unwilling, reluctant.

glamorous *adj* smart, elegant, attractive, beautiful, gorgeous, enchanting, captivating, alluring, appealing, fascinating, exciting, dazzling, glossy, colourful.
☒ plain, drab, boring.

glamour *n* attraction, allure, appeal, fascination, charm, magic, beauty, elegance, glitter, prestige.

glance *v* peep, peek, glimpse, view,

look, scan, skim, leaf, flip, thumb,
dip, browse.
n peep, peek, glimpse, look.

glare *v* **1** GLOWER, look daggers,
frown, scowl, stare. **2** DAZZLE,
blaze, flame, flare, shine, reflect.
n **1** BLACK LOOK, dirty look (*infml*),
frown, scowl, stare, look.
2 BRIGHTNESS, brilliance, blaze,
flame, dazzle, spotlight.

glaring *adj* blatant, flagrant, open,
conspicuous, manifest, patent,
obvious, outrageous, gross.
🔁 hidden, concealed, minor.

glassy *adj* **1** GLASSLIKE, smooth,
slippery, icy, shiny, glossy,
transparent, clear. **2** *a glassy stare*:
expressionless, blank, empty, vacant,
dazed, fixed, glazed, cold, lifeless,
dull.

glaze *v* coat, enamel, gloss, varnish,
lacquer, polish, burnish.
n coat, coating, finish, enamel,
varnish, lacquer, polish, shine, lustre,
gloss.

gleam *n* glint, flash, beam, ray,
flicker, glimmer, shimmer, sparkle,
glitter, gloss, glow.
v glint, flash, glance, flare, shine,
glisten, glimmer, glitter, sparkle,
shimmer, glow.

glib *adj* fluent, easy, facile, quick,
ready, talkative, plausible, insincere,
smooth, slick, suave, smooth-
tongued.
🔁 tongue-tied, implausible.

glide *v* slide, slip, skate, skim, fly,
float, drift, sail, coast, roll, run, flow.

glimmer *v* glow, shimmer, glisten,
glitter, sparkle, twinkle, wink, blink,
flicker, gleam, shine.
n **1** GLOW, shimmer, sparkle,
twinkle, flicker, glint, gleam.
2 TRACE, hint, suggestion, grain.

glimpse *n* peep, peek, squint,
glance, look, sight, sighting, view.
v spy, espy, spot, catch sight of, sight,
view.

glint *v* flash, gleam, shine, reflect,

glitter, sparkle, twinkle, glimmer.
n flash, gleam, shine, reflection,
glitter, sparkle, twinkle, glimmer.

glisten *v* shine, gleam, glint, glitter,
sparkle, twinkle, glimmer, shimmer.

glitter *v* sparkle, spangle, scintillate,
twinkle, shimmer, glimmer, glisten,
glint, gleam, flash, shine.
n sparkle, coruscation, scintillation,
twinkle, shimmer, glimmer, glint,
gleam, flash, shine, lustre, sheen,
brightness, radiance, brilliance,
splendour, showiness, glamour, tinsel.

gloat *v* triumph, glory, exult, rejoice,
revel in, relish, crow, boast, vaunt,
rub it in (*infml*).

global *adj* universal, worldwide,
international, general, all-
encompassing, total, thorough,
exhaustive, comprehensive, all-
inclusive, encyclopedic, wide-ranging.
🔁 parochial, limited.

globe *n* world, earth, planet, sphere,
ball, orb, round.

gloom *n* **1** DEPRESSION, low spirits,
despondency, dejection, sadness,
unhappiness, glumness, melancholy,
misery, desolation, despair. **2** DARK,
darkness, shade, shadow, dusk,
twilight, dimness, obscurity, cloud,
cloudiness, dullness.
🔁 **1** cheerfulness, happiness.
2 brightness.

gloomy *adj* **1** DEPRESSED, down,
low, despondent, dejected, downcast,
dispirited, down-hearted, sad,
miserable, glum, morose, pessimistic,
cheerless, dismal, depressing.
2 DARK, sombre, shadowy, dim,
obscure, overcast, dull, dreary.
🔁 **1** cheerful. **2** bright.

glorious *adj* **1** ILLUSTRIOUS,
eminent, distinguished, famous,
renowned, noted, great, noble,
splendid, magnificent, grand,
majestic, triumphant. **2** FINE, bright,
radiant, shining, brilliant, dazzling,
beautiful, gorgeous, superb,
excellent, wonderful, marvellous,

delightful, heavenly.
☒ 1 unknown.

glory n 1 FAME, renown, celebrity, illustriousness, greatness, eminence, distinction, honour, prestige, kudos, triumph. 2 PRAISE, homage, tribute, worship, veneration, adoration, exaltation, blessing, thanksgiving, gratitude. 3 BRIGHTNESS, radiance, brilliance, beauty, splendour, resplendence, magnificence, grandeur, majesty, dignity.

gloss[1] n polish, varnish, lustre, sheen, shine, brightness, brilliance, show, appearance, semblance, surface, front, façade, veneer, window-dressing.

gloss over conceal, hide, veil, mask, disguise, camouflage, cover up, whitewash, explain away.

gloss[2] n annotation, note, footnote, explanation, elucidation, interpretation, translation, definition, comment, commentary.
v annotate, define, explain, elucidate, interpret, construe, translate, comment.

glossy adj shiny, sheeny, lustrous, sleek, silky, smooth, glassy, polished, burnished, glazed, enamelled, bright, shining, brilliant.
☒ matt.

glow n 1 LIGHT, gleam, glimmer, radiance, luminosity, brightness, vividness, brilliance, splendour. 2 ARDOUR, fervour, intensity, warmth, passion, enthusiasm, excitement. 3 FLUSH, blush, rosiness, redness, burning.
v 1 SHINE, radiate, gleam, glimmer, burn, smoulder. 2 their faces glowed: flush, blush, colour, redden.

glower v glare, look daggers, frown, scowl.
n glare, black look, dirty look (infml), frown, scowl, stare, look.

glowing adj 1 BRIGHT, luminous, vivid, vibrant, rich, warm, flushed, red, flaming. 2 a glowing review:

complimentary, enthusiastic, ecstatic, rhapsodic, rave (infml).
☒ 1 dull, colourless. 2 restrained.

glue n adhesive, gum, paste, size, cement.
v stick, affix, gum, paste, seal, bond, cement, fix.

glut n surplus, excess, superfluity, surfeit, overabundance, superabundance, saturation, overflow.
☒ scarcity, lack.

glutton n gourmand, gormandizer, guzzler, gorger, gobbler, pig.
☒ ascetic.

gluttony n gourmandise, gourmandism, greed, greediness, voracity, insatiability, piggishness.
☒ abstinence, asceticism.

gnarled adj gnarly, knotted, knotty, twisted, contorted, distorted, rough, rugged, weather-beaten.

gnaw v 1 BITE, nibble, munch, chew, eat, devour, consume, erode, wear, haunt. 2 WORRY, niggle, fret, trouble, plague, nag, prey.

go v 1 MOVE, pass, advance, progress, proceed, make for, travel, journey, start, begin, depart, leave, take one's leave, retreat, withdraw, disappear, vanish. 2 OPERATE, function, work, run, act, perform. 3 EXTEND, spread, stretch, reach, span, continue, unfold. 4 time goes quickly: pass, elapse, lapse, roll on.
☒ break down, fail.
n (infml) 1 have a go: attempt, try, shot (infml), bash (infml), stab (infml), turn. 2 ENERGY, get-up-and-go (infml), vitality, life, spirit, dynamism, effort.

go about approach, begin, set about, address, tackle, attend to, undertake, engage in, perform.

go ahead begin, proceed, carry on, continue, advance, progress, move.

go away depart, leave, clear off (infml), withdraw, retreat, disappear, vanish.

go back return, revert, backslide, retreat.

go by 1 PASS, elapse, flow. **2** *go by the rules*: observe, follow, comply with, heed.

go down descend, sink, set, fall, drop, decrease, decline, deteriorate, degenerate, fail, founder, go under, collapse, fold (*infml*).

go for 1 (*infml*) CHOOSE, prefer, favour, like, admire, enjoy. **2** ATTACK, assail, set about, lunge at.

go in for enter, take part in, participate in, engage in, take up, embrace, adopt, undertake, practise, pursue, follow.

go into discuss, consider, review, examine, study, scrutinize, investigate, inquire into, check out, probe, delve into, analyse, dissect.

go off 1 DEPART, leave, quit, abscond, vanish, disappear. **2** EXPLODE, blow up, detonate. **3** *the milk has gone off*: deteriorate, turn, sour, go bad, rot.

go on 1 CONTINUE, carry on, proceed, persist, stay, endure, last. **2** CHATTER, rabbit (*infml*), witter (*infml*), ramble on. **3** HAPPEN, occur, take place.

go out exit, depart, leave.

go over examine, peruse, study, revise, scan, read, inspect, check, review, repeat, rehearse, list.

go through 1 SUFFER, undergo, experience, bear, tolerate, endure, withstand. **2** INVESTIGATE, check, examine, look, search, hunt, explore. **3** USE, consume, exhaust, spend, squander.

go together match, harmonize, accord, fit.

go with 1 MATCH, harmonize, co-ordinate, blend, complement, suit, fit, correspond. **2** ACCOMPANY, escort, take, usher.
F∃ **1** clash.

go without abstain, forgo, do without, manage without, lack, want.

goad *v* prod, prick, spur, impel, push, drive, provoke, incite, instigate, arouse, stimulate, prompt, urge, nag, hound, harass, annoy, irritate, vex.

go-ahead *n* permission, authorization, clearance, green light (*infml*), sanction, assent, consent, OK (*infml*), agreement.
F∃ ban, veto, embargo.
adj enterprising, pioneering, progressive, ambitious, up-and-coming, dynamic, energetic.
F∃ unenterprising, sluggish.

goal *n* target, mark, objective, aim, intention, object, purpose, end, ambition, aspiration.

gobble *v* bolt, guzzle, gorge, cram, stuff, devour, consume, put away (*infml*), swallow, gulp.

go-between *n* intermediary, mediator, liaison, contact, middleman, broker, dealer, agent, messenger, medium.

God *n* Supreme Being, Creator, Providence, Lord, Almighty, Holy One, Jehovah, Yahweh, Allah, Brahma, Zeus.

god, goddess *n* deity, divinity, idol, spirit, power.

god-forsaken *adj* remote, isolated, lonely, bleak, desolate, abandoned, deserted, forlorn, dismal, dreary, gloomy, miserable, wretched.

godless *adj* ungodly, atheistic, heathen, pagan, irreligious, unholy, impious, sacrilegious, profane, irreverent, bad, evil, wicked.
F∃ godly, pious.

godly *adj* religious, holy, pious, devout, God-fearing, righteous, good, virtuous, pure, innocent.
F∃ godless, impious.

godsend *n* blessing, boon, stroke of luck, windfall, miracle.
F∃ blow, setback.

golden *adj* **1** GOLD, gilded, gilt, yellow, blond(e), fair, bright, shining, lustrous, resplendent. **2** PROSPEROUS, successful, glorious, excellent, happy, joyful, favourable, auspicious, promising, rosy.

good *adj* **1** ACCEPTABLE,

satisfactory, pleasant, agreeable, nice, enjoyable, pleasing, commendable, excellent, great (*infml*), super (*infml*), first-class, first-rate, superior, advantageous, beneficial, favourable, auspicious, helpful, useful, worthwhile, profitable, appropriate, suitable, fitting. **2** *good at her job*: competent, proficient, skilled, expert, accomplished, professional, skilful, clever, talented, gifted, fit, able, capable, dependable, reliable. **3** KIND, considerate, gracious, benevolent, charitable, philanthropic. **4** VIRTUOUS, exemplary, moral, upright, honest, trustworthy, worthy, righteous. **5** WELL-BEHAVED, obedient, well-mannered. **6** THOROUGH, complete, whole, substantial, considerable. ⊞ **1** bad, poor. **2** incompetent. **3** unkind, inconsiderate. **4** wicked, immoral. **5** naughty, disobedient. *n* **1** VIRTUE, morality, goodness, righteousness, right. **2** USE, purpose, avail, advantage, profit, gain, worth, merit, usefulness, service. **3** *for your own good*: welfare, wellbeing, interest, sake, behalf, benefit, convenience.

good-bye *n* farewell, adieu, au revoir, valediction, leave-taking, parting.

good-humoured *adj* cheerful, happy, jovial, genial, affable, amiable, friendly, congenial, pleasant, good-tempered, approachable. ⊞ ill-humoured.

good-looking *adj* attractive, handsome, beautiful, fair, pretty, personable, presentable. ⊞ ugly, plain.

good-natured *adj* kind, kindly, kind-hearted, sympathetic, benevolent, helpful, neighbourly, gentle, good-tempered, approachable, friendly, tolerant, patient.

⊞ ill-natured.

goodness *n* virtue, uprightness, rectitude, honesty, probity, kindness, compassion, graciousness, goodwill, benevolence, unselfishness, generosity, friendliness, helpfulness. ⊞ badness, wickedness.

goods *n* **1** PROPERTY, chattels, effects, possessions, belongings, paraphernalia, stuff, things, gear (*infml*). **2** MERCHANDISE, wares, commodities, stock, freight.

goodwill *n* benevolence, kindness, generosity, favour, friendliness, friendship, zeal. ⊞ ill-will.

gore *v* pierce, penetrate, stab, spear, stick, impale, wound.

gorge *n* canyon, ravine, gully, defile, chasm, abyss, cleft, fissure, gap, pass. *v* feed, guzzle, gobble, devour, bolt, wolf, gulp, swallow, cram, stuff, fill, sate, surfeit, glut, overeat. ⊞ fast.

gorgeous *adj* magnificent, splendid, grand, glorious, superb, fine, rich, sumptuous, luxurious, brilliant, dazzling, showy, glamorous, attractive, beautiful, handsome, good-looking, delightful, pleasing, lovely, enjoyable, good. ⊞ dull, plain.

gory *adj* bloody, sanguinary, bloodstained, blood-soaked, grisly, brutal, savage, murderous.

gossip *n* **1** IDLE TALK, prattle, chitchat, tittle-tattle, rumour, hearsay, report, scandal. **2** GOSSIP-MONGER, scandalmonger, whisperer, prattler, babbler, chatterbox, nosey parker (*infml*), busybody, talebearer, tell-tale, tattler. *v* talk, chat, natter, chatter, gabble, prattle, tattle, tell tales, whisper, rumour.

gouge *v* chisel, cut, hack, incise, score, groove, scratch, claw, gash, slash, dig, scoop, hollow, extract.

gourmet *n* gastronome, epicure,

epicurean, connoisseur, bon vivant.

govern v **1** RULE, reign, direct, manage, superintend, supervise, oversee, preside, lead, head, command, influence, guide, conduct, steer, pilot. **2** *govern one's temper*: dominate, master, control, regulate, curb, check, restrain, contain, quell, subdue, tame, discipline.

government n **1** *blame the government*: administration, executive, ministry, Establishment, authorities, powers that be, state, régime. **2** RULE, sovereignty, sway, direction, management, superintendence, supervision, surveillance, command, charge, authority, guidance, conduct, domination, dominion, control, regulation, restraint.

government systems

> *Government systems include*: absolutism, autocracy, commonwealth, communism, democracy, despotism, dictatorship, empire, federation, hierocracy, junta, kingdom, monarchy, plutocracy, puppet government, republic, theocracy, triumvirate. *see also* **parliaments and political assemblies**

governor n ruler, commissioner, administrator, executive, director, manager, leader, head, chief, commander, superintendent, supervisor, overseer, controller, boss.

gown n robe, dress, frock, dressing-gown, habit, costume.

grab v seize, snatch, take, nab (*infml*), pluck, snap up, catch hold of, grasp, clutch, grip, catch, bag, capture, collar (*infml*), commandeer, appropriate, usurp, annex.

grace n **1** GRACEFULNESS, poise, beauty, attractiveness, loveliness, shapeliness, elegance, tastefulness, refinement, polish, breeding, manners, etiquette, decorum,

decency, courtesy, charm. **2** KINDNESS, kindliness, compassion, consideration, goodness, virtue, generosity, charity, benevolence, goodwill, favour, forgiveness, indulgence, mercy, leniency, pardon, reprieve. **3** *say grace*: blessing, benediction, thanksgiving, prayer.
F₃ **2** cruelty, harshness.
v favour, honour, dignify, distinguish, embellish, enhance, set off, trim, garnish, decorate, ornament, adorn.
F₃ spoil, detract from.

graceful adj easy, flowing, smooth, supple, agile, deft, natural, slender, fine, tasteful, elegant, beautiful, charming, suave.
F₃ graceless, awkward, clumsy, ungainly.

gracious adj elegant, refined, polite, courteous, well-mannered, considerate, sweet, obliging, accommodating, kind, compassionate, kindly, benevolent, generous, magnanimous, charitable, hospitable, forgiving, indulgent, lenient, mild, clement, merciful.
F₃ ungracious.

grade n rank, status, standing, station, place, position, level, stage, degree, step, rung, notch, mark, brand, quality, standard, condition, size, order, group, class, category.
v sort, arrange, categorize, order, group, class, rate, size, rank, range, classify, evaluate, assess, value, mark, brand, label, pigeonhole, type.

gradient n slope, incline, hill, bank, rise, declivity.

gradual adj slow, leisurely, unhurried, easy, gentle, moderate, regular, even, measured, steady, continuous, progressive, step-by-step.
F₃ sudden, precipitate.

gradually adv little by little, bit by bit, imperceptibly, inch by inch, step by step, progressively, by degrees, piecemeal, slowly, gently, cautiously, gingerly, moderately, evenly,

grass

steadily.

graduate *v* **1** *graduate from medical school*: pass, qualify. **2** CALIBRATE, mark off, measure out, proportion, grade, arrange, range, order, rank, sort, group, classify.

graft *n* implant, implantation, transplant, splice, bud, sprout, shoot, scion.
v engraft, implant, insert, transplant, join, splice.

grain *n* **1** BIT, piece, fragment, scrap, morsel, crumb, granule, particle, molecule, atom, jot, iota, mite, speck, modicum, trace. **2** SEED, kernel, corn, cereals. **3** TEXTURE, fibre, weave, pattern, marking, surface.

grand *adj* **1** MAJESTIC, regal, stately, splendid, magnificent, glorious, superb, sublime, fine, excellent, outstanding, first-rate, impressive, imposing, striking, monumental, large, noble, lordly, lofty, pompous, pretentious, grandiose, ambitious. **2** SUPREME, pre-eminent, leading, head, chief, arch, highest, senior, great, illustrious.

🔁 **1** humble, common, poor.

grandeur *n* majesty, stateliness, pomp, state, dignity, splendour, magnificence, nobility, greatness, illustrious, importance.

🔁 humbleness, lowliness, simplicity.

grandiose *adj* pompous, pretentious, high-flown, lofty, ambitious, extravagant, ostentatious, showy, flamboyant, grand, majestic, stately, magnificent, impressive, imposing, monumental.

🔁 unpretentious.

grant *v* **1** GIVE, donate, present, award, confer, bestow, impart, transmit, dispense, apportion, assign, allot, allocate, provide, supply.
2 ADMIT, acknowledge, concede, allow, permit, consent to, agree to, accede to.

🔁 **1** withhold. **2** deny.
n allowance, subsidy, concession, award, bursary, scholarship, gift, donation, endowment, bequest, annuity, pension, honorarium.

granular *adj* grainy, granulated, gritty, sandy, lumpy, rough, crumbly, friable.

graph *n* diagram, chart, table, grid.

graphic *adj* vivid, descriptive, expressive, striking, telling, lively, realistic, explicit, clear, lucid, specific, detailed, blow-by-blow, visual, pictorial, diagrammatic, illustrative.

🔁 vague, impressionistic.

grapple *v* seize, grasp, snatch, grab, grip, clutch, clasp, hold, wrestle, tussle, struggle, contend, fight, combat, clash, engage, encounter, face, confront, tackle, deal with, cope with.

🔁 release, avoid, evade.

grasp *v* **1** HOLD, clasp, clutch, grip, grapple, seize, snatch, grab, catch.
2 *grasp a concept*: understand, comprehend, get (*infml*), follow, see, realize.
n **1** GRIP, clasp, hold, embrace, clutches, possession, control, power.
2 UNDERSTANDING, comprehension, apprehension, mastery, familiarity, knowledge.

grasping *adj* avaricious, greedy, rapacious, acquisitive, mercenary, mean, selfish, miserly, close-fisted, tight-fisted, parsimonious.

🔁 generous.

grass *n* turf, lawn, green, grassland, field, meadow, pasture, prairie, pampas, savanna, steppe.

Types of grass include: bamboo, barley, beard grass, bent, buckwheat, cane, cocksfoot, corn, couch grass, English ryegrass, esparto, fescue, Italian ryegrass, Kentucky bluegrass, kangaroo grass, knot grass, maize, marijuana, marram grass, meadow

grate 242

foxtail, meadow grass, millet, oats,
paddy, pampas grass, papyrus,
rattan, reed, rice, rye, ryegrass,
sorghum, squirrel-tail grass, sugar
cane, switch grass, twitch grass,
wheat, wild oat.

grate v 1 GRIND, shred, mince,
pulverize, rub, rasp, scrape. 2 JAR,
set one's teeth on edge, annoy,
irritate, aggravate (*infml*), get on
one's nerves, vex, irk, exasperate.

grateful adj thankful, appreciative,
indebted, obliged, obligated,
beholden.
E3 ungrateful.

gratify v satisfy, fulfil, indulge,
pander to, humour, favour, please,
gladden, delight, thrill.
E3 frustrate, thwart.

grating[1] adj harsh, rasping,
scraping, squeaky, strident,
discordant, jarring, annoying,
irritating, unpleasant, disagreeable.
E3 harmonious, pleasing.

grating[2] n grate, grill, grid, lattice,
trellis.

gratitude n gratefulness,
thankfulness, thanks, appreciation,
acknowledgement, recognition,
indebtedness, obligation.
E3 ingratitude, ungratefulness.

gratuitous adj wanton, unnecessary,
needless, superfluous, unwarranted,
unjustified, groundless, undeserved,
unprovoked, uncalled-for, unasked-
for, unsolicited, voluntary, free,
gratis, complimentary.
E3 justified, provoked.

gratuity n tip, bonus, perk (*infml*),
gift, present, donation, reward,
recompense.

grave[1] n burial-place, tomb, vault,
crypt, sepulchre, mausoleum, pit,
barrow, tumulus, cairn.

grave[2] adj 1 *a grave mistake*:
important, significant, weighty,
momentous, serious, critical, vital,
crucial, urgent, acute, severe,

dangerous, hazardous. 2 SOLEMN,
dignified, sober, sedate, serious,
thoughtful, pensive, grim, long-faced,
quiet, reserved, subdued, restrained.
E3 1 trivial, light, slight. 2 cheerful.

graveyard n cemetery, burial-
ground, churchyard.

gravity n 1 IMPORTANCE,
significance, seriousness, urgency,
acuteness, severity, danger. 2
SOLEMNITY, dignity, sobriety,
seriousness, thoughtfulness,
sombreness, reserve, restraint.
3 GRAVITATION, attraction, pull,
weight, heaviness.
E3 1 triviality. 2 levity.

graze v scratch, scrape, skin,
abrade, rub, chafe, shave, brush,
skim, touch.
n scratch, scrape, abrasion.

grease n oil, lubrication, fat, lard,
dripping, tallow.

greasy adj oily, fatty, lardy,
buttery, smeary, slimy, slippery,
smooth, waxy.

great adj 1 LARGE, big, huge,
enormous, massive, colossal,
gigantic, mammoth, immense, vast,
impressive. 2 *with great care*:
considerable, pronounced, extreme,
excessive, inordinate. 3 FAMOUS,
renowned, celebrated, illustrious,
eminent, distinguished, prominent,
noteworthy, notable, remarkable,
outstanding, grand, glorious, fine.
4 IMPORTANT, significant, serious,
major, principal, primary, main,
chief, leading. 5 (*infml*) EXCELLENT,
first-rate, superb, wonderful,
marvellous, tremendous, terrific,
fantastic, fabulous.
E3 1 small. 2 slight. 3 unknown. 4
unimportant, insignificant.

greed n 1 HUNGER, ravenousness,
gluttony, gourmandism, voracity,
insatiability. 2 ACQUISITIVENESS,
covetousness, desire, craving,
longing, eagerness, avarice,
selfishness.

Ε∃ 1 abstemiousness, self-restraint.

greedy *adj* **1** HUNGRY, starving, ravenous, gluttonous, gormandizing, voracious, insatiable. **2** ACQUISITIVE, covetous, desirous, craving, eager, impatient, avaricious, grasping, selfish.

Ε∃ 1 abstemious.

green *adj* **1** GRASSY, leafy, verdant, unripe, unseasoned, tender, fresh, budding, blooming, flourishing. **2** *green with envy*: envious, covetous, jealous, resentful. **3** IMMATURE, naïve, unsophisticated, ignorant, inexperienced, untrained, raw, new, recent, young. **4** ECOLOGICAL, environmental, eco-friendly, environmentally aware.

n common, lawn, grass, turf.

greenhouse *n* glasshouse, hothouse, conservatory, pavilion, vinery, orangery.

greet *v* hail, salute, acknowledge, address, accost, meet, receive, welcome.

Ε∃ ignore.

greeting *n* salutation, acknowledgement, wave, hallo, the time of day, address, reception, welcome.

greetings *n* regards, respects, compliments, salutations, best wishes, good wishes, love.

gregarious *adj* sociable, outgoing, extrovert, friendly, affable, social, convivial, cordial, warm.

Ε∃ unsociable.

grey *adj* **1** NEUTRAL, colourless, pale, ashen, leaden, dull, cloudy, overcast, dim, dark, murky. **2** GLOOMY, dismal, cheerless, depressing, dreary, bleak.

grief *n* sorrow, sadness, unhappiness, depression, dejection, desolation, distress, misery, woe, heartbreak, mourning, bereavement, heartache, anguish, agony, pain, suffering, affliction, trouble, regret, remorse.

Ε∃ happiness, delight.

grievance *n* complaint, moan (*infml*), grumble (*infml*), resentment, objection, protest, charge, wrong, injustice, injury, damage, trouble, affliction, hardship, trial, tribulation.

grieve *v* **1** SORROW, mope, lament, mourn, wail, cry, weep. **2** SADDEN, upset, dismay, distress, afflict, pain, hurt, wound.

Ε∃ 1 rejoice. **2** please, gladden.

grim *adj* **1** UNPLEASANT, horrible, horrid, ghastly, gruesome, grisly, sinister, frightening, fearsome, terrible, shocking. **2** STERN, severe, harsh, dour, forbidding, surly, sullen, morose, gloomy, depressing, unattractive.

Ε∃ 1 pleasant. **2** attractive.

grimace *n* frown, scowl, pout, smirk, sneer, face.

v make a face, pull a face, frown, scowl, pout, smirk, sneer.

grime *n* dirt, muck, filth, soot, dust.

grimy *adj* dirty, mucky, grubby, soiled, filthy, sooty, smutty, dusty, smudgy.

Ε∃ clean.

grind *v* crush, pound, pulverize, powder, mill, grate, scrape, gnash, rut, abrade, sand, file, smooth, polish, sharpen, whet.

grip *n* hold, grasp, clasp, embrace, clutches, control, power.

v **1** HOLD, grasp, clasp, clutch, seize, grab, catch. **2** FASCINATE, thrill, enthral, spellbind, mesmerize, hypnotize, rivet, engross, absorb, involve, engage, compel.

grisly *adj* gruesome, gory, grim, macabre, horrid, horrible, ghastly, awful, frightful, terrible, dreadful, abominable, appalling, shocking.

Ε∃ delightful.

grit *n* gravel, pebbles, shingle, sand, dust.

v clench, gnash, grate, grind.

groan *n* moan, sigh, cry, whine, wail, lament, complaint, objection, protest, outcry.

🔁 cheer.

v moan, sigh, cry, whine, wail, lament, complain, object, protest.

🔁 cheer.

groom *v* **1** SMARTEN, neaten, tidy, spruce up, clean, brush, curry, preen, dress. **2** *groomed for her new post*: PREPARE, train, school, educate, drill.

groove *n* furrow, rut, track, slot, channel, gutter, trench, hollow, indentation, score.

🔁 ridge.

grope *v* feel, fumble, scrabble, flounder, cast about, fish, search, probe.

gross *adj* **1** *gross misconduct*: serious, grievous, blatant, flagrant, glaring, obvious, plain, sheer, utter, outright, shameful, shocking. **2** OBSCENE, lewd, improper, indecent, offensive, rude, coarse, crude, vulgar, tasteless. **3** FAT, obese, overweight, big, large, huge, colossal, hulking, bulky, heavy. **4** *gross earnings*: inclusive, all-inclusive, total, aggregate, entire, complete, whole.

🔁 **3** slight. **4** net.

grotesque *adj* bizarre, odd, weird, unnatural, freakish, monstrous, hideous, ugly, unsightly, misshapen, deformed, distorted, twisted, fantastic, fanciful, extravagant, absurd, surreal, macabre.

🔁 normal, graceful.

ground *n* **1** BOTTOM, foundation, surface, land, terrain, dry land, terra firma, earth, soil, clay, loam, dirt, dust. **2** *football ground*: field, pitch, stadium, arena, park.

v **1** BASE, found, establish, set, fix, settle. **2** PREPARE, introduce, initiate, familiarize with, acquaint with, inform, instruct, teach, train, drill, coach, tutor.

groundless *adj* baseless, unfounded, unsubstantiated,

unsupported, empty, imaginary, false, unjustified, unwarranted, unprovoked, uncalled-for.

🔁 well-founded, reasonable, justified.

grounds[1] *n* land, terrain, holding, estate, property, territory, domain, gardens, park, campus, surroundings, fields, acres.

grounds[2] *n* base, foundation, justification, excuse, vindication, reason, motive, inducement, cause, occasion, call, score, account, argument, principle, basis.

group *n* band, gang, pack, team, crew, troop, squad, detachment, party, faction, set, circle, clique, club, society, association, organization, company, gathering, congregation, crowd, collection, bunch, clump, cluster, conglomeration, constellation, batch, lot, combination, formation, grouping, class, classification, category, genus, species.

v **1** GATHER, collect, assemble, congregate, mass, cluster, clump, bunch. **2** *group them according to size*: sort, range, arrange, marshal, organize, order, class, classify, categorize, band, link, associate.

grovel *v* crawl, creep, ingratiate oneself, toady, suck up (*sl*), flatter, fawn, cringe, cower, kowtow, defer, demean oneself.

grow *v* **1** INCREASE, rise, expand, enlarge, swell, spread, extend, stretch, develop, proliferate, mushroom. **2** ORIGINATE, arise, issue, spring, germinate, shoot, sprout, bud, flower, mature, develop, progress, thrive, flourish, prosper. **3** CULTIVATE, farm, produce, propagate, breed, raise. **4** *grow cold*: become, get, go, turn.

🔁 **1** decrease, shrink.

growl *v* snarl, snap, yap, rumble, roar.

grown-up *adj* adult, mature, of age, full-grown, fully-fledged.

young, immature.
n adult, man, woman.
■ child.

growth *n* **1** INCREASE, rise, extension, enlargement, expansion, spread, proliferation, development, evolution, progress, advance, improvement, success, prosperity. **2** TUMOUR, lump, swelling, protuberance, outgrowth.
■ **1** decrease, decline, failure.

grub *v* dig, burrow, delve, probe, root, rummage, forage, ferret, hunt, search, scour, explore.
n maggot, worm, larva, pupa, caterpillar, chrysalis.

grubby *adj* dirty, soiled, unwashed, mucky, grimy, filthy, squalid, seedy, scruffy.
■ clean.

grudge *n* resentment, bitterness, envy, jealousy, spite, malice, enmity, antagonism, hate, dislike, animosity, ill-will, hard feelings, grievance.
■ favour.
v begrudge, resent, envy, covet, dislike, take exception to, object to, mind.

grudging *adj* reluctant, unwilling, hesitant, half-hearted, unenthusiastic, resentful, envious, jealous.

gruelling *adj* hard, difficult, taxing, demanding, tiring, exhausting, laborious, arduous, strenuous, backbreaking, harsh, severe, tough, punishing.
■ easy.

gruesome *adj* horrible, disgusting, repellent, repugnant, repulsive, hideous, grisly, macabre, grim, ghastly, awful, terrible, horrific, shocking, monstrous, abominable.
■ pleasant.

gruff *adj* **1** CURT, brusque, abrupt, blunt, rude, surly, sullen, grumpy, bad-tempered. **2** *a gruff voice*: rough, harsh, rasping, guttural, throaty, husky, hoarse.
■ **1** friendly, courteous.

grumble *v* complain, moan, whine, bleat, grouch, gripe, mutter, murmur, carp, find fault.

grumpy *adj* bad-tempered, ill-tempered, crotchety, crabbed, cantankerous, cross, irritable, surly, sullen, sulky, grouchy, discontented.
■ contented.

guarantee *n* warranty, insurance, assurance, promise, word of honour, pledge, oath, bond, security, collateral, surety, endorsement, testimonial.
v assure, promise, pledge, swear, vouch for, answer for, warrant, certify, underwrite, endorse, secure, protect, insure, ensure, make sure, make certain.

guard *v* protect, safeguard, save, preserve, shield, screen, shelter, cover, defend, patrol, police, escort, supervise, oversee, watch, look out, mind, beware.
n **1** PROTECTOR, defender, custodian, warder, escort, bodyguard, minder (*sl*), watchman, lookout, sentry, picket, patrol, security. **2** PROTECTION, safeguard, defence, wall, barrier, screen, shield, bumper, buffer, pad.

guarded *adj* cautious, wary, careful, watchful, discreet, non-committal, reticent, reserved, secretive, cagey (*infml*).
■ communicative, frank.

guardian *n* trustee, curator, custodian, keeper, warden, protector, preserver, defender, champion, guard, warder, escort, attendant.

guess *v* speculate, conjecture, predict, estimate, judge, reckon, work out, suppose, assume, surmise, think, believe, imagine, fancy, feel, suspect.
n prediction, estimate, speculation, conjecture, supposition, assumption, belief, fancy, idea, notion, theory, hypothesis, opinion, feeling, suspicion, intuition.

guesswork n speculation, conjecture, estimation, reckoning, supposition, assumption, surmise, intuition.

guest n visitor, caller, boarder, lodger, resident, patron, regular.

guidance n leadership, direction, management, control, teaching, instruction, advice, counsel, counselling, help, instructions, directions, guidelines, indications, pointers, recommendations.

guide v lead, conduct, direct, navigate, point, steer, pilot, manoeuvre, usher, escort, accompany, attend, control, govern, manage, oversee, supervise, superintend, advise, counsel, influence, educate, teach, instruct, train.

n **1** LEADER, courier, navigator, pilot, helmsman, steersman, usher, escort, chaperon, attendant, companion, adviser, counsellor, mentor, guru, teacher, instructor. **2** MANUAL, handbook, guidebook, catalogue, directory. **3** GUIDELINE, example, model, standard, criterion, indication, pointer, signpost, sign, marker.

guilt n **1** *he confessed his guilt*: culpability, responsibility, blame, disgrace, dishonour. **2** *a feeling of guilt*: guilty conscience, conscience, shame, self-condemnation, self-reproach, regret, remorse, contrition.
F3 1 innocence, righteousness.
2 shamelessness.

guilty adj **1** CULPABLE, responsible, blamable, blameworthy, offending, wrong, sinful, wicked, criminal, convicted. **2** CONSCIENCE-STRICKEN, ashamed, shamefaced, sheepish, sorry, regretful, remorseful, contrite, penitent, repentant.
F3 1 innocent, guiltless, blameless.
2 shameless.

gulf n bay, bight, basin, gap, opening, separation, rift, split, breach, cleft, chasm, gorge, abyss, void.

gullible adj credulous, suggestible, impressionable, trusting, unsuspecting, foolish, naïve, green, unsophisticated, innocent.
F3 astute.

gully n channel, watercourse, gutter, ditch, ravine.

gulp v swallow, swig, swill, knock back (*infml*), bolt, wolf (*infml*), gobble, guzzle, devour, stuff.
F3 sip, nibble.
n swallow, swig, draught, mouthful.

gum n adhesive, glue, paste, cement.
v stick, glue, paste, fix, cement, seal, clog.

gun n firearm, handgun, pistol, revolver, shooter (*sl*), shooting iron (*sl*), rifle, shotgun, bazooka, howitzer, cannon.

gurgle v bubble, babble, burble, murmur, ripple, lap, splash, crow.
n babble, murmur, ripple.

gush v **1** FLOW, run, pour, stream, cascade, flood, rush, burst, spurt, spout, jet. **2** ENTHUSE, chatter, babble, jabber, go on (*infml*), drivel.
n flow, outflow, stream, torrent, cascade, flood, tide, rush, burst, outburst, spurt, spout, jet.

gust n blast, burst, rush, flurry, blow, puff, breeze, wind, gale, squall.

gusto n zest, relish, appreciation, enjoyment, pleasure, delight, enthusiasm, exuberance, élan, verve, zeal.
F3 distaste, apathy.

gut v *gut fish*: disembowel, draw, clean (out). **2** STRIP, clear, empty, rifle, ransack, plunder, loot, sack, ravage.

guts n **1** INTESTINES, bowels, viscera, entrails, insides, innards (*infml*), belly, stomach. **2** (*infml*) COURAGE, bravery, pluck, grit, nerve, mettle.

gutter n drain, sluice, ditch, trench, trough, channel, duct, conduit, passage, pipe, tube.

guy (*infml*) *n* fellow, bloke (*infml*), chap (*infml*), man, boy, youth, person, individual.

gypsy, gipsy *n* Romany, traveller, wanderer, nomad, tinker.

gyrate *v* turn, revolve, rotate, twirl, pirouette, spin, whirl, wheel, circle, spiral.

H

habit *n* custom, usage, practice, routine, rule, second nature, way, manner, mode, wont, inclination, tendency, bent, mannerism, quirk, addiction, dependence, fixation, obsession, weakness.

habitat *n* home, abode, domain, element, environment, surroundings, locality, territory, terrain.

habitual *adj* **1** CUSTOMARY, traditional, wonted, routine, usual, ordinary, common, natural, normal, standard, regular, recurrent, fixed, established, familiar. **2** *habitual drinker*: confirmed, inveterate, hardened, addicted, dependent, persistent.

Ea 1 occasional, infrequent.

hack¹ *v* cut, chop, hew, notch, gash, slash, lacerate, mutilate, mangle.

hack² *n* scribbler, journalist, drudge, slave.

hackneyed *adj* stale, overworked, tired, worn-out, time-worn, threadbare, unoriginal, corny (*infml*), clichéd, stereotyped, stock, banal, trite, commonplace, common, pedestrian, uninspired.

Ea original, new, fresh.

hag *n* crone, witch, battle-axe (*infml*), shrew, termagant, vixen.

haggard *adj* drawn, gaunt, careworn, thin, wasted, shrunken, pinched, pale, wan, ghastly.

Ea hale.

haggle *v* bargain, negotiate, barter, wrangle, squabble, bicker, quarrel, dispute.

hail¹ *n* barrage, bombardment, volley, torrent, shower, rain, storm.   *v* pelt, bombard, shower, rain, batter, attack, assail.

hail² *v* greet, address, acknowledge, salute, wave, signal to, flag down, shout, call, acclaim, cheer, applaud, honour, welcome.

hair *n* locks, tresses, shock, mop, mane.

hairdresser *n* hairstylist, stylist, barber, coiffeur, coiffeuse.

hairless *adj* bald, bald-headed, shorn, tonsured, shaven, clean-shaven, beardless.

Ea hairy, hirsute.

hair-raising *adj* frightening, scary, terrifying, horrifying, shocking, bloodcurdling, spine-chilling, eerie, alarming, startling, thrilling.

hairstyle *n* style, coiffure, hairdo (*infml*), cut, haircut, set, perm (*infml*).

> *Hairstyles include*: Afro, backcombed, bangs, beehive, bob, bouffant, braid, bun, chignon, corn rows, cowlick, crewcut, crimped, crop, curled, dreadlocks, Eton crop, French pleat, fringe, frizette, marcel wave, mohican, pageboy, perm, pigtail, plait, pompadour, ponytail, pouffe, quiff, ringlets, shingle, short back and sides, sideboards, sideburns, skinhead, tonsure, topknot, undercut; hair-piece, toupee, wig.

hairy *adj* hirsute, bearded, shaggy, bushy, fuzzy, furry, woolly.
F3 bald, clean-shaven.

half *n* fifty per cent, bisection, hemisphere, semicircle, section, segment, portion, share, fraction.
adj semi-, halved, divided, fractional, part, partial, incomplete, moderate, limited.
F3 whole.
adv partly, partially, incompletely, moderately, slightly.
F3 completely.

half-hearted *adj* lukewarm, cool, weak, feeble, passive, apathetic, uninterested, indifferent, neutral.
F3 whole-hearted, enthusiastic.

halfway *adv* midway, in the middle, centrally.
adj middle, central, equidistant, mid, midway, intermediate.

hall *n* hallway, corridor, passage, passageway, entrance-hall, foyer, vestibule, lobby, concert-hall, auditorium, chamber, assembly room.

hallmark *n* stamp, mark, trademark, brand-name, sign, indication, symbol, emblem, device, badge.

hallucinate *v* dream, imagine, see things, daydream, fantasize, freak out (*sl*), trip (*sl*).

hallucination *n* illusion, mirage, vision, apparition, dream, daydream, fantasy, figment, delusion, freak-out (*sl*), trip (*sl*).

halt *v* stop, draw up, pull up, pause, wait, rest, break off, discontinue, cease, desist, quit, end, terminate, check, stem, curb, obstruct, impede.
F3 start, continue.
n stop, stoppage, arrest, interruption, break, pause, rest, standstill, end, close, termination.
F3 start, continuation.

halting *adj* hesitant, stuttering, stammering, faltering, stumbling, broken, imperfect, laboured, awkward.

F3 fluent.

halve *v* bisect, cut in half, split in two, divide, split, share, cut down, reduce, lessen.

hammer *v* hit, strike, beat, drum, bang, bash, pound, batter, knock, drive, shape, form, make.
n mallet, gavel.

hammer out settle, sort out, negotiate, thrash out, produce, bring about, accomplish, complete, finish.

hamper *v* hinder, impede, obstruct, slow down, hold up, frustrate, thwart, prevent, handicap, hamstring, shackle, cramp, restrict, curb, restrain.
F3 aid, facilitate.

hand *n* **1** FIST, palm, paw (*infml*), mitt (*sl*). **2** *give me a hand*: help, aid, assistance, support, participation, part, influence. **3** WORKER, employee, operative, workman, labourer, farm-hand, hireling.
v give, pass, offer, submit, present, yield, deliver, transmit, conduct, convey.

at hand near, close, to hand, handy, accessible, available, ready, imminent.

hand down bequeath, will, pass on, transfer, give, grant.

hand out distribute, deal out, give out, share out, dish out (*infml*), mete out, dispense.

hand over yield, relinquish, surrender, turn over, deliver, release, give, donate, present.
F3 keep, retain.

handbook *n* manual, instruction book, guide, guidebook, companion.

handful *n* few, sprinkling, scattering, smattering.
F3 a lot, many.

handicap *n* obstacle, block, barrier, impediment, stumbling-block, hindrance, drawback, disadvantage, restriction, limitation, penalty, disability, impairment, defect, shortcoming.
F3 assistance, advantage.

v impede, hinder, disadvantage, hold back, retard, hamper, burden, encumber, restrict, limit, disable.
⊞ help, assist.

handicraft *n* craft, art, craftwork, handwork, handiwork.

handiwork *n* work, doing, responsibility, achievement, product, result, design, invention, creation, production, skill, workmanship, craftsmanship, artisanship.

handle *n* grip, handgrip, knob, stock, shaft, hilt.
v 1 TOUCH, finger, feel, fondle, pick up, hold, grasp. 2 *handle a situation*: tackle, treat, deal with, manage, cope with, control, supervise.

handout *n* 1 CHARITY, alms, dole, largess(e), share, issue, free sample, freebie (*sl*). 2 LEAFLET, circular, bulletin, statement, press release, literature.

hands *n* care, custody, possession, charge, authority, command, power, control, supervision.

handsome *adj* 1 GOOD-LOOKING, attractive, fair, personable, elegant. 2 GENEROUS, liberal, large, considerable, ample.
⊞ 1 ugly, unattractive. 2 mean.

handwriting *n* writing, script, hand, fist (*infml*), penmanship, calligraphy.

handy *adj* 1 AVAILABLE, to hand, ready, at hand, near, accessible, convenient, practical, useful, helpful. 2 SKILFUL, proficient, expert, skilled, clever, practical.
⊞ 1 inconvenient. 2 clumsy.

hang *v* 1 SUSPEND, dangle, swing, drape, drop, flop, droop, sag, trail. 2 FASTEN, attach, fix, stick. 3 *hang in the air*: float, drift, hover, linger, remain, cling.

hang about hang around, linger, loiter, dawdle, waste time, associate with, frequent, haunt.

hang back hold back, demur, hesitate, shy away, recoil.

hang on 1 WAIT, hold on, remain, hold out, endure, continue, carry on, persevere, persist. 2 GRIP, grasp, hold fast. 3 DEPEND ON, hinge on, turn on.
⊞ 1 give up.

hanger-on *n* follower, minion, lackey, toady, sycophant, parasite, sponger, dependant.

hang-up *n* inhibition, difficulty, problem, obsession, preoccupation, thing (*infml*), block, mental block.

hanker for hanker after, crave, hunger for, thirst for, want, wish for, desire, covet, yearn for, long for, pine for, itch for.

hankering *n* craving, hunger, thirst, wish, desire, yearning, longing, itch, urge.

haphazard *adj* random, chance, casual, arbitrary, hit-or-miss, unsystematic, disorganized, disorderly, careless, slapdash, slipshod.
⊞ methodical, orderly.

happen *v* occur, take place, arise, crop up, develop, materialize (*infml*), come about, result, ensue, follow, turn out, transpire.

happening *n* occurrence, phenomenon, event, incident, episode, occasion, adventure, experience, accident, chance, circumstance, case, affair.

happiness *n* joy, joyfulness, gladness, cheerfulness, contentment, pleasure, delight, glee, elation, bliss, ecstasy, euphoria.
⊞ unhappiness, sadness.

happy *adj* 1 JOYFUL, jolly, merry, cheerful, glad, pleased, delighted, thrilled, elated, satisfied, content, contented. 2 *a happy coincidence*: lucky, fortunate, felicitous, favourable, appropriate, apt, fitting.
⊞ 1 unhappy, sad, discontented. 2 unfortunate, inappropriate.

harangue *n* diatribe, tirade, lecture, speech, address.
v lecture, preach, hold forth, spout, declaim, address.

harass v pester, badger, harry, plague, torment, persecute, exasperate, vex, annoy, irritate, bother, disturb, hassle (*infml*), trouble, worry, stress, tire, wear out, exhaust, fatigue.

harbour n port, dock, quay, wharf, marina, mooring, anchorage, haven, shelter.

v 1 HIDE, conceal, protect, shelter.
2 *harbour a feeling*: hold, retain, cling to, entertain, foster, nurse, nurture, cherish, believe, imagine.

hard adj 1 SOLID, firm, unyielding, tough, strong, dense, impenetrable, stiff, rigid, inflexible. 2 DIFFICULT, arduous, strenuous, laborious, tiring, exhausting, backbreaking, complex, complicated, involved, knotty, baffling, puzzling, perplexing.
3 HARSH, severe, strict, callous, unfeeling, unsympathetic, cruel, pitiless, merciless, ruthless, unrelenting, distressing, painful, unpleasant.

E7 1 soft, yielding. 2 easy, simple.
3 kind, pleasant.

adv industriously, diligently, assiduously, doggedly, steadily, laboriously, strenuously, earnestly, keenly, intently, strongly, violently, intensely, energetically, vigorously.

hard up poor, broke (*infml*), penniless, impoverished, in the red, bankrupt, bust, short, lacking.

E7 rich.

harden v solidify, set, freeze, bake, stiffen, strengthen, reinforce, fortify, buttress, brace, steel, nerve, toughen, season, accustom, train.

E7 soften, weaken.

hard-headed adj shrewd, astute, businesslike, level-headed, clear-thinking, sensible, realistic, pragmatic, practical, hard-boiled, tough, unsentimental.

E7 unrealistic.

hard-hearted adj callous, unfeeling, cold, hard, stony, heartless,

unsympathetic, cruel, inhuman, pitiless, merciless.

E7 soft-hearted, kind, merciful.

hard-hitting adj condemnatory, critical, unsparing, no-holds-barred, vigorous, forceful, tough.

E7 mild.

hardly adv barely, scarcely, just, only just, not quite, not at all, by no means.

hardship n misfortune, adversity, trouble, difficulty, affliction, distress, suffering, trial, tribulation, want, need, privation, austerity, poverty, destitution, misery.

E7 ease, comfort, prosperity.

hard-wearing adj durable, lasting, strong, tough, sturdy, stout, rugged, resilient.

E7 delicate.

hard-working adj industrious, diligent, assiduous, conscientious, zealous, busy, energetic.

E7 idle, lazy.

hardy adj strong, tough, sturdy, robust, vigorous, fit, sound, healthy.

E7 weak, unhealthy.

harm n damage, loss, injury, hurt, detriment, ill, misfortune, wrong, abuse.

E7 benefit.

v damage, impair, blemish, spoil, mar, ruin, hurt, injure, wound, ill-treat, maltreat, abuse, misuse.

E7 benefit, improve.

harmful adj damaging, detrimental, pernicious, noxious, unhealthy, unwholesome, injurious, dangerous, hazardous, poisonous, toxic, destructive.

E7 harmless.

harmless adj safe, innocuous, non-toxic, inoffensive, gentle, innocent.

E7 harmful, dangerous, destructive.

harmonious adj 1 MELODIOUS, tuneful, musical, sweet-sounding.
2 MATCHING, co-ordinated, balanced, compatible, like-minded, agreeable, cordial, amicable, friendly,

hate

sympathetic.

F3 1 discordant.

harmonize v match, co-ordinate, balance, fit in, suit, tone, blend, correspond, agree, reconcile, accommodate, adapt, arrange, compose.

F3 clash.

harmony n 1 TUNEFULNESS, tune, melody, euphony. 2 *live in harmony*: agreement, unanimity, accord, concord, unity, compatibility, like-mindedness, peace, goodwill, rapport, sympathy, understanding, amicability, friendliness, co-operation, co-ordination, balance, symmetry, correspondence, conformity.

F3 1 discord. 2 conflict.

harness n tackle, gear, equipment, reins, straps, tack.

v control, channel, use, utilize, exploit, make use of, employ, mobilize, apply.

harrowing adj distressing, upsetting, heart-rending, disturbing, alarming, frightening, terrifying, nerve-racking, traumatic, agonizing, excruciating.

harry v badger, pester, nag, chivvy, harass, plague, torment, persecute, annoy, vex, worry, trouble, bother, hassle (*infml*), disturb, molest.

harsh adj 1 SEVERE, strict, Draconian, unfeeling, cruel, hard, pitiless, austere, Spartan, bleak, grim, comfortless. 2 *a harsh sound*: rough, coarse, rasping, croaking, guttural, grating, jarring, discordant, strident, raucous, sharp, shrill, unpleasant. 3 BRIGHT, dazzling, glaring, gaudy, lurid.

F3 1 lenient. 2 soft.

harvest n 1 HARVEST-TIME, ingathering, reaping, collection. 2 CROP, yield, return, produce, fruits, result, consequence.

v reap, mow, pick, gather, collect, accumulate, amass.

hash n mess, botch, muddle, mix-up, jumble, confusion, hotchpotch, mishmash.

haste n hurry, rush, hustle, bustle, speed, velocity, rapidity, swiftness, quickness, briskness, urgency, rashness, recklessness, impetuosity.

F3 slowness.

hasten v hurry, rush, make haste, run, sprint, dash, tear, race, fly, bolt, accelerate, speed (up), quicken, expedite, dispatch, precipitate, urge, press, advance, step up.

F3 dawdle, delay.

hasty adj hurried, rushed, impatient, headlong, rash, reckless, heedless, thoughtless, impetuous, impulsive, hot-headed, fast, quick, rapid, swift, speedy, brisk, prompt, short, brief, cursory.

F3 slow, careful, deliberate.

hat

> *Hats include*: trilby, bowler, fedora, top-hat, Homburg, derby (*US*), pork-pie hat, flat-cap, beret, bonnet, Tam o'Shanter, tammy, deerstalker, hunting-cap, stovepipe hat, stetson, ten-gallon hat, boater, sunhat, panama, straw hat, picture-hat, pill-box, cloche, beanie (*US*), poke-bonnet, mob-cap, turban, fez, sombrero, sou'wester, glengarry, bearskin, busby, peaked cap, sailor-hat, baseball cap, balaclava, hood, snood, toque, helmet, mortar-board, skullcap, yarmulka, mitre, biretta.

hatch v 1 INCUBATE, brood, breed. 2 CONCOCT, formulate, originate, think up, dream up, conceive, devise, contrive, plot, scheme, design, plan, project.

hate v dislike, despise, detest, loathe, abhor, abominate, execrate.

F3 like, love.

n hatred, aversion, dislike, loathing, abhorrence, abomination.

F3 liking, love.

hatred n hate, aversion, dislike, detestation, loathing, repugnance, revulsion, abhorrence, abomination, execration, animosity, ill-will, antagonism, hostility, enmity, antipathy.
E3 liking, love.

haughty adj lofty, imperious, high and mighty, supercilious, cavalier, snooty (infml), contemptuous, disdainful, scornful, superior, snobbish, arrogant, proud, stuck-up (infml), conceited.
E3 humble, modest.

haul v 1 pull, heave, tug, draw, tow, drag, trail, move, transport, convey, carry, cart, lug, hump (infml).
E3 push.
n LOOT, booty, plunder, swag (sl), spoils, takings, gain, yield, find.

haunt v 1 FREQUENT, patronize, visit. 2 memories haunted her: plague, torment, trouble, disturb, recur, prey on, beset, obsess, possess.
n resort, hangout (infml), stamping-ground, den, meeting-place, rendezvous.

haunting adj memorable, unforgettable, persistent, recurrent, evocative, nostalgic, poignant.
E3 unmemorable.

have v 1 OWN, possess, get, obtain, gain, acquire, procure, secure, receive, accept, keep, hold. 2 FEEL, experience, enjoy, suffer, undergo, endure, put up with. 3 CONTAIN, include, comprise, incorporate, consist of. 4 have a baby: give birth to, bear.
E3 1 lack.
  have to must, be forced, be compelled, be obliged, be required, ought, should.

haven n harbour, port, anchorage, shelter, refuge, sanctuary, asylum, retreat.

havoc n chaos, confusion, disorder, disruption, damage, destruction, ruin, wreck, rack and ruin, devastation, waste, desolation.

haywire (infml) adj wrong, tangled, out of control, crazy, mad, wild, chaotic, confused, disordered, disorganized, topsy-turvy.

hazard n risk, danger, peril, jeopardy, threat, death-trap, accident, chance.
E3 safety.
v 1 RISK, endanger, jeopardize, expose. 2 CHANCE, gamble, stake, venture, suggest, speculate.

hazardous adj risky, dangerous, unsafe, perilous, precarious, insecure, chancy, difficult, tricky.
E3 safe, secure.

haze n mist, fog, cloud, steam, vapour, film, mistiness, smokiness, dimness, obscurity.

hazy adj misty, foggy, smoky, clouded, cloudy, milky, fuzzy, blurred, ill-defined, veiled, obscure, dim, faint, unclear, indistinct, vague, indefinite, uncertain.
E3 clear, bright, definite.

head n 1 SKULL, cranium, brain, mind, mentality, brains (infml), intellect, intelligence, understanding, thought. 2 TOP, peak, summit, crown, tip, apex, height, climax, front, fore, lead. 3 LEADER, chief, captain, commander, boss, director, manager, superintendent, principal, head teacher, ruler.
E3 1 foot, tail. 2 base, foot. 3 subordinate.
adj leading, front, foremost, first, chief, main, prime, principal, top, highest, supreme, premier, dominant, pre-eminent.
v lead, rule, govern, command, direct, manage, run, superintend, oversee, supervise, control, guide, steer.
  head for make for, go towards, direct towards, aim for, point to, turn for, steer for.
  head off forestall, intercept, intervene, interpose, deflect, divert, fend off, ward off, avert, prevent, stop.

heading n title, name, headline, rubric, caption, section, division, category, class.

headland n promontory, cape, head, point, foreland.

headlong adj hasty, precipitate, impetuous, impulsive, rash, reckless, dangerous, breakneck, head-first. adv head first, hurriedly, hastily, precipitately, rashly, recklessly, heedlessly, thoughtlessly, wildly.

headquarters n HQ, base (camp), head office, nerve centre.

headstrong adj stubborn, obstinate, intractable, pigheaded, wilful, self-willed, perverse, contrary.

☒ tractable, docile.

headway n advance, progress, way, improvement.

heady adj intoxicating, strong, stimulating, exhilarating, thrilling, exciting.

heal v cure, remedy, mend, restore, treat, soothe, salve, settle, reconcile, patch up.

health n fitness, constitution, form, shape, trim, fettle, condition, tone, state, healthiness, good condition, wellbeing, welfare, soundness, robustness, strength, vigour.

☒ illness, infirmity.

healthy adj 1 WELL, fit, good, fine, in condition, in good shape, in fine fettle, sound, sturdy, robust, strong, vigorous, hale and hearty, blooming, flourishing, thriving. 2 healthy food: wholesome, nutritious, nourishing, bracing, invigorating, healthful.

☒ 1 ill, sick, infirm.

heap n pile, stack, mound, mountain, lot, mass, accumulation, collection, hoard, stockpile, store. v pile, stack, mound, bank, build, amass, accumulate, collect, gather, hoard, stockpile, store, load, burden, shower, lavish.

hear v 1 LISTEN, catch, pick up, overhear, eavesdrop, heed, pay attention. 2 LEARN, find out,

discover, ascertain, understand, gather. 3 JUDGE, try, examine, investigate.

hearing n 1 EARSHOT, sound, range, reach, ear, perception. 2 TRIAL, inquiry, investigation, inquest, audition, interview, audience.

hearsay n rumour, word of mouth, talk, gossip, tittle-tattle, report, buzz (*infml*).

heart n 1 SOUL, mind, character, disposition, nature, temperament, feeling, emotion, sentiment, love, tenderness, compassion, sympathy, pity. 2 lose heart: courage, bravery, boldness, spirit, resolution, determination. 3 CENTRE, middle, core, kernel, nucleus, nub, crux, essence.

☒ 2 cowardice. 3 periphery.

by heart by rote, parrot-fashion, pat, off pat, word for word, verbatim.

Parts of the heart include: aortic valve, ascending aorta, bicuspid valve, carotid artery, descending thoracic aorta, inferior vena cava, left atrium, left pulmonary artery, left pulmonary veins, left ventricle, mitral valve, myocardium, papillary muscle, pulmonary valve, right atrium, right pulmonary artery, right pulmonary veins, right ventricle, superior vena cava, tricuspid valve, ventricular septum.

heartbreaking adj distressing, sad, tragic, harrowing, heart-rending, pitiful, agonizing, grievous, bitter, disappointing.

☒ heartwarming, heartening.

heartbroken adj broken-hearted, desolate, sad, miserable, dejected, despondent, downcast, crestfallen, disappointed, dispirited, grieved, crushed.

☒ delighted, elated.

hearten v comfort, console, reassure, cheer (up), buck up (*infml*).

encourage, boost, inspire, stimulate, rouse, pep up (*infml*).
🖅 dishearten, depress, dismay.

heartfelt *adj* deep, profound, sincere, honest, genuine, earnest, ardent, fervent, whole-hearted, warm.
🖅 insincere, false.

heartless *adj* unfeeling, uncaring, cold, hard, hard-hearted, callous, unkind, cruel, inhuman, brutal, pitiless, merciless.
🖅 kind, considerate, sympathetic, merciful.

heart-rending *adj* harrowing, heartbreaking, agonizing, pitiful, piteous, pathetic, tragic, sad, distressing, moving, affecting, poignant.

heartwarming *adj* pleasing, gratifying, satisfying, cheering, heartening, encouraging, touching, moving, affecting.
🖅 heartbreaking.

hearty *adj* 1 ENTHUSIASTIC, whole-hearted, unreserved, heartfelt, sincere, genuine, warm, friendly, cordial, jovial, cheerful, ebullient, exuberant, boisterous, energetic, vigorous. 2 *a hearty breakfast*: large, sizable, substantial, filling, ample, generous.
🖅 1 half-hearted, cool, cold.

heat *n* 1 HOTNESS, warmth, sultriness, closeness, high temperature, fever. 2 ARDOUR, fervour, fieriness, passion, intensity, vehemence, fury, excitement, impetuosity, earnestness, zeal.
🖅 1 cold(ness). 2 coolness.
v warm, boil, toast, cook, bake, roast, reheat, warm up, inflame, excite, animate, rouse, stimulate, flush, glow.
🖅 cool, chill.

heated *adj* angry, furious, raging, passionate, fiery, stormy, tempestuous, bitter, fierce, intense, vehement, violent, frenzied,

🖅 calm.

heave *v* 1 PULL, haul, drag, tug, raise, lift, hitch, hoist, lever, rise, surge. 2 THROW, fling, hurl, cast, toss, chuck, let fly. 3 RETCH, vomit, throw up (*infml*), spew.

heaven *n* sky, firmament, next world, hereafter, after-life, paradise, utopia, ecstasy, rapture, bliss, happiness, joy.
🖅 hell.

heavenly *adj* 1 BLISSFUL, wonderful, glorious, beautiful, lovely, delightful, out of this world. 2 CELESTIAL, unearthly, supernatural, spiritual, divine, godlike, angelic, immortal, sublime, blessed.
🖅 1 hellish. 2 infernal.

heavy *adj* 1 WEIGHTY, hefty, ponderous, burdensome, massive, large, bulky, solid, dense, stodgy. 2 *heavy work*: hard, difficult, tough, arduous, laborious, strenuous, demanding, taxing, harsh, severe. 3 OPPRESSIVE, intense, serious, dull, tedious.
🖅 1 light. 2 easy.

heavy-handed *adj* clumsy, awkward, unsubtle, tactless, insensitive, thoughtless, oppressive, overbearing, domineering, autocratic.

hectic *adj* busy, frantic, frenetic, chaotic, fast, feverish, excited, heated, furious, wild.
🖅 leisurely.

hedge *n* hedgerow, screen, windbreak, barrier, fence, dike, boundary.
v 1 SURROUND, enclose, hem in, confine, restrict, fortify, guard, shield, protect, safeguard, cover. 2 STALL, temporize, equivocate, dodge, sidestep, evade, duck.

heed *v* listen, pay attention, mind, note, regard, observe, follow, obey.
🖅 ignore, disregard.

heedless *adj* oblivious, unthinking, careless, negligent, rash, reckless, inattentive, unobservant, thoughtless, unconcerned.

F3 heedful, mindful, attentive.

hefty adj heavy, weighty, big, large, burly, hulking, beefy, brawny, strong, powerful, vigorous, robust, strapping, solid, substantial, massive, colossal, bulky, unwieldy.

F3 slight, small.

height n **1** HIGHNESS, altitude, elevation, tallness, loftiness, stature. **2** TOP, summit, peak, pinnacle, apex, crest, crown, zenith, apogee, culmination, climax, extremity, maximum, limit, ceiling.

F3 1 depth.

heighten v raise, elevate, increase, add to, magnify, intensify, strengthen, sharpen, improve, enhance.

F3 lower, decrease, diminish.

hell n **1** heaven and hell: underworld, Hades, inferno, lower regions, nether world, abyss. **2** SUFFERING, anguish, agony, torment, ordeal, nightmare, misery.

F3 1 heaven.

hellish adj INFERNAL, devilish, diabolical, fiendish, accursed, damnable, monstrous, abominable, atrocious, dreadful.

F3 heavenly.

helm n tiller, wheel, driving seat, reins, saddle, command, control, leadership, direction.

help v **1** AID, assist, lend a hand, serve, be of use, collaborate, co-operate, back, stand by, support. **2** IMPROVE, ameliorate, relieve, alleviate, mitigate, ease, facilitate.

F3 1 hinder. **2** worsen.

n aid, assistance, collaboration, co-operation, support, advice, guidance, service, use, utility, avail, benefit.

F3 hindrance.

helper n assistant, deputy, auxiliary, subsidiary, attendant, right-hand man, PA, mate, partner, associate, colleague, collaborator, accomplice, ally, supporter, second.

helpful adj **1** USEFUL, practical, constructive, worthwhile, valuable, beneficial, advantageous. **2** a helpful person: co-operative, obliging, neighbourly, friendly, caring, considerate, kind, sympathetic, supportive.

F3 useless, futile.

helping n serving, portion, share, ration, amount, plateful, piece, dollop (infml).

helpless adj weak, feeble, powerless, dependent, vulnerable, exposed, unprotected, defenceless, abandoned, friendless, destitute, forlorn, incapable, incompetent, infirm, disabled, paralysed.

F3 strong, independent, competent.

hem n edge, border, margin, fringe, trimming.

hem in surround, enclose, box in, confine, restrict.

henpecked adj dominated, subjugated, browbeaten, bullied, intimidated, meek, timid.

F3 dominant.

herald n messenger, courier, harbinger, forerunner, precursor, omen, token, signal, sign, indication. v announce, proclaim, broadcast, advertise, publicize, trumpet, pave the way, precede, usher in, show, indicate, promise.

heraldry

Heraldic terms include: shield, crest, mantling, helmet, supporters, field, charge, compartment, motto, dexter, centre, sinister, annulet, fleur-de-lis, martlet, mullet, rampant, passant, sejant, caboched, statant, displayed, couchant, dormant, urinant, volant, chevron, pile, pall, saltire, quarter, orle, bordure, gyronny, lozenge, impale, escutcheon, antelope, camelopard, cockatrice, eagle, griffin, lion, phoenix, unicorn, wivern, addorsed, bezant, blazon, canton, cinquefoil, quatrefoil, roundel, semé, tierced, undee, urdé.

herbs and spices

Herbs and spices include: angelica, anise, basil, bay, bergamot, borage, camomile, catmint, chervil, chives, comfrey, cumin, dill, fennel, garlic, hyssop, lavender, lemon balm, lovage, marjoram, mint, oregano, parsley, rosemary, sage, savory, sorrel, tarragon, thyme; allspice, caper, caraway seeds, cardamon, cayenne pepper, chilli, cinnamon, cloves, coriander, curry, ginger, mace, mustard, nutmeg, paprika, pepper, saffron, sesame, turmeric, vanilla.

herd *n* drove, flock, swarm, pack, press, crush, mass, horde, throng, multitude, crowd, mob, the masses, rabble.

v **1** FLOCK, congregate, gather, collect, assemble, rally. **2** LEAD, guide, shepherd, round up, drive, force.

hereditary *adj* inherited, bequeathed, handed down, family, ancestral, inborn, inbred, innate, natural, congenital, genetic.

heresy *n* heterodoxy, unorthodoxy, free-thinking, apostasy, dissidence, schism, blasphemy.
Ea orthodoxy.

heretic *n* free-thinker, nonconformist, apostate, dissident, dissenter, revisionist, separatist, schismatic, sectarian, renegade.
Ea conformist.

heretical *adj* heterodox, unorthodox, free-thinking, rationalistic, schismatic, impious, irreverent, iconoclastic, blasphemous.
Ea orthodox, conventional, conformist.

heritage *n* **1** INHERITANCE, legacy, bequest, endowment, lot, portion, share, birthright, due. **2** HISTORY,

past, tradition, culture.

hermit *n* recluse, solitary, monk, ascetic, anchorite.

hero *n* protagonist, lead, celebrity, star, superstar, idol, paragon, goody (*infml*), champion, conqueror.

heroic *adj* brave, courageous, fearless, dauntless, undaunted, lion-hearted, stout-hearted, valiant, bold, daring, intrepid, adventurous, gallant, chivalrous, noble, selfless.
Ea cowardly, timid.

heroism *n* bravery, courage, valour, boldness, daring, intrepidity, gallantry, prowess, selflessness.
Ea cowardice, timidity.

hesitant *adj* hesitating, reluctant, half-hearted, uncertain, unsure, indecisive, irresolute, vacillating, wavering, tentative, wary, shy, timid, halting, stammering, stuttering.
Ea decisive, resolute, confident, fluent.

hesitate *v* pause, delay, wait, be reluctant, be unwilling, think twice, hold back, shrink from, scruple, boggle, demur, vacillate, waver, be uncertain, dither, shilly-shally, falter, stumble, halt, stammer, stutter.
Ea decide.

hesitation *n* pause, delay, reluctance, unwillingness, hesitance, scruple(s), qualm(s), misgivings, doubt, second thoughts, vacillation, uncertainty, indecision, irresolution, faltering, stumbling, stammering, stuttering.
Ea eagerness, assurance.

hew *v* cut, fell, axe, lop, chop, hack, sever, split, carve, sculpt, sculpture, fashion, model, form, shape, make.

heyday *n* peak, prime, flush, bloom, flowering, golden age, boom time.

hidden *adj* **1** *a hidden door:* concealed, covered, shrouded, veiled, disguised, camouflaged, unseen, secret. **2** OBSCURE, dark, occult, secret, covert, close, cryptic, mysterious, abstruse, mystical, latent, ulterior.

☒ 1 showing, apparent. 2 obvious.

hide[1] *v* 1 CONCEAL, cover, cloak, shroud, veil, screen, mask, disguise, camouflage, obscure, shadow, eclipse, bury, stash (*infml*), secrete, withhold, keep dark, suppress.
2 TAKE COVER, shelter, lie low, go to ground, hole up (*infml*).
☒ 1 reveal, show, display.

hide[2] *n* skin, pelt, fell, fur, leather.

hidebound *adj* set, rigid, entrenched, narrow-minded, strait-laced, conventional, ultra-conservative.
☒ liberal, progressive.

hideous *adj* ugly, repulsive, grotesque, monstrous, horrid, ghastly, awful, dreadful, frightful, terrible, grim, gruesome, macabre, terrifying, shocking, appalling, disgusting, revolting, horrible.
☒ beautiful, attractive.

hiding[1] *n* beating, flogging, whipping, caning, spanking, thrashing, walloping (*infml*).

hiding[2] *n* concealment, cover, veiling, screening, disguise, camouflage.

hiding-place *n* hide-away, hideout, lair, den, hole, hide, cover, refuge, haven, sanctuary, retreat.

hierarchy *n* pecking order, ranking, grading, scale, series, ladder, echelons, strata.

high *adj* 1 TALL, lofty, elevated, soaring, towering. 2 GREAT, strong, intense, extreme. 3 IMPORTANT, influential, powerful, eminent, distinguished, prominent, chief, leading, senior. 4 HIGH-PITCHED, soprano, treble, sharp, shrill, piercing. 5 *a high price*: expensive, dear, costly, exorbitant, excessive.
☒ 1 low, short. 3 lowly. 4 deep.
5 cheap.

high-born *adj* noble, aristocratic, blue-blooded, thoroughbred.
☒ low-born.

highbrow *n* intellectual, egghead

(*infml*), scholar, academic.
adj intellectual, sophisticated, cultured, cultivated, academic, bookish, brainy (*infml*), deep, serious, classical.
☒ low-brow.

high-class *adj* upper-class, posh (*infml*), classy (*infml*), top-class, top-flight, high-quality, quality, de luxe, superior, excellent, first-rate, choice, select, exclusive.
☒ ordinary, mediocre.

high-flown *adj* florid, extravagant, exaggerated, elaborate, flamboyant, ostentatious, pretentious, high-standing, grandiose, pompous, bombastic, turgid, artificial, stilted, affected, lofty, highfalutin, la-di-da (*infml*), supercilious.

high-handed *adj* overbearing, domineering, bossy (*infml*), imperious, dictatorial, autocratic, despotic, tyrannical, oppressive, arbitrary.

highlight *n* high point, high spot, peak, climax, best, cream.
v underline, emphasize, stress, accentuate, play up, point up, spotlight, illuminate, show up, set off, focus on, feature.

highly *adv* very, greatly, considerably, decidedly, extremely, immensely, tremendously, exceptionally, extraordinarily, enthusiastically, warmly, well.

highly-strung *adj* sensitive, neurotic, nervy, jumpy, edgy, temperamental, excitable, restless, nervous, tense.
☒ calm.

high-minded *adj* lofty, noble, moral, ethical, principled, idealistic, virtuous, upright, righteous, honourable, worthy.
☒ immoral, unscrupulous.

high-powered *adj* powerful, forceful, driving, aggressive, dynamic, go-ahead, enterprising, energetic, vigorous.

high-spirited *adj* boisterous, bouncy, exuberant, effervescent, frolicsome, ebullient, sparkling, vibrant, vivacious, lively, energetic, spirited, dashing, bold, daring.
E3 quiet, sedate.

hijack *v* commandeer, expropriate, skyjack, seize, take over.

hike *v* ramble, walk, trek, tramp, trudge, plod.
n ramble, walk, trek, tramp, march.

hilarious *adj* funny, amusing, comical, side-splitting, hysterical (*infml*), uproarious, noisy, rollicking, merry, jolly, jovial.
E3 serious, grave.

hilarity *n* mirth, laughter, fun, amusement, levity, frivolity, merriment, jollity, conviviality, high spirits, boisterousness, exuberance, exhilaration.
E3 seriousness, gravity.

hill *n* **1** HILLOCK, knoll, mound, prominence, eminence, elevation, foothill, down, fell, mountain, height. **2** *a steep hill*: slope, incline, gradient, ramp, rise, ascent, acclivity, drop, descent, declivity.

hinder *v* hamper, obstruct, impede, encumber, handicap, hamstring, hold up, delay, retard, slow down, hold back, check, curb, stop, prevent, frustrate, thwart, oppose.
E3 help, aid, assist.

hindrance *n* obstruction, impediment, handicap, encumbrance, obstacle, stumbling-block, barrier, bar, check, restraint, restriction, limitation, difficulty, drag, snag, hitch, drawback, disadvantage, inconvenience, deterrent.
E3 help, aid, assistance.

hinge *v* centre, turn, revolve, pivot, hang, depend, rest.

hint *n* **1** TIP, advice, suggestion, help, clue, inkling, suspicion, tip-off, reminder, indication, sign, pointer, mention, allusion, intimation, insinuation, implication, innuendo.

2 *a hint of garlic*: touch, trace, tinge, taste, dash, soupçon, speck.
v suggest, prompt, tip off, indicate, imply, insinuate, intimate, allude, mention.

hire *v* rent, let, lease, charter, commission, book, reserve, employ, take on, sign up, engage, appoint, retain.
E3 dismiss, fire.
n rent, rental, fee, charge, cost, price.

hiss *v* **1** WHISTLE, shrill, whizz, sizzle. **2** JEER, mock, ridicule, deride, boo, hoot.

historic *adj* momentous, consequential, important, significant, epoch-making, notable, remarkable, outstanding, extraordinary, celebrated, renowned, famed, famous.
E3 unimportant, insignificant, unknown.

historical *adj* real, actual, authentic, factual, documented, recorded, attested, verifiable.
E3 legendary, fictional.

history *n* **1** PAST, olden days, days of old, antiquity. **2** CHRONICLE, record, annals, archives, chronology, account, narrative, story, tale, saga, biography, life, autobiography, memoirs.

hit *v* **1** STRIKE, knock, tap, smack, slap, thrash, whack (*infml*), bash, thump, clout, punch, belt (*infml*), wallop (*infml*), beat, batter. **2** BUMP, collide with, bang, crash, smash, damage, harm.
n **1** STROKE, shot, blow, knock, tap, slap, smack, bash, bump, collision, impact, crash, smash. **2** SUCCESS, triumph, winner (*sl*).
E3 2 failure.

hit back retaliate, reciprocate, counter-attack, strike back.

hit on chance on, stumble on, light on, discover, invent, realize, arrive at, guess.

hit out lash out, assail, attack, rail,

denounce, condemn, criticize.

hitch v 1 FASTEN, attach, tie, harness, yoke, couple, connect, join, unite. 2 PULL, heave, yank (*infml*), tug, jerk, hoist, hike (up) (*infml*). ⏴ 1 unhitch, unfasten.
n delay, hold-up, trouble, problem, difficulty, mishap, setback, hiccup, drawback, snag, catch, impediment, hindrance.

hoard n collection, accumulation, mass, heap, pile, fund, reservoir, supply, reserve, store, stockpile, cache, treasure-trove.
v collect, gather, amass, accumulate, save, put by, lay up, store, stash away (*infml*), stockpile, keep, treasure.
⏴ use, squander.

hoarse adj husky, croaky, throaty, guttural, gravelly, gruff, growling, rough, harsh, rasping, grating, raucous, discordant.
⏴ clear, smooth.

hoax n trick, prank, practical joke, put-on, joke, leg-pull (*infml*), spoof, fake, fraud, deception, bluff, humbug, cheat, swindle, con (*infml*).
v trick, deceive, take in, fool, dupe, gull, delude, have on (*infml*), pull someone's leg (*infml*), con (*infml*), swindle, take for a ride (*infml*), cheat, hoodwink, bamboozle (*infml*), bluff.

hobble v limp, stumble, falter, stagger, totter, dodder, shuffle.

hobby n pastime, diversion, recreation, relaxation, pursuit, sideline.

hoist v lift, elevate, raise, erect, jack up, winch up, heave, rear, uplift.
n jack, winch, crane, tackle, lift, elevator.

hold v 1 GRIP, grasp, clutch, clasp, embrace, have, own, possess, keep, retain. 2 *hold a meeting*: conduct, carry on, continue, call, summon, convene, assemble. 3 CONSIDER, regard, deem, judge, reckon, think, believe, maintain. 4 BEAR, support, sustain, carry, comprise, contain,

accommodate. 5 IMPRISON, detain, stop, arrest, check, curb, restrain. 6 CLING, stick, adhere, stay.
⏴ 1 drop. 5 release, free, liberate.
n 1 GRIP, grasp, clasp, embrace. 2 INFLUENCE, power, sway, mastery, dominance, authority, control, leverage.

hold back 1 CONTROL, curb, check, restrain, suppress, stifle, retain, withhold, repress, inhibit. 2 HESITATE, delay, desist, refrain, shrink, refuse.
⏴ 1 release.

hold forth speak, talk, lecture, discourse, orate, preach, declaim.

hold off 1 FEND OFF, ward off, stave off, keep off, repel, rebuff. 2 PUT OFF, postpone, defer, delay, wait.

hold out 1 OFFER, give, present, extend. 2 LAST, continue, persist, endure, persevere, stand fast, hang on.
⏴ 2 give in, yield.

hold up 1 SUPPORT, sustain, brace, shore up, lift, raise. 2 DELAY, detain, retard, slow, hinder, impede.

hold with agree with, go along with, approve of, countenance, support, subscribe to, accept.

holder n 1 *holders of British passports*: bearer, owner, possessor, proprietor, keeper, custodian, occupant, incumbent. 2 CONTAINER, receptacle, case, housing, cover, sheath, rest, stand.

hold-up n 1 DELAY, wait, hitch, setback, snag, difficulty, trouble, obstruction, stoppage, (traffic) jam, bottle-neck. 2 ROBBERY, heist (*sl*), stick-up (*sl*).

hole n aperture, opening, orifice, pore, puncture, perforation, eyelet, tear, split, vent, outlet, shaft, slot, gap, breach, break, crack, fissure, fault, defect, flaw, dent, dimple, depression, hollow, cavity, crater, pit, excavation, cavern, cave, chamber, pocket, niche, recess, burrow, nest, lair, retreat.

holiday *n* vacation, recess, leave, time off, day off, break, rest, half-term, bank-holiday, feast-day, festival, celebration, anniversary.

holiness *n* sacredness, sanctity, spirituality, divinity, piety, devoutness, godliness, saintliness, virtuousness, righteousness, purity.
🔁 impiety.

hollow *adj* **1** CONCAVE, indented, depressed, sunken, deep, cavernous, empty, vacant, unfilled. **2** FALSE, artificial, deceptive, insincere, meaningless, empty, vain, futile, fruitless, worthless.
🔁 **1** solid. **2** real.
n hole, pit, well, cavity, crater, excavation, cavern, cave, depression, concavity, basin, bowl, cup, dimple, dent, indentation, groove, channel, trough, valley.
v dig, excavate, burrow, tunnel, scoop, gouge, channel, groove, furrow, pit, dent, indent.

holy *adj* **1** *holy ground*: sacred, hallowed, consecrated, sanctified, dedicated, blessed, venerated, revered, spiritual, divine, evangelical. **2** PIOUS, religious, devout, godly, God-fearing, saintly, virtuous, good, righteous, faithful, pure, perfect.
🔁 **1** unsanctified. **2** impious, irreligious.

homage *n* recognition, acknowledgement, tribute, honour, praise, adulation, admiration, regard, esteem, respect, deference, reverence, adoration, awe, veneration, worship, devotion.

home *n* residence, domicile, dwelling-place, abode, base, house, pied-à-terre, fireside, birthplace, home town, home ground, territory, habitat, element.
adj domestic, household, family, internal, local, national, inland.
🔁 foreign, international.
at home 1 COMFORTABLE, relaxed, at ease. **2** FAMILIAR, knowledgeable,

experienced, skilled.

homeland *n* native land, native country, fatherland, motherland.

homeless *adj* itinerant, travelling, nomadic, wandering, vagrant, rootless, unsettled, displaced, dispossessed, evicted, exiled, outcast, abandoned, forsaken, destitute, down-and-out.
n travellers, vagabonds, vagrants, tramps, down-and-outs, dossers (*sl*), squatters.

homely *adj* homelike, homey, comfortable, cosy, snug, relaxed, informal, friendly, intimate, familiar, everyday, ordinary, domestic, natural, plain, simple, modest, unassuming, unpretentious, unsophisticated, folksy, homespun.
🔁 grand, formal.

homicide *n* murder, manslaughter, assassination, killing, bloodshed.

homogeneous *adj* uniform, consistent, unvarying, identical, similar, alike, akin, kindred, analogous, comparable, harmonious, compatible.
🔁 different.

homosexual *n* gay, queer (*sl*), poof (*sl*), lesbian, dike (*sl*).
🔁 heterosexual, straight (*sl*).
adj gay, queer (*sl*), lesbian.

hone *v* sharpen, whet, point, edge, grind, file, polish.

honest *adj* **1** TRUTHFUL, sincere, frank, candid, blunt, outspoken, direct, straight, outright, forthright, straightforward, plain, simple, open, above-board, legitimate, legal, lawful, on the level (*infml*), fair, just, impartial, objective. **2** LAW-ABIDING, virtuous, upright, ethical, moral, high-minded, scrupulous, honourable, reputable, respectable, reliable, trustworthy, true, genuine, real.
🔁 **1** dishonest. **2** dishonourable.

honestly *adv* truly, really, truthfully, sincerely, frankly, directly, outright, plainly, openly, legitimately, legally, lawfully, on the level, fairly, justly, objectively, honourably, in good faith.

F3 dishonestly, dishonourably.

honesty n 1 TRUTHFULNESS, sincerity, frankness, candour, bluntness, outspokenness, straightforwardness, plain-speaking, explicitness, openness, legitimacy, legality, equity, fairness, justness, objectivity, even-handedness. 2 VIRTUE, uprightness, honour, integrity, morality, scrupulousness, trustworthiness, genuineness, veracity.

F3 1 dishonesty.

honorary adj unpaid, unofficial, titular, nominal, in name only, honorific, formal.

F3 paid.

honour n 1 REPUTATION, good name, repute, renown, distinction, esteem, regard, respect, credit, dignity, self-respect, pride, integrity, morality, decency, rectitude, probity. 2 AWARD, accolade, commendation, acknowledgement, recognition, tribute, privilege. 3 PRAISE, acclaim, homage, admiration, reverence, worship, adoration.

F3 1 dishonour, disgrace.

v 1 PRAISE, acclaim, exalt, glorify, pay homage to, decorate, crown, celebrate, commemorate, remember, admire, esteem, respect, revere, worship, prize, value. 2 honour a promise: keep, observe, respect, fulfil, carry out, discharge, execute, perform.

F3 1 dishonour, disgrace.

honourable adj great, eminent, distinguished, renowned, respected, worthy, prestigious, trusty, reputable, respectable, virtuous, upright, upstanding, straight, honest, trustworthy, true, sincere, noble, high-minded, principled, moral, ethical, fair, just, right, proper, decent.

F3 dishonourable, unworthy, dishonest.

hoodwink v deceive, dupe, fool, take in, delude, bamboozle (infml), have on (infml), mislead, hoax, trick, cheat, con (infml), rook, gull, swindle.

hook n crook, sickle, peg, barb, trap, snare, catch, fastener, clasp, hasp.
v 1 BEND, crook, curve, curl. 2 CATCH, capture, bag, grab, trap, snare, ensnare, entangle. 3 FASTEN, clasp, hitch, fix, secure.

hooligan n ruffian, rowdy, hoodlum, mobster, bovver boy (sl), thug, tough, lout, yob (sl), vandal, delinquent.

hoop n ring, circle, round, loop, wheel, band, girdle, circlet.

hoot n, v call, cry, shout, shriek, whoop, toot, beep, whistle, boo, jeer, laugh, howl.

hop v jump, leap, spring, bound, vault, skip, dance, prance, frisk, limp, hobble.
n jump, leap, spring, bound, vault, bounce, step, skip, dance.

hope n hopefulness, optimism, ambition, aspiration, wish, desire, longing, dream, expectation, anticipation, prospect, promise, belief, confidence, assurance, conviction, faith.

F3 pessimism, despair.

v aspire, wish, desire, long, expect, await, look forward, anticipate, contemplate, foresee, believe, trust, rely, reckon on, assume.

F3 despair.

hopeful adj 1 OPTIMISTIC, bullish (infml), confident, assured, expectant, sanguine, cheerful, buoyant. 2 a hopeful sign: encouraging, heartening, reassuring, favourable, auspicious, promising, rosy, bright.

F3 1 pessimistic, despairing. 2 discouraging.

hopeless *adj* **1** PESSIMISTIC, defeatist, negative, despairing, demoralized, downhearted, dejected, despondent, forlorn, wretched. **2** UNATTAINABLE, unachievable, impracticable, impossible, vain, foolish, futile, useless, pointless, worthless, poor, helpless, lost, irremediable, irreparable, incurable.
F3 1 hopeful, optimistic. **2** curable.

horde *n* band, gang, pack, herd, drove, flock, swarm, crowd, mob, throng, multitude, host.

horizon *n* skyline, vista, prospect, compass, range, scope, perspective.

horrible *adj* unpleasant, disagreeable, nasty, unkind, horrid, disgusting, revolting, offensive, repulsive, hideous, grim, ghastly, awful, dreadful, frightful, fearful, terrible, abominable, shocking, appalling, horrific.
F3 pleasant, agreeable, lovely, attractive.

horrific *adj* horrifying, shocking, appalling, awful, dreadful, ghastly, gruesome, terrifying, frightening, scary, harrowing, bloodcurdling.

horrify *v* shock, outrage, scandalize, appal, disgust, sicken, dismay, alarm, startle, scare, frighten, terrify.
F3 please, delight.

horror *n* **1** *recoil in horror*: shock, outrage, disgust, revulsion, repugnance, abhorrence, loathing, dismay, consternation, alarm, fright, fear, terror, panic, dread, apprehension. **2** GHASTLINESS, awfulness, frightfulness, hideousness.
F3 1 approval, delight.

horseman, horsewoman *n* equestrian, rider, jockey, cavalryman, hussar.

horseplay *n* clowning, buffoonery, foolery, tomfoolery, skylarking, pranks, capers, high jinks, fun and games, rough-and-tumble.

hospitable *adj* friendly, sociable, welcoming, receptive, cordial, amicable, congenial, convivial, genial, kind, gracious, generous, liberal.
F3 inhospitable, unfriendly, hostile.

hospitality *n* friendliness, sociability, welcome, accommodation, entertainment, conviviality, warmth, cheer, generosity, open-handedness.
F3 unfriendliness.

host[1] *n* **1** COMPÈRE, master of ceremonies, presenter, announcer, anchorman, anchorwoman, linkman. **2** PUBLICAN, innkeeper, landlord, proprietor.
v present, introduce, compère.

host[2] *n* multitude, myriad, array, army, horde, crowd, throng, swarm, pack, band.

hostage *n* prisoner, captive, pawn, surety, security, pledge.

hostel *n* youth hostel, residence, dosshouse (*sl*), boarding-house, guest-house, hotel, inn.

hostile *adj* belligerent, warlike, ill-disposed, unsympathetic, unfriendly, inhospitable, inimical, antagonistic, opposed, adverse, unfavourable, contrary, opposite.
F3 friendly, welcoming, favourable.

hostilities *n* war, warfare, battle, fighting, conflict, strife, bloodshed.

hostility *n* opposition, aggression, belligerence, enmity, estrangement, antagonism, animosity, ill-will, malice, resentment, hate, hatred, dislike, aversion, abhorrence.
F3 friendliness, friendship.

hot *adj* **1** WARM, heated, fiery, burning, scalding, blistering, scorching, roasting, baking, boiling, steaming, sizzling, sweltering, sultry, torrid, tropical. **2** SPICY, peppery, piquant, sharp, pungent, strong.
F3 1 cold, cool. **2** mild.

hotchpotch *n* mishmash, medley, miscellany, collection, mix, mixture, jumble, confusion, mess.

hotel *n* boarding-house, guest-house,

pension, motel, inn, public house, pub (*infml*), hostel.

hotheaded *adj* headstrong, impetuous, impulsive, hasty, rash, reckless, fiery, volatile, hot-tempered, quick-tempered.
E3 cool, calm.

hothouse *n* greenhouse, glasshouse, conservatory, orangery, vinery.

hound *v* chase, pursue, hunt (down), drive, goad, prod, chivvy, nag, pester, badger, harry, harass, persecute.

house *n* 1 BUILDING, dwelling, residence, home. 2 DYNASTY, family, clan, tribe.

> *Types of house include*: semi-detached, semi (*infml*), detached, terraced, town-house, council house, cottage, thatched cottage, prefab (*infml*), pied-à-terre, bungalow, chalet bungalow; flat, bedsit, apartment, studio, maisonette, penthouse, granny flat, duplex (*US*), condominium (*US*); manor, hall, lodge, grange, villa, mansion, rectory, vicarage, parsonage, manse, croft, farmhouse, homestead, ranchhouse, chalet, log cabin, shack, shanty, hut, igloo, hacienda.

v 1 LODGE, quarter, billet, board, accommodate, put up, take in, shelter, harbour. 2 HOLD, contain, protect, cover, sheathe, place, keep, store.

household *n* family, family circle, house, home, ménage, establishment, set-up.
adj domestic, home, family, ordinary, plain, everyday, common, familiar, well-known, established.

householder *n* resident, tenant, occupier, occupant, owner, landlady, freeholder, leaseholder, proprietor, landlord, home-owner, head of the household.

housing *n* 1 ACCOMMODATION, houses, homes, dwellings, habitation, shelter. 2 CASING, case, container,

holder, covering, cover, sheath, protection.

hovel *n* shack, shanty, cabin, hut, shed, dump, hole (*infml*).

hover *v* 1 HANG, poise, float, drift, fly, flutter, flap. 2 *he hovered by the door*: pause, linger, hang about, hesitate, waver, fluctuate, seesaw.

however *conj* nevertheless, nonetheless, still, yet, even so, notwithstanding, though, anyhow.

howl *n, v* wail, cry, shriek, scream, shout, yell, roar, bellow, bay, yelp, hoot, moan, groan.

hub *n* centre, middle, focus, focal point, axis, pivot, linchpin, nerve centre, core, heart.

hubbub *n* noise, racket, din, clamour, commotion, disturbance, riot, uproar, hullaballoo, rumpus, confusion, disorder, tumult, hurly-burly, chaos, pandemonium.
E3 peace, quiet.

huddle *n* 1 CLUSTER, clump, knot, mass, crowd, muddle, jumble. 2 CONCLAVE, conference, meeting. *v* cluster, gravitate, converge, meet, gather, congregate, crowd, flock, throng, press, cuddle, snuggle, nestle, curl up, crouch, hunch.
E3 disperse.

hue *n* colour, shade, tint, dye, tinge, nuance, tone, complexion, aspect, light.

huff *n* pique, sulks, mood, bad mood, anger, rage, passion.

hug *v* embrace, cuddle, squeeze, enfold, hold, clasp, clutch, grip, cling to, enclose.
n embrace, cuddle, squeeze, clasp, hold, clinch.

huge *adj* immense, vast, enormous, massive, colossal, titanic, giant, gigantic, mammoth, monumental, tremendous, great, big, large, bulky, unwieldy.
E3 tiny, minute.

hulking *adj* massive, heavy, unwieldy, bulky, awkward, ungainly.

hull

⊞ small, delicate.

hull n body, frame, framework, structure, casing, covering.

hullabaloo n fuss, palaver, to-do (infml), outcry, furore, hue and cry, uproar, pandemonium, rumpus, disturbance, commotion, hubbub.

⊞ calm, peace.

hum v buzz, whirr, purr, drone, thrum, croon, sing, murmur, mumble, throb, pulse, vibrate.

n buzz, whirr, purring, drone, murmur, mumble, throb, pulsation, vibration.

human adj 1 MORTAL, fallible, susceptible, reasonable, rational. 2 KIND, considerate, understanding, humane, compassionate.

⊞ 2 inhuman.

n human being, mortal, homo sapiens, man, woman, child, person, individual, body, soul.

humane adj kind, compassionate, sympathetic, understanding, kind-hearted, good-natured, gentle, tender, loving, mild, lenient, merciful, forgiving, forbearing, kindly, benevolent, charitable, humanitarian, good.

⊞ inhumane, cruel.

humanitarian adj benevolent, charitable, philanthropic, public-spirited, compassionate, humane, altruistic, unselfish.

⊞ selfish, self-seeking.

n philanthropist, benefactor, good Samaritan, do-gooder, altruist.

⊞ egoist, self-seeker.

humanity n 1 HUMAN RACE, humankind, mankind, womankind, mortality, people. 2 HUMANENESS, kindness, compassion, fellow-feeling, understanding, tenderness, benevolence, generosity, goodwill.

⊞ 2 inhumanity.

humanize v domesticate, tame, civilize, cultivate, educate, enlighten, edify, improve, better, polish, refine.

humble adj 1 MEEK, submissive,

unassertive, self-effacing, polite, respectful, deferential, servile, subservient, sycophantic, obsequious. 2 LOWLY, low, mean, insignificant, unimportant, common, commonplace, ordinary, plain, simple, modest, unassuming, unpretentious, unostentatious.

⊞ 1 proud, assertive. 2 important, pretentious.

v bring down, lower, bring low, abase, demean, sink, discredit, disgrace, shame, humiliate, mortify, chasten, crush, deflate, subdue.

⊞ exalt.

humbug n 1 DECEPTION, pretence, sham, found, swindle, trick, hoax, deceit, trickery. 2 NONSENSE, rubbish, baloney (sl), bunkum (infml), claptrap (infml), eye-wash (infml), bluff, cant, hypocrisy.

humdrum adj boring, tedious, monotonous, routine, dull, dreary, uninteresting, uneventful, ordinary, mundane, everyday, commonplace.

⊞ lively, unusual, exceptional.

humid adj damp, moist, dank, clammy, sticky, muggy, sultry, steamy.

⊞ dry.

humiliate v mortify, embarrass, confound, crush, break, deflate, chasten, shame, disgrace, discredit, degrade, demean, humble, bring low.

⊞ dignify, exalt.

humiliation n mortification, embarrassment, shame, disgrace, dishonour, ignominy, abasement, deflation, put-down, snub, rebuff, affront.

⊞ gratification, triumph.

humility n meekness, submissiveness, deference, self-abasement, servility, humbleness, lowliness, modesty, unpretentiousness.

⊞ pride, arrogance, assertiveness.

humorist n wit, satirist, comedian, comic, joker, wag, jester, clown.

humorous *adj* funny, amusing, comic, entertaining, witty, satirical, jocular, facetious, playful, waggish, droll, whimsical, comical, farcical, zany (*infml*), ludicrous, absurd, hilarious, side-splitting.
🔁 serious, humourless.

humour *n* 1 WIT, drollery, jokes, jesting, badinage, repartee, facetiousness, satire, comedy, farce, fun, amusement. 2 *in a bad humour*: mood, temper, frame of mind, spirits, disposition, temperament.
v go along with, comply with, accommodate, gratify, indulge, pamper, spoil, favour, please, mollify, flatter.

humourless *adj* boring, tedious, dull, dry, solemn, serious, glum, morose.
🔁 humorous, witty.

hump *n* hunch, lump, knob, bump, projection, protuberance, bulge, swelling, mound, prominence.

hunch *n* premonition, presentiment, intuition, suspicion, feeling, impression, idea, guess.
v hump, bend, curve, arch, stoop, crouch, squat, huddle, draw in, curl up.

hunger *n* 1 HUNGRINESS, emptiness, starvation, malnutrition, famine, appetite, ravenousness, voracity, greed, greediness. 2 *hunger for power*: desire, craving, longing, yearning, itch, thirst.
v starve, want, wish, desire, crave, hanker, long, yearn, pine, ache, itch, thirst.

hungry *adj* 1 STARVING, underfed, undernourished, peckish (*infml*), empty, hollow, famished, ravenous, greedy. 2 *hungry for knowledge*: desirous, craving, longing, aching, thirsty, eager, avid.
🔁 1 satisfied, full.

hunk *n* chunk, lump, piece, block, slab, wedge, mass, clod.

hunt *v* 1 CHASE, pursue, hound, dog, stalk, track, trail. 2 SEEK, look for, search, scour, rummage, forage, investigate.
n chase, pursuit, search, quest, investigation.

hurdle *n* jump, fence, wall, hedge, barrier, barricade, obstacle, obstruction, stumbling-block, hindrance, impediment, handicap, problem, snag, difficulty, complication.

hurl *v* throw, toss, fling, sling, catapult, project, propel, fire, launch, send.

hurricane *n* gale, tornado, typhoon, cyclone, whirlwind, squall, storm, tempest.

hurried *adj* rushed, hectic, hasty, precipitate, speedy, quick, swift, rapid, passing, brief, short, cursory, superficial, shallow, careless, slapdash.
🔁 leisurely.

hurry *v* rush, dash, fly, get a move on (*infml*), hasten, quicken, speed up, hustle, push.
🔁 slow down, delay.
n rush, haste, quickness, speed, urgency, hustle, bustle, flurry, commotion.
🔁 leisureliness, calm.

hurt *v* 1 *my leg hurts*: ache, pain, throb, sting. 2 INJURE, wound, maltreat, ill-treat, bruise, cut, burn, torture, maim, disable. 3 DAMAGE, impair, harm, mar, spoil. 4 UPSET, sadden, grieve, distress, afflict, offend, annoy.
n pain, soreness, discomfort, suffering, injury, wound, damage, harm, distress, sorrow.
adj 1 INJURED, wounded, bruised, grazed, cut, scarred, maimed.
2 UPSET, sad, saddened, distressed, aggrieved, annoyed, offended, affronted.

hurtful *adj* 1 UPSETTING, wounding, vicious, cruel, mean, unkind, nasty, malicious, spiteful, catty, derogatory,

scathing, cutting. **2** HARMFUL, damaging, injurious, pernicious, destructive.
ᴙ **1** kind.

hurtle v dash, tear, race, fly, shoot, speed, rush, charge, plunge, dive, crash, rattle.

husband n spouse, partner, mate, better half, hubby (*infml*), groom, married man.

hush v quieten, silence, still, settle, compose, calm, soothe, subdue.
ᴙ disturb, rouse.
n quietness, silence, peace, stillness, repose, calm, calmness, tranquillity, serenity.
ᴙ noise, clamour.
interj quiet, hold your tongue, shut up, not another word.
hush up keep dark, suppress, conceal, cover up, stifle, gag.
ᴙ publicize.

hush-hush adj secret, confidential, classified, restricted, under wraps (*infml*), top-secret.
ᴙ open, public.

husk n covering, case, shell, pod, hull, rind, bran, chaff.

husky adj hoarse, croaky, croaking, low, throaty, guttural, gruff, rasping, rough, harsh.

hustle v hasten, rush, hurry, bustle, force, push, shove, thrust, bundle, elbow, jostle.

hut n cabin, shack, shanty, booth, shed, lean-to, shelter, den.

hybrid n cross, crossbreed, half-breed, mongrel, composite, combination, mixture, amalgam, compound.
adj crossbred, mongrel, composite, combined, mixed, heterogeneous, compound.
ᴙ pure-bred.

hygiene n sanitariness, sanitation, sterility, disinfection, cleanliness,

purity, wholesomeness.
ᴙ insanitariness.

hygienic adj sanitary, sterile, aseptic, germ-free, disinfected, clean, pure, salubrious, healthy, wholesome.
ᴙ unhygienic, insanitary.

hyperbole n overstatement, exaggeration, magnification, extravagance.
ᴙ understatement.

hypnotic adj mesmerizing, soporific, sleep-inducing, spellbinding, fascinating, compelling, irresistible, magnetic.

hypnotism n hypnosis, mesmerism, suggestion.

hypnotize v mesmerize, spellbind, bewitch, enchant, entrance, fascinate, captivate, magnetize.

hypocrisy n insincerity, double-talk, double-dealing, falsity, deceit, deception, pretence.
ᴙ sincerity.

hypocritical adj insincere, two-faced, self-righteous, double-dealing, false, hollow, deceptive, spurious, deceitful, dissembling, pharisaic(al).
ᴙ sincere, genuine.

hypothesis n theory, thesis, premise, postulate, proposition, supposition, conjecture, speculation.

hypothetical adj theoretical, imaginary, supposed, assumed, proposed, conjectural, speculative.
ᴙ real, actual.

hysteria n agitation, frenzy, panic, hysterics, neurosis, mania, madness.
ᴙ calm, composure.

hysterical adj **1** FRANTIC, frenzied, berserk, uncontrollable, mad, raving, crazed, demented, overwrought, neurotic. **2** (*infml*) HILARIOUS, uproarious, side-splitting, priceless (*infml*), rich (*infml*).
ᴙ **1** calm, composed, self-possessed.

I

ice *n* frost, rime, icicle, glacier, iciness, frostiness, coldness, chill.
v freeze, refrigerate, chill, cool, frost, glaze.

icon *n* idol, portrait, image, representation, symbol.

icy *adj* 1 ICE-COLD, arctic, polar, glacial, freezing, frozen, raw, bitter, biting, cold, chill, chilly. 2 *icy roads*: frosty, slippery, glassy, frozen, icebound, frostbound. 3 HOSTILE, cold, stony, cool, indifferent, aloof, distant, formal.
🔁 1 hot. 3 friendly, warm.

idea *n* 1 THOUGHT, concept, notion, theory, hypothesis, guess, conjecture, belief, opinion, view, viewpoint, judgement, conception, vision, image, impression, perception, interpretation, understanding, inkling, suspicion, clue. 2 *a good idea*: brainwave, suggestion, proposal, proposition, recommendation, plan, scheme, design. 3 AIM, intention, purpose, reason, point, object.

ideal *n* perfection, epitome, acme, paragon, exemplar, example, model, pattern, archetype, prototype, type, image, criterion, standard.
adj 1 PERFECT, dream, utopian, best, optimum, optimal, supreme, highest, model, archetypal.
2 UNREAL, imaginary, theoretical, hypothetical, unattainable, impractical, idealistic.

idealist *n* perfectionist, romantic, visionary, dreamer, optimist.
🔁 realist, pragmatist.

idealistic *adj* perfectionist, utopian, visionary, romantic, quixotic, starry-eyed, optimistic, unrealistic,
impractical, impracticable.
🔁 realistic, pragmatic.

idealize *v* utopianize, romanticize, glamorize, glorify, exalt, worship, idolize.
🔁 caricature.

identical *adj* same, self-same, indistinguishable, interchangeable, twin, duplicate, like, alike, corresponding, matching, equal, equivalent.
🔁 different.

identification *n* 1 RECOGNITION, detection, diagnosis, naming, labelling, classification. 2 EMPATHY, association, involvement, rapport, relationship, sympathy, fellow-feeling. 3 IDENTITY CARD, documents, papers, credentials.

identify *v* recognize, know, pick out, single out, distinguish, perceive, make out, discern, notice, detect, diagnose, name, label, tag, specify, pinpoint, place, catalogue, classify.
identify with empathize with, relate to, associate with, respond to, sympathize with, feel for.

identity *n* 1 INDIVIDUALITY, particularity, singularity, uniqueness, self, personality, character, existence. 2 SAMENESS, likeness.

ideology *n* philosophy, world-view, ideas, principles, tenets, doctrine(s), convictions, belief(s), faith, creed, dogma.

idiocy *n* folly, stupidity, silliness, senselessness, lunacy.
🔁 wisdom, sanity.

idiom *n* phrase, expression, colloquialism, language, turn of phrase, phraseology, style, usage, jargon, vernacular.

idiosyncrasy n characteristic, peculiarity, singularity, oddity, eccentricity, freak, quirk, habit, mannerism, trait, feature.

idiosyncratic adj personal, individual, characteristic, distinctive, peculiar, singular, odd, eccentric, quirky.

🖝 general, common.

idiot n fool, blockhead, ass (infml), nitwit (infml), dimwit, halfwit, imbecile, moron, cretin, simpleton, dunce, ignoramus.

idiotic adj foolish, stupid, silly, absurd, senseless, daft (infml), lunatic, insane, foolhardy, harebrained, halfwitted, moronic, cretinous, crazy.

🖝 sensible, sane.

idle adj 1 INACTIVE, inoperative, unused, unoccupied, unemployed, jobless, redundant. 2 LAZY, work-shy, indolent. 3 idle talk: empty, trivial, casual, futile, vain, pointless, unproductive.

🖝 1 active. 2 busy.

v do nothing, laze, lounge, take it easy, kill time, potter, loiter, dawdle, fritter, waste, loaf, slack, skive (infml).

🖝 work.

idol n icon, effigy, image, graven image, god, deity, fetish, favourite, darling, hero, heroine, pin-up.

idolize v hero-worship, lionize, exalt, glorify, worship, venerate, revere, admire, adore, love, dote on.

🖝 despise.

idyllic adj perfect, idealized, heavenly, delightful, charming, picturesque, pastoral, rustic, unspoiled, peaceful, happy.

🖝 unpleasant.

ignite v set fire to, set alight, catch fire, flare up, burn, conflagrate, fire, kindle, touch off, spark off.

🖝 quench.

ignoble adj low, mean, petty, base, vulgar, wretched, contemptible, despicable, vile, heinous, infamous,

disgraceful, dishonourable, shameless.

🖝 noble, worthy, honourable.

ignominious adj humiliating, mortifying, degrading, undignified, shameful, dishonourable, disreputable, disgraceful, despicable, scandalous.

🖝 triumphant, honourable.

ignorance n unintelligence, illiteracy, unawareness, unconsciousness, oblivion, unfamiliarity, inexperience, innocence, naïvety.

🖝 knowledge, wisdom.

ignorant adj uneducated, illiterate, unread, untaught, untrained, inexperienced, stupid, clueless (infml), uninitiated, unenlightened, uninformed, ill-informed, unwitting, unaware, unconscious, oblivious.

🖝 educated, knowledgeable, clever, wise.

ignore v disregard, take no notice of, shut one's eyes to, overlook, pass over, neglect, omit, reject, snub, cold-shoulder.

🖝 notice, observe.

ill adj 1 SICK, poorly, unwell, indisposed, laid up, ailing, off-colour, out of sorts (infml), under the weather (infml), seedy, queasy, diseased, unhealthy, infirm, frail. 2 an ill omen: bad, evil, damaging, harmful, injurious, detrimental, adverse, unfavourable, inauspicious, unpromising, sinister, ominous, threatening, unlucky, unfortunate, difficult, harsh, severe, unkind, unfriendly, antagonistic.

🖝 1 well. 2 good, favourable, fortunate.

ill-advised adj imprudent, injudicious, unwise, foolish, ill-considered, thoughtless, hasty, rash, short-sighted, misguided, inappropriate.

🖝 wise, sensible, well-advised.

ill-bred adj bad-mannered, ill-

mannered, discourteous, impolite,
rude, coarse, indelicate.
F3 well-bred, polite.

illegal *adj* unlawful, illicit, criminal,
wrong, forbidden, prohibited,
banned, outlawed, unauthorized,
under-the-counter, black-market,
unconstitutional, wrongful.
F3 legal, lawful.

illegible *adj* unreadable,
indecipherable, scrawled, obscure,
faint, indistinct.
F3 legible.

illegitimate *adj* **1** *an illegitimate
child*: natural, bastard, born out of
wedlock (*fml*). **2** ILLEGAL, unlawful,
illicit, unauthorized, unwarranted,
improper, incorrect, inadmissible,
spurious, invalid, unsound.
F3 **1** legitimate. **2** legal.

ill-fated *adj* doomed, ill-starred, ill-
omened, unfortunate, unlucky,
luckless, unhappy.
F3 lucky.

illicit *adj* illegal, unlawful, criminal,
wrong, illegitimate, improper,
forbidden, prohibited, unauthorized,
unlicensed, black-market,
contraband, ill-gotten, under-the-
counter, furtive, clandestine.
F3 legal, permissible.

illness *n* disease, disorder,
complaint, ailment, sickness, ill
health, ill-being, indisposition,
infirmity, disability, affliction.

illogical *adj* irrational,
unreasonable, unscientific, invalid,
unsound, faulty, fallacious, specious,
sophistical, inconsistent, senseless,
meaningless, absurd.
F3 logical.

ill-treat *v* maltreat, abuse, injure,
harm, damage, neglect, mistreat,
mishandle, misuse, wrong, oppress.

illuminate *v* **1** LIGHT, light up,
brighten, decorate. **2** ENLIGHTEN,
edify, instruct, elucidate, illustrate,
explain, clarify, clear up.
F3 **1** darken. **2** mystify.

illumination *n* light, lights, lighting,
beam, ray, brightness, radiance,
decoration, ornamentation.
F3 darkness.

illusion *n* apparition, mirage,
hallucination, figment, fantasy,
fancy, delusion, misapprehension,
misconception, error, fallacy.
F3 reality, truth.

illusory *adj* illusive, deceptive,
misleading, apparent, seeming,
deluding, delusive, unreal,
unsubstantial, sham, false, fallacious,
untrue, mistaken.
F3 real.

illustrate *v* draw, sketch, depict,
picture, show, exhibit, demonstrate,
exemplify, explain, interpret, clarify,
elucidate, illuminate, decorate,
ornament, adorn.

illustration *n* **1** PICTURE, plate,
half-tone, photograph, drawing,
sketch, figure, representation,
decoration. **2** EXAMPLE, specimen,
instance, case, analogy,
demonstration, explanation,
interpretation.

illustrious *adj* great, noble,
eminent, distinguished, celebrated,
famous, famed, renowned, noted,
prominent, outstanding, remarkable,
notable, brilliant, excellent, splendid,
magnificent, glorious, exalted.
F3 ignoble, inglorious.

ill-will *n* hostility, antagonism, bad
blood, enmity, unfriendliness,
malevolence, malice, spite,
animosity, ill-feeling, resentment,
hard feelings, grudge, dislike,
aversion, hatred.
F3 goodwill, friendship.

image *n* **1** IDEA, notion, concept,
impression, perception.
2 REPRESENTATION, likeness,
picture, portrait, icon, effigy, figure,
statue, idol, replica, reflection.

imaginable *adj* conceivable,
thinkable, believable, credible,
plausible, likely, possible.

ɛɜ unimaginable.

imaginary *adj* imagined, fanciful, illusory, hallucinatory, visionary, pretend, make-believe, unreal, non-existent, fictional, fabulous, legendary, mythological, made-up, invented, fictitious, assumed, supposed, hypothetical.

ɛɜ real.

imagination *n* imaginativeness, creativity, inventiveness, originality, inspiration, insight, ingenuity, resourcefulness, enterprise, wit, vision, mind's eye, fancy, illusion.

ɛɜ unimaginativeness, reality.

imaginative *adj* creative, inventive, innovative, original, inspired, visionary, ingenious, clever, resourceful, enterprising, fanciful, fantastic, vivid.

ɛɜ unimaginative.

imagine *v* **1** PICTURE, visualize, envisage, conceive, fancy, fantasize, pretend, make believe, conjure up, dream up, think up, invent, devise, create, plan, project. **2** *I imagine so*: think, believe, judge, suppose, guess, conjecture, assume, take it, gather.

imbalance *n* unevenness, inequality, disparity, disproportion, unfairness, partiality, bias.

ɛɜ balance, parity.

imbecile *n* idiot, halfwit, simpleton, moron, cretin, fool, blockhead, bungler.

imbue *v* permeate, impregnate, pervade, suffuse, fill, saturate, steep, inculcate, instil, tinge, tint.

imitate *v* copy, emulate, follow, ape, mimic, impersonate, take off, caricature, parody, send up, spoof, mock, parrot, repeat, echo, mirror, duplicate, reproduce, simulate, counterfeit, forge.

imitation *n* **1** MIMICRY, impersonation, impression, take-off, caricature, parody, send-up, spoof, mockery, travesty. **2** COPY, duplicate, reproduction, replica, simulation, counterfeit, fake, forgery, sham, likeness, resemblance, reflection, dummy.

adj artificial, synthetic, man-made, ersatz, fake, phoney (*infml*), mock, pseudo, reproduction, simulated, sham, dummy.

ɛɜ genuine.

imitative *adj* copying, mimicking, parrot-like, unoriginal, derivative, plagiarized, second-hand, simulated, mock.

imitator *n* mimic, impersonator, impressionist, parrot, copycat (*infml*), copier, emulator, follower.

immaculate *adj* perfect, unblemished, flawless, faultless, impeccable, spotless, clean, spick and span, pure, unsullied, undefiled, untainted, stainless, blameless, innocent.

ɛɜ blemished, stained, contaminated.

immaterial *adj* irrelevant, insignificant, unimportant, minor, trivial, trifling, inconsequential.

ɛɜ relevant, important.

immature *adj* young, under-age, adolescent, juvenile, childish, puerile, infantile, babyish, raw, crude, callow, inexperienced, green, unripe, undeveloped.

ɛɜ mature.

immeasurable *adj* vast, immense, infinite, limitless, unlimited, boundless, unbounded, endless, bottomless, inexhaustible, incalculable, inestimable.

ɛɜ limited.

immediate *adj* **1** INSTANT, instantaneous, direct, prompt, swift, current, present, existing, urgent, pressing. **2** NEAREST, next, adjacent, near, close, recent.

ɛɜ **1** delayed. **2** distant.

immediately *adv* now, straight away, right away, at once, instantly, directly, forthwith, without delay, promptly, unhesitatingly.

ɛɜ eventually, never.

immense adj vast, great, huge, enormous, massive, giant, gigantic, tremendous, monumental.
☒ tiny, minute.

immensity n magnitude, bulk, expanse, vastness, greatness, hugeness, enormousness, massiveness.
☒ minuteness.

immerse v plunge, submerge, submerse, sink, duck, dip, douse, bathe.

immigrant n incomer, settler, newcomer, alien.
☒ emigrant.

imminent adj impending, forthcoming, in the offing, approaching, coming, near, close, looming, menacing, threatening, brewing, in the air.
☒ remote, far-off.

immobile adj stationary, motionless, unmoving, still, stock-still, static, immovable, rooted, fixed, frozen, rigid, stiff.
☒ mobile, moving.

immobilize v stop, halt, fix, freeze, transfix, paralyse, cripple, disable.
☒ mobilize.

immodest adj indecent, revealing, shameless, forward, improper, immoral, obscene, lewd, coarse, risqué.

immoral adj unethical, wrong, bad, sinful, evil, wicked, unscrupulous, unprincipled, dishonest, corrupt, depraved, degenerate, dissolute, lewd, indecent, pornographic, obscene, impure.
☒ moral, right, good.

immortal adj undying, imperishable, eternal, everlasting, perpetual, endless, ceaseless, lasting, enduring, abiding, timeless, ageless.
☒ mortal.

immortalize v celebrate, commemorate, memorialize, perpetuate, enshrine.

immovable adj fixed, rooted,

immobile, stuck, fast, secure, stable, constant, firm, set, determined, resolute, adamant, unshakable, obstinate, unyielding.
☒ movable.

immune adj invulnerable, unsusceptible, resistant, proof, protected, safe, exempt, free, clear.
☒ susceptible.

immunity n resistance, protection, exemption, indemnity, impunity, exoneration, freedom, liberty, licence, franchise, privilege, right.
☒ susceptibility.

immunize v vaccinate, inoculate, inject, protect, safeguard.

impact n 1 *the impact of the reforms*: effect, consequences, repercussions, impression, power, influence, significance, meaning. 2 COLLISION, crash, smash, bang, bump, blow, knock, contact, jolt, shock, brunt.

impair v damage, harm, injure, hinder, mar, spoil, worsen, undermine, weaken, reduce, lessen, diminish, blunt.
☒ improve, enhance.

impale v pierce, puncture, perforate, run through, spear, lance, spike, skewer, spit, stick, transfix.

impart v tell, relate, communicate, make known, disclose, divulge, reveal, convey, pass on, give, grant, confer, offer, contribute, lend.
☒ withhold.

impartial adj objective, dispassionate, detached, disinterested, neutral, non-partisan, unbiased, unprejudiced, open-minded, fair, just, equitable, even-handed, equal.
☒ biased, prejudiced.

impasse n deadlock, stalemate, dead end, cul-de-sac, blind alley, halt, standstill.

impassive adj expressionless, calm, composed, unruffled, unconcerned, cool, unfeeling, unemotional, unmoved, imperturbable, unexcitable, stoical, indifferent, dispassionate.

☒ responsive, moved.

impatience n eagerness, keenness, restlessness, agitation, anxiety, nervousness, irritability, intolerance, shortness, brusqueness, haste, rashness.

☒ patience.

impatient adj eager, keen, restless, fidgety, fretful, edgy, irritable, snappy, hot-tempered, quick-tempered, intolerant, brusque, abrupt, impetuous, hasty, precipitate, headlong.

☒ patient.

impeach v accuse, charge, indict, arraign, denounce, impugn, disparage, criticize, censure, blame.

impeccable adj perfect, faultless, precise, exact, flawless, unblemished, stainless, immaculate, pure, irreproachable, blameless, innocent.

☒ faulty, flawed, corrupt.

impede v hinder, hamper, obstruct, block, clog, slow, retard, hold up, delay, check, curb, restrain, thwart, disrupt, stop, bar.

☒ aid, promote, further.

impediment n hindrance, obstacle, obstruction, barrier, bar, block, stumbling-block, snag, difficulty, handicap, check, curb, restraint, restriction.

☒ aid.

impel v urge, force, oblige, compel, constrain, drive, propel, push, spur, goad, prompt, stimulate, excite, instigate, motivate, inspire, move.

☒ deter, dissuade.

impending adj imminent, forthcoming, approaching, coming, close, near, looming, menacing, threatening.

☒ remote.

impenetrable adj 1 impenetrable jungle: solid, thick, dense, impassable. 2 UNINTELLIGIBLE, incomprehensible, unfathomable,

baffling, mysterious, cryptic, enigmatic, obscure, dark, inscrutable.

☒ 2 accessible, understandable.

imperative adj compulsory, obligatory, essential, vital, crucial, pressing, urgent.

☒ optional, unimportant.

imperceptible adj inappreciable, indiscernible, inaudible, faint, slight, negligible, infinitesimal, microscopic, minute, tiny, small, fine, subtle, gradual.

☒ perceptible.

imperfect adj faulty, flawed, defective, damaged, broken, chipped, deficient, incomplete.

☒ perfect.

imperfection n fault, flaw, defect, blemish, deficiency, shortcoming, weakness, failing.

☒ perfection.

imperial adj sovereign, supreme, royal, regal, majestic, grand, magnificent, great, noble.

imperil v endanger, jeopardize, risk, hazard, expose, compromise, threaten.

imperious adj overbearing, domineering, autocratic, despotic, tyrannical, dictatorial, high-handed, commanding, arrogant, haughty.

☒ humble.

impersonal adj formal, official, businesslike, bureaucratic, faceless, aloof, remote, distant, detached, neutral, objective, dispassionate, cold, frosty, glassy.

☒ informal, friendly.

impersonate v imitate, mimic, take off, parody, caricature, mock, masquerade as, pose as, act, portray.

impertinence n rudeness, impoliteness, disrespect, insolence, impudence, cheek (infml), brass (sl), effrontery, nerve (infml), audacity, boldness, brazenness, forwardness, presumption.

☒ politeness, respect.

impertinent adj rude, impolite, ill-mannered, discourteous, disrespectful, insolent, impudent, cheeky (*infml*), saucy (*infml*), pert, bold, brazen, forward, presumptuous, fresh.

🔄 polite, respectful.

imperturbable *adj* unexcitable, unflappable (*infml*), calm, tranquil, composed, collected, self-possessed, cool, unmoved, unruffled.

impervious *adj* 1 IMPERMEABLE, waterproof, damp-proof, watertight, hermetic, closed, sealed, impenetrable. 2 *impervious to criticism*: immune, invulnerable, untouched, unaffected, unmoved, resistant.

🔄 1 porous, pervious. 2 responsive, vulnerable.

impetuous *adj* impulsive, spontaneous, unplanned, unpremeditated, hasty, precipitate, rash, reckless, thoughtless, unthinking.

🔄 cautious, wary, circumspect.

impetus *n* impulse, momentum, force, energy, power, drive, boost, push, spur, stimulus, incentive, motivation.

impinge *v* hit, touch (on), affect, influence, encroach, infringe, intrude, trespass, invade.

implacable *adj* inexorable, relentless, remorseless, merciless, pitiless, cruel, ruthless, intransigent, inflexible.

🔄 compassionate.

implant *v* graft, engraft, embed, sow, plant, fix, root, insert, instil, inculcate.

implausible *adj* improbable, unlikely, far-fetched, dubious, suspect, unconvincing, weak, flimsy, thin, transparent.

🔄 plausible, likely, reasonable.

implement *n* tool, instrument, utensil, gadget, device, apparatus, appliance.

v enforce, effect, bring about, carry out, execute, discharge, perform, do, fulfil, complete, accomplish, realize.

implicate *v* involve, embroil, entangle, incriminate, compromise, include, concern, connect, associate.

🔄 exonerate.

implication *n* 1 INFERENCE, insinuation, suggestion, meaning, significance, ramification, repercusssion. 2 INVOLVEMENT, entanglement, incrimination, connection, association.

implicit *adj* 1 IMPLIED, inferred, insinuated, indirect, unsaid, unspoken, tacit, understood. *implicit belief*: unquestioning, utter, total, full, complete, absolute, unqualified, unreserved, wholehearted.

🔄 1 explicit. 2 half-hearted.

imply *v* suggest, insinuate, hint, intimate, mean, signify, point to, indicate, involve, require.

🔄 state.

impolite *adj* rude, discourteous, bad-mannered, ill-mannered, ill-bred, disrespectful, insolent, rough, coarse, vulgar, abrupt.

🔄 polite, courteous.

importance *n* momentousness, significance, consequence, substance, matter, concern, interest, usefulness, value, worth, weight, influence, mark, prominence, eminence, distinction, esteem, prestige, status, standing.

🔄 unimportance.

important *adj* 1 MOMENTOUS, noteworthy, significant, meaningful, relevant, material, salient, urgent, vital, essential, key, primary, major, substantial, valuable, seminal, weighty, serious, grave, far-reaching. 2 LEADING, foremost, high-level, high-ranking, influential, powerful, pre-eminent, prominent, outstanding, eminent, noted.

🔄 1 unimportant, insignificant, trivial.

impose v **1** INTRODUCE, institute, enforce, promulgate, exact, levy, set, fix, put, place, lay, inflict, burden, encumber, saddle. **2** INTRUDE, butt in, encroach, trespass, obtrude, force oneself, presume, take liberties.

imposing adj impressive, striking, grand, stately, majestic, dignified. 🖙 unimposing, modest.

imposition n **1** INTRODUCTION, infliction, exaction, levying. **2** INTRUSION, encroachment, liberty, burden, constraint, charge, duty, task, punishment.

impossible adj hopeless, impracticable, unworkable, unattainable, unachievable, unobtainable, insoluble, unreasonable, unacceptable, inconceivable, unthinkable, preposterous, absurd, ludicrous, ridiculous. 🖙 possible.

impostor n fraud, fake, phoney (infml), quack, charlatan, impersonator, pretender, con man (infml), swindler, cheat, rogue.

impotent adj powerless, helpless, unable, incapable, ineffective, incompetent, inadequate, weak, feeble, frail, infirm, disabled, incapacitated, paralysed. 🖙 potent, strong.

impoverished adj poor, needy, impecunious, poverty-stricken, destitute, bankrupt, ruined. 🖙 rich.

impracticable adj unworkable, unfeasible, unattainable, unachievable, impossible, unviable, useless, unserviceable, inoperable. 🖙 practicable.

impractical adj unrealistic, idealistic, romantic, starry-eyed, impracticable, unworkable, impossible, awkward, inconvenient. 🖙 practical, realistic, sensible.

imprecise adj inexact, inaccurate, approximate, estimated, rough,

loose, indefinite, vague, woolly, hazy, ill-defined, sloppy, ambiguous, equivocal. 🖙 precise, exact.

impregnable adj impenetrable, unconquerable, invincible, unbeatable, unassailable, indestructible, fortified, strong, solid, secure, safe, invulnerable. 🖙 vulnerable.

impregnate v **1** SOAK, steep, saturate, fill, permeate, pervade, suffuse, imbue. **2** INSEMINATE, fertilize.

impress v **1** I'm not impressed: strike, move, touch, affect, influence, stir, inspire, excite, grab (sl). **2** STAMP, imprint, mark, indent, instil, inculcate.

impression n **1** FEELING, awareness, consciousness, sense, illusion, idea, notion, opinion, belief, conviction, suspicion, hunch, memory, recollection. **2** STAMP, mark, print, dent, outline. **3** IMPERSONATION, imitation, take-off, parody, send-up. **4** make a good impression: effect, impact, influence.

impressionable adj naïve, gullible, susceptible, vulnerable, sensitive, responsive, open, receptive.

impressive adj striking, imposing, grand, powerful, effective, stirring, exciting, moving, touching. 🖙 unimpressive, uninspiring.

imprint n print, mark, stamp, impression, sign, logo. v print, mark, brand, stamp, impress, engrave, etch.

imprison v jail, incarcerate, intern, detain, send down (infml), put away (infml), lock up, cage, confine, shut in. 🖙 release, free.

imprisonment n incarceration, internment, detention, custody, confinement. 🖙 freedom, liberty.

improbable adj uncertain,

questionable, doubtful, unlikely, dubious, implausible, unconvincing, far-fetched, preposterous, unbelievable, incredible.
Ea probable, likely, convincing.

impromptu *adj* improvised, extempore, ad-lib, off the cuff, unscripted, unrehearsed, unprepared, spontaneous.
Ea rehearsed.
adv extempore, ad lib, off the cuff, off the top of one's head, spontaneously, on the spur of the moment.

improper *adj* wrong, incorrect, irregular, unsuitable, inappropriate, inopportune, incongruous, out of place, indecent, rude, vulgar, unseemly, unbecoming, shocking.
Ea proper, appropriate, decent.

improve *v* better, ameliorate, enhance, polish, touch up, mend, rectify, correct, amend, reform, upgrade, increase, rise, pick up, develop, look up, advance, progress, get better, recover, recuperate, rally, perk up, mend one's ways, turn over a new leaf.
Ea worsen, deteriorate, decline.

improvement *n* betterment, amelioration, enhancement, rectification, correction, amendment, reformation, increase, rise, upswing, gain, development, advance, progress, furtherance, recovery, rally.
Ea deterioration, decline.

improvise *v* 1 CONTRIVE, devise, concoct, invent, throw together, make do. 2 EXTEMPORIZE, ad-lib, play by ear, vamp.

imprudent *adj* unwise, ill-advised, foolish, short-sighted, rash, reckless, hasty, irresponsible, careless, heedless, impolitic, indiscreet.
Ea prudent, wise, cautious.

impudence *n* impertinence, cheek (*infml*), effrontery, nerve (*infml*), face (*infml*), boldness, insolence, rudeness, presumption.

Ea politeness.

impudent *adj* impertinent, cheeky (*infml*), saucy (*infml*), bold, forward, shameless, cocky, insolent, rude, presumptuous, fresh.
Ea polite.

impulse *n* 1 URGE, wish, desire, inclination, whim, notion, instinct, feeling, passion. 2 IMPETUS, momentum, force, pressure, drive, thrust, push, incitement, stimulus, motive.

impulsive *adj* impetuous, rash, reckless, hasty, quick, spontaneous, automatic, instinctive, intuitive.
Ea cautious, premeditated.

impure *adj* 1 UNREFINED, adulterated, diluted, contaminated, polluted, tainted, infected, corrupt, debased, unclean, dirty, foul.
2 OBSCENE, indecent, immodest.
Ea 1 pure. 2 chaste, decent.

impurity *n* adulteration, contamination, pollution, infection, corruption, dirtiness, contaminant, dirt, filth, foreign body, mark, spot.
Ea purity.

inability *n* incapability, incapacity, powerlessness, impotence, inadequacy, weakness, handicap, disability.
Ea ability.

inaccessible *adj* isolated, remote, unfrequented, unapproachable, unreachable, unget-at-able (*infml*), unattainable.
Ea accessible.

inaccuracy *n* mistake, error, miscalculation, slip, blunder, fault, defect, imprecision, inexactness, unreliability.
Ea accuracy, precision.

inaccurate *adj* incorrect, wrong, erroneous, mistaken, faulty, flawed, defective, imprecise, inexact, loose, unreliable, unfaithful, untrue.
Ea accurate, correct.

inaction *n* inactivity, immobility, inertia, rest, idleness, lethargy, torpor, stagnation.

Ea action.

inactive *adj* immobile, inert, idle,
unused, inoperative, dormant,
passive, sedentary, lazy, lethargic,
sluggish, torpid, sleepy.

Ea active, working, busy.

inadequacy *n* **1** INSUFFICIENCY,
lack, shortage, dearth, want,
deficiency, scantiness, meagreness,
defectiveness, ineffectiveness,
inability, incompetence. **2** *the
inadequacies of the system*: fault,
defect, imperfection, weakness,
failing, shortcoming.

Ea 1 adequacy.

inadequate *adj* **1** INSUFFICIENT,
short, wanting, deficient, scanty,
sparse, meagre, niggardly.
2 INCOMPETENT, incapable,
unequal, unqualified, ineffective,
faulty, defective, imperfect,
unsatisfactory.

Ea 1 adequate. **2** satisfactory.

inadmissible *adj* unacceptable,
irrelevant, immaterial, inappropriate,
disallowed, prohibited.

Ea admissible.

inadvertent *adj* accidental, chance,
unintentional, unintended,
unplanned, unpremeditated, careless.

Ea deliberate, conscious, careful.

inadvisable *adj* unwise, imprudent,
injudicious, foolish, silly, ill-advised,
misguided, indiscreet.

Ea advisable, wise.

inane *adj* senseless, foolish, stupid,
unintelligent, silly, idiotic, fatuous,
frivolous, trifling, puerile, mindless,
vapid, empty, vacuous, vain,
worthless, futile.

Ea sensible.

inanimate *adj* lifeless, dead,
defunct, extinct, unconscious,
inactive, inert, dormant, immobile,
stagnant, spiritless, dull.

Ea animate, living, alive.

inappropriate *adj* unsuitable, inapt,
ill-suited, ill-fitted, irrelevant,

incongruous, out of place, untimely,
ill-timed, tactless, improper,
unseemly, unbecoming, unfitting.

Ea appropriate, suitable.

inarticulate *adj* incoherent,
unintelligible, incomprehensible,
unclear, indistinct, hesitant, faltering,
halting, tongue-tied, speechless,
dumb, mute.

Ea articulate.

inattention *n* carelessness,
negligence, disregard, absent-
mindedness, forgetfulness,
daydreaming, preoccupation.

inattentive *adj* distracted, dreamy,
daydreaming, preoccupied, absent-
minded, unmindful, heedless,
regardless, careless, negligent.

Ea attentive.

inaudible *adj* silent, noiseless,
imperceptible, faint, indistinct,
muffled, muted, low, mumbled.

Ea audible, loud.

inaugural *adj* opening,
introductory, first, initial.

inaugurate *v* institute, originate,
begin, commence, start, set up, open,
launch, introduce, usher in, initiate,
induct, ordain, invest, install,
commission, dedicate, consecrate.

inauspicious *adj* unfavourable,
bad, unlucky, unfortunate,
unpromising, discouraging,
threatening, ominous, black.

Ea auspicious, promising.

inborn *adj* innate, inherent, natural,
native, congenital, inbred, hereditary,
inherited, ingrained, instinctive,
intuitive.

Ea learned.

incalculable *adj* countless, untold,
inestimable, limitless, unlimited,
immense, vast.

Ea limited, restricted.

incapable *adj* unable, powerless,
impotent, helpless, weak, feeble,
unfit, unsuited, unqualified,
incompetent, inept, inadequate,
ineffective.

include

❷ capable.

incapacitate *v* disable, cripple, paralyse, immobilize, impotence, put out of action, lay up, scupper (*infml*).

incapacity *n* incapability, inability, disability, powerlessness, impotence, ineffectiveness, weakness, feebleness, inadequacy, incompetency.

❷ capability.

incarnation *n* personification, embodiment, manifestation, impersonation.

incautious *adj* careless, imprudent, injudicious, ill-judged, unthinking, thoughtless, inconsiderate, rash, reckless, hasty, impulsive.

❷ cautious, careful.

incense *v* anger, enrage, infuriate, madden, exasperate, irritate, rile, provoke, excite.

❷ calm.

incentive *n* bait, lure, enticement, carrot (*infml*), sweetener (*sl*), reward, encouragement, inducement, reason, motive, impetus, spur, stimulus, motivation.

❷ disincentive, discouragement, deterrent.

incessant *adj* ceaseless, unceasing, endless, never-ending, interminable, continual, persistent, constant, perpetual, eternal, everlasting, continuous, unbroken, unremitting, non-stop.

❷ intermittent, sporadic, periodic, temporary.

incidence *n* frequency, commonness, prevalence, extent, range, amount, degree, rate, occurrence.

incident *n* **1** OCCURRENCE, happening, event, episode, adventure, affair, occasion, instance. **2** CONFRONTATION, clash, fight, skirmish, commotion, disturbance, scene, upset, mishap.

incidental *adj* accidental, chance, random, minor, non-essential, secondary, subordinate, subsidiary,

ancillary, supplementary, accompanying, attendant, related, contributory.

❷ important, essential.

incinerate *v* burn, cremate, reduce to ashes.

incision *n* cut, opening, slit, gash, notch.

incisive *adj* cutting, keen, sharp, acute, trenchant, piercing, penetrating, biting, caustic, acid, astute, perceptive.

❷ vague.

incite *v* prompt, instigate, rouse, foment, stir up, whip up, work up, excite, animate, provoke, stimulate, spur, goad, impel, drive, urge, encourage, egg on (*infml*).

❷ restrain.

incitement *n* prompting, instigation, agitation, provocation, spur, goad, impetus, stimulus, motivation, encouragement, inducement, incentive.

❷ discouragement.

inclement *adj* intemperate, harsh, severe, stormy, tempestuous, rough.

❷ fine.

inclination *n* **1** LIKING, fondness, taste, predilection, preference, partiality, bias, tendency, trend, disposition, propensity, leaning. **2** *an inclination of 45 degrees*: angle, slope, gradient, incline, pitch, slant, tilt, bend, bow, nod.

❷ disinclination, dislike.

incline *v* **1** DISPOSE, influence, persuade, affect, bias, prejudice. **2** LEAN, slope, slant, tilt, tip, bend, bow, tend, veer.

n slope, gradient, ramp, hill, rise, ascent, acclivity, dip, descent, declivity.

inclined *adj* liable, likely, given, apt, disposed, of a mind, willing.

include *v* comprise, incorporate, embody, comprehend, contain, enclose, embrace, encompass, cover, subsume, take in, add, allow for, take into account, involve, rope in.

Ex exclude, omit, eliminate.

inclusion *n* incorporation, involvement, addition, insertion.
Ex exclusion.

inclusive *adj* comprehensive, full, all-in, all-inclusive, all-embracing, blanket, across-the-board, general, catch-all, overall, sweeping.
Ex exclusive, narrow.

incognito *adj* in disguise, disguised, masked, veiled, unmarked, unidentified, unrecognizable, unknown.
Ex undisguised.

incoherent *adj* unintelligible, incomprehensible, inarticulate, rambling, stammering, stuttering, unconnected, disconnected, broken, garbled, scrambled, confused, muddled, jumbled, disordered.
Ex coherent, intelligible.

income *n* revenue, returns, proceeds, gains, profits, interest, takings, receipts, earnings, pay, salary, wages, means.
Ex expenditure, expenses.

incoming *adj* arriving, entering, approaching, coming, homeward, returning, ensuing, succeeding, next, new.
Ex outgoing.

incomparable *adj* matchless, unmatched, unequalled, unparalleled, unrivalled, peerless, supreme, superlative, superb, brilliant.
Ex ordinary, run-of-the-mill, poor.

incompatible *adj* irreconcilable, contradictory, conflicting, at variance, inconsistent, clashing, mismatched, unsuited.
Ex compatible.

incompetent *adj* incapable, unable, unfit, inefficient, inexpert, unskilful, bungling, stupid, useless, ineffective.
Ex competent, able.

incomplete *adj* deficient, lacking, short, unfinished, abridged, partial, part, fragmentary, broken, imperfect, defective.

Ex complete, exhaustive.

incomprehensible *adj* unintelligible, impenetrable, unfathomable, above one's head, puzzling, perplexing, baffling, mysterious, inscrutable, obscure, opaque.
Ex comprehensible, intelligible.

inconceivable *adj* unthinkable, unimaginable, mind-boggling (*infml*), staggering, unheard-of, unbelievable, incredible, implausible.
Ex conceivable.

inconclusive *adj* unsettled, undecided, open, uncertain, indecisive, ambiguous, vague, unconvincing, unsatisfying.
Ex conclusive.

incongruous *adj* inappropriate, unsuitable, out of place, out of keeping, inconsistent, conflicting, incompatible, irreconcilable, contradictory, contrary.
Ex consistent, compatible.

inconsequential *adj* minor, trivial, trifling, unimportant, insignificant, immaterial.
Ex important.

inconsiderable *adj* small, slight, negligible, trivial, petty, minor, unimportant, insignificant.
Ex considerable, large.

inconsiderate *adj* unkind, uncaring, unconcerned, selfish, self-centred, intolerant, insensitive, tactless, rude, thoughtless, unthinking, careless, heedless.
Ex considerate.

inconsistent *adj* **1** CONFLICTING, at variance, at odds, incompatible, contradictory, contrary, incongruous, discordant. **2** CHANGEABLE, variable, irregular, unpredictable, varying, unstable, unsteady, inconstant, fickle.
Ex **2** constant.

inconsolable *adj* heartbroken, brokenhearted, devastated, desolate, despairing, wretched.

inconspicuous adj hidden, concealed, camouflaged, plain, ordinary, unobtrusive, discreet, low-key, modest, unassuming, quiet, retiring, insignificant.
🔁 conspicuous, noticeable, obtrusive.

incontrovertible adj indisputable, unquestionable, irrefutable, undeniable, certain, clear, self-evident.
🔁 questionable, uncertain.

inconvenience n awkwardness, difficulty, annoyance, nuisance, hindrance, drawback, bother, trouble, fuss, upset, disturbance, disruption.
🔁 convenience.
v bother, disturb, disrupt, put out, trouble, upset, irk.
🔁 convenience.

inconvenient adj awkward, ill-timed, untimely, inopportune, unsuitable, difficult, embarrassing, annoying, troublesome, unwieldy, unmanageable.
🔁 convenient.

incorporate v include, embody, contain, subsume, take in, absorb, assimilate, integrate, combine, unite, merge, blend, mix, fuse, coalesce, consolidate.
🔁 separate.

incorrect adj wrong, mistaken, erroneous, inaccurate, imprecise, inexact, false, untrue, faulty, ungrammatical, improper, illegitimate, inappropriate, unsuitable.
🔁 correct.

incorrigible adj irredeemable, incurable, inveterate, hardened, hopeless.

incorruptible adj honest, straight, upright, moral, honourable, trustworthy, unbribable, just.
🔁 corruptible.

increase v raise, boost, add to, improve, enhance, advance, step up, intensify, strengthen, heighten, grow, develop, build up, wax, enlarge, extend, prolong, expand, spread, swell, magnify, multiply, proliferate, rise, mount, soar, escalate.
🔁 decrease, reduce, decline.
n rise, surge, upsurge, upturn, gain, boost, addition, increment, advance, step-up, intensification, growth, development, enlargement, extension, expansion, spread, proliferation, escalation.
🔁 decrease, reduction, decline.

incredible adj unbelievable, improbable, implausible, far-fetched, preposterous, absurd, impossible, inconceivable, unthinkable, unimaginable, extraordinary, amazing, astonishing, astounding.
🔁 credible, believable.

incredulity n unbelief, disbelief, scepticism, doubt, distrust, mistrust.
🔁 credulity.

incredulous adj unbelieving, disbelieving, unconvinced, sceptical, doubting, distrustful, suspicious, dubious, doubtful, uncertain.
🔁 credulous.

incriminate v inculpate, implicate, involve, accuse, charge, impeach, indict, point the finger at, blame.
🔁 exonerate.

incur v suffer, sustain, provoke, arouse, bring upon oneself, expose oneself to, meet with, run up, gain, earn.

incurable adj 1 an incurable disease: terminal, fatal, untreatable, inoperable, hopeless. 2 INCORRIGIBLE, inveterate, hardened, dyed-in-the-wool.
🔁 1 curable.

indebted adj obliged, grateful, thankful.

indecency n immodesty, indecorum, impurity, obscenity, pornography, lewdness, vulgarity, coarseness, crudity, foulness, grossness.
🔁 decency, modesty.

indecent adj improper, immodest,

impure, indelicate, offensive, obscene, pornographic, lewd, licentious, vulgar, coarse, crude, dirty, filthy, foul, gross, outrageous, shocking.

E3 decent, modest.

indecision n indecisiveness, irresolution, vacillation, wavering, hesitation, hesitancy, ambivalence, uncertainty, doubt.

E3 decisiveness, resolution.

indecisive adj undecided, irresolute, undetermined, vacillating, wavering, in two minds, hesitating, faltering, tentative, uncertain, unsure, doubtful, inconclusive, indefinite, indeterminate, unclear.

E3 decisive.

indeed adv really, actually, in fact, certainly, positively, truly, undeniably, undoubtedly, to be sure.

indefensible adj unjustifiable, inexcusable, unforgivable, unpardonable, insupportable, untenable, wrong, faulty.

E3 defensible, excusable.

indefinite adj unknown, uncertain, unsettled, unresolved, undecided, undetermined, undefined, unspecified, unlimited, ill-defined, vague, indistinct, unclear, obscure, ambiguous, imprecise, inexact, loose, general.

E3 definite, limited, clear.

indefinitely adv for ever, eternally, endlessly, continually, ad infinitum.

indelible adj lasting, enduring, permanent, fast, ineffaceable, ingrained, indestructible.

E3 erasable.

indemnity n compensation, reimbursement, remuneration, reparation, insurance, guarantee, security, protection, immunity, amnesty.

indentation n notch, nick, cut, serration, dent, groove, furrow, depression, dip, hollow, pit, dimple.

independence n autonomy, self-government, self-determination, self-rule, home rule, sovereignty, freedom, liberty, individualism, separation.

E3 dependence.

independent adj 1 AUTONOMOUS, self-governing, self-determining, sovereign, absolute, non-aligned, neutral, impartial, unbiased. 2 FREE, liberated, unconstrained, individualistic, unconventional, self-sufficient, self-supporting, self-reliant, unaided. 3 INDIVIDUAL, self-contained, separate, unconnected, unrelated.

E3 1 dependent.

indescribable adj indefinable, inexpressible, unutterable, unspeakable.

E3 describable.

indestructible adj unbreakable, durable, tough, strong, lasting, enduring, abiding, permanent, eternal, everlasting, immortal, imperishable.

E3 breakable, mortal.

indeterminate adj unspecified, unstated, undefined, unfixed, imprecise, inexact, indefinite, vague, open-ended, undecided, undetermined, uncertain.

E3 known, specified, fixed.

index n 1 index of names: table, key, list, catalogue, directory, guide. 2 INDICATOR, pointer, needle, hand, sign, token, mark, indication, clue.

indicate v register, record, show, reveal, display, manifest, point to, designate, specify, point out, mark, signify, mean, denote, express, suggest, imply.

indication n mark, sign, manifestation, evidence, symptom, signal, warning, omen, intimation, suggestion, hint, clue, note, explanation.

indicator n pointer, needle, marker, sign, symbol, token, signal, display, dial, gauge, meter, index, guide, signpost.

indict *v* charge, accuse, arraign, impeach, summon, summons, prosecute, incriminate.
🗲 exonerate.

indifference *n* apathy, unconcern, coldness, coolness, inattention, disregard, negligence, neutrality, disinterestedness.
🗲 interest, concern.

indifferent *adj* **1** UNINTERESTED, unenthusiastic, unexcited, apathetic, unconcerned, unmoved, uncaring, unsympathetic, cold, cool, distant, aloof, detached, uninvolved, neutral, disinterested. **2** MEDIOCRE, average, middling, passable, moderate, fair, ordinary.
🗲 **1** interested, caring. **2** excellent.

indigenous *adj* native, aboriginal, original, local, home-grown.
🗲 foreign.

indignant *adj* annoyed, angry, irate, heated, fuming, livid, furious, incensed, infuriated, exasperated, outraged.
🗲 pleased, delighted.

indignation *n* annoyance, anger, ire, wrath, rage, fury, exasperation, outrage, scorn, contempt.
🗲 pleasure, delight.

indirect *adj* **1** ROUNDABOUT, circuitous, wandering, rambling, winding, meandering, zigzag, tortuous. **2** *an indirect effect*: secondary, incidental, unintended, subsidiary, ancillary.
🗲 **1** direct. **2** primary.

indiscreet *adj* tactless, undiplomatic, impolitic, injudicious, imprudent, unwise, foolish, rash, reckless, hasty, careless, heedless, unthinking.
🗲 discreet, cautious.

indiscretion *n* mistake, error, slip, boob (*infml*), faux pas, gaffe, tactlessness, rashness, recklessness, foolishness, folly.

indiscriminate *adj* general,

sweeping, wholesale, random, haphazard, hit or miss, aimless, unsystematic, unmethodical, mixed, motley, miscellaneous.
🗲 selective, specific, precise.

indispensable *adj* vital, essential, basic, key, crucial, imperative, required, requisite, needed, necessary.
🗲 dispensable, unnecessary.

indisposed *adj* ill, sick, unwell, poorly, ailing, laid up.
🗲 well.

indisputable *adj* incontrovertible, unquestionable, irrefutable, undeniable, absolute, undisputed, definite, positive, certain, sure.
🗲 doubtful.

indistinct *adj* unclear, ill-defined, blurred, fuzzy, misty, hazy, shadowy, obscure, dim, faint, muffled, confused, unintelligible, vague, woolly, ambiguous, indefinite.
🗲 distinct, clear.

individual *n* person, being, creature, party, body, soul, character, fellow. *adj* distinctive, characteristic, idiosyncratic, peculiar, singular, unique, exclusive, special, personal, own, proper, respective, several, separate, distinct, specific, personalized, particular, single.
🗲 collective, shared, general.

individuality *n* character, personality, distinctiveness, peculiarity, singularity, uniqueness, separateness, distinction.
🗲 sameness.

indoctrinate *v* brainwash, teach, instruct, school, ground, train, drill.

induce *v* **1** CAUSE, effect, bring about, occasion, give rise to, lead to, incite, instigate, prompt, provoke, produce, generate. **2** COAX, prevail upon, encourage, press, persuade, talk into, move, influence, draw, tempt.
🗲 **2** discourage, deter.

inducement *n* lure, bait, attraction,

indulge

enticement, encouragement, incentive, reward, spur, stimulus, motive, reason. ❐ disincentive.

indulge *v* gratify, satisfy, humour, pander to, go along with, give in to, yield to, favour, pet, cosset, mollycoddle, pamper, spoil, treat, regale.

indulgence *n* extravagance, luxury, excess, immoderation, intemperance, favour, tolerance.

indulgent *adj* tolerant, easy-going (*infml*), lenient, permissive, generous, liberal, kind, fond, tender, understanding, patient. ❐ strict, harsh.

industrialist *n* manufacturer, producer, magnate, tycoon, baron, captain of industry, capitalist, financier.

industrious *adj* busy, productive, hard-working, diligent, assiduous, conscientious, zealous, active, energetic, tireless, persistent, persevering. ❐ lazy, idle.

industry *n* **1** *the steel industry*: business, trade, commerce, manufacturing, production. **2** INDUSTRIOUSNESS, diligence, application, effort, labour, toil, persistence, perseverance, determination.

inebriated *adj* drunk, intoxicated, tipsy, merry. ❐ sober.

inedible *adj* uneatable, unpalatable, indigestible, harmful, noxious, poisonous, deadly. ❐ edible.

ineffective *adj* useless, worthless, vain, idle, futile, unavailing, fruitless, unproductive, unsuccessful, powerless, impotent, ineffectual, inadequate, weak, feeble, inept, incompetent. ❐ effective, effectual.

inefficient *adj* uneconomic,

wasteful, money-wasting, time-wasting, incompetent, inexpert, unworkmanlike, slipshod, sloppy, careless, negligent. ❐ efficient.

inelegant *adj* graceless, ungraceful, clumsy, awkward, laboured, ugly, unrefined, crude, unpolished, rough, unsophisticated, uncultivated, uncouth. ❐ elegant.

ineligible *adj* disqualified, ruled out, unacceptable, undesirable, unworthy, unsuitable, unfit, unqualified, unequipped. ❐ eligible.

inept *adj* awkward, clumsy, bungling, incompetent, unskilful, inexpert, foolish, stupid. ❐ competent, skilful.

inequality *n* unequalness, difference, diversity, dissimilarity, disparity, unevenness, disproportion, bias, prejudice. ❐ equality.

inert *adj* immobile, motionless, unmoving, still, inactive, inanimate, lifeless, dead, passive, unresponsive, apathetic, dormant, idle, lazy, lethargic, sluggish, torpid, sleepy. ❐ lively, animated.

inertia *n* immobility, stillness, inactivity, passivity, unresponsiveness, apathy, idleness, laziness, lethargy, torpor. ❐ activity, liveliness.

inescapable *adj* inevitable, unavoidable, destined, fated, certain, sure, irrevocable, unalterable. ❐ escapable.

inevitable *adj* unavoidable, inescapable, necessary, definite, certain, sure, decreed, ordained, destined, fated, automatic, assured, fixed, unalterable, irrevocable, inexorable. ❐ avoidable, uncertain, alterable.

inexcusable *adj* indefensible, unforgivable, unpardonable, intolerable, unacceptable, outrageous, shameful, blameworthy, reprehensible.

☒ excusable, justifiable.

inexhaustible adj **1** an inexhaustible supply: unlimited, limitless, boundless, unbounded, infinite, endless, never-ending, abundant. **2** INDEFATIGABLE, tireless, untiring, unflagging, unwearied, unwearying.

☒ 1 limited.

inexpensive adj cheap, low-priced, reasonable, modest, bargain, budget, low-cost, economical.

☒ expensive, dear.

inexperience n inexpertness, ignorance, unfamiliarity, strangeness, newness, rawness, naïveness, innocence.

☒ experience.

inexperienced adj inexpert, untrained, unskilled, amateur, probationary, apprentice, unacquainted, unfamiliar, unaccustomed, new, fresh, raw, callow, young, immature, naïve, unsophisticated, innocent.

☒ experienced, mature.

inexplicable adj unexplainable, unaccountable, strange, mystifying, puzzling, baffling, mysterious, enigmatic, unfathomable, incomprehensible, incredible, unbelievable, miraculous.

☒ explicable.

inexpressive adj unexpressive, expressionless, deadpan, inscrutable, blank, vacant, empty, emotionless, impassive.

☒ expressive.

infallible adj accurate, unerring, unfailing, foolproof, fail-safe, sure-fire (infml), certain, sure, reliable, dependable, trustworthy, sound, perfect, faultless, impeccable.

☒ fallible.

infamous adj notorious, ill-famed, disreputable, disgraceful, shameful,

shocking, outrageous, scandalous, wicked, iniquitous.

☒ illustrious, glorious.

infamy n notoriety, disrepute, disgrace, shame, dishonour, discredit, ignominy, wickedness.

☒ glory.

infancy n **1** BABYHOOD, childhood, youth. **2** BEGINNING, start, commencement, inception, outset, birth, dawn, genesis, emergence, origins, early stages.

☒ 1 adulthood.

infant n baby, toddler, tot (infml), child, babe (fml), babe in arms (fml).

☒ adult.

adj newborn, baby, young, youthful, juvenile, immature, growing, developing, rudimentary, early, initial, new.

☒ adult, mature.

infantile adj babyish, childish, puerile, juvenile, young, youthful, adolescent, immature.

☒ adult, mature.

infatuated adj besotted, obsessed, enamoured, smitten (infml), crazy (infml), spellbound, mesmerized, captivated, fascinated, enraptured, ravished.

☒ indifferent, disenchanted.

infatuation n besottedness, obsession, fixation, passion, crush (sl), love, fondness, fascination.

☒ indifference, disenchantment.

infect v contaminate, pollute, defile, taint, blight, poison, corrupt, pervert, influence, affect, touch, inspire.

infection n illness, disease, virus, epidemic, contagion, pestilence, contamination, pollution, defilement, taint, blight, poison, corruption, influence.

infectious adj contagious, communicable, transmissible, infective, catching, spreading, epidemic, virulent, deadly, contaminating, polluting, defiling, corrupting.

infer v derive, extrapolate, deduce, conclude, assume, presume, surmise, gather, understand.

inference n deduction, conclusion, corollary, consequence, assumption, presumption, surmise, conjecture, extrapolation, construction, interpretation, reading.

inferior adj **1** LOWER, lesser, minor, secondary, junior, subordinate, subsidiary, second-class, low, humble, menial. **2** *inferior work*: substandard, second-rate, mediocre, bad, poor, unsatisfactory, slipshod, shoddy.
🔁 **1** superior. **2** excellent.
n subordinate, junior, underling (*infml*), minion, vassal, menial.
🔁 superior.

inferiority n **1** SUBORDINATION, subservience, humbleness, lowliness, meanness, insignificance.
2 MEDIOCRITY, imperfection, inadequacy, slovenliness, shoddiness.
🔁 **1** superiority. **2** excellence.

infernal adj hellish, satanic, devilish, diabolical, fiendish, accursed, damned.
🔁 heavenly.

infertile adj barren, sterile, childless, unproductive, unfruitful, arid, parched, dried-up.
🔁 fertile, fruitful.

infest v swarm, teem, throng, flood, overrun, invade, infiltrate, penetrate, permeate, pervade, ravage.

infidelity n adultery, unfaithfulness, faithlessness, disloyalty, duplicity, treachery, betrayal, cheating, falseness.
🔁 fidelity, faithfulness.

infiltrate v penetrate, enter, creep into, insinuate, intrude, pervade, permeate, filter, percolate.

infinite adj limitless, unlimited, boundless, unbounded, endless, never-ending, inexhaustible, bottomless, innumerable, numberless, uncountable, countless, untold, incalculable, inestimable, immeasurable, unfathomable, vast, immense, enormous, huge, absolute, total.
🔁 finite, limited.

infinitesimal adj tiny, minute, microscopic, minuscule, inconsiderable, insignificant, negligible, inappreciable, imperceptible.
🔁 great, large, enormous.

infinity n eternity, perpetuity, limitlessness, boundlessness, endlessness, inexhaustibility, countlessness, immeasurableness, vastness, immensity.
🔁 finiteness, limitation.

infirm adj weak, feeble, frail, ill, unwell, poorly, sickly, failing, faltering, unsteady, shaky, wobbly, doddery, lame.
🔁 healthy, strong.

inflame v anger, enrage, infuriate, incense, exasperate, madden, provoke, stimulate, excite, rouse, arouse, agitate, foment, kindle, ignite, fire, heat, fan, fuel, increase, intensify, worsen, aggravate.
🔁 cool, quench.

inflamed adj sore, swollen, septic, infected, poisoned, red, hot, heated, fevered, feverish.

inflammable adj flammable, combustible, burnable.
🔁 non-flammable, incombustible, flameproof.

inflammation n soreness, painfulness, tenderness, swelling, abscess, infection, redness, heat, rash, sore, irritation.

inflate v blow up, pump up, blow out, puff out, swell, distend, bloat, expand, enlarge, increase, boost, exaggerate.
🔁 deflate.

inflation n expansion, increase, rise, escalation, hyperinflation.
🔁 deflation.

inflexible adj rigid, stiff, hard, solid,

set, fixed, fast, immovable, firm, strict, stringent, unbending, unyielding, adamant, resolute, relentless, implacable, uncompromising, stubborn, obstinate, intransigent, entrenched, dyed-in-the-wool.
⊟ flexible, yielding, adaptable.

inflict v impose, enforce, perpetrate, wreak, administer, apply, deliver, deal, mete out, lay, burden, exact, levy.

influence n power, sway, rule, authority, domination, mastery, hold, control, direction, guidance, bias, prejudice, pull, pressure, effect, impact, weight, importance, prestige, standing.
v dominate, control, manipulate, direct, guide, manoeuvre, change, alter, modify, affect, impress, move, stir, arouse, rouse, sway, persuade, induce, incite, instigate, prompt, motivate, dispose, incline, bias, prejudice, predispose.

influential adj dominant, controlling, leading, authoritative, charismatic, persuasive, convincing, compelling, inspiring, moving, powerful, potent, effective, telling, strong, weighty, momentous, important, significant, instrumental, guiding.
⊟ ineffective, unimportant.

influx n inflow, inrush, invasion, arrival, stream, flow, rush, flood, inundation.

inform v tell, advise, notify, communicate, impart, leak, tip off, acquaint, fill in (infml), brief, instruct, enlighten, illuminate.

inform on betray, incriminate, shop (sl), tell on (infml), squeal (sl), blab, grass (sl), denounce.

informal adj unofficial, unceremonious, casual, relaxed, easy, free, natural, simple, unpretentious, familiar, colloquial.
⊟ formal, solemn.

information n facts, data, input, gen (infml), bumf (sl), intelligence, news, report, bulletin, communiqué, message, word, advice, notice, briefing, instruction, knowledge, dossier, database, databank, clues, evidence.

informative adj educational, instructive, edifying, enlightening, illuminating, revealing, forthcoming, communicative, chatty, gossipy, newsy, helpful, useful, constructive.
⊟ uninformative.

informed adj **1** we'll keep you informed: familiar, conversant, acquainted, enlightened, briefed, primed, posted, up to date, abreast, au fait, in the know (infml). **2** an informed opinion: well-informed, authoritative, expert, versed, well-read, erudite, learned, knowledgeable, well-researched.
⊟ **1** ignorant, unaware.

informer n informant, grass (sl), supergrass (sl), betrayer, traitor, Judas, tell-tale, sneak, spy, mole (infml).

infringe v **1** BREAK, violate, contravene, transgress, overstep, disobey, defy, flout, ignore.
2 INTRUDE, encroach, trespass, invade.

infuriate v anger, vex, enrage, incense, exasperate, madden, provoke, rouse, annoy, irritate, rile, antagonize.
⊟ calm, pacify.

ingenious adj clever, shrewd, cunning, crafty, skilful, masterly, imaginative, creative, inventive, resourceful, original, innovative.
⊟ unimaginative.

ingenuous adj artless, guileless, innocent, honest, sincere, frank, open, plain, simple, unsophisticated, naïve, trusting.
⊟ artful, sly.

ingrained adj fixed, rooted, deep-rooted, deep-seated, entrenched, immovable, ineradicable, permanent, inbuilt, inborn, inbred.

ingratiate *v* curry favour, flatter, creep, crawl, grovel, fawn, get in with.

ingratitude *n* ungratefulness, thanklessness, unappreciativeness, ungraciousness.
🔃 gratitude, thankfulness.

ingredient *n* constituent, element, factor, component, part.

inhabit *v* live, dwell, reside, occupy, possess, colonize, settle, people, populate, stay.

inhabitant *n* resident, dweller, citizen, native, occupier, occupant, inmate, tenant, lodger.

inherent *adj* inborn, inbred, innate, inherited, hereditary, native, natural, inbuilt, built-in, intrinsic, ingrained, essential, fundamental, basic.

inherit *v* succeed to, accede to, assume, come into, be left, receive.

inheritance *n* legacy, bequest, heritage, birthright, heredity, descent, succession.

inheritor *n* heir, heiress, successor, beneficiary, recipient.

inhibit *v* discourage, repress, hold back, suppress, curb, check, restrain, hinder, impede, obstruct, interfere with, frustrate, thwart, prevent, stop, stanch, stem.
🔃 encourage, assist.

inhibited *adj* repressed, self-conscious, shy, reticent, withdrawn, reserved, guarded, subdued.
🔃 uninhibited, open, relaxed.

inhibition *n* repression, hang-up (*sl*), self-consciousness, shyness, reticence, reserve, restraint, curb, check, hindrance, impediment, obstruction, bar.
🔃 freedom.

inhuman *adj* barbaric, barbarous, animal, bestial, vicious, savage, sadistic, cold-blooded, brutal, cruel, inhumane.
🔃 human.

inhumane *adj* unkind, insensitive, callous, unfeeling, heartless, cold-hearted, hard-hearted, pitiless, ruthless, cruel, brutal, inhuman.
🔃 humane, kind, compassionate.

initial *adj* first, beginning, opening, introductory, inaugural, original, primary, early, formative.
🔃 final, last.

initially *adv* at first, at the beginning, to begin with, to start with, originally, first, firstly, first of all.
🔃 finally, in the end.

initiate *v* begin, start, commence, originate, pioneer, institute, set up, introduce, launch, open, inaugurate, instigate, activate, trigger, prompt, stimulate, cause.

initiation *n* admission, reception, entrance, entry, debut, introduction, enrolment, induction, investiture, installation, inauguration, inception.

initiative *n* **1** ENERGY, drive, dynamism, get-up-and-go (*infml*), ambition, enterprise, resourcefulness, inventiveness, originality, innovativeness. **2** SUGGESTION, recommendation, action, lead, first move, first step.

inject *v* **1** *inject drugs*: inoculate, vaccinate, shoot (*sl*). **2** INTRODUCE, insert, add, bring, infuse, instil.

injection *n* inoculation, vaccination, jab (*infml*), shot (*infml*), fix (*sl*), dose, insertion, introduction.

injunction *n* command, order, directive, ruling, mandate, direction, instruction, precept.

injure *v* hurt, harm, damage, impair, spoil, mar, ruin, disfigure, deface, mutilate, wound, cut, break, fracture, maim, disable, cripple, lame, ill-treat, maltreat, abuse, offend, wrong, upset, put out.

injury *n* wound, cut, lesion, fracture, trauma, hurt, mischief, ill, harm, damage, impairment, ruin, disfigurement, mutilation, ill-treatment, abuse, insult, offence, wrong, injustice.

injustice n unfairness, inequality, disparity, discrimination, oppression, bias, prejudice, one-sidedness, partisanship, partiality, favouritism, wrong, iniquity.
🖪 justice, fairness.

inkling n suspicion, idea, notion, faintest (*infml*), glimmering, clue, hint, intimation, suggestion, allusion, indication, sign, pointer.

inlet n bay, cove, creek, fiord, opening, entrance, passage.

inn n public house, pub (*infml*), local (*infml*), tavern, hostelry, hotel.

innate adj inborn, inbred, inherent, intrinsic, native, natural, instinctive, intuitive.
🖪 acquired, learnt.

inner adj internal, interior, inside, inward, innermost, central, middle, concealed, hidden, secret, private, personal, intimate, mental, psychological, spiritual, emotional.
🖪 outer, outward.

innocence n **1** GUILTLESSNESS, blamelessness, honesty, virtue, righteousness, purity, chastity, virginity, incorruptibility, harmlessness, innocuousness. **2** ARTLESSNESS, guilelessness, naïveness, inexperience, ignorance, naturalness, simplicity, unsophistication, unworldliness, credulity, gullibility, trustfulness.
🖪 **1** guilt. **2** experience.

innocent adj **1** *innocent of the crime*: guiltless, blameless, irreproachable, unimpeachable, honest, upright, virtuous, righteous, sinless, faultless, impeccable, stainless, spotless, immaculate, unsullied, untainted, uncontaminated, pure, chaste, virginal, incorrupt, inoffensive, harmless, innocuous. **2** ARTLESS, guileless, ingenuous, naïve, green, inexperienced, fresh, natural, simple, unsophisticated, unworldly, childlike,

credulous, gullible, trusting.
🖪 **1** guilty. **2** experienced.

innocuous adj harmless, safe, inoffensive, unobjectionable, innocent.
🖪 harmful.

innovation n newness, novelty, neologism, modernization, progress, reform, change, alteration, variation, departure.

innovative adj new, fresh, original, creative, imaginative, inventive, resourceful, enterprising, go-ahead, progressive, reforming, bold, daring, adventurous.
🖪 conservative, unimaginative.

innuendo n insinuation, aspersion, slur, whisper, hint, intimation, suggestion, implication.

innumerable adj numberless, unnumbered, countless, uncountable, untold, incalculable, infinite, numerous, many.

inoculation n vaccination, immunization, protection, injection, shot (*infml*), jab (*infml*).

inoffensive adj harmless, innocuous, innocent, peaceable, mild, unobtrusive, unassertive, quiet, retiring.
🖪 offensive, harmful, provocative.

inordinate adj excessive, immoderate, unwarranted, undue, unreasonable, disproportionate, great.
🖪 moderate, reasonable.

inquire, enquire v ASK, question, quiz, query, investigate, look into, probe, examine, inspect, scrutinize, search, explore.

inquiry, enquiry n question, query, investigation, inquest, hearing, inquisition, examination, inspection, scrutiny, study, survey, poll, search, probe, exploration.

inquisitive adj curious, questioning, probing, searching, prying, peeping, snooping, nosey, interfering, meddlesome, intrusive.

insane adj **1** MAD, crazy, mentally ill, lunatic, mental (sl), demented, deranged, unhinged, disturbed. **2** FOOLISH, stupid, senseless, impractical.
E3 **1** sane. **2** sensible.

insanity n madness, craziness, lunacy, mental illness, neurosis, psychosis, mania, dementia, derangement, folly, stupidity, senselessness, irresponsibility.
E3 sanity.

insatiable adj unquenchable, unsatisfiable, ravenous, voracious, immoderate, inordinate.

inscribe v engrave, etch, carve, cut, incise, imprint, impress, stamp, print, write, sign, autograph, dedicate.

inscription n engraving, epitaph, caption, legend, lettering, words, writing, signature, autograph, dedication.

inscrutable adj incomprehensible, unfathomable, impenetrable, deep, inexplicable, unexplainable, baffling, mysterious, enigmatic, cryptic, hidden.
E3 comprehensible, expressive.

insect

Insects include: fly, gnat, midge, mosquito, tsetse-fly, locust, dragonfly, cranefly, daddy longlegs (infml), horsefly, mayfly, butterfly, red admiral, cabbage-white, moth, tiger moth, bee, bumblebee, wasp, hornet, aphid, blackfly, greenfly, whitefly, froghopper, ladybird, water boatman, lacewing; beetle, cockroach, roach (US), earwig, stick insect, grasshopper, cricket, cicada, flea, louse, nit, leatherjacket, termite, glowworm, woodworm, weevil, woodlouse.
Arachnids include: spider, black widow, tarantula, scorpion, mite, tick.

Parts of an insect: abdomen, antenna, cercus, compound eye, forewing, head, hindwing, legs, mandible, mouthpart, ocellus, ovipositor, segment, spiracle, thorax.

insecure adj **1** ANXIOUS, worried, nervous, uncertain, unsure, afraid. **2** UNSAFE, dangerous, hazardous, perilous, precarious, unsteady, shaky, loose, unprotected, defenceless, exposed, vulnerable.
E3 **1** confident, self-assured. **2** secure, safe.

insensible adj numb, anaesthetized, dead, cold, insensitive, unresponsive, blind, deaf, unconscious, unaware, oblivious, unmindful.
E3 conscious.

insensitive adj hardened, tough, resistant, impenetrable, impervious, immune, unsusceptible, thick-skinned, unfeeling, impassive, indifferent, unaffected, unmoved, untouched, uncaring, unconcerned, callous, thoughtless, tactless, crass.
E3 sensitive.

inseparable adj indivisible, indissoluble, inextricable, close, intimate, bosom, devoted.
E3 separable.

insert v put, place, put in, stick in, push in, introduce, implant, embed, engraft, set, inset, let in, interleave, intercalate, interpolate, interpose.
n insertion, enclosure, inset, notice, advertisement, supplement, addition.

inside n interior, content, contents, middle, centre, heart, core.
E3 outside.
adv within, indoors, internally, inwardly, secretly, privately.
E3 outside.
adj interior, internal, inner, innermost, inward, secret, classified, confidential, private.

insides n entrails, guts, intestines, bowels, innards (infml), organs, viscera, belly, stomach.

insidious adj subtle, sly, crafty, cunning, wily, deceptive, devious,

stealthy, surreptitious, furtive, sneaking, treacherous.
⊠ direct, straightforward.

insight n awareness, knowledge, comprehension, understanding, grasp, apprehension, perception, intuition, sensitivity, discernment, judgement, acumen, penetration, observation, vision, wisdom, intelligence.

insignificant adj unimportant, irrelevant, meaningless, inconsequential, minor, trivial, trifling, petty, paltry, small, tiny, insubstantial, inconsiderable, negligible, non-essential.
⊠ significant, important.

insincere adj hypocritical, two-faced, double-dealing, lying, untruthful, dishonest, deceitful, devious, unfaithful, faithless, untrue, false, feigned, pretended, phoney (*infml*), hollow.
⊠ sincere.

insinuate v imply, suggest, allude, hint, intimate, get at (*infml*), indicate.

insipid adj tasteless, flavourless, unsavoury, unappetizing, watery, weak, bland, wishy-washy (*infml*), colourless, drab, dull, monotonous, boring, uninteresting, tame, flat, lifeless, spiritless, characterless, trite, unimaginative, dry.
⊠ tasty, spicy, piquant, appetizing.

insist v demand, require, urge, stress, emphasize, repeat, reiterate, dwell on, harp on, assert, maintain, claim, contend, hold, vow, swear, persist, stand firm.

insistence n demand, entreaty, exhortation, urging, stress, emphasis, repetition, reiteration, assertion, claim, contention, persistence, determination, resolution, firmness.

insistent adj demanding, importunate, emphatic, forceful, pressing, urgent, dogged, tenacious, persistent, persevering, relentless, unrelenting, unremitting, incessant.

insolent adj rude, abusive, insulting, disrespectful, cheeky (*infml*), impertinent, impudent, saucy (*infml*), bold, forward, fresh, presumptuous, arrogant, defiant, insubordinate.
⊠ polite, respectful.

insoluble adj unsolvable, unexplainable, inexplicable, incomprehensible, unfathomable, impenetrable, obscure, mystifying, puzzling, perplexing, baffling.
⊠ explicable.

insolvent adj bankrupt, bust, failed, ruined, broke (*infml*), penniless, destitute.
⊠ solvent.

inspect v check, vet, look over, examine, search, investigate, scrutinize, study, scan, survey, superintend, supervise, oversee, visit.

inspection n check, check-up, examination, scrutiny, scan, study, survey, review, search, investigation, supervision, visit.

inspector n supervisor, superintendent, overseer, surveyor, controller, scrutineer, checker, tester, examiner, investigator, reviewer, critic.

inspiration n **1** CREATIVITY, imagination, genius, muse, influence, encouragement, stimulation, motivation, spur, stimulus. **2** IDEA, brainwave, insight, illumination, revelation, awakening.

inspire v encourage, hearten, influence, impress, animate, enliven, quicken, galvanize, fire, kindle, stir, arouse, trigger, spark off, prompt, spur, motivate, provoke, stimulate, excite, exhilarate, thrill, enthral, enthuse, imbue, infuse.

inspiring adj encouraging, heartening, uplifting, invigorating, stirring, rousing, stimulating, exciting, exhilarating, thrilling, enthralling, moving, affecting, memorable, impressive.
⊠ uninspiring, dull.

instability n unsteadiness, shakiness, vacillation, wavering, irresolution, uncertainty, unpredictability, changeableness, variability, fluctuation, volatility, capriciousness, fickleness, inconstancy, unreliability, insecurity, unsafeness, unsoundness.
≠ stability.

install v fix, fit, lay, put, place, position, locate, site, situate, station, plant, settle, establish, set up, introduce, institute, inaugurate, invest, induct, ordain.

instalment n **1** *pay in instalments*: payment, repayment, portion. **2** EPISODE, chapter, part, section, division.

instant n flash, twinkling, trice, moment, tick (*infml*), split second, second, minute, time, occasion. *adj* instantaneous, immediate, on-the-spot, direct, prompt, urgent, unhesitating, quick, fast, rapid, swift. **≠** slow.

instead adv alternatively, preferably, rather.
instead of in place of, in lieu of, on behalf of, in preference to, rather than.

instigate v initiate, set on, start, begin, cause, generate, inspire, move, influence, encourage, urge, spur, prompt, provoke, stimulate, incite, stir up, whip up, foment, rouse, excite.

instil v infuse, imbue, insinuate, introduce, inject, implant, inculcate, impress, din into (*infml*).

instinct n intuition, sixth sense, gut reaction (*infml*), impulse, urge, feeling, hunch, flair, knack, gift, talent, feel, faculty, ability, aptitude, predisposition, tendency.

instinctive adj natural, native, inborn, innate, inherent, intuitive, impulsive, involuntary, automatic, mechanical, reflex, spontaneous, immediate, unthinking, unpremeditated, gut (*infml*), visceral.

≠ conscious, voluntary, deliberate.

institute v originate, initiate, introduce, enact, begin, start, commence, create, establish, set up, organize, found, inaugurate, open, launch, appoint, install, invest, induct, ordain.
≠ cancel, discontinue, abolish.
n school, college, academy, conservatory, foundation, institution.

institution n **1** CUSTOM, tradition, usage, practice, ritual, convention, rule, law. **2** ORGANIZATION, association, society, guild, concern, corporation, foundation, establishment, institute, hospital, home. **3** INITIATION, introduction, enactment, inception, creation, establishment, formation, founding, foundation, installation.

instruct v **1** TEACH, educate, tutor, coach, train, drill, ground, school, discipline. **2** ORDER, command, direct, mandate, tell, inform, notify, advise, counsel, guide.

instruction n **1** *follow the instructions*: direction, recommendation, advice, guidance, information, order, command, injunction, mandate, directive, ruling. **2** EDUCATION, schooling, lesson(s), tuition, teaching, training, coaching, drilling, grounding, preparation.

instructive adj informative, educational, edifying, enlightening, illuminating, helpful, useful.
≠ unenlightening.

instructor n teacher, master, mistress, tutor, coach, trainer, demonstrator, exponent, adviser, mentor, guide, guru.

instrument n **1** TOOL, implement, utensil, appliance, gadget, contraption, device, contrivance, apparatus, mechanism. **2** AGENT, agency, vehicle, organ, medium, factor, channel, way, means.

instrumental adj active, involved,

contributory, conducive, influential, useful, helpful, auxiliary, subsidiary.
₣ obstructive, unhelpful.

insufferable *adj* intolerable, unbearable, detestable, loathsome, dreadful, impossible.
₣ pleasant, tolerable.

insufficiency *n* inadequacy, shortage, deficiency, lack, scarcity, dearth, want, need, poverty.
₣ sufficiency, excess.

insufficient *adj* inadequate, short, deficient, lacking, sparse, scanty, scarce.
₣ sufficient, excessive.

insular *adj* parochial, provincial, cut off, detached, isolated, remote, withdrawn, inward-looking, blinkered, closed, narrow-minded, narrow, limited, petty.

insulate *v* cushion, pad, lag, cocoon, protect, shield, shelter, isolate, separate, cut off.

insult *v* abuse, call names, disparage, revile, libel, slander, slight, snub, injure, affront, offend, outrage.
₣ compliment, praise.
n abuse, rudeness, insolence, defamation, libel, slander, slight, snub, affront, indignity, offence, outrage.
₣ compliment, praise.

insurance *n* cover, protection, safeguard, security, provision, assurance, indemnity, guarantee, warranty, policy, premium.

insure *v* cover, protect, assure, underwrite, indemnify, guarantee, warrant.

∗ **insurmountable** *adj* insuperable, unconquerable, invincible, overwhelming, hopeless, impossible.
₣ surmountable.

insurrection *n* rising, uprising, insurgence, riot, rebellion, mutiny, revolt, revolution, coup, putsch.

intact *adj* unbroken, all in one piece, whole, complete, integral, entire, perfect, sound, undamaged, unhurt, uninjured.
₣ broken, incomplete, damaged.

intangible *adj* insubstantial, imponderable, elusive, fleeting, airy, shadowy, vague, indefinite, abstract, unreal, invisible.
₣ tangible, real.

integral *adj* **1** *an integral part*: intrinsic, constituent, elemental, basic, fundamental, necessary, essential, indispensable.
2 COMPLETE, entire, full, whole, undivided.
₣ **1** extra, additional, unnecessary.

integrate *v* assimilate, merge, join, unite, combine, amalgamate, incorporate, coalesce, fuse, knit, mesh, mix, blend, harmonize.
₣ divide, separate.

integrity *n* **1** HONESTY, uprightness, probity, incorruptibility, purity, morality, principle, honour, virtue, goodness, righteousness.
2 COMPLETENESS, wholeness, unity, coherence, cohesion.
₣ **1** dishonesty. **2** incompleteness.

intellect *n* mind, brain(s), brainpower, intelligence, genius, reason, understanding, sense, wisdom, judgement.
₣ stupidity.

intellectual *adj* academic, scholarly, intelligent, studious, thoughtful, cerebral, mental, highbrow, cultural.
₣ low-brow.
n thinker, academic, highbrow, egghead, mastermind, genius.
₣ low-brow.

intelligence *n* **1** INTELLECT, reason, wit(s), brain(s) (*infml*), brainpower, cleverness, brightness, aptitude, quickness, alertness, discernment, perception, understanding, comprehension.
2 INFORMATION, facts, data, low-down (*sl*), knowledge, findings, news, report, warning, tip-off.
₣ **1** stupidity, foolishness.

intelligent *adj* clever, bright, smart,

brainy (*infml*), quick, alert, quick-witted, sharp, acute, knowing, knowledgeable, well-informed, thinking, rational, sensible.
E3 unintelligent, stupid, foolish.

intend *v* aim, have a mind, contemplate, mean, propose, plan, project, scheme, plot, design, purpose, resolve, determine, destine, mark out, earmark, set apart.

intense *adj* great, deep, profound, strong, powerful, forceful, fierce, harsh, severe, acute, sharp, keen, eager, earnest, ardent, fervent, fervid, passionate, vehement, energetic, violent, intensive, concentrated, heightened.
E3 moderate, mild, weak.

intensify *v* increase, step up, escalate, heighten, hot up (*infml*), fire, boost, fuel, aggravate, add to, strengthen, reinforce, sharpen, whet, quicken, deepen, concentrate, emphasize, enhance.
E3 reduce, weaken.

intensive *adj* concentrated, thorough, exhaustive, comprehensive, detailed, in-depth, thoroughgoing, all-out, intense.
E3 superficial.

intent *adj* determined, resolved, resolute, set, bent, concentrated, eager, earnest, committed, steadfast, fixed, alert, attentive, concentrating, preoccupied, engrossed, wrapped up, absorbed, occupied.
E3 absent-minded, distracted.

intention *n* aim, purpose, object, end, point, target, goal, objective, idea, plan, design, view, intent, meaning.

intentional *adj* designed, wilful, conscious, planned, deliberate, prearranged, premeditated, calculated, studied, intended, meant.
E3 unintentional, accidental.

intercede *v* mediate, arbitrate, intervene, plead, entreat, beseech, speak.

intercept *v* head off, ambush, interrupt, cut off, stop, arrest, catch, take, seize, check, block, obstruct, delay, frustrate, thwart.

interchangeable *adj* reciprocal, equivalent, similar, identical, the same, synonymous, standard.
E3 different.

interest *n* **1** IMPORTANCE, significance, note, concern, care, attention, notice, curiosity, involvement, participation. **2** *leisure interests*: activity, pursuit, pastime, hobby, diversion, amusement. **3** ADVANTAGE, benefit, profit, gain.
E3 1 boredom.
v concern, involve, touch, move, attract, appeal to, divert, amuse, occupy, engage, absorb, engross, fascinate, intrigue.
E3 bore.

interested *adj* **1** ATTENTIVE, curious, absorbed, engrossed, fascinated, enthusiastic, keen, attracted. **2** CONCERNED, involved, affected.
E3 1 uninterested, indifferent, apathetic. **2** disinterested, unaffected.

interesting *adj* attractive, appealing, entertaining, engaging, absorbing, engrossing, fascinating, intriguing, compelling, gripping, stimulating, thought-provoking, curious, unusual.
E3 uninteresting, boring, monotonous, tedious.

interfere *v* **1** INTRUDE, poke one's nose in, pry, butt in, interrupt, intervene, meddle, tamper. **2** HINDER, hamper, obstruct, block, impede, handicap, cramp, inhibit, conflict, clash.
E3 2 assist.

interference *n* **1** INTRUSION, prying, interruption, intervention, meddling. **2** OBSTRUCTION, opposition, conflict, clashing.
E3 2 assistance.

interim *adj* temporary, provisional,

stopgap, makeshift, improvised, stand-in, acting, caretaker.

n meantime, meanwhile, interval.

interior *adj* **1** INTERNAL, inside, inner, central, inward, mental, spiritual, private, secret, hidden. **2** HOME, domestic, inland, up-country, remote.

F3 **1** exterior, external.

n inside, centre, middle, core, heart, depths.

F3 exterior, outside.

interjection *n* exclamation, ejaculation, cry, shout, call, interpolation.

intermediary *n* mediator, go-between, middleman, broker, agent.

intermediate *adj* midway, halfway, in-between, middle, mid, median, mean, intermediary, intervening, transitional.

F3 extreme.

interminable *adj* endless, never-ending, ceaseless, perpetual, limitless, unlimited, long, long-winded, long-drawn-out, dragging, wearisome.

F3 limited, brief.

intermission *n* interval, entr'acte, interlude, break, recess, rest, respite, breather (*infml*), breathing-space, pause, lull, let-up (*infml*), remission, suspension, interruption, halt, stop, stoppage, cessation.

intermittent *adj* occasional, periodic, sporadic, spasmodic, fitful, erratic, irregular, broken.

F3 continuous, constant.

internal *adj* inside, inner, interior, inward, intimate, private, personal, domestic, in-house.

F3 external.

international *adj* global, worldwide, intercontinental, cosmopolitan, universal, general.

F3 national, local, parochial.

interplay *n* exchange, interchange, interaction, reciprocation, give-and-take.

interpose *v* insert, introduce,

interject, interpolate, put in, thrust in, interrupt, intrude, interfere, come between, intervene, step in, mediate.

interpret *v* explain, expound, elucidate, clarify, throw light on, define, paraphrase, translate, render, decode, decipher, solve, make sense of, understand, construe, read, take.

interpretation *n* explanation, clarification, analysis, translation, rendering, version, performance, reading, understanding, sense, meaning.

interrogate *v* question, quiz, examine, cross-examine, grill, give the third degree, pump, debrief.

interrogation *n* questioning, cross-questioning, examination, cross-examination, grilling, third degree, inquisition, inquiry, inquest.

interrupt *v* intrude, barge in (*infml*), butt in, interject, break in, heckle, disturb, disrupt, interfere, obstruct, check, hinder, hold up, stop, halt, suspend, discontinue, cut off, disconnect, punctuate, separate, divide, cut, break.

interruption *n* intrusion, interjection, disturbance, disruption, obstruction, impediment, obstacle, hitch, pause, break, halt, stop, stoppage, suspension, discontinuance, disconnection, separation, division.

intersect *v* cross, criss-cross, cut across, bisect, divide, meet, converge.

intersection *n* junction, interchange, crossroads, crossing.

intertwine *v* entwine, interweave, interlace, interlink, twist, twine, cross, weave.

interval *n* interlude, intermission, break, rest, pause, delay, wait, interim, meantime, meanwhile, gap, opening, space, distance, period, spell, time, season.

intervene *v* **1** STEP IN, mediate, arbitrate, interfere, interrupt, intrude. **2** OCCUR, happen, elapse, pass.

intervention *n* involvement, interference, intrusion, mediation, agency, intercession.

interview *n* audience, consultation, talk, dialogue, meeting, conference, press conference, oral examination, viva.

v question, interrogate, examine, vet.

intestines *n* bowels, guts, entrails, insides, innards (*infml*), offal, viscera, vitals.

intimacy *n* friendship, closeness, familiarity, confidence, confidentiality, privacy.
⊟ distance.

intimate[1] *v* hint, insinuate, imply, suggest, indicate, communicate, impart, tell, state, declare, announce.

intimate[2] *adj* friendly, informal, familiar, cosy, warm, affectionate, dear, bosom, close, near, confidential, secret, private, personal, internal, innermost, deep, penetrating, detailed, exhaustive.
⊟ unfriendly, cold, distant.
n friend, bosom friend, confidant(e), associate.
⊟ stranger.

intimidate *v* daunt, cow, overawe, appal, dismay, alarm, scare, frighten, terrify, threaten, menace, terrorize, bully, browbeat, bulldoze, coerce, pressure, pressurize, lean on (*sl*).

intolerable *adj* unbearable, unendurable, insupportable, unacceptable, insufferable, impossible.
⊟ tolerable.

intolerant *adj* impatient, prejudiced, bigoted, narrow-minded, small-minded, opinionated, dogmatic, illiberal, uncharitable.
⊟ tolerant.

intonation *n* modulation, tone, accentuation, inflection.

intoxicated *adj* 1 DRUNK, drunken, inebriated, tipsy. 2 EXCITED, elated, exhilarated, thrilled.

intoxicating *adj* 1 *intoxicating liquor*: alcoholic, strong.
2 EXCITING, stimulating, heady, exhilarating, thrilling.
⊟ 1 sobering.

intoxication *n* 1 DRUNKENNESS, inebriation, tipsiness.
2 EXCITEMENT, elation, exhilaration, euphoria.
⊟ 1 sobriety.

intrepid *adj* bold, daring, brave, courageous, plucky, valiant, lion-hearted, fearless, dauntless, undaunted, stout-hearted, stalwart, gallant, heroic.
⊟ cowardly, timid.

intricate *adj* elaborate, fancy, ornate, rococo, complicated, complex, sophisticated, involved, convoluted, tortuous, tangled, entangled, knotty, perplexing, difficult.
⊟ simple, plain, straightforward.

intrigue *n* 1 PLOT, scheme, conspiracy, collusion, machination, manoeuvre, stratagem, ruse, wile, trickery, double-dealing, sharp practice. 2 ROMANCE, liaison, affair, amour, intimacy.
v 1 FASCINATE, rivet, puzzle, tantalize, attract, charm, captivate.
2 PLOT, scheme, conspire, connive, machinate, manoeuvre.
⊟ 1 bore.

introduce *v* 1 INSTITUTE, begin, start, commence, establish, found, inaugurate, launch, open, bring in, announce, present, acquaint, familiarize, initiate. 2 PUT FORWARD, advance, submit, offer, propose, suggest.
⊟ 1 end, conclude. 2 remove, take away.

introduction *n* 1 INSTITUTION, beginning, start, commencement, establishment, inauguration, launch, presentation, debut, initiation.
2 FOREWORD, preface, preamble,

prologue, preliminaries, overture,
prelude, lead-in, opening.
E3 1 removal, withdrawal. **2** appendix,
conclusion.

introductory *adj* preliminary,
preparatory, opening, inaugural,
first, initial, early, elementary, basic.

introspective *adj* inward-looking,
contemplative, meditative, pensive,
thoughtful, brooding, introverted,
self-centred, reserved, withdrawn.
E3 outward-looking.

introverted *adj* introspective,
inward-looking, self-centred,
withdrawn, shy, reserved, quiet.
E3 extroverted.

intrude *v* interrupt, butt in, meddle,
interfere, violate, infringe, encroach,
trespass.
E3 withdraw, stand back.

intruder *n* trespasser, prowler,
burglar, raider, invader, infiltrator,
interloper, gatecrasher.

intrusion *n* interruption,
interference, violation, infringement,
encroachment, trespass, invasion,
incursion.
E3 withdrawal.

intuition *n* instinct, sixth sense,
perception, discernment, insight,
hunch, feeling, gut feeling (*infml*).
E3 reasoning.

intuitive *adj* instinctive,
spontaneous, involuntary, innate,
untaught.
E3 reasoned.

inundate *v* flood, deluge, swamp,
engulf, submerge, immerse, drown,
bury, overwhelm, overrun.

invade *v* enter, penetrate, infiltrate,
burst in, descend on, attack, raid,
seize, occupy, overrun, swarm over,
infest, pervade, encroach, infringe,
violate.
E3 withdraw, evacuate.

invalid[1] *adj* sick, ill, poorly, ailing,
sickly, weak, feeble, frail, infirm,
disabled, bedridden.
E3 healthy.

n patient, convalescent.

invalid[2] *adj* **1** FALSE, fallacious,
unsound, ill-founded, unfounded,
baseless, illogical, irrational,
unscientific, wrong, incorrect.
2 ILLEGAL, null, void, worthless.
E3 1 valid. **2** legal.

invaluable *adj* priceless,
inestimable, incalculable, precious,
valuable, useful.
E3 worthless, cheap.

invariable *adj* fixed, set, unvarying,
unchanging, unchangeable,
permanent, constant, steady,
unwavering, uniform, rigid,
inflexible, habitual, regular.
E3 variable.

invariably *adv* always, without
exception, without fail, unfailingly,
consistently, regularly, habitually.
E3 never.

invasion *n* attack, offensive,
onslaught, raid, incursion, foray,
breach, penetration, infiltration,
intrusion, encroachment,
infringement, violation.
E3 withdrawal, evacuation.

invent *v* conceive, think up, design,
discover, create, originate, formulate,
frame, devise, contrive, improvise,
fabricate, make up, concoct, cook up,
trump up, imagine, dream up.

invention *n* **1** *her latest invention*:
design, creation, brainchild,
discovery, development, device,
gadget. **2** LIE, falsehood, deceit,
fabrication, fiction, tall story,
fantasy, figment. **3** INVENTIVENESS,
imagination, creativity, innovation,
originality, ingenuity, inspiration,
genius.
E3 2 truth.

inventive *adj* imaginative, creative,
innovative, original, ingenious,
resourceful, fertile, inspired, gifted,
clever.

inventor *n* designer, discoverer,
creator, originator, author, architect,
maker, scientist, engineer.

inverse *adj* inverted, upside down, transposed, reversed, opposite, contrary, reverse, converse.

invert *v* upturn, turn upside down, overturn, capsize, upset, transpose, reverse.

☐ right.

invertebrate

Invertebrates include: sponges: calcareous, glass, horny; *jellyfish, corals and sea anemones:* Portuguese man-of-war, box jellyfish, sea wasp, dead-men's fingers, sea pansy, sea gooseberry, Venus's girdle; *echinoderms:* sea lily, feather star, starfish, crown-of-thorns, brittle star, sea urchin, sand dollar, sea cucumber; *worms:* annelid worm, arrow worm, blood fluke, bristle worm, earthworm, eelworm, flatworm, fluke, hookworm, leech, liver fluke, lugworm, peanut worm, pinworm, ragworm, ribbonworm, roundworm, sea mouse, tapeworm, threadworm; *crustaceans:* acorn barnacle, barnacle, brine shrimp, crayfish, daphnia, fairy shrimp, fiddler crab, fish louse, goose barnacle, hermit crab, krill, lobster, mantis shrimp, mussel shrimp, pill bug, prawn, sand hopper, seed shrimp, spider crab, spiny lobster, tadpole shrimp, water flea, whale louse, woodlouse; centipede, millipede, velvet worm.

---

invest *v* **1** SPEND, lay out, put in, sink. **2** PROVIDE, supply, endow, vest, empower, authorize, sanction.

investigate *v* inquire into, look into, consider, examine, study, inspect, scrutinize, analyse, go into, probe, explore, search, sift.

investigation *n* inquiry, inquest, hearing, examination, study, research, survey, review, inspection, scrutiny, analysis, probe, exploration, search.

investigator *n* examiner, researcher, detective, sleuth (*infml*), private detective, private eye (*infml*).

investment *n* asset, speculation, venture, stake, contribution, outlay, expenditure, transaction.

invigorate *v* vitalize, energize, animate, enliven, liven up, quicken, strengthen, fortify, brace, stimulate, inspire, exhilarate, perk up, refresh, freshen, revitalize, rejuvenate.

☐ tire, weary, dishearten.

invincible *adj* unbeatable, unconquerable, insuperable, unsurmountable, indomitable, unassailable, impregnable, impenetrable, invulnerable, indestructible.

☐ beatable.

invisible *adj* unseen, out of sight, hidden, concealed, disguised, inconspicuous, indiscernible, imperceptible, infinitesimal, microscopic, imaginary, non-existent.

☐ visible.

invitation *n* request, solicitation, call, summons, temptation, enticement, allurement, come-on (*infml*), encouragement, inducement, provocation, incitement, challenge.

invite *v* ask, call, summon, welcome, encourage, lead, draw, attract, tempt, entice, allure, bring on, provoke, ask for, request, solicit, seek.

inviting *adj* welcoming, appealing, attractive, tempting, seductive, enticing, alluring, pleasing, delightful, captivating, fascinating, intriguing, tantalizing.

☐ uninviting, unappealing.

invoke *v* call upon, conjure, appeal to, petition, solicit, implore, entreat, beg, beseech, supplicate, pray.

involuntary *adj* spontaneous, unconscious, automatic, mechanical, reflex, instinctive, conditioned, impulsive, unthinking, blind, uncontrolled, unintentional.

☐ deliberate, intentional.

involve v **1** REQUIRE, necessitate, mean, imply, entail, include, incorporate, embrace, cover, take in, affect, concern. **2** IMPLICATE, incriminate, inculpate, draw in, mix up, embroil, associate. **3** ENGAGE, occupy, absorb, engross, preoccupy, hold, grip, rivet.
✲ 1 exclude.

involved adj **1** CONCERNED, implicated, mixed up, caught up, in on (sl), participating. **2** an involved explanation: complicated, complex, intricate, elaborate, tangled, knotty, tortuous, confusing.
✲ 1 uninvolved. **2** simple.

involvement n concern, interest, responsibility, association, connection, participation, implication, entanglement.

invulnerable adj safe, secure, unassailable, impenetrable, invincible, indestructible.
✲ vulnerable.

inward adj incoming, entering, inside, interior, internal, inner, innermost, inmost, personal, private, secret, confidential.
✲ outward, external.

iota n scrap, bit, mite, jot, speck, trace, hint, grain, particle, atom.

irate adj annoyed, irritated, indignant, up in arms, angry, enraged, mad (infml), furious, infuriated, incensed, worked up, fuming, livid, exasperated.
✲ calm, composed.

iron adj rigid, inflexible, adamant, determined, hard, steely, tough, strong.
✲ pliable, weak.
v press, smooth, flatten.

iron out resolve, settle, sort out, straighten out, clear up, put right, reconcile, deal with, get rid of, eradicate, eliminate.

ironic adj ironical, sarcastic, sardonic, scornful, contemptuous, derisive, sneering, scoffing, mocking, satirical, wry, paradoxical.

irony n sarcasm, mockery, satire, paradox, contrariness, incongruity.

irrational adj unreasonable, unsound, illogical, absurd, crazy, wild, foolish, silly, senseless, unwise.
✲ rational.

irreconcilable adj incompatible, opposed, conflicting, clashing, contradictory, inconsistent.
✲ reconcilable.

irrefutable adj undeniable, incontrovertible, indisputable, incontestable, unquestionable, unanswerable, certain, sure.

irregular adj **1** ROUGH, bumpy, uneven, crooked. **2** VARIABLE, fluctuating, wavering, erratic, fitful, intermittent, sporadic, spasmodic, occasional, random, haphazard, disorderly, unsystematic.
3 ABNORMAL, unconventional, unorthodox, improper, unusual, exceptional, anomalous.
✲ 1 smooth, level. **2** regular.
3 conventional.

irrelevant adj immaterial, beside the point, inapplicable, inappropriate, unrelated, unconnected, inconsequent, peripheral, tangential.
✲ relevant.

irreplaceable adj indispensable, essential, vital, unique, priceless, peerless, matchless, unmatched.
✲ replaceable.

irrepressible adj ebullient, bubbly, uninhibited, buoyant, resilient, boisterous, uncontrollable, ungovernable, unstoppable.

irreproachable adj irreprehensible, blameless, unimpeachable, faultless, impeccable, perfect, unblemished, immaculate, stainless, spotless, pure.
✲ blameworthy, culpable.

irresistible adj overwhelming, overpowering, unavoidable, inevitable, inescapable, uncontrollable, potent, compelling,

imperative, pressing, urgent,
tempting, seductive, ravishing,
enchanting, charming, fascinating.
ᴇ﹖ resistible, avoidable.

irresponsible *adj* unreliable,
untrustworthy, careless, negligent,
thoughtless, heedless, ill-considered,
rash, reckless, wild, carefree, light-
hearted, immature.
ᴇ﹖ responsible, cautious.

irreverent *adj* **1** IMPIOUS, godless,
irreligious, profane, sacrilegious,
blasphemous. **2** DISRESPECTFUL,
discourteous, rude, impudent,
impertinent, mocking, flippant.
ᴇ﹖ 1 reverent. 2 respectful.

irreversible *adj* irrevocable,
unalterable, final, permanent, lasting,
irreparable, irremediable,
irretrievable, incurable, hopeless.
ᴇ﹖ reversible, remediable, curable.

irrevocable *adj* unalterable,
unchangeable, changeless, invariable,
immutable, final, fixed, settled,
predetermined, irreversible,
irretrievable.
ᴇ﹖ alterable, flexible, reversible.

irrigate *v* water, flood, inundate,
wet, moisten, dampen.

irritable *adj* cross, bad-tempered,
ill-tempered, crotchety, crusty,
cantankerous, crabby, testy, short-
tempered, snappish, snappy, short,
impatient, touchy, edgy, thin-
skinned, hypersensitive, prickly,
peevish, fretful, fractious.
ᴇ﹖ good-tempered, cheerful.

irritate *v* **1** ANNOY, get on one's
nerves, aggravate (*infml*), bother,
harass, rouse, provoke, rile, anger,
enrage, infuriate, incense, exasperate,
peeve, put out. **2** INFLAME, chafe,
rub, tickle, itch.
ᴇ﹖ 1 please, gratify.

irritation *n* displeasure,
dissatisfaction, annoyance,
aggravation, provocation, anger,
vexation, indignation, fury,
exasperation, irritability, crossness,

testiness, snappiness, impatience.
ᴇ﹖ pleasure, satisfaction, delight.

isolate *v* set apart, sequester,
seclude, keep apart, segregate,
quarantine, insulate, cut off, detach,
remove, disconnect, separate,
divorce, alienate, shut out, ostracize,
exclude.
ᴇ﹖ assimilate, incorporate.

isolated *adj* **1** REMOTE, out-of-the-
way, outlying, god-forsaken,
deserted, unfrequented, secluded,
detached, cut off, lonely, solitary,
single. **2** *an isolated occurrence*:
unique, special, exceptional, atypical,
unusual, freak, abnormal,
anomalous.
ᴇ﹖ 1 populous. 2 typical.

isolation *n* quarantine, solitude,
solitariness, loneliness, remoteness,
seclusion, retirement, withdrawal,
exile, segregation, insulation,
separation, detachment,
disconnection, dissociation,
alienation.

issue *n* **1** MATTER, affair, concern,
problem, point, subject, topic,
question, debate, argument, dispute,
controversy. **2** PUBLICATION,
release, distribution, supply, delivery,
circulation, promulgation, broadcast,
announcement. **3** *last week's issue*:
copy, number, instalment, edition,
impression, printing.
v **1** PUBLISH, release, distribute,
supply, deliver, give out, deal out,
circulate, promulgate, broadcast,
announce, put out, emit, produce.
2 ORIGINATE, stem, spring, rise,
emerge, burst forth, gush, flow,
proceed, emanate, arise.

itch *v* tickle, irritate, tingle, prickle,
crawl.
n **1** ITCHINESS, tickle, irritation,
prickling. **2** EAGERNESS, keenness,
desire, longing, yearning, hankering,
craving.

item *n* **1** OBJECT, article, thing,
piece, component, ingredient,

element, factor, point, detail, particular, aspect, feature, consideration, matter. **2** *an item in the local paper*: article, piece, report, account, notice, entry, paragraph.

itinerant *adj* travelling, peripatetic, roving, roaming, wandering,

rambling, nomadic, migratory, rootless, unsettled.
F∃ stationary, settled.

itinerary *n* route, course, journey, tour, circuit, plan, programme, schedule.

J

jab *v* poke, prod, dig, nudge, stab, push, elbow, lunge, punch, tap, thrust.

jackpot *n* prize, winnings, kitty, pool, pot, reward, award, big time (*infml*), bonanza, stakes.

jaded *adj* fatigued, exhausted, dulled, played-out, tired, tired out, weary, spent, bored, fagged (*infml*).
F∃ fresh, refreshed.

jagged *adj* uneven, irregular, notched, indented, rough, serrated, saw-edged, toothed, ragged, pointed, ridged, craggy, barbed, broken.
F∃ even, smooth.

jail, gaol *n* prison, jailhouse, custody, lock-up, penitentiary, guardhouse, inside (*infml*), nick (*sl*), clink (*sl*).
v imprison, incarcerate, lock up, put away, send down, confine, detain, intern, impound, immure.

jailer, gaoler *n* prison officer, warden, warder, guard, screw (*sl*), keeper, captor.

jam¹ *v* **1** CRAM, pack, wedge, squash, squeeze, press, crush, crowd, congest, ram, stuff, confine, force. **2** BLOCK, clog, obstruct, stall, stick.
n **1** CRUSH, crowd, press, congestion, pack, mob, throng, bottle-neck, traffic jam. **2** PREDICAMENT, trouble, quandary, plight, fix (*infml*).

jam² *n* conserve, preserve, jelly, spread, marmalade.

jangle *v* clank, clash, jar, clatter,

jingle, chime, rattle, vibrate.
n clang, clash, rattle, jar, cacophony, dissonance, din, discord, racket, reverberation.
F∃ euphony.

jar¹ *n* pot, container, vessel, receptacle, crock, pitcher, urn, vase, flagon, jug, mug.

jar² *v* **1** JOLT, agitate, rattle, shake, vibrate, jangle, rock, disturb, discompose. **2** ANNOY, irritate, grate, nettle (*infml*), offend, upset, irk. **3** BICKER, quarrel, clash, disagree.

jargon *n* **1** PARLANCE, cant, argot, vernacular, idiom. **2** NONSENSE, gobbledegook (*infml*), mumbo-jumbo (*infml*), gibberish.

jarring *adj* discordant, jangling, harsh, grating, irritating, cacophonous, rasping, strident, upsetting, disturbing, jolting.

jaundiced *adj* **1** BITTER, cynical, pessimistic, sceptical, distrustful, disbelieving, envious, jealous, hostile, jaded, suspicious, resentful. **2** DISTORTED, biased, prejudiced, preconceived.

jaunty *adj* sprightly, lively, perky, breezy, buoyant, high-spirited, self-confident, carefree, airy, cheeky, debonair, dapper, smart, showy, spruce.
F∃ depressed, dowdy.

jaw (*infml*) *v* chat, chatter, gossip, natter (*infml*), talk, rabbit (on) (*infml*), gabble, babble.

n talk, gossip, chat, conversation, discussion, chinwag, natter (*infml*).

jealous *adj* 1 ENVIOUS, covetous, grudging, resentful, green (*infml*), green-eyed (*infml*). 2 SUSPICIOUS, wary, distrustful, anxious, possessive, protective.

F3 1 contented, satisfied.

jealousy *n* 1 ENVY, covetousness, grudge, resentment, spite, ill-will. 2 SUSPICION, distrust, mistrust, possessiveness.

jeer *v* mock, scoff, taunt, jibe, ridicule, sneer, deride, make fun of, chaff, barrack, twit, knock (*infml*), heckle, banter.

n mockery, derision, ridicule, taunt, jibe, sneer, scoff, abuse, catcall, dig (*infml*), hiss, hoot.

jell see gel.

jeopardize *v* endanger, imperil, risk, hazard, venture, gamble, chance, threaten, menace, expose, stake.

F3 protect, safeguard.

jeopardy *n* danger, peril, risk, hazard, endangerment, venture, vulnerability, precariousness, insecurity, exposure, liability.

F3 safety, security.

jerk *n* jolt, tug, twitch, jar, jog, yank, wrench, pull, pluck, lurch, throw, thrust, shrug.

v jolt, tug, twitch, jog, yank, wrench, pull, jiggle, lurch, pluck, thrust, shrug, throw, bounce.

jerky *adj* fitful, twitchy, spasmodic, jumpy, jolting, convulsive, disconnected, bumpy, bouncy, shaky, rough, unco-ordinated, uncontrolled, incoherent.

F3 smooth.

jest *n* joke, quip, wisecrack (*infml*), witticism, crack (*infml*), banter, fooling, gag (*infml*), prank, kidding (*infml*), leg-pull (*infml*), trick, hoax.

v joke, quip, fool, kid (*infml*), tease, mock, jeer.

jet[1] *n* gush, spurt, spout, spray,

spring, sprinkler, sprayer, fountain, flow, stream, squirt.

jet[2] *adj* black, pitch-black, ebony, sable, sooty.

jetty *n* breakwater, pier, dock, groyne, quay, wharf.

jewel *n* 1 GEM, precious stone, gemstone, ornament, rock (*sl*). 2 TREASURE, find, prize, rarity, paragon, pearl.

jewellery

> *Types of jewellery include*: bangle, bracelet, charm bracelet, anklet, cufflink, tiepin, hatpin, brooch, cameo, earring, nose-ring, ring, signet-ring, solitaire ring, necklace, necklet, choker, pendant, locket, chain, beads, amulet, torque, tiara, coronet, diadem.

Jewish calendar

> *The Jewish calendar and its Gregorian equivalents*: Tishri (September-October), Hesshvan (October-November), Kislev (November-December), Tevet (December-January), Shevat (January-February), Adar (February-March), Adar Sheni (leap years only), Nisan (March-April), Iyar (April-May), Sivan (May-June), Tammuz (June-July), Av (July-August), Elul (August-September).

jibe see gibe.

jig *v* jerk, prance, caper, hop, jump, twitch, skip, bounce, bob, wiggle, shake, wobble.

jilt *v* abandon, reject, desert, discard, brush off, ditch (*infml*), drop, spurn, betray.

jingle *v* clink, tinkle, ring, chime, chink, jangle, clatter, rattle.

n 1 CLINK, tinkle, ringing, clang, rattle, clangour. 2 RHYME, verse, song, tune, ditty, doggerel, melody, poem, chant, chorus.

jingoism n chauvinism, flag-waving, patriotism, nationalism, imperialism, warmongering, insularity.

jinx (*infml*) n spell, curse, evil eye, hex, voodoo, hoodoo, black magic, gremlin (*infml*), charm, plague.
v curse, bewitch, bedevil, doom, plague.

job n **1** *she has a good job*: work, employment, occupation, position, post, situation, profession, career, calling, vocation, trade, métier, capacity, business, livelihood. **2** *it's a difficult job*: task, chore, duty, responsibility, charge, commission, mission, activity, affair, concern, proceeding, project, enterprise, office, pursuit, role, undertaking, venture, province, part, place, share, errand, function, contribution, stint, assignment, consignment.

jobless adj unemployed, out of work, laid off, on the dole, inactive, redundant.
◼ employed.

jocular adj joking, jesting, funny, jocose (*fml*), humorous, jovial, amusing, comical, entertaining, facetious, droll, whimsical, teasing, witty.
◼ serious.

jog v **1** JOLT, jar, bump, jostle, jerk, joggle, nudge, poke, shake, prod, bounce, push, rock. **2** PROMPT, remind, stir, arouse, activate, stimulate. **3** RUN, trot.
n **1** JOLT, bump, jerk, nudge, shove, push, poke, prod, shake. **2** RUN, trot.

join v **1** UNITE, connect, combine, conjoin, attach, link, amalgamate, fasten, merge, marry, couple, yoke, tie, splice, knit, cement, add, adhere, annex. **2** ABUT, adjoin, border (on), verge on, touch, meet, coincide, march with. **3** ASSOCIATE, affiliate, accompany, ally, enlist, enrol, enter, sign up, team.
◼ **1** divide, separate. **3** leave.

joint n junction, connection, union, juncture, intersection, hinge, knot, articulation, seam.
adj combined, common, communal, joined, shared, united, collective, amalgamated, mutual, co-operative, co-ordinated, consolidated, concerted.

joke n **1** JEST, quip, crack (*infml*), gag (*infml*), witticism, wisecrack (*infml*), one-liner (*infml*), pun, hoot, whimsy, yarn. **2** TRICK, jape, lark, prank, spoof, fun.
v jest, quip, clown, fool, pun, wisecrack (*infml*), kid (*infml*), tease, banter, mock, laugh, frolic, gambol.

joker n comedian, comic, wit, humorist, jester, trickster, wag, clown, buffoon, kidder, droll, card (*infml*), character, sport.

jolly adj jovial, merry, cheerful, playful, hearty, happy, exuberant.
◼ sad.

jolt v **1** JAR, jerk, jog, bump, jostle, knock, bounce, shake, push. **2** UPSET, startle, shock, surprise, stun, discompose, disconcert, disturb.
n **1** JAR, jerk, jog, bump, blow, impact, lurch, shake. **2** SHOCK, surprise, reversal, setback, start.

jostle v push, shove, jog, bump, elbow, hustle, jolt, crowd, shoulder, joggle, shake, squeeze, throng.

jot down write down, take down, note, list, record, scribble, register, enter.

journal n newspaper, periodical, magazine, paper, publication, review, weekly, monthly, register, chronicle, diary, gazette, daybook, log, record.

journalist n reporter, news-writer, hack, correspondent, editor, columnist, feature-writer, commentator, broadcaster, contributor.

journey n voyage, trip, travel, expedition, passage, trek, tour, ramble, outing, wanderings, safari, progress.
v travel, voyage, go, trek, tour, roam,

rove, proceed, wander, tramp, ramble, range, gallivant.

jovial *adj* jolly, cheery, merry, affable, cordial, genial.
🖅 gloomy.

joy *n* happiness, gladness, delight, pleasure, bliss, ecstasy, elation, joyfulness, exultation, gratification, rapture.
🖅 despair, grief.

joyful *adj* happy, pleased, delighted, glad, elated, ecstatic, triumphant.
🖅 sorrowful.

jubilant *adj* joyful, rejoicing, overjoyed, delighted, elated, triumphant, exuberant, excited, euphoric, thrilled.

jubilee *n* celebration, commemoration, anniversary, festival, festivity, gala, fête, carnival.

judge *n* **1** JUSTICE, Law Lord, magistrate, arbiter, adjudicator, arbitrator, mediator, moderator, referee, umpire, beak (*sl*).
2 CONNOISSEUR, authority, expert, evaluator, assessor, critic.
v **1** ADJUDICATE, arbitrate, try, referee, umpire, decree, mediate, examine, sentence, review, rule, find.
2 ASCERTAIN, determine, decide, assess, appraise, evaluate, estimate, value, distinguish, discern, reckon, believe, think, consider, conclude, rate. **3** CONDEMN, criticize, doom.

judgement *n* **1** VERDICT, sentence, ruling, decree, conclusion, decision, arbitration, finding, result, mediation, order. **2** DISCERNMENT, discrimination, understanding, wisdom, prudence, common sense, sense, intelligence, taste, shrewdness, penetration, enlightenment.
3 ASSESSMENT, evaluation, appraisal, estimate, opinion, view, belief, diagnosis. **4** CONVICTION, damnation, punishment, retribution, doom, fate, misfortune.

judicial *adj* legal, judiciary, magistral, forensic, official,

discriminating, critical, impartial.

judicious *adj* wise, prudent, careful, cautious, astute, discerning, informed, shrewd, thoughtful, reasonable, sensible, sound, well-judged, well-advised, considered.
🖅 injudicious.

jug *n* pitcher, carafe, ewer, flagon, urn, jar, vessel, container.

juggle *v* alter, change, manipulate, falsify, rearrange, rig, doctor (*infml*), cook (*infml*), disguise.

juice *n* liquid, fluid, extract, essence, sap, secretion, nectar, liquor.

juicy *adj* **1** SUCCULENT, moist, lush, watery. **2** (*infml*) INTERESTING, colourful, sensational, racy, risqué, suggestive, lurid.
🖅 **1** dry.

jumble *v* disarrange, confuse, disorganize, mix (up), muddle, shuffle, tangle.
🖅 order.
n disorder, disarray, confusion, mess, chaos, mix-up, muddle, clutter, mixture, hotch-potch, mishmash (*infml*), medley.

jump *v* **1** LEAP, spring, bound, vault, clear, bounce, skip, hop, prance, frolic, gambol. **2** START, flinch, jerk, recoil, jump out of one's skin (*infml*), wince, quail. **3** OMIT, leave out, miss, skip, pass over, bypass, disregard, ignore, avoid, digress.
4 RISE, increase, gain, appreciate, ascend, escalate, mount, advance, surge, spiral.
n **1** LEAP, spring, bound, vault, hop, skip, bounce, prance, frisk, frolic, pounce. **2** START, jerk, jolt, jar, lurch, shock, spasm, quiver, shiver, twitch.
3 BREAK, gap, interruption, lapse, omission, interval, breach, switch. **4** RISE, increase, escalation, boost, advance, increment, upsurge, upturn, mounting. **5** HURDLE, fence, gate, hedge, barricade, obstacle.

jumpy *adj* nervous, anxious, agitated, apprehensive, jittery, tense,

edgy, fidgety, shaky.
⊟ calm, composed.

junction *n* joint, join, joining,
connection, juncture, union,
intersection, linking, coupling,
meeting-point, confluence.

junior *adj* younger, minor, lesser,
lower, subordinate, secondary,
subsidiary, inferior.
⊟ senior.

junk *n* rubbish, refuse, trash, debris,
garbage, waste, scrap, litter, clutter,
oddments, rummage, dregs,
wreckage.

jurisdiction *n* power, authority,
control, influence, dominion,
province, sovereignty, command,
domination, rule, prerogative (*fml*),
sway, orbit, bounds, area, field,
scope, range, reach, sphere, zone.

just *adj* **1** *a just ruler*: fair, equitable,
impartial, unbiased, unprejudiced,
fair-minded, even-handed, objective,
righteous, upright, virtuous,
honourable, good, honest,
irreproachable. **2** *a just punishment*:
deserved, merited, fitting, well-
deserved, appropriate, suitable, due,
proper, reasonable, rightful, lawful,
legitimate.
⊟ **1** unjust. **2** undeserved.

justice *n* **1** FAIRNESS, equity,
impartiality, objectivity,
equitableness, justness, legitimacy,
honesty, right, rightfulness, rightness,
justifiableness, reasonableness,

rectitude. **2** LEGALITY, law, penalty,
recompense, reparation, satisfaction.
3 JUDGE, Justice of the Peace, JP,
magistrate.
⊟ **1** injustice, unfairness.

justifiable *adj* defensible, excusable,
warranted, reasonable, justified,
lawful, legitimate, acceptable,
explainable, forgivable, pardonable,
understandable, valid, well-founded,
right, proper, explicable, fit, tenable.
⊟ unjustifiable.

justification *n* defence, plea,
mitigation, apology, explanation,
excuse, vindication, warrant,
rationalization, reason, grounds.

justify *v* vindicate, exonerate,
warrant, substantiate, defend, acquit,
absolve, excuse, forgive, explain,
pardon, validate, uphold, sustain,
support, maintain, establish.

jut (out) *v* project, protrude, stick
out, overhang, extend.
⊟ recede.

juvenile *n* child, youth, minor,
young person, youngster, adolescent,
teenager, boy, girl, kid (*infml*),
infant.
adj young, youthful, immature,
childish, puerile, infantile, adolescent,
babyish, unsophisticated.
⊟ mature.

juxtaposition *n* contiguity,
proximity, nearness, closeness,
contact, vicinity, immediacy.

K

karate

*Karate belts include: junior grades
(Kyu): red belt (beginner), white belt
(8th Kyu), yellow belt (7th Kyu),
orange belt (6th Kyu), green belt (5th
Kyu), brown belt (4th-1st Kyu),*
*black belt (1st Dan); senior grades
(Dans): black belts (1st-8th Dan).*

keel over 1 OVERTURN, capsize,
founder, collapse, upset. **2** FAINT,
pass out, swoon, fall, drop, stagger,
topple over.

keen *adj* **1** EAGER, avid, fervent, enthusiastic, earnest, devoted, diligent, industrious. **2** ASTUTE, shrewd, clever, perceptive, wise, discerning, quick, deep, sensitive. **3** SHARP, piercing, penetrating, incisive, acute, pointed, intense, pungent, trenchant.

Ea 1 apathetic. **2** superficial. **3** dull.

keep *v* **1** RETAIN, hold, preserve, hold on to, hang on to, store, stock, possess, amass, accumulate, collect, stack, conserve, deposit, heap, pile, place, maintain, furnish. **2** CARRY ON, keep on, continue, persist, remain. **3** LOOK AFTER, tend, care for, have charge of, have custody of, maintain, provide for, subsidize, support, sustain, be responsible for, foster, mind, protect, shelter, guard, defend, watch (over), shield, safeguard, feed, nurture, manage. **4** DETAIN, delay, retard, check, hinder, hold (up), impede, obstruct, prevent, block, curb, interfere with, restrain, limit, inhibit, deter, hamper, keep back, control, constrain, arrest, withhold. **5** OBSERVE, comply with, respect, obey, fulfil, adhere to, recognize, keep up, keep faith with, commemorate, celebrate, hold, maintain, perform, perpetuate, mark, honour.

n **1** SUBSISTENCE, board, livelihood, living, maintenance, support, upkeep, means, food, nourishment, nurture. **2** FORT, fortress, tower, castle, citadel, stronghold, dungeon.

keep back 1 RESTRAIN, check, constrain, curb, impede, limit, prohibit, retard, stop, control, delay. **2** HOLD BACK, restrict, suppress, withhold, conceal, censor, hide, hush up, stifle, reserve, retain.

keep in 1 REPRESS, keep back, inhibit, bottle up, conceal, stifle, suppress, hide, control, restrain, quell, stop up. **2** CONFINE, detain, shut in, coop up.

Ea 1 declare. **2** release.

keep on continue, carry on, endure, persevere, persist, keep at it, last, remain, stay, stay the course, soldier on (*infml*), hold on, retain, maintain.

keep up keep pace, equal, contend, compete, vie, rival, match, emulate, continue, maintain, persevere, support, sustain, preserve.

keeper *n* guard, custodian, curator, caretaker, attendant, guardian, overseer, steward, warder, jailer, gaoler, warden, supervisor, minder (*infml*), inspector, conservator (*fml*), defender, governor, superintendent, surveyor.

keepsake *n* memento, souvenir, remembrance, relic, reminder, token, pledge, emblem.

kernel *n* core, grain, seed, nucleus, heart, nub, essence, germ, marrow, substance, nitty-gritty (*infml*), gist.

key *n* **1** CLUE, cue, indicator, pointer, explanation, sign, answer, solution, interpretation, means, secret. **2** GUIDE, glossary, translation, legend, code, table, index.

adj important, essential, vital, crucial, necessary, principal, decisive, central, chief, main, major, leading, basic, fundamental.

keynote *n* core, centre, heart, substance, theme, gist, essence, emphasis, accent, stress.

keystone *n* cornerstone, core, crux, base, basis, foundation, ground, linchpin, principle, root, mainspring, source, spring, motive.

kick *v* **1** BOOT, hit, strike, jolt. **2** (*infml*) GIVE UP, quit, stop, leave off, abandon, desist from, break.

n **1** BLOW, recoil, jolt, striking. **2** (*infml*) STIMULATION, thrill, excitement.

kick off begin, commence, start, open, get under way, open the proceedings, set the ball rolling, introduce, inaugurate, initiate.

kick out eject, evict, expel, oust,

remove, chuck out (*infml*), discharge, dismiss, get rid of, sack (*infml*), throw out, reject.

kid[1] *n* child, youngster, youth, juvenile, infant, girl, boy, teenager, lad, nipper (*infml*), tot (*infml*).

kid[2] *v* tease, joke, have on (*infml*), hoax, fool, pull someone's leg (*infml*), pretend, trick, delude, dupe, con (*infml*), jest, hoodwink, humbug, bamboozle.

kidnap *v* abduct, capture, seize, hold to ransom, snatch, hijack, steal.

kill *v* 1 SLAUGHTER, murder, slay, put to death, exterminate, assassinate, do to death, do in (*infml*), bump off (*infml*), finish off, massacre, smite (*fml*), execute, eliminate (*sl*), destroy, dispatch (*infml*), do away with, butcher, annihilate, liquidate (*sl*), knock off (*infml*), rub out (*sl*). 2 STIFLE, deaden, smother, quash, quell, suppress.

killer *n* murderer, assassin, executioner, destroyer, slaughterer, exterminator, butcher (*infml*), cut-throat, gunman, hatchet man (*sl*), hit-man (*sl*).

killing *n* 1 SLAUGHTER, murder, massacre, homicide, assassination, execution, slaying, manslaughter, extermination, carnage, bloodshed, elimination, fatality, liquidation. 2 (*infml*) GAIN, fortune, windfall, profit, lucky break, coup, clean-up (*infml*), success, stroke of luck, bonanza (*infml*), hit, big hit.
adj (*infml*) 1 FUNNY, hilarious, comical, amusing, side-splitting (*infml*), ludicrous. 2 EXHAUSTING, hard, taxing, arduous.

kind *n* sort, type, class, category, set, variety, character, genus, genre, style, brand, family, breed, race, nature, persuasion, description, species, stamp, temperament, manner.
adj benevolent, kind-hearted, kindly, good-hearted, good-natured, helpful, obliging, humane, generous, compassionate, charitable, amiable, friendly, congenial, soft-hearted, thoughtful, warm, warm-hearted, considerate, courteous, sympathetic, tender-hearted, understanding, lenient, mild, hospitable, gentle, indulgent, neighbourly, tactful, giving, good, loving, gracious.
■ cruel, inconsiderate, unhelpful.

kindle *v* 1 IGNITE, light, set alight, set on fire. 2 INFLAME, fire, stir, thrill, stimulate, rouse, arouse, awaken, excite, fan, incite, inspire, induce, provoke.

kindly *adj* benevolent, kind, compassionate, charitable, good-natured, helpful, warm, generous, cordial, favourable, giving, indulgent, pleasant, sympathetic, tender, gentle, mild, patient, polite.
■ cruel, uncharitable.

kindness *n* 1 BENEVOLENCE, kindliness, charity, magnanimity, compassion, generosity, hospitality, humanity, loving-kindness (*fml*), courtesy, friendliness, good will, goodness, grace, indulgence, tolerance, understanding, gentleness. 2 FAVOUR, good turn, assistance, help, service.
■ 1 cruelty, inhumanity. 2 disservice.

king *n* monarch, ruler, sovereign, majesty, emperor, chief, chieftain, prince, supremo, leading light (*infml*).

kingdom *n* monarchy, sovereignty, reign, realm, empire, dominion, commonwealth, nation, principality, state, country, domain, dynasty, province, sphere, territory, land, division.

kink *n* 1 CURL, twist, bend, dent, indentation, knot, loop, crimp, coil, tangle, wrinkle. 2 QUIRK, eccentricity, idiosyncracy, foible, perversion.

kinship *n* 1 KIN, blood, relation. 2

AFFINITY, similarity, association, alliance, connection, correspondence, relationship, tie, community, conformity.

kiosk *n* booth, stall, stand, newsstand, bookstall, cabin, box, counter.

kiss *v* **1** CARESS, peck (*infml*), smooch (*infml*), neck (*infml*), snog (*sl*). **2** TOUCH, graze, glance, brush, lick, scrape, fan.
n peck (*infml*), smack (*infml*), smacker (*sl*).

kit *n* equipment, gear, apparatus, supplies, tackle, provisions, outfit, implements, set, tools, trappings, rig, instruments, paraphernalia, utensils, effects, luggage, baggage.

kit out equip, fit out, outfit, supply, fix up, furnish, prepare, arm, deck out, dress.

knack *n* flair, faculty, facility, hang (*infml*), bent, skill, talent, genius, gift, trick, propensity, ability, expertise, skilfulness, forte, capacity, handiness, dexterity, quickness, turn.

knapsack *n* bag, pack, haversack, rucksack, backpack.

knead *v* manipulate, press, massage, work, ply, squeeze, shape, rub, form, mould, knuckle.

knell *n* toll, ringing, chime, peel, knoll.

knick-knack *n* trinket, trifle, bauble, gewgaw, gimcrack, bric-à-brac, plaything.

knife *n* blade, cutter, carver, dagger, pen-knife, pocket-knife, switchblade, jack-knife, flick-knife, machete.
v cut, rip, slash, stab, pierce, wound.

knit *v* **1** JOIN, unite, secure, connect, tie, fasten, link, mend, interlace, intertwine. **2** KNOT, loop, crotchet, weave. **3** WRINKLE, furrow.

knock *v* hit, strike, rap, thump, pound, slap, smack.
n blow, box, rap, thump, cuff, clip, pounding, hammering, slap, smack.

knock about 1 WANDER, travel, roam, rove, saunter, traipse, ramble, range.

2 ASSOCIATE, go around. **3** BEAT UP, batter, abuse, mistreat, hurt, hit, bash, damage, maltreat, manhandle, bruise, buffet.

knock down demolish, destroy, fell, floor, level, wreck, raze, pound, batter, clout, smash, wallop.

knock off 1 (*infml*) FINISH, cease, stop, pack (it) in, clock off, clock out, terminate. **2** (*infml*) STEAL, rob, pilfer, pinch (*infml*), nick (*infml*), filch. **3** DEDUCT, take away. **4** (*sl*) KILL, murder, slay, assassinate, do away with, bump off (*infml*), do in (*infml*), waste (*sl*).

knockout (*infml*) *n* success, triumph, sensation, hit, smash (*infml*), smash-hit (*infml*), winner, stunner (*infml*). ⊟ flop, loser.

knot *v* tie, secure, bind, entangle, tangle, knit, entwine, ravel, weave.
n **1** TIE, bond, joint, fastening, loop, splice, hitch. **2** BUNCH, cluster, clump, group.

Types of knot include: bend, Blackwall hitch, blood knot, bow, bowline, running bowline, carrick bend, clove hitch, common whipping, double-overhang, Englishman's tie (or knot), figure of eight, fisherman's bend, fisherman's knot, flat knot, granny knot, half hitch, highwayman's hitch, hitch, Hunter's bend, loop knot, overhand knot or thumb knot, reef knot or square knot, rolling hitch, round turn and two half hitches, seizing, sheepshank, sheet bend or common bend or swab hitch, slipknot, spade-end knot, surgeon's knot, tie, timber hitch, Turk's head, turle knot, wall knot, weaver's knot, Windsor knot.

know *v* **1** *know French:* understand, comprehend, apprehend, perceive, notice, be aware, fathom, experience, realize, see, undergo. **2** *I know George:* be acquainted with, be

familiar with, recognize, identify.
3 *know a good wine*: distinguish,
discriminate, discern, differentiate,
make out, tell.

knowledge n **1** LEARNING,
scholarship, erudition, education,
schooling, instruction, tuition,
information, enlightenment, know-
how. **2** ACQUAINTANCE, familiarity,
awareness, cognizance, intimacy,
consciousness. **3** UNDERSTANDING,
comprehension, cognition,
apprehension, recognition,
judgement, discernment, ability,
grasp, wisdom, intelligence.
1 ignorance. **2** unawareness.

knowledgeable adj **1** EDUCATED,
scholarly, learned, well-informed,
lettered, intelligent. **2** AWARE,
acquainted, conscious, familiar, au
fait, in the know (*infml*), conversant,
experienced.
1 ignorant.

known adj acknowledged,
recognized, well-known, noted,
obvious, patent, plain, admitted,
familiar, avowed, commonplace,
published, confessed, celebrated,
famous.

kowtow v defer, cringe, fawn,
grovel, pander, suck up (*infml*),
toady (*infml*), flatter, kneel.

L

label n **1** TAG, ticket, docket, mark,
marker, sticker, trademark.
2 DESCRIPTION, categorization,
identification, characterization,
classification, badge, brand.
v **1** TAG, mark, stamp. **2** DEFINE,
describe, classify, categorize,
characterize, identify, class, designate,
brand, call, dub, name.

laborious adj **1** HARD, arduous,
difficult, strenuous, tough,
backbreaking, wearisome, tiresome,
uphill, onerous, heavy, toilsome.
2 HARD-WORKING, industrious,
painstaking, indefatigable, diligent.
1 easy, effortless. **2** lazy.

labour n **1** WORK, task, job, chore,
toil, effort, exertion, drudgery, grind
(*infml*), slog (*infml*), sweat (*infml*).
2 WORKERS, employees, workforce,
labourers. **3** CHILDBIRTH, birth,
delivery, labour pains, contractions.
1 ease, leisure. **2** management.
v **1** WORK, toil, drudge, slave, strive,
endeavour, struggle, grind (*infml*),
sweat (*infml*), plod, travail (*fml*).
2 TOSS, pitch, roll. **3** OVERDO,

overemphasize, dwell on, elaborate,
overstress, strain.
1 laze, idle, lounge.

labourer n manual worker, blue-
collar worker, navvy, hand, worker,
drudge, hireling.

labyrinth n maze, complexity,
intricacy, complication, puzzle,
riddle, windings, tangle, jungle.

lace n **1** NETTING, mesh-work,
open-work, tatting, crochet.
2 STRING, cord, thong, tie, shoelace,
bootlace.
v **1** TIE, do up, fasten, thread, close,
bind, attach, string, intertwine,
interweave. **2** ADD TO, mix in, spike
(*infml*), fortify.

lacerate v tear, rip, rend, cut, gash,
slash, wound, claw, mangle, maim,
torture, torment, distress, afflict.

lack n need, want, scarcity, shortage,
insufficiency, dearth, deficiency,
absence, scantiness, vacancy, void,
privation, deprivation, destitution,
emptiness.
**abundance, profusion.
v need, want, require, miss.

lacking *adj* needing, wanting, without, short of, missing, minus, inadequate, deficient, defective, flawed.

lacklustre *adj* drab, dull, flat, boring, leaden, lifeless, unimaginative, dim.
🔁 brilliant, inspired.

laconic *adj* terse, succinct, pithy, concise, crisp, taciturn, short, curt, brief.
🔁 verbose, wordy.

lad *n* boy, youth, youngster, kid (*infml*), schoolboy, chap, guy (*infml*), fellow.

lag *v* dawdle, loiter, hang back, linger, straggle, trail, saunter, delay, shuffle, tarry, idle.
🔁 hurry, lead.

lair *n* den, burrow, hole, nest, earth, form, roost, retreat, hideout, refuge, sanctuary, stronghold.

lake *n* lagoon, reservoir, loch, mere, tarn.

lame *adj* **1** DISABLED, handicapped, crippled, limping, hobbling. **2** WEAK, feeble, flimsy, inadequate, unsatisfactory, poor.
🔁 **1** able-bodied. **2** convincing.

lament *v* mourn, bewail, bemoan, grieve, sorrow, weep, wail, complain, deplore, regret.
🔁 rejoice, celebrate.
n lamentation, dirge, elegy, requiem, threnody (*fml*), complaint, moan, wail.

lamentable *adj* **1** DEPLORABLE, regrettable, mournful, distressing, tragic, unfortunate, sorrowful. **2** MEAGRE, low, inadequate, insufficient, mean, unsatisfactory, pitiful, miserable, poor, disappointing.

lampoon *n* satire, skit, caricature, parody, send-up (*infml*), spoof, take-off (*infml*), burlesque.
v satirize, caricature, parody, send up, take off (*infml*), spoof, make fun of, ridicule, mock, burlesque.

land *n* **1** EARTH, ground, soil, terra firma. **2** PROPERTY, grounds, estate, real estate, country, countryside, farmland, tract. **3** COUNTRY, nation, region, territory, province.
v **1** ALIGHT, disembark, dock, berth, touch down, come to rest, arrive, deposit, wind up, end up, drop, settle, turn up. **2** OBTAIN, secure, gain, get, acquire, net, capture, achieve, win.

landlord *n* owner, proprietor, host, publican, innkeeper, hotelier, restaurateur, hotel-keeper, freeholder.
🔁 tenant.

landmark *n* feature, monument, signpost, turning-point, watershed, milestone, beacon, cairn.

landscape *n* scene, scenery, view, panorama, outlook, vista, prospect, countryside, aspect.

landslide *n* landslip, earthfall, rock-fall, avalanche.
adj overwhelming, decisive, emphatic, runaway.

language *n* **1** SPEECH, vocabulary, terminology, parlance. **2** TALK, conversation, discourse. **3** WORDING, style, phraseology, phrasing, expression, utterance, diction.

Language terms include: brogue, dialect, idiom, patois, tongue, pidgin, creole, lingua franca, vernacular, argot, cant, jargon, doublespeak, gobbledegook, buzzword, journalese, lingo (*infml*), patter, slang, cockney rhyming slang; etymology, lexicography, linguistics, phonetics, semantics, syntax, usage, grammar, orthography, sociolinguistics.

---

languages

Languages of the world include: Aborigine, Afghan, Afrikaans, Arabic, Balinese, Bantu, Basque, Bengali, Burmese, Belorussian, Catalan, Celtic,

Chinese, Cornish, Czech, Danish, Dutch, English, Esperanto, Estonian, Ethiopian, Farsi, Finnish, Flemish, French, Gaelic, German, Greek, Haitian, Hawaiian, Hebrew, Hindi, Hindustani, Hottentot, Hungarian, Icelandic, Indonesian, Inuit, Irish, Iranian, Iraqi, Italian, Japanese, Kurdish, Lapp, Latin, Latvian, Lithuanian, Magyar, Malay, Maltese, Mandarin, Manx, Maori, Nahuatl, Navajo, Norwegian, Persian, Polish, Portuguese, Punjabi, Quechua, Romany, Romanian, Russian, Sanskrit, Scots, Serbo-Croat, Siamese, Sinhalese, Slavonic, Slovak, Slovenian, Somali, Spanish, Swahili, Swedish, Swiss, Tamil, Thai, Tibetan, Tupi, Turkish, Ukrainian, Urdu, Vietnamese, Volapük, Welsh, Yiddish, Zulu.

languish *v* **1** WILT, droop, fade, fail, flag, wither, waste away, weaken, sink, faint, decline, mope, waste, grieve, sorrow, sigh, sicken. **2** PINE, yearn, want, long, desire, hanker, hunger.
F3 1 flourish.

lanky *adj* gaunt, gangling, scrawny, tall, thin, scraggy, weedy.
F3 short, squat.

lap[1] *v* drink, sip, sup, lick.

lap[2] *n* circuit, round, orbit, tour, loop, course, circle, distance.
v wrap, fold, envelop, enfold, swathe, surround, cover, swaddle, overlap.

lapse *n* **1** ERROR, slip, mistake, negligence, omission, oversight, fault, failing, indiscretion, aberration, backsliding, relapse. **2** FALL, descent, decline, drop, deterioration. **3** BREAK, gap, interval, lull, interruption, intermission, pause.
v **1** DECLINE, fall, sink, drop, deteriorate, slide, slip, fail, worsen, degenerate, backslide. **2** EXPIRE, run out, end, stop, terminate.

large *adj* **1** BIG, huge, immense, massive, vast, sizable, great, giant, gigantic, bulky, enormous, king-sized, broad, considerable, monumental, substantial. **2** FULL, extensive, generous, liberal, roomy, plentiful, spacious, grand, sweeping, grandiose.
F3 1 small, tiny.
at large free, at liberty, on the loose, on the run, independent.

largely *adv* mainly, principally, chiefly, generally, primarily, predominantly, mostly, considerably, by and large, widely, extensively, greatly.

lark *n* escapade, antic, fling, prank, romp, skylark (*infml*), revel, mischief, frolic, caper, game.

lash[1] *n* blow, whip, stroke, swipe, hit.
v **1** WHIP, flog, beat, hit, thrash, strike, scourge. **2** ATTACK, criticize, lay into, scold.

lash[2] *v* tie, bind, fasten, secure, make fast, join, affix, rope, tether, strap.

last[1] *adj* final, ultimate, closing, latest, rearmost, terminal, furthest, concluding, remotest, utmost, extreme, conclusive, definitive.
F3 first, initial.
adv finally, ultimately, behind, after.
F3 first, firstly.
at last eventually, finally, in the end, in due course, at length.

last[2] *v* continue, endure, remain, persist, keep (on), survive, hold out, carry on, wear, stay, hold on, stand up, abide (*fml*).
F3 cease, stop, fade.

lasting *adj* enduring, unchanging, unceasing, unending, continuing, permanent, perpetual, lifelong, long-standing, long-term.
F3 brief, fleeting, short-lived.

latch *n* fastening, catch, bar, bolt, lock, hook, hasp.

late *adj* **1** OVERDUE, behind, behind-hand, slow, unpunctual, delayed, last-minute. **2** FORMER, previous,

departed, dead, deceased, past, preceding, old. **3** RECENT, up-to-date, current, fresh, new.
🞝 1 early, punctual.

lately *adv* recently, of late, latterly.

latent *adj* potential, dormant, undeveloped, unrealized, lurking, unexpressed, unseen, secret, concealed, hidden, invisible, underlying, veiled.
🞝 active, conspicuous.

later *adv* next, afterwards, subsequently, after, successively.
🞝 earlier.

lateral *adj* sideways, side, oblique, sideward, edgeways, marginal, flanking.

lather *n* **1** FOAM, suds, soap-suds, froth, bubbles, soap, shampoo.
2 AGITATION, fluster, fuss, dither, state (*infml*), flutter, flap (*infml*), fever.
v foam, froth, soap, shampoo, whip up.

latitude *n* **1** SCOPE, range, room, space, play, clearance, breadth, width, spread, sweep, reach, span, field, extent. **2** FREEDOM, liberty, licence, leeway, indulgence.

latter *adj* last-mentioned, last, later, closing, concluding, ensuing, succeeding, successive, second.
🞝 former.

laugh *v* chuckle, giggle, guffaw, snigger, titter, chortle, split one's sides, fall about (*infml*), crease up (*infml*).
n giggle, chuckle, snigger, titter, guffaw, chortle, lark, scream (*infml*), hoot (*infml*), joke.

laugh at mock, ridicule, deride, jeer, make fun of, scoff at, scorn, taunt.

laughable *adj* **1** FUNNY, amusing, comical, humorous, hilarious, droll, farcical, diverting. **2** RIDICULOUS, absurd, ludicrous, preposterous, nonsensical, derisory, derisive.
🞝 1 serious.

laughing-stock *n* figure of fun,

butt, victim, target, fair game.

laughter *n* laughing, giggling, chuckling, chortling, guffawing, tittering, hilarity, amusement, merriment, mirth, glee, convulsions.

launch *v* **1** PROPEL, dispatch, discharge, send off, project, float, set in motion, throw, fire. **2** BEGIN, commence, start, embark on, establish, found, open, initiate, inaugurate, introduce, instigate.

lavatory *n* toilet, loo (*infml*), WC, bathroom, cloakroom, washroom, water-closet, public convenience, Ladies (*infml*), Gents (*infml*), bog (*sl*), urinal, powder-room.

lavish *adj* **1** ABUNDANT, lush, luxuriant, plentiful, profuse, unlimited, prolific. **2** GENEROUS, liberal, open-handed, extravagant, thriftless, prodigal, immoderate, intemperate, unstinting.
🞝 1 scant. 2 frugal, thrifty.

law *n* **1** RULE, act, decree, edict, order, statute, regulation, command, ordinance, charter, constitution, enactment. **2** PRINCIPLE, axiom, criterion, standard, precept, formula, code, canon. **3** JURISPRUDENCE, legislation, litigation.

law-abiding *adj* obedient, upright, orderly, lawful, honest, honourable, decent, good.
🞝 lawless.

lawful *adj* legal, legitimate, permissible, legalized, authorized, allowable, warranted, valid, proper, rightful.
🞝 illegal, unlawful, illicit.

lawless *adj* disorderly, rebellious, anarchic(al), unruly, riotous, mutinous, unrestrained, chaotic, wild, reckless.
🞝 law-abiding.

lawsuit *n* litigation, suit, action, proceedings, case, prosecution, dispute, process, trial, argument, contest, cause.

lawyer *n* solicitor, barrister,

advocate, attorney, counsel, QC.

lax *adj* **1** CASUAL, careless, easy-going, slack, lenient, negligent, remiss. **2** IMPRECISE, inexact, indefinite, loose.
⊟ 1 strict. **2** exact.

lay¹ *v* **1** PUT, place, deposit, set down, settle, lodge, plant, set, establish, leave. **2** ARRANGE, position, set out, locate, work out, devise, prepare, present, submit. **3** ATTRIBUTE, ascribe, assign, charge.

lay in store (up), stock up, amass, accumulate, hoard, stockpile, gather, collect, build up, glean.

lay into (*infml*) attack, assail, pitch into, set about, tear into, let fly at.

lay off 1 DISMISS, discharge, make redundant, sack (*infml*), pay off, let go. **2** (*infml*) GIVE UP, drop, stop, quit, cease, desist, leave off, leave alone, let up.

lay on provide, supply, cater, furnish, give, set up.

lay out 1 DISPLAY, set out, spread out, exhibit, arrange, plan, design. **2** (*infml*) KNOCK OUT, fell, flatten, demolish. **3** (*infml*) SPEND, pay, shell out (*infml*), fork out (*infml*), give, invest.

lay up store up, hoard, accumulate, amass, keep, save, put away.

lay² *adj* **1** LAIC, secular. **2** AMATEUR, non-professional, non-specialist.
⊟ 1 clergy. **2** expert.

layer *n* **1** COVER, coating, coat, covering, film, blanket, mantle, sheet, lamina. **2** STRATUM, seam, thickness, tier, bed, plate, row, ply.

layman *n* **1** LAYPERSON, parishioner. **2** AMATEUR, outsider.
⊟ 1 clergyman. **2** expert.

layout *n* arrangement, design, outline, plan, sketch, draft, map.

laze *v* idle, loaf (*infml*), lounge, sit around, lie around, loll.

lazy *adj* idle, slothful, slack, work-shy, inactive, lethargic.
⊟ industrious.

lead *v* **1** GUIDE, conduct, escort, steer, pilot, usher. **2** RULE, govern, head, preside over, direct, supervise. **3** INFLUENCE, persuade, incline. **4** SURPASS, outdo, excel, outstrip, transcend. **5** PASS, spend, live, undergo.
⊟ follow.
n **1** PRIORITY, precedence, first place, start, van, vanguard, advantage, edge, margin. **2** LEADERSHIP, guidance, direction, example, model. **3** CLUE, hint, indication, guide, tip, suggestion. **4** TITLE ROLE, starring part, principal.

lead off begin, commence, open, get going, start (off), inaugurate, initiate, kick off (*infml*), start the ball rolling.

lead on entice, lure, seduce, tempt, draw on, beguile, persuade, string along, deceive, trick.

lead to cause, result in, produce, bring about, bring on, contribute to, tend towards.

lead up to prepare (the way) for, approach, introduce, make overtures, pave the way.

leader *n* head, chief, director, ruler, principal, commander, captain, boss (*infml*), superior, chieftain, ringleader, guide, conductor.
⊟ follower.

leadership *n* direction, control, command, management, authority, guidance, domination, pre-eminence, premiership, administration, sway, directorship.

leading *adj* main, principal, chief, primary, first, supreme, outstanding, foremost, dominant, ruling, superior, greatest, highest, governing, pre-eminent, number one.
⊟ subordinate.

leaflet *n* pamphlet, booklet, brochure, circular, handout.

league *n* **1** ASSOCIATION, confederation, alliance, union, federation, confederacy, coalition,

leak 312

combination, band, syndicate, guild,
consortium, cartel, combine,
partnership, fellowship, compact.
2 CATEGORY, class, level, group.
in league allied, collaborating,
conspiring.

leak *n* 1 CRACK, hole, opening,
puncture, crevice, chink. 2 LEAKAGE,
leaking, seepage, drip, oozing,
percolation. 3 DISCLOSURE,
divulgence.
v 1 SEEP, drip, ooze, escape, spill,
trickle, percolate, exude, discharge.
2 DIVULGE, disclose, reveal, let slip,
make known, make public, tell, give
away, pass on.

leaky *adj* leaking, holey, perforated,
punctured, split, cracked, porous,
permeable.

lean[1] *v* 1 SLANT, slope, bend, tilt,
list, tend. 2 RECLINE, prop, rest.
3 INCLINE, favour, prefer.

lean[2] *adj* 1 THIN, skinny, bony,
gaunt, lank, angular, slim, scraggy,
scrawny, emaciated. 2 SCANTY,
inadequate, bare, barren.
⧉ 1 fat.

leaning *n* tendency, inclination,
propensity, partiality, liking, bent,
bias, disposition, aptitude.

leap *v* 1 JUMP (OVER), bound,
spring, vault, clear, skip, hop,
bounce, caper, gambol. 2 SOAR,
surge, increase, rocket, escalate, rise.
⧉ 2 drop, fall.
n 1 JUMP, bound, spring, vault, hop,
skip, caper. 2 INCREASE, upsurge,
upswing, surge, rise, escalation.

learn *v* 1 GRASP, comprehend,
understand, master, acquire, pick up,
gather, assimilate, discern.
2 MEMORIZE, learn by heart.
3 DISCOVER, find out, ascertain,
hear, detect, determine.

learned *adj* scholarly, erudite, well-
informed, well-read, cultured,
academic, lettered, literate,
intellectual, versed.
⧉ uneducated, illiterate.

learner *n* novice, beginner, student,
trainee, pupil, scholar, apprentice.

learning *n* scholarship, erudition,
education, schooling, knowledge,
information, letters, study, wisdom,
tuition, culture, edification, research.

lease *v* let, loan, rent, hire, sublet,
charter.

least *adj* smallest, lowest, minimum,
fewest, slightest, poorest.
⧉ most.

leave[1] *v* 1 DEPART, go, go away, set
out, take off, decamp, exit, move,
quit, retire, withdraw, disappear, do
a bunk (*infml*). 2 ABANDON, desert,
forsake, give up, drop, relinquish,
renounce, pull out, surrender, desist,
cease. 3 ASSIGN, commit, entrust,
consign, bequeath, will, hand down,
leave behind, give over, transmit.
⧉ 1 arrive. 1 receive.

leave off stop, cease, discontinue,
desist, abstain, refrain, lay off, quit,
terminate, break off, end, halt, give
over.

leave out omit, exclude, overlook,
ignore, except, disregard, pass over,
count out, cut (out), eliminate, neglect,
reject, cast aside, bar.

leave[2] *n* 1 PERMISSION,
authorization, consent, allowance,
sanction, concession, dispensation,
indulgence, liberty, freedom.
2 HOLIDAY, time off, vacation,
sabbatical, furlough.
⧉ 1 refusal, rejection.

lecture *n* 1 DISCOURSE, address,
lesson, speech, talk, instruction.
2 REPRIMAND, rebuke, reproof,
scolding, harangue, censure, chiding,
telling-off (*infml*), talking-to (*infml*),
dressing-down (*infml*).
v 1 TALK, teach, hold forth, speak,
expound, address. 2 REPRIMAND,
reprove, scold, admonish, harangue,
chide, censure, tell off (*infml*).

ledge *n* shelf, sill, mantle, ridge,
projection, step.

leeway *n* space, room, latitude,

elbow-room, play, scope.

left adj **1** LEFT-HAND, port, sinistral.
2 LEFT-WING, socialist, radical,
progressive, revolutionary, liberal,
communist, red (infml).
≠ **1** right. **2** right-wing.

left-overs n leavings, remainder,
remains, remnants, residue, surplus,
scraps, sweepings, refuse, dregs,
excess.

leg n **1** LIMB, member, shank, pin
(infml), stump (infml). **2** SUPPORT,
prop, upright, brace. **3** STAGE, part,
section, portion, stretch, segment,
lap.

legacy n bequest, endowment, gift,
heritage, heritance, inheritance,
birthright, estate, heirloom.

legal adj **1** LAWFUL, legitimate,
permissible, sanctioned, allowed,
authorized, allowable, legalized,
constitutional, valid, warranted,
above-board, proper, rightful.
2 JUDICIAL, forensic. **3** judiciary.
≠ **1** illegal.

Legal terms include: courts: county
court, courthouse, courtroom, Court
of Appeal, Court of Protection,
Court of Session, Crown Court,
European Court of Human Rights,
European Court of Justice, High
Court of Justice, House of Lords,
International Court of Justice,
juvenile court, magistrates' court,
Old Bailey, small claims court,
Supreme Court (*North Amer.*);
criminal law: acquittal, age of
consent, alibi, arrest, bail, caution,
charge, confession, contempt of
court, dock, fine, guilty, indictment,
innocent, malice aforethought,
pardon, parole, plead guilty, plead
not guilty, prisoner, probation,
remand, reprieve, sentence; *marriage
and divorce*: adultery, alimony,
annulment, bigamy, decree absolute,
decree nisi, divorce, maintenance,
settlement; *people*: accessory,

accomplice, accused, advocate,
Attorney General, barrister, brief
(*infml*), clerk of the court, client,
commissioner for oaths, convict,
coroner, criminal, defendant,
Director of Public Prosecutions,
DPP, executor, felon, judge, jury,
justice of the peace, JP, juvenile, Law
Lord, lawyer, Lord Advocate, Lord
Chancellor, Lord Chief Justice,
liquidator, magistrate, notary public,
offender, plaintiff, procurator fiscal,
receiver, Queen's Counsel, QC,
sheriff, solicitor, witness, young
offender; *property or ownership*:
asset, conveyance, copyright, deed,
easement, endowment, estate,
exchange of contracts, fee simple,
foreclosure, freehold, inheritance,
intestacy, lease, leasehold, legacy,
local search, mortgage, patent,
tenancy, title, trademark, will;
miscellaneous: act of God, Act of
Parliament, adjournment, affidavit,
agreement, allegation, amnesty,
appeal, arbitration, bar, Bill of
Rights, bench, brief, by-law, charter,
civil law, claim, codicil, common law,
constitution, contract covenant,
cross-examine, courtcase, court
martial, custody, damages, defence,
demand, equity, eviction, evidence,
extradition, grant, hearing, hung
jury, indemnity, injunction, inquest,
inquiry, judgment, judiciary, lawsuit,
legal aid, liability, mandate,
misadventure, miscarriage of justice,
oath, party, penalty, power of
attorney, precedent, probate,
proceedings, proof, proxy, public
inquiry, repeal, sanction, settlement,
statute, subpoena, sue, summons,
testimony, trial, tribunal, verdict,
waiver, ward of court, warrant, will,
writ. *see also* crime.

legalize v legitimize, license, permit,
sanction, allow, authorize, warrant,
validate, approve.

legend n 1 MYTH, story, tale, folk-tale, fable, fiction, narrative.
2 INSCRIPTION, caption, key, motto.

legendary adj 1 MYTHICAL, fabulous, story-book, fictitious, traditional. 2 FAMOUS, celebrated, renowned, well-known, illustrious.

legible adj readable, intelligible, decipherable, clear, distinct, neat.
🔁 illegible.

legislate v enact, ordain, authorize, codify, constitutionalize, prescribe, establish.

legislation n 1 LAW, statute, regulation, bill, act, charter, authorization, ruling, measure.
2 LAW-MAKING, enactment, codification.

legislative adj law-making, law-giving, judicial, parliamentary, congressional, senatorial.

legislator n law-maker, law-giver, member of parliament, parliamentarian.

legislature n assembly, chamber, house, parliament, congress, senate.

legitimate adj 1 LEGAL, lawful, authorized, statutory, rightful, proper, correct, real, acknowledged.
2 REASONABLE, sensible, admissible, acceptable, justifiable, warranted, well-founded, valid, true.
🔁 1 illegal. 2 invalid.

leisure n relaxation, rest, spare time, time off, ease, freedom, liberty, recreation, retirement, holiday, vacation.
🔁 work.

leisurely adj unhurried, slow, relaxed, comfortable, easy, unhasty, tranquil, restful, gentle, carefree, laid-back (infml), lazy, loose.
🔁 rushed, hectic.

lend v 1 LOAN, advance. 2 GIVE, grant, bestow, provide, furnish, confer, supply, impart, contribute.
🔁 1 borrow.

length n 1 EXTENT, distance, measure, reach, piece, portion, section, segment. 2 DURATION, period, term, stretch, space, span.

lengthen v stretch, extend, elongate, draw out, prolong, protract, spin out, eke (out), pad out, increase, expand, continue.
🔁 reduce, shorten.

lengthy adj long, prolonged, protracted, extended, lengthened, overlong, long-drawn-out, long-winded, rambling, diffuse, verbose, drawn-out, interminable.
🔁 brief, concise.

lenient adj tolerant, forbearing, sparing, indulgent, merciful, forgiving, soft-hearted, kind, mild, gentle, compassionate.
🔁 strict, severe.

lessen v decrease, reduce, diminish, lower, ease, abate, contract, die down, dwindle, lighten, slow down, weaken, shrink, abridge, de-escalate, erode, minimize, narrow, moderate, slack, flag, fail, deaden, impair.
🔁 grow, increase.

lesser adj lower, secondary, inferior, smaller, subordinate, slighter, minor.
🔁 greater.

lesson n 1 CLASS, period, instruction, lecture, tutorial, teaching, coaching. 2 ASSIGNMENT, exercise, homework, practice, task, drill. 3 EXAMPLE, model, warning, deterrent.

let v 1 PERMIT, allow, give leave, give permission, authorize, consent to, agree to, sanction, grant, OK, enable, tolerate. 2 LEASE, hire, rent.
🔁 1 prohibit, forbid.

let in admit, accept, receive, take in, include, incorporate, welcome.
🔁 prohibit, bar, forbid.

let off 1 EXCUSE, absolve, pardon, exempt, forgive, acquit, exonerate, spare, reprieve, liberate, release. 2 DISCHARGE, detonate, fire, explode, emit.
🔁 1 punish.

let out 1 FREE, release, let go, discharge, leak (*infml*). **2** REVEAL, disclose, make known, utter, betray, let slip.
E3 **1** keep in.

let up abate, subside, ease (up), moderate, slacken, diminish, decrease, stop, end, cease, halt.
E3 continue.

let-down *n* anticlimax, disappointment, disillusionment, set-back, betrayal, desertion, wash-out (*infml*).

lethal *adj* fatal, deadly, deathly, mortal, dangerous, poisonous, noxious, destructive, devastating.
E3 harmless, safe.

lethargy *n* lassitude, listlessness, sluggishness, torpor, dullness, inertia, slowness, apathy, inaction, indifference, sleepiness, drowsiness, stupor.
E3 liveliness.

letter *n* **1** NOTE, message, line, missive, epistle (*fml*), dispatch, communication, chit, acknowledgement. **2** CHARACTER, symbol, sign, grapheme.

level *adj* **1** FLAT, smooth, even, flush, horizontal, aligned, plane. **2** EQUAL, balanced, even, on a par, neck and neck, matching, uniform.
E3 **1** uneven. **2** unequal.
v **1** DEMOLISH, destroy, devastate, flatten, knock down, raze, pull down, bulldoze, tear down, lay low. **2** EVEN OUT, flush, plane, smooth, equalize. **3** DIRECT, point.
n **1** HEIGHT, elevation, altitude. **2** POSITION, rank, status, class, degree, grade, standard, standing, plane, echelon, layer, stratum, storey, stage, zone.

level-headed *adj* calm, balanced, even-tempered, sensible, steady, reasonable, composed, cool, unflappable, sane, self-possessed, dependable.

lever *n* bar, crowbar, jemmy, joy-stick, handle.
v force, prise, pry, raise, dislodge, jemmy, shift, move, heave.

levity *n* light-heartedness, frivolity, facetiousness, flippancy, irreverence, triviality, silliness.
E3 seriousness.

levy *v* tax, impose, exact, demand, charge.
n tax, toll, subscription, contribution, duty, fee, tariff, collection.

lewd *adj* obscene, smutty, indecent, bawdy, pornographic, salacious, licentious, lascivious, impure, vulgar, unchaste, lustful.
E3 decent, chaste.

liability *n* **1** ACCOUNTABILITY, duty, obligation, responsibility, onus. **2** DEBT, arrears, indebtedness. **3** DRAWBACK, disadvantage, hindrance, impediment, drag (*infml*).

liable *adj* **1** INCLINED, likely, apt, disposed, prone, tending, susceptible. **2** RESPONSIBLE, answerable, accountable, amenable.

liaison *n* **1** CONTACT, connection, go-between, link. **2** LOVE AFFAIR, affair, romance, intrigue, amour, entanglement.

liar *n* falsifier, perjurer, deceiver, fibber (*infml*).

libel *n* defamation, slur, smear, slander, vilification, aspersion, calumny.
v defame, slur, smear, slander, vilify, malign.

libellous *adj* defamatory, vilifying, slanderous, derogatory, maligning, injurious, scurrilous, untrue.

liberal *adj* **1** BROAD-MINDED, open-minded, tolerant, lenient. **2** PROGRESSIVE, reformist, moderate. **3** GENEROUS, ample, bountiful, lavish, plentiful, handsome.
E3 **1** narrow-minded. **2** conservative. **3** mean, miserly.

liberate *v* free, emancipate, release,

let loose, let go, let out, set free,
deliver, unchain, discharge, rescue,
ransom.
≢ imprison, enslave.
liberty n **1** FREEDOM, emancipation,
release, independence, autonomy.
2 LICENCE, permission, sanction,
right, authorization, dispensation,
franchise. **3** FAMILIARITY,
disrespect, overfamiliarity,
presumption, impertinence,
impudence.
≢ **1** imprisonment. **3** respect.
at liberty free, unconstrained,
unrestricted, not confined.
licence n **1** PERMISSION, permit,
leave, warrant, authorization,
authority, certificate, charter, right,
imprimatur, entitlement, privilege,
dispensation, carte blanche, freedom,
liberty, exemption, independence.
2 ABANDON, dissipation, excess,
immoderation, indulgence,
lawlessness, unruliness, anarchy,
disorder, debauchery, dissoluteness,
impropriety, irresponsibility.
≢ **1** prohibition, restriction.
2 decorum, moderation.
license v permit, allow, authorize,
certify, warrant, entitle, empower,
sanction, commission, accredit.
≢ ban, prohibit.
licentious adj debauched, dissolute,
profligate, lascivious, immoral,
abandoned, lewd, promiscuous,
libertine, impure, lax, lustful,
disorderly, wanton, unchaste.
≢ modest, chaste.
lick v tongue, touch, wash, lap, taste,
dart, flick, flicker, play over, smear,
brush.
lie¹ v perjure, misrepresent,
fabricate, falsify, fib (infml), invent,
equivocate, prevaricate, forswear
oneself (fml).
n falsehood, untruth, falsification,
fabrication, invention, fiction, deceit,
fib (infml), falsity, white lie,
prevarication, whopper (infml).

≢ truth.
lie² v be, exist, dwell, belong, extend,
remain.
lie down repose, rest, recline, stretch
out, lounge, couch, laze.
life n **1** BEING, existence, animation,
breath, viability, entity, soul.
2 DURATION, course, span, career.
3 LIVELINESS, vigour, vitality,
vivacity, verve, zest, energy, élan,
spirit, sparkle, activity.
lifeless adj **1** DEAD, deceased,
defunct, cold, unconscious,
inanimate, insensible, stiff.
2 LETHARGIC, listless, sluggish, dull,
apathetic, passive, insipid, colourless,
slow. **3** BARREN, bare, empty,
desolate, arid.
≢ **1** alive. **2** lively.
lifelike adj realistic, true-to-life,
real, true, vivid, natural, authentic,
faithful, exact, graphic.
≢ unrealistic, unnatural.
lifelong adj lifetime, long-lasting,
long-standing, persistent, lasting,
enduring, abiding, permanent,
constant.
≢ impermanent, temporary.
lift v **1** she lifted the chair: raise,
elevate, hoist, upraise. **2** he lifted
their spirits: uplift, exalt, buoy up,
boost. **3** the ban has been lifted:
revoke, cancel, relax.
≢ **1** drop. **2** lower.
light¹ n **1** ILLUMINATION,
brightness, brilliance, luminescence,
radiance, glow, ray, shine, glare,
gleam, glint, lustre, flash, blaze.
2 LAMP, lantern, lighter, match,
torch, candle, bulb, beacon. **3** DAY,
daybreak, daylight, daytime, dawn,
sunrise. **4** ENLIGHTENMENT,
explanation, elucidation,
understanding.
≢ **1** darkness. **3** night.
v **1** IGNITE, fire, set alight, set fire to,
kindle. **2** ILLUMINATE, light up,
lighten, brighten, animate, cheer,
switch on, turn on, put on.

⊟ **1** extinguish. **2** darken.

adj **1** ILLUMINATED, bright, brilliant, luminous, glowing, shining, well-lit, sunny. **2** PALE, pastel, fair, blond, blonde, bleached, faded, faint. **1** dark. **2** black.

light² *adj* **1** WEIGHTLESS, insubstantial, delicate, airy, buoyant, flimsy, feathery, slight. **2** TRIVIAL, inconsiderable, trifling, inconsequential, worthless. **3** CHEERFUL, cheery, carefree, lively, merry, blithe. **4** ENTERTAINING, amusing, funny, humorous, frivolous, witty, pleasing.
⊟ **1** heavy, weighty. **2** important, serious. **3** solemn. **4** serious.

lighten¹ *v* illuminate, illumine, brighten, light up, shine.
⊟ darken.

lighten² *v* **1** EASE, lessen, unload, lift, relieve, reduce, mitigate, alleviate. **2** BRIGHTEN, cheer, encourage, hearten, inspirit, uplift, gladden, revive, elate, buoy up, inspire.
⊟ **1** burden. **2** depress.

light-headed *adj* **1** FAINT, giddy, dizzy, woozy (*infml*), delirious. **2** FLIGHTY, scatter-brained (*infml*), foolish, frivolous, silly, superficial, shallow, feather-brained (*infml*), flippant, vacuous, trifling.
⊟ **2** level-headed, solemn.

light-hearted *adj* cheerful, joyful, jolly, happy-go-lucky, bright, carefree, untroubled, merry, sunny, glad, elated, jovial, playful.
⊟ sad, unhappy, serious.

likable *adj* loveable, pleasing, appealing, agreeable, charming, engaging, winsome, pleasant, amiable, congenial, attractive, sympathetic.
⊟ unpleasant, disagreeable.

like¹ *adj* similar, resembling, alike, same, identical, equivalent, akin, corresponding, related, relating, parallel, allied, analogous, approximating.
⊟ unlike, dissimilar.

like² *v* **1** ENJOY, delight in, care for, admire, appreciate, love, adore, hold dear, esteem, cherish, prize, relish, revel in, approve, take (kindly) to. **2** PREFER, choose, select, feel inclined, go for (*infml*), desire, want, wish.
⊟ **1** dislike. **2** reject.

likelihood *n* likeliness, probability, possibility, chance, prospect, liability.
⊟ improbability, unlikeliness.

likely *adj* **1** PROBABLE, possible, anticipated, expected, liable, prone, tending, predictable, odds-on (*infml*), inclined, foreseeable. **2** CREDIBLE, believable, plausible, feasible, reasonable. **3** PROMISING, hopeful, pleasing, appropriate, proper, suitable.
⊟ **1** unlikely. **3** unsuitable.
adv probably, presumably, like as not, in all probability, no doubt, doubtlessly.

liken *v* compare, equate, match, parallel, relate, juxtapose, associate, set beside.

likeness *n* **1** SIMILARITY, resemblance, affinity, correspondence. **2** REPRESENTATION, image, copy, reproduction, replica, facsimile, effigy, picture, portrait, photograph, counterpart. **3** SEMBLANCE, guise, appearance, form.
⊟ **1** dissimilarity, unlikeness.

likewise *adv* moreover, furthermore, in addition, similarly, also, further, besides, by the same token, too.

liking *n* fondness, love, affection, preference, partiality, affinity, predilection, penchant, taste, attraction, appreciation, proneness, propensity, inclination, tendency, bias, desire, weakness, fancy, soft spot.

dislike, aversion, hatred.

limb n arm, leg, member, appendage, branch, projection, offshoot, wing, fork, extension, part, spur, extremity, bough.

limber up v loosen up, warm up, work out, exercise, prepare.

limelight n fame, celebrity, spotlight, stardom, recognition, renown, attention, prominence, publicity, public eye.

limit n 1 BOUNDARY, bound, border, frontier, confines, edge, brink, threshold, verge, brim, end, perimeter, rim, compass, termination, ultimate, utmost, terminus, extent. 2 CHECK, curb, restraint, restriction, limitation, ceiling, maximum, cut-off point, saturation point, deadline.
v check, curb, restrict, restrain, constrain, confine, demarcate, delimit, bound, hem in, ration, specify, hinder.

limitation n 1 CHECK, restriction, curb, control, constraint, restraint, delimitation, demarcation, block. 2 INADEQUACY, shortcoming, disadvantage, drawback, condition, qualification, reservation.
extension.

limited adj restricted, circumscribed, constrained, controlled, confined, checked, defined, finite, fixed, minimal, narrow, inadequate, insufficient.
limitless.

limitless adj unlimited, unbounded, boundless, illimited, undefined, immeasurable, incalculable, infinite, countless, endless, never-ending, unending, inexhaustible, untold, vast.
limited.

limp¹ v hobble, falter, stumble, hop, shuffle, shamble.

limp² adj 1 FLABBY, drooping, flaccid, floppy, loose, slack, relaxed, lax, soft, flexible, pliable, limber. 2 TIRED, weary, exhausted, spent,

weak, worn out, lethargic, debilitated, enervated.
1 stiff. 2 vigorous.

line¹ n 1 STROKE, band, bar, stripe, mark, strip, rule, dash, strand, streak, underline, score, scratch. 2 ROW, rank, queue, file, column, sequence, series, procession, chain, trail. 3 LIMIT, boundary, border, borderline, edge, frontier, demarcation. 4 STRING, rope, cord, cable, thread, filament, wire. 5 PROFILE, contour, outline, silhouette, figure, formation, configuration. 6 CREASE, wrinkle, furrow, groove, corrugation. 7 COURSE, path, direction, track, route, axis. 8 APPROACH, avenue, course (of action), belief, ideology, policy, system, position, practice, procedure, method, scheme. 9 OCCUPATION, business, trade, profession, vocation, job, activity, interest, employment, department, calling, field, province, forte, area, pursuit, specialization, specialty, specialism, speciality. 10 ANCESTRY, family, descent, extraction, lineage, pedigree, stock, race, breed.

line up 1 ALIGN, range, straighten, marshal, order, regiment, queue up, form ranks, fall in, array, assemble. 2 ORGANIZE, lay on, arrange, prepare, produce, procure, secure, obtain.

line² v encase, cover, fill, pad, stuff, reinforce.

lineage n (fml) ancestry, descent, extraction, genealogy, family, line, pedigree, race, stock, birth, breed, house, heredity, ancestors, forebears, descendants, offspring, succession.

lined adj 1 RULED, feint. 2 WRINKLED, furrowed, wizened, worn.
1 unlined. 2 smooth.

line-up n array, arrangement, queue, row, selection, cast, team, bill.

linger v loiter, delay, dally, tarry, wait, remain, stay, hang on, lag, procrastinate, dawdle, dilly-dally (*infml*), idle, stop, endure, hold out, last, persist, survive.

F3 leave, rush.

lining n inlay, interfacing, padding, backing, encasement, stiffening.

link n **1** CONNECTION, bond, tie, association, joint, relationship, tie-up, union, knot, liaison, attachment, communication. **2** PART, piece, element, member, constituent, component, division.

v connect, join, couple, tie, fasten, unite, bind, amalgamate, merge, associate, ally, bracket, identify, relate, yoke, attach, hook up, join forces, team up.

F3 separate, unfasten.

lip n edge, brim, border, brink, rim, margin, verge.

liquid n liquor, fluid, juice, drink, sap, solution, lotion.

adj fluid, flowing, liquefied, watery, wet, runny, melted, molten, thawed, clear, smooth.

F3 solid.

liquidate v **1** ANNIHILATE, terminate, do away with, dissolve, kill, murder, massacre, assassinate, destroy, dispatch, abolish, eliminate, exterminate, remove, finish off, rub out (*infml*). **2** PAY (OFF), close down, clear, discharge, wind up, sell.

liquor n alcohol, intoxicant, strong drink, spirits, drink, hard stuff (*infml*), booze (*infml*).

list¹ n catalogue, roll, inventory, register, enumeration, schedule, index, listing, record, file, directory, table, tabulation, tally, series, syllabus, invoice.

v enumerate, register, itemize, catalogue, index, tabulate, record, file, enrol, enter, note, bill, book, set down, write down.

list² v lean, incline, tilt, slope, heel (over), tip.

listen v hark, attend, pay attention, hear, heed, hearken, hang on

(someone's) words, prick up one's ears, take notice, lend an ear, eavesdrop, overhear, give ear.

listless adj sluggish, lethargic, languid, torpid, enervated, spiritless, limp, lifeless, inert, inactive, impassive, indifferent, uninterested, vacant, apathetic, indolent, depressed, bored, heavy.

F3 energetic, enthusiastic.

literal adj **1** VERBATIM, word-for-word, strict, close, actual, precise, faithful, exact, accurate, factual, true, genuine, unexaggerated.

2 PROSAIC, unimaginative, uninspired, matter-of-fact, down-to-earth, humdrum.

F3 1 imprecise, loose. **2** imaginative.

literary adj educated, well-read, bookish, learned, erudite, scholarly, lettered, literate, cultured, cultivated, refined, formal.

F3 ignorant, illiterate.

literature n **1** WRITINGS, letters, paper(s). **2** INFORMATION, leaflet(s), pamphlet(s), circular(s), brochure(s), hand-out(s), bumf (*infml*).

> *Types of literature include*: allegory, anti-novel, autobiography, belles-lettres (*fml*), biography, classic novel, criticism, drama, epic, epistle, essay, fiction, Gothic novel, lampoon, libretto, magnum opus, non-fiction, novel, novella, parody, pastiche, penny dreadful (*infml*), picaresque novel, poetry, polemic, postil, prose, roman novel, saga, satire, thesis, tragedy, treatise, triad, trilogy, verse. *see also* **poem**; **story**.

litigation n lawsuit, action, suit, case, prosecution, process, contention.

litter n **1** RUBBISH, debris, refuse, waste, mess, disorder, clutter, confusion, disarray, untidiness, junk (*infml*), muck, jumble, fragments,

shreds. **2** OFFSPRING, young, progeny (*fml*), brood, family.
v strew, scatter, mess up, disorder, clutter.
Ⓔ tidy.

little *adj* **1** SMALL, short, tiny, wee (*infml*), minute, teeny (*infml*), diminutive, miniature, infinitesimal, mini, microscopic, petite, pint-size(d) (*infml*), slender. **2** SHORT-LIVED, brief, fleeting, passing, transient.
3 INSUFFICIENT, sparse, scant, meagre, paltry, skimpy.
4 INSIGNIFICANT, inconsiderable, negligible, trivial, petty, trifling, unimportant.
Ⓔ 1 big. **2** lengthy. **3** ample.
4 considerable.
adv barely, hardly, scarcely, rarely, seldom, infrequently, not much.
Ⓔ frequently.
n bit, dash, pinch, spot, trace, drop, dab, speck, touch, taste, particle, hint, fragment, modicum, trifle.
Ⓔ lot.

live¹ *v* **1** BE, exist, breathe, draw breath. **2** LAST, endure, continue, remain, persist, survive. **3** DWELL, inhabit, reside, lodge, abide. **4** PASS, spend, lead.
Ⓔ 1 die. **2** cease.

live² *adj* **1** ALIVE, living, existent.
2 LIVELY, vital, active, energetic, dynamic, alert, vigorous.
3 BURNING, glowing, blazing, ignited. **4** RELEVANT, current, topical, pertinent, controversial.
Ⓔ 1 dead. **2** apathetic.

livelihood *n* occupation, employment, job, living, means, income, maintenance, work, support, subsistence, sustenance.

lively *adj* **1** ANIMATED, alert, active, energetic, spirited, vivacious, vigorous, sprightly, spry, agile, nimble, quick, keen. **2** CHEERFUL, blithe, merry, frisky, perky, breezy, chirpy (*infml*), frolicsome. **3** BUSY, bustling, brisk, crowded, eventful,

exciting, buzzing. **4** VIVID, bright, colourful, stimulating, stirring, invigorating, racy, refreshing, sparkling.
Ⓔ 1 moribund, apathetic. **3** inactive.

liven (up) enliven, vitalize, put life into, rouse, invigorate, animate, energize, brighten, stir (up), buck up (*infml*), pep up (*infml*), perk up (*infml*), hot up (*infml*).
Ⓔ dishearten.

livery *n* uniform, costume, regalia, dress, clothes, clothing, apparel (*fml*), attire, vestments, suit, garb, habit.

livid *adj* **1** LEADEN, black-and-blue, bruised, discoloured, greyish, purple.
2 PALE, pallid, ashen, blanched, bloodless, wan, waxy, pasty.
3 (*infml*) ANGRY, furious, infuriated, irate, outraged, enraged, raging, fuming, indignant, incensed, exasperated, mad (*infml*).
Ⓔ 3 calm.

living *adj* alive, breathing, existing, live, current, extant, operative, strong, vigorous, active, lively, vital, animated.
Ⓔ dead, sluggish.
n **1** BEING, life, animation, existence.
2 LIVELIHOOD, maintenance, support, income, subsistence, sustenance, work, job, occupation, profession, benefice, way of life.

load *n* **1** BURDEN, onus, encumbrance, weight, pressure, oppression, millstone. **2** CARGO, consignment, shipment, goods, lading, freight.
v **1** BURDEN, weigh down, encumber, overburden, oppress, trouble, weight, saddle with. **2** PACK, pile, heap, freight, fill, stack.

loaded *adj* burdened, charged, laden, full, weighted.

loafer *n* (*infml*) idler, layabout (*infml*), shirker, skiver (*infml*), sluggard, wastrel, lounger, ne'er-do-well, lazybones (*infml*).

loan *n* advance, credit, mortgage,

allowance.

v lend, advance, credit, allow.

loathe *v* hate, detest, abominate, abhor, despise, dislike.

F3 adore, love.

loathing *n* hatred, detestation, abhorrence, abomination, repugnance, revulsion, repulsion, dislike, disgust, aversion, horror.

F3 affection, love.

loathsome *adj* detestable, abhorrent, odious, repulsive, abominable, hateful, repugnant, repellent, offensive, horrible, disgusting, vile, revolting, nasty.

lobby *v* campaign for, press for, demand, persuade, call for, urge, push for, influence, solicit, pressure, promote.

n **1** VESTIBULE, foyer, porch, anteroom, hall, hallway, waiting-room, entrance hall, corridor, passage. **2** PRESSURE GROUP, campaign, ginger group.

local *adj* regional, provincial, community, district, neighbourhood, parochial, vernacular, small-town, limited, narrow, restricted, parish(-pump).

F3 national.

n **1** INHABITANT, citizen, resident, native. **2** (*infml*) PUB.

locality *n* neighbourhood, vicinity, district, area, locale, region, position, place, site, spot, scene, setting.

locate *v* **1** FIND, discover, unearth, run to earth (*infml*), track down, detect, lay one's hands on (*infml*), pin-point, identify. **2** SITUATE, settle, fix, establish, place, put, set, seat.

location *n* position, situation, place, locus, whereabouts, venue, site, locale, bearings, spot, point.

lock *n* fastening, bolt, clasp, padlock.

v **1** FASTEN, secure, bolt, latch, seal, shut. **2** JOIN, unite, engage, link, mesh, entangle, entwine, clench.

3 CLASP, hug, embrace, grasp, encircle, enclose, clutch, grapple.

F3 unlock.

lock out shut out, refuse admittance to, keep out, exclude, bar, debar.

lock up imprison, jail, confine, shut in, shut up, incarcerate, secure, cage, pen, detain, close up.

F3 free.

lodge *n* hut, cabin, cottage, chalet, shelter, retreat, den, gatehouse, house, hunting-lodge, meeting-place, club, haunt.

v **1** ACCOMMODATE, put up (*infml*), quarter, board, billet, shelter. **2** LIVE, stray, reside. **3** FIX, imbed, implant, get stuck. **4** DEPOSIT, place, put, submit, register.

lodger *n* boarder, paying guest, resident, tenant, roomer, inmate, guest.

lodgings *n* accommodation, digs (*infml*), dwelling, quarters, billet, abode, boarding-house, rooms, pad (*infml*), residence.

log *n* **1** TIMBER, trunk, block, chunk. **2** RECORD, diary, journal, logbook, daybook, account, tally.

v record, register, write up, note, book, chart, tally.

logic *n* reasoning, reason, sense, deduction, rationale, argumentation.

logical *adj* reasonable, rational, reasoned, coherent, consistent, valid, sound, well-founded, clear, sensible, deducible, methodical, well-organized.

F3 illogical, irrational.

loiter *v* dawdle, hang about, idle, linger, dally, dilly-dally (*infml*), delay, mooch, lag, saunter.

lone *adj* single, sole, one, only, isolated, solitary, separate, separated, unattached, unaccompanied, unattended.

F3 accompanied.

loneliness *n* aloneness, isolation, lonesomeness, solitariness, solitude, seclusion, desolation.

lonely adj **1** ALONE, friendless, lonesome, solitary, abandoned, forsaken, companionless, unaccompanied, destitute.
2 ISOLATED, uninhabited, remote, out-of-the-way, unfrequented, secluded, abandoned, deserted, forsaken, desolate.
🔁 **1** popular. **2** crowded, populous.

long adj lengthy, extensive, extended, expanded, prolonged, protracted, stretched, spread out, sustained, expansive, far-reaching, long-drawn-out, interminable, slow.
🔁 brief, short, fleeting, abbreviated.
long for yearn for, crave, want, wish, desire, dream of, hanker for, pine, thirst for, lust after, covet, itch for, yen for (*infml*).

longing n craving, desire, yearning, hungering, hankering, yen, thirst, wish, urge, coveting, aspiration, ambition.

long-lasting adj permanent, imperishable, enduring, unchanging, unfading, continuing, abiding, long-standing, prolonged, protracted.
🔁 short-lived, ephemeral, transient.

long-standing adj established, long-established, long-lived, long-lasting, enduring, abiding, time-honoured, traditional.

long-suffering adj uncomplaining, forbearing, forgiving, tolerant, easy-going, patient, stoical.

long-winded adj lengthy, overlong, prolonged, diffuse, verbose, wordy, voluble, long-drawn-out, discursive, repetitious, rambling, tedious.
🔁 brief, terse.

look v **1** WATCH, see, observe, view, survey, regard, gaze, study, stare, examine, inspect, scrutinize, glance, contemplate, scan, peep, gawp (*infml*). **2** SEEM, appear, show, exhibit, display.
n **1** VIEW, survey, inspection, examination, observation, sight, review, once-over (*infml*), glance, glimpse, gaze, peek. **2** APPEARANCE, aspect, manner, semblance, mien, expression, bearing, face, complexion.

look after take care of, mind, care for, attend to, take charge of, tend, keep an eye on, watch over, protect, supervise, guard.
🔁 neglect.

look down on despise, scorn, sneer at, hold in contempt, disdain, look down one's nose at (*infml*), turn one's nose up at (*infml*).
🔁 esteem, approve.

look forward to anticipate, await, expect, hope for, long for, envisage, envision, count on, wait for, look for.

look into investigate, probe, research, study, go into, examine, enquire about, explore, check out, inspect, scrutinize, look over, plumb, fathom.

look out pay attention, watch out, beware, be careful, keep an eye out.

look over inspect, examine, check, give a once-over (*infml*), cast an eye over, look through, scan, view.

look up 1 SEARCH FOR, research, hunt for, find, track down. **2** VISIT, call on, drop in on, look in on, pay a visit to, stop by, drop by. **3** IMPROVE, get better, pick up, progress, come on.

look up to admire, esteem, respect, revere, honour, have a high opinion of.

look-alike n double, replica, twin, spitting image (*infml*), living image, clone, spit (*infml*), ringer (*infml*), doppelgänger.

look-out n **1** GUARD, sentry, watch, watch-tower, watchman, sentinel, tower, post. **2** (*infml*) CONCERN, responsibility, worry, affair, business, problem.

loom v appear, emerge, take shape, menace, threaten, impend, hang over, dominate, tower, overhang, rise, soar, overshadow, overtop.

loop n hoop, ring, circle, noose, coil, eyelet, loophole, spiral, curve, curl, kink, twist, whorl, twirl, turn, bend.
v coil, encircle, roll, bend, circle,

curve round, turn, twist, spiral, connect, join, knot, fold, braid.

loophole n let-out, escape, evasion, excuse, pretext, plea, pretence.

loose adj 1 FREE, unfastened, untied, movable, unattached, insecure, wobbly. 2 SLACK, lax, baggy, hanging. 3 IMPRECISE, vague, inexact, ill-defined, indefinite, inaccurate, indistinct.

F3 1 firm, secure. 2 tight. 3 precise.

loosen v 1 EASE, relax, loose, slacken, undo, unbind, untie, unfasten. 2 FREE, set free, release, let go, let out, deliver.

F3 1 tighten.

loot n spoils, booty, plunder, haul, swag (infml), prize.
v plunder, pillage, rob, sack, rifle, raid, maraud, ransack, ravage.

lop-sided adj asymmetrical, unbalanced, askew, off balance, uneven.

F3 balanced, symmetrical.

lord n 1 PEER, noble, earl, duke, count, baron. 2 MASTER, ruler, superior, overlord, leader, commander, governor, king.

lordly adj 1 NOBLE, dignified, aristocratic. 2 PROUD, arrogant, disdainful, haughty, imperious, condescending, high-handed, domineering, overbearing.

F3 1 low(ly). 2 humble.

lore n knowledge, wisdom, learning, erudition, scholarship, traditions, teaching, beliefs, sayings.

lose v 1 MISLAY, misplace, forget, miss, forfeit. 2 WASTE, squander, dissipate, use up, exhaust, expend, drain. 3 FAIL, fall short, suffer defeat.

F3 1 gain. 2 make. 3 win.

loser n failure, also-ran, runner-up, flop (infml), no-hoper.

F3 winner.

loss n 1 DEPRIVATION, disadvantage, defeat, failure, losing, bereavement, damage, destruction,

ruin, hurt. 2 WASTE, depletion, disappearance, deficiency, deficit.

F3 1 gain.

lost adj 1 MISLAID, missing, vanished, disappeared, misplaced, astray. 2 CONFUSED, disoriented, bewildered, puzzled, baffled, perplexed, preoccupied. 3 WASTED, squandered, ruined, destroyed.

F3 1 found.

lot n 1 COLLECTION, batch, assortment, quantity, group, set, crowd. 2 SHARE, portion, allowance, ration, quota, part, piece, parcel.

lotion n ointment, balm, cream, salve.

lottery n 1 DRAW, raffle, sweepstake. 2 SPECULATION, venture, risk, gamble.

loud adj 1 NOISY, deafening, booming, resounding, ear-piercing, ear-splitting, piercing, thundering, blaring, clamorous, vociferous. 2 GARISH, gaudy, glaring, flashy, brash, showy, ostentatious, tasteless.

F3 1 quiet. 2 subdued.

lounge v relax, loll, idle, laze, waste time, kill time, lie about, take it easy, sprawl, recline, lie back, slump.
n sitting-room, living-room, drawing-room, day-room, parlour.

lovable adj adorable, endearing, winsome, captivating, charming, engaging, attractive, fetching, sweet, lovely, pleasing, delightful.

F3 detestable, hateful.

love v 1 he loves his wife: adore, cherish, dote on, treasure, hold dear, idolize, worship. 2 I love macaroons: like, take pleasure in, enjoy, delight in, appreciate, desire, fancy.

F3 detest, hate.

n adoration, affection, fondness, attachment, regard, liking, amorousness, ardour, devotion, adulation, passion, rapture, tenderness, warmth, inclination, infatuation, delight, enjoyment, soft spot (infml), weakness, taste,

friendship.
🔁 detestation, hate, loathing.

love affair n affair, romance, liaison, relationship, love, passion.

lovely adj beautiful, charming, delightful, attractive, enchanting, pleasing, pleasant, pretty, adorable, agreeable, enjoyable, sweet, winning, exquisite.
🔁 ugly, hideous.

lover n beloved, admirer, boyfriend, girlfriend, sweetheart, suitor, mistress, fiancé(e), flame (infml).

loving adj amorous, affectionate, devoted, doting, fond, ardent, passionate, warm, warm-hearted, tender.

low adj **1** SHORT, small, squat, stunted, little, shallow, deep, depressed, sunken. **2** INADEQUATE, deficient, poor, sparse, meagre, paltry, scant, insignificant.
3 UNHAPPY, depressed, downcast, gloomy. **4** BASE, coarse, vulgar, mean, contemptible. **5** CHEAP, inexpensive, reasonable. **6** subdued, muted, soft.
🔁 **1** high. **2** high. **3** cheerful.
4 honourable. **5** exorbitant. **6** loud.

lower adj inferior, lesser, subordinate, secondary, minor, second-class, low-level, lowly, junior.
🔁 higher.
v **1** DROP, depress, sink, descend, let down. **2** REDUCE, decrease, cut, lessen, diminish.
🔁 **1** raise. **2** increase.

lowly adj humble, low-born, obscure, poor, plebeian, plain, simple, modest, ordinary, inferior, meek, mild, mean, submissive, subordinate.
🔁 lofty, noble.

low-spirited adj depressed, gloomy, heavy-hearted, low, down, down-hearted, despondent, fed up (infml), sad, unhappy, miserable, moody.
🔁 high-spirited, cheerful.

loyal adj true, faithful, steadfast,

staunch, devoted, trustworthy, sincere, patriotic.
🔁 disloyal, treacherous.

loyalty n allegiance, faithfulness, fidelity, devotion, steadfastness, constancy, trustworthiness, reliability, patriotism.
🔁 disloyalty, treachery.

lubricate v oil, grease, smear, wax, lard.

luck n **1** CHANCE, fortune, accident, fate, fortuity (fml), fluke (infml), destiny. **2** GOOD FORTUNE, success, break (infml), godsend.
🔁 **1** design. **2** misfortune.

luckily adv fortunately, happily, providentially.
🔁 unfortunately.

lucky adj fortunate, favoured, auspicious, successful, prosperous, timely.
🔁 unlucky.

lucrative adj profitable, well-paid, remunerative, advantageous.
🔁 unprofitable.

ludicrous adj absurd, ridiculous, preposterous, nonsensical, laughable, farcical, silly, comical, funny, outlandish, crazy (infml).
🔁 serious.

lug v pull, drag, haul, carry, tow, heave, hump.

luggage

> *Types of luggage include*: case, suitcase, vanity-case, bag, holdall, portmanteau, valise, overnight-bag, kit-bag, flight bag, hand-luggage, travel bag, Gladstone bag, grip, rucksack, knapsack, haversack, backpack, briefcase, attaché case, portfolio, satchel, basket, hamper, trunk, chest, box.

lukewarm adj cool, half-hearted, apathetic, tepid, indifferent, unenthusiastic, uninterested, unresponsive, unconcerned.

lull v soothe, subdue, calm, hush,

pacify, quieten down, quiet, quell, compose.
🔳 agitate.
n calm, peace, quiet, tranquillity, stillness, let-up, pause, hush, silence.
🔳 agitation.

lumber¹ *n* clutter, jumble, rubbish, bits and pieces, odds and ends, junk.

lumber² *v* clump, shamble, plod, shuffle, stump, trundle.

luminous *adj* glowing, illuminated, lit, lighted, radiant, shining, fluorescent, brilliant, lustrous, bright.

lump *n* **1** MASS, cluster, clump, clod, ball, bunch, piece, chunk, cake, hunk, nugget, wedge. **2** SWELLING, growth, bulge, bump, protuberance, protrusion, tumour.
v collect, mass, gather, cluster, combine, coalesce, group, consolidate, unite.

lunacy *n* madness, insanity, aberration, derangement, mania, craziness (*infml*), idiocy, imbecility, folly, absurdity, stupidity.
🔳 sanity.

lunatic *n* psychotic, psychopath, madman, maniac, loony (*infml*), nutcase (*infml*), nutter (*infml*), fruitcake (*infml*).
adj mad, insane, deranged, psychotic, irrational, crazy (*infml*), bonkers (*infml*).
🔳 sane.

lunge *v* thrust, jab, stab, pounce, plunge, pitch into, charge, dart, dash, dive, poke, strike (at), fall upon, grab (at), hit (at), leap.
n thrust, stab, pounce, charge, jab, pass, cut, spring.

lurch *v* roll, rock, pitch, sway, stagger, reel, list.

lure *v* tempt, entice, draw, attract, allure, seduce, ensnare, lead on.
n temptation, enticement, attraction, bait, inducement.

lurid *adj* **1** SENSATIONAL, shocking, startling, graphic, exaggerated.

2 MACABRE, gruesome, gory, ghastly, grisly. **3** BRIGHTLY COLOURED, garish, glaring, loud, vivid.

lurk *v* skulk, prowl, lie in wait, crouch, lie low, hide, snoop.

luscious *adj* delicious, juicy, succulent, appetizing, mouth-watering, sweet, tasty, savoury, desirable.

lush *adj* **1** FLOURISHING, luxuriant, abundant, prolific, overgrown, green, verdant. **2** SUMPTUOUS, opulent, ornate, plush, rich.

lust *n* **1** SENSUALITY, libido, lechery, licentiousness, lewdness. **2** CRAVING, desire, appetite, longing, passion, greed, covetousness.
lust after desire, crave, yearn for, want, need, hunger for, thirst for.

lustre *n* **1** SHINE, gloss, sheen, gleam, glow, brilliance, brightness, radiance, sparkle, resplendence, burnish, glitter, glint. **2** GLORY, honour, prestige, illustriousness.

lusty *adj* robust, strong, sturdy, vigorous, hale, hearty, healthy, gutsy (*infml*), energetic, strapping, rugged, powerful.

luxurious *adj* sumptuous, opulent, lavish, de luxe, plush, magnificent, splendid, expensive, costly, self-indulgent, pampered.
🔳 austere, spartan.

luxury *n* sumptuousness, opulence, hedonism, splendour, affluence, richness, magnificence, pleasure, indulgence, gratification, comfort, extravagance, satisfaction.
🔳 austerity.

lying *adj* deceitful, dishonest, false, untruthful, double-dealing, two-faced (*infml*).
🔳 honest, truthful.
n dishonesty, untruthfulness, deceit, falsity, fibbing (*infml*), perjury, duplicity, fabrication, double-dealing.
🔳 honesty, truthfulness.

M

macabre *adj* gruesome, grisly, grim, horrible, frightful, dreadful, ghostly, eerie.

machine *n* 1 INSTRUMENT, device, contrivance, tool, mechanism, engine, apparatus, appliance.
2 AGENCY, organization, structure, system.

machinery *n* 1 INSTRUMENTS, mechanism, tools, apparatus, equipment, tackle, gear.
2 ORGANIZATION, channels, structure, system, procedure.

mad *adj* 1 INSANE, lunatic, unbalanced, psychotic, deranged, demented, out of one's mind, crazy (*infml*), nuts (*infml*), barmy (*infml*), bonkers (*infml*). 2 (*infml*) ANGRY, furious, enraged, infuriated, incensed. 3 IRRATIONAL, illogical, unreasonable, absurd, preposterous, foolish. 4 FANATICAL, enthusiastic, infatuated, ardent.
Ea 1 sane. 2 calm. 3 sensible.
4 apathetic.

madden *v* anger, enrage, infuriate, incense, exasperate, provoke, annoy, irritate.
Ea calm, pacify.

madly *adv* 1 *he rolled his eyes madly*: insanely, dementedly, hysterically, wildly. 2 *madly cleaning up*: excitedly, frantically, furiously, recklessly, violently, energetically, rapidly, hastily, hurriedly. 3 *madly in love*: intensely, extremely, exceedingly, fervently, devotedly.

madman, madwoman *n* lunatic, psychotic, psychopath, maniac, loony (*infml*), nutcase (*infml*), fruitcake (*infml*).

magazine *n* 1 JOURNAL, periodical, paper, weekly, monthly, quarterly.
2 ARSENAL, storehouse, ammunition dump, depot, ordnance.

magic *n* 1 SORCERY, enchantment, occultism, black art, witchcraft, spell.
2 CONJURING, illusion, sleight of hand, trickery. 3 CHARM, fascination, glamour, allure.
adj charming, enchanting, bewitching, fascinating, spellbinding.

magician *n* sorcerer, miracle-worker, conjuror, enchanter, wizard, witch, warlock, spellbinder, wonder-worker.

magnanimous *adj* generous, liberal, open-handed, benevolent, selfless, charitable, big-hearted, kind, noble, unselfish, ungrudging.
Ea mean.

magnate *n* tycoon, captain of industry, industrialist, mogul, entrepreneur, plutocrat, baron, personage, notable.

magnetic *adj* attractive, alluring, fascinating, charming, mesmerizing, seductive, irresistible, entrancing, captivating, gripping, absorbing, charismatic.
Ea repellent, repulsive.

magnetism *n* attraction, allure, fascination, charm, lure, appeal, drawing power, draw, pull, hypnotism, mesmerism, charisma, grip, magic, power, spell.

magnificent *adj* splendid, grand, imposing, impressive, glorious, gorgeous, brilliant, excellent, majestic, superb, sumptuous, noble, elegant, fine, rich.
Ea modest, humble, poor.

magnify *v* enlarge, amplify, increase, expand, intensify, boost, enhance,

greaten, heighten, deepen, build up, exaggerate, dramatize, overemphasize, overplay, overstate, overdo, blow up (*infml*).
🔄 belittle, play down.

magnitude *n* 1 SIZE, extent, measure, amount, expanse, dimensions, mass, proportions, quantity, volume, bulk, largeness, space, strength, amplitude.
2 IMPORTANCE, consequence, significance, weight, greatness, moment, intensity.

maiden *n* girl, virgin, lass, lassie, damsel (*fml*), miss.

mail *n* post, letters, correspondence, packages, parcels, delivery.
v post, send, dispatch, forward.

maim *v* mutilate, wound, incapacitate, injure, disable, hurt, impair, cripple, lame.

main *adj* principal, chief, leading, first, foremost, predominant, pre-eminent, primary, prime, supreme, paramount, central, cardinal, outstanding, essential, critical, crucial, necessary, vital.
🔄 minor, unimportant, insignificant.
n pipe, duct, conduit, channel, cable, line.

mainly *adv* primarily, principally, chiefly, in the main, mostly, on the whole, for the most part, generally, in general, especially, as a rule, above all, largely, overall.

mainstay *n* support, buttress, bulwark, linchpin, prop, pillar, backbone, foundation.

maintain *v* 1 CARRY ON, continue, keep (up), sustain, retain. 2 CARE FOR, conserve, look after, take care of, preserve, support, finance, supply. 3 ASSERT, affirm, claim, contend, declare, hold, state, insist, believe, fight for.
🔄 2 neglect. 3 deny.

maintenance *n* 1 CONTINUATION, continuance, perpetuation. 2 CARE, conservation, preservation, support, repairs, protection, upkeep, running. 3 KEEP, subsistence, living, livelihood, allowance, alimony.
🔄 2 neglect.

majestic *adj* magnificent, grand, dignified, noble, royal, stately, splendid, imperial, impressive, exalted, imposing, regal, sublime, superb, lofty, monumental, pompous.
🔄 lowly, unimpressive, unimposing.

majesty *n* grandeur, glory, dignity, magnificence, nobility, royalty, resplendence, splendour, stateliness, pomp, exaltedness, impressiveness, loftiness.

major *adj* greater, chief, main, larger, bigger, higher, leading, outstanding, notable, supreme, uppermost, significant, crucial, important, key, keynote, great, senior, older, superior, pre-eminent, vital, weighty.
🔄 minor, unimportant, trivial.

majority *n* 1 BULK, mass, preponderance, most, greater part. 2 ADULTHOOD, maturity, manhood, womanhood, years of discretion.
🔄 1 minority.

make *v* 1 CREATE, manufacture, fabricate, construct, build, produce, put together, originate, compose, form, shape. 2 CAUSE, bring about, effect, accomplish, occasion, give rise to, generate, render, perform. 3 COERCE, force, oblige, constrain, compel, prevail upon, pressurize, press, require. 4 APPOINT, elect, designate, nominate, ordain, install. 5 EARN, gain, net, obtain, acquire. 6 CONSTITUTE, compose, comprise, add up to, amount to.
🔄 1 dismantle. 5 spend.
n brand, sort, type, style, variety, manufacture, model, mark, kind, form, structure.

make off run off, run away, depart, bolt, leave, fly, cut and run (*infml*), beat a hasty retreat (*infml*), clear off (*infml*).

make out 1 DISCERN, perceive,

decipher, distinguish, recognize, see, detect, discover, understand, work out, grasp, follow, fathom. **2** DRAW UP, complete, fill in, write out. **3** MAINTAIN, imply, claim, assert, describe, demonstrate, prove.
4 MANAGE, get on, progress, succeed, fare (*fml*).

make up 1 CREATE, invent, devise, fabricate, construct, originate, formulate, dream up, compose. **2** COMPLETE, fill, supply, meet, supplement. **3** COMPRISE, constitute, compose, form. **4** BE RECONCILED, make peace, settle differences, bury the hatchet (*infml*), forgive and forget, call it quits (*infml*).

make up for compensate for, make good, make amends for, redress, recompense, redeem, atone for.

make-believe *n* pretence, imagination, fantasy, unreality, play-acting, role-play, dream, charade.
Ea reality.

maker *n* creator, manufacturer, constructor, builder, producer, director, architect, author.

makeshift *adj* temporary, improvised, rough and ready, provisional, substitute, stop-gap, expedient, make-do.
Ea permanent.

make-up *n* **1** COSMETICS, paint, powder, maquillage, war paint (*infml*). **2** CONSTITUTION, nature, composition, character, construction, form, format, formation, arrangement, organization, style, structure, assembly.

maladjusted *adj* disturbed, unstable, confused, alienated, neurotic, estranged.
Ea well-adjusted.

male *adj* masculine, manly, virile, boyish, he-.
Ea female.

Male terms include: boy, lad, youth, man, gentleman, gent (*infml*),

bachelor, chap (*infml*), bloke (*infml*), guy (*infml*), son, brother, boyfriend, beau, toy boy (*sl*), fiancé, bridegroom, husband, father, uncle, nephew, grandfather, patriarch, godfather, widower, sugar daddy (*sl*), hunk (*sl*), gigolo, homosexual, gay, rent boy, male chauvinist pig (MCP) (*sl*); bull, dog, buck, tup, cock, cockerel, stallion, billy-goat, boar, dog fox, stag, ram, tom cat, drake, gander.

malevolent *adj* malicious, malign, spiteful, vindictive, ill-natured, hostile, vicious, venomous, evil-minded.
Ea benevolent, kind.

malformation *n* irregularity, deformity, distortion, warp.

malformed *adj* misshapen, irregular, deformed, distorted, twisted, warped, crooked, bent.
Ea perfect.

malfunction *n* fault, defect, failure, breakdown.
v break down, go wrong, fail.

malice *n* malevolence, enmity, animosity, ill-will, hatred, hate, spite, vindictiveness, bitterness.
Ea love.

malicious *adj* malevolent, ill-natured, malign, spiteful, venomous, vicious, vengeful, evil-minded, bitter, resentful.
Ea kind, friendly.

malign *adj* malignant, malevolent, bad, evil, harmful, hurtful, injurious, destructive, hostile.
Ea benign.
v defame, slander, libel, disparage, abuse, run down (*infml*), harm, injure.
Ea praise.

malignant *adj* **1** MALEVOLENT, malicious, spiteful, evil, hostile, vicious, venomous, destructive, harmful, hurtful, pernicious. **2** FATAL, deadly, incurable, dangerous, cancerous, uncontrollable, virulent.

⋯ 1 kind. **2** benign.

malpractice *n* misconduct, mismanagement, negligence, impropriety, dereliction of duty (*fml*), abuse, misdeed.

maltreat *v* ill-treat, mistreat, misuse, abuse, injure, harm, hurt.
⋯ care for.

mammal

Mammals include: aardvark, African black rhinoceros, African elephant, anteater, antelope, armadillo, baboon, Bactrian camel, badger, bat, bear, beaver, bushbaby, cat, chimpanzee, chipmunk, cow, deer, dog, dolphin, duck-billed platypus, dugong, echidna, flying lemur, fox, gerbil, gibbon, giraffe, goat, gorilla, guinea pig, hamster, hare, hedgehog, hippopotamus, horse, human being, hyena, Indian elephant, kangaroo, koala, lemming, leopard, lion, manatee, marmoset, marmot, marsupial mouse, mole, mouse, opossum, orang utan, otter, pig, porcupine, porpoise, rabbit, raccoon, rat, sea cow, sea lion, seal, sheep, shrew, sloth, squirrel, tamarin, tapir, tiger, vole, wallaby, walrus, weasel, whale, wolf, zebra. *see also* **cat**; **cattle**; **dog**; **marsupial**; **monkey**; **rodent**.

---

mammoth *adj* enormous, huge, vast, colossal, gigantic, giant, massive, immense, monumental, mighty.
⋯ tiny, minute.

man *n* **1** MALE, gentleman, fellow, bloke (*infml*), chap (*infml*), guy (*infml*). **2** HUMAN BEING, person, individual, adult, human. **3** HUMANITY, humankind, mankind, human race, people, Homo sapiens, mortals. **4** MANSERVANT, servant, worker, employee, hand, soldier, valet, houseman, houseboy.
v staff, crew, take charge of, operate, occupy.

manacle *v* handcuff, shackle, restrain, fetter, chain, put in chains, bind, curb, check, hamper, inhibit.
⋯ free, unshackle.

manage *v* **1** ACCOMPLISH, succeed, bring about, bring off, effect. **2** ADMINISTER, direct, run, command, govern, preside over, rule, superintend, oversee, conduct. **3** CONTROL, influence, deal with, handle, operate, manipulate, guide. **4** COPE, fare, survive, get by, get along, get on, make do.
⋯ **1** fail. **2** mismanage.

manageable *adj* tractable, governable, controllable, amenable, submissive, docile.
⋯ unmanageable.

management *n* **1** ADMINISTRATION, direction, control, government, command, running, superintendence, supervision, charge, care, handling. **2** MANAGERS, directors, directorate, executive, executives, governors, board, bosses (*infml*), supervisors.
⋯ **1** mismanagement. **2** workers.

manager *n* director, executive, administrator, controller, superintendent, supervisor, overseer, governor, organizer, head, boss.

mandate *n* order, command, decree, edict, injunction, charge, directive, warrant, authorization, authority, instruction, commission, sanction.

mandatory *adj* obligatory, compulsory, binding, required, necessary, requisite, essential.
⋯ optional.

mangle *v* mutilate, disfigure, mar, maim, spoil, butcher, destroy, deform, wreck, twist, maul, distort, crush, cut, hack, tear, rend.

mangy *adj* seedy, shabby, scruffy, scabby, tatty (*infml*), shoddy, moth-eaten, dirty, mean.

manhandle *v* **1** *the porters*

manhandled the baggage: haul, heave, hump, pull, push, shove, tug. **2** *the police manhandled the demonstrators*: maul, mistreat, maltreat, misuse, abuse, knock about (*infml*), rough up (*infml*).

manhood *n* **1** ADULTHOOD, maturity. **2** MASCULINITY, virility, manliness, manfulness, machismo (*infml*).

mania *n* **1** MADNESS, insanity, lunacy, psychosis, derangement, disorder, aberration, craziness (*infml*), frenzy. **2** PASSION, craze, rage, obsession, compulsion, enthusiasm, fad (*infml*), infatuation, fixation, craving.

Manias (by name of disorder) include: dipsomania (*alcohol*), bibliomania (*books*), ailuromania (*cats*), demomania (*crowds*), necromania (*dead bodies*), thanatomania (*death*), cynomania (*dogs*), narcomania (*drugs*), pyromania (*fire-raising*), anthomania (*flowers*), hippomania (*horses*), mythomania (*lying and exaggerating*), egomania (*oneself*), ablutomania (*personal cleanliness*), hedonomania (*pleasure*), megalomania (*power*), theomania (*religion*), nymphomania (*sex*), monomania (*single idea or thing*), kleptomania (*stealing*), tomomania (*surgery*), logomania (*talking*), ergomania (*work*). *see also* **phobia**.

maniac *n* **1** LUNATIC, madman, madwoman, psychotic, psychopath, loony (*infml*). **2** ENTHUSIAST, fan (*infml*), fanatic, fiend (*infml*), freak (*infml*).

manifest *adj* obvious, evident, clear, apparent, plain, open, patent, noticeable, conspicuous, unmistakable, visible, unconcealed. ◼ unclear.
v show, exhibit, display, demonstrate, reveal, set forth, expose, prove, illustrate, establish. ◼ conceal.

manifestation *n* display, exhibition, demonstration, show, revelation, exposure, disclosure, appearance, expression, sign, indication.

manifesto *n* statement, declaration, policies, platform.

manifold *adj* (*fml*) many, numerous, varied, various, diverse, multiple, kaleidoscopic, abundant, copious.

manipulate *v* **1** HANDLE, control, wield, operate, use, manoeuvre, influence, engineer, guide, direct, steer, negotiate, work. **2** FALSIFY, rig, juggle with, doctor (*infml*), cook (*infml*), fiddle (*infml*).

mankind *n* humankind, humanity, human race, man, Homo sapiens, people.

manly *adj* masculine, male, virile, manful, macho (*infml*), robust.

man-made *adj* synthetic, manufactured, simulated, imitation, artificial. ◼ natural.

manner *n* **1** WAY, method, means, fashion, style, procedure, process, form. **2** BEHAVIOUR, conduct, bearing, demeanour, air, appearance, look, character.

mannerism *n* idiosyncrasy, peculiarity, characteristic, quirk, trait, feature, foible, habit.

manners *n* behaviour, conduct, demeanour, etiquette, politeness, bearing, courtesy, formalities, social graces, p's and q's.

manoeuvre *n* move, movement, operation, action, exercise, plan, ploy, plot, ruse, strategem, machination, gambit, tactic, trick, scheme, dodge (*infml*).
v **1** MOVE, manipulate, handle, guide, pilot, steer, navigate, jockey, direct, drive, exercise. **2** CONTRIVE, engineer, plot, scheme, wangle (*infml*), pull strings (*infml*), manipulate,

manage, plan, devise, negotiate.

mantle n cloak, cover, covering, cape, hood, blanket, shawl, veil, wrap, shroud, screen.

manual n handbook, guide, guidebook, instructions, Bible, vade mecum, directions.
adj hand-operated, by hand, physical, human.

manufacture v 1 MAKE, produce, construct, build, fabricate, create, assemble, mass-produce, turn out, process, forge, form. 2 INVENT, make up, concoct, fabricate, think up.
n production, making, construction, fabrication, mass-production, assembly, creation, formation.

manufacturer n maker, producer, industrialist, constructor, factory-owner, builder, creator.

manure n fertilizer, compost, muck, dung.

many adj numerous, countless, lots of (infml), manifold (fml), various, varied, sundry, diverse, umpteen (infml).
Fa few.

map n chart, plan, street plan, atlas, graph, plot.

mar v spoil, impair, harm, hurt, damage, deface, disfigure, mutilate, injure, maim, scar, detract from, mangle, ruin, wreck, tarnish.
Fa enhance.

marauder n bandit, brigand, robber, raider, plunderer, pillager, pirate, buccaneer, outlaw, ravager, predator.

march v walk, stride, parade, pace, file, tread, stalk.
n 1 STEP, pace, stride. 2 WALK, trek, hike, footslog (infml). 3 PROCESSION, parade, demonstration, demo (infml). 4 ADVANCE, development, progress, evolution, passage.

margin n 1 BORDER, edge, boundary, bound, periphery, perimeter, rim, brink, limit, confine,

verge, side, skirt. 2 ALLOWANCE, play, leeway, latitude, scope, room, space, surplus, extra.

marginal adj borderline, peripheral, negligible, minimal, insignificant, minor, slight, doubtful, low, small.
Fa central, core.

marine adj sea, maritime, naval, nautical, seafaring, sea-going, ocean-going, salt-water.

mariner n sailor, seaman, seafarer, deckhand, navigator, tar (infml), sea-dog (infml), salt (infml).

marital adj conjugal, matrimonial, married, wedded, nuptial (fml), connubial (fml).

maritime adj marine, nautical, naval, seafaring, sea, seaside, oceanic, coastal.

mark n 1 SPOT, stain, blemish, blot, blotch, smudge, dent, impression, scar, scratch, bruise, line. 2 SYMBOL, sign, indication, emblem, brand, stamp, token, characteristic, feature, proof, evidence, badge. 3 TARGET, goal, aim, objective, purpose.
v 1 STAIN, blemish, blot, smudge, dent, scar, scratch, bruise. 2 BRAND, label, stamp, characterize, identify, distinguish. 3 EVALUATE, assess, correct, grade. 4 HEED, listen, mind, note, observe, regard, notice, take to heart.

marked adj 1 NOTICEABLE, obvious, conspicuous, evident, pronounced, distinct, decided, emphatic, considerable, remarkable, apparent, clearing. 2 SUSPECTED, watched, doomed.
Fa 1 unnoticeable, slight.

market n mart, marketplace, bazaar, fair, exchange, outlet.
v sell, retail, hawk, peddle.
Fa buy.

maroon v abandon, cast away, desert, put ashore, strand, leave, isolate.

marriage n 1 MATRIMONY,

wedlock, wedding, nuptials (*fml*).
2 UNION, alliance, merger, coupling, amalgamation, link, association, confederation.
🔁 1 divorce. 2 separation.

marrow *n* essence, heart, nub, kernel, core, soul, spirit, substance, quick, stuff, gist.

marry *v* 1 WED, join in matrimony, tie the knot (*infml*), get hitched (*infml*), get spliced (*infml*). 2 UNITE, ally, join, merge, match, link, knit.
🔁 1 divorce. 2 separate.

marsh *n* marshland, bog, swamp, fen, morass, quagmire, slough.

marshal *v* 1 ARRANGE, dispose, order, line up, align, array, rank, organize, assemble, gather, muster, group, collect, draw up, deploy.
2 GUIDE, lead, escort, conduct, usher.

marsupial

Marsupials include: bandicoot, cuscus, kangaroo, rat kangaroo, tree kangaroo, wallaroo, koala, marsupial anteater, marsupial mouse, marsupial mole, marsupial rat, opossum, pademelon, phalanger, Tasmanian Devil, Tasmanian wolf, wallaby, rock wallaby, wombat.

martial *adj* warlike, military, belligerent, soldierly, militant, heroic, brave.

marvel *n* wonder, miracle, phenomenon, prodigy, spectacle, sensation, genius.
v wonder, gape, gaze, be amazed at.

marvellous *adj* 1 WONDERFUL, excellent, splendid, superb, magnificent, terrific (*infml*), super, fantastic (*infml*).
2 EXTRAORDINARY, amazing, astonishing, astounding, miraculous, remarkable, surprising, unbelievable, incredible, glorious.
🔁 1 terrible, awful. 2 ordinary, run-of-the-mill.

masculine *adj* 1 MALE, manlike, manly, mannish, virile, macho.
2 VIGOROUS, strong, strapping, robust, powerful, muscular, red-blooded, bold, brave, gallant, resolute, stout-hearted.
🔁 1 feminine.

mash *v* crush, pulp, beat, pound, pulverize, pummel, grind, smash.

mask *n* disguise, camouflage, façade, front, concealment, cover-up, cover, guise, pretence, semblance, cloak, veil, blind, show, veneer, visor.
v disguise, camouflage, cover, conceal, cloak, veil, hide, obscure, screen, shield.
🔁 expose, uncover.

masquerade *n* 1 MASQUE, masked ball, costume ball, fancy dress party.
2 DISGUISE, counterfeit, cover-up, cover, deception, front, pose, pretence, guise, cloak.
v disguise, impersonate, pose, pass oneself off, mask, play, pretend, profess, dissimulate.

mass *n* 1 HEAP, pile, load, accumulation, aggregate, collection, conglomeration, combination, entirety, whole, totality, sum, lot, group, batch, bunch. 2 QUANTITY, multitude, throng, troop, crowd, band, horde, mob. 3 MAJORITY, body, bulk. 4 SIZE, dimension, magnitude, immensity. 5 LUMP, piece, chunk, block, hunk.
adj widespread, large-scale, extensive, comprehensive, general, indiscriminate, popular, across-the-board, sweeping, wholesale, blanket.
🔁 limited, small-scale.
v collect, gather, assemble, congregate, crowd, rally, cluster, muster, swarm, throng.
🔁 separate.

massacre *n* slaughter, murder, extermination, carnage, butchery, holocaust, blood bath, annihilation, killing.
v slaughter, butcher, murder, mow

down, wipe out, exterminate, annihilate, kill, decimate.

massage n manipulation, kneading, rubbing, rub-down.
  v manipulate, knead, rub (down).

massive adj huge, immense, enormous, vast, colossal, gigantic, big, bulky, monumental, solid, substantial, heavy, large-scale, extensive.
  ⏴ tiny, small.

master n 1 RULER, chief, governor, head, lord, captain, boss (infml), employer, commander, controller, director, manager, superintendent, overseer, principal, overlord, owner. 2 EXPERT, genius, virtuoso, past master, maestro, dab hand (infml), ace (infml), pro (infml). 3 TEACHER, tutor, instructor, schoolmaster, guide, guru, preceptor (fml).
  ⏴ 1 servant, underling. 2 amateur. 3 learner, pupil.
  adj 1 CHIEF, principal, main, leading, foremost, prime, predominant, controlling, great, grand. 2 EXPERT, masterly, skilled, skilful, proficient.
  ⏴ 1 subordinate. 2 inept.
  v 1 CONQUER, defeat, subdue, subjugate, vanquish, triumph over, overcome, quell, rule, control. 2 LEARN, grasp, acquire, get the hang of (infml), manage.

masterful adj 1 ARROGANT, authoritative, domineering, overbearing, high-handed, despotic, dictatorial, autocratic, bossy (infml), tyrannical, powerful. 2 EXPERT, masterly, skilful, skilled, dexterous, first-rate, professional.
  ⏴ 1 humble. 2 inept, unskilful.

masterly adj expert, skilled, skilful, dexterous, adept, adroit, first-rate, ace (infml), excellent, superb, superior, supreme.
  ⏴ inept, clumsy.

masterpiece n master-work, magnum opus, pièce de résistance,

chef d'oeuvre, jewel.

mastery n 1 PROFICIENCY, skill, ability, command, expertise, virtuosity, knowledge, know-how, dexterity, familiarity, grasp. 2 CONTROL, command, domination, supremacy, upper hand, dominion, authority.
  ⏴ 1 incompetence. 2 subjugation.

match n 1 CONTEST, competition, bout, game, test, trial. 2 EQUAL, equivalent, peer, counterpart, fellow, mate, rival, copy, double, replica, look-alike, twin, duplicate. 3 MARRIAGE, alliance, union, partnership, affiliation.
  v 1 EQUAL, compare, measure up to, rival, compete, oppose, contend, vie, pit against. 2 FIT, go with, accord, agree, suit, correspond, harmonize, tally, co-ordinate, blend, adapt, go together, relate, tone with, accompany. 3 JOIN, marry, unite, mate, link, couple, combine, ally, pair, yoke, team.
  ⏴ 2 clash. 3 separate.

matching adj corresponding, comparable, equivalent, like, identical, co-ordinating, similar, duplicate, same, twin.
  ⏴ clashing.

matchless adj unequalled, peerless, incomparable, unmatched, unparalleled, unsurpassed, unrivalled, inimitable, unique.

mate n 1 FRIEND, companion, comrade, pal (infml), colleague, partner, fellow-worker, co-worker, associate. 2 SPOUSE, husband, wife. 3 ASSISTANT, helper, subordinate. 4 MATCH, fellow, twin.
  v 1 COUPLE, pair, breed, copulate. 2 JOIN, match, marry, wed.

material n 1 STUFF, substance, body, matter. 2 FABRIC, textile, cloth. 3 INFORMATION, facts, data, evidence, constituents, work, notes.
  adj 1 PHYSICAL, concrete, tangible, substantial. 2 RELEVANT, significant,

important, meaningful, pertinent, essential, vital, indispensable, serious. **☒ 1** abstract. **2** irrelevant.

materialize v appear, arise, take shape, turn up, happen, occur. **☒** disappear.

mathematical terms

Mathematical terms include: acute angle, addition, algebra, algorithm, analysis, angle, apex, approximate, arc, area, argument, arithmetic, arithmetic progression, asymmetrical, average, axis, axis of symmetry, bar chart, bar graph, base, bearing, binary, binomial, breadth, calculus, capacity, cardinal number, Cartesian coordinates, chance, chord, circumference, coefficient, combination, commutative operation, complement, complementary angle, complex number, concave, concentric circles, congruent, conjugate angles, constant, continuous distribution, converse, convex, coordinate, correlation, cosine, covariance, cross section, cube, cube root, curve, decimal, degree, denominator, depth, derivative, determinant, diagonal, diameter, differentiation, directed number, distribution, dividend, division, divisor, edge, equal, equation, equidistant, even number, exponent, exponential, face, factor, factorial, Fibonacci sequence, formula, fraction, function, geometric progression, geometry, gradient, graph, greater than, group, harmonic progression, height, helix, histogram, horizontal, hyperbola, hypotenuse, identity, infinity, integer, integration, irrational number, latitude, length, less than, linear, line, locus, logarithm, longitude, magic square, matrix, maximum, mean, measure, median, minimum, minus, mirror image, mirror symmetry, Möbius strip, mode, modulus, multiple, multiplication, natural

logarithm, natural number, negative number, number, numerator, oblique, obtuse angle, odd number, operation, ordinal number, origin, parabola, parallel lines, parallel planes, parameter, percentage, percentile, perimeter, permutation, perpendicular, pi, pie chart, place value, plane figure, plus, point, positive number, prime number, probability, product, proportion, protractor, Pythagoras's theorem, quadrant, quadratic equation, quadrilateral, quartile, quotient, radian, radius, random sample, ratio, rational number, real numbers, reciprocal, recurring decimal, reflection, reflex angle, regression, remainder, right-angle, right-angled triangle, root, rotation, rotational symmetry, sample, scalar segment, secant, sector, set, side, simultaneous equation, sine, speed, spiral, square, square root, standard deviation, straight line, subset, subtractor, supplementary angles, symmetry, tangent, three-dimensional, total, transcendental number, triangulation, trigonometry, unit, universal set, variable, variance, vector, velocity, Venn diagram, vertex, vertical, volume, whole number, width, zero.

matrimonial adj marital, nuptial, marriage, wedding, married, wedded, conjugal.

matter n **1** SUBJECT, issue, topic, question, affair, business, concern, event, episode, incident. **2** IMPORTANCE, significance, consequence, note. **3** TROUBLE, problem, difficulty, worry. **4** SUBSTANCE, stuff, material, body, content.
v count, be important, make a difference, mean something.

matter-of-fact adj unemotional, prosaic, emotionless, straightforward, sober,

unimaginative, flat, deadpan (*infml*).
 emotional.

mature *adj* **1** ADULT, grown-up,
grown, full-grown, fully fledged,
complete, perfect, perfected, well-
thought-out. **2** RIPE, ripened,
seasoned, mellow, ready.
 1 childish. **2** immature.
v grow up, come of age, develop,
mellow, ripen, perfect, age, bloom,
fall due.

maturity *n* **1** ADULTHOOD,
majority, womanhood, manhood,
wisdom, experience. **2** RIPENESS,
readiness, mellowness, perfection.
 1 childishness. **2** immaturity.

maul *v* abuse, ill-treat, manhandle,
maltreat, molest, paw, beat (up),
knock about, rough up, claw,
lacerate, batter.

maxim *n* saying, proverb, adage,
axiom, aphorism, epigram, motto,
byword, precept, rule.

maximum *adj* greatest, highest,
largest, biggest, most, utmost,
supreme.
 minimum.
n most, top (point), utmost, upper
limit, peak, pinnacle, summit, height,
ceiling, extremity, zenith (*fml*).
 mimimum.

maybe *adv* perhaps, possibly,
perchance (*fml*).
 definitely.

maze *n* labyrinth, network, tangle,
web, complex, confusion, puzzle,
intricacy.

meadow *n* field, grassland, pasture,
lea.

meagre *adj* **1** SCANTY, sparse,
inadequate, deficient, skimpy, paltry,
negligible, poor. **2** THIN, puny,
insubstantial, bony, emaciated,
scrawny, slight.
 1 ample. **2** fat.

meal

Meals include: breakfast, wedding
breakfast, elevenses (*infml*), brunch,
lunch, luncheon, tea, tea-break, tea-
party, tiffin, afternoon tea, cream-tea,
high-tea, evening meal, dinner, TV
dinner, supper, harvest supper, fork
supper, banquet, feast, blow-out (*sl*),
barbecue, buffet, spread, picnic,
snack, take-away.

mean[1] *adj* **1** MISERLY, niggardly,
parsimonious, selfish, tight (*infml*),
tight-fisted, stingy (*infml*), penny-
pinching (*infml*). **2** UNKIND,
unpleasant, nasty, bad-tempered,
cruel. **3** LOWLY, base, poor, humble,
wretched.
 1 generous. **2** kind. **3** splendid.

mean[2] *v* **1** SIGNIFY, represent,
denote, stand for, symbolize, suggest,
indicate, imply. **2** INTEND, aim,
propose, design. **3** CAUSE, give rise
to, involve, entail.

mean[3] *adj* average, intermediate,
middle, halfway, median, normal.
 extreme.
n average, middle, mid-point, norm,
median, compromise, middle course,
middle way, happy medium, golden
mean.
 extreme.

meander *v* **1** WIND, zigzag, turn,
twist, snake, curve. **2** WANDER,
stray, amble, ramble, stroll.

meaning *n* **1** SIGNIFICANCE, sense,
import, implication, gist, trend,
explanation, interpretation. **2** AIM,
intention, purpose, object, idea.
3 VALUE, worth, point.

meaningful *adj* **1** IMPORTANT,
significant, relevant, valid, useful,
worthwhile, material, purposeful,
serious. **2** EXPRESSIVE, speaking,
suggestive, warning, pointed.
 1 unimportant, worthless.

meaningless *adj* **1** SENSELESS,
pointless, purposeless, useless,
insignificant, aimless, futile,
insubstantial, trifling, trivial.
2 EMPTY, hollow, vacuous, vain,
worthless, nonsensical, absurd.

⊞ 1 important, meaningful.
2 worthwhile.

means *n* **1** METHOD, mode, way, medium, course, agency, process, instrument, channel, vehicle. **2** RESOURCES, funds, money, income, wealth, riches, substance, wherewithal, fortune, affluence.

measure *n* **1** PORTION, ration, share, allocation, quota. **2** SIZE, quantity, magnitude, amount, degree, extent, range, scope, proportion. **3** RULE, gauge, scale, standard, criterion, norm, touchstone, yardstick, test, meter. **4** STEP, course, action, deed, procedure, method, act, bill, statute.
v quantify, evaluate, assess, weigh, value, gauge, judge, sound, fathom, determine, calculate, estimate, plumb, survey, compute, measure out, measure off.
measure up to equal, meet, match, compare with, touch, rival, make the grade.

measured *adj* deliberate, planned, reasoned, slow, unhurried, steady, studied, well-thought-out, calculated, careful, considered, precise.

measurement *n* **1** DIMENSION, size, extent, amount, magnitude, area, capacity, height, depth, length, width, weight, volume. **2** ASSESSMENT, evaluation, estimation, computation, calculation, calibration, gauging, judgement, appraisal, appreciation, survey.

SI (Système International d'Unités) base units include: ampere, candela, kelvin, kilogram, metre, mole, second.
SI derivatives and other measurements include: acre, angstrom, atmosphere, bar, barrel, becquerel, bushel, cable, calorie, centimetre, century, chain, coulomb, cubic centimetre, cubic foot, cubic inch, cubic metre, cubic yard, day, decade, decibel, degree, dyne, erg, farad, fathom, fluid ounce, fresnel, foot, foot-pound, furlong, gallon, gill, gram, hand, hectare, hertz, horsepower, hour, hundredweight, inch, joule, kilometre, knot, league, litre, lumen, micrometre, mile, millennium, millibar, millilitre, minute, month, nautical mile, newton, ohm, ounce, pascal, peak, pint, pound, pound per square inch, radian, rod, siemens, span, square centimetre, square foot, square inch, square kilometre, square metre, square mile, square yard, steradian, stone, therm, ton, tonne, volt, watt, week, yard, year.

meat *n* **1** FLESH. **2** (*infml*) FOOD, rations, provisions, nourishment, sustenance, subsistence, eats (*infml*).

Kinds of meat include: beef, pork, lamb, mutton, ham, bacon, gammon, chicken, turkey, goose, duck, rabbit, hare, venison, pheasant, grouse, partridge, pigeon, quail; offal, liver, heart, tongue, kidney, brains, brawn, pig's knuckle, trotters, oxtail, sweetbread, tripe; steak, minced beef, sausage, rissole, faggot, beefburger, hamburger, black pudding, paté.

Cuts of meat include: shoulder, collar, hand, loin, hock, leg, chop, shin, knuckle, rib, spare-rib, breast, brisket, chine, cutlet, fillet, rump, scrag, silverside, topside, sirloin, flank, escalope, neck, saddle.

mechanical *adj* automatic, involuntary, instinctive, routine, habitual, impersonal, emotionless, cold, matter-of-fact, unfeeling, lifeless, dead, dull.
⊞ conscious.

mechanism *n* **1** MACHINE, machinery, engine, appliance,

instrument, tool, motor, works, workings, gadget, device, apparatus, contrivance, gears, components.
2 MEANS, method, agency, process, procedure, system, technique, medium, structure, operation, functioning, performance.

meddle *v* interfere, intervene, pry, snoop (*infml*), intrude, butt in, tamper.

meddlesome *adj* interfering, meddling, prying, intrusive, intruding, mischievous.

mediate *v* arbitrate, conciliate, intervene, referee, umpire, intercede, moderate, reconcile, negotiate, resolve, settle, step in.

mediator *n* arbitrator, referee, umpire, intermediary, negotiator, go-between, interceder, judge, moderator, intercessor, conciliator, peacemaker, Ombudsman.

medical terms

Medical terms include: abortion, allergy, amputation, analgesic, antibiotics, antiseptic, bandage, barium meal, biopsy, blood bank, blood count, blood donor, blood group, blood pressure, blood test, caesarean, cardiopulmonary resuscitation (CPR), case history, casualty, cauterization, cervical smear, check-up, childbirth, circulation, circumcision, clinic, complication, compress, consultant, consultation, contraception, convulsion, cure, diagnosis, dialysis, dislocate, dissection, doctor, donor, dressings, enema, examination, gene, health screening, home visit, hormone replacement therapy (HRT), hospice, hospital, immunization, implantation, incubation, infection, inflammation, injection, injury, inoculation, intensive care, labour, miscarriage, mouth-to-mouth, nurse, ointment, operation, paraplegia, post-mortem,

pregnancy, prescription, prognosis, prosthesis, psychosomatic, quarantine, radiotherapy, recovery, rehabilitation, relapse, remission, respiration, resuscitation, scan, side effect, sling, smear test, specimen, splint, sterilization, steroid, surgery, suture, symptom, syndrome, therapy, tourniquet, tranquillizer, transfusion, transplant, trauma, treatment, tumour, ultrasound scanning, vaccination, vaccine, virus, x-ray.

medicinal *adj* therapeutic, healing, remedial, curative, restorative, medical.

medicine *n* medication, drug, cure, remedy, medicament, prescription, pharmaceutical, panacea.

Types of medicine include: tablet, capsule, pill, painkiller, lozenge, pastille, gargle, linctus, tonic, laxative, suppository, antacid, ointment, arnica, eye drops, ear drops, nasal spray, inhaler, Ventolin, antibiotic, penicillin, emetic, gripe-water, paregoric. *see also* **drug**.

Forms of alternative medicine include: acupuncture, aromatherapy, chiropractic, herbal remedies, homeopathy, naturopathy, osteopathy, reflexology.

mediocre *adj* ordinary, average, middling, medium, indifferent, unexceptional, undistinguished, so-so (*infml*), run-of-the-mill, commonplace, insignificant, second-rate, inferior, uninspired.
◼ exceptional, extraordinary, distinctive.

mediocrity *n* **1** ORDINARINESS, unimportance, insignificance, poorness, inferiority, indifference. **2** NONENTITY, nobody.

meditate *v* **1** REFLECT, ponder,

ruminate, contemplate, muse, brood, think. **2** THINK OVER, consider, deliberate, mull over, study, speculate, scheme, plan, devise, intend.

medium *adj* average, middle, median, mean, medial, intermediate, middling, midway, standard, fair.
n **1** AVERAGE, middle, mid-point, middle ground, compromise, centre, happy medium, golden mean.
2 MEANS, agency, channel, vehicle, instrument, way, mode, form, avenue, organ. **3** PSYCHIC, spiritualist, spiritist, clairvoyant.

medley *n* assortment, mixture, miscellany, pot-pourri, hotchpotch, hodge-podge, collection, jumble.

meek *adj* modest, long-suffering, forbearing, humble, docile, patient, unassuming, unpretentious, resigned, gentle, peaceful, tame, timid, submissive, spiritless.
F3 arrogant, assertive, rebellious.

meet *v* **1** ENCOUNTER, come across, run across, run into, chance on, bump into (*infml*). **2** EXPERIENCE, encounter, face, go through, undergo, endure. **3** GATHER, collect, assemble, congregate, convene.
4 FULFIL, satisfy, match, answer, measure up to, equal, discharge, perform. **5** JOIN, converge, come together, connect, cross, intersect, touch, abut, unite.
F3 3 scatter. **5** diverge.

meeting *n* **1** ENCOUNTER, confrontation, rendezvous, engagement, assignation, introduction, tryst (*fml*).
2 ASSEMBLY, gathering, congregation, conference, convention, rally, get-together, forum, conclave, session.
3 CONVERGENCE, confluence, junction, intersection, union.

melancholy *adj* depressed, dejected, downcast, down, down-hearted, gloomy, low, low-spirited, heavy-hearted, sad, unhappy, despondent, dispirited, miserable, mournful, dismal, sorrowful, moody.
F3 cheerful, elated, joyful.
n depression, dejection, gloom, despondency, low spirits, blues (*infml*), sadness, unhappiness, sorrow.
F3 elation, joy.

mellow *adj* **1** MATURE, ripe, juicy, full-flavoured, sweet, tender, mild.
2 GENIAL, cordial, affable, pleasant, relaxed, placid, serene, tranquil, cheerful, happy, jolly. **3** SMOOTH, melodious, rich, rounded, soft.
F3 1 unripe. **2** cold. **3** harsh.
v mature, ripen, improve, sweeten, soften, temper, season, perfect.

melodious *adj* tuneful, musical, melodic, harmonious, dulcet, sweet-sounding, euphonious (*fml*), silvery.
F3 discordant, grating, harsh.

melodramatic *adj* histrionic, theatrical, overdramatic, exaggerated, overemotional, sensational, hammy (*infml*).

melody *n* tune, music, song, refrain, harmony, theme, air, strain.

melt *v* liquefy, dissolve, thaw, fuse, deliquesce (*fml*).
F3 freeze, solidify.
melt away disappear, vanish, fade, evaporate, dissolve, disperse.

member *n* adherent, associate, subscriber, representative, comrade, fellow.

memento *n* souvenir, keepsake, remembrance, reminder, token, memorial, record, relic.

memoirs *n* reminiscences, recollections, autobiography, life story, diary, chronicles, annals, journals, records, confessions, experiences.

memorable *adj* unforgettable, remarkable, significant, impressive, notable, noteworthy, extraordinary, important, outstanding, momentous.
F3 forgettable, trivial, unimportant.

memorial *n* remembrance,

monument, souvenir, memento, record, stone, plaque, mausoleum. adj commemorative, celebratory.

memorize v learn, learn by heart, commit to memory, remember.
🔁 forget.

memory n recall, retention, recollection, remembrance, reminiscence, commemoration.
🔁 forgetfulness.

menace v threaten, frighten, alarm, intimidate, terrorize, loom.
n 1 INTIMIDATION, threat, terrorism, warning. 2 DANGER, peril, hazard, jeopardy, risk. 3 NUISANCE, annoyance, pest.

mend v 1 REPAIR, renovate, restore, refit, fix, patch, cobble, darn, heal.
2 RECOVER, get better, improve.
3 REMEDY, correct, rectify, reform, revise.
🔁 1 break. 2 deteriorate. 3 destroy.

menial adj low, lowly, humble, base, dull, humdrum, routine, degrading, demeaning, ignominious, unskilled, subservient, servile, slavish.
n servant, domestic, labourer, minion, attendant, drudge, slave, underling, skivvy (infml), dog's-body (infml).

mental adj 1 INTELLECTUAL, abstract, conceptual, cognitive, cerebral, theoretical, rational.
2 (infml) MAD, insane, lunatic, crazy, unbalanced, deranged, psychotic, disturbed, loony (infml).
🔁 1 physical. 2 sane.

mentality n 1 INTELLECT, brains, understanding, faculty, rationality.
2 FRAME OF MIND, character, disposition, personality, psychology, outlook.

mention v refer to, speak of, allude to, touch on, name, cite, acknowledge, bring up, report, make known, impart, declare, communicate, broach, divulge, disclose, intimate, point out, reveal, state, hint at, quote.

n reference, allusion, citation, observation, recognition, remark, acknowledgement, announcement, notification, tribute, indication.

mercenary adj 1 GREEDY, avaricious, covetous, grasping, acquisitive, materialistic. 2 HIRED, paid, venal.

merchandise n goods, commodities, stock, produce, products, wares, cargo, freight, shipment.

merchant n trader, dealer, broker, trafficker, wholesaler, retailer, seller, shopkeeper, vendor.

merciful adj compassionate, forgiving, forbearing, humane, lenient, sparing, tender-hearted, pitying, gracious, humanitarian, kind, liberal, sympathetic, generous, mild.
🔁 hard-hearted, merciless.

merciless adj pitiless, relentless, unmerciful, ruthless, hard-hearted, hard, heartless, implacable, inhumane, unforgiving, remorseless, unpitying, unsparing, severe, cruel, callous, inhuman.
🔁 compassionate, merciful.

mercy n 1 COMPASSION, clemency, forgiveness, forbearance, leniency, pity, humanitarianism, kindness, grace. 2 BLESSING, godsend, good luck, relief.
🔁 1 cruelty, harshness.

mere adj sheer, plain, simple, bare, utter, pure, absolute, complete, stark, unadulterated, common, paltry, petty.

merge v join, unite, combine, converge, amalgamate, blend, coalesce, mix, intermix, mingle, melt into, fuse, meet, meld, incorporate, consolidate.

merger n amalgamation, union, fusion, combination, coalition, consolidation, confederation, incorporation.

merit n worth, excellence, value,

quality, good, goodness, virtue, asset, credit, advantage, strong point, talent, justification, due, claim.
F3 fault.
v deserve, be worthy of, earn, justify, warrant.

merriment *n* fun, jollity, mirth, hilarity, laughter, conviviality, festivity, amusement, revelry, frolic, liveliness, joviality.
F3 gloom, seriousness.

merry *adj* jolly, light-hearted, mirthful, joyful, happy, convivial, festive, cheerful, glad.
F3 gloomy, melancholy, sober.

mesh *n* net, network, netting, lattice, web, tangle, entanglement, snare, trap.
v engage, interlock, dovetail, fit, connect, harmonize, co-ordinate, combine, come together.

mess *n* **1** CHAOS, untidiness, disorder, disarray, confusion, muddle, jumble, clutter, disorganization, mix-up, shambles (*infml*). **2** DIFFICULTY, trouble, predicament, fix (*infml*).
F3 1 order, tidiness.

mess about mess around, fool around, play, play around, play about, muck about (*infml*), interfere, tamper, trifle.

mess up 1 DISARRANGE, jumble, muddle, tangle, dishevel, disrupt. **2** BOTCH, bungle, spoil, muck up (*infml*).

message *n* **1** COMMUNICATION, bulletin, dispatch, communiqué, report, missive (*fml*), errand, letter, memorandum, note, notice, cable. **2** MEANING, idea, point, theme, moral.

messenger *n* courier, emissary (*fml*), envoy, go-between, herald, runner, carrier, bearer, harbinger, agent, ambassador.

messy *adj* untidy, unkempt, dishevelled, disorganized, chaotic, sloppy, slovenly, confused, dirty, grubby, muddled, cluttered.

F3 neat, ordered, tidy.

metamorphosis *n* change, alteration, transformation, rebirth, regeneration, transfiguration, conversion, modification, change-over.

metaphor *n* figure of speech, allegory, analogy, symbol, picture, image.

metaphorical *adj* figurative, allegorical, symbolic.

mete out allot, apportion, deal out, dole out, hand out, measure out, share out, ration out, portion, distribute, dispense, divide out, assign, administer.

meteoric *adj* rapid, speedy, swift, sudden, overnight, instantaneous, momentary, brief, spectacular, brilliant, dazzling.

method *n* **1** WAY, approach, means, course, manner, mode, fashion, process, procedure, route, technique, style, plan, scheme, programme. **2** ORGANIZATION, order, structure, system, pattern, form, planning, regularity, routine.

methodical *adj* systematic, structured, organized, ordered, orderly, tidy, regular, planned, efficient, disciplined, businesslike, deliberate, neat, scrupulous, precise, meticulous, painstaking.
F3 chaotic, irregular, confused.

meticulous *adj* precise, scrupulous, exact, punctilious, fussy, detailed, accurate, thorough, fastidious, painstaking, strict.
F3 careless, slapdash.

metropolis *n* capital, city, municipality, megalopolis.

mettle *n* **1** CHARACTER, temperament, disposition. **2** SPIRIT, courage, vigour, nerve, boldness, daring, indomitability, pluck, resolve, valour, bravery, fortitude.

microbe *n* micro-organism, bacterium, bacillus, germ, virus, pathogen, bug (*infml*).

microscopic *adj* minute, tiny, minuscule, infinitesimal, indiscernible, imperceptible, negligible.
$\quad$ ⊟ huge, enormous.

middle *adj* central, halfway, mean, median, intermediate, inner, inside, intervening.
$\quad$ *n* centre, halfway point, midpoint, mean, heart, core, midst, inside, bull's eye.
$\quad$ ⊟ extreme, end, edge, beginning, border.

middling *adj* mediocre, medium, ordinary, moderate, average, unexceptional, unremarkable, run-of-the-mill, indifferent, modest, passable, tolerable, so-so (*infml*), OK (*infml*).

midget *n* person of restricted growth, pygmy, dwarf, Tom Thumb, gnome.
$\quad$ ⊟ giant.
$\quad$ *adj* tiny, small, miniature, little, pocket, pocket-sized.
$\quad$ ⊟ giant.

midst *n* middle, centre, mid-point, heart, hub, interior.

migrant *n* traveller, wanderer, itinerant, emigrant, immigrant, rover, nomad, globe-trotter, drifter, gypsy, tinker, vagrant.

migrate *v* move, resettle, relocate, wander, roam, rove, journey, emigrate, travel, voyage, trek, drift.

mild *adj* **1** *mild manners*: gentle, calm, peaceable, placid, tender, soft, good-natured, kind, amiable, lenient, compassionate. **2** *mild weather*: calm, temperate, warm, balmy, clement, fair, pleasant. **3** *mild coffee*: bland, mellow, smooth, subtle, soothing.
$\quad$ ⊟ **1** harsh, fierce. **2** stormy. **3** strong.

militant *adj* aggressive, belligerent, vigorous, fighting, warring.
$\quad$ ⊟ pacifist, peaceful.
$\quad$ *n* activist, combatant, fighter, struggler, warrior, aggressor, belligerent.

military *adj* martial, armed, soldierly, warlike, service.
$\quad$ *n* army, armed forces, soldiers, forces, services.

militate against oppose, counter, counteract, count against, tell against, weigh against, contend, resist.

milk *v* drain, bleed, tap, extract, draw off, exploit, use, express, press, pump, siphon, squeeze, wring.

milky *adj* white, milk-white, chalky, opaque, clouded, cloudy.

mill *n* **1** FACTORY, plant, works, workshop, foundry. **2** GRINDER, crusher, quern, roller.
$\quad$ *v* grind, pulverize, powder, pound, crush, roll, press, grate.

mime *n* dumb show, pantomime, gesture, mimicry.
$\quad$ *v* gesture, signal, act out, represent, simulate, impersonate, mimic.

mimic *v* imitate, parody, caricature, take-off (*infml*), ape, parrot, impersonate, echo, mirror, simulate, look like.
$\quad$ *n* imitator, impersonator, impressionist, caricaturist, copy-cat (*infml*), copy.

mimicry *n* imitation, imitating, impersonation, copying, parody, impression, caricature, take-off (*infml*), burlesque.

mince *v* **1** CHOP, cut, hash, dice, grind, crumble. **2** DIMINISH, suppress, play down, tone down, hold back, moderate, weaken, soften, spare.

mind *n* **1** INTELLIGENCE, intellect, brains, reason, sense, understanding, wits, mentality, thinking, thoughts, grey matter (*infml*), head, genius, concentration, attention, spirit, psyche. **2** MEMORY, remembrance, recollection. **3** OPINION, view, point of view, belief, attitude, judgement, feeling, sentiment. **4** INCLINATION, disposition, tendency, will, wish, intention, desire.

v **1** CARE, object, take offence, resent, disapprove, dislike.
2 REGARD, heed, pay attention, pay heed to, note, obey, listen to, comply with, follow, observe, be careful, watch. **3** LOOK AFTER, take care of, watch over, guard, have charge of, keep an eye on (*infml*).
bear in mind consider, remember, note.
make up one's mind decide, choose, determine, settle, resolve.

mindful *adj* aware, conscious, alive (to), alert, attentive, careful, watchful, wary.
🖃 heedless, inattentive.

mindless *adj* **1** THOUGHTLESS, senseless, illogical, irrational, stupid, foolish, gratuitous, negligent.
2 MECHANICAL, automatic, tedious.
🖃 **1** thoughtful, intelligent.

mine *n* **1** PIT, colliery, coalfield, excavation, vein, seam, shaft, trench, deposit. **2** SUPPLY, source, stock, store, reserve, fund, hoard, treasury, wealth.
v excavate, dig for, dig up, delve, quarry, extract, unearth, tunnel, remove, undermine.

minerals

Minerals include: alabaster, albite, anhydrite, asbestos, aventurine, azurite, bentonite, blacklead, bloodstone, blue john, borax, cairngorm, calamine, calcite, calcspar, cassiterite, chalcedony, chlorite, chrysoberyl, cinnabar, corundum, dolomite, emery, feldspar, fluorite, fluorspar, fool's gold, French chalk, galena, graphite, gypsum, haematite, halite, haüyne, hornblende, hyacinth, idocrase, jacinth, jargoon, jet, kandite, kaolinite, lapis lazuli, lazurite, magnetite, malachite, meerschaum, mica, microcline, montmorillonite, orthoclase, plumbago, pyrites, quartz, rock salt, rutile, saltpetre, sanidine, silica, smithsonite, sodalite, spar,

sphalerite, spinel, talc, uralite, uranite, vesuvianite, wurtzite, zircon.

mingle *v* **1** MIX, intermingle, intermix, combine, blend, merge, unite, alloy, coalesce, join, compound. **2** ASSOCIATE, socialize, circulate, hobnob (*infml*), rub shoulders (*infml*).

miniature *adj* tiny, small, scaled-down, minute, diminutive, baby, pocket-sized, pint-size(d) (*infml*), little, mini (*infml*).
🖃 giant.

minimal *adj* least, smallest, minimum, slightest, littlest, negligible, minute, token.

minimize *v* **1** REDUCE, decrease, diminish. **2** BELITTLE, make light of, make little of, disparage, deprecate, discount, play down, underestimate, underrate.
🖃 **1** maximize.

minimum *n* least, lowest point, slightest, bottom.
🖃 maximum.
adj minimal, least, lowest, slightest, smallest, littlest, tiniest.
🖃 maximum.

minion *n* **1** ATTENDANT, follower, underling, lackey, hireling.
2 DEPENDANT, hanger-on, favourite, darling, sycophant, yes-man (*infml*), bootlicker (*infml*).

minister *n* **1** OFFICIAL, office-holder, politician, dignitary, diplomat, ambassador, delegate, envoy, consul, cabinet minister, agent, aide, administrator, executive.
2 CLERGYMAN, churchman, cleric, parson, priest, pastor, vicar, preacher, ecclesiastic (*fml*), divine.
v attend, serve, tend, take care of, wait on, cater to, accommodate, nurse.

ministry *n* **1** GOVERNMENT, cabinet, department, office, bureau, administration. **2** THE CHURCH, holy orders, the priesthood.

minor *adj* lesser, secondary, smaller, inferior, subordinate, subsidiary, junior, younger, insignificant, inconsiderable, negligible, petty, trivial, trifling, second-class, unclassified, slight, light.
🔁 major, significant, important.

mint *v* coin, stamp, strike, cast, forge, punch, make, manufacture, produce, construct, devise, fashion, invent, make up.
adj perfect, brand-new, fresh, immaculate, unblemished, excellent, first-class.

minute[1] *n* moment, second, instant, flash, jiffy (*infml*), tick (*infml*).

minute[2] *adj* **1** TINY, infinitesimal, minuscule, microscopic, miniature, inconsiderable, negligible, small. **2** DETAILED, precise, meticulous, painstaking, close, critical, exhaustive.
🔁 **1** gigantic, huge. **2** cursory, superficial.

minutes *n* proceedings, record(s), notes, memorandum, transcript, transactions, details, tapes.

miracle *n* wonder, marvel, prodigy, phenomenon.

miraculous *adj* wonderful, marvellous, phenomenal, extraordinary, amazing, astounding, astonishing, unbelievable, supernatural, incredible, inexplicable, unaccountable, superhuman.
🔁 natural, normal.

mirage *n* illusion, optical illusion, hallucination, fantasy, phantasm.

mirror *n* **1** GLASS, looking-glass, reflector. **2** REFLECTION, likeness, image, double, copy.
v reflect, echo, imitate, copy, represent, show, depict, mimic.

mirth *n* merriment, hilarity, gaiety, fun, laughter, jollity, jocularity, amusement, revelry, glee, cheerfulness.
🔁 gloom, melancholy.

misapprehension *n*

misunderstanding, misconception, misinterpretation, misreading, error, mistake, fallacy, delusion.

misappropriate *v* steal, embezzle, peculate, pocket, swindle (*infml*), misspend, misuse, misapply, abuse, pervert.

misbehave *v* offend, transgress, trespass, get up to mischief, mess about, muck about (*infml*), play up, act up (*infml*).

misbehaviour *n* misconduct, misdemeanour, impropriety, disobedience, naughtiness, insubordination.

miscalculate *v* misjudge, get wrong, slip up, blunder, boob (*infml*), miscount, overestimate, underestimate.

miscarriage *n* failure, breakdown, abortion, mishap, mismanagement, error, disappointment.
🔁 success.

miscarry *v* fail, abort, come to nothing, fall through, misfire, founder, come to grief.
🔁 succeed.

miscellaneous *adj* mixed, varied, various, assorted, diverse, diversified, sundry, motley, jumbled, indiscriminate.

miscellany *n* mixture, variety, assortment, collection, anthology, medley, mixed bag, pot-pourri, hotch-potch, jumble, diversity.

mischief *n* **1** TROUBLE, harm, evil, damage, injury, disruption. **2** MISBEHAVIOUR, naughtiness, impishness, pranks.

mischievous *adj* **1** MALICIOUS, evil, spiteful, vicious, wicked, pernicious, destructive, injurious. **2** NAUGHTY, impish, rascally, roguish, playful, teasing.
🔁 **1** kind. **2** well-behaved, good.

misconception *n* misapprehension, misunderstanding, misreading, error, fallacy, delusion, the wrong end of the stick (*infml*).

misconduct n misbehaviour, impropriety, misdemeanour, malpractice, mismanagement, wrongdoing.

miser n niggard, skinflint, penny-pincher (*infml*), Scrooge.
☒ spendthrift.

miserable adj 1 UNHAPPY, sad, dejected, despondent, downcast, heartbroken, wretched, distressed, crushed. 2 CHEERLESS, depressing, dreary, impoverished, shabby, gloomy, dismal, forlorn, joyless, squalid. 3 CONTEMPTIBLE, despicable, ignominious, detestable, disgraceful, deplorable, shameful. 4 MEAGRE, paltry, niggardly, worthless, pathetic, pitiful.
☒ 1 cheerful, happy. 2 pleasant. 4 generous.

miserly adj mean, niggardly, tight, stingy (*infml*), sparing, parsimonious, cheese-paring, beggarly, penny-pinching (*infml*), mingy (*infml*).
☒ generous, spendthrift.

misery n 1 UNHAPPINESS, sadness, suffering, distress, depression, despair, gloom, grief, wretchedness, affliction. 2 PRIVATION, hardship, deprivation, poverty, want, oppression, destitution. 3 (*infml*) SPOILSPORT, pessimist, killjoy, wet blanket (*infml*).
☒ 1 contentment. 2 comfort.

misfire v miscarry, go wrong, abort, fail, fall through, flop (*infml*), founder, fizzle out, come to grief.
☒ succeed.

misfit n individualist, nonconformist, eccentric, maverick, drop-out, loner, lone wolf.
☒ conformist.

misfortune n bad luck, mischance, mishap, ill-luck, setback, reverse, calamity, catastrophe, disaster, blow, accident, tragedy, trouble, hardship, trial, tribulation.
☒ luck, success.

misgiving n doubt, uncertainty,

hesitation, qualm, reservation, apprehension, scruple, suspicion, second thoughts, niggle, anxiety, worry, fear.
☒ confidence.

misguided adj misled, misconceived, ill-considered, ill-advised, ill-judged, imprudent, rash, misplaced, deluded, foolish, erroneous.
☒ sensible, wise.

mishap n misfortune, ill-fortune, misadventure, accident, setback, calamity, disaster, adversity.

misinterpret v misconstrue, misread, misunderstand, mistake, distort, garble.

misjudge v miscalculate, mistake, misinterpret, misconstrue, misunderstand, overestimate, underestimate.

mislay v lose, misplace, miss, lose sight of.

mislead v misinform, misdirect, deceive, delude, lead astray, fool.

misleading adj deceptive, confusing, unreliable, ambiguous, biased, loaded, evasive, tricky (*infml*).
☒ unequivocal, authoritative, informative.

mismanage v mishandle, botch, bungle, make a mess of, mess up, misrule, misspend, misjudge, foul up, mar, waste.

misprint n mistake, error, erratum, literal, typo (*infml*).

misrepresent v distort, falsify, slant, pervert, twist, garble, misquote, exaggerate, minimize, misconstrue, misinterpret.

miss v 1 FAIL, miscarry, lose, let slip, let go, omit, overlook, pass over, slip, leave out, mistake, trip, misunderstand, err. 2 AVOID, escape, evade, dodge, forego, skip, bypass, circumvent. 3 PINE FOR, long for, yearn for, regret, grieve for, mourn, sorrow for, want, wish, need, lament.

misuse

n failure, error, blunder, mistake, omission, oversight, fault, flop (*infml*), fiasco.

misshapen *adj* deformed, distorted, twisted, malformed, warped, contorted, crooked, crippled, grotesque, ugly, monstrous.
E3 regular, shapely.

missile *n* projectile, shot, guided missile, arrow, shaft, dart, rocket, bomb, shell, flying bomb, grenade, torpedo, weapon.

missing *adj* absent, lost, lacking, gone, mislaid, unaccounted-for, wanting, disappeared, astray, strayed, misplaced.
E3 found, present.

mission *n* 1 TASK, undertaking, assignment, operation, campaign, crusade, business, errand.
2 CALLING, duty, purpose, vocation, raison d'être, aim, charge, office, job, work. 3 COMMISSION, ministry, delegation, deputation, legation, embassy.

missionary *n* evangelist, campaigner, preacher, proselytizer, apostle, crusader, propagandist, champion, promoter, emissary, envoy, ambassador.

mist *n* haze, fog, vapour, smog, cloud, condensation, film, spray, drizzle, dew, steam, veil, dimness.
mist over cloud over, fog, dim, blur, steam up, obscure, veil.
E3 clear.

mistake *n* error, inaccuracy, slip, slip-up, oversight, lapse, blunder, Ilanger (*infml*), boob (*infml*), gaffe, fault, faux pas, solecism (*fml*), indiscretion, misjudgement, miscalculation, misunderstanding, misprint, misspelling, misreading, mispronunciation, howler (*infml*).
v misunderstand, misapprehend, misconstrue, misjudge, misread, miscalculate, confound, confuse, slip up, blunder, err, boob (*infml*).

mistaken *adj* wrong, incorrect,

erroneous, inaccurate, inexact, untrue, inappropriate, ill-judged, inauthentic, false, deceived, deluded, misinformed, misled, faulty.
E3 correct, right.

mistreat *v* abuse, ill-treat, ill-use, maltreat, harm, hurt, batter, injure, knock about, molest.

mistress *n* 1 LOVER, live-in lover, kept woman, concubine, courtesan, girlfriend, paramour, woman, lady-love. 2 TEACHER, governess, tutor.

mistrust *n* distrust, doubt, suspicion, wariness, misgiving, reservations, qualm, hesitancy, chariness, caution, uncertainty, scepticism, apprehension.
E3 trust.
v distrust, doubt, suspect, be wary of, beware, have reservations, fear.
E3 trust.

misty *adj* hazy, foggy, cloudy, blurred, fuzzy, murky, smoky, unclear, dim, indistinct, obscure, opaque, vague, veiled.
E3 clear.

misunderstand *v* misapprehend, misconstrue, misinterpret, misjudge, mistake, get wrong, miss the point, mishear, get hold of the wrong end of the stick (*infml*).
E3 understand.

misunderstanding *n* 1 MISTAKE, error, misapprehension, misconception, misjudgement, misinterpretation, misreading, mix-up. 2 DISAGREEMENT, argument, dispute, conflict, clash, difference, breach, quarrel, discord, rift.
E3 1 understanding. 2 agreement.

misuse *n* mistreatment, maltreatment, abuse, harm, ill-treatment, misapplication, misappropriation, waste, perversion, corruption, exploitation.
v abuse, misapply, misemploy, ill-use, ill-treat, harm, mistreat, wrong, distort, injure, corrupt, pervert, waste, squander, misappropriate, exploit,

dissipate.

mitigating *adj* extenuating, justifying, vindicating, modifying, qualifying.

mix *v* COMBINE, blend, mingle, intermingle, intermix, amalgamate, compound, homogenize, synthesize, merge, join, unite, coalesce, fuse, incorporate, fold in. 2 ASSOCIATE, consort, fraternize, socialize, mingle, join, hobnob (*infml*).
F3 1 divide, separate.
n mixture, blend, amalgam, assortment, combination, conglomerate, compound, fusion, synthesis, medley, composite, mishmash (*infml*).

mix up confuse, bewilder, muddle, perplex, puzzle, confound, mix, jumble, complicate, garble, involve, implicate, disturb, upset, snarl up.

mixed *adj* 1 *mixed race*: combined, hybrid, mingled, crossbred, mongrel, blended, composite, compound, incorporated, united, alloyed, amalgamated, fused. 2 *mixed biscuits*: assorted, varied, miscellaneous, diverse, diversified, motley. 3 *mixed feelings*: ambivalent, equivocal, conflicting, contradicting, uncertain.

mixture *n* mix, blend, combination, amalgamation, amalgam, compound, conglomeration, composite, coalescence, alloy, brew, synthesis, union, fusion, concoction, cross, hybrid, assortment, variety, miscellany, medley, mélange, mixed bag, pot-pourri, jumble, hotchpotch.

moan *n* lament, lamentation, sob, wail, howl, whimper, whine, grumble, complaint, grievance, groan.
v 1 LAMENT, wail, sob, weep, howl, groan, whimper, mourn, grieve. 2 (*infml*) COMPLAIN, grumble, whine, whinge (*infml*), gripe (*infml*), carp.
F3 1 rejoice.

mob *n* 1 CROWD, mass, throng,

multitude, horde, host, swarm, gathering, group, collection, flock, herd, pack, set, tribe, troop, company, crew, gang. 2 POPULACE, rabble, masses, hoi polloi, plebs (*infml*), riff-raff (*infml*).
v crowd, crowd round, surround, swarm round, jostle, overrun, set upon, besiege, descend on, throng, pack, pester, charge.

mobile *adj* 1 MOVING, movable, portable, peripatetic, travelling, roaming, roving, itinerant, wandering, migrant. 2 FLEXIBLE, agile, active, energetic, nimble. 3 CHANGING, changeable, ever-changing, expressive, lively.
F3 1 immobile.

mobilize *v* assemble, marshal, rally, conscript, muster, call up, enlist, activate, galvanize, organize, prepare, ready, summon, animate.

mock *v* 1 RIDICULE, jeer, make fun of, laugh at, disparage, deride, scoff, sneer, taunt, scorn, tease. 2 IMITATE, simulate, mimic, ape, caricature, satirize.
adj imitation, counterfeit, artificial, sham, simulated, synthetic, false, fake, forged, fraudulent, bogus, phoney (*infml*), pseudo, spurious, feigned, faked, pretended, dummy.

mockery *n* 1 RIDICULE, jeering, scoffing, scorn, derision, contempt, disdain, disrespect, sarcasm. 2 PARODY, satire, sham, travesty.

mocking *adj* scornful, derisive, contemptuous, sarcastic, satirical, taunting, scoffing, sardonic, snide (*infml*), insulting, irreverent, impudent, disrespectful, disdainful, cynical.

model *n* 1 COPY, replica, representation, facsimile, imitation, mock-up. 2 EXAMPLE, exemplar, pattern, standard, ideal, mould, prototype, template. 3 DESIGN, style, type, version, mark. 4 MANNEQUIN, dummy, sitter, subject, poser.

adj exemplary, perfect, typical, ideal.
v **1** MAKE, form, fashion, mould,
sculpt, carve, cast, shape, work,
create, design, plan. **2** DISPLAY, wear,
show off.

moderate *adj* **1** MEDIOCRE,
medium, ordinary, fair, indifferent,
average, middle-of-the-road.
2 REASONABLE, restrained, sensible,
calm, controlled, cool, mild, well-
regulated.
1 exceptional. **2** immoderate.
v control, regulate, decrease, lessen,
soften, restrain, tone down, play
down, diminish, ease, curb, calm,
check, modulate, repress, subdue,
soft-pedal, tame, subside, pacify,
mitigate, allay, alleviate, abate,
dwindle.

moderately *adv* somewhat, quite,
rather, fairly, slightly, reasonably,
passably, to some extent.
extremely.

moderation *n* **1** DECREASE,
reduction. **2** RESTRAINT, self-
control, caution, control, composure,
sobriety, abstemiousness,
temperance, reasonableness.

modern *adj* current, contemporary,
up-to-date, new, fresh, latest, late,
novel, present, present-day, recent,
up-to-the-minute, newfangled
(*infml*), advanced, avant-garde,
progressive, modernistic, innovative,
inventive, state-of-the-art, go-ahead,
fashionable, stylish, in vogue, in
style, modish, trendy (*infml*).
old-fashioned, old, out-of-date,
antiquated.

modernize *v* renovate, refurbish,
rejuvenate, regenerate, streamline,
revamp, renew, update, improve, do
up, redesign, reform, remake,
remodel, refresh, transform, modify,
progress.
regress.

modest *adj* **1** UNASSUMING,
humble, self-effacing, quiet, reserved,
retiring, unpretentious, discreet,
bashful, shy. **2** MODERATE, ordinary,
unexceptional, fair, reasonable,
limited, small.
1 immodest, conceited.
2 exceptional, excessive.

modesty *n* humility, humbleness,
self-effacement, reticence, reserve,
quietness, decency, propriety,
demureness, shyness, bashfulness,
coyness.
immodesty, vanity, conceit.

modify *v* **1** CHANGE, alter, redesign,
revise, vary, adapt, adjust,
transform, reform, convert, improve,
reorganize. **2** MODERATE, reduce,
temper, tone down, limit, soften,
qualify.

modulate *v* modify, adjust, balance,
alter, soften, lower, regulate, vary,
harmonize, inflect, tune.

moist *adj* damp, clammy, humid,
wet, dewy, rainy, muggy, marshy,
drizzly, watery, soggy.
dry, arid.

moisten *v* moisturize, dampen,
damp, wet, water, lick, irrigate.
dry.

moisture *n* water, liquid, wetness,
wateriness, damp, dampness,
dankness, humidity, vapour, dew,
mugginess, condensation, steam,
spray.
dryness.

molest *v* **1** ANNOY, disturb, bother,
harass, irritate, persecute, pester,
plague, tease, torment, hound, upset,
worry, trouble, badger. **2** ATTACK,
accost, assail, hurt, ill-treat, maltreat,
mistreat, abuse, harm, injure.

mollusc

Molluscs include: abalone, conch,
cowrie, cuttlefish, clam, cockle,
limpet, mussel, nautilus, nudibranch,
octopus, oyster, periwinkle, scallop,
sea slug, slug, freshwater snail, land
snail, marine snail, squid, tusk shell,
whelk.

moment n second, instant, minute, split second, trice, jiffy (*infml*), tick (*infml*).

momentary adj brief, short, short-lived, temporary, transient, transitory, fleeting, ephemeral, hasty, quick, passing.
Ea lasting, permanent.

momentous adj significant, important, critical, crucial, decisive, weighty, grave, serious, vital, fateful, historic, earth-shaking, epoch-making, eventful, major.
Ea insignificant, unimportant, trivial.

momentum n impetus, force, energy, impulse, drive, power, thrust, speed, velocity, impact, incentive, stimulus, urge, strength, push.

monarch n sovereign, crowned head, ruler, king, queen, emperor, empress, prince, princess, tsar, potentate.

monarchy n **1** KINGDOM, empire, principality, realm, domain, dominion. **2** ROYALISM, sovereignty, autocracy, monocracy, absolutism, despotism, tyranny.

monastery n friary, priory, abbey, cloister, charterhouse.

monastic adj reclusive, withdrawn, secluded, cloistered, austere, ascetic, celibate, contemplative.
Ea secular, worldly.

monetary adj financial, fiscal, pecuniary (*fml*), budgetary, economic, capital, cash.

money n currency, cash, legal tender, banknotes, coin, funds, capital, dough (*infml*), dosh (*infml*), riches, wealth.

mongrel n cross, crossbreed, hybrid, half-breed.
adj crossbred, hybrid, half-breed, bastard, mixed, ill-defined.
Ea pure-bred, pedigree.

monitor n **1** SCREEN, display, VDU, recorder, scanner. **2** SUPERVISOR, watchdog, overseer, invigilator, adviser, prefect.

v check, watch, keep track of, keep under surveillance, keep an eye on, follow, track, supervise, observe, note, survey, trace, scan, record, plot, detect.

monkey n **1** PRIMATE, simian, ape. **2** (*infml*) SCAMP, imp, urchin, brat, rogue, scallywag (*infml*), rascal.

Monkeys include: ape, baboon, capuchin, colobus monkey, drill and mandrill, guenon, guereza, howler monkey, langur, leaf monkey, macaque, mangabey, marmoset, night monkey (or douroucouli), proboscis monkey, rhesus monkey, saki, spider monkey, squirrel money, tamarin, titi, toque, uakari (or cacajou), woolly monkey.

monopolize v dominate, take over, appropriate, corner, control, hog (*infml*), engross, occupy, preoccupy, take up, tie up.
Ea share.

monotonous adj boring, dull, tedious, uninteresting, tiresome, wearisome, unchanging, uneventful, unvaried, uniform, toneless, flat, colourless, repetitive, routine, plodding, humdrum, soul-destroying.
Ea lively, varied, colourful.

monotony n tedium, dullness, boredom, sameness, tiresomeness, uneventfulness, flatness, wearisomeness, uniformity, routine, repetitiveness.
Ea liveliness, colour.

monster n **1** BEAST, fiend, brute, barbarian, savage, villain, giant, ogre, ogress, troll, mammoth. **2** FREAK, monstrosity, mutant.
adj huge, gigantic, giant, colossal, enormous, immense, massive, monstrous, jumbo, mammoth, vast, tremendous.
Ea tiny, minute.

monstrous adj **1** WICKED, evil, vicious, cruel, criminal, heinous,

outrageous, scandalous, disgraceful,
atrocious, abhorrent, dreadful,
frightful, horrible, horrifying,
terrible. **2** UNNATURAL, inhuman,
freakish, grotesque, hideous,
deformed, malformed, misshapen.
3 HUGE, enormous, colossal,
gigantic, vast, immense, massive,
mammoth.

monument n memorial, cenotaph,
headstone, gravestone, tombstone,
shrine, mausoleum, cairn, barrow,
cross, marker, obelisk, pillar, statue,
relic, remembrance, commemoration,
testament, reminder, record,
memento, evidence, token.

monumental adj **1** IMPRESSIVE,
imposing, awe-inspiring, awesome,
overwhelming, significant,
important, epoch-making, historic,
magnificent, majestic, memorable,
notable, outstanding, abiding,
immortal, lasting, classic. **2** HUGE,
immense, enormous, colossal, vast,
tremendous, massive, great.
3 COMMEMORATIVE, memorial.
Ea 1 insignificant, unimportant.

mood n **1** DISPOSITION, frame of
mind, state of mind, temper, humour,
spirit, tenor, whim. **2** BAD TEMPER,
sulk, the sulks, pique, melancholy,
depression, blues (*infml*), doldrums,
dumps (*infml*).

moody adj changeable,
temperamental, unpredictable,
capricious, irritable, moody,
crabby (*infml*), crotchety, crusty
(*infml*), testy, touchy, morose, angry,
broody, mopy, sulky, sullen, gloomy,
melancholy, miserable, downcast,
doleful, glum, impulsive, fickle,
flighty.
Ea equable, cheerful.

moon v idle, loaf, mooch, languish,
pine, mope, brood, daydream,
dream, fantasize.

moor¹ v fasten, secure, tie up, drop
anchor, anchor, berth, dock, make
fast, fix, hitch, bind.

Ea loose.

moor² n moorland, heath, fell,
upland.

mop n head of hair, shock, mane,
tangle, thatch, mass.
v swab, sponge, wipe, clean, wash,
absorb, soak.

mope v brood, fret, sulk, pine,
languish, droop, despair, grieve, idle.

moral adj ethical, virtuous, good,
right, principled, honourable, decent,
upright, upstanding, straight,
righteous, high-minded, honest,
incorruptible, proper, blameless,
chaste, clean-living, pure, just, noble.
Ea immoral.
n lesson, message, teaching, dictum,
meaning, maxim, adage, precept,
saying, proverb, aphorism, epigram.

morale n confidence, spirits, esprit
de corps, self-esteem, state of mind,
heart, mood.

morality n ethics, morals, ideals,
principles, standards, virtue,
rectitude, righteousness, decency,
goodness, honesty, integrity, justice,
uprightness, propriety, conduct,
manners.
Ea immorality.

morals n morality, ethics, principles,
standards, ideals, integrity, scruples,
behaviour, conduct, habits, manners.

morbid adj **1** GHOULISH, ghastly,
gruesome, macabre, hideous, horrid,
grim. **2** GLOOMY, pessimistic,
melancholy, sombre. **3** SICK,
unhealthy, unwholesome,
insalubrious.

more adj further, extra, additional,
added, new, fresh, increased, other,
supplementary, repeated, alternative,
spare.
Ea less.
adv further, longer, again, besides,
moreover, better.
Ea less.

moreover adv furthermore, further,
besides, in addition, as well as, also,
additionally, what is more.

morning n daybreak, daylight, dawn, sunrise, break of day, before noon.

morose adj ill-tempered, bad-tempered, moody, sullen, sulky, surly, gloomy, grim, gruff, sour, taciturn, glum, grouchy (*infml*), crabby (*infml*), saturnine.
₣ cheerful, communicative.

morsel n bit, scrap, piece, fragment, crumb, bite, mouthful, nibble, taste, soupçon, titbit, slice, fraction, modicum, grain, atom, part.

mortal adj **1** WORLDLY, earthly, bodily, human, perishable, temporal. **2** FATAL, lethal, deadly. **3** EXTREME, great, severe, intense, grave, awful.
₣ **1** immortal.
n human being, human, individual, person, being, body, creature.
₣ immortal, god.

mortality n **1** HUMANITY, death, impermanence, perishability. **2** FATALITY, death rate.
₣ **1** immortality.

mortified adj humiliated, shamed, ashamed, humbled, embarrassed, crushed.

mostly adv mainly, on the whole, principally, chiefly, generally, usually, largely, for the most part, as a rule.

mother n **1** PARENT, procreator (*fml*), progenitress (*fml*), dam, mamma, mum (*infml*), mummy (*infml*), matriarch, ancestor, matron, old woman (*infml*). **2** ORIGIN, source.
v **1** BEAR, produce, nurture, raise, rear, nurse, care for, cherish. **2** PAMPER, spoil, baby, indulge, overprotect, fuss over.

motherly adj maternal, caring, comforting, affectionate, kind, loving, protective, warm, tender, gentle, fond.
₣ neglectful, uncaring.

motif n theme, idea, topic, concept, pattern, design, figure, form, logo, shape, device, ornament, decoration.

motion n **1** MOVEMENT, action, mobility, moving, activity, locomotion, travel, transit, passage, passing, progress, change, flow, inclination. **2** GESTURE, gesticulation, signal, sign, wave, nod. **3** PROPOSAL, suggestion, recommendation, proposition.
v signal, gesture, gesticulate, sign, wave, nod, beckon, direct, usher.

motionless adj unmoving, still, stationary, static, immobile, at a standstill, fixed, halted, at rest, resting, standing, paralysed, inanimate, lifeless, frozen, rigid, stagnant.
₣ active, moving.

motivate v prompt, incite, impel, spur, provoke, stimulate, drive, lead, stir, urge, push, propel, persuade, move, inspire, encourage, cause, trigger, induce, kindle, draw, arouse, bring.
₣ deter, discourage.

motive n ground(s), cause, reason, purpose, motivation, object, intention, influence, rationale, thinking, incentive, impulse, stimulus, inspiration, incitement, urge, encouragement, design, desire, consideration.
₣ deterrent, disincentive.

mottled adj speckled, dappled, blotchy, flecked, piebald, stippled, streaked, tabby, spotted, freckled, variegated.
₣ monochrome, uniform.

motto n saying, slogan, maxim, watchword, catchword, byword, precept, proverb, adage, formula, rule, golden rule, dictum.

mould[1] n **1** CAST, form, die, template, pattern, matrix. **2** SHAPE, form, format, pattern, structure, style, type, build, construction, cut, design, kind, model, sort, stamp, arrangement, brand, frame,

character, nature, quality, line, make.
v **1** FORGE, cast, shape, stamp, make, form, create, design, construct, sculpt, model, work. **2** INFLUENCE, direct, control.

mould² n mildew, fungus, mouldiness, mustiness, blight.

mouldy adj mildewed, blighted, musty, decaying, corrupt, rotten, fusty, putrid, bad, spoiled, stale.
🔁 fresh, wholesome.

mound n **1** HILL, hillock, hummock, rise, knoll, bank, dune, elevation, ridge, embankment, earthwork. **2** HEAP, pile, stack.

mount v **1** PRODUCE, put on, set up, prepare, stage, exhibit, display, launch. **2** INCREASE, grow, accumulate, multiply, rise, intensify, soar, swell. **3** CLIMB, ascend, get up, go up, get on, clamber up, scale, get astride.
🔁 **2** decrease, descend. **3** descend, dismount, go down.
n horse, steed, support, mounting.

mountain n **1** HEIGHT, elevation, mount, peak, mound, alp, tor, massif. **2** HEAP, pile, stack, mass, abundance, backlog.

mountainous adj **1** CRAGGY, rocky, hilly, high, highland, upland, alpine, soaring, steep. **2** HUGE, towering, enormous, immense.
🔁 **1** flat. **2** tiny.

mourn v grieve, lament, sorrow, bemoan, miss, regret, deplore, weep, wail.
🔁 rejoice.

mournful adj sorrowful, sad, unhappy, desolate, grief-stricken, heavy-hearted, heartbroken, broken-hearted, cast-down, downcast, miserable, tragic, woeful, melancholy, sombre, depressed, dejected, gloomy, dismal.
🔁 joyful.

mourning n bereavement, grief, grieving, lamentation, sadness, sorrow, desolation, weeping.

🔁 rejoicing.

mouth n **1** LIPS, jaws, trap (infml), gob (sl). **2** OPENING, aperture, orifice, cavity, entrance, gateway, inlet, estuary.
v enunciate, articulate, utter, pronounce, whisper, form.

> *Parts of the mouth and types of teeth include*: cleft palate, gum, hard palate, hare lip, inferior dental arch, isthmus of fauces, labial commissure, lower lip, palatoglossal arch, palato-pharyngeal arch, softpalate, superior dental arch, tongue, tonsil, upper lip, uvula.

movable adj mobile, portable, transportable, changeable, alterable, adjustable, flexible, transferable.
🔁 fixed, immovable.

move v **1** STIR, go, advance, budge, change, proceed, progress, make strides. **2** TRANSPORT, carry, transfer. **3** DEPART, go away, leave, decamp, migrate, remove, move house, relocate. **4** PROMPT, stimulate, urge, impel, drive, propel, motivate, incite, persuade, induce, inspire. **5** AFFECT, touch, agitate, stir, impress, excite.
n **1** MOVEMENT, motion, step, manoeuvre, action, device, stratagem. **2** REMOVAL, relocation, migration, transfer.

movement n **1** REPOSITIONING, move, moving, relocation, activity, act, action, agitation, stirring, transfer, passage. **2** CHANGE, development, advance, evolution, current, drift, flow, shift, progress, progression, trend, tendency. **3** CAMPAIGN, crusade, drive, group, organization, party, faction.

moving adj **1** MOBILE, active, in motion. **2** TOUCHING, affecting, poignant, impressive, emotive, arousing, stirring, inspiring, inspirational, exciting, thrilling, persuasive, stimulating.

₤ 1 immobile. 2 unemotional.

mow v cut, trim, crop, clip, shear, scythe.

much adv greatly, considerably, a lot, frequently, often.
adj copious, plentiful, ample, considerable, a lot, abundant, great, substantial.
n plenty, a lot, lots (*infml*), loads (*infml*), heaps (*infml*), lashings (*infml*).
₤ little.

muck n dirt, dung, manure, mire, filth, mud, sewage, slime, gunge (*infml*), ordure, scum, sludge.
muck up ruin, wreck, spoil, mess up, make a mess of, botch, bungle, cock up (*sl*).

mud n clay, mire, ooze, dirt, sludge, silt.

muddle v 1 DISORGANIZE, disorder, mix up, mess up, jumble, scramble, tangle. 2 CONFUSE, bewilder, bemuse, perplex.
n chaos, confusion, disorder, mess, mix-up, jumble, clutter, tangle.

muddy adj 1 DIRTY, foul, miry, mucky, marshy, boggy, swampy, quaggy, grimy. 2 CLOUDY, indistinct, obscure, opaque, murky, hazy, blurred, fuzzy, dull.
₤ 1 clean. 2 clear.

muffle v 1 WRAP, envelop, cloak, swathe, cover. 2 DEADEN, dull, quieten, silence, stifle, dampen, muzzle, suppress.
₤ 2 amplify.

mug¹ n cup, beaker, pot, tankard.

mug² v set upon, attack, assault, waylay, set from, rob, beat up, jump (on).

muggy adj humid, sticky, stuffy, sultry, close, clammy, oppressive, sweltering, moist, damp.
₤ dry.

mull over v reflect on, ponder, contemplate, think over, think about, ruminate, consider, weigh up, chew over, meditate, study, examine,

deliberate.

multiple adj many, numerous, manifold, various, several, sundry, collective.

multiply v increase, proliferate, expand, spread, reproduce, propagate, breed, accumulate, intensify, extend, build up, augment, boost.
₤ decrease, lessen.

multitude n crowd, throng, horde, swarm, mass, herd, congregation, host, lot, lots, legion, public, people, populace.
₤ few, scattering.

munch v eat, chew, crunch, masticate (*fml*).

mundane adj banal, ordinary, everyday, commonplace, prosaic, humdrum, workaday, routine.
₤ extraordinary.

municipal adj civic, city, town, urban, borough, community, public.

murder n homicide, killing, manslaughter, slaying, assassination, massacre, bloodshed.
v kill, slaughter, slay, assassinate, butcher, massacre.

murderer n killer, homicide, slayer, slaughterer, assassin, butcher, cut-throat.

murderous adj 1 HOMICIDAL, brutal, barbarous, bloodthirsty, bloody, cut-throat, killing, lethal, cruel, savage, ferocious, deadly. 2 (*infml*) DIFFICULT, exhausting, strenuous, unpleasant, dangerous.

murky adj dark, dismal, gloomy, dull, overcast, misty, foggy, dim, cloudy, obscure, veiled, grey.
₤ bright, clear.

murmur n mumble, muttering, whisper, undertone, humming, rumble, drone, grumble.
v mutter, mumble, whisper, buzz, hum, rumble, purr, burble.

muscular adj brawny, beefy (*infml*), sinewy, athletic, powerfully built, strapping, hefty, powerful, husky,

robust, stalwart, vigorous, strong.
🔁 puny, flabby, weak.

mushrooms and toadstools

*Types of mushroom and toadstool
include*: *edible*: beefsteak fungus,
blewits, boletus, chestnut boletus,
button mushroom, cep, champignon,
chanterelle, clouded agaric, common
morel, cultivated mushroom, dingy
agaric, fairy ring, the goat's lip,
gypsy mushroom, honey fungus, horn
of plenty, horse mushroom, lawyer's
wig, man on horseback, march
mushroom, oyster mushroom,
parasol mushroom, penny bun,
saffron milk cap, shaggy parasol,
slippery jack, sweetbread mushroom,
truffle, trumpet agaric, velvet shank,
winter mushroom, wood hedgehog;
inedible/poisonous: amanita,
common ink cap, copper trumpet,
death cap, destroying angel, devil's
boletus, earth ball, false morel, fly
agaric, mower's mushroom, panther
cap, purple boletus, satan's
mushroom, shaggy milk cap, stinking
parasol, sulphur tuft, verdigris agaric,
woolly milk cap, yellow-staining
mushroom.

music

Types of music include: acid house,
ambient, ballet, ballroom, bluegrass,
blues, boogie-woogie, chamber,
choral, classical, country-and-
western, dance, disco, Dixieland,
doo-wop, drum and bass, electronic,
folk, folk rock, funk, gangsta, garage,
gospel, grunge, hardcore, hard rock,
heavy metal, hip-hop, honky-tonk,
house, incidental, instrumental, jazz,
jazz-funk, jazz-pop, jazz-rock, jive,
jungle, karaoke, operatic, orchestral,
pop, punk rock, ragtime, rap, reggae,
rhythm and blues (R & B), rock and
roll, rock, sacred, ska, skiffle, soft
rock, soul, swing, techno, thrash
metal, trance, trip-hop.

musical *adj* tuneful, melodious,
melodic, harmonious, dulcet, sweet-
sounding, lyrical.
🔁 discordant, unmusical.

musical instruments

Musical instruments include:
balalaika, banjo, cello, double-bass,
guitar, harp, hurdy-gurdy, lute, lyre,
mandolin, sitar, spinet, ukulele, viola,
violin, fiddle (*infml*); zither;
accordion, concertina, squeeze-box
(*infml*), clavichord, harmonium,
harpsichord, keyboard, melodeon,
organ, Wurlitzer®, piano, grand
piano, Pianola®, player-piano,
synthesizer, virginals; bagpipes,
bassoon, bugle, clarinet, cor anglais,
cornet, didgeridoo, euphonium, fife,
flugelhorn, flute, French horn,
harmonica, horn, kazoo, mouth-
organ, oboe, Pan-pipes, piccolo,
recorder, saxophone, sousaphone,
trombone, trumpet, tuba; castanets,
cymbal, glockenspiel, maracas,
marimba, tambourine, triangle,
tubular bells, xylophone; bass-drum,
bongo, kettle-drum, snare-drum,
tenor-drum, timpani, tom-tom.

musical terms

Musical terms include: accelerando,
acciaccatura, accidental,
accompaniment, acoustic, adagio, ad
lib, a due, affettuoso, agitato, al fine,
al segno, alla breve, alla cappella,
allargando, allegretto, allegro, al
segno, alto, amoroso, andante,
animato, appoggiatura, arco,
arpeggio, arrangement, a tempo,
attacca, bar, bar line, double bar line,
baritone, bass, beat, bis, breve, buffo,
cadence, cantabile, cantilena, chord,
chromatic, clef, alto clef, bass clef,
tenor clef, treble clef, coda, col canto,
con brio, concert, con fuoco, con

moto, consonance, contralto, counterpoint, crescendo, crotchet, cross-fingering, cue, da capo, decrescendo, demisemiquaver, descant, diatonic, diminuendo, dissonance, dolce, doloroso, dominant, dotted note, dotted rest, downbeat, drone, duplet, triplet, quadruplet, quintuplet, sextuplet, encore, ensemble, expression, finale, fine, fingerboard, flat, double flat, forte, fortissimo, fret, glissando, grave, harmonics, harmony, hemidemisemiquaver, hold, imitation, improvisation, interval, augmented interval, diminished interval, second interval, third interval, fourth interval, fifth interval, sixth interval, seventh interval, major interval, minor interval, perfect interval, intonation, key, key signature, langsam, larghetto, largo, leading note, ledger line, legato, lento, lyric, maestoso, major, manual, marcato, mediant, medley, melody, metre, mezza voce, mezzo forte, microtone, middle C, minim, minor, moderato, mode, modulation, molto, mordent, movement, mute, natural, non troppo, note, obbligato, octave, orchestra, ostinato, part, pause, pedal point, pentatonic, perdendo, phrase, pianissimo, piano, piece, pitch, pizzicato, presto, quarter tone, quaver, rallentando, recital, refrain, resolution, rest, rhythm, ritenuto, root, scale, score, semibreve, semiquaver, semitone, semplice, sempre, senza, sequence, sforzando, shake, sharp, double sharp, slur, smorzando, solo, soprano, sostenuto, sotto voce, spiritoso, staccato, staff, stave, subdominant, subito, submediant, sul ponticello, supertonic, swell, syncopation, tablature, tacet, tanto, tempo, tenor, tenuto, theme, tie, timbre, time signature, compound time, simple time, two-two time, three-four time, four-four time, six-eight time, tone, tonic sol-fa, transposition, treble, tremolo, triad, trill, double trill, tune, tuning, turn, tutti, upbeat, unison, vibrato, vigoroso, virtuoso, vivace.

musician

Musicians include: instrumentalist, accompanist, performer, player; bugler, busker, cellist, clarinettist, drummer, flautist, fiddler, guitarist, harpist, oboist, organist, pianist, piper, soloist, trombonist, trumpeter, violinist; singer, vocalist, balladeer, diva, prima donna; conductor, maestro; band, orchestra, group, backing group, ensemble, chamber orchestra, choir, duo, duet, trio, quartet, quintet, sextet, octet, nonet.

muster *v* assemble, convene, gather, call together, mobilize, round up, marshal, come together, congregate, collect, group, meet, rally, mass, throng, call up, summon, enrol.

musty *adj* mouldy, mildewy, stale, stuffy, fusty, dank, airless, decayed, smelly.

mutation *n* change, alteration, variation, modification, transformation, deviation, anomaly, evolution.

mute *adj* silent, dumb, voiceless, wordless, speechless, mum (*infml*), unspoken, noiseless, unexpressed, unpronounced.
F∃ vocal, talkative.
v tone down, subdue, muffle, lower, moderate, dampen, deaden, soften, silence.

mutilate *v* **1** MAIM, injure, dismember, disable, disfigure, lame, mangle, cut to pieces, cut up, butcher. **2** SPOIL, mar, damage, cut, censor.

mutinous *adj* rebellious, insurgent, insubordinate, disobedient, seditious, revolutionary, riotous, subversive, bolshie (*infml*), unruly.

◼ obedient, compliant.

mutiny *n* rebellion, insurrection, revolt, revolution, rising, uprising, insubordination, disobedience, defiance, resistance, riot, strike.
v rebel, revolt, rise up, resist, protest, disobey, strike.

mutter *v* 1 MUMBLE, murmur, rumble. 2 COMPLAIN, grumble, grouse (*infml*).

mutual *adj* reciprocal, shared, common, joint, interchangeable, interchanged, exchanged, complementary.

muzzle *v* restrain, stifle, suppress, gag, mute, silence, censor, choke.

mysterious *adj* enigmatic, cryptic, mystifying, inexplicable, incomprehensible, puzzling, perplexing, obscure, strange, unfathomable, unsearchable, mystical, baffling, curious, hidden, insoluble, secret, weird, secretive, veiled, dark, furtive.

◼ straightforward, comprehensible.

mystery *n* 1 ENIGMA, puzzle, secret, riddle, conundrum, question.
2 OBSCURITY, secrecy, ambiguity.

mystical *adj* occult, arcane, mystic, esoteric, supernatural, paranormal, transcendental, metaphysical, hidden, mysterious.

mystify *v* puzzle, bewilder, baffle, perplex, confound, confuse.

myth *n* legend, fable, fairytale, allegory, parable, saga, story, fiction, tradition, fancy, fantasy, superstition.

mythical *adj* 1 MYTHOLOGICAL, legendary, fabled, fairytale.
2 FICTITIOUS, imaginary, made-up, invented, make-believe, non-existent, unreal, pretended, fanciful.

◼ 1 historical. 2 actual, real.

mythology *n* legend, myths, lore, tradition(s), folklore, folk-tales, tales.

Mythological creatures and spirits include: abominable snowman (or yeti), afrit, basilisk, bunyip, Cecrops, centaur, Cerberus, Chimera, cockatrice, Cyclops, dragon, dryad, Echidna, elf, Erinyes (or Furies), Fafnir, fairy, faun, Frankenstein's monster, genie, Geryon, Gigantes, gnome, goblin, golem, Gorgon, griffin, Harpies, hippocampus, hippogriff, hobgoblin, imp, kelpie, kraken, lamia, leprechaun, Lilith, Loch Ness monster, mermaid, merman, Minotaur, naiad, nereid, nymph, ogre, ogress, orc, oread, Pegasus, phoenix, pixie, roc, salamander, sasquatch, satyr, sea serpent, Siren, Sphinx, sylph, troll, Typhoeus, unicorn, werewolf, wivern.

N

nag *v* scold, berate, irritate, annoy, pester, badger, plague, torment, harass, henpeck (*infml*), harry, vex, upbraid, goad.

nail *v* fasten, attach, secure, pin, tack, fix, join.
n 1 FASTENER, pin, tack, spike, skewer. 2 TALON, claw.

naïve *adj* unsophisticated, ingenuous, innocent, unaffected, artless, guileless, simple, natural, childlike, open, trusting, unsuspecting, gullible, credulous, wide-eyed.

◼ experienced, sophisticated.

naïvety *n* ingenuousness, innocence,

inexperience, naturalness, simplicity, openness, frankness, gullibility, credulity.
E3 experience, sophistication.

naked adj 1 NUDE, bare, undressed, unclothed, uncovered, stripped, stark-naked, disrobed, denuded, in the altogether (*infml*). 2 OPEN, unadorned, undisguised, unqualified, plain, stark, overt, blatant, exposed.
E3 1 clothed, covered. 2 concealed.

name n 1 TITLE, appellation (*fml*), designation, label, term, epithet, handle (*infml*). 2 REPUTATION, character, repute, renown, esteem, eminence, fame, honour, distinction, note.
v 1 CALL, christen, baptize, term, title, entitle, dub, label, style.
2 DESIGNATE, nominate, cite, choose, select, specify, classify, commission, appoint.

nameless adj 1 UNNAMED, anonymous, unidentified, unknown, obscure. 2 INEXPRESSIBLE, indescribable, unutterable, unspeakable, unmentionable, unheard-of.
E3 1 named.

namely adv that is, ie, specifically, viz, that is to say.

nap v doze, sleep, snooze (*infml*), nod (off), drop off, rest, kip (*infml*).
n rest, sleep, siesta, catnap, forty winks (*infml*), kip (*infml*).

narcotic n drug, opiate, sedative, tranquillizer, pain-killer.
adj soporific, hypnotic, sedative, analgesic, pain-killing, numbing, dulling, calming, stupefying.

narrate v tell, relate, report, recount, describe, unfold, recite, state, detail.

narrative n story, tale, chronicle, account, history, report, detail, statement.

narrator n storyteller, chronicler, reporter, raconteur, commentator, writer.

narrow adj 1 TIGHT, confined, constricted, cramped, slim, slender, thin, fine, tapering, close. 2 LIMITED, restricted, circumscribed. 3 NARROW-MINDED, biased, bigoted, exclusive, dogmatic.
E3 1 wide. 2 broad. 3 broad-minded, tolerant.
v constrict, limit, tighten, reduce, diminish, simplify.
E3 broaden, widen, increase.

narrow-minded adj illiberal, biased, bigoted, prejudiced, reactionary, small-minded, conservative, intolerant, insular, petty.
E3 broad-minded.

nasty adj 1 UNPLEASANT, repellent, repugnant, repulsive, objectionable, offensive, disgusting, sickening, horrible, filthy, foul, polluted, obscene. 2 MALICIOUS, mean, spiteful, vicious, malevolent.
E3 1 agreeable, pleasant, decent. 2 benevolent, kind.

nation n country, people, race, state, realm, population, community, society.

national adj countrywide, civil, domestic, nationwide, state, internal, general, governmental, public, widespread, social.
n citizen, native, subject, inhabitant, resident.

nationalism n patriotism, allegiance, loyalty, chauvinism, xenophobia, jingoism.

nationality n race, nation, ethnic group, birth, tribe, clan.

native adj 1 LOCAL, indigenous, domestic, vernacular, home, aboriginal, autochthonous (*fml*), mother, original. 2 INBORN, inherent, innate, inbred, hereditary, inherited, congenital, instinctive, natural, intrinsic, natal.
n inhabitant, resident, national, citizen, dweller, aborigine, autochthon (*fml*).

foreigner, outsider, stranger.

natural adj **1** ORDINARY, normal, common, regular, standard, usual, typical. **2** INNATE, inborn, instinctive, intuitive, inherent, congenital, native, indigenous. **3** GENUINE, pure, authentic, unrefined, unprocessed, unmixed, real. **4** SINCERE, unaffected, genuine, artless, ingenuous, guileless, simple, unsophisticated, open, candid, spontaneous.

1 unnatural. **2** acquired. **3** affected, disingenuous.

naturalistic adj natural, realistic, true-to-life, representational, lifelike, graphic, real-life, photographic.

naturally adj **1** OF COURSE, as a matter of course, simply, obviously, logically, typically, certainly, absolutely. **2** NORMALLY, genuinely, instinctively, spontaneously.

nature n **1** ESSENCE, quality, character, features, disposition, attributes, personality, make-up, constitution, temperament, mood, outlook, temper. **2** KIND, sort, type, description, category, variety, style, species. **3** UNIVERSE, world, creation, earth, environment. **4** COUNTRYSIDE, country, landscape, scenery, natural history.

naughty adj **1** BAD, badly behaved, mischievous, disobedient, wayward, exasperating, playful, roguish. **2** INDECENT, obscene, bawdy, risqué, smutty.

1 good, well-behaved. **2** decent.

nausea n **1** VOMITING, sickness, retching, queasiness, biliousness. **2** DISGUST, revulsion, loathing, repugnance.

nauseate v sicken, disgust, revolt, repel, offend, turn one's stomach (infml).

nautical adj naval, marine, maritime, sea-going, seafaring, sailing, oceanic, boating.

navigate v steer, drive, direct, pilot,

guide, handle, manoeuvre, cruise, sail, skipper, voyage, journey, cross, helm, plot, plan.

navigation n sailing, steering, cruising, voyaging, seamanship, helmsmanship.

navy n fleet, ships, flotilla, armada, warships.

near adj **1** NEARBY, close, bordering, adjacent, adjoining, alongside, neighbouring. **2** IMMINENT, impending, forthcoming, coming, approaching. **3** DEAR, familiar, close, related, intimate, akin.

1 far. **2** distant. **3** remote.

nearby adj near, neighbouring, adjoining, adjacent, accessible, convenient, handy.

faraway.

adv near, within reach, at close quarters, close at hand, not far away.

nearly adv almost, practically, virtually, closely, approximately, more or less, as good as, just about, roughly, well-nigh.

completely, totally.

neat adj **1** TIDY, orderly, smart, spruce, trim, clean, spick-and-span (infml), shipshape. **2** DEFT, clever, adroit, skilful, expert. **3** UNDILUTED, unmixed, unadulterated, straight, pure.

1 untidy. **2** clumsy. **3** diluted.

nebulous adj vague, hazy, imprecise, indefinite, indistinct, cloudy, misty, obscure, uncertain, unclear, dim, ambiguous, confused, fuzzy, shapeless, amorphous.

clear.

necessary adj needed, required, essential, compulsory, indispensable, vital, imperative, mandatory, obligatory, needful, unavoidable, inevitable, inescapable, inexorable, certain.

unnecessary, inessential, unimportant.

necessitate v require, involve,

entail, call for, demand, oblige, force, constrain, compel.

necessity n **1** REQUIREMENT, obligation, prerequisite, essential, fundamental, need, want, compulsion, demand. **2** INDISPENSABILITY, inevitability, needfulness. **3** POVERTY, destitution, hardship.

need v miss, lack, want, require, demand, call for, necessitate, have need of, have to, crave.
n **1** a need for caution: call, demand, obligation, requirement. **2** the country's needs: essential, necessity, requisite, prerequisite, desideratum. **3** a need for equipment: want, lack, insufficiency, inadequacy, neediness, shortage.

needless adj unnecessary, gratuitous, uncalled-for, unwanted, redundant, superfluous, useless, pointless, purposeless.
■ necessary, essential.

needy adj poor, destitute, impoverished, penniless, disadvantaged, deprived, poverty-stricken, underprivileged.
■ affluent, wealthy, well-off.

negate v **1** NULLIFY, annul, cancel, invalidate, undo, countermand, abrogate (fml), neutralize, quash, retract, reverse, revoke, rescind, wipe out, void, repeal. **2** DENY, contradict, oppose, disprove, refute, repudiate.
■ affirm.

negative adj **1** CONTRADICTORY, contrary, denying, opposing, invalidating, neutralizing, nullifying, annulling. **2** UNCO-OPERATIVE, cynical, pessimistic, unenthusiastic, uninterested, unwilling.
■ **1** affirmative, positive.
2 constructive, positive.
n contradiction, denial, opposite, refusal.

neglect v **1** DISREGARD, ignore, leave alone, abandon, pass by, rebuff, scorn, disdain, slight, spurn.

2 FORGET, fail (in), omit, overlook, let slide, shirk, skimp.
■ **1** cherish, appreciate. **2** remember.
n negligence, disregard, carelessness, failure, inattention, indifference, slackness, dereliction of duty, forgetfulness, heedlessness, oversight, slight, disrespect.
■ care, attention, concern.

negligence n inattentiveness, carelessness, laxity, neglect, slackness, thoughtlessness, forgetfulness, indifference, omission, oversight, disregard, failure, default.
■ attentiveness, care, regard.

negligent adj neglectful, inattentive, remiss, thoughtless, casual, lax, careless, indifferent, offhand, nonchalant, slack, uncaring, forgetful.
■ attentive, careful, scrupulous.

negligible adj unimportant, insignificant, small, imperceptible, trifling, trivial, minor, minute.
■ significant.

negotiate v **1** CONFER, deal, mediate, arbitrate, bargain, arrange, transact, work out, manage, settle, consult, contract. **2** GET ROUND, cross, surmount, traverse, pass.

negotiation n mediation, arbitration, debate, discussion, diplomacy, bargaining, transaction.

negotiator n arbitrator, go-between, mediator, intermediary, moderator, intercessor, adjudicator, broker, ambassador, diplomat.

neighbourhood n district, locality, vicinity, community, locale, environs, confines, surroundings, region, proximity.

neighbouring adj adjacent, bordering, near, nearby, adjoining, connecting, next, surrounding.
■ distant, remote.

neighbourly adj sociable, friendly, amiable, kind, helpful, genial, hospitable, obliging, considerate, companionable.

nerve n **1** COURAGE, bravery, mettle, pluck, guts (infml), spunk (infml), spirit, vigour, intrepidity, daring, fearlessness, firmness, resolution, fortitude, steadfastness, will, determination, endurance, force. **2** (infml) AUDACITY, impudence, cheek (infml), effrontery, brazenness, boldness, chutzpah (infml), impertinence, insolence.
1 weakness. **2** timidity.

nerve-racking adj harrowing, distressing, trying, stressful, tense, maddening, worrying, difficult, frightening.

nerves n nervousness, tension, stress, anxiety, worry, strain, fretfulness.

nervous adj highly-strung, excitable, anxious, agitated, nervy (infml), on edge, edgy, jumpy (infml), jittery (infml), tense, fidgety, apprehensive, neurotic, shaky, uneasy, worried, flustered, fearful.
calm, relaxed.

nest n **1** BREEDING-GROUND, den, roost, eyrie, lair. **2** RETREAT, refuge, haunt, hideaway.

nestle v snuggle, huddle, cuddle, curl up.

net¹ n mesh, web, network, netting, open-work, lattice, lace.
v catch, trap, capture, bag, ensnare, entangle, nab (infml).

net² adj nett, clear, after tax, final, lowest.
v bring in, clear, earn, make, realize, receive, gain, obtain, accumulate.

network n system, organization, arrangement, structure, interconnections, complex, grid, net, maze, mesh, labyrinth, channels, circuitry, convolution, grill, tracks.

neurosis n disorder, affliction, abnormality, disturbance, derangement, deviation, obsession, phobia.

neurotic adj disturbed, maladjusted, anxious, nervous, overwrought, unstable, unhealthy, deviant, abnormal, compulsive, obsessive.

neuter v castrate, emasculate, doctor, geld, spay.

neutral adj **1** IMPARTIAL, uncommitted, unbia(s)sed, non-aligned, disinterested, unprejudiced, undecided, non-partisan, non-committal, objective, indifferent, dispassionate, even-handed. **2** DULL, nondescript, colourless, drab, expressionless, indistinct.
1 biased, partisan. **2** colourful.

neutralize v counteract, counterbalance, offset, negate, cancel, nullify, invalidate, undo, frustrate.

never-ending adj everlasting, eternal, non-stop, perpetual, unceasing, uninterrupted, unremitting, interminable, incessant, unbroken, permanent, persistent, unchanging, relentless.
fleeting, transitory.

nevertheless adv nonetheless, notwithstanding, still, anyway, even so, yet, however, anyhow, but, regardless.

new adj **1** NOVEL, original, fresh, different, unfamiliar, unusual, brand-new, mint, unknown, unused, virgin, newborn. **2** MODERN, contemporary, current, latest, recent, up-to-date, up-to-the-minute, topical, trendy (infml), ultra-modern, advanced, newfangled (infml). **3** CHANGED, altered, modernized, improved, renewed, restored, redesigned. **4** ADDED, additional, extra, more, supplementary.
1 usual. **2** outdated, out-of-date. **3** old.

newcomer n immigrant, alien, foreigner, incomer, colonist, settler, arrival, outsider, stranger, novice, beginner.

news n report, account, information, intelligence, dispatch, communiqué, bulletin, gossip, hearsay, rumour, statement, story, word, tidings, latest, release, scandal, revelation, lowdown (*infml*), exposé, disclosure, gen (*infml*) advice.

next *adj* 1 ADJACENT, adjoining, neighbouring, nearest, closest.
2 FOLLOWING, subsequent, succeeding, ensuing, later.
✑ 2 previous, preceding.
adv afterwards, subsequently, later, then.

nibble *n* bite, morsel, taste, titbit, bit, crumb, snack, piece.
v bite, eat, peck, pick at, nosh (*sl*), munch, gnaw.

nice *adj* 1 PLEASANT, agreeable, delightful, charming, likable, attractive, good, kind, friendly, well-mannered, polite, respectable.
2 SUBTLE, delicate, fine, fastidious, discriminating, scrupulous, precise, exact, accurate, careful, strict.
✑ 1 nasty, disagreeable, unpleasant.
2 careless.

nicety *n* 1 DELICACY, refinement, subtlety, distinction, nuance.
2 PRECISION, accuracy, meticulousness, scrupulousness, minuteness, finesse.

niche *n* 1 RECESS, alcove, hollow, nook, cubby-hole, corner, opening.
2 POSITION, place, vocation, calling, métier, slot.

nick *n* 1 NOTCH, indentation, chip, cut, groove, dent, scar, scratch, mark. 2 (*sl*) PRISON, jail, police station.
v 1 NOTCH, cut, dent, indent, chip, score, scratch, scar, mark, damage, snick. 2 (*sl*) STEAL, pilfer, knock off (*infml*), pinch (*infml*).

nickname *n* pet name, sobriquet, epithet, diminutive.

night *n* night-time, darkness, dark, dead of night.
✑ day, daytime.

nightfall *n* sunset, dusk, twilight, evening, gloaming.
✑ dawn, sunrise.

nightmare *n* 1 BAD DREAM, hallucination. 2 ORDEAL, horror, torment, trial.

nil *n* nothing, zero, none, nought, naught, love, duck, zilch (*sl*).

nimble *adj* agile, active, lively, sprightly, spry, smart, quick, brisk, nippy (*infml*), deft, alert, light-footed, prompt, ready, swift, quick-witted.
✑ clumsy, slow.

nip[1] *v* bite, pinch, squeeze, snip, clip, tweak, catch, grip, nibble.

nip[2] *n* dram, draught, shot, swallow, mouthful, drop, sip, taste, portion.

nobility *n* 1 NOBLENESS, dignity, grandeur, illustriousness, stateliness, majesty, magnificence, eminence, excellence, superiority, uprightness, honour, virtue, worthiness. 2 ARISTOCRACY, peerage, nobles, gentry, élite, lords, high society.
✑ 1 baseness. 2 proletariat.

Titles of the nobility include: aristocrat, baron, baroness, baronet, count, countess, dame, dowager, duchess, duke, earl, grand duke, governor, knight, lady, laird, liege, liege lord, life peer, lord, marchioness, marquess, marquis, noble, nobleman, noblewoman, peer, peeress, ruler, seigneur, squire, thane, viscount, viscountess.

noble *n* aristocrat, peer, lord, lady, nobleman, noblewoman.
✑ commoner.
adj 1 ARISTOCRATIC, high-born, titled, high-ranking, patrician, blue-blooded (*infml*). 2 MAGNIFICENT, magnanimous, splendid, stately, generous, dignified, distinguished, eminent, grand, great, honoured, honourable, imposing, impressive, majestic, virtuous, worthy, excellent, elevated, fine, gentle.
✑ 1 low-born. 2 ignoble, base, contemptible.

nobody *n* no-one, nothing, nonentity, menial, cipher.
F3 somebody.

nod *v* **1** GESTURE, indicate, sign, signal, salute, acknowledge. **2** AGREE, assent. **3** SLEEP, doze, drowse, nap.
n gesture, indication, sign, signal, salute, greeting, beck, acknowledgement.

noise *n* sound, din, racket, row, clamour, clash, clatter, commotion, outcry, hubbub, uproar, cry, blare, talk, pandemonium, tumult, babble.
F3 quiet, silence.
v report, rumour, publicize, announce, circulate.

noiseless *adj* silent, inaudible, soundless, quiet, mute, still, hushed.
F3 loud, noisy.

noisy *adj* loud, deafening, ear-splitting, clamorous, piercing, vocal, vociferous, tumultuous, boisterous, obstreperous.
F3 quiet, silent, peaceful.

nomad *n* traveller, wanderer, itinerant, rambler, roamer, rover, migrant.

nominal *adj* **1** TITULAR, supposed, purported, professed, ostensible, so-called, theoretical, self-styled, puppet, symbolic. **2** TOKEN, minimal, trifling, trivial, insignificant, small.
F3 **1** actual, genuine, real.

nominate *v* propose, choose, select, name, designate, submit, suggest, recommend, put up, present, elect, appoint, assign, commission, elevate, term.

nomination *n* proposal, choice, selection, submission, suggestion, recommendation, designation, election, appointment.

nominee *n* candidate, entrant, contestant, appointee, runner, assignee.

nonchalant *adj* unconcerned, detached, dispassionate, offhand, blasé, indifferent, casual, cool, collected, apathetic, careless, insouciant.
F3 concerned, careful.

non-committal *adj* guarded, unrevealing, cautious, wary, reserved, ambiguous, discreet, equivocal, evasive, circumspect, careful, neutral, indefinite, politic, tactful, tentative, vague.

nonconformist *n* dissenter, rebel, individualist, dissident, radical, protester, heretic, iconoclast, eccentric, maverick, secessionist.
F3 conformist.

nondescript *adj* featureless, indeterminate, undistinctive, undistinguished, unexceptional, ordinary, commonplace, plain, dull, uninspiring, uninteresting, unclassified.
F3 distinctive, remarkable.

none *pron* no-one, not any, not one, nobody, nil, zero.

nonplussed *adj* disconcerted, confounded, taken aback, stunned, bewildered, astonished, astounded, dumbfounded, perplexed, stumped, flabbergasted, flummoxed, puzzled, baffled, dismayed, embarrassed.

nonsense *n* rubbish, trash, drivel, balderdash, gibberish, gobbledygook, senselessness, stupidity, silliness, foolishness, folly, rot (*infml*), blather, twaddle, ridiculousness, claptrap (*infml*), cobblers (*sl*).
F3 sense, wisdom.

nonsensical *adj* ridiculous, meaningless, senseless, foolish, inane, irrational, silly, incomprehensible, ludicrous, absurd, fatuous, crazy (*infml*).
F3 reasonable, sensible, logical.

non-stop *adj* never-ending, uninterrupted, continuous, incessant, constant, endless, interminable, unending, unbroken, round-the-clock, on-going.
F3 intermittent, occasional.

nook *n* recess, alcove, corner, cranny, niche, cubby-hole, hide-out, retreat, shelter, cavity.

norm *n* average, mean, standard, rule, pattern, criterion, model, yardstick, benchmark, measure, reference.

normal *adj* usual, standard, general, common, ordinary, conventional, average, regular, routine, typical, mainstream, natural, accustomed, well-adjusted, straight, rational, reasonable.
🗲 abnormal, irregular, peculiar.

normality *n* usualness, commonness, ordinariness, regularity, routine, conventionality, balance, adjustment, typicality, naturalness, reason, rationality.
🗲 abnormality, irregularity, peculiarity.

normally *adv* ordinarily, usually, as a rule, typically, commonly, characteristically.
🗲 abnormally, exceptionally.

nosegay *n* bouquet, posy, spray, bunch.

nosey (*infml*) *adj* inquisitive, meddlesome, prying, interfering, snooping, curious, eavesdropping.

nostalgia *n* yearning, longing, regretfulness, remembrance, reminiscence, homesickness, pining.

nostalgic *adj* yearning, longing, wistful, emotional, regretful, sentimental, homesick.

notable *adj* noteworthy, remarkable, noticeable, striking, extraordinary, impressive, outstanding, marked, unusual, celebrated, distinguished, famous, eminent, well-known, notorious, renowned, rare.
🗲 ordinary, commonplace, usual.
n celebrity, notability, VIP, personage, somebody, dignitary, luminary, worthy.
🗲 nobody, nonentity.

notably *adv* markedly, noticeably, particularly, remarkably, strikingly, conspicuously, distinctly, especially, impressively, outstandingly, eminently.

notation *n* symbols, characters, code, signs, alphabet, system, script, noting, record, shorthand.

notch *n* cut, nick, indentation, incision, score, groove, cleft, mark, snip, degree, grade, step.
v cut, nick, score, scratch, indent, mark.

note *n* **1** COMMUNICATION, letter, message, memorandum, reminder, memo (*infml*), line, jotting, record. **2** ANNOTATION, comment, gloss, remark. **3** INDICATION, signal, token, mark, symbol. **4** EMINENCE, distinction, consequence, fame, renown, reputation. **5** HEED, attention, regard, notice, observation.
v **1** NOTICE, observe, perceive, heed, detect, mark, remark, mention, see, witness. **2** RECORD, register, write down, enter.

noted *adj* famous, well-known, renowned, notable, celebrated, eminent, prominent, great, acclaimed, illustrious, distinguished, respected, recognized.
🗲 obscure, unknown.

notes *n* jottings, record, impressions, report, sketch, outline, synopsis, draft.

noteworthy *adj* remarkable, significant, important, notable, memorable, exceptional, extraordinary, unusual, outstanding.
🗲 commonplace, unexceptional, ordinary.

nothing *n* nought, zero, nothingness, zilch (*sl*), nullity, non-existence, emptiness, void, nobody, nonentity.
🗲 something.

notice *v* note, remark, perceive, observe, mind, see, discern, distinguish, mark, detect, heed, spot.
🗲 ignore, overlook.

n **1** NOTIFICATION, announcement, information, declaration, communication, intelligence, news, warning, instruction. **2** ADVERTISEMENT, poster, sign, bill. **3** REVIEW, comment, criticism. **4** ATTENTION, observation, awareness, note, regard, consideration, heed.

noticeable *adj* perceptible, observable, appreciable, unmistakable, conspicuous, evident, manifest, clear, distinct, significant, striking, plain, obvious, measurable.
☒ inconspicuous, unnoticeable.

notification *n* announcement, information, notice, declaration, advice, warning, intelligence, message, publication, statement, communication.

notify *v* inform, tell, advise, announce, declare, warn, acquaint, alert, publish, disclose, reveal.

notion *n* **1** IDEA, thought, concept, conception, belief, impression, view, opinion, understanding, apprehension. **2** INCLINATION, wish, whim, fancy, caprice.

notoriety *n* infamy, disrepute, dishonour, disgrace, scandal.

notorious *adj* infamous, disreputable, scandalous, dishonourable, disgraceful, ignominious, flagrant, well-known.

nought *n* zero, nil, zilch, naught, nothing, nothingness.

nourish *v* **1** NURTURE, feed, foster, care for, provide for, sustain, support, tend, nurse, maintain, cherish. **2** STRENGTHEN, encourage, promote, cultivate, stimulate.

nourishment *n* nutrition, food, sustenance, diet.

novel *adj* new, original, fresh, innovative, unfamiliar, unusual, uncommon, different, imaginative, unconventional, strange.
☒ hackneyed, familiar, ordinary.
n fiction, story, tale, narrative,

romance.

novelty *n* **1** NEWNESS, originality, freshness, innovation, unfamiliarity, uniqueness, difference, strangeness. **2** GIMMICK, gadget, trifle, memento, knick-knack, curiosity, souvenir, trinket, bauble, gimcrack.

novice *n* beginner, tiro, learner, pupil, trainee, probationer, apprentice, neophyte (*fml*), amateur, newcomer.
☒ expert.

now *adv* **1** IMMEDIATELY, at once, directly, instantly, straight away, promptly, next. **2** AT PRESENT, nowadays, these days.

noxious *adj* harmful, poisonous, pernicious, toxic, injurious, unhealthy, deadly, destructive, noisome, foul.
☒ innocuous, wholesome.

nuance *n* subtlety, suggestion, shade, hint, suspicion, gradation, distinction, overtone, refinement, touch, trace, tinge, degree, nicety.

nub *n* centre, heart, core, nucleus, kernel, crux, gist, pith, point, essence.

nucleus *n* centre, heart, nub, core, focus, kernel, pivot, basis, crux.

nude *adj* naked, bare, undressed, unclothed, stripped, stark-naked, uncovered, starkers (*infml*), in one's birthday suit (*infml*).
☒ clothed, dressed.

nudge *v, n* poke, prod, shove, dig, jog, prompt, push, elbow, bump.

nuisance *n* annoyance, inconvenience, bother, irritation, pest, pain (*infml*), drag (*infml*), bore, problem, trial, trouble, drawback.

null *adj* void, invalid, ineffectual, useless, vain, worthless, powerless, inoperative.
☒ valid.

nullify *v* annul, revoke, cancel, invalidate, abrogate, abolish, negate, rescind, quash, repeal, counteract.
☒ validate.

numb *adj* benumbed, insensible,

number

unfeeling, deadened, insensitive, frozen, immobilized.

☒ sensitive.

v deaden, anaesthetize, freeze, immobilize, paralyse, dull, stun.

☒ sensitize.

number *n* **1** FIGURE, numeral, digit, integer, unit. **2** TOTAL, sum, aggregate, collection, amount, quantity, several, many, company, crowd, multitude, throng, horde. **3** COPY, issue, edition, impression, volume, printing.

v count, calculate, enumerate, reckon, total, add, compute, include.

numerous *adj* many, abundant, several, plentiful, copious, profuse, sundry.

☒ few.

nurse *v* **1** TEND, care for, look after, treat. **2** BREAST-FEED, feed, suckle, nurture, nourish. **3** PRESERVE, sustain, support, cherish, encourage, keep, foster, promote.

n sister, matron, nursemaid, nanny.

nurture *n* **1** FOOD, nourishment. **2** REARING, upbringing, training, care, cultivation, development, education, discipline.

v **1** FEED, nourish, nurse, tend, care for, foster, support, sustain. **2** BRING UP, rear, cultivate, develop, educate, instruct, train, school, discipline.

nut

Varieties of nut include: almond, beech nut, brazil nut, cashew, chestnut, cobnut, coconut, filbert, hazelnut, macadamia, monkey nut, peanut, pecan, pistachio, walnut.

nutrition *n* food, nourishment, sustenance.

nutritious *adj* nourishing, nutritive, wholesome, healthful, health-giving, good, beneficial, strengthening, substantial, invigorating.

☒ bad, unwholesome.

O

oasis *n* **1** SPRING, watering-hole. **2** REFUGE, haven, island, sanctuary, retreat.

oath *n* **1** VOW, pledge, promise, word, affirmation, assurance, word of honour. **2** CURSE, imprecation, swear-word, profanity, expletive, blasphemy.

obedient *adj* compliant, docile, acquiescent, submissive, tractable, yielding, dutiful, law-abiding, deferential, respectful, subservient, observant.

☒ disobedient, rebellious, wilful.

obesity *n* fatness, overweight, corpulence, stoutness, grossness, plumpness, portliness, bulk.

☒ thinness, slenderness, skinniness.

obey *v* **1** COMPLY, submit, surrender, yield, be ruled by, bow to, take orders from, defer (to), give way, follow, observe, abide by, adhere to, conform, heed, keep, mind, respond. **2** CARRY OUT, discharge, execute, act upon, fulfil, perform.

☒ **1** disobey.

object[1] *n* **1** THING, entity, article, body. **2** AIM, objective, purpose, goal, target, intention, motive, end, reason, point, design. **3** TARGET, recipient, butt, victim.

object[2] *v* protest, oppose, demur, take exception, disapprove, refuse, complain, rebut, repudiate.

☒ agree, acquiesce.

objection n protest, dissent, disapproval, opposition, demur, complaint, challenge, scruple.
≠ agreement, assent.

objectionable adj unacceptable, unpleasant, offensive, obnoxious, repugnant, disagreeable, abhorrent, detestable, deplorable, despicable.
≠ acceptable.

objective adj impartial, unbiased, detached, unprejudiced, open-minded, equitable, dispassionate, even-handed, neutral, disinterested, just, fair.
≠ subjective.
n object, aim, goal, end, purpose, ambition, mark, target, intention, design.

obligation n duty, responsibility, onus, charge, commitment, liability, requirement, bond, contract, debt, burden, trust.

obligatory adj compulsory, mandatory, statutory, required, binding, essential, necessary, enforced.
≠ optional.

oblige v 1 COMPEL, constrain, coerce, require, make, necessitate, force, bind. 2 HELP, assist, accommodate, do a favour, serve, gratify, please.

obliging adj accommodating, co-operative, helpful, considerate, agreeable, friendly, kind, civil.
≠ unhelpful.

oblique adj slanting, sloping, inclined, angled, tilted.

obliterate v eradicate, destroy, annihilate, delete, blot out, wipe out, erase.

oblivion n obscurity, nothingness, unconsciousness, void, limbo.
≠ awareness.

oblivious adj unaware, unconscious, inattentive, careless, heedless, blind, insensible, negligent.
≠ aware.

obnoxious adj unpleasant, disagreeable, disgusting, loathsome, nasty, horrid, odious, repulsive, revolting, repugnant, sickening, nauseating.
≠ pleasant.

obscene adj indecent, improper, immoral, impure, filthy, dirty, bawdy, lewd, licentious, pornographic, scurrilous, suggestive, disgusting, foul, shocking, shameless, offensive.
≠ decent, wholesome.

obscenity n 1 INDECENCY, immodesty, impurity, impropriety, lewdness, licentiousness, suggestiveness, pornography, dirtiness, filthiness, foulness, grossness, indelicacy, coarseness. 2 ATROCITY, evil, outrage, offence. 3 PROFANITY, expletive, swear-word, four-letter word.

obscure adj 1 UNKNOWN, unimportant, little-known, unheard-of, undistinguished, nameless, inconspicuous, humble, minor. 2 INCOMPREHENSIBLE, enigmatic, cryptic, recondite, esoteric, accrue, mysterious, deep, abstruse, confusing. 3 INDISTINCT, unclear, indefinite, shadowy, blurred, cloudy, faint, hazy, dim, misty, shady, vague, murky, gloomy, dusky.
≠ 1 famous, renowned. 2 intelligible, straightforward. 3 clear, definite.
v conceal, cloud, obfuscate, hide, cover, blur, disguise, mask, overshadow, shadow, shade, cloak, veil, shroud, darken, dim, eclipse, screen, block out.
≠ clarify, illuminate.

obsequious adj servile, ingratiating, grovelling, fawning, sycophantic, cringing, deferential, flattering, smarmy (*infml*), unctuous, oily, submissive, subservient, slavish.

observance n 1 ADHERENCE, compliance, observation, performance, obedience, fulfilment, honouring, notice, attention.

2 RITUAL, custom, ceremony, practice, celebration.

observant *adj* attentive, alert, vigilant, watchful, perceptive, eagle-eyed, wide-awake, heedful.
≠ unobservant.

observation *n* 1 ATTENTION, notice, examination, inspection, scrutiny, monitoring, study, watching, consideration, discernment. 2 REMARK, comment, utterance, thought, statement, pronouncement, reflection, opinion, finding, note.

observe *v* 1 WATCH, see, study, notice, contemplate, keep an eye on, perceive. 2 REMARK, comment, say, mention. 3 ABIDE BY, comply with, honour, keep, fulfil, celebrate, perform.
≠ 1 miss. 3 break, violate.

observer *n* watcher, spectator, viewer, witness, looker-on, onlooker, eyewitness, commentator, bystander, beholder.

obsess *v* preoccupy, dominate, rule, monopolize, haunt, grip, plague, prey on, possess.

obsession *n* preoccupation, fixation, idée fixe, ruling passion, compulsion, fetish, hang-up (*infml*), infatuation, mania, enthusiasm.

obsessive *adj* consuming, compulsive, gripping, fixed, haunting, tormenting, maddening.

obsolete *adj* outmoded, disused, out of date, old-fashioned, passé, dated, outworn, old, antiquated, antique, dead, extinct.
≠ modern, current, up-to-date.

obstacle *n* barrier, bar, obstruction, impediment, hurdle, hindrance, check, snag, stumbling-block, drawback, difficulty, hitch, catch, stop, interference, interruption.
≠ advantage, help.

obstinate *adj* stubborn, inflexible, immovable, intractable, pig-headed (*infml*), unyielding, intransigent,

persistent, dogged, headstrong, bloody-minded (*sl*), strong-minded, self-willed, steadfast, firm, determined, wilful.
≠ flexible, tractable.

obstruct *v* block, impede, hinder, prevent, check, frustrate, hamper, clog, choke, bar, barricade, stop, stall, retard, restrict, thwart, inhibit, hold up, curb, arrest, slow down, interrupt, interfere with, shut off, cut off, obscure.
≠ assist, further.

obstruction *n* barrier, blockage, bar, barricade, hindrance, impediment, check, stop, stoppage, difficulty.
≠ help.

obstructive *adj* hindering, delaying, blocking, stalling, unhelpful, awkward, difficult, restrictive, inhibiting.
≠ co-operative, helpful.

obtain *v* 1 ACQUIRE, get, gain, come by, attain, procure, secure, earn, achieve. 2 PREVAIL, exist, hold, be in force, be the case, stand, reign, rule, be prevalent.

obtrusive *adj* 1 PROMINENT, protruding, noticeable, obvious, blatant, forward. 2 INTRUSIVE, interfering, prying, meddling, nosey (*infml*), pushy (*infml*).
≠ 1 unobtrusive.

obtuse *adj* slow, stupid, thick (*infml*), dull, dense, crass, dumb (*infml*), stolid, dull-witted, thick-skinned.
≠ bright, sharp.

obvious *adj* evident, self-evident, manifest, patent, clear, plain, distinct, transparent, undeniable, unmistakable, conspicuous, glaring, apparent, open, unconcealed, visible, noticeable, perceptible, pronounced, recognizable, self-explanatory, straightforward, prominent.
≠ unclear, indistinct, obscure.

obviously *adv* plainly, clearly,

evidently, manifestly, undeniably, unmistakably, without doubt, certainly, distinctly, of course.

occasion n 1 EVENT, occurrence, incident, time, instance, chance, case, opportunity. 2 REASON, cause, excuse, justification, ground(s). 3 CELEBRATION, function, affair, party.

occasional adj periodic, intermittent, irregular, sporadic, infrequent, uncommon, incidental, odd, rare, casual.

≠ frequent, regular, constant.

occasionally adv sometimes, on occasion, from time to time, at times, at intervals, now and then, now and again, irregularly, periodically, every so often, once in a while, off and on, infrequently.

≠ frequently, often, always.

occult adj mystical, supernatural, magical, esoteric, mysterious, concealed, arcane, recondite, obscure, secret, hidden, veiled.

occupant n occupier, holder, inhabitant, resident, householder, tenant, user, lessee, squatter, inmate.

occupation n 1 JOB, profession, work, vocation, employment, trade, post, calling, business, line, pursuit, craft, walk of life, activity. 2 INVASION, seizure, conquest, control, takeover. 3 OCCUPANCY, possession, holding, tenancy, tenure, residence, habitation, use.

occupy v 1 INHABIT, live in, possess, reside in, stay in, take possession of, own. 2 ABSORB, take up, engross, engage, hold, involve, preoccupy, amuse, busy, interest. 3 INVADE, seize, capture, overrun, take over. 4 FILL, take up, use.

occur v happen, come about, take place, transpire, chance, come to pass, materialize, befall, develop, crop up, arise, appear, turn up, obtain, result, exist, be present, be found.

occurrence n 1 INCIDENT, event, happening, affair, circumstance, episode, instance, case, development, action. 2 INCIDENCE, existence, appearance, manifestation.

odd adj 1 UNUSUAL, strange, uncommon, peculiar, abnormal, exceptional, curious, atypical, different, queer, bizarre, eccentric, remarkable, unconventional, weird, irregular, extraordinary, outlandish, rare. 2 OCCASIONAL, incidental, irregular, random, casual. 3 UNMATCHED, unpaired, single, spare, surplus, left-over, remaining, sundry, various, miscellaneous.

≠ 1 normal, usual. 2 regular.

oddity n 1 ABNORMALITY, peculiarity, rarity, eccentricity, idiosyncrasy, phenomenon, quirk. 2 CURIOSITY, character, freak, misfit.

oddment n bit, scrap, left-over, fragment, offcut, end, remnant, shred, snippet, patch.

odds n 1 LIKELIHOOD, probability, chances. 2 ADVANTAGE, edge, lead, superiority.

odious adj offensive, loathsome, unpleasant, obnoxious, disgusting, hateful, repulsive, revolting, repugnant, foul, execrable, detestable, abhorrent, horrible, horrid, abominable.

≠ pleasant.

odour n smell, scent, fragrance, aroma, perfume, redolence, stench, stink (infml).

off adj 1 ROTTEN, bad, sour, turned, rancid, mouldy, decomposed. 2 CANCELLED, postponed. 3 AWAY, absent, gone. 4 SUBSTANDARD, below par, disappointing, unsatisfactory, slack.
adv away, elsewhere, out, at a distance, apart, aside.

off-colour adj indisposed, off form, under the weather, unwell, sick, out of sorts, ill, poorly.

offence n 1 MISDEMEANOUR, transgression, violation, wrong, wrong-doing, infringement, crime, misdeed, sin, trespass. 2 AFFRONT, insult, injury. 3 RESENTMENT, indignation, pique, umbrage, outrage, hurt, hard feelings.

offend v 1 HURT, insult, injure, affront, wrong, wound, displease, snub, upset, annoy, outrage.
2 DISGUST, repel, sicken.
3 TRANSGRESS, sin, violate, err.
🖝 1 please.

offender n transgressor, wrong-doer, culprit, criminal, miscreant, guilty party, law-breaker, delinquent.

offensive adj 1 DISAGREEABLE, unpleasant, objectionable, displeasing, disgusting, odious, obnoxious, repellent, repugnant, revolting, loathsome, vile, nauseating, nasty, detestable, abominable. 2 INSOLENT, abusive, rude, insulting, impertinent.
🖝 1 pleasant. 2 polite.
n attack, assault, onslaught, invasion, raid, sortie.

offer v 1 PRESENT, make available, advance, extend, put forward, submit, suggest, hold out, provide, sell. 2 PROFFER, propose, bid, tender. 3 VOLUNTEER, come forward, show willing (infml).
n proposal, bid, submission, tender, suggestion, proposition, overture, approach, attempt, presentation.

offering n present, gift, donation, contribution, subscription.

offhand adj casual, unconcerned, uninterested, take-it-or-leave-it (infml), brusque, abrupt, perfunctory, informal, cavalier, careless.
adv impromptu, off the cuff, extempore (fml), off the top of one's head, immediately.
🖝 calculated, planned.

office n 1 RESPONSIBILITY, duty, obligation, charge, commission, occupation, situation, post, employment, function, appointment, business, role, service.
2 WORKPLACE, workroom, bureau.

officer n official, office-holder, public servant, functionary, dignitary, bureaucrat, administrator, representative, executive, agent, appointee.

official adj authorized, authoritative, legitimate, formal, licensed, accredited, certified, approved, authenticated, authentic, bona fide, proper.
🖝 unofficial.
n office-bearer, officer, functionary, bureaucrat, executive, representative, agent.

Officials include: agent, ambassador, bailiff, bureaucrat, captain, chairman, chairwoman, chairperson, chancellor, chief, clerk, commander, commissar, commissioner, congressman, congresswoman, consul, coroner, councillor, delegate, diplomat, director, elder, envoy, equerry, Eurocrat, executive, Euro-MP, gauleiter, governor, hakim, inspector, justice of the peace (JP), magistrate, manager, mandarin, marshal, mayor, mayoress, member of parliament, minister, monitor, notary, ombudsman, overseer, prefect, president, principal, proctor, proprietor, public prosecutor, registrar, senator (*North Amer.*), sheriff, steward, superintendent, supervisor, usher.

---

officiate v preside, superintend, conduct, chair, manage, oversee, run.

officious adj obtrusive, dictatorial, intrusive, bossy (infml), interfering, meddlesome, over-zealous, self-important, pushy (infml), forward, bustling, importunate (fml).

offload v unburden, unload, jettison, dump, drop, deposit, get rid of, discharge.

off-putting *adj* intimidating, daunting, disconcerting, discouraging, disheartening, formidable, unnerving, unsettling, demoralizing, disturbing.

offset *v* counterbalance, compensate for, cancel out, counteract, make up for, balance out, neutralize.

offshoot *n* branch, outgrowth, limb, arm, development, spin-off, by-product, appendage.

offspring *n* child, children, young, issue, progeny (*fml*), brood, heirs, successors, descendants.
⊡ parent(s).

often *adv* frequently, repeatedly, regularly, generally, again and again, time after time, time and again, much.
⊡ rarely, seldom, never.

ogre *n* giant, monster, fiend, bogeyman, demon, devil, troll.

oil *v* grease, lubricate, anoint.

oily *adj* **1** GREASY, fatty. **2** UNCTUOUS, smooth, obsequious, ingratiating, smarmy (*infml*), glib, flattering.

ointment *n* salve, balm, cream, lotion, liniment, embrocation.

OK (*infml*) *adj* acceptable, all right, fine, permitted, in order, fair, satisfactory, reasonable, tolerable, passable, not bad, good, adequate, convenient, correct, accurate.
n authorization, approval, endorsement, go-ahead, permission, green light, consent, agreement.
v approve, authorize, pass, give the go-ahead to, give the green light to (*infml*), rubber-stamp, agree to.
interj all right, fine, very well, agreed, right, yes.

old *adj* **1** AGED, elderly, advanced in years, grey, senile. **2** ANCIENT, original, primitive, antiquated, mature. **3** LONG-STANDING, long-established, time-honoured, traditional. **4** OBSOLETE, old-

fashioned, out of date, worn-out, decayed, decrepit. **5** FORMER, previous, earlier, one-time, ex-.
⊡ 1 young. **2** new. **4** modern. **5** current.

old-fashioned *adj* outmoded, out of date, outdated, dated, unfashionable, obsolete, behind the times, antiquated, archaic, passé, obsolescent.
⊡ modern, up-to-date.

omen *n* portent, sign, warning, premonition, foreboding, augury, indication.

ominous *adj* portentous, inauspicious, foreboding, menacing, sinister, fateful, unpromising, threatening.
⊡ auspicious, favourable.

omission *n* exclusion, gap, oversight, failure, lack, neglect, default, avoidance.

omit *v* leave out, exclude, miss out, pass over, overlook, drop, skip, eliminate, forget, neglect, leave undone, fail, disregard, edit out.
⊡ include.

once *adv* formerly, previously, in the past, at one time, long ago, in times past, once upon a time, in the old days.
at once 1 IMMEDIATELY, instantly, directly, right away, straightaway, without delay, now, promptly, forthwith. **2** SIMULTANEOUSLY, together, at the same time.

oncoming *adj* approaching, advancing, upcoming, looming, onrushing, gathering.

one *adj* **1** SINGLE, solitary, lone, individual, only. **2** UNITED, harmonious, like-minded, whole, entire, complete, equal, identical, alike.

onerous (*fml*) *adj* oppressive, burdensome, demanding, laborious, hard, taxing, difficult, troublesome, exacting, exhausting, heavy, weighty.
⊡ easy, light.

one-sided *adj* **1** UNBALANCED, unequal, lopsided. **2** UNFAIR, unjust, prejudiced, biased, partial, partisan. **3** UNILATERAL, independent.
■ 1 balanced. **2** impartial. **3** bilateral, multilateral.

ongoing *adj* **1** CONTINUING, continuous, unbroken, uninterrupted, constant. **2** DEVELOPING, evolving, progressing, growing, in progress, unfinished, unfolding.

onlooker *n* bystander, observer, spectator, looker-on, eye-witness, witness, watcher, viewer.

only *adv* just, at most, merely, simply, purely, barely, exclusively, solely.
adj sole, single, solitary, lone, unique, exclusive, individual.

onset *n* **1** BEGINNING, start, commencement, inception, outset, outbreak. **2** ASSAULT, attack, onslaught, onrush.
■ 1 end, finish.

onslaught *n* attack, assault, offensive, charge, bombardment, blitz.

onus *n* burden, responsibility, load, obligation, duty, liability, task.

onward(s) *adv* forward, on, ahead, in front, beyond, forth.
■ backward(s).

ooze *v* seep, exude, leak, percolate, escape, dribble, drip, drop, discharge, bleed, secrete, emit, overflow with, filter, drain.

opaque *adj* **1** CLOUDY, clouded, murky, dull, dim, hazy, muddied, muddy, turbid. **2** OBSCURE, unclear, impenetrable, incomprehensible, unintelligible, enigmatic, difficult.
■ 1 transparent. **2** clear, obvious.

open *adj* **1** UNCLOSED, ajar, gaping, uncovered, unfastened, unlocked, unsealed, yawning, lidless. **2** UNRESTRICTED, free, unobstructed, clear, accessible, exposed, unprotected, unsheltered, vacant, wide, available. **3** OVERT, obvious, plain, evident, manifest, noticeable, flagrant, conspicuous. **4** UNDECIDED, unresolved, unsettled, debatable, problematic, moot. **5** FRANK, candid, honest, guileless, natural, ingenuous, unreserved.
■ 1 shut. **2** restricted. **3** hidden. **4** decided. **5** reserved.
v **1** UNFASTEN, undo, unlock, uncover, unseal, unblock, uncork, clear, expose. **2** EXPLAIN, divulge, disclose, lay bare. **3** EXTEND, spread (out), unfold, separate, split. **4** BEGIN, start, commence, inaugurate, initiate, set in motion, launch.
■ 1 close, shut. **2** hide. **4** end, finish.

open-air *adj* outdoor, alfresco.
■ indoor.

opening *n* **1** APERTURE, breach, gap, orifice, break, chink, crack, fissure, cleft, chasm, hole, split, vent, rupture. **2** START, onset, beginning, inauguration, inception, birth, dawn, launch. **3** OPPORTUNITY, chance, occasion, break (*infml*), place, vacancy.
■ 2 close, end.
adj beginning, commencing, starting, first, inaugural, introductory, initial, early, primary.
■ closing.

openly *adv* overtly, frankly, candidly, blatantly, flagrantly, plainly, unashamedly, unreservedly, glaringly, in public, in full view, shamelessly.
■ secretly, slyly.

operate *v* **1** *it operates on batteries*: function, act, perform, run, work, go. **2** *she can operate that machine*: control, handle, manage, use, utilize, manoeuvre.

operation *n* **1** FUNCTIONING, action, running, motion, movement, performance, working. **2** INFLUENCE, manipulation, handling, management, use, utilization. **3** UNDERTAKING,

optimum

enterprise, affair, procedure, proceeding, process, business, deal, transaction, effort. **4** CAMPAIGN, action, task, manoeuvre, exercise.

operational *adj* working, in working order, usable, functional, going, viable, workable, ready, prepared, in service.
🔁 out of order.

operative *adj* **1** OPERATIONAL, in operation, in force, functioning, active, effective, efficient, in action, workable, viable, serviceable, functional. **2** KEY, crucial, important, relevant, significant.
🔁 **1** inoperative, out of service.

opinion *n* belief, judgement, view, point of view, idea, perception, stance, theory, impression, feeling, sentiment, estimation, assessment, conception, mind, notion, way of thinking, persuasion, attitude.

opinionated *adj* dogmatic, doctrinaire, dictatorial, arrogant, inflexible, obstinate, stubborn, uncompromising, single-minded, prejudiced, biased, bigoted.
🔁 open-minded.

opponent *n* adversary, enemy, antagonist, foe, competitor, contestant, challenger, opposer, opposition, rival, objector, dissident.
🔁 ally.

opportunity *n* chance, opening, break (*infml*), occasion, possibility, hour, moment.

oppose *v* **1** RESIST, withstand, counter, attack, combat, contest, stand up to, take a stand against, take issue with, confront, defy, face, fight, fly in the face of, hinder, obstruct, bar, check, prevent, thwart. **2** COMPARE, contrast, match, offset, counterbalance, play off.
🔁 **1** defend, support.

opposed *adj* in opposition, against, hostile, conflicting, opposing, opposite, antagonistic, clashing, contrary, incompatible, anti.
🔁 in favour.

opposite *adj* **1** FACING, fronting, corresponding. **2** OPPOSED, antagonistic, conflicting, contrary, hostile, adverse, contradictory, antithetical, irreconcilable, unlike, reverse, inconsistent, different, contrasted, differing.
🔁 **2** same.
n reverse, converse, contrary, antithesis, contradiction, inverse.
🔁 same.

opposition *n* **1** ANTAGONISM, hostility, resistance, obstructiveness, unfriendliness, disapproval. **2** OPPONENT, antagonist, rival, foe, other side.
🔁 **1** co-operation, support. **2** ally, supporter.

oppress *v* **1** BURDEN, afflict, lie heavy on, harass, depress, sadden, torment, vex. **2** SUBJUGATE, suppress, subdue, overpower, overwhelm, crush, trample, tyrannize, persecute, maltreat, abuse.

oppression *n* tyranny, subjugation, subjection, repression, despotism, suppression, injustice, cruelty, brutality, abuse, persecution, maltreatment, harshness, hardship.

oppressive *adj* **1** AIRLESS, stuffy, close, stifling, suffocating, sultry, muggy, heavy. **2** TYRANNICAL, despotic, overbearing, overwhelming, repressive, harsh, unjust, inhuman, cruel, brutal, burdensome, onerous, intolerable.
🔁 **1** airy. **2** just, gentle.

oppressor *n* tyrant, bully, taskmaster, slave-driver, despot, dictator, persecutor, tormentor, intimidator, autocrat.

optimistic *adj* confident, assured, sanguine, hopeful, positive, cheerful, buoyant, bright, idealistic, expectant.
🔁 pessimistic.

optimum *adj* best, ideal, perfect, optimal, superlative, top, choice.
🔁 worst.

option *n* choice, alternative, preference, possibility, selection.

optional *adj* voluntary, discretionary, elective, free, unforced. 🔁 compulsory.

oral *adj* verbal, spoken, unwritten, vocal. 🔁 written.

orbit *n* **1** CIRCUIT, cycle, circle, course, path, trajectory, track, revolution, rotation. **2** RANGE, scope, domain, influence, sphere of influence, compass.

v revolve, circle, encircle, circumnavigate.

ordeal *n* trial, test, tribulation(s), affliction, trouble(s), suffering, anguish, agony, pain, persecution, torture, nightmare.

order *n* **1** COMMAND, directive, decree, injunction, instruction, direction, edict, ordinance, mandate, regulation, rule, precept, law. **2** REQUISITION, request, booking, commission, reservation, application, demand. **3** ARRANGEMENT, organization, grouping, disposition, sequence, categorization, classification, method, pattern, plan, system, array, layout, line-up, structure. **4** PEACE, quiet, calm, tranquillity, harmony, law and order, discipline. **5** ASSOCIATION, society, community, fraternity, brotherhood, sisterhood, lodge, guild, company, organization, denomination, sect, union. **6** CLASS, kind, sort, type, rank, species, hierarchy, family. 🔁 **3** confusion, disorder. **4** anarchy.

v **1** COMMAND, instruct, direct, bid, decree, require, authorize. **2** REQUEST, reserve, book, apply for, requisition. **3** ARRANGE, organize, dispose, classify, group, marshal, sort out, lay out, manage, control, catalogue.

out of order **1** BROKEN, broken down, not working, inoperative.

2 DISORDERED, disorganized, out of sequence. **3** UNSEEMLY, improper, un-called-for, incorrect, wrong.

orderly *adj* **1** ORDERED, systematic, neat, tidy, regular, methodical, in order, well-organized, well-regulated. **2** WELL-BEHAVED, controlled, disciplined, law-abiding. 🔁 **1** chaotic. **2** disorderly.

ordinary *adj* common, commonplace, regular, routine, standard, average, everyday, run-of-the-mill, usual, unexceptional, unremarkable, typical, normal, customary, common-or-garden, plain, familiar, habitual, simple, conventional, modest, mediocre, indifferent, pedestrian, prosaic, undistinguished. 🔁 extraordinary, unusual.

organ *n* **1** DEVICE, instrument, implement, tool, element, process, structure, unit, member. **2** MEDIUM, agency, forum, vehicle, voice, mouthpiece, publication, newspaper, periodical, journal.

organic *adj* natural, biological, living, animate.

organization *n* **1** ASSOCIATION, institution, society, company, firm, corporation, federation, group, league, club, confederation, consortium. **2** ARRANGEMENT, system, classification, methodology, order, formation, grouping, method, plan, structure, pattern, composition, configuration, design.

organize *v* **1** STRUCTURE, co-ordinate, arrange, order, group, marshal, classify, systematize, tabulate, catalogue. **2** ESTABLISH, found, set up, develop, form, frame, construct, shape, run. 🔁 **1** disorganize.

orgy *n* debauch, carousal, revelry, bout, bacchanalia, indulgence, excess, spree.

orientation *n* **1** SITUATION, bearings, location, direction, position, alignment, placement, attitude. **2** INITIATION, training, acclimatization, familiarization, adaptation, adjustment, settling in.

origin n **1** SOURCE, spring, fount, foundation, base, cause, derivation, provenance, roots, well-spring. **2** BEGINNING, commencement, start, inauguration, launch, dawning, creation, emergence. **3** ANCESTRY, descent, extraction, heritage, family, lineage, parentage, pedigree, birth, paternity, stock.

F3 2 end, termination.

original adj **1** FIRST, early, earliest, initial, primary, archetypal, rudimentary, embryonic, starting, opening, commencing, first-hand. **2** NOVEL, innovative, new, creative, fresh, imaginative, inventive, unconventional, unusual, unique.

F3 1 latest. 2 hackneyed, unoriginal. n prototype, master, paradigm, model, pattern, archetype, standard, type.

originate v **1** RISE, arise, spring, stem, issue, flow, proceed, derive, come, evolve, emerge, be born. **2** CREATE, invent, inaugurate, introduce, give birth to, develop, discover, establish, begin, commence, start, set up, launch, pioneer, conceive, form, produce, generate.

F3 1 end, terminate.

ornament n decoration, adornment, embellishment, garnish, trimming, accessory, frill, trinket, bauble, jewel. v decorate, adorn, embellish, garnish, trim, beautify, brighten, dress up, deck, gild.

ornamental adj decorative, embellishing, adorning, attractive, showy.

ornate adj elaborate, ornamented, fancy, decorated, baroque, rococo, florid, flowery, fussy, busy, sumptuous.

F3 plain.

orthodox adj conformist, conventional, accepted, official,

traditional, usual, well-established, established, received, customary, conservative, recognized, authoritative.

F3 nonconformist, unorthodox.

ostensible adj alleged, apparent, presumed, seeming, supposed, so-called, professed, outward, pretended, superficial.

F3 real.

ostentatious adj showy, flashy, pretentious, vulgar, loud, garish, gaudy, flamboyant, conspicuous, extravagant.

F3 restrained.

ostracize v exclude, banish, exile, expel, excommunicate, reject, segregate, send to Coventry, shun, snub, boycott, avoid, cold-shoulder (infml), cut.

F3 accept, welcome.

other adj **1** DIFFERENT, dissimilar, unlike, separate, distinct, contrasting. **2** MORE, further, extra, additional, supplementary, spare, alternative.

oust v expel, eject, depose, displace, turn out, throw out, overthrow, evict, drive out, unseat, dispossess, disinherit, replace, topple.

F3 install, settle.

out adj **1** AWAY, absent, elsewhere, not at home, gone, outside, abroad. **2** REVEALED, exposed, disclosed, public, evident, manifest. **3** FORBIDDEN, unacceptable, impossible, disallowed, excluded. **4** OUT OF DATE, unfashionable, old-fashioned, dated, passé, antiquated. **5** EXTINGUISHED, finished, expired, dead, used up.

F3 1 in. 2 concealed. 3 allowed. 4 up to date.

outbreak n eruption, outburst, explosion, flare-up, upsurge, flash, rash, burst, epidemic.

outburst n outbreak, eruption, explosion, flare-up, outpouring, burst, fit, gush, surge, storm, spasm, seizure, gale, attack, fit of temper.

outcast n castaway, exile, pariah, outsider, untouchable, refugee, reject, persona non grata.

outcome n result, consequence, upshot, conclusion, effect, end result.

outcry n protest, complaint, protestation, objection, dissent, indignation, uproar, cry, exclamation, clamour, row, commotion, noise, hue and cry, hullaballoo (*infml*), outburst.

outdated adj out of date, old-fashioned, dated, unfashionable, outmoded, behind the times, obsolete, obsolescent, antiquated, archaic.
ε∃ fashionable, modern.

outdo v surpass, exceed, beat, excel, outstrip, outshine, get the better of, overcome, outclass, outdistance.

outdoor adj out-of-door(s), outside, open-air.
ε∃ indoor.

outer adj 1 EXTERNAL, exterior, outside, outward, surface, superficial, peripheral. 2 OUTLYING, distant, remote, further.
ε∃ 1 internal. 2 inner.

outfit n 1 CLOTHES, costume, ensemble, get-up (*infml*), togs (*infml*), garb. 2 EQUIPMENT, gear (*infml*), kit, rig, trappings, paraphernalia. 3 (*infml*) ORGANIZATION, firm, business, corporation, company, group, team, unit, set, set-up, crew, gang, squad.

outgoing adj 1 SOCIABLE, friendly, unreserved, amiable, warm, approachable, expansive, open, extrovert, cordial, easy-going, communicative, demonstrative, sympathetic. 2 DEPARTING, retiring, former, last, past, ex-.
ε∃ 1 reserved. 2 incoming.

outing n excursion, expedition, jaunt, pleasure trip, trip, spin, picnic.

outlandish adj unconventional, unfamiliar, bizarre, strange, odd, weird, eccentric, alien, exotic,

barbarous, foreign, extraordinary.
ε∃ familiar, ordinary.

outlaw n bandit, brigand, robber, desperado, highwayman, criminal, marauder, pirate, fugitive.
v ban, disallow, forbid, prohibit, exclude, embargo, bar, debar, banish, condemn.
ε∃ allow, legalize.

outlay n expenditure, expenses, outgoings, disbursement (*fml*), cost, spending.
ε∃ income.

outlet n 1 EXIT, way out, vent, egress, escape, opening, release, safety valve, channel. 2 RETAILER, shop, store, market.
ε∃ 1 entry, inlet.

outline n 1 SUMMARY, synopsis, précis, bare facts, sketch, thumbnail sketch, abstract. 2 PROFILE, form, contour, silhouette, shape.
v sketch, summarize, draft, trace, rough out.

outlook n 1 VIEW, viewpoint, point of view, attitude, perspective, frame of mind, angle, slant, standpoint, opinion. 2 EXPECTATIONS, future, forecast, prospect, prognosis.

outlying adj distant, remote, far-off, far-away, far-flung, outer, provincial.
ε∃ inner.

out-of-the-way adj remote, isolated, far-flung, far-off, far-away, distant, inaccessible, little-known, obscure, unfrequented.

output n production, productivity, product, yield, manufacture, achievement.

outrage n 1 ANGER, fury, rage, indignation, shock, affront, horror. 2 ATROCITY, offence, injury, enormity, barbarism, crime, violation, evil, scandal.
v anger, infuriate, affront, incense, enrage, madden, disgust, injure, offend, shock, scandalize.

outrageous adj 1 ATROCIOUS, abominable, shocking, scandalous,

over

offensive, disgraceful, monstrous, heinous, unspeakable, horrible.
2 EXCESSIVE, exorbitant, immoderate, unreasonable, extortionate, inordinate, preposterous.
Ez 2 acceptable, reasonable.

outright *adj* total, utter, absolute, complete, downright, out-and-out, unqualified, unconditional, perfect, pure, thorough, direct, definite, categorical, straightforward.
Ez ambiguous, indefinite.
adv **1** TOTALLY, absolutely, completely, utterly, thoroughly, openly, without restraint, straightforwardly, positively, directly, explicitly. **2** *killed outright*: instantaneously, at once, there and then, instantly, immediately.

outset *n* start, beginning, opening, inception, commencement, inauguration, kick-off (*infml*).
Ez end, conclusion.

outside *adj* **1** EXTERNAL, exterior, outer, surface, superficial, outward, extraneous, outdoor, outermost, extreme. **2** *an outside chance*: remote, marginal, distant, faint, slight, slim, negligible.
Ez 1 inside.
n exterior, façade, front, surface, face, appearance, cover.
Ez inside.

outsider *n* stranger, intruder, alien, non-member, non-resident, foreigner, newcomer, visitor, intruder, interloper, misfit, odd man out.

outskirts *n* suburbs, vicinity, periphery, fringes, borders, boundary, edge, margin.
Ez centre.

outspoken *adj* candid, frank, forthright, blunt, unreserved, plain-spoken, direct, explicit.
Ez diplomatic, reserved.

outstanding *adj* **1** EXCELLENT, distinguished, eminent, pre-eminent, celebrated, exceptional, superior, remarkable, prominent, superb,

great, notable, impressive, striking, superlative, important, noteworthy, memorable, special, extraordinary. **2** OWING, unpaid, due, unsettled, unresolved, uncollected, pending, payable, remaining, ongoing, leftover.
Ez 1 ordinary, unexceptional. **2** paid, settled.

outstrip *v* surpass, exceed, better, outdo, beat, top, transcend, outshine, pass, gain on, leave behind, leave standing, outrun, outdistance, overtake, eclipse.

outward *adj* external, exterior, outer, outside, surface, superficial, visible, apparent, observable, evident, supposed, professed, public, obvious, ostensible.
Ez inner, private.

outwardly *adv* apparently, externally, to all appearances, visibly, superficially, supposedly, seemingly, on the surface, at first sight.

outweigh *v* override, prevail over, overcome, take precedence over, cancel out, make up for, compensate for, predominate.

outwit *v* outsmart, outthink, get the better of, trick, better, beat, dupe, cheat, deceive, defraud, swindle.

outworn *adj* outdated, out of date, outmoded, stale, discredited, defunct, old-fashioned, hackneyed, rejected, obsolete, disused, exhausted.
Ez fresh, new.

oval *adj* egg-shaped, elliptical, ovoid, ovate.

ovation *n* applause, acclaim, acclamation, praises, plaudits (*fml*), tribute, clapping, cheering, bravos.
Ez abuse, catcalls.

over *adj* finished, ended, done with, concluded, past, gone, completed, closed, in the past, settled, up, forgotten, accomplished.
adv **1** ABOVE, beyond, overhead, on high. **2** EXTRA, remaining, surplus, superfluous, left, unclaimed, unused,

unwanted, in excess, in addition.
prep **1** ABOVE, on, on top of, upon,
in charge of, in command of.
2 EXCEEDING, more than, in excess
of.

overact *v* overplay, exaggerate,
overdo, ham (*infml*).
◼ underact, underplay.

overall *adj* total, all-inclusive, all-
embracing, comprehensive, inclusive,
general, universal, global, broad,
blanket, complete, all-over.
◼ narrow, specific.
adv in general, on the whole, by and
large, broadly, generally speaking.

overbearing *adj* imperious,
domineering, arrogant, dictatorial,
tyrannical, high-handed, haughty,
bossy (*infml*), cavalier, autocratic,
oppressive.
◼ meek, unassertive.

overcast *adj* cloudy, grey, dull,
dark, sombre, sunless, hazy,
lowering.
◼ bright, clear.

overcharge *v* surcharge, short-
change, cheat, extort, rip off (*infml*),
sting (*infml*), do (*infml*), diddle
(*infml*).
◼ undercharge.

overcome *v* conquer, defeat, beat,
surmount, triumph over, vanquish,
rise above, master, overpower,
overwhelm, overthrow, subdue.

overcrowded *adj* congested, packed
(out), jam-packed, crammed full,
chock-full, overpopulated,
overloaded, swarming.
◼ deserted, empty.

overdo *v* exaggerate, go too far,
carry to excess, go overboard (*infml*),
lay it on thick (*infml*), overindulge,
overstate, overact, overplay,
overwork.

overdue *adj* late, behindhand,
behind schedule, delayed, owing,
unpunctual, slow.
◼ early.

overeat *v* gorge, binge, overindulge,

guzzle, stuff oneself, make a pig of
oneself, pig out (*infml*), gormandize.
◼ abstain, starve.

overflow *v* spill, overrun, run over,
pour over, well over, brim over,
bubble over, surge, flood, inundate,
deluge, shower, submerge, soak,
swamp, teem.
n overspill, spill, inundation, flood,
overabundance, surplus.

overhang *v* jut, project, bulge,
protrude, stick out, extend.

overhaul *v* **1** RENOVATE, repair,
service, recondition, mend, examine,
inspect, check, survey, re-examine,
fix. **2** OVERTAKE, pull ahead of,
outpace, outstrip, gain on, pass.
n reconditioning, repair, renovation,
check, service, examination,
inspection, going-over (*infml*).

overhead *adv* above, up above, on
high, upward.
◼ below, underfoot.
adj elevated, aerial, overhanging,
raised.

overjoyed *adj* delighted, elated,
euphoric, ecstatic, in raptures,
enraptured, thrilled, jubilant, over
the moon (*infml*).
◼ sad, disappointed.

overload *v* burden, oppress, strain,
tax, weigh down, overcharge,
encumber.

overlook *v* **1** FRONT ON TO, face,
look on to, look over, command a
view of. **2** MISS, disregard, ignore,
omit, neglect, pass over, let pass, let
ride, slight. **3** EXCUSE, forgive,
pardon, condone, wink at, turn a
blind eye to.
◼ **2** notice. **3** penalize.

overpower *v* overcome, conquer,
overwhelm, vanquish, defeat, beat,
subdue, overthrow, quell, master,
crush, immobilize, floor.

overpowering *adj* overwhelming,
powerful, strong, forceful,
irresistible, uncontrollable,
compelling, extreme, oppressive,

suffocating, unbearable, nauseating, sickening.

overrate v overestimate, overvalue, overpraise, magnify, blow up, make too much of.
Fa underrate.

overrule v overturn, override, countermand, revoke, reject, rescind, reverse, invalidate, cancel, vote down.

overrun v **1** INVADE, occupy, infest, overwhelm, inundate, run riot, spread over, swamp, swarm over, surge over, ravage, overgrow. **2** EXCEED, overshoot, overstep, overreach.

overseer n supervisor, boss (*infml*), chief, foreman, forewoman, manager, superintendent.

overshadow v **1** OBSCURE, cloud, darken, dim, spoil, veil. **2** OUTSHINE, eclipse, excel, surpass, dominate, dwarf, put in the shade, rise above, tower above.

oversight n **1** LAPSE, omission, fault, error, slip-up, mistake, blunder, carelessness, neglect. **2** SUPERVISION, responsibility, care, charge, control, custody, keeping, administration, management, direction.

overt adj open, manifest, plain, evident, observable, obvious, apparent, public, professed, unconcealed.
Fa covert, secret.

overtake v **1** PASS, catch up with, outdistance, outstrip, draw level with, pull ahead of, overhaul. **2** COME UPON, befall, happen, strike, engulf.

overthrow v depose, oust, bring down, topple, unseat, displace, dethrone, conquer, vanquish, beat, defeat, crush, overcome, overpower, overturn, overwhelm, subdue, master, abolish, upset.
Fa install, protect, reinstate, restore.
n ousting, unseating, defeat,

deposition, dethronement, fall, rout, undoing, suppression, downfall, end, humiliation, destruction, ruin.

overtone n suggestion, intimation, nuance, hint, undercurrent, insinuation, connotation, association, feeling, implication, sense, flavour.

overture n **1** APPROACH, advance, offer, invitation, proposal, proposition, suggestion, signal, move, motion. **2** PRELUDE, opening, introduction, opening move, (opening) gambit.

overturn v **1** CAPSIZE, upset, upturn, tip over, topple, overbalance, keel over, knock over, spill. **2** OVERTHROW, repeal, rescind, reverse, annul, abolish, destroy, quash, set aside.

overwhelm v **1** OVERCOME, overpower, destroy, defeat, crush, rout, devastate. **2** OVERRUN, inundate, snow under, submerge, swamp, engulf. **3** CONFUSE, bowl over, stagger, floor.

overwork v overstrain, overload, exploit, exhaust, overuse, overtax, strain, wear out, oppress, burden, weary.

overwrought adj tense, agitated, keyed up, on edge, worked up, wound up, frantic, overcharged, overexcited, excited, beside oneself, uptight (*infml*).
Fa calm.

owing adj unpaid, due, owed, in arrears, outstanding, payable, unsettled, overdue.

owing to because of, as a result of, on account of, thanks to.

own adj personal, individual, private, particular, idiosyncratic.
v possess, have, hold, retain, keep, enjoy.

own up admit, confess, come clean (*infml*), tell the truth, acknowledge.

owner n possessor, holder, landlord, landlady, proprietor, proprietress, master, mistress, freeholder.

P

pace n step, stride, walk, gait, tread, movement, motion, progress, rate, speed, velocity, celerity, quickness, rapidity, tempo, measure.
v step, stride, walk, march, tramp, pound, patrol, mark out, measure.

pacifist n peace-lover, pacificist, conscientious objector, peacemaker, peace-monger, dove.
🖃 warmonger, hawk.

pacify v appease, conciliate, placate, mollify, calm, compose, soothe, assuage, allay, moderate, soften, lull, still, quiet, silence, quell, crush, put down, tame, subdue.
🖃 anger.

pack n 1 PACKET, box, carton, parcel, package, bundle, burden, load, backpack, rucksack, haversack, knapsack, kitbag. 2 GROUP, company, troop, herd, flock, band, crowd, gang, mob.
v 1 WRAP, parcel, package, bundle, stow, store. 2 FILL, load, charge, cram, stuff, crowd, throng, press, ram, wedge, compact, compress.

package n parcel, pack, packet, box, carton, bale, consignment.
v parcel (up), wrap (up), pack (up), box, batch.

packed adj filled, full, jam-packed, chock-a-block, crammed, crowded, congested.
🖃 empty, deserted.

packet n pack, carton, box, bag, package, parcel, case, container, wrapper, wrapping, packing.

pact n treaty, convention, covenant, bond, alliance, cartel, contract, deal, bargain, compact, agreement, arrangement, understanding.
🖃 disagreement, quarrel.

pad n 1 CUSHION, pillow, wad, buffer, padding, protection.
2 WRITING-PAD, note-pad, jotter, block.
v fill, stuff, wad, pack, wrap, line, cushion, protect.

pad out expand, inflate, fill out, augment, amplify, elaborate, flesh out, lengthen, stretch, protract, spin out.

padding n 1 FILLING, stuffing, wadding, packing, protection.
2 VERBIAGE, verbosity, wordiness, waffle (*infml*), bombast, hot air.

paddle¹ n oar, scull.
v row, oar, scull, propel, steer.

paddle² v wade, splash, slop, dabble.

pagan n heathen, atheist, unbeliever, infidel, idolater.
🖃 believer.
adj heathen, irreligious, atheistic, godless, infidel, idolatrous.

page¹ n leaf, sheet, folio, side.

page² n page-boy, attendant, messenger, bell-boy, footman, servant.
v call, send for, summon, bid, announce.

pageant n procession, parade, show, display, tableau, scene, play, spectacle, extravaganza.

pageantry n pomp, ceremony, grandeur, magnificence, splendour, glamour, glitter, spectacle, parade, display, show, extravagance, theatricality, drama, melodrama.

pain n 1 HURT, ache, throb, cramp, spasm, twinge, pang, stab, sting, smart, soreness, tenderness, discomfort, distress, suffering, affliction, trouble, anguish, agony, torment, torture. 2 (*infml*)

NUISANCE, bother, bore (*infml*), annoyance, vexation, burden, headache (*infml*).

v hurt, afflict, torment, torture, agonize, distress, upset, sadden, grieve.

⯍ please, delight, gratify.

pained *adj* hurt, injured, wounded, stung, offended, aggrieved, reproachful, distressed, upset, saddened, grieved.

⯍ pleased, gratified.

painful *adj* **1** SORE, tender, aching, throbbing, smarting, stabbing, agonizing, excruciating. **2** *a painful experience*: unpleasant, disagreeable, distressing, upsetting, saddening, harrowing, traumatic. **3** HARD, difficult, laborious, tedious.

⯍ **1** painless, soothing. **2** pleasant, agreeable. **3** easy.

pain-killer *n* analgesic, anodyne, anaesthetic, palliative, sedative, drug, remedy.

painless *adj* pain-free, trouble-free, effortless, easy, simple, undemanding.

⯍ painful, difficult.

pains *n* trouble, bother, effort, labour, care, diligence.

painstaking *adj* careful, meticulous, scrupulous, thorough, conscientious, diligent, assiduous, industrious, hardworking, dedicated, devoted, persevering.

⯍ careless, negligent.

paint *n* colour, colouring, pigment, dye, tint, stain.

Paints include: acrylic paint, colourwash, distemper, eggshell, emulsion, enamel, gloss paint, gouache, glaze, lacquer, masonry paint, matt paint, oil paint, oils, pastel, poster paint, primer, undercoat, varnish, watercolour, whitewash.

---

v **1** COLOUR, dye, tint, stain, lacquer,

varnish, glaze, apply, daub, coat, cover, decorate. **2** PORTRAY, depict, describe, recount, picture, represent.

painting *n* oil painting, oil, watercolour, picture, portrait, landscape, still life, miniature, illustration, fresco, mural.

pair *n* couple, brace, twosome, duo, twins, two of a kind.

v match (up), twin, team, mate, marry, wed, splice, join, couple, link, bracket, put together.

⯍ separate, part.

palace *n* castle, château, mansion, stately home, basilica, dome.

palatable *adj* tasty, appetizing, eatable, edible, acceptable, satisfactory, pleasant, agreeable, enjoyable, attractive.

⯍ unpalatable, unacceptable, unpleasant, disagreeable.

palate *n* taste, appreciation, liking, relish, enjoyment, appetite, stomach, heart.

palatial *adj* grand, magnificent, splendid, majestic, regal, stately, grandiose, imposing, luxurious, de luxe, sumptuous, opulent, plush, spacious.

pale *adj* **1** PALLID, livid, ashen, ashy, white, chalky, pasty, pasty-faced, waxen, waxy, wan, sallow, anaemic. **2** *pale blue*: light, pastel, faded, washed-out, bleached, colourless, insipid, vapid, weak, feeble, faint, dim.

⯍ **1** ruddy. **2** dark.

v whiten, blanch, bleach, fade, dim.

⯍ colour, blush.

pall[1] *n* shroud, veil, mantle, cloak, cloud, shadow, gloom, damper.

pall[2] *v* tire, weary, jade, sate, satiate, cloy, sicken.

palm *n* hand, paw (*infml*), mitt (*sl*).

v take, grab, snatch, appropriate.

palm off foist, impose, fob off, offload, unload, pass off.

palpable *adj* solid, substantial, material, real, touchable, tangible visible, apparent, clear, plain, obvious, evident, manifest, conspicuous, blatant, unmistakable. 🔁 impalpable, imperceptible, intangible, elusive.

palpitate v flutter, quiver, tremble, shiver, vibrate, beat, pulsate, pound, thump, throb.

paltry adj meagre, derisory, contemptible, mean, low, miserable, wretched, poor, sorry, small, slight, trifling, inconsiderable, negligible, trivial, minor, petty, unimportant, insignificant, worthless. 🔁 substantial, significant, valuable.

pamper v cosset, coddle, mollycoddle, humour, gratify, indulge, overindulge, spoil, pet, fondle. 🔁 neglect, ill-treat.

pamphlet n leaflet, brochure, booklet, folder, circular, handout, notice.

pan n saucepan, frying-pan, pot, casserole, container, vessel.

panache n flourish, flamboyance, ostentation, style, flair, élan, dash, spirit, enthusiasm, zest, energy, vigour, verve.

pandemonium n chaos, disorder, confusion, commotion, rumpus, turmoil, turbulence, tumult, uproar, din, bedlam, hubbub, hullabaloo, hue and cry, to-do (*infml*). 🔁 order, calm, peace.

pander to humour, indulge, pamper, please, gratify, satisfy, fulfil, provide, cater to.

panel n board, committee, jury, team.

pang n pain, ache, twinge, stab, sting, prick, stitch, gripe, spasm, throe, agony, anguish, discomfort, distress.

panic n agitation, flap (*infml*), alarm, dismay, consternation, fright, fear, horror, terror, frenzy, hysteria. 🔁 calmness, confidence.
v lose one's nerve, lose one's head, go

to pieces, flap (*infml*), overreact. 🔁 relax.

panic-stricken adj alarmed, frightened, horrified, terrified, petrified, scared stiff, in a cold sweat, panicky, frantic, frenzied, hysterical. 🔁 relaxed, confident.

panorama n view, vista, prospect, scenery, landscape, scene, spectacle, perspective, overview, survey.

panoramic adj scenic, wide, sweeping, extensive, far-reaching, widespread, overall, general, universal. 🔁 narrow, restricted, limited.

pant v puff, blow, gasp, wheeze, breathe, sigh, heave, throb, palpitate.

pants n 1 UNDERPANTS, drawers, panties, briefs, knickers (*infml*), Y-fronts, boxer shorts, trunks, shorts. 2 TROUSERS, slacks, jeans.

paper n 1 NEWSPAPER, daily, broadsheet, tabloid, rag (*sl*), journal, organ. 2 DOCUMENT, credential, authorization, identification, certificate, deed. 3 *a paper on alternative medicine*: essay, composition, dissertation, thesis, treatise, article, report.

Types of paper include: art paper, bank, blotting paper, bond, carbon paper, cartridge paper, crêpe paper, greaseproof paper, graph paper, manila, notepaper, parchment, rice paper, silver paper, sugar paper, tissue paper, toilet paper, tracing paper, vellum, wallpaper, wrapping paper, writing-paper; card, cardboard, pasteboard; A4, foolscap, quarto, atlas, crown.

---

parable n fable, allegory, lesson, moral tale, story.

parade n procession, cavalcade, motorcade, march, column, file, train, review, ceremony, spectacle, pageant, show, display, exhibition.
v 1 MARCH, process, file past.

2 SHOW, display, exhibit, show off, vaunt, flaunt, brandish.

paradise n heaven, Utopia, Shangri-La, Elysium, Eden, bliss, delight.
Ea hell, Hades.

paradox n contradiction, inconsistency, incongruity, absurdity, oddity, anomaly, mystery, enigma, riddle, puzzle.

paradoxical adj self-contradictory, contradictory, conflicting, inconsistent, incongruous, absurd, illogical, improbable, impossible, mysterious, enigmatic, puzzling, baffling.

paragon n ideal, exemplar, epitome, quintessence, model, pattern, archetype, prototype, standard, criterion.

paragraph n passage, section, part, portion, subsection, subdivision, clause, item.

parallel adj equidistant, aligned, coextensive, alongside, analogous, equivalent, corresponding, matching, like, similar, resembling.
Ea divergent, different.
n **1** MATCH, equal, twin, duplicate, analogue, equivalent, counterpart.
2 SIMILARITY, resemblance, likeness, correspondence, correlation, equivalence, analogy, comparison.
v match, echo, conform, agree, correspond, correlate, compare, liken.
Ea diverge, differ.

paralyse v cripple, lame, disable, incapacitate, immobilize, anaesthetize, numb, deaden, freeze, transfix, halt, stop.

paralysed adj paralytic, paraplegic, quadriplegic, crippled, lame, disabled, incapacitated, immobilized, numb.
Ea able-bodied.

paralysis n paraplegia, quadriplegia, palsy, numbness, deadness, immobility, halt, standstill, stoppage, shutdown.

parameter n variable, guideline, indication, criterion, specification, limitation, restriction, limit, boundary.

paramount adj supreme, highest, topmost, predominant, pre-eminent, prime, principal, main, chief, cardinal, primary, first, foremost.
Ea lowest, last.

paraphernalia n equipment, gear, tackle, apparatus, accessories, trappings, bits and pieces, odds and ends, belongings, effects, stuff, things, baggage.

paraphrase n rewording, rephrasing, restatement, version, interpretation, rendering, translation.
v reword, rephrase, restate, interpret, render, translate.

parasite n sponger, scrounger, cadger, hanger-on, leech, bloodsucker.

parcel n package, packet, pack, box, carton, bundle.
v package, pack, wrap, bundle, tie up.

parcel out divide, carve up, apportion, allocate, allot, share out, distribute, dispense, dole out, deal out, mete out.

parch v dry (up), desiccate, dehydrate, bake, burn, scorch, sear, blister, wither, shrivel.

parched adj **1** ARID, waterless, dry, dried up, dehydrated, scorched, withered, shrivelled. **2** (infml) THIRSTY, gasping (infml).

pardon v forgive, condone, overlook, excuse, vindicate, acquit, absolve, remit, let off, reprieve, free, liberate, release.
Ea punish, discipline.
n forgiveness, mercy, clemency, indulgence, amnesty, excuse, acquittal, absolution, reprieve, release, discharge.
Ea punishment, condemnation.

pardonable adj forgivable, excusable, justifiable, warrantable, understandable, allowable,

pare 382

permissible, minor, venial.
🔁 inexcusable.

pare *v* peel, skin, shear, clip, trim, crop, cut, dock, lop, prune, cut back, reduce, decrease.

parent *n* father, mother, dam, sire, progenitor, begetter, procreator, guardian.

parish *n* district, community, parishioners, church, churchgoers, congregation, flock, fold.

park *n* grounds, estate, parkland, gardens, woodland, reserve, pleasure-ground.
v put, position, deposit, leave.

parliament *n* legislature, senate, congress, house, assembly, convocation, council, diet.

parliaments and political assemblies

Names of parliaments and political assemblies include: House of Representatives, Senate (Australia); Nationalrat, Bundesrat (Austria); Narodno Sobraniye (Bulgaria); House of Commons, Senate (Canada); National People's Congress (China); Folketing (Denmark); People's Assembly (Egypt); Eduskunta (Finland); National Assembly, Senate (France); Bundesrat, Bundestag, Landtag (Germany); Althing (Iceland); Lok Sabha, Rajya Sabha (India); Majlis (Iran); Dáil, Seanad (Ireland); Knesset (Israel); Camera dei Deputati, Senato (Italy); Diet (Japan); Staten-Generaal (Netherlands); House of Representatives (New Zealand); Storting (Norway); Sejm (Poland); Cortes (Portugal); State Duma, Federation Council (Russia); House of Assembly (South Africa); Cortes (Spain); Riksdag (Sweden); Nationalrat, Ständerat, Bundesrat (Switzerland); Porte (Turkey); House of Commons, House of Lords (UK); House of Representatives, Senate (US); National Assembly (Vietnam).

parliamentary *adj* governmental, senatorial, congressional, legislative, law-making.

parochial *adj* insular, provincial, parish-pump, petty, small-minded, narrow-minded, inward-looking, blinkered, limited, restricted, confined.
🔁 national, international.

parody *n* caricature, lampoon, burlesque, satire, send-up, spoof, skit, mimicry, imitation, take-off, travesty, distortion.
v caricature, lampoon, burlesque, satirize, send up, spoof, mimic, imitate, ape, take off.

paroxysm *n* fit, seizure, spasm, convulsion, attack, outbreak, outburst, explosion.

parry *v* ward off, fend off, repel, repulse, field, deflect, block, avert, avoid, evade, duck, dodge, sidestep, shun.

parson *n* vicar, rector, priest, minister, pastor, preacher, clergyman, reverend, cleric, churchman.

part *n* **1** COMPONENT, constituent, element, factor, piece, bit, particle, fragment, scrap, segment, fraction, portion, share, section, division, department, branch, sector, district, region, territory. **2** ROLE, character, duty, task, responsibility, office, function, capacity.
🔁 **1** whole, totality.
v separate, detach, disconnect, sever, split, tear, break, break up, take apart, dismantle, come apart, split up, divide, disunite, part company, disband, disperse, scatter, leave, depart, withdraw, go away.

part with relinquish, let go of, give up, yield, surrender, renounce, forgo, abandon, discard, jettison.

partial *adj* **1** *a partial victory*: incomplete, limited, restricted,

imperfect, fragmentary, unfinished.
2 BIASED, prejudiced, partisan, one-sided, discriminatory, unfair, unjust, predisposed, coloured, affected.
☒ **1** complete, total. **2** impartial, disinterested, unbiased, fair.
partial to fond of, keen on, crazy about (*infml*), mad about (*infml*).

partiality *n* liking, fondness, predilection (*fml*), proclivity, inclination, preference, predisposition.

participant *n* entrant, contributor, participator, member, party, co-operator, helper, worker.

participate *v* take part, join in, contribute, engage, be involved, enter, share, partake, co-operate, help, assist.

participation *n* involvement, sharing, partnership, co-operation, contribution, assistance.

particle *n* bit, piece, fragment, scrap, shred, sliver, speck, morsel, crumb, iota, whit, jot, tittle, atom, grain, drop.

particular *adj* **1** *on that particular day*: specific, precise, exact, distinct, special, peculiar. **2** EXCEPTIONAL, remarkable, notable, marked, thorough, unusual, uncommon.
3 FUSSY, discriminating, choosy (*infml*), finicky, fastidious.
☒ **1** general.
n detail, specific, point, feature, item, fact, circumstance.

particularly *adv* especially, exceptionally, remarkably, notably, extraordinarily, unusually, uncommonly, surprisingly, in particular, specifically, explicitly, distinctly.

parting *n* **1** DEPARTURE, going, leave-taking, farewell, goodbye, adieu. **2** DIVERGENCE, separation, division, partition, rift, split, rupture, breaking.
☒ **1** meeting. **2** convergence.
adj departing, farewell, last, dying,

final, closing, concluding.
☒ first.

partisan *n* devotee, adherent, follower, disciple, backer, supporter, champion, stalwart, guerrilla, irregular.
adj biased, prejudiced, partial, predisposed, discriminatory, one-sided, factional, sectarian.
☒ impartial.

partition *n* **1** DIVIDER, barrier, wall, panel, screen, room-divider.
2 DIVISION, break-up, splitting, separation, parting, severance.
v **1** SEPARATE, divide, subdivide, wall off, fence off, screen. **2** SHARE, divide, split up, parcel out.

partly *adv* somewhat, to some extent, to a certain extent, up to a point, slightly, fractionally, moderately, relatively, in part, partially, incompletely.
☒ completely, totally.

partner *n* associate, ally, confederate, colleague, team-mate, collaborator, accomplice, helper, mate, sidekick (*infml*), oppo (*infml*), companion, comrade, consort, spouse, husband, wife.

partnership *n* **1** ALLIANCE, confederation, affiliation, combination, union, syndicate, co-operative, association, society, corporation, company, firm, fellowship, fraternity, brotherhood.
2 COLLABORATION, co-operation, participation, sharing.

party *n* **1** CELEBRATION, festivity, social, do (*infml*), knees-up (*sl*), rave-up (*sl*), get-together, gathering, reunion, function, reception, at-home, housewarming. **2** *a search party*: team, squad, crew, gang, band, group, company, detachment.
3 *a political party*: faction, side, league, cabal, alliance, association, grouping, combination. **4** PERSON, individual, litigant, plaintiff, defendant.

> *Types of party include*: acid-house
> party, barbecue, bash (*sl*), beanfeast
> (*infml*), beano (*infml*), birthday
> party, bunfight (*infml*), ceilidh,
> dinner party, disco, discotheque, do
> (*infml*), flatwarming, garden party,
> gathering of the clan (*infml*),
> Hallowe'en party, hen party, hooley,
> hootnanny (*North Amer. infml*),
> housewarming, orgy, picnic, pyjama
> party, rave, rave-up (*sl*), social,
> soirée, stag party, stag night, supper
> party, tea party, thrash (*infml*),
> welcoming party.

pass¹ *v* 1 SURPASS, exceed, go
beyond, outdo, outstrip, overtake,
leave behind. 2 *pass time*: spend,
while away, fill, occupy. 3 GO PAST,
go by, elapse, lapse, proceed, roll,
flow, run, move, go, disappear,
vanish. 4 GIVE, hand, transfer,
transmit. 5 ENACT, ratify, validate,
adopt, authorize, sanction, approve.
6 *pass an exam*: succeed, get through,
qualify, graduate.
n 1 THROW, kick, move, lunge,
swing. 2 PERMIT, passport,
identification, ticket, licence,
authorization, warrant, permission.
pass away die, pass on, expire,
decease, give up the ghost.
pass off 1 FEIGN, counterfeit, fake,
palm off. 2 HAPPEN, occur, take place,
go off.
pass out 1 FAINT, lose consciousness,
black out, collapse, flake out, keel over
(*infml*), drop. 2 GIVE OUT, hand out,
dole out, distribute, deal out, share out.
pass over disregard, ignore, overlook,
miss, omit, leave, neglect.
pass² *n* col, defile, gorge, ravine,
canyon, gap, passage.
passable *adj* 1 SATISFACTORY,
acceptable, allowable, tolerable,
average, ordinary, unexceptional,
moderate, fair, adequate, all right,
OK (*infml*), mediocre. 2 CLEAR,

unobstructed, unblocked, open,
navigable.
ЕⱫ 1 unacceptable, excellent.
2 obstructed, blocked, impassable.
passage *n* 1 PASSAGEWAY, aisle,
corridor, hall, hallway, lobby,
vestibule, doorway, opening,
entrance, exit. 2 THOROUGHFARE,
way, route, road, avenue, path, lane,
alley. 3 EXTRACT, excerpt,
quotation, text, paragraph, section,
piece, clause, verse. 4 JOURNEY,
voyage, trip, crossing.
passenger *n* traveller, voyager,
commuter, rider, fare, hitch-hiker.
passer-by *n* bystander, witness,
looker-on, onlooker, spectator.
passing *adj* ephemeral, transient,
short-lived, temporary, momentary,
fleeting, brief, short, cursory, hasty,
quick, slight, superficial, shallow,
casual, incidental.
ЕⱫ lasting, permanent.
passion *n* feeling, emotion, love,
adoration, infatuation, fondness,
affection, lust, itch, desire, craving,
fancy, mania, obsession, craze,
eagerness, keenness, avidity, zest,
enthusiasm, fanaticism, zeal, ardour,
fervour, warmth, heat, fire, spirit,
intensity, vehemence, anger,
indignation, fury, rage, outburst.
ЕⱫ coolness, indifference, self-
possession.
passionate *adj* 1 ARDENT, fervent,
eager, keen, avid, enthusiastic,
fanatical, zealous, warm, hot, fiery,
inflamed, aroused, excited,
impassioned, intense, strong, fierce,
vehement, violent, stormy,
tempestuous, wild, frenzied.
2 EMOTIONAL, excitable, hot-
headed, impetuous, impulsive, quick-
tempered, irritable. 3 LOVING,
affectionate, lustful, erotic, sexy,
sensual, sultry.
ЕⱫ 1 phlegmatic, laid back (*infml*).
3 frigid.
passive *adj* receptive, unassertive,

385

pathetic

submissive, docile, unresisting, non-violent, patient, resigned, long-suffering, indifferent, apathetic, lifeless, inert, inactive, non-participating.

F3 active, lively, responsive, involved.

past adj **1** OVER, ended, finished, completed, done, over and done with. **2** FORMER, previous, preceding, foregoing, late, recent. **3** ANCIENT, bygone, olden, early, gone, no more, extinct, defunct, forgotten.

F3 2 future.

n **1** in the past: history, former times, olden days, antiquity. **2** LIFE, background, experience, track record.

F3 1 future.

pasta

Forms and shapes of pasta include: agnolotti, anelli, angel's hair, bombolotti, bucatini, cannelloni, capelletti, casarecci, conchiglie, crescioni, ditali, elbow macaroni, farfalline, fedelini, fettuccine, fiochetti, fusilli, gnocchi, lasagne, lasagne verde, linguini, lumache, macaroni, mafalde, manicotti, maruzze, mezzani, noodle, noodle farfel, penne, pennine, ravioli, rigatoni, ruoti, spaghetti, spaghetti bolognese, stelline, tagliatelle, tortellini, trofie, vermicelli, ziti.

paste n adhesive, glue, gum, mastic, putty, cement.

v stick, glue, gum, cement, fix.

pastel adj delicate, soft, soft-hued, light, pale, subdued, faint.

pastime n hobby, activity, game, sport, recreation, play, fun, amusement, entertainment, diversion, distraction, relaxation.

F3 work, employment.

pastoral adj **1** RURAL, country, rustic, bucolic, agricultural, agrarian, idyllic. **2** ECCLESIASTICAL, clerical, priestly, ministerial.

F3 1 urban.

pastry

Types of pastry include: American crust pastry, biscuit-crumb pastry, cheese pastry, choux, Danish pastry, filo pastry, flaky pastry, flan pastry, hot-water crust pastry, one-stage pastry, pâte à savarin, pâte brisée, pâte frolle, pâte sablée, pâte sucrée, plain pastry, pork-pie pastry, puff pastry, rich shortcrust pastry, rough-puff pastry, short pastry, shortcrust pastry, suetcrust pastry, sweet pastry.

pasture n grass, grassland, meadow, field, paddock, pasturage, grazing.

pasty adj pale, pallid, wan, anaemic, pasty-faced, sickly, unhealthy.

F3 ruddy, healthy.

pat v tap, dab, slap, touch, stroke, caress, fondle, pet.

n tap, dab, slap, touch, stroke, caress.

adv precisely, exactly, perfectly, flawlessly, faultlessly, fluently.

F3 imprecisely, inaccurately, wrongly.

adj glib, fluent, smooth, slick, ready, easy, facile, simplistic.

patch n piece, bit, scrap, spot, area, stretch, tract, plot, lot, parcel.

v mend, repair, fix, cover, reinforce.

patchy adj uneven, irregular, inconsistent, variable, random, fitful, erratic, sketchy, bitty, spotty, blotchy.

F3 even, uniform, regular, consistent.

patent adj obvious, evident, conspicuous, manifest, clear, transparent, apparent, visible, palpable, unequivocal, open, overt, blatant, flagrant, glaring.

F3 hidden, opaque.

path n route, course, direction, way, passage, road, avenue, lane, footpath, bridleway, trail, track, walk.

pathetic adj **1** PITIABLE, poor, sorry, lamentable, miserable, sad, distressing, moving, touching, poignant, plaintive, heart-rending,

heartbreaking. **2** (*infml*)
CONTEMPTIBLE, derisory,
deplorable, useless, worthless,
inadequate, meagre, feeble.
F3 1 cheerful. **2** admirable, excellent,
valuable.

patience *n* calmness, composure,
self-control, restraint, tolerance,
forbearance, endurance, fortitude,
long-suffering, submission,
resignation, stoicism, persistence,
perseverance, diligence.
F3 impatience, intolerance,
exasperation.

patient *adj* calm, composed, self-
possessed, self-controlled, restrained,
even-tempered, mild, lenient,
indulgent, understanding, forgiving,
tolerant, accommodating, forbearing,
long-suffering, uncomplaining,
submissive, resigned, philosophical,
stoical, persistent, persevering.
F3 impatient, restless, intolerant,
exasperated.
n invalid, sufferer, case, client.

patriotic *adj* nationalistic,
chauvinistic, jingoistic, loyal, flag-
waving.

patrol *n* **1** GUARD, sentry, sentinel,
watchman. **2** *on patrol*: watch,
surveillance, policing, protection,
defence.
v police, guard, protect, defend, go
the rounds, tour, inspect.

patron *n* **1** BENEFACTOR,
philanthropist, sponsor, backer,
supporter, sympathizer, advocate,
champion, defender, protector,
guardian, helper. **2** CUSTOMER,
client, frequenter, regular, shopper,
buyer, purchaser, subscriber.

patronage *n* custom, business,
trade, sponsorship, backing, support.

patronize *v* **1** SPONSOR, fund, back,
support, maintain, help, assist,
promote, foster, encourage. **2**
FREQUENT, shop at, buy from, deal
with.

patronizing *adj* condescending,

stooping, overbearing, high-handed,
haughty, superior, snobbish,
supercilious, disdainful.
F3 humble, lowly.

patter *v* tap, pat, pitter-patter, beat,
pelt, scuttle, scurry.
n **1** PATTERING, tapping, pitter-
patter, beating. **2** *a salesman's patter*:
chatter, gabble, jabber, line, pitch,
spiel (*sl*), jargon, lingo (*infml*).

pattern *n* **1** SYSTEM, method, order,
plan. **2** DECORATION,
ornamentation, ornament, figure,
motif, design, style. **3** MODEL,
template, stencil, guide, original,
prototype, standard, norm.

patterned *adj* decorated,
ornamented, figured, printed.
F3 plain.

paunch *n* abdomen, belly, pot-belly,
beer-belly, corporation (*infml*).

pause *v* halt, stop, cease,
discontinue, break off, interrupt, take
a break, rest, wait, delay, hesitate.
n halt, stoppage, interruption, break,
rest, breather (*infml*), lull, let-up
(*infml*), respite, gap, interval, interlude,
intermission, wait, delay, hesitation.

pave *v* flag, tile, floor, surface,
cover, asphalt, tarmac, concrete.

paw *v* maul, manhandle, mishandle,
molest.
n foot, pad, forefoot, hand.

pawn[1] *n* dupe, puppet, tool,
instrument, toy, plaything.

pawn[2] *v* deposit, pledge, stake,
mortgage, hock (*sl*), pop (*sl*).

pay *v* **1** REMIT, settle, discharge,
reward, remunerate, recompense,
reimburse, repay, refund, spend, pay
out. **2** BENEFIT, profit, pay off, bring
in, yield, return. **3** ATONE, make
amends, compensate, answer, suffer.
n remuneration, wages, salary,
earnings, income, fee, stipend,
honorarium, emoluments, payment,
reward, recompense, compensation,
reimbursement.

pay back 1 REPAY, refund, reimburse,

recompense, settle, square.
2 RETALIATE, get one's own back, take revenge, get even with, reciprocate, counter-attack.
pay off 1 DISCHARGE, settle, square, clear. **3** *the preparations paid off*: succeed, work.
pay out spend, disburse, hand over, fork out (*infml*), shell out (*infml*), lay out.
payable *adj* owed, owing, unpaid, outstanding, in arrears, due, mature.
payment *n* remittance, settlement, discharge, premium, outlay, advance, deposit, instalment, contribution, donation, allowance, reward, remuneration, pay, fee, hire, fare, toll.
peace *n* **1** SILENCE, quiet, hush, stillness, rest, relaxation, tranquillity, calm, calmness, composure, contentment. **2** ARMISTICE, truce, cease-fire, conciliation, concord, harmony, agreement, treaty.
1 noise, disturbance. **2** war, disagreement.
peaceable *adj* pacific, peace-loving, unwarlike, non-violent, conciliatory, friendly, amicable, inoffensive, gentle, placid, easy-going (*infml*), mild.
belligerent, aggressive.
peaceful *adj* quiet, still, restful, relaxing, tranquil, serene, calm, placid, unruffled, undisturbed, untroubled, friendly, amicable, peaceable, pacific, gentle.
noisy, disturbed, troubled, violent.
peacemaker *n* appeaser, conciliator, mediator, arbitrator, intercessor, peace-monger, pacifist.
peak *n* top, summit, pinnacle, crest, crown, zenith, height, maximum, climax, culmination, apex, tip, point.
nadir, trough.
v climax, culminate, come to a head.
peal *n* chime, carillon, toll, knell, ring, clang, ringing, reverberation, rumble, roar, crash, clap.
v chime, toll, ring, clang, resonate, reverberate, resound, rumble, roll, roar, crash.
peasant *n* rustic, provincial, yokel, bumpkin, oaf, boor, lout.
peculiar *adj* **1** *a peculiar sound*: strange, odd, curious, funny, weird, bizarre, extraordinary, unusual, abnormal, exceptional, unconventional, offbeat, eccentric, way-out (*sl*), outlandish, exotic.
2 CHARACTERISTIC, distinctive, specific, particular, special, individual, personal, idiosyncratic, unique, singular.
1 ordinary, normal. **2** general.
peculiarity *n* oddity, bizarreness, abnormality, exception, eccentricity, quirk, mannerism, feature, trait, mark, quality, attribute, characteristic, distinctiveness, particularity, idiosyncrasy.
pedantic *adj* stilted, fussy, particular, precise, exact, punctilious, hair-splitting, nit-picking, finical, academic, bookish, erudite.
imprecise, informal, casual.
peddle *v* sell, vend, flog (*infml*), hawk, tout, push, trade, traffic, market.
pedestal *n* plinth, stand, support, mounting, foot, base, foundation, platform, podium.
pedestrian *n* walker, foot-traveller.
adj dull, boring, flat, uninspired, banal, mundane, run-of-the-mill, commonplace, ordinary, mediocre, indifferent, prosaic, stodgy, plodding.
exciting, imaginative.
pedigree *n* genealogy, family tree, lineage, ancestry, descent, line, family, parentage, derivation, extraction, race, breed, stock, blood.
peel *v* pare, skin, strip, scale, flake (off).
n skin, rind, zest, peeling.
peep *v* look, peek, glimpse, spy, squint, peer, emerge, issue, appear.

n look, peek, glimpse, glance, squint.

peephole *n* spyhole, keyhole, pinhole, hole, opening, aperture, slit, chink, crack, fissure, cleft, crevice.

peer¹ *v* look, gaze, scan, scrutinize, examine, inspect, spy, snoop, peep, squint.

peer² *n* **1** ARISTOCRAT, noble, nobleman, lord, duke, marquess, marquis, earl, count, viscount, baron. **2** EQUAL, counterpart, equivalent, match, fellow.

peerage *n* aristocracy, nobility, upper crust.

peeress *n* aristocrat, noble, noblewoman, lady, dame, duchess, marchioness, countess, viscountess, baroness.

peevish *adj* petulant, querulous, fractious, fretful, touchy, irritable, cross, grumpy, ratty (*infml*), crotchety, ill-tempered, crabbed, cantankerous, crusty, snappy, short-tempered, surly, sullen, sulky.
F3 good-tempered.

peg *v* **1** FASTEN, secure, fix, attach, join, mark. **2** *peg prices*: control, stabilize, limit, freeze, fix, set.
n pin, dowel, hook, knob, marker, post, stake.

pejorative *adj* derogatory, disparaging, belittling, slighting, unflattering, uncomplimentary, unpleasant, bad, negative.
F3 complimentary.

pelt *v* **1** THROW, hurl, bombard, shower, assail, batter, beat, hit, strike. **2** POUR, teem, rain cats and dogs (*infml*). **3** RUSH, hurry, charge, belt (*infml*), tear, dash, speed, career.

pen¹ *n* fountain-pen, ballpoint, Biro®, felt-tip pen.
v write, compose, draft, scribble, jot down.

pen² *n* enclosure, fold, stall, sty, coop, cage, hutch.
v enclose, fence, hedge, hem in, confine, cage, coop, shut up.

penalize *v* punish, discipline,

correct, fine, handicap.
F3 reward.

penalty *n* punishment, retribution, fine, forfeit, handicap, disadvantage.
F3 reward.

penance *n* atonement, reparation, punishment, penalty, mortification.

pendant *n* medallion, locket, necklace.

pending *adj* impending, in the offing, forthcoming, imminent, undecided, in the balance.
F3 finished, settled.

penetrate *v* pierce, stab, prick, puncture, probe, sink, bore, enter, infiltrate, permeate, seep, pervade, suffuse.

penetrating *adj* piercing, stinging, biting, incisive, sharp, keen, acute, shrewd, discerning, perceptive, observant, profound, deep, searching, probing.
F3 blunt.

penitence *n* repentance, contrition, remorse, regret, shame, self-reproach.

penitent *adj* repentant, contrite, sorry, apologetic, remorseful, regretful, conscience-stricken, shamefaced, humble.
F3 unrepentant, hard-hearted, callous.

penniless *adj* poor, poverty-stricken, impoverished, destitute, bankrupt, ruined, bust, broke (*infml*), stony-broke (*sl*).
F3 rich, wealthy, affluent.

pension *n* annuity, superannuation, allowance, benefit.

pensive *adj* thoughtful, reflective, contemplative, meditative, ruminative, absorbed, preoccupied, absent-minded, wistful, solemn, serious, sober.
F3 carefree.

pent-up *adj* repressed, inhibited, restrained, bottled-up, suppressed, stifled.

people *n* persons, individuals, humans, human beings, mankind,

humanity, folk, public, general
public, populace, rank and file,
population, inhabitants, citizens,
community, society, race, nation.
v populate, inhabit, occupy, settle,
colonize.

pep (*infml*) *n* energy, vigour, verve,
spirit, vitality, liveliness, get-up-and-
go (*infml*), exuberance, high spirits.

pep up (*infml*) invigorate, vitalize,
liven up, quicken, stimulate, excite,
exhilarate, inspire.
☒ tone down.

perceive *v* **1** SEE, discern, make out,
detect, discover, spot, catch sight of,
notice, observe, view, remark, note,
distinguish, recognize. **2** SENSE, feel,
apprehend, learn, realize, appreciate,
be aware of, know, grasp,
understand, gather, deduce,
conclude.

perceptible *adj* perceivable,
discernible, detectable, appreciable,
distinguishable, observable,
noticeable, obvious, evident,
conspicuous, clear, plain, apparent,
visible.
☒ imperceptible, inconspicuous.

perception *n* sense, feeling,
impression, idea, conception,
apprehension, awareness,
consciousness, observation,
recognition, grasp, understanding,
insight, discernment, taste.

perceptive *adj* discerning,
observant, sensitive, responsive,
aware, alert, quick, sharp, astute,
shrewd.
☒ unobservant.

perch *v* land, alight, settle, sit, roost,
balance, rest.

percolate *v* filter, strain, seep, ooze,
leak, drip, penetrate, permeate,
pervade.

peremptory *adj* imperious,
commanding, dictatorial, autocratic,
authoritative, assertive, high-handed,
overbearing, domineering, bossy
(*infml*), abrupt, curt, summary,

arbitrary.

perennial *adj* lasting, enduring,
everlasting, eternal, immortal,
undying, imperishable, unceasing,
incessant, never-ending, constant,
continual, uninterrupted, perpetual,
persistent, unfailing.

perfect *adj* **1** FAULTLESS,
impeccable, flawless, immaculate,
spotless, blameless, pure, superb,
excellent, matchless, incomparable.
2 EXACT, precise, accurate, right,
correct, true. **3** IDEAL, model,
exemplary, ultimate, consummate,
expert, accomplished, experienced,
skilful. **4** *perfect strangers*: utter,
absolute, sheer, complete, entire,
total.
☒ **1** imperfect, flawed, blemished.
2 inaccurate, wrong. **3** inexperienced,
unskilled.
v fulfil, consummate, complete,
finish, polish, refine, elaborate.
☒ spoil, mar.

perfection *n* faultlessness,
flawlessness, excellence, superiority,
ideal, model, paragon, crown,
pinnacle, acme, consummation,
completion.
☒ imperfection, flaw.

perfectionist *n* idealist, purist,
pedant, stickler.

perfectly *adv* **1** UTTERLY,
absolutely, quite, thoroughly,
completely, entirely, wholly, totally,
fully. **2** FAULTLESSLY, flawlessly,
impeccably, ideally, exactly,
correctly.
☒ **1** partially. **2** imperfectly, badly.

perforate *v* hole, punch, drill, bore,
pierce, prick, stab, puncture,
penetrate.

perforation *n* hole, bore, prick,
puncture, dotted line.

perform *v* **1** DO, carry out, execute,
discharge, fulfil, satisfy, complete,
achieve, accomplish, bring off, pull
off, effect, bring about. **2** *perform a
play*: stage, put on, present, enact,

represent, act, play, appear as.
3 FUNCTION, work, operate, behave,
produce.

performance *n* **1** SHOW, act, play,
appearance, gig (*sl*), presentation,
production, interpretation, rendition,
representation, portrayal, acting.
2 ACTION, deed, doing, carrying out,
execution, implementation,
discharge, fulfilment, completion,
achievement, accomplishment.
3 FUNCTIONING, operation,
behaviour, conduct.

> *Types of performance include*: act,
> audition, benefit, box-office hit,
> bomb (*North Amer. colloq.*), charity
> concert, commandperformance,
> concert, début, dress rehearsal, dry
> run, encore, entertainment,
> exhibition, farewell performance, first
> house, firstnight, flop (*colloq.*), full
> house, gala night, gig, last night, last
> night at the Proms, matinée, one-
> night stand, opening night, play, pop
> concert, première, preview,
> production, readthrough, recital,
> rehearsal, rendition, runthrough,
> second house, sell-out, shortrun,
> show, sketch, smash hit (*colloq.*),
> sneak preview, theatre, turn. *see also*
> **theatrical**.

performer *n* actor, actress, player,
artiste, entertainer.
perfume *n* scent, fragrance, smell,
odour, aroma, bouquet, sweetness,
balm, essence, cologne, toilet water,
incense.
perhaps *adv* maybe, possibly,
conceivably, feasibly.
peril *n* danger, hazard, risk,
jeopardy, uncertainty, insecurity,
threat, menace.
E3 safety, security.
perilous *adj* dangerous, unsafe,
hazardous, risky, chancy, precarious,
insecure, unsure, vulnerable,
exposed, menacing, threatening, dire.

E3 safe, secure.
perimeter *n* circumference, edge,
border, boundary, frontier, limit,
bounds, confines, fringe, margin,
periphery.
E3 middle, centre, heart.
period *n* era, epoch, age, generation,
date, years, time, term, season, stage,
phase, stretch, turn, session, interval,
space, span, spell, cycle.
periodic *adj* occasional, infrequent,
sporadic, intermittent, recurrent,
repeated, regular, periodical,
seasonal.
periodical *n* magazine, journal,
publication, weekly, monthly,
quarterly.
peripheral *adj* **1** MINOR, secondary,
incidental, unimportant, irrelevant,
unnecessary, marginal, borderline,
surface, superficial. **2** OUTLYING,
outer, outermost.
E3 1 major, crucial. **2** central.
perish *v* rot, decay, decompose,
disintegrate, crumble, collapse, fall,
die, expire, pass away.
perishable *adj* destructible,
biodegradable, decomposable, short-
lived.
E3 imperishable, durable.
perk (*infml*) *n* perquisite, fringe
benefit, benefit, bonus, dividend,
gratuity, tip, extra, plus (*infml*).
perk up (*infml*) brighten, cheer up,
buck up (*infml*), revive, liven up, pep up
(*infml*), rally, recover, improve, look
up.
permanence *n* fixedness, stability,
imperishability, perpetuity,
constancy, endurance, durability.
E3 impermanence, transience.
permanent *adj* fixed, stable,
unchanging, imperishable,
indestructible, unfading, eternal,
everlasting, lifelong, perpetual,
constant, steadfast, perennial, long-
lasting, lasting, enduring, durable.
E3 temporary, ephemeral, fleeting.
permeable *adj* porous, absorbent,

absorptive, penetrable.

🖅 impermeable, watertight.

permeate v pass through, soak through, filter through, seep through, penetrate, infiltrate, pervade, imbue, saturate, impregnate, fill.

permissible adj permitted, allowable, allowed, admissible, all right, acceptable, proper, authorized, sanctioned, lawful, legal, legitimate.

🖅 prohibited, banned, forbidden.

permission n consent, assent, agreement, approval, go-ahead, green light (infml), authorization, sanction, leave, warrant, permit, licence, dispensation, freedom, liberty.

🖅 prohibition.

permissive adj liberal, broad-minded, tolerant, forbearing, lenient, easy-going (infml), indulgent, overindulgent, lax, free.

🖅 strict, rigid.

permit v allow, let, consent, agree, admit, grant, authorize, sanction, warrant, license.

🖅 prohibit, forbid.

n pass, passport, visa, licence, warrant, authorization, sanction, permission.

🖅 prohibition.

perpendicular adj vertical, upright, erect, straight, sheer, plumb.

🖅 horizontal.

perpetrate v commit, carry out, execute, do, perform, inflict, wreak.

perpetual adj eternal, everlasting, infinite, endless, unending, never-ending, interminable, ceaseless, unceasing, incessant, continuous, uninterrupted, constant, persistent, continual, repeated, recurrent, perennial, permanent, lasting, enduring, abiding, unchanging.

🖅 intermittent, temporary, ephemeral, transient.

perpetuate v continue, keep up, maintain, preserve, keep alive, immortalize, commemorate.

perplex v puzzle, baffle, mystify, stump, confuse, muddle, confound, bewilder, dumbfound.

persecute v hound, pursue, hunt, bother, worry, annoy, pester, harass, molest, abuse, ill-treat, maltreat, oppress, tyrannize, victimize, martyr, distress, afflict, torment, torture, crucify.

🖅 pamper, spoil.

persecution n harassment, molestation, abuse, maltreatment, discrimination, oppression, subjugation, suppression, tyranny, punishment, torture, martyrdom.

perseverance n persistence, determination, resolution, doggedness, tenacity, diligence, assiduity, dedication, commitment, constancy, steadfastness, stamina, endurance, indefatigability.

persevere v continue, carry on, stick at it (infml), keep going, soldier on, persist, plug away (infml), remain, stand firm, stand fast, hold on, hang on.

🖅 give up, stop, discontinue.

persist v remain, linger, last, endure, abide, continue, carry on, keep at it, persevere, insist.

🖅 desist, stop.

persistent adj **1** INCESSANT, endless, never-ending, interminable, continuous, unrelenting, relentless, unremitting, constant, steady, continual, repeated, perpetual, lasting, enduring. **2** persistent effort: persevering, determined, resolute, dogged, tenacious, stubborn, obstinate, steadfast, zealous, tireless, unflagging, indefatigable.

person n individual, being, human being, human, man, woman, body, soul, character, type.

personal adj own, private, confidential, intimate, special, particular, individual, exclusive, idiosyncratic, distinctive.

🖅 public, general, universal.

personality n 1 CHARACTER,
nature, disposition, temperament,
individuality, psyche, traits, make-
up, charm, charisma, magnetism.
2 CELEBRITY, notable, personage,
public figure, VIP (*infml*), star.

personify v embody, epitomize,
typify, exemplify, symbolize,
represent, mirror.

personnel n staff, workforce,
workers, employees, crew, human
resources, manpower, people,
members.

perspective n aspect, angle, slant,
attitude, standpoint, viewpoint, point
of view, view, vista, scene, prospect,
outlook, proportion, relation.

perspiration n sweat, secretion,
moisture, wetness.

perspire v sweat, exude, secrete,
swelter, drip.

persuade v coax, prevail upon, lean
on, cajole, wheedle, inveigle, talk
into, induce, bring round, win over,
convince, convert, sway, influence,
lead on, incite, prompt, urge.
E₃ dissuade, deter, discourage.

persuasion n 1 COAXING, cajolery,
wheedling, inducement, enticement,
pull, power, influence, conviction,
conversion. 2 OPINION, school (of
thought), party, faction, side,
conviction, faith, belief,
denomination, sect.

persuasive adj convincing,
plausible, cogent, sound, valid,
influential, forceful, weighty,
effective, telling, potent, compelling,
moving, touching.
E₃ unconvincing.

pertinent adj appropriate, suitable,
fitting, apt, apposite, relevant, to the
point, material, applicable.
E₃ inappropriate, unsuitable,
irrelevant.

perturb v disturb, bother, trouble,
upset, worry, alarm, disconcert,
unsettle, discompose, ruffle, fluster,
agitate, vex.

E₃ reassure, compose.

peruse v study, pore over, read,
browse, look through, scan,
scrutinize, examine, inspect, check.

pervade v affect, penetrate,
permeate, percolate, charge, fill,
imbue, infuse, suffuse, saturate,
impregnate.

pervasive adj prevalent, common,
extensive, widespread, general,
universal, inescapable, omnipresent,
ubiquitous.

perverse adj contrary, wayward,
wrong-headed, wilful, headstrong,
stubborn, obstinate, unyielding,
intransigent, disobedient, rebellious,
troublesome, unmanageable, ill-
tempered, cantankerous,
unreasonable, incorrect, improper.
E₃ obliging, co-operative, reasonable.

perversion n 1 CORRUPTION,
depravity, debauchery, immorality,
vice, wickedness, deviance, kinkiness
(*infml*), abnormality. 2 TWISTING,
distortion, misrepresentation,
travesty, misinterpretation,
aberration, deviation, misuse,
misapplication.

pervert v 1 *pervert the truth*: twist,
warp, distort, misrepresent, falsify,
garble, misinterpret. 2 CORRUPT,
lead astray, deprave, debauch,
debase, degrade, abuse, misuse,
misapply.
n deviant, debauchee, degenerate,
weirdo (*infml*).

perverted adj twisted, warped,
distorted, deviant, kinky (*infml*),
unnatural, abnormal, unhealthy,
corrupt, depraved, debauched,
debased, immoral, evil, wicked.
E₃ natural, normal.

pessimistic adj negative, cynical,
fatalistic, defeatist, resigned,
hopeless, despairing, despondent,
dejected, downhearted, glum,
morose, melancholy, depressed,
dismal, gloomy, bleak.
E₃ optimistic.

pest *n* nuisance, bother, annoyance, irritation, vexation, trial, curse, scourge, bane, plague, blight, bug.

pester *v* nag, badger, hound, hassle (*infml*), harass, plague, torment, provoke, worry, bother, disturb, annoy, irritate, pick on, get at (*infml*).

pet *n* favourite, darling, idol, treasure, jewel.
adj favourite, favoured, preferred, dearest, cherished, special, particular, personal.
v stroke, caress, fondle, cuddle, kiss, neck (*sl*), snog (*sl*).

peter out dwindle, taper off, fade, wane, ebb, fail, cease, stop.

petition *n* appeal, round robin, application, request, solicitation, plea, entreaty, prayer, supplication, invocation.
v appeal, call upon, ask, crave, solicit, bid, urge, press, implore, beg, plead, entreat, beseech, supplicate, pray.

petrify *v* terrify, horrify, appal, paralyse, numb, stun, dumbfound.

petty *adj* **1** MINOR, unimportant, insignificant, trivial, secondary, lesser, small, little, slight, trifling, paltry, inconsiderable, negligible.
2 SMALL-MINDED, mean, ungenerous, grudging, spiteful.
◨ 1 important, significant.
2 generous.

petulant *adj* fretful, peevish, cross, irritable, snappish, bad-tempered, ill-humoured, moody, sullen, sulky, sour, ungracious.

phantom *n* ghost, spectre, spirit, apparition, vision, hallucination, illusion, figment.

phase *n* stage, step, time, period, spell, season, chapter, position, point, aspect, state, condition.
phase out wind down, run down, ease off, taper off, eliminate, dispose of, get rid of, remove, withdraw, close, terminate.

phenomenal *adj* marvellous, sensational, stupendous, amazing, remarkable, extraordinary, exceptional, unusual, unbelievable, incredible.

phenomenon *n* **1** OCCURRENCE, happening, event, incident, episode, fact, appearance, sight. **2** WONDER, marvel, miracle, prodigy, rarity, curiosity, spectacle, sensation.

philanthropic *adj* humanitarian, public-spirited, altruistic, unselfish, benevolent, kind, charitable, alms-giving, generous, liberal, open-handed.
◨ misanthropic.

philanthropist *n* humanitarian, benefactor, patron, sponsor, giver, donor, contributor, altruist.
◨ misanthrope.

philanthropy *n* humanitarianism, public-spiritedness, altruism, unselfishness, benevolence, kind-heartedness, charity, alms-giving, patronage, generosity, liberality, open-handedness.
◨ misanthropy.

philosophical *adj* **1** *a philosophical discussion*: metaphysical, abstract, theoretical, analytical, rational, logical, erudite, learned, wise, thoughtful. **2** RESIGNED, patient, stoical, unruffled, calm, composed.

philosophy *n* metaphysics, rationalism, reason, logic, thought, thinking, wisdom, knowledge, ideology, world-view, doctrine, beliefs, convictions, values, principles, attitude, viewpoint.

Philosophical terms include: absolutism, aesthetics, agnosticism, altruism, antinomianism, a posteriori, a priori, ascetism, atheism, atomism, behaviourism, deduction, deism, deontology, determinism, dialectical materialism, dogmatism, dualism, egoism, empiricism, entailment, Epicureanism, epistemology, ethics, existentialism, fatalism, hedonism, historicism, humanism, idealism, identity, induction, instrumentalism, interactionism, intuition, jurisprudence, libertarianism, logic, logical positivism, materialism, metaphysics, monism, naturalism, nihilism, nominalism, objectivism, ontology, pantheism, phenomenalism, phenomenology, positivism, pragmatism, prescriptivism, rationalism, realism, reductionism, relativism, scepticism, scholasticism, sensationalism, sense data, solipsism, stoicism, structuralism, subjectivism, substance, syllogism, teleology, theism, transcendentalism, utilitarianism.

phlegmatic *adj* placid, stolid, impassive, unemotional, unconcerned, indifferent, matter-of-fact, stoical.

🖃 emotional, passionate.

phobia *n* fear, terror, dread, anxiety, neurosis, obsession, hang-up (*infml*), thing (*infml*), aversion, dislike, hatred, horror, loathing, revulsion, repulsion.

🖃 love, liking.

Phobias (by name of fear) include: zoophobia (*animals*), apiphobia (*bees*), ailurophobia (*cats*), necrophobia (*corpses*), scotophobia (*darkness*), cynophobia (*dogs*), claustrophobia (*enclosed places*), panphobia (*everything*), pyrophobia (*fire*), xenophobia (*foreigners*), phasmophobia (*ghosts*), acrophobia (*high places*), hippophobia (*horses*), entomophobia (*insects*), astraphobia (*lightning*), autophobia (*loneliness*), agoraphobia (*open spaces*), toxiphobia (*poison*), herpetophobia (*reptiles*), ophiophobia (*snakes*), tachophobia (*speed*), arachnophobia

(*spiders*), triskaidekaphobia (*thirteen*), brontophobia (*thunder*), hydrophobia (*water*).

phone *v* telephone, ring (up), call (up), dial, contact, get in touch, give a buzz (*infml*), give a tinkle (*infml*).

phoney (*infml*) *adj* fake, counterfeit, forged, bogus, trick, false, spurious, assumed, affected, put-on, sham, pseudo, imitation.

🖃 real, genuine.

photocopy *v* copy, duplicate, Photostat®, Xerox®, print, run off. *n* copy, duplicate, Photostat®, Xerox®.

photograph *n* photo, snap, snapshot, print, shot, slide, transparency, picture, image, likeness.

v snap, take, film, shoot, video, record.

Photographic accessories include: air-shutter release, battery, cable release, camera bag, eye-cup, eyepiece magnifier, film, cartridge film, cassette film, disc film, film pack, filter, colour filter, heat filter, polarizing filter, skylight filter, flashbulb, flashcube, flashgun, flash unit, hot shoe, lens, afocal lens, auxiliary lens, close-up lens, fish-eye lens, macro lens, supplementary lens, telephoto lens, teleconverter, wide-angle lens, zoom lens, lens cap, lens hood, lens shield, light meter, exposure meter, spot meter, diffuser, barn doors, honeycomb diffuser, parabolic reflector, snoot, slide mount, viewfinder, right-angle finder; camcorder battery discharger/charger/tester, cassette adaptor, remote control, tele-cine converter, video editor, video light, video mixer. *see also* **camera**.

Photographic equipment includes: camera, stand, tripod, flash umbrella, boom arm; developer bath, developing tank, dry mounting press, easel, enlarger, enlarger timer, film-drying cabinet, fixing bath, focus magnifier, light-box, negative carrier, print washer, contact printer, print-drying rack, paper drier, safelight, stop bath, Vertoscope®, viewer; slide viewer, slide projector, film projector, screen.

phrase n construction, clause, idiom, expression, saying, utterance, remark.

v word, formulate, frame, couch, present, put, express, say, utter, pronounce.

physical adj bodily, corporeal, fleshy, incarnate, mortal, earthly, material, concrete, solid, substantial, tangible, visible, real, actual.

Fa mental, spiritual.

physics

Terms used in physics include: absolute zero, acceleration, acoustics, alpha particles, analogue signal, applied physics, Archimedes principle, area, atom, beta particles, Big Bang theory, boiling point, bubble-chamber, capillary action, centre of gravity, centre of mass, centrifugal force, chain reaction, charge, charged particle, circuit, circuit-breaker, couple, critical mass, cryogenics, density, diffraction, digital, dynamics, efficiency, elasticity, electric current, electric discharge, electricity, electrodynamics, electromagnetic spectrum, electromagnetic waves, electron, energy, engine, entropy, equation, equilibrium, evaporation, field, flash point, force, formula, freezing point, frequency, friction, fundamental constant, gamma ray, gas, gate, grand united theory (GUT), gravity, half-life, heat, heavy water, hydraulics, hydrodynamics,

hydrostatics, incandescence, indeterminacy principle, inertia, infrared, interference, ion, kinetic energy, kinetic theory, Kelvin effect, laser (light amplification by stimulated emission of radiation), latent heat, law, laws of motion, laws of reflection, laws of refraction, laws of thermodynamics, lens, lever, light, light emission, light intensity, light source, liquid, longitudinal wave, luminescence, Mach number, magnetic field, magnetism, mass, mechanics, microwaves, mirror, Mohs scale, molecule, moment, momentum, motion, neutron, nuclear, nuclear fission, nuclear fusion, nuclear physics, nucleus, optical centre, optics, oscillation, parallel motion, particle, periodic law, perpetual motion, phonon, photon, photosensitivity, polarity, potential energy, power, pressure, principle, process, proton, quantum chromodynamics (QCD), quantum electrodynamics (QED), quantum mechanics, quantum theory, quark, radiation, radioactive element, radioactivity, radioisotope, radio wave, ratio, reflection, refraction, relativity, resistance, resonance, rule, semiconductor, sensitivity, separation, SI unit, sound, sound wave, specific gravity, specific heat capacity, spectroscopy, spectrum, speed, states of matter, statics, substance, superstring theory, supersymmetry, surface tension, temperature, tension, theory, theory of relativity, thermodynamics, Thomson effect, transverse wave, ultrasound, ultraviolet, uncertainty principle, velocity, visible spectrum, viscosity, volume, wave, wave property, weight, white heat, work, X-ray. see also **atom**.

physician n doctor, medical practitioner, medic (infml), general practitioner, GP, houseman, intern, registrar, consultant, specialist, healer.

physique *n* body, figure, shape, form, build, frame, structure, constitution, make-up.

pick *v* 1 SELECT, choose, opt for, decide on, settle on, single out. 2 GATHER, collect, pluck, harvest, cull.
n 1 CHOICE, selection, option, decision, preference. 2 BEST, cream, flower, élite, elect.

pick on bully, torment, persecute, nag, get at (*infml*), needle (*infml*), bait.

pick out spot, notice, perceive, recognize, distinguish, tell apart, separate, single out, hand-pick, choose, select.

pick up 1 LIFT, raise, hoist. 2 *I'll pick you up at eight*: call for, fetch, collect. 3 LEARN, master, grasp, gather. 4 IMPROVE, rally, recover, perk up (*infml*). 5 BUY, purchase. 6 OBTAIN, acquire, gain. 7 *pick up an infection*: catch, contract, get.

picket *n* picketer, protester, demonstrator, striker.
v protest, demonstrate, boycott, blockade, enclose, surround.

pickle *v* preserve, conserve, souse, marinade, steep, cure, salt.

pictorial *adj* graphic, diagrammatic, schematic, representational, vivid, striking, expressive, illustrated, picturesque, scenic.

picture *n* 1 PAINTING, portrait, landscape, drawing, sketch, illustration, engraving, photograph, print, representation, likeness, image, effigy. 2 DEPICTION, portrayal, description, account, report, impression. 3 *the picture of health*: embodiment, personification, epitome, archetype, essence. 4 FILM, movie (*infml*), motion picture.
v 1 IMAGINE, envisage, envision, conceive, visualize, see. 2 DEPICT, describe, represent, show, portray,

draw, sketch, paint, photograph, illustrate.

picturesque *adj* 1 ATTRACTIVE, beautiful, pretty, charming, quaint, idyllic, scenic. 2 DESCRIPTIVE, graphic, vivid, colourful, striking.
F∃ 1 unattractive. 2 dull.

piece *n* 1 FRAGMENT, bit, scrap, morsel, mouthful, bite, lump, chunk, slice, sliver, snippet, shred, offcut, sample, component, constituent, element, part, segment, section, division, fraction, share, portion, quantity. 2 ARTICLE, item, study, work, composition, creation, specimen, example.

pier *n* 1 JETTY, breakwater, landing-stage, quay, wharf. 2 SUPPORT, upright, pillar, post.

pierce *v* penetrate, enter, stick into, puncture, drill, bore, probe, perforate, punch, prick, stab, lance, bayonet, run through, spear, skewer, spike, impale, transfix.

piercing *adj* 1 *a piercing cry*: shrill, high-pitched, loud, ear-splitting, sharp. 2 PENETRATING, probing, searching. 3 COLD, bitter, raw, biting, keen, fierce, severe, wintry, frosty, freezing. 4 PAINFUL, agonizing, excruciating, stabbing, lacerating.

piety *n* piousness, devoutness, godliness, saintliness, holiness, sanctity, religion, faith, devotion, reverence.
F∃ impiety, irreligion.

pig *n* swine, hog, sow, boar, animal, beast, brute, glutton, gourmand.

pigeonhole *n* compartment, niche, slot, cubby-hole, cubicle, locker, box, place, section, class, category, classification.
v compartmentalize, label, classify, sort, file, catalogue, alphabetize, shelve, defer.

pigment *n* colour, hue, tint, dye, stain, paint, colouring, tincture.

pile[1] *n* stack, heap, mound,

mountain, mass, accumulation, collection, assortment, hoard, stockpile.

v stack, heap, mass, amass, accumulate, build up, gather, assemble, collect, hoard, stockpile, store, load, pack, jam, crush, crowd, flock, flood, stream, rush, charge.

pile² *n* post, column, upright, support, bar, beam, foundation.

pile³ *n* nap, shag, plush, fur, hair, fuzz, down.

pilfer *v* steal, pinch (*infml*), nick (*infml*), knock off (*sl*), filch, lift, shoplift, rob, thieve.

pilgrim *n* crusader, traveller, wanderer.

pilgrimage *n* crusade, mission, expedition, journey, trip, tour.

pill *n* tablet, capsule, pellet.

pillar *n* column, shaft, post, mast, pier, upright, pile, support, prop, mainstay, bastion, tower of strength.

pilot *n* 1 FLYER, aviator, airman. 2 NAVIGATOR, steersman, helmsman, coxswain, captain, leader, director, guide.

v fly, drive, steer, direct, control, handle, manage, operate, run, conduct, lead, guide, navigate.

adj experimental, trial, test, model.

pimple *n* spot, zit (*sl*), blackhead, boil, swelling.

pin *v* tack, nail, fix, affix, attach, join, staple, clip, fasten, secure, hold down, restrain, immobilize.

n tack, nail, screw, spike, rivet, bolt, peg, fastener, clip, staple, brooch.

pin down 1 PINPOINT, identify, determine, specify. 2 FORCE, make, press, pressurize.

pinch *v* 1 SQUEEZE, compress, crush, press, tweak, nip, hurt, grip, grasp. 2 (*infml*) STEAL, nick, pilfer, filch, snatch.

n 1 SQUEEZE, tweak, nip. 2 DASH, soupçon, taste, bit, speck, jot, mite. 3 EMERGENCY, crisis, predicament, difficulty, hardship, pressure, stress.

pine *v* long, yearn, ache, sigh, grieve, mourn, wish, desire, crave, hanker, hunger, thirst.

pinnacle *n* 1 PEAK, summit, top, cap, crown, crest, apex, vertex, acme, zenith, height, eminence. 2 SPIRE, steeple, turret, pyramid, cone, obelisk, needle.

pinpoint *v* identify, spot, distinguish, locate, place, home in on, zero in on (*infml*), pin down, determine, specify, define.

pioneer *n* colonist, settler, frontiersman, frontierswoman, explorer, developer, pathfinder, trailblazer, leader, innovator, inventor, discoverer, founder.

v invent, discover, originate, create, initiate, instigate, begin, start, launch, institute, found, establish, set up, develop, open up.

pious *adj* 1 DEVOUT, godly, saintly, holy, spiritual, religious, reverent, good, virtuous, righteous, moral. 2 SANCTIMONIOUS, holier-than-thou, self-righteous, goody-goody (*infml*), hypocritical.

E3 1 impious, irreligious, irreverent.

pipe *n* tube, hose, piping, tubing, pipeline, line, main, flue, duct, conduit, channel, passage, conveyor.

v 1 CHANNEL, funnel, siphon, carry, convey, conduct, transmit, supply, deliver. 2 WHISTLE, chirp, tweet, cheep, peep, twitter, sing, warble, trill, play, sound.

piquant *adj* 1 *piquant sauce*: spicy, tangy, savoury, salty, peppery, pungent, sharp, biting, stinging. 2 LIVELY, spirited, stimulating, provocative, interesting, sparkling.

E3 1 bland, insipid. 2 dull, banal.

pique *n* annoyance, irritation, vexation, displeasure, offence, huff (*infml*), resentment, grudge.

piqued *adj* annoyed, irritated, vexed, riled, angry, displeased, offended, miffed (*infml*), peeved (*infml*), put out, resentful.

pit n mine, coalmine, excavation, trench, ditch, hollow, depression, indentation, dent, hole, cavity, crater, pothole, gulf, chasm, abyss.

pitch v **1** THROW, fling, toss, chuck (*infml*), lob, bowl, hurl, heave, sling, fire, launch, aim, direct. **2** PLUNGE, dive, plummet, drop, fall headlong, tumble, lurch, roll, wallow. **3** *pitch camp*: erect, put up, set up, place, station, settle, plant, fix.

n **1** *cricket pitch*: ground, field, playing-field, arena, stadium. **2** SOUND, tone, timbre, modulation, frequency, level. **3** GRADIENT, incline, slope, tilt, angle, degree, steepness.

piteous adj poignant, moving, touching, distressing, heart-rending, plaintive, mournful, sad, sorrowful, woeful, wretched, pitiful, pitiable, pathetic.

pitfall n danger, peril, hazard, trap, snare, stumbling-block, catch, snag, drawback, difficulty.

pith n importance, significance, moment, weight, value, consequence, substance, matter, marrow, meat, gist, essence, crux, nub, heart, core, kernel.

pithy adj succinct, concise, compact, terse, short, brief, pointed, trenchant, forceful, cogent, telling.

🔁 wordy, verbose.

pitiful adj **1** CONTEMPTIBLE, despicable, low, mean, vile, shabby, deplorable, lamentable, woeful, inadequate, hopeless, pathetic (*infml*), insignificant, paltry, worthless. **2** PITEOUS, doleful, mournful, distressing, heart-rending, pathetic, pitiable, sad, miserable, wretched, poor, sorry.

pitiless adj merciless, cold-hearted, unsympathetic, unfeeling, uncaring, hard-hearted, callous, cruel, inhuman, brutal, cold-blooded, ruthless, relentless, unremitting, inexorable, harsh.

🔁 merciful, compassionate, kind, gentle.

pittance n modicum, crumb, drop (in the ocean), chicken-feed (*infml*), peanuts (*sl*), trifle.

pitted adj dented, holey, potholed, pockmarked, blemished, scarred, marked, notched, indented, rough.

pity n **1** SYMPATHY, commiseration, regret, understanding, fellow-feeling, compassion, kindness, tenderness, mercy, forbearance. **2** *what a pity!*: shame, misfortune, bad luck.

🔁 cruelty, anger, scorn.

v feel sorry for, feel for, sympathize with, commiserate with, grieve for, weep for.

pivot n axis, hinge, axle, spindle, kingpin, linchpin, swivel, hub, focal point, centre, heart.

v **1** SWIVEL, turn, spin, revolve, rotate, swing. **2** DEPEND, rely, hinge, hang, lie.

placard n poster, bill, notice, sign, advertisement.

placate v appease, pacify, conciliate, mollify, calm, assuage, soothe, lull, quiet.

🔁 anger, enrage, incense, infuriate.

place n **1** SITE, locale, venue, location, situation, spot, point, position, seat, space, room. **2** CITY, town, village, locality, neighbourhood, district, area, region. **3** BUILDING, property, dwelling, residence, house, flat, apartment, home.

v put, set, plant, fix, position, locate, situate, rest, settle, lay, stand, deposit, leave.

in place of instead of, in lieu of, as a replacement for, as a substitute for, as an alternative to.

out of place inappropriate, unsuitable, unfitting, unbecoming, unseemly.

take place happen, occur, come about.

placid adj calm, composed, unruffled, untroubled, cool, self-possessed, level-headed,

imperturbable, mild, gentle, equable, even-tempered, serene, tranquil, still, quiet, peaceful, restful.
■ excitable, agitated, disturbed.

plagiarize v crib, copy, reproduce, imitate, counterfeit, pirate, infringe copyright, poach, steal, lift, appropriate, borrow.

plague n 1 PESTILENCE, epidemic, disease, infection, contagion, infestation. 2 NUISANCE, annoyance, curse, scourge, trial, affliction, torment, calamity.
v annoy, vex, bother, disturb, trouble, distress, upset, pester, harass, hound, haunt, bedevil, afflict, torment, torture, persecute.

plain adj 1 plain cookery: ordinary, basic, simple, unpretentious, modest, unadorned, unelaborate, restrained.
2 OBVIOUS, evident, patent, clear, understandable, apparent, visible, unmistakable. 3 FRANK, candid, blunt, outspoken, direct, forthright, straightforward, unambiguous, plain-spoken, open, honest, truthful.
4 UNATTRACTIVE, ugly, unprepossessing, unlovely. 5 plain fabric: unpatterned, unvariegated, uncoloured, self-coloured.
■ 1 fancy, elaborate. 2 unclear, obscure. 3 devious, deceitful.
4 attractive, good-looking.
5 patterned.
n grassland, prairie, steppe, lowland, flat, plateau, tableland.

plaintive adj doleful, mournful, melancholy, wistful, sad, sorrowful, grief-stricken, piteous, heart-rending, high-pitched.

plan n 1 BLUEPRINT, layout, diagram, chart, map, drawing, sketch, representation, design.
2 IDEA, suggestion, proposal, proposition, project, scheme, plot, system, method, procedure, strategy, programme, schedule, scenario.
v 1 PLOT, scheme, design, invent, devise, contrive, formulate, frame,

draft, outline, prepare, organize, arrange. 2 AIM, intend, propose, contemplate, envisage, foresee.

planet

> *Planets within the Earth's solar system (nearest the sun shown first) are:* Mercury, Venus, Earth, Mars, Jupiter, Saturn, Uranus, Neptune, Pluto.

plant

> *Plants include:* annual, biennial, perennial, herbaceous plant, evergreen, succulent, cultivar, hybrid, house plant, pot plant; flower, herb, shrub, bush, tree, vegetable, grass, vine, weed, cereal, wild flower, air-plant, water-plant, cactus, fern, moss, algae, lichen, fungus; bulb, corm, seedling, sapling, bush, climber. *see also* **flower**; **shrub**.

n factory, works, foundry, mill, shop, yard, workshop, machinery, apparatus, equipment, gear.
v 1 SOW, seed, bury, transplant. 2 INSERT, put, place, set, fix, lodge, root, settle, found, establish.

plaster n sticking-plaster, dressing, bandage, plaster of Paris, mortar, stucco.
v daub, smear, coat, cover, spread.

plastic adj soft, pliable, flexible, supple, malleable, mouldable, ductile, receptive, impressionable, manageable.
■ rigid, inflexible.

> *Types of plastic include:* Bakelite®, Biopol®, celluloid®, epoxy resin, Perspex®, phenolic resin, plexiglass, polyester, polyethylene, polymethyl methacrylate, polynorbornene, polypropylene, polystyrene, polythene, polyurethane, PTFE (polytetrafluoroethylene), PVC (polyvinyl chloride), uPVC, silicone,

plate 400

Teflon®, transpolyisoprene, urea formaldehyde, vinyl.

plate n **1** DISH, platter, salver, helping, serving, portion. **2** ILLUSTRATION, picture, print, lithograph.
v coat, cover, overlay, veneer, laminate, electroplate, anodize, galvanize, platinize, gild, silver, tin.

platform n **1** STAGE, podium, dais, rostrum, stand. **2** POLICY, party line, principles, tenets, manifesto, programme, objectives.

platitude n banality, commonplace, truism, cliché, chestnut.

plausible adj credible, believable, reasonable, logical, likely, possible, probable, convincing, persuasive, smooth-talking, glib.
✏ implausible, unlikely, improbable.

play v **1** AMUSE ONESELF, have fun, enjoy oneself, revel, sport, romp, frolic, caper. **2** PARTICIPATE, take part, join in, compete. **3** France played Italy: oppose, vie with, challenge, take on. **4** ACT, perform, portray, represent, impersonate.
✏ **1** work.
n **1** FUN, amusement, entertainment, diversion, recreation, sport, game, hobby, pastime. **2** DRAMA, tragedy, comedy, farce, show, performance. **3** MOVEMENT, action, flexibility, give, leeway, latitude, margin, scope, range, room, space.
✏ **1** work.

play down minimize, make light of, gloss over, underplay, understate, undervalue, underestimate.
✏ exaggerate.

play on exploit, take advantage of, turn to account, profit by, trade on, capitalize on.

play up 1 EXAGGERATE, highlight, spotlight, accentuate, emphasize, stress. **2** MISBEHAVE, malfunction, trouble, bother, annoy, hurt.

playboy n philanderer, womanizer,

ladies' man, rake, libertine.

player n **1** CONTESTANT, competitor, participant, sportsman, sportswoman. **2** PERFORMER, entertainer, artiste, actor, actress, musician, instrumentalist.

playful adj sportive, frolicsome, lively, spirited, mischievous, roguish, impish, puckish, kittenish, good-natured, jesting, teasing, humorous, tongue-in-cheek.
✏ serious.

playwright n dramatist, scriptwriter, screenwriter.

plea n **1** APPEAL, petition, request, entreaty, supplication, prayer, invocation. **2** DEFENCE, justification, excuse, explanation, claim.

plead v **1** BEG, implore, beseech, entreat, appeal, petition, ask, request. **2** plead ignorance: assert, maintain, claim, allege.

pleasant adj agreeable, nice, fine, lovely, delightful, charming, likable, amiable, friendly, affable, good-humoured, cheerful, congenial, enjoyable, amusing, pleasing, gratifying, satisfying, acceptable, welcome, refreshing.
✏ unpleasant, nasty, unfriendly.

please v **1** DELIGHT, charm, captivate, entertain, amuse, cheer, gladden, humour, indulge, gratify, satisfy, content, suit. **2** WANT, will, wish, desire, like, prefer, choose, think fit.
✏ **1** displease, annoy, anger, sadden.

pleased adj contented, satisfied, gratified, glad, happy, delighted, thrilled, euphoric.
✏ displeased, annoyed.

pleasing adj gratifying, satisfying, acceptable, good, pleasant, agreeable, nice, delightful, charming, attractive, engaging, winning.
✏ unpleasant, disagreeable.

pleasure n amusement, entertainment, recreation, fun, enjoyment, gratification, satisfaction, contentment, happiness, joy, delight, comfort, solace.

◨ sorrow, pain, trouble, displeasure.

pleat v tuck, fold, crease, flute, crimp, gather, pucker.

pledge n **1** PROMISE, vow, word of honour, oath, bond, covenant, guarantee, warrant, assurance, undertaking. **2** DEPOSIT, security, surety, bail.

v promise, vow, swear, contract, engage, undertake, vouch, guarantee, secure.

plentiful adj ample, abundant, profuse, copious, overflowing, lavish, generous, liberal, bountiful, fruitful, productive.

◨ scarce, scanty, rare.

plenty n abundance, profusion, plethora, lots (infml), loads (infml), masses (infml), heaps (infml), piles (infml), stacks (infml), enough, sufficiency, quantity, mass, volume, fund, mine, store.

◨ scarcity, lack, want, need.

pliable adj pliant, flexible, bendable, bendy (infml), supple, lithe, malleable, plastic, yielding, adaptable, accommodating, manageable, tractable, docile, compliant, biddable, persuadable, responsive, receptive, impressionable, susceptible.

◨ rigid, inflexible, headstrong.

plight n predicament, quandary, dilemma, extremity, trouble, difficulty, straits, state, condition, situation, circumstances, case.

plod v **1** TRUDGE, tramp, stump, lumber, plough through. **2** DRUDGE, labour, toil, grind, slog, persevere, soldier on.

plot n **1** CONSPIRACY, intrigue, machination, scheme, plan, stratagem. **2** STORY, narrative, subject, theme, storyline, thread, outline, scenario. **3** plot of land: patch, tract, area, allotment, lot, parcel.

v **1** CONSPIRE, intrigue, machinate, scheme, hatch, lay, cook up, devise, contrive, plan, project, design, draft. **2** CHART, map, mark, locate, draw, calculate.

plotter n conspirator, intriguer, machinator, schemer.

ploy n manoeuvre, strategem, tactic, move, device, contrivance, scheme, game, trick, artifice, dodge, wile, ruse, subterfuge.

pluck n courage, bravery, spirit, mettle, nerve (infml), guts (infml), grit, backbone, fortitude, resolution, determination.

◨ cowardice.

v **1** PULL, draw, tug, snatch, pull off, remove, pick, collect, gather, harvest. **2** pluck a guitar: pick, twang, strum.

plucky adj brave, courageous, bold, daring, intrepid, heroic, valiant, spirited.

◨ cowardly, weak, feeble.

plug n **1** STOPPER, bung, cork, spigot. **2** (infml) ADVERTISEMENT, publicity, mention, puff.

v **1** STOP (UP), bung, cork, block, choke, close, seal, fill, pack, stuff. **2** (infml) ADVERTISE, publicize, promote, push, mention.

plumb adv **1** VERTICALLY, perpendicularly. **2** PRECISELY, exactly, dead, slap (infml), bang (infml).

v sound, fathom, measure, gauge, penetrate, probe, search, explore.

plummet v plunge, dive, nose-dive, descend, drop, fall, tumble.

◨ soar.

plump adj fat, obese, dumpy, tubby, stout, round, rotund, portly, chubby, podgy, fleshy, full, ample, buxom.

◨ thin, skinny.

plump for opt for, choose, select, favour, back, support.

plunder v loot, pillage, ravage, devastate, sack, raid, ransack, rifle, steal, rob, strip.

n loot, pillage, booty, swag (sl),

spoils, pickings, ill-gotten gains, prize.

plunge *v* **1** DIVE, jump, nose-dive, swoop, dive-bomb, plummet, descend, go down, sink, drop, fall, pitch, tumble, hurtle, career, charge, dash, rush, tear. **2** IMMERSE, submerge, dip.
n dive, swoop, descent, drop, fall, tumble, immersion, submersion.

ply *n* layer, fold, thickness, strand, sheet, leaf.

poach *v* steal, pilfer, appropriate, trespass, encroach, infringe.

pocket *n* pouch, bag, envelope, receptacle, compartment, hollow, cavity.
adj small, little, mini (*infml*), concise, compact, portable, miniature.
v take, appropriate, help oneself to, lift, pilfer, filch, steal, nick (*infml*), pinch (*infml*).

pod *n* shell, husk, case, hull.

poem

Types of poem include: ballad, elegy, epic, haiku, idyll, lay, limerick, lyric, madrigal, nursery-rhyme, ode, pastoral, roundelay, sonnet, tanka.

poet *n* versifier, rhymer, rhymester, lyricist, bard, minstrel.

poetic *adj* poetical, lyrical, moving, artistic, graceful, flowing, metrical, rhythmical, rhyming. ✒ prosaic.

poignant *adj* moving, touching, affecting, tender, distressing, upsetting, heartbreaking, heart-rending, piteous, pathetic, sad, painful, agonizing.

point *n* **1** FEATURE, attribute, aspect, facet, detail, particular, item, subject, topic. **2** *what's the point?*: use, purpose, motive, reason, object, intention, aim, end, goal, objective. **3** ESSENCE, crux, core, pith, gist, thrust, meaning, drift, burden. **4** PLACE, position, situation, location, site, spot. **5** MOMENT,

instant, juncture, stage, time, period. **6** DOT, spot, mark, speck, full stop.
v **1** *point a gun*: aim, direct, train, level. **2** INDICATE, signal, show, signify, denote, designate.

point of view opinion, view, belief, judgement, attitude, position, standpoint, viewpoint, outlook, perspective, approach, angle, slant.

point out show, indicate, draw attention to, point to, reveal, identify, specify, mention, bring up, allude to, remind.

point-blank *adj* direct, forthright, straightforward, plain, explicit, open, unreserved, blunt, frank, candid.
adv directly, forthrightly, straightforwardly, plainly, explicitly, openly, bluntly, frankly, candidly.

pointed *adj* sharp, keen, edged, barbed, cutting, incisive, trenchant, biting, penetrating, telling.

pointer *n* **1** ARROW, indicator, needle, hand. **2** TIP, recommendation, suggestion, hint, guide, indication, advice, warning, caution.

pointless *adj* useless, futile, vain, fruitless, unproductive, unprofitable, worthless, senseless, absurd, meaningless, aimless. ✒ useful, profitable, meaningful.

poise *n* calmness, composure, self-possession, presence of mind, coolness, equanimity, aplomb, assurance, dignity, elegance, grace, balance, equilibrium.
v balance, position, hover, hang, suspend.

poised *adj* **1** DIGNIFIED, graceful, calm, composed, unruffled, collected, self-possessed, cool, self-confident, assured. **2** *poised for action*: prepared, ready, set, waiting, expectant.

poison *n* toxin, venom, bane, blight, cancer, malignancy, contagion, contamination, corruption.
v infect, contaminate, pollute, taint,

adulterate, corrupt, deprave, pervert, warp.

poisonous *adj* toxic, venomous, lethal, deadly, fatal, mortal, noxious, pernicious, malicious.

poke *v* prod, stab, jab, stick, thrust, push, shove, nudge, elbow, dig, butt, hit, punch.

n prod, jab, thrust, shove, nudge, dig, butt, punch.

pole¹ *n* bar, rod, stick, shaft, spar, upright, post, stake, mast, staff.

pole² *n* antipode, extremity, extreme, limit.

poles apart irreconcilable, worlds apart, incompatible, like chalk and cheese.

police *n* police force, constabulary, the Law (*infml*), the Bill (*sl*), the fuzz (*sl*).

v check, control, regulate, monitor, watch, observe, supervise, oversee, patrol, guard, protect, defend, keep the peace.

policeman, policewoman *n* officer, constable, PC, cop (*sl*), copper (*infml*), bobby (*infml*).

policy *n* **1** CODE OF PRACTICE, rules, guidelines, procedure, method, practice, custom, protocol. **2** COURSE OF ACTION, line, course, plan, programme, scheme, stance, position.

polish *v* **1** SHINE, brighten, smooth, rub, buff, burnish, clean, wax. **2** IMPROVE, enhance, brush up, touch up, finish, perfect, refine, cultivate.

E3 1 tarnish, dull.

n **1** *a tin of polish*: wax, varnish. **2** SHINE, gloss, sheen, lustre, brightness, brilliance, sparkle, smoothness, finish, glaze, veneer. **3** REFINEMENT, cultivation, class, breeding, sophistication, finesse, style, elegance, grace, poise.

E3 2 dullness. 3 clumsiness.

polished *adj* **1** SHINING, shiny, glossy, lustrous, gleaming, burnished,

smooth, glassy, slippery. **2** FAULTLESS, flawless, impeccable, perfect, outstanding, superlative, masterly, expert, professional, skilful, accomplished, perfected. **3** REFINED, cultivated, genteel, well-bred, polite, sophisticated, urbane, suave, elegant, graceful.

E3 1 tarnished. 2 inexpert. 3 gauche.

polite *adj* courteous, well-mannered, respectful, civil, well-bred, refined, cultured, gentlemanly, ladylike, gracious, obliging, thoughtful, considerate, tactful, diplomatic.

E3 impolite, discourteous, rude.

political ideologies

> *Political ideologies include*:
> absolutism, anarchism,
> authoritarianism, Bolshevism,
> Christian democracy, collectivism,
> communism, conservatism,
> democracy, egalitarianism, fascism,
> federalism, holism, imperialism,
> individualism, liberalism, Maoism,
> Marxism, nationalism, Nazism,
> neocolonialism, neo-fascism, neo-
> nazism, pluralism, republicanism,
> social democracy, socialism,
> syndicalism, Thatcherism, theocracy,
> totalitarianism, unilateralism,
> Trotskyism, Whiggism.

politician *n* Member of Parliament, MP, minister, statesman, stateswoman, legislator.

politics *n* public affairs, civics, affairs of state, statecraft, government, diplomacy, statesmanship, political science.

> *Terms used in politics include*:
> alliance, apartheid, ballot, bill,
> blockade, cabinet, campaign, civil
> service, coalition, constitution,
> council, coup d'état, détente,
> election, electoral register, ethnic
> cleansing, general election, glasnost,
> go to the country, government, green

paper, Hansard, judiciary, left wing, lobby, local government, majority, mandate, manifesto, nationalization, parliament, party, party line, perestroika, prime minister's question time, privatization, propaganda, proportional representation, rainbow coalition, referendum, right wing, sanction, shadow cabinet, sovereignty, state, summit, summit conference, term of office, trade union, veto, vote, welfare state, whip, three-line whip, white paper. *People in politics include*: activist, ambassador, Black Rod, capitalist, Communist, commie (*infml*), comrade, Conservative, Democrat, Deputy Speaker, dictator, dissident, dry (*infml*), extremist, Green, high commissioner, independent, lefty (*infml*), Liberal, Liberal Democrat, loyalist, Marxist, Marxist-Leninist, member of parliament, minister, moderate, MP, party chairman, party member, party worker, pinko (*infml*), politician, premier, president, prime minister, radical, red (*infml*), Republican, revolutionary, secretary of state, Social Democrat, Socialist, speaker, Tory, Trotskyite, true-blue, wet (*infml*), Whig. *Political parties include*: Alliance, Co-operative, Communist, Conservative and Unionist, Democratic, Democratic Left, Democratic Unionist, Fianna Fáil, Fine Gael, Green, Labour, Liberal, Liberal Democratic, Militant Labour, National Front, Parliamentary, Parliamentary Labour, Plaid Cymru, Progressive Democrats, Republican, Scottish Conservative and Unionist, Scottish Liberal Democratic, Scottish National, Sinn Féin, Social and Liberal Democratic, Social Democratic and Labour, Ulster Popular Unionist, Ulster Unionist, Welsh Liberal Democratic. *see also*

government systems;
parliaments and assemblies;
political ideologies.

poll *n* ballot, vote, voting, plebiscite, referendum, straw-poll, sampling, canvass, opinion poll, survey, census, count, tally.

pollute *v* contaminate, infect, poison, taint, adulterate, debase, corrupt, dirty, foul, soil, defile, sully, stain, mar, spoil.

pollution *n* impurity, contamination, infection, taint, adulteration, corruption, dirtiness, foulness, defilement.
◳ purification, purity, cleanness.

pomp *n* ceremony, ceremonial, ritual, solemnity, formality, ceremoniousness, state, grandeur, splendour, magnificence, pageantry, show, display, parade, ostentation, flourish.
◳ austerity, simplicity.

pompous *adj* self-important, arrogant, grandiose, supercilious, overbearing, imperious, magisterial, bombastic, high-flown, overblown, windy, affected, pretentious, ostentatious.
◳ unassuming, modest, simple, unaffected.

pool¹ *n* puddle, pond, lake, mere, tarn, watering-hole, paddling-pool, swimming-pool.

pool² *n* **1** FUND, reserve, accumulation, bank, kitty, purse, pot, jackpot. **2** SYNDICATE, cartel, ring, combine, consortium, collective, group, team.
v contribute, chip in (*infml*), combine, amalgamate, merge, share, muck in (*infml*).

poor *adj* **1** IMPOVERISHED, poverty-stricken, badly off, hard-up, broke (*infml*), stony-broke (*sl*), skint (*sl*), bankrupt, penniless, destitute, miserable, wretched, distressed, straitened, needy, lacking, deficient, insufficient, scanty, skimpy, meagre, sparse, depleted, exhausted. **2** BAD, substandard, unsatisfactory, inferior, mediocre, below par, low-grade, second-rate, third-rate, shoddy, imperfect, faulty, weak, feeble, pathetic (*infml*), sorry, worthless, fruitless. **3** UNFORTUNATE, unlucky, luckless, ill-fated, unhappy, miserable, pathetic, pitiable, pitiful. **Ea 1** rich, wealthy, affluent. **2** superior, impressive. **3** fortunate, lucky.

poorly *adj* ill, sick, unwell, indisposed, ailing, sickly, off colour, below par, out of sorts (*infml*), under the weather (*infml*), seedy, groggy, rotten (*infml*).
Ea well, healthy.

pop *v* burst, explode, go off, bang, crack, snap.
n bang, crack, snap, burst, explosion.

popular *adj* well-liked, favourite, liked, favoured, approved, in demand, sought-after, fashionable, modish, trendy (*infml*), prevailing, current, accepted, conventional, standard, stock, common, prevalent, widespread, universal, general, household, famous, well-known, celebrated, idolized.
Ea unpopular.

popularise *v* spread, propagate, universalize, democratize, simplify.

popularly *adv* commonly, widely, universally, generally, usually, customarily, conventionally, traditionally.

populate *v* people, occupy, settle, colonize, inhabit, live in, overrun.

population *n* inhabitants, natives, residents, citizens, occupants, community, society, people, folk.

populous *n* crowded, packed, swarming, teeming, crawling, overpopulated.
Ea deserted.

pornographic *adj* obscene, indecent, dirty, filthy, blue, risqué, bawdy, coarse, gross, lewd, erotic, titillating.

porous *adj* permeable, pervious, penetrable, absorbent, spongy, honeycombed, pitted.
Ea impermeable, impervious.

portable *adj* movable, transportable, compact, lightweight, manageable, handy, convenient.
Ea fixed, immovable.

porter[1] *n* bearer, carrier, baggage-attendant, baggage-handler.

porter[2] *n* doorman, commissionaire, door-keeper, gatekeeper, janitor, caretaker, concierge.

portion *n* share, allocation, allotment, parcel, allowance, ration, quota, measure, part, section, division, fraction, percentage, bit, fragment, morsel, piece, segment, slice, serving, helping.

portly *adj* stout, corpulent, rotund, round, fat, plump, obese, overweight, heavy, large.
Ea slim, thin, slight.

portrait *n* picture, painting, drawing, sketch, caricature, miniature, icon, photograph, likeness, image, representation, vignette, profile, characterization, description, depiction, portrayal.

portray *v* draw, sketch, paint, illustrate, picture, represent, depict, describe, evoke, play, impersonate, characterize, personify.

portrayal *n* representation, characterization, depiction, description, evocation, presentation, performance, interpretation, rendering.

pose *v* **1** MODEL, sit, position. **2** PRETEND, feign, affect, put on an act, masquerade, pass oneself off, impersonate. **3** *pose a question*: set, put forward, submit, present.
n **1** POSITION, stance, air, bearing, posture, attitude. **2** PRETENCE, sham, affectation, façade, front, masquerade, role, act.

poser[1] *n* puzzle, riddle, conundrum,

brain-teaser, mystery, enigma, problem, vexed question.

poser[2] *n* poseur, poseuse, posturer, attitudinizer, exhibitionist, show-off, pseud (*infml*), phoney (*infml*).

posh (*infml*) *adj* smart, stylish, fashionable, high-class, upper-class, la-di-da (*sl*), grand, luxurious, lavish, swanky (*infml*), luxury, deluxe, up-market, exclusive, select, classy (*infml*), swish (*infml*).
Ea inferior, cheap.

position *n* **1** PLACE, situation, location, site, spot, point.
2 POSTURE, stance, pose, arrangement, disposition. **3** JOB, post, occupation, employment, office, duty, function, role. **4** RANK, grade, level, status, standing. **5** OPINION, point of view, belief, view, outlook, viewpoint, standpoint, stand.
v put, place, set, fix, stand, arrange, dispose, lay out, deploy, station, locate, situate, site.

positive *adj* **1** SURE, certain, convinced, confident, assured.
2 *positive criticism:* helpful, constructive, practical, useful, optimistic, hopeful, promising.
3 DEFINITE, decisive, conclusive, clear, unmistakable, explicit, unequivocal, express, firm, emphatic, categorical, undeniable, irrefutable, indisputable, incontrovertible.
4 ABSOLUTE, utter, sheer, complete, perfect.
Ea 1 uncertain. **2** negative.
3 indefinite, vague.

possess *v* **1** OWN, have, hold, enjoy, be endowed with. **2** SEIZE, take, obtain, acquire, take over, occupy, control, dominate, bewitch, haunt.

possession *n* ownership, title, tenure, occupation, custody, control, hold, grip.

possessions *n* belongings, property, things, paraphernalia,

effects, goods, chattels, movables, assets, estate, wealth, riches.

possessive *adj* selfish, clinging, overprotective, domineering, dominating, jealous, covetous, acquisitive, grasping.
Ea unselfish, sharing.

possibility *n* likelihood, probability, odds, chance, risk, danger, hope, prospect, potentiality, conceivability, practicability, feasibility.
Ea impossibility, impracticability.

possible *adj* potential, promising, likely, probable, imaginable, conceivable, practicable, feasible, viable, tenable, workable, achievable, attainable, accomplishable, realizable.
Ea impossible, unthinkable, impracticable, unattainable.

possibly *adv* perhaps, maybe, hopefully (*infml*), by any means, at all, by any chance.

post[1] *n* pole, stake, picket, pale, pillar, column, shaft, support, baluster, upright, stanchion, strut, leg.
v display, stick up, pin up, advertise, publicize, announce, make known, report, publish.

post[2] *n* office, job, employment, position, situation, place, vacancy, appointment, assignment, station, beat.
v station, locate, situate, position, place, put, appoint, assign, second, transfer, move, send.

post[3] *n* mail, letters, dispatch, collection, delivery.
v mail, send, dispatch, transmit.

poster *n* notice, bill, sign, placard, sticker, advertisement, announcement.

posterity *n* descendants, successors, progeny, issue, offspring, children.

postpone *v* put off, defer, put back, hold over, delay, adjourn, suspend, shelve, pigeonhole, freeze, put on ice.
Ea advance, forward.

postscript n PS (*infml*), addition, supplement, afterthought, addendum, codicil, appendix, afterword, epilogue.
■ introduction, prologue.

postulate v theorize, hypothesize, suppose, assume, propose, advance, lay down, stipulate.

posture n position, stance, pose, attitude, disposition, bearing, carriage, deportment.

posy n bouquet, spray, buttonhole, corsage.

pot n receptacle, vessel, teapot, coffee pot, urn, jar, vase, bowl, basin, pan, cauldron, crucible.

potent adj powerful, mighty, strong, intoxicating, pungent, effective, impressive, cogent, convincing, persuasive, compelling, forceful, dynamic, vigorous, authoritative, commanding, dominant, influential, overpowering.
■ impotent, weak.

potential adj possible, likely, probable, prospective, future, aspiring, would-be, promising, budding, embryonic, undeveloped, dormant, latent, hidden, concealed, unrealized.
n possibility, ability, capability, capacity, aptitude, talent, powers, resources.

potion n mixture, concoction, brew, beverage, drink, draught, dose, medicine, tonic, elixir.

potpourri n medley, mixture, jumble, hotchpotch, miscellany, collection.

potter v tinker, fiddle, mess about (*infml*), dabble, loiter, fritter.

pottery n earthenware, stoneware, terracotta, ceramics, crockery, china, porcelain.

> *Terms used in pottery include*:
> armorial, art pottery, basalt, blanc-de-chine, bronzing, celadon, ceramic, china clay, cloisonné, crackleware, crazing, creamware, delft, earthenware, enamel, faïence, fairing, figure, firing, flambé, flatback, glaze, grotesque, ground, ironstone, jasper, kiln, lustre, maiolica, majolica, maker's mark, mandarin palette, model, monogram, overglaze, porcelain, sagger, scratch blue, sgraffito, slip, slip-cast, spongeware, Staffordshire, stoneware, terracotta, tin-glazed earthenware, transfer printing, underglaze, Willow pattern.

pounce v fall on, dive on, swoop, drop, attack, strike, ambush, spring, jump, leap, snatch, grab.

pound[1] v **1** STRIKE, thump, beat, drum, pelt, hammer, batter, bang, bash, smash. **2** PULVERIZE, powder, grind, mash, crush. **3** *his heart was pounding*: throb, pulsate, palpitate, thump, thud.

pound[2] n enclosure, compound, corral, yard, pen, fold.

pour v **1** *pour a drink*: serve, decant, tip. **2** SPILL, issue, discharge, flow, stream, run, rush, spout, spew, gush, cascade, crowd, throng, swarm.

pout v scowl, glower, grimace, pull a face, sulk, mope.
■ grin, smile.
n scowl, glower, grimace, long face.
■ grin, smile.

poverty n poorness, impoverishment, insolvency, bankruptcy, pennilessness, penury, destitution, distress, hardship, privation, need, necessity, want, lack, deficiency, shortage, inadequacy, insufficiency, depletion, scarcity, meagreness, paucity, dearth.
■ wealth, richness, affluence, plenty.

powdery adj dusty, sandy, grainy, granular, powdered, pulverized, ground, fine, loose, dry, crumbly, friable, chalky.

power n **1** COMMAND, authority, sovereignty, rule, dominion, control, influence. **2** RIGHT, privilege,

prerogative, authorization, warrant.
3 POTENCY, strength, intensity,
force, vigour, energy. **4** ABILITY,
capability, capacity, potential,
faculty, competence.
Ea 1 subjection. **3** weakness.
4 inability.

powerful *adj* dominant, prevailing,
leading, influential, high-powered,
authoritative, commanding, potent,
effective, strong, mighty, robust,
muscular, energetic, forceful, telling,
impressive, convincing, persuasive,
compelling, winning, overwhelming.
Ea impotent, ineffective, weak.

powerless *adj* impotent, incapable,
ineffective, weak, feeble, frail, infirm,
incapacitated, disabled, paralysed,
helpless, vulnerable, defenceless,
unarmed.
Ea powerful, potent, able.

practicable *adj* possible, feasible,
performable, achievable, attainable,
viable, workable, practical, realistic.
Ea impracticable.

practical *adj* **1** REALISTIC, sensible,
commonsense, practicable, workable,
feasible, down-to-earth, matter-of-
fact, pragmatic, hardnosed (*infml*),
hard-headed, businesslike,
experienced, trained, qualified,
skilled, accomplished, proficient,
hands on, applied. **2** USEFUL, handy,
serviceable, utilitarian, functional,
working, everyday, ordinary.
Ea 1 impractical, unskilled,
theoretical.

practically *adv* **1** ALMOST, nearly,
well-nigh, virtually, pretty well, all
but, just about, in principle, in effect,
essentially, fundamentally, to all
intents and purposes. **2**
REALISTICALLY, sensibly,
reasonably, rationally, pragmatically.

practice *n* **1** CUSTOM, tradition,
convention, usage, habit, routine,
way, method, system, procedure,
policy. **2** REHEARSAL, run-through,
dry run, dummy run, try-out,

training, drill, exercise, work-out,
study, experience. **3** *in practice*:
effect, reality, actuality, action,
operation, performance, use,
application.
Ea 3 theory, principle.

practise *v* **1** DO, perform, execute,
implement, carry out, apply, put into
practice, follow, pursue, engage in,
undertake. **2** REHEARSE, run
through, repeat, drill, exercise, train,
study, perfect.

practised *adj* experienced, seasoned,
veteran, trained, qualified,
accomplished, skilled, versed,
knowledgeable, able, proficient,
expert, masterly, consummate,
finished.
Ea unpractised, inexperienced,
inexpert.

pragmatic *adj* practical, realistic,
sensible, matter-of-fact, businesslike,
efficient, hard-headed, hardnosed
(*infml*), unsentimental.
Ea unrealistic, idealistic, romantic.

praise *n* approval, admiration,
commendation, congratulation,
compliment, flattery, adulation,
eulogy, applause, ovation, cheering,
acclaim, recognition, testimonial,
tribute, accolade, homage, honour,
glory, worship, adoration, devotion,
thanksgiving.
Ea criticism, revilement.
v commend, congratulate, admire,
compliment, flatter, eulogize, wax
lyrical, rave over (*infml*), extol,
promote, applaud, cheer, acclaim,
hail, recognize, acknowledge, pay
tribute to, honour, laud, glorify,
magnify, exalt, worship, adore, bless.
Ea criticize, revile.

praiseworthy *adj* commendable,
fine, excellent, admirable, worthy,
deserving, honourable, reputable,
estimable, sterling.
Ea blameworthy, dishonourable,
ignoble.

prank *n* trick, practical joke, joke,

stunt, caper, frolic, lark, antic, escapade.

pray v invoke, call on, supplicate, entreat, implore, plead, beg, beseech, petition, ask, request, crave, solicit.

prayer n collect, litany, devotion, communion, invocation, supplication, entreaty, plea, appeal, petition, request.

preach v address, lecture, harangue, pontificate, sermonize, evangelize, moralize, exhort, urge, advocate.

precarious adj unsafe, dangerous, treacherous, risky, hazardous, chancy, uncertain, unsure, dubious, doubtful, unpredictable, unreliable, unsteady, unstable, shaky, wobbly, insecure, vulnerable.
F3 safe, certain, stable, secure.

precaution n safeguard, security, protection, insurance, providence, forethought, caution, prudence, foresight, anticipation, preparation, provision.

precautionary adj safety, protective, preventive, provident, cautious, prudent, judicious, preparatory, preliminary.

precede v come before, lead, come first, go before, take precedence, introduce, herald, usher in.
F3 follow, succeed.

precedence n priority, preference, pride of place, superiority, supremacy, pre-eminence, lead, first place, seniority, rank.

precedent n example, instance, pattern, model, standard, criterion.

precinct n **1** ZONE, area, district, quarter, sector, division, section.
2 BOUNDARY, limit, bound, confine.

precious adj **1** VALUED, treasured, prized, cherished, beloved, dearest, darling, favourite, loved, adored, idolized. **2** VALUABLE, expensive, costly, dear, priceless, inestimable, rare, choice, fine.

precipitate v hasten, hurry, speed, accelerate, quicken, expedite, advance, further, bring on, induce, trigger, cause, occasion.
adj sudden, unexpected, abrupt, quick, swift, rapid, brief, hasty, hurried, headlong, breakneck, frantic, violent, impatient, hot-headed, impetuous, impulsive, rash, reckless, heedless, indiscreet.
F3 cautious, careful.

precipitous adj steep, sheer, perpendicular, vertical, high.
F3 gradual.

precise adj exact, accurate, right, punctilious, correct, factual, faithful, authentic, literal, word-for-word, express, definite, explicit, unequivocal, unambiguous, clear-cut, distinct, detailed, blow-by-blow, minute, nice, particular, specific, fixed, rigid, strict, careful, meticulous, scrupulous, fastidious.
F3 imprecise, inexact, ambiguous, careless.

precisely adv exactly, absolutely, just so, accurately, correctly, literally, verbatim, word for word, strictly, minutely, clearly, distinctly.

precision n exactness, accuracy, correctness, faithfulness, explicitness, distinctness, detail, particularity, rigour, care, meticulousness, scrupulousness, neatness.
F3 imprecision, inaccuracy.

precocious adj forward, ahead, advanced, early, premature, mature, developed, gifted, clever, bright, smart, quick, fast.
F3 backward.

preconceive v presuppose, presume, assume, anticipate, project, imagine, conceive, envisage, expect, visualize, picture.

preconception n presupposition, presumption, assumption, conjecture, anticipation, expectation, prejudgement, bias, prejudice.

precondition n condition, stipulation, requirement, prerequisite, essential, necessity, must.

precursor n antecedent, forerunner, sign, indication, herald, harbinger, messenger, usher, pioneer, trail-blazer.

F3 follower, successor.

predecessor n ancestor, forefather, forebear, antecedent, forerunner, precursor.

F3 successor, descendant.

predestination n destiny, fate, lot, doom, predetermination, foreordination.

predetermined adj 1 PREDESTINED, destined, fated, doomed, ordained, foreordained. 2 PREARRANGED, arranged, agreed, fixed, set.

predicament n situation, plight, trouble, mess, fix, spot (*infml*), quandary, dilemma, impasse, crisis, emergency.

predict v foretell, prophesy, foresee, forecast, prognosticate, project.

predictable adj foreseeable, expected, anticipated, likely, probable, imaginable, foreseen, foregone, certain, sure, reliable, dependable.

F3 unpredictable, uncertain.

prediction n prophecy, forecast, prognosis, augury, divination, fortune-telling, soothsaying.

predispose v dispose, incline, prompt, induce, make, sway, influence, affect, bias, prejudice.

predominant adj dominant, prevailing, preponderant, chief, main, principal, primary, capital, paramount, supreme, sovereign, ruling, controlling, leading, powerful, potent, prime, important, influential, forceful, strong.

F3 minor, lesser, weak.

pre-eminent adj supreme, unsurpassed, unrivalled, unequalled, unmatched, matchless, incomparable, inimitable, chief, foremost, leading, eminent, distinguished, renowned, famous, prominent, outstanding, exceptional, excellent, superlative, transcendent, superior.

F3 inferior, unknown.

preface n foreword, introduction, preamble, prologue, prelude, preliminaries.

F3 epilogue, postscript.

v precede, prefix, lead up to, introduce, launch, open, begin, start.

F3 end, finish, complete.

prefer v favour, like better, would rather, would sooner, want, wish, desire, choose, select, pick, opt for, go for, plump for, single out, advocate, recommend, back, support, fancy, elect, adopt.

F3 reject.

preferable adj better, superior, nicer, preferred, favoured, chosen, desirable, advantageous, advisable, recommended.

F3 inferior, undesirable.

preference n 1 FAVOURITE, first choice, choice, pick, selection, option, wish, desire. 2 LIKING, fancy, inclination, predilection, partiality, favouritism, preferential treatment.

preferential adj better, superior, favoured, privileged, special, favourable, advantageous.

F3 equal.

pregnant adj 1 *a pregnant woman*: expectant, expecting, with child (*fml*). 2 *a pregnant pause*: meaningful, significant, eloquent, expressive, suggestive, charged, loaded, full.

prejudice n 1 BIAS, partiality, partisanship, discrimination, unfairness, injustice, intolerance, narrow-mindedness, bigotry, chauvinism, racism, sexism. 2 HARM, damage, impairment, hurt, injury, detriment, disadvantage, loss, ruin.

F3 1 fairness, tolerance. 2 benefit, advantage.

v 1 BIAS, predispose, incline, sway,

influence, condition, colour, slant, distort, load, weight. **2** HARM, damage, impair, hinder, undermine, hurt, injure, mar, spoil, ruin, wreck.
F2 benefit, help, advance.

prejudiced *adj* biased, partial, predisposed, subjective, partisan, one-sided, discriminatory, unfair, unjust, loaded, weighted, intolerant, narrow-minded, bigoted, chauvinist, racist, sexist, jaundiced, distorted, warped, influenced, conditioned.
F3 impartial, fair, tolerant.

prejudicial *adj* harmful, damaging, hurtful, injurious, detrimental, disadvantageous, unfavourable, inimical.
F2 beneficial, advantageous.

preliminaries *n* preparation, groundwork, foundations, basics, rudiments, formalities, introduction, preface, prelude, opening, beginning, start.

preliminary *adj* preparatory, prior, advance, exploratory, experimental, trial, test, pilot, early, earliest, first, initial, primary, qualifying, inaugural, introductory, opening.
F2 final, closing.

prelude *n* overture, introduction, preface, foreword, preamble, prologue, opening, opener, preliminary, preparation, beginning, start, commencement, precursor, curtain raiser.
F3 finale, epilogue.

premature *adj* early, immature, green, unripe, embryonic, half-formed, incomplete, undeveloped, abortive, hasty, ill-considered, rash, untimely, inopportune, ill-timed.
F2 late, tardy.

premeditated *adj* planned, intended, intentional, deliberate, wilful, conscious, cold-blooded, calculated, considered, contrived, preplanned, prearranged, predetermined.
F3 unpremeditated, spontaneous.

première *n* first performance, opening, opening night, first night, début.

premise *n* proposition, statement, assertion, postulate, thesis, argument, basis, supposition, hypothesis, presupposition, assumption.

premises *n* building, property, establishment, office, grounds, estate, site, place.

premonition *n* presentiment, feeling, intuition, hunch, idea, suspicion, foreboding, misgiving, fear, apprehension, anxiety, worry, warning, omen, sign.

preoccupation *n* **1** OBSESSION, fixation, hang-up (*infml*), concern, interest, enthusiasm, hobby-horse. **2** DISTRACTION, absent-mindedness, reverie, obliviousness, oblivion.

preoccupied *adj* **1** OBSESSED, intent, immersed, engrossed, engaged, taken up, wrapped up, involved. **2** DISTRACTED, abstracted, absent-minded, daydreaming, absorbed, faraway, heedless, oblivious, pensive.

preparation *n* **1** READINESS, provision, precaution, safeguard, foundation, groundwork, spadework, basics, rudiments, preliminaries, plans, arrangements. **2** MIXTURE, compound, concoction, potion, medicine, lotion, application.

preparatory *adj* preliminary, introductory, opening, initial, primary, basic, fundamental, rudimentary, elementary.

prepare *v* **1** GET READY, warm up, train, coach, study, make ready, adapt, adjust, plan, organize, arrange, pave the way. **2** *prepare a meal*: make, produce, construct, assemble, concoct, contrive, devise, draft, draw up, compose. **3** PROVIDE, supply, equip, fit out, rig out.

prepare oneself brace oneself, steel

oneself, gird oneself, fortify oneself.

prepared *adj* ready, waiting, set, fit, inclined, disposed, willing, planned, organized, arranged.
🔁 unprepared, unready.

preponderant *adj* greater, larger, superior, predominant, prevailing, overriding, overruling, controlling, foremost, important, significant.

preposterous *adj* incredible, unbelievable, absurd, ridiculous, ludicrous, foolish, crazy, nonsensical, unreasonable, monstrous, shocking, outrageous, intolerable, unthinkable, impossible.
🔁 sensible, reasonable, acceptable.

prerequisite *n* precondition, condition, proviso, qualification, requisite, requirement, imperative, necessity, essential, must.
🔁 extra.

prescribe *v* ordain, decree, dictate, rule, command, order, require, direct, assign, specify, stipulate, lay down, set, appoint, impose, fix, define, limit.

prescription *n* 1 INSTRUCTION, direction, formula. 2 MEDICINE, drug, preparation, mixture, remedy, treatment.

presence *n* 1 ATTENDANCE, company, occupancy, residence, existence. 2 AURA, air, demeanour, bearing, carriage, appearance, poise, self-assurance, personality, charisma. 3 NEARNESS, closeness, proximity, vicinity.
🔁 1 absence. 3 remoteness.

present¹ *adj* 1 ATTENDING, here, there, near, at hand, to hand, available, ready. 2 *at the present time*: current, contemporary, present-day, immediate, instant, existent, existing.
🔁 1 absent. 2 past, out-of-date.

present² *v* 1 SHOW, display, exhibit, demonstrate, mount, stage, put on, introduce, announce. 2 AWARD, confer, bestow, grant, give, donate,

hand over, entrust, extend, hold out, offer, tender, submit.

present³ *n* gift, prezzie (*infml*), offering, donation, grant, endowment, benefaction, bounty, largess, gratuity, tip, favour.

presentable *adj* neat, tidy, clean, respectable, decent, proper, suitable, acceptable, satisfactory, tolerable.
🔁 unpresentable, untidy, shabby.

presentation *n* 1 SHOW, performance, production, staging, representation, display, exhibition, demonstration, talk, delivery, appearance, arrangement. 2 AWARD, conferral, bestowal, investiture.

present-day *adj* current, present, existing, living, contemporary, modern, up-to-date, fashionable.
🔁 past, future.

presently *adv* 1 SOON, shortly, in a minute, before long, by and by. 2 CURRENTLY, at present, now.

preserve *v* 1 PROTECT, safeguard, guard, defend, shield, shelter, care for, maintain, uphold, sustain, continue, perpetuate, keep, retain, conserve, save, store. 2 *preserve food*: bottle, tin, can, pickle, salt, cure, dry.
🔁 destroy, ruin.
n 1 *home-made preserves*: conserve, jam, marmalade, jelly, pickle. 2 DOMAIN, realm, sphere, area, field, speciality. 3 RESERVATION, sanctuary, game reserve, safari park.

preside *v* chair, officiate, conduct, direct, manage, administer, control, run, head, lead, govern, rule.

press *v* 1 CRUSH, squash, squeeze, compress, stuff, cram, crowd, push, depress. 2 *press clothes*: iron, smooth, flatten. 3 HUG, embrace, clasp, squeeze. 4 URGE, plead, petition, campaign, demand, insist on, compel, constrain, force, pressure, pressurize, harass.
n 1 CROWD, throng, multitude, mob, horde, swarm, pack, crush, push. 2 JOURNALISTS, reporters,

correspondents, the media, newspapers, papers, Fleet Street, fourth estate.

pressing adj urgent, high-priority, burning, crucial, vital, essential, imperative, serious, important.
🔁 unimportant, trivial.

pressure n 1 FORCE, power, load, burden, weight, heaviness, compression, squeezing, stress, strain. 2 DIFFICULTY, problem, demand, constraint, obligation, urgency.

pressurize v force, compel, constrain, oblige, drive, bulldoze, coerce, press, pressure, lean on (infml), browbeat, bully.

prestige n status, reputation, standing, stature, eminence, distinction, esteem, regard, importance, authority, influence, fame, renown, kudos, credit, honour.
🔁 humbleness, unimportance.

prestigious adj esteemed, respected, reputable, important, influential, great, eminent, prominent, illustrious, renowned, celebrated, exalted, imposing, impressive, up-market.
🔁 humble, modest.

presume v 1 ASSUME, take it, think, believe, suppose, surmise, infer, presuppose, take for granted, count on, rely on, depend on, bank on, trust. 2 presume to criticize: dare, make so bold, go so far, venture, undertake.

presumption n 1 ASSUMPTION, belief, opinion, hypothesis, presupposition, supposition, surmise, conjecture, guess, likelihood, probability. 2 PRESUMPTUOUSNESS, boldness, audacity, impertinence, cheek (infml), nerve (infml), impudence, insolence, forwardness, assurance.
🔁 2 humility.

presumptuous adj bold, audacious, impertinent, impudent, insolent,

over-familiar, forward, pushy, arrogant, over-confident, conceited.
🔁 humble, modest.

pretence n show, display, appearance, cover, front, façade, veneer, cloak, veil, mask, guise, sham, feigning, faking, simulation, deception, trickery, wile, ruse, excuse, pretext, bluff, falsehood, deceit, fabrication, invention, make-believe, charade, acting, play-acting, posturing, posing, affectation, pretension, pretentiousness.
🔁 honesty, openness.

pretend v 1 AFFECT, put on, assume, feign, sham, counterfeit, fake, simulate, bluff, impersonate, pass oneself off, act, play-act, mime, go through the motions. 2 CLAIM, allege, profess, purport. 3 IMAGINE, make believe, suppose.

pretender n claimant, aspirant, candidate.

pretension n 1 PRETENTIOUSNESS, pomposity, self-importance, airs, conceit, vanity, snobbishness, affectation, pretence, show, showiness, ostentation. 2 CLAIM, profession, demand, aspiration, ambition.
🔁 1 modesty, humility, simplicity.

pretentious adj pompous, self-important, conceited, immodest, snobbish, affected, mannered, showy, ostentatious, extravagant, over-the-top, exaggerated, magniloquent, high-sounding, inflated, grandiose, ambitious, overambitious.
🔁 modest, humble, simple, straightforward.

pretext n excuse, ploy, ruse, cover, cloak, mask, guise, semblance, appearance, pretence, show.

pretty adj attractive, good-looking, beautiful, fair, lovely, bonny, cute, winsome, appealing, charming, dainty, graceful, elegant, fine, delicate, nice.
🔁 plain, unattractive, ugly.

adv fairly, somewhat, rather, quite, reasonably, moderately, tolerably.

prevail *v* **1** PREDOMINATE, preponderate, abound. **2** WIN, triumph, succeed, overcome, overrule, reign, rule.
🔁 **2** lose.

prevail upon persuade, talk into, prompt, induce, incline, sway, influence, convince, win over.

prevailing *adj* predominant, preponderant, main, principal, dominant, controlling, powerful, compelling, influential, reigning, ruling, current, fashionable, popular, mainstream, accepted, established, set, usual, customary, common, prevalent, widespread.
🔁 minor, subordinate.

prevalent *adj* widespread, extensive, rampant, rife, frequent, general, customary, usual, universal, ubiquitous, common, everyday, popular, current, prevailing.
🔁 uncommon, rare.

prevaricate *v* hedge, equivocate, quibble, cavil, dodge, evade, shift, shuffle, lie, deceive.

prevent *v* stop, avert, avoid, head off, ward off, stave off, intercept, forestall, anticipate, frustrate, thwart, check, restrain, inhibit, hinder, hamper, impede, obstruct, block, bar.
🔁 cause, help, foster, encourage, allow.

prevention *n* avoidance, frustration, check, hindrance, impediment, obstruction, obstacle, bar, elimination, precaution, safeguard, deterrence.
🔁 cause, help.

preventive *adj* preventative, anticipatory, pre-emptive, inhibitory, obstructive, precautionary, protective, counteractive, deterrent.
🔁 causative.

previous *adj* preceding, foregoing, earlier, prior, past, former, ex-, one-

time, sometime, erstwhile.
🔁 following, subsequent, later.

previously *adv* formerly, once, earlier, before, beforehand.
🔁 later.

prey *n* quarry, victim, game, kill.
prey on 1 HUNT, kill, devour, feed on, live off, exploit. **2** *prey on one's mind*: haunt, trouble, distress, worry, burden, weigh down, oppress.

price *n* value, worth, cost, expense, outlay, expenditure, fee, charge, levy, toll, rate, bill, assessment, valuation, estimate, quotation, figure, amount, sum, payment, reward, penalty, forfeit, sacrifice, consequences.
v value, rate, cost, evaluate, assess, estimate.

priceless *adj* **1** INVALUABLE, inestimable, incalculable, expensive, costly, dear, precious, valuable, prized, treasured, irreplaceable. **2** (*infml*) FUNNY, amusing, comic, hilarious, riotous, side-splitting, killing (*infml*), rich (*infml*).
🔁 **1** cheap, run-of-the-mill.

prick *v* pierce, puncture, perforate, punch, jab, stab, sting, bite, prickle, itch, tingle.
n puncture, perforation, pinhole, stab, pang, twinge, sting, bite.

prickle *n* thorn, spine, barb, spur, point, spike, needle.
v tingle, itch, smart, sting, prick.

prickly *adj* **1** THORNY, brambly, spiny, barbed, spiky, bristly, rough, scratchy. **2** IRRITABLE, edgy, touchy, grumpy, short-tempered.
🔁 **1** smooth. **2** relaxed, easy-going (*infml*).

pride *n* **1** CONCEIT, vanity, egotism, bigheadedness, boastfulness, smugness, arrogance, self-importance, presumption, haughtiness, superciliousness, snobbery, pretentiousness.
2 DIGNITY, self-respect, self-esteem, honour. **3** SATISFACTION, gratification, pleasure, delight.

Ea 1 humility, modesty. 2 shame.

priest *n* minister, vicar, padre, father, man of God, man of the cloth, clergyman, churchman.

priggish *adj* smug, self-righteous, goody-goody (*infml*), sanctimonious, holier-than-thou, puritanical, prim, prudish, narrow-minded.
Ea broadminded.

prim *adj* prudish, strait-laced, formal, demure, proper, priggish, prissy, fussy, particular, precise, fastidious.
Ea informed, relaxed, easy-going (*infml*).

primarily *adv* chiefly, principally, mainly, mostly, basically, fundamentally, especially, particularly, essentially.

primary *adj* 1 FIRST, earliest, original, initial, introductory, beginning, basic, fundamental, essential, radical, rudimentary, elementary, simple. 2 CHIEF, principal, main, dominant, leading, foremost, supreme, cardinal, capital, paramount, greatest, highest, ultimate.
Ea 2 secondary, subsidiary, minor.

prime *adj* best, choice, select, quality, first-class, first-rate, excellent, top, supreme, pre-eminent, superior, senior, leading, ruling, chief, principal, main, predominant, primary.
Ea second-rate, secondary.
n height, peak, zenith, heyday, flower, bloom, maturity, perfection.

primeval *adj* earliest, first, original, primordial, early, old, ancient, prehistoric, primitive, instinctive.
Ea modern.

primitive *adj* 1 CRUDE, rough, unsophisticated, uncivilized, barbarian, savage. 2 EARLY, elementary, rudimentary, primary, first, original, earliest.
Ea 1 advanced, sophisticated, civilized.

princely *adj* 1 SOVEREIGN, imperial, royal, regal, majestic, stately, grand, noble. 2 *princely sum*: generous, liberal, lavish, sumptuous, magnificent, handsome.

principal *adj* main, chief, key, essential, cardinal, primary, first, foremost, leading, dominant, prime, paramount, pre-eminent, supreme, highest.
Ea minor, subsidiary, lesser, least.
n head, head teacher, headmaster, headmistress, chief, leader, boss, director, manager, superintendent.

principally *adv* mainly, mostly, chiefly, primarily, predominantly, above all, particularly, especially.

principle *n* 1 RULE, formula, law, canon, axiom, dictum, precept, maxim, truth, tenet, doctrine, creed, dogma, code, standard, criterion, proposition, fundamental, essential. 2 *a man of principle*: HONOUR, integrity, rectitude, uprightness, virtue, decency, morality, morals, ethics, standards, scruples, conscience.

print *v* mark, stamp, imprint, impress, engrave, copy, reproduce, run off, publish, issue.
n 1 LETTERS, characters, lettering, type, typescript, typeface, fount. 2 MARK, impression, fingerprint, footprint. 3 COPY, reproduction, picture, engraving, lithograph, photograph, photo.

prior *adj* earlier, preceding, foregoing, previous, former.
Ea later.
prior to before, preceding, earlier than.
Ea after, following.

priority *n* right of way, precedence, seniority, rank, superiority, pre-eminence, supremacy, the lead, first place, urgency.
Ea inferiority.

prison *n* jail, nick (*sl*), clink (*sl*), cooler (*sl*), penitentiary, cell, lock-up, cage, dungeon, imprisonment, confinement, detention, custody.

prisoner n captive, hostage, convict, jail-bird (*infml*), inmate, internee, detainee.

privacy n secrecy, confidentiality, independence, solitude, isolation, seclusion, concealment, retirement, retreat.

private adj secret, classified, hush-hush (*infml*), off the record, unofficial, confidential, intimate, personal, individual, own, exclusive, particular, special, separate, independent, solitary, isolated, secluded, hidden, concealed, reserved, withdrawn.
🔁 public, open.

in private privately, in confidence, secretly, in secret, behind closed doors, in camera.
🔁 publicly, openly.

privilege n advantage, benefit, concession, birthright, title, due, right, prerogative, entitlement, freedom, liberty, franchise, licence, sanction, authority, immunity, exemption.
🔁 disadvantage.

privileged adj advantaged, favoured, special, sanctioned, authorized, immune, exempt, élite, honoured, ruling, powerful.
🔁 disadvantaged, under-privileged.

prize n reward, trophy, medal, award, winnings, jackpot, purse, premium, stake(s), honour, accolade.
adj best, top, first-rate, excellent, outstanding, champion, winning, prize-winning, award-winning.
🔁 second-rate.
v treasure, value, appreciate, esteem, revere, cherish, hold dear.
🔁 despise.

probability n likelihood, odds, chances, expectation, prospect, chance, possibility.
🔁 improbability.

probable adj likely, odds-on, expected, credible, believable,

plausible, feasible, possible, apparent, seeming.
🔁 improbable, unlikely.

probation n apprenticeship, trial period, trial, test.

probe v prod, poke, pierce, penetrate, sound, plumb, explore, examine, scrutinize, investigate, go into, look into, search, sift, test.
n 1 BORE, drill. 2 INQUIRY, inquest, investigation, exploration, examination, test, scrutiny, study, research.

problem n 1 TROUBLE, worry, predicament, quandary, dilemma, difficulty, complication, snag.
2 QUESTION, poser, puzzle, brain-teaser, conundrum, riddle, enigma.
adj difficult, unmanageable, uncontrollable, unruly, delinquent.
🔁 well-behaved, manageable.

procedure n routine, process, method, system, technique, custom, practice, policy, formula, course, scheme, strategy, plan of action, move, step, action, conduct, operation, performance.

proceed v 1 *the permission to proceed*: advance, go ahead, move on, progress, continue, carry on, press on. 2 ORIGINATE, derive, flow, start, stem, spring, arise, issue, result, ensue, follow, come.
🔁 1 stop, retreat.

proceedings n 1 MATTERS, affairs, business, dealings, transactions, report, account, minutes, records, archives, annals. 2 EVENTS, happenings, deeds, doings, moves, steps, measures, action, course of action.

proceeds n revenue, income, returns, receipts, takings, earnings, gain, profit, yield, produce.
🔁 expenditure, outlay.

process n 1 PROCEDURE, operation, practice, method, system, technique, means, manner, mode, way, stage, step. 2 COURSE,

progression, advance, progress, development, evolution, formation, growth, movement, action, proceeding.
v deal with, handle, treat, prepare, refine, transform, convert, change, alter.

procession *n* march, parade, cavalcade, motorcade, cortège, file, column, train, succession, series, sequence, course, run.

proclaim *v* announce, declare, pronounce, affirm, give out, publish, advertise, make known, profess, testify, show, indicate.

proclamation *n* announcement, declaration, pronouncement, affirmation, publication, promulgation, notice, notification, manifesto, decree, edict.

procrastinate *v* defer, put off, postpone, delay, retard, stall, temporize, play for time, dally, dilly-dally (*infml*), drag one's feet, prolong, protract.
🔄 advance, proceed.

procure *v* acquire, buy, purchase, get, obtain, find, come by, pick up, lay hands on, earn, gain, win, secure, appropriate, requisition.
🔄 lose.

prod *v* poke, jab, dig, elbow, nudge, push, shove, goad, spur, urge, egg on (*infml*), prompt, stimulate, motivate.
n poke, jab, dig, elbow, nudge, push, shove, prompt, reminder, stimulus, motivation.

prodigy *n* genius, virtuoso, wonder, marvel, miracle, phenomenon, sensation, freak, curiosity, rarity, child genius, wonder child, whizz kid (*infml*).

produce *v* **1** CAUSE, occasion, give rise to, provoke, bring about, result in, effect, create, originate, invent, make, manufacture, fabricate, construct, compose, generate, yield, bear, deliver. **2** ADVANCE, put forward, present, offer, give, supply,

provide, furnish, bring out, bring forth, show, exhibit, demonstrate. **3** *produce a play*: direct, stage, mount, put on.
n crop, harvest, yield, output, product.

product *n* **1** COMMODITY, merchandise, goods, end-product, artefact, work, creation, invention, production, output, yield, produce, fruit, return. **2** RESULT, consequence, outcome, issue, upshot, offshoot, spin-off, by-product, legacy.
🔄 **2** cause.

production *n* **1** MAKING, manufacture, fabrication, construction, assembly, creation, origination, preparation, formation. **2** *an amateur production*: staging, presentation, direction, management.
🔄 **1** consumption.

productive *adj* fruitful, profitable, rewarding, valuable, worthwhile, useful, constructive, creative, inventive, fertile, rich, teeming, busy, energetic, vigorous, efficient, effective.
🔄 unproductive, fruitless, useless.

productivity *n* productiveness, yield, output, work rate, efficiency.

profane *adj* secular, temporal, lay, unconsecrated, unhallowed, unsanctified, unholy, irreligious, impious, sacrilegious, blasphemous, ungodly, irreverent, disrespectful, abusive, crude, coarse, foul, filthy, unclean.
🔄 sacred, religious, respectful.
v desecrate, pollute, contaminate, defile, debase, pervert, abuse, misuse.
🔄 revere, honour.

profess *v* admit, confess, acknowledge, own, confirm, certify, declare, announce, proclaim, state, assert, affirm, maintain, claim, allege, make out, pretend.

profession *n* **1** CAREER, job, occupation, employment, business, line (of work), trade, vocation,

calling, métier, craft, office, position.
2 ADMISSION, confession,
acknowledgement, declaration,
announcement, statement, testimony,
assertion, affirmation, claim.

professional adj qualified, licensed,
trained, experienced, practised,
skilled, expert, masterly, proficient,
competent, businesslike, efficient.
☒ amateur, unprofessional.
n expert, authority, specialist, pro
(*infml*), master, virtuoso, dab hand
(*infml*).
☒ amateur.

proficiency n skill, skilfulness,
expertise, mastery, talent, knack,
dexterity, finesse, aptitude, ability,
competence.
☒ incompetence.

proficient adj able, capable, skilled,
qualified, trained, experienced,
accomplished, expert, masterly,
gifted, talented, clever, skilful,
competent, efficient.
☒ unskilled, incompetent.

profile n **1** SIDE VIEW, outline,
contour, silhouette, shape, form,
figure, sketch, drawing, diagram,
chart, graph. **2** BIOGRAPHY,
curriculum vitae, thumbnail sketch,
vignette, portrait, study, analysis,
examination, survey, review.

profit n gain, surplus, excess, bottom
line, revenue, return, yield, proceeds,
receipts, takings, earnings, winnings,
interest, advantage, benefit, use,
avail, value, worth.
☒ loss.
v gain, make money, pay, serve, avail,
benefit.
☒ lose.

profit by, profit from exploit, take
advantage of, use, utilize, turn to
advantage, capitalize on, cash in on,
reap the benefit of.

profitable adj cost-effective,
economic, commercial, money-
making, lucrative, remunerative,
paying, rewarding, successful,
fruitful, productive, advantageous,
beneficial, useful, valuable,
worthwhile.
☒ unprofitable, loss-making, non-
profit-making.

profound adj **1** DEEP, great, intense,
extreme, heartfelt, marked, far-
reaching, extensive, exhaustive. **2** a
profound remark: serious, weighty,
penetrating, thoughtful,
philosophical, wise, learned, erudite,
abstruse.
☒ **1** shallow, slight, mild.

profuse adj ample, abundant,
plentiful, copious, generous, liberal,
lavish, rich, luxuriant, excessive,
immoderate, extravagant,
overabundant, superabundant,
overflowing.
☒ inadequate, sparse.

profusion n abundance, plenty,
wealth, multitude, plethora, glut,
excess, surplus, superfluity,
extravagance.
☒ inadequacy, scarcity.

programme n **1** SCHEDULE,
timetable, agenda, calendar, order of
events, listing, line-up, plan, scheme,
project, syllabus, curriculum. **2** *radio
programme*: broadcast, transmission,
show, performance, production,
presentation.

progress n movement, progression,
passage, journey, way, advance,
headway, step forward,
breakthrough, development,
evolution, growth, increase,
improvement, betterment,
promotion.
☒ recession, deterioration, decline.
v proceed, advance, go forward,
forge ahead, make progress, make
headway, come on, develop, grow,
mature, blossom, improve, better,
prosper, increase.
☒ deteriorate, decline.

progression n cycle, chain, string,
succession, series, sequence, order,
course, advance, headway, progress,

development.

progressive *adj* 1 MODERN, avant-garde, advanced, forward-looking, enlightened, liberal, radical, revolutionary, reformist, dynamic, enterprising, go-ahead, up-and-coming. 2 ADVANCING, continuing, developing, growing, increasing, intensifying.
🔁 1 regressive.

prohibit *v* forbid, ban, bar, veto, proscribe, outlaw, rule out, preclude, prevent, stop, hinder, hamper, impede, obstruct, restrict.
🔁 permit, allow, authorize.

project *n* assignment, contract, task, job, work, occupation, activity, enterprise, undertaking, venture, plan, scheme, programme, design, proposal, idea, conception.
v 1 PREDICT, forecast, extrapolate, estimate, reckon, calculate. 2 THROW, fling, hurl, launch, propel. 3 PROTRUDE, stick out, bulge, jut out, overhang.

projection *n* 1 PROTUBERANCE, bulge, overhang, ledge, sill, shelf, ridge. 2 PREDICTION, forecast, extrapolation, estimate, reckoning, calculation, computation.

proliferate *v* multiply, reproduce, breed, increase, build up, intensify, escalate, mushroom, snowball, spread, expand, flourish, thrive.
🔁 dwindle.

prolific *adj* productive, fruitful, fertile, profuse, copious, abundant.
🔁 unproductive.

prolong *v* lengthen, extend, stretch, protract, draw out, spin out, drag out, delay, continue, perpetuate.
🔁 shorten.

prominence *n* 1 FAME, celebrity, renown, eminence, distinction, greatness, importance, reputation, name, standing, rank, prestige. 2 BULGE, protuberance, bump, hump, lump, mound, rise, elevation, projection, process, headland, promontory, cliff, crag.
🔁 1 unimportance, insignificance.

prominent *adj* 1 NOTICEABLE, conspicuous, obvious, unmistakable, striking, eye-catching. 2 BULGING, protuberant, projecting, jutting, protruding, obtrusive. 3 *a prominent writer*: famous, well-known, celebrated, renowned, noted, eminent, distinguished, respected, leading, foremost, chief, main, important, popular, outstanding.
🔁 1 inconspicuous. 3 unknown, unimportant, insignificant.

promiscuity *n* looseness, laxity, permissiveness, wantonness, immorality, licentiousness, debauchery, depravity.
🔁 chastity, morality.

promiscuous *adj* loose, immoral, licentious, dissolute, casual, random, haphazard, indiscriminate.
🔁 chaste, moral.

promise *v* 1 VOW, pledge, swear, take an oath, contract, undertake, give one's word, vouch, warrant, guarantee, assure. 2 AUGUR, presage, indicate, suggest, hint at.
n 1 VOW, pledge, oath, word of honour, bond, compact, covenant, guarantee, assurance, undertaking, engagement, commitment. 2 POTENTIAL, ability, capability, aptitude, talent.

promising *adj* auspicious, propitious, favourable, rosy, bright, encouraging, hopeful, talented, gifted, budding, up-and-coming.
🔁 unpromising, inauspicious, discouraging.

promote *v* 1 ADVERTISE, plug (*infml*), publicize, hype (*sl*), popularize, market, sell, push, recommend, advocate, champion, endorse, sponsor, support, back, help, aid, assist, foster, nurture, further, forward, encourage, boost, stimulate, urge. 2 UPGRADE, advance, move up, raise, elevate, exalt, honour.

Ea 1 disparage, hinder. **2** demote.

promotion n **1** ADVANCEMENT, upgrading, rise, preferment, elevation, exaltation.
2 ADVERTISING, plugging (*infml*), publicity, hype (*sl*), campaign, progaganda, marketing, pushing, support, backing, furtherance, development, encouragement, boosting.

Ea 1 demotion. **2** disparagement, obstruction.

prompt¹ adj punctual, on time, immediate, instantaneous, instant, direct, quick, swift, rapid, speedy, unhesitating, willing, ready, alert, responsive, timely, early.

Ea slow, hesitant, late.

adv promptly, punctually, exactly, on the dot, to the minute, sharp.

prompt² v cause, give rise to, result in, occasion, produce, instigate, call forth, elicit, provoke, incite, urge, encourage, inspire, move, stimulate, motivate, spur, prod, remind.

Ea deter, dissuade.

n reminder, cue, hint, help, prod, spur, stimulus.

prone adj **1** LIKELY, given, inclined, disposed, predisposed, bent, apt, liable, subject, susceptible, vulnerable. **2** *she lay prone*: face down, prostrate, flat, horizontal, full-length, stretched, recumbent.

Ea 1 unlikely, immune. **2** upright, supine.

pronounce v **1** SAY, utter, speak, express, voice, vocalize, sound, enunciate, articulate, stress.
2 DECLARE, announce, proclaim, decree, judge, affirm, assert.

pronounced adj clear, distinct, definite, positive, decided, marked, noticeable, conspicuous, evident, obvious, striking, unmistakable, strong, broad.

Ea faint, vague.

pronunciation n speech, diction,

elocution, enunciation, articulation, delivery, accent, stress, inflection, intonation, modulation.

proof n evidence, documentation, demonstration, verification, confirmation, corroboration, substantiation.

prop v **1** SUPPORT, sustain, uphold, maintain, shore, stay, buttress, bolster, underpin, set. **2** *propped against the wall*: lean, rest, stand.
n support, stay, mainstay, strut, buttress, brace, truss.

propaganda n advertising, publicity, hype (*sl*), indoctrination, brainwashing, disinformation.

propagate v **1** SPREAD, transmit, broadcast, diffuse, disseminate, circulate, publish, promulgate, publicize, promote. **2** INCREASE, multiply, proliferate, generate, produce, breed, beget, spawn, procreate, reproduce.

propel v move, drive, impel, force, thrust, push, shove, launch, shoot, send.

Ea stop.

proper adj **1** RIGHT, correct, accurate, exact, precise, true, genuine, real, actual. **2** ACCEPTED, correct, suitable, appropriate, fitting, decent, respectable, polite, formal.

Ea 1 wrong. **2** improper, indecent.

property n **1** ESTATE, land, real estate, acres, premises, buildings, house(s), wealth, riches, resources, means, capital, assets, holding(s), belongings, possessions, effects, goods, chattels. **2** FEATURE, trait, quality, attribute, characteristic, idiosyncrasy, peculiarity, mark.

prophecy n prediction, augury, forecast, prognosis.

prophesy v predict, foresee, augur, foretell, forewarn, forecast.

prophet n seer, soothsayer, foreteller, forecaster, oracle, clairvoyant, fortune-teller.

proportion n **1** PERCENTAGE,

fraction, part, division, share, quota, amount. **2** RATIO, relationship, correspondence, symmetry, balance, distribution.

F∃ 2 disproportion, imbalance.

proportional *adj* proportionate, relative, commensurate, consistent, corresponding, analogous, comparable, equitable, even.

F∃ disproportionate.

proportions *n* dimensions, measurements, size, magnitude, volume, capacity.

proposal *n* proposition, suggestion, recommendation, motion, plan, scheme, project, design, programme, manifesto, presentation, bid, offer, tender, terms.

propose *v* **1** SUGGEST, recommend, move, advance, put forward, introduce, bring up, table, submit, present, offer, tender. **2** INTEND, mean, aim, purpose, plan, design. **3** NOMINATE, put up.

F∃ 1 withdraw.

proprietor, proprietress *n* landlord, landlady, title-holder, freeholder, leaseholder, landowner, owner, possessor.

prosecute *v* accuse, indict, sue, prefer charges, take to court, litigate, summon, put on trial, try.

F∃ defend.

prosody

Forms of prosody include: abstract verse, Alcaic verse, alexandrine, alliteration, amphibrach, amphimacer, Anacreontic verse, anacrusis, analysed rhyme, anapaest, antibacchius, antispast, Archilochian verse, asclepiad, assonance, asynartete, ballade, blank verse, broken rhyme, bouts rimés, caesura, canto, catalexis, choliamb, choree, choriamb, cinquain, couplet, dactyl, decastich, dipody, dispondee, distich, ditrochee, dizain, dochmius, elision, enjambment, envoy, epitrite, epode, eye rhyme, false quantity, feminine caesura, feminine ending, feminine rhyme, foot, free verse, galliambic, glyconic, heptameter, heptapody, heroic couplet, hexameter, hexastich, hypermetrical, iamb, ictus, Ionic, kyrielle, laisse, Leonine rhyme, linked verse, long-measure, macaronic, masculine ending, masculine rhyme, metre, miurus, monometer, monorhyme, paeon, pantoum, pentameter, pentastich, Petrarchan sonnet, Pherecratean, Pindaric, poulters' measure, pyrrhic, Pythian verse, quatorzain, quatrain, reported verses, rhopalic, rhyme royal, rime riche, rime suffisante, rondeau, rondel, rove-over, Sapphic, senarius, septenarius, sonnet, Spencerian stanza, spondee, sprung rhythm, strophe, substituion, synaphea, tetrameter, tetrapody, tetrastich, tribrach, trimeter, triolet, tripody, triseme, trochee, villanelle, virelay.

prospect *n* chance, odds, probability, likelihood, possibility, hope, expectation, anticipation, outlook, future.

F∃ unlikelihood.

prospective *adj* future, -to-be, intended, designate, destined, forthcoming, approaching, coming, imminent, awaited, expected, anticipated, likely, possible, probable, potential, aspiring, would-be.

F∃ current.

prospectus *n* plan, scheme, programme, syllabus, manifesto, outline, synopsis, pamphlet, leaflet, brochure, catalogue, list.

prosper *v* boom, thrive, flourish, flower, bloom, succeed, get on, advance, progress, grow rich.

F∃ fail.

prosperity *n* boom, plenty, affluence, wealth, riches, fortune, well-being, luxury, the good life,

success, good fortune.
Ea adversity, poverty.
prosperous adj booming, thriving,
flourishing, blooming, successful,
fortunate, lucky, rich, wealthy,
affluent, well-off, well-to-do.
Ea unfortunate, poor.
prostrate adj flat, horizontal, prone,
fallen, overcome, overwhelmed,
crushed, paralysed, powerless,
helpless, defenceless.
Ea triumphant.
v lay low, overcome, overwhelm,
crush, overthrow, tire, wear out,
fatigue, exhaust, drain, ruin.
Ea strengthen.
prostrate oneself bow down, kneel,
kowtow, submit, grovel, cringe, abase
oneself.
protagonist n hero, heroine, lead,
principal, leader, prime mover,
champion, advocate, supporter,
proponent, exponent.
protect v safeguard, defend, guard,
escort, cover, screen, shield, secure,
watch over, look after, care for,
support, shelter, harbour, keep,
conserve, preserve, save.
Ea attack, neglect.
protection n 1 protection of the
environment: care, custody, charge,
guardianship, safekeeping,
conservation, preservation, safety,
safeguard. 2 BARRIER, buffer,
bulwark, defence, guard, shield,
armour, screen, cover, shelter,
refuge, security, insurance.
Ea 1 neglect, attack.
protective adj 1 POSSESSIVE,
defensive, motherly, maternal,
fatherly, paternal, watchful, vigilant,
careful. 2 protective clothing:
waterproof, fireproof, insulating.
Ea 1 aggressive, threatening.
protest n objection, disapproval,
opposition, dissent, complaint,
protestation, outcry, appeal,
demonstration.
Ea acceptance.

v 1 OBJECT, take exception,
complain, appeal, demonstrate,
oppose, disapprove, disagree, argue.
2 protest one's innocence: assert,
maintain, contend, insist, profess.
Ea 1 accept.
protester n demonstrator, agitator,
rebel, dissident, dissenter.
protocol n procedure, formalities,
convention, custom, etiquette,
manners, good form, propriety.
protracted adj long, lengthy,
prolonged, extended, drawn-out,
long-drawn-out, overlong,
interminable.
Ea brief, shortened.
protrude v stick out, poke out, come
through, bulge, jut out, project,
extend, stand out, obtrude.
proud adj 1 CONCEITED, vain,
egotistical, bigheaded, boastful,
smug, complacent, arrogant, self-
important, cocky, presumptuous,
haughty, high and mighty,
overbearing, supercilious, snooty
(infml), snobbish, toffee-nosed
(infml), stuck-up (infml).
2 SATISFIED, contented, gratified,
pleased, delighted, honoured.
3 DIGNIFIED, noble, honourable,
worthy, self-respecting.
Ea 1 humble, modest, unassuming.
2 ashamed. 3 deferential, ignoble.
prove v show, demonstrate, attest,
verify, confirm, corroborate,
substantiate, bear out, document,
certify, authenticate, validate, justify,
establish, determine, ascertain, try,
test, check, examine, analyse.
Ea disprove, discredit, falsify.
proverb n saying, adage, aphorism,
maxim, byword, dictum, precept.
proverbial adj axiomatic, accepted,
conventional, traditional, customary,
time-honoured, famous, well-known,
legendary, notorious, typical,
archetypal.
provide v 1 SUPPLY, furnish, stock,
equip, outfit, prepare for, cater,

serve, present, give, contribute, yield, lend, add, bring. **2 PLAN FOR**, allow, make provision, accommodate, arrange for, take precautions. **3 STATE**, specify, stipulate, lay down, require.
ⅇ 1 take, remove.

providence n **1 FATE**, destiny, divine intervention, God's will, fortune, luck. **2 PRUDENCE**, far-sightedness, foresight, caution, care, thrift.
ⅇ 2 improvidence.

provident adj prudent, far-sighted, judicious, cautious, careful, thrifty, economical, frugal.
ⅇ improvident.

providential adj timely, opportune, convenient, fortunate, lucky, happy, welcome, heaven-sent.
ⅇ untimely.

providing conj provided, with the proviso, given, as long as, on condition, on the understanding.

province n **1 REGION**, area, district, zone, county, shire, department, territory, colony, dependency. **2 RESPONSIBILITY**, concern, duty, office, role, function, field, sphere, domain, department, line.

provincial adj regional, local, rural, rustic, country, home-grown, small-town, parish-pump, parochial, insular, inward-looking, limited, narrow, narrow-minded, small-minded.
ⅇ national, cosmopolitan, urban, sophisticated.

provision n **1 PLAN**, arrangement, preparation, measure, precaution. **2 STIPULATION**, specification, proviso, condition, term, requirement.

provisional adj temporary, interim, transitional, stopgap, makeshift, conditional, tentative.
ⅇ permanent, fixed, definite.

provisions n food, foodstuff, groceries, eatables (infml),

sustenance, rations, supplies, stocks, stores.

proviso n condition, term, requirement, stipulation, qualification, reservation, restriction, limitation, provision, clause, rider.

provocation n cause, grounds, justification, reason, motive, stimulus, motivation, incitement, instigation, annoyance, aggravation (infml), vexation, grievance, offence, insult, affront, injury, taunt, challenge, dare.

provocative adj **1 ANNOYING**, aggravating (infml), galling, outrageous, offensive, insulting, abusive. **2 STIMULATING**, exciting, challenging. **3 EROTIC**, titillating, arousing, sexy, seductive, alluring, tempting, inviting, tantalizing, teasing, suggestive.
ⅇ 1 conciliatory.

provoke v **1 ANNOY**, irritate, rile, aggravate (infml), offend, insult, anger, enrage, infuriate, incense, madden, exasperate, tease, taunt. **2 CAUSE**, occasion, give rise to, produce, generate, induce, elicit, evoke, excite, inspire, move, stir, prompt, stimulate, motivate, incite, instigate.
ⅇ 1 please, pacify. **2** result.

prowess n accomplishment, attainment, ability, aptitude, skill, expertise, mastery, command, talent, genius.

proximity n closeness, nearness, vicinity, neighbourhood, adjacency, juxtaposition.
ⅇ remoteness.

proxy n agent, factor, deputy, stand-in, substitute, representative, delegate, attorney.

prudent adj wise, sensible, politic, judicious, shrewd, discerning, careful, cautious, wary, vigilant, circumspect, discreet, provident, far-sighted, thrifty.
ⅇ imprudent, unwise, careless, rash.

pry v meddle, interfere, poke one's nose in, intrude, peep, peer, snoop, nose, ferret, dig, delve.

🞂 mind one's own business.

pseudonym n false name, assumed name, alias, incognito, pen name, nom de plume, stage name.

psychic adj spiritual, supernatural, occult, mystic(al), clairvoyant, extrasensory, telepathic, mental, psychological, intellectual, cognitive.

psychological adj mental, cerebral, intellectual, cognitive, emotional, subjective, subconscious, unconscious, psychosomatic, irrational, unreal.

🞂 physical, real.

puberty n pubescence, adolescence, teens, youth, growing up, maturity.

🞂 childhood, immaturity, old age.

public adj **1** public buildings: state, national, civil, community, social, collective, communal, common, general, universal, open, unrestricted. **2** KNOWN, well-known, recognized, acknowledged, overt, open, exposed, published.

🞂 **1** private, personal. **2** secret.

n people, nation, country, population, populace, masses, citizens, society, community, voters, electorate, followers, supporters, fans, audience, patrons, clientèle, customers, buyers, consumers.

public house pub (infml), local (infml), bar, saloon, inn, tavern.

publication n **1** BOOK, newspaper, magazine, periodical, booklet, leaflet, pamphlet, handbill. **2** ANNOUNCEMENT, declaration, notification, disclosure, release, issue, printing, publishing.

publicity n advertising, plug (infml), hype (sl), promotion, build-up, boost, attention, limelight, splash.

publicize v advertise, plug (infml), hype (sl), promote, push, spotlight, broadcast, make known, blaze.

publish v **1** ANNOUNCE, declare, communicate, make known, divulge, disclose, reveal, release, publicize, advertise. **2** publish a book: produce, print, issue, bring out, distribute, circulate, spread, diffuse.

pucker v gather, ruffle, wrinkle, shrivel, crinkle, crumple, crease, furrow, purse, screw up, contract, compress.

puerile adj childish, babyish, infantile, juvenile, immature, irresponsible, silly, foolish, inane, trivial.

🞂 mature.

puff **1** BREATH, waft, whiff, draught, flurry, gust, blast. **2** a puff on a cigarette: pull, drag.

v **1** BREATHE, pant, gasp, gulp, wheeze, blow, waft, inflate, expand, swell. **2** puff a cigarette: smoke, pull, drag, draw, suck.

puffy adj puffed up, inflated, swollen, bloated, distended, enlarged.

pugnacious adj hostile, aggressive, belligerent, contentious, disputatious, argumentative, quarrelsome, hot-tempered.

🞂 peaceable.

pull v **1** TOW, drag, haul, draw, tug, jerk, yank (infml). **2** REMOVE, take out, extract, pull out, pluck, uproot, pull up, rip, tear. **3** ATTRACT, draw, lure, allure, entice, tempt, magnetize. **4** DISLOCATE, sprain, wrench, strain.

🞂 **1** push, press. **3** repel, deter, discourage.

n **1** TOW, drag, tug, jerk, yank (infml). **2** ATTRACTION, lure, allurement, drawing power, magnetism, influence, weight.

pull apart separate, part, dismember, dismantle, take to pieces.

🞂 join.

pull down destroy, demolish, knock down, bulldoze.

🞂 build, erect, put up.

pull off 1 ACCOMPLISH, achieve, bring off, succeed, manage, carry out.

2 DETACH, remove.

1 fail. **2** attach.

pull out retreat, withdraw, leave, depart, quit, move out, evacuate, desert, abandon.
 join, arrive.

pull through recover, rally, recuperate, survive, weather.

pull together co-operate, work together, collaborate, team up.
 fight.

pull up 1 STOP, halt, park, draw up, pull in, pull over, brake. **2** REPRIMAND, tell off (*infml*), tick off (*infml*), take to task, rebuke, criticize.

pulp *n* flesh, marrow, paste, purée, mash, mush, pap.
 v crush, squash, pulverize, mash, purée, liquidize.

pulsate *v* pulse, beat, throb, pound, hammer, drum, thud, thump, vibrate, oscillate, quiver.

pulse *n* beat, stroke, rhythm, throb, pulsation, beating, pounding, drumming, vibration, oscillation.

pulverize *v* **1** CRUSH, pound, grind, mill, powder. **2** DEFEAT, destroy, demolish, annihilate.

pump *v* push, drive, force, inject, siphon, draw, drain.

pump up blow up, inflate, puff up, fill.

pun *n* play on words, double entendre, witticism, quip.

punch[1] *v* hit, strike, pummel, jab, bash, clout, cuff, box, thump, sock (*sl*), wallop (*infml*).
 n **1** BLOW, jab, bash, clout, thump, wallop (*infml*). **2** FORCE, impact, effectiveness, drive, vigour, verve, panache.

punch[2] *v* perforate, pierce, puncture, prick, bore, drill, stamp, cut.

punctilious *adj* scrupulous, conscientious, meticulous, careful, exact, precise, strict, formal, proper, particular, finicky, fussy.
 lax, informal.

punctual *adj* prompt, on time, on the dot, exact, precise, early, in good time.
 unpunctual, late.

punctuation

> *Punctuation marks include*: comma, full stop, period, colon, semicolon, brackets, parentheses, square brackets, inverted commas, speech marks, quotation marks, quotes (*infml*), exclamation mark, question mark, apostrophe, asterisk, star, hyphen, dash, oblique stroke, solidus, backslash.

puncture *n* **1** FLAT TYRE, flat (*infml*), blow-out. **2** LEAK, hole, perforation, cut, nick.
 v prick, pierce, penetrate, perforate, hole, cut, nick, burst, rupture, flatten, deflate.

pungent *adj* strong, hot, peppery, spicy, aromatic, tangy, piquant, sharp, keen, acute, sour, bitter, acrid, caustic, stinging, biting, cutting, incisive, pointed, piercing, penetrating, sarcastic, scathing.
 mild, bland, tasteless.

punish *v* penalize, discipline, correct, chastise, castigate, scold, beat, flog, lash, cane, spank, fine, imprison.
 reward.

punishment *n* discipline, correction, chastisement, beating, flogging, penalty, fine, imprisonment, sentence, deserts, retribution, revenge.
 reward.

punitive *adj* penal, disciplinary, retributive, retaliatory, vindictive, punishing.

puny *adj* weak, feeble, frail, sickly, undeveloped, underdeveloped, stunted, undersized, diminutive, little, tiny, insignificant.
 strong, sturdy, large, important.

pupil *n* student, scholar, schoolboy, schoolgirl, learner, apprentice, beginner, novice, disciple, protégé(e).
 teacher.

purchase v buy, pay for, invest in (*infml*), procure, acquire, obtain, get, secure, gain, earn, win.
🔼 sell.
n acquisition, buy (*infml*), investment, asset, possession, property.
🔼 sale.

purchaser n buyer, consumer, shopper, customer, client.
🔼 seller, vendor.

pure adj **1** *pure gold*: unadulterated, unalloyed, unmixed, undiluted, neat, solid, simple, natural, real, authentic, genuine, true. **2** STERILE, uncontaminated, unpolluted, germ-free, aseptic, antiseptic, disinfected, sterilized, hygienic, sanitary, clean, immaculate, spotless, clear. **3** SHEER, utter, complete, total, thorough, absolute, perfect, unqualified. **4** CHASTE, virginal, undefiled, unsullied, moral, upright, virtuous, blameless, innocent. **5** *pure mathematics*: theoretical, abstract, conjectural, speculative, academic.
🔼 **1** impure, adulterated. **2** contaminated, polluted. **4** immoral. **5** applied.

purely adv **1** UTTERLY, completely, totally, entirely, wholly, thoroughly, absolutely. **2** ONLY, simply, merely, just, solely, exclusively.

purge v **1** PURIFY, cleanse, clean out, scour, clear, absolve. **2** OUST, remove, get rid of, eject, expel, root out, eradicate, exterminate, wipe out, kill.
n removal, ejection, expulsion, witch hunt, eradication, extermination.

purify v refine, filter, clarify, clean, cleanse, decontaminate, sanitize, disinfect, sterilize, fumigate, deodorize.
🔼 contaminate, pollute, defile.

purist n pedant, literalist, formalist, stickler, quibbler, nit-picker.

puritanical adj puritan, moralistic, disciplinarian, ascetic, abstemious, austere, severe, stern, strict, strait-laced, prim, proper, prudish, disapproving, stuffy, stiff, rigid, narrow-minded, bigoted, fanatical, zealous.
🔼 hedonistic, liberal, indulgent, broad-minded.

purity n **1** CLEARNESS, clarity, cleanness, cleanliness, untaintedness, wholesomeness. **2** SIMPLICITY, authenticity, genuineness, truth. **3** CHASTITY, decency, morality, integrity, rectitude, uprightness, virtue, innocence, blamelessness.
🔼 **1** impurity. **3** immorality.

purpose n **1** INTENTION, aim, objective, end, goal, target, plan, design, vision, idea, point, object, reason, motive, rationale, principle, result, outcome. **2** DETERMINATION, resolve, resolution, drive, single-mindedness, dedication, devotion, constancy, steadfastness, persistence, tenacity, zeal. **3** USE, function, application, good, advantage, benefit, value.
on purpose purposely, deliberately, intentionally, consciously, knowingly, wittingly, wilfully.
🔼 accidentally, impulsively, spontaneously.

purposeful adj determined, decided, resolved, resolute, single-minded, constant, steadfast, persistent, persevering, tenacious, strong-willed, positive, firm, deliberate.
🔼 purposeless, aimless.

purse n **1** MONEY-BAG, wallet, pouch. **2** MONEY, means, resources, finances, funds, coffers, treasury, exchequer. **3** REWARD, award, prize.
v pucker, wrinkle, draw together, close, tighten, contract, compress.

pursue v **1** *pursue an activity*: perform, engage in, practise, conduct, carry on, continue, keep on, keep up, maintain, persevere in, persist in, hold to, aspire to, aim for, strive for, try for. **2** CHASE, go after, follow, track, trail, shadow, tail, dog, harass, harry, hound, hunt, seek, search for, investigate, inquire into.

pursuit *n* **1** CHASE, hue and cry, tracking, stalking, trail, hunt, quest, search, investigation. **2** ACTIVITY, interest, hobby, pastime, occupation, trade, craft, line, speciality, vocation.

push *v* **1** PROPEL, thrust, ram, shove, jostle, elbow, prod, poke, press, depress, squeeze, squash, drive, force, constrain. **2** PROMOTE, advertise, publicize, boost, encourage, urge, egg on (*infml*), incite, spur, influence, persuade, pressurize, bully.

F3 **1** pull. **2** discourage, dissuade.

n **1** KNOCK, shove, nudge, jolt, prod, poke, thrust. **2** ENERGY, vigour, vitality, go (*infml*), drive, effort, dynamism, enterprise, initiative, ambition, determination.

pushy *adj* assertive, self-assertive, ambitious, forceful, aggressive, over-confident, forward, bold, brash, arrogant, presumptuous, assuming, bossy (*infml*).

F3 unassertive, unassuming.

put *v* **1** PLACE, lay, deposit, plonk (*infml*), set, fix, settle, establish, stand, position, dispose, situate, station, post. **2** APPLY, impose, inflict, levy, assign, subject. **3** WORD, phrase, formulate, frame, couch, express, voice, utter, state. **4** *put a suggestion*: submit, present, offer, suggest, propose.

put across put over, communicate, convey, express, explain, spell out, bring home to, get through to.

put aside put by, set aside, keep, retain, save, reserve, store, stow, stockpile, stash (*infml*), hoard, salt away.

put away (*infml*) **1** CONSUME, devour, eat, drink. **2** IMPRISON, jail, lock up, commit, certify.

put back 1 DELAY, defer, postpone, reschedule. **2** REPLACE, return.

F3 **1** bring forward.

put down 1 WRITE DOWN, transcribe, enter, log, register, record, note. **2** CRUSH, quash, suppress, defeat, quell, silence, snub, slight, squash, deflate, humble, take down a peg, shame, humiliate, mortify. **3** *put down a sick dog*: kill, put to sleep. **4** ASCRIBE, attribute, blame, charge.

put forward advance, suggest, recommend, nominate, propose, move, table, introduce, present, submit, offer, tender.

put in insert, enter, input, submit, install, fit.

put off 1 DELAY, defer, postpone, reschedule. **2** DETER, dissuade, discourage, dishearten, demoralize, daunt, dismay, intimidate, disconcert, confuse, distract.

F3 **2** encourage.

put on 1 ATTACH, affix, apply, place, add, impose. **2** PRETEND, feign, sham, fake, simulate, affect, assume. **3** STAGE, mount, produce, present, do, perform.

put out 1 PUBLISH, announce, broadcast, circulate. **2** EXTINGUISH, quench, douse, smother, switch off, turn off. **3** INCONVENIENCE, impose on, bother, disturb, trouble, upset, hurt, offend, annoy, irritate, irk, anger, exasperate.

F3 **2** light.

put through accomplish, achieve, complete, conclude, finalize, execute, manage, bring off.

put up 1 ERECT, build, construct, assemble. **2** ACCOMMODATE, house, lodge, shelter. **3** *put up prices*: raise, increase. **4** PAY, invest, give, advance, float, provide, supply, pledge, offer.

put up to prompt, incite, encourage, egg on (*infml*), urge, goad.

F3 discourage, dissuade.

put up with stand, bear, abide, stomach, endure, suffer, tolerate, allow, accept, stand for, take, take lying down.

object to, reject.

putrid adj rotten, decayed,
decomposed, mouldy, off, bad,
rancid, addled, corrupt,
contaminated, tainted, polluted, foul,
rank, fetid, stinking.
 fresh, wholesome.

put-upon adj imposed on, taken
advantage of, exploited, used,
abused, maltreated, persecuted.

puzzle v 1 BAFFLE, mystify, perplex,
confound, stump (infml), floor
(infml), confuse, bewilder, flummox
(infml). 2 THINK, ponder, meditate,
consider, mull over, deliberate,
figure, rack one's brains.

n question, poser, brain-teaser,
mind-bender, crossword, rebus,
anagram, riddle, conundrum, mystery,
enigma, paradox.

puzzle out solve, work out, figure out,
decipher, decode, crack, unravel,
untangle, sort out, resolve, clear up.

puzzled adj baffled, mystified,
perplexed, confounded, at a loss,
beaten, stumped (infml), confused,
bewildered, nonplussed, lost, at sea,
flummoxed (infml).
 clear.

pyromaniac n arsonist, incendiary,
fire-raiser, firebug (infml).

Q

quagmire n bog, marsh, quag, fen,
swamp, morass, mire, quicksand.

quail v recoil, back away, shy away,
shrink, flinch, cringe, cower, tremble,
quake, shudder, falter.

quaint adj picturesque, charming,
twee (infml), old-fashioned,
antiquated, old-world, olde-worlde
(infml), unusual, strange, odd,
curious, bizarre, fanciful, whimsical.
 modern.

quake v shake, tremble, shudder,
quiver, shiver, quail, vibrate, wobble,
rock, sway, move, convulse, heave.

qualification n 1 CERTIFICATE,
diploma, training, skill, competence,
ability, capability, capacity, aptitude,
suitability, fitness, eligibility.
2 RESTRICTION, limitation,
reservation, exception, exemption,
condition, caveat, provision, proviso,
stipulation, modification.

qualified adj 1 CERTIFIED,
chartered, licensed, professional,
trained, experienced, practised,
skilled, accomplished, expert,
knowledgeable, skilful, talented,

proficient, competent, efficient, able,
capable, fit, eligible. 2 qualified
praise: reserved, guarded, cautious,
restricted, limited, bounded,
contingent, conditional, provisional,
equivocal.
 1 unqualified. 2 unconditional,
whole-hearted.

qualify v 1 TRAIN, prepare, equip,
fit, pass, graduate, certify, empower,
entitle, authorize, sanction, permit.
2 MODERATE, reduce, lessen,
diminish, temper, soften, weaken,
mitigate, ease, adjust, modify,
restrain, restrict, limit, delimit,
define, classify.
 disqualify.

quality n 1 PROPERTY,
characteristic, peculiarity, attribute,
aspect, feature, trait, mark. 2 of poor
quality: standard, grade, class, kind,
sort, nature, character, calibre,
status, rank, value, worth, merit,
condition. 3 EXCELLENCE,
superiority, pre-eminence,
distinction, refinement.

qualm n misgiving, apprehension,

fear, anxiety, worry, disquiet, uneasiness, scruple, hesitation, reluctance, uncertainty, doubt.

quandary *n* dilemma, predicament, impasse, perplexity, bewilderment, confusion, mess, fix, hole (*infml*), problem, difficulty.

quantity *n* amount, number, sum, total, aggregate, mass, lot, share, portion, quota, allotment, measure, dose, proportion, part, content, capacity, volume, weight, bulk, size, magnitude, expanse, extent, length, breadth.

quarrel *n* row, argument, slanging match (*infml*), wrangle, squabble, tiff, misunderstanding, disagreement, dispute, dissension, controversy, difference, conflict, clash, contention, strife, fight, scrap, brawl, feud, vendetta, schism.
E3 agreement, harmony.
v row, argue, bicker, squabble, wrangle, be at loggerheads, fall out, disagree, dispute, dissent, differ, be at variance, clash, contend, fight, scrap, feud.
E3 agree.

quarrelsome *adj* argumentative, disputatious, contentious, belligerent, ill-tempered, irritable.
E3 peaceable, placid.

quarry *n* prey, victim, object, goal, target, game, kill, prize.

quarter *n* district, sector, zone, neighbourhood, locality, vicinity, area, region, province, territory, division, section, part, place, spot, point, direction, side.
v station, post, billet, accommodate, put up, lodge, board, house, shelter.

quarters *n* accommodation, lodgings, billet, digs (*infml*), residence, dwelling, habitation, domicile, rooms, barracks, station, post.

quash *v* annul, revoke, rescind, overrule, cancel, nullify, void, invalidate, reverse, set aside, squash,

crush, quell, suppress, subdue, defeat, overthrow.
E3 confirm, vindicate, reinstate.

quaver *v* shake, tremble, quake, shudder, quiver, vibrate, pulsate, oscillate, flutter, flicker, trill, warble.

quay *n* wharf, pier, jetty, dock, harbour.

queasy *adj* sick, ill, unwell, queer, groggy, green, nauseated, sickened, bilious, squeamish, faint, dizzy, giddy.

queen *n* **1** monarch, sovereign, ruler, majesty, princess, empress, consort. **2** beauty, belle.

queer *adj* **1** ODD, mysterious, strange, unusual, uncommon, weird, unnatural, bizarre, eccentric, peculiar, funny, puzzling, curious, remarkable. **2** *I feel queer*: unwell, ill, sick, queasy, light-headed, faint, giddy, dizzy. **3** SUSPECT, suspicious, shifty, dubious, shady (*infml*). **4** (*sl*) HOMOSEXUAL, gay, lesbian.
E3 **1** ordinary, usual, common. **2** well.

quell *v* subdue, quash, crush, squash, suppress, put down, overcome, conquer, defeat, overpower, moderate, mitigate, allay, alleviate, soothe, calm, pacify, hush, quiet, silence, stifle, extinguish.

quench *v* **1** *quench one's thirst*: slake, satisfy, sate, cool. **2** EXTINGUISH, douse, put out, snuff out.

querulous *adj* peevish, fretful, fractious, cantankerous, cross, irritable, complaining, grumbling, discontented, dissatisfied, critical, carping, captious, fault-finding, fussy.
E3 placid, uncomplaining, contented.

query *v* ask, inquire, question, challenge, dispute, quarrel with, doubt, suspect, distrust, mistrust, disbelieve.
E3 accept.
n question, inquiry, problem, uncertainty, doubt, suspicion,

scepticism, reservation, hesitation.

quest n search, hunt, pursuit, investigation, inquiry, mission, crusade, enterprise, undertaking, venture, journey, voyage, expedition, exploration, adventure.

question v interrogate, quiz, grill, pump, interview, examine, cross-examine, debrief, ask, inquire, investigate, probe, query, challenge, dispute, doubt, disbelieve.
n 1 QUERY, inquiry, poser, problem, difficulty. 2 ISSUE, matter, subject, topic, point, proposal, proposition, motion, debate, dispute, controversy.

questionable adj debatable, disputable, unsettled, undetermined, unproven, uncertain, arguable, controversial, vexed, doubtful, dubious, suspicious, suspect, shady (infml), fishy (infml), iffy (sl).
☒ unquestionable, indisputable, certain.

questionnaire n quiz, test, survey, opinion poll.

queue n line, tailback, file, crocodile, procession, train, string, succession, series, sequence, order.

quibble v carp, cavil, split hairs, nit-pick, equivocate, prevaricate.
n complaint, objection, criticism, query.

quick adj 1 FAST, swift, rapid, speedy, express, hurried, hasty, cursory, fleeting, brief, prompt, ready, immediate, instant, instantaneous, sudden, brisk, nimble, sprightly, agile. 2 CLEVER, intelligent, quick-witted, smart, sharp, keen, shrewd, astute, discerning, perceptive, responsive, receptive.
☒ 1 slow, sluggish, lethargic.
2 unintelligent, dull.

quicken v 1 ACCELERATE, speed, hurry, hasten, precipitate, expedite, dispatch, advance. 2 ANIMATE, enliven, invigorate, energize, galvanize, activate, rouse, arouse,

stimulate, excite, inspire, revive, refresh, reinvigorate, reactivate.
☒ 1 slow, retard. 2 dull.

quiet adj 1 SILENT, noiseless, inaudible, hushed, soft, low.
2 PEACEFUL, still, tranquil, serene, calm, composed, undisturbed, untroubled, placid. 3 SHY, reserved, reticent, uncommunicative, taciturn, unforthcoming, retiring, withdrawn, thoughtful, subdued, meek. 4 a quiet spot: isolated, unfrequented, lonely, secluded, private.
☒ 1 noisy, loud. 2 excitable.
3 extrovert.
n quietness, silence, hush, peace, lull, stillness, tranquillity, serenity, calm, rest, repose.
☒ noise, loudness, disturbance, bustle.

quieten v 1 SILENCE, hush, mute, soften, lower, diminish, reduce, stifle, muffle, deaden, dull. 2 SUBDUE, pacify, quell, quiet, still, smooth, calm, soothe, compose, sober.
☒ 2 disturb, agitate.

quilt n bedcover, coverlet, bedspread, counterpane, eiderdown, duvet.

quip n joke, jest, crack, gag (infml), witticism, riposte, retort, gibe.

quirk n freak, eccentricity, curiosity, oddity, peculiarity, idiosyncrasy, mannerism, habit, trait, foible, whim, caprice, turn, twist.

quit v 1 LEAVE, depart, go, exit, decamp, desert, forsake, abandon, renounce, relinquish, surrender, give up, resign, retire, withdraw. 2 quit smoking: stop, cease, end, discontinue, desist, drop, give up, pack in (sl).

quite adv 1 MODERATELY, rather, somewhat, fairly, relatively, comparatively. 2 UTTERLY, absolutely, totally, completely, entirely, wholly, fully, perfectly, exactly, precisely.

quiver v shake, tremble, shudder,

shiver, quake, quaver, vibrate, palpitate, flutter, flicker, oscillate, wobble.

n shake, tremble, shudder, shiver, tremor, vibration, palpitation, flutter, flicker, oscillation, wobble.

quiz *n* questionnaire, test, examination, competition.

v. question, interrogate, grill, pump, examine, cross-examine.

quizzical *adj* questioning, inquiring, curious, amused, humorous, teasing, mocking, satirical, sardonic, sceptical.

quota *n* ration, allowance, allocation, assignment, share, portion, part, slice, cut (*infml*), percentage, proportion.

quotation *n* 1 CITATION, quote (*infml*), extract, excerpt, passage, piece, cutting, reference. 2 ESTIMATE, quote (*infml*), tender, figure, price, cost, charge, rate.

quote *v* cite, refer to, mention, name, reproduce, echo, repeat, recite, recall, recollect.

R

rabble *n* crowd, throng, horde, herd, mob, masses, populace, riff-raff.

rabble-rouser *n* agitator, troublemaker, incendiary, demagogue, ringleader.

race[1] *n* sprint, steeplechase, marathon, scramble, regatta, competition, contest, contention, rivalry, chase, pursuit, quest.

v run, sprint, dash, tear, fly, gallop, speed, career, dart, zoom, rush, hurry, hasten.

Types of race and famous races include: cycle race, cyclo-cross, road race, time trial, Milk Race, Tour de France; greyhound race, Greyhound Derby; horserace, Cheltenham Gold Cup, the Classics (Derby, Oaks, One Thousand Guineas, St. Leger, Two Thousand Guineas), Grand National, Kentucky Derby, Melbourne Cup, Prix de l'Arc de Triomphe, steeplechase, trotting race, harness race; motorcycle race, motocross, scramble, speedway, Isle of Man Tourist Trophy (TT); motor-race, GrandPrix, Indianapolis 500, Le Mans, Monte Carlo rally, RAC Rally, stock car race; rowing, regatta,

Boat Race; running, cross-country, dash (*NorthAmer.*), hurdles, marathon, London Marathon, relay, sprint, steeplechase, track event; ski race, downhill, slalom; swimming race; walking race, walkathon; yacht race, Admiral's Cup, America's Cup; egg-and-spoon race, pancake race, sack race, wheelbarrow race.

race[2] *n* nation, people, tribe, clan, house, dynasty, family, kindred, ancestry, line, blood, stock, genus, species, breed.

race-course *n* racetrack, course, track, circuit, lap, turf, speedway.

racial *adj* national, tribal, ethnic, folk, genealogical, ancestral, inherited, genetic.

racism *n* racialism, xenophobia, chauvinism, jingoism, discrimination, prejudice, bias.

rack *n* shelf, stand, support, structure, frame, framework.

racket *n* 1 NOISE, din, uproar, row, fuss, outcry, clamour, commotion, disturbance, pandemonium, hurly-burly, hubbub. 2 SWINDLE, con (*infml*), fraud, fiddle, deception, trick, dodge, scheme, business, game.

racy *adj* **1** RIBALD, bawdy, risqué, naughty, indecent, indelicate, suggestive. **2** LIVELY, animated, spirited, energetic, dynamic, buoyant, boisterous.

radiance *n* light, luminosity, incandescence, radiation, brightness, brilliance, shine, lustre, gleam, glow, glitter, resplendence, splendour, happiness, joy, pleasure, delight, rapture.

radiant *adj* bright, luminous, shining, gleaming, glowing, beaming, glittering, sparkling, brilliant, resplendent, splendid, glorious, happy, joyful, delighted, ecstatic.
Ea dull, miserable.

radiate *v* shine, gleam, glow, beam, shed, pour, give off, emit, emanate, diffuse, issue, disseminate, scatter, spread (out), diverge, branch.

radical *adj* **1** BASIC, fundamental, primary, essential, natural, native, innate, intrinsic, deep-seated, profound. **2** *radical changes*: drastic, comprehensive, thorough, sweeping, far-reaching, thoroughgoing, complete, total, entire. **3** FANATICAL, militant, extreme, extremist, revolutionary.
Ea 1 superficial. **3** moderate.
n fanatic, militant, extremist, revolutionary, reformer, reformist, fundamentalist.

raffle *n* draw, lottery, sweepstake, sweep, tombola.

rage *n* **1** ANGER, wrath, fury, frenzy, tantrum, temper. **2** (*infml*) *all the rage*: craze, fad, thing (*infml*), fashion, vogue, style, passion, enthusiasm, obsession.
v fume, seethe, rant, rave, storm, thunder, explode, rampage.

ragged *adj* **1** *ragged clothes*: frayed, torn, ripped, tattered, worn-out, threadbare, tatty, shabby, scruffy, unkempt, down-at-heel. **2** JAGGED, serrated, indented, notched, rough, uneven, irregular, fragmented,

erratic, disorganized.

raid *n* attack, onset, onslaught, invasion, inroad, incursion, foray, sortie, strike, blitz, swoop, bust (*sl*), robbery, break-in, hold-up.
v loot, pillage, plunder, ransack, rifle, maraud, attack, descend on, invade, storm.

raider *n* attacker, invader, looter, plunderer, ransacker, marauder, robber, thief, brigand, pirate.

railing *n* fence, paling, barrier, parapet, rail, balustrade.

railway *n* track, line, rails, underground, tube (*infml*), subway, metro.

rain *n* rainfall, precipitation, raindrops, drizzle, shower, cloudburst, downpour, deluge, torrent, storm, thunderstorm, squall.
v spit, drizzle, shower, pour, teem, pelt, bucket (*infml*), deluge.

rainy *adj* wet, damp, showery, drizzly.
Ea dry.

raise *v* **1** LIFT, elevate, hoist, jack up, erect, build, construct.
2 INCREASE, augment, escalate, magnify, heighten, strengthen, intensify, amplify, boost, enhance. **3** *raise funds*: get, obtain, collect, gather, assemble, rally, muster, recruit. **4** *raise a subject*: bring up, broach, introduce, present, put forward, moot, suggest.
Ea 1 lower. **2** decrease, reduce.
5 suppress.

rake *v* hoe, scratch, scrape, graze, comb, scour, search, hunt, ransack, gather, collect, amass, accumulate.

rally *v* **1** GATHER, collect, assemble, congregate, convene, muster, summon, round up, unite, marshal, organize, mobilize, reassemble, regroup, reorganize. **2** RECOVER, recuperate, revive, improve, pick up.
n **1** GATHERING, assembly,

convention, convocation, conference, meeting, jamboree, reunion, march, demonstration. **2** RECOVERY, recuperation, revival, comeback, improvement, resurgence, renewal.

ram v **1** HIT, strike, butt, hammer, pound, drum, crash, smash, slam. **2** FORCE, drive, thrust, cram, stuff, pack, crowd, jam, wedge.

ramble v **1** WALK, hike, trek, tramp, traipse, stroll, amble, saunter, straggle, wander, roam, rove, meander, wind, zigzag. **2** CHATTER, babble, rabbit (on) (*infml*), witter (on) (*infml*), expatiate, digress, drift.
n walk, hike, trek, tramp, stroll, saunter, tour, trip, excursion.

rambler n hiker, walker, stroller, rover, roamer, wanderer, wayfarer.

rambling adj **1** SPREADING, sprawling, straggling, trailing. **2** CIRCUITOUS, roundabout, digressive, wordy, long-winded, long-drawn-out, disconnected, incoherent.
◻ 2 direct.

ramification n branch, offshoot, development, complication, result, consequence, upshot, implication.

ramp n slope, incline, gradient, rise.

rampage v run wild, run amok, run riot, rush, tear, storm, rage, rant, rave.
n rage, fury, frenzy, storm, uproar, violence, destruction.
on the rampage wild, amok, berserk, violent, out of control.

rampant adj unrestrained, uncontrolled, unbridled, unchecked, wanton, excessive, fierce, violent, raging, wild, riotous, rank, profuse, rife, widespread, prevalent.

ramshackle adj dilapidated, tumbledown, broken-down, crumbling, ruined, derelict, jerry-built, unsafe, rickety, shaky, unsteady, tottering, decrepit.
◻ solid, stable.

rancid adj sour, off, bad, musty, stale, rank, foul, fetid, putrid, rotten.

◻ sweet.

random adj arbitrary, chance, fortuitous, casual, incidental, haphazard, irregular, unsystematic, unplanned, accidental, aimless, purposeless, indiscriminate, stray.
◻ systematic, deliberate.

range n **1** SCOPE, compass, scale, gamut, spectrum, sweep, spread, extent, distance, reach, span, limits, bounds, parameters, area, field, domain, province, sphere, orbit. **2** *a range of fittings*: variety, diversity, assortment, selection, sort, kind, class, order, series, string, chain.
v **1** EXTEND, stretch, reach, spread, vary, fluctuate. **2** ALIGN, arrange, order, rank, classify, catalogue.

rank¹ n **1** GRADE, degree, class, caste, status, standing, position, station, condition, estate, echelon, level, stratum, tier, classification, sort, type, group, division. **2** ROW, line, range, column, file, series, order, formation.

Ranks in the armed services include: *air force*: aircraftsman, aircraftswoman, corporal, sergeant, warrant officer, pilot officer, flying officer, flight lieutenant, squadron-leader, wing commander, group-captain, air-commodore, air-vice-marshal, air-marshal, air-chief-marshal, marshal of the Royal Air Force; *army*: private, lance-corporal, corporal, sergeant, warrant officer, lieutenant, captain, major, lieutenant-colonel, colonel, brigadier, major general, lieutenant-general, general, field marshal; *navy*: able seaman, rating, petty officer, chief petty officer, sublieutenant, lieutenant, lieutenant-commander, commander, captain, commodore, rear admiral, vice-admiral, admiral, admiral of the fleet.
see also **soldier**.

---

v grade, class, rate, place, position,

range, sort, classify, categorize, order, arrange, organize, marshal.

rank² *adj* **1** UTTER, total, complete, absolute, unmitigated, thorough, sheer, downright, out-and-out, arrant, gross, flagrant, glaring, outrageous. **2** FOUL, repulsive, disgusting, revolting, stinking, putrid, rancid, stale.

rankle *v* annoy, irritate, rile, nettle, gall, irk, anger.

ransack *v* search, scour, comb, rummage, rifle, raid, sack, strip, despoil, ravage, loot, plunder, pillage.

ransom *n* price, money, payment, pay-off, redemption, deliverance, rescue, liberation, release.
v buy off, redeem, deliver, rescue, liberate, free, release.

rant *v* shout, cry, yell, roar, bellow, declaim, bluster, rave.

rap *v* **1** KNOCK, hit, strike, tap, thump. **2** (*sl*) REPROVE, reprimand, criticize, censure.
n **1** KNOCK, blow, tap, thump. **2** (*sl*) REBUKE, reprimand, censure, blame, punishment.

rape *n* violation, assault, abuse, maltreatment.
v violate, assault, abuse, maltreat.

rapid *adj* swift, speedy, quick, fast, express, lightning, prompt, brisk, hurried, hasty, precipitate, headlong.
🔁 slow, leisurely, sluggish.

rapport *n* bond, link, affinity, relationship, empathy, sympathy, understanding, harmony.

rapt *adj* engrossed, absorbed, preoccupied, intent, gripped, spellbound, enthralled, captivated, fascinated, entranced, charmed, enchanted, entranced, delighted, ravished, enraptured, transported.

rapture *n* delight, happiness, joy, bliss, ecstasy, euphoria, exaltation.

rare *adj* **1** UNCOMMON, unusual, scarce, sparse, sporadic, infrequent. **2** EXQUISITE, superb, excellent,

superlative, incomparable, exceptional, remarkable, precious.
🔁 **1** common, abundant, frequent.

rarefied *adj* exclusive, select, private, esoteric, refined, high, noble, sublime.

rarely *adv* seldom, hardly ever, infrequently, little.
🔁 often, frequently.

raring *adj* eager, keen, enthusiastic, ready, willing, impatient, longing, itching, desperate.

rarity *n* **1** CURIOSITY, curio, gem, pearl, treasure, find.
2 UNCOMMONNESS, unusualness, strangeness, scarcity, shortage, sparseness, infrequency.
🔁 **2** commonness, frequency.

rascal *n* rogue, scoundrel, scamp, scallywag, imp, devil, villain, good-for-nothing, wastrel.

rash¹ *adj* reckless, ill-considered, foolhardy, ill-advised, madcap, hare-brained, hot-headed, headstrong, impulsive, impetuous, hasty, headlong, unguarded, unwary, indiscreet, imprudent, careless, heedless, unthinking.
🔁 cautious, wary, careful.

rash² *n* eruption, outbreak, epidemic, plague.

rasp *n* grating, scrape, grinding, scratch, harshness, hoarseness, croak.
v grate, scrape, grind, file, sand, scour, abrade, rub.

rate *n* **1** SPEED, velocity, tempo, time, ratio, proportion, relation, degree, grade, rank, rating, standard, basis, measure, scale. **2** CHARGE, fee, hire, toll, tariff, price, cost, value, worth, tax, duty, amount, figure, percentage.
v **1** JUDGE, regard, consider, deem, count, reckon, figure, estimate, evaluate, assess, weigh, measure, grade, rank, class, classify. **2** ADMIRE, respect, esteem, value, prize. **3** DESERVE, merit.

rather *adv* **1** MODERATELY, relatively, slightly, a bit, somewhat, fairly, quite, pretty, noticeably, significantly, very. **2** PREFERABLY, sooner, instead.

ratify *v* approve, uphold, endorse, sign, legalize, sanction, authorize, establish, affirm, confirm, certify, validate, authenticate.
🔁 repudiate, reject.

rating *n* class, rank, degree, status, standing, position, placing, order, grade, mark, evaluation, assessment, classification, category.

ratio *n* percentage, fraction, proportion, relation, relationship, correspondence, correlation.

ration *n* quota, allowance, allocation, allotment, share, portion, helping, part, measure, amount.
v apportion, allot, allocate, share, deal out, distribute, dole out, dispense, supply, issue, control, restrict, limit, conserve, save.

rational *adj* logical, reasonable, sound, well-founded, realistic, sensible, clear-headed, judicious, wise, sane, normal, balanced, lucid, reasoning, thinking, intelligent, enlightened.
🔁 irrational, illogical, insane, crazy.

rationale *n* logic, reasoning, philosophy, principle, basis, grounds, explanation, reason, motive, motivation, theory.

rationalize *v* **1** JUSTIFY, excuse, vindicate, explain, account for. **2** REORGANIZE, streamline.

rations *n* food, provisions, supplies, stores.

rattle *v* clatter, jingle, jangle, clank, shake, vibrate, jolt, jar, bounce, bump.
rattle off reel off, list, run through, recite, repeat.

raucous *adj* harsh, rough, hoarse, husky, rasping, grating, jarring, strident, noisy, loud.

ravage *v* destroy, devastate, lay waste, demolish, raze, wreck, ruin, spoil, damage, loot, pillage, plunder, sack, despoil.
n destruction, devastation, havoc, damage, ruin, desolation, wreckage, pillage, plunder.

rave *v* rage, storm, thunder, roar, rant, ramble, babble, splutter.
adj (*infml*) enthusiastic, rapturous, favourable, excellent, wonderful.

ravenous *adj* hungry, starving, starved, famished, greedy, voracious, insatiable.

ravine *n* canyon, gorge, gully, pass.

raving *adj* mad, insane, crazy, hysterical, delirious, wild, frenzied, furious, berserk.

ravish *v* enrapture, delight, overjoy, enchant, charm, captivate, entrance, fascinate, spellbind.

ravishing *adj* delightful, enchanting, charming, lovely, beautiful, gorgeous, stunning, radiant, dazzling, alluring, seductive.

raw *adj* **1** *raw vegetables*: uncooked, fresh. **2** UNPROCESSED, unrefined, untreated, crude, natural. **3** PLAIN, bare, naked, basic, harsh, brutal, realistic. **4** SCRATCHED, grazed, scraped, open, bloody, sore, tender, sensitive. **5** COLD, chilly, bitter, biting, piercing, freezing, bleak. **6** *a raw recruit*: new, green, immature, callow, inexperienced, untrained, unskilled.
🔁 **1** cooked, done. **2** processed, refined. **5** warm. **6** experienced, skilled.

ray *n* beam, shaft, flash, gleam, flicker, glimmer, glint, spark, trace, hint, indication.

raze *v* demolish, pull down, tear down, bulldoze, flatten, level, destroy.

re *prep* about, concerning, regarding, with regard to, with reference to.

reach *v* arrive at, get to, attain, achieve, make, amount to, hit, strike, touch, contact, stretch, extend, grasp.

n range, scope, compass, distance, spread, extent, stretch, grasp, jurisdiction, command, power, influence.

react *v* respond, retaliate, reciprocate, reply, answer, acknowledge, act, behave.

reaction *n* response, effect, reply, answer, acknowledgement, feedback, counteraction, reflex, recoil, reciprocation, retaliation.

reactionary *adj* conservative, right-wing, rightist, die-hard, counter-revolutionary.
◨ progressive, revolutionary.
n conservative, right-winger, rightist, die-hard, counter-revolutionary.
◨ progressive, revolutionary.

read *v* **1** STUDY, peruse, pore over, scan, skim, decipher, decode, interpret, construe, understand, comprehend. **2** RECITE, declaim, deliver, speak, utter. **3** *the gauge read zero*: indicate, show, display, register, record.

readable *adj* **1** LEGIBLE, decipherable, intelligible, clear, understandable, comprehensible. **2** INTERESTING, enjoyable, entertaining, gripping, unputdownable (*infml*).
◨ **1** illegible. **2** unreadable.

readily *adv* willingly, unhesitatingly, gladly, eagerly, promptly, quickly, freely, smoothly, easily, effortlessly.
◨ unwillingly, reluctantly.

reading *n* **1** STUDY, perusal, scrutiny, examination, inspection, interpretation, understanding, rendering, version, rendition, recital. **2** *a reading from the Bible*: passage, lesson.

ready *adj* **1** *ready to go*: prepared, waiting, set, fit, arranged, organized, completed, finished. **2** WILLING, inclined, disposed, happy, game (*infml*), eager, keen. **3** AVAILABLE, to hand, present, near, accessible, convenient, handy. **4** PROMPT,

immediate, quick, sharp, astute, perceptive, alert.
◨ **1** unprepared. **2** unwilling, reluctant, disinclined. **3** unavailable, inaccessible. **4** slow.

real *adj* actual, existing, physical, material, substantial, tangible, genuine, authentic, bona fide, official, rightful, legitimate, valid, true, factual, certain, sure, positive, veritable, honest, sincere, heartfelt, unfeigned, unaffected.
◨ unreal, imaginary, false.

realistic *adj* **1** PRACTICAL, down-to-earth, commonsense, sensible, level-headed, clear-sighted, businesslike, hard-headed, pragmatic, matter-of-fact, rational, logical, objective, detached, unsentimental, unromantic. **2** LIFELIKE, faithful, truthful, true, genuine, authentic, natural, real, real-life, graphic, representational.
◨ unrealistic, impractical, irrational, idealistic.

reality *n* truth, fact, certainty, realism, actuality, existence, materiality, tangibility, genuineness, authenticity, validity.

realize *v* **1** UNDERSTAND, comprehend, grasp, catch on, cotton on (*infml*), recognize, accept, appreciate. **2** ACHIEVE, accomplish, fulfil, complete, implement, perform. **3** SELL FOR, fetch, make, earn, produce, net, clear.

really *adv* actually, truly, honestly, sincerely, genuinely, positively, certainly, absolutely, categorically, very, indeed.

realm *n* kingdom, monarchy, principality, empire, country, state, land, territory, area, region, province, domain, sphere, orbit, field, department.

rear *n* back, stern, end, tail, rump, buttocks, posterior, behind, bottom, backside (*infml*).
◨ front.

adj back, hind, hindmost, rearmost, last.

🔁 front.

v **1** *rear a child*: bring up, raise, breed, grow, cultivate, foster, nurse, nurture, train, educate. **2** RISE, tower, soar, raise, lift.

reason *n* **1** CAUSE, motive, incentive, rationale, explanation, excuse, justification, defence, warrant, ground, basis, case, argument, aim, intention, purpose, object, end, goal. **2** SENSE, logic, reasoning, rationality, sanity, mind, wit, brain, intellect, understanding, wisdom, judgement, common sense, gumption.

v work out, solve, resolve, conclude, deduce, infer, think.

reason with urge, persuade, move, remonstrate with, argue with, debate with, discuss with.

reasonable *adj* **1** SENSIBLE, wise, well-advised, sane, intelligent, rational, logical, practical, sound, reasoned, well-thought-out, plausible, credible, possible, viable. **2** *a reasonable price*: acceptable, satisfactory, tolerable, moderate, average, fair, just, modest, inexpensive.

🔁 **1** irrational. **2** exorbitant.

reasoning *n* logic, thinking, thought, analysis, interpretation, deduction, supposition, hypothesis, argument, case, proof.

reassure *v* comfort, cheer, encourage, hearten, inspirit, brace, bolster.

🔁 alarm.

rebate *n* refund, repayment, reduction, discount, deduction, allowance.

rebel *v* revolt, mutiny, rise up, run riot, dissent, disobey, defy, resist, recoil, shrink.

🔁 conform.

n revolutionary, insurrectionist, mutineer, dissenter, nonconformist, schismatic, heretic.

rebellion *n* revolt, revolution, rising, uprising, insurrection, insurgence, mutiny, resistance, opposition, defiance, disobedience, insubordination, dissent, heresy.

rebellious *adj* revolutionary, insurrectionary, insurgent, seditious, mutinous, resistant, defiant, disobedient, insubordinate, unruly, disorderly, ungovernable, unmanageable, intractable, obstinate.

🔁 obedient, submissive.

rebirth *n* reincarnation, resurrection, renaissance, regeneration, renewal, restoration, revival, revitalization, rejuvenation.

rebound *v* recoil, backfire, return, bounce, ricochet, boomerang.

rebuff *v* spurn, reject, refuse, decline, turn down, repulse, discourage, snub, slight, cut, cold-shoulder.

n rejection, refusal, repulse, check, discouragement, snub, brush-off (*infml*), slight, put-down, cold shoulder.

rebuke *v* reprove, castigate, chide, scold, tell off (*infml*), admonish, tick off (*infml*), reprimand, upbraid, rate, censure, blame, reproach.

🔁 praise, compliment.

n reproach, reproof, reprimand, lecture, dressing-down (*infml*), telling-off (*infml*), ticking-off (*infml*), admonition, censure, blame.

🔁 praise, commendation.

recall *v* remember, recollect, cast one's mind back, evoke, bring back.

recapitulate *v* recap, summarize, review, repeat, reiterate, restate, recount.

recede *v* go back, return, retire, withdraw, retreat, ebb, wane, sink, decline, diminish, dwindle, decrease, lessen, shrink, slacken, subside, abate.

🔁 advance.

receipt *n* **1** VOUCHER, ticket, slip, counterfoil, stub, acknowledgement.

2 RECEIVING, reception, acceptance, delivery.

receipts n takings, income, proceeds, profits, gains, return.

receive v 1 TAKE, accept, get, obtain, derive, acquire, pick up, collect, inherit. 2 receive guests: admit, let in, greet, welcome, entertain, accommodate. 3 EXPERIENCE, undergo, suffer, sustain, meet with, encounter. 4 REACT TO, respond to, hear, perceive, apprehend.
F3 1 give, donate.

recent adj late, latest, current, present-day, contemporary, modern, up-to-date, new, novel, fresh, young.
F3 old, out-of-date.

recently adv lately, newly, freshly.

receptacle n container, vessel, holder.

reception n 1 ACCEPTANCE, admission, greeting, recognition, welcome, treatment, response, reaction, acknowledgement, receipt. 2 PARTY, function, do (infml), entertainment.

receptive adj open-minded, amenable, accommodating, suggestible, susceptible, sensitive, responsive, open, accessible, approachable, friendly, hospitable, welcoming, sympathetic, favourable, interested.
F3 narrow-minded, resistant, unresponsive.

recess n 1 BREAK, interval, intermission, rest, respite, holiday, vacation. 2 ALCOVE, niche, nook, corner, bay, cavity, hollow, depression, indentation.

recession n slump, depression, downturn, decline.
F3 boom, upturn.

recipe n formula, prescription, ingredients, instructions, directions, method, system, procedure, technique.

reciprocal adj mutual, joint, shared, give-and-take, complementary, alternating, corresponding, equivalent, interchangeable.

reciprocate v respond, reply, requite, return, exchange, swap, trade, match, equal, correspond, interchange, alternate.

recital n performance, concert, recitation, reading, narration, account, rendition, interpretation, repetition.

recitation n passage, piece, party piece, poem, monologue, narration, story, tale, recital, telling.

recite v repeat, tell, narrate, relate, recount, speak, deliver, articulate, declaim, perform, reel off, itemize, enumerate.

reckless adj heedless, thoughtless, mindless, careless, negligent, irresponsible, imprudent, ill-advised, indiscreet, rash, hasty, foolhardy, daredevil, wild.
F3 cautious, wary, careful, prudent.

reckon v 1 CALCULATE, compute, figure out, work out, add up, total, tally, count, number, enumerate. 2 DEEM, regard, consider, esteem, value, rate, judge, evaluate, assess, estimate, gauge. 3 THINK, believe, imagine, fancy, suppose, surmise, assume, guess, conjecture.
reckon on rely on, depend on, bank on, count on, trust in, hope for, expect, anticipate, foresee, plan for, bargain for, figure on, take into account, face.

reckoning n 1 by my reckoning: calculation, computation, estimate. 2 BILL, account, charge, due, score, settlement. 3 JUDGEMENT, retribution, doom.

reclaim v recover, regain, recapture, retrieve, salvage, rescue, redeem, restore, reinstate, regenerate.

recline v rest, repose, lean back, lie, lounge, loll, sprawl, stretch out.

recognition n 1 IDENTIFICATION, detection, discovery, recollection, recall, remembrance, awareness, perception, realization, understanding. **2** CONFESSION, admission, acceptance, acknowledgement, gratitude, appreciation, honour, respect, greeting, salute.

recognize *v* **1** IDENTIFY, know, remember, recollect, recall, place, see, notice, spot, perceive. **2** CONFESS, own, acknowledge, accept, admit, grant, concede, allow, appreciate, understand, realize.

recollect *v* recall, remember, cast one's mind back, reminisce.

recollection *n* recall, remembrance, memory, souvenir, reminiscence, impression.

recommend *v* advocate, urge, exhort, advise, counsel, suggest, propose, put forward, advance, praise, commend, plug (*infml*), endorse, approve, vouch for.
Fa disapprove.

recommendation *n* advice, counsel, suggestion, proposal, advocacy, endorsement, approval, sanction, blessing, praise, commendation, plug (*infml*), reference, testimonial.
Fa disapproval.

recompense *n* compensation, indemnification, damages, reparation, restitution, amends, requital, repayment, reward, payment, remuneration, pay, wages.

reconcile *v* reunite, conciliate, pacify, appease, placate, propitiate, accord, harmonize, accommodate, adjust, resolve, settle, square.
Fa estrange, alienate.

reconciliation *n* reunion, conciliation, pacification, appeasement, propitiation, rapprochement, détente, settlement, agreement, harmony, accommodation, adjustment, compromise.
Fa estrangement, separation.

reconnoitre *v* explore, survey, scan,

spy out, recce (*sl*), inspect, examine, scrutinize, investigate, patrol.

reconstruct *v* remake, rebuild, reassemble, re-establish, refashion, remodel, reform, reorganize, recreate, restore, renovate, regenerate.

record *n* **1** REGISTER, log, report, account, minutes, memorandum, note, entry, document, file, dossier, diary, journal, memoir, history, annals, archives, documentation, evidence, testimony, trace. **2** RECORDING, disc, single, CD, compact disc, album, release, LP. **3** *break the record*: fastest time, best performance, personal best, world record. **4** BACKGROUND, track record, curriculum vitae, career.
v **1** NOTE, enter, inscribe, write down, transcribe, register, log, put down, enrol, report, minute, chronicle, document, keep, preserve. **2** TAPE-RECORD, tape, videotape, video, cut.

recording *n* release, performance, record, disc, CD, cassette, tape, video.

Types of recording include: album, audiotape, cassette, CD, compact disc, digital recording, disc, EP (extended play), 45, gramophone record, long-playing record, LP, magnetic tape, mono recording, record, 78, single, stereo recording, tape, tape-recording, tele-recording, video, videocassette, video disc, videotape, vinyl (*infml*).

recount *v* tell, relate, impart, communicate, report, narrate, describe, depict, portray, detail, repeat, rehearse, recite.

recoup *v* recover, retrieve, regain, get back, make good, repay, refund, reimburse, compensate.

recover *v* **1** *recover from illness*: get better, improve, pick up, rally, mend,

heal, pull through, get over,
recuperate, revive, convalesce, come
round. **2** REGAIN, get back, recoup,
retrieve, retake, recapture, repossess,
reclaim, restore.
⊞ 1 worsen. **2** lose, forfeit.

recovery n **1** RECUPERATION,
convalescence, rehabilitation,
mending, healing, improvement,
upturn, rally, revival, restoration.
2 RETRIEVAL, salvage, reclamation,
repossession, recapture.
⊞ 1 worsening. **2** loss, forfeit.

recreation n fun, enjoyment,
pleasure, amusement, diversion,
distraction, entertainment, hobby,
pastime, game, sport, play, leisure,
relaxation, refreshment.

recrimination n countercharge,
accusation, counter-attack,
retaliation, reprisal, retort, quarrel,
bickering.

recruit v enlist, draft, conscript,
enrol, sign up, engage, take on,
mobilize, raise, gather, obtain,
procure.
n beginner, novice, initiate, learner,
trainee, apprentice, conscript, convert.

rectify v correct, put right, right,
remedy, cure, repair, fix, mend,
improve, amend, adjust, reform.

recuperate v recover, get better,
improve, pick up, rally, revive, mend,
convalesce.
⊞ worsen.

recur v repeat, persist, return,
reappear.

recurrent adj recurring, chronic,
persistent, repeated, repetitive,
regular, periodic, frequent,
intermittent.

recycle v reuse, reprocess, reclaim,
recover, salvage, save.

red adj **1** SCARLET, vermilion,
cherry, ruby, crimson, maroon, pink,
reddish, bloodshot, inflamed.
2 RUDDY, florid, glowing, rosy,
flushed, blushing, embarrassed,
shamefaced. **3** *red hair*: ginger,

carroty, auburn, chestnut, Titian.

redden v blush, flush, colour, go
red, crimson.

redeem v **1** BUY BACK, repurchase,
cash (in), exchange, change, trade,
ransom, reclaim, regain, repossess,
recoup, recover, recuperate, retrieve,
salvage. **2** COMPENSATE FOR, make
up for, offset, outweigh, atone for,
expiate, absolve, acquit, discharge,
release, liberate, emancipate, free,
deliver, rescue, save.

reduce v **1** LESSEN, decrease,
contract, shrink, slim, shorten,
curtail, trim, cut, slash, discount,
rebate, lower, moderate, weaken,
diminish, impair. **2** DRIVE, force,
degrade, downgrade, demote,
humble, humiliate, impoverish,
subdue, overpower, master,
vanquish.
⊞ 1 increase, raise, boost.

reduction n decrease, drop, fall,
decline, lessening, moderation,
weakening, diminution, contraction,
compression, shrinkage, narrowing,
shortening, curtailment, restriction,
limitation, cutback, cut, discount,
rebate, devaluation, depreciation,
deduction, subtraction, loss.
⊞ increase, rise, enlargement.

redundant adj **1** UNEMPLOYED, out
of work, laid off, dismissed.
2 SUPERFLUOUS, surplus, excess,
extra, supernumerary, unneeded,
unnecessary, unwanted. **3** WORDY,
verbose, repetitious, tautological.
⊞ 2 necessary, essential. **3** concise.

reel v stagger, totter, wobble, rock,
sway, waver, falter, stumble, lurch,
pitch, roll, revolve, gyrate, spin,
wheel, twirl, whirl, swirl.

refer v **1** SEND, direct, point, guide,
pass on, transfer, commit, deliver.
2 *refer to a catalogue*: consult, look
up, turn to, resort to. **3** ALLUDE,
mention, touch on, speak of, bring
up, recommend, cite, quote.
4 APPLY, concern, relate, belong,

pertain.

referee *n* umpire, judge, adjudicator, arbitrator, mediator, ref (*infml*).

v umpire, judge, adjudicate, arbitrate.

reference *n* **1** ALLUSION, remark, mention, citation, quotation, illustration, instance, note. **2** TESTIMONIAL, recommendation, endorsement, character. **3** RELATION, regard, respect, connection, bearing.

refine *v* process, treat, purify, clarify, filter, distil, polish, hone, improve, perfect, elevate, exalt.

refined *adj* civilized, cultured, cultivated, polished, sophisticated, urbane, genteel, gentlemanly, ladylike, well-bred, well-mannered, polite, civil, elegant, fine, delicate, subtle, precise, exact, sensitive, discriminating.

☒ coarse, vulgar, rude.

refinement *n* **1** MODIFICATION, alteration, amendment, improvement. **2** CULTIVATION, sophistication, urbanity, gentility, breeding, style, elegance, taste, discrimination, subtlety, finesse.

☒ **1** deterioration. **2** coarseness, vulgarity.

reflect *v* **1** MIRROR, echo, imitate, reproduce, portray, depict, show, reveal, display, exhibit, manifest, demonstrate, indicate, express, communicate. **2** THINK, ponder, consider, mull (over), deliberate, contemplate, meditate, muse.

reflection *n* **1** IMAGE, likeness, echo, impression, indication, manifestation, observation, view, opinion. **2** THINKING, thought, study, consideration, deliberation, contemplation, meditation, musing.

reform *v* change, amend, improve, ameliorate, better, rectify, correct, mend, repair, rehabilitate, rebuild, reconstruct, remodel, revamp, renovate, restore, regenerate,

reconstitute, reorganize, shake up (*infml*), revolutionize, purge.

n change, amendment, improvement, rectification, correction, rehabilitation, renovation, reorganization, shake-up (*infml*), purge.

refrain *v* stop, cease, quit, leave off, renounce, desist, abstain, forbear, avoid.

refresh *v* **1** COOL, freshen, enliven, invigorate, fortify, revive, restore, renew, rejuvenate, revitalize, reinvigorate. **2** *refresh one's memory*: jog, stimulate, prompt, prod.

☒ **1** tire, exhaust.

refreshing *adj* cool, thirst-quenching, bracing, invigorating, energizing, stimulating, inspiring, fresh, new, novel, original.

refreshment *n* sustenance, food, drink, snack, revival, restoration, renewal, reanimation, reinvigoration, revitalization.

refuge *n* sanctuary, asylum, shelter, protection, security, retreat, hideout, hide-away, resort, harbour, haven.

refugee *n* exile, émigré, displaced person, fugitive, runaway, escapee.

refund *v* repay, reimburse, rebate, return, restore.

n repayment, reimbursement, rebate, return.

refusal *n* rejection, no, rebuff, repudiation, denial, negation.

☒ acceptance.

refuse[1] *v* reject, turn down, decline, spurn, repudiate, rebuff, repel, deny, withhold.

☒ accept, allow, permit.

refuse[2] *n* rubbish, waste, trash, garbage, junk, litter.

refute *v* disprove, rebut, confute, give the lie to, discredit, counter, negate.

regain *v* recover, get back, recoup, reclaim, repossess, retake, recapture, retrieve, return to.

regal *adj* majestic, kingly, queenly,

princely, imperial, royal, sovereign, stately, magnificent, noble, lordly.

regard *v* consider, deem, judge, rate, value, think, believe, suppose, imagine, look upon, view, observe, watch.
n care, concern, consideration, attention, notice, heed, respect, deference, honour, esteem, admiration, affection, love, sympathy.
≠ disregard, contempt.

regarding *prep* with regard to, as regards, concerning, with reference to, re, about, as to.

regardless *adj* disregarding, heedless, unmindful, neglectful, inattentive, unconcerned, indifferent.
≠ heedful, mindful, attentive.
adv anyway, nevertheless, nonetheless, despite everything, come what may.

regime *n* government, rule, administration, management, leadership, command, control, establishment, system.

regimented *adj* strict, disciplined, controlled, regulated, standardized, ordered, methodical, systematic, organized.
≠ free, lax, disorganized.

region *n* land, terrain, territory, country, province, area, district, zone, sector, neighbourhood, range, scope, expanse, domain, realm, sphere, field, division, section, part, place.

> *Types of geographical region and community include*: antarctic, arctic, area, bailiwick, banana republic, basin, belt, Black Country, borough, built-up area, burgh, capital city, catchment area, city, coast, colony, commune, continent, country, countryside, county, county town, desert, development area, diocese, district, dockland, domain, dominion, duchy, East End, emirate, empire, estate, The Fens, forest, free state, ghetto, ghost town, grassland, green belt, hamlet, health resort, heartland, heath, hemisphere, home-town, hundred, industrial park, inner city, interior, jungle, kibbutz, kingdom, lowlands, manor, market town, marshland, metropolis, The Midlands, mission, municipality, nation, new town, no-man's land, old country, orient, outback, outpost, outskirts, pampas, parish, plain, port, postal district, prairie, principality, protectorate, province, quarter, realm, red-light district, region, republic, reservation, resort, riding, riviera, rural district, satellite town, savannah, scrubland, seaside, settlement, shanty town, shire, spa, state, steppe, subcontinent, suburb, territory, Third World, time zone, town, township, tract, tropics, tundra, urban district, veld, village, wasteland, West Country, West End, wilderness, woodland, zone.

register *n* roll, roster, list, index, catalogue, directory, log, record, chronicle, annals, archives, file, ledger, schedule, diary, almanac.
v **1** RECORD, note, log, enter, inscribe, mark, list, catalogue, chronicle, enrol, enlist, sign on, check in. **2** SHOW, reveal, betray, display, exhibit, manifest, express, say, read, indicate.

regret *v* rue, repent, lament, mourn, grieve, deplore.
n remorse, contrition, compunction, self-reproach, shame, sorrow, grief, disappointment, bitterness.

regretful *adj* remorseful, rueful, repentant, contrite, penitent, conscience-stricken, ashamed, sorry, apologetic, sad, sorrowful, disappointed.
≠ impenitent, unashamed.

regrettable *adj* unfortunate, unlucky, unhappy, sad, disappointing, upsetting, distressing,

lamentable, deplorable, shameful, wrong, ill-advised.
☒ fortunate, happy.

regular *adj* **1** ROUTINE, habitual, typical, usual, customary, time-honoured, conventional, orthodox, correct, official, standard, normal, ordinary, common, commonplace, everyday. **2** PERIODIC, rhythmic, steady, constant, fixed, set, unvarying, uniform, even, level, smooth, balanced, symmetrical, orderly, systematic, methodical.
☒ **1** unusual, unconventional. **2** irregular.

regulate *v* control, direct, guide, govern, rule, administer, manage, handle, conduct, run, organize, order, arrange, settle, square, monitor, set, adjust, tune, moderate, balance.

regulation *n* rule, statute, law, ordinance, edict, decree, order, commandment, precept, dictate, requirement, procedure.
adj standard, official, statutory, prescribed, required, orthodox, accepted, customary, usual, normal.

rehearsal *n* practice, drill, exercise, dry run, run-through, preparation, reading, recital, narration, account, enumeration, list.

rehearse *v* practise, drill, train, go over, prepare, try out, repeat, recite, recount, relate.

reign *n* rule, sway, monarchy, empire, sovereignty, supremacy, power, command, dominion, control, influence.
v rule, govern, command, prevail, predominate, influence.

reimburse *v* refund, repay, return, restore, recompense, compensate, indemnify, remunerate.

reinforce *v* strengthen, fortify, toughen, harden, stiffen, steel, brace, support, buttress, shore, prop, stay, supplement, augment, increase, emphasize, stress, underline.

☒ weaken, undermine.

reinforcements *n* auxiliaries, reserves, back-up, support, help.

reinstate *v* restore, return, replace, recall, reappoint, reinstall, re-establish.

reject *v* refuse, deny, decline, turn down, veto, disallow, condemn, despise, spurn, rebuff, jilt, exclude, repudiate, repel, renounce, eliminate, scrap, discard, jettison, cast off.
☒ accept, choose, select.
n failure, second, discard, cast-off.

rejection *n* refusal, denial, veto, dismissal, rebuff, brush-off, exclusion, repudiation, renunciation, elimination.
☒ acceptance, choice, selection.

rejoice *v* celebrate, revel, delight, glory, exult, triumph.

rejoicing *n* celebration, revelry, merrymaking, festivity, happiness, gladness, joy, delight, elation, jubilation, exultation, triumph.

relapse *v* worsen, deteriorate, degenerate, weaken, sink, fail, lapse, revert, regress, backslide.
n worsening, deterioration, setback, recurrence, weakening, lapse, reversion, regression, backsliding.

relate *v* **1** LINK, connect, join, couple, ally, associate, correlate. **2** REFER, apply, concern, pertain, appertain. **3** *relate an anecdote*: tell, recount, narrate, report, describe, recite. **4** IDENTIFY, sympathize, empathize, understand, feel for.

related *adj* kindred, akin, affiliated, allied, associated, connected, linked, interrelated, interconnected, accompanying, concomitant, joint, mutual.
☒ unrelated, unconnected.

relation *n* **1** LINK, connection, bond, relationship, correlation, comparison, similarity, affiliation, interrelation, interconnection, interdependence, regard, reference. **2** RELATIVE, family, kin, kindred.

relations n 1 RELATIVES, family, kin, kindred. 2 RELATIONSHIP, terms, rapport, liaison, intercourse, affairs, dealings, interaction, communications, contact, associations, connections.

relationship n bond, link, connection, association, liaison, rapport, affinity, closeness, similarity, parallel, correlation, ratio, proportion.

relative adj comparative, proportional, proportionate, commensurate, corresponding, respective, appropriate, relevant, applicable, related, connected, interrelated, reciprocal, dependent.
n relation, family, kin.

relax v slacken, loosen, lessen, reduce, diminish, weaken, lower, soften, moderate, abate, remit, relieve, ease, rest, unwind, calm, tranquillize, sedate.
F3 tighten, intensify.

relaxation n 1 REST, repose, refreshment, leisure, recreation, fun, amusement, entertainment, enjoyment, pleasure. 2 SLACKENING, lessening, reduction, moderation, abatement, let-up (infml), détente, easing.
F3 2 tension, intensification.

relaxed adj informal, casual, laid-back (infml), easy-going (infml), carefree, happy-go-lucky, cool, calm, composed, collected, unhurried, leisurely.
F3 tense, nervous, formal.

relay n 1 BROADCAST, transmission, programme, communication, message, dispatch. 2 work in relays: shift, turn.
v broadcast, transmit, communicate, send, spread, carry, supply.

release v loose, unloose, unleash, unfasten, extricate, free, liberate, deliver, emancipate, acquit, absolve, exonerate, excuse, exempt, discharge, issue, publish, circulate, distribute,

present, launch, unveil.
F3 imprison, detain, check.
n freedom, liberty, liberation, deliverance, emancipation, acquittal, absolution, exoneration, exemption, discharge, issue, publication, announcement, proclamation.
F3 imprisonment, detention.

relent v give in, give way, yield, capitulate, unbend, relax, slacken, soften, weaken.

relentless adj unrelenting, unremitting, incessant, persistent, unflagging, ruthless, remorseless, implacable, merciless, pitiless, unforgiving, cruel, harsh, fierce, grim, hard, punishing, uncompromising, inflexible, unyielding, inexorable.
F3 merciful, yielding.

relevant adj pertinent, material, significant, germane, related, applicable, apposite, apt, appropriate, suitable, fitting, proper, admissible.
F3 irrelevant, inapplicable, inappropriate, unsuitable.

reliable adj unfailing, certain, sure, dependable, responsible, trusty, trustworthy, honest, true, faithful, constant, staunch, solid, safe, sound, stable, predictable, regular.
F3 unreliable, doubtful, untrustworthy.

reliance n dependence, trust, faith, belief, credit, confidence, assurance.

relic n memento, souvenir, keepsake, token, survival, remains, remnant, scrap, fragment, vestige, trace.

relief n reassurance, consolation, comfort, ease, alleviation, cure, remedy, release, deliverance, help, aid, assistance, support, sustenance, refreshment, diversion, relaxation, rest, respite, break, breather (infml), remission, let-up (infml), abatement.

relieve v reassure, console, comfort, ease, soothe, alleviate, mitigate, cure, release, deliver, free, unburden, lighten, soften, slacken, relax, calm,

help, aid, assist, support, sustain.
🔁 aggravate, intensify.

religion

> *Religions include*: Christianity,
> Church of England (C of E), Church
> of Scotland, Baptists, Catholicism,
> Methodism, Protestantism,
> Presbyterianism, Anglicanism,
> Congregationalism, Calvinism,
> evangelicalism, Free Church,
> Jehovah's Witnesses, Mormonism,
> Quakerism, Amish; Baha'ism,
> Buddhism, Confucianism, Hinduism,
> Islam, Jainism, Judaism, Sikhism,
> Taoism, Shintoism, Zen,
> Zoroastrianism, voodoo, druidism.

religious *adj* **1** SACRED, holy,
divine, spiritual, devotional,
scriptural, theological, doctrinal. **2** *a
religious person*: devout, godly,
pious, God-fearing, church-going,
reverent, righteous.
🔁 **1** secular. **2** irreligious, ungodly.

religious officer

> *Religious officers include*: abbess,
> abbot, archbishop, archdeacon,
> bishop, canon, cardinal, chancellor,
> chaplain, clergy, clergyman,
> clergywoman, curate, deacon,
> deaconess, dean, elder, father, friar,
> minister, monk, Monsignor, mother
> superior, nun, padre, parson, pastor,
> pope, prelate, priest, prior, proctor,
> rector, vicar; ayatollah, Dalai Lama,
> guru, imam, rabbi.

relinquish *n* let go, release, hand
over, surrender, yield, cede, give up,
resign, renounce, repudiate, waive,
forgo, abandon, desert, forsake,
drop, discard.
🔁 keep, retain.

relish *v* like, enjoy, savour,
appreciate, revel in.
n **1** SEASONING, condiment, sauce,
pickle, spice, piquancy, tang.

2 ENJOYMENT, pleasure, delight,
gusto, zest.

reluctant *adj* unwilling, disinclined,
indisposed, hesitant, slow, backward,
loth, averse, unenthusiastic,
grudging.
🔁 willing, ready, eager.

rely *v* depend, lean, count, bank,
reckon, trust, swear by.

remain *v* stay, rest, stand, dwell,
abide, last, endure, survive, prevail,
persist, continue, linger, wait.
🔁 go, leave, depart.

remainder *n* rest, balance, surplus,
excess, remnant, remains.

remaining *adj* left, unused, unspent,
unfinished, residual, outstanding,
surviving, persisting, lingering,
lasting, abiding.

remains *n* rest, remainder, residue,
dregs, leavings, leftovers, scraps,
crumbs, fragments, remnants,
oddments, traces, vestiges, relics,
body, corpse, carcase, ashes, debris.

remark *v* comment, observe, note,
mention, say, state, declare.
n comment, observation, opinion,
reflection, mention, utterance,
statement, assertion, declaration.

remarkable *adj* striking, impressive,
noteworthy, surprising, amazing,
strange, odd, unusual, uncommon,
extraordinary, phenomenal,
exceptional, outstanding, notable,
conspicuous, prominent,
distinguished.
🔁 average, ordinary, commonplace,
usual.

remedy *n* cure, antidote,
countermeasure, corrective,
restorative, medicine, treatment,
therapy, relief, solution, answer,
panacea.
v correct, rectify, put right, redress,
counteract, cure, heal, restore, treat,
help, relieve, soothe, ease, mitigate,
mend, repair, fix, solve.

remember *v* **1** RECALL, recollect,
summon up, think back, reminisce,

recognize, place. **2** MEMORIZE, learn, retain.

■ **1** forget.

remind v prompt, nudge, hint, jog one's memory, refresh one's memory, bring to mind, call to mind, call up.

reminder n prompt, nudge, hint, suggestion, memorandum, memo, souvenir, memento.

reminiscence n memory, remembrance, memoir, anecdote, recollection, recall, retrospection, review, reflection.

reminiscent adj suggestive, evocative, nostalgic.

remit v send, transmit, dispatch, post, mail, forward, pay, settle. n brief, orders, instructions, guidelines, terms of reference, scope, authorization, responsibility.

remittance n sending, dispatch, payment, fee, allowance, consideration.

remnant n scrap, piece, bit, fragment, end, off cut, leftover, remainder, balance, residue, shred, trace, vestige.

remorse n regret, compunction, ruefulness, repentance, penitence, contrition, self-reproach, shame, guilt, bad conscience, sorrow, grief.

remote adj **1** DISTANT, far, faraway, far-off, outlying, out-of-the-way, inaccessible, god-forsaken, isolated, secluded, lonely.

2 DETACHED, aloof, standoffish, uninvolved, reserved, withdrawn. **3** a remote possibility: slight, small, slim, slender, faint, negligible, unlikely, improbable.

■ **1** close, nearby, accessible. **2** friendly.

remove v detach, pull off, amputate, cut off, extract, pull out, withdraw, take away, take off, strip, shed, doff, expunge, efface, erase, delete, strike out, get rid of, abolish, purge, eliminate, dismiss, discharge, eject, throw out, oust, depose, displace,

dislodge, shift, move, transport, transfer, relocate.

remuneration n pay, wages, salary, emolument, stipend, fee, retainer, earnings, income, profit, reward, recompense, payment, remittance, repayment, reimbursement, compensation, indemnity.

render v **1** they rendered it harmless: make, cause to be, leave. **2** GIVE, provide, supply, tender, present, submit, hand over, deliver.
3 TRANSLATE, transcribe, interpret, explain, clarify, represent, perform, play, sing.

renew v **1** RENOVATE, modernize, refurbish, refit, recondition, mend, repair, overhaul, remodel, reform, transform, recreate, reconstitute, re-establish, regenerate, revive, resuscitate, refresh, rejuvenate, reinvigorate, revitalize, restore, replace, replenish, restock.
2 REPEAT, restate, reaffirm, extend, prolong, continue, recommence, restart, resume.

renounce v abandon, forsake, give up, resign, relinquish, surrender, discard, reject, spurn, disown, repudiate, disclaim, deny, recant, abjure.

renovate v restore, renew, recondition, repair, overhaul, modernize, refurbish, refit, redecorate, do up, remodel, reform, revamp, improve.

renown n fame, celebrity, stardom, acclaim, glory, eminence, illustriousness, distinction, note, mark, esteem, reputation, honour.

■ obscurity, anonymity.

renowned adj famous, well-known, celebrated, acclaimed, famed, noted, eminent, distinguished, illustrious, notable.

■ unknown, obscure.

rent n rental, lease, hire, payment, fee.
v let, sublet, lease, hire, charter.

repair *v* mend, fix, patch up, overhaul, service, rectify, redress, restore, renovate, renew.
n mend, patch, darn, overhaul, service, maintenance, restoration, adjustment, improvement.

repartee *n* banter, badinage, jesting, wit, riposte, retort.

repay *v* refund, reimburse, compensate, recompense, reward, remunerate, pay, settle, square, get even with, retaliate, reciprocate, revenge, avenge.

repeal *v* revoke, rescind, abrogate, quash, annul, nullify, void, invalidate, cancel, countermand, reverse, abolish.
✗ enact.

repeat *v* restate, reiterate, recapitulate, echo, quote, recite, relate, retell, reproduce, duplicate, renew, rebroadcast, reshow, replay, rerun, redo.
n repetition, echo, reproduction, duplicate, rebroadcast, reshowing, replay, rerun.

repeatedly *adv* time after time, time and (time) again, again and again, over and over, frequently, often.

repel *v* **1** DRIVE BACK, repulse, check, hold off, ward off, parry, resist, oppose, fight, refuse, decline, reject, rebuff. **2** DISGUST, revolt, nauseate, sicken, offend.
✗ 1 attract. **2** delight.

repent *v* regret, rue, sorrow, lament, deplore, atone.

repentance *n* penitence, contrition, remorse, compunction, regret, sorrow, grief, guilt, shame.

repentant *adj* penitent, contrite, sorry, apologetic, remorseful, regretful, rueful, chastened, ashamed.
✗ unrepentant.

repercussion *n* result, consequence, backlash, reverberation, echo, rebound, recoil.

repetition *n* restatement, reiteration, recapitulation, echo,

return, reappearance, recurrence, duplication, tautology.

repetitive *adj* recurrent, monotonous, tedious, boring, dull, mechanical, unchanging, unvaried.

replace *v* **1** *replace the lid*: put back, return, restore, make good, reinstate, re-establish. **2** SUPERSEDE, succeed, follow, supplant, oust, deputize, substitute.

replacement *n* substitute, stand-in, understudy, fill-in, supply, proxy, surrogate, successor.

replenish *v* refill, restock, reload, recharge, replace, restore, renew, supply, provide, furnish, stock, fill, top up.

replica *n* model, imitation, reproduction, facsimile, copy, duplicate, clone.

reply *v* answer, respond, retort, rejoin, react, acknowledge, return, echo, reciprocate, counter, retaliate.
n answer, response, retort, rejoinder, riposte, repartee, reaction, comeback, acknowledgement, return, echo, retaliation.

report *n* article, piece, write-up, record, account, relation, narrative, description, story, tale, gossip, hearsay, rumour, talk, statement, communiqué, declaration, announcement, communication, information, news, word, message, note.
v state, announce, declare, proclaim, air, broadcast, relay, publish, circulate, communicate, notify, tell, recount, relate, narrate, describe, detail, cover, document, record, note.

reporter *n* journalist, correspondent, columnist, newspaperman, newspaperwoman, hack, newscaster, commentator, announcer.

represent *v* stand for, symbolize, designate, denote, mean, express, evoke, depict, portray, describe, picture, draw, sketch, illustrate, exemplify, typify, epitomize, embody, personify, appear as, act as, enact, perform, show, exhibit, be, amount to, constitute.

representation n 1 LIKENESS, image, icon, picture, portrait, illustration, sketch, model, statue, bust, depiction, portrayal, description, account, explanation. 2 PERFORMANCE, production, play, show, spectacle.

representative n delegate, deputy, proxy, stand-in, spokesperson, spokesman, spokeswoman, ambassador, commissioner, agent, salesman, saleswoman, rep (*infml*), traveller.
adj typical, illustrative, exemplary, archetypal, characteristic, usual, normal, symbolic.
◙ unrepresentative, atypical.

repress v inhibit, check, control, curb, restrain, suppress, bottle up, hold back, stifle, smother, muffle, silence, quell, crush, quash, subdue, overpower, overcome, master, subjugate, oppress.

repression n inhibition, restraint, suppression, suffocation, gagging, censorship, authoritarianism, despotism, tyranny, oppression, domination, control, constraint, coercion.

repressive adj oppressive, authoritarian, despotic, tyrannical, dictatorial, autocratic, totalitarian, absolute, harsh, severe, tough, coercive.

reprieve v pardon, let off, spare, rescue, redeem, relieve, respite.
n pardon, amnesty, suspension, abeyance, postponement, deferment, remission, respite, relief, let-up (*infml*), abatement.

reprimand n rebuke, reproof, reproach, admonition, telling-off (*infml*), ticking-off (*infml*), lecture, talking-to (*infml*), dressing-down (*infml*), censure, blame.

v rebuke, reprove, reproach, admonish, scold, chide, tell off (*infml*), tick off (*infml*), lecture, criticize, slate (*infml*), censure, blame.

reprisal n retaliation, counter-attack, retribution, requital, revenge, vengeance.

reproach v rebuke, reprove, reprimand, upbraid, scold, chide, reprehend, blame, censure, condemn, criticize, disparage, defame.
n rebuke, reproof, reprimand, scolding, blame, censure, condemnation, criticism, disapproval, scorn, contempt, shame, disgrace.

reproachful adj reproving, upbraiding, scolding, censorious, critical, fault-finding, disapproving, scornful.
◙ complimentary.

reproduce v 1 COPY, transcribe, print, duplicate, mirror, echo, repeat, imitate, emulate, match, simulate, recreate, reconstruct. 2 BREED, spawn, procreate, generate, propagate, multiply.

reproduction n 1 COPY, print, picture, duplicate, facsimile, replica, clone, imitation. 2 BREEDING, procreation, generation, propagation, multiplication.
◙ 1 original.

reproductive adj procreative, generative, sexual, sex, genital.

reproof n rebuke, reproach, reprimand, admonition, upbraiding, dressing-down (*infml*), scolding, telling-off (*infml*), ticking-off (*infml*), censure, condemnation, criticism.
◙ praise.

reprove v rebuke, reproach, reprimand, upbraid, scold, chide, tell off (*infml*), reprehend, admonish, censure, condemn, criticize.
◙ praise.

reptile n

Reptiles include: adder, puff adder, grass snake, tree snake, asp, viper, rattlesnake, sidewinder, anaconda, boa constrictor, cobra, king cobra, mamba, python; lizard, frilled lizard, chameleon, gecko, iguana, skink, slow-worm; turtle, green turtle, hawksbill turtle, terrapin, tortoise, giant tortoise; alligator, crocodile.

repugnance n reluctance, distaste, dislike, aversion, hatred, loathing, abhorrence, horror, repulsion, revulsion, disgust.
🔁 liking, pleasure, delight.

repulsive adj repellent, repugnant, revolting, disgusting, nauseating, sickening, offensive, distasteful, objectionable, obnoxious, foul, vile, loathsome, abominable, abhorrent, hateful, horrid, unpleasant, disagreeable, ugly, hideous, forbidding.
🔁 attractive, pleasant, delightful.

reputable adj respectable, reliable, dependable, trustworthy, upright, honourable, creditable, worthy, good, excellent, irreproachable.
🔁 disreputable, infamous.

reputation n honour, character, standing, stature, esteem, opinion, credit, repute, fame, renown, celebrity, distinction, name, good name, bad name, infamy, notoriety.

reputed adj alleged, supposed, said, rumoured, believed, thought, considered, regarded, estimated, reckoned, held, seeming, apparent, ostensible.
🔁 actual, true.

request v ask for, solicit, demand, require, seek, desire, beg, entreat, supplicate, petition, appeal.
n appeal, call, demand, requisition, desire, application, solicitation, suit, petition, entreaty, supplication, prayer.

require v **1** NEED, want, wish, desire, lack, miss. **2** *you are required to attend*: oblige, force, compel, constrain, make, ask, request, instruct, direct, order, demand,

necessitate, take, involve.

requirement n need, necessity, essential, must, requisite, prerequisite, demand, stipulation, condition, term, specification, proviso, qualification, provision.

requisite adj required, needed, necessary, essential, obligatory, compulsory, set, prescribed.

requisition v request, put in for, demand, commandeer, appropriate, take, confiscate, seize, occupy.

rescue v save, recover, salvage, deliver, free, liberate, release, redeem, ransom.
🔁 capture, imprison.
n saving, recovery, salvage, deliverance, liberation, release, redemption, salvation.
🔁 capture.

research n investigation, inquiry, fact-finding, groundwork, examination, analysis, scrutiny, study, search, probe, exploration, experimentation.
v investigate, examine, analyse, scrutinize, study, search, probe, explore, experiment.

resemblance n likeness, similarity, sameness, parity, conformity, closeness, affinity, parallel, comparison, analogy, correspondence, image, facsimile.
🔁 dissimilarity.

resemble v be like, look like, take after, favour, mirror, echo, duplicate, parallel, approach.
🔁 differ from.

resent v grudge, begrudge, envy, take offence at, take umbrage at, take amiss, object to, grumble at, take exception to, dislike.
🔁 accept, like.

resentful adj grudging, envious, jealous, bitter, embittered, hurt, wounded, offended, aggrieved, put out, miffed (*infml*), peeved (*infml*), indignant, angry, vindictive.
🔁 satisfied, contented.

resentment *n* grudge, envy, jealousy, bitterness, spite, malice, ill-will, ill-feeling, animosity, hurt, umbrage, pique, displeasure, irritation, indignation, vexation, anger, vindictiveness.
🖪 contentment, happiness.

reservation *n* **1** DOUBT, scepticism, misgiving, qualm, scruple, hesitation, second thought. **2** PROVISO, stipulation, qualification. **3** RESERVE, preserve, park, sanctuary, homeland, enclave. **4** BOOKING, engagement, appointment.

reserve *v* **1** SET APART, earmark, keep, retain, hold back, save, store, stockpile. **2** *reserve a seat*: book, engage, order, secure.
🖪 use up.
n **1** STORE, stock, supply, fund, stockpile, cache, hoard, savings. **2** SHYNESS, reticence, secretiveness, coolness, aloofness, modesty, restraint. **3** RESERVATION, preserve, park, sanctuary. **4** REPLACEMENT, substitute, stand-in.
🖪 **2** friendliness, openness.

reserved *adj* **1** BOOKED, engaged, taken, spoken for, set aside, earmarked, meant, intended, designated, destined, saved, held, kept, retained. **2** SHY, retiring, reticent, unforthcoming, uncommunicative, secretive, silent, taciturn, unsociable, cool, aloof, standoffish, unapproachable, modest, restrained, cautious.
🖪 **1** unreserved, free, available. **2** friendly, open.

reside *v* live, inhabit, dwell, lodge, stay, sojourn, settle, remain.

residence *n* dwelling, habitation, domicile, abode, seat, place, home, house, lodgings, quarters, hall, manor, mansion, palace, villa, country-house, country-seat.

resident *n* inhabitant, citizen, local, householder, occupier, tenant, lodger, guest.

🖪 non-resident.

residual *adj* remaining, leftover, unused, unconsumed, net.

resign *v* stand down, leave, quit, abdicate, vacate, renounce, relinquish, forgo, waive, surrender, yield, abandon, forsake.
🖪 join.

resign oneself reconcile oneself, accept, bow, submit, yield, comply, acquiesce.
🖪 resist.

resignation *n* **1** STANDING-DOWN, abdication, retirement, departure, notice, renunciation, relinquishment, surrender. **2** ACCEPTANCE, acquiescence, submission, non-resistance, passivity, patience, stoicism, defeatism.
🖪 **2** resistance.

resigned *adj* reconciled, philosophical, stoical, patient, unprotesting, unresisting, submissive, defeatist.
🖪 resistant.

resilient *adj* **1** *resilient material*: flexible, pliable, supple, plastic, elastic, springy, bouncy. **2** STRONG, tough, hardy, adaptable, buoyant.
🖪 **1** rigid, brittle.

resist *v* oppose, defy, confront, fight, combat, weather, withstand, repel, counteract, check, avoid, refuse.
🖪 submit, accept.

resistant *adj* **1** OPPOSED, antagonistic, defiant, unyielding, intransigent, unwilling. **2** PROOF, impervious, immune, invulnerable, tough, strong.
🖪 **1** compliant, yielding.

resolute *adj* determined, resolved, set, fixed, unwavering, staunch, firm, steadfast, relentless, single-minded, persevering, dogged, tenacious, stubborn, obstinate, strong-willed, undaunted, unflinching, bold.
🖪 irresolute, weak-willed, half-hearted.

resolution *n* **1** DETERMINATION, resolve, willpower, commitment, dedication, devotion, firmness, steadfastness, persistence, perseverance, doggedness, tenacity, zeal, courage, boldness. **2** DECISION, judgement, finding, declaration, proposition, motion.
☒ **1** half-heartedness, uncertainty, indecision.

resolve *v* decide, make up one's mind, determine, fix, settle, conclude, sort out, work out, solve.

resort *v* go, visit, frequent, patronize, haunt.
n recourse, refuge, course (of action), alternative, option, chance, possibility.
resort to turn to, use, utilize, employ, exercise.

resound *v* resonate, reverberate, echo, re-echo, ring, boom, thunder.

resounding *adj* **1** RESONANT, reverberating, echoing, ringing, sonorous, booming, thunderous, full, rich, vibrant. **2** *a resounding victory*: decisive, conclusive, crushing, thorough.
☒ **1** faint.

resource *n* **1** SUPPLY, reserve, stockpile, source, expedient, contrivance, device. **2** RESOURCEFULNESS, initiative, ingenuity, inventiveness, talent, ability, capability.

resourceful *adj* ingenious, imaginative, creative, inventive, innovative, original, clever, bright, sharp, quick-witted, able, capable, talented.

resources *n* materials, supplies, reserves, holdings, funds, money, wealth, riches, capital, assets, property, means.

respect *n* **1** ADMIRATION, esteem, appreciation, recognition, honour, deference, reverence, veneration, politeness, courtesy. **2** *in every respect*: point, aspect, facet, feature, characteristic, particular, detail, sense, way, regard, reference, relation, connection.
☒ **1** disrespect.
v **1** ADMIRE, esteem, regard, appreciate, value. **2** OBEY, observe, heed, follow, honour, fulfil.
☒ **1** despise, scorn. **2** ignore, disobey.

respectable *adj* **1** HONOURABLE, worthy, respected, dignified, upright, honest, decent, clean-living. **2** ACCEPTABLE, tolerable, passable, adequate, fair, reasonable, appreciable, considerable.
☒ **1** dishonourable, disreputable. **2** inadequate, paltry.

respectful *adj* deferential, reverential, humble, polite, well-mannered, courteous, civil.
☒ disrespectful.

respective *adj* corresponding, relevant, various, several, separate, individual, personal, own, particular, special.

respond *v* answer, reply, retort, acknowledge, react, return, reciprocate.

response *n* answer, reply, retort, comeback, acknowledgement, reaction, feedback.
☒ query.

responsibility *n* fault, blame, guilt, culpability, answerability, accountability, duty, obligation, burden, onus, charge, care, trust, authority, power.

responsible *adj* **1** *a responsible citizen*: GUILTY, culpable, at fault, to blame, liable, answerable, accountable. **2** dependable, reliable, conscientious, trustworthy, honest, sound, steady, sober, mature, sensible, rational. **3** IMPORTANT, authoritative, executive, decision-making.
☒ **2** irresponsible, unreliable, untrustworthy.

rest¹ *n* **1** LEISURE, relaxation, repose, lie-down, sleep, snooze, nap, siesta, idleness, inactivity,

rest

motionlessness, standstill, stillness, tranquillity, calm. **2** BREAK, pause, breathing-space, breather (*infml*), intermission, interlude, interval, recess, holiday, vacation, halt, cessation, lull, respite. **3** SUPPORT, prop, stand, base.

Ea 1 action, activity. **2** work.

v **1** PAUSE, halt, stop, cease.
2 RELAX, repose, sit, recline, lounge, laze, lie down, sleep, snooze, doze.
3 DEPEND, rely, hinge, hang, lie.
4 LEAN, prop, support, stand.

Ea 1 continue. **2** work.

rest[2] *n* remainder, others, balance, surplus, excess, residue, remains, leftovers, remnants.

restaurant *n* eating-house, bistro, steakhouse, grill room, dining-room, snack-bar, buffet, cafeteria, café.

restful *adj* relaxing, soothing, calm, tranquil, serene, peaceful, quiet, undisturbed, relaxed, comfortable, leisurely, unhurried.

Ea tiring, restless.

restless *adj* fidgety, unsettled, disturbed, troubled, agitated, nervous, anxious, worried, uneasy, fretful, edgy, jumpy, restive, unruly, turbulent, sleepless.

Ea calm, relaxed, comfortable.

restore *v* **1** REPLACE, return, reinstate, rehabilitate, re-establish, reintroduce, re-enforce. **2** *restore a building*: renovate, renew, rebuild, reconstruct, refurbish, retouch, recondition, repair, mend, fix.
3 REVIVE, refresh, rejuvenate, revitalize, strengthen.

Ea 1 remove. **2** damage. **3** weaken.

restrain *v* hold back, keep back, suppress, subdue, repress, inhibit, check, curb, bridle, stop, arrest, prevent, bind, tie, chain, fetter, manacle, imprison, jail, confine, restrict, regulate, control, govern.

Ea encourage, liberate.

restrained *adj* moderate, temperate, mild, subdued, muted, quiet, soft,

low-key, unobtrusive, discreet, tasteful, calm, controlled, steady, self-controlled.

Ea unrestrained.

restraint *n* moderation, inhibition, self-control, self-discipline, hold, grip, check, curb, rein, bridle, suppression, bondage, captivity, confinement, imprisonment, bonds, chains, fetters, straitjacket, restriction, control, constraint, limitation, tie, hindrance, prevention.

Ea liberty.

restrict *v* limit, bound, demarcate, control, restrain, confine, contain, cramp, constrain, impede, hinder, hamper, handicap, tie, restrain, curtail.

Ea broaden, free.

restriction *n* limit, bound, confine, limitation, constraint, handicap, check, curb, restraint, ban, embargo, control, regulation, rule, stipulation, condition, proviso.

Ea freedom.

result *n* effect, consequence, sequel, repercussion, reaction, outcome, upshot, issue, end-product, fruit, score, answer, verdict, judgement, decision, conclusion.

Ea cause.

v follow, ensue, happen, occur, issue, emerge, arise, spring, derive, stem, flow, proceed, develop, end, finish, terminate, culminate.

Ea cause.

resume *v* restart, recommence, reopen, reconvene, continue, carry on, go on, proceed.

Ea cease.

resumption *n* restart, recommencement, reopening, renewal, resurgence, continuation.

Ea cessation.

resurrect *v* restore, revive, resuscitate, reactivate, bring back, reintroduce, renew.

Ea kill, bury.

resurrection *n* restoration, revival,

453   **revelation**

resuscitation, renaissance, rebirth, renewal, resurgence, reappearance, return, comeback.

resuscitate v revive, resurrect, save, rescue, reanimate, quicken, reinvigorate, revitalize, restore, renew.

retain v **1** KEEP, hold, reserve, hold back, save, preserve. **2** *retain information*: remember, memorize. **3** EMPLOY, engage, hire, commission.
 1 release. **2** forget. **3** dismiss.

retaliate v reciprocate, counter-attack, hit back, strike back, fight back, get one's own back, get even with, take revenge.

retaliation n reprisal, counter-attack, revenge, vengeance, retribution.

reticent adj reserved, shy, uncommunicative, unforthcoming, tight-lipped, secretive, taciturn, silent, quiet.
 communicative, forward, frank.

retire v leave, depart, withdraw, retreat, recede.
 join, enter, advance.

retirement n withdrawal, retreat, solitude, loneliness, seclusion, privacy, obscurity.

retiring adj shy, bashful, timid, shrinking, quiet, reticent, reserved, self-effacing, unassertive, modest, unassuming, humble.
 bold, forward, assertive.

retort v answer, reply, respond, rejoin, return, counter, retaliate. n answer, reply, response, rejoinder, riposte, repartee, quip.

retract v take back, withdraw, recant, reverse, revoke, rescind, cancel, repeal, repudiate, disown, disclaim, deny.
 assert, maintain.

retreat v draw back, recoil, shrink, turn tail (*infml*), withdraw, retire, leave, depart, quit.
 advance.
n **1** WITHDRAWAL, departure,

evacuation, flight. **2** SECLUSION, privacy, hideaway, den, refuge, asylum, sanctuary, shelter, haven.
 1 advance, charge.

retrieve v fetch, bring back, regain, get back, recapture, repossess, recoup, recover, salvage, save, rescue, redeem, restore, return.
 lose.

retrograde adj retrogressive, backward, reverse, negative, downward, declining, deteriorating.
 progressive.

retrospect n hindsight, afterthought, re-examination, review, recollection, remembrance.
 prospect.

return v **1** COME BACK, reappear, recur, go back, backtrack, regress, revert. **2** GIVE BACK, hand back, send back, deliver, put back, replace, restore. **3** *return a favour*: reciprocate, requite, repay, refund, reimburse, recompense.
 1 leave, depart. **2** take.
n **1** REAPPEARANCE, recurrence, comeback, home-coming.
2 REPAYMENT, recompense, replacement, restoration, reinstatement, reciprocation.
3 REVENUE, income, proceeds, takings, yield, gain, profit, reward, advantage, benefit.
 1 departure, disappearance.
2 removal. **3** payment, expense, loss.

reveal v expose, uncover, unveil, unmask, show, display, exhibit, manifest, disclose, divulge, betray, leak, tell, impart, communicate, broadcast, publish, announce, proclaim.
 hide, conceal, mask.

revel in enjoy, relish, savour, delight in, thrive on, bask in, glory in, lap up, indulge in, wallow in, luxuriate in.

revelation n uncovering, unveiling, exposure, unmasking, show, display, exhibition, manifestation, disclosure, confession, admission, betrayed, giveaway, leak, news, information, communication, broadcasting, publication, announcement, proclamation.

revelry n celebration, festivity, party, merrymaking, jollity, fun, carousal, debauchery.
∃ sobriety.

revenge n vengeance, satisfaction, reprisal, retaliation, requital, retribution.
v avenge, repay, retaliate, get one's own back.

revenue n income, return, yield, interest, profit, gain, proceeds, receipts, takings.
∃ expenditure.

reverberate v echo, re-echo, resound, resonate, ring, boom, vibrate.

revere v respect, esteem, honour, pay homage to, venerate, worship, adore, exalt.
∃ despise, scorn.

reverence n respect, deference, honour, homage, admiration, awe, veneration, worship, adoration, devotion.
∃ contempt, scorn.

reverent adj reverential, respectful, deferential, humble, dutiful, awed, solemn, pious, devout, adoring, loving.
∃ irreverent, disrespectful.

reversal n negation, cancellation, annulment, nullification, countermanding, revocation, rescinding, repeal, reverse, turnabout, turnaround, U-turn, volte-face, upset.
∃ advancement, progress.

reverse v 1 BACK, retreat, backtrack, undo, negate, cancel, annul, invalidate, countermand, overrule, revoke, rescind, repeal, retract, quash, overthrow.
2 TRANSPOSE, turn round, invert, up-end, overturn, upset, change,

alter.
∃ 1 advance, enforce.
n 1 UNDERSIDE, back, rear, inverse, converse, contrary, opposite, antithesis. 2 MISFORTUNE, mishap, misadventure, adversity, affliction, hardship, trial, blow, disappointment, setback, check, delay, problem, difficulty, failure, defeat.
adj opposite, contrary, converse, inverse, inverted, backward, back, rear.

revert v return, go back, resume, lapse, relapse, regress.

review v 1 CRITICIZE, assess, evaluate, judge, weigh, discuss, examine, inspect, scrutinize, study, survey, recapitulate. 2 *review the situation*: reassess, re-evaluate, re-examine, reconsider, rethink, revise.
n 1 CRITICISM, critique, assessment, evaluation, judgement, report, commentary, examination, scrutiny, analysis, study, survey, recapitulation, reassessment, re-evaluation, re-examination, revision. 2 MAGAZINE, periodical, journal.

revise v 1 *revise one's opinion*: change, alter, modify, amend, correct, update, edit, rewrite, reword, recast, revamp, reconsider, re-examine, review. 2 STUDY, learn, swot up (infml), cram (infml).

revival n resuscitation, revitalization, restoration, renewal, renaissance, rebirth, reawakening, resurgence, upsurge.

revive v resuscitate, reanimate, revitalize, restore, renew, refresh, animate, invigorate, quicken, rouse, awaken, recover, rally, reawaken, rekindle, reactivate.
∃ weary.

revoke v repeal, rescind, quash, abrogate, annul, nullify, invalidate, negate, cancel, countermand, reverse, retract, withdraw.
∃ enforce.

revolt n revolution, rebellion,

mutiny, rising, uprising, insurrection,
putsch, coup (d'état), secession,
defection.

v **1** REBEL, mutiny, rise, riot, resist,
dissent, defect. **2** DISGUST, sicken,
nauseate, repel, offend, shock,
outrage, scandalize.

Ea **1** submit. **2** please, delight.

revolting *adj* disgusting, sickening,
nauseating, repulsive, repellent,
obnoxious, nasty, horrible, foul,
loathsome, abhorrent, distasteful,
offensive, shocking, appalling.

Ea pleasant, delightful, attractive,
palatable.

revolution *n* **1** REVOLT, rebellion,
mutiny, rising, uprising, insurrection,
putsch, coup (d'état), reformation,
change, transformation, innovation,
upheaval, cataclysm. **2** ROTATION,
turn, spin, cycle, circuit, round,
circle, orbit, gyration.

revolutionary *n* rebel, mutineer,
insurgent, anarchist, revolutionist.
adj **1** REBEL, rebellious, mutinous,
insurgent, subversive, seditious,
anarchic. **2** *revolutionary ideas*: new,
innovative, avant-garde, different,
drastic, radical, thoroughgoing.

Ea **1** conservative.

revolve *v* rotate, turn, pivot, swivel,
spin, wheel, whirl, gyrate, circle,
orbit.

revulsion *n* repugnance, disgust,
distaste, dislike, aversion, hatred,
loathing, abhorrence, abomination.

Ea delight, pleasure, approval.

reward *n* prize, honour, medal,
decoration, bounty, pay-off, bonus,
premium, payment, remuneration,
recompense, repayment, requital,
compensation, gain, profit, return,
benefit, merit, desert, retribution.

Ea punishment.

v pay, remunerate, recompense,
repay, requite, compensate, honour,
decorate.

Ea punish.

rewarding *adj* profitable,

remunerative, lucrative, productive,
fruitful, worthwhile, valuable,
advantageous, beneficial, satisfying,
gratifying, pleasing, fulfilling,
enriching.

Ea unrewarding.

rhetoric *n* eloquence, oratory,
grandiloquence, magniloquence,
bombast, pomposity, hyperbole,
verbosity, wordiness.

> *Rhetorical devices include*:
> abscission, alliteration, amplification,
> anacoluthon, anadiplosis, anaphora,
> anastrophe, anticlimax, antimetabole,
> antimetathesis, antiphrasis,
> antithesis, antonomasia, aporia,
> apostrophe, asyndeton, auxesis,
> bathos, catachresis, chiasmus, climax,
> diallage, diegesis, dissimile, double
> entendre, dramatic irony,
> dysphemism, ellipsis, enantiosis,
> enumeration, epanadiplosis,
> epanalepsis, epanaphora, epanodos,
> epanorthosis, epigram, epiphonema,
> epistrophe, epizeuxis, erotema,
> erotetic, euphemism, figure of speech,
> hendiadys, hypallage, hyperbole,
> hypostrophe, hypotyposis, hysteron-
> proteron, increment, innuendo, irony,
> litotes, meiosis, metalepsis,
> metaphor, mixed metaphor,
> metonymy, onomatopoeia,
> oxymoron, parabole, paradox,
> paraleipsis, parenthesis, pathetic
> fallacy, personification, prolepsis,
> pun, rhetorical question, simile,
> syllepsis, symploce, synchoresis,
> synchrysis, synecdoche, synoeciosis,
> tautology, transferred epithet, trope,
> vicious circle, zeugma.

rhetorical *adj* oratorical,
grandiloquent, magniloquent,
bombastic, declamatory, pompous,
high-sounding, grand, high-flown,
flowery, florid, flamboyant, showy,
pretentious, artificial, insincere.

Ea simple.

rhyme n poetry, verse, poem, ode, limerick, jingle, song, ditty.

rhythm n beat, pulse, time, tempo, metre, measure, movement, flow, lilt, swing, accent, cadence, pattern.

rhythmic adj rhythmical, metric, metrical, pulsating, throbbing, flowing, lilting, periodic, regular, steady.

rich adj **1** WEALTHY, affluent, moneyed, prosperous, well-to-do, well-off, loaded (sl). **2** PLENTIFUL, abundant, copious, profuse, prolific, ample, full. **3** FERTILE, fruitful, productive, lush. **4** rich food: creamy, fatty, full-bodied, heavy, full-flavoured, strong, spicy, savoury, tasty, delicious, luscious, juicy, sweet. **5** rich colours: deep, intense, vivid, bright, vibrant, warm. **6** EXPENSIVE, precious, valuable, lavish, sumptuous, opulent, luxurious, splendid, gorgeous, fine, elaborate, ornate.
F3 **1** poor, impoverished. **3** barren. **4** plain, bland. **5** dull, soft. **6** plain.

riches n wealth, affluence, money, gold, treasure, fortune, assets, property, substance, resources, means.
F3 poverty.

rickety adj unsteady, wobbly, shaky, unstable, insecure, flimsy, jerry-built, decrepit, ramshackle, broken-down, dilapidated, derelict.
F3 stable, strong.

rid v clear, purge, free, deliver, relieve, unburden.

riddle[1] n enigma, mystery, conundrum, brain-teaser, puzzle, poser, problem.

riddle[2] v **1** PERFORATE, pierce, puncture, pepper, fill, permeate, pervade, infest. **2** SIFT, sieve, strain, filter, mar, winnow.

ride v sit, move, progress, travel, journey, gallop, trot, pedal, drive, steer, control, handle, manage.
n journey, trip, outing, jaunt, spin, drive, lift.

ridicule n satire, irony, sarcasm, mockery, jeering, scorn, derision, taunting, teasing, chaff, banter, badinage, laughter.
F3 praise.
v satirize, send up, caricature, lampoon, burlesque, parody, mock, make fun of, jeer, scoff, deride, sneer, tease, rib (infml), humiliate, taunt.
F3 praise.

ridiculous adj ludicrous, absurd, nonsensical, silly, foolish, stupid, contemptible, derisory, laughable, farcical, comical, funny, hilarious, outrageous, preposterous, incredible, unbelievable.
F3 sensible.

rife adj abundant, rampant, teeming, raging, epidemic, prevalent, widespread, general, common, frequent.
F3 scarce.

rift n **1** SPLIT, breach, break, fracture, crack, fault, chink, cleft, cranny, crevice, gap, space, opening. **2** DISAGREEMENT, difference, separation, division, schism, alienation.
F3 **2** unity.

rig n equipment, kit, outfit, gear, tackle, apparatus, machinery, fittings, fixtures.
rig out equip, kit out, outfit, fit (out), supply, furnish, clothe, dress (up).

right adj **1** the right answer: correct, accurate, exact, precise, true, factual, actual, real. **2** PROPER, fitting, seemly, becoming, appropriate, suitable, fit, admissible, satisfactory, reasonable, desirable, favourable, advantageous. **3** FAIR, just, equitable, lawful, honest, upright, good, virtuous, righteous, moral, ethical, honourable. **4** RIGHT-WING, conservative, Tory.
F3 **1** wrong, incorrect. **2** improper, unsuitable. **3** unfair, wrong. **4** left-wing.

adv **1** CORRECTLY, accurately, exactly, precisely, factually, properly, satisfactorily, well, fairly. **2** *right to the bottom*: straight, directly, completely, utterly.

Ea 1 wrongly, incorrectly, unfairly.

n **1** PRIVILEGE, prerogative, due, claim, business, authority, power. **2** JUSTICE, legality, good, virtue, righteousness, morality, honour, integrity, uprightness.

Ea 2 wrong.

v rectify, correct, put right, fix, repair, redress, vindicate, avenge, settle, straighten, stand up.

right away straight away, immediately, at once, now, instantly, directly, forthwith, without delay, promptly.

Ea later, eventually.

rightful *adj* legitimate, lawful, legal, just, bona fide, true, real, genuine, valid, authorized, correct, proper, suitable, due.

Ea wrongful, unlawful.

rigid *adj* stiff, inflexible, unbending, cast-iron, hard, firm, set, fixed, unalterable, invariable, austere, harsh, severe, unrelenting, strict, rigorous, stringent, stern, uncompromising, unyielding.

Ea flexible, elastic.

rigorous *adj* strict, stringent, rigid, firm, exact, precise, accurate, meticulous, painstaking, scrupulous, conscientious, thorough.

Ea lax, superficial.

rile *v* annoy, irritate, nettle, pique, peeve (*infml*), put out, upset, irk, vex, anger, exasperate.

Ea calm, soothe.

rim *n* lip, edge, brim, brink, verge, margin, border, circumference.

Ea centre, middle.

rind *n* peel, skin, husk, crust.

ring¹ *n* **1** CIRCLE, round, loop, hoop, halo, band, girdle, collar, circuit, arena, enclosure. **2** GROUP, cartel, syndicate, association,

organization, gang, crew, mob, band, cell, clique, coterie.

v surround, encircle, gird, circumscribe, encompass, enclose.

ring² *v* **1** CHIME, peal, toll, tinkle, clink, jingle, clang, sound, resound, resonate, reverberate, buzz. **2** TELEPHONE, phone, call, ring up.

n **1** CHIME, peal, toll, tinkle, clink, jingle, clang. **2** PHONE CALL, call, buzz (*infml*), tinkle (*infml*).

rinse *v* swill, bathe, wash, clean, cleanse, flush, wet, dip.

riot *n* insurrection, rising, uprising, revolt, rebellion, anarchy, lawlessness, affray, disturbance, turbulence, disorder, confusion, commotion, tumult, turmoil, uproar, row, quarrel, strife.

Ea order, calm.

v revolt, rebel, rise up, run riot, run wild, rampage.

rip *v* tear, rend, split, separate, rupture, burst, cut, slit, slash, gash, lacerate, hack.

n tear, rent, split, cleavage, rupture, cut, slit, slash, gash, hole.

rip off (*sl*) overcharge, swindle, defraud, cheat, diddle, do (*infml*), fleece, sting (*sl*), con (*infml*), trick, dupe, exploit.

ripe *adj* **1** RIPENED, mature, mellow, seasoned, grown, developed, complete, finished, perfect. **2** READY, suitable, right, favourable, auspicious, propitious, timely, opportune.

Ea 2 untimely, inopportune.

ripen *v* develop, mature, mellow, season, age.

rise *v* **1** GO UP, ascend, climb, mount, slope (up), soar, tower, grow, increase, escalate, intensify. **2** STAND UP, get up, arise, jump up, spring up. **3** ADVANCE, progress, improve, prosper. **4** ORIGINATE, spring, flow, issue, emerge, appear.

Ea 1 fall, descend. **2** sit down. **3** declare.

n **1** ASCENT, climb, slope, incline, hill, elevation. **2** INCREASE, increment, upsurge, upturn, advance, progress, improvement, advancement, promotion.

F3 1 descent, valley. **2** fall.

risk *n* danger, peril, jeopardy, hazard, chance, possibility, uncertainty, gamble, speculation, venture, adventure.

F3 safety, certainty.

v endanger, imperil, jeopardize, hazard, chance, gamble, venture, dare.

risky *adj* dangerous, unsafe, perilous, hazardous, chancy, uncertain, touch-and-go, dicey (*infml*), tricky, precarious.

F3 safe.

risqué *adj* indecent, improper, indelicate, suggestive, coarse, crude, earthy, bawdy, racy, naughty, blue.

F3 decent, proper.

ritual *n* custom, tradition, convention, usage, practice, habit, wont, routine, procedure, ordinance, prescription, form, formality, ceremony, ceremonial, solemnity, rite, sacrament, service, liturgy, observance, act.

adj customary, traditional, conventional, habitual, routine, procedural, prescribed, set, formal, ceremonial.

F3 informal.

rival *n* competitor, contestant, contender, challenger, opponent, adversary, antagonist, match, equal, peer.

F3 colleague, associate.

adj competitive, competing, opposed, opposing, conflicting.

F3 associate.

v compete with, contend with, vie with, oppose, emulate, match, equal.

F3 co-operate.

rivalry *n* competitiveness, competition, contest, contention, conflict, struggle, strife, opposition, antagonism.

F3 co-operation.

river *n* waterway, watercourse, tributary, stream, brook, beck, creek, estuary.

road *n* roadway, motorway, bypass, highway, thoroughfare, street, avenue, boulevard, crescent, drive, lane, track, route, course, way, direction.

roam *v* wander, rove, range, travel, walk, ramble, stroll, amble, prowl, drift, stray.

F3 stay.

roar *v, n* bellow, yell, shout, cry, bawl, howl, hoot, guffaw, thunder, crash, blare, rumble.

F3 whisper.

rob *v* steal from, hold up, raid, burgle, loot, pillage, plunder, sack, rifle, ransack, swindle, rip off (*sl*), do (*infml*), cheat, defraud, deprive.

robbery *n* theft, stealing, larceny, hold-up, stick-up (*sl*), heist (*sl*), raid, burglary, pillage, plunder, fraud, embezzlement, swindle, rip-off (*sl*).

robot *n* automaton, machine, android, zombie.

robust *adj* strong, sturdy, tough, hardy, vigorous, powerful, muscular, athletic, fit, healthy, well.

F3 weak, feeble, unhealthy.

rock¹ *n* boulder, stone, pebble, crag, outcrop.

Rocks include: basalt, breccia, chalk, coal, conglomerate, flint, gabbro, gneiss, granite, gravel, lava, limestone, marble, marl, obsidian, ore, porphyry, pumice stone, sandstone, schist, serpentine, shale, slate.

rock² *v* **1** SWAY, swing, tilt, tip, shake, wobble, roll, pitch, toss, lurch, reel, stagger, totter. **2** *news that rocked the nation*: shock, stun, daze, dumbfound, astound, astonish, surprise, startle.

rocky¹ *adj* stony, pebbly, craggy, rugged, rough, hard, flinty.

☒ smooth, soft.

rocky[2] *adj* unsteady, shaky, wobbly, staggering, tottering, unstable, unreliable, uncertain, weak.

☒ steady, stable, dependable, strong.

rod *n* bar, shaft, strut, pole, stick, baton, wand, cane, switch, staff, mace, sceptre.

rodent

Rodents include: agouti, bandicoot, beaver, black rat, brown rat, cane rat, capybara, cavy, chinchilla, chipmunk, cony, coypu, dormouse, fieldmouse, ferret, gerbil, gopher, grey squirrel, groundhog, guinea pig, hamster, hare, harvest mouse, hedgehog, jerboa, kangaroo rat, lemming, marmot, meerkat, mouse, muskrat, musquash, pika, porcupine, prairie dog, rabbit, rat, red squirrel, sewer-rat, squirrel, vole, water rat, water vole, woodchuck.

rogue *n* scoundrel, rascal, scamp, villain, miscreant, crook (*infml*), swindler, fraud, cheat, con man (*infml*), reprobate, wastrel, ne'er-do-well.

role *n* part, character, representation, portrayal, impersonation, function, capacity, task, duty, job, post, position.

roll *v* 1 ROTATE, revolve, turn, spin, wheel, twirl, whirl, gyrate, move, run, pass. 2 WIND, coil, furl, twist, curl, wrap, envelop, enfold, bind. 3 *the ship rolled:* rock, sway, swing, pitch, toss, lurch, reel, wallow, undulate. 4 PRESS, flatten, smooth, level. 5 RUMBLE, roar, thunder, boom, resound, reverberate.

n 1 ROLLER, cylinder, drum, reel, spool, bobbin, scroll. 2 REGISTER, roster, census, list, inventory, index, catalogue, directory, schedule, record, chronicle, annals. 3 ROTATION, revolution, cycle, turn, spin, wheel, twirl, whirl, gyration, undulation.

4 RUMBLE, roar, thunder, boom, resonance, reverberation.

roll up (*infml*) arrive, assemble, gather, congregate, convene.

☒ leave.

romance *n* 1 LOVE AFFAIR, affair, relationship, liaison, intrigue, passion. 2 LOVE STORY, novel, story, tale, fairytale, legend, idyll, fiction, fantasy. 3 ADVENTURE, excitement, melodrama, mystery, charm, fascination, glamour, sentiment.

v lie, fantasize, exaggerate, overstate.

romantic *adj* 1 IMAGINARY, fictitious, fanciful, fantastic, legendary, fairy-tale, idyllic, utopian, idealistic, quixotic, visionary, starry-eyed, dreamy, unrealistic, impractical, improbable, wild, extravagant, exciting, fascinating. 2 SENTIMENTAL, loving, amorous, passionate, tender, fond, lovey-dovey (*infml*), soppy, mushy, sloppy.

☒ 1 real, practical. 2 unromantic, unsentimental.

n sentimentalist, dreamer, visionary, idealist, utopian.

☒ realist.

room

Types of room include: attic, loft, box-room, bedroom, boudoir, spare room, dressing-room, guest room, nursery, playroom, sitting-room, lounge, front room, living-room, drawing-room, salon, reception room, chamber, lounge-diner, dining-room, study, den (*infml*), library, kitchen, kitchen-diner, kitchenette, breakfast room, larder, pantry, scullery, bathroom, en suite bathroom, toilet, lavatory, WC, loo (*infml*), cloakroom, laundry, utility room, porch, hall, landing, basement, conservatory, sun lounge, cellar, basement; classroom, music-room, laboratory, office, sick-room, dormitory, workroom, studio, workshop, storeroom, waiting-room, anteroom, foyer, mezzanine, family room, games room.

n space, volume, capacity, headroom, legroom, elbow-room, scope, range, extent, leeway, latitude, margin, allowance, chance, opportunity.

roomy *adj* spacious, capacious, large, sizable, broad, wide, extensive, ample, generous.
 F3 cramped, small, tiny.

root[1] *n* 1 TUBER, rhizome, stem. 2 ORIGIN, source, derivation, cause, starting point, fount, fountainhead, seed, germ, nucleus, heart, core, nub, essence, seat, base, bottom, basis, foundation.
 v anchor, moor, fasten, fix, set, stick, implant, embed, entrench, establish, ground, base.
 root out unearth, dig out, uncover, discover, uproot, eradicate, extirpate, eliminate, exterminate, destroy, abolish, clear away, remove.

root[2] *v* dig, delve, burrow, forage, hunt, rummage, ferret, poke, pry, nose.

roots *n* beginning(s), origins, family, heritage, background, birthplace, home.

rope *n* line, cable, cord, string, strand.
 v tie, bind, lash, fasten, hitch, moor, tether.
 rope in enlist, engage, involve, persuade, inveigle.

roster *n* rota, schedule, register, roll, list.

rostrum *n* platform, stage, dais, podium.

rot *v* decay, decompose, putrefy, fester, perish, corrode, spoil, go bad, go off, degenerate, deteriorate, crumble, disintegrate, taint, corrupt.
 n 1 DECAY, decomposition, putrefaction, corrosion, rust, mould. 2 (*infml*) NONSENSE, rubbish, poppycock (*infml*), drivel, claptrap.

rotary *adj* rotating, revolving, turning, spinning, whirling, gyrating.

F3 fixed.

rotate *v* revolve, turn, spin, gyrate, pivot, swivel, roll.

rotation *n* revolution, turn, spin, gyration, orbit, cycle, sequence, succession, turning, spinning.

rotten *adj* 1 DECAYED, decomposed, putrid, addled, bad, off, mouldy, fetid, stinking, rank, foul, rotting, decaying, disintegrating.
 2 INFERIOR, bad, poor, inadequate, low-grade, lousy, crummy (*sl*), ropy (*sl*), mean, nasty, beastly, dirty, despicable, contemptible, dishonourable, wicked. 3 (*infml*) ILL, sick, unwell, poorly, grotty (*sl*), rough (*infml*).
 F3 1 fresh. 2 good. 3 well.

rough *adj* 1 UNEVEN, bumpy, lumpy, rugged, craggy, jagged, irregular, coarse, bristly, scratchy. 2 HARSH, severe, tough, hard, cruel, brutal, drastic, extreme, brusque, curt, sharp. 3 APPROXIMATE, estimated, imprecise, inexact, vague, general, cursory, hasty, incomplete, unfinished, crude, rudimentary. 4 *rough sea*: choppy, agitated, turbulent, stormy, tempestuous, violent, wild. 5 (*infml*) ILL, sick, unwell, poorly, off colour, rotten (*infml*).
 F3 1 smooth. 2 mild. 3 accurate. 4 calm. 5 well.

round *adj* 1 SPHERICAL, globular, ball-shaped, circular, ring-shaped, disc-shaped, cylindrical, rounded, curved. 2 ROTUND, plump, stout, portly.
 n 1 CIRCLE, ring, band, disc, sphere, ball, orb. 2 CYCLE, series, sequence, succession, period, bout, session. 3 BEAT, circuit, lap, course, routine.
 v circle, skirt, flank, bypass.
 round off finish (off), complete, end, close, conclude, cap, crown.
 F3 begin.
 round on turn on, attack, lay into, abuse.

round up herd, marshal, assemble, gather, rally, collect, group.
🔁 disperse, scatter.

roundabout adj circuitous, tortuous, twisting, winding, indirect, oblique, devious, evasive.
🔁 straight, direct.

rouse v wake (up), awaken, arouse, call, stir, move, start, disturb, agitate, anger, provoke, stimulate, instigate, incite, inflame, excite, galvanize, whip up.
🔁 calm.

rout n defeat, conquest, overthrow, beating, thrashing, flight, stampede.
🔁 win.
v defeat, conquer, overthrow, crush, beat, hammer (infml), thrash, lick, put to flight, chase, dispel, scatter.

route n course, run, path, road, avenue, way, direction, itinerary, journey, passage, circuit, round, beat.

routine n 1 PROCEDURE, way, method, system, order, pattern, formula, practice, usage, custom, habit. 2 comedy routine: act, piece, programme, performance.
adj customary, habitual, usual, typical, ordinary, run-of-the-mill, normal, standard, conventional, unoriginal, predictable, familiar, everyday, banal, humdrum, dull, boring, monotonous, tedious.
🔁 unusual, different, exciting.

row¹ n line, tier, bank, rank, range, column, file, queue, string, series, sequence.

row² n 1 ARGUMENT, quarrel, dispute, controversy, squabble, tiff, slanging match (infml), fight, brawl. 2 NOISE, racket, din, uproar, commotion, disturbance, rumpus, fracas.
🔁 2 calm.
v argue, quarrel, wrangle, bicker, squabble, fight, scrap.

rowdy adj noisy, loud, rough, boisterous, disorderly, unruly, riotous, wild.
🔁 quiet, peaceful.

royal adj regal, majestic, kingly, queenly, princely, imperial, monarchical, sovereign, august, grand, stately, magnificent, splendid, superb.

rub v apply, spread, smear, stroke, caress, massage, knead, chafe, grate, scrape, abrade, scour, scrub, clean, wipe, smooth, polish, buff, shine.
rub out erase, efface, obliterate, delete, cancel.

rubbish n 1 REFUSE, garbage, trash, junk, litter, waste, dross, debris, flotsam and jetsam. 2 NONSENSE, drivel, claptrap, twaddle, gibberish, gobbledegook, balderdash, poppycock, rot (infml), cobblers (sl).
🔁 2 sense.

ruddy adj red, scarlet, crimson, blushing, flushed, rosy, glowing, healthy, blooming, florid, sunburnt.
🔁 pale.

rude adj 1 IMPOLITE, discourteous, disrespectful, impertinent, impudent, cheeky (infml), insolent, offensive, insulting, abusive, ill-mannered, ill-bred, uncouth, uncivilized, unrefined, unpolished, uneducated, untutored, uncivil, curt, brusque, abrupt, sharp, short. 2 a rude joke: obscene, vulgar, coarse, dirty, naughty, gross.
🔁 1 polite, courteous, civil. 2 clean, decent.

rudimentary adj primary, initial, introductory, elementary, basic, fundamental, primitive, undeveloped, embryonic.
🔁 advanced, developed.

rudiments n basics, fundamentals, essentials, principles, elements, ABC, beginnings, foundations.

rugged adj 1 ROUGH, bumpy, uneven, irregular, jagged, rocky, craggy, stark. 2 STRONG, robust, hardy, tough, muscular, weather-beaten.
🔁 1 smooth.

ruin *n* destruction, devastation, wreckage, havoc, damage, disrepair, decay, disintegration, breakdown, collapse, fall, downfall, failure, defeat, overthrow, ruination, undoing, insolvency, bankruptcy, crash.

F3 development, reconstruction.

v spoil, mar, botch, mess up (*infml*), damage, break, smash, shatter, wreck, destroy, demolish, raze, devastate, overwhelm, overthrow, defeat, crush, impoverish, bankrupt.

F3 develop, restore.

rule *n* 1 REGULATION, law, statute, ordinance, decree, order, direction, guide, precept, tenet, canon, maxim, axiom, principle, formula, guideline, standard, criterion. 2 REIGN, sovereignty, supremacy, dominion, mastery, power, authority, command, control, influence, regime, government, leadership. 3 CUSTOM, convention, practice, routine, habit, wont.

v 1 *rule a country*: reign, govern, command, lead, administer, manage, direct, guide, control, regulate, prevail, dominate. 2 JUDGE, adjudicate, decide, find, determine, resolve, establish, decree, pronounce.

as a rule usually, normally, ordinarily, generally.

rule out exclude, eliminate, reject, dismiss, preclude, prevent, ban, prohibit, forbid, disallow.

ruler

Titles of rulers include: Aga, begum, caesar, caliph, consul, duce, emir, emperor, empress, Führer, governor, governor-general, head of state, kaiser, khan, king, maharajah, maharani, mikado, monarch, nawab, nizam, pharaoh, president, prince, princess, queen, rajah, rani, regent, shah, sheikh, shogun, sovereign, sultan, sultana, suzerain, tsar, viceroy.

ruling *n* judgement, adjudication, verdict, decision, finding, resolution, decree, pronouncement.

adj reigning, sovereign, supreme, governing, commanding, leading, main, chief, principal, dominant, predominant, controlling.

rumour *n* hearsay, gossip, talk, whisper, word, news, report, story, grapevine, bush telegraph.

run *v* 1 SPRINT, jog, race, career, tear, dash, hurry, rush, speed, bolt, dart, scoot, scuttle. 2 GO, pass, move, proceed, issue. 3 FUNCTION, work, operate, perform. 4 *run a company*: head, lead, administer, direct, manage, superintend, supervise, oversee, control, regulate.

5 COMPETE, contend, stand, challenge. 6 LAST, continue, extend, reach, stretch, range. 7 FLOW, stream, pour, gush.

n 1 JOG, gallop, race, sprint, spurt, dash, rush. 2 DRIVE, ride, spin, jaunt, excursion, outing, trip, journey. 3 SEQUENCE, series, string, chain, course.

run after chase, pursue, follow, tail.

F3 flee.

run away escape, flee, abscond, bolt, scarper (*sl*), beat it (*infml*), run off, make off, clear off (*infml*).

F3 stay.

run down 1 CRITICIZE, belittle, disparage, denigrate, defame. 2 RUN OVER, knock over, hit, strike. 3 TIRE, weary, exhaust, weaken. 4 *run down production*: reduce, decrease, drop, cut, trim, curtail.

F3 1 praise. 4 increase.

run into meet, encounter, run across, bump into, hit, strike, collide with.

F3 miss.

run out expire, terminate, end, cease, close, finish, dry up, fail.

runaway *n* escaper, escapee, fugitive, absconder, deserter, refugee.

adj escaped, fugitive, loose, uncontrolled.

rundown n 1 REDUCTION, decrease, decline, drop, cut. 2 SUMMARY, résumé, synopsis, outline, review, recap, run-through.

runner n jogger, sprinter, athlete, competitor, participant, courier, messenger.

running adj successive, consecutive, unbroken, uninterrupted, continuous, constant, perpetual, incessant, unceasing, moving, flowing.
🖛 broken, occasional.
n 1 ADMINISTRATION, direction, management, organization, co-ordination, superintendency, supervision, leadership, charge, control, regulation, functioning, working, operation, performance, conduct. 2 out of the running: contention, contest, competition.

runny adj flowing, fluid, liquid, liquefied, melted, molten, watery, diluted.
🖛 solid.

run-of-the-mill adj ordinary, common, everyday, average, unexceptional, unremarkable, undistinguished, unimpressive, mediocre.
🖛 exceptional.

rupture n split, tear, burst, puncture, break, breach, fracture, crack, separation, division, estrangement, schism, rift, disagreement, quarrel, falling-out, bust-up (infml).
v split, tear, burst, puncture, break, fracture, crack, sever, separate, divide.

rural adj country, rustic, pastoral, agricultural, agrarian.
🖛 urban.

rush v hurry, hasten, quicken, accelerate, speed (up), press, push, dispatch, bolt, dart, shoot, fly, tear, career, dash, race, run, sprint, scramble, stampede, charge.
n hurry, haste, urgency, speed, swiftness, dash, race, scramble, stampede, charge, flow, surge.

rust n corrosion, oxidation.
v corrode, decay, rot, oxidize, tarnish, deteriorate, decline.

rustic adj 1 PASTORAL, sylvan, bucolic, countrified, country, rural. 2 PLAIN, simple, rough, crude, coarse, rude, clumsy, awkward, artless, unsophisticated, unrefined, uncultured, provincial, uncouth, boorish, oafish.
🖛 1 urban. 2 urbane, sophisticated, cultivated, polished.

rustle v, n crackle, whoosh, swish, whisper.

rusty adj 1 CORRODED, rusted, rust-covered, oxidized, tarnished, discoloured, dull. 2 UNPRACTISED, weak, poor, deficient, dated, old-fashioned, outmoded, antiquated, stale, stiff, creaking.

ruthless adj merciless, pitiless, hard-hearted, hard, heartless, unfeeling, callous, cruel, inhuman, brutal, savage, cut-throat, fierce, ferocious, relentless, unrelenting, inexorable, implacable, harsh, severe.
🖛 merciful, compassionate.

S

sabotage v damage, spoil, mar, disrupt, vandalize, wreck, destroy, thwart, scupper, cripple, incapacitate, disable, undermine, weaken.
n vandalism, damage, impairment, disruption, wrecking, destruction.

sack (infml) v dismiss, fire, discharge, axe (infml), lay off, make redundant.

n dismissal, discharge, one's cards, notice, the boot (*infml*), the push (*infml*), the elbow (*infml*), the axe (*infml*), the chop (*infml*).

sacred *adj* holy, divine, heavenly, blessed, hallowed, sanctified, consecrated, dedicated, religious, devotional, ecclesiastical, priestly, saintly, godly, venerable, revered, sacrosanct, inviolable.
🔁 temporal, profane.

sacred writing

Sacred writings include: Holy Bible, the Gospel, Old Testament, New Testament, Epistle, Torah, Pentateuch, Talmud, Koran, Bhagavad-Gita, Veda, Granth, Zend-Avesta.

sacrifice *v* surrender, forfeit, relinquish, let go, abandon, renounce, give up, forgo, offer, slaughter.
n offering, immolation, slaughter, destruction, surrender, renunciation, loss.

sacrilege *n* blasphemy, profanity, heresy, desecration, profanation, violation, outrage, irreverence, disrespect, mockery.
🔁 piety, reverence, respect.

sacrosanct *adj* sacred, hallowed, untouchable, inviolable, impregnable, protected, secure.

sad *adj* 1 UNHAPPY, sorrowful, tearful, grief-stricken, heavy-hearted, upset, distressed, miserable, low-spirited, downcast, glum, long-faced, crestfallen, dejected, down-hearted, despondent, melancholy, depressed, low, gloomy, dismal. 2 *sad news*: upsetting, distressing, painful, depressing, touching, poignant, heart-rending, tragic, grievous, lamentable, regrettable, sorry, unfortunate, serious, grave, disastrous.
🔁 1 happy, cheerful. 2 fortunate, lucky.

sadden *v* upset, distress, grieve, depress, dismay, discourage, dishearten.
🔁 cheer, please, gratify, delight.

saddle *v* burden, encumber, lumber, impose, tax, charge, load (*infml*).

sadistic *adj* cruel, inhuman, brutal, savage, vicious, merciless, pitiless, barbarous, bestial, unnatural, perverted.

safe *adj* 1 HARMLESS, innocuous, non-toxic, non-poisonous, uncontaminated. 2 UNHARMED, undamaged, unscathed, uninjured, unhurt, intact, secure, protected, guarded, impregnable, invulnerable, immune. 3 UNADVENTUROUS, cautious, prudent, conservative, sure, proven, tried, tested, sound, dependable, reliable, trustworthy.
🔁 1 dangerous, harmful. 2 vulnerable, exposed. 3 risky.

safeguard *v* protect, preserve, defend, guard, shield, screen, shelter, secure.
🔁 endanger, jeopardize.
n protection, defence, shield, security, surety, guarantee, assurance, insurance, cover, precaution.

safe-keeping *n* protection, care, custody, keeping, charge, trust, guardianship, surveillance, supervision.

safety *n* protection, refuge, sanctuary, shelter, cover, security, safeguard, immunity, impregnability, safeness, harmlessness, reliability, dependability.
🔁 danger, jeopardy, risk.

sag *v* bend, give, bag, droop, hang, fall, drop, sink, dip, decline, slump, flop, fail, flag, weaken, wilt.
🔁 bulge, rise.

sail *v* 1 *sail for France*: embark, set sail, weigh anchor, put to sea, cruise, voyage. 2 CAPTAIN, skipper, pilot, navigate, steer. 3 GLIDE, plane, sweep, float, skim, scud, fly.

sailor *n* seafarer, mariner, seaman,

marine, rating, yachtsman, yachtswoman.

saintly *adj* godly, pious, devout, God-fearing, holy, religious, blessed, angelic, pure, spotless, innocent, blameless, sinless, virtuous, upright, worthy, righteous.
✷ godless, unholy, wicked.

sake *n* benefit, advantage, good, welfare, wellbeing, gain, profit, behalf, interest, account, regard, respect, cause, reason.

salary *n* pay, remuneration, emolument, stipend, wages, earnings, income.

sale *n* selling, marketing, vending, disposal, trade, traffic, transaction, deal, auction.

> *Types of sale include*: auction, autumn sale, bargain offer, bazaar, bazumble, boot-sale, bring-and-buy, car-boot sale, charity sale, church bazaar, clearance sale, closing-down sale, cold-call, end-of-line sale, end-of-season sale, exhibition, exposition, fair, fleamarket, forced sale, garage sale, grand opening sale, introductory offer, January sale, jumble sale, mail order, market, mid-season sale, on-promotion, open market, private sale, public sale, pyramid selling, remainder sale, rummage sale, sale of bankrupt stock, sale of the century, sale of work, second-hand sale, special offer, spring sale, stocktaking sale, summer sale, tabletop sale, telesales, trade show, trash and treasure sale, winter sale.

salesperson *n* salesman, saleswoman, sales assistant, shop assistant, shop-boy, shop-girl, shopkeeper, representative, rep (*infml*).

salient *adj* important, significant, chief, main, principal, striking, conspicuous, noticeable, obvious, prominent, outstanding, remarkable.

sallow *adj* yellowish, pale, pallid, wan, pasty, sickly, unhealthy, anaemic, colourless.
✷ rosy, healthy.

salt *n* seasoning, taste, flavour, savour, relish, piquancy.

salty *adj* salt, salted, saline, briny, brackish, savoury, spicy, piquant, tangy.
✷ fresh, sweet.

salubrious *adj* sanitary, hygienic, health-giving, healthy, wholesome, pleasant.

salutary *adj* good, beneficial, advantageous, profitable, valuable, helpful, useful, practical, timely.

salute *v* greet, acknowledge, recognize, wave, hail, address, nod, bow, honour.
n greeting, acknowledgement, recognition, wave, gesture, hail, address, handshake, nod, bow, tribute, reverence.

salvage *v* save, preserve, conserve, rescue, recover, recuperate, retrieve, reclaim, redeem, repair, restore.
✷ waste, abandon.

salvation *n* deliverance, liberation, rescue, saving, preservation, redemption, reclamation.
✷ loss, damnation.

salve *n* ointment, lotion, cream, balm, liniment, embrocation, medication, preparation, application.

same *adj* identical, twin, duplicate, indistinguishable, equal, selfsame, very, alike, like, similar, comparable, equivalent, matching, corresponding, mutual, reciprocal, interchangeable, substitutable, synonymous, consistent, uniform, unvarying, changeless, unchanged.
✷ different, inconsistent, variable, changeable.

sample *n* specimen, example, cross-section, model, pattern, swatch, piece, demonstration, illustration, instance, sign, indication, foretaste.
v try, test, taste, sip, inspect,

experience.

adj representative, specimen, demonstrative, illustrative, dummy, trial, test, pilot.

sanctify *v* hallow, consecrate, bless, anoint, dedicate, cleanse, purify, exalt, canonize.

F3 desecrate, defile.

sanctimonious *adj* self-righteous, holier-than-thou, pious, moralizing, smug, superior, hypocritical, pharisaical.

F3 humble.

sanction *n* authorization, permission, agreement, OK (*infml*), approval, go-ahead, ratification, confirmation, support, backing, endorsement, licence, authority.

F3 veto, disapproval.

v authorize, allow, permit, approve, ratify, confirm, support, back, endorse, underwrite, accredit, license, warrant.

F3 veto, forbid, disapprove.

sanctions *n* restrictions, boycott, embargo, ban, prohibition, penalty.

sanctity *n* holiness, sacredness, inviolability, piety, godliness, religiousness, devotion, grace, spirituality, purity, goodness, righteousness.

F3 unholiness, secularity, worldliness, godlessness, impurity.

sanctuary *n* **1** CHURCH, temple, tabernacle, shrine, altar. **2** ASYLUM, refuge, protection, shelter, haven, retreat.

sand *n* beach, shore, strand, sands, grit.

sane *adj* normal, rational, right-minded, all there (*infml*), balanced, stable, sound, sober, level-headed, sensible, judicious, reasonable, moderate.

F3 insane, mad, crazy, foolish.

sanitary *adj* clean, pure, uncontaminated, unpolluted, aseptic, germ-free, disinfected, hygienic, salubrious, healthy, wholesome.

F3 insanitary, unwholesome.

sanity *n* normality, rationality, reason, sense, common sense, balance of mind, stability, soundness, level-headedness, judiciousness.

F3 insanity, madness.

sap *v* bleed, drain, exhaust, weaken, undermine, deplete, reduce, diminish, impair.

F3 strengthen, build up, increase.

sarcasm *n* irony, satire, mockery, sneering, derision, scorn, contempt, cynicism, bitterness.

sarcastic *adj* ironical, satirical, mocking, taunting, sneering, derisive, scathing, disparaging, cynical, incisive, cutting, biting, caustic.

sardonic *adj* mocking, jeering, sneering, derisive, scornful, sarcastic, biting, cruel, heartless, malicious, cynical, bitter.

sash *n* belt, girdle, cummerbund, waistband.

satanic *adj* satanical, diabolical, devilish, demonic, fiendish, hellish, infernal, inhuman, malevolent, wicked, evil, black.

F3 holy, divine, godly, saintly, benevolent.

satire *n* ridicule, irony, sarcasm, wit, burlesque, skit, send-up, spoof, take-off, parody, caricature, travesty.

satirical *adj* ironical, sarcastic, mocking, irreverent, taunting, derisive, sardonic, incisive, cutting, biting, caustic, cynical, bitter.

satirize *v* ridicule, mock, make fun of, burlesque, lampoon, send up, take off, parody, caricature, criticize, deride.

F3 acclaim, honour.

satisfaction *n* **1** GRATIFICATION, contentment, happiness, pleasure, enjoyment, comfort, ease, well-being, fulfilment, self-satisfaction, pride. **2** SETTLEMENT, compensation, reimbursement, indemnification, damages, reparation, amends, redress, recompense, requital,

vindication.
⇄ 1 dissatisfaction, displeasure.

satisfactory adj acceptable, passable, up to the mark, all right, OK (infml), fair, average, competent, adequate, sufficient, suitable, proper.
⇄ unsatisfactory, unacceptable, inadequate.

satisfy v 1 GRATIFY, indulge, content, please, delight, quench, slake, sate, satiate, surfeit. 2 satisfy requirements: meet, fulfil, discharge, settle, answer, fill, suffice, serve, qualify. 3 ASSURE, convince, persuade.
⇄ 1 dissatisfy. 2 fail.

saturate v soak, steep, souse, drench, waterlog, impregnate, permeate, imbue, suffuse, fill.

saucy (infml) adj cheeky (infml), impertinent, impudent, insolent, disrespectful, pert, forward, presumptuous, flippant.
⇄ polite, respectful.

saunter v stroll, amble, mosey (infml), mooch (infml), wander, ramble (sl), meander.
n stroll, walk, constitutional, ramble.

savage adj wild, untamed, undomesticated, uncivilized, primitive, barbaric, barbarous, fierce, ferocious, vicious, beastly, cruel, inhuman, brutal, sadistic, bloodthirsty, bloody, murderous, pitiless, merciless, ruthless, harsh.
⇄ tame, civilized, humane, mild.
n brute, beast, barbarian.
v attack, bite, claw, tear, maul, mangle.

save v 1 ECONOMIZE, cut back, conserve, preserve, keep, retain, hold, reserve, store, lay up, set aside, put by, hoard, stash (infml), collect, gather. 2 RESCUE, deliver, liberate, free, salvage, recover, reclaim. 3 PROTECT, guard, screen, shield, safeguard, spare, prevent, hinder.
⇄ 1 spend, squander, waste, discard.
n economy, thrift, discount,

reduction, bargain, cut, conservation, preservation.
⇄ expense, waste, loss.

savings n capital, investments, nest egg, fund, store, reserves, resources.

saviour n rescuer, deliverer, redeemer, liberator, emancipator, guardian, protector, defender, champion.
⇄ destroyer.

savour n taste, flavour, smack, smell, tang, piquancy, salt, spice, relish, zest.
v relish, enjoy, delight in, revel in, like, appreciate.
⇄ shrink from.

savoury adj 1 TASTY, appetizing, delicious, mouthwatering, luscious, palatable. 2 savoury pancakes: salty, spicy, aromatic, piquant, tangy.
⇄ 1 unappetizing, tasteless, insipid. 2 sweet.

say v 1 EXPRESS, phrase, put, render, utter, voice, articulate, enunciate, pronounce, deliver, speak, orate, recite, repeat, read, indicate. 2 ANSWER, reply, respond, rejoin, retort, exclaim, ejaculate, comment, remark, observe, mention, add, drawl, mutter, grunt. 3 TELL, instruct, order, communicate, convey, intimate, report, announce, declare, state, assert, affirm, maintain, claim, allege, rumour, suggest, imply, signify, reveal, disclose, divulge. 4 GUESS, estimate, reckon, judge, imagine, suppose, assume, presume, surmise.

Other words for say include:
accuse, acknowledge, add, admit, admonish, advise, affirm, agree, allege, announce, answer, argue, ask, assert, assume, babble, banter, bark, bawl, beg, begin, bellow, blare, blaspheme, blurt, boast, brag, call, chant, chatter, claim, coax, command, comment, complain, conclude, confide, continue,

contradict, correct, counter, croak, cry, curse, declare, demand, deny, describe, detail, disclose, dispute, divulge, echo, elaborate, elucidate, emphasize, enjoin, enquire, estimate, exclaim, expostulate, express, falter, finish, flounder, gasp, greet, groan, growl, grumble, grunt, guess, hint, howl, imagine, implore, imply, indicate, infer, inform, insinuate, instruct, interrogate, interrupt, intervene, intimate, jeer, jest, joke, laugh, lecture, lie, mention, mimic, moan, mock, mouth, mumble, murmur, mutter, nag, observe, offer, orate, order, persist, persuade, phrase, pipe, plead, point out, predict, press, presume, proclaim, profess, proffer, prompt, pronounce, propose, protest, query, question, quote, rage, rail, rant, read, reassure, rebuke, recite, recommend, reckon, rehearse, reiterate, rejoice, relate, remark, remonstrate, renounce, repeat, reply, report, respond, request, resolve, respond, retaliate, retort, retract, reveal, roar, scoff, scold, scream, screech, shout, shriek, snap, snarl, speak, specify, squeak, stammer, state, storm, stutter, submit, suggest, surmise, swear, sympathize, taunt, tease, tell, testify, thunder, urge, utter, venture, voice, volunteer, vow, whine, whisper, wonder, yell.

saying n adage, proverb, dictum, precept, axiom, aphorism, maxim, motto, slogan, phrase, expression, quotation, statement, remark.

scale[1] n ratio, proportion, measure, degree, extent, spread, reach, range, scope, compass, spectrum, gamut, sequence, series, progression, order, hierarchy, ranking, ladder, steps, gradation, graduation, calibration, register.
v climb, ascend, mount, clamber, scramble, shin up, conquer, surmount.

scale[2] n encrustation, deposit, crust, layer, film, lamina, plate, flake, scurf.

scamp n rogue, rascal, scallywag, monkey, imp, devil.

scamper v scuttle, scurry, scoot, dart, dash, run, sprint, rush, hurry, hasten, fly, romp, frolic, gambol.

scan v 1 EXAMINE, scrutinize, study, search, survey, investigate, check. 2 SKIM, glance at, flick through, thumb through.
n screening, examination, scrutiny, search, probe, check, investigation, survey, review.

scandal n outrage, offence, outcry, uproar, furore, gossip, rumours, smear, dirt, discredit, dishonour, disgrace, shame, embarrassment, ignominy.

scandalize v shock, horrify, appal, dismay, disgust, repel, revolt, offend, affront, outrage.

scandalous adj shocking, appalling, atrocious, abominable, monstrous, unspeakable, outrageous, disgraceful, shameful, disreputable, infamous, improper, unseemly, defamatory, scurrilous, slanderous, libellous, untrue.

scanty adj deficient, short, inadequate, insufficient, scant, little, limited, restricted, narrow, poor, meagre, insubstantial, thin, skimpy, sparse, bare.
▪ adequate, sufficient, ample, plentiful, substantial.

scar n mark, lesion, wound, injury, blemish, stigma.
v mark, disfigure, spoil, damage, brand, stigmatize.

scarce adj few, rare, infrequent, uncommon, unusual, sparse, scanty, insufficient, deficient, lacking.
▪ plentiful, common.

scarcely adv hardly, barely, only just.

scarcity n lack, shortage, dearth, deficiency, insufficiency, paucity, rareness, rarity, infrequency, uncommonness, sparseness, scantiness.

F3 glut, plenty, abundance, sufficiency, enough.

scare v frighten, startle, alarm, dismay, daunt, intimidate, unnerve, threaten, menace, terrorize, shock, appal, panic, terrify.

F3 reassure, calm.

n fright, start, shock, alarm, panic, hysteria, terror.

F3 reassurance, comfort.

scared adj frightened, fearful, nervous, anxious, worried, startled, shaken, panic-stricken, terrified.

F3 confident, reassured.

scary adj frightening, alarming, daunting, intimidating, disturbing, shocking, horrifying, terrifying, hair-raising, bloodcurdling, spine-chilling, chilling, creepy, eerie, spooky (infml).

scathing adj sarcastic, scornful, critical, trenchant, cutting, biting, caustic, acid, vitriolic, bitter, harsh, brutal, savage, unsparing.

F3 complimentary.

scatter v disperse, dispel, dissipate, disband, disunite, separate, divide, break up, disintegrate, diffuse, broadcast, disseminate, spread, sprinkle, sow, strew, fling, shower.

F3 gather, collect.

scatterbrained adj forgetful, absent-minded, empty-headed, feather-brained, scatty (infml), careless, inattentive, thoughtless, unreliable, irresponsible, frivolous.

F3 sensible, sober, efficient, careful.

scattering n sprinkling, few, handful, smattering.

F3 mass, abundance.

scavenge v forage, rummage, rake, search, scrounge.

scenario n outline, synopsis, summary, résumé, storyline, plot, scheme, plan, programme, projection, sequence, situation, scene.

scene n **1** PLACE, area, spot, locale, site, situation, position, whereabouts,

location, locality, environment, milieu, setting, contact, background, backdrop, set, stage. **2** LANDSCAPE, panorama, view, vista, prospect, sight, spectacle, picture, tableau, pageant. **3** EPISODE, incident, part, division, act, clip. **4** don't make a scene: fuss, commotion, to-do (infml), performance, drama, exhibition, display, show.

scenery n landscape, terrain, panorama, view, vista, outlook, scene, background, setting, surroundings, backdrop, set.

scenic adj panoramic, picturesque, attractive, pretty, beautiful, grand, striking, impressive, spectacular, breathtaking, awe-inspiring.

F3 dull, dreary.

scent n **1** PERFUME, fragrance, aroma, bouquet, smell, odour. **2** follow the scent: track, trail.

F3 1 stink.

v smell, sniff (out), nose (out), sense, perceive, detect, discern, recognize.

scented adj perfumed, fragrant, sweet-smelling, aromatic.

F3 malodorous, stinking.

sceptic n doubter, unbeliever, disbeliever, agnostic, atheist, rationalist, questioner, scoffer, cynic.

F3 believer.

sceptical adj doubting, doubtful, unconvinced, unbelieving, disbelieving, questioning, distrustful, mistrustful, hesitating, dubious, suspicious, scoffing, cynical, pessimistic.

F3 convinced, confident, trusting.

scepticism n doubt, unbelief, disbelief, agnosticism, atheism, rationalism, distrust, suspicion, cynicism, pessimism.

F3 belief, faith.

schedule n timetable, programme, agenda, diary, calendar, itinerary, plan, scheme, list, inventory, catalogue, table, form.

v timetable, time, table, programme,

plan, organize, arrange, appoint, assign, book, list.

schematic *adj* diagrammatic, representational, symbolic, illustrative, graphic.

scheme *n* **1** PROGRAMME, schedule, plan, project, idea, proposal, proposition, suggestion, draft, outline, blueprint, schema, diagram, chart, layout, pattern, design, shape, configuration, arrangement. **2** INTRIGUE, plot, conspiracy, device, stratagem, ruse, ploy, shift, manoeuvre, tactic(s), strategy, procedure, system, method.
v plot, conspire, connive, collude, intrigue, machinate, manoeuvre, manipulate, pull strings, mastermind, plan, project, contrive, devise, frame, work out.

schism *n* **1** DIVISION, split, rift, rupture, break, breach, disunion, separation, severance, estrangement, discord. **2** SPLINTER GROUP, faction, sect.

scholar *n* pupil, student, academic, intellectual, egghead (*infml*), authority, expert.
Ea dunce, ignoramus.

scholarly *adj* learned, erudite, lettered, academic, scholastic, school, intellectual, highbrow, bookish, studious, knowledgeable, well-read, analytical, scientific.
Ea uneducated, illiterate.

scholarship *n* **1** ERUDITION, learnedness, learning, knowledge, wisdom, education, schooling. **2** *a scholarship to a public school*: grant, award, bursary, endowment, fellowship, exhibition.

school *n* college, academy, institute, institution, seminary, faculty, department, discipline, class, group, pupils, students.
v educate, teach, instruct, tutor, coach, train, discipline, drill, verse, prime, prepare, indoctrinate.

schooling *n* education, book-

learning, teaching, instruction, tuition, coaching, training, drill, preparation, grounding, guidance, indoctrination.

science *n* technology, discipline, specialization, knowledge, skill, proficiency, technique, art.

Sciences include: acoustics, aerodynamics, aeronautics, agricultural science, anatomy, anthropology, archaeology, astronomy, astrophysics, behavioural science, biochemistry, biology, biophysics, botany, chemistry, chemurgy, climatology, computer science, cybernetics, diagnostics, dietetics, domestic science, dynamics, earth science, ecology, economics, electrodynamics, electronics, engineering, entomology, environmental science, food science, genetics, geochemistry, geographical science, geology, geophysics, graphology, hydraulics, information technology, inorganic chemistry, life science, linguistics, macrobiotics, materials science, mathematics, mechanical engineering, mechanics, medical science, metallurgy, meteorology, microbiology, mineralogy, morphology, natural science, nuclear physics, organic chemistry, ornithology, pathology, pharmacology, physics, physiology, political science, psychology, radiochemistry, robotics, sociology, space technology, telecommunications, thermodynamics, toxicology, ultrasonics, veterinary science, zoology.

scientific *adj* methodical, systematic, controlled, regulated, analytical, mathematical, exact, precise, accurate, scholarly, thorough.

scintillating *adj* sparkling,

glittering, flashing, bright, shining, brilliant, dazzling, exciting, stimulating, lively, animated, vivacious, ebullient, witty.

Ea dull.

scoff[1] *v* mock, ridicule, poke fun, taunt, tease, rib (*sl*), jeer, sneer, pooh-pooh, scorn, despise, revile, deride, belittle, disparage, knock (*infml*).

Ea praise, compliment, flatter.

scoff[2] *v* eat, consume, devour, put away (*infml*), gobble, guzzle, wolf (*infml*), bolt, gulp.

Ea fast, abstain.

scold *v* chide, tell off (*infml*), tick off (*infml*), reprimand, reprove, rebuke, take to task, admonish, upbraid, reproach, blame, censure, lecture, nag.

Ea praise, commend.

scolding *n* castigation, telling-off, ticking-off (*infml*), dressing-down, reprimand, reproof, rebuke, lecture, talking-to, earful (*infml*).

Ea praise, commendation.

scoop *n* 1 LADLE, spoon, dipper, bailer, bucket, shovel. 2 EXCLUSIVE, coup, inside story, revelation, exposé, sensation, latest (*infml*).

v gouge, scrape, hollow, empty, excavate, dig, shovel, ladle, spoon, dip, bail.

scope *n* 1 RANGE, compass, field, area, sphere, ambit, terms of reference, confines, reach, extent, span, breadth, coverage. 2 *scope for improvement*: room, space, capacity, elbow-room, latitude, leeway, freedom, liberty, opportunity.

scorch *v* burn, singe, char, blacken, scald, roast, sear, parch, shrivel, wither.

scorching *adj* burning, boiling, baking, roasting, sizzling, blistering, sweltering, torrid, tropical, searing, red-hot.

score *n* 1 RESULT, total, sum, tally, points, marks. 2 SCRATCH, line, groove, mark, nick, notch.

v 1 RECORD, register, chalk up, notch up, count, total, make, earn, gain, achieve, attain, win, have the advantage, have the edge, be one up. 2 SCRATCH, scrape, graze, mark, groove, gouge, cut, incise, engrave, indent, nick, slash.

scorn *n* contempt, scornfulness, disdain, sneering, derision, mockery, ridicule, sarcasm, disparagement, disgust.

Ea admiration, respect.

v despise, look down on, disdain, sneer at, scoff at, deride, mock, laugh at, slight, spurn, refuse, reject, dismiss.

Ea admire, respect.

scornful *adj* contemptuous, disdainful, supercilious, haughty, arrogant, sneering, scoffing, derisive, mocking, jeering, sarcastic, scathing, disparaging, insulting, slighting, dismissive.

Ea admiring, respectful.

scour[1] *v* scrape, abrade, rub, polish, burnish, scrub, clean, wash, cleanse, purge, flush.

scour[2] *v* search, hunt, comb, drag, ransack, rummage, forage, rake.

scourge *n* 1 AFFLICTION, misfortune, torment, terror, bane, evil, curse, plague, penalty, punishment. 2 WHIP, lash.

Ea 1 blessing, godsend, boon.

v 1 AFFLICT, torment, curse, plague, devastate, punish, chastise, discipline. 2 WHIP, flog, beat, lash, cane, flail, thrash.

scout *v* spy out, reconnoitre, explore, investigate, check out, survey, case (*sl*), spy, snoop, search, seek, hunt, probe, look, watch, observe.

n spy, reconnoitre, vanguard, outrider, escort, lookout, recruiter, spotter.

scowl *v*, *n* frown, glower, glare, grimace, pout.

⊟ smile, grin, beam.

scraggy *adj* scrawny, skinny, thin, lean, lanky, bony, angular, gaunt, undernourished, emaciated, wasted.
⊟ plump, sleek.

scramble *v* **1** CLIMB, scale, clamber, crawl, shuffle, scrabble, grope. **2** RUSH, hurry, hasten, run, push, jostle, struggle, strive, vie, contend. *n* rush, hurry, race, dash, hustle, bustle, commotion, confusion, muddle, struggle, free-for-all, mêlée.

scrap[1] *n* bit, piece, fragment, part, fraction, crumb, morsel, bite, mouthful, sliver, shred, snippet, atom, iota, grain, particle, mite, trace, vestige, remnant, leftover, waste, junk.
v discard, throw away, jettison, shed, abandon, drop, dump, ditch (*sl*), cancel, axe, demolish, break up, write off.
⊟ recover, restore.

scrap[2] *n* fight, scuffle, brawl, dust-up (*infml*), quarrel, row, argument, squabble, wrangle, dispute, disagreement.
⊟ peace, agreement.
v fight, brawl, quarrel, argue, fall out, squabble, bicker, wrangle, disagree.
⊟ agree.

scrape *v* grate, grind, rasp, file, abrade, scour, rub, clean, remove, erase, scrabble, claw, scratch, graze, skin, bark, scuff.

scrappy *adj* bitty, disjointed, piecemeal, fragmentary, incomplete, sketchy, superficial, slapdash, slipshod.
⊟ complete, finished.

scratch *v* claw, gouge, score, mark, cut, incise, etch, engrave, scrape, rub, scuff, graze, gash, lacerate.
n mark, line, scrape, scuff, abrasion, graze, gash, laceration.

scrawny *adj* scraggy, skinny, thin, lean, lanky, angular, bony, underfed, undernourished, emaciated.

⊟ fat, plump.

scream *v, n* shriek, screech, cry, shout, yell, bawl, roar, howl, wail, squeal, yelp.

screen *v* **1** *screen a film*: show, present, broadcast. **2** SHIELD, protect, safeguard, defend, guard, cover, mask, veil, cloak, shroud, hide, conceal, shelter, shade. **3** SORT, grade, sift, sieve, filter, process, evaluate, gauge, examine, scan, vet.
⊟ **2** uncover, expose.
n partition, divider, shield, guard, cover, mask, veil, cloak, shroud, concealment, shelter, shade, awning, canopy, net, mesh.

screw *v* fasten, adjust, tighten, contract, compress, squeeze, extract, extort, force, constrain, pressurize, turn, wind, twist, wring, distort, wrinkle.

scribble *v* write, pen, jot, dash off, scrawl, doodle.

scribe *n* writer, copyist, amanuensis, secretary, clerk.

script *n* **1** *a film script*: text, lines, words, dialogue, screenplay, libretto, book. **2** WRITING, handwriting, hand, longhand, calligraphy, letters, manuscript, copy.

scrounge *v* cadge, beg, sponge.

scrounger *n* cadger, sponger, parasite.

scrub *v* **1** *scrub the floor*: rub, brush, clean, wash, cleanse, scour. **2** (*infml*) ABOLISH, cancel, delete, abandon, give up, drop, discontinue.

scruffy *adj* untidy, messy, unkempt, dishevelled, bedraggled, run-down, tattered, shabby, disreputable, worn-out, ragged, seedy, squalid, slovenly.
⊟ tidy, well-dressed.

scruple *n* reluctance, hesitation, doubt, qualm, misgiving, uneasiness, difficulty, perplexity.
v hesitate, think twice, hold back, shrink.

scruples *n* standards, principles,

morals, ethics.

scrupulous adj **1** PAINSTAKING, meticulous, conscientious, careful, rigorous, strict, exact, precise, minute, nice. **2** PRINCIPLED, moral, ethical, honourable, upright.

F3 1 superficial, careless, reckless. **2** unscrupulous, unprincipled.

scrutinize v examine, inspect, study, scan, analyse, sift, investigate, probe, search, explore.

scrutiny n examination, inspection, study, analysis, investigation, inquiry, search, exploration.

scuff v scrape, scratch, graze, abrade, rub, brush, drag.

scuffle v fight, scrap, tussle, brawl, grapple, struggle, contend, clash. n fight, scrap, tussle, brawl, fray, set-to, rumpus, commotion, disturbance, affray.

sculpt v sculpture, carve, chisel, hew, cut, model, mould, cast, form, shape, fashion.

scum n froth, foam, film, impurities, dross, dregs, rubbish, trash.

scurrilous adj rude, vulgar, coarse, foul, obscene, indecent, salacious, offensive, abusive, insulting, disparaging, defamatory, slanderous, libellous, scandalous.

F3 polite, courteous, complimentary.

scurry v dash, rush, hurry, hasten, bustle, scramble, scuttle, scamper, scoot, dart, run, sprint, trot, race, fly, skim, scud.

sea n **1** OCEAN, main, deep, briny (infml). **2** a sea of faces: multitude, abundance, profusion, mass. adj marine, maritime, ocean, oceanic, salt, saltwater, aquatic, seafaring.

F3 land, air.

at sea adrift, lost, confused, bewildered, baffled, puzzled, perplexed, mystified.

seafaring adj sea-going, ocean-going, sailing, nautical, naval, marine, maritime.

seal v **1** seal a jar: close, shut, stop, plug, cork, stopper, waterproof, fasten, secure. **2** SETTLE, conclude, finalize, stamp.

F3 1 unseal.

n stamp, signet, insignia, imprimatur, authentication, assurance, attestation, confirmation, ratification.

seal off block up, close off, shut off, fence off, cut off, segregate, isolate, quarantine.

F3 open up.

seam n **1** JOIN, joint, weld, closure, line. **2** coal seam: layer, stratum, vein, lode.

seamy adj disreputable, sleazy, sordid, squalid, unsavoury, rough, dark, low, nasty, unpleasant.

F3 respectable, wholesome, pleasant.

sear v burn, scorch, brown, fry, sizzle, seal, cauterize, brand, parch, shrivel, wither.

search v seek, look, hunt, rummage, rifle, ransack, scour, comb, sift, probe, explore, frisk (sl), examine, scrutinize, inspect, check, investigate, inquire, pry. n hunt, quest, pursuit, rummage, probe, exploration, examination, scrutiny, inspection, investigation, inquiry, research, survey.

searching adj penetrating, piercing, keen, sharp, close, intent, probing, thorough, minute.

F3 vague, superficial.

seaside n coast, shore, beach, sands.

season n period, spell, phase, term, time, span, interval. v **1** season food: flavour, spice, salt. **2** AGE, mature, ripen, harden, toughen, train, prepare, condition, treat, temper.

seasonable adj timely, well-timed, welcome, opportune, convenient, suitable, appropriate, fitting.

F3 unseasonable, inopportune.

seasoned adj mature, experienced,

practised, well-versed, veteran, old, hardened, toughened, conditioned, acclimatized, weathered.
F3 inexperienced, novice.

seasoning *n* flavouring, spice, condiment, salt, pepper, relish, sauce, dressing.

seat *n* **1** CHAIR, bench, pew, stool, throne. **2** *country seat*: residence, abode, house, mansion. **3** PLACE, site, situation, location, headquarters, centre, heart, hub, axis, source, cause, bottom, base, foundation, footing, ground.
v sit, place, set, locate, install, fit, fix, settle, accommodate, hold, contain, take.

seating *n* seats, chairs, places, room, accommodation.

secluded *adj* private, cloistered, sequestered, shut away, cut off, isolated, lonely, solitary, remote, out-of-the-way, sheltered, hidden, concealed.
F3 public, accessible.

seclusion *n* privacy, retirement, retreat, isolation, solitude, remoteness, shelter, hiding, concealment.

second¹ *adj* duplicate, twin, double, repeated, additional, further, extra, supplementary, alternative, other, alternate, next, following, subsequent, succeeding, secondary, subordinate, lower, inferior, lesser, supporting.
n helper, assistant, backer, supporter.
v approve, agree with, endorse, back, support, help, assist, aid, further, advance, forward, promote, encourage.

second² *n* minute, tick (*infml*), moment, instant, flash, jiffy (*infml*).

secondary *adj* subsidiary, subordinate, lower, inferior, lesser, minor, unimportant, ancillary, auxiliary, supporting, relief, back-up, reserve, spare, extra, second, alternative, indirect, derived, resulting.
F3 primary, main, major.

second-hand *adj* used, old, worn, hand-me-down, borrowed, derivative, secondary, indirect, vicarious.
F3 new.

second-rate *adj* inferior, substandard, second-class, second-best, poor, low-grade, shoddy, cheap, tawdry, mediocre, undistinguished, uninspired, uninspiring.
F3 first-rate.

secrecy *n* privacy, seclusion, confidentiality, confidence, covertness, concealment, disguise, camouflage, furtiveness, surreptitiousness, stealthiness, stealth, mystery.
F3 openness.

secret *adj* **1** PRIVATE, discreet, covert, hidden, concealed, unseen, shrouded, covered, disguised, camouflaged, undercover, furtive, surreptitious, stealthy, sly, underhand, under-the-counter, hole-and-corner, cloak-and-dagger, clandestine, underground, backstairs, back-door. **2** CLASSIFIED, restricted, confidential, hush-hush (*infml*), unpublished, undisclosed, unrevealed, unknown. **3** CRYPTIC, mysterious, occult, arcane, recondite, deep. **4** SECRETIVE, close, retired, secluded, out-of-the-way.
F3 1 public, open. **2** well-known.
n confidence, mystery, enigma, code, key, formula, recipe.

secretary *n* personal assistant, PA, typist, stenographer, clerk.

secrete¹ *v* hide, conceal, stash away (*infml*), bury, cover, screen, shroud, veil, disguise, take, appropriate.
F3 uncover, reveal, disclose.

secrete² *v* exude, discharge, release, give off, emit, emanate, produce.

secretion *n* exudation, discharge, release, emission.

secretive *adj* tight-lipped, close,

cagey (*infml*), uncommunicative, unforthcoming, reticent, reserved, withdrawn, quiet, deep, cryptic, enigmatic.

🔁 open, communicative, forthcoming.

sect *n* denomination, cult, division, subdivision, group, splinter group, faction, camp, wing, party, school.

sectarian *adj* factional, partisan, cliquish, exclusive, narrow, limited, parochial, insular, narrow-minded, bigoted, fanatical, doctrinaire, dogmatic, rigid.

🔁 non-sectarian, cosmopolitan, broad-minded.

section *n* division, subdivision, chapter, paragraph, passage, instalment, part, component, fraction, fragment, bit, piece, slice, portion, segment, sector, zone, district, area, region, department, branch, wing.

🔁 whole.

sector *n* zone, district, quarter, area, region, section, division, subdivision, part.

🔁 whole.

secular *adj* lay, temporal, worldly, earthly, civil, state, non-religious, profane.

🔁 religious.

secure *adj* **1** SAFE, unharmed, undamaged, protected, sheltered, shielded, immune, impregnable, fortified, fast, tight, fastened, locked, fixed, immovable, stable, steady, solid, firm, well-founded, reliable, dependable, steadfast, certain, sure, conclusive, definite. **2** CONFIDENT, assured, reassured.

🔁 **1** insecure, vulnerable. **2** uneasy, ill at ease.

v **1** OBTAIN, acquire, gain, get. **2** FASTEN, attach, fix, make fast, tie, moor, lash, chain, lock (up), padlock, bolt, batten down, nail, rivet.

🔁 **1** lose. **2** unfasten.

security *n* **1** SAFETY, immunity,

asylum, sanctuary, refuge, cover, protection, defence, surveillance, safe-keeping, preservation, care, custody. **2** *security for a loan*: collateral, surety, pledge, guarantee, warranty, assurance, insurance, precautions, safeguards.

3 CONFIDENCE, conviction, certainty, positiveness.

🔁 **1** insecurity.

sedate *adj* staid, dignified, solemn, grave, serious, sober, decorous, proper, seemly, demure, composed, unruffled, serene, tranquil, calm, quiet, cool, collected, imperturbable, unflappable (*infml*), deliberate, slow-moving.

🔁 undignified, lively, agitated.

sedative *adj* calming, soothing, anodyne, lenitive, tranquillizing, relaxing, soporific, depressant.

🔁 rousing.

n tranquillizer, sleeping-pill, narcotic, barbiturate.

sedentary *adj* sitting, seated, desk-bound, inactive, still, stationary, immobile, unmoving.

🔁 active.

sediment *n* deposit, residue, grounds, lees, dregs.

sedition *n* agitation, rabble-rousing, subversion, disloyalty, treachery, treason, insubordination, mutiny, rebellion, revolt.

🔁 calm, loyalty.

seduce *v* entice, lure, allure, attract, tempt, charm, beguile, ensnare, lead astray, mislead, deceive, corrupt, dishonour, ruin.

🔁 repel.

seduction *n* enticement, lure, attraction, temptation, come-on (*infml*), corruption, ruin.

seductive *adj* enticing, alluring, attractive, tempting, tantalizing, inviting, come-hither (*infml*), flirtatious, sexy, provocative, beguiling, captivating, bewitching, irresistible.

Ᏼ unattractive, repulsive.

see *v* **1** PERCEIVE, glimpse, discern, spot, make out, distinguish, identify, sight, notice, observe, watch, view, look at, mark, note. **2** IMAGINE, picture, visualize, envisage, foresee, anticipate. **3** *I see your point*: understand, comprehend, grasp, fathom, follow, realize, recognize, appreciate, regard, consider, deem. **4** DISCOVER, find out, learn, ascertain, determine, decide. **5** LEAD, usher, accompany, escort, court, go out with, date. **6** VISIT, consult, interview, meet.

see to attend to, deal with, take care of, look after, arrange, organize, manage, do, fix, repair, sort out.

seed *n* pip, stone, kernel, nucleus, grain, germ, sperm, ovum, egg, ovule, spawn, embryo, source, start, beginning.

seedy *adj* **1** SHABBY, scruffy, tatty, mangy, sleazy, squalid, grotty (*infml*), crummy (*sl*), run-down, dilapidated, decaying. **2** UNWELL, ill, sick, poorly, ailing, off-colour. **Ᏼ 2** well.

seek *v* look for, search for, hunt, pursue, follow, inquire, ask, invite, request, solicit, petition, entreat, want, desire, aim, aspire, try, attempt, endeavour, strive.

seem *v* appear, look, feel, sound, pretend to be.

seeming *adj* apparent, ostensible, outward, superficial, surface, quasi-, pseudo, specious. **Ᏼ** real.

seep *v* ooze, leak, exude, well, trickle, dribble, percolate, permeate, soak.

seethe *v* **1** BOIL, simmer, bubble, effervesce, fizz, foam, froth, ferment, rise, swell, surge, teem, swarm. **2** RAGE, fume, smoulder, storm.

see-through *adj* transparent, translucent, sheer, filmy, gauzy, gossamer(y), flimsy.

Ᏼ opaque.

segment *n* section, division, compartment, part, bit, piece, slice, portion, wedge. **Ᏼ** whole.

segregate *v* separate, keep apart, cut off, isolate, quarantine, impound, exclude. **Ᏼ** unite, join.

segregation *n* separation, isolation, quarantine, apartheid, discrimination. **Ᏼ** unification.

seize *v* grab, snatch, grasp, clutch, grip, hold, take, confiscate, impound, appropriate, commandeer, hijack, annex, abduct, catch, capture, arrest, apprehend, nab (*infml*), collar (*infml*). **Ᏼ** let go, release, hand back.

seizure *n* **1** FIT, attack, convulsion, paroxysm, spasm. **2** TAKING, confiscation, appropriation, hijack, annexation, abduction, capture, arrest, apprehension. **Ᏼ 2** release, liberation.

seldom *adv* rarely, infrequently, occasionally, hardly ever. **Ᏼ** often, usually.

select *v* choose, pick, single out, decide on, appoint, elect, prefer, opt for. *adj* selected, choice, top, prime, first-class, first-rate, hand-picked, élite, exclusive, limited, privileged, special, excellent, superior, posh (*infml*). **Ᏼ** second-rate, ordinary, general.

selection *n* choice, pick, option, preference, assortment, variety, range, line-up, miscellany, medley, potpourri, collection, anthology.

selective *adj* particular, choosy (*infml*), careful, discerning, discriminating. **Ᏼ** indiscriminate.

self *n* ego, personality, identity, person.

self-centred *adj* selfish, self-seeking, self-serving, self-interested,

egotistic(al), narcissistic, self-absorbed, egocentric.
🞂 altruistic.

self-confident *adj* confident, self-reliant, self-assured, assured, self-possessed, cool, fearless.
🞂 unsure, self-conscious.

self-conscious *adj* uncomfortable, ill at ease, awkward, embarrassed, shamefaced, sheepish, shy, bashful, coy, retiring, shrinking, self-effacing, nervous, insecure.
🞂 natural, unaffected, confident.

self-control *n* calmness, composure, cool, patience, self-restraint, restraint, self-denial, temperance, self-discipline, self-mastery, will-power.

self-denial *n* moderation, temperance, abstemiousness, asceticism, self-sacrifice, unselfishness, selflessness.
🞂 self-indulgence.

self-evident *adj* obvious, manifest, clear, undeniable, axiomatic, unquestionable, incontrovertible, inescapable.

self-government *n* autonomy, independence, home rule, democracy.
🞂 subjection.

self-indulgent *adj* hedonistic, dissolute, dissipated, profligate, extravagant, intemperate, immoderate.
🞂 abstemious.

selfish *adj* self-interested, self-seeking, self-serving, mean, miserly, mercenary, greedy, covetous, self-centred, egocentric, egotistic(al).
🞂 unselfish, selfless, generous, considerate.

selfless *adj* unselfish, altruistic, self-denying, self-sacrificing, generous, philanthropic.
🞂 selfish, self-centred.

self-respect *n* pride, dignity, self-esteem, self-assurance, self-confidence.

self-righteous *adj* smug,

complacent, superior, goody-goody (*infml*), pious, sanctimonious, holier-than-thou, pietistic, hypocritical, pharisaical.

self-sacrifice *n* self-denial, self-renunciation, selflessness, altruism, unselfishness, generosity.
🞂 selfishness.

self-satisfied *adj* smug, complacent, self-congratulatory, self-righteous.
🞂 humble.

self-styled *adj* self-appointed, professed, so-called, would-be.

self-supporting *adj* self-sufficient, self-financing, independent, self-reliant.
🞂 dependent.

sell *v* barter, exchange, trade, auction, vend, retail, stock, handle, deal in, trade in, traffic in, merchandise, hawk, peddle, push, advertise, promote, market.
🞂 buy.

seller *n* vendor, merchant, trader, dealer, supplier, stockist, retailer, shopkeeper, salesman, saleswoman, agent, representative, rep (*infml*), traveller.
🞂 buyer, purchaser.

semblance *n* appearance, air, show, pretence, guise, mask, front, façade, veneer, apparition, image, resemblance, likeness, similarity.

send *v* **1** POST, mail, dispatch, consign, remit, forward, convey, deliver. **2** TRANSMIT, broadcast, communicate. **3** PROPEL, drive, move, throw, fling, hurl, launch, fire, shoot, discharge, emit, direct.
send for summon, call for, request, order, command.
🞂 dismiss.
send up satirize, mock, ridicule, parody, take off, mimic, imitate.

send-off *n* farewell, leave-taking, departure, start, goodbye.
🞂 arrival.

senile *adj* old, aged, doddering,

decrepit, failing, confused.

senior *adj* older, elder, higher, superior, high-ranking, major, chief. ⊟ junior.

seniority *n* priority, precedence, rank, standing, status, age, superiority, importance.

sensation *n* **1** FEELING, sense, impression, perception, awareness, consciousness, emotion. **2** *the report caused a sensation*: commotion, stir, agitation, excitement, thrill, furore, outrage, scandal.

sensational *adj* **1** EXCITING, thrilling, electrifying, breathtaking, startling, amazing, astounding, staggering, dramatic, spectacular, impressive, exceptional, excellent, wonderful, marvellous, smashing (*infml*). **2** SCANDALOUS, shocking, horrifying, revealing, melodramatic, lurid.
⊟ **1** ordinary, run-of-the-mill.

sense *n* **1** FEELING, sensation, impression, perception, awareness, consciousness, appreciation, faculty. **2** REASON, logic, mind, brain(s), wit(s), wisdom, intelligence, cleverness, understanding, discernment, judgement, intuition. **3** MEANING, significance, definition, interpretation, implication, point, purpose, substance.
⊟ **2** foolishness. **3** nonsense.
v feel, suspect, intuit, perceive, detect, notice, observe, realize, appreciate, understand, comprehend, grasp.

senseless *adj* **1** FOOLISH, stupid, unwise, silly, idiotic, mad, crazy, daft (*infml*), ridiculous, ludicrous, absurd, meaningless, nonsensical, fatuous, irrational, illogical, unreasonable, pointless, purposeless, futile. **2** UNCONSCIOUS, out, stunned, anaesthetized, deadened, numb, unfeeling.
⊟ **1** sensible, meaningful. **2** conscious.

sensible *adj* wise, prudent, judicious, well-advised, shrewd, far-sighted, intelligent, level-headed, down-to-earth, commonsense, sober, sane, rational, logical, reasonable, realistic, practical, functional, sound.
⊟ senseless, foolish, unwise.

sensitive *adj* **1** SUSCEPTIBLE, vulnerable, impressionable, tender, emotional, thin-skinned, temperamental, touchy, irritable, sensitized, responsive, aware, perceptive, discerning, appreciative. **2** DELICATE, fine, exact, precise.
⊟ **1** insensitive, thick-skinned. **2** imprecise, approximate.

sensual *adj* self-indulgent, voluptuous, worldly, physical, animal, carnal, fleshly, bodily, sexual, erotic, sexy, lustful, randy (*infml*), lecherous, lewd, licentious.
⊟ ascetic.

sensuous *adj* pleasurable, gratifying, voluptuous, rich, lush, luxurious, sumptuous.
⊟ ascetic, plain, simple.

sentence *n* judgement, decision, verdict, condemnation, pronouncement, ruling, decree, order.
v judge, pass judgement on, condemn, doom, punish, penalize.

sentiment *n* **1** THOUGHT, idea, feeling, opinion, view, judgement, belief, persuasion, attitude. **2** EMOTION, sensibility, tenderness, soft-heartedness, romanticism, sentimentality, mawkishness.

sentimental *adj* tender, soft-hearted, emotional, gushing, touching, pathetic, tear-jerking, weepy (*infml*), maudlin, mawkish, nostalgic, romantic, lovey-dovey (*infml*), slushy, mushy, sloppy, schmaltzy, soppy, corny (*infml*).
⊟ unsentimental, realistic, cynical.

sentry *n* sentinel, guard, picket, watchman, watch, look-out.

separable *adj* divisible, detachable, removable, distinguishable, distinct.

Ea inseparable.

separate v divide, sever, part, split (up) divorce, part company, diverge, disconnect, uncouple, disunite, disaffiliate, disentangle, segregate, isolate, cut off, abstract, remove, detach, withdraw, secede.

Ea join, unite, combine.

adj single, individual, particular, independent, alone, solitary, segregated, isolated, apart, divorced, divided, disunited, disconnected, disjointed, detached, unattached, unconnected, unrelated, different, disparate, distinct, discrete, several, sundry.

Ea together, attached.

separation n division, severance, parting, leave-taking, farewell, split-up, break-up, divorce, split, rift, gap, divergence, disconnection, disengagement, dissociation, estrangement, segregation, isolation, detachment.

Ea unification.

septic adj infected, poisoned, festering, putrefying, putrid.

sequel n follow-up, continuation, development, result, consequence, outcome, issue, upshot, pay-off, end, conclusion.

sequence n succession, series, run, progression, chain, string, train, line, procession, order, arrangement, course, track, cycle, set.

serene adj calm, tranquil, cool, composed, placid, untroubled, undisturbed, still, quiet, peaceful.

Ea troubled, disturbed.

series n set, cycle, succession, sequence, run, progression, chain, string, line, train, order, arrangement, course.

serious adj 1 IMPORTANT, significant, weighty, momentous, crucial, critical, urgent, pressing, acute, grave, worrying, difficult, dangerous, grim, severe, deep, far-reaching. 2 UNSMILING, long-faced,

humourless, solemn, sober, stern, thoughtful, pensive, earnest, sincere.

Ea 1 trivial, slight. 2 smiling, facetious, frivolous.

sermon n address, discourse, lecture, harangue, homily, talking-to (infml).

serrated adj toothed, notched, indented, jagged.

Ea smooth.

servant n domestic, maid, valet, steward, attendant, retainer, hireling, lackey, menial, skivvy (infml), slave, help, helper, assistant, ancillary.

Ea master, mistress.

serve v 1 WAIT ON, attend, minister to, work for, help, aid, assist, benefit, further. 2 serve a purpose: fulfil, complete, answer, satisfy, discharge, perform, act, function. 3 DISTRIBUTE, dole out, present, deliver, provide, supply.

service n 1 EMPLOYMENT, work, labour, business, duty, function, performance. 2 USE, usefulness, utility, advantage, benefit, help, assistance. 3 SERVICING, maintenance, overhaul, check. 4 church service: worship, observance, ceremony, rite. v maintain, overhaul, check, repair, recondition, tune.

serviceable adj usable, useful, helpful, profitable, advantageous, beneficial, utilitarian, simple, plain, unadorned, strong, tough, durable, hard-wearing, dependable, efficient, functional, practical, convenient.

Ea unserviceable, unusable.

servile adj obsequious, sycophantic, toadying, cringing, fawning, grovelling, bootlicking, slavish, subservient, subject, submissive, humble, abject, low, mean, base, menial.

Ea assertive, aggressive.

session n sitting, hearing, meeting, assembly, conference, discussion, period, time, term, semester, year.

set v **1** PUT, place, locate, situate,
position, arrange, prepare, lodge, fix,
stick, park, deposit. **2** SCHEDULE,
appoint, designate, specify, name,
prescribe, ordain, assign, allocate,
impose, fix, establish, determine,
decide, conclude, settle, resolve.
3 ADJUST, regulate, synchronize, co-
ordinate. **4** *the sun sets*: go down,
sink, dip, subside, disappear, vanish.
5 CONGEAL, thicken, gel, gel, stiffen,
solidify, harden, crystallize.
Fa 4 rise.
n batch, series, sequence, kit, outfit,
compendium, assortment, collection,
class, category, group, band, gang,
crowd, circle, clique, faction.
adj scheduled, appointed, arranged,
prepared, prearranged, fixed,
established, definite, decided, agreed,
settled, firm, strict, rigid, inflexible,
prescribed, formal, conventional,
traditional, customary, usual, routine,
regular, standard, stock, stereotyped,
hackneyed.
Fa movable, free, spontaneous,
undecided.
set about begin, start, embark on,
undertake, tackle, attack.
set aside 1 PUT ASIDE, lay aside, keep
(back), save, reserve, set apart,
separate, select, earmark. **2** ANNUL,
abrogate, cancel, revoke, reverse,
overturn, overrule, reject, discard.
set back delay, hold up, slow, retard,
hinder, impede.
set off 1 LEAVE, depart, set out, start
(out), begin. **2** DETONATE, light,
ignite, touch off, trigger off, explode.
3 DISPLAY, show off, enhance,
contrast.
set on set upon, attack, turn on, go for,
fall upon, lay into, beat up (*infml*).
set out 1 LEAVE, depart, set off, start
(out), begin. **2** LAY OUT, arrange,
display, exhibit, present, describe,
explain.
set up raise, elevate, erect, build,
construct, assemble, compose, form,

create, establish, institute, found,
inaugurate, initiate, begin, start,
introduce, organize, arrange, prepare.
setback n delay, hold-up, problem,
snag, hitch, hiccup, reverse,
misfortune, upset, disappointment,
defeat.
Fa boost, advance, help, advantage.
setting n mounting, frame,
surroundings, milieu, environment,
background, context, perspective,
period, position, location, locale, site,
scene, scenery.
settle v **1** ARRANGE, order, adjust,
reconcile, resolve, complete,
conclude. **2** SINK, subside, drop, fall,
descend, land, alight. **3** CHOOSE,
appoint, fix, establish, determine,
decide, agree, confirm. **4** COLONIZE,
occupy, populate, people, inhabit,
live, reside. **5** *settle a bill*: pay, clear,
discharge.
settlement n **1** RESOLUTION,
agreement, arrangement, decision,
conclusion, termination, satisfaction.
2 PAYMENT, clearance, clearing,
discharge. **3** COLONY, outpost,
community, kibbutz, camp,
encampment, hamlet, village.
settler n colonist, colonizer, pioneer,
frontiersman, frontierswoman,
planter, immigrant, incomer,
newcomer, squatter.
Fa native.
set-up n system, structure,
organization, arrangement, business,
conditions, circumstances.
sever v cut, cleave, split, rend, part,
separate, divide, cut off, amputate,
detach, disconnect, disjoin, disunite,
dissociate, estrange, alienate, break
off, dissolve, end, terminate.
Fa join, unite, combine, attach.
several adj some, many, various,
assorted, sundry, diverse, different,
distinct, separate, particular,
individual.
severe adj **1** STERN, disapproving,
sober, strait-laced, strict, rigid,

unbending, harsh, tough, hard, difficult, demanding, arduous, punishing, rigorous, grim, forbidding, cruel, biting, cutting, scathing, pitiless, merciless, oppressive, relentless, inexorable, acute, bitter, intense, extreme, fierce, violent, distressing, serious, grave, critical, dangerous. **2** PLAIN, simple, unadorned, unembellished, functional, restrained, austere, ascetic.

F3 **1** kind, compassionate, sympathetic, lenient, mild. **2** decorated, ornate.

sew *v* stitch, tack, baste, hem, darn, embroider.

sex *n* **1** GENDER, sexuality. **2** SEXUAL INTERCOURSE, intercourse, sexual relations, copulation, coitus, lovemaking, fornication, reproduction, union, intimacy.

sexual *adj* sex, reproductive, procreative, genital, coital, venereal, carnal, sensual, erotic.

> *Sexual orientations include*: bisexual, AC/DC (*sl*), hermaphrodite, unisexual, heterosexual, homosexual, gay, queer (*sl*), cissy (*sl*), pretty boy (*sl*), nancy (*sl*), nancy boy (*sl*), pansy (*sl*), faggot (*sl*), rent boy, lesbian, lez (*sl*), dyke (*sl*), butch (*sl*), transsexual, transvestite, cross-dresser.

sexy *adj* sensual, voluptuous, nubile, beddable (*infml*), seductive, inviting, flirtatious, arousing, provoking, provocative, titillating, pornographic, erotic, salacious, suggestive.

F3 sexless.

shabby *adj* **1** RAGGED, tattered, frayed, worn, worn-out, mangy, moth-eaten, scruffy, tatty, disreputable, dilapidated, run-down, seedy, dirty, dingy, poky. **2** *a shabby*

trick: contemptible, despicable, rotten, mean, low, cheap, shoddy, shameful, dishonourable.

F3 **1** smart. **2** honourable, fair.

shack *n* hut, cabin, shanty, hovel, shed, lean-to.

shade *n* **1** SHADINESS, shadow, darkness, obscurity, semi-darkness, dimness, gloom, gloominess, twilight, dusk, gloaming. **2** AWNING, canopy, cover, shelter, screen, blind, curtain, shield, visor, umbrella, parasol. **3** COLOUR, hue, tint, tone, tinge. **4** TRACE, dash, hint, suggestion, suspicion, nuance, gradation, degree, amount, variety. **5** GHOST, spectre, phantom, spirit, apparition, semblance.

v shield, screen, protect, cover, shroud, veil, hide, conceal, obscure, cloud, dim, darken, shadow, overshadow.

shadow *n* **1** SHADE, darkness, obscurity, semi-darkness, dimness, gloom, twilight, dusk, gloaming, cloud, cover, protection. **2** SILHOUETTE, shape, image, representation. **3** TRACE, hint, suggestion, suspicion, vestige, remnant.

v **1** OVERSHADOW, overhang, shade, shield, screen, obscure, darken. **2** FOLLOW, tail, dog, stalk, trail, watch.

shadowy *adj* dark, gloomy, murky, obscure, dim, faint, indistinct, ill-defined, vague, hazy, nebulous, intangible, unsubstantial, ghostly, spectral, illusory, dreamlike, imaginary, unreal.

shady *adj* **1** SHADED, shadowy, dim, dark, cool, leafy. **2** (*infml*) DUBIOUS, questionable, suspect, suspicious, fishy (*infml*), dishonest, crooked, unreliable, untrustworthy, disreputable, unscrupulous, unethical, underhand.

F3 **1** sunny, sunlit, bright. **2** honest, trustworthy, honourable.

shaft

shaft *n* handle, shank, stem, upright, pillar, pole, rod, bar, stick, arrow, dart, beam, ray, duct, passage.

shaggy *adj* hairy, long-haired, hirsute, bushy, woolly, unshorn, dishevelled, unkempt.
₣ bald, shorn, close-cropped.

shake *v* **1** WAVE, flourish, brandish, wag, waggle, agitate, rattle, joggle, jolt, jerk, twitch, convulse, heave, throb, vibrate, oscillate, fluctuate, waver, wobble, totter, sway, rock, tremble, quiver, quake, shiver, shudder. **2** *the news shook her*: upset, distress, shock, frighten, unnerve, intimidate, disturb, discompose, unsettle, agitate, stir, rouse.

shake off get rid of, dislodge, lose, elude, give the slip, leave behind, outdistance, outstrip.

shake-up (*infml*) *n* reorganization, rearrangement, reshuffle, disturbance, upheaval.

shaky *adj* **1** TREMBLING, quivering, faltering, tentative, uncertain.
2 UNSTABLE, unsteady, insecure, precarious, wobbly, rocky, tottery, rickety, weak. **3** DUBIOUS, questionable, suspect, unreliable, unsound, unsupported.
₣ **2** firm, strong.

shallow *adj* superficial, surface, skin-deep, slight, flimsy, trivial, frivolous, foolish, idle, empty, meaningless, unscholarly, ignorant, simple.
₣ deep, profound.

sham *n* pretence, fraud, counterfeit, forgery, fake, imitation, simulation, hoax, humbug.
adj false, fake, counterfeit, spurious, bogus, phoney (*infml*), pretended, feigned, put-on, simulated, artificial, mock, imitation, synthetic.
₣ genuine, authentic, real.
v pretend, feign, affect, put on, simulate, imitate, fake, counterfeit.

shame *n* disgrace, dishonour, discredit, stain, stigma, disrepute, infamy, scandal, ignominy, humiliation, degradation, shamefacedness, remorse, guilt, embarrassment, mortification.
₣ honour, credit, distinction, pride.
v embarrass, mortify, abash, confound, humiliate, ridicule, humble, put to shame, show up, disgrace, dishonour, discredit, debase, degrade, sully, taint, stain.

shamefaced *adj* ashamed, conscience-stricken, remorseful, contrite, apologetic, sorry, sheepish, red-faced, blushing, embarrassed, mortified, abashed, humiliated, uncomfortable.
₣ unashamed, proud.

shameful *adj* **1** *a shameful waste of money*: disgraceful, outrageous, scandalous, indecent, abominable, atrocious, wicked, mean, low, vile, reprehensible, contemptible, unworthy, ignoble.
2 EMBARRASSING, mortifying, humiliating, ignominious.
₣ **1** honourable, creditable, worthy.

shameless *adj* **1** UNASHAMED, unabashed, unrepentant, impenitent barefaced, flagrant, blatant, brazen, brash, audacious, insolent, defiant, hardened, incorrigible. **2** IMMODEST, indecent, improper, unprincipled, wanton, dissolute, corrupt, depraved.
₣ **1** ashamed, shamefaced, contrite. **2** modest.

shape *n* **1** FORM, outline, silhouette, profile, model, mould, pattern, cut, lines, contours, figure, physique, build, frame, format, configuration. **2** APPEARANCE, guise, likeness, semblance. **3** *in good shape*: condition, state, form, health, trim, fettle.

> Geometrical shapes include:
> polygon, circle, semicircle, quadrant, oval, ellipse, crescent, triangle, equilateral triangle, isosceles triangle, scalene triangle, quadrilateral, square,

rectangle, oblong, rhombus, diamond, kite, trapezium, parallelogram, pentagon, hexagon, heptagon, octagon, nonagon, decagon; polyhedron, cube, cuboid, prism, pyramid, tetrahedron, pentahedron, octahedron, cylinder, cone, sphere, hemisphere.

v form, fashion, model, mould, cast, forge, sculpt, carve, whittle, make, produce, construct, create, devise, frame, plan, prepare, adapt, adjust, regulate, accommodate, modify, remodel.

shapeless *adj* formless, amorphous, unformed, nebulous, unstructured, irregular, misshapen, deformed, dumpy.

share *v* divide, split, go halves, partake, participate, share out, distribute, dole out, give out, deal out, apportion, allot, allocate, assign. *n* portion, ration, quota, allowance, allocation, allotment, lot, part, division, proportion, percentage, cut (*infml*), dividend, due, contribution, whack (*infml*).

sharp *adj* **1** *a sharp needle*: pointed, keen, edged, knife-edged, razor-sharp, cutting, serrated, jagged, barbed, spiky. **2** CLEAR, clear-cut, well-defined, distinct, marked, crisp. **3** QUICK-WITTED, alert, shrewd, astute, perceptive, observant, discerning, penetrating, clever, crafty, cunning, artful, sly. **4** SUDDEN, abrupt, violent, fierce, intense, extreme, severe, acute, piercing, stabbing. **5** PUNGENT, piquant, sour, tart, vinegary, bitter, acerbic, acid. **6** TRENCHANT, incisive, cutting, biting, caustic, sarcastic, sardonic, scathing, vitriolic, acrimonious.

🔁 **1** blunt. **2** blurred. **3** slow, stupid. **4** gentle. **5** bland. **6** mild.

adv punctually, promptly, on the dot, exactly, precisely, abruptly, suddenly,

unexpectedly.

🔁 approximately, roughly.

sharpen *v* edge, whet, hone, grind, file.

🔁 blunt.

shatter *v* break, smash, splinter, shiver, crack, split, burst, explode, blast, crush, demolish, destroy, devastate, wreck, ruin, overturn, upset.

sheath *n* SCABBARD, case, sleeve, envelope, shell, casing, covering. **2** CONDOM, rubber (*sl*), French letter (*sl*).

shed[1] *v* cast (off), moult, slough, discard, drop, spill, pour, shower, scatter, diffuse, emit, radiate, shine, throw.

shed[2] *n* outhouse, lean-to, hut, shack.

sheen *n* lustre, gloss, shine, shimmer, brightness, brilliance, shininess, polish, burnish.

🔁 dullness, tarnish.

sheepish *adj* ashamed, shamefaced, embarrassed, mortified, chastened, abashed, uncomfortable, self-conscious, silly, foolish.

🔁 unabashed, brazen, bold.

sheer *adj* **1** UTTER, complete, total, absolute, thorough, mere, pure, unadulterated, downright, out-and-out, rank, thoroughgoing, unqualified, unmitigated. **2** *a sheer drop*: vertical, perpendicular, precipitous, abrupt, steep. **3** THIN, fine, flimsy, gauzy, gossamer, translucent, transparent, see-through.

🔁 **2** gentle, gradual. **3** thick, heavy.

sheet *n* cover, blanket, covering, coating, coat, film, layer, stratum, skin, membrane, lamina, veneer, overlay, plate, leaf, page, folio, piece, panel, slab, pane, expanse, surface.

shelf *n* ledge, mantelpiece, sill, step, bench, counter, bar, bank, sandbank, reef, terrace.

shell *n* covering, hull, husk, pod, rind, crust, case, casing, body, chassis, frame, framework, structure, skeleton.

v 1 *shell nuts*: hull, husk, pod. 2 BOMB, bombard, barrage, blitz, attack.

shelter v cover, shroud, screen, shade, shadow, protect, safeguard, defend, guard, shield, harbour, hide, accommodate, put up.

◨ expose.

n cover, roof, shade, shadow, protection, defence, guard, security, safety, sanctuary, asylum, haven, refuge, retreat, accommodation, lodging.

◨ exposure.

sheltered adj covered, shaded, shielded, protected, cosy, snug, warm, quiet, secluded, isolated, retired, withdrawn, reclusive, cloistered, unworldly.

◨ exposed.

shelve v postpone, defer, put off, suspend, halt, put aside, pigeonhole, put on ice, mothball.

◨ expedite, implement.

shield n buckler, escutcheon, defence, bulwark, rampart, screen, guard, cover, shelter, protection, safeguard.

v defend, guard, protect, safeguard, screen, shade, shadow, cover, shelter.

◨ expose.

shift v change, vary, fluctuate, alter, adjust, move, budge, remove, dislodge, displace, relocate, reposition, rearrange, transpose, transfer, switch, swerve, veer.

n change, fluctuation, alteration, modification, move, removal, displacement, rearrangement, transposition, transfer, switch.

shifty adj untrustworthy, dishonest, deceitful, scheming, contriving, tricky, wily, crafty, cunning, devious, evasive, slippery, furtive, underhand, dubious, shady (*infml*).

◨ dependable, honest, open.

shimmer v glisten, gleam, glitter, scintillate, twinkle.

n lustre, gleam, glimmer, glitter, glow.

shine v 1 BEAM, radiate, glow, flash, glare, gleam, glint, glitter, sparkle, twinkle, shimmer, glisten, glimmer.

2 POLISH, burnish, buff, brush, rub. 3 *shine at athletics*: excel, stand out.

n 1 LIGHT, radiance, glow, brightness, glare, gleam, sparkle, shimmer. 2 GLOSS, polish, burnish, sheen, lustre, glaze.

shining adj 1 BRIGHT, radiant, glowing, beaming, flashing, gleaming, glittering, glistening, shimmering, twinkling, sparkling, brilliant, resplendent, splendid, glorious. 2 *a shining example*: conspicuous, outstanding, leading, eminent, celebrated, distinguished, illustrious.

◨ 1 dark.

shiny adj polished, burnished, sheeny, lustrous, glossy, sleek, bright, gleaming, glistening.

◨ dull, matt.

ship n vessel, craft, liner, steamer, tanker, trawler, ferry, boat, yacht.

shirk v dodge, evade, avoid, duck (*infml*), shun, slack, skive (*infml*).

shiver v shudder, tremble, quiver, quake, shake, vibrate, palpitate, flutter.

n shudder, quiver, shake, tremor, twitch, start, vibration, flutter.

shock v disgust, revolt, sicken, offend, appal, outrage, scandalize, horrify, astound, stagger, stun, stupefy, numb, paralyse, traumatize, jolt, jar, shake, agitate, unsettle, disquiet, unnerve, confound, dismay.

◨ delight, please, gratify, reassure.

n fright, start, jolt, impact, collision, surprise, bombshell, thunderbolt, blow, trauma, upset, distress, dismay, consternation, disgust, outrage.

◨ delight, pleasure, reassurance.

shocking adj appalling, outrageous, scandalous, horrifying, disgraceful, deplorable, intolerable, unbearable, atrocious, abominable, monstrous, unspeakable, detestable, abhorrent, dreadful, awful, terrible, frightful, ghastly, hideous, horrible, disgusting, revolting, repulsive, sickening, nauseating, offensive, distressing. **E3** acceptable, satisfactory, pleasant, delightful.

shoddy *adj* inferior, second-rate, cheap, tawdry, tatty, trashy, rubbishy, poor, careless, slipshod, slapdash.
E3 superior, well-made.

shoot *v* 1 FIRE, discharge, launch, propel, hurl, fling, project. 2 DART, bolt, dash, tear, rush, race, sprint, speed, charge, hurtle. 3 HIT, kill, blast, bombard, gun down, snipe at, pick off.
n sprout, bud, offshoot, branch, twig, sprig, slip, scion.

shop

Types of shop include: bazaar, market, indoor market, mini-market, corner shop, shopping mall, department store, supermarket, superstore, hypermarket, cash-and-carry; butcher, baker, grocer, greengrocer, fishmonger, dairy, delicatessen, health-food shop, farm shop, fish and chip shop, take-away, off-licence, tobacconist, sweet shop, confectioner, tuck shop; bookshop, newsagent, stationer, chemist, pharmacy, tailor, outfitter, dress shop, boutique, milliner, shoe shop, haberdasher, draper, florist, jeweller, toy shop, hardware shop, ironmonger, saddler, radio and TV shop, video shop; launderette, hairdresser, barber, betting shop, bookmaker, bookie (*infml*), pawnbroker, post office.

shore[1] *n* seashore, beach, sand(s), shingle, strand, waterfront, front, promenade, coast, seaboard, lakeside, bank.

shore[2] *v* support, hold, prop, stay, underpin, buttress, brace, strengthen, reinforce.

short *adj* 1 BRIEF, cursory, fleeting, momentary, transitory, ephemeral, concise, succinct, terse, pithy, compact, compressed, shortened, curtailed, abbreviated, abridged, summarized. 2 BRUSQUE, curt, gruff, snappy, sharp, abrupt, blunt, direct, rude, impolite, discourteous, uncivil. 3 SMALL, little, low, petite, diminutive, squat, dumpy. 4 INADEQUATE, insufficient, deficient, lacking, wanting, low, poor, meagre, scant, sparse.
E3 1 long, lasting. 2 polite. 3 tall. 4 adequate, ample.

shortage *n* inadequacy, insufficiency, deficiency, shortfall, deficit, lack, want, need, scarcity, paucity, poverty, dearth, absence.
E3 sufficiency, abundance, surplus.

shortcoming *n* defect, imperfection, fault, flaw, drawback, failing, weakness, foible.

shorten *v* cut, trim, prune, crop, dock, curtail, truncate, abbreviate, abridge, reduce, lessen, decrease, diminish, take up.
E3 lengthen, enlarge, amplify.

shortly *adv* soon, before long, presently, by and by.

short-sighted *adj* 1 MYOPIC, near-sighted. 2 IMPROVIDENT, imprudent, injudicious, unwise, impolitic, ill-advised, careless, hasty, ill-considered.
E3 1 long-sighted, far-sighted.

shot *n* 1 BULLET, missile, projectile, ball, pellet, slug (*infml*), discharge, blast. 2 (*infml*) ATTEMPT, try, effort, endeavour, go (*infml*), bash (*infml*), crack (*infml*), stab (*infml*), guess, turn.

shoulder *v* 1 PUSH, shove, jostle, thrust, press. 2 ACCEPT, assume, take on, bear, carry, sustain.

shout *n, v* call, cry, scream, shriek, yell, roar, bellow, bawl, howl, bay, cheer.

shove v push, thrust, drive, propel, force, barge, jostle, elbow, shoulder, press, crowd.

shovel n spade, scoop, bucket.
v dig, scoop, dredge, clear, move, shift, heap.

show v **1** REVEAL, expose, uncover, disclose, divulge, present, offer, exhibit, manifest, display, indicate, register, demonstrate, prove, illustrate, exemplify, explain, instruct, teach, clarify, elucidate. **2** *show him out*: lead, guide, conduct, usher, escort, accompany, attend. **F3** hide, cover.
n **1** OSTENTATION, parade, display, flamboyance, panache, pizzazz (*infml*), showiness, exhibitionism, affectation, pose, pretence, illusion, semblance, façade, impression, appearance, air. **2** DEMONSTRATION, presentation, exhibition, exposition, fair, display, parade, pageant, extravaganza, spectacle, entertainment, performance, production, staging, showing, representation.

show off parade, strut, swagger, brag, boast, swank (*infml*), flaunt, brandish, display, exhibit, demonstrate, advertise, set off, enhance.

show up 1 (*infml*) ARRIVE, come, turn up, appear, materialize (*infml*). **2** HUMILIATE, embarrass, mortify, shame, disgrace, let down. **3** REVEAL, show, expose, unmask, lay bare, highlight, pinpoint.

showdown n confrontation, clash, crisis, climax, culmination.

shower n rain, stream, torrent, deluge, hail, volley, barrage.
v spray, sprinkle, rain, pour, deluge, inundate, overwhelm, load, heap, lavish.

show-off n swaggerer, braggart, boaster, swanker (*infml*), exhibitionist, peacock, poser, poseur, egotist.

showy adj flashy, flamboyant, ostentatious, gaudy, garish, loud, tawdry, fancy, ornate, pretentious, pompous, swanky (*infml*), flash (*infml*).
F3 quiet, restrained.

shred n ribbon, tatter, rag, scrap, snippet, sliver, bit, piece, fragment, jot, iota, atom, grain, mite, whit, trace.

shrewd adj astute, judicious, well-advised, calculated, far-sighted, smart, clever, intelligent, sharp, keen, acute, alert, perceptive, observant, discerning, discriminating, knowing, calculating, cunning, crafty, artful, sly.
F3 unwise, obtuse, naïve, unsophisticated.

shriek v, n scream, screech, squawk, squeal, cry, shout, yell, wail, howl.

shrill adj high, high-pitched, treble, sharp, acute, piercing, penetrating, screaming, screeching, strident, ear-splitting.
F3 deep, low, soft, gentle.

shrink v **1** CONTRACT, shorten, narrow, decrease, lessen, diminish, dwindle, shrivel, wrinkle, wither. **2** RECOIL, back away, shy away, withdraw, retire, balk, quail, cower, cringe, wince, flinch, shun.
F3 1 expand, stretch. **2** accept, embrace.

shrivel v wrinkle, pucker, wither, wilt, shrink, dwindle, parch, dehydrate, desiccate, scorch, sear, burn, frizzle.

shroud v wrap, envelop, swathe, cloak, veil, screen, hide, conceal, blanket, cover.
F3 uncover, expose.
n winding-sheet, pall, mantle, cloak, veil, screen, blanket, covering.

shrub

Shrubs include: azalea, berberis, broom, buddleia, camellia, clematis, cotoneaster, daphne, dogwood,

euonymus, firethorn, flowering
currant, forsythia, fuchsia, heather,
hebe, holly, honeysuckle, hydrangea,
ivy, japonica, jasmine, laburnum,
laurel, lavender, lilac, magnolia,
mallow, mimosa, mock orange, peony,
privet, musk rose, rhododendron, rose,
spiraea, viburnum, weigela, witch
hazel, wistaria. *see also* **flower**;
plant.

shudder v shiver, shake, tremble,
quiver, quake, heave, convulse.
n shiver, quiver, tremor, spasm,
convulsion.

shuffle v **1** MIX (UP), intermix,
jumble, confuse, disorder, rearrange,
reorganize, shift around, switch.
2 *shuffle across the room*: shamble,
scuffle, scrape, drag, limp, hobble.

shun v avoid, evade, elude, steer
clear of, shy away from, spurn,
ignore, cold-shoulder, ostracize.
Ea accept, embrace.

shut v close, slam, seal, fasten,
secure, lock, latch, bolt, bar.
Ea open.
shut down close, stop, cease,
terminate, halt, discontinue, suspend,
switch off, inactivate.
shut in enclose, box in, hem in, fence in,
immure, confine, imprison, cage.
shut off seclude, isolate, cut off,
separate, segregate.
shut out 1 EXCLUDE, bar, debar, lock
out, ostracize, banish. **2** HIDE,
conceal, cover, mask, screen, veil.
shut up 1 SILENCE, gag, quiet, hush up,
pipe down (*infml*), hold one's tongue,
clam up (*infml*). **2** CONFINE, coop up,
imprison, incarcerate, jail, intern.

shy adj timid, bashful, reticent,
reserved, retiring, diffident, coy, self-
conscious, inhibited, modest, self-
effacing, shrinking, hesitant,
cautious, chary, suspicious, nervous.
Ea bold, assertive, confident.

sick adj **1** ILL, unwell, indisposed,
laid up, poorly, ailing, sickly, under

the weather, weak, feeble. **2**
VOMITING, queasy, bilious, seasick,
airsick. **3** *sick of waiting*: bored, fed
up (*infml*), tired, weary, disgusted,
nauseated.
Ea 1 well, healthy.

sicken v nauseate, revolt, disgust,
repel, put off, turn off (*sl*).
Ea delight, attract.

sickening adj nauseating, revolting,
disgusting, offensive, distasteful,
foul, vile, loathsome, repulsive.
Ea delightful, pleasing, attractive.

sickly adj **1** UNHEALTHY, infirm,
delicate, weak, feeble, frail, wan,
pallid, ailing, indisposed, sick,
bilious, faint, languid.
2 NAUSEATING, revolting, sweet,
syrupy, cloying, mawkish.
Ea 1 healthy, robust, sturdy, strong.

sickness n **1** ILLNESS, disease,
malady, ailment, complaint,
affliction, ill-health, indisposition,
infirmity. **2** VOMITING, nausea,
queasiness, biliousness.
Ea 1 health.

side n **1** EDGE, margin, fringe,
periphery, border, boundary, limit,
verge, brink, bank, shore, quarter,
region, flank, hand, face, facet,
surface. **2** STANDPOINT, viewpoint,
view, aspect, angle, slant. **3** TEAM,
party, faction, camp, cause, interest.
adj lateral, flanking, marginal,
secondary, subsidiary, subordinate,
lesser, minor, incidental, indirect,
oblique.
side with agree with, team up with,
support, vote for, favour, prefer.

sidestep v avoid, dodge, duck,
evade, elude, skirt, bypass.
Ea tackle, deal with.

sidetrack v deflect, head off, divert,
distract.

sideways adv sidewards, edgeways,
laterally, obliquely.
adj sideward, side, lateral, slanted,
oblique, indirect, sidelong.

sidle v slink, edge, inch, creep,

sneak.

sieve v sift, strain, separate, remove. n colander, strainer, sifter, riddle, screen.

sift v **1** SIEVE, strain, filter, riddle, screen, winnow, separate, sort. **2** EXAMINE, scrutinize, investigate, analyse, probe, review.

sigh v breathe, exhale, moan, complain, lament, grieve.

sight n **1** VISION, eyesight, seeing, observation, perception. **2** VIEW, look, glance, glimpse, range, field of vision, visibility. **3** APPEARANCE, spectacle, show, display, exhibition, scene, eyesore, monstrosity, fright (*infml*).
v see, observe, spot, glimpse, perceive, discern, distinguish, make out.

sightseer n tourist, visitor, holidaymaker, tripper, excursionist.

sign n **1** SYMBOL, token, character, figure, representation, emblem, badge, insignia, logo. **2** INDICATION, mark, signal, gesture, evidence, manifestation, clue, pointer, hint, suggestion, trace. **3** NOTICE, poster, board, placard. **4** PORTENT, omen, forewarning, foreboding.
v autograph, initial, endorse, write.

sign up enlist, enrol, join (up), volunteer, register, sign on, recruit, take on, hire, engage, employ.

signal n sign, indication, mark, gesture, cue, go-ahead, password, light, indicator, beacon, flare, rocket, alarm, alert, warning, tip-off.
v wave, gesticulate, gesture, beckon, motion, nod, sign, indicate, communicate.

signature n autograph, initials, mark, endorsement, inscription.

significance n importance, relevance, consequence, matter, interest, consideration, weight, force, meaning, implication, sense, point, message.
F3 insignificance, unimportance,

pettiness.

significant adj **1** IMPORTANT, relevant, consequential, momentous, weighty, serious, noteworthy, critical, vital, marked, considerable, appreciable. **2** MEANINGFUL, symbolic, expressive, suggestive, indicative, symptomatic.
F3 1 insignificant, unimportant, trivial. 2 meaningless.

signify v **1** MEAN, denote, symbolize, represent, stand for, indicate, show, express, convey, transmit, communicate, intimate, imply, suggest. **2** MATTER, count.

silence n quiet, quietness, hush, peace, stillness, calm, lull, noiselessness, soundlessness, muteness, dumbness, speechlessness, taciturnity, uncommunicativeness, reticence, reserve.
F3 noise, sound, din, uproar.
v quiet, quieten, hush, mute, deaden, muffle, stifle, gag, muzzle, suppress, subdue, quell, still, dumbfound.

silent adj inaudible, noiseless, soundless, quiet, peaceful, still, hushed, muted, mute, dumb, speechless, tongue-tied, taciturn, mum, reticent, reserved, tacit, unspoken, unexpressed, understood, voiceless, wordless.
F3 noisy, loud, talkative.

silhouette n outline, contour, delineation, shape, form, configuration, profile, shadow.

silky adj silken, fine, sleek, lustrous, glossy, satiny, smooth, soft, velvety.

silly adj foolish, stupid, imprudent, senseless, pointless, idiotic, daft (*infml*), ridiculous, ludicrous, preposterous, absurd, meaningless, irrational, illogical, childish, puerile, immature, irresponsible, scatterbrained.
F3 wise, sensible, sane, mature, clever, intelligent.

silt n sediment, deposit, alluvium, sludge, mud, ooze.

silt up block, clog, choke.

similar *adj* like, alike, close, related, akin, corresponding, equivalent, analogous, comparable, uniform, homogeneous.
🔁 dissimilar, different.

similarity *n* likeness, resemblance, similitude, closeness, relation, correspondence, congruence, equivalence, analogy, comparability, compatibility, agreement, affinity, homogeneity, uniformity.
🔁 dissimilarity, difference.

simmer *v* boil, bubble, seethe, stew, burn, smoulder, fume, rage.

simmer down calm down, cool down, control oneself, collect oneself.

simple *adj* **1** *a simple question*: easy, elementary, straightforward, uncomplicated, uninvolved, clear, lucid, plain, understandable, comprehensible.
2 UNSOPHISTICATED, natural, innocent, artless, guileless, ingenuous, naïve, green, foolish, stupid, silly, idiotic, half-witted, simple-minded, feeble-minded, backward.
🔁 **1** difficult, hard, complicated, intricate. **2** sophisticated, worldly, artful, clever.

simplicity *n* simpleness, ease, straightforwardness, uncomplicatedness, clarity, purity, plainness, restraint, naturalness, innocence, artlessness, candour, openness, sincerity, directness.
🔁 difficulty, complexity, intricacy, sophistication.

simplify *v* disentangle, untangle, decipher, clarify, paraphrase, abridge, reduce, streamline.
🔁 complicate, elaborate.

simplistic *adj* oversimplified, superficial, shallow, sweeping, facile, simple, naïve.
🔁 analytical, detailed.

simply *adv* **1** MERELY, just, only, solely, purely, utterly, completely,
totally, wholly, absolutely, quite, really, undeniably, unquestionably, clearly, plainly, obviously. **2** EASILY, straightforwardly, directly, intelligibly.

simulate *v* pretend, affect, assume, put on, act, feign, sham, fake, counterfeit, reproduce, duplicate, copy, imitate, mimic, parrot, echo, reflect.

simultaneous *adj* synchronous, synchronic, concurrent, contemporaneous, coinciding, parallel.
🔁 asynchronous.

sin *n* wrong, offence, transgression, trespass, misdeed, lapse, fault, error, crime, wrongdoing, sinfulness, wickedness, iniquity, evil, impiety, ungodliness, unrighteousness, guilt.
v offend, transgress, trespass, lapse, err, misbehave, stray, go astray, fall, fall from grace.

sincere *adj* honest, truthful, candid, frank, open, direct, straightforward, plain-spoken, serious, earnest, heartfelt, wholehearted, real, true, genuine, pure, unadulterated, unmixed, natural, unaffected, artless, guileless, simple.
🔁 insincere, hypocritical, affected.

sincerity *n* honour, integrity, probity, uprightness, honesty, truthfulness, candour, frankness, openness, directness, straightforwardness, seriousness, earnestness, wholeheartedness, genuineness.
🔁 **1, 3** insincerity.

sinewy *adj* muscular, brawny, strong, sturdy, robust, vigorous, athletic, wiry, stringy.

sinful *adj* wrong, wrongful, criminal, bad, wicked, iniquitous, erring, fallen, immoral, corrupt, depraved, impious, ungodly, unholy, irreligious, guilty.
🔁 sinless, righteous, godly.

sing *v* chant, intone, vocalize, croon,

serenade, yodel, trill, warble, chirp,
pipe, whistle, hum.

singe v scorch, char, blacken, burn,
sear.

singer

> *Singers include*: balladeer, minstrel,
> troubadour, opera singer, diva, prima
> donna, soloist, precentor, choirboy,
> choirgirl, chorister, chorus, folk-singer,
> pop star, crooner, carol-singer;
> soprano, coloratura soprano, castrato,
> tenor, treble, contralto, alto, baritone,
> bass; songster, vocalist.

single adj one, unique, singular,
individual, particular, exclusive, sole,
only, lone, solitary, separate, distinct,
free, unattached, unmarried, celibate,
unshared, undivided, unbroken,
simple, one-to-one, man-to-man.
F3 multiple.

single out choose, select, pick, hand-
pick, distinguish, identify, separate, set
apart, isolate, highlight, pinpoint.

single-handed adj, adv solo, alone,
unaccompanied, unaided, unassisted,
independent(ly).

single-minded adj determined,
resolute, dogged, persevering, tireless,
unwavering, fixed, unswerving,
undeviating, steadfast, dedicated,
devoted.

sinister adj ominous, menacing,
threatening, disturbing, disquieting,
unlucky, inauspicious, malevolent,
evil.
F3 auspicious, harmless, innocent.

sink v 1 DESCEND, slip, fall, drop,
slump, lower, stoop, succumb, droop,
droop, sag, dip, set, disappear,
vanish. 2 DECREASE, lessen, subside,
abate, dwindle, diminish, ebb, fade,
flag, weaken, fail, decline, worsen,
degenerate, degrade, decay, collapse.
3 FOUNDER, dive, plunge, plummet,
submerge, immerse, engulf, drown.
4 *sink a well*: bore, drill, penetrate,
dig, excavate, lay, conceal.

F3 1 rise. 2 increase. 3 float.

sinner n wrong-doer, miscreant,
offender, transgressor, trespasser,
backslider, reprobate, evil-doer,
malefactor.

sinuous adj lithe, slinky, curved,
wavy, undulating, tortuous, twisting,
winding, meandering, serpentine,
coiling.
F3 straight.

sip v taste, sample, drink, sup.
n taste, drop, spoonful, mouthful.

sit v 1 SETTLE, rest, perch, roost,
brood, pose. 2 SEAT, accommodate,
hold, contain. 3 MEET, assemble,
gather, convene, deliberate.

site n location, place, spot, position,
situation, station, setting, scene, plot,
lot, ground, area.
v locate, place, position, situate,
station, set, install.

sitting n session, period, spell,
meeting, assembly, hearing,
consultation.

situation n 1 SITE, location,
position, place, spot, seat, locality,
locale, setting, scenario. 2 STATE OF
AFFAIRS, case, circumstances,
predicament, state, condition, status,
rank, station, post, office, job,
employment.

sizable adj large, substantial,
considerable, respectable, goodly,
largish, biggish, decent, generous.
F3 small, tiny.

size n magnitude, measurement(s),
dimensions, proportions, volume,
bulk, mass, height, length, extent,
range, scale, amount, greatness,
largeness, bigness, vastness,
immensity.

size up gauge, assess, evaluate, weigh
up, measure.

sizzle v hiss, crackle, spit, sputter,
fry, frizzle.

skeleton n bones, frame, structure,
framework, bare bones, outline,
draft, sketch.

sketch v draw, depict, portray,

represent, pencil, paint, outline, delineate, draft, rough out, block out.

n drawing, vignette, design, plan, diagram, outline, delineation, skeleton, draft.

sketchy *adj* rough, vague, incomplete, unfinished, scrappy, bitty, imperfect, inadequate, insufficient, slight, superficial, cursory, hasty.

🖝 full, complete.

skilful *adj* able, capable, adept, competent, proficient, deft, adroit, handy, expert, masterly, accomplished, skilled, practised, experienced, professional, clever, tactical, cunning.

🖝 inept, clumsy, awkward.

skill *n* skilfulness, ability, aptitude, facility, handiness, talent, knack, art, technique, training, experience, expertise, expertness, mastery, proficiency, competence, accomplishment, cleverness, intelligence.

skilled *adj* trained, schooled, qualified, professional, experienced, practised, accomplished, expert, masterly, proficient, able, skilful.

🖝 unskilled, inexperienced.

skim *v* **1** BRUSH, touch, skate, plane, float, sail, glide, fly. **2** SCAN, look through, skip. **3** CREAM, separate.

skimp *v* economize, scrimp, pinch, cut corners, stint, withhold.

🖝 squander, waste.

skin *n* hide, pelt, membrane, film, coating, surface, outside, peel, rind, husk, casing, crust.

v flay, fleece, strip, peel, scrape, graze.

skinny *adj* thin, lean, scrawny, scraggy, skeletal, skin-and-bone, emaciated, underfed, undernourished.

🖝 fat, plump.

skip *v* **1** HOP, jump, leap, dance, gambol, frisk, caper, prance. **2** *skip a*

page: miss, omit, leave out, cut.

skirmish *n* fight, combat, battle, engagement, encounter, conflict, clash, brush, scrap, tussle, set-to, dust-up (*infml*).

skirt *v* circle, circumnavigate, border, edge, flank, bypass, avoid, evade, circumvent.

skit *n* satire, parody, caricature, spoof, take-off, sketch.

skulk *v* lurk, hide, prowl, sneak, creep, slink.

sky *n* space, atmosphere, air, heavens, blue.

slab *n* piece, block, lump, chunk, hunk, wodge (*infml*), wedge, slice, portion.

slack *adj* **1** LOOSE, limp, sagging, baggy. **2** LAZY, sluggish, slow, quiet, idle, inactive. **3** NEGLECTFUL, negligent, careless, inattentive, remiss, permissive, lax, relaxed, easy-going (*infml*).

🖝 **1** tight, taut, stiff, rigid. **2** busy. **3** diligent.

n looseness, give, play, room, leeway, excess.

v idle, shirk, skive (*infml*), neglect.

slacken off loosen, release, relax, ease, moderate, reduce, lessen, decrease, diminish, abate, slow (down).

🖝 tighten, increase, intensify, quicken.

slacker *n* idler, shirker, skiver (*infml*), dawdler, clock-watcher, good-for-nothing, layabout.

slam *v* **1** BANG, crash, dash, smash, throw, hurl, fling. **2** (*infml*) CRITICIZE, slate (*infml*), pan (*infml*).

slander *n* defamation, calumny, misrepresentation, libel, scandal, smear, slur, aspersion, backbiting.

v defame, vilify, malign, denigrate, disparage, libel, smear, slur, backbite.

🖝 praise, compliment.

slanderous *adj* defamatory, false, untrue, libellous, damaging, malicious, abusive, insulting.

slant *v* **1** TILT, slope, incline, lean,

list, skew, angle. **2** DISTORT, twist, warp, bend, weight, bias, colour.

n **1** SLOPE, incline, gradient, ramp, camber, pitch, tilt, angle, diagonal. **2** BIAS, emphasis, attitude, viewpoint.

slanting *adj* sloping, tilted, oblique, diagonal.

slap *n* smack, spank, cuff, blow, bang, clap.

v **1** SMACK, spank, hit, strike, cuff, clout, bang, clap. **2** DAUB, plaster, spread, apply.

slash *v* cut, slit, gash, lacerate, rip, tear, rend.

n cut, incision, slit, gash, laceration, rip, tear, rent.

slate *v* scold, rebuke, reprimand, berate, censure, blame, criticize, slam (*infml*).

⊡ praise.

slaughter *n* killing, murder, massacre, extermination, butchery, carnage, blood-bath, bloodshed.

v kill, slay, murder, massacre, exterminate, liquidate, butcher.

slave *n* servant, drudge, vassal, serf, villein, captive.

v toil, labour, drudge, sweat, grind, slog.

slaver *v* dribble, drivel, slobber, drool, salivate.

slavery *n* servitude, bondage, captivity, enslavement, serfdom, thraldom, subjugation.

⊡ freedom, liberty.

slavish *adj* **1** UNORIGINAL, imitative, unimaginative, uninspired, literal, strict. **2** SERVILE, abject, submissive, sycophantic, grovelling, cringing, fawning, menial, low, mean.

⊡ **1** original, imaginative. **2** independent, assertive.

sleek *adj* shiny, glossy, lustrous, smooth, silky, well-groomed.

⊡ rough, unkempt.

sleep *v* doze, snooze, slumber, kip (*sl*), doss (down) (*sl*), hibernate, drop off, nod off, rest, repose.

n doze, snooze, nap, forty winks,

shut-eye (*infml*), kip (*sl*), slumber, hibernation, rest, repose, siesta.

sleepless *adj* unsleeping, awake, wide-awake, alert, vigilant, watchful, wakeful, restless, disturbed, insomniac.

sleepy *adj* drowsy, somnolent, tired, weary, heavy, slow, sluggish, torpid, lethargic, inactive, quiet, dull, soporific, hypnotic.

⊡ awake, alert, wakeful, restless.

slender *adj* **1** SLIM, thin, lean, slight, svelte, graceful. **2** *a slender chance*: faint, remote, slight, inconsiderable, tenuous, flimsy, feeble, inadequate, insufficient, meagre, scanty.

⊡ **1** fat. **2** appreciable, considerable, ample.

slice *n* piece, sliver, wafer, rasher, tranche, slab, wedge, segment, section, share, portion, helping, cut (*infml*), whack (*infml*).

v carve, cut, chop, divide, segment.

slick *adj* **1** GLIB, plausible, deft, adroit, dexterous, skilful, professional. **2** SMOOTH, sleek, glossy, shiny, polished.

slide *v* slip, slither, skid, skate, ski, toboggan, glide, plane, coast, skim.

slight *adj* **1** MINOR, unimportant, insignificant, negligible, trivial, paltry, modest, small, little, inconsiderable, insubstantial. **2** SLENDER, slim, diminutive, petite, delicate.

⊡ **1** major, significant, noticeable, considerable. **2** large, muscular.

v scorn, despise, disdain, disparage, insult, affront, offend, snub, cut, cold-shoulder, ignore, disregard, neglect.

⊡ respect, praise, compliment, flatter.

n insult, affront, slur, snub, rebuff, rudeness, discourtesy, disrespect, contempt, disdain, indifference, disregard, neglect.

slim *adj* **1** SLENDER, thin, lean, svelte, trim. **2** SLIGHT, remote, faint, poor.

🔳 1 fat, chubby. **2** strong, considerable.

v lose weight, diet, reduce.

slimy *adj* **1** MUDDY, miry, mucous, viscous, oily, greasy, slippery. **2** SERVILE, obsequious, sycophantic, toadying, smarmy, oily, unctuous.

sling *v* **1** THROW, hurl, fling, catapult, heave, pitch, lob, toss, chuck (*infml*). **2** HANG, suspend, dangle, swing.

slink *v* sneak, steal, creep, sidle, slip, prowl, skulk.

slinky *adj* close-fitting, figure-hugging, clinging, skin-tight, sleek, sinuous.

slip^1 *v* slide, glide, skate, skid, stumble, trip, fall, slither, slink, sneak, steal, creep.

n mistake, error, slip-up (*infml*), bloomer (*infml*), blunder, fault, indiscretion, boob (*infml*), omission, oversight, failure.

slip^2 *n* piece, strip, voucher, chit, coupon, certificate.

slippery *adj* **1** SLIPPY, icy, greasy, glassy, smooth, dangerous, treacherous, perilous. **2** *a slippery character*: dishonest, untrustworthy, false, duplicitous, two-faced, crafty, cunning, devious, evasive, smooth, smarmy.

🔳 1 rough. **2** trustworthy, reliable.

slipshod *adj* careless, slap-dash, sloppy, slovenly, untidy, negligent, lax, casual.

🔳 careful, fastidious, neat, tidy.

slit *v* cut, gash, slash, slice, split, rip, tear.

n opening, aperture, vent, cut, incision, gash, slash, split, tear, rent.

slither *v* slide, slip, glide, slink, creep, snake, worm.

sliver *n* flake, shaving, paring, slice, wafer, shred, fragment, chip, splinter, shiver, shard.

slobber *v* dribble, drivel, slaver, drool, salivate.

slogan *n* jingle, motto, catch-phrase, catchword, watchword, battle-cry, war cry.

slop *v* spill, overflow, slosh, splash, splatter, spatter.

slope *v* slant, lean, tilt, tip, pitch, incline, rise, fall.

n incline, gradient, ramp, hill, ascent, descent, slant, tilt, pitch, inclination.

sloppy *adj* **1** WATERY, wet, liquid, runny, mushy, slushy. **2** *sloppy work*: careless, hit-or-miss, slap-dash, slipshod, slovenly, untidy, messy, clumsy, amateurish. **3** SOPPY, sentimental, schmaltzy, slushy, mushy.

🔳 1 solid. **2** careful, exact, precise.

slot *n* hole, opening, aperture, slit, vent, groove, channel, gap, space, time, vacancy, place, spot, position, niche.

v insert, fit, place, position, assign, pigeonhole.

slouch *v* stoop, hunch, droop, slump, lounge, loll, shuffle, shamble.

slovenly *adj* sloppy, careless, slipshod, untidy, scruffy, slatternly, sluttish.

🔳 neat, smart.

slow *adj* **1** LEISURELY, unhurried, lingering, loitering, dawdling, lazy, sluggish, slow-moving, creeping, gradual, deliberate, measured, plodding, delayed, late, unpunctual. **2** STUPID, slow-witted, dim, thick (*infml*). **3** PROLONGED, protracted, long-drawn-out, tedious, boring, dull, uninteresting, uneventful.

🔳 1 quick, fast, swift, rapid, speedy. **2** clever, intelligent. **3** brisk, lively, exciting.

v brake, decelerate, delay, hold up, retard, handicap, check, curb, restrict.

🔳 speed, accelerate.

sluggish *adj* lethargic, listless, torpid, heavy, dull, slow, slow-moving, slothful, lazy, idle, inactive, lifeless, unresponsive.

🔳 brisk, vigorous, lively, dynamic.

slump v 1 COLLAPSE, fall, drop, plunge, plummet, sink, decline, deteriorate, worsen, crash, fail. 2 DROOP, sag, bend, stoop, slouch, loll, lounge, flop.
n recession, depression, stagnation, downturn, low, trough, decline, deterioration, worsening, fall, drop, collapse, crash, failure.
€ boom.

sly adj wily, foxy, crafty, cunning, artful, guileful, clever, canny, shrewd, astute, knowing, subtle, devious, shifty, tricky, furtive, stealthy, surreptitious, underhand, covert, secretive, scheming, conniving, mischievous, roguish.
€ honest, frank, candid, open.

smack v hit, strike, slap, spank, whack (infml), thwack (infml), clap, box, cuff, pat, tap.
n blow, slap, spank, whack (infml), thwack (infml), box, cuff, pat, tap.
adv bang, slap-bang, right, plumb, straight, directly, exactly, precisely.

small adj 1 LITTLE, tiny, minute, minuscule, short, slight, puny, petite, diminutive, pint-size(d) (infml), miniature, mini, pocket, pocket-sized, young. 2 PETTY, trifling, trivial, unimportant, insignificant, minor, inconsiderable, negligible. 3 INADEQUATE, insufficient, scanty, meagre, paltry, mean, limited.
€ 1 large, big, huge. 2 great, considerable. 3 ample.

small-minded adj petty, mean, ungenerous, illiberal, intolerant, bigoted, narrow-minded, parochial, insular, rigid, hidebound.
€ liberal, tolerant, broad-minded.

smarmy adj smooth, oily, unctuous, servile, obsequious, sycophantic, toadying, ingratiating, crawling, fawning.

smart adj 1 smart clothes: elegant, stylish, chic, fashionable, modish, neat, tidy, spruce, trim, well-groomed. 2 CLEVER, intelligent, bright, sharp, acute, shrewd, astute.
€ 1 dowdy, unfashionable, untidy, scruffy. 2 stupid, slow.
v sting, hurt, prick, burn, tingle, twinge, throb.

smarten v neaten, tidy, spruce up, groom, clean, polish, beautify.

smash v 1 smash a window: break, shatter, shiver, ruin, wreck, demolish, destroy, defeat, crush. 2 CRASH, collide, strike, bang, bash, thump.
n accident, crash, collision, pile-up.

smattering n bit, modicum, dash, sprinkling, basics, rudiments, elements.

smear v 1 DAUB, plaster, spread, cover, coat, rub, smudge, streak. 2 DEFAME, malign, vilify, blacken, sully, stain, tarnish.
n 1 STREAK, smudge, blot, blotch, splodge, daub. 2 DEFAMATION, slander, libel, mudslinging, muck-raking.

smell n odour, whiff, scent, perfume, fragrance, bouquet, aroma, stench, stink, pong (infml).
v sniff, nose, scent, stink, reek, pong (infml).

> *Ways of describing smells include:*
> *pleasant*: aroma, bouquet, fragrance, incense, nose, odour, pot pourri, perfume, redolence, scent;
> *unpleasant*: b.o. (body odour), fetor, funk (*North Amer.*), hum, malodour, mephitis, miasma, niff (*slang*), pong (*colloq.*), pungency, reek, sniff, stench, stink, whiff.

smelly adj malodorous, pongy (infml), stinking, reeking, foul, bad, off, fetid, putrid, high, strong.

smile n, v grin, beam, simper, smirk, leer, laugh.

smoke n fumes, exhaust, gas, vapour, mist, fog, smog.
v fume, smoulder, cure, dry.

smoky adj sooty, black, grey, grimy, murky, cloudy, hazy, foggy.

smooth adj 1 LEVEL, plane, even, flat, horizontal, flush. 2 STEADY, unbroken, flowing, regular, uniform, rhythmic, easy, effortless. 3 SHINY, polished, glossy, silky, glassy, calm, undisturbed, serene, tranquil, peaceful. 4 SUAVE, agreeable, smooth-talking, glib, plausible, persuasive, slick, smarmy, unctuous, ingratiating.
☒ 1 rough, lumpy. 2 irregular, erratic, unsteady. 3 rough, choppy.
v 1 IRON, press, roll, flatten, level, plane, file, sand, polish. 2 EASE, alleviate, assuage, allay, mitigate, calm, mollify.
☒ 1 roughen, wrinkle, crease.

smother v suffocate, asphyxiate, strangle, throttle, choke, stifle, extinguish, snuff, muffle, suppress, repress, hide, conceal, cover, shroud, envelop, wrap.

smoulder v burn, smoke, fume, rage, seethe, simmer.

smudge v blur, smear, daub, mark, spot, stain, dirty, soil.
n blot, stain, spot, blemish, blur, smear, streak.

smug adj complement, self-satisfied, superior, holier-than-thou, self-righteous, priggish, conceited.
☒ humble, modest.

snack n refreshment(s), bite, nibble, titbit, elevenses (infml).

snag n disadvantage, inconvenience, drawback, catch, problem, difficulty, complication, setback, hitch, obstacle, stumbling-block.
v catch, rip, tear, hole, ladder.

snap v 1 the twig snapped: break, crack, split, separate. 2 BITE, nip, bark, growl, snarl, retort, crackle, pop. 3 SNATCH, seize, catch, grasp, grip.
n break, crack, bite, nip, flick, fillip, crackle, pop.
adj immediate, instant, on-the-spot, abrupt, sudden.

snappy adj 1 SMART, stylish, chic,

fashionable, modish, trendy (infml). 2 QUICK, hasty, brisk, lively, energetic. 3 CROSS, irritable, edgy, touchy, brusque, quick-tempered, ill-natured, crabbed, testy.
☒ 1 dowdy. 2 slow.

snare v trap, ensnare, entrap, catch, net.
n trap, wire, net, noose, catch, pitfall.

snarl[1] v growl, grumble, complain.

snarl[2] v tangle, knot, ravel, entangle, enmesh, embroil, confuse, muddle, complicate.

snatch v grab, seize, kidnap, take, nab (infml), pluck, pull, wrench, wrest, gain, win, clutch, grasp, grip.

sneak v 1 CREEP, steal, slip, slink, sidle, skulk, lurk, prowl, smuggle, spirit. 2 TELL TALES, split (sl), inform on, grass on (sl).
n tell-tale, informer, grass (sl).

sneaking adj private, secret, furtive, surreptitious, hidden, lurking, suppressed, grudging, nagging, niggling, persistent, worrying, uncomfortable, intuitive.

sneer v scorn, disdain, look down on, deride, scoff, jeer, mock, ridicule, gibe, laugh, snigger.
n scorn, disdain, derision, jeer, mockery, ridicule, gibe, snigger.

snide adj derogatory, disparaging, sarcastic, cynical, scornful, sneering, hurtful, unkind, nasty, mean, spiteful, malicious, ill-natured.
☒ complimentary.

sniff v breathe, inhale, snuff, snuffle, smell, nose, scent.

snigger v, n laugh, giggle, titter, chuckle, sneer.

snip v cut, clip, trim, crop, dock, slit, nick, notch.

snippet n piece, scrap, cutting, clipping, fragment, particle, shred, snatch, part, portion, segment, section.

snobbery n snobbishness, superciliousness, snootiness (infml), airs, loftiness, arrogance, pride, pretension, condescension.

snobbish *adj* supercilious, disdainful, snooty (*infml*), stuck-up (*infml*), toffee-nosed (*infml*), superior, lofty, high and mighty, arrogant, pretentious, affected, condescending, patronizing.

snoop *v* spy, sneak, pry, nose, interfere, meddle.

snooze *v* nap, doze, sleep, kip (*sl*). *n* nap, catnap, forty winks, doze, siesta, sleep, kip (*sl*)

snub *v* rebuff, brush off, cut, cold-shoulder, slight, rebuke, put down, squash, humble, shame, humiliate, mortify.
n rebuff, brush-off, slight, affront, insult, rebuke, put-down, humiliation.

snug *adj* cosy, warm, comfortable, homely, friendly, intimate, sheltered, secure, tight, close-fitting.

soak *v* wet, drench, saturate, penetrate, permeate, infuse, bathe, marinate, souse, steep, submerge, immerse.

soaking *adj* soaked, drenched, sodden, waterlogged, saturated, sopping, wringing, dripping, streaming.
✍ dry.

soar *v* fly, wing, glide, plane, tower, rise, ascend, climb, mount, escalate, rocket.
✍ fall, plummet.

sob *v* cry, weep, bawl, howl, blubber, snivel.

sober *adj* **1** TEETOTAL, temperate, moderate, abstinent, abstemious. **2** SOLEMN, dignified, serious, staid, steady, sedate, quiet, serene, calm, composed, unruffled, unexcited, cool, dispassionate, level-headed, practical, realistic, reasonable, rational, clear-headed. **3** *sober dress*: sombre, drab, dull, plain, subdued, restrained.
✍ 1 drunk, intemperate. **2** frivolous, excited, unrealistic, irrational. **3** flashy, garish.

so-called *adj* alleged, supposed,

purported, ostensible, nominal, self-styled, professed, would-be, pretended.

sociable *adj* outgoing, gregarious, friendly, affable, companionable, genial, convivial, cordial, warm, hospitable, neighbourly, approachable, accessible, familiar.
✍ unsociable, withdrawn, unfriendly, hostile.

social *adj* communal, public, community, common, general, collective, group, organized.
n party, do (*infml*), get-together, gathering.

socialize *v* mix, mingle, fraternize, get together, go out, entertain.

society *n* **1** COMMUNITY, population, culture, civilization, nation, people, mankind, humanity. **2** CLUB, circle, group, association, organization, company, corporation, league, union, guild, fellowship, fraternity, brotherhood, sisterhood, sorority. **3** FRIENDSHIP, companionship, camaraderie, fellowship, company. **4** UPPER CLASSES, aristocracy, gentry, nobility, elite.

soft *adj* **1** YIELDING, pliable, flexible, elastic, plastic, malleable, spongy, squashy, pulpy. **2** *soft colours*: pale, light, pastel, delicate, subdued, muted, quiet, low, dim, faint, diffuse, mild, bland, gentle, soothing, sweet, mellow, melodious, dulcet, pleasant. **3** FURRY, downy, velvety, silky, smooth. **4** LENIENT, lax, permissive, indulgent, tolerant, easy-going (*infml*), kind, generous, gentle, merciful, soft-hearted, tender, sensitive, weak, spineless.
✍ 1 hard. **2** harsh. **3** rough. **4** strict, severe.

soften *v* **1** MODERATE, temper, mitigate, lessen, diminish, abate, alleviate, ease, soothe, palliate, quell, assuage, subdue, mollify, appease, calm, still, relax. **2** MELT, liquefy,

dissolve, reduce. **3** CUSHION, pad,
muffle, quicken, lower, lighten.

soft-hearted *adj* sympathetic,
compassionate, kind, benevolent,
charitable, generous, warm-hearted,
tender, sentimental.

☒ hard-hearted, callous.

soggy *adj* wet, damp, moist, soaked,
drenched, sodden, waterlogged,
saturated, sopping, dripping, heavy,
boggy, spongy, pulpy.

soil[1] *n* earth, clay, loam, humus,
dirt, dust, ground, land, region,
country.

soil[2] *v* dirty, begrime, stain, spot,
smudge, smear, foul, muddy, pollute,
defile, besmirch, sully, tarnish.

solace *n* comfort, consolation,
relief, alleviation, support, cheer.

soldier

> *Types of soldier include*: cadet,
> private, sapper, NCO, orderly, officer,
> gunner, infantryman, trooper, fusilier,
> rifleman, paratrooper, sentry,
> guardsman, marine, commando,
> tommy, dragoon, cavalryman, lancer,
> hussar, conscript, recruit, regular,
> Territorial, GI (*US*), warrior,
> mercenary, legionnaire, guerrilla,
> partisan, centurion; troops;
> serviceman, servicewoman, fighter.
> *see also* rank.

sole *adj* only, unique, exclusive,
individual, single, singular, one, lone,
solitary, alone.

☒ shared, multiple.

solemn *adj* **1** *a solemn expression*:
serious, grave, sober, sedate, sombre,
glum, thoughtful, earnest, awed,
reverential. **2** GRAND, stately,
majestic, ceremonial, ritual, formal,
ceremonious, pompous, dignified,
august, venerable, awe-inspiring,
impressive, imposing, momentous.

☒ **1** light-hearted. **2** frivolous.

solicit *v* ask, request, seek, crave,
beg, beseech, entreat, implore, pray,

supplicate, sue, petition, canvass,
importune.

solicitor *n* lawyer, advocate,
attorney, barrister, QC.

solicitous *adj* caring, attentive,
considerate, concerned, anxious,
worried.

solid *adj* **1** HARD, firm, dense,
compact, strong, sturdy, substantial,
sound, unshakable. **2** *a solid white
line*: unbroken, continuous,
uninterrupted. **3** RELIABLE,
dependable, trusty, worthy, decent,
upright, sensible, level-headed,
stable, serious, sober. **4** REAL,
genuine, pure, concrete, tangible.

☒ **1** liquid, gaseous, hollow. **2** broken,
dotted. **3** unreliable, unstable.
4 unreal.

solidarity *n* unity, agreement,
accord, unanimity, consensus,
harmony, concord, cohesion, like-
mindedness, camaraderie, team
spirit, soundness, stability.

☒ discord, division, schism.

solidify *v* harden, set, jell, congeal,
coagulate, clot, cake, crystallize.

☒ soften, liquefy, dissolve.

solitary *adj* sole, single, lone, alone,
lonely, lonesome, friendless,
unsociable, reclusive, withdrawn,
retired, sequestered, cloistered,
secluded, separate, isolated, remote,
out-of-the-way, inaccessible,
unfrequented, unvisited, untrodden.

☒ accompanied, gregarious, busy.

solitude *n* aloneness, loneliness,
reclusiveness, retirement, privacy,
seclusion, isolation, remoteness.

☒ companionship.

solution *n* **1** ANSWER, result,
explanation, resolution, key, remedy.
2 MIXTURE, blend, compound,
suspension, emulsion, liquid.

solve *v* work out, figure out, puzzle
out, decipher, crack, disentangle,
unravel, answer, resolve, settle, clear
up, clarify, explain, interpret.

sombre *adj* dark, funereal, drab,

dull, dim, obscure, shady, shadowy, gloomy, dismal, melancholy, mournful, sad, joyless, sober, serious, grave.

Ea bright, cheerful, happy.

someday *adv* sometime, one day, eventually, ultimately.

Ea never.

sometimes *adv* occasionally, now and again, now and then, once in a while, from time to time.

Ea always, never.

song *n* ballad, madrigal, lullaby, shanty, anthem, hymn, carol, chant, chorus, air, tune, melody, lyric, number, ditty.

Types of song include: air, anthem, aria, ballad, barcarole, bird call, bird song, blues, calypso, cantata, canticle, cantilena, canzone, canzonet, carol, chanson, chansonette, chant, chorus, descant, dirge, ditty, elegy, epinikion, epithalamium, folk-song, gospel song, hymn, jingle, love-song, lied, lilt, lullaby, madrigal, nursery rhyme, ode, plainchant, plainsong, pop song, psalm, recitative, requiem, rock and roll, roundelay, serenade, shanty, spiritual, Negro spiritual, war song, wassail, yodel.

soon *adv* shortly, presently, in a minute, before long, in the near future.

soothe *v* alleviate, relieve, ease, salve, comfort, allay, calm, compose, tranquillize, settle, still, quiet, hush, lull, pacify, appease, mollify, assuage, mitigate, soften.

Ea aggravate, irritate, annoy, vex.

sophisticated *adj* **1** URBANE, cosmopolitan, worldly, worldly-wise, cultured, cultivated, refined, polished. **2** *sophisticated technology:* advanced, highly-developed, complicated, complex, intricate, elaborate, delicate, subtle.

Ea 1 unsophisticated, naïve. **2** primitive, simple.

soporific *adj* sleep-inducing, hypnotic, sedative, tranquillizing, sleepy, somnolent.

Ea stimulating, invigorating.

soppy *adj* sentimental, lovey-dovey (*infml*), weepy (*infml*), sloppy, slushy, mushy, corny (*infml*), mawkish, cloying, soft, silly, daft (*infml*).

sorcery *n* magic, black magic, witchcraft, wizardry, necromancy, voodoo, spell, incantation, charm, enchantment.

sordid *adj* dirty, filthy, unclean, foul, vile, squalid, sleazy, seamy, seedy, disreputable, shabby, tawdry, corrupt, degraded, degenerate, debauched, low, base, despicable, shameful, wretched, mean, miserly, niggardly, grasping, mercenary, selfish, self-seeking.

Ea pure, honourable, upright.

sore *adj* **1** PAINFUL, hurting, aching, smarting, stinging, tender, sensitive, inflamed, red, raw. **2** ANNOYED, irritated, vexed, angry, upset, hurt, wounded, afflicted, aggrieved, resentful.

Ea 2 pleased, happy.

n wound, lesion, swelling, inflammation, boil, abscess, ulcer.

sorrow *n* sadness, unhappiness, grief, mourning, misery, woe, distress, affliction, anguish, heartache, heartbreak, misfortune, hardship, trouble, worry, trial, tribulation, regret, remorse.

Ea happiness, joy.

sorry *adj* **1** APOLOGETIC, regretful, remorseful, contrite, penitent, repentant, conscience-stricken, guilt-ridden, shamefaced. **2** *in a sorry state:* pathetic, pitiful, poor, wretched, miserable, sad, unhappy, dismal. **3** SYMPATHETIC, compassionate, understanding, pitying, concerned, moved.

Ea 1 impenitent, unashamed. **2** happy,

cheerful. **3** uncaring.

sort *n*   kind, type, genre, ilk, family, race, breed, species, genus, variety, order, class, category, group, denomination, style, make, brand, stamp, quality, nature, character, description.

v   class, group, categorize, distribute, divide, separate, segregate, sift, screen, grade, rank, order, classify, catalogue, arrange, organize, systematize.

sort out   resolve, clear up, clarify, tidy up, neaten, choose, select.

soul *n*   **1** SPIRIT, psyche, mind, reason, intellect, character, inner being, essence, life, vital force.
2 INDIVIDUAL, person, man, creature. **3** woman.

sound^1 *n*   noise, din, report, resonance, reverberation, tone, timbre, tenor, description.

v   **1** RING, toll, chime, peal, resound, resonate, reverberate, echo.
2 ARTICULATE, enunciate, pronounce, voice, express, utter, say, declare, announce.

sound^2 *adj*   **1** FIT, well, healthy, vigorous, robust, sturdy, firm, solid, whole, complete, intact, perfect, unbroken, undamaged, unimpaired, unhurt, uninjured. **2** VALID, well-founded, reasonable, rational, logical, orthodox, right, true, proven, reliable, trustworthy, secure, substantial, thorough, good.

   1 unfit, ill, shaky. **2** unsound, unreliable, poor.

sound^3 *v*   measure, plumb, fathom, probe, examine, test, inspect, investigate.

sour *adj*   **1** TART, sharp, acid, pungent, vinegary, bitter, rancid.
2 EMBITTERED, acrimonious, ill-tempered, peevish, crabbed, crusty, disagreeable.

   1 sweet, sugary. **2** good-natured, generous.

source *n*   origin, derivation, beginning, start, commencement, cause, root, rise, spring, fountainhead, wellhead, supply, mine, originator, authority, informant.

souvenir *n*   memento, reminder, remembrance, keepsake, relic, token.

sovereign *n*   ruler, monarch, king, queen, emperor, empress, potentate, chief.

adj   ruling, royal, imperial, absolute, unlimited, supreme, paramount, predominant, principal, chief, dominant, independent, autonomous.

sow *v*   plant, seed, scatter, strew, spread, disseminate, lodge, implant.

space *n*   **1** ROOM, place, seat, accommodation, capacity, volume, extent, expansion, scope, range, play, elbow-room, leeway, margin.
2 BLANK, omission, gap, opening, lacuna, interval, intermission, chasm.

spacious *adj*   roomy, capacious, ample, big, large, sizable, broad, wide, huge, vast, extensive, open, uncrowded.

   small, narrow, cramped, confined.

span *n*   spread, stretch, reach, range, scope, compass, extent, length, distance, duration, term, period, spell.

v   arch, vault, bridge, link, cross, traverse, extend, cover.

spank *v*   smack, slap, wallop (*infml*), whack (*infml*), thrash, slipper, cane.

spare *adj*   reserve, emergency, extra, additional, leftover, remaining, unused, over, surplus, superfluous, supernumerary, unwanted, free, unoccupied.

   necessary, vital, used.

v   **1** PARDON, let off, reprieve, release, free. **2** GRANT, allow, afford, part with.

sparing *adj*   economical, thrifty, careful, prudent, frugal, meagre, miserly.

   unsparing, liberal, lavish.

spark *n*   flash, flare, gleam, glint, flicker, hint, trace, vestige, scrap, atom, jot.

v kindle, set off, trigger, start, cause, occasion, prompt, provoke, stimulate, stir, excite, inspire.

sparkle *v* **1** TWINKLE, glitter, scintillate, flash, gleam, glint, glisten, shimmer, coruscate, shine, beam.
2 EFFERVESCE, fizz, bubble.

n twinkle, glitter, flash, gleam, glint, flicker, spark, radiance, brilliance, dazzle, spirit, vitality, life, animation.

sparse *adj* scarce, scanty, meagre, scattered, infrequent, sporadic.
E₃ plentiful, thick, dense.

spartan *adj* austere, harsh, severe, rigorous, strict, disciplined, ascetic, abstemious, temperate, frugal, plain, simple, bleak, joyless.
E₃ luxurious, self-indulgent.

spasm *n* burst, eruption, outburst, frenzy, fit, convulsion, seizure, attack, contraction, jerk, twitch, tic.

spasmodic *adj* sporadic, occasional, intermittent, erratic, irregular, fitful, jerky.
E₃ continuous, uninterrupted.

spate *n* flood, deluge, torrent, rush, outpouring, flow.

speak *v* talk, converse, say, state, declare, express, utter, voice, articulate, enunciate, pronounce, tell, communicate, address, lecture, harangue, hold forth, declaim, argue, discuss.

speaker *n* lecturer, orator, spokesperson, spokesman, spokeswoman.

special *adj* **1** *a special occasion*: important, significant, momentous, major, noteworthy, distinguished, memorable, remarkable, extraordinary, exceptional.
2 DIFFERENT, distinctive, characteristic, peculiar, singular, individual, unique, exclusive, select, choice, particular, specific, unusual, precise, detailed.
E₃ 1 normal, ordinary, usual.
2 general, common.

specialist *n* consultant, authority, expert, master, professional, connoisseur.

speciality *n* strength, forte, talent, field, specialty, pièce de résistance.

specific *adj* precise, exact, fixed, limited, particular, special, definite, unequivocal, clear-cut, explicit, express, unambiguous.
E₃ vague, approximate.

specification *n* requirement, condition, qualification, description, listing, item, particular, detail.

specify *v* stipulate, spell out, define, particularize, detail, itemize, enumerate, list, mention, cite, name, designate, indicate, describe, delineate.

specimen *n* sample, example, instance, illustration, model, pattern, paradigm, exemplar, representative, copy, exhibit.

spectacle *n* show, performance, display, exhibition, parade, pageant, extravaganza, scene, sight, curiosity, wonder, marvel, phenomenon.

spectacular *adj* grand, splendid, magnificent, sensational, impressive, striking, stunning, staggering, amazing, remarkable, dramatic, daring, breathtaking, dazzling, eye-catching, colourful.
E₃ unimpressive, ordinary.

spectator *n* watcher, viewer, onlooker, looker-on, bystander, passer-by, witness, eye-witness, observer.
E₃ player, participant.

spectre *n* ghost, phantom, spirit, wraith, apparition, vision, presence.

speculate *v* wonder, contemplate, meditate, muse, reflect, consider, deliberate, theorize, suppose, guess, conjecture, surmise, gamble, risk, hazard, venture.

speculative *adj* conjectural, hypothetical, theoretical, notional, abstract, academic, tentative, risky, hazardous, uncertain, unpredictable.

speech n **1** DICTION, articulation, enunciation, elocution, delivery, utterance, voice, language, tongue, parlance, dialect, jargon. **2** *make a speech*: oration, address, discourse, talk, lecture, harangue, spiel (*sl*), conversation, dialogue, monologue, soliloquy.

speechless adj dumbfounded, thunderstruck, amazed, aghast, tongue-tied, inarticulate, mute, dumb, silent, mum.
F3 talkative.

speed n velocity, rate, pace, tempo, quickness, swiftness, rapidity, celerity, alacrity, haste, hurry, dispatch, rush, acceleration.
F3 slowness, delay.
v race, tear, belt (*infml*), zoom, career, bowl along, sprint, gallop, hurry, rush, hasten, accelerate, quicken, put one's foot down (*infml*), step on it (*infml*).
F3 slow, delay.

speedy adj fast, quick, swift, rapid, nimble, express, prompt, immediate, hurried, hasty, precipitate, cursory.
F3 slow, leisurely.

spell[1] n period, time, bout, session, term, season, interval, stretch, patch, turn, stint.

spell[2] n charm, incantation, magic, sorcery, witchery, bewitchment, enchantment, fascination, glamour.

spellbound adj transfixed, hypnotized, mesmerized, fascinated, enthralled, gripped, entranced, captivated, bewitched, enchanted, charmed.

spend v **1** *spend money*: disburse, pay out, fork out (*infml*), shell out (*infml*), invest, lay out, splash out (*infml*), waste, squander, fritter, expend, consume, use up, exhaust. **2** PASS, fill, occupy, use, employ, apply, devote.
F3 **1** save, hoard.

spendthrift n squanderer, prodigal, profligate, wastrel.

F3 miser.
adj improvident, extravagant, prodigal, wasteful.

sphere n **1** BALL, globe, orb, round. **2** DOMAIN, realm, province, department, territory, field, range, scope, compass, rank, function, capacity.

spherical adj round, rotund, ball-shaped, globe-shaped.

spicy adj **1** PIQUANT, hot, pungent, tangy, seasoned, aromatic, fragrant. **2** RACY, risqué, ribald, suggestive, indelicate, improper, indecorous, unseemly, scandalous, sensational.
F3 **1** bland, insipid. **2** decent.

spike n point, prong, tine, spine, barb, nail, stake.
v impale, stick, spear, skewer, spit.

spill v overturn, upset, slop, overflow, disgorge, pour, tip, discharge, shed, scatter.

spin v turn, revolve, rotate, twist, gyrate, twirl, pirouette, wheel, whirl, swirl, reel.
n **1** TURN, revolution, twist, gyration, twirl, pirouette, whirl, swirl. **2** COMMOTION, agitation, panic, flap (*infml*), state (*infml*), tizzy (*infml*). **3** DRIVE, ride, run.
spin out prolong, protract, extend, lengthen, amplify, pad out.

spindle n axis, pivot, pin, rod, axle.

spine n **1** BACKBONE, spinal column, vertebral column, vertebrae. **2** THORN, barb, prickle, bristle, quill.

spineless adj weak, feeble, irresolute, ineffective, cowardly, faint-hearted, lily-livered, yellow (*sl*), soft, wet, submissive, weak-kneed.
F3 strong, brave.

spiral adj winding, coiled, corkscrew, helical, whorled, scrolled, circular.
n coil, helix, corkscrew, screw, whorl, convolution.

spire n steeple, pinnacle, peak, summit, top, tip, point, spike.

spirit n **1** SOUL, psyche, mind,

breath, life. **2** GHOST, spectre, phantom, apparition, angel, demon, fairy, sprite. **3** LIVELINESS, vivacity, animation, sparkle, vigour, energy, zest, fire, ardour, motivation, enthusiasm, zeal, enterprise, resolution, willpower, courage, backbone, mettle. **4** *the spirit of the law*: meaning, sense, substance, essence, gist, tenor, character, quality. **5** MOOD, humour, temper, disposition, temperament, feeling, morale, attitude, outlook.

spirited *adj* lively, vivacious, animated, sparkling, high-spirited, vigorous, energetic, active, ardent, zealous, bold, courageous, mettlesome, plucky.
■ spiritless, lethargic, cowardly.

spiritual *adj* unworldly, incorporeal, immaterial, otherwordly, heavenly, divine, holy, sacred, religious, ecclesiastical.
■ physical, material.

spit *v* expectorate, eject, discharge, splutter, hiss.
n spittle, saliva, slaver, drool, dribble, sputum, phlegm, expectoration.

spite *n* spitefulness, malice, venom, gall, bitterness, rancour, animosity, ill feeling, grudge, malevolence, malignity, ill nature, hate, hatred.
■ goodwill, compassion, affection.
v annoy, irritate, irk, vex, provoke, gall, hurt, injure, offend, put out.

spiteful *adj* malicious, venomous, catty, bitchy, snide, barbed, cruel, vindictive, vengeful, malevolent, malignant, ill-natured, ill-disposed, nasty.
■ charitable, affectionate.

splash *v* **1** BATHE, wallow, paddle, wade, dabble, plunge, wet, wash, shower, spray, squirt, sprinkle, spatter, splatter, splodge, spread, daub, plaster, slop, slosh, plop, surge, break, dash, strike, buffet, smack. **2** PUBLICIZE, flaunt, blazon, trumpet.

n **1** SPOT, patch, splatter, splodge, burst, touch, dash. **2** PUBLICITY, display, ostentation, effect, impact, stir, excitement, sensation.

splendid *adj* brilliant, dazzling, glittering, lustrous, bright, radiant, glowing, glorious, magnificent, gorgeous, resplendent, sumptuous, luxurious, lavish, rich, fine, grand, stately, imposing, impressive, great, outstanding, remarkable, exceptional, sublime, supreme, superb, excellent, first-class, wonderful, marvellous, admirable.
■ drab, ordinary, run-of-the-mill.

splendour *n* brightness, radiance, brilliance, dazzle, lustre, glory, resplendence, magnificence, richness, grandeur, majesty, solemnity, pomp, ceremony, display, show, spectacle.
■ drabness, squalor.

splice *v* join, unite, wed, marry, bind, tie, plait, braid, interweave, interlace, intertwine, entwine, mesh, knit, graft.

splinter *n* sliver, shiver, chip, shard, fragment, flake, shaving, paring.
v split, fracture, smash, shatter, shiver, fragment, disintegrate.

split *v* divide, separate, partition, part, disunite, disband, open, gape, fork, diverge, break, splinter, shiver, snap, crack, burst, rupture, tear, rend, rip, slit, slash, cleave, halve, slice up, share, distribute, parcel out.
n **1** DIVISION, separation, partition, break, breach, gap, cleft, crevice, crack, fissure, rupture, tear, rent, rip, rift, slit, slash. **2** SCHISM, disunion, dissension, discord, difference, divergence, break-up.
adj divided, cleft, cloven, bisected, dual, twofold, broken, fractured, cracked, ruptured.

split up part, part company, disband, break up, separate, divorce.

spoil *v* **1** MAR, upset, wreck, ruin, destroy, damage, impair, harm, hurt, injure, deface, disfigure, blemish.

2 *spoil a child*: indulge, pamper, cosset, coddle, mollycoddle, baby, spoon-feed. **3** DETERIORATE, go bad, go off, sour, turn, curdle, decay, decompose.

spoils *n* plunder, loot, booty, haul, swag (*sl*), pickings, gain, acquisitions, prizes, winnings.

sponge *v* **1** WIPE, mop, clean, wash. **2** CADGE, scrounge.

sponger *n* cadger, scrounger, parasite, hanger-on.

spongy *adj* soft, cushioned, yielding, elastic, springy, porous, absorbent, light.

sponsor *n* patron, backer, angel (*infml*), promoter, underwriter, guarantor, surety.
v finance, fund, bankroll, subsidize, patronize, back, promote, underwrite, guarantee.

spontaneous *adj* natural, unforced, untaught, instinctive, impulsive, unpremeditated, free, willing, unhesitating, voluntary, unprompted, impromptu, extempore.
🔁 forced, studied, planned, deliberate.

sporadic *adj* occasional, intermittent, infrequent, isolated, spasmodic, erratic, irregular, uneven, random, scattered.
🔁 frequent, regular.

sport *n* **1** GAME, exercise, activity, pastime, amusement, entertainment, diversion, recreation, play. **2** FUN, mirth, humour, joking, jesting, banter, teasing, mockery, ridicule.

Sports include: badminton, fives, lacrosse, squash, table-tennis, ping-pong (*infml*); tennis; American football, baseball, basketball, billiards, boules, bowls, cricket, croquet, football, golf, handball, hockey, netball, pétanque, pitch and putt, polo, pool, putting, rounders, Rugby, snooker, soccer, tenpin bowling, volleyball; athletics, cross-country, decathlon, discus, high-jump, hurdling, javelin, long-jump, marathon, pentathlon, pole vault, running, shot put, triple-jump; angling, canoeing, diving, fishing, rowing, sailing, skin-diving, surfing, swimming, synchronized swimming, water polo, water-skiing, windsurfing, yachting; bobsleigh, curling, ice-hockey, ice-skating, skiing, speed skating, tobogganing (luging); aerobics, fencing, gymnastics, jogging, keep-fit, roller-skating, trampolining; archery, darts, quoits; boxing, judo, jujitsu, karate, tae kwon do, weightlifting, wrestling; climbing, mountaineering, rock-climbing, walking, orienteering, pot-holing; cycle racing, drag-racing, go-karting, motor racing, speedway racing, stock-car racing, greyhound-racing, horse-racing, show-jumping, trotting, hunting, shooting, clay-pigeon shooting; gliding, sky-diving.

Types of sports equipment include: ball, basketball, boule, bowl, jack, wood, football, netball, rugby ball, tenpin bowling ball, volleyball; fishing-rod, fly rod, spinning rod, fishing-line, paternoster, reel, fly reel, hook, gaff, gang-hook, jig, trace, lure, bait, fly, float, net, keep-net, priest, disgorger; bow, arrow, crossbow, bolt; badminton racket, shuttlecock, net; baseball bat, baseball, mitt, catcher's glove; boxing glove, gum shield, punch-bag, punch-ball; cricket bat, cricket ball, wicket, stump, bail, nets; épée, foil, sabre, face-guard, mask; discus, hammer, javelin, shot; golf club, golf ball, tee, golfing glove; asymmetrical bars, horizontal bar, isometric bar, parallel-bars, beam, balance-beam, mat, pommel horse, vaulting horse, rings, rope, springboard, trampoline; hockey stick, hockey ball, ice-hockey stick, puck, hockey skate; curling stone; ice-skate, roller-skate, rollerblade, roller boot, speed skate, skateboard; ski, ski stick, snow board, toboggan; snooker ball; billiard ball, cue ball, table, cue, rest, bridge, rack, chalk; squash racket, squash ball; table-tennis bat, table-tennis ball, net; tennis racket, tennis ball, net, racket press; oar, aqualung, snorkel, water-ski, sailboard, surfboard.

v wear, display, exhibit, show off.

sporting *adj* sportsmanlike, gentlemanly, decent, considerate, fair.

F∃ unsporting, ungentlemanly, unfair.

sporty *adj* **1** ATHLETIC, fit, energetic, outdoor. **2** STYLISH, trendy (*infml*), jaunty, natty (*infml*), snazzy (*infml*), showy, loud, flashy, casual, informal.

spot *n* **1** DOT, speckle, fleck, mark, speck, blotch, blot, smudge, daub, splash, stain, discoloration, blemish, flaw, pimple. **2** PLACE, point, position, situation, location, site, scene, locality. **3** (*infml*) PLIGHT, predicament, quandary, difficulty, trouble, mess.

v see, notice, observe, detect, discern, identify, recognize.

spotless *adj* immaculate, clean, white, gleaming, spick and span, unmarked, unstained, unblemished, unsullied, pure, chaste, virgin, untouched, innocent, blameless, faultless, irreproachable.

F∃ dirty, impure.

spotted *adj* dotted, speckled, flecked, mottled, dappled, pied.

spotty *adj* pimply, pimpled, blotchy, spotted.

spouse *n* husband, wife, partner, mate, better half (*infml*).

spout *v* jet, spurt, squirt, spray, shoot, gush, stream, surge, erupt, emit, discharge.

n jet, fountain, geyser, gargoyle, outlet, nozzle, rose, spray.

sprawl *v* spread, straggle, trail, ramble, flop, slump, slouch, loll, lounge, recline, repose.

spray[1] *v* shower, spatter, sprinkle, scatter, diffuse, wet, drench.

n **1** MOISTURE, drizzle, mist, foam, froth. **2** AEROSOL, atomizer, sprinkler.

spray[2] *n* sprig, branch, corsage, posy, bouquet, garland, wreath.

spread *v* **1** STRETCH, extend, sprawl, broaden, widen, dilate, expand, swell, mushroom, proliferate, escalate, open, unroll, unfurl, unfold, fan out, cover, lay out, arrange. **2** SCATTER, strew, diffuse, radiate, disseminate, broadcast, transmit, communicate, promulgate, propagate, publicize, advertise, publish, circulate, distribute.

F∃ **1** close, fold. **2** suppress.

n **1** STRETCH, reach, span, extent, expanse, sweep, compass. **2** *the spread of disease*: advance, development, expansion, increase, proliferation, escalation, diffusion, dissemination, dispersion.

spree *n* bout, fling, binge, splurge, orgy, revel.

sprightly *adj* agile, nimble, spry, active, energetic, lively, spirited, vivacious, hearty, brisk, jaunty, cheerful, blithe, airy.

F∃ doddering, inactive, lifeless.

spring[1] *v* **1** JUMP, leap, vault, bound, hop, bounce, rebound, recoil. **2** ORIGINATE, derive, come, stem, arise, start, proceed, issue, emerge, emanate, appear, sprout, grow, develop.

n **1** JUMP, leap, vault, bound, bounce. **2** SPRINGINESS, resilience, give, flexibility, elasticity, buoyancy.

spring[2] *n* source, origin, beginning, cause, root, fountainhead, wellhead, wellspring, well, geyser, spa.

springy adj bouncy, resilient, flexible, elastic, stretchy, rubbery, spongy, buoyant.
🔄 hard, stiff.

sprinkle v shower, spray, spatter, scatter, strew, dot, pepper, dust, powder.

sprint v run, race, dash, tear, belt (infml), dart, shoot.

sprout v shoot, bud, germinate, grow, develop, come up, spring up.

spruce adj smart, elegant, neat, trim, dapper, well-dressed, well-turned-out, well-groomed, sleek.
🔄 scruffy, untidy.

spruce up neaten, tidy, smarten up, groom.

spur v goad, prod, poke, prick, stimulate, prompt, incite, drive, propel, impel, urge, encourage, motivate.
🔄 curb, discourage.
n incentive, encouragement, inducement, motive, stimulus, incitement, impetus, fillip.
🔄 curb, disincentive.

spurious adj false, fake, counterfeit, forged, bogus, phoney (infml), mock, sham, feigned, pretended, simulated, imitation, artificial.
🔄 genuine, authentic, real.

spurn v reject, turn down, scorn, despise, disdain, rebuff, repulse, slight, snub, cold-shoulder, ignore, disregard.
🔄 accept, embrace.

spurt v gush, squirt, jet, shoot, burst, erupt, surge.
n burst, rush, surge, spate, fit, access.

spy n secret agent, undercover agent, double agent, mole (infml), fifth columnist, scout, snooper.
v spot, glimpse, notice, observe, discover.

squabble v bicker, wrangle, quarrel, row, argue, dispute, clash, brawl, scrap, fight.

squad n crew, team, gang, band, group, company, brigade, troop, force, outfit.

squalid adj dirty, filthy, unclean, foul, disgusting, repulsive, sordid, seedy, dingy, untidy, slovenly, unkempt, broken-down, run-down, neglected, uncared-for, low, mean, nasty.
🔄 clean, pleasant, attractive.

squander v waste, misspend, misuse, lavish, blow (sl), fritter away, throw away, dissipate, scatter, spend, expend, consume.

square v settle, reconcile, tally, agree, accord, harmonize, correspond, match, balance, straighten, level, align, adjust, regulate, adapt, tailor, fit, suit.
adj 1 QUADRILATERAL, rectangular, right-angled, perpendicular, straight, true, even, level. 2 FAIR, equitable, just, ethical, honourable, honest, genuine, above-board, on the level (infml).

squash v 1 CRUSH, flatten, press, squeeze, compress, crowd, trample, stamp, pound, pulp, smash, distort. 2 SUPPRESS, silence, quell, quash, annihilate, put down, snub, humiliate.
🔄 1 stretch, expand.

squat adj short, stocky, thickset, dumpy, chunky, stubby.
🔄 slim, lanky.
v crouch, stoop, bend, sit.

squawk v, n screech, shriek, cry, croak, cackle, crow, hoot.

squeak v, n squeal, whine, creak, peep, cheep.

squeal v, n cry, shout, yell, yelp, wail, scream, screech, shriek, squawk.

squeamish adj queasy, nauseated, sick, delicate, fastidious, particular, prudish.

squeeze v 1 PRESS, squash, crush, pinch, nip, compress, grip, clasp, clutch, hug, embrace, enfold, cuddle. 2 squeeze into a corner: cram, stuff, pack, crowd, wedge, jam, force, ram, push, thrust, shove, jostle. **3** WRING, wrest, extort, milk, bleed, force, lean on (*infml*).

n **1** PRESS, squash, crush, crowd, congestion, jam. **2** HUG, embrace, hold, grasp, clasp.

squirt *v* spray, spurt, jet, shoot, spout, gush, ejaculate, discharge, emit, eject, expel.

n spray, spurt, jet.

stab *v* pierce, puncture, cut, wound, injure, gore, knife, spear, stick, jab, thrust.

n **1** ACHE, pang, twinge, prick, puncture, cut, incision, gash, wound, jab. **2** (*infml*) TRY, attempt, endeavour, bash (*infml*).

stability *n* steadiness, firmness, soundness, constancy, steadfastness, strength, sturdiness, solidity, durability, permanence.

F3 instability, unsteadiness, insecurity, weakness.

stable *adj* steady, firm, secure, fast, sound, sure, constant, steadfast, reliable, established, well-founded, deep-rooted, strong, sturdy, durable, lasting, enduring, abiding, permanent, unchangeable, unalterable, invariable, immutable, fixed, static, balanced.

F3 unstable, wobbly, shaky, weak.

stack *n* heap, pile, mound, mass, load, accumulation, hoard, stockpile.

v heap, pile, load, amass, accumulate, assemble, gather, save, hoard, stockpile.

staff *n* **1** *member of staff*: personnel, workforce, employees, workers, crew, team, teachers, officers. **2** STICK, cane, rod, baton, wand, pole, prop.

stage *n* point, juncture, step, phase, period, division, lap, leg, length, level, floor.

v mount, put on, present, produce, give, do, perform, arrange, organize, stage-manage, orchestrate, engineer.

stagger *v* **1** LURCH, totter, teeter, wobble, sway, rock, reel, falter,

hesitate, waver. **2** SURPRISE, amaze, astound, astonish, stun, stupefy, dumbfound, flabbergast (*infml*), shake, shock, confound, overwhelm.

stagnant *adj* still, motionless, standing, brackish, stale, sluggish, torpid, lethargic.

F3 fresh, moving.

stagnate *v* vegetate, idle, languish, decline, deteriorate, degenerate, decay, rot, rust.

staid *adj* sedate, calm, composed, sober, demure, solemn, serious, grave, quiet, steady.

F3 jaunty, debonair, frivolous, adventurous.

stain *v* **1** MARK, spot, blemish, blot, smudge, discolour, dirty, soil, taint, contaminate, sully, tarnish, blacken, disgrace. **2** DYE, tint, tinge, colour, paint, varnish.

n mark, spot, blemish, blot, smudge, discoloration, smear, slur, disgrace, shame, dishonour.

stake[1] *n* post, pole, standard, picket, pale, paling, spike, stick.

stake[2] *n* bet, wager, pledge, interest, concern, involvement, share, investment, claim.

v gamble, bet, wager, pledge, risk, chance, hazard, venture.

stale *adj* **1** *stale bread*: dry, hard, old, musty, fusty, flat, insipid, tasteless. **2** OVERUSED, hackneyed, clichéed, stereotyped, jaded, worn-out, unoriginal, trite, banal, commonplace.

F3 1 crisp. **2** new.

stalemate *n* draw, tie, deadlock, impasse, standstill, halt.

F3 progress.

stalk[1] *v* track, trail, hunt, follow, pursue, shadow, tail, haunt.

stalk[2] *n* stem, twig, branch, trunk.

stall *v* temporize, play for time, delay, hedge, equivocate, obstruct, stonewall.

stalwart *adj* strong, sturdy, robust, rugged, stout, strapping, muscular,

athletic, vigorous, valiant, daring, intrepid, indomitable, determined, resolute, staunch, steadfast, reliable, dependable.
F3 weak, feeble, timid.

stamina *n* energy, vigour, strength, power, force, grit, resilience, resistance, endurance, indefatigability, staying power.
F3 weakness.

stammer *v* stutter, stumble, falter, hesitate, splutter.

stamp *v* **1** TRAMPLE, crush, beat, pound. **2** IMPRINT, impress, print, inscribe, engrave, emboss, mark, brand, label, categorize, identify, characterize.
n print, imprint, impression, seal, signature, authorization, mark, hallmark, attestation, brand, cast, mould, cut, form, fashion, sort, kind, type, breed, character, description.

stampede *n* charge, rush, dash, sprint, flight, rout.
v charge, rush, dash, tear, run, sprint, gallop, shoot, fly, flee, scatter.

stance *n* posture, deportment, carriage, bearing, position, standpoint, viewpoint, angle, point of view, attitude.

stand *v* **1** PUT, place, set, erect, up-end, position, station. **2** *I can't stand it*: bear, tolerate, abide, endure, suffer, experience, undergo, withstand, weather. **3** RISE, get up, stand up.
n base, pedestal, support, frame, rack, table, stage, platform, place, stall, booth.
stand by support, back, champion, defend, stick up for, uphold, adhere to, hold to, stick by.
F3 let down.
stand down step down, resign, abdicate, quit, give up, retire, withdraw.
F3 join.
stand for represent, symbolize, mean, signify, denote, indicate.

stand in for deputize for, cover for, understudy, replace, substitute for.
stand out show, catch the eye, stick out, jut out, project.
stand up for defend, stick up for, side with, fight for, support, protect, champion, uphold.
F3 attack.
stand up to defy, oppose, resist, withstand, endure, face, confront, brave.
F3 give in to.

standard *n* **1** NORM, average, type, model, pattern, example, sample, guideline, benchmark, touchstone, yardstick, rule, measure, gauge, level, criterion, requirement, specification, grade, quality. **2** FLAG, ensign, pennant, pennon, colours, banner.
adj normal, average, typical, stock, classic, basic, staple, usual, customary, popular, prevailing, regular, approved, accepted, recognized, official, orthodox, set, established, definitive.
F3 abnormal, unusual, irregular.

standardize *v* normalize, equalize, homogenize, stereotype, mass-produce.
F3 differentiate.

standards *n* principles, ideals, morals, ethics.

standoffish *adj* aloof, remote, distant, unapproachable, unsociable, uncommunicative, reserved, cold.
F3 friendly.

standpoint *n* position, station, vantagepoint, stance, viewpoint, angle, point of view.

standstill *n* stop, halt, pause, lull, rest, stoppage, jam, log-jam, hold-up, impasse, deadlock, stalemate.
F3 advance, progress.

staple *adj* basic, fundamental, primary, key, main, chief, major, principal, essential, necessary, standard.
F3 minor.

star *n* celebrity, personage,

luminary, idol, lead, leading man, leading lady, superstar.

> *Types of star include:* nova, supernova, pulsar, falling-star, shooting-star, meteor, comet, Halley's comet, red giant, supergiant, white dwarf, red dwarf, brown dwarf, neutron star, Pole Star, Polaris, North Star.

stare *v* gaze, look, watch, gape, gawp, gawk, goggle, glare.
n gaze, look, glare.

stark *adj* **1** *stark landscape:* bare, barren, bleak, bald, plain, simple, austere, harsh, severe, grim, dreary, gloomy, depressing. **2** UTTER, unmitigated, total, consummate, absolute, sheer, downright, out-and-out, flagrant, arrant.

start *v* **1** BEGIN, commence, originate, initiate, introduce, pioneer, create, found, establish, set up, institute, inaugurate, launch, open, kick off (*infml*), instigate, activate, trigger, set off, set out, leave, depart, appear, arise, issue. **2** JUMP, jerk, twitch, flinch, recoil.
F3 **1** stop, finish, end.
n **1** BEGINNING, commencement, outset, inception, dawn, birth, break, outburst, onset, origin, initiation, introduction, foundation, inauguration, launch, opening, kick-off (*infml*). **2** JUMP, jerk, twitch, spasm, convulsion, fit.
F3 **1** stop, finish, end.

startle *v* surprise, amaze, astonish, astound, shock, scare, frighten, alarm, agitate, upset, disturb.
F3 calm.

starvation *n* hunger, undernourishment, malnutrition, famine.
F3 plenty, excess.

starve *v* hunger, fast, diet, deprive, refuse, deny, die, perish.
F3 feed, gorge.

starving *adj* hungry, underfed, undernourished, ravenous, famished.

state *v* say, declare, announce, report, communicate, assert, aver, affirm, specify, present, express, put, formulate, articulate, voice.
n **1** CONDITION, shape, situation, position, circumstances, case.
2 NATION, country, land, territory, kingdom, republic, government.
3 (*infml*) PANIC, flap (*infml*), tizzy (*infml*), bother, plight, predicament.
4 POMP, ceremony, dignity, majesty, grandeur, glory, splendour.
adj national, governmental, public, official, formal, ceremonial, pompous, stately.

stately *adj* grand, imposing, impressive, elegant, majestic, regal, royal, imperial, noble, august, lofty, pompous, dignified, measured, deliberate, solemn, ceremonious.
F3 informal, unimpressive.

statement *n* account, report, bulletin, communiqué, announcement, declaration, proclamation, communication, utterance, testimony.

static *adj* stationary, motionless, immobile, unmoving, still, inert, resting, fixed, constant, changeless, unvarying, stable.
F3 dynamic, mobile, varying.

station *n* place, location, position, post, headquarters, base, depot.
v locate, set, establish, install, garrison, post, send, appoint, assign.

stationary *adj* motionless, immobile, unmoving, still, static, inert, standing, resting, parked, moored, fixed.
F3 mobile, moving, active.

statue *n* figure, head, bust, effigy, idol, statuette, carving, bronze.

status *n* rank, grade, degree, level, class, station, standing, position, state, condition, prestige, eminence, distinction, importance, consequence, weight.

🞂 unimportance, insignificance.

staunch *adj* loyal, faithful, hearty, strong, stout, firm, sound, sure, true, trusty, reliable, dependable, steadfast.

🞂 unfaithful, weak, unreliable.

stay *v* **1** LAST, continue, endure, abide, remain, linger, persist. **2** RESIDE, dwell, live, settle, sojourn, stop, halt, pause, wait.

🞂 **1** go, leave.

n visit, holiday, stopover, sojourn.

steady *adj* stable, balanced, poised, fixed, immovable, firm, poised, settled, still, calm, imperturbable, equable, even, uniform, consistent, unvarying, unchanging, constant, persistent, unremitting, incessant, uninterrupted, unbroken, regular, rhythmic, steadfast, unwavering.

🞂 unsteady, unstable, variable, wavering.

v balance, stabilize, fix, secure, brace, support.

steal *v* **1** *steal a car*: thieve, pilfer, filch, pinch (*infml*), nick (*infml*), take, appropriate, snatch, swipe, shoplift, poach, embezzle, lift, plagiarize. **2** CREEP, tiptoe, slip, slink, sneak.

🞂 **1** return, give back.

stealthy *adj* surreptitious, clandestine, covert, secret, unobtrusive, secretive, quiet, furtive, sly, cunning, sneaky, underhand.

🞂 open.

steam *n* vapour, mist, haze, condensation, moisture, dampness.

steep *adj* **1** *a steep slope*: sheer, precipitous, headlong, abrupt, sudden, sharp. **2** (*infml*) EXCESSIVE, extreme, stiff, unreasonable, high, exorbitant, extortionate, overpriced.

🞂 **1** gentle, gradual. **2** moderate, low.

steer *v* pilot, guide, direct, control, govern, conduct.

stem¹ *n* stalk, shoot, stock, branch, trunk.

stem² *v* stop, halt, arrest, stanch,

staunch, block, dam, check, curb, restrain, contain, resist, oppose.

🞂 encourage.

stench *n* stink, reek, pong (*infml*), smell, odour.

step *n* **1** PACE, stride, footstep, tread, footprint, print, trace, track. **2** MOVE, act, action, deed, measure, procedure, process, proceeding, progression, movement, stage, phase, degree. **3** RUNG, stair, level, rank, point.

v pace, stride, tread, stamp, walk, move.

step down stand down, resign, abdicate, quit, leave, retire, withdraw.

🞂 join.

step up increase, raise, augment, boost, build up, intensify, escalate, accelerate, speed up.

🞂 decrease.

stereotype *n* formula, convention, mould, pattern, model.

v categorize, pigeonhole, typecast, standardize, formalize, conventionalize, mass-produce.

🞂 differentiate.

sterile *adj* **1** GERM-FREE, aseptic, sterilized, disinfected, antiseptic, uncontaminated. **2** INFERTILE, barren, arid, bare, unproductive, fruitless, pointless, useless, abortive.

🞂 **1** septic. **2** fertile, fruitful.

sterilize *v* disinfect, fumigate, purify, clean, cleanse.

🞂 contaminate, infect.

stern *adj* strict, severe, authoritarian, rigid, inflexible, unyielding, hard, tough, rigorous, stringent, harsh, cruel, unsparing, relentless, unrelenting, grim, forbidding, stark, austere.

🞂 kind, gentle, mild, lenient.

stew *v* boil, simmer, braise, casserole.

stick¹ *v* **1** THRUST, poke, stab, jab, pierce, penetrate, puncture, spear, transfix. **2** GLUE, gum, paste, cement, bond, fuse, weld, solder,

adhere, cling, hold. **3** ATTACH, affix, fasten, secure, fix, pin, join, bind.
4 put, place, position, set, install, deposit, drop.

stick at persevere, plug away (*infml*), persist, continue.

🔁 give up.

stick out protrude, jut out, project, extend.

stick up for stand up for, speak up for, defend, champion, support, uphold.

🔁 attack.

stick² *n* branch, twig, wand, baton, staff, sceptre, cane, birch, rod, pole, stake.

sticky *adj* **1** ADHESIVE, gummed, tacky, gluey, gummy, viscous, glutinous, gooey (*infml*). **2** (*infml*) *a sticky situation*: difficult, tricky, thorny, unpleasant, awkward, embarrassing, delicate. **3** HUMID, clammy, muggy, close, oppressive, sultry.

🔁 **1** dry. **2** easy. **3** fresh, cool.

stiff *adj* **1** RIGID, inflexible, unbending, unyielding, hard, solid, hardened, solidified, firm, tight, taut, tense. **2** FORMAL, ceremonious, pompous, stand-offish, cold, prim, priggish, austere, strict, severe, harsh. **3** DIFFICULT, hard, tough, arduous, laborious, awkward, exacting, rigorous.

🔁 **1** flexible. **2** informal. **3** easy.

stiffen *v* harden, solidify, tighten, tense, brace, reinforce, starch, thicken, congeal, coagulate, jell, set.

stifle *v* smother, suffocate, asphyxiate, strangle, choke, extinguish, muffle, dampen, deaden, silence, hush, suppress, quell, check, curb, restrain, repress.

🔁 encourage.

stigma *n* brand, mark, stain, blot, spot, blemish, disgrace, shame, dishonour.

🔁 credit, honour.

still *adj* stationary, motionless, lifeless, stagnant, smooth,

undisturbed, unruffled, calm, tranquil, serene, restful, peaceful, hushed, quiet, silent, noiseless.

🔁 active, disturbed, agitated, noisy.

v calm, soothe, allay, tranquillize, subdue, restrain, hush, quieten, silence, pacify, settle, smooth.

🔁 agitate, stir up.

adv yet, even so, nevertheless, nonetheless, notwithstanding, however.

stilted *adj* artificial, unnatural, stiff, wooden, forced, constrained.

🔁 fluent, flowing.

stimulate *v* rouse, arouse, animate, quicken, fire, inflame, inspire, motivate, encourage, induce, urge, impel, spur, prompt, goad, provoke, incite, instigate, trigger off.

🔁 discourage, hinder, prevent.

stimulus *n* incentive, encouragement, inducement, spur, goad, provocation, incitement.

🔁 discouragement.

sting *v* *bees sting*: bite, prick, hurt, injure, wound. **2** SMART, tingle, burn, pain.

n bite, nip, prick, smart, tingle.

stingy *adj* mean, miserly, niggardly, tight-fisted (*infml*), parsimonious, penny-pinching.

🔁 generous, liberal.

stink *v* smell, reek, pong (*infml*), hum (*sl*).

n smell, odour, stench, pong (*infml*), niff (*sl*).

stint *n* spell, stretch, period, time, shift, turn, bit, share, quota.

stipulate *v* specify, lay down, require, demand, insist on.

stipulation *n* specification, requirement, demand, condition, proviso.

stir *v* **1** MOVE, budge, touch, affect, inspire, excite, thrill, disturb, agitate, shake, tremble, quiver, flutter, rustle. **2** MIX, blend, beat.

n activity, movement, bustle, flurry, commotion, ado, fuss, to-do (*infml*).

uproar, tumult, disturbance, disorder, agitation, excitement, ferment.

Ea calm.

stir up rouse, arouse, awaken, animate, quicken, kindle, fire, inflame, stimulate, spur, prompt, provoke, incite, instigate, agitate.

Ea calm, discourage.

stock n **1** GOODS, merchandise, wares, commodities, capital, assets, inventory, repertoire, range, variety, assortment, source, supply, fund, reservoir, store, reserve, stockpile, hoard. **2** PARENTAGE, ancestry, descent, extraction, family, line, lineage, pedigree, race, breed, species, blood. **3** LIVESTOCK, animals, cattle, horses, sheep, herds, flocks.

adj standard, basic, regular, routine, ordinary, run-of-the-mill, usual, customary, traditional, conventional, set, stereotyped, hackneyed, overused, banal, trite.

Ea original, unusual.

v keep, carry, sell, trade in, deal in, handle, supply, provide.

stock up gather, accumulate, amass, lay in, provision, fill, replenish, store (up), save, hoard, pile up.

stocky *adj* sturdy, solid, thickset, chunky, short, squat, dumpy, stubby.

Ea tall, skinny.

stoical *adj* patient, long-suffering, uncomplaining, resigned, philosophical, indifferent, impassive, unemotional, phlegmatic, dispassionate, cool, calm, imperturbable.

Ea excitable, anxious.

stolid *adj* slow, heavy, dull, bovine, wooden, blockish, lumpish, impassive, phlegmatic, unemotional.

Ea lively, interested.

stomach n tummy (*infml*), gut, inside(s), belly, abdomen, paunch, pot.

v tolerate, bear, stand, abide, endure, suffer, submit to, take.

stony *adj* **1** BLANK, expressionless, hard, cold, frigid, icy, indifferent, unfeeling, heartless, callous, merciless, pitiless, inexorable, hostile. **2** *stony beach*: pebbly, shingly, rocky.

Ea **1** warm, soft-hearted, friendly.

stoop *v* **1** HUNCH, bow, bend, incline, lean, duck, squat, crouch, kneel. **2** *stoop to blackmail*: descend, sink, lower oneself, resort, go so far as, condescend, deign.

stop *v* **1** HALT, cease, end, finish, conclude, terminate, discontinue, suspend, interrupt, pause, quit, refrain, desist, pack in (*sl*).
2 PREVENT, bar, frustrate, thwart, intercept, hinder, impede, check, restrain. **3** SEAL, close, plug, block, obstruct, arrest, stem, stanch.

Ea **1** start, continue.

n **1** STATION, terminus, destination. **2** REST, break, pause, stage. **3** HALT, standstill, stoppage, cessation, end, finish, conclusion, termination, discontinuation.

Ea **3** start, beginning, continuation.

stoppage *n* stop, halt, standstill, arrest, blockage, obstruction, check, hindrance, interruption, shutdown, closure, strike, walk-out, sit-in.

Ea start, continuation.

stopper *n* cork, bung, plug.

store *v* save, keep, put aside, lay by, reserve, stock, lay in, deposit, lay down, lay up, accumulate, hoard, salt away, stockpile, stash (*infml*).

Ea use.

n **1** STOCK, supply, provision, fund, reserve, mine, reservoir, hoard, cache, stockpile, accumulation, quantity, abundance, plenty, lot.

2 STOREROOM, storehouse, warehouse, repository, depository.

Ea **1** scarcity.

storey *n* floor, level, stage, tier, flight, deck.

storm n **1** TEMPEST, thunderstorm, squall, blizzard, gale, hurricane, whirlwind, tornado, cyclone.

Kinds of storm include: blizzard, buran, cloudburst, cyclone, downpour, dust-devil, dust-storm, electrical storm, gale, haboob, hailstorm, hurricane, monsoon, rainstorm, sand storm, snow storm, squall, tempest, thunderstorm, tornado, typhoon, whirlwind. *see also* **wind**.

2 OUTBURST, uproar, furore, outcry, row, rumpus, commotion, tumult, disturbance, turmoil, stir, agitation, rage, outbreak, attack, assault.
F3 2 calm.

v charge, rush, attack, assault, assail, roar, thunder, rage, rant, rave, fume.

stormy *adj* tempestuous, squally, rough, choppy, turbulent, wild, raging, windy, gusty, blustery, foul.
F3 calm.

story *n* **1** TALE, fairy-tale, fable, myth, legend, novel, romance, fiction, yarn, anecdote, episode, plot, narrative, history, chronicle, record, account, relation, recital, report, article, feature.

Types of story include: adventure story, bedtime story, blockbuster (*infml*), children's story, comedy, black comedy, crime story, detective story, fable, fairy-tale, fantasy, folk tale, ghost story, historical novel, horror story, legend, love story, Mills & Boon®, mystery, myth, parable, romance, saga, science fiction, sci-fi (*infml*), short story, spiel, spine-chiller, supernatural tale, tall story, thriller, western, whodunit (*infml*).

2 LIE, falsehood, untruth.

stout *adj* **1** FAT, plump, fleshy, portly, corpulent, overweight, heavy, bulky, big, brawny, beefy, hulking, burly, muscular, athletic. **2** *stout packaging*: strong, tough, durable, thick, sturdy, robust, hardy, vigorous. **3** BRAVE, courageous, valiant, plucky, fearless, bold, intrepid, dauntless, resolute, stalwart.
F3 1 thin, lean, slim. **2** weak.
3 cowardly, timid.

stow *v* put away, store, load, pack, cram, stuff, stash (*infml*).
F3 unload.

straight *adj* **1** *a straight line*: level, even, flat, horizontal, upright, vertical, aligned, direct, undeviating, unswerving, true, right. **2** TIDY, neat, orderly, shipshape, organized.
3 HONOURABLE, honest, law-abiding, respectable, upright, trustworthy, reliable, straightforward, fair, just. **4** FRANK, candid, blunt, forthright, direct. **5** *straight whisky*: undiluted, neat, unadulterated, unmixed.
F3 1 bent, crooked. **2** untidy.
3 dishonest. **4** evasive. **5** diluted.
adv directly, point-blank, honestly, frankly, candidly.
straight away at once, immediately, instantly, right away, directly, now, there and then.
F3 later, eventually.

straighten *v* unbend, align, tidy, neaten, order, arrange.
F3 bend, twist.

straighten out clear up, sort out, settle, resolve, correct, rectify, disentangle, regularize.
F3 confuse, muddle.

straightforward *adj* **1** EASY, simple, uncomplicated, clear, elementary.
2 HONEST, truthful, sincere, genuine, open, frank, candid, direct, forthright.
F3 1 complicated. **2** evasive, devious.

strain¹ *v* **1** PULL, wrench, twist, sprain, tear, stretch, extend, tighten, tauten. **2** SIEVE, sift, screen, separate, filter, purify, drain, wring, squeeze, compress, express. **3** WEAKEN, tire, tax, overtax, overwork, labour, try, endeavour, struggle, strive, exert, force, drive.

n stress, anxiety, burden, pressure, tension, tautness, pull, sprain, wrench, injury, exertion, effort, struggle, force.
🖝 relaxation.

strain² *n* 1 STOCK, ancestry, descent, extraction, family, lineage, pedigree, blood, variety, type. 2 TRAIT, streak, vein, tendency, trace, suggestion, suspicion.

strained *adj* forced, constrained, laboured, false, artificial, unnatural, stiff, tense, unrelaxed, uneasy, uncomfortable, awkward, embarrassed, self-conscious.
🖝 natural, relaxed.

strait-laced *adj* prudish, stuffy, starchy, prim, proper, strict, narrow, narrow-minded, puritanical, moralistic.
🖝 broad-minded.

strand *n* fibre, filament, wire, thread, string, piece, length.

stranded *adj* marooned, high and dry, abandoned, forsaken, in the lurch, helpless, aground, grounded, beached, shipwrecked, wrecked.

strange *adj* 1 ODD, peculiar, funny (*infml*), curious, queer, weird, bizarre, eccentric, abnormal, irregular, uncommon, unusual, exceptional, remarkable, extraordinary, mystifying, perplexing, unexplained. 2 NEW, novel, untried, unknown, unheard-of, unfamiliar, unacquainted, foreign, alien, exotic.
🖝 1 ordinary, common. 2 well-known, familiar.

stranger *n* newcomer, visitor, guest, non-member, outsider, foreigner, alien.
🖝 local, native.

strangle *n* throttle, choke, asphyxiate, suffocate, stifle, smother, suppress, gag, repress, inhibit.

strap *n* thong, tie, band, belt, leash.
v 1 BEAT, lash, whip, flog, belt. 2 FASTEN, secure, tie, bind.

stratagem *n* plan, scheme, plot, intrigue, ruse, ploy, trick, dodge, manoeuvre, device, artifice, wile, subterfuge.

strategic *adj* important, key, critical, decisive, crucial, vital, tactical, planned, calculated, deliberate, politic, diplomatic.
🖝 unimportant.

strategy *n* tactics, planning, policy, approach, procedure, plan, programme, design, scheme.

stray *v* wander (off), get lost, err, ramble, roam, rove, range, meander, straggle, drift, diverge, deviate, digress.
adj 1 LOST, abandoned, homeless, wandering, roaming. 2 RANDOM, chance, accidental, freak, odd, erratic.

streak *n* line, stroke, smear, band, stripe, strip, layer, vein, trace, dash, touch, element, strain.
v 1 BAND, stripe, fleck, striate, smear, daub. 2 SPEED, tear, hurtle, sprint, gallop, fly, dart, flash, whistle, zoom, whizz, sweep.

stream *n* 1 RIVER, creek, brook, beck, burn, rivulet, tributary. 2 CURRENT, drift, flow, run, gush, flood, deluge, cascade, torrent.
v issue, well, surge, run, flow, course, pour, spout, gush, flood, cascade.

streamer *n* ribbon, banner, pennant, pennon, flag, ensign, standard.

streamlined *adj* aerodynamic, smooth, sleek, graceful, efficient, well-run, smooth-running, rationalized, time-saving, organized, slick.
🖝 clumsy, inefficient.

strength *n* toughness, robustness, sturdiness, lustiness, brawn, muscle, sinew, power, might, force, vigour, energy, stamina, health, fitness, courage, fortitude, spirit, resolution, firmness, effectiveness, potency, concentration, intensity, vehemence.
🖝 weakness, feebleness, impotence.

strengthen v reinforce, brace, steel, fortify, buttress, bolster, support, toughen, harden, stiffen, consolidate, substantiate, corroborate, confirm, encourage, hearten, refresh, restore, invigorate, nourish, increase, heighten, intensify.
E3 weaken, undermine.

strenuous adj 1 *strenuous work*: hard, tough, demanding, gruelling, taxing, laborious, uphill, arduous, tiring, exhausting. 2 ACTIVE, energetic, vigorous, eager, earnest, determined, resolute, spirited, tireless, indefatigable.
E3 1 easy, effortless.

stress n 1 PRESSURE, strain, tension, worry, anxiety, weight, burden, trauma, hassle (*infml*). 2 EMPHASIS, accent, accentuation, beat, force, weight, importance, significance.
E3 1 relaxation.
v emphasize, accentuate, highlight, underline, underscore, repeat.
E3 understate, downplay.

stretch n 1 EXPANSE, spread, sweep, reach, extent, distance, space, area, tract. 2 PERIOD, time, term, spell, stint, run.
v pull, tighten, tauten, strain, tax, extend, lengthen, elongate, expand, spread, unfold, unroll, inflate, swell, reach.
E3 compress.

stretch out extend, relax, hold out, put out, lie down, reach.
E3 draw back.

strict adj 1 *a strict teacher*: stern, authoritarian, no-nonsense, firm, rigid, inflexible, stringent, rigorous, harsh, severe, austere. 2 EXACT, precise, accurate, literal, faithful, true, absolute, utter, total, complete, thoroughgoing, meticulous, scrupulous, particular, religious.
E3 1 easy-going (*infml*), flexible. 2 loose.

strident adj loud, clamorous,

vociferous, harsh, raucous, grating, rasping, shrill, screeching, unmusical, discordant, clashing, jarring, jangling.
E3 quiet, soft.

strife n conflict, discord, dissension, controversy, animosity, friction, rivalry, contention, quarrel, row, wrangling, struggle, fighting, combat, battle, warfare.
E3 peace.

strike n 1 INDUSTRIAL ACTION, work-to-rule, go-slow, stoppage, sit-in, walk-out, mutiny, revolt. 2 HIT, blow, stroke, raid, attack.
v 1 STOP WORK, down tools, work to rule, walk out, protest, mutiny, revolt. 2 HIT, knock, collide with, slap, smack, cuff, clout, thump, wallop (*infml*), beat, pound, hammer, buffet, raid, attack, afflict. 3 IMPRESS, affect, touch, register. 4 FIND, discover, unearth, uncover, encounter, reach.

strike out cross out, delete, strike through, cancel, strike off, remove.
E3 add.

striking adj noticeable, conspicuous, salient, outstanding, remarkable, extraordinary, memorable, impressive, dazzling, arresting, astonishing, stunning.
E3 unimpressive.

string n 1 *a piece of string*: twine, cord, rope, cable, line, strand, fibre. 2 SERIES, succession, sequence, chain, line, row, file, queue, procession, train.
v thread, link, connect, tie up, hang, suspend, festoon, loop.

stringent adj binding, strict, severe, rigorous, tough, rigid, inflexible, tight.
E3 lax, flexible.

strip¹ v peel, skin, flay, denude, divest, deprive, undress, disrobe, unclothe, uncover, expose, lay bare, bare, empty, clear, gut, ransack, pillage, plunder, loot.
E3 dress, clothe, cover.

study

strip[2] *n* ribbon, thong, strap, belt, sash, band, stripe, lath, slat, piece, bit, slip, shred.

stripe *n* band, line, bar, chevron, flash, streak, fleck, strip, belt.

strive *v* try, attempt, endeavour, struggle, strain, work, toil, labour, fight, contend, compete.

stroke *n* **1** CARESS, pat, rub. **2** BLOW, hit, knock, swipe. **3** SWEEP, flourish, movement, action, move, line.
v caress, fondle, pet, touch, pat, rub, massage.

stroll *v* saunter, amble, dawdle, ramble, wander.
n saunter, amble, walk, constitutional, turn, ramble.

strong *adj* **1** TOUGH, resilient, durable, hard-wearing, heavy-duty, robust, sturdy, firm, sound, lusty, strapping, stout, burly, well-built, beefy, brawny, muscular, sinewy, athletic, fit, healthy, hardy, powerful, mighty, potent. **2** INTENSE, deep, vivid, fierce, violent, vehement, keen, eager, zealous, fervent, ardent, dedicated, staunch, stalwart, determined, resolute, tenacious, strong-minded, strong-willed, self-assertive. **3** HIGHLY-FLAVOURED, piquant, hot, spicy, highly-seasoned, sharp, pungent, undiluted, concentrated. **4** *strong argument*: convincing, persuasive, cogent, effective, telling, forceful, weighty, compelling, urgent.
E3 **1** weak, feeble. **2** indecisive. **3** mild, bland. **4** unconvincing.

stronghold *n* citadel, bastion, fort, fortress, castle, keep, refuge.

structure *n* construction, erection, building, edifice, fabric, framework, form, shape, design, configuration, conformation, make-up, formation, arrangement, organization, set-up.
v construct, assemble, build, form, shape, design, arrange, organize.

struggle *v* strive, work, toil, labour, strain, agonize, fight, battle, wrestle, grapple, contend, compete, vie.
E3 yield, give in.
n difficulty, problem, effort, exertion, pains, agony, work, labour, toil, clash, conflict, strife, fight, battle, skirmish, encounter, combat, hostilities, contest.
E3 ease, submission, co-operation.

stub *n* end, stump, remnant, fag-end (*infml*), dog-end (*infml*), butt, counterfoil.

stubborn *adj* obstinate, stiff-necked, mulish, pig-headed, obdurate, intransigent, rigid, inflexible, unbending, unyielding, dogged, persistent, tenacious, headstrong, self-willed, wilful, refractory, difficult, unmanageable.
E3 compliant, flexible, yielding.

stuck *adj* **1** FAST, jammed, firm, fixed, fastened, joined, glued, cemented. **2** BEATEN, stumped (*infml*), baffled.
E3 **1** loose.

stuck-up (*infml*) *adj* snobbish, toffee-nosed (*infml*), supercilious, snooty (*infml*), haughty, high and mighty, condescending, proud, arrogant, conceited, bigheaded (*infml*).
E3 humble, modest.

student *n* undergraduate, postgraduate, scholar, schoolboy, schoolgirl, pupil, disciple, learner, trainee, apprentice.

studied *adj* deliberate, conscious, wilful, intentional, premeditated, planned, calculated, contrived, forced, unnatural, over-elaborate.
E3 unplanned, impulsive, natural.

studio *n* workshop, workroom.

studious *adj* scholarly, academic, intellectual, bookish, serious, thoughtful, reflective, diligent, hard-working, industrious, assiduous, careful, attentive, earnest, eager.
E3 lazy, idle, negligent.

study *v* read, learn, revise, cram, swot (*infml*), mug up (*infml*), read up, research, investigate, analyse, survey, scan, examine, scrutinize, peruse, pore over, contemplate, meditate, ponder, consider, deliberate.

n 1 READING, homework, preparation, learning, revision, cramming, swotting (*infml*), research, investigation, inquiry, analysis, examination, scrutiny, inspection, contemplation, consideration, attention. 2 REPORT, essay, thesis, paper, monograph, survey, review, critique. 3 OFFICE, den (*infml*).

Subjects of study include:
accountancy, agriculture, anatomy, anthropology, archaeology, architecture, art, astrology, astronomy, biology, botany, building studies, business studies, calligraphy, chemistry, CDT (craft, design and technology), civil engineering, the Classics, commerce, computer studies, cosmology, craft, dance, design, domestic science, drama, dressmaking, driving, ecology, economics, education, electronics, engineering, environmental studies, ethnology, eugenics, fashion, fitness, food technology, forensics, genetics, geography, geology, heraldry, history, home economics, horticulture, information technology (IT), journalism, languages, law, leisure studies, lexicography, linguistics, literature, logistics, management studies, marketing, mathematics, mechanics, media studies, medicine, metallurgy, metaphysics, meteorology, music, mythology, natural history, oceanography, ornithology, pathology, penology, personal and social education (PSE); personal, health and social education (PHSE), pharmacology, philosophy, photography, physics, physiology, politics, pottery, psychology,

religious studies, science, shorthand, social sciences, sociology, sport, statistics, surveying, technology, theology, typewriting, visual arts, word processing, writing, zoology.

stuff v 1 PACK, stow, load, fill, cram, crowd, force, push, shove, ram, wedge, jam, squeeze, compress. 2 GORGE, gormandise, overindulge, guzzle, gobble, sate, satiate.
🔄 unload, empty. 🔄 nibble.
n 1 MATERIAL, fabric, matter, substance, essence. 2 (*infml*) BELONGINGS, possessions, things, objects, articles, goods, luggage, paraphernalia, gear (*infml*), clobber (*infml*), kit, tackle, equipment, materials.

stuffing n padding, wadding, quilting, filling, force-meat.

stuffy adj 1 *a stuffy room*: musty, stale, airless, unventilated, suffocating, stifling, oppressive, heavy, close, muggy, sultry. 2 STAID, strait-laced, prim, conventional, old-fashioned, pompous, dull, dreary, uninteresting, stodgy.
🔄 1 airy, well-ventilated. 2 informal, modern, lively.

stumble v 1 TRIP, slip, fall, lurch, reel, stagger, flounder, blunder. 2 STAMMER, stutter, hesitate, falter.
stumble on come across, chance upon, happen upon, find, discover, encounter.

stumbling-block n obstacle, hurdle, barrier, bar, obstruction, hindrance, impediment, difficulty, snag.

stump n end, remnant, trunk, stub.
v (*infml*) defeat, outwit, confound, perplex, puzzle, baffle, mystify, confuse, bewilder, flummox (*infml*), bamboozle (*infml*), dumbfound.
🔄 assist.
stump up (*infml*) pay, hand over, fork out (*infml*), shell out (*infml*), donate, contribute, cough up (*infml*).
🔄 receive.

stun v amaze, astonish, astound, stagger, shock, daze, stupefy, dumbfound, flabbergast (infml), overcome, confound, confuse, bewilder.

stunning (infml) adj beautiful, lovely, gorgeous, ravishing, dazzling, brilliant, striking, impressive, spectacular, remarkable, wonderful, marvellous, great, sensational.
🖅 ugly, awful.

stunt[1] n feat, exploit, act, deed, enterprise, trick, turn, performance.

stunt[2] v stop, arrest, check, restrict, slow, retard, hinder, impede, dwarf.
🖅 promote, encourage.

stupefy v daze, stun, numb, dumbfound, shock, stagger, amaze, astound.

stupendous adj huge, enormous, gigantic, colossal, vast, prodigious, phenomenal, tremendous, breathtaking, overwhelming, staggering, stunning, amazing, astounding, fabulous, fantastic, superb, wonderful, marvellous.
🖅 ordinary, unimpressive.

stupid adj 1 SILLY, foolish, irresponsible, ill-advised, indiscreet, foolhardy, rash, senseless, mad, lunatic, brainless, half-witted, idiotic, imbecilic, moronic, feeble-minded, simple-minded, slow, dim, dull, dense, thick, dumb, dopey, crass, inane, puerile, mindless, futile, pointless, meaningless, nonsensical, absurd, ludicrous, ridiculous, laughable. 2 DAZED, groggy, stupefied, stunned, sluggish, semiconscious.
🖅 1 sensible, wise, clever, intelligent. 2 alert.

stupor n daze, stupefaction, torpor, lethargy, inertia, trance, coma, numbness, insensibility, unconsciousness.
🖅 alertness, consciousness.

sturdy adj strong, robust, durable, well-made, stout, substantial, solid, well-built, powerful, muscular, athletic, hardy, vigorous, flourishing, hearty, staunch, stalwart, steadfast, firm, resolute, determined.
🖅 weak, flimsy, puny.

stutter v stammer, hesitate, falter, stumble, mumble.

style n 1 APPEARANCE, cut, design, pattern, shape, form, sort, type, kind, genre, variety, category. 2 ELEGANCE, smartness, chic, flair, panache, stylishness, taste, polish, refinement, sophistication, urbanity, fashion, vogue, trend, mode, dressiness, flamboyance, affluence, luxury, grandeur. 3 style of working: technique, approach, method, manner, mode, fashion, way, custom. 4 WORDING, phrasing, expression, tone, tenor.
🖅 2 inelegance, tastelessness.
v 1 DESIGN, cut, tailor, fashion, shape, adapt. 2 DESIGNATE, term, name, call, address, title, dub, label.

stylish adj chic, fashionable, á la mode, modish, in vogue, voguish, trendy (infml), snappy, natty (infml), snazzy (infml), dressy, smart, elegant, classy (infml), polished, refined, sophisticated, urbane.
🖅 old-fashioned, shabby.

suave adj polite, courteous, charming, agreeable, affable, soft-spoken, smooth, unctuous, sophisticated, urbane, worldly.
🖅 rude, unsophisticated.

subconscious adj subliminal, unconscious, intuitive, inner, innermost, hidden, latent, repressed, suppressed.
🖅 conscious.

subdue v overcome, quell, suppress, repress, overpower, crush, defeat, conquer, vanquish, overrun, subject, subjugate, humble, break, tame, master, discipline, control, check, moderate, reduce, soften, quieten, damp, mellow.
🖅 arouse, awaken.

subdued adj 1 SAD, downcast, dejected, crestfallen, quiet, serious, grave, solemn. 2 QUIET, muted, hushed, soft, dim, shaded, sombre, sober, restrained, unobtrusive, low-key, subtle.
F3 1 lively, excited. 2 striking, obtrusive.

subject n 1 TOPIC, theme, matter, issue, question, point, case, affair, business, discipline, field. 2 NATIONAL, citizen, participant, client, patient, victim.
F3 1 monarch, ruler, master.
adj 1 LIABLE, disposed, prone, susceptible, vulnerable, open, exposed. 2 SUBJUGATED, captive, bound, obedient, answerable, subordinate, inferior, subservient, submissive. 3 DEPENDENT, contingent, conditional.
F3 1 vulnerable. 2 free, superior. 3 unconditional.
v expose, lay open, submit, subjugate, subdue.

subjection n subjugation, defeat, captivity, bondage, chains, shackles, slavery, enslavement, oppression, domination, mastery.

subjective adj biased, prejudiced, personal, individual, idiosyncratic, emotional, intuitive, instinctive.
F3 objective, unbiased, impartial.

sublime adj exalted, elevated, high, lofty, noble, majestic, great, grand, imposing, magnificent, glorious, transcendent, spiritual.
F3 lowly, base.

submerge v submerse, immerse, plunge, duck, dip, sink, drown, engulf, overwhelm, swamp, flood, inundate, deluge.
F3 surface.

submerged adj submersed, immersed, underwater, sunk, sunken, drowned, swamped, inundated, hidden, concealed, unseen.

submission n 1 SURRENDER, capitulation, resignation, acquiescence, assent, compliance, obedience, deference, submissiveness, meekness, passivity. 2 PRESENTATION, offering, contribution, entry, suggestion, proposal.
F3 1 intransigence, intractability.

submissive adj yielding, unresisting, resigned, patient, uncomplaining, accommodating, biddable, obedient, deferential, ingratiating, subservient, humble, meek, docile, subdued, passive.
F3 intransigent, intractable.

submit v 1 YIELD, give in, surrender, capitulate, knuckle under, bow, bend, stoop, succumb, agree, comply. 2 PRESENT, tender, offer, put forward, suggest, propose, table, state, claim, argue.
F3 1 resist. 2 withdraw.

subordinate adj secondary, auxiliary, ancillary, subsidiary, dependent, inferior, lower, junior, minor, lesser.
F3 superior, senior.
n inferior, junior, assistant, attendant, second, aide, dependant, underling (infml).
F3 superior, boss.

subscribe v 1 subscribe to a theory: support, endorse, back, advocate, approve, agree. 2 GIVE, donate, contribute.

subscription n membership fee, dues, payment, donation, contribution, offering, gift.

subsequent adj following, later, future, next, succeeding, consequent, resulting, ensuing.
F3 previous, earlier.

subside v sink, collapse, settle, descend, fall, drop, lower, decrease, lessen, diminish, dwindle, decline, wane, ebb, recede, moderate, abate, die down, quieten, slacken, ease.
F3 rise, increase.

subsidiary adj auxiliary, supplementary, additional, ancillary, assistant, supporting, contributory, secondary, subordinate, lesser, minor.
🔁 primary, chief, major.
n branch, offshoot, division, section, part.

subsidize v support, back, underwrite, sponsor, finance, fund, aid, promote.

subsidy n grant, allowance, assistance, help, aid, contribution, sponsorship, finance, support, backing.

subsistence n living, survival, existence, livelihood, maintenance, support, keep, sustenance, nourishment, food, provisions, rations.

substance n **1** MATTER, material, stuff, fabric, essence, pith, entity, body, solidity, concreteness, reality, actuality, ground, foundation. **2** SUBJECT, subject-matter, theme, gist, meaning, significance, force.

substandard adj second-rate, inferior, imperfect, damaged, shoddy, poor, inadequate, unacceptable.
🔁 first-rate, superior, perfect.

substantial adj large, big, sizable, ample, generous, great, considerable, significant, important, worthwhile, massive, bulky, hefty, well-built, stout, sturdy, strong, sound, durable.
🔁 small, insignificant, weak.

substantiate v prove, verify, confirm, support, corroborate, authenticate, validate.
🔁 disprove, refute.

substitute v **1** CHANGE, exchange, swap, switch, interchange, replace. **2** STAND IN, fill in (infml), cover, deputize, understudy, relieve.
n reserve, stand-by, temp (infml), supply, locum, understudy, stand-in, replacement, relief, surrogate, proxy, agent, deputy, makeshift, stopgap.
adj reserve, temporary, acting,

surrogate, proxy, replacement, alternative.

subterfuge n trick, stratagem, scheme, ploy, ruse, dodge, manoeuvre, machination, deviousness, evasion, deception, artifice, pretence, excuse.
🔁 openness, honesty.

subtle adj **1** DELICATE, understated, implied, indirect, slight, tenuous, faint, mild, fine, nice, refined, sophisticated, deep, profound. **2** ARTFUL, cunning, crafty, sly, devious, shrewd, astute.
🔁 **1** blatant, obvious. **2** artless, open.

subtract v deduct, take away, remove, withdraw, debit, detract, diminish.
🔁 add.

suburbs n suburbia, commuter belt, residential area, outskirts.
🔁 centre, heart.

subversive adj seditious, treasonous, treacherous, traitorous, inflammatory, incendiary, disruptive, riotous, weakening, undermining, destructive.
🔁 loyal.
n seditionist, terrorist, freedom fighter, dissident, traitor, quisling, fifth columnist.

succeed v **1** TRIUMPH, make it, get on, thrive, flourish, prosper, make good, manage, work. **2** winter succeeds autumn: follow, replace, result, ensue.
🔁 **1** fail. **2** precede.

succeeding adj following, next, subsequent, ensuing, coming, to come, later, successive.
🔁 previous, earlier.

success n **1** TRIUMPH, victory, luck, fortune, prosperity, fame, eminence, happiness. **2** CELEBRITY, star, somebody, winner, bestseller, hit, sensation.
🔁 **1** failure, disaster.

successful adj **1** VICTORIOUS, winning, lucky, fortunate, prosperous, wealthy, thriving, flourishing, booming, moneymaking, lucrative, profitable, rewarding, satisfying, fruitful, productive. **2** *a successful writer*: famous, well-known, popular, leading, bestselling, top, unbeaten.

≢ 1 unsuccessful, unprofitable, fruitless. **2** unknown.

succession *n* sequence, series, order, progression, run, chain, string, cycle, continuation, flow, course, line, train, procession.

successive *adj* consecutive, sequential, following, succeeding.

succinct *adj* short, brief, terse, pithy, concise, compact, condensed, summary.

≢ long, lengthy, wordy, verbose.

succulent *adj* fleshy, juicy, moist, luscious, mouthwatering, lush, rich, mellow.

≢ dry.

succumb *v* give way, yield, give in, submit, knuckle under, surrender, capitulate, collapse, fall.

≢ overcome, master.

suck *v* draw in, imbibe, absorb, soak up, extract, drain.

sudden *adj* unexpected, unforeseen, surprising, startling, abrupt, sharp, quick, swift, rapid, prompt, hurried, hasty, rash, impetuous, impulsive, snap (*infml*).

≢ expected, predictable, gradual, slow.

sue *v* prosecute, charge, indict, summon, solicit, appeal.

suffer *v* **1** HURT, ache, agonize, grieve, sorrow. **2** BEAR, support, tolerate, endure, sustain, experience, undergo, go through, feel.

suffering *n* pain, discomfort, agony, anguish, affliction, distress, misery, hardship, ordeal, torment, torture.

≢ ease, comfort.

sufficient *adj* enough, adequate, satisfactory, effective.

≢ insufficient, inadequate.

suffocate *v* asphyxiate, smother, stifle, choke, strangle, throttle.

suggest *v* **1** PROPOSE, put forward, advocate, recommend, advise, counsel. **2** IMPLY, insinuate, hint, intimate, evoke, indicate.

suggestion *n* **1** PROPOSAL, proposition, motion, recommendation, idea, plan. **2** IMPLICATION, insinuation, innuendo, hint, intimation, suspicion, trace, indication.

suggestive *adj* **1** EVOCATIVE, reminiscent, expressive, meaning, indicative. **2** *a suggestive remark*: indecent, immodest, improper, indelicate, off-colour, risqué, bawdy, dirty, smutty, provocative.

≢ 1 inexpressive. **2** decent, clean.

suit *v* **1** SATISFY, gratify, please, answer, match, tally, agree, correspond, harmonize. **2** FIT, befit, become, tailor, adapt, adjust, accommodate, modify.

≢ 1 displease, clash.

n outfit, costume, dress, clothing.

suitable *adj* appropriate, fitting, convenient, opportune, suited, due, apt, apposite, relevant, applicable, fit, adequate, satisfactory, acceptable, befitting, becoming, seemly, proper, right.

≢ unsuitable, inappropriate.

sulk *v* mope, brood, pout.

sulky *adj* brooding, moody, morose, resentful, grudging, disgruntled, put out, cross, bad-tempered, sullen, aloof, unsociable.

≢ cheerful, good-tempered, sociable.

sullen *adj* **1** SULKY, moody, morose, glum, gloomy, silent, surly, sour, perverse, obstinate, stubborn. **2** DARK, gloomy, sombre, dismal, cheerless, dull, leaden, heavy.

≢ 1 cheerful, happy. **2** fine, clear.

sully *v* dirty, soil, defile, pollute, contaminate, taint, spoil, mar, spot, blemish, besmirch, stain, tarnish, disgrace, dishonour.

cleanse, honour.

sultry adj hot, sweltering, stifling, stuffy, oppressive, close, humid, muggy, sticky.
cool, cold.

sum n total, sum total, aggregate, whole, entirety, number, quantity, amount, tally, reckoning, score, result.

sum up summarize, review, recapitulate, conclude, close.

summarize v outline, précis, condense, abridge, abbreviate, shorten, sum up, encapsulate, review.
expand (on).

summary n synopsis, résumé, outline, abstract, précis, condensation, digest, compendium, abridgement, summing-up, review, recapitulation.
adj short, succinct, brief, cursory, hasty, prompt, direct, unceremonious, arbitrary.
lengthy, careful.

summit n top, peak, pinnacle, apex, point, crown, head, zenith, acme, culmination, height.
bottom, foot, nadir.

summon v call, send for, invite, bid, beckon, gather, assemble, convene, rally, muster, mobilize, rouse, arouse.
dismiss.

sumptuous adj luxurious, plush, lavish, extravagant, opulent, rich, costly, expensive, dear, splendid, magnificent, gorgeous, superb, grand.
plain, poor.

sunbathe v sun, bask, tan, brown, bake.

sunburnt adj brown, tanned, bronzed, weather-beaten, burnt, red, blistered, peeling.
pale.

sundry adj various, diverse, miscellaneous, assorted, varied, different, several, some, a few.

sunken adj submerged, buried, recessed, lower, depressed, concave,
hollow, haggard, drawn.

sunny adj **1** FINE, cloudless, clear, summery, sunshiny, sunlit, bright, brilliant. **2** CHEERFUL, happy, joyful, smiling, beaming, radiant, light-hearted, buoyant, optimistic, pleasant.
1 sunless, dull. **2** gloomy.

sunrise n dawn, crack of dawn, daybreak, daylight.

sunset n sundown, dusk, twilight, gloaming, evening, nightfall.

superb adj excellent, first-rate, first-class, superior, choice, fine, exquisite, gorgeous, magnificent, splendid, grand, wonderful, marvellous, admirable, impressive, breathtaking.
bad, poor, inferior.

superficial adj surface, external, exterior, outward, apparent, seeming, cosmetic, skin-deep, shallow, slight, trivial, lightweight, frivolous, casual, cursory, sketchy, hasty, hurried, passing.
internal, deep, thorough.

superfluous adj extra, spare, excess, surplus, remaining, redundant, supernumerary, unnecessary, needless, unwanted, uncalled-for, excessive.
necessary, needed, wanted.

superintend v supervise, oversee, overlook, inspect, run, manage, administer, direct, control, handle.

superior adj **1** EXCELLENT, first-class, first-rate, top-notch (*infml*), top-flight (*infml*), high-class, exclusive, choice, select, fine, de luxe, admirable, distinguished, exceptional, unrivalled, par excellence. **2** BETTER, preferred, greater, higher, senior. **3** HAUGHTY, lordly, pretentious, snobbish, snooty (*infml*), supercilious, disdainful, condescending, patronizing.
1 inferior, average. **2** worse, lower. **3** humble.
n senior, elder, better, boss, chief, principal, director, manager, foreman,

supervisor.

■ inferior, junior, assistant.

superiority n advantage, lead, edge, supremacy, ascendancy, pre-eminence, predominance.

■ inferiority.

superlative adj best, greatest, highest, supreme, transcendent, unbeatable, unrivalled, unparalleled, matchless, peerless, unsurpassed, unbeaten, consummate, excellent, outstanding.

■ poor, average.

supernatural adj paranormal, unnatural, abnormal, metaphysical, spiritual, psychic, mystic, occult, hidden, mysterious, miraculous, magical, phantom, ghostly.

■ natural, normal.

supersede v succeed, replace, supplant, usurp, oust, displace, remove.

superstition n myth, old wives' tale, fallacy, delusion, illusion.

superstitious adj mythical, false, fallacious, irrational, groundless, delusive, illusory.

■ rational, logical.

supervise v oversee, watch over, look after, superintend, run, manage, administer, direct, conduct, preside over, control, handle.

supervision n surveillance, care, charge, superintendence, oversight, running, management, administration, direction, control, guidance, instruction.

supervisor n overseer, inspector, superintendent, boss, chief, director, administrator, manager, foreman, forewoman.

supplant v replace, supersede, usurp, oust, displace, remove, overthrow, topple, unseat.

supple adj flexible, bending, pliant, pliable, plastic, lithe, graceful, loose-limbed, double-jointed, elastic.

■ stiff, rigid, inflexible.

supplement n addition, extra,

insert, pull-out, addendum, appendix, codicil, postscript, sequel.

v add to, augment, boost, reinforce, fill up, top up, complement, extend, eke out.

■ deplete, use up.

supplementary adj additional, extra, auxiliary, secondary, complementary, accompanying.

supplier n dealer, seller, vendor, wholesaler, retailer.

supplies n stores, provisions, food, equipment, materials, necessities.

supply v provide, furnish, equip, outfit, stock, fill, replenish, give, donate, grant, endow, contribute, yield, produce, sell.

■ take, receive.

n source, amount, quantity, stock, fund, reservoir, store, reserve, stockpile, hoard, cache.

■ lack.

support v **1** BACK, second, defend, champion, advocate, promote, foster, help, aid, assist, rally round, finance, fund, subsidize, underwrite. **2** HOLD UP, bear, carry, sustain, brace, reinforce, strengthen, prop, buttress, bolster. **3** MAINTAIN, keep, provide for, feed, nourish. **4** support a statement: endorse, confirm, verify, authenticate, corroborate, substantiate, document.

■ **1** oppose. **3** live off. **4** contradict.

n **1** BACKING, allegiance, loyalty, defence, protection, patronage, sponsorship, approval, encouragement, comfort, relief, help, aid, assistance. **2** PROP, stay, post, pillar, brace, crutch, foundation, underpinning.

■ **1** opposition, hostility.

supporter n fan, follower, adherent, advocate, champion, defender, seconder, patron, sponsor, helper, ally, friend.

■ opponent.

supportive adj helpful, caring, attentive, sympathetic,

understanding, comforting, reassuring, encouraging.

≠ discouraging.

suppose v assume, presume, expect, infer, conclude, guess, conjecture, surmise, believe, think, consider, judge, imagine, conceive, fancy, pretend, postulate, hypothesize.

≠ know.

supposed adj alleged, reported, rumoured, assumed, presumed, reputed, putative, imagined, hypothetical.

≠ known, certain.

supposed to meant to, intended to, expected to, required to, obliged to.

supposition n assumption, presumption, guess, conjecture, speculation, theory, hypothesis, idea, notion.

≠ knowledge.

suppress v crush, stamp out, quash, quell, subdue, stop, silence, censor, stifle, smother, strangle, conceal, withhold, hold back, contain, restrain, check, repress, inhibit.

≠ encourage, incite.

supreme adj best, greatest, highest, top, crowning, culminating, first, leading, foremost, chief, principal, head, sovereign, pre-eminent, predominant, prevailing, world-beating, unsurpassed, second-to-none, incomparable, matchless, consummate, transcendent, superlative, prime, ultimate, extreme, final.

≠ lowly, poor.

sure adj **1** CERTAIN, convinced, assured, confident, decided, positive, definite, unmistakable, clear, accurate, precise, unquestionable, indisputable, undoubted, undeniable, irrevocable, inevitable, bound. **2** SAFE, secure, fast, solid, firm, steady, stable, guaranteed, reliable, dependable, trustworthy, steadfast, unwavering, unerring, unfailing, infallible, effective.

≠ **1** unsure, uncertain, doubtful. **2** unsafe, insecure.

surface n outside, exterior, façade, veneer, covering, skin, top, side, face, plane.

≠ inside, interior.

v rise, arise, come up, emerge, appear, materialise, come to light.

≠ sink, disappear, vanish.

surly adj gruff, brusque, churlish, ungracious, bad-tempered, cross, crabbed, grouchy, crusty, sullen, sulky, morose.

≠ friendly, polite.

surpass v beat, outdo, exceed, outstrip, better, excel, transcend, outshine, eclipse.

surplus n excess, residue, remainder, balance, superfluity, glut, surfeit.

≠ lack, shortage.

adj excess, superfluous, redundant, extra, spare, remaining, unused.

surprise v startle, amaze, astonish, astound, stagger, flabbergast (infml), bewilder, confuse, nonplus, disconcert, dismay.

n amazement, astonishment, incredulity, wonder, bewilderment, dismay, shock, start, bombshell, revelation.

≠ composure.

surprised adj startled, amazed, astonished, astounded, staggered, flabbergasted (infml), thunderstruck, dumbfounded, speechless, shocked, nonplussed.

≠ unsurprised, composed.

surprising adj amazing, astonishing, astounding, staggering, stunning, incredible, extraordinary, remarkable, startling, unexpected, unforeseen.

≠ unsurprising, expected.

surrender v capitulate, submit, resign, concede, yield, give in, cede, give up, quit, relinquish, abandon, renounce, forgo, waive.

n capitulation, resignation,

submission, yielding, relinquishment, renunciation.

surreptitious adj furtive, stealthy, sly, covert, veiled, hidden, secret, clandestine, underhand, unauthorized.

Ea open, obvious.

surround v encircle, ring, girdle, encompass, envelop, encase, enclose, hem in, besiege.

surrounding adj encircling, bordering, adjacent, adjoining, neighbouring, nearby.

surroundings n neighbourhood, vicinity, locality, setting, environment, background, milieu, ambience.

survey v view, contemplate, observe, supervise, scan, scrutinize, examine, inspect, study, research, review, consider, estimate, evaluate, assess, measure, plot, plan, map, chart, reconnoitre.

n review, overview, scrutiny, examination, inspection, study, pull, appraisal, assessment, measurement.

survive v outlive, outlast, endure, last, stay, remain, live, exist, withstand, weather.

Ea succumb, die.

susceptible adj liable, prone, inclined, disposed, given, subject, receptive, responsive, impressionable, suggestible, weak, vulnerable, open, sensitive, tender.

Ea resistant, immune.

suspect v 1 DOUBT, distrust, mistrust, call into question. 2 *I suspect you're right*: believe, fancy, feel, guess, conjecture, speculate, surmise, suppose, consider, conclude, infer.

adj suspicious, doubtful, dubious, questionable, debatable, unreliable, iffy (*sl*), dodgy (*infml*), fishy (*infml*).

Ea acceptable, reliable.

suspend v 1 HANG, dangle, swing. 2 ADJOURN, interrupt, discontinue, cease, delay, defer, postpone, put off,

shelve. 3 EXPEL, dismiss, exclude, debar.

Ea 2 continue. 3 restore, reinstate.

suspense n uncertainty, insecurity, anxiety, tension, apprehension, anticipation, expectation, expectancy, excitement.

Ea certainty, knowledge.

suspension n adjournment, interruption, break, intermission, respite, remission, stay, moratorium, delay, deferral, postponement, abeyance.

Ea continuation.

suspicion n 1 DOUBT, scepticism, distrust, mistrust, wariness, caution, misgiving, apprehension. 2 TRACE, hint, suggestion, soupçon, touch, tinge, shade, glimmer, shadow. 3 IDEA, notion, hunch.

Ea 1 trust.

suspicious adj 1 DOUBTFUL, sceptical, unbelieving, suspecting, distrustful, mistrustful, wary, chary, apprehensive, uneasy. 2 DUBIOUS, questionable, suspect, irregular, shifty, shady (*infml*), dodgy (*infml*), fishy (*infml*).

Ea 1 trustful, confident. 2 trustworthy, innocent.

sustain v 1 NOURISH, provide for, nurture, foster, help, aid, assist, comfort, relieve, support, uphold, endorse, bear, carry. 2 MAINTAIN, keep going, keep up, continue, prolong, hold.

sustained adj prolonged, protracted, long-drawn-out, steady, continuous, constant, perpetual, unremitting.

Ea broken, interrupted, intermittent, spasmodic.

sustenance n nourishment, food, provisions, fare, maintenance, subsistence, livelihood.

swagger v bluster, boast, crow, brag, swank (*infml*), parade, strut.

n bluster, show, ostentation, arrogance.

swallow v **1** CONSUME, devour, eat, gobble up, guzzle, drink, quaff, knock back (*infml*), gulp, down (*infml*). **2** ENGULF, enfold, envelop, swallow up, absorb, assimilate, accept, believe.

swamp n bog, marsh, fen, slough, quagmire, quicksand, mire, mud. v flood, inundate, deluge, engulf, submerge, sink, drench, saturate, waterlog, overload, overwhelm, besiege, beset.

swap, swop v exchange, transpose, switch, interchange, barter, trade, traffic.

swarm n crowd, throng, mob, mass, multitude, myriad, host, army, horde, herd, flock, drove, shoal. v **1** flock, flood, stream, mass, congregate, crowd, throng. **2** *swarming with tourists*: teem, crawl, bristle, abound.

swarthy adj dark, dark-skinned, dark-complexioned, dusky, black, brown, tanned.
🖪 fair, pale.

sway v **1** ROCK, roll, lurch, swing, wave, oscillate, fluctuate, bend, incline, lean, divert, veer, swerve. **2** INFLUENCE, affect, persuade, induce, convince, convert, overrule, dominate, govern.

swear v **1** VOW, promise, pledge, avow, attest, asseverate, testify, affirm, assert, declare, insist. **2** CURSE, blaspheme.

swear-word n expletive, four-letter word, curse, oath, imprecation, obscenity, profanity, blasphemy, swearing, bad language.

sweat n **1** PERSPIRATION, moisture, stickiness. **2** ANXIETY, worry, agitation, panic. **3** TOIL, labour, drudgery, chore.
v perspire, swelter, exude.

sweaty adj damp, moist, clammy, sticky, sweating, perspiring.
🖪 dry, cool.

sweep v **1** *sweep the floor*: brush, dust, clean, clear, remove. **2** PASS, sail, fly, glide, scud, skim, glance, whisk, tear, hurtle.
n arc, curve, bend, swing, stroke, movement, gesture, compass, scope, range, extent, span, stretch, expanse, vista.

sweeping adj general, global, all-inclusive, all-embracing, blanket, across-the-board, broad, wide-ranging, extensive, far-reaching, comprehensive, thoroughgoing, radical, wholesale, indiscriminate, oversimplified, simplistic.
🖪 specific, narrow.

sweet adj **1** SUGARY, syrupy, sweetened, honeyed, saccharine, luscious, delicious. **2** PLEASANT, delightful, lovely, attractive, beautiful, pretty, winsome, cute, appealing, lovable, charming, agreeable, amiable, affectionate, tender, kind, treasured, precious, dear, darling. **3** FRESH, clean, wholesome, pure, clear, perfumed, fragrant, aromatic, balmy. **4** *sweet music*: melodious, tuneful, harmonious, euphonious, musical, dulcet, soft, mellow.
🖪 **1** savoury, salty, sour, bitter. **2** unpleasant, nasty, ugly. **3** foul. **4** discordant.
n dessert, pudding, afters (*infml*).

sweets

Sweets include: barley sugar, bull's eye, butterscotch, caramel, chewing-gum, chocolate, fondant, fruit pastille, fudge, gobstopper, gumdrop, humbug, jelly, jelly bean, liquorice, liquorice allsort, lollipop, Mars®, marshmallow, marzipan, nougat, peppermint, praline, rock, Edinburgh rock, toffee, toffee apple, truffle, Turkish delight.

sweeten v sugar, honey, mellow, soften, soothe, appease, temper, cushion.

swell *v* expand, dilate, inflate, blow up, puff up, bloat, distend, fatten, bulge, balloon, billow, surge, rise, mount, increase, enlarge, extend, grow, augment, heighten, intensify.
F3 shrink, contract, decrease, dwindle.
n billow, wave, undulation, surge, rise, increase, enlargement.

swelling *n* lump, tumour, bump, bruise, blister, boil, inflammation, bulge, protuberance, puffiness, distension, enlargement.

sweltering *adj* hot, tropical, baking, scorching, stifling, suffocating, airless, oppressive, sultry, steamy, sticky, humid.
F3 cold, cool, fresh, breezy, airy.

swerve *v* turn, bend, incline, veer, swing, shift, deviate, stray, wander, diverge, deflect, sheer.

swift *adj* fast, quick, rapid, speedy, express, flying, hurried, hasty, short, brief, sudden, prompt, ready, agile, nimble, nippy (*infml*).
F3 slow, sluggish, unhurried.

swimsuit *n* swimming costume, bathing-costume, bathing-suit, bikini, trunks.

swindle *v* cheat, defraud, diddle, do (*infml*), overcharge, fleece, rip off (*sl*), trick, deceive, dupe, con (*infml*), bamboozle (*infml*).
n fraud, fiddle, racket, sharp practice, double-dealing, trickery, deception, con (*infml*), rip-off (*sl*).

swindler *n* cheat, fraud, impostor, con man (*infml*), trickster, shark, rogue, rascal.

swing *v* hang, suspend, dangle, wave, brandish, sway, rock, oscillate, vibrate, fluctuate, vary, veer, swerve, turn, whirl, twirl, spin, rotate.
n sway, rock, oscillation, vibration, fluctuation, variation, change, shift, movement, motion, rhythm.

swingeing *adj* harsh, severe, stringent, drastic, punishing, devastating, excessive, extortionate, oppressive, heavy.
F3 mild.

swipe *v* **1** HIT, strike, lunge, lash out, slap, wallop (*infml*), sock (*sl*). **2** (*infml*) STEAL, pilfer, lift, pinch (*infml*).
n stroke, blow, slap, smack, clout, whack (*infml*), wallop (*infml*).

swirl *v* churn, agitate, spin, twirl, whirl, wheel, eddy, twist, curl.

switch *v* change, exchange, swap, trade, interchange, transpose, substitute, replace, shift, rearrange, turn, veer, deviate, divert, deflect.
n change, alteration, shift, exchange, swap, interchange, substitution, replacement.

swivel *v* pivot, spin, rotate, revolve, turn, twirl, pirouette, gyrate, wheel.

swollen *adj* bloated, distended, inflated, tumid, puffed up, puffy, inflamed, enlarged, bulbous, bulging.
F3 shrunken, shrivelled.

swoop *v* dive, plunge, drop, fall, descend, stoop, pounce, lunge, rush.
n dive, plunge, drop, descent, pounce, lunge, rush, attack, onslaught.

swop *see* **swap**.

sword *n* blade, foil, rapier, sabre, scimitar.

swot (*infml*) *v* study, work, learn, memorize, revise, cram, mug up (*infml*), bone up (*sl*).

syllabus *n* curriculum, course, programme, schedule, plan.

symbol *n* sign, token, representation, mark, emblem, badge, logo, character, ideograph, figure, image.

> *Symbols include*: badge, brand, cipher, coat of arms, crest, emblem, hieroglyph, icon, ideogram, insignia, logo, logogram, monogram, motif, pictograph, swastika, token, totem, trademark; ampersand, asterisk, caret, dagger, double-dagger, obelus.

symbolic *adj* symbolical, representative, emblematic, token, figurative, metaphorical, allegorical, meaningful, significant.

symbolize *v* represent, stand for, denote, mean, signify, typify, exemplify, epitomize, personify.

symmetrical *adj* balanced, even, regular, parallel, corresponding, proportional.
⊟ asymmetrical, irregular.

symmetry *n* balance, evenness, regularity, parallelism, correspondence, proportion, harmony, agreement.
⊟ asymmetry, irregularity.

sympathetic *adj* understanding, appreciative, supportive, comforting, consoling, commiserating, pitying, interested, concerned, solicitous, caring, compassionate, tender, kind, warm-hearted, well-disposed, affectionate, agreeable, friendly, congenial, like-minded, compatible.
⊟ unsympathetic, indifferent, callous, antipathetic.

sympathize *v* understand, comfort, commiserate, pity, feel for, empathize, identify with, respond to.
⊟ ignore, disregard.

sympathy *n* **1** UNDERSTANDING, comfort, consolation, condolences, commiseration, pity, compassion, tenderness, kindness, warmth, thoughtfulness, empathy, fellow-feeling, affinity, rapport.
2 AGREEMENT, accord, correspondence, harmony.
⊟ **1** indifference, insensitivity, callousness. **2** disagreement.

symptom *n* sign, indication, evidence, manifestation, expression, feature, characteristic, mark, token, warning.

symptomatic *adj* indicative, typical, characteristic, associated, suggestive.

synonymous *adj* interchangeable, substitutable, the same, identical, similar, comparable, tantamount, equivalent, corresponding.
⊟ antonymous, opposite.

synopsis *n* outline, abstract, summary, résumé, précis, condensation, digest, abridgement, review, recapitulation.

synthesize *v* unite, combine, amalgamate, integrate, merge, blend, compound, alloy, fuse, weld, coalesce, unify.
⊟ separate, analyse, resolve.

synthetic *adj* manufactured, man-made, simulated, artificial, ersatz, imitation, fake, bogus, mock, sham, pseudo.
⊟ genuine, real, natural.

system *n* **1** METHOD, mode, technique, procedure, process, routine, practice, usage, rule.
2 ORGANIZATION, structure, set-up, systematization, co-ordination, orderliness, methodology, logic, classification, arrangement, order, plan, scheme.

systematic *adj* methodical, logical, ordered, well-ordered, planned, well-planned, organized, well-organized, structured, systematized, standardized, orderly, businesslike, efficient.
⊟ unsystematic, arbitrary, disorderly, inefficient.

T

tab *n* flap, tag, marker, label, sticker, ticket.

table *n* **1** BOARD, slab, counter, worktop, desk, bench, stand.

2 DIAGRAM, chart, graph, timetable, schedule, programme, list, inventory, catalogue, index, register, record.
v propose, suggest, submit, put forward.

taboo *adj* forbidden, prohibited, banned, proscribed, unacceptable, unmentionable, unthinkable.
▪ permitted, acceptable.
n ban, interdiction, prohibition, restriction, anathema, curse.

tacit *adj* unspoken, unexpressed, unvoiced, silent, understood, implicit, implied, inferred.
▪ express, explicit.

taciturn *adj* silent, quiet, uncommunicative, unforthcoming, reticent, reserved, withdrawn, aloof, distant, cold.
▪ talkative, communicative, forthcoming.

tack *n* **1** NAIL, pin, drawing-pin, staple. **2** COURSE, path, bearing, heading, direction, line, approach, method, way, technique, procedure, plan, tactic, attack.
v add, append, attach, affix, fasten, fix, nail, pin, staple, stitch, baste.

tackle *n* **1** *a rugby tackle*: attack, challenge, interception, intervention, block. **2** EQUIPMENT, tools, implements, apparatus, rig, outfit, gear, trappings, paraphernalia.
v **1** BEGIN, embark on, set about, try, attempt, undertake, take on, challenge, confront, encounter, face up to, grapple with, deal with, attend to, handle, grab, seize, grasp. **2** INTERCEPT, block, halt, stop.
▪ **1** avoid, sidestep.

tact *n* tactfulness, diplomacy, discretion, prudence, delicacy, sensitivity, perception, discernment, judgement, understanding, thoughtfulness, consideration, skill, adroitness, finesse.
▪ tactlessness, indiscretion.

tactful *adj* diplomatic, discreet, politic, judicious, prudent, careful,

delicate, subtle, sensitive, perceptive, discerning, understanding, thoughtful, considerate, polite, skilful, adroit.
▪ tactless, indiscreet, thoughtless, rude.

tactic *n* approach, course, way, means, method, procedure, plan, stratagem, scheme, ruse, ploy, subterfuge, trick, device, shift, move, manoeuvre.

tactical *adj* strategic, planned, calculated, artful, cunning, shrewd, skilful, clever, smart, prudent, politic, judicious.

tactics *n* strategy, campaign, plan, policy, approach, line of attack, moves, manoeuvres.

tactless *adj* undiplomatic, indiscreet, indelicate, inappropriate, impolitic, imprudent, careless, clumsy, blundering, insensitive, unfeeling, hurtful, unkind, thoughtless, inconsiderate, rude, impolite, discourteous.
▪ tactful, diplomatic, discreet.

tag *n* label, sticker, tab, ticket, mark, identification, note, slip, docket.
v **1** LABEL, mark, identify, designate, term, call, name, christen, nickname, style, dub. **2** ADD, append, annex, adjoin, affix, fasten.

tag along follow, shadow, tail, trail, accompany.

tail *n* end, extremity, rear, rear end, rump, behind (*infml*), posterior (*infml*), appendage.
v follow, pursue, shadow, dog, stalk, track, trail.

tail off decrease, decline, drop, fall away, fade, wane, dwindle, taper off, peter out, die (out).
▪ increase, grow.

tailor *n* outfitter, dressmaker.
v fit, suit, cut, trim, style, fashion, shape, mould, alter, modify, adapt, adjust, accommodate.

tailor-made *adj* made-to-measure, custom-built, ideal, perfect, right, suited, fitted.

☒ unsuitable.

taint *v* contaminate, infect, pollute, adulterate, corrupt, deprave, stain, blemish, blot, smear, tarnish, blacken, dirty, soil, muddy, defile, sully, harm, damage, blight, spoil, ruin, shame, disgrace, dishonour. *n* contamination, infection, pollution, corruption, stain, blemish, fault, flaw, defect, spot, blot, smear, stigma, shame, disgrace, dishonour.

take *v* **1** SEIZE, grab, snatch, grasp, hold, catch, capture, get, obtain, acquire, secure, gain, win, derive, adopt, assume, pick, choose, select, accept, receive. **2** REMOVE, eliminate, take away, subtract, deduct, steal, filch, purloin, nick (*infml*), pinch (*infml*), appropriate, abduct, carry off. **3** NEED, necessitate, require, demand, call for. **4** *take me home*: convey, carry, bring, transport, ferry, accompany, escort, lead, guide, conduct, usher. **5** BEAR, tolerate, stand, stomach, abide, endure, suffer, undergo, withstand.

☒ **1** leave, refuse. **2** replace, put back.

take aback surprise, astonish, astound, stagger, stun, startle, disconcert, bewilder, dismay, upset.

take apart take to pieces, dismantle, disassemble, analyse.

take back reclaim, repossess, withdraw, retract, recant, repudiate, deny, eat one's words.

take down 1 DISMANTLE, disassemble, demolish, raze, level, lower. **2** NOTE, record, write down, put down, set down, transcribe.

take in 1 ABSORB, assimilate, digest, realize, appreciate, understand, comprehend, grasp, admit, receive, shelter, accommodate, contain, include, comprise, incorporate, embrace, encompass, cover. **2** DECEIVE, fool, dupe, con (*infml*), mislead, trick, hoodwink, bamboozle (*infml*), cheat, swindle.

take off 1 REMOVE, doff, divest, shed, discard, drop. **2** LEAVE, depart, go, decamp, disappear. **3** IMITATE, mimic, parody, caricature, satirize, mock, send up.

take on 1 ACCEPT, assume, acquire, undertake, tackle, face, contend with, fight, oppose. **2** *take on staff*: employ, hire, enlist, recruit, engage, retain.

take up 1 OCCUPY, fill, engage, engross, absorb, monopolize, use up. **2** *take up a hobby*: start, begin, embark on, pursue, carry on, continue. **3** RAISE, lift. **4** ACCEPT, adopt, assume.

take-off *n* imitation, mimicry, impersonation, parody, caricature, spoof, send-up, travesty.

takeover *n* merger, amalgamation, combination, incorporation, coup.

takings *n* receipts, gate, proceeds, profits, gain, returns, revenue, yield, income, earnings, pickings.

tale *n* story, yarn, anecdote, spiel (*sl*), narrative, account, report, rumour, tall story, old wives' tale, superstition, fable, myth, legend, saga, lie, fib, falsehood, untruth, fabrication.

talent *n* gift, endowment, genius, flair, feel, knack, bent, aptitude, faculty, skill, ability, capacity, power, strength, forte.

☒ inability, weakness.

talented *adj* gifted, brilliant, well-endowed, versatile, accomplished, able, capable, proficient, adept, adroit, deft, clever, skilful.

☒ inept.

talk *v* speak, utter, articulate, say, communicate, converse, chat, gossip, natter (*infml*), chatter, discuss, confer, negotiate.

n **1** CONVERSATION, dialogue, discussion, conference, meeting, consultation, negotiation, chat, chatter, natter (*infml*), gossip, hearsay, rumour, tittle-tattle. **2** *give a talk*: lecture, seminar, symposium, speech,

address, discourse, sermon, spiel (*sl*).
3 LANGUAGE, dialect, slang, jargon, speech, utterance, words.

talk into encourage, coax, sway, persuade, convince, bring round, win over.

F3 dissuade.

talk out of discourage, deter, put off, dissuade.

F3 persuade, convince.

talkative *adj* garrulous, voluble, vocal, communicative, forthcoming, unreserved, expansive, chatty, gossipy, verbose, wordy.

F3 taciturn, quiet, reserved.

talking-to (*infml*) *n* lecture, dressing-down (*infml*), telling-off (*infml*), ticking-off (*infml*), scolding, reprimand, rebuke, reproof, reproach, criticism.

F3 praise, commendation.

tall *adj* high, lofty, elevated, soaring, towering, big, great, giant, gigantic.

F3 short, low, small.

tally *v* **1** AGREE, concur, tie in, square, accord, harmonize, coincide, correspond, match, conform, suit, fit. **2** ADD (UP), total, count, reckon, figure.

F3 1 disagree, differ.

n record, count, total, score, reckoning, account.

tame *adj* **1** *a tame rabbit*: domesticated, broken in, trained, disciplined, manageable, tractable, amenable, gentle, docile, meek, submissive, unresisting, obedient, biddable. **2** DULL, boring, tedious, uninteresting, humdrum, flat, bland, insipid, weak, feeble, uninspired, unadventurous, unenterprising, lifeless, spiritless.

F3 1 wild, unmanageable, rebellious. **2** exciting.

v domesticate, house-train, break in, train, discipline, master, subjugate, conquer, bridle, curb, repress, suppress, quell, subdue, temper, soften, mellow, calm, pacify, humble.

tamper *v* interfere, meddle, mess (*infml*), tinker, fiddle, fix, rig, manipulate, juggle, alter, damage.

tang *n* sharpness, bite, piquancy, pungency, taste, flavour, savour, smack, smell, aroma, scent, whiff, tinge, touch, trace, hint, suggestion, overtone.

tangible *adj* touchable, tactile, palpable, solid, concrete, material, substantial, physical, real, actual, perceptible, discernible, evident, manifest, definite, positive.

F3 intangible, abstract, unreal.

tangle *n* knot, snarl-up, twist, coil, convolution, mesh, web, maze, labyrinth, mess, muddle, jumble, mix-up, confusion, entanglement, embroilment, complication.

v entangle, knot, snarl, ravel, twist, coil, interweave, interlace, intertwine, catch, ensnare, entrap, enmesh, embroil, implicate, involve, muddle, confuse.

F3 disentangle.

tangled *adj* knotty, snarled, matted, tousled, dishevelled, messy, muddled, jumbled, confused, twisted, convoluted, tortuous, involved, complicated, complex, intricate.

tangy *adj* sharp, biting, acid, tart, spicy, piquant, pungent, strong, fresh.

F3 tasteless, insipid.

tank *n* container, reservoir, cistern, aquarium, vat, basin.

tantalize *v* tease, taunt, torment, torture, provoke, lead on, titillate, tempt, entice, bait, balk, frustrate, thwart.

F3 gratify, satisfy, fulfil.

tantamount *adj* as good as, equivalent, commensurate, equal, synonymous, the same as.

tantrum *n* temper, rage, fury, storm, outburst, fit, scene, paddy (*infml*).

tap¹ *v* hit, strike, knock, rap, beat, drum, pat, touch.

n knock, rap, beat, pat, touch.

tap² *n* **1** STOPCOCK, valve, faucet, spigot, spout. **2** STOPPER, plug, bung.

v use, utilize, exploit, mine, quarry, siphon, bleed, milk, drain.

tape *n* band, strip, binding, ribbon, video, cassette.

v record, video, bind, secure, stick, seal.

taper *v* narrow, attenuate, thin, slim, decrease, reduce, lessen, dwindle, fade, wane, peter out, tail off, die away.

E3 widen, flare, swell, increase.

n spill, candle, wick.

target *n* aim, object, end, purpose, intention, ambition, goal, destination, objective, butt, mark, victim, prey, quarry.

tariff *n* price list, schedule, charges, rate, toll, tax, levy, customs, excise, duty.

tarnish *v* discolour, corrode, rust, dull, dim, darken, blacken, sully, taint, stain, blemish, spot, blot, mar, spoil.

E3 polish, brighten.

tart¹ *n* pie, flan, pastry, tartlet, patty.

tart² *adj* sharp, acid, sour, bitter, vinegary, tangy, piquant, pungent, biting, cutting, trenchant, incisive, caustic, astringent, acerbic, scathing, sardonic.

E3 bland, sweet.

task *n* job, chore, duty, charge, imposition, assignment, exercise, mission, errand, undertaking, enterprise, business, occupation, activity, employment, work, labour, toil, burden.

taste *n* **1** FLAVOUR, savour, relish, smack, tang. **2** SAMPLE, bit, piece, morsel, titbit, bite, nibble, mouthful, sip, drop, dash, soupçon. **3** *a taste for adventure*: liking, fondness, partiality, preference, inclination, leaning, desire, appetite.

4 DISCRIMINATION, discernment, judgement, perception, appreciation, sensitivity, refinement, polish, culture, cultivation, breeding, decorum, finesse, style, elegance, tastefulness.

E3 1 blandness. **3** distaste.

4 tastelessness.

v savour, relish, sample, nibble, sip, try, test, differentiate, distinguish, discern, perceive, experience, undergo, feel, encounter, meet, know.

> *Ways of describing taste include:*
> acid, acrid, appetizing, bitter,
> bittersweet, citrus, creamy, delicious,
> flavoursome, fruity, hot, meaty,
> moreish, peppery, piquant, pungent,
> sapid, salty, savoury, scrumptious
> (*infml*), sharp, sour, spicy, sugary,
> sweet, tangy, tart, tasty, yummy
> (*infml*).

tasteful *adj* refined, polished, cultured, cultivated, elegant, smart, stylish, aesthetic, artistic, harmonious, beautiful, exquisite, delicate, graceful, restrained, well-judged, judicious, correct, fastidious, discriminating.

E3 tasteless, garish, tawdry.

tasteless *adj* **1** FLAVOURLESS, insipid, bland, mild, weak, watery, flat, stale, dull, boring, uninteresting, vapid. **2** INELEGANT, graceless, unseemly, improper, indiscreet, crass, rude, crude, vulgar, kitsch, naff (*sl*), cheap, tawdry, flashy, gaudy, garish, loud.

E3 1 tasty. **2** tasteful, elegant.

tasty *adj* luscious, palatable, appetizing, mouthwatering, delicious, flavoursome, succulent, scrumptious (*infml*), yummy (*sl*), tangy, piquant, savoury, sweet.

E3 tasteless, insipid.

tattered *adj* ragged, frayed, threadbare, ripped, torn, tatty, shabby, scruffy.

E3 smart, neat.

tatters *n* rags, shreds, ribbons,

taunt

taunt 532

pieces.

taunt v tease, torment, provoke, bait, goad, jeer, mock, ridicule, gibe, rib (sl), deride, sneer, insult, revile, reproach.

n jeer, catcall, gibe, dig, sneer, insult, reproach, taunting, teasing, provocation, ridicule, sarcasm, derision, censure.

taut adj tight, stretched, contracted, strained, tense, unrelaxed, stiff, rigid.
🆎 slack, loose, relaxed.

tautological adj repetitive, superfluous, redundant, pleonastic, verbose, wordy.
🆎 succinct, economical.

tautology n repetition, duplication, superfluity, redundancy, pleonasm.

tawdry adj cheap, vulgar, tasteless, fancy, showy, flashy, gaudy, garish, tinselly, glittering.
🆎 fine, tasteful.

tax n levy, charge, rate, tariff, customs, contribution, imposition, burden, load.

Taxes include: airport tax, capital gains tax, capital transfer tax, community charge, corporation tax, council tax, customs, death duty, estate duty, excise, income tax, inheritance tax, PAYE, poll tax, property tax, rates, surtax, tithe, toll, value added tax (VAT).

v levy, charge, demand, exact, assess, impose, burden, load, strain, stretch, try, tire, weary, exhaust, drain, sap, weaken.

teach v instruct, train, coach, tutor, lecture, drill, ground, verse, discipline, school, educate, enlighten, edify, inform, impart, inculcate, advise, counsel, guide, direct, show, demonstrate.
🆎 learn.

teacher n schoolteacher, schoolmaster, master, schoolmistress, mistress, educator, pedagogue, tutor,

lecturer, professor, don, instructor, trainer, coach, adviser, counsellor, mentor, guide, guru.
🆎 pupil.

teaching n **1** INSTRUCTION, tuition, training, grounding, schooling, education, pedagogy, indoctrination. **2** DOGMA, doctrine, tenet, precept, principle.

team n side, line-up, squad, shift, crew, gang, band, group, company, stable.

team up join, unite, couple, combine, band together, co-operate, collaborate, work together.

tear v **1** RIP, rend, divide, rupture, sever, shred, scratch, claw, gash, lacerate, mutilate, mangle. **2** PULL, snatch, grab, seize, wrest. **3** *tear down the street*: dash, rush, hurry, speed, race, run, sprint, fly, shoot, dart, bolt, belt (infml), career, charge.

n rip, rent, slit, hole, split, rupture, scratch, gash, laceration.

tearful adj crying, weeping, sobbing, whimpering, blubbering, sad, sorrowful, upset, distressed, emotional, weepy (infml).
🆎 happy, smiling, laughing.

tears n crying, weeping, sobbing, wailing, whimpering, blubbering, sorrow, distress.

tease v taunt, provoke, bait, annoy, irritate, aggravate (infml), needle (infml), badger, worry, pester, plague, torment, tantalize, mock, ridicule, gibe, banter, rag (sl), rib (sl).

technical adj mechanical, scientific, technological, electronic, computerized, specialized, expert, professional.

technique n method, system, procedure, manner, fashion, style, mode, way, means, approach, course, performance, execution, delivery, artistry, craftsmanship, skill, facility, proficiency, expertise, know-how (infml), art, craft, knack, touch.

tedious adj boring, monotonous, uninteresting, unexciting, dull, dreary, drab, banal, humdrum, tiresome, wearisome, tiring, laborious, long-winded, long-drawn-out.
☒ lively, interesting, exciting.

teeming adj swarming, crawling, alive, bristling, seething, full, packed, brimming, overflowing, bursting, replete, abundant, fruitful, thick.
☒ lacking, sparse, rare.

teenage adj teenaged, adolescent, young, youthful, juvenile, immature.

teenager n adolescent, youth, boy, girl, minor, juvenile.

teetotal adj temperate, abstinent, abstemious, sober, on the wagon (sl).

telepathy n mind-reading, thought transference, sixth sense, ESP, clairvoyance.

telephone n phone, handset, receiver, blower (infml).
v phone, ring (up), call (up), dial, buzz (infml), contact, get in touch.

telescope v contract, shrink, compress, condense, abridge, squash, crush, shorten, curtail, truncate, abbreviate, reduce, cut, trim.

television n TV, receiver, set, telly (infml), the box (infml), goggle-box (infml), idiot box (infml), small screen.

tell v 1 INFORM, notify, let know, acquaint, impart, communicate, speak, utter, say, state, confess, divulge, disclose, reveal. 2 tell a story: narrate, recount, relate, report, announce, describe, portray, mention. 3 ORDER, command, direct, instruct, authorize.
4 DIFFERENTIATE, distinguish, discriminate, discern, recognize, identify, discover, see, understand, comprehend.

tell off (infml) scold, chide, tick off (infml), upbraid, reprimand, rebuke, reprove, lecture, berate, dress down (infml), reproach, censure.

temerity n impudence, impertinence, cheek (infml), gall, nerve (infml), audacity, boldness, daring, rashness, recklessness, impulsiveness.
☒ caution, prudence.

temper n 1 MOOD, humour, nature, temperament, character, disposition, constitution. 2 ANGER, rage, fury, passion, tantrum, paddy (infml), annoyance, irritability, ill-humour.
3 CALM, composure, self-control, cool (sl).
☒ 2 calmness, self-control. 3 anger, rage.
v 1 MODERATE, lessen, reduce, calm, soothe, allay, assuage, palliate, mitigate, modify, soften. 2 HARDEN, toughen, strengthen.

temperament n nature, character, personality, disposition, tendency, bent, constitution, make-up, soul, spirit, mood, humour, temper, state of mind, attitude, outlook.

temperamental adj 1 MOODY, emotional, neurotic, highly-strung, sensitive, touchy, irritable, impatient, passionate, fiery, excitable, explosive, volatile, mercurial, capricious, unpredictable, unreliable.
2 NATURAL, inborn, innate, inherent, constitutional, ingrained.
☒ 1 calm, level-headed, steady.

temperance n teetotalism, prohibition, abstinence, abstemiousness, sobriety, continence, moderation, restraint, self-restraint, self-control, self-discipline, self-denial.
☒ intemperance, excess.

temperate adj 1 temperate climate: mild, clement, balmy, fair, equable, balanced, stable, gentle, pleasant, agreeable. 2 TEETOTAL, abstinent, abstemious, sober, continent, moderate, restrained, controlled, even-tempered, calm, composed, reasonable, sensible.
☒ 2 intemperate, extreme, excessive.

tempestuous adj stormy, windy,

temple 534

gusty, blustery, squally, turbulent,
tumultuous, rough, wild, violent,
furious, raging, heated, passionate,
intense.
F3 calm.

temple *n* shrine, sanctuary, church,
tabernacle, mosque, pagoda.

tempo *n* time, rhythm, metre, beat,
pulse, speed, velocity, rate, pace.

temporal *adj* secular, profane,
worldly, earthly, terrestrial, material,
carnal, fleshly, mortal.
F3 spiritual.

temporary *adj* impermanent,
provisional, interim, makeshift,
stopgap, temporal, transient,
transitory, passing, ephemeral,
evanescent, fleeting, brief, short-
lived, momentary.
F3 permanent, everlasting.

tempt *v* entice, coax, persuade, woo,
bait, lure, allure, attract, draw,
seduce, invite, tantalize, provoke,
incite.
F3 discourage, dissuade, repel.

temptation *n* enticement,
inducement, coaxing, persuasion,
bait, lure, allure, appeal, attraction,
draw, pull, seduction, invitation.

tenable *adj* credible, defensible,
justifiable, reasonable, rational,
sound, arguable, believable,
defendable, plausible, viable, feasible.
F3 untenable, indefensible,
unjustifiable.

tenant *n* renter, lessee, leaseholder,
occupier, occupant, resident,
inhabitant.

tend¹ *v* incline, lean, bend, bear,
head, aim, lead, go, move, gravitate.

tend² *v* look after, care for, cultivate,
keep, maintain, manage, handle,
guard, protect, watch, mind, nurture,
nurse, minister to, serve, attend.
F3 neglect, ignore.

tendency *n* trend, drift, movement,
course, direction, bearing, heading,
bias, partiality, predisposition,
propensity, readiness, liability,

susceptibility, proneness, inclination,
leaning, bent, disposition.

tender¹ *adj* 1 KIND, gentle, caring,
humane, considerate, compassionate,
sympathetic, warm, fond,
affectionate, loving, amorous,
romantic, sentimental, emotional,
sensitive, tender-hearted, soft-
hearted. 2 YOUNG, youthful,
immature, green, raw, new,
inexperienced, impressionable,
vulnerable. 3 SOFT, succulent, fleshy,
dainty, delicate, fragile, frail, weak,
feeble. 4 SORE, painful, aching,
smarting, bruised, inflamed, raw.
F3 1 hard-hearted, callous. 2 mature.
3 tough, hard.

tender² *v* offer, proffer, extend, give,
present, submit, propose, suggest,
advance, volunteer.
n 1 *legal tender*: currency, money. 2
OFFER, bid, estimate, quotation,
proposal, proposition, suggestion,
submission.

tense *adj* 1 TIGHT, taut, stretched,
strained, stiff, rigid. 2 NERVOUS,
anxious, worried, jittery, uneasy,
apprehensive, edgy, fidgety, restless,
jumpy, overwrought, keyed up.
3 STRESSFUL, exciting, worrying,
fraught.
F3 1 loose, slack. 2 calm, relaxed.
v tighten, contract, brace, stretch,
strain.
F3 loosen, relax.

tension *n* 1 TIGHTNESS, tautness,
stiffness, strain, stress, pressure.
2 NERVOUSNESS, anxiety, worry,
uneasiness, apprehension, edginess,
restlessness, suspense.
F3 1 looseness. 2 calm(ness),
relaxation.

tent *n* tepee, wigwam, marquee, big
top.

tentative *adj* experimental,
exploratory, speculative, hesitant,
faltering, cautious, unsure, uncertain,
doubtful, undecided, provisional,
indefinite, unconfirmed.

■ definite, decisive, conclusive, final.

tenuous *adj* thin, slim, slender, fine, slight, insubstantial, flimsy, fragile, delicate, weak, shaky, doubtful, dubious, questionable.
■ strong, substantial.

tepid *adj* lukewarm, cool, half-hearted, unenthusiastic, apathetic.
■ cold, hot, passionate.

term *n* **1** WORD, name, designation, appellation, title, epithet, phrase, expression. **2** TIME, period, course, duration, spell, span, stretch, interval, space, semester, session, season.
v call, name, dub, style, designate, label, tag, title, entitle.

terminal *adj* **1** LAST, final, concluding, ultimate, extreme, utmost. **2** *terminal illness*: FATAL, deadly, lethal, mortal, incurable.
■ **1** initial.

terminate *v* finish, complete, conclude, cease, end, stop, close, discontinue, wind up, cut off, abort, lapse, expire.
■ begin, start, initiate.

terminology *n* language, jargon, phraseology, vocabulary, words, terms, nomenclature.

terminus *n* end, close, termination, extremity, limit, boundary, destination, goal, target, depot, station, garage, terminal.

terms *n* **1** *on good terms*: relations, relationship, footing, standing, position. **2** CONDITIONS, specifications, stipulations, provisos, provisions, qualifications, particulars. **3** RATES, charges, fees, prices, tariff.

terrain *n* land, ground, territory, country, countryside, landscape, topography.

terrestrial *adj* earthly, worldly, global, mundane.
■ cosmic, heavenly.

terrible *adj* bad, awful, frightful, dreadful, shocking, appalling, outrageous, disgusting, revolting, repulsive, offensive, abhorrent, hateful, horrid, horrible, unpleasant, obnoxious, foul, vile, hideous, gruesome, horrific, harrowing, distressing, grave, serious, severe, extreme, desperate.
■ excellent, wonderful, superb.

terribly (*infml*) *adv* very, much, greatly, extremely, exceedingly, awfully, frightfully, decidedly, seriously.

terrific (*infml*) *adj* **1** EXCELLENT, wonderful, marvellous, super, smashing (*infml*), outstanding, brilliant, magnificent, superb, fabulous (*infml*), fantastic (*infml*), sensational, amazing, stupendous, breathtaking. **2** HUGE, enormous, gigantic, tremendous, great, intense, extreme, excessive.
■ **1** awful, terrible, appalling.

terrify *v* petrify, horrify, appal, shock, terrorize, intimidate, frighten, scare, alarm, dismay.

territory *n* country, land, state, dependency, province, domain, preserve, jurisdiction, sector, region, area, district, zone, tract, terrain.

terror *n* fear, panic, dread, trepidation, horror, shock, fright, alarm, dismay, consternation, terrorism, intimidation.

terrorize *v* threaten, menace, intimidate, oppress, coerce, bully, browbeat, frighten, scare, alarm, terrify, petrify, horrify, shock.

terse *adj* short, brief, succinct, concise, compact, condensed, epigrammatic, pithy, incisive, snappy, curt, brusque, abrupt, laconic.
■ long-winded, verbose.

test *v* try, experiment, examine, assess, evaluate, check, investigate, analyse, screen, prove, verify.
n trial, try-out, experiment, examination, assessment, evaluation, check, investigation, analysis, proof,

probation, ordeal.

testify v give evidence, depose, state, declare, assert, swear, avow, attest, vouch, certify, corroborate, affirm, show, bear witness.

testimonial n reference, character, credential, certificate, recommendation, endorsement, commendation, tribute.

testimony n evidence, statement, affidavit, submission, deposition, declaration, profession, attestation, affirmation, support, proof, verification, confirmation, witness, demonstration, manifestation, indication.

tether n chain, rope, cord, line, lead, leash, bond, fetter, shackle, restraint, fastening.
v tie, fasten, secure, restrain, chain, rope, leash, bind, lash, fetter, shackle, manacle.

text n words, wording, content, matter, body, subject, topic, theme, reading, passage, paragraph, sentence, book, textbook, source.

texture n consistency, feel, surface, grain, weave, tissue, fabric, structure, composition, constitution, character, quality.

thank v say thank you, be grateful, appreciate, acknowledge, recognize, credit.

thankful adj grateful, appreciative, obliged, indebted, pleased, contented, relieved.
Ea ungrateful, unappreciative.

thankless adj unrecognized, unappreciated, unrequited, unrewarding, unprofitable, fruitless.
Ea rewarding, worthwhile.

thanks n gratitude, gratefulness, appreciation, acknowledgement, recognition, credit, thanksgiving, thank-offering.

thanks to because of, owing to, due to, on account of, as a result of, through.

thaw v melt, defrost, defreeze, de-ice, soften, liquefy, dissolve, warm, heat

up.
Ea freeze.

theatrical adj **1** DRAMATIC, thespian. **2** MELODRAMATIC, histrionic, mannered, affected, artificial, pompous, ostentatious, showy, extravagant, exaggerated, overdone.

> *Theatrical forms include*: ballet, burlesque, cabaret, circus, comedy, black comedy, comedy of humours, comedy of manners, comedy of menace, commedia dell'arte, duologue, farce, fringe theatre, Grand Guignol, kabuki, Kensington gore, Kitchen-Sink, legitimate drama, masque, melodrama, mime, miracle play, monologue, morality play, mummery, music hall, musical, musical comedy, mystery play, Noh, opera, operetta, pageant, pantomime, play, Punch and Judy, puppet theatre, revue, street theatre, tableau, theatre-in-the-round, Theatre of the Absurd, Theatre of Cruelty, tragedy. *see also* **performance**.

theft n robbery, thieving, stealing, pilfering, larceny, shop-lifting, kleptomania, fraud, embezzlement.

theme n subject, topic, thread, motif, keynote, idea, gist, essence, burden, argument, thesis, dissertation, composition, essay, text, matter.

theorem n formula, principle, rule, statement, deduction, proposition, hypothesis.

theoretical adj hypothetical, conjectural, speculative, abstract, academic, doctrinaire, pure, ideal.
Ea practical, applied, concrete.

theorize v hypothesize, suppose, guess, conjecture, speculate, postulate, propound, formulate.

theory n hypothesis, supposition, assumption, presumption, surmise, guess, conjecture, speculation, idea, notion, abstraction, philosophy, thesis, plan, proposal, scheme, system.

≡ certainty, practice.

therapeutic *adj* remedial, curative, healing, restorative, tonic, medicinal, corrective, good, beneficial.

≡ harmful, detrimental.

therapy *n* treatment, remedy, cure, healing, tonic.

therefore *adv* so, then, consequently, as a result.

thesis *n* **1** *doctoral thesis*: dissertation, essay, composition, treatise, paper, monograph. **2** SUBJECT, topic, theme, idea, opinion, view, theory, hypothesis, proposal, proposition, premise, statement, argument, contention.

thick *adj* **1** WIDE, broad, fat, heavy, solid, dense, impenetrable, close, compact, concentrated, condensed, viscous, coagulated, clotted. **2** FULL, packed, crowded, chock-a-block, swarming, teeming, bristling, brimming, bursting, numerous, abundant. **3** (*infml*) STUPID, foolish, slow, dull, dim-witted, brainless, simple.

≡ **1** thin, slim, slender, slight. **2** sparse. **3** clever, brainy (*infml*).

thicken *v* condense, stiffen, congeal, coagulate, clot, cake, gel, jell, set.

≡ thin.

thicket *n* wood, copse, coppice, grove, spinney.

thickness *n* **1** WIDTH, breadth, diameter, density, viscosity, bulk, body. **2** LAYER, stratum, ply, sheet, coat.

≡ **1** thinness.

thick-skinned *adj* insensitive, unfeeling, callous, tough, hardened, hard-boiled.

≡ thin-skinned, sensitive.

thief *n* robber, bandit, mugger, pickpocket, shop-lifter, burglar, house-breaker, plunderer, poacher, stealer, pilferer, filcher,

kleptomaniac, swindler, embezzler.

thin *adj* **1** LEAN, slim, slender, narrow, attenuated, slight, skinny, bony, skeletal, scraggy, scrawny, lanky, gaunt, spare, underweight, undernourished, emaciated. **2** *thin fabric*: fine, delicate, light, flimsy, filmy, gossamer, sheer, see-through, transparent, translucent. **3** SPARSE, scarce, scattered, scant, meagre, poor, inadequate, deficient, scanty, skimpy. **4** WEAK, feeble, runny, watery, diluted.

≡ **1** fat, broad. **2** thick, dense, solid. **3** plentiful, abundant. **4** strong.

v **1** NARROW, attenuate, diminish, reduce, trim, weed out. **2** WEAKEN, dilute, water down, rarefy, refine.

thing *n* **1** ARTICLE, object, entity, creature, body, substance, item, detail, particular, feature, factor, element, point, fact, concept, thought. **2** DEVICE, contrivance, gadget, tool, implement, instrument, apparatus, machine, mechanism. **3** ACT, deed, feat, action, task, responsibility, problem. **4** CIRCUMSTANCE, eventuality, happening, occurrence, event, incident, phenomenon, affair, proceeding. **5** (*infml*) OBSESSION, preoccupation, fixation, fetish, phobia, hang-up (*infml*).

things *n* belongings, possessions, effects, paraphernalia, stuff (*infml*), goods, luggage, baggage, equipment, gear (*infml*), clobber (*infml*), odds and ends, bits and pieces.

think *v* **1** BELIEVE, hold, consider, regard, esteem, deem, judge, estimate, reckon, calculate, determine, conclude, reason. **2** CONCEIVE, imagine, suppose, presume, surmise, expect, foresee, envisage, anticipate. **3** *think it over*: ponder, mull over, chew over, ruminate, meditate, contemplate, muse, cogitate, reflect, deliberate, weigh up, recall, recollect, remember.

think up devise, contrive, dream up, imagine, conceive, visualize, invent, design, create, concoct.

thinker n philosopher, theorist, ideologist, brain, intellect, mastermind.

thinking n reasoning, philosophy, thoughts, conclusions, theory, idea, opinion, view, outlook, position, judgement, assessment.
adj reasoning, rational, intellectual, intelligent, cultured, sophisticated, philosophical, analytical, reflective, contemplative, thoughtful.

third-rate adj low-grade, poor, bad, inferior, mediocre, indifferent, shoddy, cheap and nasty.
E3 first-rate.

thirst n 1 THIRSTINESS, dryness, drought. 2 DESIRE, longing, yearning, hankering, craving, hunger, appetite, lust, passion, eagerness, keenness.

thirsty adj 1 DRY, parched (infml), gasping (infml), dehydrated, arid. 2 thirsty for knowledge: desirous, longing, yearning, hankering, craving, hungry, burning, itching, dying, eager, avid, greedy.

thorn n spike, point, barb, prickle, spine, bristle, needle.

thorough adj full, complete, total, entire, utter, absolute, perfect, pure, sheer, unqualified, unmitigated, out-and-out, downright, sweeping, all-embracing, comprehensive, all-inclusive, exhaustive, thoroughgoing, intensive, in-depth, conscientious, efficient, painstaking, scrupulous, meticulous, careful.
E3 partial, superficial, careless.

though conj although, even if, notwithstanding, while, allowing, granted.
adv however, nevertheless, nonetheless, yet, still, even so, all the same, for all that.

thought n 1 THINKING, attention, heed, regard, consideration, study, scrutiny, introspection, meditation, contemplation, cogitation, reflection, deliberation. 2 IDEA, notion, concept, conception, belief, conviction, opinion, view, judgement, assessment, conclusion, plan, design, intention, purpose, aim, hope, dream, expectation, anticipation. 3 THOUGHTFULNESS, consideration, kindness, care, concern, compassion, sympathy, gesture, touch.

thoughtful adj 1 PENSIVE, wistful, dreamy, abstracted, reflective, contemplative, introspective, thinking, absorbed, studious, serious, solemn. 2 CONSIDERATE, kind, unselfish, helpful, caring, attentive, heedful, mindful, careful, prudent, cautious, wary.
E3 2 thoughtless, insensitive, selfish.

thoughtless adj 1 INCONSIDERATE, unthinking, insensitive, unfeeling, tactless, undiplomatic, unkind, selfish, uncaring. 2 absent-minded, inattentive, heedless, mindless, foolish, stupid, silly, rash, reckless, ill-considered, imprudent, careless, negligent, remiss.
E3 1 thoughtful, considerate. 2 careful.

thrash v 1 PUNISH, beat, whip, lash, flog, scourge, cane, belt, spank, clobber, wallop (infml), lay into. 2 DEFEAT, beat, trounce, hammer (infml), slaughter (infml), crush, overwhelm, rout. 3 THRESH, flail, toss, jerk.

thrash out discuss, debate, negotiate, settle, resolve.

thread n 1 COTTON, yarn, strand, fibre, filament, string, line. 2 COURSE, direction, drift, tenor, theme, motif, plot, storyline.

threadbare adj 1 threadbare clothes: worn, frayed, ragged, moth-eaten, scruffy, shabby. 2 HACKNEYED, overused, old, stale, tired, trite, commonplace, stock, stereotyped.
E3 1 new. 2 fresh.

threat *n* menace, warning, omen, portent, presage, foreboding, danger, risk, hazard, peril.

threaten *v* menace, intimidate, browbeat, pressurize, bully, terrorize, warn, portend, presage, forebode, foreshadow, endanger, jeopardize, imperil.

threatening *adj* menacing, intimidatory, warning, cautionary, ominous, inauspicious, sinister, grim, looming, impending.

threshold *n* doorstep, sill, doorway, door, entrance, brink, verge, starting-point, dawn, beginning, start, outset, opening.

thrift *n* economy, husbandry, saving, conservation, frugality, prudence, carefulness.
F3 extravagance, waste.

thrifty *adj* economical, saving, frugal, sparing, prudent, careful.
F3 extravagant, profligate, prodigal, wasteful.

thrill *n* excitement, adventure, pleasure, stimulation, charge, kick, buzz (*sl*), sensation, glow, tingle, throb, shudder, quiver, tremor.
v excite, electrify, galvanize, exhilarate, rouse, arouse, move, stir, stimulate, flush, glow, tingle, throb, shudder, tremble, quiver, shake.
F3 bore.

thrive *v* flourish, prosper, boom, grow, increase, advance, develop, bloom, blossom, gain, profit, succeed.
F3 languish, stagnate, fail, die.

throb *v* pulse, pulsate, beat, palpitate, vibrate, pound, thump.
n pulse, pulsation, beat, palpitation, vibration, pounding, thumping.

throttle *v* strangle, choke, asphyxiate, suffocate, smother, stifle, gag, silence, suppress, inhibit.

through *prep* **1** BETWEEN, by, via, by way of, by means of, using. **2** *all through the night*: throughout, during, in. **3** BECAUSE OF, as a result of, thanks to.
adj **1** FINISHED, ended, completed, done. **2** *through train*: direct, express, non-stop.

throw *v* **1** HURL, heave, lob, pitch, chuck (*infml*), sling, cast, fling, toss, launch, propel, send. **2** *throw light*: shed, cast, project, direct. **3** BRING DOWN, floor, upset, overturn, dislodge, unseat, unsaddle, unhorse. **4** (*infml*) PERPLEX, baffle, confound, confuse, disconcert, astonish, dumbfound.
n heave, lob, cast, sling, fling, toss, cast.

throw away 1 DISCARD, jettison, dump, ditch (*sl*), scrap, dispose of, throw out. **2** WASTE, squander, fritter away, blow (*sl*).
F3 1 keep, preserve, salvage, rescue.

throw off shed, cast off, drop, abandon, shake off, get rid of, elude.

throw out 1 EVICT, turn out, expel, turf out (*infml*), eject, emit, radiate, give off. **2** REJECT, discard, dismiss, turn down, jettison, dump, ditch (*sl*), throw away, scrap.

throw up 1 (*infml*) VOMIT, spew, regurgitate, disgorge, retch, heave. **2** abandon, renounce, relinquish, resign, quit, leave. **3** GIVE UP.

thrust *v* push, shove, butt, ram, jam, wedge, stick, poke, prod, jab, lunge, pierce, stab, plunge, press, force, impel, drive, propel.
n push, shove, poke, prod, lunge, stab, drive, impetus, momentum.

thud *n, v* thump, clump, knock, clunk, smack, wallop (*infml*), crash, bang, thunder.

thug *n* ruffian, tough, robber, bandit, mugger, killer, murderer, assassin, gangster, hooligan.

thump *n* knock, blow, punch, clout, box, cuff, smack, whack (*infml*), wallop (*infml*), crash, bang, thud, beat, throb.
v hit, strike, knock, punch, clout, box, cuff, smack, thrash, whack

(*infml*), wallop (*infml*), crash, bang, thud, batter, pound, hammer, beat, throb.

thunder *n* boom, reverberation, crash, bang, crack, clap, peal, rumble, roll, roar, blast, explosion.
v boom, resound, reverberate, crash, bang, crack, clap, peal, rumble, roll, roar, blast.

thunderous *adj* booming, resounding, reverberating, roaring, loud, noisy, deafening, ear-splitting.

thus *adv* so, hence, therefore, consequently, then, accordingly, like this, in this way, as follows.

thwart *v* frustrate, foil, stymie, defeat, hinder, impede, obstruct, block, check, baffle, stop, prevent, oppose.
☒ help, assist, aid.

tick *n* 1 CLICK, tap, stroke, tick-tock. 2 (*infml*) *wait a tick*: moment, instant, flash, jiffy (*infml*), second, minute.
v 1 MARK, indicate, choose, select. 2 CLICK, tap, beat.

tick off (*infml*) scold, chide, reprimand, rebuke, reproach, reprove, upbraid, tell off (*infml*).
☒ praise, compliment.

ticket *n* pass, card, certificate, token, voucher, coupon, docket, slip, label, tag, sticker.

tickle *v* excite, thrill, delight, please, gratify, amuse, entertain, divert.

ticklish *adj* sensitive, touchy, delicate, thorny, awkward, difficult, tricky, critical, risky, hazardous, dodgy (*infml*).
☒ easy, simple.

tide *n* current, ebb, flow, stream, flux, movement, course, direction, drift, trend, tendency.

tidy *adj* 1 NEAT, orderly, methodical, systematic, organized, clean, spick-and-span, shipshape, smart, spruce, trim, well-kept, ordered, uncluttered.
2 (*infml*) *a tidy sum*: large, substantial, sizable, considerable,

good, generous, ample.
☒ 1 untidy, messy, disorganized.
2 small, insignificant.
v neaten, straighten, order, arrange, clean, smarten, spruce up, groom.

tie *v* knot, fasten, secure, moor, tether, attach, join, connect, link, unite, rope, lash, strap, bind, restrain, restrict, confine, limit, hamper, hinder.
n 1 KNOT, fastening, joint, connection, link, liaison, relationship, bond, affiliation, obligation, commitment, duty, restraint, restriction, limitation, hindrance.
2 DRAW, dead heat, stalemate, deadlock.

tie up 1 MOOR, tether, attach, secure, rope, lash, bind, truss, wrap up, restrain. 2 CONCLUDE, terminate, wind up, settle. 3 OCCUPY, engage, engross.

tier *n* floor, storey, level, stage, stratum, layer, belt, zone, band, echelon, rank, row, line.

tight *adj* 1 TAUT, stretched, tense, rigid, stiff, firm, fixed, fast, secure, close, cramped, constricted, compact, snug, close-fitting. 2 SEALED, hermetic, -proof, impervious, airtight, watertight. 3 (*infml*) MEAN, stingy, miserly, niggardly, parsimonious, tight-fisted (*infml*).
4 *tight security*: strict, severe, stringent, rigorous.
☒ 1 loose, slack. 2 open. 3 generous.
4 lax.

tighten *v* tauten, stretch, tense, stiffen, fix, fasten, secure, narrow, close, cramp, constrict, crush, squeeze.
☒ loosen, relax.

tight-fisted (*infml*) *adj* mean, stingy, miserly, mingy (*infml*), niggardly, penny-pinching, sparing, parsimonious, tight (*infml*), grasping.
☒ generous, charitable.

till *v* cultivate, work, plough, dig, farm.

tire

tilt v slope, incline, slant, pitch, list,
tip, lean.
  n slope, incline, angle, inclination,
slant, pitch, list.

timber n wood, trees, forest, beam,
lath, plank, board, log.

time n 1 SPELL, stretch, period,
term, season, session, span, duration,
interval, space, while. 2 TEMPO, beat,
rhythm, metre, measure. 3 MOMENT,
point, juncture, stage, instance,
occasion, date, day, hour. 4 AGE, era,
epoch, life, lifetime, generation,
heyday, peak.

> *Periods of time include*: eternity,
> eon, era, age, generation, epoch,
> millennium, chiliad, century, lifetime,
> decade, decennium, quinquennium,
> year, light-year, yesteryear, quarter,
> month, fortnight, week, midweek,
> weekend, long weekend, day, today,
> tonight, yesterday, tomorrow,
> morrow, weekday, hour, minute,
> second, moment, instant, millisecond,
> microsecond, nanosecond; dawn,
> sunrise, sun-up, the early hours, wee
> small hours (*infml*), morning, morn,
> a.m., daytime, midday, noon, high
> noon, p.m., afternoon, tea-time,
> evening, twilight, dusk, sunset,
> nightfall, bedtime, night, night-time;
> season, spring, summer, midsummer,
> autumn, fall, (*North Amer.*) winter.

  v clock, measure, meter, regulate,
control, set, schedule, timetable.

timeless adj ageless, immortal,
everlasting, eternal, endless,
permanent, changeless, unchanging.

timely adj well-timed, seasonable,
suitable, appropriate, convenient,
opportune, propitious, prompt,
punctual.
  ⊟ ill-timed, unsuitable,
inappropriate.

timetable n schedule, programme,
agenda, calendar, diary, rota, roster,
list, listing, curriculum.

timid adj shy, bashful, modest,
shrinking, retiring, nervous,
apprehensive, afraid, timorous,
fearful, cowardly, faint-hearted,
spineless, irresolute.
  ⊟ brave, bold, audacious.

tinge n tint, dye, colour, shade,
touch, trace, suggestion, hint, smack,
flavour, pinch, drop, dash, bit,
sprinkling, smattering.
  v tint, dye, stain, colour, shade,
suffuse, imbue.

tingle v sting, prickle, tickle, itch,
thrill, throb, quiver, vibrate.
  n stinging, prickling, pins and
needles, tickle, tickling, itch, itching,
thrill, throb, quiver, shiver, gooseflesh,
goose-pimples.

tinker v fiddle, play, toy, trifle,
potter, dabble, meddle, tamper.

tint n dye, stain, rinse, wash, colour,
hue, shade, tincture, tinge, tone, cast,
streak, trace, touch.
  v dye, colour, tinge, streak, stain,
taint, affect.

tiny adj minute, microscopic,
infinitesimal, teeny (*infml*), small,
little, slight, negligible, insignificant,
diminutive, petite, dwarfish, pint-
sized (*infml*), pocket, miniature, mini
(*infml*).
  ⊟ huge, enormous, immense.

tip¹ n end, extremity, point, nib,
apex, peak, pinnacle, summit, acme,
top, cap, crown, head.
  v cap, crown, top, surmount.

tip² v lean, incline, slant, list, tilt,
topple over, capsize, upset, overturn,
spill, pour out, empty, unload, dump.
  n dump, rubbish-heap, refuse-heap.

tip³ n 1 CLUE, pointer, hint,
suggestion, advice, warning, tip-off,
information, inside information,
forecast. 2 GRATUITY, gift,
perquisite.
  v 1 ADVISE, suggest, warn, caution,
forewarn, tip off, inform, tell. 2 *tip the
driver*: reward, remunerate.

tire v weary, fatigue, wear out,

exhaust, drain, enervate.

☒ enliven, invigorate, refresh.

tired adj **1** WEARY, drowsy, sleepy, flagging, fatigued, worn out, exhausted, dog-tired, drained, fagged (*sl*), bushed (*infml*), whacked (*infml*), shattered (*infml*), beat (*infml*), dead-beat (*infml*), all in (*infml*), knackered (*infml*). **2** *tired of waiting*: fed up, bored, sick.

☒ **1** lively, energetic, rested, refreshed. **3** new.

tireless adj untiring, unwearied, unflagging, indefatigable, energetic, vigorous, diligent, industrious, resolute, determined.

☒ tired, lazy.

tiresome adj troublesome, trying, annoying, irritating, exasperating, wearisome, dull, boring, tedious, monotonous, uninteresting, tiring, fatiguing, laborious.

☒ interesting, stimulating, easy.

tiring adj wearying, fatiguing, exhausting, draining, demanding, exacting, taxing, arduous, strenuous, laborious.

tissue n substance, matter, material, fabric, stuff, gauze, web, mesh, network, structure, texture.

titbit n morsel, scrap, appetizer, snack, delicacy, dainty, treat.

titillate v stimulate, arouse, turn on (*sl*), excite, thrill, tickle, provoke, tease, tantalize, intrigue, interest.

title n **1** NAME, appellation, denomination, term, designation, label, epithet, nickname, pseudonym, rank, status, office, position. **2** HEADING, headline, caption, legend, inscription. **3** RIGHT, prerogative, privilege, claim, entitlement, ownership, deeds.

v entitle, name, call, dub, style, term, designate, label.

titter v laugh, chortle, chuckle, giggle, snigger, mock.

titular adj honorary, formal, official, so-called, nominal, token.

toast v grill, brown, roast, heat, warm.

n drink, pledge, tribute, salute, compliment, health.

together adv jointly, in concert, side by side, shoulder to shoulder, in unison, as one, simultaneously, at the same time, all at once, collectively, en masse, closely, continuously, consecutively, successively, in succession, in a row, hand in hand.

☒ separately, individually, alone.

toil n labour, hard work, donkey-work, drudgery, sweat, graft (*infml*), industry, application, effort, exertion, elbow grease.

v labour, work, slave, drudge, sweat, grind, slog, graft (*infml*), plug away (*infml*), persevere, strive, struggle.

toilet n lavatory, WC, loo (*infml*), bog (*sl*), bathroom, cloakroom, washroom, rest room, public convenience, Ladies (*infml*), Gents (*infml*), urinal, convenience, powder room.

token n **1** SYMBOL, emblem, representation, mark, sign, indication, manifestation, demonstration, expression, evidence, proof, clue, warning, reminder, memorial, memento, souvenir, keepsake. **2** *gift token*: voucher, coupon, counter, disc.

adj symbolic, emblematic, nominal, minimal, perfunctory, superficial, cosmetic, hollow, insincere.

tolerable adj bearable, endurable, sufferable, acceptable, passable, adequate, reasonable, fair, average, all right, OK (*infml*), not bad, mediocre, indifferent, so-so (*infml*), unexceptional, ordinary, run-of-the-mill.

☒ intolerable, unbearable, insufferable.

tolerance n **1** TOLERATION, patience, forbearance, open-mindedness, broad-mindedness, magnanimity, sympathy,

understanding, lenity, indulgence, permissiveness. **2** VARIATION, fluctuation, play, allowance, clearance. **3** RESISTANCE, resilience, toughness, endurance, stamina.
🔁 intolerance, prejudice, bigotry, narrow-mindedness.

tolerant *adj* patient, forbearing, long-suffering, open-minded, fair, unprejudiced, broad-minded, liberal, charitable, kind-hearted, sympathetic, understanding, forgiving, lenient, indulgent, easy-going (*infml*), permissive, lax, soft.
🔁 intolerant, biased, prejudiced, bigoted, unsympathetic.

tolerate *v* endure, suffer, put up with, bear, stand, abide, stomach, swallow, take, receive, accept, admit, allow, permit, condone, countenance, indulge.

toll[1] *v* ring, peal, chime, knell, sound, strike, announce, call.

toll[2] *n* charge, fee, payment, levy, tax, duty, tariff, rate, cost, penalty, demand, loss.

tomb *n* grave, burial-place, vault, crypt, sepulchre, catacomb, mausoleum, cenotaph.

tone *n* **1** *tone of voice*: note, timbre, pitch, volume, intonation, modulation, inflection, accent, stress, emphasis, force, strength. **2** TINT, tinge, colour, hue, shade, cast, tonality. **3** AIR, manner, attitude, mood, spirit, humour, temper, character, quality, feel, style, effect, vein, tenor, drift.
v match, co-ordinate, blend, harmonize.
tone down moderate, temper, subdue, restrain, soften, dim, dampen, play down, reduce, alleviate, assuage, mitigate.

tongue *n* language, speech, discourse, talk, utterance, articulation, parlance, vernacular, idiom, dialect, patois.

tongue-tied *adj* speechless,

dumbstruck, inarticulate, silent, mute, dumb, voiceless.
🔁 talkative, garrulous, voluble.

tonic *n* cordial, pick-me-up, restorative, refresher, bracer, stimulant, shot in the arm (*infml*), boost, fillip.

too *adv* **1** ALSO, as well, in addition, besides, moreover, likewise. **2** EXCESSIVELY, inordinately, unduly, over, overly, unreasonably, ridiculously, extremely, very.

tool *n* **1** IMPLEMENT, instrument, utensil, gadget, device, contrivance, contraption, apparatus, appliance, machine, means, vehicle, medium, agency, agent, intermediary. **2** PUPPET, pawn, dupe, stooge, minion, hireling.

Types of tool include: bolster, caulking-iron, crowbar, hod, jackhammer, jointer, mattock, pick, pick-axe, plumb-line, sledgehammer; chaser, clamp, dividers, dolly, drill, hacksaw, jack, pincers, pliers, protractor, punch, rule, sander, scriber, snips, socket-wrench, soldering-iron, spraygun, tommy bar, vice; auger, awl, brace and bit, bradawl, chisel, file, fretsaw, hammer, handsaw, jack-plane, jig-saw, level, mallet, plane, rasp, saw, screwdriver, set-square, spirit level, tenon-saw, T-square; billhook, chainsaw, chopper, dibber, fork, grass-rake, hay fork, hoe, pitchfork, plough, pruning-knife, pruning-shears, rake, scythe, secateurs, shears, shovel, sickle, spade, thresher, trowel; needle, scissors, pinking-shears, bodkin, crochet hook, forceps, scalpel, tweezers, tongs, cleaver, steel, gimlet, mace, mortar, pestle, paper-cutter, paper-knife, stapler, pocket-knife, penknife.

---

top *n* **1** HEAD, tip, vertex, apex, crest, crown, peak, pinnacle, summit, acme, zenith, culmination, height. **2**

topic

LID, cap, cover, cork, stopper.

E 1 bottom, base, nadir.

adj highest, topmost, upmost, uppermost, upper, superior, head, chief, leading, first, foremost, principal, sovereign, ruling, pre-eminent, dominant, prime, paramount, greatest, maximum, best, finest, supreme, crowning, culminating.

E bottom, lowest, inferior.

v 1 TIP, cap, crown, cover, finish (off), decorate, garnish. 2 BEAT, exceed, outstrip, better, excel, best, surpass, eclipse, outshine, outdo, surmount, transcend. 3 HEAD, lead, rule, command.

topic *n* subject, theme, issue, question, matter, point, thesis, text.

topical *adj* current, contemporary, up-to-date, up-to-the-minute, recent, newsworthy, relevant, popular, familiar.

topple *v* totter, overbalance, tumble, fall, collapse, upset, overturn, capsize, overthrow, oust.

torment *v* tease, provoke, annoy, vex, trouble, worry, harass, hound, pester, bother, bedevil, plague, afflict, distress, harrow, pain, torture, persecute.

n provocation, annoyance, vexation, bane, scourge, trouble, bother, nuisance, harassment, worry, anguish, distress, misery, affliction, suffering, pain, agony, ordeal, torture, persecution.

torrent *n* stream, volley, outburst, gush, rush, flood, spate, deluge, cascade, downpour.

E trickle.

tortuous *adj* twisting, winding, meandering, serpentine, zigzag, circuitous, roundabout, indirect, convoluted, complicated, involved.

E straight, straightforward.

torture *v* pain, agonize, excruciate, crucify, rack, martyr, persecute, torment, afflict, distress.

n pain, agony, suffering, affliction, distress, misery, anguish, torment, martyrdom, persecution.

toss *v* 1 FLIP, cast, fling, throw, chuck (*infml*), sling, hurl, lob. 2 ROLL, heave, pitch, lurch, jolt, shake, agitate, rock, thrash, squirm, wriggle.

n flip, cast, fling, throw, pitch.

total *n* sum, whole, entirety, totality, all, lot, mass, aggregate, amount.

adj full, complete, entire, whole, integral, all-out, utter, absolute, unconditional, unqualified, outright, undisputed, perfect, consummate, thoroughgoing, sheer, downright, thorough.

E partial, limited, restricted.

v add (up), sum (up), tot (up), count (up), reckon, amount to, come to, reach.

totter *v* stagger, reel, lurch, stumble, falter, waver, teeter, sway, rock, shake, quiver, tremble.

touch *n* 1 FEEL, texture, brush, stroke, caress, pat, tap, contact. 2 *a touch of garlic*: trace, spot, dash, pinch, soupçon, suspicion, hint, suggestion, speck, jot, tinge, smack. 3 SKILL, art, knack, flair, style, method, manner, technique, approach.

v 1 FEEL, handle, finger, brush, graze, stroke, caress, fondle, pat, tap, hit, strike, contact, meet, abut, adjoin, border. 2 MOVE, stir, upset, disturb, impress, inspire, influence, affect, concern, regard. 3 REACH, attain, equal, match, rival, better.

touch on mention, broach, speak of, remark on, refer to, allude to, cover, deal with.

touched *adj* 1 MOVED, stirred, affected, disturbed, impressed. 2 MAD, crazy, deranged, disturbed, eccentric, dotty (*infml*), daft (*infml*), barmy (*infml*).

touching *adj* moving, stirring, affecting, poignant, pitiable, pitiful, pathetic, sad, emotional, tender.

touchy adj irritable, irascible, quick-tempered, bad-tempered, grumpy, grouchy, crabbed, cross, peevish, captious, edgy, over-sensitive.
🔄 calm, imperturbable.

tough adj **1** STRONG, durable, resilient, resistant, hardy, sturdy, solid, rigid, stiff, inflexible, hard, leathery. **2** tough criminal: rough, violent, vicious, callous, hardened, obstinate. **3** HARSH, severe, strict, stern, firm, resolute, determined, tenacious. **4** ARDUOUS, laborious, exacting, hard, difficult, puzzling, perplexing, baffling, knotty, thorny, troublesome.
🔄 **1** fragile, delicate, weak, tender. **2** gentle, soft. **3** gentle. **4** easy, simple.
n brute, thug, bully, ruffian, hooligan, lout, yob (sl).

tour n circuit, round, visit, expedition, journey, trip, outing, excursion, drive, ride, course.
v visit, go round, sightsee, explore, travel, journey, drive, ride.

tourist n holidaymaker, visitor, sightseer, tripper, excursionist, traveller, voyager, globetrotter.

tournament n championship, series, competition, contest, match, event, meeting.

tow v pull, tug, draw, trail, drag, lug, haul, transport.

towards prep **1** TO, approaching, nearing, close to, nearly, almost. **2** his feelings towards her: regarding, with regard to, with respect to, concerning, about, for.

tower n steeple, spire, belfry, turret, fortification, bastion, citadel, fort, fortress, castle, keep.
v rise, rear, ascend, mount, soar, loom, overlook, dominate, surpass, transcend, exceed, top.

Types of tower and famous towers include: barbican, bastille, bastion, belfry, bell tower, belvedere, campanile, castle, church tower, citadel, column, demi-bastion, donjon, Eiffel Tower, fort, fortification, fortress, gate-tower, high-rise building, hill-fort, keep, lookout tower, martello tower, minar, minaret, mirador, pagoda, peel-tower, scaffold tower, skyscraper, smock mill, spire, steeple, tower block, tower mill, Tower of London, Tower of Pisa, turret, watchtower, water tower.

towering adj soaring, tall, high, lofty, elevated, monumental, colossal, gigantic, great, magnificent, imposing, impressive, sublime, supreme, surpassing, overpowering, extreme, inordinate.
🔄 small, tiny, minor, trivial.

toxic adj poisonous, harmful, noxious, unhealthy, dangerous, deadly, lethal.
🔄 harmless, safe.

toy n plaything, game, doll, knick-knack.
v play, tinker, fiddle, sport, trifle, dally.

trace n trail, track, spoor, footprint, footmark, mark, token, sign, indication, evidence, record, relic, remains, remnant, vestige, shadow, hint, suggestion, suspicion, soupçon, dash, drop, spot, bit, jot, touch, tinge, smack.
v **1** COPY, draw, sketch, outline, delineate, depict, mark, record, map, chart. **2** FIND, discover, detect, unearth, track (down), trail, stalk, hunt, seek, follow, pursue, shadow.

track n footstep, footprint, footmark, scent, spoor, trail, wake, mark, trace, slot, groove, rail, path, way, route, orbit, line, course, drift, sequence.
v stalk, trail, hunt, trace, follow, pursue, chase, dog, tail, shadow.
track down find, discover, trace, hunt down, run to earth, sniff out, ferret out,

tract 546

dig up, unearth, expose, catch, capture.

tract *n* stretch, extent, expanse, plot, lot, territory, area, region, zone, district, quarter.

trade *n* **1** COMMERCE, traffic, business, dealing, buying, selling, shopkeeping, barter, exchange, transactions, custom.
2 OCCUPATION, job, business, profession, calling, craft, skill.
v traffic, peddle, do business, deal, transact, buy, sell, barter, exchange, swap, switch, bargain.

trademark *n* brand, label, name, sign, symbol, logo, insignia, crest, emblem, badge, hallmark.

trader *n* merchant, tradesman, broker, dealer, buyer, seller, vendor, supplier, wholesaler, retailer, shopkeeper, trafficker, peddler.

tradition *n* convention, custom, usage, way, habit, routine, ritual, institution, folklore.

traditional *adj* conventional, customary, habitual, usual, accustomed, established, fixed, long-established, time-honoured, old, historic, folk, oral, unwritten.
⊟ unconventional, innovative, new, modern, contemporary.

traffic *n* **1** VEHICLES, shipping, transport, transportation, freight, passengers. **2** TRADE, commerce, business, dealing, trafficking, barter, exchange. **3** COMMUNICATION, dealings, relations.
v peddle, buy, sell, trade, do business, deal, bargain, barter, exchange.

tragedy *n* adversity, misfortune, unhappiness, affliction, blow, calamity, disaster, catastrophe.

tragic *adj* sad, sorrowful, miserable, unhappy, unfortunate, unlucky, ill-fated, pitiable, pathetic, heartbreaking, shocking, appalling, dreadful, awful, dire, calamitous, disastrous, catastrophic, deadly, fatal.

⊟ happy, comic, successful.

trail *v* **1** DRAG, pull, tow, droop, dangle, extend, stream, straggle, dawdle, lag, loiter, linger. **2** TRACK, stalk, hunt, follow, pursue, chase, shadow, tail.
n track, footprints, footmarks, scent, trace, path, footpath, road, route, way.

train *v* **1** TEACH, instruct, coach, tutor, educate, improve, school, discipline, prepare, drill, exercise, work out, practise, rehearse.
2 POINT, direct, aim, level.
n **1** *train of events*: sequence, succession, series, progression, order, string, chain, line, file, procession, convoy, cortège, caravan. **2** RETINUE, entourage, attendants, court, household, staff, followers, following.

trainer *n* teacher, instructor, coach, tutor, handler.

training *n* teaching, instruction, coaching, tuition, education, schooling, discipline, preparation, grounding, drill, exercise, working-out, practice, learning, apprenticeship.

trait *n* feature, attribute, quality, characteristic, idiosyncrasy, peculiarity, quirk.

traitor *n* betrayer, informer, deceiver, double-crosser, turncoat, renegade, deserter, defector, quisling, collaborator.
⊟ loyalist, supporter, defender.

tramp *v* walk, march, tread, stamp, stomp, stump, plod, trudge, traipse, trail, trek, hike, ramble, roam, rove.
n vagrant, vagabond, hobo, down-and-out, dosser (*sl*).

trample *v* tread, stamp, crush, squash, flatten.

trance *n* dream, reverie, daze, stupor, unconsciousness, spell, ecstasy, rapture.

tranquil *adj* calm, composed, cool, imperturbable, unexcited, placid, sedate, relaxed, laid-back (*infml*), serene, peaceful, restful, still, undisturbed, untroubled, quiet, hushed, silent.

F3 agitated, disturbed, troubled, noisy.

tranquillizer *n* sedative, opiate, narcotic, barbiturate.

transaction *n* deal, bargain, agreement, arrangement, negotiation, business, affair, matter, proceeding, enterprise, undertaking, deed, action, execution, discharge.

transcend *v* surpass, excel, outshine, eclipse, outdo, outstrip, beat, surmount, exceed, overstep.

transcribe *v* write out, copy, reproduce, rewrite, transliterate, translate, render, take down, note, record.

transcript *n* transcription, copy, reproduction, duplicate, transliteration, translation, version, note, record, manuscript.

transfer *v* change, transpose, move, shift, remove, relocate, transplant, transport, carry, convey, transmit, consign, grant, hand over.
n change, changeover, transposition, move, shift, removal, relocation, displacement, transmission, handover, transference.

transfix *v* 1 FASCINATE, spellbind, mesmerize, hypnotize, paralyse.
2 IMPALE, spear, skewer, spike, stick.

transform *v* change, alter, adapt, convert, remodel, reconstruct, transfigure, revolutionize.

F3 preserve, maintain.

transformation *n* change, alteration, mutation, conversion, metamorphosis, transfiguration, revolution.

F3 preservation, conservation.

transient *adj* transitory, passing, flying, fleeting, brief, short, momentary, ephemeral, short-lived, temporary, short-term.

F3 lasting, permanent.

transit *n* passage, journey, travel, movement, transfer, transportation, conveyance, carriage, haulage,

shipment.

transition *n* passage, passing, progress, progression, development, evolution, flux, change, alteration, conversion, transformation, shift.

transitional *adj* provisional, temporary, passing, intermediate, developmental, changing, fluid, unsettled.

F3 initial, final.

translate *v* interpret, render, paraphrase, simplify, decode, decipher, transliterate, transcribe, change, alter, convert, transform, improve.

translation *n* rendering, version, interpretation, gloss, crib, rewording, rephrasing, paraphrase, simplification, transliteration, transcription, change, alteration, conversion, transformation.

transmission *n* 1 BROADCASTING, diffusion, spread, communication, conveyance, carriage, transport, shipment, sending, dispatch, relaying, transfer. 2 *a live transmission*: broadcast, programme, show, signal.

F3 1 reception.

transmit *v* communicate, impart, convey, carry, bear, transport, send, dispatch, forward, relay, transfer, broadcast, radio, disseminate, network, diffuse, spread.

F3 receive.

transparency *n* slide, photograph, picture.

transparent *adj* 1 *transparent plastic*: clear, see-through, translucent, sheer. 2 PLAIN, distinct, clear, lucid, explicit, unambiguous, unequivocal, apparent, visible, obvious, evident, manifest, patent, undisguised, open, candid, straightforward.

F3 1 opaque. 2 unclear, ambiguous.

transplant *v* move, shift, displace, remove, uproot, transfer, relocate, resettle, repot.

F3 leave.

transport *v* convey, carry, bear, take, fetch, bring, move, shift, transfer, ship, haul, remove, deport.
n conveyance, carriage, transfer, transportation, shipment, shipping, haulage, removal.

transpose *v* swap, exchange, switch, interchange, transfer, shift, rearrange, reorder, change, alter, move, substitute.

transverse *adj* cross, crosswise, transversal, diagonal, oblique.

trap *n* snare, net, noose, springe, gin, booby-trap, pitfall, danger, hazard, ambush, trick, wile, ruse, stratagem, device, trickery, artifice, deception.
v snare, net, entrap, ensnare, enmesh, catch, take, ambush, corner, trick, deceive, dupe.

trash *n* rubbish, garbage, refuse, junk, waste, litter, sweepings, offscourings, scum, dregs.

trauma *n* injury, wound, hurt, damage, pain, suffering, anguish, agony, torture, ordeal, shock, jolt, upset, disturbance, upheaval, strain, stress.
F3 healing.

traumatic *adj* painful, hurtful, injurious, wounding, shocking, upsetting, distressing, disturbing, unpleasant, frightening, stressful.
F3 healing, relaxing.

travel *v* journey, voyage, go, wend, move, proceed, progress, wander, ramble, roam, rove, tour, cross, traverse.
F3 stay, remain.

> *Methods of travel include*: fly, aviate, pilot, shuttle, sail, cruise, punt, paddle, row, steam, ride, cycle, bike (*infml*), freewheel, drive, motor, bus, walk, hike, march, ramble, trek, orienteer, hitch-hike, commute.

n travelling, touring, tourism, globetrotting.

> *Forms of travel include*: flight, cruise, sail, voyage, ride, drive, march, walk, hike, ramble, excursion, holiday, jaunt, outing, tour, trip, visit, expedition, safari, trek, circumnavigation, exploration, journey, migration, mission, pilgrimage.

traveller *n* **1** TOURIST, explorer, voyager, globetrotter, holidaymaker, tripper (*infml*), excursionist, passenger, commuter, wanderer, rambler, hiker, wayfarer, migrant, nomad, gypsy, itinerant, tinker, vagrant. **2** SALESMAN, saleswoman, representative, rep (*infml*), agent.

travelling *adj* touring, wandering, roaming, roving, wayfaring, migrant, migratory, nomadic, itinerant, peripatetic, mobile, moving, vagrant, homeless.
F3 fixed.

travels *n* voyage, expedition, passage, journey, trip, excursion, tour, wanderings.

travesty *n* mockery, parody, take-off, send-up, farce, caricature, distortion, sham, apology.

treacherous *adj* **1** TRAITOROUS, disloyal, unfaithful, faithless, unreliable, untrustworthy, false, untrue, deceitful, double-crossing. **2** *treacherous roads*: dangerous, hazardous, risky, perilous, precarious, icy, slippery.
F3 **1** loyal, faithful, dependable. **2** safe, stable.

treachery *n* treason, betrayal, disloyalty, infidelity, falseness, duplicity, double-dealing.
F3 loyalty, dependability.

tread *v* walk, step, pace, stride, march, tramp, trudge, plod, stamp, trample, walk on, press, crush, squash.
n walk, footfall, footstep, step, pace, stride.

treason *n* treachery, perfidy, disloyalty, duplicity, subversion, sedition, mutiny, rebellion.

☒ loyalty.

treasonable *adj* traitorous, perfidious, disloyal, false, subversive, seditious, mutinous.

☒ loyal.

treasure *n* fortune, wealth, riches, money, cash, gold, jewels, hoard, cache.

v prize, value, esteem, revere, worship, love, adore, idolize, cherish, preserve, guard.

☒ disparage, belittle.

treat *n* indulgence, gratification, pleasure, delight, enjoyment, fun, entertainment, excursion, outing, party, celebration, feast, banquet, gift, surprise, thrill.

v 1 DEAL WITH, manage, handle, use, regard, consider, discuss, cover.
2 TEND, nurse, minister to, attend to, care for, heal, cure. 3 PAY FOR, buy, stand, give, provide, entertain, regale, feast.

treatise *n* essay, dissertation, thesis, monograph, paper, pamphlet, tract, study, exposition.

treatment *n* 1 HEALING, cure, remedy, medication, therapy, surgery, care, nursing.
2 MANAGEMENT, handling, use, usage, conduct, discussion, coverage.

treaty *n* pact, convention, agreement, covenant, compact, negotiation, contract, bond, alliance.

tree *n* bush, shrub, evergreen, conifer.

Trees include: acacia, acer, alder, almond, apple, ash, aspen, balsa, bay, beech, birch, blackthorn, blue gum, box, cedar, cherry, chestnut, coconut palm, cottonwood, cypress, date palm, dogwood, Dutch elm, ebony, elder, elm, eucalyptus, fig, fir, gum, hawthorn, hazel, hickory, hornbeam, horse chestnut, Japanese maple, larch, laurel, lime, linden, mahogany, maple, monkey puzzle, mountain ash, oak, palm, pear, pine, plane, plum, poplar, prunus, pussy willow, redwood, rowan, rubber tree, sandalwood, sapele, sequoia, silver birch, silver maple, spruce, sycamore, teak, walnut, weeping willow, whitebeam, willow, witch hazel, yew, yucca; bonsai, conifer, deciduous, evergreen, fruit, hardwood, ornamental, palm, softwood.

trek *n* hike, walk, march, tramp, journey, expedition, safari.

v hike, walk, march, tramp, trudge, plod, journey, rove, roam.

tremble *v* shake, vibrate, quake, shiver, shudder, quiver, wobble, rock.

n shake, vibration, quake, shiver, shudder, quiver, tremor, wobble.

tremendous *adj* wonderful, marvellous, stupendous, sensational, spectacular, extraordinary, amazing, incredible, terrific, impressive, huge, immense, vast, colossal, gigantic, towering, formidable.

☒ ordinary, unimpressive.

tremor *n* shake, quiver, tremble, shiver, quake, quaver, wobble, vibration, agitation, thrill, shock, earthquake.

☒ steadiness.

trend *n* course, flow, drift, tendency, inclination, leaning, craze, rage (*infml*), fashion, vogue, mode, style, look.

trespass *v* invade, intrude, encroach, poach, infringe, violate, offend, wrong.

☒ obey, keep to.

n invasion, intrusion, encroachment, poaching, infringement, violation, contravention, offence, misdemeanour.

trespasser *n* intruder, poacher, offender, criminal.

trial *n* 1 LITIGATION, lawsuit, hearing, inquiry, tribunal.

2 EXPERIMENT, test, examination, check, dry run, dummy run, practice, rehearsal, audition, contest. **3** AFFLICTION, suffering, grief, misery, distress, adversity, hardship, ordeal, trouble, nuisance, vexation, tribulation.

F3 3 relief, happiness.

adj experimental, test, pilot, exploratory, provisional, probationary.

tribe *n* race, nation, people, clan, family, house, dynasty, blood, stock, group, caste, class, division, branch.

tribute *n* **1** PRAISE, commendation, compliment, accolade, homage, respect, honour, credit, acknowledgement, recognition, gratitude. **2** PAYMENT, levy, charge, tax, duty, gift, offering, contribution.

trick *n* fraud, swindle, deception, deceit, artifice, illusion, hoax, practical joke, joke, leg-pull (*infml*), prank, antic, caper, frolic, feat, stunt, ruse, wile, dodge, subterfuge, trap, device, knack, technique, secret. *adj* false, mock, artificial, imitation, ersatz, fake, forged, counterfeit, feigned, sham, bogus.

F3 real, genuine.

v deceive, delude, dupe, fool, hoodwink, beguile, mislead, bluff, hoax, pull someone's leg (*infml*), cheat, swindle, diddle, defraud, con (*infml*), trap, outwit.

trickery *n* deception, illusion, sleight-of-hand, pretence, artifice, guile, deceit, dishonesty, cheating, swindling, fraud, imposture, double-dealing, monkey business, funny business (*sl*), chicanery, skulduggery, hocus-pocus.

F3 straightforwardness, honesty.

trickle *v* dribble, run, leak, seep, ooze, exude, drip, drop, filter, percolate.

F3 stream, gush.

n dribble, drip, drop, leak, seepage.

F3 stream, gush.

tricky *adj* **1** *a tricky problem*:

difficult, awkward, problematic, complicated, knotty, thorny, delicate, ticklish. **2** CRAFTY, artful, cunning, sly, wily, foxy, subtle, devious, slippery, scheming, deceitful.

F3 1 easy, simple. 2 honest.

trifle *n* **1** LITTLE, bit, spot, drop, dash, touch, trace. **2** TOY, plaything, trinket, bauble, knick-knack, triviality, nothing.

v toy, play, sport, flirt, dally, dabble, fiddle, meddle, fool.

trifling *adj* small, paltry, slight, negligible, inconsiderable, unimportant, insignificant, minor, trivial, petty, silly, frivolous, idle, empty, worthless.

F3 important, significant, serious.

trigger *v* cause, start, initiate, activate, set off, spark off, provoke, prompt, elicit, generate, produce. *n* lever, catch, switch, spur, stimulus.

trim *adj* **1** NEAT, tidy, orderly, shipshape, spick-and-span, spruce, smart, dapper. **2** SLIM, slender, streamlined, compact.

F3 1 untidy, scruffy.

v **1** CUT, clip, crop, dock, prune, pare, shave. **2** DECORATE, ornament, embellish, garnish, dress, array, adjust, arrange, order, neaten, tidy. *n* condition, state, order, form, shape, fitness, health.

trimmings *n* **1** GARNISH, decorations, ornaments, frills, extras, accessories. **2** CUTTINGS, clippings, parings, ends.

trinket *n* bauble, jewel, ornament, knick-knack.

trio *n* threesome, triad, triumvirate, trinity, triplet, trilogy.

trip *n* outing, excursion, tour, jaunt, ride, drive, spin, journey, voyage, expedition, foray. *v* stumble, slip, fall, tumble, stagger, totter, blunder.

triple *adj* treble, triplicate, threefold, three-ply, three-way. *v* treble, triplicate.

trite *adj* banal, commonplace, ordinary, run-of-the-mill, stale, tired, worn, threadbare, unoriginal, hackneyed, overused, stock, stereotyped, clichéed, corny (*infml*).
🔁 original, new, fresh.

triumph *n* **1** WIN, victory, conquest, walk-over, success, achievement, accomplishment, feat, coup, masterstroke, hit, sensation.
2 EXULTATION, jubilation, rejoicing, celebration, elation, joy, happiness.
🔁 **1** failure.
v win, succeed, prosper, conquer, vanquish, overcome, overwhelm, prevail, dominate, celebrate, rejoice, glory, gloat.
🔁 lose, fail.

triumphant *adj* winning, victorious, conquering, successful, exultant, jubilant, rejoicing, celebratory, glorious, elated, joyful, proud, boastful, gloating, swaggering.
🔁 defeated, humble.

trivial *adj* unimportant, insignificant, inconsequential, incidental, minor, petty, paltry, trifling, small, little, inconsiderable, negligible, worthless, meaningless, frivolous, banal, trite, commonplace, everyday.
🔁 important, significant, profound.

triviality *n* unimportance, insignificance, pettiness, smallness, worthlessness, meaninglessness, frivolity, trifle, detail, technicality.
🔁 importance, essential.

troop *n* contingent, squadron, unit, division, company, squad, team, crew, gang, band, bunch, group, body, pack, herd, flock, horde, crowd, throng, multitude.
v go, march, parade, stream, flock, swarm, throng.

troops *n* army, military, soldiers, servicemen, servicewomen.

trophy *n* cup, prize, award, souvenir, memento.

tropical *adj* hot, torrid, sultry,

sweltering, stifling, steamy, humid.
🔁 arctic, cold, cool, temperate.

trot *v* jog, run, scamper, scuttle, scurry.

trouble *n* **1** PROBLEM, difficulty, struggle, annoyance, irritation, bother, nuisance, inconvenience, misfortune, adversity, trial, tribulation, pain, suffering, affliction, distress, grief, woe, heartache, concern, uneasiness, worry, anxiety, agitation. **2** UNREST, strife, tumult, commotion, disturbance, disorder, upheaval. **3** *back trouble*: disorder, complaint, ailment, illness, disease, disability, defect. **4** EFFORT, exertion, pains, care, attention, thought.
🔁 **1** relief, calm. **2** order. **3** health.
v annoy, vex, harass, torment, bother, inconvenience, disturb, upset, distress, sadden, pain, afflict, burden, worry, agitate, disconcert, perplex.
🔁 reassure, help.

troublemaker *n* agitator, rabble-rouser, incendiary, instigator, ringleader, stirrer, mischief-maker.
🔁 peacemaker.

troublesome *adj* **1** ANNOYING, irritating, vexatious, irksome, bothersome, inconvenient, difficult, hard, tricky, thorny, taxing, demanding, laborious, tiresome, wearisome. **2** UNRULY, rowdy, turbulent, trying, unco-operative, insubordinate, rebellious.
🔁 **1** easy, simple. **2** helpful.

trough *n* gutter, conduit, trench, ditch, gully, channel, groove, furrow, hollow, depression.

trousers *n* pants, slacks, jeans, denims, Levis®, flannels, bags (*infml*), dungarees, breeches, shorts.

truancy *n* absence, absenteeism, shirking, skiving (*infml*).
🔁 attendance.

truant *n* absentee, deserter, runaway, idler, shirker, skiver (*infml*), dodger.
adj absent, missing, runaway.

truce *n* cease-fire, peace, armistice,

truck 552

cessation, moratorium, suspension, stay, respite, let-up (*infml*), lull, rest, break, interval, intermission.
F3 war, hostilities.

truck *n* lorry, van, wagon, trailer, float, cart, barrow.

trudge *v* tramp, plod, clump, stump, lumber, traipse, slog, labour, trek, hike, walk, march.
n tramp, traipse, slog, haul, trek, hike, walk, march.

true *adj* **1** REAL, genuine, authentic, actual, veritable, exact, precise, accurate, correct, right, factual, truthful, veracious, sincere, honest, legitimate, valid, rightful, proper. **2** FAITHFUL, loyal, constant, steadfast, staunch, firm, trustworthy, trusty, honourable, dedicated, devoted.
F3 1 false, wrong, incorrect, inaccurate. **2** unfaithful, faithless.

truism *n* truth, platitude, commonplace, cliché.

truly *adv* very, greatly, extremely, really, genuinely, sincerely, honestly, truthfully, undeniably, indubitably, indeed, in fact, in reality, exactly, precisely, correctly, rightly, properly.
F3 slightly, falsely, incorrectly.

trumpet *n* bugle, horn, clarion, blare, blast, roar, bellow, cry, call.
v blare, blast, roar, bellow, shout, proclaim, announce, broadcast, advertise.

truncate *v* shorten, abbreviate, curtail, cut, lop, dock, prune, pare, clip, trim, crop.
F3 lengthen, extend.

trunk *n* **1** CASE, suitcase, chest, coffer, box, crate. **2** TORSO, body, frame, shaft, stock, stem, stalk.

truss *v* tie, strap, bind, pinion, fasten, secure, bundle, pack.
F3 untie, loosen.
n binding, bandage, support, brace, prop, stay, shore, strut, joist.

trust *n* **1** FAITH, belief, credence, credit, hope, expectation, reliance,

confidence, assurance, conviction, certainty. **2** CARE, charge, custody, safekeeping, guardianship, protection, responsibility, duty.
F3 1 distrust, mistrust, scepticism, doubt.
v **1** BELIEVE, imagine, assume, presume, suppose, surmise, hope, expect, rely on, depend on, count on, bank on, swear by. **2** ENTRUST, commit, consign, confide, give, assign, delegate.
F3 1 distrust, mistrust, doubt, disbelieve.

trusting *adj* trustful, credulous, gullible, naïve, innocent, unquestioning, unsuspecting, unguarded, unwary.
F3 distrustful, suspicious, cautious.

trustworthy *adj* honest, upright, honourable, principled, dependable, reliable, steadfast, true, responsible, sensible.
F3 untrustworthy, dishonest, unreliable, irresponsible.

truth *n* **1** TRUTHFULNESS, veracity, candour, frankness, honesty, sincerity, genuineness, authenticity, realism, exactness, precision, accuracy, validity, legitimacy, honour, integrity, uprightness, faithfulness, fidelity, loyalty, constancy. **2** *tell the truth*: facts, reality, actuality, fact, axiom, maxim, principle, truism.
F3 1 deceit, dishonesty, falseness. **2** lie, falsehood.

truthful *adj* veracious, frank, candid, straight, honest, sincere, true, veritable, exact, precise, accurate, correct, realistic, faithful, trustworthy, reliable.
F3 untruthful, deceitful, false, untrue.

try *v* **1** ATTEMPT, endeavour, venture, undertake, seek, strive. **2** HEAR, judge. **3** EXPERIMENT, test, sample, taste, inspect, examine, investigate, evaluate, appraise.
n **1** ATTEMPT, endeavour, effort, go

(*infml*), bash (*infml*), crack (*infml*), shot (*infml*), stab (*infml*). **2** EXPERIMENT, test, trial, ample, taste.

trying *adj* annoying, irritating, aggravating (*infml*), vexatious, exasperating, troublesome, tiresome, wearisome, difficult, hard, tough, arduous, taxing, demanding, testing.
☒ easy.

tub *n* bath, basin, vat, tun, butt, cask, barrel, keg.

tube *n* hose, pipe, cylinder, duct, conduit, spout, channel.

tuck *v* **1** INSERT, push, thrust, stuff, cram. **2** FOLD, pleat, gather, crease.
n fold, pleat, gather, pucker, crease.

tuft *n* crest, beard, tassel, knot, clump, cluster, bunch.

tug *v* pull, draw, tow, haul, drag, lug, heave, wrench, jerk, pluck.
n pull, tow, haul, heave, wrench, jerk, pluck.

tuition *n* teaching, instruction, coaching, training, lessons, schooling, education.

tumble *v* fall, stumble, trip, topple, overthrow, drop, flop, collapse, plummet, pitch, roll, toss.
n fall, stumble, trip, drop, plunge, roll, toss.

tumult *n* commotion, turmoil, disturbance, upheaval, stir, agitation, unrest, disorder, chaos, pandemonium, noise, clamour, din, racket, hubbub, hullabaloo, row, rumpus, uproar, riot, fracas, brawl, affray, strife.
☒ peace, calm, composure.

tumultuous *adj* turbulent, stormy, raging, fierce, violent, wild, hectic, boisterous, rowdy, noisy, disorderly, unruly, riotous, restless, agitated, troubled, disturbed, excited.
☒ calm, peaceful, quiet.

tune *n* melody, theme, motif, song, air, strain.
v pitch, harmonize, set, regulate, adjust, adapt, temper, attune, synchronize.

tuneful *adj* melodious, melodic, catchy, musical, euphonious, harmonious, pleasant, mellow, sonorous.
☒ tuneless, discordant.

tunnel *n* passage, passageway, gallery, subway, underpass, burrow, hole, mine, shaft, chimney.
v burrow, dig, excavate, mine, bore, penetrate, undermine, sap.

turbulent *adj* rough, choppy, stormy, blustery, tempestuous, raging, furious, violent, wild, tumultuous, unbridled, boisterous, rowdy, disorderly, unruly, undisciplined, obstreperous, rebellious, mutinous, riotous, agitated, unsettled, unstable, confused, disordered.
☒ calm, composed.

turmoil *n* confusion, disorder, tumult, commotion, disturbance, trouble, disquiet, agitation, turbulence, stir, ferment, flurry, bustle, chaos, pandemonium, bedlam, noise, din, hubbub, row, uproar.
☒ calm, peace, quiet.

turn *v* **1** REVOLVE, circle, spin, twirl, whirl, twist, gyrate, pivot, hinge, swivel, rotate, roll, move, shift, invert, reverse, bend, veer, swerve, divert. **2** MAKE, transform, change, alter, modify, convert, adapt, adjust, fit, mould, shape, form, fashion, remodel. **3** *turn cold*: go, become, grow. **4** RESORT, have recourse, apply, appeal. **5** SOUR, curdle, spoil, go off, go bad.
n **1** REVOLUTION, cycle, round, circle, rotation, spin, twirl, twist, gyration, bend, curve, loop, reversal. **2** CHANGE, alteration, shift, deviation. **3** *it's your turn*: go, chance, opportunity, occasion, stint, period, spell. **4** ACT, performance, performer.

turn away reject, avert, deflect, deviate, depart.
☒ accept, receive.

turn down 1 *turn down an offer*: reject, decline, refuse, spurn, rebuff, repudiate. **2** LOWER, lessen, quieten, soften, mute, muffle.
■ **1** accept. **2** turn up.

turn in 1 GO TO BED, retire. **2** HAND OVER, give up, surrender, deliver, hand in, tender, submit, return, give back.
■ **1** get up. **2** keep.

turn off 1 BRANCH OFF, leave, quit, depart from, deviate, divert.
2 SWITCH OFF, turn out, stop, shut down, unplug, disconnect. **3** (*sl*) REPEL, sicken, nauseate, disgust, offend, displease, disenchant, alienate, bore, discourage, put off.
■ **1** join. **2** turn on. **3** turn on (*sl*).

turn on 1 SWITCH ON, start (up), activate, connect. **2** (*sl*) AROUSE, stimulate, excite, thrill, please, attract. **3** HINGE ON, depend on, rest on. **4** ATTACK, round on, fall on.
■ **1** turn off. **2** turn off (*sl*).

turn out 1 HAPPEN, come about, transpire, ensue, result, end up, become, develop, emerge. **2** SWITCH OFF, turn off, unplug, disconnect. **3** APPEAR, present, dress, clothe. **4** PRODUCE, make, manufacture, fabricate, assemble. **5** EVICT, throw out, expel, deport, banish, dismiss, discharge, drum out, kick out, sack (*infml*). **6** *turn out the attic*: empty, clear, clean out.
■ **2** turn on. **5** admit. **6** fill.

turn over 1 THINK OVER, think about, mull over, ponder, deliberate, reflect on, contemplate, consider, examine. **2** HAND OVER, surrender, deliver, transfer. **3** OVERTURN, upset, upend, invert, capsize, keel over.

turn up 1 ATTEND, come, arrive, appear, show up (*infml*). **2** AMPLIFY, intensify, raise, increase. **3** DISCOVER, find, unearth, dig up, expose, disclose, reveal, show.
■ **1** stay away. **2** turn down.

turning *n* turn-off, junction, crossroads, fork, bend, curve, turn.

turning-point *n* crossroads, watershed, crux, crisis.

turnout *n* **1** ATTENDANCE, audience, gate, crowd, assembly, congregation. **2** APPEARANCE, outfit, dress, clothes.

tutor *n* teacher, instructor, coach, educator, lecturer, supervisor, guide, mentor, guru, guardian.
v teach, instruct, train, drill, coach, educate, school, lecture, supervise, direct, guide.

tweak *v*, *n* twist, pinch, squeeze, nip, pull, tug, jerk, twitch.

twee (*infml*) *adj* sweet, cute, pretty, dainty, quaint, sentimental, affected, precious.

twiddle *v* turn, twirl, swivel, twist, wiggle, adjust, fiddle, finger.

twilight *n* dusk, half-light, gloaming, gloom, dimness, sunset, evening.

twin *n* double, look-alike, likeness, duplicate, clone, match, counterpart, corollary, fellow, mate.
adj identical, matching, corresponding, symmetrical, parallel, matched, paired, double, dual, duplicate, twofold.
v match, pair, couple, link, join.

twine *n* string, cord, thread, yarn.
v wind, coil, spiral, loop, curl, bend, twist, wreathe, wrap, surround, encircle, entwine, plait, braid, knit, weave.

twinge *n* pain, pang, throb, spasm, throe, stab, stitch, pinch, prick.

twinkle *v* sparkle, glitter, shimmer, glisten, glimmer, flicker, wink, flash, glint, gleam, shine.
n sparkle, scintillation, glitter, shimmer, glisten, glimmer, flicker, wink, flash, glint, gleam, light.

twirl *v* spin, whirl, pirouette, wheel, rotate, revolve, swivel, pivot, turn, twist, gyrate, wind, coil.
n spin, whirl, pirouette, rotation, revolution, turn, twist, gyration, convlution, spiral, coil.

twist *v* **1** TURN, screw, wring, spin,

swivel, wind, zigzag, bend, coil,
spiral, curl, wreathe, twine, entwine,
intertwine, weave, entangle, wriggle,
squirm, writhe. **2** *twist one's ankle*:
wrench, rick, sprain, strain. **3**
CHANGE, alter, garble, misquote,
misrepresent, distort, contort, warp,
pervert.
n **1** TURN, screw, spin, roll, bend,
curve, arc, curl, loop, zigzag, coil,
spiral, convolution, squiggle, tangle. **2**
CHANGE, variation, break.
3 PERVERSION, distortion,
contortion. **4** SURPRISE, quirk,
oddity, peculiarity.

twisted *adj* warped, perverted,
deviant, unnatural.
F∃ straight.

twitch *v* jerk, jump, start, blink,
tremble, shake, pull, tug, tweak,
snatch, pluck.
n spasm, convulsion, tic, tremor,
jerk, jump, start.

twitter *v* chirp, chirrup, tweet, cheep,
sing, warble, whistle, chatter.

two-faced *adj* hypocritical,
insincere, false, lying, deceitful,
treacherous, double-dealing, devious,
untrustworthy.
F∃ honest, candid, frank.

tycoon *n* industrialist, entrepreneur,
captain of industry, magnate, mogul,
baron, supremo, capitalist, financier.

type *n* **1** SORT, kind, form, genre,
variety, strain, species, breed, group,
class, category, subdivision,
classification, description.

designation, stamp, mark, order,
standard. **2** ARCHETYPE,
embodiment, prototype, original,
model, pattern, specimen, example.
3 PRINT, printing, characters, letters,
lettering, face, fount, font.

typhoon *n* whirlwind, cyclone,
tornado, twister (*infml*), hurricane,
tempest, storm, squall.

typical *adj* standard, normal, usual,
average, conventional, orthodox,
stock, model, representative,
illustrative, indicative, characteristic,
distinctive.
F∃ atypical, unusual.

typify *v* embody, epitomize,
encapsulate, personify, characterize,
exemplify, symbolize, represent,
illustrate.

tyrannical *adj* dictatorial, despotic,
autocratic, absolute, arbitrary,
authoritarian, domineering,
overbearing, high-handed, imperious,
magisterial, ruthless, harsh, severe,
oppressive, overpowering, unjust,
unreasonable.
F∃ liberal, tolerant.

tyranny *n* dictatorship, despotism,
autocracy, absolutism,
authoritarianism, imperiousness,
ruthlessness, harshness, severity,
oppression, injustice.
F∃ democracy, freedom.

tyrant *n* dictator, despot, autocrat,
absolutist, authoritarian, bully,
oppressor, slave-driver, taskmaster.

U

ubiquitous *adj* omnipresent, ever-
present, everywhere, universal,
global, pervasive, common, frequent.
F∃ rare, scarce.

ugly *adj* **1** UNATTRACTIVE,
unsightly, plain, unprepossessing, ill-

favoured, hideous, monstrous,
misshapen, deformed.
2 UNPLEASANT, disagreeable, nasty,
horrid, objectionable, offensive,
disgusting, revolting, repulsive, vile,
frightful, terrible.

æ 1 attractive, beautiful, handsome, pretty. **2** pleasant.

ulterior *adj* secondary, hidden, concealed, undisclosed, unexpressed, covert, secret, private, personal, selfish.

æ overt.

ultimate *adj* final, last, closing, concluding, eventual, terminal, furthest, remotest, extreme, utmost, greatest, highest, supreme, superlative, perfect, radical, fundamental, primary.

ultimately *adv* finally, eventually, at last, in the end, after all.

umpire *n* referee, linesman, judge, adjudicator, arbiter, arbitrator, mediator, moderator.
v referee, judge, adjudicate, arbitrate, mediate, moderate, control.

umpteen (*infml*) *adj* a good many, numerous, plenty, millions, countless, innumerable.

æ few.

unabashed *adj* unashamed, unembarrassed, brazen, blatant, bold, confident, undaunted, unconcerned, undismayed.

æ abashed, sheepish.

unable *adj* incapable, powerless, impotent, unequipped, unqualified, unfit, incompetent, inadequate.

æ able, capable.

unacceptable *adj* intolerable, inadmissible, unsatisfactory, undesirable, unwelcome, objectionable, offensive, unpleasant.

æ acceptable, satisfactory.

unaccompanied *adj* alone, unescorted, unattended, lone, solo, single-handed.

æ accompanied.

unaccountable *adj* inexplicable, unexplainable, unfathomable, impenetrable, incomprehensible, baffling, puzzling, mysterious, astonishing, extraordinary, strange, odd, peculiar, singular, unusual, uncommon, unheard-of.

æ explicable, explainable.

unaccustomed *adj* **1** *unaccustomed to such luxury*: unused, unacquainted, unfamiliar, unpractised, inexperienced.
2 STRANGE, unusual, uncommon, different, new, unexpected, surprising, uncharacteristic, unprecedented.

æ 1 accustomed, familiar.
2 customary.

unaffected *adj* **1** UNMOVED, unconcerned, indifferent, impervious, untouched, unchanged, unaltered.
2 UNSOPHISTICATED, artless, naïve, ingenuous, unspoilt, plain, simple, straightforward, unpretentious, unassuming, sincere, honest, genuine.

æ 1 moved, influenced. **2** affected, pretentious, insincere.

unalterable *adj* unchangeable, invariable, unchanging, immutable, final, inflexible, unyielding, rigid, fixed, permanent.

æ alterable, flexible.

unanimity *n* consensus, unity, agreement, concurrence, accord, like-mindedness, concord, harmony, unison, concert.

æ disagreement, disunity.

unanimous *adj* united, concerted, joint, common, as one, in agreement, in accord, harmonious.

æ disunited, divided.

unapproachable *adj* inaccessible, remote, distant, aloof, standoffish, withdrawn, reserved, unsociable, unfriendly, forbidding.

æ approachable, friendly.

unarmed *adj* defenceless, unprotected, exposed, open, vulnerable, weak, helpless.

æ armed, protected.

unashamed *adj* shameless, unabashed, impenitent, unrepentant, unconcealed, undisguised, open, blatant.

unasked *adj* uninvited, unbidden,

unrequested, unsought, unsolicited, unwanted, voluntary, spontaneous.
Ea invited, wanted.

unassuming *adj* unassertive, self-effacing, retiring, modest, humble, meek, unobtrusive, unpretentious, simple, restrained.
Ea presumptuous, assertive, pretentious.

unattached *adj* unmarried, single, free, available, footloose, fancy-free, independent, unaffiliated.
Ea engaged, committed.

unattended *adj* ignored, disregarded, unguarded, unwatched, unsupervised, unaccompanied, unescorted, alone.
Ea attended, escorted.

unauthorized *adj* unofficial, unlawful, illegal, illicit, illegitimate, irregular, unsanctioned.
Ea authorized, legal.

unavoidable *adj* inevitable, inescapable, inexorable, certain, sure, fated, destined, obligatory, compulsory, mandatory, necessary.
Ea avoidable.

unaware *adj* oblivious, unconscious, ignorant, uninformed, unknowing, unsuspecting, unmindful, heedless, blind, deaf.
Ea aware, conscious.

unbalanced *adj* **1** INSANE, mad, crazy, lunatic, deranged, disturbed, demented, irrational, unsound. **2** *an unbalanced report*: biased, prejudiced, one-sided, partisan, unfair, unjust, unequal, uneven, asymmetrical, lopsided, unsteady, unstable.
Ea **1** sane. **2** unbiased.

unbearable *adj* intolerable, unacceptable, insupportable, insufferable, unendurable, excruciating.
Ea bearable, acceptable.

unbeatable *adj* invincible, unconquerable, unstoppable, unsurpassable, matchless, supreme,

excellent.

unbecoming *adj* unseemly, improper, unsuitable, inappropriate, unbefitting, ungentlemanly, unladylike, unattractive, unsightly.
Ea suitable, attractive.

unbelief *n* atheism, agnosticism, scepticism, doubt, incredulity, disbelief.
Ea belief, faith.

unbelievable *adj* incredible, inconceivable, unthinkable, unimaginable, astonishing, staggering, extraordinary, impossible, improbable, unlikely, implausible, unconvincing, far-fetched, preposterous.
Ea believable, credible.

unborn *adj* embryonic, expected, awaited, coming, future.

unbounded *adj* boundless, limitless, unlimited, unrestricted, unrestrained, unchecked, unbridled, infinite, endless, immeasurable, vast.
Ea limited, restrained.

unbreakable *adj* indestructible, shatterproof, toughened, resistant, proof, durable, strong, tough, rugged, solid.
Ea breakable, fragile.

unbridled *adj* immoderate, excessive, uncontrolled, unrestrained, unchecked.

unbroken *adj* **1** INTACT, whole, entire, complete, solid, undivided. **2** UNINTERRUPTED, continuous, endless, ceaseless, incessant, unceasing, constant, perpetual, progressive, successive. **3** *unbroken record*: unbeaten, unsurpassed, unequalled, unmatched.
Ea **1** broken. **2** intermittent, fitful.

uncalled-for *adj* gratuitous, unprovoked, unjustified, unwarranted, undeserved, unnecessary, needless.
Ea timely.

uncanny *adj* weird, strange, queer, bizarre, mysterious, unaccountable, incredible, remarkable, extraordinary, fantastic, unnatural, unearthly, supernatural, eerie, creepy, spooky (*infml*).

uncaring *adj* unconcerned, unmoved, unsympathetic, inconsiderate, unfeeling, cold, callous, indifferent, uninterested.
E3 caring, concerned.

unceasing *adj* ceaseless, incessant, unending, endless, never-ending, non-stop, continuous, unbroken, constant, perpetual, continual, persistent, relentless, unrelenting, unremitting.
E3 intermittent, spasmodic.

uncertain *adj* **1** UNSURE, unconvinced, doubtful, dubious, undecided, ambivalent, hesitant, wavering, vacillating.
2 INCONSTANT, changeable, variable, erratic, irregular, shaky, unsteady, unreliable.
3 UNPREDICTABLE, unforeseeable, undetermined, unsettled, unresolved, unconfirmed, indefinite, vague, insecure, risky, iffy (*sl*).
E3 1 certain, sure. **2** steady.
3 predictable.

uncertainty *n* doubt, scepticism, irresolution, dilemma, hesitation, misgiving, confusion, bewilderment, perplexity, puzzlement, unreliability, unpredictability, insecurity.
E3 certainty.

unchanging *adj* unvarying, changeless, steady, steadfast, constant, perpetual, lasting, enduring, abiding, eternal, permanent.
E3 changing, changeable.

uncharitable *adj* unkind, cruel, hard-hearted, callous, unfeeling, insensitive, unsympathetic, unfriendly, mean, ungenerous.
E3 kind, sensitive, charitable, generous.

uncharted *adj* unexplored, undiscovered, unplumbed, foreign,
alien, strange, unfamiliar, new, virgin.
E3 familiar.

uncivilized *adj* primitive, barbaric, savage, wild, untamed, uncultured, unsophisticated, unenlightened, uneducated, illiterate, uncouth, antisocial.
E3 civilized, cultured.

unclean *adj* dirty, soiled, filthy, foul, polluted, contaminated, tainted, impure, unhygienic, unwholesome, corrupt, defiled, sullied.
E3 clean, hygienic.

unclear *adj* indistinct, hazy, dim, obscure, vague, indefinite, ambiguous, equivocal, uncertain, unsure, doubtful, dubious.
E3 clear, evident.

uncomfortable *adj* **1** CRAMPED, hard, cold, ill-fitting, irritating, painful, disagreeable. **2** AWKWARD, embarrassed, self-conscious, uneasy, troubled, worried, disturbed, distressed, disquieted, conscience-stricken.
E3 1 comfortable. **2** relaxed.

uncommon *adj* rare, scarce, infrequent, unusual, abnormal, atypical, unfamiliar, strange, odd, curious, bizarre, extraordinary, remarkable, notable, outstanding, exceptional, distinctive, special.
E3 common, usual, normal.

uncommunicative *adj* silent, taciturn, tight-lipped, close, secretive, unforthcoming, unresponsive, curt, brief, reticent, reserved, shy, retiring, withdrawn, unsociable.
E3 communicative, forthcoming.

uncompromising *adj* unyielding, unbending, inflexible, unaccommodating, rigid, firm, strict, tough, hard-line, inexorable, intransigent, stubborn, obstinate, die-hard.
E3 flexible.

unconcealed *adj* open, patent, obvious, evident, manifest, blatant, conspicuous, noticeable, visible, apparent.

🗲 hidden, secret.

unconcerned *adj* indifferent, apathetic, uninterested, nonchalant, carefree, relaxed, complacent, cool, composed, untroubled, unworried, unruffled, unmoved, uncaring, unsympathetic, callous, aloof, remote, distant, detached, dispassionate, uninvolved, oblivious.

🗲 concerned, worried, interested.

unconditional *adj* unqualified, unreserved, unrestricted, unlimited, absolute, utter, full, total, complete, entire, whole-hearted, thoroughgoing, downright, outright, positive, categorical, unequivocal.

🗲 conditional, qualified, limited.

unconnected *adj* **1** IRRELEVANT, unrelated, unattached, detached, separate, independent.

2 DISCONNECTED, incoherent, irrational, illogical.

🗲 **1** connected, relevant.

unconscious *adj* **1** STUNNED, knocked out, out cold, out for the count, concussed, comatose, senseless, insensible. **2** UNAWARE, oblivious, blind, deaf, heedless, unmindful, ignorant. **3** *an unconscious reaction*: involuntary, automatic, reflex, instinctive, impulsive, innate, subconscious, subliminal, repressed, suppressed, latent, unwitting, inadvertent, accidental, unintentional.

🗲 **1** conscious. **2** aware. **3** intentional.

uncontrollable *adj* ungovernable, unmanageable, unruly, wild, mad, furious, violent, strong, irrepressible.

🗲 controllable, manageable.

uncontrolled *adj* unrestrained, unbridled, unchecked, rampant, wild, unruly, undisciplined.

🗲 controlled, restrained.

unconventional *adj* unorthodox, alternative, different, offbeat, eccentric, idiosyncratic, individual,

original, odd, unusual, irregular, abnormal, bizarre, way-out (*sl*).

🗲 conventional, orthodox.

unconvincing *adj* implausible, unlikely, improbable, questionable, doubtful, dubious, suspect, weak, feeble, flimsy, lame.

🗲 convincing, plausible.

unco-ordinated *adj* clumsy, awkward, ungainly, ungraceful, inept, disjointed.

🗲 graceful.

uncouth *adj* coarse, crude, vulgar, rude, ill-mannered, unseemly, improper, clumsy, awkward, gauche, graceless, unrefined, uncultivated, uncultured, uncivilized, rough.

🗲 polite, refined, urbane.

uncover *v* unveil, unmask, unwrap, strip, bare, open, expose, reveal, show, disclose, divulge, leak, unearth, exhume, discover, detect.

🗲 cover, conceal, suppress.

uncritical *adj* undiscerning, undiscriminating, unselective, unquestioning, credulous, accepting, trusting, gullible, naive.

🗲 discerning, discriminating, sceptical.

uncultivated *adj* fallow, wild, rough, natural.

🗲 cultivated.

uncultured *adj* unsophisticated, unrefined, uncultivated, uncivilized, rough, uncouth, boorish, rustic, coarse, crude, ill-bred.

🗲 cultured, sophisticated.

undaunted *adj* undeterred, undiscouraged, undismayed, unbowed, resolute, steadfast, brave, courageous, fearless, bold, intrepid, dauntless, indomitable.

🗲 discouraged, timorous.

undecided *adj* uncertain, unsure, in two minds, ambivalent, doubtful, hesitant, wavering, irresolute, uncommitted, indefinite, vague, dubious, debatable, moot, unsettled, open.

decided, certain, definite.

undemonstrative *adj* aloof,
distant, remote, withdrawn, reserved,
reticent, uncommunicative, stiff,
formal, cool, cold, unemotional,
restrained, impassive, phlegmatic.
demonstrative, communicative.

undeniable *adj* irrefutable,
unquestionable, incontrovertible,
sure, certain, undoubted, proven,
clear, obvious, patent, evident,
manifest, unmistakable.
questionable.

under *prep* below, underneath,
beneath, lower than, less than,
inferior to, subordinate to.
over, above.

under way moving, in motion, going,
in operation, started, begun, in
progress, afoot.

undercover *adj* secret, hush-hush
(*infml*), private, confidential, spy,
intelligence, underground,
clandestine, surreptitious, furtive,
covert, hidden, concealed.
open, unconcealed.

undercurrent *n* undertone,
overtone, hint, suggestion, tinge,
flavour, aura, atmosphere, feeling,
sense, movement, tendency, trend,
drift.

underestimate *v* underrate,
undervalue, misjudge, miscalculate,
minimize, belittle, disparage, dismiss.
overestimate, exaggerate.

undergo *v* experience, suffer,
sustain, submit to, bear, stand,
endure, weather, withstand.

underground *adj* 1 *an underground
passage*: subterranean, buried,
sunken, covered, hidden, concealed.
2 SECRET, covert, undercover,
revolutionary, subversive, radical,
experimental, avant-garde,
alternative, unorthodox, unofficial.

undergrowth *n* brush, scrub,
vegetation, ground cover, bracken,
bushes, brambles, briars.

underhand *adj* unscrupulous,

unethical, immoral, improper, sly,
crafty, sneaky, stealthy,
surreptitious, furtive, clandestine,
devious, dishonest, deceitful,
deceptive, fraudulent, crooked
(*infml*), shady (*infml*).
honest, open, above board.

underline *v* mark, underscore,
stress, emphasize, accentuate,
italicize, highlight, point up.
play down, soft-pedal.

underlying *adj* basic, fundamental,
essential, primary, elementary, root,
intrinsic, latent, hidden, lurking,
veiled.

undermine *v* mine, tunnel,
excavate, erode, wear away, weaken,
sap, sabotage, subvert, vitiate, mar,
impair.
strengthen, fortify.

underprivileged *adj*
disadvantaged, deprived, poor,
needy, impoverished, destitute,
oppressed.
privileged, fortunate, affluent.

underrate *v* underestimate,
undervalue, belittle, disparage,
depreciate, dismiss.
overrate, exaggerate.

undersized *adj* small, tiny, minute,
miniature, pygmy, dwarf, stunted,
underdeveloped, underweight, puny.
oversized, big, overweight.

understand *v* 1 *I don't understand*:
grasp, comprehend, take in, follow,
get (*infml*), cotton on (*infml*),
fathom, penetrate, make out, discern,
perceive, see, realize, recognize,
appreciate, accept. 2 SYMPATHIZE,
empathize, commiserate. 3 BELIEVE,
think, know, hear, learn, gather,
assume, presume, suppose, conclude.
1 misunderstand.

understanding *n* 1 GRASP,
comprehension, knowledge, wisdom,
intelligence, intellect, sense,
judgement, discernment, insight,
appreciation, awareness, impression,
perception, belief, idea, notion,

opinion, interpretation.
2 AGREEMENT, arrangement, pact, accord, harmony. **3** SYMPATHY, empathy.

adj sympathetic, compassionate, kind, considerate, sensitive, tender, loving, patient, tolerant, forbearing, forgiving.

🖅 unsympathetic, insensitive, impatient, intolerant.

understate *v* underplay, play down, soft-pedal, minimize, make light of, belittle, dismiss.

🖅 exaggerate.

understood *adj* accepted, assumed, presumed, implied, implicit, inferred, tacit, unstated, unspoken, unwritten.

understudy *n* stand-in, double, substitute, replacement, reserve, deputy.

undertake *v* **1** PLEDGE, promise, guarantee, agree, contract, covenant. **2** BEGIN, commence, embark on, tackle, try, attempt, endeavour, take on, accept, assume.

undertaking *n* **1** ENTERPRISE, venture, business, affair, task, project, operation, attempt, endeavour, effort. **2** PLEDGE, commitment, promise, vow, word, assurance.

undertone *n* hint, suggestion, whisper, murmur, trace, tinge, touch, flavour, feeling, atmosphere, undercurrent.

undervalue *v* underrate, underestimate, misjudge, minimize, depreciate, disparage, dismiss.

🖅 overrate, exaggerate.

underwater *adj* subaquatic, undersea, submarine, submerged, sunken.

underwear *n* underclothes, undergarments, lingerie, undies (*infml*), smalls (*infml*).

underweight *adj* thin, undersized, underfed, undernourished, half-starved.

🖅 overweight.

underwrite *v* endorse, authorize, sanction, approve, back, guarantee, insure, sponsor, fund, finance, subsidize, subscribe, sign, initial, countersign.

undesirable *adj* unwanted, unwelcome, unacceptable, unsuitable, unpleasant, disagreeable, distasteful, repugnant, offensive, objectionable, obnoxious.

🖅 desirable, pleasant.

undignified *adj* inelegant, ungainly, clumsy, foolish, unseemly, improper, unsuitable, inappropriate.

🖅 dignified, elegant.

undisguised *adj* unconcealed, open, overt, explicit, frank, genuine, apparent, patent, obvious, evident, manifest, blatant, naked, unadorned, stark, utter, outright, thoroughgoing.

🖅 secret, concealed, hidden.

undisputed *adj* uncontested, unchallenged, unquestioned, undoubted, indisputable, incontrovertible, undeniable, irrefutable, accepted, acknowledged, recognized, sure, certain, conclusive.

🖅 debatable, uncertain.

undistinguished *adj* unexceptional, unremarkable, unimpressive, ordinary, run-of-the-mill, everyday, banal, indifferent, mediocre, inferior.

🖅 distinguished, exceptional.

undivided *adj* solid, unbroken, intact, whole, entire, full, complete, combined, united, unanimous, concentrated, exclusive, whole-hearted.

undo *v* **1** UNFASTEN, untie, unbuckle, unbutton, unzip, unlock, unwrap, unwind, open, loose, loosen, separate. **2** ANNUL, nullify, invalidate, cancel, offset, neutralize, reverse, overturn, upset, quash, defeat, undermine, subvert, mar, spoil, ruin, wreck, shatter, destroy.

🖅 **1** fasten, do up.

undoing *n* downfall, ruin, ruination, collapse, destruction, defeat,

overthrow, reversal, weakness,
shame, disgrace.

undone adj **1** UNACCOMPLISHED,
unfulfilled, unfinished, uncompleted,
incomplete, outstanding, left,
omitted, neglected, forgotten.
2 UNFASTENED, untied, unlaced,
unbuttoned, unlocked, open, loose.
E **1** done, accomplished, complete.
2 fastened.

undoubted adj unchallenged,
undisputed, acknowledged,
unquestioned, indisputable,
incontrovertible, undesirable,
indubitable, sure, certain, definite,
obvious, patent.

undress v strip, peel off (infml),
disrobe, take off, divest, remove,
shed.

undressed adj unclothed, disrobed,
stripped, naked, stark naked, nude.
E clothed.

undue adj unnecessary, needless,
uncalled-for, unwarranted,
undeserved, unreasonable,
disproportionate, excessive,
immoderate, inordinate, extreme,
extravagant, improper.
E reasonable, moderate, proper.

unduly adv too, over, excessively,
immoderately, inordinately,
disproportionately, unreasonably,
unjustifiably, unnecessarily.
E moderately, reasonably.

unearth v dig up, exhume, disinter,
excavate, uncover, expose, reveal,
find, discover, detect.
E bury.

unearthly adj **1** SUPERNATURAL,
ghostly, eerie, uncanny, weird,
strange, spine-chilling. **2** at this
unearthly hour: unreasonable,
outrageous, ungodly.
E **2** reasonable.

uneasy adj uncomfortable, anxious,
worried, apprehensive, tense,
strained, nervous, agitated, shaky,
jittery, edgy, upset, troubled,
disturbed, unsettled, restless,

impatient, unsure, insecure.
E calm, composed.

uneducated adj unschooled,
untaught, unread, ignorant, illiterate,
uncultivated, uncultured, philistine,
benighted.
E educated.

unemotional adj cool, cold,
unfeeling, impassive, indifferent,
apathetic, unresponsive,
undemonstrative, unexcitable,
phlegmatic, objective, dispassionate.
E emotional, excitable.

unemployed adj jobless, out of
work, laid off, redundant, unwaged,
on the dole (infml), idle, unoccupied.
E employed, occupied.

unending adj endless, never-ending,
unceasing, ceaseless, incessant,
interminable, constant, continual,
perpetual, everlasting, eternal,
undying.
E transient, intermittent.

unenviable adj undesirable,
unpleasant, disagreeable,
uncongenial, uncomfortable,
thankless, difficult.
E enviable, desirable.

unequal adj different, varying,
dissimilar, unlike, unmatched,
uneven, unbalanced,
disproportionate, asymmetrical,
irregular, unfair, unjust, biased,
discriminatory.
E equal.

unequivocal adj unambiguous,
explicit, clear, plain, evident, distinct,
unmistakable, express, direct,
straight, definite, positive,
categorical, incontrovertible,
absolute, unqualified, unreserved.
E ambiguous, vague, qualified.

unethical adj unprofessional,
immoral, improper, wrong,
unscrupulous, unprincipled,
dishonourable, disreputable, illegal,
illicit, dishonest, underhand, shady
(infml).
E ethical.

uneven *adj* **1** *uneven ground*: rough, bumpy. **2** ODD, unequal, inequitable, unfair, unbalanced, one-sided, asymmetrical, lopsided, crooked. **3** IRREGULAR, intermittent, spasmodic, fitful, jerky, unsteady, variable, changeable, fluctuating, erratic, inconsistent, patchy.
Fa **1** flat, level. **2** even, equal. **3** regular.

uneventful *adj* uninteresting, unexciting, quiet, unvaried, boring, monotonous, tedious, dull, routine, humdrum, ordinary, commonplace, unremarkable, unexceptional, unmemorable.
Fa eventful, memorable.

unexceptional *adj* unremarkable, unmemorable, typical, average, normal, usual, ordinary, indifferent, mediocre, unimpressive.
Fa exceptional, impressive.

unexpected *adj* unforeseen, unanticipated, unpredictable, chance, accidental, fortuitous, sudden, abrupt, surprising, startling, amazing, astonishing, unusual.
Fa expected, predictable.

unfair *adj* unjust, inequitable, partial, biased, prejudiced, bigoted, discriminatory, unbalanced, one-sided, partisan, arbitrary, undeserved, unmerited, unwarranted, uncalled-for, unethical, unscrupulous, unprincipled, wrongful, dishonest.
Fa fair, just, unbiased, deserved.

unfaithful *adj* disloyal, treacherous, false, untrue, deceitful, dishonest, untrustworthy, unreliable, fickle, inconstant, adulterous, two-timing, duplicitous, double-dealing, faithless, unbelieving, godless.
Fa faithful, loyal, reliable.

unfamiliar *adj* strange, unusual, uncommon, curious, alien, foreign, uncharted, unexplored, unknown, different, new, novel, unaccustomed, unacquainted, inexperienced,

unpractised, unskilled, unversed.
Fa familiar, customary, conversant.

unfashionable *adj* unmoded, dated, out of date, out, passé, old-fashioned, antiquated, obsolete.
Fa fashionable.

unfasten *v* undo, untie, loosen, unlock, open, uncouple, disconnect, separate, detach.
Fa fasten.

unfavourable *adj* inauspicious, unpromising, ominous, threatening, discouraging, inopportune, untimely, unseasonable, ill-suited, unfortunate, unlucky, disadvantageous, bad, poor, adverse, contrary, negative, hostile, unfriendly, uncomplimentary.
Fa favourable, auspicious, promising.

unfeeling *adj* insensitive, cold, hard, stony, callous, heartless, hard-hearted, cruel, inhuman, pitiless, uncaring, unsympathetic, apathetic.
Fa sensitive, sympathetic.

unfinished *adj* incomplete, uncompleted, half-done, sketchy, rough, crude, imperfect, lacking, wanting, deficient, undone, unaccomplished, unfulfilled.
Fa finished, perfect.

unfit *adj* **1** UNSUITABLE, inappropriate, unsuited, ill-equipped, unqualified, ineligible, untrained, unprepared, unequal, incapable, incompetent, inadequate, ineffective, useless. **2** UNHEALTHY, out of condition, flabby, feeble, decrepit.
Fa **1** fit, suitable, competent. **2** healthy.

unfold *v* **1** DEVELOP, evolve. **2** REVEAL, disclose, show, present, describe, explain, clarify, elaborate. **3** *unfold a map*: open, spread, flatten, straighten, stretch out, undo, unfurl, unroll, uncoil, unwrap, uncover.
Fa **2** withhold, suppress. **3** fold, wrap.

unforeseen *adj* unpredicted, unexpected, unanticipated, surprising, startling, sudden, unavoidable.
Fa expected, predictable.

unforgettable adj memorable, momentous, historic, noteworthy, notable, impressive, remarkable, exceptional, extraordinary.
 unmemorable, unexceptional.

unforgivable adj unpardonable, inexcusable, unjustifiable, indefensible, reprehensible, shameful, disgraceful, deplorable.
 forgivable, venial.

unfortunate adj 1 UNLUCKY, luckless, hapless, unsuccessful, poor, wretched, unhappy, doomed, ill-fated, hopeless, calamitous, disastrous, ruinous.
2 REGRETTABLE, lamentable, deplorable, adverse, unfavourable, unsuitable, inappropriate, inopportune, untimely, ill-timed.
 1 fortunate, happy. 2 favourable, appropriate.

unfounded adj baseless, groundless, unsupported, unsubstantiated, unproven, unjustified, idle, false, spurious, trumped-up, fabricated.
 substantiated, justified.

unfriendly adj unsociable, standoffish, aloof, distant, unapproachable, inhospitable, uncongenial, unneighbourly, unwelcoming, cold, chilly, hostile, aggressive, quarrelsome, inimical, antagonistic, ill-disposed, disagreeable, surly, sour.
 friendly, amiable, agreeable.

ungainly adj clumsy, awkward, gauche, inelegant, gawky, unco-ordinated, lumbering, unwieldy.
 graceful, elegant.

ungodly adj 1 UNREASONABLE, outrageous, intolerable, unearthly, unsocial. 2 IMPIOUS, irreligious, godless, blasphemous, profane, immoral, corrupt, depraved, sinful, wicked.

ungrateful adj unthankful, unappreciative, ill-mannered, ungracious, selfish, heedless.
 grateful, thankful.

unguarded adj 1 *in an unguarded moment*: unwary, careless, incautious, imprudent, impolitic, indiscreet, undiplomatic, thoughtless, unthinking, heedless, foolish, foolhardy, rash, ill-considered.
2 UNDEFENDED, unprotected, exposed, vulnerable, defenceless.
 1 guarded, cautious. 2 defended, protected.

unhappy adj 1 SAD, sorrowful, miserable, melancholy, depressed, dispirited, despondent, dejected, downcast, crestfallen, long-faced, gloomy. 2 UNFORTUNATE, unlucky, ill-fated, unsuitable, inappropriate, inapt, ill-chosen, tactless, awkward, clumsy.
 1 happy. 2 fortunate, suitable.

unharmed adj undamaged, unhurt, uninjured, unscathed, whole, intact, safe, sound.
 harmed, damaged.

unhealthy adj 1 UNWELL, sick, ill, poorly, ailing, sickly, infirm, invalid, weak, feeble, frail, unsound.
2 UNWHOLESOME, insanitary, unhygienic, harmful, detrimental, morbid, unnatural.
 1 healthy, fit. 2 wholesome, hygienic, natural.

unheard-of adj 1 UNTHINKABLE, inconceivable, unimaginable, undreamed-of, unprecedented, unacceptable, offensive, shocking, outrageous, preposterous.
2 UNKNOWN, unfamiliar, new, unusual, obscure.
 1 normal, acceptable. 2 famous.

unheeded adj ignored, disregarded, disobeyed, unnoticed, unobserved, unremarked, overlooked, neglected, forgotten.
 noted, observed.

unhesitating adj immediate, instant, instantaneous, prompt, ready, automatic, spontaneous, unquestioning, unwavering, unfaltering, whole-hearted, implicit.

◧ hesitant, tentative.

unholy *adj* **1** IMPIOUS, irreligious, sinful, iniquitous, immoral, corrupt, depraved, wicked, evil. **2** (*infml*) *an unholy mess*: unreasonable, shocking, outrageous, ungodly, unearthly.

◧ **1** holy, pious, godly. **2** reasonable.

unhurried *adj* slow, leisurely, deliberate, easy, relaxed, calm, easy-going (*infml*), laid-back (*sl*).

◧ hurried, hasty, rushed.

unidentified *adj* unknown, unrecognized, unmarked, unnamed, nameless, anonymous, incognito, unfamiliar, strange, mysterious.

◧ identified, known, named.

uniform *n* outfit, costume, livery, insignia, regalia, robes, dress, suit.
adj same, identical, like, alike, similar, homogeneous, consistent, regular, equal, smooth, even, flat, monotonous, unvarying, unchanging, constant, unbroken.

◧ different, varied, changing.

unify *v* unite, join, bind, combine, integrate, merge, amalgamate, consolidate, coalesce, fuse, weld.

◧ separate, divide, split.

unimaginable *adj* inconceivable, mind-boggling (*infml*), unbelievable, incredible, impossible, fantastic, undreamed-of, unthinkable, unheard-of.

unimaginative *adj* uninspired, unoriginal, predictable, hackneyed, banal, ordinary, dull, boring, routine, matter-of-fact, dry, barren, lifeless, unexciting, tame.

◧ imaginative, creative, original.

unimportant *adj* insignificant, inconsequential, irrelevant, immaterial, minor, trivial, trifling, petty, slight, negligible, worthless.

◧ important, significant, relevant, vital.

unimpressive *adj* unspectacular, undistinguished, unexceptional, unremarkable, uninteresting, dull, average, commonplace, indifferent, mediocre.

◧ impressive, memorable, notable.

uninhabited *adj* unoccupied, vacant, empty, deserted, abandoned, unpeopled, unpopulated.

uninhibited *adj* unconstrained, unreserved, unselfconscious, liberated, free, unrestricted, uncontrolled, unrestrained, abandoned, natural, spontaneous, frank, candid, open, relaxed, informal.

◧ inhibited, repressed, constrained, restrained.

unintelligible *adj* incomprehensible, incoherent, inarticulate, double Dutch, garbled, scrambled, jumbled, muddled, indecipherable, illegible.

◧ intelligible, comprehensible, clear.

unintentional *adj* unintended, accidental, fortuitous, inadvertent, unplanned, unpremeditated, involuntary, unconscious, unwitting.

◧ intentional, deliberate.

uninterested *adj* indifferent, unconcerned, uninvolved, bored, listless, apathetic, unenthusiastic, blasé, impassive, unresponsive.

◧ interested, concerned, enthusiastic, responsive.

uninteresting *adj* boring, tedious, monotonous, humdrum, dull, drab, dreary, dry, flat, tame, uneventful, unexciting, uninspiring, unimpressive.

◧ interesting, exciting.

uninterrupted *adj* unbroken, continuous, non-stop, unending, constant, continual, steady, sustained, undisturbed, peaceful.

◧ broken, intermittent.

uninvited *adj* unasked, unsought, unsolicited, unwanted, unwelcome.

◧ invited.

union *n* alliance, coalition, league, association, federation, confederation, confederacy, merger, combination, amalgamation, blend,

unique 566

mixture, synthesis, fusion, unification, unity.
₣ separation, alienation, estrangement.

unique *adj* single, one-off, sole, only, lone, solitary, unmatched, matchless, peerless, unequalled, unparalleled, unrivalled, incomparable, inimitable.
₣ common.

unison *n* concert, co-operation, unanimity, unity.

unit *n* item, part, element, constituent, piece, component, module, section, segment, portion, entity, whole, one, system, assembly.

unite *v* join, link, couple, marry, ally, co-operate, band, associate, federate, confederate, combine, pool, amalgamate, merge, blend, unify, consolidate, coalesce, fuse.
₣ separate, sever.

united *adj* allied, affiliated, corporate, unified, combined, pooled, collective, concerted, one, unanimous, agreed, in agreement, in accord, like-minded.
₣ disunited.

unity *n* agreement, accord, concord, harmony, peace, consensus, unanimity, solidarity, integrity, oneness, wholeness, union, unification.
₣ disunity, disagreement, discord, strife.

universal *adj* worldwide, global, all-embracing, all-inclusive, general, common, across-the-board, total, whole, entire, all-round, unlimited.

unjust *adj* unfair, inequitable, wrong, partial, biased, prejudiced, one-sided, partisan, unreasonable, unjustified, undeserved.
₣ just, fair, reasonable.

unjustifiable *adj* indefensible, inexcusable, unforgivable, unreasonable, unwarranted, immoderate, excessive, unacceptable, outrageous.

₣ justifiable, acceptable.

unkempt *adj* dishevelled, tousled, rumpled, uncombed, ungroomed, untidy, messy, scruffy, shabby, slovenly.
₣ well-groomed, tidy.

unkind *adj* cruel, inhuman, inhumane, callous, hard-hearted, unfeeling, insensitive, thoughtless, inconsiderate, uncharitable, nasty, malicious, spiteful, mean, malevolent, unfriendly, uncaring, unsympathetic.
₣ kind, considerate.

unknown *adj* unfamiliar, unheard-of, strange, alien, foreign, mysterious, dark, obscure, hidden, concealed, undisclosed, secret, untold, new, uncharted, unexplored, undiscovered, unidentified, unnamed, nameless, anonymous, incognito.
₣ known, familiar.

unlawful *adj* illegal, criminal, illicit, illegitimate, unconstitutional, outlawed, banned, prohibited, forbidden, unauthorized.
₣ lawful, legal.

unlikely *adj* **1** IMPROBABLE, implausible, far-fetched, unconvincing, unbelievable, incredible, unimaginable, unexpected, doubtful, dubious, questionable, suspect, suspicious. **2** SLIGHT, faint, remote, distant.
₣ **1** likely, plausible.

unlimited *adj* limitless, unrestricted, unbounded, boundless, infinite, endless, countless, incalculable, immeasurable, vast, immense, extensive, great, indefinite, absolute, unconditional, unqualified, all-encompassing, total, complete, full, unconstrained, unhampered.
₣ limited.

unload *v* unpack, empty, discharge, dump, offload, unburden, relieve.
₣ load.

unlock *v* unbolt, unlatch, unfasten, undo, open, free, release.

lock, fasten.

unloved *adj* unpopular, disliked, hated, detested, unwanted, rejected, spurned, loveless, uncared-for, neglected.

loved.

unlucky *adj* unfortunate, luckless, unhappy, miserable, wretched, ill-fated, ill-starred, jinxed, doomed, cursed, unfavourable, inauspicious, ominous, unsuccessful, disastrous.

lucky.

unmanageable *adj* **1** UNWIELDY, bulky, cumbersome, awkward, inconvenient, unhandy.
2 UNCONTROLLABLE, wild, unruly, disorderly, difficult.

1 manageable. **2** controllable.

unmarried *adj* single, unwed, celibate, unattached, available.

married.

unmask *v* unveil, uncloak, uncover, bare, expose, reveal, show, disclose, discover, detect.

mask, conceal.

unmentionable *adj* unspeakable, unutterable, taboo, immodest, indecent, shocking, scandalous, shameful, disgraceful, abominable.

unmistakable *adj* clear, plain, distinct, pronounced, obvious, evident, manifest, patent, glaring, explicit, unambiguous, unequivocal, positive, definite, sure, certain, unquestionable, indisputable, undeniable.

unclear, ambiguous.

unmoved *adj* unaffected, untouched, unshaken, dry-eyed, unfeeling, cold, dispassionate, indifferent, impassive, unresponsive, unimpressed, firm, adamant, inflexible, unbending, undeviating, unwavering, steady, unchanged, resolute, resolved, determined.

moved, affected, shaken.

unnatural *adj* **1** ABNORMAL, anomalous, freakish, irregular, unusual, strange, odd, peculiar, queer, bizarre, extraordinary, uncanny, supernatural, inhuman, perverted. **2** AFFECTED, feigned, artificial, false, insincere, unspontaneous, contrived, laboured, stilted, forced, strained, self-conscious, stiff.

1 natural, normal. **2** sincere, fluent.

unnecessary *adj* unneeded, needless, uncalled-for, unwanted, non-essential, dispensable, expendable, superfluous, redundant, tautological.

necessary, essential, indispensable.

unnerve *v* daunt, intimidate, frighten, scare, discourage, demoralize, dismay, disconcert, upset, worry, shake, rattle (*infml*), confound, fluster.

nerve, brace, steel.

unnoticed *adj* unobserved, unremarked, unseen, unrecognized, undiscovered, overlooked, ignored, disregarded, neglected, unheeded.

noticed, noted.

unobtrusive *adj* inconspicuous, unnoticeable, unassertive, self-effacing, humble, modest, unostentatious, unpretentious, restrained, low-key, subdued, quiet, retiring.

obtrusive, ostentatious.

unoccupied *adj* uninhabited, vacant, empty, free, idle, inactive, workless, jobless, unemployed.

occupied, busy.

unofficial *adj* unauthorized, illegal, informal, off-the-record, personal, private, confidential, undeclared, unconfirmed.

official.

unorthodox *adj* unconventional, nonconformist, heterodox, alternative, fringe, irregular, abnormal, unusual.

orthodox, conventional.

unpaid *adj* **1** *unpaid bills*: outstanding, overdue, unsettled, owing, due, payable. **2** *unpaid work*:

voluntary, honorary, unsalaried, unwaged, unremunerative, free.
E 1 paid.

unpalatable *adj* 1 UNAPPETIZING, distasteful, insipid, bitter, uneatable, inedible. 2 UNPLEASANT, disagreeable, unattractive, offensive, repugnant.
E 1 palatable. 2 pleasant.

unparalleled *adj* unequalled, unmatched, matchless, peerless, incomparable, unrivalled, unsurpassed, supreme, superlative, rare, exceptional, unprecedented.

unpleasant *adj* disagreeable, ill-natured, nasty, objectionable, offensive, distasteful, unpalatable, unattractive, repulsive, bad, troublesome.
E pleasant, agreeable, nice.

unpopular *adj* disliked, hated, detested, unloved, unsought-after, unfashionable, undesirable, unwelcome, unwanted, rejected, shunned, avoided, neglected.
E popular, fashionable.

unprecedented *adj* new, original, revolutionary, unknown, unheard-of, exceptional, remarkable, extraordinary, abnormal, unusual, freakish, unparalleled, unrivalled.
E usual.

unpredictable *adj* unforeseeable, unexpected, changeable, variable, inconstant, unreliable, fickle, unstable, erratic, random, chance.
E predictable, foreseeable, constant.

unprepared *adj* unready, surprised, unsuspecting, ill-equipped, unfinished, incomplete, half-baked, unplanned, unrehearsed, spontaneous, improvised, ad-lib, off-the-cuff.
E prepared, ready.

unpretentious *adj* unaffected, natural, plain, simple, unobtrusive, honest, straightforward, humble, modest, unassuming, unostentatious.
E pretentious.

unproductive *adj* infertile, sterile, barren, dry, arid, unfruitful, fruitless, futile, vain, idle, useless, ineffective, unprofitable, unremunerative, unrewarding.
E productive, fertile.

unprofessional *adj* amateurish, inexpert, unskilled, sloppy, incompetent, inefficient, casual, negligent, lax, unethical, unprincipled, improper, unseemly, unacceptable, inadmissible.
E professional, skilful.

unprotected *adj* unguarded, unattended, undefended, unfortified, unarmed, unshielded, unsheltered, uncovered, exposed, open, naked, vulnerable, defenceless, helpless.
E protected, safe, immune.

unqualified *adj* 1 UNTRAINED, inexperienced, amateur, ineligible, unfit, incompetent, incapable, unprepared, ill-equipped.
2 ABSOLUTE, categorical, utter, total, complete, thorough, consummate, downright, unmitigated, unreserved, whole-hearted, outright, unconditional, unrestricted.
E 1 qualified, professional.
2 conditional, tentative.

unravel *v* unwind, undo, untangle, disentangle, free, extricate, separate, resolve, sort out, solve, work out, figure out, puzzle out, penetrate, interpret, explain.
E tangle, complicate.

unreal *adj* false, artificial, synthetic, mock, fake, sham, imaginary, visionary, fanciful, make-believe, pretend (*infml*), fictitious, made-up, fairy-tale, legendary, mythical, fantastic, illusory, immaterial, insubstantial, hypothetical.
E real, genuine.

unrealistic *adj* impractical, idealistic, romantic, quixotic, impracticable, unworkable, unreasonable, impossible.

realistic, pragmatic.

unreasonable *adj* **1** UNFAIR, unjust, biased, unjustifiable, unjustified, unwarranted, undue, uncalled-for. **2** IRRATIONAL, illogical, inconsistent, arbitrary, absurd, nonsensical, far-fetched, preposterous, mad, senseless, silly, foolish, stupid, headstrong, opinionated, perverse. **3** *unreasonable prices*: excessive, immoderate, extravagant, exorbitant, extortionate.
1 reasonable, fair. **2** rational, sensible. **3** moderate.

unrecognizable *adj* unidentifiable, disguised, incognito, changed, altered.

unrefined *adj* raw, untreated, unprocessed, unfinished, unpolished, crude, coarse, vulgar, unsophisticated, uncultivated, uncultured.
refined, finished.

unrelated *adj* unconnected, unassociated, irrelevant, extraneous, different, dissimilar, unlike, disparate, distinct, separate, independent.
related, similar.

unrelenting *adj* relentless, unremitting, uncompromising, inexorable, incessant, unceasing, ceaseless, endless, unbroken, continuous, constant, continual, perpetual, steady, unabated, remorseless, unmerciful, merciless, pitiless, unsparing.
spasmodic, intermittent.

unreliable *adj* unsound, fallible, deceptive, false, mistaken, erroneous, inaccurate, unconvincing, implausible, uncertain, undependable, untrustworthy, unstable, fickle, irresponsible.
reliable, dependable, trustworthy.

unrepentant *adj* impenitent, unapologetic, unabashed, unashamed, shameless, incorrigible, confirmed, hardened, obdurate.
repentant, penitent, ashamed.

unrest *n* protest, rebellion, turmoil, agitation, restlessness, dissatisfaction, dissension, disaffection, worry.
peace, calm.

unrestricted *adj* unlimited, unbounded, unopposed, unhindered, unimpeded, unobstructed, clear, free, open, public, unconditional, absolute.
restricted, limited.

unripe *adj* unripened, green, immature, undeveloped, unready.
ripe, mature.

unrivalled *adj* unequalled, unparalleled, unmatched, matchless, peerless, incomparable, inimitable, unsurpassed, supreme, superlative.

unruffled *adj* undisturbed, untroubled, imperturbable, collected, composed, cool, calm, tranquil, serene, peaceful, smooth, level, even.
troubled, anxious.

unruly *adj* uncontrollable, unmanageable, ungovernable, intractable, disorderly, wild, rowdy, riotous, rebellious, mutinous, lawless, insubordinate, disobedient, wayward, wilful, headstrong, obstreperous.
manageable, orderly.

unsafe *adj* dangerous, perilous, risky, hazardous, treacherous, unreliable, uncertain, unsound, unstable, precarious, insecure, vulnerable, exposed.
safe, secure.

unsatisfactory *adj* unacceptable, imperfect, defective, faulty, inferior, poor, weak, inadequate, insufficient, deficient, unsuitable, displeasing, dissatisfying, unsatisfying, frustrating, disappointing.
satisfactory, pleasing.

unscathed *adj* unhurt, uninjured, unharmed, undamaged, untouched, whole, intact, safe, sound.
hurt, injured.

unscrupulous *adj* unprincipled, ruthless, shameless, dishonourable, dishonest, crooked (*infml*), corrupt, immoral, unethical, improper.
⊟ scrupulous, ethical, proper.

unseemly *adj* improper, indelicate, indecorous, unbecoming, undignified, unrefined, disreputable, discreditable, undue, inappropriate, unsuitable.
⊟ seemly, decorous.

unseen *adj* unnoticed, unobserved, undetected, invisible, hidden, concealed, veiled, obscure.
⊟ visible.

unselfish *adj* selfless, altruistic, self-denying, self-sacrificing, disinterested, noble, magnanimous, generous, liberal, charitable, philanthropic, public-spirited, humanitarian, kind.
⊟ selfish.

unsentimental *adj* realistic, practical, pragmatic, hard-headed, tough, unromantic, level-headed.
⊟ sentimental, idealistic.

unsettle *v* disturb, upset, trouble, bother, discompose, ruffle, fluster, unbalance, shake, agitate, rattle (*infml*), disconcert, confuse, throw.

unsettled *adj* **1** DISTURBED, upset, troubled, agitated, anxious, uneasy, tense, edgy, flustered, shaken, unnerved, disoriented, confused. **2** UNRESOLVED, undetermined, undecided, open, uncertain, doubtful. **3** *unsettled weather*: changeable, variable, unpredictable, inconstant, unstable, insecure, unsteady, shaky. **4** UNPAID, outstanding, owing, payable, overdue.
⊟ 1 composed. **2** certain. **3** settled. **4** paid.

unshakable *adj* firm, well-founded, fixed, stable, immovable, unassailable, unwavering, constant, steadfast, staunch, sure, resolute, determined.
⊟ insecure.

unsightly *adj* ugly, unattractive, unprepossessing, hideous, repulsive, repugnant, off-putting, unpleasant, disagreeable.
⊟ attractive.

unskilled *adj* untrained, unqualified, inexperienced, unpractised, inexpert, unprofessional, amateurish, incompetent.
⊟ skilled.

unsociable *adj* unfriendly, aloof, distant, standoffish, withdrawn, introverted, reclusive, retiring, reserved, taciturn, unforthcoming, uncommunicative, cold, chilly, uncongenial, unneighbourly, inhospitable, hostile.
⊟ sociable, friendly.

unsolicited *adj* unrequested, unsought, uninvited, unasked, unwanted, unwelcome, uncalled-for, gratuitous, voluntary, spontaneous.
⊟ requested, invited.

unsophisticated *adj* artless, guileless, innocent, ingenuous, naïve, inexperienced, unworldly, childlike, natural, unaffected, unpretentious, unrefined, plain, simple, straightforward, uncomplicated, uninvolved.
⊟ sophisticated, worldly, complex.

unsound *adj* **1** *unsound reasoning*: faulty, flawed, defective, ill-founded, fallacious, false, erroneous, invalid, illogical. **2** UNHEALTHY, unwell, ill, diseased, weak, frail, unbalanced, deranged, unhinged. **3** UNSTABLE, unsteady, wobbly, shaky, insecure, unsafe.
⊟ 1 sound. **2** well. **3** stable.

unspeakable *adj* unutterable, inexpressible, indescribable, awful, dreadful, frightful, terrible, horrible, shocking, appalling, monstrous, inconceivable, unbelievable.

unspoilt *adj* preserved, unchanged, untouched, natural, unaffected, unsophisticated, unharmed, undamaged, unimpaired, unblemished, perfect.

■ spoilt, affected.

unspoken *adj* unstated, undeclared, unuttered, unexpressed, unsaid, voiceless, wordless, silent, tacit, implicit, implied, inferred, understood, assumed.
■ stated, explicit.

unstable *adj* **1** CHANGEABLE, variable, fluctuating, vacillating, wavering, fitful, erratic, inconsistent, volatile, capricious, inconstant, unpredictable, unreliable, untrustworthy. **2** UNSTEADY, wobbly, shaky, rickety, insecure, unsafe, risky, precarious, tottering, unbalanced.
■ **1** stable. **2** steady.

unsteady *adj* unstable, wobbly, shaky, rickety, insecure, unsafe, treacherous, precarious, tottering, unreliable, inconstant, irregular, flickering.
■ steady, firm.

unsuccessful *adj* failed, abortive, vain, futile, useless, ineffective, unavailing, fruitless, unproductive, sterile, luckless, unlucky, unfortunate, losing, beaten, defeated, frustrated, thwarted.
■ successful, effective, fortunate, winning.

unsuitable *adj* inappropriate, inapt, unsuited, unfit, unacceptable, improper, unseemly, unbecoming, incompatible, incongruous.
■ suitable, appropriate.

unsung *adj* unhonoured, unpraised, unacknowledged, unrecognized, overlooked, disregarded, neglected, forgotten, unknown, obscure.
■ honoured, famous, renowned.

unsure *adj* uncertain, doubtful, dubious, suspicious, sceptical, unconvinced, unpersuaded, undecided, hesitant, tentative.
■ sure, certain, confident.

unsurpassed *adj* surpassing, supreme, transcendent, unbeaten, unexcelled, unequalled, unparalleled, unrivalled, incomparable, matchless, superlative, exceptional.

unsuspecting *adj* unwary, unaware, unconscious, trusting, trustful, unsuspicious, credulous, gullible, ingenuous, naïve, innocent.
■ suspicious, knowing.

unsympathetic *adj* unpitying, unconcerned, unmoved, unresponsive, indifferent, insensitive, unfeeling, cold, heartless, soulless, hard-hearted, callous, cruel, inhuman, unkind, hard, stony, hostile, antagonistic.
■ sympathetic, compassionate.

untangle *v* disentangle, extricate, unravel, undo, resolve, solve.
■ tangle, complicate.

unthinkable *adj* inconceivable, unimaginable, unheard-of, unbelievable, incredible, impossible, improbable, unlikely, implausible, unreasonable, illogical, absurd, preposterous, outrageous, shocking.

unthinking *adj* thoughtless, inconsiderate, insensitive, tactless, indiscreet, rude, heedless, careless, negligent, rash, impulsive, instinctive, unconscious, automatic, mechanical.
■ considerate, conscious.

untidy *adj* messy, cluttered, disorderly, muddled, jumbled, unsystematic, chaotic, topsy-turvy, scruffy, dishevelled, unkempt, slovenly, sloppy, slipshod.
■ tidy, neat.

untie *v* undo, unfasten, unknot, unbind, free, release, loose, loosen.
■ tie, fasten.

untimely *adj* early, premature, unseasonable, ill-timed, inopportune, inconvenient, awkward, unsuitable, inappropriate, unfortunate, inauspicious.
■ timely, opportune.

untiring *adj* unflagging, tireless, indefatigable, dogged, persevering, persistent, tenacious, determined, resolute, devoted, dedicated,

untold

constant, incessant, unremitting, steady, staunch, unfailing.
≠ inconstant, wavering.

untold *adj* uncounted, unnumbered, unreckoned, incalculable, innumerable, uncountable, countless, infinite, measureless, boundless, inexhaustible, undreamed-of, unimaginable.

untouched *adj* unharmed, undamaged, unimpaired, unhurt, uninjured, unscathed, safe, intact, unchanged, unaltered, unaffected.
≠ damaged, affected.

untrained *adj* unskilled, untaught, unschooled, uneducated, inexperienced, unqualified, amateur, unprofessional, inexpert.
≠ trained, expert.

untried *adj* untested, unproved, experimental, exploratory, new, novel, innovative, innovatory.
≠ tried, tested, proven.

untrue *adj* **1** FALSE, fallacious, deceptive, misleading, wrong, incorrect, inaccurate, mistaken, erroneous. **2** UNFAITHFUL, disloyal, untrustworthy, dishonest, deceitful, untruthful.
≠ **1** true, correct. **2** faithful, honest.

untrustworthy *adj* dishonest, deceitful, untruthful, disloyal, unfaithful, faithless, treacherous, false, untrue, capricious, fickle, fly-by-night, unreliable, untrusty.
≠ trustworthy, reliable.

untruth *n* lie, fib, whopper (*infml*), story, tale, fiction, invention, fabrication, falsehood, lying, untruthfulness, deceit, perjury.
≠ truth.

untruthful *adj* lying, deceitful, dishonest, crooked (*infml*), hypocritical, two-faced, insincere, false, untrue.
≠ truthful, honest.

unused *adj* leftover, remaining, surplus, extra, spare, available, new, fresh, blank, clean, untouched, unexploited, unemployed, idle.
≠ used.

unusual *adj* uncommon, rare, unfamiliar, strange, odd, curious, queer, bizarre, unconventional, irregular, abnormal, extraordinary, remarkable, exceptional, different, surprising, unexpected.
≠ usual, normal, ordinary.

unveil *v* uncover, expose, bare, reveal, disclose, divulge, discover.
≠ cover, hide.

unwanted *adj* undesired, unsolicited, uninvited, unwelcome, outcast, rejected, unrequired, unneeded, unnecessary, surplus, extra, superfluous, redundant.
≠ wanted, needed, necessary.

unwarranted *adj* unjustified, undeserved, unprovoked, uncalled-for, groundless, unreasonable, unjust, wrong.
≠ warranted, justifiable, deserved.

unwary *adj* unguarded, incautious, careless, imprudent, indiscreet, thoughtless, unthinking, heedless, reckless, rash, hasty.
≠ wary, cautious.

unwelcome *adj* **1** UNWANTED, undesirable, unpopular, uninvited, excluded, rejected. **2** *unwelcome news*: unpleasant, disagreeable, upsetting, worrying, distasteful, unpalatable, unacceptable.
≠ **1** welcome, desirable. **2** pleasant.

unwell *adj* ill, sick, poorly, indisposed, off-colour, ailing, sickly, unhealthy.
≠ well, healthy.

unwieldy *adj* unmanageable, inconvenient, awkward, clumsy, ungainly, bulky, massive, hefty, weighty, ponderous, cumbersome.
≠ handy, dainty.

unwilling *adj* reluctant, disinclined, indisposed, resistant, opposed, averse, loath, slow, unenthusiastic, grudging.
≠ willing, enthusiastic.

unwind v 1 UNROLL, unreel, unwrap, undo, uncoil, untwist, unravel, disentangle. 2 (*infml*) RELAX, wind down, calm down.
🔁 1 wind, roll.

unwitting *adj* unaware, unknowing, unsuspecting, unthinking, unconscious, involuntary, accidental, chance, inadvertent, unintentional, unintended, unplanned.
🔁 knowing, conscious, deliberate.

unworldly *adj* spiritual, transcendental, metaphysical, otherworldly, visionary, idealistic, impractical, unsophisticated, inexperienced, innocent, naïve.
🔁 worldly, materialistic, sophisticated.

unworthy *adj* undeserving, inferior, ineligible, unsuitable, inappropriate, unfitting, unbecoming, unseemly, improper, unprofessional, shameful, disgraceful, dishonourable, discreditable, ignoble, base, contemptible, despicable.
🔁 worthy, commendable.

unwritten *adj* verbal, oral, word-of-mouth, unrecorded, tacit, implicit, understood, accepted, recognized, traditional, customary, conventional.
🔁 written, recorded.

upbraid v reprimand, admonish, rebuke, reprove, reproach, scold, chide, castigate, berate, criticize, censure.
🔁 praise, commend.

upbringing n bringing-up, raising, rearing, breeding, parenting, care, nurture, cultivation, education, training, instruction, teaching.

update v modernize, revise, amend, correct, renew, renovate, revamp.

upgrade v promote, advance, elevate, raise, improve, enhance.
🔁 downgrade, demote.

upheaval n disruption, disturbance, upset, chaos, confusion, disorder, turmoil, shake-up (*infml*), revolution, overthrow.

uphill *adj* hard, difficult, arduous, tough, taxing, strenuous, laborious, tiring, wearisome, exhausting, gruelling, punishing.
🔁 easy.

uphold v support, maintain, hold to, stand by, defend, champion, advocate, promote, back, endorse, sustain, fortify, strengthen, justify, vindicate.
🔁 abandon, reject.

upkeep n maintenance, preservation, conservation, care, running, repair, support, sustenance, subsistence, keep.
🔁 neglect.

upper *adj* higher, loftier, superior, senior, top, topmost, uppermost, high, elevated, exalted, eminent, important.
🔁 lower, inferior, junior.

uppermost *adj* highest, loftiest, top, topmost, greatest, supreme, first, primary, foremost, leading, principal, main, chief, dominant, predominant, paramount, pre-eminent.
🔁 lowest.

upright *adj* 1 VERTICAL, perpendicular, erect, straight. 2 RIGHTEOUS, good, virtuous, upstanding, noble, honourable, ethical, principled, incorruptible, honest, trustworthy.
🔁 1 horizontal, flat. 2 dishonest.

uprising n rebellion, revolt, mutiny, rising, insurgence, insurrection, revolution.

uproar n noise, din, racket, hubbub, hullabaloo, pandemonium, tumult, turmoil, turbulence, commotion, confusion, disorder, clamour, outcry, furore, riot, rumpus.

uproot v pull up, rip up, root out, weed out, remove, displace, eradicate, destroy, wipe out.

upset v 1 DISTRESS, grieve, dismay, trouble, worry, agitate, disturb, bother, fluster, ruffle, discompose, shake, unnerve, disconcert, confuse,

upshot

disorganize. **2** TIP, spill, overturn, capsize, topple, overthrow, destabilize, unsteady.

n **1** TROUBLE, worry, agitation, disturbance, bother, disruption, upheaval, shake-up (*infml*), reverse, surprise, shock. **2** *stomach upset*: disorder, complaint, bug (*infml*), illness, sickness.

adj distressed, grieved, hurt, annoyed, dismayed, troubled, worried, agitated, disturbed, bothered, shaken, disconcerted, confused.

upshot *n* result, consequence, outcome, issue, end, conclusion, finish, culmination.

upside down inverted, upturned, wrong way up, upset, overturned, disordered, muddled, jumbled, confused, topsy-turvy, chaotic.

up-to-date *adj* current, contemporary, modern, fashionable, trendy (*infml*), latest, recent, new.
E3 out-of-date, old-fashioned.

upturn *n* revival, recovery, upsurge, upswing, rise, increase, boost, improvement.
E3 downturn, drop.

urban *adj* town, city, inner-city, metropolitan, municipal, civic, built-up.
E3 country, rural.

urge *v* advise, counsel, recommend, advocate, encourage, exhort, implore, beg, beseech, entreat, plead, press, constrain, compel, force, push, drive, impel, goad, spur, hasten, induce, incite, instigate.
E3 discourage, dissuade, deter, hinder.
n desire, wish, inclination, fancy, longing, yearning, itch, impulse, compulsion, impetus, drive, eagerness.
E3 disinclination.

urgency *n* hurry, haste, pressure, stress, importance, seriousness, gravity, imperativeness, need, necessity.

urgent *adj* immediate, instant, top-priority, important, critical, crucial, imperative, exigent, pressing, compelling, persuasive, earnest, eager, insistent, persistent.
E3 unimportant.

usable *adj* working, operational, serviceable, functional, practical, exploitable, available, current, valid.
E3 unusable, useless.

usage *n* **1** TREATMENT, handling, management, control, running, operation, employment, application, use. **2** TRADITION, custom, practice, habit, convention, etiquette, rule, regulation, form, routine, procedure, method.

use *v* utilize, employ, exercise, practise, operate, work, apply, wield, handle, treat, manipulate, exploit, enjoy, consume, exhaust, expend, spend.
n utility, usefulness, value, worth, profit, advantage, benefit, good, avail, help, service, point, object, end, purpose, reason, cause, occasion, need, necessity, usage, application, employment, operation, exercise.

use up finish, exhaust, drain, sap, deplete, consume, devour, absorb, waste, squander, fritter.

used *adj* second-hand, cast-off, hand-me-down, nearly new, worn, dog-eared, soiled.
E3 unused, new, fresh.

useful *adj* handy, convenient, all-purpose, practical, effective, productive, fruitful, profitable, valuable, worthwhile, advantageous, beneficial, helpful.
E3 useless, ineffective, worthless.

useless *adj* futile, fruitless, unproductive, vain, idle, unavailing, hopeless, pointless, worthless, unusable, broken-down, clapped-out (*sl*), unworkable, impractical, ineffective, inefficient, incompetent, weak.
E3 useful, helpful, effective.

usher n usherette, doorkeeper, attendant, escort, guide.
v escort, accompany, conduct, lead, direct, guide, show, pilot, steer.

usual adj normal, typical, stock, standard, regular, routine, habitual, customary, conventional, accepted, recognized, accustomed, familiar, common, everyday, general, ordinary, unexceptional, expected, predictable.
🖅 unusual, strange, rare.

usually adv normally, generally, as a rule, ordinarily, typically, traditionally, regularly, commonly, by and large, on the whole, mainly, chiefly, mostly.
🖅 exceptionally.

usurp v take over, assume, arrogate, seize, take, annex, appropriate, commandeer, steal.

utensil n tool, implement, instrument, device, contrivance, gadget, apparatus, appliance.

utility n usefulness, use, value, profit, advantage, benefit, avail, service, convenience, practicality, efficacy, efficiency, fitness, serviceableness.

utmost adj 1 with the utmost care: extreme, maximum, greatest, highest, supreme, paramount. 2 FARTHEST, furthermost, remotest, outermost, ultimate, final, last.
n best, hardest, most, maximum.

utter[1] adj absolute, complete, total, entire, thoroughgoing, out-and-out, downright, sheer, stark, arrant, unmitigated, unqualified, perfect, consummate.

utter[2] v speak, say, voice, vocalize, verbalize, express, articulate, enunciate, sound, pronounce, deliver, state, declare, announce, proclaim, tell, reveal, divulge.

utterance n statement, remark, comment, expression, articulation, delivery, speech, declaration, announcement, proclamation, pronouncement.

utterly adv absolutely, completely, totally, fully, entirely, wholly, thoroughly, downright, perfectly.

U-turn n about-turn, volte-face, reversal, backtrack.

V

vacancy n opportunity, opening, position, post, job, place, room, situation.

vacant adj 1 EMPTY, unoccupied, unfilled, free, available, void, not in use, unused, uninhabited. 2 BLANK, expressionless, vacuous, inane, inattentive, absent, absent-minded, unthinking, dreamy.
🖅 1 occupied, engaged.

vacate v leave, depart, evacuate, abandon, withdraw, quit.

vacuum n emptiness, void, nothingness, vacuity, space, chasm, gap.

vague adj 1 ILL-DEFINED, blurred, indistinct, hazy, dim, shadowy, misty, fuzzy, nebulous, obscure. 2 INDEFINITE, imprecise, unclear, uncertain, undefined, undetermined, unspecific, generalized, inexact, ambiguous, evasive, loose, woolly.
🖅 1 clear. 2 definite.

vain adj 1 a vain attempt: useless, worthless, futile, abortive, fruitless, pointless, unproductive, unprofitable, unavailing, hollow, groundless, empty, trivial, unimportant. 2 CONCEITED, proud, self-satisfied, arrogant, self-important, egotistical, bigheaded (*infml*), swollen-headed (*infml*), stuck-up (*infml*), affected, pretentious, ostentatious, swaggering.

🗙 1 fruitful, successful. 2 modest, self-effacing.

valiant *adj* brave, courageous, gallant, fearless, intrepid, bold, dauntless, heroic, plucky, indomitable, staunch.

🗙 cowardly, fearful.

valid *adj* 1 LOGICAL, well-founded, well-grounded, sound, good, cogent, convincing, telling, conclusive, reliable, substantial, weighty, powerful, just. 2 OFFICIAL, legal, lawful, legitimate, authentic, bona fide, genuine, binding, proper.

🗙 1 false, weak. 2 unofficial, invalid.

valley *n* dale, vale, dell, glen, hollow, cwm, depression, gulch.

valuable *adj* 1 *valuable necklace*: precious, prized, valued, costly, expensive, dear, high-priced, treasured, cherished, estimable. 2 *valuable suggestions*: helpful, worthwhile, useful, beneficial, invaluable, constructive, fruitful, profitable, important, serviceable, worthy, handy.

🗙 1 worthless. 2 useless.

value *n* 1 COST, price, rate, worth. 2 WORTH, use, usefulness, utility, merit, importance, desirability, benefit, advantage, significance, good, profit.
v 1 PRIZE, appreciate, treasure, esteem, hold dear, respect, cherish. 2 EVALUATE, assess, estimate, price, appraise, survey, rate.

🗙 1 disregard, neglect. 2 undervalue.

vanish *v* disappear, fade, dissolve, evaporate, disperse, melt, die out, depart, exit, fizzle out, peter out.

🗙 appear, materialize.

vanity *n* 1 CONCEIT, conceitedness, pride, arrogance, self-conceit, self-love, self-satisfaction, narcissism, egotism, pretension, ostentation,

affectation, airs, bigheadedness (*infml*), swollen-headedness (*infml*). 2 WORTHLESSNESS, uselessness, emptiness, futility, pointlessness, unreality, hollowness, fruitlessness, triviality.

🗙 1 modesty, worth.

vapour *n* steam, mist, fog, smoke, breath, fumes, haze, damp, dampness, exhalation.

variable *adj* changeable, inconstant, varying, shifting, mutable, unpredictable, fluctuating, fitful, unstable, unsteady, wavering, vacillating, temperamental, fickle, flexible.

🗙 fixed, invariable, stable.

variance *n* 1 VARIATION, difference, discrepancy, divergence, inconsistency, disagreement. 2 DISAGREEMENT, disharmony, conflict, discord, division, dissent, dissension, quarrelling, strife.

🗙 1 agreement. 2 harmony.

variation *n* diversity, variety, deviation, discrepancy, diversification, alteration, change, difference, departure, modification, modulation, inflection, novelty, innovation.

🗙 monotony, uniformity.

varied *adj* assorted, diverse, miscellaneous, mixed, various, sundry, heterogeneous (*fml*), different, wide-ranging.

🗙 standardized, uniform.

variegated *adj* multicoloured, many-coloured, parti-coloured, varicoloured, speckled, mottled, dappled, pied, streaked, motley.

🗙 monochrome, plain.

variety *n* 1 ASSORTMENT, miscellany, mixture, collection, medley, pot-pourri, range. 2 DIFFERENCE, diversity, dissimilarity, discrepancy, variation, multiplicity. 3 SORT, kind, class, category, species, type, breed, brand, make, strain.

2 uniformity, similitude.

various *adj* different, differing, diverse, varied, varying, assorted, miscellaneous, heterogeneous (*fml*), distinct, diversified, mixed, many, several.

varnish *n* lacquer, glaze, resin, polish, gloss, coating.

vary *v* **1** CHANGE, alter, modify, modulate, diversify, reorder, transform, alternate, inflect, permutate. **2** DIVERGE, differ, disagree, depart, fluctuate.

vast *adj* huge, immense, massive, gigantic, enormous, great, colossal, extensive, tremendous, sweeping, unlimited, fathomless, immeasurable, never-ending, monumental, monstrous, far-flung.

vault¹ *v* leap, spring, bound, clear, jump, hurdle, leap-frog.

vault² *n* **1** CELLAR, crypt, strongroom, repository, cavern, depository, wine-cellar, tomb, mausoleum. **2** ARCH, roof, span, concave.

vaunt (*fml*) *v* boast, brag, exult in, flaunt, show off, parade, trumpet, crow.

2 belittle, minimize.

veer *v* swerve, swing, change, shift, diverge, deviate, wheel, turn, sheer, tack.

vegetable

Vegetables include: artichoke, aubergine, bean, beetroot, broad bean, broccoli, Brussel's sprout, butter bean, cabbage, calabrese, capsicum, carrot, cauliflower, celeriac, celery, chicory, courgette, cress, cucumber, eggplant (*US*), endive, fennel, French bean, garlic, kale, leek, lentil, lettuce, mange tout, marrow, mushroom, okra, onion, parsnip, pea, pepper, petit pois, potato, spud (*infml*), pumpkin, radish, runner bean, shallot, soya bean, spinach, spring onion, swede, sweetcorn, sweet potato, turnip, watercress, yam, zucchini (*US*).

Vegetable dishes include: aubergine roll, baba ganoush, bhaji, onion bhaji, bubble and squeak, cauliflower cheese, champ, chillada, colcannon, coleslaw, couscous, crudités, dal, dolma, duchesse potatoes, fasolia, felafel, fondue, gado-gado, gnocchi, guacamole, gumbo, hummus, imam bayildi, latke, macaroni cheese, macédoine, mushy peas, nut cutlet, paella, pakora, pease pudding, peperonata, pilau, pissaladière, polenta, ratatouille, raita, risotto, rösti, salad, caesar salad, green salad, warm salad, mixed salad, salade niçoise, Waldorf salad, winter salad, sauerkraut, stovies, stuffed marrow, stuffed mushroom, succotash, tabbouleh, tahina, tsatsiki, vegetable chilli, vegetable curry, vegetable soup, vegetarian goulash, vichyssoise.

vegetate *v* stagnate, degenerate, deteriorate, rusticate, go to seed, idle, rust, languish.

vehement *adj* impassioned, passionate, ardent, fervent, intense, forceful, emphatic, heated, strong, powerful, urgent, enthusiastic, animated, eager, earnest, forcible, fierce, violent, zealous.

2 apathetic, indifferent.

vehicle *n* **1** CONVEYANCE, transport. **2** MEANS, agency, channel, medium, mechanism, organ.

Vehicles include: plane, boat, ship, car, taxi, hackney-carriage, bicycle, bike (*infml*), cycle, tandem, tricycle, boneshaker (*infml*), penny-farthing, motor-cyclemotor-bike, scooter, bus, omnibus, minibus, double-decker (*infml*), coach, charabanc, caravan, caravanette, camper, train, Pullman, sleeper, wagon-lit, tube, tram, monorail, maglev, trolleybus; van,

Transit®, lorry, truck, juggernaut,
pantechnicon, trailer, tractor, fork-lift
truck, steam-roller, tank, wagon;
bobsleigh, sled, sledge, sleigh,
toboggan, troika; barouche,
brougham, dog-cart, dray, four-in-
hand, gig, hansom, landau, phaeton,
post-chaise, stagecoach, sulky, surrey,
trap; rickshaw, sedan-chair, litter. *see
also* **aircraft**; **boats and ships**; **car**.

veil *v* screen, cloak, cover, mask,
shadow, shield, obscure, conceal,
hide, disguise, shade.
E3 expose, uncover.
n cover, cloak, curtain, mask, screen,
disguise, film, blind, shade, shroud.

vein *n* **1** STREAK, stripe, stratum,
seam, lode, blood vessel. **2** MOOD,
tendency, bent, strain, temper, tenor,
tone, frame of mind, mode, style.

Veins and arteries include: aorta,
axillary, brachial, carotid, femoral,
frontal, gastric, hepatic, iliac, jugular,
portal, pulmonary, radial, renal,
saphena, subclavian, superior,
temporal, tibial.

vendetta *n* feud, blood-feud,
enmity, rivalry, quarrel, bad blood,
bitterness.

veneer *n* front, façade, appearance,
coating, surface, show, mask, gloss,
pretence, guise, finish.

venerable *adj* respected, revered,
esteemed, honoured, venerated,
dignified, grave, wise, august, aged,
worshipped.

venerate *v* revere, respect, honour,
esteem, worship, hallow (*fml*), adore.
E3 despise, anathematize.

vengeance *n* retribution, revenge,
retaliation, reprisal, requital, tit for
tat.
E3 forgiveness.

venom *n* **1** POISON, toxin. **2**
RANCOUR, ill-will, malice,
malevolence, spite, bitterness,
acrimony, hate, virulence.

venomous *adj* **1** POISONOUS, toxic,
virulent, harmful, noxious.
2 MALICIOUS, spiteful, vicious,
vindictive, baleful, hostile,
malignant, rancorous, baneful.
E3 1 harmless.

vent *n* opening, hole, aperture,
outlet, passage, orifice, duct.
v air, express, voice, utter, release,
discharge, emit.

ventilate *v* **1** *ventilate a room*: air,
aerate, freshen. **2** *ventilate one's
feelings*: air, broadcast, debate,
discuss.

venture *v* **1** DARE, advance, make
bold, put forward, presume, suggest,
volunteer. **2** RISK, hazard, endanger,
imperil, jeopardize, speculate, wager,
stake.
n risk, chance, hazard, speculation,
gamble, undertaking, project,
adventure, endeavour, enterprise,
operation, fling.

verbal *adj* spoken, oral, verbatim,
unwritten, word-of-mouth.

verbatim *adv* word for word,
exactly, literally, to the letter,
precisely.

verbose *adj* long-winded, wordy,
prolix, loquacious, diffuse,
circumlocutory.
E3 succinct, brief.

verdict *n* decision, judgement,
conclusion, finding, adjudication,
assessment, opinion, sentence.

verge *n* border, edge, margin, limit,
rim, brim, brink, boundary,
threshold, extreme, edging.
verge on approach, border on, come
close to, near.

verify *v* confirm, corroborate,
substantiate, authenticate, bear out,
prove, support, validate, testify,
attest.
E3 invalidate, discredit.

vernacular *adj* indigenous, local,
native, popular, vulgar, informal,
colloquial, common.

n language, speech, tongue, parlance, dialect, idiom, jargon.

versatile *adj* adaptable, flexible, all-round, multipurpose, multifaceted, adjustable, many-sided, general-purpose, functional, resourceful, handy, variable.
Ⓔ inflexible.

verse *n* poetry, rhyme, stanza, metre, doggerel, jingle.

versed *adj* skilled, proficient, practised, experienced, familiar, acquainted, learned, knowledgeable, conversant, seasoned, qualified, competent, accomplished.

version *n* **1** RENDERING, reading, interpretation, account, translation, paraphrase, adaptation, portrayal. **2** TYPE, kind, variant, form, model, style, design.

vertical *adj* upright, perpendicular, upstanding, erect, on end.
Ⓔ horizontal.

vertigo *n* dizziness, giddiness, light-headedness.

verve *n* vitality, vivacity, animation, energy, dash, élan, liveliness, sparkle, vigour, enthusiasm, gusto, life, relish, spirit, force.
Ⓔ apathy, lethargy.

very *adv* extremely, greatly, highly, deeply, truly, terribly (*infml*), remarkably, excessively, exceeding(ly), acutely, particularly, really, absolutely, noticeably, unusually.
Ⓔ slightly, scarcely.
adj actual, real, same, selfsame, identical, true, genuine, simple, utter, sheer, pure, perfect, plain, mere, bare, exact, appropriate.

vestige *n* trace, suspicion, indication, sign, hint, evidence, whiff, inkling, glimmer, token, scrap, remains, remainder, remnant, residue.

vet *v* investigate, examine, check, scrutinize, scan, inspect, survey, review, appraise, audit.

veteran *n* master, pastmaster, old hand, old stager, old-timer, pro (*infml*), war-horse.
Ⓔ novice, recruit.
adj experienced, practised, seasoned, long-serving, expert, adept, proficient, old.
Ⓔ inexperienced.

veto *v* reject, turn down, forbid, disallow, ban, prohibit, rule out, block.
Ⓔ approve, sanction.
n rejection, ban, embargo, prohibition, thumbs down (*infml*).
Ⓔ approval, assent.

vex *v* irritate, annoy, provoke, pester, trouble, upset, worry, bother, put out (*infml*), harass, hassle (*infml*), aggravate (*infml*), needle (*infml*), disturb, distress, agitate, exasperate, torment, fret.
Ⓔ calm, soothe.

vexed *adj* **1** IRRITATED, annoyed, provoked, upset, troubled, worried, nettled, put out, exasperated, bothered, confused, perplexed, aggravated (*infml*), harassed, hassled (*infml*), ruffled, riled, disturbed, distressed, displeased, agitated. **2** *a vexed question*: difficult, controversial, contested, disputed.

viable *adj* feasible, practicable, possible, workable, usable, operable, achievable, sustainable.
Ⓔ impossible, unworkable.

vibrant *adj* **1** ANIMATED, vivacious, vivid, bright, brilliant, colourful, lively, responsive, sparkling, spirited, sensitive. **2** THRILLING, dynamic, electrifying, electric.

vibrate *v* quiver, pulsate, shudder, shiver, resonate, reverberate, throb, oscillate, tremble, undulate, sway, swing, shake.

vice *n* **1** EVIL, evil-doing, depravity, immorality, wickedness, sin, corruption, iniquity (*fml*), profligacy (*fml*), degeneracy. **2** FAULT, failing, defect, shortcoming, weakness,

imperfection, blemish, bad habit, besetting sin.
⊟ 1 virtue, morality.

vicinity *n* neighbourhood, area, locality, district, precincts, environs, proximity.

vicious *adj* **1** WICKED, bad, wrong, immoral, depraved, unprincipled, diabolical, corrupt, debased, perverted, profligate (*fml*), vile, heinous. **2** MALICIOUS, spiteful, vindictive, virulent, cruel, mean, nasty, slanderous, venomous, defamatory. **3** SAVAGE, wild, violent, barbarous, brutal, dangerous.
⊟ 1 virtuous. **2** kind.

victim *n* sufferer, casualty, prey, scapegoat, martyr, sacrifice, fatality.
⊟ offender, attacker.

victimize *v* **1** OPPRESS, persecute, discriminate against, pick on, prey on, bully, exploit. **2** CHEAT, deceive, defraud, swindle (*infml*), dupe, hoodwink, fool.

victorious *adj* conquering, champion, triumphant, winning, unbeaten, successful, prize-winning, top, first.
⊟ defeated, unsuccessful.

victory *n* conquest, win, triumph, success, superiority, mastery, vanquishment, subjugation, overcoming.
⊟ defeat, loss.

vie *v* strive, compete, contend, struggle, contest, fight, rival.

view *n* **1** OPINION, attitude, belief, judgement, estimation, feeling, sentiment, impression, notion. **2** SIGHT, scene, vision, vista, outlook, prospect, perspective, panorama, landscape. **3** SURVEY, inspection, examination, observation, scrutiny, scan. **4** GLIMPSE, look, sight, perception.
v **1** CONSIDER, regard, contemplate, judge, think about, speculate. **2** OBSERVE, watch, see, examine, inspect, look at, scan, survey, witness,

perceive.

viewer *n* spectator, watcher, observer, onlooker.

viewpoint *n* attitude, position, perspective, slant, standpoint, stance, opinion, angle, feeling.

vigilant *adj* watchful, alert, attentive, observant, on one's guard, on the lookout, cautious, wide-awake, sleepless, unsleeping.
⊟ careless.

vigorous *adj* energetic, active, lively, healthy, strong, strenuous, robust, lusty, sound, vital, brisk, dynamic, forceful, forcible, powerful, stout, spirited, full-blooded, effective, efficient, enterprising, flourishing, intense.
⊟ weak, feeble.

vigour *n* energy, vitality, liveliness, health, robustness, stamina, strength, resilience, soundness, spirit, verve, gusto, activity, animation, power, potency, force, forcefulness, might, dash, dynamism.
⊟ weakness.

vile *adj* **1** *a vile sinner*: base, contemptible, debased, depraved, degenerate, bad, wicked, wretched, worthless, sinful, miserable, mean, evil, impure, corrupt, despicable, disgraceful, degrading, vicious, appalling. **2** *a vile meal*: disgusting, foul, nauseating, sickening, repulsive, repugnant, revolting, noxious, offensive, nasty, loathsome, horrid.
⊟ 1 pure, worthy. **2** pleasant, lovely.

villain *n* evil-doer, miscreant (*fml*), scoundrel, rogue, malefactor (*fml*), criminal, reprobate, rascal.

villainous *adj* wicked, bad, criminal, evil, sinful, vicious, notorious, cruel, inhuman, vile, depraved, disgraceful, terrible.
⊟ good.

vindicate (*fml*) *v* **1** CLEAR, acquit, excuse, exonerate, absolve, rehabilitate. **2** JUSTIFY, uphold, support, maintain, defend, establish, advocate, assert, verify.

vindictive *adj* spiteful, unforgiving, implacable, vengeful, relentless, unrelenting, revengeful, resentful, punitive, venomous, malevolent, malicious.

🖙 forgiving.

vintage *n* year, period, era, epoch, generation, origin, harvest, crop.
adj choice, best, fine, prime, select, superior, rare, mature, old, ripe, classic, venerable, veteran.

violate *v* **1** CONTRAVENE, disobey, disregard, transgress, break, flout, infringe. **2** OUTRAGE, debauch, defile, rape, ravish, dishonour, desecrate, profane, invade.

🖙 1 observe.

violence *n* **1** FORCE, strength, power, vehemence, might, intensity, ferocity, fierceness, severity, tumult, turbulence, wildness. **2** BRUTALITY, destructiveness, cruelty, bloodshed, murderousness, savagery, passion, fighting, frenzy, fury, hostilities.

violent *adj* **1** INTENSE, strong, severe, sharp, acute, extreme, harmful, destructive, devastating, injurious, powerful, painful, agonizing, forceful, forcible, harsh, ruinous, rough, vehement, tumultuous, turbulent. **2** CRUEL, brutal, aggressive, bloodthirsty, impetuous, hot-headed, headstrong, murderous, savage, wild, vicious, unrestrained, uncontrollable, ungovernable, passionate, furious, intemperate, maddened, outrageous, riotous, fiery.

🖙 1 calm, moderate. **2** peaceful, gentle.

virgin *n* girl, maiden, celibate, vestal.
adj virginal, chaste, intact, immaculate, maidenly, pure, modest, new, fresh, spotless, stainless, undefiled, untouched, unsullied.

virile *adj* man-like, masculine, male, manly, macho (*infml*), robust,

vigorous, potent, lusty, red-blooded, forceful, strong, rugged.

🖙 effeminate, impotent.

virtual *adj* effective, essential, practical, implied, implicit, potential.

virtually *adv* practically, in effect, almost, nearly, as good as, in essence.

virtue *n* **1** GOODNESS, morality, rectitude, uprightness, worthiness, righteousness, probity (*fml*), integrity, honour, incorruptibility, justice, high-mindedness, excellence. **2** QUALITY, worth, merit, advantage, asset, credit, strength.

🖙 1 vice.

virtuoso *n* expert, master, maestro, prodigy, genius.

virtuous *adj* good, moral, righteous, upright, worthy, honourable, irreproachable, incorruptible, exemplary, unimpeachable, high-principled, blameless, clean-living, excellent, innocent.

🖙 immoral, vicious.

virulent *adj* **1** POISONOUS, toxic, venomous, deadly, lethal, malignant, injurious, pernicious, intense. **2** HOSTILE, resentful, spiteful, acrimonious, bitter, vicious, vindictive, malevolent, malicious.

🖙 1 harmless.

visible *adj* perceptible, discernible, detectable, apparent, noticeable, observable, distinguishable, discoverable, evident, unconcealed, undisguised, unmistakable, conspicuous, clear, obvious, manifest, open, palpable, plain, patent.

🖙 invisible, indiscernible, hidden.

vision *n* **1** APPARITION, hallucination, illusion, delusion, mirage, phantom, ghost, chimera, spectre, wraith. **2** IDEA, ideal, conception, insight, view, picture, image, fantasy, dream, daydream. **3** SIGHT, seeing, eyesight, perception, discernment, far-sightedness, foresight, penetration.

visionary *adj* idealistic, impractical, romantic, dreamy, unrealistic, utopian, unreal, fanciful, prophetic, speculative, unworkable, illusory, imaginary.

n idealist, romantic, dreamer, daydreamer, fantasist, prophet, mystic, seer, utopian, rainbow-chaser, theorist.

🠪 pragmatist.

visit *v* call on, call in, stay with, stay at, drop in on (*infml*), stop by (*infml*), look in, look up, pop in (*infml*), see.

n call, stay, stop, excursion, sojourn (*fml*).

visitor *n* caller, guest, company, tourist, holidaymaker.

vista *n* view, prospect, panorama, perspective, outlook, scene.

visualize *v* picture, envisage, imagine, conceive.

vital *adj* 1 CRITICAL, crucial, important, imperative, key, significant, basic, fundamental, essential, necessary, requisite, indispensable, urgent, life-or-death, decisive, forceful. 2 LIVING, alive, lively, life-giving, invigorating, spirited, vivacious, vibrant, vigorous, dynamic, animated, energetic, quickening (*fml*).

🠪 1 inessential, peripheral. 2 dead.

vitality *n* life, liveliness, animation, vigour, energy, vivacity, spirit, sparkle, exuberance, go (*infml*), strength, stamina.

vitamin

Vitamins include: aneurin (thiamine), ascorbic acid, bioflavonoid/citrin, biotin, calciferol, cholecalciferol, cyanocobalamin, ergocalciferol, folic acid, linoleic acid, linolenic acid, menadione, nicotinic acid (niacin), pantothenic acid, phylloquinone, pteroic acid, pyridoxine (adermin), retinol, riboflavin, tocopherol.

vitriolic *adj* bitter, abusive, virulent, vicious, venomous, malicious, caustic, biting, sardonic, scathing, destructive.

vivacious *adj* lively, animated, spirited, high-spirited, effervescent, ebullient, cheerful, sparkling, bubbly, light-hearted.

vivid *adj* 1 BRIGHT, colourful, intense, strong, rich, vibrant, brilliant, glowing, dazzling, vigorous, expressive, dramatic, flamboyant, animated, lively, lifelike, spirited. 2 MEMORABLE, powerful, graphic, clear, distinct, striking, sharp, realistic.

🠪 1 colourless, dull. 2 vague.

vocabulary *n* language, words, glossary, lexicon, dictionary, word-book, thesaurus, idiom.

vocal *adj* 1 SPOKEN, said, oral, uttered, voiced. 2 ARTICULATE, eloquent, expressive, noisy, clamorous, shrill, strident, outspoken, frank, forthright, plain-spoken.

🠪 1 unspoken. 2 inarticulate.

vocation *n* calling, pursuit, career, métier, mission, profession, trade, employment, work, role, post, job, business, office.

vociferous *adj* noisy, vocal, clamorous, loud, obstreperous, strident, vehement, thundering, shouting.

🠪 quiet.

vogue *n* fashion, mode, style, craze, popularity, trend, prevalence, acceptance, custom, fad (*infml*), the latest (*infml*), the rage (*infml*), the thing (*infml*).

voice *n* 1 SPEECH, utterance, articulation, language, words, sound, tone, intonation, inflection, expression, mouthpiece, medium, instrument, organ. 2 SAY, vote, opinion, view, decision, option, will.

v express, say, utter, air, articulate, speak of, verbalize, assert, convey, disclose, divulge, declare, enunciate.

void *adj* **1** EMPTY, emptied, free, unfilled, unoccupied, vacant, clear, bare, blank, drained. **2** ANNULLED, inoperative, invalid, cancelled, ineffective, futile, useless, vain, worthless.

◨ **1** full. **2** valid.

n emptiness, vacuity, vacuum, chasm, blank, blankness, space, lack, want, cavity, gap, hollow, opening.

volatile *adj* changeable, inconstant, unstable, variable, erratic, temperamental, unsteady, unsettled, fickle, mercurial, unpredictable, capricious, restless, giddy, flighty, up and down (*infml*), lively.

◨ constant, steady.

volley *n* barrage, bombardment, hail, shower, burst, blast, discharge, explosion.

voluble *adj* fluent, glib, articulate, loquacious (*fml*), talkative, forthcoming, garrulous.

volume *n* **1** BULK, size, capacity, dimensions, amount, mass, quantity, aggregate, amplitude, body. **2** BOOK, tome, publication.

voluminous *adj* roomy, capacious, ample, spacious, billowing, vast, bulky, huge, large.

voluntary *adj* **1** FREE, gratuitous, optional, spontaneous, unforced, willing, unpaid, honorary. **2** CONSCIOUS, deliberate, purposeful, intended, intentional, wilful.

◨ **1** compulsory. **2** involuntary.

volunteer *v* offer, propose, put forward, present, suggest, step forward, advance.

voluptuous *adj* **1** SENSUAL, licentious, luxurious. **2** EROTIC, shapely, sexy (*infml*), seductive, provocative, enticing.

vomit *v* be sick, bring up, heave, retch, throw up (*infml*), puke (*infml*).

vote *n* ballot, poll, election, franchise, referendum.

v elect, ballot, choose, opt, plump for, declare, return.

vouch for guarantee, support, back, endorse, confirm, certify, affirm, assert, attest to, speak for, swear to, uphold.

vow *v* promise, pledge, swear, dedicate, devote, profess, consecrate, affirm.

n promise, oath, pledge.

voyage *n* journey, trip, passage, expedition, crossing.

vulgar *adj* **1** TASTELESS, flashy, gaudy, tawdry, cheap and nasty (*infml*). **2** UNREFINED, uncouth, coarse, common, crude, ill-bred, impolite, indecorous. **3** INDECENT, suggestive, risqué, rude, indelicate. **4** ORDINARY, general, popular, vernacular.

◨ **1** tasteful. **2** correct. **3** decent.

vulnerable *adj* unprotected, exposed, defenceless, susceptible, weak, sensitive, wide open.

◨ protected, strong.

W

wad *n* chunk, plug, roll, ball, wodge (*infml*), lump, hunk, mass, block.

waddle *v* toddle, totter, wobble, sway, rock, shuffle.

waffle *v* jabber, prattle, blather, rabbit on (*infml*), witter on (*infml*).

n blather, prattle, wordiness, padding, nonsense, gobbledegook (*infml*), hot air (*infml*).

waft *v* drift, float, blow, transport,

transmit.

n breath, puff, draught, current, breeze, scent, whiff.

wag *v* shake, waggle, wave, sway, swing, bob, nod, wiggle, oscillate, flutter, vibrate, quiver, rock.

wage *n* pay, fee, earnings, salary, wage-packet, payment, stipend, remuneration, emolument (*fml*), allowance, reward, hire, compensation, recompense.

v carry on, conduct, engage in, undertake, practise, pursue.

waif *n* orphan, stray, foundling.

wail *v* moan, cry, howl, lament, weep, complain, yowl (*infml*).

n moan, cry, howl, lament, complaint, weeping.

wait *v* delay, linger, hold back, hesitate, pause, hang around, hang fire, remain, rest, stay.

F3 proceed, go ahead.

n hold-up, hesitation, delay, interval, pause, halt.

waive *v* renounce, relinquish, forgo, resign, surrender, yield.

wake[1] *v* **1** RISE, get up, arise, rouse, came to, bring round. **2** STIMULATE, stir, activate, arouse, animate, excite, fire, galvanize.

F3 1 sleep.

n funeral, death-watch, vigil, watch.

wake[2] *n* trail, track, path, aftermath, backwash, wash, rear, train, waves.

walk *v* step, stride, pace, proceed, advance, march, plod, tramp, traipse, trek, trudge, saunter, amble, stroll, tread, hike, promenade, move, hoof it, accompany, escort.

n **1** *he has an odd walk*: carriage, gait, step, pace, stride. **2** *go for a walk*: stroll, amble, ramble, saunter, march, hike, tramp, trek, traipse, trudge, trail. **3** *a tree-lined walk*: footpath, path, walkway, avenue, pathway, promenade, alley, esplanade, lane, pavement, sidewalk.

walk of life field, area, sphere, line, activity, arena, course, pursuit, calling,

métier, career, vocation, profession, trade.

walker *n* pedestrian, rambler, hiker.

walk-out *n* strike, stoppage, industrial action, protest, rebellion, revolt.

walk-over *n* pushover (*infml*), doddle (*infml*), child's play, piece of cake (*infml*), cinch (*infml*).

wall *n* **1** PARTITION, screen, panel, divider, fence, hedge, enclosure, membrane, bulk-head.

2 FORTIFICATION, barricade, rampart, parapet, stockade, embankment, bulwark, palisade.

3 OBSTACLE, obstruction, barrier, block, impediment.

wallow *v* **1** *wallow in mud*: loll, lie, roll, wade, welter, lurch, flounder, splash. **2** *wallow in nostalgia*: indulge, luxuriate, relish, revel, bask, enjoy, glory, delight.

wand *n* rod, baton, staff, stick, sprig, mace, sceptre, twig.

wander *v* **1** ROAM, rove, ramble, meander, saunter, stroll, prowl, drift, range, stray, straggle. **2** DIGRESS, diverge, deviate, depart, go astray, swerve, veer, err. **3** RAMBLE, rave, babble, gibber.

n excursion, ramble, stroll, saunter, meander, prowl, cruise.

wanderer *n* itinerant, traveller, voyager, drifter, rover, rambler, stroller, stray, straggler, ranger, nomad, gypsy, vagrant, vagabond, rolling stone (*infml*).

wane *v* diminish, decrease, decline, weaken, subside, fade, dwindle, ebb, lessen, abate, sink, drop, taper off, dim, droop, contract, shrink, fail, wither.

F3 increase, wax.

wangle (*infml*) *v* manipulate, arrange, contrive, engineer, fix, scheme, manoeuvre, work, pull off, manage, fiddle (*infml*).

want *v* **1** DESIRE, wish, crave, covet, fancy, long for, pine for, yearn for,

warm

hunger for, thirst for. **2** NEED, require, demand, lack, miss, call for.

n 1 DESIRE, demand, longing, requirement, wish, need, appetite. **2** LACK, dearth, insufficiency, deficiency, shortage, inadequacy. **3** POVERTY, privation, destitution.

wanting adj **1** ABSENT, missing, lacking, short, insufficient. **2** INADEQUATE, imperfect, faulty, defective, substandard, poor, deficient, unsatisfactory.

Ea **1** sufficient. **2** adequate.

wanton adj malicious, immoral, shameless, arbitrary, unprovoked, unjustifiable, unrestrained, rash, reckless, wild.

war n warfare, hostilities, fighting, battle, combat, conflict, strife, struggle, bloodshed, contest, contention, enmity.

Ea peace, cease-fire.

Types of war include: ambush, armed conflict, assault, attack, battle, biological warfare, blitz, blitzkrieg, bombardment, chemical warfare, civil war, Cod wars, cold war, counter-attack, engagement, germ warfare, guerrilla warfare, holy war, hot war, invasion, jihad, jungle warfare, limited war, manoeuvres, nuclear war, Opium Wars, private war, resistance, skirmish, state of siege, struggle, total war, trade war, war of attrition, war of nerves, world war.
Famous wars include: American Civil War (Second American Revolution), American Revolution (War of Independence), Boer War, Crimean War, Crusades, English Civil War, Falklands War, Franco-Prussian War, Gulf War, Hundred Years War, Indian Wars, Iran-Iraq War, Korean War, Mexican War, Napoleonic War, Peasants' War, Russo-Finnish War (Winter War), Russo-Japanese War, Russo-Turkish Wars, Seven Years War, Six-Day War, Spanish-American War, Spanish-American Wars of Independence, Spanish Civil War, Suez Crisis, Thirty Years War, Vietnam War, War of 1812, War of the Pacific, Wars of the Roses, World War I (the Great War), World War II.

v wage war, fight, take up arms, battle, clash, combat, strive, skirmish, struggle, contest, contend.

ward n **1** ROOM, apartment, unit. **2** DIVISION, area, district, quarter, precinct, zone. **3** CHARGE, dependant, protégé(e), minor.

ward off avert, fend off, deflect, parry, repel, stave off, thwart, beat off, forestall, evade, turn away, block, avoid.

warden n keeper, custodian, guardian, warder, caretaker, curator, ranger, steward, watchman, superintendent, administrator, janitor.

warder n jailer, keeper, prison officer, guard, wardress, custodian.

wardrobe n **1** CUPBOARD, closet. **2** CLOTHES, outfit, attire.

warehouse n store, storehouse, depot, depository, repository, stockroom, entrepot.

wares n goods, merchandise, commodities, stock, products, produce, stuff.

warfare n war, fighting, hostilities, battle, arms, combat, strife, struggle, passage of arms, contest, conflict, contention, discord, blows.

Ea peace.

warlike adj belligerent, aggressive, bellicose, pugnacious, combative, bloodthirsty, war-mongering, militaristic, hostile, antagonistic, unfriendly.

Ea friendly, peaceable.

warm adj **1** HEATED, tepid, lukewarm. **2** ARDENT, passionate,

fervent, vehement, earnest, zealous.
3 *warm colours*: rich, intense,
mellow, cheerful. **4** FRIENDLY,
amiable, cordial, affable, kindly,
genial, hearty, hospitable,
sympathetic, affectionate, tender.
5 FINE, sunny, balmy, temperate,
close.
F3 1 cool. 2 indifferent. 3 cold. 4
unfriendly. 5 cool.
v **1** HEAT (UP), reheat, melt, thaw. **2**
ANIMATE, interest, please, delight,
stimulate, stir, rouse, excite.
F3 1 cool.

warmth *n* **1** WARMNESS, heat. **2**
FRIENDLINESS, affection, cordiality,
tenderness. **3** ARDOUR, enthusiasm,
passion, fervour, zeal, eagerness.
F3 1 coldness. 2 unfriendliness.
3 indifference.

warn *v* caution, alert, admonish,
advise, notify, counsel, put on one's
guard, inform, tip off (*infml*).

warning *n* **1** CAUTION, alert,
admonition, advice, notification,
notice, advance notice, counsel, hint,
lesson, alarm, threat, tip-off (*infml*).
2 OMEN, augury, premonition,
presage, sign, signal, portent.

warp *v* twist, bend, contort, deform,
distort, kink, misshape, pervert,
corrupt, deviate.
F3 straighten.
n twist, bend, contortion,
deformation, distortion, bias, kink,
irregularity, turn, bent, defect,
deviation, quirk, perversion.

warrant *n* authorization, authority,
sanction, permit, permission, licence,
guarantee, warranty, security, pledge,
commission, voucher.
v **1** GUARANTEE, pledge, certify,
assure, declare, affirm, vouch for,
answer for, underwrite, uphold,
endorse. **2** AUTHORIZE, entitle,
empower, sanction, allow,
license, justify, excuse, approve, call
for, commission, necessitate, require.

wary *adj* cautious, guarded, careful,

chary, on one's guard, on the
lookout, prudent, distrustful,
suspicious, heedful, attentive, alert,
watchful, vigilant, wide-awake.
F3 unwary, careless, heedless.

wash *v* **1** CLEAN, cleanse, launder,
scrub, swab down, rinse, swill.
2 BATHE, bath, shower, douche,
shampoo.
n **1** CLEANING, cleansing, bath,
bathe, laundry, laundering, scrub,
shower, shampoo, washing, rinse.
2 FLOW, sweep, wave, swell.

wash-out (*infml*) *n* failure, disaster,
disappointment, fiasco, flop (*infml*),
debacle.
F3 success, triumph.

waste *v* **1** SQUANDER, misspend,
misuse, fritter away, dissipate, lavish,
spend, throw away, blow (*infml*).
2 CONSUME, erode, exhaust, drain,
destroy, spoil.
F3 1 economize. 2 preserve.
n **1** SQUANDERING, dissipation,
prodigality, wastefulness,
extravagance, loss.
2 MISAPPLICATION, misuse, abuse,
neglect. **3** RUBBISH, refuse, trash,
garbage, leftovers, debris, dregs,
effluent, litter, scrap, slops,
offscouring(s), dross.
adj **1** USELESS, worthless, unwanted,
unused, left-over, superfluous,
supernumerary, extra. **2** BARREN,
desolate, empty, uninhabited, bare,
devastated, uncultivated, unprofitable,
wild, dismal, dreary.

wasted *adj* **1** UNNECESSARY,
needless, useless. **2** EMACIATED,
withered, shrivelled, shrunken, gaunt,
washed-out, spent.
F3 1 necessary. 2 robust.

wasteful *adj* extravagant,
spendthrift, prodigal, profligate,
uneconomical, thriftless, unthrifty,
ruinous, lavish, improvident.
F3 economical, thrifty.

wasteland *n* wilderness, desert,
barrenness, waste, wild(s), void.

watch v 1 OBSERVE, see, look at, regard, note, notice, mark, stare at, peer at, gaze at, view. 2 GUARD, look after, keep an eye on, mind, protect, superintend, take care of, keep. 3 PAY ATTENTION, be careful, take heed, look out.
n 1 TIMEPIECE, wristwatch, clock, chronometer. 2 VIGILANCE, watchfulness, vigil, observation, surveillance, notice, lookout, attention, heed, alertness, inspection, supervision.
watch out notice, be vigilant, look out, keep one's eyes open.
watch over guard, protect, stand guard over, keep an eye on, look after, mind, shield, defend, preserve.
watchdog n 1 GUARD DOG, house-dog. 2 MONITOR, inspector, scrutineer, vigilante, ombudsman, guardian, custodian, protector.
watcher n spectator, observer, onlooker, looker-on, viewer, lookout, spy, witness.
watchful adj vigilant, attentive, heedful, observant, alert, guarded, on one's guard, wide awake, suspicious, wary, chary, cautious.
🔁 unobservant, inattentive.
watchman n guard, security guard, caretaker, custodian.
water n rain, sea, ocean, lake, river, stream.
v wet, moisten, dampen, soak, spray, sprinkle, irrigate, drench, flood, hose.
🔁 dry out, parch.
water down dilute, thin, water, weaken, adulterate, mix, tone down, soften, qualify.
waterfall n fall, cascade, chute, cataract, torrent.
watertight adj 1 WATERPROOF, sound, hermetic. 2 IMPREGNABLE, unassailable, airtight, flawless, foolproof, firm, incontrovertible.
🔁 1 leaky.
watery adj 1 LIQUID, fluid, moist, wet, damp. 2 WEAK, watered-down,

diluted, insipid, tasteless, thin, runny, soggy, flavourless, washy, wishy-washy (infml).
🔁 1 dry.
wave v 1 BECKON, gesture, gesticulate, indicate, sign, signal, direct. 2 BRANDISH, flourish, flap, flutter, shake, sway, swing, waft, quiver, ripple.
n 1 BREAKER, roller, billow, ripple, tidal wave, wavelet, undulation, white horse (infml). 2 SURGE, sweep, swell, upsurge, ground swell, current, drift, movement, rush, tendency, trend, stream, flood, outbreak, rash.
waver v 1 VACILLATE, falter, hesitate, dither, fluctuate, vary, seesaw. 2 OSCILLATE, shake, sway, wobble, tremble, totter, rock.
🔁 1 decide.
wavy adj undulating, rippled, curly, curvy, ridged, sinuous, winding, zigzag.
wax v grow, increase, rise, swell, develop, enlarge, expand, magnify, mount, fill out, become.
🔁 decrease, wane.
way n 1 METHOD, approach, manner, technique, procedure, means, mode, system, fashion. 2 CUSTOM, practice, habit, usage, characteristic, idiosyncrasy, trait, style, conduct, nature. 3 DIRECTION, course, route, path, road, channel, access, avenue, track, passage, highway, street, thoroughfare, lane.
by the way incidentally, in passing.
wayward adj wilful, capricious, perverse, contrary, changeable, fickle, unpredictable, stubborn, self-willed, unmanageable, headstrong, obstinate, disobedient, rebellious, insubordinate, intractable, unruly, incorrigible.
🔁 tractable, good-natured.
weak adj 1 FEEBLE, frail, infirm, unhealthy, sickly, delicate, debilitated, exhausted, fragile, flimsy. 2 VULNERABLE, unprotected,

unguarded, defenceless, exposed.
3 POWERLESS, impotent, spineless, cowardly, indecisive, ineffectual, irresolute, poor, lacking, lame, inadequate, defective, deficient, inconclusive, unconvincing, untenable. **4** FAINT, slight, low, soft, muffled, dull, imperceptible. **5** INSIPID, tasteless, watery, thin, diluted, runny.

F3 1 strong. 2 secure. 3 powerful. 4 strong. 5 strong.

weaken v **1** ENFEEBLE, exhaust, debilitate, sap, undermine, dilute, diminish, lower, lessen, reduce, moderate, mitigate, temper, soften (up), thin, water down. **2** TIRE, flag, fail, give way, droop, fade, abate, ease up, dwindle.

F3 1 strengthen.

weakness n **1** FEEBLENESS, debility, infirmity, impotence, frailty, powerlessness, vulnerability. **2** FAULT, failing, flaw, shortcoming, blemish, defect, deficiency, foible. **3** LIKING, inclination, fondness, penchant, passion, soft spot (infml).

F3 1 strength. 2 strength. 3 dislike.

wealth n **1** MONEY, cash, riches, assets, affluence, prosperity, funds, mammon, fortune, capital, opulence, means, substance, resources, goods, possessions, property, estate. **2** ABUNDANCE, plenty, bounty, fullness, profusion, store.

F3 1 poverty.

wealthy adj rich, prosperous, affluent, well-off, moneyed, opulent, comfortable, well-heeled, well-to-do, flush (infml), loaded (sl), rolling in it (infml).

F3 poor, impoverished.

weapon

Weapons include: gun, airgun, pistol, revolver, automatic, Colt®, Luger®, magnum, Mauser, six-gun, six-shooter, rifle, air rifle, Winchester® rifle, carbine, shotgun, blunderbuss, musket, elephant gun, machine-gun, kalashnikov, submachine-gun, Uzi, tommy-gun, sten gun, Bren gun, cannon, field gun, gatling-gun, howitzer, mortar, turret-gun; knife, bowie knife, flick-knife, stiletto, dagger, dirk, poniard, sword, épée, foil, rapier, sabre, scimitar, bayonet, broadsword, claymore, lance, spear, pike, machete; bomb, atom bomb, H-bomb, cluster-bomb, depth-charge, incendiary bomb, Mills bomb, mine, land-mine, napalm bomb, time-bomb; bow and arrow, longbow, crossbow, blowpipe, catapult, boomerang, sling, harpoon, bolas, rocket, bazooka, ballistic missile, Cruise missile, Exocet®, Scud (infml), torpedo, hand grenade, flame-thrower; battleaxe, pole-axe, halberd, tomahawk, cosh, cudgel, knuckleduster, shillelagh, truncheon; gas, CS gas, mustard gas, tear-gas.

wear v **1** DRESS IN, have on, put on, don, sport, carry, bear, display, show. **2** DETERIORATE, erode, corrode, consume, fray, rub, abrade, waste, grind.
n **1** CLOTHES, clothing, dress, garments, outfit, costume, attire. **2** DETERIORATION, erosion, corrosion, wear and tear, friction, abrasion.

wear off decrease, abate, dwindle, diminish, subside, wane, weaken, fade, lessen, ebb, peter out, disappear.

F3 increase.

wear out 1 EXHAUST, fatigue, tire (out), enervate, sap. **2** DETERIORATE, wear through, erode, impair, consume, fray.

wearing adj exhausting, fatiguing, tiresome, tiring, wearisome, trying, taxing, oppressive, irksome, exasperating.

F3 refreshing.

weary adj tired, exhausted, fatigued, sleepy, worn out, drained, drowsy,

jaded, all in (*infml*), done in (*infml*), fagged out (*infml*), knackered (*infml*), dead beat (*infml*), dog-tired (*infml*), whacked (*infml*).
Ⓕ refreshed.

wearying *adj* tiring, fatiguing, exhausting, wearisome, wearing, taxing, trying.
Ⓕ refreshing.

weather *n* climate, conditions, temperature.

> *Types of weather include*: breeze, wind, squall, gale, hurricane, tornado, typhoon, monsoon, cyclone, whirlwind, chinook, mistral, cloud, mist, dew, fog, smog, rain, drizzle, shower, deluge, downpour, rainbow, sunshine, heatwave, haze, drought, storm, tempest, thunder, lightning, frost, hoar frost, hail, sleet, snow, snowstorm, ice, black ice, thaw, slush.

v 1 ENDURE, survive, live through, come through, ride out, rise above, stick out, withstand, surmount, stand, brave, overcome, resist, pull through, suffer. 2 EXPOSE, toughen, season, harden.
Ⓕ 1 succumb.

weave *v* 1 INTERLACE, lace, plait, braid, intertwine, spin, knit, entwine, intercross, fuse, merge, unite. 2 CREATE, compose, construct, contrive, put together, fabricate. 3 WIND, twist, zigzag, criss-cross.

web *n* network, net, netting, lattice, mesh, webbing, interlacing, weft, snare, tangle, trap.

wedding *n* marriage, matrimony, nuptials (*fml*), wedlock, bridal.
Ⓕ divorce.

wedge *n* lump, block, chunk, wodge, chock.
v jam, cram, pack, ram, squeeze, stuff, push, lodge, block, thrust, crowd, force.

weedy (*infml*) *adj* thin, skinny, puny, scrawny, undersized, weak,

feeble, frail, weak-kneed, insipid, wet (*infml*), wimpish (*infml*).
Ⓕ strong.

weep *v* cry, sob, moan, lament, wail, mourn, grieve, bawl, blubber, snivel, whimper, blub (*infml*).
Ⓕ rejoice.

weigh *v* 1 BEAR DOWN, oppress. 2 CONSIDER, contemplate, evaluate, meditate on, mull over, ponder, think over, examine, reflect on, deliberate.

weigh down oppress, overload, load, burden, bear down, weigh upon, press down, get down (*infml*), depress, afflict, trouble, worry.
Ⓕ lighten, hearten.

weigh up assess, examine, size up, balance, consider, contemplate, deliberate, mull over, ponder, think over, discuss, chew over (*infml*).

weight *n* 1 HEAVINESS, gravity, burden, load, pressure, mass, force, ballast, tonnage, poundage. 2 IMPORTANCE, significance, substance, consequence, impact, moment, influence, value, authority, clout (*infml*), power, preponderance, consideration.
Ⓕ 1 lightness.
v 1 LOAD, weigh down, oppress, handicap. 2 BIAS, unbalance, slant, prejudice.

weighty *adj* 1 HEAVY, burdensome, substantial, bulky. 2 IMPORTANT, significant, consequential, crucial, critical, momentous, serious, grave, solemn. 3 DEMANDING, difficult, exacting, taxing.
Ⓕ 1 light. 2 unimportant.

weird *adj* strange, uncanny, bizarre, eerie, creepy, supernatural, unnatural, ghostly, freakish, mysterious, queer, grotesque, spooky (*infml*), far-out (*infml*), way-out (*infml*).
Ⓕ normal, usual.

welcome *adj* acceptable, desirable, pleasing, pleasant, agreeable, gratifying, appreciated, delightful, refreshing.

☒ unwelcome.

n reception, greeting, salutation (*infml*), acceptance, hospitality, red carpet (*infml*).

v greet, receive, salute, meet, accept, approve of, embrace.

☒ reject, snub.

weld *v* fuse, unite, bond, join, solder, bind, connect, seal, link, cement.

☒ separate.

welfare *n* well-being, health, prosperity, happiness, benefit, good, advantage, interest, profit, success.

well[1] *n* spring, well-spring, fountain, fount, source, reservoir, well-head, waterhole.

v flow, spring, surge, gush, stream, brim over, jet, spout, spurt, swell, pour, flood, ooze, run, trickle, rise, seep.

well[2] *adv* rightly, correctly, properly, skilfully, ably, expertly, successfully, adequately, sufficiently, suitably, easily, satisfactorily, thoroughly, greatly, fully, considerably, completely, agreeably, pleasantly, happily, kindly, favourably, splendidly, substantially, comfortably, readily, carefully, clearly, highly, deeply, justly.

☒ badly, inadequately, incompetently, wrongly.

adj 1 HEALTHY, in good health, fit, able-bodied, sound, robust, strong, thriving, flourishing.

2 SATISFACTORY, right, all right, good, pleasing, proper, agreeable, fine, lucky, fortunate.

☒ 1 ill. 2 bad.

well-balanced *adj* 1 RATIONAL, reasonable, level-headed, well-adjusted, stable, sensible, sane, sound, sober, together (*sl*).

2 SYMMETRICAL, even, harmonious.

☒ 1 unbalanced. 2 asymmetrical.

well-being *n* welfare, happiness, comfort, good.

well-bred *adj* well-mannered, polite,

well-brought-up, mannerly, courteous, civil, refined, cultivated, cultured, genteel.

☒ ill-bred.

well-dressed *adj* smart, well-groomed, elegant, fashionable, chic, stylish, neat, trim, spruce, tidy.

☒ badly dressed, scruffy.

well-known *adj* famous, renowned, celebrated, famed, eminent, notable, noted, illustrious, familiar.

☒ unknown.

well-off *adj* rich, wealthy, affluent, prosperous, well-to-do, moneyed, thriving, successful, comfortable, fortunate.

☒ poor, badly-off.

well-thought-of *adj* respected, highly regarded, esteemed, admired, honoured, revered.

☒ despised.

well-worn *adj* timeworn, stale, tired, trite, overused, unoriginal, hackneyed, commonplace, stereotyped, threadbare, corny (*infml*).

☒ original.

wet *adj* 1 DAMP, moist, soaked, soaking, sodden, saturated, soggy, sopping, watery, waterlogged, drenched, dripping, spongy, dank, clammy. 2 RAINING, rainy, showery, teeming, pouring, drizzling, humid. 3 (*infml*) WEAK, feeble, weedy, wimpish (*infml*), spineless, soft, ineffectual, namby-pamby, irresolute, timorous.

☒ 1 dry. 2 dry. 3 strong.

n wetness, moisture, damp, dampness, liquid, water, clamminess, condensation, humidity, rain, drizzle.

☒ dryness.

v moisten, damp, dampen, soak, saturate, drench, steep, water, irrigate, spray, splash, sprinkle, imbue, dip.

☒ dry.

whack *v* hit, strike, smack, thrash, slap, beat, bash (*infml*), bang, cuff, thump, box, buffet, rap, wallop (*infml*), belt (*infml*), clobber (*infml*), clout (*infml*), sock (*infml*).

n smack, slap, blow, hit, rap, stroke, thump, cuff, box, bang, clout (*infml*), bash (*infml*), wallop (*infml*).

wharf *n* dock, quay, quayside, jetty, landing-stage, dockyard, marina, pier.

wheedle *v* cajole, coax, persuade, inveigle, charm, flatter, entice, court, draw.

Ea force.

wheel *n* turn, revolution, circle, rotation, gyration, pivot, roll, spin, twirl, whirl.

v turn, rotate, circle, gyrate, orbit, spin, twirl, whirl, swing, roll, swivel.

wheeze *v* pant, gasp, cough, hiss, rasp, whistle.

whereabouts *n* location, position, place, situation, site, vicinity.

whet *v* **1** SHARPEN, hone, file, grind. **2** STIMULATE, stir, rouse, arouse, provoke, kindle, quicken, incite, awaken, increase.

Ea **1** blunt. **2** dampen.

whiff *n* breath, puff, hint, trace, blast, draught, odour, smell, aroma, sniff, scent, reek, stink, stench.

whim *n* fancy, caprice, notion, quirk, freak, humour, conceit, fad, vagary, urge.

whimper *v* cry, sob, weep, snivel, whine, grizzle, mewl, moan, whinge (*infml*).

n sob, snivel, whine, moan.

whimsical *adj* fanciful, capricious, playful, impulsive, eccentric, funny, droll, curious, queer, unusual, weird, odd, peculiar, quaint, dotty (*infml*).

whine *n* **1** CRY, sob, whimper, moan, wail. **2** COMPLAINT, grumble, grouse, gripe (*infml*), grouch (*infml*).

v **1** CRY, sob, whimper, grizzle, moan, wail. **2** COMPLAIN, carp, grumble, whinge (*infml*), gripe (*infml*), grouch (*infml*).

whip *v* **1** BEAT, flog, lash, flagellate,

scourge, birch, cane, strap, thrash, punish, chastise, discipline, castigate (*fml*). **2** PULL, jerk, snatch, whisk, dash, dart, rush, tear, flit, flash, fly. **3** GOAD, drive, spur, push, urge, stir, rouse, agitate, incite, provoke, instigate.

n lash, scourge, switch, birch, horsewhip, riding-crop, cat-o'-nine-tails.

whirl *v* swirl, spin, turn, twist, twirl, pivot, pirouette, swivel, wheel, rotate, revolve, reel, roll, gyrate, circle.

n **1** SPIN, twirl, twist, gyration, revolution, pirouette, swirl, turn, wheel, rotation, circle, reel, roll. **2** CONFUSION, daze, flurry, commotion, agitation, bustle, hubbub, hurly-burly, giddiness, tumult, uproar.

whirlwind *n* tornado, cyclone, vortex.

adj hasty, impulsive, quick, rapid, speedy, swift, lightning, headlong, impetuous, rash.

Ea deliberate, slow.

whisk *v* **1** WHIP, beat. **2** DART, dash, rush, hurry, speed, hasten, race. **3** BRUSH, sweep, flick, wipe, twitch.

whisper *v* **1** MURMUR, mutter, mumble, breathe, hiss, rustle, sigh. **2** HINT, intimate, insinuate, gossip, divulge.

Ea **1** shout.

n **1** MURMUR, undertone, sigh, hiss, rustle. **2** HINT, suggestion, suspicion, breath, whiff, rumour, report, innuendo, insinuation, trace, tinge, soupçon, buzz.

white *adj* **1** PALE, pallid, wan, ashen, colourless, anaemic, pasty. **2** LIGHT, snowy, milky, creamy, ivory, hoary, silver, grey. **3** PURE, immaculate, spotless, stainless, undefiled.

Ea **1** ruddy. **2** dark. **3** defiled.

whiten *v* bleach, blanch, whitewash, pale, fade.

▪ blacken, darken.

whittle v 1 CARVE, cut, scrape, shave, trim, pare, hew, shape.
2 ERODE, eat away, wear away, diminish, consume, reduce, undermine.

whole adj 1 COMPLETE, entire, integral, full, total, unabridged, uncut, undivided, unedited.
2 INTACT, unharmed, undamaged, unbroken, inviolate, perfect, in one piece, mint, unhurt. 3 WELL, healthy, fit, sound, strong.
▪ 1 partial. 2 damaged. 3 ill.
n total, aggregate, sum total, entirety, all, fullness, totality, ensemble, entity, unit, lot, piece, everything.
▪ part.
on the whole generally, mostly, in general, generally speaking, as a rule, for the most part, all in all, all things considered, by and large.

whole-hearted adj unreserved, unstinting, unqualified, passionate, enthusiastic, earnest, committed, dedicated, devoted, heartfelt, emphatic, warm, sincere, unfeigned, genuine, complete, true, real, zealous.
▪ half-hearted.

wholesale adj comprehensive, far-reaching, extensive, sweeping, wide-ranging, mass, broad, outright, total, massive, indiscriminate.
▪ partial.

wholesome adj 1 wholesome food: healthy, hygienic, salubrious, sanitary, nutritious, nourishing, beneficial, salutary, invigorating, bracing. 2 wholesome entertainment: moral, decent, clean, proper, improving, edifying, uplifting, pure, virtuous, righteous, honourable, respectable.
▪ 1 unhealthy. 2 unwholesome.

wholly adv completely, entirely, fully, purely, absolutely, totally, utterly, comprehensively, altogether, perfectly, thoroughly, all, exclusively, only.

▪ partly.

wicked adj 1 EVIL, sinful, immoral, depraved, corrupt, vicious, unprincipled, iniquitous, heinous, debased, abominable, ungodly, unrighteous, shameful. 2 BAD, unpleasant, harmful, offensive, vile, worthless, difficult, dreadful, distressing, awful, atrocious, severe, intense, nasty, injurious, troublesome, terrible, foul, fierce.
3 NAUGHTY, mischievous, roguish.
▪ 1 good, upright. 2 harmless.

wide adj 1 BROAD, roomy, spacious, vast, immense. 2 DILATED, expanded, full. 3 EXTENSIVE, wide-ranging, comprehensive, far-reaching, general. 4 LOOSE, baggy.
5 OFF-TARGET, distant, remote.
▪ 1 narrow. 3 restricted. 5 near.
adv 1 ASTRAY, off course, off target, off the mark. 2 FULLY, completely, all the way.
▪ 1 on target.

widen v distend, dilate, expand, extend, spread, stretch, enlarge, broaden.
▪ narrow.

widespread adj extensive, prevalent, rife, general, sweeping, universal, wholesale, far-reaching, unlimited, broad, common, pervasive, far-flung.
▪ limited.

width n breadth, diameter, wideness, compass, thickness, span, scope, range, measure, girth, beam, amplitude, extent, reach.

wield v 1 wield a weapon: brandish, flourish, swing, wave, handle, ply, manage, manipulate. 2 wield power: have, hold, possess, employ, exert, exercise, use, utilize, maintain, command.

wife n partner, spouse, mate, better half, bride.

wild adj 1 UNTAMED, undomesticated, feral, savage, barbarous, primitive, uncivilized,

natural, ferocious, fierce.
2 UNCULTIVATED, desolate, waste, uninhabited. **3** unrestrained, unruly, unmanageable, violent, turbulent, rowdy, lawless, disorderly, riotous, boisterous. **4** STORMY, tempestuous, rough, blustery, choppy. **5** UNTIDY, unkempt, messy, dishevelled, tousled. **6** RECKLESS, rash, imprudent, foolish, foolhardy, impracticable, irrational, outrageous, preposterous, wayward, extravagant. **7** MAD, crazy (*infml*), frenzied, distraught, demented.

🔁 **1** civilized, tame. **2** cultivated. **3** restrained. **4** calm. **5** tidy. **6** sensible. **7** sane.

wilderness *n* desert, wasteland, waste, wilds, jungle.

wiles *n* trick, stratagem, ruse, ploy, device, contrivance, guile, manoeuvre, subterfuge, cunning, dodge (*infml*), deceit, cheating, trickery, fraud, craftiness, chicanery.

🔁 guilelessness.

wilful *adj* **1** DELIBERATE, conscious, intentional, voluntary, premeditated. **2** SELF-WILLED, obstinate, stubborn, pig-headed, obdurate, intransigent, inflexible, perverse, wayward, contrary.

🔁 **1** unintentional. **2** good-natured.

will *n* **1** VOLITION, choice, option, preference, decision, discretion. **2** WISH, desire, inclination, feeling, fancy, disposition, mind. **3** PURPOSE, resolve, resolution, determination, will-power, aim, intention, command.

v **1** WANT, desire, choose, compel, command, decree, order, ordain. **2** BEQUEATH, leave, hand down, pass on, transfer, confer, dispose of.

willing *adj* disposed, inclined, agreeable, compliant, ready, prepared, consenting, content, amenable, biddable, pleased, well-disposed, favourable, happy, eager, enthusiastic.

🔁 unwilling, disinclined, reluctant.

wilt *v* droop, sag, wither, shrivel, flop, flag, dwindle, weaken, diminish, fail, fade, languish, ebb, sink, wane.

🔁 perk up.

wily *adj* shrewd, cunning, scheming, artful, crafty, foxy, intriguing, tricky, underhand, shifty, deceitful, deceptive, astute, sly, guileful, designing, crooked, fly (*infml*).

🔁 guileless.

win *v* **1** BE VICTORIOUS, triumph, succeed, prevail, overcome, conquer, come first, carry off, finish first. **2** GAIN, acquire, achieve, attain, accomplish, receive, procure, secure, obtain, get, earn, catch, net.

🔁 **1** fail, lose.

n victory, triumph, conquest, success, mastery.

🔁 defeat.

win over persuade, prevail upon, convince, influence, convert, sway, talk round, charm, allure, attract.

wind¹ *n* air, breeze, draught, gust, puff, breath, air-current, blast, current, bluster, gale, hurricane, tornado, cyclone.

Types of wind include: anticyclone, austral wind, berg wind, bise, bora, Cape doctor, chinook, cyclone, doctor, east wind, El Niño, etesian, Favonian wind, föhn, gregale, harmattan, helm wind, khamsin, levant, libeccio, meltemi, mistral, monsoon, north wind, nor'wester, pampero, prevailing wind, samiel, simoom, sirocco, snoweater, southerly, southerly buster, trade wind, tramontana, westerly, wet chinook, williwaw, willy-willy, zephyr, zonda. *see also* **storm**.

wind² *v* coil, twist, turn, curl, curve, bend, loop, spiral, zigzag, twine, encircle, furl, deviate, meander, ramble, wreath, roll, reel.

wind down 1 SLOW (DOWN), slacken

windfall 594

off, lessen, reduce, subside, diminish, dwindle, decline. **2** RELAX, unwind, quieten down, ease up, calm down.

E∃ 1 increase.

wind up 1 CLOSE (DOWN), end, conclude, terminate, finalize, finish, liquidate. **2** END UP, finish up, find oneself, settle. **3** (*infml*) ANNOY, irritate, disconcert, fool, trick, kid (*infml*).

E∃ 1 begin.

windfall *n* bonanza, godsend, jackpot, treasure-trove, stroke of luck, find.

window *n* pane, light, opening, skylight, rose-window, casement, oriel, dormer.

windy *adj* breezy, blowy, blustery, squally, windswept, stormy, tempestuous, gusty.

E∃ calm.

wine

Types of wine include: alcohol-free, dry, brut, sec, demi-sec, sweet, sparkling, table wine, house wine; red wine, house red (*infml*), white wine, house white (*infml*), rosé, blush wine, fortified wine, mulled wine, tonic wine, vintage wine, plonk (*infml*); sherry, dry sherry, fino, medium sherry, amontillado, sweet sherry, oloroso; port, ruby, tawny, white port, vintage port.

Varieties of wine include: Alsace, Asti, Auslese, Beaujolais, Beaujolais Nouveau, Beaune, Bordeaux, Burgundy, cabernet sauvignon, Chablis, Chambertin, champagne, Chardonnay, Chianti, claret, Côtes du Rhône, Dão, Douro, Frascati, Graves, hock, Lambrusco, Liebfraumilch, Mâcon, Madeira, Malaga, Marsala, Mateus Rosé, Médoc, Merlot, moselle, Muscadet, muscatel, Niersteiner, retsina, Riesling, Rioja, Sauterne, Sekt,

Soave, Spätlese, Tarragona, Valpolicella, vinho verde.

wing *n* branch, arm, section, faction, group, grouping, flank, circle, coterie, set, segment, side, annexe, adjunct, extension.

wink *v* blink, flutter, glimmer, glint, twinkle, gleam, sparkle, flicker, flash. *n* **1** BLINK, flutter, sparkle, twinkle, glimmering, gleam, glint. **2** INSTANT, second, split second, flash.

winner *n* champion, victor, prizewinner, medallist, title-holder, world-beater, conqueror.

E∃ loser.

winning *adj* **1** CONQUERING, triumphant, unbeaten, undefeated, victorious, successful. **2** WINSOME, charming, attractive, captivating, engaging, fetching, enchanting, endearing, delightful, amiable, alluring, lovely, pleasing, sweet.

E∃ 1 losing. **2** unappealing.

winnow *v* sift, separate, screen, divide, cull, select, part, fan.

wintry *adj* cold, chilly, bleak, cheerless, desolate, dismal, harsh, snowy, frosty, freezing, frozen, icy.

wipe *v* **1** RUB, clean, dry, dust, brush, mop, swab, sponge, clear. **2** REMOVE, erase, take away, take off.

wipe out eradicate, obliterate, destroy, massacre, exterminate, annihilate, erase, expunge, raze, abolish, blot out, efface.

wiry *adj* muscular, sinewy, lean, tough, strong.

E∃ puny.

wisdom *n* discernment, penetration, sagacity, reason, sense, astuteness, comprehension, enlightenment, judgement, judiciousness, understanding, knowledge, learning, intelligence, erudition, foresight, prudence.

E∃ folly, stupidity.

wise *adj* **1** DISCERNING, sagacious,

perceptive, rational, informed, well-informed, understanding, erudite, enlightened, knowing, intelligent, clever, aware, experienced. **2** WELL-ADVISED, judicious, prudent, reasonable, sensible, sound, long-sighted, shrewd.

🔁 **1** foolish, stupid. **2** ill-advised.

wish *v* **1** DESIRE, want, yearn, long, hanker, covet, crave, aspire, hope, hunger, thirst, prefer, need. **2** ASK, bid, require, order, instruct, direct, command.

n **1** DESIRE, want, hankering, aspiration, inclination, hunger, thirst, liking, preference, yearning, urge, whim, hope. **2** REQUEST, bidding, order, command, will.

wisp *n* shred, strand, thread, twist, piece, lock.

wispy *adj* thin, straggly, frail, fine, attenuated, insubstantial, light, flimsy, fragile, delicate, ethereal, gossamer, faint.

🔁 substantial.

wistful *adj* **1** THOUGHTFUL, pensive, musing, reflective, wishful, contemplative, dreamy, dreaming, meditative. **2** MELANCHOLY, sad, forlorn, disconsolate, longing, mournful.

wit *n* **1** HUMOUR, repartee, facetiousness, drollery, banter, jocularity, levity. **2** INTELLIGENCE, cleverness, brains, sense, reason, common sense, wisdom, understanding, judgement, insight, intellect. **3** HUMORIST, comedian, comic, satirist, joker, wag.

🔁 **1** seriousness. **2** stupidity.

witch *n* sorceress, enchantress, occultist, magician, hag.

witchcraft *n* sorcery, magic, wizardry, occultism, the occult, the black art, black magic, enchantment, necromancy, voodoo, spell, incantation, divination, conjuration.

withdraw *v* **1** RECOIL, shrink back, draw back, pull back. **2** RECANT,

disclaim, take back, revoke, rescind, retract, cancel, abjure, recall, take away. **3** DEPART, go (away), absent oneself, retire, remove, leave, back out, fall back, drop out, retreat, secede. **4** DRAW OUT, extract, pull out.

withdrawal *n* **1** REPUDIATION, recantation, disclaimer, disavowal, revocation, recall, secession, abjuration. **2** DEPARTURE, exit, exodus, retirement, retreat. **3** EXTRACTION, removal.

withdrawn *adj* **1** RESERVED, unsociable, shy, introvert, quiet, retiring, aloof, detached, shrinking, uncommunicative, unforthcoming, taciturn, silent. **2** REMOTE, isolated, distant, secluded, out-of-the-way, private, hidden, solitary.

🔁 **1** extrovert, outgoing.

wither *v* shrink, shrivel, dry, wilt, droop, decay, disintegrate, wane, perish, fade, languish, decline, waste.

🔁 flourish, thrive.

withering *adj* **1** DESTRUCTIVE, deadly, death-dealing, devastating. **2** SCORNFUL, contemptuous, scathing, snubbing, humiliating, mortifying, wounding.

🔁 **2** encouraging, supportive.

withhold *v* keep back, retain, hold back, suppress, restrain, repress, control, check, reserve, deduct, refuse, hide, conceal.

🔁 give, accord.

withstand *v* resist, oppose, stand fast, stand one's ground, stand, stand up to, confront, brave, face, cope with, take on, thwart, defy, hold one's ground, hold out, last out, hold off, endure, bear, tolerate, put up with, survive, weather.

🔁 give in, yield.

witness *n* **1** TESTIFIER, attestant, deponent (*fml*). **2** ONLOOKER, eye-witness, looker-on, observer, spectator, viewer, watcher, bystander.

v **1** SEE, observe, notice, note, view, watch, look on, mark, perceive. **2** TESTIFY, attest, bear witness, depose (*fml*), confirm, bear out, corroborate. **3** ENDORSE, sign, countersign.

witty *adj* humorous, amusing, comic, sharp-witted, droll, whimsical, original, brilliant, clever, ingenious, lively, sparkling, funny, facetious, fanciful, jocular.

$\boxminus$ dull, unamusing.

wizard *n* **1** SORCERER, magician, warlock, enchanter, necromancer, occultist, witch, conjurer. **2** (*infml*) EXPERT, adept, virtuoso, ace, master, maestro, prodigy, genius, star (*infml*), whiz (*infml*), hotshot (*infml*).

wizened *adj* shrivelled, shrunken, dried up, withered, wrinkled, gnarled, thin, worn, lined.

wobble *v* shake, oscillate, tremble, quake, sway, teeter, totter, rock, seesaw, vibrate, waver, dodder, fluctuate, hesitate, dither, vacillate, shilly-shally.

wobbly *adj* unstable, shaky, rickety, unsteady, wonky (*infml*), teetering, tottering, doddering, doddery, uneven, unbalanced, unsafe.

$\boxminus$ stable, steady.

woman *n* female, lady, girl, matriarch, maiden, maid.

womanly *adj* feminine, female, ladylike, womanish.

wonder *n* **1** MARVEL, phenomenon, miracle, prodigy, sight, spectacle, rarity, curiosity. **2** AWE, amazement, astonishment, admiration, wonderment, fascination, surprise, bewilderment.

v **1** MEDITATE, speculate, ponder, ask oneself, question, conjecture, puzzle, enquire, query, doubt, think. **2** MARVEL, gape, be amazed, be surprised.

wonderful *adj* **1** MARVELLOUS, magnificent, oustanding, excellent,

superb, admirable, delightful, phenomenal, sensational, stupendous, tremendous, super (*infml*), terrific (*infml*), brilliant (*infml*), great (*infml*), fabulous (*infml*), fantastic (*infml*). **2** AMAZING, astonishing, astounding, startling, surprising, extraordinary, incredible, remarkable, staggering, strange.

$\boxminus$ **1** appalling, dreadful. **2** ordinary.

woo *v* **1** (*fml*) *woo a lover*: court, chase, pursue. **2** *woo custom*: encourage, cultivate, attract, look for, seek.

wood *n* **1** TIMBER, lumber, planks. **2** FOREST, woods, woodland, trees, plantation, thicket, grove, coppice, copse, spinney.

Types of wood include: timber, lumber (*North Amer.*), hardwood, softwood, heartwood, sapwood, seasoned wood, green wood, bitterwood, brushwood, cordwood, firewood, kindling, matchwood, plywood, pulpwood, whitewood, chipboard, hardboard, wood veneer; afrormosia, ash, balsa, beech, cedar, cherry, chestnut, cottonwood, deal, ebony, elm, mahogany, African mahogany, maple, oak, pine, redwood, rosewood, sandalwood, sapele, satinwood, teak, walnut, willow. *see also* **tree**.

wooded *adj* forested, timbered, woody, tree-covered, sylvan (*fml*).

wooden *adj* **1** TIMBER, woody. **2** EMOTIONLESS, expressionless, awkward, clumsy, stilted, lifeless, spiritless, unemotional, stiff, rigid, leaden, deadpan, blank, empty, slow.

$\boxminus$ **2** lively.

wool *n* fleece, down, yarn.

woolly *adj* **1** WOOLLEN, fleecy, woolly-haired, downy, shaggy, fuzzy, frizzy. **2** UNCLEAR, ill-defined, hazy, blurred, confused, muddled, vague, indefinite, nebulous.

⊟ 2 clear, distinct.

n jumper, sweater, jersey, pullover, cardigan.

word *n* **1** NAME, term, expression, designation, utterance, vocable (*fml*). **2** CONVERSATION, chat, talk, discussion, consultation.

3 INFORMATION, news, report, communication, notice, message, bulletin, communiqué, statement, dispatch, declaration, comment, assertion, account, remark, advice, warning. **4** PROMISE, pledge, oath, assurance, vow, guarantee.

5 COMMAND, order, decree, commandment, go-ahead (*infml*), green light (*infml*).

v phrase, express, couch, put, say, explain, write.

words *n* **1** ARGUMENT, dispute, quarrel, disagreement, altercation, bickering, row, squabble. **2** LYRICS, libretto, text, book.

wordy *adj* verbose, long-winded, loquacious (*fml*), garrulous, prolix, rambling, diffuse, discursive.

⊟ concise.

work *n* **1** OCCUPATION, job, employment, profession, trade, business, career, calling, vocation, line, métier, livelihood, craft, skill. **2** TASK, assignment, undertaking, job, chore, responsibility, duty, commission. **3** TOIL, labour, drudgery, effort, exertion, industry, slog (*infml*), graft (*infml*), elbow grease (*infml*). **4** CREATION, production, achievement, composition, opus.

⊟ 1 play, rest, hobby.

v **1** BE EMPLOYED, have a job, earn one's living. **2** LABOUR, toil, drudge, slave. **3** FUNCTION, go, operate, perform, run, handle, manage, use, control. **4** BRING ABOUT, accomplish, achieve, create, cause, pull off (*infml*). **5** CULTIVATE, farm, dig, till. **6** MANIPULATE, knead,

mould, shape, form, fashion, make, process.

⊟ 1 be unemployed. **2** play, rest. **3** fail.

work out 1 SOLVE, resolve, calculate, figure out, puzzle out, sort out, understand, clear up. **2** DEVELOP, evolve, go well, succeed, prosper, turn out, pan out (*infml*). **3** PLAN, devise, arrange, contrive, invent, construct, put together. **4** ADD UP TO, amount to, total, come out.

work up incite, stir up, rouse, arouse, animate, excite, move, stimulate, inflame, spur, instigate, agitate, generate.

worker *n* employee, labourer, working man, working woman, artisan, craftsman, tradesman, hand, operative, wage-earner, breadwinner, proletarian.

workforce *n* workers, employees, personnel, labour force, staff, labour, work-people, shop-floor.

working *n* functioning, operation, running, routine, manner, method, action.

adj **1** FUNCTIONING, operational, running, operative, going.

2 EMPLOYED, active.

⊟ 1 inoperative. **2** idle.

workmanship *n* skill, craft, craftsmanship, expertise, art, handicraft, handiwork, technique, execution, manufacture, work, finish.

works *n* **1** FACTORY, plant, workshop, mill, foundry, shop. **2** ACTIONS, acts, doings. **3** PRODUCTIONS, output, oeuvre, writings, books. **4** MACHINERY, mechanism, workings, action, movement, parts, installations.

workshop *n* **1** WORKS, workroom, atelier, studio, factory, plant, mill, shop. **2** STUDY GROUP, seminar, symposium, discussion group, class.

world *n* **1** EARTH, globe, planet, star, universe, cosmos, creation, nature. **2** EVERYBODY, everyone, people, human race, humankind, humanity. **3** SPHERE, realm, field, area, domain, division, system, society, province, kingdom. **4** TIMES, epoch, era, period, age, days, life.

worldly *adj* **1** TEMPORAL, earthly, mundane, terrestrial, physical, secular, unspiritual, profane. **2** WORLDLY-WISE, sophisticated, urbane, cosmopolitan, experienced, knowing, streetwise (*infml*). **3** MATERIALISTIC, selfish, ambitious, grasping, greedy, covetous, avaricious.
ᴇᴀ 1 spiritual, eternal.
2 unsophisticated.

worn *adj* **1** SHABBY, threadbare, worn-out, tatty, tattered, frayed, ragged. **2** EXHAUSTED, tired, weary, spent, fatigued, careworn, drawn, haggard, jaded.
ᴇᴀ 1 new, unused. **2** fresh.

worn out 1 SHABBY, threadbare, useless, used, tatty, tattered, on its last legs, ragged, moth-eaten, frayed, decrepit. **2** TIRED OUT, exhausted, weary, done in (*infml*), all in (*infml*), dog-tired (*infml*), knackered (*infml*).
ᴇᴀ 1 new, unused. **2** fresh.

worried *adj* anxious, troubled, uneasy, ill at ease, apprehensive, concerned, bothered, upset, fearful, afraid, frightened, on edge, overwrought, tense, strained, nervous, disturbed, distraught, distracted, fretful, distressed, agonized.
ᴇᴀ calm, unworried, unconcerned.

worry *v* **1** BE ANXIOUS, be troubled, be distressed, agonize, fret.
2 IRRITATE, plague, pester, torment, upset, unsettle, annoy, bother, disturb, vex, tease, nag, harass, harry, perturb, hassle (*infml*).
3 ATTACK, go for, savage.
ᴇᴀ 1 be unconcerned. **2** comfort.
n **1** PROBLEM, trouble, responsibility, burden, concern, care, trial, annoyance, irritation, vexation.

2 ANXIETY, apprehension, unease, misgiving, fear, disturbance, agitation, torment, misery, perplexity.
ᴇᴀ 2 comfort, reassurance.

worsen *v* **1** EXACERBATE, aggravate, intensify, heighten. **2** GET WORSE, weaken, deteriorate, degenerate, decline, sink, go downhill (*infml*).
ᴇᴀ improve.

worship *v* venerate, revere, reverence, adore, exalt, glorify, honour, praise, idolize, adulate, love, respect, pray to, deify.
ᴇᴀ despise, hate.
n veneration, reverence, adoration, devotion(s), homage, honour, glory, glorification, exaltation, praise, prayer(s), respect, regard, love, adulation, deification, idolatry.

worth *n* worthiness, merit, value, benefit, advantage, importance, significance, use, usefulness, utility, quality, good, virtue, excellence, credit, desert(s), cost, rate, price, help, assistance, avail.
ᴇᴀ worthlessness.

worthless *adj* **1** VALUELESS, useless, pointless, meaningless, futile, unavailing, unimportant, insignificant, trivial, unusable, cheap, poor, rubbishy, trashy, trifling, paltry. **2** CONTEMPTIBLE, despicable, good-for-nothing, vile.
ᴇᴀ 1 valuable. **2** worthy.

worthwhile *adj* profitable, useful, valuable, worthy, good, helpful, beneficial, constructive, gainful, justifiable, productive.
ᴇᴀ worthless.

worthy *adj* praiseworthy, laudable, creditable, commendable, valuable, worthwhile, admirable, fit, deserving, appropriate, respectable, reputable, good, honest, honourable, excellent, decent, upright, righteous.
ᴇᴀ unworthy, disreputable.

wound *n* **1** INJURY, trauma, hurt, cut, gash, lesion, laceration, scar.

2 HURT, distress, trauma, torment, heartbreak, harm, damage, anguish, grief, shock.

v **1** DAMAGE, harm, hurt, injure, hit, cut, gash, lacerate, slash, pierce.

2 DISTRESS, offend, insult, pain, mortify, upset, slight, grieve.

wrangle *n* argument, quarrel, dispute, controversy, squabble, tiff, row (*infml*), bickering, disagreement, clash, altercation, contest, slanging match (*infml*), set-to (*infml*).

🔁 agreement.

v argue, quarrel, disagree, dispute, bicker, altercate, contend, fall out (*infml*), row (*infml*), squabble, scrap, fight, spar.

🔁 agree.

wrap *v* envelop, fold, enclose, cover, pack, shroud, wind, surround, package, muffle, cocoon, cloak, roll up, bind, bundle up, immerse.

🔁 unwrap.

wrap up 1 WRAP, pack up, package, parcel. **2** (*infml*) CONCLUDE, finish off, end, bring to a close, terminate, wind up, complete, round off.

wrapper *n* wrapping, packaging, envelope, cover, jacket, dust jacket, sheath, sleeve, paper.

wreak *v* inflict, exercise, create, cause, bring about, perpetrate, vent, unleash, express, execute, carry out, bestow.

wreath *n* garland, coronet, chaplet, festoon, crown, band, ring.

wreck *v* destroy, ruin, demolish, devastate, shatter, smash, break, spoil, play havoc with, ravage, write off.

🔁 conserve, repair.

n ruin, destruction, devastation, mess, demolition, ruination, write-off, disaster, loss, disruption.

wreckage *n* debris, remains, rubble, ruin, fragments, flotsam, pieces.

wrench *v* yank, wrest, jerk, pull, tug, force, sprain, strain, rick, tear, twist, wring, rip, distort.

v struggle, strive, fight, scuffle, grapple, tussle, combat, contend, contest, vie, battle.

wretch *n* scoundrel, rogue, villain, good-for-nothing, ruffian, rascal, vagabond, miscreant, outcast.

wretched *adj* **1** ATROCIOUS, awful, deplorable, appalling. **2** UNHAPPY, sad, miserable, melancholy, depressed, dejected, disconsolate, downcast, forlorn, gloomy, doleful, distressed, broken-hearted, crestfallen.

3 PATHETIC, pitiable, pitiful, unfortunate, sorry, hopeless, poor.

4 CONTEMPTIBLE, despicable, vile, worthless, shameful, inferior, low, mean, paltry.

🔁 **1** excellent. **2** happy. **3** enviable. **4** worthy.

wriggle *v* squirm, writhe, wiggle, worm, twist, snake, slink, crawl, edge, sidle, manoeuvre, squiggle, dodge, extricate, zigzag, waggle, turn.

n wiggle, twist, squirm, jiggle, jerk, turn, twitch.

wring *v* **1** SQUEEZE, twist, wrench, wrest, extract, mangle, screw.

2 EXACT, extort, coerce, force.

3 DISTRESS, pain, hurt, rack, rend, pierce, torture, wound, stab, tear.

wrinkle *n* furrow, crease, corrugation, line, fold, gather, pucker, crumple.

v crease, corrugate, furrow, fold, crinkle, crumple, shrivel, gather, pucker.

write *v* pen, inscribe, record, jot down, set down, take down, transcribe, scribble, scrawl, correspond, communicate, draft, draw up, copy, compose, create.

write off 1 DELETE, cancel, cross out, disregard. **2** WRECK, destroy, crash, smash up.

writer *n* author, scribe, wordsmith, novelist, dramatist, essayist, playwright, columnist, diarist, hack, penpusher, scribbler, secretary, copyist, clerk.

> *Writers include*: annalist, author,
> autobiographer, bard, biographer,
> calligraphist, chronicler, clerk,
> columnist, composer, contributor,
> copyist, copywriter, correspondent,
> court reporter, diarist, dramatist,
> editor, essayist, fabler, fiction writer,
> ghost writer, hack, historian,
> journalist, leader-writer,
> lexicographer, librettist, lyricist,
> novelist, pen-friend, penman, pen-
> pal, penpusher (*infml*), penwoman,
> playwright, poet, poet laureate,
> reporter, rhymer, satirist, scribbler,
> scribe, scriptwriter, short-story
> writer, sonneteer, stenographer,
> storyteller (*infml*).

writhe *v* squirm, wriggle, thresh,
thrash, twist, wiggle, toss, coil,
contort, struggle.

writing *n* **1** HANDWRITING,
calligraphy, script, penmanship,
scrawl, scribble, hand, print.
2 DOCUMENT, letter, book,
composition, letters, literature, work,
publication.

wrong *adj* **1** INACCURATE,
incorrect, mistaken, erroneous, false,
fallacious, in error, imprecise. **2**
INAPPROPRIATE, unsuitable,
unseemly, improper, indecorous,
unconventional, unfitting,
incongruous, inapt. **3** UNJUST,
unethical, unfair, unlawful, immoral,
illegal, illicit, dishonest, criminal,
crooked (*infml*), reprehensible,
blameworthy, guilty, to blame, bad,
wicked, sinful, iniquitous, evil.
4 DEFECTIVE, faulty, out of order,
amiss, awry.

E₹ 1 correct, right. **2** suitable, right.
3 good, moral.

adv amiss, astray, awry, inaccurately,
incorrectly, wrongly, mistakenly,
faultily, badly, erroneously, improperly.

E₹ right.

n sin, misdeed, offence, crime,
immorality, sinfulness, transgression,
wickedness, wrong-doing, trespass
(*fml*), injury, grievance, abuse,
injustice, iniquity, inequity,
infringement, unfairness, error.

E₹ right.

v abuse, ill-treat, mistreat, maltreat,
injure, ill-use, hurt, harm, discredit,
dishonour, misrepresent, malign,
oppress, cheat.

wrongdoer *n* offender, law-breaker,
transgressor, criminal, delinquent,
felon, miscreant, evil-doer, sinner,
trespasser, culprit.

wrongful *adj* immoral, improper,
unfair, unethical, unjust, unlawful,
illegal, illegitimate, illicit, dishonest,
criminal, blameworthy,
dishonourable, wrong, reprehensible,
wicked, evil.

E₹ rightful.

wry *adj* **1** *wry humour*: ironic,
sardonic, dry, sarcastic, mocking,
droll. **2** TWISTED, distorted,
deformed, contorted, warped,
uneven, crooked.

E₹ 2 straight.

Y

yank *v, n* jerk, tug, pull, wrench,
snatch, haul, heave.

yap *v* **1** BARK, yelp. **2** (*infml*)
CHATTER, jabber, babble, prattle,
yatter, jaw (*infml*).

yardstick *n* measure, gauge,
criterion, standard, benchmark,
touchstone, comparison.

yarn n **1** THREAD, fibre, strand. **2** STORY, tale, anecdote, fable, fabrication, tall story, cock-and-bull story (*infml*).

yawning adj gaping, wide, wide-open, huge, vast, cavernous.

yearly adj annual, per year, per annum, perennial.
adv annually, every year, once a year, perennially.

yearn for long for, pine for, desire, want, wish for, crave, covet, hunger for, hanker for, ache for, languish for, itch for.

yell v shout, scream, bellow, roar, bawl, shriek, squeal, howl, holler (*infml*), screech, squall, yelp, yowl, whoop.
F3 whisper.
n shout, scream, cry, roar, bellow, shriek, howl, screech, squall, whoop.
F3 whisper.

yelp v yap, bark, squeal, cry, yell, yowl, bay.
n yap, bark, yip, squeal, cry, yell, yowl.

yield v **1** SURRENDER, renounce, abandon, abdicate, cede, part with, relinquish. **2** GIVE WAY, capitulate, concede, submit, succumb, give (in), admit defeat, bow, cave in, knuckle under, resign oneself, go along with, permit, allow, acquiesce, accede, agree, comply, consent. **3** PRODUCE, bear, supply, provide, generate, bring in, bring forth, furnish, return, earn, pay.
F3 **1** hold. **2** resist, withstand.
n return, product, earnings, harvest, crop, produce, output, profit, revenue, takings, proceeds, income.

yoke n **1** HARNESS, bond, link. **2** BURDEN, bondage, enslavement, slavery, oppression, subjugation, servility.
v couple, link, join, tie, harness, hitch, bracket, connect, unite.

young adj **1** YOUTHFUL, juvenile, baby, infant, junior, adolescent. **2** IMMATURE, early, new, recent, green, growing, fledgling, unfledged, inexperienced.
F3 **1** adult, old. **2** mature, old.
n offspring, babies, issue, litter, progeny, brood, children, family.

youngster n child, boy, girl, toddler, youth, teenager, kid (*infml*).

youth n **1** ADOLESCENT, youngster, juvenile, teenager, kid (*infml*), boy, young man. **2** YOUNG PEOPLE, the young, younger generation. **3** ADOLESCENCE, childhood, immaturity, boyhood, girlhood.
F3 **3** adulthood.

youthful adj young, boyish, girlish, childish, immature, juvenile, inexperienced, fresh, active, lively, well-preserved.
F3 aged.

Z

zany (*infml*) adj comical, funny, amusing, eccentric, droll, crazy (*infml*), clownish, loony (*infml*), wacky (*infml*).
F3 serious.

zeal n ardour, fervour, passion, warmth, fire, enthusiasm, devotion, spirit, keenness, zest, eagerness, earnestness, dedication, fanaticism, gusto, verve.
F3 apathy, indifference.

zealot n fanatic, extremist, bigot, militant, partisan.

zealous adj ardent, fervent, impassioned, passionate, devoted, burning, enthusiastic, intense,

fanatical, militant, keen, eager, earnest, spirited.
🔁 apathetic, indifferent.

zenith *n* summit, peak, height, pinnacle, apex, high point, top, optimum, climax, culmination, acme, meridian, vertex.
🔁 nadir.

zero *n* nothing, nought, nil, nadir, bottom, cipher, zilch (*infml*), duck, love.

zest *n* **1** GUSTO, appetite, enthusiasm, enjoyment, keenness, zeal, exuberance, interest.
2 FLAVOUR, taste, relish, savour, spice, tang, piquancy.
🔁 1 apathy.

zigzag *v* meander, snake, wind, twist, curve.

adj meandering, crooked, serpentine, sinuous, twisting, winding.
🔁 straight.

zodiac

> *The signs of the zodiac (with their symbols) are:* Aries (Ram), Taurus (Bull), Gemini (Twins), Cancer (Crab), Leo (Lion), Virgo (Virgin), Libra (Balance), Scorpio (Scorpion), Sagittarius (Archer), Capricorn (Goat), Aquarius (Water-bearer), Pisces (Fishes).

zone *n* region, area, district, territory, section, sector, belt, sphere, tract, stratum.

zoom *v* race, rush, tear, dash, speed, fly, hurtle, streak, flash, shoot, whirl, dive, buzz, zip.